Organizational Behaviour

◎ CONCEPTS   ◎ CONTROVERSIES   ◎ APPLICATIONS

FOURTH CANADIAN EDITION

Organizational Behaviour

◎ CONCEPTS ◎ CONTROVERSIES ◎ APPLICATIONS

NANCY LANGTON
University of British Columbia

STEPHEN ROBBINS
San Diego State University

PEARSON

Prentice
Hall

Toronto

Library and Archives Canada Cataloguing in Publication

Langton, Nancy
    Organizational behaviour : concepts, controversies, applications / Nancy Langton, Stephen P. Robbins. — 4th Canadian ed.

Order of authors reversed on 3rd Canadian ed.
Includes indexes.

ISBN 0-13-197110-7

1. Organizational behaviour—Textbooks. 2. Management— Textbooks. I. Robbins, Stephen P., 1943– II. Title.

HD58.7.37 2007   658   C2005-904211-7

Vice President, Editorial Director: Michael J. Young
Editor-in-Chief: Gary Bennett
Acquisitions Editor: Karen Elliott
Executive Marketing Manager: Cas Shields
Developmental Editor: Su Mei Ku
Production Editor: Jennifer Handel
Copy Editor: Claudia Forgas
Proofreader: Sheila Wawanash
Senior Production Coordinator: Patricia Ciardullo
Page Layout: Carolyn E. Sebestyen
Permissions and Photo Research: Lisa Brant
Art Director: Mary Opper
Interior and Cover Design: Alex Li
Cover Image: © José Ortega/Stock Illustration Source

3 4 5   11 10 09 08 07

Printed and bound in the United States of America.

BRIEF CONTENTS

CONTENTS

PART 4

PART 5
REORGANIZING THE WORKPLACE 474

CHAPTER 13 Organizational Structure 474

PREFACE

Welcome to the fourth Canadian edition of *Organizational Behaviour*. Since its arrival in Canada, *Organizational Behaviour* has enjoyed widespread acclaim across the country for its rich Canadian content and has quickly established itself as the leading textbook in the field.

Organizational Behaviour, Fourth Canadian Edition, is truly a Canadian product. While it draws upon the strongest aspects of its American cousin, it expresses its own vision and voice. It provides the context for understanding organizational behaviour (OB) in the Canadian workplace and highlights the many Canadian contributions to the field. Indeed, it goes a step further than most OB textbooks prepared for the Canadian marketplace. Specifically, it asks, in many instances:

- How does this theory apply in the Canadian workplace of today?

- What are the implications of the theory for managers and employees working in the twenty-first century?

- What are the implications of the theory for everyday life? OB, after all, is not something that applies only in the workplace.

This textbook is sensitive to important Canadian issues. Subject matter reflects the broad multicultural flavour of Canada, and also highlights the roles of women and other visible minorities. Examples reflect the broad range of organizations in Canada: large, small, public and private sector, unionized and non-unionized.

Organizational Behaviour continues to be a vibrant and relevant text because it is a product of the Canadian classroom. It is used in Canada by the first author and her colleagues. Thus, there is a "frontline" approach to considering revisions. We also solicit considerable feedback from OB instructors and students throughout the country. While we have kept the features of the previous edition that adopters continue to say they like, there is also a lot that is new.

OUR PEDAGOGICAL APPROACH IN WRITING THE TEXTBOOK

- *Relevance.* The text reminds both teacher and student alike that we have entered the twenty-first century and must contend with a new paradigm of work that may be considerably different from the past. The new paradigm is more globally focused and competitive, relies more heavily on part-time and contract jobs, and places a higher premium on being entrepreneurial, either within the traditional workplace structure, as an individual seeking out an alternative job, or as the creator of your own new business.

    When the first Canadian edition appeared, it was the first text to emphasize that OB is for everyone, from the bottom-rung employee to the CEO, as well as to anyone who has to interact with others to accomplish a task. We continue to emphasize this theme. We remind readers of the material's relevance beyond a "9-to-5" job by concluding each chapter with a summary that outlines the implications not only for the workplace, but also for individuals in their daily lives. We also include the feature **OB in the Street**, which further emphasizes how OB applies outside the workplace.

- *Writing style.* We continue to make clarity and readability the hallmarks of this text. Our reviewers find the text "conversational," "interesting," "student-friendly," and "very clear and understandable." Students say they really like the informal style and personal examples.

- *Examples, examples, examples.* From our teaching experience, we know that students may not remember a concept, but they will remember an example. This textbook is packed full of recent real-world examples drawn from a variety of organizations: business and not-for-profit, large and small, and local and international. We also use examples taken from the world at large, to illustrate the broader applicability of OB material.

- *Comprehensive literature coverage.* This textbook is regularly singled out for its comprehensive and up-to-date coverage of OB from both academic journals as well as business periodicals.

- *Skill-building emphasis.* Each chapter's **OB at Work** is full of exercises to help students make the connections between theories and real-world applications. Exercises at the end of each chapter reinforce critical thinking, behavioural analysis, and team building.

- *Technology.* A Companion Website for this textbook is provided at **www.pearsoned.ca/langton**. The site includes an interactive study guide, featuring quizzes with immediate feedback, Internet exercises, and links to websites of many of the organizations mentioned in the text.

HIGHLIGHTS OF THE FOURTH EDITION

The fourth edition takes a fresh approach to organizational behaviour coverage through more relevant examples, updated theory coverage, and a continued emphasis on pedagogically sound design. Based on reviews from numerous instructors and students across Canada, we have found that many potential users want chapters that have the right balance of theory, research, and application material, while being relevant to student learning. To accomplish this, we have done the following:

- Shortened chapters to allow more focused theoretical discussions

- Shortened the opening vignettes and then allowed them to unfold throughout the chapter at the start of most major sections

- Introduced **OB in Action** to provide "take-aways" from each chapter, things that readers can put into action right now, based on what they have learned in the chapter

- Increased the number of **Focus on Research** vignettes and also highlighted research findings with a margin icon to help instructors identify key research findings. These features provide students with greater awareness of the research base that underlies OB

- Introduced **OB for You** at the end of each chapter, to highlight the relevance of the chapter to one's everyday life

- Doubled the number of end-of-chapter cases, and included two integrated cases at the end of the textbook

- Continued our **OB on the Edge** feature, which highlights what's new and hot in OB. OB on the Edge is unique to the Canadian edition, and unique to any organizational behaviour textbook in the market. The feature provides an opportunity to explore challenging issues, and encourages students to read more about these hot topics. In this edition, we cover four topics in this innovative feature: *Stress; The Toxic Workplace; Trust;* and *Spirituality in the Workplace*.

CHAPTER-BY-CHAPTER HIGHLIGHTS: WHAT'S NEW

The goal of this revision was to continue the emphasis on providing an up-to-date research base, including the latest topics in OB, and illustrating concepts through a broad array of examples and application material. These changes make this text the strongest application of OB material on the market. Each chapter brings new examples, new research, improved discussions of current issues, and a wide variety of application material. The key *changes* are listed below.

Chapter 1: What Is Organizational Behaviour?

- Included a lengthier discussion of organizational citizenship behaviour

- Added a section on "putting people first"

- Introduced *OB in Action—Practices of Successful Organizations* to show what companies do to put people first

- Added a discussion and an exhibit on research methods in OB

Chapter 2: Perception, Personality, and Emotions

- Added a number of new sections, including

    - Self-fulfilling prophecy

    - Self-esteem

    - Proactive personality

    - Personality and national culture

    - Affective events theory

- Provided additional discussion on the effects of locus of control on performance

Chapter 3: Values, Attitudes, and Diversity in the Workplace

- Significantly restructured the chapter to highlight the importance of knowing how to manage diversity in the workplace

- Included a section on Kent Hodgson's general moral principles

- Expanded discussion of the Rokeach Value Survey

- Extensively revised the section on assessing cultural values. We emphasize the GLOBE research program and its relation to Hofstede's work

- Expanded discussion on the multicultural aspects of Canada

- Added a discussion on how job satisfaction affects customer satisfaction

- Brought back the discussion on how employees can express dissatisfaction through the exit-voice-loyalty-neglect model

- Introduced the idea of "cultural intelligence" and also provided a self-test to measure it

Chapter 4: Theories of Motivation

- Divided the topic of motivation into two chapters, one on theory (Chapter 4) and the other on motivation practices in the workplace (Chapter 5)
- Expanded discussion of needs theories, including increased coverage of Alderfer's ERG theory and McClelland's theory of needs
- Expanded the discussion on goal-setting theory, including
  - How goal setting motivates
  - SMART goals
  - The research findings related to goal setting
  - Contingency factors in goal setting, including the impact of self-efficacy
- Added the following new discussions:
  - What influences an employee's expectancy
  - The ranges for expectancy, instrumentality, and valence
  - Intrinsic and extrinsic rewards, including related research findings
  - Reinforcement theory, including a discussion of how reinforcement is used in the workplace
  - *Motivation for whom?*, which looks at whether motivation theories serve managers and employees equally well

Chapter 5: Motivation in Action

This new chapter looks at the practical aspects of motivation, including the role of money as a motivator, creating an effective reward system, and how jobs can be designed to increase motivation. It also includes a section on how to increase intrinsic motivation

Chapter 6: Groups and Teamwork

- Added a number of new discussions, including
  - How groups become teams
  - Additional tips for managing virtual teams
  - How to use virtual workspaces to improve the productivity of virtual teams
  - Role ambiguity
  - The characteristics of ineffective and effective teams
- Restructured the discussion on conditions needed to create effective teams
- Increased the discussion of the role of friendships in teams
- Expanded the discussion of group cohesiveness, including tips for increasing cohesiveness
- Expanded coverage of dealing with team conflict
- Included tips for creating a team charter

Chapter 7: Communication

- Introduced a new model of the communication process, indicating its interactive nature
- Reorganized the chapter for better flow
- Included the following new discussions:
    - Information overload
    - The grapevine patterns in the workplace, and how the grapevine is used
    - The use of instant messaging in the workplace
    - How to communicate more effectively when under stress
    - Silence as a form of communication
- Expanded discussion of email in the workplace

Chapter 8: Power and Politics

- Shortened, focused section on bases of power with new discussion on ways that individuals can respond to influence tactics
- Updated discussion of influence tactics based on current research
- Provided a section on research findings regarding organizational politics
- Significantly increased discussion of workplace bullying both in the main part of text and in **HR Implications**
- Added a new discussion on how obedience is related to power, including a discussion of the classic Milgram experiment

Chapter 9: Conflict and Negotiation

- Significantly revised and reorganized the chapter
- Strengthened the introductory section on conflict
- Created an exhibit focusing on dealing with personality conflicts
- Added a discussion on win-win vs. win-lose solutions
- Included a discussion on the desired outcomes of conflict
- Expanded the description of conflict management styles
- Added a new section on conflict resolution
- Added new material on the negotiation process
- Expanded the discussion of cross-cultural issues in negotiations
- Created an exhibit on negotiation attitudes across cultures

Chapter 10: Organizational Culture

- Reorganized the chapter to increase the understanding of the purposes of organizational culture
- Focused more attention on strategies for merging organizational cultures

- Added a discussion on bicultural audits
- Extended discussion on changing organizational culture, including more examples
- Created an exhibit that provides tips for changing organizational culture

Chapter 11: Leadership

- Added the following new discussions and sections:
  - Trait theories of leadership, reflecting the latest research on this topic
  - Leadership traits across cultures (includes an exhibit)
  - Research findings for behavioural theories of leadership
  - Revisions to Path-Goal theory
  - Mentoring
  - How to create self-leaders
  - The effectiveness of women's style of leadership
  - Online leadership
- Expanded discussion of Fiedler's contingency model of leadership

Chapter 12: Decision Making, Creativity, and Ethics

- Shortened and focused the discussion on decision biases
- Included a section on knowledge management
- Added "focus on care" as a fourth ethical decision criterion
- Provided a definition of corporate social responsibility

Chapter 13: Organizational Structure

- Focused discussion on newer organizational structures
- Expanded coverage of the family business as an organizational structure, and some of the challenges these businesses face

Chapter 14: Organizational Change

- Completely rewrote and significantly reorganized the chapter
- Added several new sections:
  - Change agents
  - Kotter's eight-step plan for implementing change
  - Action research
  - Contemporary change issues for today's managers
  - Technology in the workplace
  - Stimulating innovation
  - Creating a learning organization

- Introduced appreciative inquiry, an approach to managing change

- Focused discussion on resistance to change

Throughout, we also significantly revised many of the **HR Implications** sections, as well as included new exercises and new cases in many chapters.

PEDAGOGICAL FEATURES

The pedagogical features of *Organizational Behaviour: Concepts, Controversies, Applications,* Fourth Canadian Edition, are designed to complement and reinforce the textual material. This textbook offers the most complete assortment of pedagogy available in any OB book on the market.

- NEW! The text is developed in a "story-line" format that emphasizes how the topics fit together. Each chapter opens with a concept map of key questions related to a main example that threads through the chapter. The opening vignette is shorter, and it is carried throughout the chapter to help students apply a story to the concepts they are learning. The questions from the concept map appear in the margin of the text, to indicate where they are addressed. The chapter ends with each of the opening questions repeated and answered, to summarize the contents of the chapter.

- Exclusive to the Canadian edition, **OB in the Street**, **OB in the Workplace**, **OB Around the Globe**, **Focus on Ethics**, **Focus on Diversity**, and **Focus on Research** help students see the links between theoretical material and applications.

- NEW! **OB in Action** features provide tips for using the concepts of OB in everyday life. For instance, **OB in Action** features include *Managing Virtual Teams, Ground Rules for Developing Business Partnerships With Aboriginal People, Practices of Successful Organizations,* and *Reducing Biases and Errors in Decision Making.*

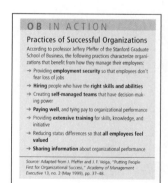

- NEW! To help instructors and students readily spot significant discussions of research findings, we have included a research icon in the margin where these discussions appear. This helps emphasize the strong research foundation that underlies OB.

- NEW! Margin definitions have been differentiated to help students separate concepts from theories. Definitions of terms and concepts appear in turquoise and definitions of theories appear in magenta, making them stand out for easier studying.

- NEW! **Integrated questions** (in the form of yellow notes) throughout the chapters encourage students to think about how OB applies to their everyday lives and engage students in their reading of the material.

- **Weblinks**, provided in the textbook margins, give students access to Internet resources for companies and organizations discussed in the text, broadening their grasp of real-world issues. To find a weblink for a particular organization, look it up in the *Name and Organization Index*, where the page on which the weblink appears in boldface. The Destinations button of the textbook's Companion Website provides hyperlinks for all weblinks (see **www.pearsoned.ca/langton**).

- Each chapter concludes with **OB at Work**, a set of resources designed to help students apply the lessons of the chapter. Included in **OB at Work** are the following continuing and new features:

  - **For Review** and **For Critical Thinking** provide thought-provoking questions to review the chapter and consider ways to apply the material presented.

  - **OB for You** (NEW) outlines how OB can be used by individuals in their daily lives.

  - **Point/Counterpoint** promotes debate on contentious OB issues. This feature has been shortened to present more focused arguments.

  - **HR Implications** spotlights those facets of each chapter topic that are relevant to human resource management.

- **Learning About Yourself Exercise, Breakout Group Exercises, Working With Others Exercise,** and **Ethical Dilemma Exercise** are valuable application exercises for the classroom. The many new exercises included here are ones that we have found particularly stimulating in our own classrooms. Our students say they like these exercises *and* they learn from them.

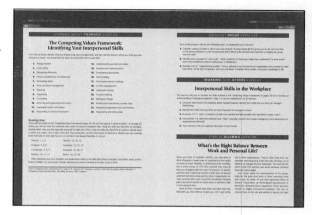

- **Case Incidents** (two per chapter) deal with real-world scenarios and require students to exercise their decision-making skills. Each case enables an instructor to quickly generate class discussion on a key theme within the chapter.

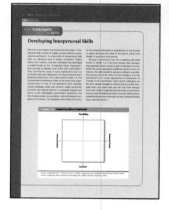

- NEW! **From Concepts to Skills** has been totally redesigned to provide a wider range of applications for students. The section begins with a practical set of tips on topics such as reading emotions, setting goals, and solving problems creatively, which demonstrate real-world applications of OB theories. These tips are followed by the features *Assessing Skills* (NEW), *Practising Skills* (NEW), and *Reinforcing Skills* (NEW). *Assessing Skills* encourages students to assess their personalities, leadership skills, conflict-handling intentions, and a variety of other traits and skills on the CD-ROM that accompanies this textbook. Students can therefore link their personal behaviours and traits to material covered in the chapter. *Practising Skills* presents an additional case or group activity to apply the chapter's learning objectives. *Reinforcing Skills* asks students to talk about the material they have learned with others, or to apply it to their own personal experiences.

- Exclusive to the Canadian edition, **OB on the Edge** (following each part) takes a close look at some of the hottest topics in the field: work-related stress, behavioural pathologies that can make an organization "toxic," trust, and spirituality in the workplace. Since this is a stand-alone feature, these topics can be introduced at the instructor's discretion.

- **CBC Video Case Incident** presents a CBC video case tied to the material in each chapter. The segments were carefully chosen by Donna Boots of the University of Saskatchewan, who also wrote the cases that appear at the end of this text. The video cases provide instructors with audiovisual material to engage students' attention.

- Our reviewers have asked for more cases, and more integrated cases. To address this request, we have added a new feature, **Integrative OB Cases**, at the end of the textbook. We include two lengthier cases, one on Wal-Mart, written by Céleste M. Brotheridge of Université du Québec à Montréal, and the other, on City Zoo, written by Nancy Langton. These cases require students to apply material from a variety of chapters.

SUPPLEMENTS

We have created an outstanding supplements package for *Organizational Behaviour, Fourth Canadian Edition*. The following materials are available:

Instructor's Resource CD-ROM (0-13-219856-8). This resource provides all of the following supplements in one convenient package:

- *Instructor's Resource Manual with CBC Video Guide.* Prepared by Nancy Langton, the Instructor's Resource Manual includes learning objectives, chapter outlines and synopses, annotated lecture outlines, teaching guides for in-text exercises, a summary and analysis of **Point/Counterpoint** features, and answers to questions found under **OB at Work**'s *For Review* and *For Critical Thinking* sections, **Case Incidents**, and **CBC Video Case Incidents**. There are additional cases, exercises, and teaching materials as well.

- *Pearson TestGen.* Prepared by Bonnie Milne (British Columbia Institute of Technology), the Pearson TestGen contains over 2000 items in TestGen format, including multiple choice, true/false, and discussion questions that relate not only to the body of the text but to **From Concepts to Skills**, **Point/Counterpoint**, and case materials. For each question we have provided the correct answer, a page reference to the text, a difficulty rating, and a classification (recall/applied). TestGen is a testing software that enables instructors to view and edit the existing questions, add questions, generate tests, and distribute the tests in a variety of formats. Powerful search and sort functions make it easy to locate questions and arrange them in any order desired. TestGen also enables instructors to administer tests on a local area network, have the tests graded electronically and have the results prepared in electronic or printed reports. TestGen is compatible with Windows and Macintosh operating systems, and can be downloaded from the TestGen website located at **www.pearsoned.com/testgen**. Contact your local sales representative for details and access.

- *Electronic Transparencies in PowerPoint®.* Prepared by Nancy Langton, this package includes nearly 500 slides of content and exhibits from the text for electronic presentation.

- *CBC/Pearson Education Canada Video Library.* The CBC and Pearson Education Canada have worked together to develop an exciting video package consisting of segments from CBC programs. These segments show students issues of organizational behaviour as they affect real Canadian individuals and companies. Teaching notes are provided in the Instructor's Resource Manual with CBC Video Guide. The videos are also available in VHS format (0-13-219851-7) and DVD format (0-13-238043-9).

Most of these instructor supplements are also available for download from a password-protected section of Pearson Education Canada's online catalogue (**vig.pearsoned.ca**). Navigate to your textbook's catalogue page to view a list of those supplements that are available. See your local sales representative for details and access.

Companion Website (**www.pearsoned.ca/langton**). The website for this textbook includes a comprehensive online study guide written by Patrick Sherlock (Nova Scotia Community College). Practice tests with true/false and multiple-choice questions offer instant feedback to students. Destinations (hyperlinks to the text's weblinks) and Internet exercises facilitate further research into key organizations and topics discussed in the text.

Colour Acetates (0-13-221464-4). This package contains a selection of the PowerPoint transparencies on full-colour acetates, highlighting key concepts for classroom presentation.

Personal Response System (0-13-219855-X). Gauge your students' course progress with this Personal Response System that enables instructors to pose questions, record results, and display those results instantly in the classroom. Questions are provided in PowerPoint® format.

VangoNotes. Study on the go with VangoNotes. Just download chapter reviews from your text and listen to them on any mp3 player. Now wherever you are—whatever you're doing—you can study by listening to the following for each chapter of your textbook:

- **Big Ideas:** Your "need to know" for each chapter

- **Practice Test:** A gut check for the Big Ideas—tells you if you need to keep studying

- **Key Terms:** Audio "flashcards" to help you review key concepts and terms

- **Rapid Review:** A quick drill session—use it right before your test

VangoNotes are **flexible**; download all the material directly to your player, or only the chapters you need. And they're **efficient**. Use them in your car, at the gym, walking to class—wherever. So get yours today. And get studying. **VangoNotes.com**.

Pearson Advantage. For qualified adopters, Pearson Education is proud to introduce the Pearson Advantage. The Pearson Advantage is the first integrated Canadian service program committed to meeting the customization, training, and support needs for your course. Our commitments are made in writing and in consultation with faculty. Your local Pearson Education sales representative can provide you with more details on this service program.

Content Media Specialists. Pearson's Content Media Specialists work with faculty and campus course designers to ensure that Pearson technology products, assessment tools, and online course materials are tailored to meet your specific needs. This highly qualified team is dedicated to helping schools take full advantage of a wide range of educational technology, by assisting in the integration of a variety of instructional materials and media formats.

ACKNOWLEDGMENTS

A number of people worked hard to give this fourth Canadian edition of *Organizational Behaviour* a new look. Su Mei Ku, who has been the developmental editor on almost all of my projects, again outdid her always excellent performance. Her wit, good humour, helpfulness, support, and organizational skills made working on this textbook immensely easier. Su Mei served as a much-valued sounding board throughout the editorial process.

I received incredible support for this project from a variety of people at Pearson Education Canada. James Bosma was Acquisitions Editor when this project started and was helpful in putting a number of important processes in place. Karen Elliott, his replacement, has worked hard in her new role to keep this project on track. Alex Li was responsible for the interior and cover design. Alex performed admirably, translating my thoughts about what this book should look like and creating an exciting new design. I particularly appreciate his responsiveness to suggestions for changes. Jen Handel was terrific in her role as the Production Editor for this project. She was very responsive and patiently and calmly handled the production process with much grace and goodwill. Steve O'Hearn, President of Higher Education, and Michael Young, Vice President, Editorial Director of Higher Education, are extremely supportive on the management side of Pearson Education Canada. This kind of support makes it much easier for an author to get work done and meet dreams and goals. Michael's support behind the scenes is particularly appreciated and valued. Lisa Brant was very helpful in doing the photo research, and made some incredible finds in her search for photos to highlight OB concepts. There are a variety of other people at Pearson who also had their hand in making sure that the manuscript would be transformed into this book and then delivered to your hands. To all of them I extend my thanks for jobs well done. The Pearson sales team is an exceptional group, and I know they will do everything possible to make this book successful. I continue to appreciate and value their support and interaction, particularly that of Cas Shields, Executive Marketing Manager.

Claudia Forgas was copyeditor for the project and did an amazing job of making sure everything was in place and written clearly. Sheila Wawanash, as the proofreader, was extremely diligent about checking for consistency throughout the text. Both performed a number of helpful fact-checking activities. I enjoyed the opportunity to work with both of them. Their keen eyes helped to make these pages as clean as they are.

I also want to acknowledge my divisional secretary, Irene Khoo, who helped to keep the project on track, doing some of the word processing, managing the courier packages and faxes, and always being attentive to detail. I could not ask for a better, more dedicated, or more cheerful assistant. She really helps keep things together.

My family and friends are often ignored during the busier parts of writing a textbook. They accept this graciously and provide food, support, and encouragement, as necessary. I am grateful for their support. A particular thanks goes to the members of the Carnavaron Quilt Guild who provided Monday night breaks from gruelling writing sessions and always asked how things were going and encouraged me along the way.

In our continuing effort to make our writing and language student-friendly, we conducted many reviews that focused on this very aspect. Special thanks to Marina Engelking, Seneca College, who helped us to consider the needs of ESL/LCD students. Many thanks to the students from across Canada who assisted us in improving the textbook's readability by reading several chapters from the textbook and providing us with suggestions. The students are Joelle Benabou (Ryerson University), Joanne Pauline Diggles (Mohawk College), Marcella Firmini (Nova Scotia Community College), Brian Kwiatkowski (Mohawk College), Tiffany McFadden (University of British Columbia), Oveeta Yasmin Ramoutar (Mohwak College), Sarah Robinson (Saskatchewan Institute of Applied Science and Technology), Pearly Tang (University of British Columbia), and Joanna Warren (University of New Brunswick).

Finally, I want to acknowledge the many reviewers of this textbook for their detailed helpful comments. I appreciate the time and care that they put into their reviewing: Amanda Bickell (St. Clair College of Applied Arts and Technology), Donna Boots (University of Saskatchewan), Robert S. Deane (University of Western Ontario), Linda Eligh (University of Guelph and University of Western Ontario), Marina Engelking (Seneca College), Genevieve Farrell (Ryerson University), Susan FitzRandolph (Ryerson University), Karen Hamilton (George Brown College), Scott Jeffrey (University of Waterloo), John Kyle (University of Victoria), Colleen Marshall (Confederation College), Bonnie Milne

(British Columbia Institute of Technology), Don Miskiman (Malaspina University-College), Beth Perry (Athabasca University), Kim Richter (Kwantlen University College), Carol Ann Samhaber (Algonquin College), and Debra Warren (Centennial College).

I dedicate this book to my father, Peter X. Langton. He was a man of many talents, and his understanding of organizational behaviour may have been greater than my own.

Nancy Langton
December 2005

ABOUT THE AUTHORS

Nancy Langton received her Ph.D. from Stanford University. Since completing her graduate studies, Dr. Langton has taught at the University of Oklahoma and the University of British Columbia. As a member of the Organizational Behaviour and Human Resources division at the Sauder School of Business, UBC, she teaches at the undergraduate, MBA and Ph.D. level and conducts executive programs on attracting and retaining employees, time management, family business issues, as well as women and management issues. Dr. Langton has received several major three-year research grants from the Social Sciences and Humanities Research Council of Canada, and her research interests have focused on human resource issues in the workplace, including pay equity, gender equity, and leadership and communication styles. She is currently conducting longitudinal research with entrepreneurs in the Greater Vancouver Region, trying to understand the relationship between their human resource practices and the success of their businesses. Her articles on these and other topics have appeared in such journals as *Administrative Science Quarterly*, *American Sociological Review*, *Sociological Quarterly*, *Journal of Management Education*, *Organization Studies*, and *Gender, Work and Organizations*. She has won Best Paper commendations from both the Academy of Management and the Administrative Sciences Association of Canada.

Dr. Langton routinely wins high marks from her students for teaching. She has been nominated many times for the Commerce Undergraduate Society Awards, and has won several honourable mention plaques. In 1998 she won the University of British Columbia Faculty of Commerce's most prestigious award for teaching innovation, The Talking Stick. The award was given for Dr. Langton's redesign of the undergraduate organizational behaviour course as well as the many activities that were a spin-off of these efforts. In 2001 she was part of the UBC MBA Core design team that won the Alan Blizzard award, a national award that recognizes innovation in teaching.

In Dr. Langton's "other life," she teaches the artistry of quiltmaking, and one day hopes to win first prize at *Visions*, the juried show for quilts as works of art. In the meantime she teaches art quilt courses on colour and design in her spare time. When she is not designing quilts, she is either reading novels (often suggested by a favourite correspondent), or studying cookbooks for new ideas. All of her friends would say that she makes from scratch the best pizza in all of Vancouver.

Stephen P. Robbins received his Ph.D. from the University of Arizona and has taught at the University of Nebraska at Omaha, Concordia University in Montreal, the University of Baltimore, Southern Illinois University at Edwardsville, and San Diego State University. Dr. Robbins' research interests have focused on conflict, power, and politics in organizations, as well as on the development of effective interpersonal skills. His articles on these and other topics have appeared in journals such as *Business Horizons*, *California Management Review*, *Business and Economic Perspectives*, *International Management*, *Management Review*, *Canadian Personnel and Industrial Relations*, and *The Journal of Management Education*.

In recent years, Dr. Robbins has been spending most of his professional time writing textbooks. These include *Essentials of Organizational Behavior*, 7th ed. (Prentice Hall,

2003); *Training in InterPersonal Skills*, 3rd ed., with Phillip Hunsaker (Prentice Hall, 2003); *Management*, 7th ed. with Mary Coulter (Prentice Hall, 2002); *Human Resource Management*, 7th ed., with David DeCenzo (Wiley, 2002); *The Self-Assessment Library 2.0* (Prentice Hall, 2002); *Fundamentals of Management*, 3rd ed., with David DeCenzo (Prentice Hall, 2001); *Supervision Today!*, 3rd ed., with David DeCenzo (Prentice Hall, 2001); *Business Today* (Harcourt, 2001); *Managing Today!* 2nd ed. (Prentice Hall, 2000); and *Organization Theory*, 3rd ed. (Prentice Hall, 1990).

In Dr. Robbins' "other life," he participates in masters' track competition. Since turning 50 in 1993, he has set numerous indoor and outdoor age-group world sprint records; won more than a dozen indoor and outdoor U.S. championships at 60, 100, 200, and 400 meters; and captured seven gold medals at the World Masters Championships. Most recently, he won gold medals at 100 and 200 meters and as the anchor on the U.S. 4 × 100 relay in the Men's 55–59 age group at the 2001 World Championships in Brisbane, Australia.

A Great Way to Learn and Instruct Online

The Pearson Education Canada Companion Website is easy to navigate and is organized to correspond to the chapters in this textbook. Whether you are a student in the classroom or a distance learner you will discover helpful resources for in-depth study and research that empower you in your quest for greater knowledge and maximize your potential for success in the course.

Companion Website

[**www.pearsoned.ca/langton**]

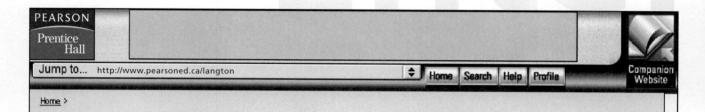

PEARSON
Prentice Hall

Jump to...   http://www.pearsoned.ca/langton   Home | Search | Help | Profile

Companion Website

Home >

Pearson Companion Website

Organizational Behaviour, Fourth Canadian Edition, by Langton and Robbins

Student Resources

The modules in this section provide students with tools for learning course material. These modules include:
- Chapter Objectives
- Destinations
- Quizzes
- Internet Exercises
- Net Search

In the quiz modules students can send answers to the grader and receive instant feedback on their progress through the Results Reporter. Coaching comments and references to the textbook may be available to ensure that students take advantage of all available resources to enhance their learning experience.

Instructor Resources

A link to this book on the Pearson online catalogue (www.pearsoned.ca) provides instructors with additional teaching tools. Downloadable PowerPoint Presentations and an Instructor's Resource Manual are just some of the materials that may be available. The catalogue is password protected. To get a password, simply contact your Pearson Education Canada Representative or call Faculty Sales and Services at 1-800-850-5813.

CHAPTER 1
What Is Organizational Behaviour?

An organization decides it will hire people with few skills and little job experience. What challenges might its managers face?

1 What is organizational behaviour?

2 What challenges do managers and employees face in today's workplace?

3 Isn't organizational behaviour common sense? Or just like psychology?

Winnipeg-based Inner City Renovation (ICR) does renovation and construction work on rundown inner city residential and commercial buildings, with the aim of revitalizing the area.[1] As part of its mission, the company employs and trains low-income residents of the inner city. ICR is a for-profit company that was created by five joint venture partners that are nonprofit organizations: North End Housing Project (NEHP), Winnipeg Partners in Housing (WPH), Spence Neighbourhood Association (SNA), West Broadway Development Corporation (WBDC), and Community Ownership Solutions (COS). The joint venture partners each have mandates to develop and implement projects and programs to help with inner city housing and job creation in Winnipeg. ICR has completed over 50 residential and commercial projects since it opened its doors in August 2002.

Because ICR hires a number of employees who have few skills and little job experience, managers must teach employees how to perform the role of employee.

Managers also teach employees about teamwork and leadership while working side by side with them on construction projects. Can a company like ICR survive as well as a company not as committed to social values?

The challenges that managers at ICR face illustrate several concepts you will find as you study the field of organizational behaviour. Let's take a look, then, at what organizational behaviour is.

DEFINING ORGANIZATIONAL BEHAVIOUR

Organizational behaviour (often abbreviated as OB) is a field of study that looks at what affects behaviour within organizations. Behaviour refers to what people do in the organization, what their attitudes are, and how they perform. OB considers the impact of individuals, groups, and structure on how organizations perform. Because the organizations studied are often business organizations, OB is frequently applied to topics such as absenteeism, turnover, productivity, motivation, working in groups, and job satisfaction. Managers often apply the knowledge gained from this research to help them manage their organizations more effectively.

Why do some people do well in organizational settings while others have difficulty?

However, much of OB is relevant beyond the workplace. The study of OB can cast light on the interactions among family members, students working as a team on a class project, the voluntary group that comes together to do something about reviving the downtown area, the parents who sit on the board of their child's daycare centre, or even the members of a lunchtime pickup basketball team.

1 What is organizational behaviour?

organizational behaviour A field of study that investigates the impact of individuals, groups, and structure on behaviour within organizations; the aim is to apply such knowledge toward improving organizational effectiveness.

What is organizational behaviour? It's a field of study that focuses on three levels of behaviour in organizations. One level is the individual, such as the Wal-Mart greeter handing out smiley balloons. Another level is the group, such as the three employees of Praxair, a distributor of bottled industrial gases, who meet to discuss their work. The third level is structure, which is depicted here by employees working in cubicles at Bloomberg, a financial media company.

What Do We Mean by Organization?

organization A consciously coordinated social unit, composed of a group of people, that functions on a relatively continuous basis to achieve a common goal or set of goals.

An **organization** is a consciously coordinated social unit, composed of a group of people, that functions on a relatively continuous basis to achieve a common goal or set of goals. Manufacturing and service firms are organizations, and so are schools, hospitals, churches, military units, retail stores, police departments, volunteer organizations, start-ups, and local, provincial, and federal government agencies. Inner City Renovation (ICR), the company discussed in this chapter's vignette, is a for-profit organization, but its partners are nonprofit organizations. Thus, when we say "organization" throughout this textbook, we are referring not only to large manufacturing firms but also to small mom-and-pop stores, as well as to the variety of other forms of organization that exist. Businesses that employ no more than 10 people make up 75 percent of the Canadian marketplace. In Canada, small and mid-sized businesses now make up 45 percent of the gross national product, up from 25 percent 20 years ago.[2]

Inner City Renovation
www.mts.net/~icri/

Hudsons Bay Company
www.hbc.com/hbc/

Air Canada
www.aircanada.com

Do you know what a "typical" organization looks like?

The examples in this textbook present various organizations so that you gain a better understanding of the many types that exist. Though you might not have considered this before, the college or university you attend is every bit as much a "real" organization as is Hudson's Bay Company or Air Canada or the Toronto Raptors. A small for-profit organization that hires unskilled workers to renovate and build in the inner city of Winnipeg is as much a real organization as is London, Ontario-based EllisDon, one of North America's largest construction companies. Therefore, the theories we cover should be considered in light of the variety of organizations you may encounter. We try to point out instances where the theory may be less applicable (or especially applicable) to a particular type of organization. For the most part, however, you should expect that the discussions in this textbook apply across the broad spectrum of organizations. Throughout, we highlight applications to a variety of organizations in our feature *OB in the Workplace*.

OB Is for Everyone

It might seem natural to think that the study of OB is for leaders and managers of organizations. After all, they often set the agenda for everyone else. However, many organizations also have informal leadership opportunities. As employees are asked to move beyond their traditional function of providing labour and play a more proactive role in achieving organizational success, the roles of managers and employees are becoming blurred in many organizations.[3] Managers are increasingly asking employees to share in their decision-making processes rather than simply follow orders. For instance, employees in some retail operations can make decisions about when to accept returned items, rather than defer the decision to the manager.

OB is not just for managers and employees. Entrepreneurs and self-employed individuals may not act as managers, but they certainly interact with other individuals and organizations as part of their work. OB applies equally well to all situations in which you interact with others: on the basketball court, at the grocery store, in school, or in church. In fact, OB is relevant anywhere that people come together and share experiences, work on goals, or meet to solve problems. To help you understand these broader connections, you will find throughout the textbook a feature called *OB in the Street*. This chapter's *CBC Video Case* helps you consider why OB is important for young entrepreneurs.

Under 21 and Self-Employed

Today's Challenges in the Canadian Workplace

Inner City Renovation (ICR) employees are different from many typical for-profit organizations.[4] Forty-seven percent have not completed high school, 58 percent have criminal records, 79 percent were unemployed before being hired by ICR, and 37 percent had not held a job for more than two years. Employees often have had jobs that last only a few days to a month; 26 percent have held 30 jobs or more. The lives of these employees are characterized by unstable employment, and thus, within the first year of employment at ICR, 42 percent were not able to work because of domestic or family issues.

Because many of its employees lack job experience, ICR needed to establish a culture that would motivate employees to show up for work. Managers recognized the need to create a supportive work environment for its employees.

Many of ICR's employees are Aboriginal peoples. To better understand the needs of these and its other employees, ICR managers conducted a formal survey of all employees and had a staff retreat near the end of the first year of operation. Because of the large number of Aboriginal peoples employed by ICR, the retreat incorporated certain Aboriginal traditions in its events. All discussions were held in a circle format, and the retreat included a sweat (a ceremony for meditation and cleansing). In addition, employees had one-on-one meetings with the ICR president and the employee support worker.

ICR is a very committed employer. The company wants to change the life circumstances of its employees. What factors affect employee motivation? How can ICR socialize its employees to perform well in their jobs? How can ICR survive in the face of competition while maintaining its goal of employing people with limited skills and experience?

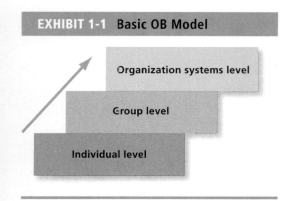

EXHIBIT 1-1 Basic OB Model

Organization systems level

Group level

Individual level

2 What challenges do managers and employees face in today's workplace?

OB considers that organizations are made up of individuals, groups, and the entire organizational structure. Each of these units represents a different level within an organization, moving from the smallest unit, the individual, to the largest, the entire organization. Each level contributes to the variety of activities that occur in today's workplace. Exhibit 1-1 presents the three levels of analysis we consider in this textbook, and shows that as we move from the individual level to the organization systems level, we deepen our understanding of behaviour in organizations. The three basic levels are like building blocks: Each level is constructed upon the previous level. Group concepts grow out of the foundation we laid out in the section on individual behaviour. We then overlay structural constraints on the individual and group in order to arrive at OB.

When we look at the different levels in the organization, we recognize that each has challenges that can affect how the levels above and/or below might operate. We consider the challenges at the individual, group, and organizational levels.

Challenges at the Individual Level

At the individual level, managers and employees need to learn how to work with people who may be different from themselves on a variety of dimensions, including personality, perception, values, and attitudes. This point is illustrated by the employee situation at ICR, where employees have a variety of experiences and come from several cultures.

Individuals also have different levels of job satisfaction and motivation, and these affect how managers manage employees. For instance, some of ICR's employees had drug and alcohol dependencies that affected their motivation and productivity. More organizations expect individuals to be empowered, with employees being asked to take on more responsibility than ever before. This expectation puts demands on both managers and employees. ICR initially created three committees where employees could give input on a variety of issues, but the managers were so busy trying to make sure the company met financial goals that they didn't have time to help the employees work on these committees.

Perhaps the greatest challenge facing individuals (and organizations) is how to behave ethically, as the findings from the Gomery Commission show.

Individual Differences

People enter groups and organizations with certain characteristics that influence their behaviour, the more obvious of these being personality characteristics, perception, values, and attitudes. These characteristics are essentially intact when an individual joins an organization, and for the most part, there is little that those in the organization can do to alter them. Yet they have a very real impact on behaviour. In this light, we look at perception, personality, values, and attitudes, and their impact on individual behaviour in Chapters 2 and 3.

Job Satisfaction

Does job satisfaction really make a difference?

Employees are increasingly demanding satisfaction out of their jobs. As we discuss in Chapter 3, overall job satisfaction in the Canadian workplace is relatively high. The belief that satisfied employees are more productive than dissatisfied employees has been a basic assumption among managers for years. Although some evidence questions that causal relationship,[5] it can be argued that society should be concerned not only with the quantity of life—that is, with con-

cerns such as higher productivity and material acquisitions—but also with its quality. Researchers with
strong humanistic values argue that satisfaction is a
legitimate objective of an organization. They believe
that organizations should be responsible for providing employees with jobs that are challenging and
intrinsically rewarding. This chapter's *Ethical Dilemma
Exercise* on page 25 questions the extent to which
organizations should be responsible for helping individuals achieve balance in their life.

Job satisfaction is also of concern because it is
negatively related to absenteeism and turnover,
which cost organizations considerable amounts of
money annually.

Toronto-based Royal Bank of Canada, Canada's largest financial institution in terms of assets, commands the respect of many business leaders. In a 2004 KPMG/Ipsos-Reid poll of 263 Canadian CEOs, the company was ranked first in six of nine categories, including "Top of Mind Most Respected," "Best Long-Term Investment Value," and "Human Resource Management."

Motivation

An Angus Reid survey showed that 29 percent of
employees do not feel they receive fair or reasonable
rewards for the work that they do.[6] To address this
concern, Chapter 4 discusses the importance of
rewards in motivating employees, while Chapter 5
describes specific rewards that can be used in the workplace. You may find the discussion of motivation and rewards particularly interesting in *Case Incident—How a UPS
Manager Cut Turnover* on page 26, where a manager faces the challenges of motivating
different types of employees in order to reduce turnover.

Empowerment

At the same time that managers are being held responsible for employee satisfaction
and happiness, they are also being asked to share more of their power. If you read any
popular business periodical nowadays, you will find that managers are referred to as
coaches, advisers, sponsors, or facilitators, rather than bosses.[7]

Employees' responsibilities are similarly increasing. In many organizations, employees have become "associates" or "teammates,"[8] and the roles of managers and workers
have blurred. Decision making is being pushed down to the operating level, where
employees solve work-related problems and are being given the freedom to make choices
about schedules and procedures.

*Are you ready
to assume more
responsibility at
work?*

In the 1980s, managers were encouraged to involve their
employees in work-related decisions.[9] Now, managers are
going considerably further by providing employees with full
control of their work. Self-managed teams, in which employees operate largely without managers, became the rage in the
1990s.[10] This trend of teamwork and employee responsibility has continued into the twenty-first century. (To help you
understand how to perform better as a team player, we discuss
the dynamics of teams in Chapter 6.)

What's going on is that managers are empowering employees. **Empowerment** means
managers are giving employees more responsibility for what they do. In the process, managers are learning how to give up control, and employees are learning how to take responsibility for their work and make appropriate decisions. The roles for both managers and
employees are changing, often without much guidance on how to perform the new functions.

empowerment Giving employees responsibility for what they do.

How widespread are these changes in the workplace? While we have no specific
Canadian data, a survey by the American Management Association of 1040 executives

found that 46 percent of their companies were still operating within a hierarchical structure, but 31 percent defined their companies as empowered.[11] *OB in the Workplace* looks at how WestJet Airlines empowers its employees.

OB IN THE WORKPLACE

WestJet Airlines' Employees Work Together

What do empowered employees do? Calgary-based WestJet Airlines employees are given lots of freedom to manage themselves.[12] Clive Beddoe, the company's president and CEO, was determined to create a company "where people wanted to manage themselves."

At WestJet, employees are asked to be responsible for their tasks, rather than rely on supervisors to tell them what to do. That includes Beddoe: "I don't direct things," he says. "We set some standards and expectations, but [I] don't interfere in how our people do their jobs." Instead, employees are given guidelines for behaviour. For instance, flight attendants are directed to serve customers in a caring, positive, and cheerful manner. How do they carry that out? It's up to them. Employees also share tasks. When a plane lands, all employees on the flight, even those who are flying off-duty, are expected to prepare the plane for its next takeoff.

Obviously, WestJet can lower its costs by keeping the number of supervisors down. The company operates with about 59 people per aircraft, while a typical full-service airline such as Air Canada needs more than 140. But allowing employees to manage themselves has a bigger benefit. Beddoe believes it encourages employees to take pride in what they do. "They are the ones making the decisions about what they're doing and how they're doing it," says Beddoe.

Throughout the textbook you will find references to empowerment. We discuss it in terms of power in Chapter 8, and how leaders contribute to empowerment in Chapter 11.

Behaving Ethically

In an organizational world characterized by cutbacks, expectations of increasing worker productivity, and tough competition in the marketplace, it's not altogether surprising that many employees feel pressured to cut corners, break rules, and engage in other forms of questionable practices.

The Enron scandal in the United States illustrated how casually some people treat the subject of ethics. Enron executives creatively changed how they reported their profits and losses. When challenged, the company's chair, Kenneth Lay, chose to look the other way. The reputation of accounting firm Arthur Andersen was destroyed because the firm failed to question Enron's accounting practices.

ethics The study of moral values or principles that guide our behaviour and inform us whether actions are right or wrong.

Ethics starts at the individual level. **Ethics** is the study of moral values or principles that guide our behaviour, and informs us whether actions are right or wrong. Ethical principles help us "do the right thing," such as not padding expense reports, or not phoning in sick to attend the opening of *Revenge of the Sith*.

As we show in Chapter 12, the study of ethics does not come with black and white answers. Rather, many factors need to be considered in determining the ethical thing to do. Those individuals who strive hard to create their own set of ethical values and those organizations that encourage an ethical climate in the face of financial and other pressures will more often do the right thing.

Throughout this textbook you will find references to ethical and unethical behaviour. The *Focus on Ethics* feature will provide you with thought-provoking illustrations of how ethics is treated in various organizations.

Challenges at the Group Level

What people-related challenges have you observed in the organizations in which you have worked?

The behaviour of people in a group is more than the sum total of all the individuals acting in their own way. People's behaviour when they are in a group differs from their behaviour when they are alone. Therefore, the next step in developing an understanding of OB is the study of group behaviour.

Chapter 6 lays the foundation for an understanding of the dynamics of group and team behaviour. That chapter discusses how individuals are influenced by the patterns of behaviour they are expected to exhibit, what the team considers to be acceptable standards of behaviour, and how to make teams more effective.

Chapters 7, 8, and 9 examine some of the more complex issues of interaction, including communication, power and politics, and conflict and negotiation. These chapters give you an opportunity to think about how communication processes sometimes become complicated because of office politicking and interpersonal and group conflict.

Few people work entirely alone, and some organizations make widespread use of teams. Therefore, most individuals interact with others during the workday. This can lead to a need for greater interpersonal skills. The workplace is also made up of people from a variety of different backgrounds. Thus, learning how to work with people from different cultures has become more important. We discuss some of the challenges that occur at the group level below.

Working With Others

Much of the success in any job involves developing good interpersonal, or "people," skills. In fact, the Conference Board of Canada identified the skills that form the foundation for a high quality workforce in today's workplace as communication, thinking, learning, and working with others. Positive attitudes and behaviours and an ability to take responsibility for one's actions are also key skills, according to the Conference Board.[13] Because many people will work in small and medium-sized firms in the future, Human Resources and Skills Development Canada has noted that additional important skills are team building and priority management.[14]

In Canada's increasingly competitive and demanding workplace, neither managers nor employees can succeed on their technical skills alone. They must also have good people skills. Management professor Jin Nam Choi of McGill University reports that research shows 40 percent of managers either leave or stop performing within 18 months of starting at an organization "because they have failed to develop relationships with bosses, colleagues or subordinates."[15] Choi's comment underscores the importance of developing interpersonal skills. This textbook has been written to help you develop those people skills, whether as an employee, manager, or potential manager. It has also been written to help you think about group behaviour from an OB perspective.

To learn more about the interpersonal skills needed in today's workplace, read *From Concepts to Skills* on pages 28–30.

Conference Board of Canada
www.conferenceboard.ca

Workforce Diversity

Why should you care about understanding other people?

The ability to adapt to many different people is one of the most important and broad-based challenges facing organizations. The term we use to describe this challenge is *workforce diversity*. **Workforce diversity** arises because organizations are becoming more heterogeneous, employing a greater variety of people in terms of gender, race, ethnicity, sexual orientation, and age. A diverse workforce, for instance, includes women, Aboriginal peoples, Asian Canadians, African Canadians, Indo-Canadians,

workforce diversity The mix of people in organizations in terms of gender, race, ethnicity, disability, sexual orientation, age, and demographic characteristics such as education and socio-economic status.

people with disabilities, gays and lesbians, and senior citizens. It also includes people with different demographic characteristics, such as education and socio-economic status. We discuss workforce diversity issues in Chapter 3.

One of the challenges in Canadian workplaces is the mix of generations—the Elders, Baby Boomers, Generation Xers, and the Net Generation work side by side. Due to their very different life experiences, they bring to the workplace different values and different expectations.

Workforce diversity is also an issue in the United States, Australia, South Africa, Japan, and Europe. The increase in female employment drives some of that diversity. However, immigration patterns and relatively open national borders in some countries have also led to changes in workforce diversity. For instance, the creation of the European Union, which opened up borders throughout much of Western Europe, has increased workforce diversity in organizations that operate in countries such as Germany, Portugal, Italy, and France.

Haven't organizations always included members of diverse groups? Yes, but they were a small percentage of the workforce and were, for the most part, ignored by large organizations. For instance, before the 1980s, the Canadian workforce was composed predominantly of male Caucasians working full-time to support nonemployed wives and school-aged children. Now such employees make up far less of the workplace. By 2010, white males will account for even fewer of the new labour-force entrants as visible minorities increase their participation in the workplace.

We used to assume that people in organizations who differed from the stereotypical employee would somehow simply fit in. We now recognize that employees don't set aside their cultural values and lifestyle preferences when they go to work. The challenge for organizations, therefore, is to accommodate diverse groups of people by addressing their different lifestyles, family needs, and work styles.[16] However, what motivates one person may not motivate another. One person may like a straightforward and open style of communication that another finds uncomfortable and threatening. To work effectively with different people, you'll need to understand their culture and how it has shaped them, and learn to adapt your interaction style.

The *Focus on Diversity* feature found throughout the textbook highlights diversity issues that arise in organizations. Our first example looks at accommodations made to help Aboriginal cadets feel welcome at the RCMP training academy in Regina.

FOCUS ON **DIVERSITY**

Bringing Aboriginal Culture to the RCMP

How does a Heritage Room promote RCMP diversity? At opening ceremonies for the Aboriginal Heritage Room in the RCMP's Regina training academy, sweet-smelling smoke from burning buffalo sage cleansed the air.[17] With cedar walls, Plains Indian artifacts, and reproductions of old photographs of Aboriginal Canadians, this is not a typical room in a police academy.

The Heritage Room was set up in 2000 to help Aboriginal cadets engage in spiritual practices while they train. They can now hold ceremonies, meet with elders, and discuss their culture in the Heritage Room. Dustin Ward, a cadet from the Mi'qmaq reserve in New Brunswick, praised the opening of the room as "one more sign that the RCMP welcomes First Nations Mounties. It shows the children hope that they can come here some day and be an RCMP cadet."

The Heritage Room is one of a series of RCMP programs to encourage diversity. In the late 1980s the RCMP decided to allow Aboriginal Mounties to wear their hair in braids, if they wanted. Saskatchewan-born Aboriginal Pauline Busch, who helped get the Heritage Room opened, remembered that decision. "There's nothing that warms a child's heart and pride as seeing another Aboriginal person in the red serge, fully outlined with the braids." 🏃

Workforce diversity has important implications for management practice. Managers need to shift their philosophy from treating everyone alike to recognizing differences. They need to respond to those differences in ways that will ensure employee retention and greater productivity, while at the same time not discriminating against certain groups. This shift includes, for instance, providing diversity training and revising benefit programs to be more "family-friendly." At ICR, managers brought in a part-time social support worker to help new employees adjust to full-time employment. Many of ICR's employees faced family issues, domestic disputes, and substance abuse issues that made it difficult for them to meet work responsibilities. The support worker helped individual employees develop steps to deal with personal issues.

Diversity, if positively managed, can increase creativity and innovation in organizations, as well as improve decision making by providing different perspectives on problems.[18] When diversity is not managed properly, there is potential for higher turnover, miscommunication, and more interpersonal conflicts.

Challenges at the Organizational Level

OB becomes more complex when we move to the organizational level of analysis. Just as groups are not just the sum of individuals, organizations are not the sum of individuals and groups. There are many more interacting factors that place constraints on individual and group behaviour. In Chapter 10 we look at organizational culture, which is generally considered the glue that holds organizations together. In Chapter 11 we consider how leadership and management affect employee behaviour. In Chapter 12 we discuss decision making and creativity, and then look at the issues of ethics and corporate social responsibility.

The design of an organization has a big impact on how effective an organization is, and we discuss organizational design in Chapter 13. If the organization is not effective, change may be in order, a topic we consider in Chapter 14. As we have noted already, and as will become clear throughout the textbook, change has become a key issue for organizations.

Canadian businesses face many challenges in the twenty-first century. Their ability to be as productive as US businesses is constantly tested. The need to develop effective, committed employees is critical. Meanwhile, Canadian businesses face greater competition because of the global economy. Many companies have expanded their operations overseas, which means they have to learn how to manage people from different cultures.

Productivity

An organization or group is productive if it achieves its goals and does so by transferring inputs (employee labour, materials used to produce goods) to outputs (finished goods or services) at the lowest cost.

Productivity implies a concern for both **effectiveness** and **efficiency**. A hospital, for example, is *effective* when it successfully meets the needs of its clientele. It is efficient when it can do so at a low cost. If a hospital manages to achieve higher output from its present staff—say, by reducing the average number of days a patient is confined to a bed, or by increasing the number of staff-patient contacts per day—we say that the hospital has gained productive *efficiency*. Similarly, a student team is effective when it puts together a group project that gets a high mark. It is efficient when all the members manage their time appropriately and aren't at each other's throats. ICR faced effectiveness issues because it started out by having one team leader for three work teams. On

productivity A performance measure including effectiveness and efficiency.

effectiveness The achievement of goals.

efficiency The ratio of effective work output to the input required to produce the work.

paper, this appeared to be an efficient strategy. However, each team needed more supervision than the manager could provide while trying to manage three teams, which decreased each team's productivity. Therefore, ICR's strategy wasn't effective.

As you study OB, you will begin to understand those factors that influence the effectiveness and efficiency of individuals, groups, and the overall organization.

Developing Effective Employees

One of the major challenges facing organizations in the twenty-first century is how to engage employees effectively so that they are committed to the organization. We use the term **organizational citizenship behaviour (OCB)** to describe discretionary behaviour that is not part of an employee's formal job requirements, but that nevertheless promotes the effective functioning of the organization.[19] Recent research has also looked at expanding the work on OCB to team behaviour.[20]

Successful organizations need employees who will go beyond their usual job duties, providing performance that is beyond expectations. In today's dynamic workplace, where tasks are increasingly done in teams and where flexibility is critical, organizations need employees who will engage in "good citizenship" behaviours, such as making constructive statements about their work group and the organization, helping others on their team, volunteering for extra job activities, avoiding unnecessary conflicts, showing care for organizational property, respecting the spirit as well as the letter of rules and regulations, and gracefully tolerating the occasional work-related impositions and nuisances.

Toronto-based BBDO Canada encourages an entrepreneurial spirit as a way of inspiring organizational citizenship behaviour. The ad agency's president and CEO, Gerry Frascione, notes that a team leader on the Campbell Soup account overheard a Campbell's representative musing about a program that would launch Campbell's Soup ads when the temperature dipped. "Instead of waiting to get approvals, she acted very entrepreneurially and took it upon herself and made the whole thing happen in one week," says Frascione. "She went back to the client, analyzed the situation, fleshed out the opportunity, came up with an integrated communication plan, came up with a budget, and it was all done within five days."[21]

Organizations want and need employees who will do those things that aren't in any job description. And the evidence indicates that organizations that have such employees outperform those that don't.[22] As a result, OB is concerned with organizational citizenship behaviour.

Putting People First

Professor Jeffery Pfeffer of the Stanford Graduate School of Business advocates that managers should spend more time recognizing the value of the people who work for them. He emphasizes the need to "put people first" in considering organizational objectives and suggests the people-first strategy not only generates a committed workforce, but also significantly affects the bottom line.[23] Pfeffer notes that research shows that when organizations concern themselves with developing their employees, they are more successful. For instance, a study of 968 US firms found that those that used people-first strategies had significantly less turnover, and significantly greater sales, market value, and profits.[24] Similar results were found in a study of 100 German companies.[25]

Pfeffer explains that people will work harder when they feel they have "more control and say in their work." They work smarter when they are "encouraged to build skills and competence." They work more responsibly when "responsibility is placed in the hands of employees farther down in the organization." *OB in Action—Practices of Successful Organizations* outlines the practices that successful people-first organizations use to encourage their employees to work harder, smarter, and more responsibly. *Case Incident—Great Plains Software: Pursuing a People-First Strategy* on page 27 asks you to consider the impact of "putting people first" in managing an organization.

organizational citizenship behaviour (OCB) Discretionary behaviour that is not part of an employee's formal job requirements, but that nevertheless promotes the effective functioning of the organization.

BBDO Canada
www.bbdo.ca

Global Competition

In recent years, Canadian businesses have faced tough competition from the United States, Europe, Japan, and even China, as well as from other companies within our borders. To survive, they have had to reduce costs, increase productivity, and improve quality. A number of Canadian companies have found it necessary to merge in order to survive. For instance, Rona, the Boucherville, Quebec-based home improvement store, bought out Lansing, Revy, and Revelstoke in recent years in order to defend its turf against the Atlanta, Georgia-based Home Depot. That may not be enough to keep it from being swallowed up by the Mooresville, North Carolina-based Lowe's home improvement company, however.

Some employers are starting to outsource jobs to other countries, where labour costs are lower. For instance, Toronto-based Dell Canada's technical service lines are handled by technicians working in India. Toronto-based Wall & Associates, a full service chartered accounting and management consulting firm, outsources document management to Uganda. Employees in Uganda are willing to work for $1 an hour to sort and record receipts. While these wages might seem low, on average, Ugandans make only $1 a day.

These changes in the workplace, and the loss of jobs to international outsourcing, mean that the actual jobs that employees perform, and even those of managers to whom employees report, are in a permanent state of flux. To stay employable under these conditions, employees need to continually update their knowledge and skills to meet new job requirements.[26] Today's managers and employees have to learn to live with flexibility, spontaneity, uncertainty, and unpredictability.

The changing and global competitive environment means that not only do individuals have to become increasingly flexible, but organizations do too. They need to learn how to adjust to shifts in demand, technology, and the economy. For example, Burnaby, BC-based George Third & Son fabricates and installs steel structures in Canada and the United States. The company was founded in 1910 and has since undergone a number of changes, including moving into different manufacturing lines. The family-owned company owes its survival to the ability to shift with the times. "Corporate survival has depended on change, a feisty willingness to leap off a cliff," says Rob Third, grandson of the founder, and the individual responsible for production and purchasing. Adds brother Brett, who is in charge of marketing, sales, and administration, "We need to make changes to keep going in the business."[27]

In order to make the changes that need to be made, organizations and people must be committed to learning new skills, new ways of thinking, and new ways of doing business.

Managing and Working in a Multicultural World

Twenty or 30 years ago, national borders insulated most firms from foreign competitive pressures. This is no longer the case. Trading blocks such as the North American Free Trade Agreement (NAFTA) and the European Union (EU) have significantly reduced tariffs and barriers to trade, and North America and Europe no longer have a monopoly on highly skilled labour. The Internet has also enabled companies to become more globally connected, by opening up international sales and by increasing the opportunities to carry on business. Even small firms can bid on projects in different countries and compete with larger firms via the Internet.

OB IN ACTION

Practices of Successful Organizations

According to professor Jeffery Pfeffer of the Stanford Graduate School of Business, the following practices characterize organizations that benefit from how they manage their employees:

→ Providing **employment security** so that employees don't fear loss of jobs

→ **Hiring** people who have the **right skills and abilities**

→ Creating **self-managed teams** that have decision-making power

→ **Paying well**, and tying pay to organizational performance

→ Providing **extensive training** for skills, knowledge, and initiative

→ Reducing status differences so that **all employees feel valued**

→ **Sharing information** about organizational performance

Source: Adapted from J. Pfeffer and J. F. Veiga, "Putting People First for Organizational Success," *Academy of Management Executive* 13, no. 2 (May 1999), pp. 37–48.

Rona
www.rona.ca

Dell Canada
www.dell.ca

Wall & Associates
www.wallca.com

George Third & Son
www.geothird.com

The world has truly become a global village. Tim Hortons, considered a Canadian icon, was bought by Wendy's International in 1995, and is now American-owned. McDonald's Canada opened the first McDonald's restaurant in Moscow. New employees at Finland-based phone maker Nokia are increasingly being recruited from India, China, and other developing countries—with non-Finns now outnumbering Finns at Nokia's renowned research centre in Helsinki. All major automobile manufacturers now build cars outside their borders: Toyota and Honda build cars in Ontario; Ford in Brazil; and both Mercedes and BMW in South Africa. Hitachi Canadian Industries in Saskatoon produces power-generating equipment components for its local market and supplies parts to the parent company in Japan.

The message? As multinational corporations develop operations worldwide, as companies develop joint ventures with foreign partners, and as employees increasingly pursue job opportunities across national borders, managers and employees must become capable of working with people from different cultures. Managing people well and understanding the interpersonal dynamics of the workplace are issues not just for companies operating in Canada.

When individuals travel to other countries to work, they may be confronted with practices different from what they're used to at home. This may present challenges, but it might also offer chances to learn from other cultures. Professor John Eggers of the Richard Ivey School of Business at the University of Western Ontario has commented on how doing business in Asia is different in some ways from doing business in Canada. He notes, "It is important to remember that business is conducted through relationships much more so than it is in Western countries. It takes years to form and develop the relationships a company needs, and to build the trust necessary to do business. Business in Asia is conducted courteously and respectfully, and at a slower pace—foreign managers who do not act in a polite manner will not be well received."[28]

The *OB Around the Globe* feature found throughout the textbook illustrates the similarities and differences of organizations throughout the world. The first such feature looks at the South African concept of *ubuntu*, or humaneness, and how it guides management activity in that country.

OB AROUND THE GLOBE

South Africa's *Ubuntu*

What happens when "youngsters" try to manage in South Africa? Values of efficiency, productivity, and increased output may drive North American firms, but they are at odds with the South African notion of *ubuntu*. *Ubuntu* is a concept that emphasizes group well-being and social harmony.[29]

A major industrial company in South Africa failed to consider *ubuntu* when it developed a training program to encourage Black employees to become managers. The first men through the program were 20 to 24 years old, and they performed well. However, when they were assigned to management positions, some individuals refused to work for them. After questioning the employees more, senior management found that older men do not work for "youngsters." The company had violated informal norms of the group by not respecting the importance of age for this culture.

Expectations about how management should be carried out are also different. An African manager who was trained in a more characteristic "Western" manner was called before his tribal elders for treating the workers as employees rather than as "brothers and sisters." 🕴

The importance of *ubuntu* in South Africa and the absence of an equivalent concept in North America underscores that behaviour and expectations are different across the world. Many of the theories that we present have been developed in North America, particularly in the United States. Therefore, we critically examine their applicability in non-North American settings throughout this textbook.

OB: MAKING SENSE OF BEHAVIOUR IN ORGANIZATIONS

The managers at Inner City Renovation (ICR) quickly noticed that some of their employees had special challenges, such as their unemployment rates, their inconsistent job records, and their low education levels.[30] Managers interviewed employees about their career interests and their needs for skill development. In addition, employees have had one-on-one meetings with the ICR president and the employee support worker. Interviews and meetings are ways of gathering data on employee behaviour. While ICR managers are not researchers, they understand the need for doing some research on their employees. How is OB research carried out, and in what areas does it apply?

We have thus far considered how OB can be applied in the workplace. In this next section we consider the discipline of OB, looking first at the fields of study that have contributed to it. We then discuss the fact that OB is a scientific discipline, with careful research that is conducted to test and evaluate theories.

3 Isn't organizational behaviour common sense? Or just like psychology?

The Building Blocks of OB

OB emerged as a distinct field in the 1940s in the United States.[31] It is an applied behavioural science that is built upon contributions from a number of behavioural disciplines. The predominant areas are psychology, sociology, social psychology, anthropology, and political science.[32] As we will learn, psychology's contributions have been mainly at the individual or micro-level of analysis. The other four disciplines have contributed to our understanding of macro concepts, such as group processes and organization. Exhibit 1-2 presents an overview of the major contributions to the study of OB.

Psychology

Psychology is the science that seeks to measure, explain, and sometimes change the behaviour of humans and other animals. Psychologists concern themselves with studying and attempting to understand individual behaviour. Those who have contributed and continue to add to the knowledge of OB are learning theorists, personality theorists, counselling psychologists, and, most important, industrial and organizational psychologists.

Early industrial and organizational psychologists concerned themselves with problems of fatigue, boredom, and other factors relevant to working conditions that could impede efficient work performance. More recently, their contributions have been expanded to include learning, perception, personality, emotions, training, leadership effectiveness, needs and motivational forces, job satisfaction, decision-making processes, performance appraisals, attitude measurement, employee selection techniques, work design, and work stress.

Sociology

Whereas psychologists focus their attention on the individual, sociologists study the social system in which individuals fill their roles; that is, sociology studies people in relation to their fellow human beings. Specifically, sociologists have made their

EXHIBIT 1-2 **Toward an OB Discipline**

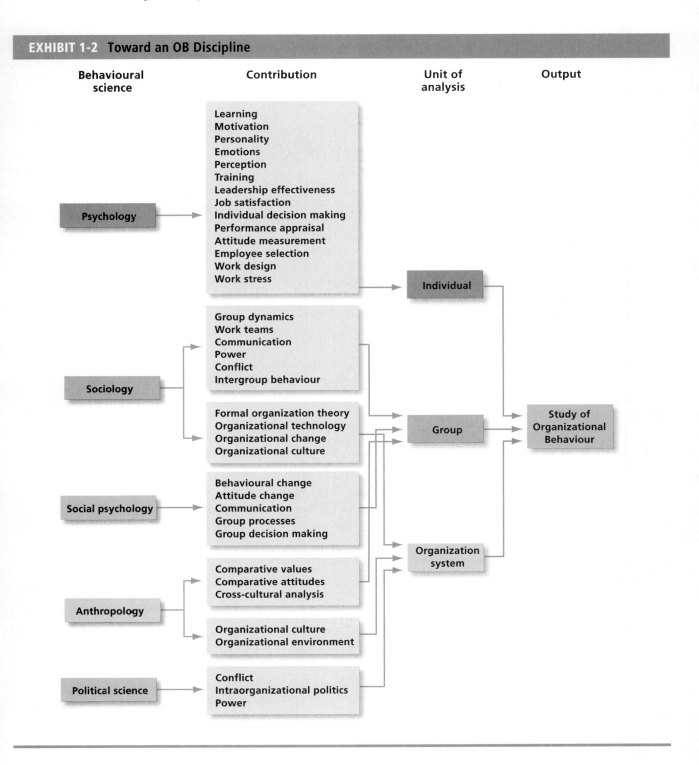

greatest contribution to OB through their study of group behaviour in organizations, particularly formal and complex organizations. Some of the areas within OB that have received valuable input from sociologists are group dynamics, design of work teams, organizational culture, formal organization theory and structure, organizational technology, communication, power, and conflict.

Social Psychology

Social psychology is an area within psychology, blending concepts from both psychology and sociology. It focuses on the influence of people on one another. One of the

Facing anticapitalism backlash from human rights and environmental activists, ExxonMobil hired anthropologist Ellen Brown (left) to help the company while building a 1000-kilometre pipeline in Africa, from Chad to Cameroon. Brown visits hundreds of villages, explaining to locals how the pipeline will affect them. She helps oversee a $1.5-million ExxonMobil initiative to build schools, fund health clinics, dig wells, advise local entrepreneurs, field an AIDS education van, and distribute anti-malaria mosquito nets.

major areas receiving considerable investigation from social psychologists has been change—how to implement it and how to reduce barriers to its acceptance. Additionally, we find social psychologists making significant contributions in such areas as communication patterns; group decision-making processes; measuring, understanding, and changing attitudes; and the ways in which group activities can satisfy individual needs.

Anthropology

Anthropology is the study of societies to learn about human beings and their activities. Anthropologists' work on cultures and environments, for instance, has helped us understand differences in fundamental values, attitudes, and behaviour between people in different countries and within different organizations. Much of our current understanding of organizational culture, organizational environments, and differences between national cultures is the result of the work of anthropologists or those using their methodologies.

Political Science

Although frequently overlooked, the contributions of political scientists are significant to the understanding of behaviour in organizations. Political science studies the behaviour of individuals and groups within a political environment. Specific topics of concern here include structuring of conflict, allocation of power, and how people manipulate power for individual self-interest.

The Rigour of OB

Whether you want to respond to the challenges of the Canadian workplace, manage well, or guarantee satisfying and rewarding employment for yourself, it pays to understand organizational behaviour. OB provides a systematic approach to the study of behaviour in organizations. Underlying this systematic approach is the belief that behaviour is not random. It stems from and is directed toward some end that the individual believes, rightly or wrongly, is in his or her best interest.

OB Looks at Consistencies

Certainly there are differences among individuals. Placed in similar situations, all people don't act exactly alike. However, there are certain fundamental consistencies underlying the behaviour of most individuals that can be identified and then modified to reflect individual differences.

These fundamental consistencies are very important because they allow predictability. When you get into your car, you make some definite and usually highly accurate predictions about how other people will behave. In North America, for instance, you predict that other drivers will stop at stop signs and red lights, drive on the right side of the road, pass on your left, and not cross the solid double line on mountain roads. Your predictions about the behaviour of people behind the wheels of their cars are almost always correct. Obviously, the rules of driving make predictions about driving behaviour fairly easy.

What may be less obvious is that there are rules (written and unwritten) in almost every setting. Therefore, it can be argued that it's possible to predict behaviour (undoubtedly, not always with 100-percent accuracy) in supermarkets, classrooms, doctors' offices, elevators, and in most structured situations. For instance, do you turn around and face the doors when you get into an elevator? Almost everyone does. Is there a sign inside the elevator that tells you to do this? Probably not! Just as we make predictions about drivers, where there are definite rules of the road, we can make predictions about the behaviour of people in elevators, where there are few written rules. This example supports a major point of this textbook: Behaviour is generally predictable, and the *systematic study* of behaviour is a means to making reasonably accurate predictions.

OB Looks Beyond Common Sense

systematic study The examination of behaviour in order to draw conclusions, based on scientific evidence, about causes and effects in relationships.

When we use the phrase **systematic study**, we mean looking at relationships, attempting to attribute causes and effects, and basing our conclusions on scientific evidence—that is, on data gathered under controlled conditions, and measured and interpreted in a reasonably rigorous manner—rather than relying on common sense. OB uses scientific research to uncover how behaviour works in organizations. Exhibit 1-3 illustrates the common methods researchers use to study topics in OB.

EXHIBIT 1-3   Research Methods in OB

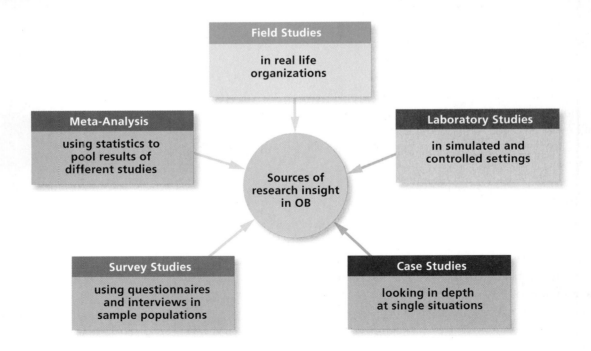

Source: J. R. Schermerhorn, J. G. Hunt, and R. N. Osborn, *Organizational Behavior*, 9th Edition, 2005, p. 4. Copyright © 2005 John Wiley & Sons, Inc. Reprinted with permission of John Wiley & Sons, Inc.

A systematic approach does not mean that those things you have come to believe in an unsystematic way are necessarily incorrect. Some of the conclusions we make in this textbook, based on solid research findings, will support what you always knew was true. You'll also be exposed to research evidence that runs counter to what you might have thought was common sense. In fact, one of the challenges to teaching a subject such as OB is to overcome the notion, held by many, that "it's all common sense."[33]

You'll find that many of the so-called common-sense views you hold about human behaviour are wrong, on closer examination. Moreover, what one person considers common sense frequently runs counter to another's version. Are leaders born or made? What is it that motivates people at work nowadays? You probably have answers to such questions, and individuals who have not reviewed the research are likely to differ on their answers. One of the objectives of this textbook is to expose you to a systematic analysis of behaviour, in the belief that such analysis will improve your accuracy in explaining and predicting behaviour. Therefore, throughout this textbook the *Focus on Research* feature will highlight some of the careful studies that form the building blocks of OB. We have also marked major research findings in every chapter with an icon (shown in the margin at right) so that you can easily see what the research says about various concepts we cover.

If understanding behaviour were simply common sense, we wouldn't observe many of the problems that occur in the workplace, because managers and employees would know how to behave. Unfortunately, as you'll see from examples throughout the textbook, many individuals and managers exhibit less than desirable behaviour in the workplace. With a stronger grounding in OB, you might be able to avoid some of these mistakes. This chapter's *Point/Counterpoint* on page 23 looks at how systematic OB is.

OB Has Few Absolutes

There are few, if any, simple and universal principles that explain OB. In contrast, the physical sciences—chemistry, astronomy, physics—have laws that are consistent and apply in a wide range of situations. They allow scientists to generalize about the pull of gravity or to confidently send astronauts into space to repair satellites. But as one noted behavioural researcher aptly concluded, "God gave all the easy problems to the physicists."

Social scientists study human problems—and human beings are complex. Because they are not alike, our ability to make simple, accurate, and sweeping generalizations is limited. Two people often act very differently in the same situation, and the same person's behaviour changes in different situations.

OB Takes a Contingency Approach

Just because people can behave differently at different times doesn't mean, of course, that we can't offer reasonably accurate explanations of human behaviour or make valid predictions. It does mean, however, that OB must consider behaviour within the context in which it occurs—known as a **contingency approach**. So, for example, OB scholars avoid stating that effective leaders should *always* seek the ideas of their employees before making a decision. Rather, we may find that in some situations a participative style is clearly superior, but, in other situations, an autocratic decision style is more effective. In other words, the effectiveness of a particular leadership style depends upon the situation in which it is used. The OB scholar therefore tries to describe the situations to which each style is suited.

contingency approach An approach taken by OB that considers behaviour within the context in which it occurs.

As you proceed through this textbook, you'll encounter a wealth of research-based theories about how people behave in organizations. You will also discover descriptions of well-designed research studies. But don't expect to find a lot of straightforward cause-and-effect relationships. There aren't many! OB theories mirror the subject matter with which they deal. People are complex and complicated, and so too must be the theories developed to explain their actions.

EXHIBIT 1-4

"I'm a social scientist, Michael. That means I can't explain
electricity or anything like that, but if you ever want to know
about people I'm your man."

Source: Drawing by Handelsman in *The New Yorker*, Copyright © 1986 by the New Yorker Magazine.
Reprinted by permission.

Consistent with the contingency approach, *Point/Counterpoint* debates are provided
in each chapter. These debates are included to highlight the fact that within OB there are
disagreements. By directly addressing some of the more controversial issues using the
Point/Counterpoint format, you gain the opportunity to explore different points of view,
discover how diverse perspectives complement and oppose each other, and gain insight
into some of the debates currently taking place within the OB field.

So in Chapter 5 you'll find the argument that money motivates, followed by the
argument that there is little evidence to support the claim that money is an important
motivator. Similarly, in other chapters you'll read both sides of debates on such controversial issues as whether leaders can be successful in any environment and whether
open communication is always desirable. These arguments are meant to demonstrate
that OB is a lively field and, like many disciplines, has disagreements over specific
findings, methods, and theories. Some of the *Point/Counterpoint* arguments are more
charged than others, but each makes some valid points that you should find thought-
provoking. The key is to be able to decipher under what conditions each argument
may be right or wrong.

SUMMARY AND IMPLICATIONS

1 **What is organizational behaviour?** Organizational behaviour (OB) is a field of
study that investigates the impact that individuals, groups, and structure have on
behaviour within an organization. It uses that knowledge to make organizations
work more effectively. Specifically, OB focuses on how to improve productivity,
reduce both absenteeism and turnover, and increase employee job satisfaction.

OB also helps us understand how people can work together more effectively in the workplace.

OB recognizes differences, helps us see the value of workforce diversity, and calls attention to practices that may need to be changed when managing and working in different countries. It can help improve quality and employee productivity by showing managers how to empower their people, as well as how to design and implement change programs. It offers specific insights to improve people skills.

② What challenges do managers and employees face in today's workplace? OB considers three levels of analysis—the individual, the group, and the organization—which, combined, help us understand behaviour in organizations. Each level has different challenges.

At the individual level, we encounter employees who have different characteristics, and thus we consider how to better understand and make the most of these differences. Because employees have become more cynical about their employers, job satisfaction and motivation have become important issues in today's organizations. Employees are also confronted with the trend toward an empowered workplace. Perhaps the greatest challenge individuals (and organizations) face is how to behave ethically.

At the group level, individuals are increasingly expected to work in teams, which means that they need to do so more effectively. Employees are expected to have good interpersonal skills. The workplace is now made up of people from many different backgrounds, requiring a greater ability to understand those different from ourselves.

At the organizational level, Canadian businesses face many challenges in the twenty-first century. They face ongoing competition from US businesses, as well as growing competition from the global marketplace. Productivity is critical. It has become essential to develop effective employees who are committed to the organization. By putting people first, organizations can generate a committed workforce, but taking this approach becomes a challenge for businesses that focus solely on the bottom line. Organizations also have to learn how to be more sensitive to cultural differences, not only because Canada is an increasingly multicultural country, but also because competitive companies often develop global alliances or set up plants in foreign countries, where being aware of other cultures becomes a key to success.

③ Isn't organizational behaviour common sense? Or just like psychology? OB is built on contributions from a number of behavioural disciplines, including psychology, sociology, social psychology, anthropology, and political science. We all hold generalizations about the behaviour of people. Some of our generalizations may provide valid insights into human behaviour, but many are wrong. If understanding behaviour were simply common sense, we would see fewer problems in the workplace, because managers and employees would know how to behave. OB provides a systematic approach to improving predictions of behaviour that would be made from common sense alone.

For Review

1. Define *organizational behaviour.*

2. What is an organization? Is the family unit an organization? Explain.

3. "Behaviour is generally predictable, so there is no need to formally study OB." Do you agree or disagree with this statement? Why?

4. What are some of the challenges and opportunities that managers face in today's workplace?

5. What are the three levels of analysis in our OB model? Are they related? If so, how?

6. Why is job satisfaction an important consideration for OB?

7. What are effectiveness and efficiency, and how are they related to OB?

8. What does it mean to say OB takes a contingency approach in its analysis of behaviour?

For Critical Thinking

1. "OB is for everyone." Build an argument to support this statement.

2. Why do you think the subject of OB might be criticized as being "only common sense," when we would rarely hear such a criticism of a course in physics or statistics? Do you think this criticism of OB is fair?

3. On a scale of 1 to 10 measuring the sophistication of a scientific discipline in predicting phenomena, mathematical physics would probably be a 10. Where do you think OB would fall on the scale? Why?

4. Can empowerment lead to greater job satisfaction?

OB For You

- As you journey through this course in OB, bear in mind that the processes we describe are as relevant to you as an individual as they are to organizations, managers, and employees.

- When you work together with student teams, join a student organization, or volunteer time to a community group, know that your ability to get along with others has an effect on your interactions with the other people in the group and the achievement of the group's goals.

- If you are aware of how your perceptions and personality affect your interactions with others, you can be more careful in forming your initial impression of others.

- By knowing how to motivate others who are working with you, how to communicate effectively, and when to negotiate and compromise, you can get along in a variety of situations that are not necessarily work-related.

 ## POINT

 ## COUNTERPOINT

| Find the Quick Fix to OB Issues | Beware of the Quick Fix! |

Find the Quick Fix to OB Issues

Walk into your nearest major bookstore. You'll undoubtedly find a large section of books devoted to management and managing human behaviour. A close look at the titles will find there is certainly no shortage of popular books on topics related to OB. To illustrate the point, consider the following book titles that are currently available on the topic of leadership:

The Leadership Secrets of Attila the Hun (Warner, 1990)

Make It So: Leadership Lessons From Star Trek, The Next Generation (Pocket Books, 1996)

The Art of Leadership by Sun Tzu (Premier, 2000)

Power Plays: Shakespeare's Lessons in Leadership and Management (Simon and Schuster, 2000)

The Leadership Teachings of Geronimo (Sterling House, 2002)

Leadership Wisdom From the Monk Who Sold His Ferrari (Hay House, 2003)

Tony Soprano on Management: Leadership Lessons Inspired by America's Favorite Mobster (Berkley, 2004)

Organizations are always looking for leaders; and managers and manager-wannabes are continually looking for ways to improve their leadership skills. Publishers respond to this demand by offering hundreds of titles that claim to provide insights into the complex subject of leadership. People hope that there are "shortcuts" to leadership success and that books like these can provide them with the secrets to leadership that others know about and which they can quickly learn through these books.

Beware of the Quick Fix!

We all want to find quick and simple solutions to our complex problems. But here's the bad news: On problems related to OB, the quick and simple solutions are often wrong because they fail to consider the diversity among organizations, situations, and individuals. As Einstein said, "Everything should be made as simple as possible, but not simpler."

When it comes to trying to understand people at work, there is no shortage of simplistic ideas that books and consultants promote. And these books aren't just on leadership. Consider three recent bestsellers. *Who Moved My Cheese?* is a metaphor about two mice that is meant to convey the benefits of accepting change. *Fish!* tells how a fish market in Seattle made its jobs motivating. And *Whale Done!* proposes that managers can learn a lot about motivating people from techniques used by whale trainers at Sea World in San Diego. Are the "insights" from these books generalizable to people working in hundreds of different countries, in a thousand different organizations, and doing a million different jobs? It's very unlikely.

Popular books on OB often have cute titles and are fun to read. But they can be dangerous. They make the job of managing people seem much simpler than it really is. They are also often based on the author's opinions rather than substantive research.

OB is a complex subject. There are few, if any, simple statements about human behaviour that are generalizable to all people in all situations. Should you really try to apply leadership insights you got from a book on Shakespeare or Attila the Hun to managing software engineers in the twenty-first century?

The capitalist system ensures that when a need exists, opportunistic individuals will surface to fill that need. When it comes to managing people at work, there is clearly a need for valid and reliable insights to guide managers and those aspiring to managerial positions. However, most of the offerings available at your local bookstore tend to be overly simplistic solutions. To the degree that people buy these books and enthusiastically expect them to provide them with the secrets to effective management, they do a disservice to themselves and those they're trying to manage.

LEARNING ABOUT **YOURSELF** EXERCISE

The Competing Values Framework: Identifying Your Interpersonal Skills

From the list below, identify what you believe to be your strongest skills, and then identify those in which you think your performance is weak. You should identify about 4 strong skills and 4 weak skills.

1. Taking initiative	**13.** Understanding yourself and others
2. Goal setting	**14.** Interpersonal communication
3. Delegating effectively	**15.** Developing subordinates
4. Personal productivity and motivation	**16.** Team building
5. Motivating others	**17.** Participative decision making
6. Time and stress management	**18.** Conflict management
7. Planning	**19.** Living with change
8. Organizing	**20.** Creative thinking
9. Controlling	**21.** Managing change
10. Receiving and organizing information	**22.** Building and maintaining a power base
11. Evaluating routine information	**23.** Negotiating agreement and commitment
12. Responding to routine information	**24.** Negotiating and selling ideas

Scoring Key:

These skills are based on the Competing Values Framework (pages 28–30) and they appear in detail in Exhibit 1-6 on page 29. Below, you will see how the individual skills relate to various managerial roles. Using the skills you identified as strongest, identify which roles you feel especially prepared for right now. Then, using the skills you identified as weakest, identify areas in which you might want to gain more skill. You should also use this information to determine whether you are currently more internally or externally focused, or oriented more toward flexibility or control.

Director: 1, 2, 3	Mentor: 13, 14, 15
Producer: 4, 5, 6	Facilitator: 16, 17, 18
Coordinator: 7, 8, 9	Innovator: 19, 20, 21
Monitor: 10, 11, 12	Broker: 22, 23, 24

After reviewing how your strengths and weaknesses relate to the skills that today's managers and leaders need, as illustrated in Exhibit 1-6, you should consider whether you need to develop a broader range of skills.

Source: Created based on material from R. E. Quinn, S. R. Faerman, M. P. Thompson, and M. R. McGrath, *Becoming a Master Manager: A Competency Framework* (New York: John Wiley & Sons, Inc. 1990), Chapter 1.

BREAKOUT **GROUP** EXERCISES

Form small groups to discuss the following topics, as assigned by your instructor:

1. Consider a group situation in which you have worked. To what extent did the group rely on the technical skills of the group members vs. their interpersonal skills? Which skills seemed most important in helping the group function well?

2. Identify some examples of "worst jobs." What conditions of these jobs made them unpleasant? To what extent were these conditions related to behaviours of individuals?

3. Develop a list of "organizational puzzles," that is, behaviour you've observed in organizations that seemed to make little sense. As the term progresses, see if you can begin to explain these puzzles, using your knowledge of OB.

WORKING WITH **OTHERS** EXERCISE

Interpersonal Skills in the Workplace

This exercise asks you to consider the skills outlined in the Competing Values Framework on pages 28–30 to develop an understanding of managerial expertise. Steps 1–4 can be completed in 15–20 minutes.

1. Using the skills listed in the *Learning About Yourself Exercise,* identify the 4 skills that you think all managers should have.

2. Identify the 4 skills that you think are least important for managers to have.

3. In groups of 5–7, reach a consensus on the most-needed and least-needed skills identified in Steps 1 and 2.

4. Using Exhibit 1-6, determine whether your "ideal" managers would have trouble managing in some dimensions of organizational demands.

5. Your instructor will lead a general discussion of your results.

ETHICAL **DILEMMA** EXERCISE

What's the Right Balance Between Work and Personal Life?

When you think of work/life conflicts, you may tend to think of people in lower levels of organizations who might not have as much flexibility in determining their workday. But a recent survey of 179 CEOs revealed that many of them are struggling with this issue. For instance, 31 percent said they have a high level of stress in their lives; 47 percent admitted that they would sacrifice some compensation for more personal time; and 16 percent considered changing jobs in the past 6 months to reduce stress or sacrifices made in their personal lives.

Most of these surveyed executives conceded that they had given up, and continue to give up, a lot to get to the top in their organizations. They're often tired from the extensive and exhausting travel their jobs demand, not to mention an average 60-hour workweek. Yet most feel the climb to the CEO position was worth whatever sacrifices they have had to make.

Jean Stone, while not representative of the group, indicates the price that some of these executives have had to pay. As senior VP and chief operating officer of Dukane Corporation, an Illinois-based manufacturer of electronic communications equipment, Stone describes herself as highly achievement-oriented. She has an intense focus on her job and admits to having lost sight of her personal life. Recently divorced after a 10-year marriage, she acknowledges that "career and work pressures were a factor in that."

How much emphasis on work is *too much*? What's the right balance between work and personal life? How much would you be willing to give up to be CEO of a major com-

pany? And if you were a CEO, what ethical responsibilities, if any, do you think you have to help your employees balance their work/family obligations?

Source: Based on M. J. Critelli, "Striking a Balance," *IndustryWeek*, November 20, 2000, pp. 26–36.

CASE INCIDENTS

How a UPS Manager Cut Turnover

In 1998, Jennifer Shroeger was promoted to district manager for UPS's operation in Buffalo, New York. She was responsible for $225 million in revenue, 2300 employees, and the processing of some 45 000 packages an hour. When she took over in Buffalo, she faced a serious problem: turnover was out of control. Part-time employees—who load, unload, and sort packages and who account for half of Buffalo's workforce—were leaving at the rate of 50 percent a year. Cutting this turnover rate became her highest priority.

The entire UPS organization relies heavily on part-time employees. In fact, it has historically been the primary inroad to becoming a full-time employee. Most of UPS's current executives, for instance, began as part-timers while attending college or university, then moved into full-time positions. In addition, UPS has always treated its part-timers well. They are given high pay, flexible work hours, full benefits, and substantial financial aid to go back to school. Yet these pluses didn't seem to be enough to keep employees at UPS in Buffalo.

Shroeger developed a comprehensive plan to reduce turnover. It focused on improving hiring, communication, the workplace, and supervisory training.

Shroeger began by modifying the hiring process to screen out people who essentially wanted full-time jobs. She reasoned that unfulfilled expectations were frustrating the hires whose preferences were for full-time work. Given that it typically took new part-timers six years to work up to a full-time job, it made sense to try to identify people who actually preferred part-time work.

Next, Shroeger analyzed the large database of information that UPS had on her district's employees. The data led her to the conclusion that she had five distinct groups working for her—differentiated by age and stages in their careers. And these groups had different needs and interests. In response, Shroeger modified the communication style and motivation techniques she used

with each employee to reflect the group to which he or she belonged. For instance, Shroeger found that college students are most interested in building skills that they can apply later in their careers. As long as these employees saw that they were learning new skills, they were content to keep working at UPS. So Shroeger began offering them Saturday classes for computer-skill development and career-planning discussions.

Many new UPS employees in Buffalo were intimidated by the huge warehouse in which they had to work. To lessen that intimidation, Shroeger improved lighting throughout the building and upgraded break rooms to make them more user-friendly. To further help new employees adjust, she turned some of her best shift supervisors into trainers who provided specific guidance during new hires' first week. She also installed more personal computers on the floor, which gave new employees easier access to training materials and human resource information on UPS's internal network.

Finally, Shroeger expanded training so supervisors had the skills to handle increased empowerment. Recognizing that her supervisors—most of whom were part-timers themselves—were the ones best equipped to understand the needs of part-time employees, supervisors learned how to assess difficult management situations, how to communicate in different ways, and how to identify the needs of different people. Supervisors learned to demonstrate interest in their employees as individuals. For instance, they were taught to inquire about employees' hobbies, where they went to school, and the like.

By 2002, Shroeger's program was showing impressive results. Her district's attrition rate had dropped from 50 percent to 6 percent. During the first quarter of 2002, not one part-timer left the night shift. Annual savings attributed to reduced turnover, based largely on lower hiring costs, are estimated to be around $1 million. Additional benefits that the Buffalo district has gained from a more stable workforce include a 20 percent reduction in lost workdays due to work-related injuries and a drop from 4 percent to 1 percent in packages delivered on the wrong day or at the wrong time.

Questions

1. In dollars-and-cents' terms, why did Jennifer Shroeger want to reduce turnover?

2. What are the implications from this case for motivating part-time employees?

3. What are the implications from this case for managing in future years when there may be a severe labour shortage?

4. Is it unethical to teach supervisors "to demonstrate interest in their employees as individuals"? Explain.

5. What facts in this case support the argument that OB should be approached from a contingency perspective?

Source: Based on K. H. Hammonds, "Handle with Care," *Fast Company,* August 2002, pp. 103–107.

Great Plains Software: Pursuing a People-First Strategy

Great Plains Software is a success story. It was begun in 1983 and bought in 2000 by Microsoft for $1.5 billion. Management attributes much of its success to the company's people-first strategy.

As the company's CEO, Doug Burgum felt that the company's growth and success could be attributed to three guiding principles. First, make the company such a great place to work that people not only won't want to leave, they'll knock down the door to get in. Second, give employees ownership at every level. Third, let people grow—as professionals and as individuals.

What did Great Plains do to facilitate its people-first culture? Managers point to the company's structure, perks, and its commitment to helping employees develop their skills and leadership. Great Plains had a flat organization structure with a minimal degree of hierarchy. Work was done mostly in teams, and there were no traditional status perks such as executive parking spaces or corner-office suites. There were stock options for everyone, casual dress standards, an on-site daycare centre, and daily extracurricular classes in everything from aerobics to personal finance. But management is most proud of its commitment to the development of its people. The company offered a long list of training and educational opportunities to its employees, run on site and designed to help employees build their skill level. Great Plains' premier training program was called *Leadership Is Everywhere.* It was designed to ensure that the company had people who could assume new leadership roles in a continuously changing environment. The company reinforced class training by placing its workers in departmental teams. At the helm of these teams were "team leaders," whose job it was to help foster their charges' ideas and projects. They also provided one-on-one job coaching and career-planning advice. Nearly all Great Plains employees were given the opportunity to become team leaders.

Burgum more than just increased revenues to support his belief that his people-first strategy works. He also succeeded in keeping employees content. Turnover, for instance, was a minuscule 5 percent a year—far below the information-technology average of 18 to 25 percent.

Questions

1. Putting people first worked for Great Plains. If the strategy is so effective, why do you think all firms haven't adopted these practices?

2. Do you think a people-first approach is more applicable to certain businesses or industries than others? If so, what might they be? Why?

3. What downside, if any, do you see in being an employee at a company like Great Plains?

4. What downside, if any, do you see in managing at a company like Great Plains?

5. Some critics have argued that "People-first policies don't lead to high profits. High profits allow people-first policies." Do you agree? Explain your position.

Source: Based on S. Boehle, "From Humble Roots," *Training,* October 2000, pp. 106–113.

From **Concepts**
            to **Skills**

Developing Interpersonal Skills

We note in the chapter that having a broad range of inter-personal skills to draw on makes us more effective organizational participants. So what kinds of interpersonal skills does an individual need in today's workplace? Robert Quinn, Kim Cameron, and their colleagues have developed a model known as the "Competing Values Framework" that can help us identify some of the most useful skills.[34] They note that the range of issues organizations face can be divided along two dimensions: an internal-external and a flexibility-control focus. This is illustrated in Exhibit 1-5. The internal-external dimension refers to the extent that organizations focus on one of two directions: either inwardly, toward employee needs and concerns and/or production processes and internal systems; or outwardly, toward such factors as the marketplace, government regulations, and the changing social, environmental, and technological conditions of the future. The flexibility-control dimension refers to the competing demands of organizations to stay focused on doing what has been done in the past vs. being more flexible in orientation and outlook.

Because organizations face the competing demands shown in Exhibit 1-5, it becomes obvious that managers and employees need a variety of skills to help them function within the various quadrants at different points in time. For instance, the skills needed to operate an efficient assembly-line process are not the same as those needed to scan the environment or to create opportunities in anticipation of changes in the environment. Quinn and his colleagues use the term *master manager* to indicate that successful managers learn and apply skills that will help them manage across the range of organizational demands; at some times moving toward flexibility, at others moving toward control, sometimes being more internally focused, sometimes being more externally driven.[35]

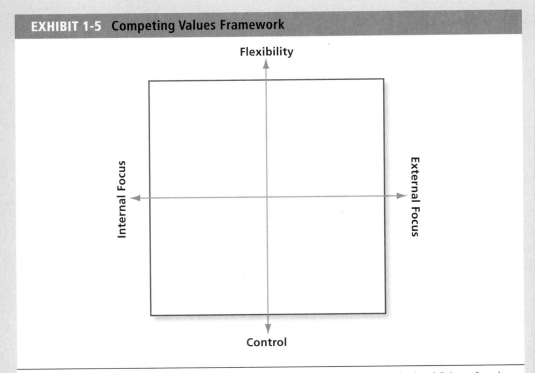

EXHIBIT 1-5   Competing Values Framework

Source: Adapted from K. Cameron and R. E. Quinn, *Diagnosing and Changing Organizational Culture: Based on the Competing Values Framework* (Reading, MA: Addison Wesley Longman, 1999).

As organizations increasingly cut their layers, reducing the number of managers while also relying more on the use of teams in the workplace, the skills of the master manager apply as well to the employee. In other words, considering the "Competing Values Framework," we can see that both managers and individual employees need to learn new skills and new ways of interpreting their organizational contexts. Continuing to use traditional skills and practices that worked in the past is not an option. The growth in self-employment also indicates a need to develop more interpersonal skills, particularly for anyone who goes on to build a business that involves hiring and managing employees.

Exhibit 1-6 outlines the many skills required of today's manager. It gives you an indication of the complex roles that managers and employees fill in the changing workplace. The skills are organized in terms of four major roles: maintaining flexibility, maintaining control, maintaining an external focus, and maintaining an internal focus. The *Learning About Yourself Exercise* on page 24 helps you identify your own strengths and weaknesses in these skill areas so that you can have a better sense of how close you

are to becoming a successful manager. For instance, on the flexibility side, organizations want to inspire their employees toward high-performance behaviour. Such behaviour includes looking ahead to the future and imagining possible new directions for the organization. To do these things, employees need to think and act like mentors and facilitators. It is also important to have the skills of innovators and brokers. On the control side, organizations need to set clear goals about productivity expectations, and they have to develop and implement systems to carry out the production process. To be effective on the production side, employees need to have the skills of monitors, coordinators, directors, and producers. The *Working With Others Exercise* on page 25 helps you better understand how closely your views on the ideal skills of managers and leaders match the skills needed to be successful in the broad range of activities that managers and leaders encounter.

At this point, you may wonder whether it is possible for people to learn all of the skills necessary to become a master manager. More important, you may wonder whether we can change our individual style, say from more controlling

EXHIBIT 1-6   Skills for Mastery in the New Workplace

Source: R. E. Quinn, *Beyond Rational Management* (San Francisco: Jossey-Bass, 1988), p. 86.

OB *AT WORK*

to more flexible. Here's what Peggy Witte, who used to be chair, president, and CEO of the now-defunct Royal Oak Mines, said about how her managerial style changed from controlling to more flexible over time: "I started out being very dictatorial. Everybody in head office reported to me. I had to learn to trust other executives so we could work out problems together."[36] So, while it is probably true that each of us has a preferred style of operating, it is also the case that we can develop new skills if that is something we choose to do.

Assessing Skills

After you've read this chapter, take the following Self-Assessments on your enclosed CD-ROM:

26. Am I Likely to Become an Entrepreneur?

47. How Motivated Am I to Manage?

48. Am I Well-Suited for a Career as a Global Manager?

Practising Skills

As the father of two young children, Marshall Rogers thought that serving on the board of Marysville Daycare would be a good way to stay in touch with those who cared for his children during the day.[37] But he never dreamed that he would become involved in union-management negotiations with daycare-centre workers.

Late one Sunday evening, in his ninth month as president of the daycare centre, Rogers received a phone call from Grace Ng, a union representative of the Provincial Government Employees' Union (PGEU). Ng informed Rogers that the daycare workers would be unionized the following week. Rogers was stunned to hear this news. Early the next morning, he had to present his new marketing plan to senior management at Techtronix Industries, where he was vice-president of marketing. Somehow he made it through the meeting, wondering why he hadn't been aware of the employees' unhappiness, and how this action would affect his children.

Following his presentation, Rogers received documentation from the Labour Relations Board indicating that the daycare employees had been working to unionize themselves for more than a year. Rogers immediately contacted Xavier Breslin, the board's vice-president, and together they determined that no one on the board had been aware that the daycare workers were unhappy, let alone prepared to join a union.

Hoping that there was some sort of misunderstanding, Rogers called Emma Reynaud, the Marysville supervisor. Reynaud attended most board meetings, but had never mentioned the union-organizing drive. Yet Reynaud now told Rogers that she had actively encouraged the other daycare workers to consider joining the PGEU because the board had not been interested in the employees' concerns, had not increased their wages sufficiently over the past two years, and had not maintained communication channels between the board and the employees.

All of the board members had full-time jobs elsewhere, and many were upper- and middle-level managers in their own companies. They were used to dealing with unhappy employees in their own workplaces, although none had experienced a union-organizing drive. Like Rogers, they had chosen to serve on the board of Marysville to stay informed about the day-to-day events of the centre. They had not really thought of themselves as the centre's employer, although, as board members, they represented all the parents of children enrolled at Marysville. Their main tasks on the daycare-centre board had been setting fees for the children and wages for the daycare employees. The board members usually saw the staff members several times a week, when they picked up their children, yet the unhappiness represented by the union-organizing drive was surprising to all of them. When they met at an emergency board meeting that evening, they tried to evaluate what had gone wrong at Marysville.

Questions

1. If you were either a board member or a parent, how would you know that the employees taking care of your children were unhappy with their jobs?

2. What might you do if you learned about their unhappiness?

3. What might Rogers have done differently as president of the board?

4. In what ways does this case illustrate that knowledge of OB can be applied beyond your own workplace?

Reinforcing Skills

1. Talk to several managers you know and ask them what skills they think are most important in today's workplace. Ask them to specifically consider the use of teams in their workplace, and what skills their team members most need to have but are least likely to have. How might you use this information to develop greater interpersonal skills?

2. Talk to several managers you know and ask them what skills they have found to be most important in doing their jobs. Why did they find these skills most important? What advice would they give a would-be manager about skills worth developing?

CHAPTER 2
Perception, Personality, and Emotions

At the Canadian Human Rights Commission, employees were unhappy with their jobs. Why would their dissatisfaction be regarded as perception rather than fact?

1 What is perception?

2 What causes people to have different perceptions of the same situation?

3 Can people be mistaken in their perceptions?

4 Does perception really affect outcomes?

5 What is personality and how does it affect behaviour?

6 Can emotions help or get in the way when we're dealing with others?

Many employees at the Canadian Human Rights Commission (CHRC) cheered in May 2001 when a commissioned report revealed widespread dissatisfaction in their workplace.[1] Ordinarily an exposé of on-the-job problems is not something to cheer about, but the CHRC workers were grateful their concerns were finally being made public.

Much to the employees' dismay, however, senior managers at CHRC suggested that the workplace problems were only a matter of employee "perception," not objective reality. Michelle Falardeau-Ramsay, who was chief commissioner at the time, even said, "It's a report that is based on perceptions and perceptions can become facts at one point."[2] The employees were left to wonder whether they and their managers were actually part of the same workplace.

All of our behaviour is somewhat shaped by our perceptions, personalities, emotions, and experiences. In this chapter, we consider the role that perception plays in affecting the way we see the world and the people around us. We also consider how personality characteristics affect our attitudes toward people and situations. We then consider how emotions shape many of our work-related behaviours.

WHAT IS PERCEPTION, AND WHY IS IT IMPORTANT?

Perception is the process by which individuals organize and interpret their impressions in order to give meaning to their environment. However, what we perceive can be substantially different from objective reality. We often disagree about what is real. As we have seen, employees and senior management at the Canadian Human Rights Commission had very different views of their workplace conditions. Michelle Falardeau-Ramsay, who was chief commissioner, even said it was all a matter of "perception."

Why is perception important in the study of organizational behaviour (OB)? Simply because people's behaviour is based on their perception of what reality is, not on reality itself. *The world as it is perceived is the world that is behaviourally important.* Paul Godfrey, president and CEO of the Toronto Blue Jays, observes that "a lot of things in life are perception." He backs this up by noting that as chair of Metropolitan Toronto for 11 years, he had little real power, but people believed he could get things done, and so he did.[3]

 **1** What is perception?

perception The process by which individuals organize and interpret their impressions in order to give meaning to their environment.

Canadian Human Rights Commission (CHRC)
www.chrc-ccdp.ca

FACTORS INFLUENCING PERCEPTION

Comments by employees and managers illustrate different perceptions of the environment at the Canadian Human Rights Commission. For example, one unnamed employee said that Chief Commissioner Michelle Falardeau-Ramsay was an absentee manager who lacked important job skills. "When she does conduct a meeting she will occupy the time describing entertainment details of the latest trip she has taken at taxpayers' expense. She's out of touch."[4]

Meanwhile, in responding to negative employee comments, Falardeau-Ramsay told reporters she felt complaints were directed against other senior managers, not her. "I was so overwhelmed, (the report) was so surprising that I didn't even think in those terms," she said.[5] Falardeau-Ramsay and her employees clearly had different perceptions of the same situation. What factors might have influenced these different perceptions?

2 What causes people to have different perceptions of the same situation?

How do we explain that individuals may look at the same thing, yet perceive it differently, and both be right? A number of factors affect perception. These factors can reside in the *perceiver*, in the object or *target* being perceived, or in the context of the *situation* in which the perception is made. Exhibit 2-1 summarizes the factors that influence perception. This chapter's *Working With Others Exercise* on page 72 will help you understand how your perceptions affect your evaluation of others.

The Perceiver

When an individual ("the perceiver") looks at something ("the target") and attempts to interpret what he or she sees, that interpretation is heavily influenced by the perceiver's personal characteristics. Have you ever bought a new car and then noticed a large number of cars like yours on the road? It's unlikely that everyone else has suddenly bought the same model. Rather, your own purchase has influenced your perception so that you are now more likely to notice the other cars. This is an example of how factors related to the perceiver influence what he or she perceives.

A variety of factors affect our perceptions. Our attitudes, motives, interests, and past experiences all shape the way we perceive an event. When chief commissioner Michelle Falardeau-Ramsay suggested that employee complaints about the CHRC were simply a matter of their perception, she was reflecting on her own interests and motives in the situation. As head of the agency, she did not want to believe that she was responsible for any of the problems the employees reported.

We often interpret others' behaviours based on our own characteristics. People who take an optimistic approach to life act as if others will be just as upbeat, while those who are dishonest suspect others are equally dishonest. Expectations can also distort our perceptions—we see what we expect to see. For example, if you expect police officers to be authoritarian, young people to be unambitious, human resource directors to "like people," or politicians to be unethical, you may perceive individuals in these categories this way, regardless of their actual traits.

Finally, perceptions are likely to vary cross-culturally. Thus, doing something that is meant to be friendly on your part may be perceived as too aggressive, or too informal, by someone from another country.

People's expectations about what employees working for a full-service web development agency should look like often leave them startled when they meet Jason Billingsley (left) and Justin Tilson (foreground), two of the founders of Vancouver-based Ekkon Global. Both men are in wheelchairs after a skiing accident for Billingsley and a mountain bike accident for Tilson. "It's an eye-opener sometimes," says Billingsley. "You've been talking on the phone for two or three weeks before you meet someone and they have no clue, and they kind of walk in and you see a little 'oh.'"

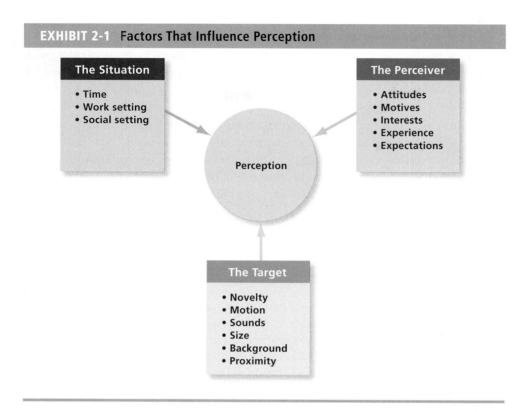

EXHIBIT 2-1 Factors That Influence Perception

The Situation
- Time
- Work setting
- Social setting

The Perceiver
- Attitudes
- Motives
- Interests
- Experience
- Expectations

Perception

The Target
- Novelty
- Motion
- Sounds
- Size
- Background
- Proximity

The Target

A target's characteristics also affect what is perceived. Loud people are more likely to be noticed in a group than are quiet ones. Extremely attractive or unattractive individuals are also more likely to be noticed. Novelty, motion, sounds, size, and other characteristics of a target shape the way we see it.

Because targets are not looked at in isolation, the relationship of a target to its background influences perception. For instance, what you see as you read this sentence is black letters on a white page. You do not see funny-shaped patches of black and white because you recognize these shapes and organize the black shapes against the white background. Exhibit 2-2 dramatizes this effect. The object may at first look like a white vase. However, if white is taken as the background, we see two purple profiles.

Objects that are close to each other tend to be perceived together rather than separately. As a result of physical or time closeness, we often group unrelated objects or events together. Employees in a particular department are seen as a group. If two people in a four-member department suddenly resign, we tend to assume that their departures were related when, in fact, they may be totally unrelated. Or perhaps a new sales manager is assigned to a territory and, soon afterward, sales in that territory skyrocket. The assignment of the new sales manager and the increase in sales may not be related—the increase may be due to the introduction of a new product line or other factors. But because of the timing we tend to perceive the two events as being related.

Persons, objects, or events that are similar to each other also tend to be grouped together. The greater the similarity, the greater the probability that we will tend to perceive them as a common group. People who are female, Aboriginal, or members of any other clearly distinguishable group will tend to be perceived as similar, not only in physical terms but also in other unrelated characteristics.

EXHIBIT 2-2 Figure-Ground Illustration

The Situation

The context in which we see objects or events is important. Elements in the surrounding environment influence our perceptions. For instance, it might be entirely appropriate to wear shorts and T-shirts in a social setting, but these clothes may not be appropriate in a work setting. Therefore, your interpretation of the same clothes will vary with the context. Similarly, you are more likely to notice your employees goofing off if your manager from the head office happens to be in town. Your employees may be acting quite "normally," but the situation affects your perception. The time at which an object or event is seen can influence attention, as can location, light, heat, or any number of situational factors. Thus, it is possible to say that truth is often in the eye of the perceiver, rather than some objective fact.

PERCEPTUAL ERRORS

> In their workplace assessment report of the Canadian Human Rights Commission, consultants Watson Wyatt Worldwide identified numerous problems reported by employees. The employees suggested that three top managers should be replaced. They also claimed that female employees were discriminated against. The problems were considered so severe that some people outside the commission thought it should be closed. Chief Commissioner Michelle Falardeau-Ramsay disagreed. She said the findings were "unpleasant"' and "painful," but suggested that those calling for the commission's closure had read the report in a "simplistic and irresponsible manner." These differences in responses might suggest that the employees, Falardeau-Ramsay, or her critics were engaged in making perceptual errors. What might have caused this to happen?

3 Can people be mistaken in their perceptions?

Perceiving and interpreting why others do what they do takes time. As a result, we develop techniques to make this task more manageable. These techniques are frequently valuable—they allow us to make accurate perceptions rapidly and provide valid data for making predictions. However, they are not foolproof. They can and do get us into trouble. Some of the errors that distort the perception process are attribution theory, selective perception, halo effect, contrast effects, projection, and stereotyping.

Attribution Theory

attribution theory The theory that when we observe what seems like atypical behaviour by an individual, we attempt to determine whether it is internally or externally caused.

Who do you tend to blame when someone makes a mistake? Ever wonder why?

Attribution theory explains how we judge people differently, depending on the meaning we attribute to a given behaviour.[6] Basically, the theory suggests that when we observe what seems like atypical behaviour by an individual, we try to make sense of it. We consider whether the individual is responsible for the behaviour (the cause is internal), or whether something outside the individual caused the behaviour (the cause is external). *Internally* caused behaviour is believed to be under the personal control of the individual. *Externally* caused behaviour is believed to result from outside causes; we see the person as having been forced into the behaviour by the situation. For example, if a student is late for class, the professor might attribute his lateness to partying into the wee hours of the morning and then oversleeping. This would be an internal attribution. But if the professor assumes a major automobile accident tied up traffic on the student's regular route to school, that is making an external attribution. In trying to determine whether behaviour is internally or externally caused, we rely on three rules about the behaviour: (1) distinctiveness, (2) consensus, and (3) consistency. Let's discuss each of these in turn.

Distinctiveness

distinctiveness A behavioural rule that considers whether an individual acts similarly across a variety of situations.

Distinctiveness refers to whether an individual acts similarly across a variety of situations. Is the student always underperforming (being late for class, goofing off in team meetings, not answering urgent emails) or is the student's behaviour in one situation uncharacteristic of behaviour usually shown in other situations? If the behaviour is unusual, the observer is likely to make an external attribution. If this action is not unusual, the observer will probably judge it as internally caused.

Consensus

Consensus considers how an individual's behaviour compares with others in the same situation. If everyone who is faced with a similar situation responds in the same way, we can say the behaviour shows **consensus**. The tardy student's behaviour would meet this criterion if all students who took the same route to school were also late. From an attribution perspective, if consensus is high, you would be expected to give an external attribution to the student's tardiness. But if other students who took the same route made it to class on time, you would conclude the cause of lateness was internal for the student in question.

consensus A behavioural rule that considers if everyone faced with a similar situation responds in the same way.

Consistency

Finally, an observer looks for **consistency** in an action that is repeated over time. If a student is usually on time for class (she has not been late all term), being 10 minutes late will be perceived differently from the way it is when the student is routinely late (almost every class). If a student is almost always late, the observer is likely to attribute lateness to internal causes. If the student is almost never late, then lateness will be attributed to external causes.

consistency A behavioural rule that considers whether the individual has been acting in the same way over time.

Exhibit 2-3 summarizes the key elements in attribution theory. It illustrates, for instance, how to evaluate an employee's behaviour on a new task. To do this, you might note that employee Kim Randolph generally performs at about the same level on other related tasks as she does on her current task (low distinctiveness). You see that other employees frequently perform differently—better or worse—than Kim does on that current task (low consensus). Finally, if Kim's performance on this current task is consistent over time (high consistency), you or anyone else who is judging Kim's work is likely to hold her primarily responsible for her task performance (internal attribution).

How Attributions Get Distorted

One of the more interesting findings from attribution theory is that there are errors or biases that distort attributions. For instance, there is substantial evidence that when we

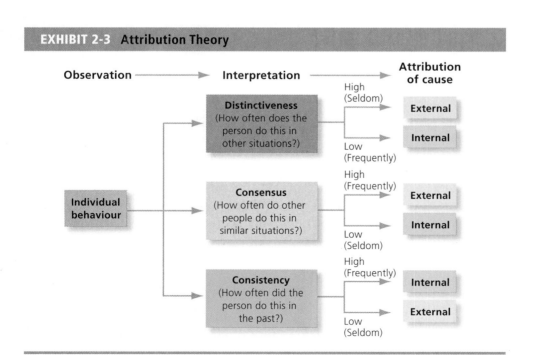

EXHIBIT 2-3   Attribution Theory

fundamental attribution error
The tendency to underestimate the influence of external factors and overestimate the influence of internal factors when making judgments about the behaviour of others.

self-serving bias The tendency for individuals to attribute their own successes to internal factors while putting the blame for failures on external factors.

judge the behaviour of other people, we tend to underestimate the influence of external factors and overestimate the influence of internal or personal factors.[7] This is called the **fundamental attribution error**. It can explain why a sales manager attributes the poor performance of his or her sales agents to laziness rather than acknowledging the impact of the innovative product line introduced by a competitor.

We use **self-serving bias** when we judge ourselves, however. This means that when we are successful, we are more likely to believe it was because of internal factors, such as ability or effort. When we fail, however, we blame external factors, such as luck. In general, people tend to believe that their own behaviour is more positive than the behaviour of those around them. Research suggests, however, that individuals tend to overestimate their own good behaviour, and underestimate the good behaviour of others.[8]

Selective Perception

Have you ever misjudged a person? Learn why.

Because it's impossible for us to see everything, any characteristic that makes a person, object, or event stand out will increase the probability that it will be perceived. This tendency explains why, as we noted earlier, you are more likely to notice cars that look like your own. It also explains why some people may be reprimanded by their manager for doing something that goes unnoticed when other employees do it. Since we cannot observe everything going on about us, we engage in **selective perception**.

selective perception People's selective interpretation of what they see based on their interests, background, experience, and attitudes.

But how does selectivity work as a shortcut in judging other people? Since we cannot take in all that we observe, we take in bits and pieces. But those bits and pieces are not chosen randomly. Rather, they are selectively chosen according to our interests, background, experience, and attitudes. Selective perception allows us to "speed-read" others, but not without the risk of coming to an inaccurate conclusion. Because we see what we want to see, we can draw unwarranted conclusions from an ambiguous situation. Suppose there is a rumour going around the office that your company's sales are down and that large layoffs may happen soon. You and your co-workers might then interpret a routine visit by a senior executive from headquarters as the first step in management's identification of people to be fired. In reality, however, such an action might be the furthest thing from the executive's mind. Selective perception can also make us draw wrong conclusions about co-workers who have suffered serious illnesses, as *Focus on Diversity* shows.

FOCUS ON **DIVERSITY**

Underestimating Employees Who Have Been Seriously Ill

Does having had a serious illness mean that you cannot do your job? Lynda Davidson learned the hard way that suffering a mental illness and then getting treatment for it does not necessarily give one a clean bill of health at work.[9] When she returned to work after treatment, though she made her targets and earned her bonuses, her contract was not renewed. She later took a job as program manager at the Canadian Mental Health Association in Toronto.

Another Toronto woman suffered a similar fate when she was diagnosed with acute leukemia. After treatment, she returned to work at a large financial services organization only to find that she could not get any promotions. "I had the sense that people no longer took me seriously. I think people looked at me and thought, 'She's going to die,'" the woman said. It took moving to a different department where no one knew her before she could get ahead in her job.

It's not uncommon for employees with critical, chronic illnesses to feel that their jobs have been harmed by their illness. Employers and co-workers apparently perceive that the employee cannot function at the same level that they had prior to the illness. Describing a recent study done in the United States by the National Coalition for Cancer Survivorship, Dr. Ross Gray, a research psychologist at the Toronto-Sunnybrook Regional Cancer Centre, noted: "The study found that employers and co-workers overestimate the impact of cancer on people's lives. Decisions get made about advancement or capability that are out of line with the realities," Dr. Gray says. 🕴

Halo Effect

When we draw a general impression of an individual on the basis of a single characteristic, such as intelligence, likeability, or appearance, a **halo effect** operates. Think about what happens when students evaluate their instructor. Students may give more weight to a single trait, such as enthusiasm, and allow their entire evaluation to be coloured by how they judge the instructor on that one trait. Thus, an instructor may be quiet, assured, knowledgeable, and highly qualified, but if his or her presentation style lacks enthusiasm, those students would probably give the instructor a low rating.

The reality of the halo effect was confirmed in a classic study. Subjects were given a list of traits and asked to evaluate the person to whom those traits applied.[10] When traits such as intelligent, skillful, practical, industrious, determined, and warm were used, the person was judged to be wise, humorous, popular, and imaginative. When cold was substituted for warm, a completely different set of perceptions was obtained, though otherwise the list was identical. Clearly, the subjects were allowing a single trait to influence their overall impression of the person being judged.

The halo effect does not operate at random. Research suggests that it is likely to be most extreme when the perceived traits are ambiguous in behavioural terms, when the traits have moral overtones, and when the perceiver has had limited experience with the traits being judged.[11]

halo effect Drawing a general impression of an individual on the basis of a single characteristic.

Contrast Effects

There's an old saying among entertainers who perform in variety shows: Never follow an act that has children or animals in it.

This example demonstrates how **contrast effects** can distort perceptions. We don't evaluate a person in isolation. Our reaction to one person is often influenced by other people we have recently encountered.

Consider what happens when a manager interviews job candidates from a pool of applicants. The evaluation of a candidate can be distorted as a result of his or her place in the interview schedule. The candidate is likely to receive a more favourable evaluation if preceded by mediocre applicants, and a less favourable evaluation if preceded by strong applicants.

contrast effects The concept that our reaction to one person is often influenced by other people we have recently encountered.

Projection

It's easy to judge others if we assume that they are similar to us. For instance, if you want challenge and responsibility in your job, you assume that others want the same. Or you are honest and trustworthy, so you take it for granted that other people are equally reliable. This tendency to attribute our own characteristics to other people is called **projection**.

People who engage in projection tend to perceive others according to what they themselves are like, rather than perceiving others as they really are. Because they always judge people as being similar to themselves, when they observe someone who is actually like them, their perceptions are naturally correct. But when they observe others who are not like them, their perceptions are not as accurate. Managers who engage in

projection Attributing one's own characteristics to other people.

projection compromise their ability to respond to individual differences. They tend to see people as more homogeneous than they really are.

Stereotyping

When we judge someone on the basis of our perception of the group to which he or she belongs, we are using the shortcut called **stereotyping**. According to a popular literary anecdote, F. Scott Fitzgerald engaged in stereotyping when he told Ernest Hemingway, "The rich are very different from you and me," implying that the wealthy have values and behaviour unlike regular people. Hemingway's reply, "Yes, they have more money," indicated that he refused to generalize characteristics of people on the basis of their wealth.

Generalization, of course, is not without advantages. It's a means of simplifying a complex world, and it permits us to maintain consistency. It's less difficult to deal with a large number of stimuli if we use stereotypes. As an example, assume you are a sales manager looking to fill a sales position in your territory and 100 people have applied. You want to hire someone who is ambitious and hard-working and who can deal well with adversity, and you do not want to spend too much time interviewing candidates. Your last five hires have been very successful and participated in athletics at university. So you eliminate from consideration candidates who have not participated in university sports, considerably reducing your search time. To the extent that athletes are ambitious, hard-working, and able to deal with adversity, the use of this stereotype can improve your decision making.

The problem, clearly, is when we inaccurately stereotype.[12] All university athletes are not necessarily ambitious, hard-working, or good at dealing with adversity, just as all accountants are not necessarily quiet and introspective. Moreover, when we stereotype like this, we run the risk of overlooking highly qualified people who do not meet our stereotypes. Recent research examining how Hollywood studio executives and producers judge the creative potential of relatively unknown screenwriters makes this clear.[13] When the screenwriters did not meet the stereotype of creative individuals in their presentation or appearance, they were judged as not creative (and often not taken seriously) without consideration of the content of their idea. The researchers noted that this could result in hiring uncreative individuals simply because they fit the creative stereotype, and failing to hire truly creative individuals who did not fit the stereotype.

Obviously, one of the problems with stereotypes is that they are widespread, despite the fact that they may not contain a shred of truth or that they may be irrelevant. Perhaps they are widespread only because many people are making the same inaccurate perception based on a false premise about a group. Stanford Graduate School of Business professor John Jost has uncovered another problem with stereotypes: They can be used to support the status quo.[14] He notes that when people buy into stereotypes about disadvantaged groups, they are less likely to challenge the consequences of the stereotype. For instance, subjects exposed to stereotypes such as "poor but happy" were less likely to respond negatively to ideas of social inequality. One implication of Jost's research is that we need to be aware of the effects of stereotypes on how we evaluate the world around us. Stereotypes can lead to strong negative reactions, such as prejudice, which we describe below.

Prejudice

Prejudice is an unfounded dislike of a person or group based on their belonging to a particular stereotyped group. For instance, an individual may dislike people of a particular religion, or state that they do not want to work with someone of a particular ethnicity. Prejudice can lead to negative consequences in the workplace and, in particular, to discrimination. For instance, an individual of a particular ethnic group might be passed over for a management position because of the belief that employees might not see that person as a good manager. In another instance, an individual in his 50s who is looking for work but cannot find a job may be discriminated against because of the belief that younger workers are more appealing than older workers. Prejudice generally starts with stereotypes and then has negative emotional content added.

WHY DO PERCEPTION AND JUDGMENT MATTER?

The employees at the Canadian Human Rights Commission (CHRC) felt that Chief Commissioner Michelle Falardeau-Ramsay was not up to her role. They cited as evidence that she spent meeting time describing entertainment details of the latest trip she had taken at taxpayers' expense. This, and other perceptions of bad management, had led to high turnover and low morale at the commission. About 63 percent of the employees had left in the previous two years and 37 percent of those still working at the time of the survey were looking for another job. Falardeau-Ramsay was unaware of employee unhappiness, because she said she had regularly met with employees and had never heard complaints of "managers openly showing favouritism, promoting men over women, and nurturing 'an anti-union culture.'"[15] Thus her perception led her to the judgment that there was nothing she needed to fix at the CHRC. It had not occurred to her that perhaps employees would be reluctant to share bad news with her or give honest opinions about their workplace. Did perceptions and judgments by both Falardeau-Ramsay and her employees lead to actions that were harmful to the organization?

People in organizations are always judging each other. For instance, people typically go through an employment interview before being hired. Interviewers make perceptual judgments during the interview that affect whether the individual is hired. Studies show that if negative information is exposed early in the interview, it tends to be more heavily weighted than if that same information comes out later.[16] If the employment interview is an important factor in the hiring decision—and it usually is—you should recognize that perceptual factors influence who is hired and, eventually, the quality of an organization's labour force.

4 Does perception really affect outcomes?

The impact of performance evaluations on behaviour will be discussed fully in *HR Implications* in Chapter 4. It should be pointed out here, though, that an employee's performance appraisal is another example of something in the workplace that depends very much on the perceptual process.[17] An employee's future is closely tied to his or her appraisal—promotions, pay raises, and continuation of employment are among the most obvious outcomes. Although the appraisal can be objective (for example, a salesperson is appraised on how many dollars of sales he or she generates in a given territory), many jobs are evaluated in subjective terms. When managers use subjective measures in appraising employees or choosing whom to promote, what the evaluator perceives to be good or bad employee characteristics or behaviours will significantly influence the outcome of the appraisal. One recent study found that managers in both Hong Kong and the United States were more likely to promote individuals who were more similar to themselves.[18] One's behaviour may also be affected by perceptions. In what follows we discuss how the self-fulfilling prophecy can lead to people engaging in behaviour that is expected of them.

Hiring and performance appraisals are not the only processes in organizations that are subject to perceptual bias. For instance, we evaluate how much effort our co-workers are putting into their jobs. When a new person joins a work team, he or she is immediately "sized up" by the other team members. Individuals even make judgments about people's virtues based on whether or not they exercise, as *Focus on Research* shows.

FOCUS ON **RESEARCH**

Exercisers Rule

Can being called an exerciser really make a difference in how others think of you? Stereotypes can strongly affect people's judgments of others, according to a study by McMaster University professor Kathleen Martin.[19] Students were given descriptions of individuals and then asked to evaluate 12 personality characteristics of "Tom" or "Mary." These characteristics included being afraid or brave, and having or lacking self-control, as well as 8 physical characteristics, including whether they were fit or unfit, sickly or healthy, ugly or good-looking. Some descriptions mentioned whether the individual exercised or not.

Students evaluated nonexercisers more negatively on every personality and physical characteristic than those described as exercisers. In fact, those described as nonexercisers were rated more negatively than those for whom no information about exercise was provided. Martin noted, "When Mary and Tom were described as exercisers, they were considered to be harder workers, more confident, braver, smarter, neater, happier and more sociable than the non-exerciser."

Self-Fulfilling Prophecy

There is an impressive amount of evidence that demonstrates that people will attempt to validate their perceptions of reality, even when those perceptions are faulty.[20] This characteristic is particularly relevant when we consider performance expectations on the job.

self-fulfilling prophecy A concept that proposes a person will behave in ways consistent with how he or she is perceived by others.

The terms **self-fulfilling prophecy** or *pygmalion effect* have evolved to characterize the fact that people's expectations determine their behaviour. In other words, if a manager expects big things from his people, they are not likely to let him down. Similarly, if a manager expects people to perform minimally, they will tend to behave so as to meet those low expectations. The result then is that the expectations become reality.

An interesting illustration of the self-fulfilling prophecy is a study undertaken with 105 soldiers in the Israeli Defense Forces who were taking a 15-week combat command course.[21] The four course instructors were told that one-third of the specific incoming trainees had high potential, one-third had normal potential, and the potential of the rest was unknown. In reality, the trainees were randomly placed into those categories by the researchers. The results confirmed the existence of a self-fulfilling prophecy. The trainees whom instructors were told had high potential scored significantly higher on objective achievement tests, exhibited more positive attitudes, and held their leaders in higher regard than did the other two groups. The instructors of the supposedly high-potential trainees got better results from them because the instructors expected them.

When managers expect big things from their employees, the self-fulfilling prophecy indicates that the employees will produce big results. That's what happened when management of Sweden's Volvo Car Corporation challenged an all-women team of designers and developers to create a concept car specifically to satisfy the needs of female car buyers. In this photo, design team members showcase their new vehicle at an international car show in Switzerland.

As you can see, perception plays a large role in how people are evaluated. Personality, which we review next, is another major factor affecting how people relate and evaluate each other in the workplace.

PERSONALITY

Why are some people quiet and passive, while others are loud and aggressive? Are certain personality types better adapted for certain job types? What do we know from theories of personality that can help us explain and predict the behaviour of leaders such as Paul Martin, Stephen Harper, or George W. Bush? How do we explain the risk-taking nature of Donald Trump, whose Trump Hotels & Casino Resorts went into bankruptcy protection, and yet he still sees himself as the greatest businessman in America? In this section, we will attempt to answer such questions.

5 What is personality and how does it affect behaviour?

What Is Personality?

When we talk of personality, we don't mean that a person has charm, a positive attitude toward life, a smiling face, or is a finalist for "Miss Congeniality." When psychologists talk of personality, they mean a dynamic concept describing the growth and development of a person's whole psychological system. Rather than looking at parts of the person, personality looks at some aggregate whole that is greater than the sum of the parts.

Gordon Allport produced the most frequently used definition of personality more than 60 years ago. He said personality is "the dynamic organization within the individual of those psychophysical systems that determine his unique adjustments to his environment."[22] For our purposes, you should think of **personality** as the stable patterns of behaviour and consistent internal states that determine how an individual reacts to and interacts with others. It's most often described in terms of measurable traits that a person exhibits. For an interesting look at how personality can affect business dealings, you might want to read this chapter's *Point/Counterpoint* discussion on page 63. The discussion centres on how flexible and inflexible personality is. In addition, this chapter's *CBC Video Case* examines the personalities of two business partners.

personality The stable patterns of behaviour and consistent internal states that determine how an individual reacts to and interacts with others.

NovaScotian Crystal

Personality Determinants

An early argument in personality research centred on whether an individual's personality was predetermined at birth, or the result of the individual's interaction with his or her environment. Clearly, there is no simple answer. Personality appears to be a result of both influences. In addition, today we recognize a third factor—the situation. Thus, an adult's personality is now generally considered to be made up of both hereditary and environmental factors, moderated by situational conditions. You may want to read the *Case Incident—The Rise and Fall of Dennis Kozlowski* to see how one man's early life may have affected how he later ran his business.

Heredity

Are people born with their personalities?

Heredity refers to those factors that were determined at conception. Physical stature, facial attractiveness, gender, temperament, muscle composition and reflexes, energy level, and biological rhythms are characteristics that are generally considered to be either completely or substantially influenced by your parents' biological, physiological, and inherent psychological makeup. The heredity approach argues that the ultimate explanation of an individual's personality is the person's genes.

Studies of young children lend strong support to the power of heredity.[23] Evidence demonstrates that traits such as shyness, fear, and distress are most likely caused by inherited genetic characteristics. This finding suggests that some personality traits may be built into the same genetic code that affects factors such as height and hair colour.

If heredity played little or no part in determining personality, you would expect to find few similarities between identical twins who were separated at birth and raised separately.

But researchers who looked at more than 100 sets of separated twins found a lot in common.[24] For almost every behavioural trait, a significant part of the variation between the twins turned out to be associated with genetic factors. For instance, one set of twins, who had been separated for 39 years and raised 70 kilometres apart, were found to drive the same model and colour car, chain-smoke the same brand of cigarette, own dogs with the same name, and regularly vacation within three blocks of each other in a beach community 2000 kilometres away. Researchers have found that genetics can explain about 50 percent of the personality differences and more than 30 percent of the variation in occupational and leisure interests found in individuals. In other words, blood-related siblings are likely to have more similar personalities, occupations, and leisure interests than unrelated people.

If personality characteristics were *completely* dictated by heredity, they would be fixed at birth and no amount of experience could alter them. If genetics resulted in your being tense and irritable as a child, for example, it would not be possible for you to change those characteristics as you grew into an adult. But personality characteristics are not completely dictated by heredity. Environmental factors and situational conditions also play a big role.

Environmental Factors

Among the factors that exert pressures on our personality formation are the culture in which we are raised; our early conditioning; the norms among our family, friends, and social groups; and other influences that we experience. The environment we are exposed to plays a substantial role in shaping our personalities.

For example, North Americans have had the themes of industriousness, success, competition, independence, and the Protestant work ethic constantly instilled in them through books, the school system, family, and friends. North Americans, as a result, tend to be ambitious and aggressive relative to individuals raised in cultures that have emphasized getting along with others, cooperation, and the priority of family over work and career.

Careful consideration of the arguments favouring either heredity or environment as the primary determinant of personality forces the conclusion that both are important. Heredity sets the parameters, or outer limits, but an individual's full potential will be determined by how well he or she adjusts to the demands and requirements of the environment.

Situational Conditions

A third factor, the situation, influences the effects of heredity and environment on personality. An individual's personality, although generally stable and consistent, does change in different situations. More specifically, the demands of different situations call forth different aspects of our personalities. We should not, therefore, look at personality patterns in isolation.[25]

It seems only logical to suppose that situations will influence an individual's personality, but a neat classification scheme that would tell us the impact of various types of situations has so far eluded us. In the words of one psychologist, "Apparently we are not yet close to developing a system for clarifying situations so that they might be systematically studied."[26] However, we do know that certain situations are more relevant than others in influencing personality. We also know that situations differ substantially in dictating appropriate behaviour. Some situations, such as a religious service or an employment interview, limit many behaviours; other situations, such as a picnic in a public park, limit relatively few.[27]

Furthermore, although certain generalizations can be made about personality, there are significant individual differences. As we will see, the study of individual differences has come to receive greater emphasis in personality research, which originally sought out more general, universal patterns.

EXHIBIT 2-4	Sixteen Primary Personality Traits		
1.	Reserved	vs.	Outgoing
2.	Less intelligent	vs.	More intelligent
3.	Affected by feelings	vs.	Emotionally stable
4.	Submissive	vs.	Dominant
5.	Serious	vs.	Happy-go-lucky
6.	Expedient	vs.	Conscientious
7.	Timid	vs.	Venturesome
8.	Tough-minded	vs.	Sensitive
9.	Trusting	vs.	Suspicious
10.	Practical	vs.	Imaginative
11.	Forthright	vs.	Shrewd
12.	Self-assured	vs.	Apprehensive
13.	Conservative	vs.	Experimenting
14.	Group-dependent	vs.	Self-sufficient
15.	Uncontrolled	vs.	Controlled
16.	Relaxed	vs.	Tense

Source: R. B. Catell, "Personality Pinned Down," *Psychology Today,* July 1973, pp. 40–46.

Personality Traits

The early work in the structure of personality revolved around attempts to identify and label enduring characteristics that describe an individual's behaviour. Popular characteristics include shy, aggressive, submissive, lazy, ambitious, loyal, and timid. Those characteristics, when they are exhibited in a large number of situations, are called **personality traits**.[28] The more consistent the characteristic and the more frequently it occurs in diverse situations, the more important that trait is in describing the individual.

personality traits Enduring characteristics that describe an individual's behaviour.

Researchers have tried to identify the different personality traits. One researcher identified 16 personality factors that he called the source, or primary, traits.[29] These 16 traits have been found to be generally steady and constant sources of behaviour, allowing prediction of an individual's behaviour in specific situations by weighing the characteristics for their situational relevance. They are shown in Exhibit 2-4. The Myers-Briggs Type Indicator and the Big Five Model, which we discuss below, are additional methods that have been used to determine personality traits.

Keep in mind that each of us reacts differently to personality traits. This is partially a function of how we perceive those traits. In Exhibit 2-5, you will note that Lucy tells Linus a few things about his personality.

The Myers-Briggs Type Indicator

One of the most widely used personality frameworks is called the **Myers-Briggs Type Indicator (MBTI)**.[30] It's essentially a 100-question personality test that asks people how they usually feel or act in particular situations.

Myers-Briggs Type Indicator (MBTI) A personality test that taps four characteristics and classifies people into 1 of 16 personality types.

The MBTI classifies people based on how they prefer to focus their attention, collect information, process and evaluate information, and orient themselves to the outer world. These classifications are then combined into 16 personality types. (These types are different from the 16 primary personality traits presented in Exhibit 2-4.) Briefly, personality is classified along the following dimensions:

- *Extraversion/Introversion (E or I).* This dimension refers to how people focus themselves: inside (introversion) or outside (extraversion).

EXHIBIT 2-5

- *Sensing/Intuiting (S or N).* This dimension refers to how people gather information: very systematically (sensing) or relying on intuition (intuiting).

- *Thinking/Feeling (T or F).* This dimension refers to how people prefer to make decisions: objectively and impersonally (thinking) or subjectively and interpersonally (feeling).

- *Judging/Perceiving (J or P).* This dimension refers to how people order their daily life: being decisive and planned (judging) or spontaneous and flexible (perceiving).

Let's take a look at three examples of MBTI personality types:

- *INTJs are visionaries.* They usually have original minds and great drive for their own ideas and purposes. They are characterized as skeptical, critical, independent, determined, and often stubborn.

- *ESTJs are organizers.* They are realistic, logical, analytical, decisive, and have a natural head for business or mechanics. They like to organize and run activities.

- *ENTPs are conceptualizers.* They are innovative, individualistic, versatile, and attracted to entrepreneurial ideas. They tend to be resourceful in solving challenging problems but may neglect routine assignments.

G. N. Landrum's *Profiles of Genius* profiled 13 contemporary business people who created super-successful firms, including Apple Computer, Federal Express, Honda Motors, Microsoft, Price Club, and Sony. He found that all 13 are intuitive thinkers (NTs).[31] This result is particularly interesting because intuitive thinkers represent only about 5 percent of the population.

Ironically, there is no hard evidence that the MBTI is a valid measure of personality. But lack of evidence does not seem to deter its use in a wide range of organizations.

One of the benefits of thinking about individuals by type is that it will give you some insight into how a particular person might react in a situation. If you browse in a library or bookstore you will find a number of popular books designed to help you identify both your own and your colleagues' "personality types." However, as we noted before in our discussion of stereotyping, relying solely on personality measures to judge people can have its problems.

The Big Five Model

The MBTI may lack valid supporting evidence, but that cannot be said for the widely accepted five-factor model of personality—more typically called the "Big Five."[32] An impressive body of research supports the notion that five basic personality dimensions underlie all others and encompass most of the significant variation in human personality. The Big Five personality factors are as follows:

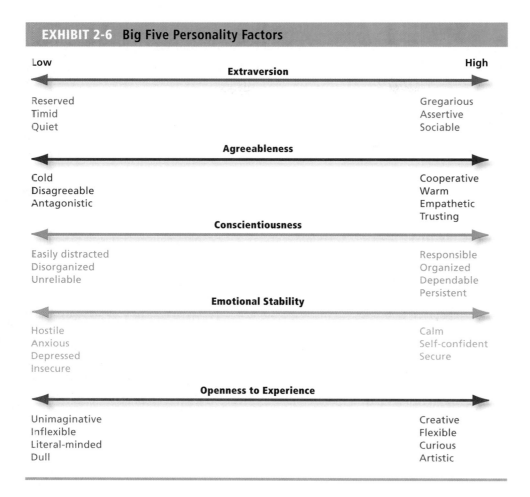

EXHIBIT 2-6   Big Five Personality Factors

	Extraversion	
Low		**High**
Reserved		Gregarious
Timid		Assertive
Quiet		Sociable

	Agreeableness	
Cold		Cooperative
Disagreeable		Warm
Antagonistic		Empathetic
		Trusting

	Conscientiousness	
Easily distracted		Responsible
Disorganized		Organized
Unreliable		Dependable
		Persistent

	Emotional Stability	
Hostile		Calm
Anxious		Self-confident
Depressed		Secure
Insecure		

	Openness to Experience	
Unimaginative		Creative
Inflexible		Flexible
Literal-minded		Curious
Dull		Artistic

- *Extraversion.* This dimension captures a person's comfort level with relationships; it describes the degree to which a person is sociable, talkative, and assertive.

- *Agreeableness.* This dimension refers to a person's propensity to defer to others; it describes the degree to which a person is good-natured, cooperative, and trusting.

- *Conscientiousness.* This dimension is a measure of reliability; it describes the degree to which a person is responsible, dependable, persistent, and achievement-oriented.

- *Emotional stability.* This dimension taps a person's ability to withstand stress; it describes the degree to which a person is calm, self-confident, and secure.

- *Openness to experience.* The final dimension addresses a person's range of interests and fascination with novelty; it describes the degree to which a person is imaginative, artistically sensitive, and intellectual.

Exhibit 2-6 shows the characteristics for the high and low dimensions of each Big Five personality factor.

RESEARCH FINDINGS

In addition to providing a unifying personality framework, the Big Five also have important implications for job performance.[33] Contemporary research has examined a broad spectrum of occupations: professionals (including engineers, architects, accountants, lawyers), police officers, managers, salespeople, and semi-skilled and skilled

extraversion A personality factor that describes the degree to which a person is sociable, talkative, and assertive.

agreeableness A personality factor that describes the degree to which a person is good-natured, cooperative, and trusting.

conscientiousness A personality factor that describes the degree to which a person is responsible, dependable, persistent, and achievement-oriented.

emotional stability A personality factor that describes the degree to which a person is calm, self-confident, and secure.

openness to experience A personality factor that describes the degree to which a person is imaginative, artistically sensitive, and intellectual.

It's not always easy for friends to share top management roles, but Anton Rabie (left), president and COO, and Ronnen Harary (right), CEO, of Toronto-based Spin Master like the arrangement. Rabie is an extravert, while Harary is an introvert. The childhood friends feel their personalities complement each other, making an ideal management team.

employees. Job performance was defined in terms of performance ratings, training proficiency (performance during training programs), and data such as salary level. All of the Big Five factors have been found to have at least some relationship to performance in some situations.[34] Exhibit 2-7 summarizes the key research findings on the relationship of the Big Five personality factors to both individual job performance and team performance.[35]

Research finds a strong relationship between some of the Big Five factors and motivation. Lower emotional stability is associated with lower motivation, while conscientiousness appears to be positively related to motivation.[36] Finally, evidence also finds a relatively strong and consistent relationship between conscientiousness and organizational citizenship behaviour (OCB).[37] Conscientiousness, however, seems to be the only personality factor that predicts OCB.

EXHIBIT 2-7 Research Results: How Big Five Personality Factors Affect Individual Job and Team Performance		
Big Five Personality Factor	**Relationship to Job Performance**	**Relationship to Team Performance**
Extraversion	• Positively related to job performance in occupations requiring social interaction • Positively related to training proficiency for all occupations	• Positively related to team performance • Positively related to degree of participation within team
Agreeableness	• Positively related to job performance in service jobs	• Most studies found no link between agreeableness and performance or productivity in team • Some found a negative link between person's likeability and team performance
Conscientiousness	• Positively related to job performance for all occupational groups • May be better than ability in predicting job performance	
Emotional Stability	• A minimal threshold amount may be necessary for adequate performance; greater degrees not related to job performance • Positively related to performance in service jobs • May be better than ability in predicting job performance across all occupational groups	
Openness to Experience	• Positively related to training proficiency	

Source: Adapted from S. L. Kichuk and W. H. Wiesner, "Work Teams: Selecting Members for Optimal Performance," *Canadian Psychology* 39, no. 1–2 (February–May 1998), pp. 24–26.

Major Personality Attributes Influencing OB

In this section, we will evaluate specific personality attributes that have been found to be powerful predictors of behaviour in organizations. The first is related to locus of control—how much power over your destiny you think you have. The others are Machiavellianism, self-esteem, self-monitoring, risk-taking, and Type A and proactive personalities. We shall briefly introduce these attributes and summarize what we know about their ability to explain and predict employee behaviour.

If you want to know more about your own personality attributes, this chapter's *Learning About Yourself Exercises* on pages 64–71 present you with a variety of personality measures to explore.

Locus of Control

Some people believe that they are in control of their own destiny. Other people see themselves as pawns of fate, believing that what happens to them in their lives is due to luck or chance. The first type, those who believe that they control their destinies, have been labelled **internals**. The latter, who see their lives as being controlled by outside forces, have been called **externals**.[38] A person's perception of the source of his or her fate is termed **locus of control**.

A large amount of research has compared internals with externals. Internals report greater well-being, and this finding appears to be universal.[39] Internals show greater motivation, believe that their efforts will result in good performance, and get higher salaries and greater salary increases than externals.[40] Externals are less satisfied with their jobs, have higher absenteeism rates, are more alienated from the work setting, and are less involved in their jobs than are internals,[41] likely because they feel they have little control over organizational outcomes. Exhibit 2-8 shows the relationship between locus of control and job performance.

If you are interested in determining your locus of control, you might want to complete *Learning About Yourself Exercise #1* on page 64.

Machiavellianism

The personality characteristic of **Machiavellianism** (Mach) is named after Niccolò Machiavelli, who wrote in the sixteenth century on how to gain and use power. An individual high in Machiavellianism is pragmatic, maintains emotional distance, and believes that ends can justify means: "If it works, use it."

A considerable amount of research has been directed toward relating high- and low-Mach personalities to certain behavioural outcomes.[42] High Machs manipulate more, win more, are persuaded less, and persuade others more than do low Machs.[43] Think of Donald Trump interacting with the characters on *The Apprentice*. Yet these high-Mach outcomes are moderated by situational factors. It has been found that high Machs do better (1) when they interact face to face with others rather than indirectly; (2) when the situation has a minimum number of rules and regulations, thus allowing room for improvising; and (3) when emotional involvement with details irrelevant to winning distracts low Machs.[44]

Should we conclude that high Machs make good employees? That answer depends on the type of job and whether you consider ethical implications in evaluating performance. In jobs that require bargaining skills (such as labour negotiation) or that offer substantial rewards for winning (as in commissioned sales), high Machs will be productive. But if the ends cannot justify the means, if there are absolute standards of behaviour, or if the three situational factors noted in the preceding paragraph are not in evidence, our ability to predict a high Mach's performance will be severely limited.

If you are interested in determining your level of Machiavellianism, you might want to complete *Learning About Yourself Exercise #2* on page 65.

internals Individuals who believe that they control their destinies.

externals Individuals who believe that their lives are controlled by outside forces, such as luck or chance.

locus of control The degree to which people believe they are in control of their own fate.

Machiavellianism The degree to which an individual is pragmatic, maintains emotional distance, and believes that ends can justify means.

EXHIBIT 2-8 The Effects of Locus of Control on Performance	
Conditions	**Performance**
Information Processing	
The work requires complex information processing and complex learning.	Internals perform better.
The work is quite simple and easy to learn.	Internals perform no better than externals.
Initiative	
The work requires initiative and independent action.	Internals perform better.
The work requires compliance and conformity.	Externals perform better.
Motivation	
The work requires high motivation and provides valued rewards in return for greater effort; it offers incentive pay for greater productivity.	Internals perform better.
The work does not require great effort and contingent rewards are lacking; hourly pay rates are determined by collective bargaining	Externals perform at least as well as internals.

Source: J. B. Miner, *Industrial-Organizational Psychology* (New York: McGraw-Hill, 1992), p. 151. Reprinted with permission of The McGraw-Hill Companies.

Self-Esteem

self-esteem The degree to which individuals like or dislike themselves.

People differ in the degree to which they like or dislike themselves. This trait is called **self-esteem**.[45] The research on self-esteem (SE) offers some interesting insights into OB. For example, self-esteem is directly related to expectations for success. High SEs believe that they possess the ability they need in order to succeed at work. Individuals with high self-esteem will take more risks in job selection and are more likely to choose unconventional jobs than are people with low self-esteem. High SEs also tend to emphasize the positive when confronted with failure.

The most generalizable finding on self-esteem is that low SEs are more susceptible to external influence than are high SEs. Low SEs are dependent on the receipt of positive evaluations from others. As a result, they are more likely than high SEs to seek approval from others and more prone to conform to the beliefs and behaviours of those they respect. In managerial positions, low SEs tend to be concerned with pleasing others and, therefore, are less likely to take unpopular stands than are high SEs.

Not surprisingly, self-esteem has also been found to be related to job satisfaction. A number of studies confirm that high SEs are more satisfied with their jobs than are low SEs.

Psychologist Nathaniel Branden suggests that people can increase their self-esteem by following his "Six Pillars of Self-Esteem," which is shown in Exhibit 2-9. By following the actions described, individuals can act with more confidence and integrity, which will lead to greater self-esteem. Branden emphasizes that self-esteem comes from the choices we make, not from how others treat us.

If you are interested in determining your self-esteem score, you might want to complete *Learning About Yourself Exercise #3* on page 66.

EXHIBIT 2-9   Branden's Six Pillars of Self-Esteem
1. *Living consciously:* Be aware of everything that affects your values and goals, and act with awareness.
2. *Self-acceptance:* Accept who you are without criticism and judgment.
3. *Personal responsibility:* Take responsibility for the decisions you make and the things you do.
4. *Self-assertiveness:* Honour your wants, needs, and values, and don't be afraid to speak up for things that are important to you.
5. *Living purposefully:* Develop short- and long-term goals, and make realistic plans to achieve your goals.
6. *Personal integrity:* Live up to your word and your values.

Source: Adapted from N. Branden, *Self-Esteem at Work: How Confident People Make Powerful Companies* (San Francisco: Jossey-Bass, 1998), pp. 33–36.

Self-Monitoring

Some people are better able to pay attention to the external environment and respond accordingly, a characteristic known as **self-monitoring**.[46] Individuals high in self-monitoring show considerable ability to adjust and adapt their behaviour to the situations they are in. They are highly sensitive to external cues and can behave differently in different situations. High self-monitors are capable of presenting striking contradictions between their public personae and their private selves.

Low self-monitors cannot disguise themselves in the same way. They tend to display their true dispositions and attitudes in every situation. There is high behavioural consistency between who they are and what they do.

Research evidence suggests that high self-monitors tend to pay closer attention to the behaviour of others and are more capable of conforming than are low self-monitors.[47] High self-monitoring managers tend to be more mobile in their careers and receive more promotions (both internal and cross-organizational).[48] Recent research found that high self-monitors are more likely to be high performers and more likely to become leaders.[49]

If you are interested in determining whether you are a high or low self-monitor, you might want to complete *Learning About Yourself Exercise #4* on page 67.

self-monitoring A personality trait that measures an individual's ability to adjust behaviour to external, situational factors.

Risk-Taking

People differ in their willingness to take chances. Matthew Barrett, the former CEO of Bank of Montreal, and Frank Stronach, chair of Magna International (and the subject of *Case Incident—Frank Stronach, Risk-Taker and Fair Enterprise Creator* on page 73), are good examples of high risk-takers. This tendency to assume or avoid risk has been shown to have an impact on how long it takes managers to make a decision and how much information they require before making their choice. In one study, 79 managers worked on simulated exercises that required them to make hiring decisions.[50] High **risk-taking** managers made more rapid decisions and used less information in making their choices than did the low risk-taking managers. Interestingly, the decision accuracy was the same for both groups.

risk-taking A person's willingness to take chances or risks.

While it's generally correct to conclude that managers in organizations prefer to avoid risk,[51] there are still individual differences on this dimension.[52] As a result, it makes sense to recognize these differences and even to consider aligning risk-taking tendencies with specific job demands. For instance, a high risk-taking tendency may lead to more effective performance for a stock trader in a brokerage firm because that type of job demands rapid decision making. On the other hand, a willingness to take risks might prove a major obstacle to an accountant who performs auditing activities.

If you are interested in determining where you stand on risk-taking, you might want to complete *Learning About Yourself Exercise #5* on page 68.

Type A Personality

Type A personality A personality with aggressive involvement in a chronic, incessant struggle to achieve more and more in less and less time and, if necessary, against the opposing efforts of other things or other people.

Do you think it is better to be a Type A or a Type B personality?

Do you know people who are excessively competitive and always seem to be chronically pushed for time? If you do, it's a good bet that those people have a Type A personality. A person with a **Type A personality** is "*aggressively* involved in a *chronic, incessant* struggle to achieve more and more in less and less time, and, if required to do so, against the opposing efforts of other things or other persons."[53] In North American culture, such characteristics tend to be highly prized and positively associated with ambition and the successful acquisition of material goods.

Type As

- Are always moving, walking, and eating rapidly
- Feel impatient with the rate at which most events take place
- Strive to think or do two or more things at once
- Cannot cope with leisure time
- Are obsessed with numbers, measuring their success in terms of how many or how much of everything they acquire

In contrast to the Type A personality is the Type B, who is exactly opposite. Research indicates that Type Bs are "rarely harried by the desire to obtain a wildly increasing number of things or participate in an endless growing series of events in an ever-decreasing amount of time."[54]

Type Bs

- Never suffer from a sense of time urgency with its accompanying impatience
- Feel no need to display or discuss either their achievements or accomplishments unless such exposure is demanded by the situation
- Play for fun and relaxation, rather than to exhibit their superiority at any cost
- Can relax without guilt

Type As are often characterized by impatience, hurriedness, competitiveness, and hostility, but these characteristics tend to emerge when a Type A individual experiences stress or challenge.[55] Type As are fast workers because they emphasize quantity over quality. In managerial positions, Type As demonstrate their competitiveness by working long hours and, not infrequently, making poor decisions because they make them too fast.

Stressed Type As are also rarely creative. Because of their concern with quantity and speed, they rely on past experiences when faced with problems. They will not take the time that is necessary to develop unique solutions to new problems. They rarely vary in their responses to specific challenges in their environment. As a result, their behaviour is easier to predict than that of Type Bs.

Are Type As or Type Bs more successful in organizations? Despite the hard work of Type As, the Type Bs are the ones who appear to make it to the top. Great salespeople are usually Type As; senior executives are usually Type Bs.

Why? The answer lies in the tendency of Type As to trade off quality of effort for quantity. Promotions in corporate and professional organizations "usually go to those who are wise rather than to those who are merely hasty, to those who are tactful rather than to those who are hostile, and to those who are creative rather than to those who are merely agile in competitive strife."[56]

More important than the simple question of promotion is the fact that Type As suffer more serious health consequences when under stress. Stressed Type A individuals tend to exhibit such negative health consequences as higher blood pressure, and their recovery from the stressful situation is slower than that of Type B personalities. These findings suggest why Type A individuals tend to have higher rates of death associated with hypertension, coronary heart disease, and coronary artery disease.[57]

Recent research has looked at the effect of job complexity on the cardiovascular health of both Type A and Type B individuals to see whether Type As always suffered negative health consequences.[58] Type A workers who faced high job complexity had higher death rates from heart-related disorders than Type As who faced lower job complexity. In contrast, Type B individuals did not suffer negative health consequences from jobs with psychological complexity. These findings suggest that healthwise, Type B workers suffer less when handling complex jobs than do Type As. It also suggests that Type As who face lower job complexity do not face the same health risks as Type As who face higher job complexity.

If you are interested in determining whether you have a Type A or Type B personality, you might want to complete *Learning About Yourself Exercise #6* on page 70.

Richard Branson's propensity to take risks aligns with his job demands of being an entrepreneur. Branson, founder and chairman of London-based Virgin Group, started risky ventures that compete against industry giants. His Virgin Atlantic airline, for example, has taken market share from British Airways and has earned a reputation as one of the financially healthiest airlines in the world. Branson's risk-taking personality extends to his leisure activities of speedboat racing, skydiving, and ballooning.

Proactive Personality

Did you ever notice that some people actively take the initiative to improve their current circumstances or create new ones while others sit by passively reacting to situations? The former individuals have been described as having a proactive personality.[59]

People with a **proactive personality** identify opportunities, show initiative, take action, and persevere until meaningful change occurs. They create positive change in their environment, regardless or even in spite of constraints or obstacles.[60] Not surprisingly, proactives have many desirable behaviours that organizations desire. For instance, the evidence indicates that proactives are more likely to be seen as leaders and more likely to act as change agents within the organization.[61] Other actions of proactives can be positive or negative, depending on the organization and the situation. For example, proactives are more likely to challenge the status quo or voice their displeasure when situations aren't to their liking.[62] If an organization requires people with entrepreneurial initiative, proactives make good candidates; however, these are people who are also more likely to leave an organization to start their own business.[63] As individuals, proactives are more likely to achieve career success.[64] This is because they select, create, and influence work situations in their favour. Proactives are more likely to seek out job and organizational information, develop contacts in high places, engage in career planning, and demonstrate persistence in the face of career obstacles.

proactive personality A person who identifies opportunities, shows initiative, takes action, and perseveres until meaningful change occurs.

Personality and National Culture

There are certainly no common personality types for a given country. You can, for instance, find high and low risk-takers in almost any culture. Yet a country's culture should influence the dominant personality characteristics of its population. Let's build this case by looking at one personality attribute—locus of control.

There is evidence that cultures differ in terms of people's relationship to their environment.[65] In some cultures, such as those in North America, people believe that they can dominate their environment. People in other societies, such as Middle Eastern countries, believe that life is essentially predetermined. Notice the close parallel to internal and external locus of control. We should expect a larger proportion of internals in the Canadian and American workforces than in the Saudi Arabian or Iranian workforces.

One caveat regarding personality tests is that they may be subject to cultural bias when used on samples of people other than those for whom the tests were designed. For instance, on common American personality tests, British people are characterized as "less dominant, achievement-orientated or flexible than Americans, but more self-controlled."[66] When these tests are used to select managers, they may result in the selection of individuals who are not as suitable in the British workplace than they would be in the American workplace. An example of a bias that can appear in such tests is that only 10 percent of British men answer "true" to the statement "I very much like hunting" while 70 percent of American men agree.[67]

Personality and Perception

Can a person's personality affect how they are perceived by others? Some research has shown that people with certain personality characteristics are perceived in a more positive light than others. For instance, people who are more open are perceived to be able to adapt more quickly and effectively to unexpected change.[68] High self-monitors have been perceived as being more successful in organizational outcomes such as performance evaluations and promotions.[69]

A recent study found that individuals tend to have more negative impressions of those who differ from them demographically (that is, those who belong to a different gender, age group, income group, ethnic group, etc.).[70] People's perceptions of those demographically different were more positive, however, when these individuals were either more extraverted, or were higher self-monitors. Why might these characteristics affect how one is perceived? Introverts may be perceived as being shyer and quieter, and thus harder to get to know. So they have more difficulty changing people's perceptions of them. Extraverts, by comparison, are seen as more friendly and open, which allows people to get to know them better.[71]

High self-monitors may also be more able to affect people's perceptions of them. In particular, they may try harder to adjust their image to the needs of those around them.[72] High self-monitors may be "particularly willing and able to tailor and fashion an image" suitable to those around them.[73]

The results of these studies suggest that people's personalities may affect how they are perceived. People who are different from their co-workers tend to be less satisfied, poorer performers, and paid less.[74] However, when those who are different are perceived in more positive ways, their job outcomes tend to be less negative. One way to be perceived more positively is to reveal more about yourself to the group.

Tony Comper, president and CEO of the Bank of Montreal (BMO), gets irritated when his personality is compared with that of former CEO Matthew Barrett. Barrett is definitely an extravert; Comper, an introvert. In 2002, three years after Comper took over the top position at BMO, the bank fell to fifth place from third in terms of assets. The perception is that it was Barrett's charismatic, risk-taking personality that drove the "excitement and stellar performance" of the bank during the 1990s.[75]

Bank of Montreal
www.bmo.com

OB in the Street examines another area where perception and personality have been linked: messy bedrooms!

OB IN THE STREET

The Case of the Messy Bedroom

Can bedrooms tell us about personality? A recent research study found that people can learn about others' personality characteristics by simply looking around their bedroom and office space.[76] Subjects observed rooms and made predictions about personality based on what they observed. Personality tests were also given to those whose spaces were observed.

The researchers found that details of the room, such as the amount of clutter, dirty laundry, and even a crooked picture frame, give clear clues to observers about the personality of the inhabitant. The researchers found that clean and organized spaces belonged to conscientious people. Extraverted people tended to have more cluttered spaces, cheerful decorating schemes, and rooms that were designed for conversation.

The researchers found that bedrooms were better predictors of personality characteristics than office space, perhaps because businesses sometimes restricted employees' abilities to freely design their workspace. They concluded that individuals may want to influence how other people perceive them by paying attention to what the space around them looks like.

EMOTIONS

Each of us has a range of personality characteristics, but we also bring with us a range of emotions. Given the obvious role that emotions play in our everyday life, it might surprise you to learn that, until very recently, the topic of emotions was given little or no attention within the field of OB. When emotions were considered, the discussion focused on strong negative emotions—especially anger—that interfered with an employee's ability to do his or her job effectively. Emotions were rarely viewed as being constructive or able to stimulate performance-enhancing behaviours.

6 Can emotions help or get in the way when we're dealing with others?

Certainly some emotions, particularly when exhibited at the wrong time, can reduce employee performance. But this does not change the reality that employees bring an emotional component with them to work every day, and that no study of OB could be comprehensive without considering the role of emotions in workplace behaviour.

What Are Emotions?

Emotions are intense feelings that are directed at someone or something.[77] By contrast, **moods** are feelings that tend to be less intense than emotions and which lack a contextual stimulus.[78]

Emotions are not enduring, but reactions to an object. You show your emotions when you are "happy about something, angry at someone, afraid of something."[79] Research has identified six universal emotions: anger, fear, sadness, happiness, disgust, and surprise.[80]

Moods, on the other hand, aren't directed at an object. Emotions can turn into moods when you stop focusing on the contextual object. So when a colleague criticizes you for the way you spoke to a client, you might become angry at that colleague. That is, you show emotion (anger) toward a specific object (your colleague). But later in the day, you might find yourself just generally dispirited. You cannot attribute this feeling to any single event; you are just not your normal, upbeat self. This state describes a mood.

emotions Intense feelings that are directed at someone or something.

moods Feelings that tend to be less intense than emotions and that lack a contextual stimulus.

Choosing Emotions: Emotional Labour

Sometimes individuals are required to manage their emotions. For instance, you may be very angry with a co-worker or manager, but you may choose to suppress that anger in the interest of keeping the peace and/or your job. You may also decide not to kiss a co-worker in a moment of overwhelming exuberance, to make sure that your intentions are not misinterpreted.

emotional labour When an employee expresses organizationally desired emotions during interpersonal interactions.

Ever wonder why the grocery clerk is always smiling?

Emotional labour refers to the requirement to express particular emotions at work (for instance, enthusiasm or loyalty) to maximize organizational productivity.[81] All employees expend physical and mental labour when they put their bodies and cognitive capabilities, respectively, into their jobs. But most jobs also require emotional labour. This term was first coined by Professor Arlie Hochschild of the University of California at Berkeley and refers to the demand organizations make on their employees to display "appropriate" emotions during interpersonal transactions.[82]

The concept of emotional labour originally developed in relation to service jobs. Studies of emotional labour have explored how smiling flight attendants, cheerful grocery clerks, gossipy hairdressers, and nasty bill collectors are expected to control their emotional expression to improve productivity, customer satisfaction, efficiency, and even profitability.[83] But today, the concept of emotional labour seems relevant to almost every job. You are expected, for example, to be courteous and not hostile in interactions with co-workers. As well, leaders are expected to draw on emotional labour to "charge the troops." Almost every great speech, for instance, contains a strong emotional component that stirs feelings in others.

As these studies show, however, managing emotions can take a toll when there is a discrepancy between the outward behaviour the person is required to display as part of his or her job and the inward feelings that the person has.[84] Therefore, while emotional labour can have positive implications within the workplace, it can also have negative personal consequences when a person consistently hides real emotions behind a work "face."[85] Flight attendants use the phrase "go robot" to describe how they separate their private feelings from their public behaviour.[86] Other researchers have discussed both the individual effects of emotional labour, such as distancing, burnout, and phoniness,[87] and the organizational effects, such as suppressed disagreements, reduced upward information flow, and loss of "voice."[88] A Vancouver Safeway employee described her company's requirement to smile at all shoppers: "My personal opinion is, they're expecting us not to be human. I just can't walk around with a smile on my face all day."[89]

Emotional labour is an important component of effective job performance at the Happy Beauty Salon in Long Island, New York. Owner Happy Nomikos, shown here serving customers strawberries and grapes, requires that her nail technicians and hairstylists build customer loyalty by being courteous and cheerful. In interacting with her employees and customers, Nomikos says, "I have to keep everyone happy." She hugs loyal customers, jokes with her staff, and offers customers pizza and cake in celebration of employees' birthdays.

As we proceed in this section, you will see that it is because of emotional labour's increasing importance in effective job performance that an understanding of emotion has gained heightened relevance within the field of OB. This chapter's *Ethical Dilemma Exercise* on page 73 considers whether it's ethical to tell employees how to manage their emotions at work.

Gender and Emotions

It's widely assumed that women are more "in touch" with their feelings than men—that they react more emotionally and are better able to read emotions in others. Is there any truth to these assumptions?

RESEARCH FINDINGS

The evidence does confirm differences between men and women when it comes to emotional reactions and ability to read others. When the genders are contrasted, women show greater emotional expression than men;[90] they experience emotions more intensely; and they display more frequent expressions of both positive and negative emotions, except anger.[91] Women also report more comfort in expressing emotions than men. Finally, women are better at reading nonverbal cues than are men.[92]

What explains these differences? Three possible answers have been suggested. One explanation is the different ways men and women have been socialized.[93] Men are taught to be tough and brave, and showing emotion is inconsistent with this image. Women, on the other hand, are socialized to be nurturing. This may account for the perception that women are generally warmer and friendlier than men. For instance, women are expected to express more positive emotions on the job (shown by smiling) than men, and they do.[94] A second explanation is that women may have more innate ability to read others and present their emotions than do men.[95] Third, women may have a greater need for social approval and, thus, a higher tendency to show positive emotions such as happiness.

Why Should We Care About Emotions in the Workplace?

There are a number of reasons to be concerned about understanding emotions in the workplace.[96] People who know their own emotions and are good at reading others' emotions may be more effective in their jobs. That, in essence, is the theme underlying contemporary research on emotional intelligence.[97] The entire workplace can be affected by positive or negative workplace emotions, another issue we consider below. Finally, we consider affective events theory, which has increased our understanding of emotions at work.

Emotional Intelligence

Emotional intelligence (EI) refers to an assortment of noncognitive skills, capabilities, and competencies that influence a person's ability to succeed in coping with environmental demands and pressures. It comprises five dimensions:

- *Self-awareness.* Being aware of what one is feeling. It's exhibited by self-confident, realistic self-assessment, and a self-deprecating sense of humour.

- *Self-management.* The ability to manage one's own emotions and impulses. It's exhibited by trustworthiness and integrity, comfort with ambiguity, and openness to change.

- *Self-motivation.* The ability to persist in the face of setbacks and failures. It's exhibited by a strong drive to achieve, optimism, and high organizational commitment.

- *Empathy.* The ability to sense how others are feeling. It's exhibited by expertise in building and retaining talent, cross-cultural sensitivity, and service to clients and customers.

- *Social skills.* The ability to handle the emotions of others. It's exhibited by persuasiveness, and expertise in building and leading groups and teams.

EI differs from emotional labour because the latter is a job requirement (the demand to smile, express enthusiasm, etc.) while the former is regarded as a personality trait. A person with low EI may control one's emotions because of a request from a manager (thus engaging in emotional labour), but might otherwise not do so.

emotional intelligence An assortment of noncognitive skills, capabilities, and competencies that influence a person's ability to succeed in coping with environmental demands and pressures.

Several studies suggest EI may play an important role in job performance. For instance, one study looked at the characteristics of Bell Labs engineers who were rated as stars by their peers. The scientists concluded that stars were better at relating to others. EI, not academic IQ, characterized high performers![98]

Another study of US Air Force recruiters generated similar findings. Top-performing recruiters exhibited high levels of EI. Using these findings, the US Air Force changed its selection criteria. A follow-up investigation found that subsequent hires who had high EI scores were 2.6 times more successful than those who did not.[99]

Corporations are acting on the results of these studies. A recent poll of human resource managers asked: How important is it for your workers to demonstrate EI to move up the corporate ladder? Forty percent replied "Very Important." Another 16 percent said "Moderately Important." Irene Taylor, a consultant with Toronto-based Praxis Canada, says her company "has conducted EQ assessments on about 300 Canadian lawyers over the past five years." She also says that demand to get into the company's EI coaching program is high. Professor John Oesch of the Joseph L. Rotman School of Management at the University of Toronto explains why coaching in EI has become popular: "It's a solid psychological construct that can be measured and, to a certain extent, taught."[100]

Tony Comper, president and CEO of the Bank of Montreal, certainly agrees with the importance of understanding EI. He cites Daniel Goleman's *Working With Emotional Intelligence*[101] as one of his favourite books on leadership.[102]

To learn more about your emotional intelligence, you might want to complete *Learning About Yourself Exercise #7* on page 70. This chapter's *From Concepts to Skills* on page 76 gives you some insight into reading the emotions of others.

Negative Workplace Emotions

Negative emotions can lead to a number of deviant workplace behaviours. Anyone who has spent much time in an organization realizes that people often engage in voluntary actions that violate established norms and threaten the organization, its members, or both. These actions are called **employee deviance**.[103] Deviant actions fall into categories such as production (leaving early, intentionally working slowly); property (stealing, sabotage); political (gossiping, blaming co-workers); and personal aggression (sexual harassment, verbal abuse).[104]

Many of these deviant behaviours can be traced to negative emotions. For instance, envy is an emotion that occurs when you resent someone for having something that you don't, and that you strongly desire.[105] It can lead to malicious deviant behaviours, such as hostility, "backstabbing," and other forms of political behaviour that negatively distort others' successes and positively distort your own accomplishments.[106]

Managing emotions in the workplace becomes important both to ward off negative behaviour and to encourage positive behaviour in those around us. *Focus on Research* looks at the issue of "catching" moods from others. You may be surprised to learn the extent to which your mood can affect the mood of others.

employee deviance Voluntary actions that violate established norms and threaten the organization, its members, or both.

FOCUS ON **RESEARCH**

Moods Affect the Success of Groups

Can you catch moods from those around you? A study of 70 work groups sought to discover whether moods could be spread throughout the group.[107] There were four to eight members in each group. While performing tasks, each group was observed by two people, who tried to judge the mood of the group from posture, facial expression, and vocal expression of group members. To assess the accuracy of the observations, group members filled out questionnaires that asked about their typical behaviour with members of their group, and their mood at the time of the observation.

The researchers found that members of groups do seem to adopt similar moods when the moods are "high-energy (e.g., cheerful enthusiasm, hostile irritability)" rather than when they are "low-energy (e.g., serene warmth, depressed sluggishness)." The entire group felt unpleasant moods the most strongly. Those who observed the work groups were able to accurately identify many of the moods the groups experienced, just by watching postures and the facial and vocal expressions of group members. The researchers also found that facial and postural cues were more likely to signal the mood of the group than vocal cues. They suggested that group members may feel it's inappropriate to express their moods verbally in some work settings, so that facial gestures become the more likely avenue of mood expression. 👤

Affective Events Theory

Understanding emotions at work has been significantly helped by a model called **affective events theory (AET)**.[108] AET demonstrates that employees react emotionally to things that happen to them at work and that this emotional reaction influences their job performance and satisfaction.

Exhibit 2-10 summarizes AET. The theory begins by recognizing that emotions are a response to an event in the work environment. The work environment includes everything surrounding the job—characteristics of the job such as the variety of tasks and degree of autonomy, job demands, and requirements for expressing emotional labour. This environment creates work events that can be hassles, uplifts, or both. Examples of events that employees frequently see as hassles are colleagues who refuse to carry their share of work, conflicting directions by different managers, and excessive time pressures.[109] Examples of uplifting events include meeting a goal, getting support from a colleague, and receiving recognition for an accomplishment. These work events trigger positive or negative emotional reactions. But the events-reaction relationship is moderated by the employee's personality and mood. Personality predisposes people to respond with greater or lesser intensity to the event. For instance, people who score low on emotional stability are more likely to react strongly to negative events. In addition, a person's

affective events theory (AET) The theory that employees react emotionally to things that happen to them at work and that this emotional reaction influences their job performance and satisfaction.

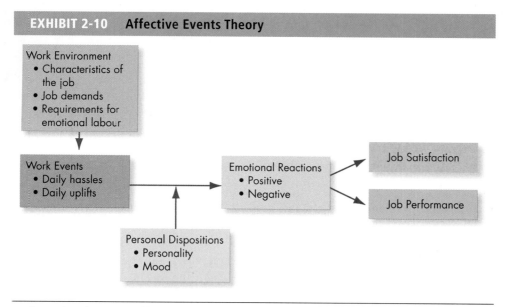

EXHIBIT 2-10   Affective Events Theory

Work Environment
- Characteristics of the job
- Job demands
- Requirements for emotional labour

Work Events
- Daily hassles
- Daily uplifts

Personal Dispositions
- Personality
- Mood

Emotional Reactions
- Positive
- Negative

Job Satisfaction

Job Performance

Source: Based on N. M. Ashkanasy and C. S. Daus, "Emotion in the Workplace: The New Challenge for Managers," *Academy of Management Executive,* February 2002, p. 77

emotional response to a given event can change depending on his or her mood. Finally, emotions influence a number of job performance and satisfaction variables such as OCB, organizational commitment, intentions to quit, and level of effort.

In addition, tests of the theory suggest that (1) an emotional episode is actually a series of emotional experiences precipitated by a single event. It reflects elements of both emotions and mood cycles. (2) Job satisfaction is influenced by current emotions at any given time along with the history of emotions surrounding the event. (3) Since moods and emotions fluctuate over time, their effect on performance also fluctuates. (4) Emotion-driven behaviours are typically short in duration and of high variability. (5) Because emotions tend to be incompatible with behaviours required to do a job, they can have a negative influence on job performance (this is the case even for positive emotions like happiness and joy).[110]

An example might help better explain AET.[111] You work as an aeronautical engineer for Bombardier. Because of the downturn in the demand for commercial jets, you have just learned that the company is considering laying off several thousand employees. This could include you. This event is likely to elicit a negative emotional reaction: You are fearful that you might lose your job and primary source of income. Also, because you are prone to worry a lot and obsess about problems, your feelings of insecurity are increased. This event also puts into place a series of subevents that create an episode: You talk with your boss and he assures you that your job is safe; you hear rumours that your department is high on the list to be eliminated; you run into a former colleague who was laid off six months ago and still has not found work. These, in turn, create emotional ups and downs. One day you are feeling more upbeat and that you will survive the cuts. The next day, you might be depressed and anxious, convinced that your department will be eliminated. These swings in your emotions take your attention away from your work and result in reduced job performance and satisfaction. Finally, your response is magnified because this is the fourth large layoff that Bombardier has initiated in the past three years.

In summary, AET offers two important messages.[112] First, emotions provide valuable insights into understanding employee behaviour. The model demonstrates how daily hassles and uplifts influence employee performance and satisfaction. Second, emotions in organizations and the events that cause them should not be ignored, even when they appear to be minor. This is because they accumulate. It's not the intensity of hassles and uplifts that lead to emotional reactions, but more the frequency with which they occur.

SUMMARY AND IMPLICATIONS

1 **What is perception?** *Perception* is the process by which individuals organize and interpret their impressions in order to give meaning to their environment. Individuals behave in a given manner based not on the way their environment actually is but, rather, on what they see or believe it to be. An organization may spend millions of dollars to create a pleasant work environment for its employees. However, despite these expenditures, an employee who believes that his or her job is lousy will behave accordingly.

2 **What causes people to have different perceptions of the same situation?** A number of factors operate to shape and sometimes distort perception. These factors can be present in the *perceiver,* in the object or *target* being perceived, or in the context of the *situation* in which the perception is made. The perceiver's attitudes, motives, interests, and past experiences all shape the way he or she sees an event. The target's characteristics also affect what is perceived. Novelty, motion, sounds, size, and other characteristics of a target shape the way it is seen. Objects or events that are unrelated are often perceived together because they are close physically or in timing. Persons, objects, or events that are similar to each other also tend to be viewed as a group. The setting in which we see objects or events also affects how they are perceived.

3 **Can people be mistaken in their perceptions?** Perceiving and interpreting what others do is difficult and takes time. As a result, we develop shortcuts to make this task more manageable. These shortcuts, described by attribution theory, selective perception, the halo effect, contrast effects, projection, and stereotyping, are often valuable—they can sometimes allow us to make accurate perceptions quickly and provide valid data for making predictions. However, they are not foolproof. They can and do get us into trouble.

4 **Does perception really affect outcomes?** The evidence suggests that what individuals perceive about their work situation influences their productivity more than the situation does. Whether a job is actually interesting or challenging is irrelevant. Whether a manager actually helps employees to structure their work more efficiently and effectively is far less important than how employees perceive the manager's efforts. Similarly, issues such as fair pay, the validity of performance appraisals, and the adequacy of working conditions are not judged "objectively." Rather, individuals interpret conditions surrounding their jobs based on how they *perceive* their jobs.

5 **What is personality and how does it affect behaviour?** *Personality* is the stable patterns of behaviour and consistent internal states that determine how an individual reacts to and interacts with others. A review of the personality literature offers general guidelines that can lead to effective job performance. As such, it can improve hiring, transfer, and promotion decisions. Personality attributes give us a framework for predicting behaviour. Personality affects how people react to others, and the types of jobs that they may desire. For example, individuals who are shy, introverted, and uncomfortable in social situations would probably make poor salespeople. Individuals who are submissive and conforming might not be effective as advertising "idea" people. Be aware, though, that measuring personality is not an exact science, and as you no doubt learned from the discussion of attribution theory, it's easy to attribute personality characteristics in error.

6 **Can emotions help or get in the way when were dealing with others?** *Emotions* are intense feelings that are directed at someone or something. Positive emotions can be motivating for everyone in the workplace. Negative emotions may make it difficult to get along with others. Can managers control the emotions of their colleagues and employees? No. Emotions are a natural part of an individual's makeup. At the same time, managers err if they ignore the emotional elements in OB and assess individual behaviour as if it were completely rational. Managers who understand the role of emotions will significantly improve their ability to explain and predict individual behaviour.

Do emotions affect job performance? Yes. Emotions, especially negative ones, can hinder performance. That's probably why organizations, for the most part, try to remove emotions from the workplace. But emotions can also enhance performance. How? Two ways.[113] First, emotions can increase arousal levels, thus acting as motivators to higher performance. Second, emotional labour recognizes that feelings can be part of a job's required behaviour. So, for instance, the ability to effectively manage emotions in leadership and sales positions may be critical to success in those positions. Research also indicates the importance of emotional intelligence, the assortment of noncognitive skills, capabilities, and competencies that influence a person's ability to succeed in coping with environmental demands and pressures.

OB AT WORK

For Review

1. Define *perception*.

2. What is attribution theory? What are its implications for explaining behaviour in organizations?

3. What is stereotyping? Give an example of how stereotyping can create perceptual distortion.

4. Give some positive results of using shortcuts when judging others.

5. Describe the factors in the Big Five model. Which factor shows the greatest value in predicting behaviour? Why does it?

6. What behavioural predictions might you make if you knew that an employee had (a) an external locus of control? (b) a low Mach score? (c) low self-esteem? (d) a Type A personality?

7. To what extent do people's personalities affect how they are perceived?

8. What is emotional labour and why is it important to understanding OB?

9. What is emotional intelligence and why is it important?

10. Explain affective events theory. What are its implications for managing emotions?

For Critical Thinking

1. How might the differences in experience of students and instructors affect each of their perceptions of classroom behaviour (e.g., students' written work and class comments)?

2. An employee does an unsatisfactory job on an assigned project. Explain the attribution process that this person's manager will use to form judgments about this employee's job performance.

3. One day your boss comes in and he's nervous, edgy, and argumentative. The next day he is calm and relaxed. Does this behaviour suggest that personality traits aren't consistent from day to day?

4. What, if anything, can managers do to manage emotions? Are there ethical implications in any of these actions? If so, what?

5. Give some examples of situations where expressing emotions might enhance job performance.

OB For You

- The discussion of perception might get you thinking about how you view the world. When we perceive someone as a troublemaker, for instance, this may be only a perception, and not a real characteristic of that person. It is always good to question your perceptions, just to be sure that you are not reading something into a situation that is not there.

- One important thing to consider when looking for a job is whether your personality will fit the organization to which you are applying. For instance, it may be a highly structured organization. If you, by nature, are much less formal, this may not be a good fit for you.

- Sometimes personalities get in the way when working in groups. You may want to see if you can figure out ways to get personality differences working in favour of group goals.

- Emotions need not always be suppressed when working with others. While emotions can sometimes hinder performance, positive emotions can motivate you and those around you.

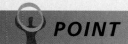 *POINT*

Traits Are Powerful Predictors of Behaviour

The essence of trait approaches in OB is that employees possess stable personality characteristics that significantly influence their attitudes toward, and behavioural reactions to, organizational settings. People with particular traits tend to be relatively consistent in their attitudes and behaviour over time and across situations.[114]

Of course, trait theorists recognize that all traits are not equally powerful. They tend to put traits into one of three categories. *Cardinal traits* are those so strong and generalized that they influence every act a person performs. *Primary traits* are generally consistent influences on behaviour, but they may not show up in all situations. Finally, *secondary traits* are those that do not form a vital part of the personality, but come into play only in particular situations. For the most part, trait theories have focused on the power of primary traits to predict employee behaviour.

Trait theorists do a fairly good job of meeting the average person's common-sense beliefs. Think of friends, relatives, and acquaintances you have known for a number of years. Do they have traits that have remained essentially stable over time? Most of us would answer that question in the affirmative. If cousin Anne was shy and nervous when we last saw her 10 years ago, we would be surprised to find her outgoing and relaxed now.

Managers seem to have a strong belief in the power of traits to predict behaviour. If managers believed that situations determined behaviour, they would hire people almost at random and put great effort into structuring situations properly. But the employee selection process in most organizations places a great deal of emphasis on how applicants perform in interviews and on tests. Assume you are an interviewer and ask yourself: What am I looking for in job candidates? If you answer with terms such as *conscientious, hard-working, persistent, confident,* and *dependable,* you are a trait theorist!

 COUNTERPOINT

Traits Reflect the Surrounding Situation

Few people would dispute that there are some stable individual attributes that affect reactions to the workplace. But trait theorists go beyond that generality and argue that individual behaviour consistencies are widespread and account for much of the difference in behaviour among people.[115]

There are two important problems with using traits to explain a large proportion of behaviour in organizations. First, organizational settings are strong situations that have a large impact on employee behaviour. Second, individuals are highly adaptive and personality traits change in response to organizational situations.

It has been well known for some time that the effects of traits are likely to be strongest in relatively weak situations, and weakest in relatively strong situations. Organizational settings tend to be strong situations because they have rules and other formal regulations that define acceptable behaviour and punish deviant behaviour; and they have informal norms that dictate appropriate behaviours. These formal and informal constraints minimize the effects of personality traits.

By arguing that employees possess stable traits that lead to cross-situational consistencies in behaviours, trait theorists are implying that individuals don't really adapt to different situations. But there is a growing body of evidence that an individual's traits are changed by the organizations in which an individual participates. If the individual's personality changes as a result of exposure to organizational settings, in what sense can that individual be said to have traits that persistently and consistently affect his or her reactions to those very settings? Moreover, people typically belong to multiple organizations, which often include very different kinds of members. They adapt to those different situations. Instead of being the prisoners of a rigid and stable personality framework, as trait theorists propose, people regularly adjust their behaviour to reflect the requirements of various situations.

LEARNING ABOUT **YOURSELF** EXERCISE #1

Assess Your Locus of Control

Read the following statements and indicate whether you agree more with choice A or choice B.

A

1. Making a lot of money is largely a matter of getting the right breaks.

2. I have noticed that there is a direct connection between how hard I study and the grades I get.

3. The number of divorces indicates that more and more people are not trying to make their marriages work.

4. It is silly to think that one can really change another person's basic attitudes.

5. Getting promoted is really a matter of being a little luckier than the next person.

6. If one knows how to deal with people, they are really quite easily led.

7. The grades I make are the result of my own efforts; luck has little or nothing to do with it.

8. People like me can change the course of world affairs if we make ourselves heard.

9. A great deal that happens to me is probably a matter of chance.

10. Getting along with people is a skill that must be practised.

B

1. Promotions are earned through hard work and persistence.

2. Many times, the reactions of teachers seem haphazard to me.

3. Marriage is largely a gamble.

4. When I am right, I can convince others.

5. In our society, a person's future earning power is dependent upon his or her ability.

6. I have little influence over the way other people behave.

7. Sometimes I feel that I have little to do with the grades I get.

8. It is only wishful thinking to believe that one can readily influence what happens in our society.

9. I am in control of my destiny.

10. It is almost impossible to figure out how to please some people.

Scoring Key:

Give yourself 1 point for each of the following selections: 1B, 2A, 3A, 4B, 5B, 6A, 7A, 8A, 9B, and 10A.
Scores can be interpreted as follows:

8–10 = High internal locus of control

6–7 = Moderate internal locus of control

5 = Mixed

3–4 = Moderate external locus of control

1–2 = High external locus of control

Source: Adapted from J. B. Rotter, "External Control and Internal Control," *Psychology Today,* June 1971, p. 42. Copyright 1971 by the American Psychological Association. Adapted with permission.

LEARNING ABOUT **YOURSELF** EXERCISE #2

How Machiavellian Are You?

For each statement, circle the number that most closely resembles your attitude.

Statement	Disagree			Agree	
	A Lot	A Little	Neutral	A Little	A Lot
1. The best way to handle people is to tell them what they want to hear.	1	2	3	4	5
2. When you ask someone to do something for you, it is best to give the real reason for wanting it rather than giving reasons that might carry more weight.	1	2	3	4	5
3. Anyone who completely trusts anyone else is asking for trouble.	1	2	3	4	5
4. It is hard to get ahead without cutting corners here and there.	1	2	3	4	5
5. It is safest to assume that all people have a vicious streak, and it will come out when they are given a chance.	1	2	3	4	5
6. One should take action only when it is morally right.	1	2	3	4	5
7. Most people are basically good and kind.	1	2	3	4	5
8. There is no excuse for lying to someone else.	1	2	3	4	5
9. Most people more easily forget the death of their father than the loss of their property.	1	2	3	4	5
10. Generally speaking, people won't work hard unless they're forced to do so.	1	2	3	4	5

Scoring Key:

To obtain your Mach score, add the number you have checked on questions 1, 3, 4, 5, 9, and 10. For the other 4 questions (2, 6, 7, and 8), reverse the numbers you have checked: 5 becomes 1, 4 is 2, 2 is 4, and 1 is 5. Total your 10 numbers to find your score. The higher your score, the more Machiavellian you are. Among a random sample of American adults, the national average was 25.

Source: R. Christie and F. L. Geis, *Studies in Machiavellianism* (New York: Academic Press, 1970). Reprinted by permission.

OB *AT WORK*

How's Your Self-Esteem?

Answer each of the following questions honestly. Next to each question write a 1, 2, 3, 4, or 5, depending on which answer best describes you.

> 1 = **Very often**
> 2 = **Fairly often**
> 3 = **Sometimes**
> 4 = **Once in a great while**
> 5 = **Practically never**

_____ **1.** How often do you have the feeling that there is nothing that you can do well?

_____ **2.** When you talk in front of a class or group of people your own age, how often do you feel worried or afraid?

_____ **3.** How often do you feel that you have handled yourself well at social gatherings?

_____ **4.** How often do you have the feeling that you can do everything well?

_____ **5.** How often are you comfortable when starting a conversation with people you don't know?

_____ **6.** How often do you feel self-conscious?

_____ **7.** How often do you feel that you are a successful person?

_____ **8.** How often are you troubled with shyness?

_____ **9.** How often do you feel inferior to most people you know?

_____ **10.** How often do you feel that you are a worthless individual?

_____ **11.** How often do you feel confident that your success in your future job or career is assured?

_____ **12.** How often do you feel sure of yourself when among strangers?

_____ **13.** How often do you feel confident that some day people will look up to you and respect you?

_____ **14.** In general, how often do you feel confident about your abilities?

_____ **15.** How often do you worry about how well you get along with other people?

_____ **16.** How often do you feel that you dislike yourself?

_____ **17.** How often do you feel so discouraged with yourself that you wonder whether anything is worthwhile?

_____ **18.** How often do you worry about whether other people like to be with you?

_____ **19.** When you talk in front of a class or a group of people of your own age, how often are you pleased with your performance?

_____ **20.** How often do you feel sure of yourself when you speak in a class discussion?

Scoring Key:

Add up your score from the left column for the following 10 items: 1, 2, 6, 8, 9, 10, 15, 16, 17, and 18. For the other 10 items, reverse your scoring (that is, 5 becomes 1, 4 is 2, 2 is 4, and 1 is 5). The higher your score, the higher your self-esteem.

Source: J. R. Robinson and P. R. Shaver, *Measures of Social Psychological Attitudes* (Ann Arbor, MI: Institute for Social Research, 1973), pp. 79–80. With permission.

LEARNING ABOUT **YOURSELF** EXERCISE #4

Are You a High Self-Monitor?

Indicate the degree to which you think the following statements are true or false by circling the appropriate number. For example, if a statement is always true, circle the 5 next to that statement.

5 = **Certainly, always true**

4 = **Generally true**

3 = **Somewhat true, but with exceptions**

2 = **Somewhat false, but with exceptions**

1 = **Generally false**

0 = **Certainly, always false**

1. In social situations, I have the ability to alter my behaviour if I feel that something else is called for.	5	4	3	2	1	0
2. I am often able to read people's true emotions correctly through their eyes.	5	4	3	2	1	0
3. I have the ability to control the way I come across to people, depending on the impression I wish to give them.	5	4	3	2	1	0
4. In conversations, I am sensitive to even the slightest change in the facial expression of the person I'm conversing with.	5	4	3	2	1	0
5. My powers of intuition are quite good when it comes to understanding others' emotions and motives.	5	4	3	2	1	0
6. I can usually tell when others consider a joke in bad taste, even though they may laugh convincingly.	5	4	3	2	1	0
7. When I feel that the image I am portraying isn't working, I can readily change it to something that does.	5	4	3	2	1	0
8. I can usually tell when I've said something inappropriate by reading the listener's eyes.	5	4	3	2	1	0
9. I have trouble changing my behaviour to suit different people and different situations.	5	4	3	2	1	0
10. I have found that I can adjust my behaviour to meet the requirements of any situation I find myself in.	5	4	3	2	1	0
11. If someone is lying to me, I usually know it at once from that person's manner of expression.	5	4	3	2	1	0
12. Even when it might be to my advantage, I have difficulty putting up a good front.	5	4	3	2	1	0
13. Once I know what the situation calls for, it is easy for me to regulate my actions accordingly.	5	4	3	2	1	0

Scoring Key:

To obtain your score, add up the numbers circled, except reverse scores for questions 9 and 12. On those, a circled 5 becomes a 0, 4 becomes 1, and so forth. High self-monitors are defined as those with scores of 53 or higher.

Source: R. D. Lennox and R. N. Wolfe, "Revision of the Self-Monitoring Scale," *Journal of Personality and Social Psychology,* June 1984, p. 1361.
Copyright © 1984 by the American Psychological Association. Reprinted by permission.

LEARNING ABOUT **YOURSELF** EXERCISE #5

Are You a Risk-Taker?

For each of the following situations, indicate the minimum odds of success you would demand before recommending that one alternative be chosen over another. Try to place yourself in the position of the adviser to the central person in each of the situations.

1. Mr. B, a 45-year-old accountant, has recently been informed by his physician that he has developed a severe heart ailment. The disease will be sufficiently serious to force Mr. B to change many of his strongest life habits—reducing his workload, drastically changing his diet, giving up favourite leisure-time pursuits. The physician suggests that a delicate medical operation could be attempted. If successful, the operation would completely relieve the heart condition. But its success cannot be assured, and, in fact, the operation might prove fatal.

   Imagine that you are advising Mr. B. Listed below are several probabilities or odds that the operation will prove successful. Check the *lowest probability* that you would consider acceptable for the operation to be performed.

   _____   Mr. B should not have the operation, no matter what the probabilities.

   _____   The chances are 9 in 10 that the operation will be a success.

   _____   The chances are 7 in 10 that the operation will be a success.

   _____   The chances are 5 in 10 that the operation will be a success.

   _____   The chances are 3 in 10 that the operation will be a success.

   _____   The chances are 1 in 10 that the operation will be a success.

2. Mr. D is the captain of University X's varsity football team. University X is playing its traditional rival, University Y, in the final game of the season. The game is in its final seconds, and Mr. D's team, University X, is behind in the score. University X has time to make one more play. Mr. D, the captain, must decide on a strategy. Would it be best to try a play that would be almost certain to work and try to settle for a tie score? Or, on the other hand, should he try a more complicated and risky play that would bring victory if it succeeded or defeat if it failed? Imagine that you are advising Mr. D. Listed below are several probabilities or odds that the risky play will work. Check the *lowest probability* that you would consider acceptable for the risky play to be attempted.

   _____   Mr. D should not attempt the risky play, no matter what the probabilities.

   _____   The chances are 9 in 10 that the risky play will work.

   _____   The chances are 7 in 10 that the risky play will work.

   _____   The chances are 5 in 10 that the risky play will work.

   _____   The chances are 3 in 10 that the risky play will work.

   _____   The chances are 1 in 10 that the risky play will work.

3. Ms. K is a successful businesswoman who has participated in a number of civic activities of considerable value to the community. Ms. K has been approached by the leaders of her political party as a possible candidate in the next provincial election. Ms. K's party is a minority party in the district, though the party has won occasional elections in the past. Ms. K would like to hold political office, but to do so would involve a serious financial sacrifice, since the party has insufficient campaign funds. She would also have to endure the attacks of her political opponents in a hot campaign.

LEARNING ABOUT **YOURSELF** EXERCISE #5 (Continued)

Imagine that you are advising Ms. K. Listed below are several probabilities or odds of Ms. K's winning the election in her district. Check the *lowest probability* that you would consider acceptable to make it worthwhile for Ms. K to run for political office.

_____   Ms. K should not run for political office, no matter what the probabilities.

_____   The chances are 9 in 10 that Ms. K will win the election.

_____   The chances are 7 in 10 that Ms. K will win the election.

_____   The chances are 5 in 10 that Ms. K will win the election.

_____   The chances are 3 in 10 that Ms. K will win the election.

_____   The chances are 1 in 10 that Ms. K will win the election.

4. Ms. L, a 30-year-old research physicist, has been given a 5-year appointment by a major university laboratory. As she contemplates the next 5 years, she realizes that she might work on a difficult long-term problem. If a solution to the problem could be found, it would resolve basic scientific issues in the field and bring high scientific honours. If no solution were found, however, Ms. L would have little to show for her 5 years in the laboratory, and it would be hard for her to get a good job afterward. On the other hand, she could, as most of her professional associates are doing, work on a series of short-term problems for which solutions would be easier to find. Those solutions, though, would be of lesser scientific importance.

Imagine that you are advising Ms. L. Listed below are several probabilities or odds that a solution will be found to the difficult long-term problem that Ms. L has in mind. Check the *lowest probability* that you would consider acceptable to make it worthwhile for Ms. L to work on the more difficult long-term problem.

_____   Ms. L should not choose the long-term, difficult problem, no matter what the probabilities.

_____   The chances are 9 in 10 that Ms. L will solve the long-term problem.

_____   The chances are 7 in 10 that Ms. L will solve the long-term problem.

_____   The chances are 5 in 10 that Ms. L will solve the long-term problem.

_____   The chances are 3 in 10 that Ms. L will solve the long-term problem.

_____   The chances are 1 in 10 that Ms. L will solve the long-term problem.

Scoring Key:

These situations were based on a longer questionnaire. Your results are an indication of your general orientation toward risk rather than a precise measure. To calculate your risk-taking score, add up the chances you were willing to take and divide by 4. (For any of the situations in which you would not take the risk, regardless of the probabilities, give yourself a 10.) The lower your number, the more risk-taking you are.

Source: Adapted from N. Kogan and M. A. Wallach, *Risk Taking: A Study in Cognition and Personality* (New York: Holt, Rinehart and Winston, 1964), pp. 256–261. Reprinted with permission of Wadsworth, a division of Thompson Learning: www.thompsonrights.com. Fax 800-730-2215.

LEARNING ABOUT **YOURSELF** EXERCISE #6

Are You a Type A?

Circle the number on the scale below that best characterizes your behaviour for each trait.

1. Casual about appointments	1	2	3	4	5	6	7	8	Never late
2. Not competitive	1	2	3	4	5	6	7	8	Very competitive
3. Never feel rushed	1	2	3	4	5	6	7	8	Always feel rushed
4. Take things one at a time	1	2	3	4	5	6	7	8	Try to do many things at once
5. Slow doing things	1	2	3	4	5	6	7	8	Fast (eating, walking, etc.)
6. Express feelings	1	2	3	4	5	6	7	8	"Sit on" feelings
7. Many interests	1	2	3	4	5	6	7	8	Few interests outside work

Scoring Key:

Total your score on the 7 questions. Now multiply the total by 3. A total of 120 or more indicates that you are a hard-core Type A. Scores below 90 indicate that you are a hard-core Type B. The following gives you more specifics:

Points	Personality type
120 or more	A1
106–119	A
100–105	A2
90–99	B1
Less than 90	B

Source: Adapted from R. W. Bortner, "Short Rating Scale as a Potential Measure of Pattern A Behavior," *Journal of Chronic Diseases,* June 1969, pp. 87–91. With permission from Elsevier.

LEARNING ABOUT **YOURSELF** EXERCISE #7

What's Your EI at Work?

Evaluating the following 25 statements will allow you to rate your social skills and self-awareness, the components of emotional intelligence (EI).

EI, the social equivalent of IQ, is complex, in no small part because it depends on some pretty slippery variables—including your innate compatibility, or lack thereof, with the people who happen to be your co-workers. But if you want to get a rough idea of how your EI stacks up, this quiz will help.

As honestly as you can, estimate how you rate in the eyes of peers, bosses, and subordinates on each of the following traits, on a scale of 1–4, with 4 representing strong agreement, and 1 representing strong disagreement.

_____   I usually stay composed, positive, and unflappable even in trying moments.

_____   I can think clearly and stay focused on the task at hand under pressure.

_____   I am able to admit my own mistakes.

_____   I usually or always meet commitments and keep promises.

LEARNING ABOUT **YOURSELF** EXERCISE #7 (Continued)

_____ I hold myself accountable for meeting my goals.

_____ I'm organized and careful in my work.

_____ I regularly seek out fresh ideas from a wide variety of sources.

_____ I'm good at generating new ideas.

_____ I can smoothly handle multiple demands and changing priorities.

_____ I'm result-oriented, with a strong drive to meet my objectives.

_____ I like to set challenging goals and take calculated risks to reach them.

_____ I'm always trying to learn how to improve my performance, including asking advice from people younger than I am.

_____ I readily make sacrifices to meet an important organizational goal.

_____ The company's mission is something I understand and can identify with.

_____ The values of my team—or of our division or department, or the company—influence my decisions and clarify the choices I make.

_____ I actively seek out opportunities to further the overall goals of the organization and enlist others to help me.

_____ I pursue goals beyond what's required or expected of me in my current job.

_____ Obstacles and setbacks may delay me a little, but they don't stop me.

_____ Cutting through red tape and bending outdated rules are sometimes necessary.

_____ I seek fresh perspectives, even if that means trying something totally new.

_____ My impulses or distressing emotions don't often get the best of me at work.

_____ I can change tactics quickly when circumstances change.

_____ Pursuing new information is my best bet for cutting down on uncertainty and finding ways to do things better.

_____ I usually don't attribute setbacks to a personal flaw (mine or someone else's).

_____ I operate from an expectation of success rather than a fear of failure.

Scoring Key:

Total your score. A score below 70 indicates very low EI. EI is not unimprovable. Says Dan Goleman, author of *Working With Emotional Intelligence,* "Emotional intelligence can be learned, and in fact we are each building it, in varying degrees, throughout life. It's sometimes called maturity. EI is nothing more or less than a collection of tools that we can sharpen to help ensure our own survival."

Source: A. Fisher, "Success Secret: A High Emotional IQ," *Fortune,* October 26, 1998, p. 298. Reprinted with the permission of Time Warner Inc. Quiz copyright Daniel Goleman.

BREAKOUT **GROUP** EXERCISES

Form small groups to discuss the following topics, as assigned by your instructor. Each person in the group should first identify 3–5 key personal values.

1. Think back to your perception of this course and your instructor on the first day of class. What factors might have affected your perceptions of what the rest of the term would be like?

2. Describe a situation where your perception turned out to be wrong. What perceptual errors did you make that might have caused this to happen?

3. Compare your scores on the *Learning About Yourself Exercises* at the end of the chapter. What conclusions could you draw about your group based on these scores?

WORKING WITH **OTHERS** EXERCISE

Evaluating Your Stereotypes

1. Your instructor will choose 4 volunteers willing to reveal an interesting true-life background fact about themselves. Examples of such background facts are as follows:

   - I can perform various dances, including polka, rumba, bossa nova, and salsa.

   - I am the youngest of four children and I attended Catholic high school.

   - Neither of my parents attended school beyond grade 8.

   - My mother is a homemaker and my father is an author.

2. The instructor will put the 4 facts on the board without revealing to which person each belongs, and the 4 students will remain in the front of the room for the first part of the group discussion below.

3. Students in the class should silently decide which person belongs to which fact.

4. Students should break into groups of about 5 or 6 and try to reach a consensus about which person belongs to which fact. Meanwhile, the 4 students can serve as observers to group discussions, listening in on rationales for how students decide to link the facts with the individuals.

5. After 15 minutes of group discussion, several groups will be asked to present their consensus to the class, with justifications.

6. The classroom discussion will focus on perceptions, assumptions, and stereotyping that led to the decisions made.

7. At the end of the discussion, the instructor will reveal which student belongs to each fact.

ETHICAL **DILEMMA** EXERCISE

Managing Emotions at Work

Our understanding of emotions at work has increased rapidly in the past decade. We are now at the point at which we are capable (or close to it) of managing the emotions of employees. For instance, companies that want to create open and friendly workplaces are using the selection process to "select out" job applicants who aren't outgoing and enthusiastic and are providing training to teach employees how to smile and appear cheerful. Some organizations are going further in attempting to create "emotionally humanistic" work environments by not only shaping the emotions that workers evoke in their daily contacts with customers, but also by selecting employee applicants with high EI, controlling the emotional atmosphere of teams and work groups, and using similar emotion-management practices.

Groucho Marx once joked that "the secret of success in show business is honesty and sincerity. Once you learn how to fake that, you've got it made." In many service organizations today, Groucho's remark is being applied. For instance, telephone sales staff in a number of insurance companies are trained to invoke positive feelings from customers—to make it easy for them to say "yes." Employees are taught to avoid words with negative connotations and replace them with upbeat and confidence-building words

such as "certainly," "rest assured," "immediate," and "great." Moreover, employees are taught to convey these "scripts" in a way that seems natural and spontaneous. To ensure that these "authentic" positive feelings are consistently evoked, the phone calls of these salespeople are often monitored.

Organizations such as McDonald's, Disney, and Starbucks select and program employees to be upbeat and friendly. They allow employees no choices. Moreover, these organizations export their emotional expectations to wherever they locate in the world. When the hamburgers or lattes come to town, the typical grimace of the Moscovite or shyness of the Finnish employee is subject to similar smile-training.

Is asking people to pretend specific job-related emotions unethical if it conflicts with their basic personality? Is exporting standardized emotional "rule books" to alien cultures unethical? What do you think?

Source: This dilemma is based on S. Fineman, "Managing Emotions at Work: Some Political Reflections" (paper presented at a symposium at the Academy of Management Conference, Washington, DC, August 2001).

CASE INCIDENTS

Frank Stronach, Risk-Taker and Fair Enterprise Creator

When people describe the personality of Frank Stronach, chair of Aurora, Ontario-based Magna International, they typically use such words as "smart aleck," "obnoxious," "canny," "arrogant," and "crazy." One of his recent actions was to help with the rescue of people in New Orleans left homeless by Hurricane Katrina. Stronach organized to transport and house 300 people in southern Florida while he builds a trailer park for them in a destination of their choice. The desire to help was obvious for Stronach, who had once been poor and hungry himself. "The great thing about a large company that makes a profit is that you have the capability to jump in and be helpful—right away." Stronach provides an excellent illustration of how an individual's personality shapes his or her behaviour.

Frank Stronach was born in Weiz, Austria, in 1932, the son of a Communist factory worker. He moved to Canada at the age of 22, with $200 in his pocket, plus his expertise as a tool-and-die maker. Within two years he had scraped together enough money to start Multimatic Investments, a small automotive tool-and-die shop, in the east end of Toronto. In the 52 years since, he has built that shop into Magna—an auto-parts giant that employs 82 000 workers and has annual sales in excess of $20.7 billion. In 2004, he was paid $52.5 million for his role as chair of Magna.

Stronach personifies the driven executive in terms of his various business acquisitions over the years. He has also taken a number of risks, some of which have resulted in huge failure. In 1990, for example, Magna reported a loss of $224.2 million, incredible by almost any standard. But Stronach turned the company around, got back to its roots, and between 1990 and 1994 share prices rose from $2.25 to $66.78. In October 1997, prices had risen to their highest yet, $101.50. However, Stronach made a number of forays into other business ventures; and by late 1999, despite rising sales and a boom in the North American auto industry, shares were trading at $61.50. Stronach stepped down as CEO in 2001, but that doesn't mean Frank Stronach is taking it easy. He is still chair of the board, and he has a new business venture: Magna Entertainment, with interests in media, sports gaming, and online betting.

Stronach believes in "fair enterprise." To him that means having a universal charter of rights for employees, and a fairer distribution of wealth. He criticizes socialist systems ("they stifle individualism"), totalitarianism ("benefits the few"), and even free enterprise ("from time to time self-destroying"). This may seem like a paradox from someone who earns more than $50 million as chair of Magna. However, as Hugh Segal, former chief of staff to Brian Mulroney and contender for leadership of the Progressive Conservative Party in 1998, explains, "If Frank were the kind of person for whom conventional orthodoxy mattered, he'd probably still be running a one-man machine shop on Dupont [in Toronto]," where he first started out in the mid-1950s.

Stronach created Magna's corporate philosophy to foster a "strong sense of ownership and entrepreneurial energy" among his employees. Ten percent of pre-tax profit is allocated to employees in the form of cash and share purchase plans, thus giving all employees a share in the profits of the company. Stronach insists that managers' salaries are to be pegged "below industry standards." At the same time, plant managers are given considerable autonomy over buying, selling, and hiring. Magna also tries to keep up with employee attitudes: Plant managers are required to meet with all their workers at least once a month, and employees return a comprehensive survey once a year.

Questions

1. To what extent would you say that Frank Stronach's personality is reflected in his corporate policy?

2. What might the study of perceptions reveal about how different people might view Stronach's personality?

3. What kind of people might be unhappy working for Frank Stronach?

4. What are the pros and cons of being a manager who works under such a strong personality?

Sources: R. MacGregor, "Stronach's Luxurious Haven for Victims of Katrina," *Globe and Mail,* September 6, 2005, p. A1; T. Van Alphen, "Stronach Paid $52 Million Last Year," *Toronto Star,* April 1, 2005, p. F2.; www.magnaint.com/magnaWeb.nsf/webpages/Company+Info?OpenDocument (accessed September 8, 2005); http://library.corporate-ir.net/library/86/863/86334/items/144107/fullar.pdf (accessed September 8, 2005); B. Simon, "Work Ethic and the Magna Carta," *Financial Post Daily,* March 20, 1997, p. 14; "Magna in Overdrive: No Canadian Has Profited From Contracting Out as Much as Stronach," *Maclean's,* September 30, 1996, pp. 50–54; "Car and Striver (Will the World's Leading Auto-Parts Supplier Become the Globe's Newest Automaker?)," *Canadian Business,* September 1996, pp. 92–94; "Magna-Mania: Resurrecting His on-the-Brink Auto Parts Empire Didn't Satisfy Frank Stronach Who Plans Growth and Monuments With Equal Flair," *Financial Post,* August 12/14, 1995, pp. 12–13; D. Steinhart, "Magna Moving into Sports Gaming: Stock on Long Slide: Auto-Parts Giant Takes 17% Drop in Third-Quarter Profit," *Financial Post,* November 9, 1999, p. C3; D. Steinhart, "Market Remains Leery of Magna," *Financial Post,* November 5, 1999, pp. D1, D3; and D. Olive, "Some Canadian CEOs Did Better Than Their US Counterparts," *Financial Post,* June 14, 1999, p. C6.

The Rise and Fall of Dennis Kozlowski

The Dennis Kozlowski story could be titled "The Good, the Bad, and the Ugly." The good: As CEO of Tyco International, Kozlowski oversaw the growth of a corporate giant. At its peak, Tyco was gobbling up 200 companies a year. Under his leadership, the value of Tyco increased 70-fold. In 2001, Kozlowski declared his desire to be remembered as the world's greatest business executive.

The bad: Things turned sour when Kozlowski and his former chief financial officer were accused of running a criminal enterprise within Tyco. The two were charged with stealing $170 million (US) directly from the company and pocketing an additional $430 million (US) through manipulated sales of stock, and found guilty in June 2005.

The ugly: Kozlowski's actions almost destroyed the company where he worked for 27 years. In 2002 alone, the value of the company's stock dropped US$90 billion!

To understand Kozlowski's behaviour, we should look at the events that shaped his personality. He spent his early years in humble circumstances. He grew up in the 1950s and 1960s in Newark, New Jersey. He said he was the son of a Newark cop turned police detective. Only after he was indicted did it come out that his father was never a police officer in Newark or anywhere else. However, his mother did work for the Newark Police Department as a school crossing guard. His father, in actuality, was a wheeler-dealer who was a practiced deceiver and an effective persuader. He had a strong personality but, for the most part, kept his misdeeds to little white lies.

Friends remember Dennis as an easygoing kid who did well in school without trying very hard. He was elected "class politician" by his high school graduating class in 1964. He went to Seton Hall, paying his way through college by playing guitar in a band. He served in Vietnam, held a few accounting jobs, and eventually joined Tyco in 1975.

Over the course of the 1980s, Kozlowski's happy-go-lucky demeanour disappeared. As he climbed the ladder at Tyco, he became a corporate tough guy, both respected and feared. He eventually become CEO in 1992 and oversaw the rapid expansion of the company.

Meanwhile, Kozlowski learned to live big. He had a $17-million apartment in New York, a $30-million mansion in Florida, and a $15-million yacht. He spent $20 million on art for his luxury homes. He took extravagance to the extreme—for instance, spending $6000 on a shower curtain! The more he made, the more he spent—and the more he allegedly stole. Although his total compensation was $170 million in 1999, it wasn't enough. He manipulated the company's employee relocation fund and Key Employee Loan Program (the latter created to help exec-

utives pay taxes due on stock options) to take hundreds of millions in interest-free funds. In 2001, for instance, he gave his wife $1.5 million to start a restaurant, spent $2.1 million on a birthday party in the Greek Islands for his wife, and gave away $43 million in corporate funds to make philanthropic contributions in his own name.

A former Harvard professor suggests Kozlowski was undone by a rampant sense of entitlement: "By entitlement I mean an aspect of a narcissistic personality who comes to believe that he and the institution are one" and thus "that he can take what he wants when he wants it."

Questions

1. How did Kozlowski's past shape his personality?

2. Does this case contradict the view that personality is largely genetically derived? Explain.

3. What does this case say about corporate ethics?

4. In the movie *Wall Street*, the Michael Douglas character says, "Greed is good." Is this true? How does this apply to Kozlowski?

5. "Kozlowski just did what anybody would do if they had the chance. The people at fault in this story are Tyco's Board of Directors for not controlling their CEO." Do you agree or disagree? Discuss.

Source: Based on A. Bianco, W. Symonds, and N. Byrnes, "The Rise and Fall of Dennis Kozlowski," *Business Week,* December 23, 2002, pp. 64–77.

From **Concepts**
to **Skills**

Reading Emotions

Understanding another person's felt emotions is very difficult. But we can learn to read others' displayed emotions.[116] We do this by focusing on verbal, nonverbal, and paralanguage cues.

The easiest way to find out what someone is feeling is to ask them. Saying something as simple as "Are you OK? What's the problem?" can often provide you with the information to assess an individual's emotional state. But relying on a verbal response has two drawbacks. First, almost all of us conceal our emotions to some extent for privacy and to reflect social expectations. So we might be unwilling to share our true feelings. Second, even if we want to verbally convey our feelings, we may be unable to do so. As we noted earlier, some people have difficulty understanding their own emotions and, hence, are unable to express them verbally. So, at best, verbal responses provide only partial information.

Let's say you are talking with a co-worker. Does the fact that his back is rigid, his teeth clenched, and his facial muscles tight tell you something about his emotional state? It probably should. Facial expressions, gestures, body movements, and physical distance are nonverbal cues that can provide additional insights into what a person is feeling. The facial expressions shown in Exhibit 2-11, for instance, are a window into a person's feelings. Notice the difference in facial features: the height of the cheeks, the raising or lowering of the brow, the turn of the mouth, the positioning of the lips, and the configuration of muscles around the eyes. Even something as subtle as the distance someone chooses to position him- or herself from you can con-

---

EXHIBIT 2-11   Facial Expressions and Emotions

Each picture portrays a different emotion. Try to identify them before looking at the answers.

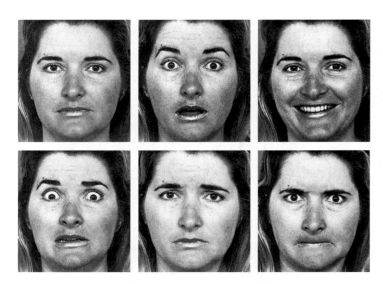

Top, left to right: neutral, surprise, happiness. Bottom: fear, sadness, anger.

Source: S. E. Taylor, L. A. Peplan, and D. O. Sears, *Social Psychology,* 9th ed. (Upper Saddle River, NJ: Prentice Hall, 1997), p. 98; photographs by Paul Ekman, Ph.D. Used with permission.

vey how much intimacy, aggressiveness, repugnance, or withdrawal that person feels.

When you speak with someone, you may notice a sharp change in the tone of her voice and the speed at which she speaks. You are tapping into the third source of information on a person's emotions—paralanguage. This is communication that goes beyond the specific spoken words. It includes pitch, amplitude, rate, and voice quality of speech. Paralanguage reminds us that people convey their feelings not only in what they say, but also in how they say it.

Assessing Skills

After you've read this chapter, take the following Self-Assessments on your enclosed CD-ROM:

1. What's My Basic Personality?
2. What's My Jungian 16-Type Personality?
3. Am I a Type A?
23. What's My Emotional Intelligence Score?

Practising Skills

Part A. Form groups of 2. Each person is to spend a couple of minutes thinking of a time in the past when he or she was emotional about something. Examples might include being upset with a parent, sibling, or friend; being excited or disappointed about an academic or athletic achievement; being angry with someone over an insult or slight; being disgusted by something someone has said or done; or being happy because of something good that happened. Do not share this event with the other person in your group.

Part B. Now you will conduct 2 role plays. Each will be an interview. In the first, 1 person will play the interviewer and the other will play the job applicant. The job is for a summer management internship with a large retail chain. Each role play will last no longer than 10 minutes. The interviewer is to conduct a normal job interview, except you are to continually rethink the emotional episode you envisioned in Part A. Try hard to convey this emotion while, at the same time, being professional in interviewing the job applicant.

Part C. Now reverse positions for the second role play. The interviewer becomes the job applicant and vice versa. The new interviewer will conduct a normal job interview, except that he or she will continually rethink the emotional episode chosen in Part A.

Part D. Spend 10 minutes analyzing the interview, with specific attention focused on these questions: What emotion(s) do you think the other person was conveying? What cues did you pick up? How accurate were you in reading those cues?

Reinforcing Skills

1. Rent a video of an emotional-laden film such as *Death of a Salesman* or *12 Angry Men.* Carefully watch the actors for clues to the emotions they are exhibiting. Try to determine the various emotions projected and explain how you arrived at your conclusion.

2. Spend a day specifically looking for emotional cues in the people with whom you interact. Did this improve communication?

CHAPTER 3

Values, Attitudes, and Diversity in the Workplace

At Procter & Gamble Canada, diversity is valued and respected. How does this affect the company's workplace?

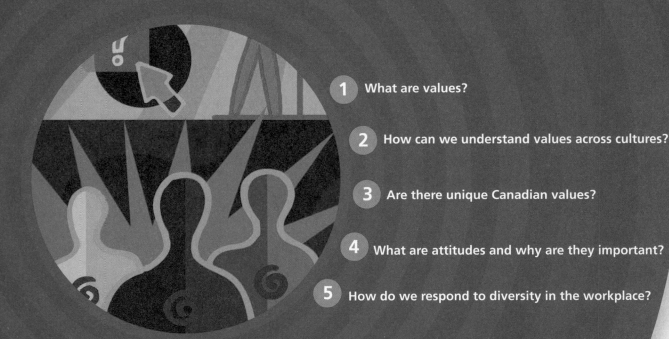

1 What are values?

2 How can we understand values across cultures?

3 Are there unique Canadian values?

4 What are attitudes and why are they important?

5 How do we respond to diversity in the workplace?

Tim Penner is president of Toronto-based Procter & Gamble (P&G) Canada. He leads a company that values diversity in its workplace. Consider P&G's statement on employee diversity:

> *Developing and managing a strong, diverse organization is essential to achieving our business purpose. We value the different perspectives that the diversity of Procter & Gamble people bring to the business. At Procter & Gamble, we operate on the fundamental belief that these diverse viewpoints are needed for organization creativity which produces genuine competitive advantage.*[1]

Generally, we expect that an organization's values, like those of an individual, will be reflected in corresponding behaviour and attitudes. If a company stated that it valued workforce diversity, and yet no behaviour followed from that statement, we would question whether that value was really so important to the company. However, in P&G's case, the company backs up its value statements with concrete policies and actions to show support for its values. Does having strong values make for a better workplace?

In this chapter, we look more carefully at how values influence behaviour, and consider the relationship between values and attitudes. We then consider two specific issues that arise from our discussion of values and attitudes: job satisfaction and workforce diversity.

VALUES

Is capital punishment right or wrong? How about racial or gender quotas in hiring—are they right or wrong? If a person likes power, is that good or bad? The answers to these questions are value-laden. Some might argue, for example, that capital punishment is right because it is an appropriate response to crimes such as murder. However, others might argue just as strongly that no government has the right to take anyone's life.

Values are concepts or beliefs that guide how we make decisions about and evaluations of behaviours and events.[2] An individual's values can be ranked according to importance. Values tend to be relatively stable and enduring.[3] Most of our values are formed in our early years—with input from parents, teachers, friends, and others. As children, we are told that certain behaviours or outcomes are always desirable or always undesirable. There were few grey areas. It is this absolute or "black-or-white" learning of values that more or less ensures their stability and endurance.

Below we examine two frameworks for understanding values: Milton Rokeach's terminal and instrumental values, and Kent Hodgson's general moral principles.

Rokeach Value Survey

Milton Rokeach classified the values that people hold into two sets, with each set containing 18 individual value items.[4] One set, called **terminal values**, refers to desirable

1 What are values?

Procter & Gamble Canada
www.pg.com/en_CA

values Concepts or beliefs that guide how we make decisions about and evaluations of behaviours and events.

terminal values Goals that individuals would like to achieve during their lifetime.

EXHIBIT 3-1   **Terminal and Instrumental Values in Rokeach Value Survey**

Terminal Values	Instrumental Values
A comfortable life (a prosperous life)	Ambitious (hard-working, aspiring)
An exciting life (a stimulating, active life)	Broad-minded (open-minded)
A sense of accomplishment (lasting contribution)	Capable (competent, effective)
A world at peace (free of war and conflict)	Cheerful (lighthearted, joyful)
A world of beauty (beauty of nature and the arts)	Clean (neat, tidy)
Equality (brotherhood, equal opportunity for all)	Courageous (standing up for your beliefs)
Family security (taking care of loved ones)	Forgiving (willing to pardon others)
Freedom (independence, free choice)	Helpful (working for the welfare of others)
Happiness (contentedness)	Honest (sincere, truthful)
Inner harmony (freedom from inner conflict)	Imaginative (daring, creative)
Mature love (sexual and spiritual intimacy)	Independent (self-reliant, self-sufficient)
National security (protection from attack)	Intellectual (intelligent, reflective)
Pleasure (an enjoyable, leisurely life)	Logical (consistent, rational)
Salvation (saved, eternal life)	Loving (affectionate, tender)
Self-respect (self-esteem)	Obedient (dutiful, respectful)
Social recognition (respect, admiration)	Polite (courteous, well-mannered)
True friendship (close companionship)	Responsible (dependable, reliable)
Wisdom (a mature understanding of life)	Self-controlled (restrained, self-disciplined)

Source: M. Rokeach, *The Nature of Human Values* (New York: Free Press, 1973), p. 56.

---

instrumental values Preferable
ways of behaving.

end-states of existence. These are the goals that individuals would like to achieve during their lifetime. The other set, called **instrumental values**, refers to preferable ways of behaving. These are the means for achieving the terminal values. Exhibit 3-1 gives common examples for each of these sets.

Several studies confirm that these sets of values vary among groups.[5] People in the same occupations or categories (e.g., corporate managers, union members, parents, stu-

---

EXHIBIT 3-2   **Value Ranking of Executives, Union Members, and Activists (Top Five Only)**

EXECUTIVES		UNION MEMBERS		ACTIVISTS	
Terminal	Instrumental	Terminal	Instrumental	Terminal	Instrumental
1. Self-respect	1. Honest	1. Family security	1. Responsible	1. Equality	1. Honest
2. Family security	2. Responsible	2. Freedom	2. Honest	2. A world of peace	2. Helpful
3. Freedom	3. Capable	3. Happiness	3. Courageous	3. Family security	3. Courageous
4. A sense of accomplishment	4. Ambitious	4. Self-respect	4. Independent	4. Self-respect	4. Responsible
5. Happiness	5. Independent	5. Mature love	5. Capable	5. Freedom	5. Capable

Source: Based on W. C. Frederick and J. Weber, "The Values of Corporate Managers and Their Critics: An Empirical Description and Normative Implications," in *Business Ethics: Research Issues and Empirical Studies,* ed. W. C. Frederick and L. E. Preston (Greenwich, CT: JAI Press, 1990), pp. 123–144.

dents) tend to hold similar values. For instance, one study compared corporate executives, members of the steelworkers' union, and members of a community activist group. Although a good deal of overlap was found among the three groups,[6] there were also some very significant differences (see Exhibit 3-2). The activists had value preferences that were quite different from those of the other two groups. They ranked "equality" as their most important terminal value; executives and union members ranked this value 12 and 13, respectively. Activists ranked "helpful" as their second-highest instrumental value. The other two groups both ranked it 14. These differences are important, because executives, union members, and activists all have a vested interest in what corporations do. These differences make it difficult when these groups have to negotiate with each other and can create serious conflicts when they try to reach agreement on the organization's economic and social policies.[7]

Ethical Values

Ethics is the study of moral values or principles that guide our behaviour and inform us whether actions are right or wrong. Thus ethical values are related to moral judgments about right and wrong.

In recent years, there has been concern that individuals are not grounded in moral values. It is believed that this lack of moral roots has resulted in a number of business scandals, such as those at WorldCom, Enron, Hollinger International, and even in the sponsorship scandal of the Canadian government.

Management consultant Kent Hodgson has identified seven general moral principles that individuals should follow when making decisions about behaviour. He calls these "the Magnificent Seven" and suggests that they are universal values that managers should use to make *principled, appropriate,* and *defensible* decisions.[8] They are presented in *OB in Action—The Magnificent Seven Principles.* We discuss the issue of ethics further in Chapter 12.

ethics The study of moral values or principles that guide our behaviour and inform us whether actions are right or wrong.

> ## OB IN ACTION
> ### The Magnificent Seven Principles
> → *Dignity of human life.* The lives of **people are to be respected**.
> → *Autonomy.* All **persons are intrinsically valuable** and **have the right to self-determination**.
> → *Honesty.* **The truth should be told** to those who have a right to know it.
> → *Loyalty.* **Promises**, **contracts**, and **commitments should be honoured**.
> → *Fairness.* **People should be treated justly.**
> → *Humaneness.* Our **actions ought to accomplish good**, and we should **avoid doing evil**.
> → *The common good.* Actions should accomplish **the greatest good for the greatest number** of people.
>
> *Source:* K. Hodgson, "Adapting Ethical Decisions to a Global Marketplace," *Management Review* 81, no. 5, May 1992, pp. 53–57. Reprinted by permission.

ASSESSING CULTURAL VALUES

> Procter & Gamble Canada's decision to value diversity in its workplace reflects a dominant value of Canada as a multicultural country. The approach to diversity is very different in the United States, which considers itself a melting pot with respect to different cultures. P&G Canada has other values that guide employees. These include integrity, trust, ownership, leadership, and passion for winning. What do we know about the values of other countries? What values make Canada unique?

In Chapter 1, we noted that managers have to become capable of working with people from different cultures. Thus it is important to understand how values differ across cultures.

One of the most widely referenced approaches for analyzing variations among cultures has come from Geert Hofstede.[9] He surveyed more than 116 000 IBM employees in 40 countries about their work-related values.

Hofstede's original findings are based on research that is nearly three decades old. However, his work was updated and reaffirmed when a Canadian researcher at the

2 How can we understand values across cultures?

Chinese University of Hong Kong, Michael Bond, conducted research on values in 22 countries on 5 continents.[10]

How do countries differ in their values?

More recently, the Global Leadership and Organizational Behavior Effectiveness (GLOBE) research program identified nine dimensions on which national cultures differ.[11] This study is an ongoing cross-cultural investigation of leadership and national culture that has used data from 825 organizations in 62 countries. The GLOBE study confirms that Hofstede's five dimensions are still valid (his four original ones, plus the long-term orientation added through the merger of Bond's research with Hofstede's).[12] However, the GLOBE study has added four dimensions and provides us with an updated measure of where countries rate on each dimension. Exhibit 3-3 presents ratings by country on each of the dimensions.

The GLOBE dimensions are defined as follows:

- *Assertiveness.* The extent to which a society encourages people to be tough, confrontational, assertive, and competitive vs. modest and tender. This is essentially equivalent to Hofstede's quantity-of-life dimension.

- *Future orientation.* The extent to which a society encourages and rewards future-oriented behaviours such as planning, investing in the future, and delaying gratification. This is essentially equivalent to Hofstede's long-term/short-term orientation.

- *Gender differentiation.* The extent to which a society maximizes gender role differences.

- *Uncertainty avoidance.* As identified by Hofstede, the GLOBE team defined this term as a society's reliance on social norms and procedures to alleviate the unpredictability of future events.

- *Power distance.* As did Hofstede, the GLOBE team defined this as the extent to which members of a society expect power to be unequally shared.

- *Individualism/collectivism.* Again, this term was defined, as was Hofstede's, as the extent to which individuals are encouraged by societal institutions to be integrated into groups within organizations and society.

- *In-group collectivism.* In contrast to focusing on societal institutions, this dimension encompasses the extent to which members of a society take pride in membership in small groups, such as their family and circle of close friends, and the organizations in which they are employed.

- *Performance orientation.* The extent to which a society encourages and rewards group members for performance improvement and excellence.

- *Humane orientation.* The extent to which a society encourages and rewards individuals for being fair, altruistic, generous, caring, and kind to others. This closely approximates Hofstede's quality-of-life dimension.

In expanding to other countries, Wal-Mart has learned the importance of understanding how differences in cultural values explain the behaviour of employees. Chinese people, for example, are accustomed to vendors hawking their goods in street markets. So it is fitting for Wal-Mart employees in China to shout out special prices for products. In contrast, this behaviour would not be acceptable in stores in other countries, like Sweden, that place a low value on assertiveness and competitiveness.

EXHIBIT 3-3 GLOBE Highlights

Dimension	Countries Rating Low	Countries Rating Moderate	Countries Rating High
Assertiveness	Sweden New Zealand Switzerland	Egypt Ireland Philippines	Spain United States Greece
Future orientation	Russia Argentina Poland	Slovenia Egypt Ireland	Denmark Canada the Netherlands
Gender differentiation	Sweden Denmark Slovenia	Italy Brazil Argentina	South Korea Egypt Morocco
Uncertainty avoidance	Russia Hungary Bolivia	Israel United States Mexico	Austria Denmark Germany
Power distance	Denmark the Netherlands South Africa	England France Brazil	Russia Spain Thailand
Individualism/collectivism*	Denmark Singapore Japan	Hong Kong United States Egypt	Greece Hungary Germany
In-group collectivism	Denmark Sweden New Zealand	Japan Israel Qatar	Egypt China Morocco
Performance orientation	Russia Argentina Greece	Sweden Israel Spain	United States Taiwan New Zealand
Humane orientation	Germany Spain France	Hong Kong Sweden Taiwan	Indonesia Egypt Malaysia

* A low score on individualism is synonymous with collectivism.

Source: M. Javidan and R. J. House, "Cultural Acumen for the Global Manager: Lessons From Project GLOBE," *Organizational Dynamics,* Spring 2001, pp. 289–305. Reprinted with permission from Elsevier.

An awareness of the GLOBE study findings reminds us that (1) not all organizational behaviour theories and concepts are universally applicable to managing people around the world, especially in countries where work values are considerably different from those in Canada; and (2) you should take into consideration cultural values when trying to understand the behaviour of people in different countries. To help you with this second point, we will regularly stop to consider the generalizability of theories and concepts presented in this book to different cultures.

In this chapter's *Working With Others Exercise* on page 106, you have the opportunity to compare the cultural values of two countries and determine how differences might affect group behaviour. The *Ethical Dilemma Exercise* on page 106 asks you to consider when something is a gift and when it is a bribe. Different cultures take different approaches to this question. This chapter's *CBC Video Case* gives you additional insights about managing in a cross-cultural world.

CBC

Managing in a Cross-Cultural World

 Are there unique
Canadian values?

VALUES IN THE CANADIAN WORKPLACE

Studies have shown that when individual values align with organizational values, the results are positive. Individuals who have an accurate understanding of the job requirements and the organization's values adjust better to their jobs, and have greater levels of satisfaction and organizational commitment.[13] In addition, shared values between the employee and the organization lead to more positive work attitudes,[14] lower turnover,[15] and greater productivity.[16]

Individual and organizational values do not always align. Moreover, within organizations, individuals can have very different values. Two major factors lead to a potential clash of values in the Canadian workplace: generational differences and cultural differences. Let's look at the implications of both factors.

Generational Differences

In his book *Sex in the Snow*, pollster Michael Adams attempted to identify the social values of today's Canadians.[17] He found that within three broad age groups of adult Canadians—the Elders (those over 60), Baby Boomers (born between the mid-1940s and the mid-1960s), and Generation Xers (born between the mid-1960s and the early 1980s)—there are at least 12 quite distinct "value tribes." We present the age groups and discuss some of their values below. For further information on these different value tribes and an opportunity to see where you might be classified in terms of your social values, visit the Environics Research Group website.

Environics Research Group
http://erg.environics.net

In the discussion of values that follows, bear in mind that we present broad generalizations, and you should certainly avoid stereotyping individuals on the basis of these generalizations. There are individual differences in values. For instance, not every Baby Boomer thinks alike, and neither does every member of Generation X. Thus, the important point about the values discussion is that you should try to understand how others might view things differently from you, even when they are exposed to the same situation.

The Elders
These individuals are characterized as "playing by the rules," and their core values are belief in order, authority, discipline, the Judeo-Christian moral code, and the Golden Rule (do unto others as you would have others do unto you). About 80 percent of the Elders resemble this description of traditional values, although there are variations within that 80 percent in the strength of fit.

Baby Boomers
The view of Baby Boomers as a somewhat spoiled, hedonistic, rebellious group belies the four categories of Boomers: autonomous rebels (25 percent), anxious communitarians (20 percent), connected enthusiasts (14 percent), and disengaged Darwinists (41 percent). So, unlike the Elders, the Boomers are a bit more fragmented in their views. Yet all but the disengaged Darwinists reflect, to some extent, the stereotypes of this generation: rejection of authority, skepticism regarding the motives of big business and government, a strong concern for the environment, and a strong desire for equality in the workplace and society. Of course, the disengaged Darwinists, the largest single group, do not fit this description well. The Darwinists are characterized as being angry, intimidated by change, and anxious about their professional and financial futures.

Generation X
Although this group is quite fragmented in its values, research shows that the common values are experience-seeking, adaptability, and concern with personal image among

peers. Despite these common values, Generation Xers can be divided into five tribes. Thrill-seeking materialists (25 percent) desire money and material possessions, as well as recognition, respect, and admiration. Aimless dependants (27 percent) seek financial independence, security, and stability. Social hedonists (15 percent) are experience-seeking, committed to their own pleasure, and seek immediate gratification. New Aquarians (13 percent) are experience-seeking, and also egalitarian and ecologically minded. Finally, autonomous post-materialists (20 percent) seek personal autonomy and self-fulfillment, and are concerned about human rights.

> Are Gen-Xers really different from their elders?

The Ne(x)t Generation

Since Adams' book appeared, another generation has been identified. Labelled the Net Generation,[18] millennials,[19] Generation Y, or the Echo Boomers, this generation, born between 1977 and 1997, consists of "creators, not recipients. And they are curious, contrarian, flexible, collaborative and high in self-esteem."[20] This generation is defined by its ease with technology, having grown up with cellphones, text messaging, and Internet access (hence the name "Net"). Individuals who belong to this generation are team players and optimists with a desire for order.[21]

In this chapter's *Learning About Yourself Exercise* on page 105, you have the opportunity to examine some of the things that you value.

The Generations Meet in the Workplace

Baby Boomers currently dominate the workplace, but their years of being in charge are limited. In 2013, half of them will be at least 55 and 18 percent will be over 60.[22] As Boomers move into head offices, the "play-by-the-rules," "boss-knows-best" Elders are being replaced by somewhat more egalitarian Boomers. They dislike the command-and-control rules that were part of their parents' lives, although the Boomers have also been described as workaholics. Meanwhile, the Generation Xers in the workplace are comfortable in adapting, but also want more experiences. They are not in awe of authority. Most important, they are not interested in copying the workaholic behaviour of their parents. Managing the expectations of each of these very different groups is not an easy task. It requires managers to be flexible, observant, and willing to adjust more to the individual needs of these different employees. Members of the Net Generation will certainly change the face of the workplace in significant ways. They have mastered a communication and information system that many of their parents have yet to understand.

Cultural Differences

Canada is a multicultural country. "One in six Canadians in their 20s are immigrants, and one in five are the children of at least one immigrant parent."[23] In 2001, 44 percent of Metropolitan Toronto's population, 38 percent of Vancouver's, and 18.6 percent of Montreal's were made up of immigrants.[24] The 2001 census found that 17 percent of Canada's population over age five spoke neither of the country's

Vancouver-based Mainframe Entertainment, the company behind *Reboot* and *Popeye's Voyage*, understands the values of its Generation X employees: experience, recognition, respect, and admiration. Mainframe's animators get leadership opportunities, including the opportunity to direct shows, which they would not get at higher-paying studios in Los Angeles. Mainframe has one of the lowest turnover rates in the animation business because of its emphasis on giving its young employees the opportunity to acquire new skills.

EXHIBIT 3-4   Canadian and American Value Differences

Statement	Percentage Who Completely Agree With Statement	
	Canadians	Americans
The impact of globalization on their country can be described as very good.	36	21
People are better off in a free market, despite inequality.	19	28
It is more important that government ensure that nobody is in need than that government stay out of the way.	52	34
It is the responsibility of government to tend to the very poor who cannot take care of themselves.	43	29
Immigrants have a very good influence on how well things are going.	19	8
Religion should be a matter of private faith, kept separate from government policy.	71	55
Homosexuality is a way of life that should be accepted by society.	69	51

Source: The Pew Research Center for the People and the Press, *Views of a Changing World 2003* (Washington, DC: The Pew Research Center for the People and the Press, June 2003).

two official languages as their first language. In Vancouver and Toronto, this rate was 38 percent and 41 percent, respectively, so considerably more than one-third of the population of those two cities does not speak either English or French as a first language.[25] Of those who speak other languages, 16 percent speak Chinese (mainly Mandarin or Cantonese). The other dominant languages in Canada are Italian (in fourth place), followed by German, Punjabi, and Spanish.[26] These figures indicate the very different cultures that are part of the Canadian fabric of life.

Though we live in a multicultural society, there are some tensions among people from different races and ethnic groups. For instance, a 2002 Statistics Canada survey on ethnic diversity found that while most Canadians (93 percent) say they have never or rarely experienced unfair treatment because of ethnic or cultural characteristics, 20 percent of visible minorities reported having been unfairly treated sometimes or often.[27]

Canadians often define themselves as "not Americans" and point out differences in the values of the two countries. A recent study, the Pew Global Attitudes Project, identified a number of differences between Canadian and American values.[28] Exhibit 3-4 shows some of the highlights of that study.

In his latest book *Fire and Ice,* Michael Adams finds that there is a growing dissimilarity between Canadian and American values. The two groups differ in 41 of the 56 values that Adams examined. For 24 values the gap has actually widened between 1992 and 2000, indicating that Canadians' social values are growing more distinct from those of Americans.[29] Adams suggests that the September 11 attacks have had an impact on the American personality. He finds Americans are more accepting of patriarchy and hierarchy these days, and he concludes that it is "the supposedly bold, individualistic Americans who are the nodding conformists, and the supposedly shy, deferential and law-abiding Canadians who are most likely to assert their personal autonomy and political agency."[30]

In what follows we identify a number of cultural values that influence workplace behaviour in Canada. Be aware that these are generalizations, and it would be a mistake to assume that everyone coming from the same cultural background acts similarly.

Rather, these overviews are meant to encourage you to think about cultural differences and similarities so that you can better understand people's behaviour.

Francophone and Anglophone Values

One of the larger issues that has confronted Canada in recent years is the question of Quebec separatism and anglophone-francophone differences. Consequently, it may be of interest to managers and employees in Canadian firms to be aware of some of the potential cultural differences when managing in francophone environments compared with anglophone environments. A number of studies have shown that English-speaking Canadians and French-speaking Canadians have distinctive value priorities. Francophones have been found to be more collectivist, or group-oriented, with a greater need for achievement, and anglophones have been found to be more individualist, or I-centred.[31] Francophones have also been shown to be more concerned about the interpersonal aspects of the workplace than task competence.[32] They have also been found to be more committed to their work organizations.[33] Anglophones have been shown to take more risks.[34] By contrast, a recent study examining work values in French- and English-speaking Canada found that French-speaking Canadians were not risk-takers and had the highest values for "reducing or avoiding ambiguity and uncertainty at work."[35]

Asked to define the fundamentals that give National Bank Financial its edge, senior vice-president and company director John Wells said he believes Montreal-based National Bank Financial's edge comes from company management that is largely French Canadian. He argues that French Canadians treat their employees well, and will try to find any means of reducing expenses rather than lay off staff, in sharp contrast to the cost-cutting mechanisms of either English Canadian or American firms.

Other studies have found that anglophone managers tended to value autonomy and intrinsic job values, such as achievement, and thus were more achievement-oriented, while francophone managers tended to value affiliation and extrinsic job values, such as technical supervision.[36] A study conducted at the University of Ottawa and Laval University suggests that some of the differences reported in previous research may be decreasing.[37] Another study indicates that French Canadians have become more like English Canadians in valuing autonomy and self-fulfillment.[38] However, there is evidence of some continuing differences in lifestyle values. A recent Canadian Institute for Health Information report noted that Quebecers experience more stress than other Canadians.[39] The study also found that Quebecers smoke more, have the highest workplace absenteeism rate, and are less physically active than the rest of the country. Another study found that French-speaking Canadians and English-speaking Canadians have different values regarding cultural activities. For example, francophones are more likely to attend symphonic, classical, or choral music performances than anglophones. Anglophones are more likely to read newspapers, magazines, and books than francophones.[40]

Despite some cultural and lifestyle value differences, both francophone and anglophone managers today would have been exposed to more of the same types of organizational theories during their training in post-secondary school, which might also influence their outlooks as managers. Thus we would not expect to find large differences in the way that firms in francophone Canada are managed, compared with those in the rest of Canada. Throughout the textbook, you will find examples of Quebec-based businesses that support this conclusion.

Aboriginal Values

What can you learn about OB from Aboriginal culture?

Entrepreneurial activity among Canada's Aboriginal peoples has been increasing at the same time that there are more partnerships and alliances between Aboriginal and non-Aboriginal businesses. Because of these business interactions, it is important to examine the types of differences we might observe in how each culture manages its businesses. Certainly the opening ceremony for the First Nations Bank of Canada's head office branch in Saskatoon in September 1997 was different from many openings of Western businesses. The ceremony was accompanied by the burning of sweet grass. "This is a blessing," Blaine Favel, chief of the Federation of Saskatchewan Indian Nations, said to a large outdoor gathering. "We are celebrating a great accomplishment by our people."[41]

"Aboriginal values are usually perceived (by non-Aboriginals) as an impediment to economic development and organizational effectiveness."[42] These values include reluctance to compete, a time orientation different from the Western one, and an emphasis on consensus decision making.[43] Aboriginal people do not necessarily agree that these values are business impediments, however.

Specifically, although Canadian businesses and government have historically assumed that "non-Native people must teach Native people how to run their own organizations," the First Nations of Canada are not convinced.[44] They believe that traditional culture, values, and languages do not have to be compromised in the building of a self-sustaining economy. Moreover, they believe that their cultural values may actually be a positive force in conducting business.[45]

In recent years, Canadian businesses facing Native land claims have met some difficulties in trying to accommodate demands for appropriate land usage. In some cases, *accommodation* can mean less logging or mining by businesses until land claims are worked out. Cliff Hickey and David Natcher, two anthropologists from the University of Alberta, collaborated with the Little Red River Cree Nation in northern Alberta to develop a new model for forestry operations on First Nations land and achieve better communication between businesses and Native leaders.[46] The anthropologists sought to balance the Native community's traditional lifestyle with the economic concerns of forestry operations. *OB in Action—Ground Rules for Developing Aboriginal and Business Partnerships* outlines several of Hickey and Natcher's recommended ground rules, which they say could be used in oil and gas developments as well. Johnson Sewepegaham, chief of the Little Red River Cree, said his community will use these recommendations to resolve difficulties on treaty lands for which Vernon, BC-based Tolko Industries and High Level, Alberta-based Footner Forest Products jointly hold forest tenure.

Lindsay Redpath of Athabasca University has noted that Aboriginal cultures are more collectivist in orientation than are non-Aboriginal cultures in Canada and the United States.[47] Aboriginal organizations are much more likely to reflect and advance the goals of the community. There is also a greater sense of family within the workplace, with greater affiliation and loyalty. Power distance in Aboriginal cultures is smaller than in non-Aboriginal cultures of Canada and the United States, and there is an emphasis on consensual decision making. Aboriginal cultures are lower on uncertainty avoidance than non-Aboriginal cultures in Canada and the United States. Aboriginal organizations and cultures tend to have fewer rules and regulations. Each of these differences suggests that businesses created by Aboriginal people will differ from non-Aboriginal businesses, and both research and anecdotal evidence support this conjecture.[48] For instance, Richard Prokopanko, director of corporate affairs for Vancouver-based Alcan, says that shifting from handling issues in a generally legalistic, contract-oriented manner to valuing more dialogue and collaboration has helped ease some of the tension that had built up over 48 years between Alcan and First Nations people.[49]

Asian Values

The largest visible minority group in Canada are the Chinese. Over 1 million Chinese live in Canada, and represent 26 percent of the country's visible minority population.[50] The Chinese in this country are a diverse group; they come from different countries, speak different languages, and practise different religions. The Chinese are only one part of the entire influence of East and Southeast Asian values that influence Canadian society. It's predicted that by 2017 almost one-half of all visible minorities in Canada will come from two groups, South Asian and Chinese, and that these groups will be represented in almost equal numbers.[51] As well, many Canadian organizations, particularly those in British Columbia, conduct significant business with Asian firms. Asian cultures differ from Canadian culture on many of the GLOBE dimensions discussed earlier. For instance, Asian cultures tend to exhibit greater power distance and greater collectivism. These differences in values can affect individual interactions.

Professor Rosalie Tung of Simon Fraser University and

What would you need to know to set up a business in Asia?

her student Irene Yeung examined the importance of *guanxi* (personal connections with the appropriate authorities or individuals) for a sample of North American, European, and Hong Kong firms doing business with companies in mainland China.[52] They suggest that their findings are also relevant in understanding how to develop relationships with firms from Japan, South Korea, and Hong Kong.

"*Guanxi* refers to the establishment of a connection between two independent individuals to enable a bilateral flow of personal or social transactions. Both parties must derive benefits from the transaction to ensure the continuation of such a relationship."[53] *Guanxi* relations are based on reciprocation, unlike Western networked relationships, which may be characterized more by self-interest. *Guanxi* relationships are meant to be long-term and enduring, in contrast with the immediate gains sometimes expected in Western relationships. *Guanxi* also relies less on institutional law, and more on personal power and authority, than do Western relationships. Finally, *guanxi* relations are governed more by the notion of shame (that is, external pressures on performance), while Western relations often rely on guilt (that is, internal pressures on performance) to maintain agreements. *Guanxi* is seen as extremely important for business success in China—more than such factors as the right location, price, or strategy, or product differentiation and quality. For Western firms wanting to do business with Asian firms, an understanding of *guanxi*, and an effort to build relationships, are important strategic advantages.

Our discussion about differences in cross-cultural values should suggest to you that understanding other cultures matters. When Canadian firms develop operations across Canada, south of the border, or overseas, employees need to understand other cultures in order to work more effectively and get along with others.

OB IN ACTION

Ground Rules for Developing Business Partnerships With Aboriginal People

→ Modify management operations to **reduce negative impact on wildlife species**.

→ Modify operations to **ensure community access** to lands and resources.

→ **Protect** all those **areas identified by community members** as having biological, cultural, and historical significance.

→ **Recognize and protect Aboriginal and treaty rights** to hunting, fishing, trapping, and gathering activities.

→ **Increase** forest-based **economic opportunities** for community members.

→ **Increase** the **involvement of community members** in decision making.

Source: D. C. Natcher and C. G. Hickey, "Putting the Community Back into Community-Based Resource Management: A Criteria and Indicators Approach to Sustainability," *Human Organization* 61, no. 4, 2002, pp. 350–363.

ATTITUDES

Managers at Procter & Gamble Canada consider diversity a competitive advantage. They "believe that a diverse company will outperform a homogeneous company by inspiring more creative and innovative solutions."[54] To help employees foster a similar attitude toward diversity, P&G conducts mandatory diversity training for all employees. Thus, P&G realizes the link between organizational values and employee attitudes. The training is meant to help employees have greater awareness of cultural and style differences. Managers are given additional training to help them improve their leadership in a diverse workplace. So how do attitudes get formed, and can they really be changed?

4 What are attitudes
and why are they
important?

attitudes Positive or negative feelings about objects, people, or events.

Mill & Ross Architects
www.millross.com

Attitudes are positive or negative feelings about objects, people, or events. When I say, "I like my job," I am expressing my attitude to work. Attitudes are thus responses to situations.

Attitudes are not the same as values because values are convictions about what is important, but the two are interrelated. In organizations, attitudes are important because they affect job behaviour. Employees may believe, for example, that supervisors, auditors, managers, and time-and-motion engineers are all conspiring to make them work harder for the same or less money. This may then lead to a negative attitude toward management when an employee is asked to stay late for help on a special project. *Case Incident—Gourmet Foods Works on Employee Attitudes* on page 107 highlights how changes in attitudes can help a company's bottom line.

Employees may be negatively affected by the attitudes of their co-workers or clients. For instance, Debra Krakow, an architect with Kingston, Ontario-based Mill & Ross Architects, notes that client attitudes toward the competency of female architects discourage women from staying in that profession. "In my experience, if you're male, you're presumed competent or you wouldn't be there. If you're female, you're presumed incompetent until proven otherwise," she says.[55] In *From Concepts to Skills* on page 108, we discuss whether it's possible to change someone's attitude, and how that might happen in the workplace. *Focus on Diversity* looks at how attitudes about who can make proper sushi affect who gets hired to be a sushi maker.

FOCUS ON **DIVERSITY**

Nontraditional Sushi Makers

What determines a good sushi maker? For many sushi restaurants in Japan and in North America, a sushi chef "should" be male.[56] It's what's expected, and it's what's observed. Yoko Ogawa, 30, a female sushi chef at Yamaguchi in Midtown Manhattan, explains the problem women face: "They say that women cannot make sushi because their hands are too warm and that will ruin the fish."

Hiromi Suzuki, whose father is the chef and owner of Mie in the East Village of New York, shared some of her father's stories about women sushi makers: "Women can't make sushi because they wear perfume and makeup, and the smell of the perfume and makeup will ruin the food."

Others believe that women can't become sushi chefs because the area behind the counter is sacred, and men traditionally fill the religious roles in Japanese society.

These attitudes have made it difficult not only for women but also for non-Japanese to become sushi makers in Japan and North America, although that is starting to change. When Toshi Sugiura started the California Sushi Academy in Venice, California, in 1998, he expected that his students would be Asian immigrants. Instead, most of the students were American. This required him to change his vision. "Sushi is becoming a worldwide food. Why can't Black people and white people make sushi?"

All of these examples suggest that who gets hired into any position can be affected by attitudes about what the "right" person should look like.

A person can have thousands of attitudes, but OB focuses our attention on a limited number of job-related attitudes. These job-related attitudes tap positive or negative evaluations that employees hold about aspects of their work environment. Below we consider two important attitudes that affect organizational performance: job satisfaction and organizational commitment.

Job Satisfaction

The term **job satisfaction** refers to an individual's general attitude toward his or her job. A person with a high level of job satisfaction holds *positive attitudes toward the job*; a person who is dissatisfied with his or her job holds *negative attitudes toward the job*. When people speak of *employee attitudes*, more often than not they mean job satisfaction. In fact, the terms are frequently used interchangeably.

A recent Canadian Policy Research Networks survey on job satisfaction found that only 40 percent of Canadian employees are very satisfied with their jobs. By comparison, 47 percent of American employees are happy with their work and 54 percent of Danish workers are highly satisfied.[57] Almost 40 percent of Canadian employees would not recommend their company as a good place to work. Forty percent also believe that they never see any of the benefits of their company making money. Almost 40 percent report that red tape and bureaucracy are among the biggest barriers to job satisfaction. A majority of the workforce (55 percent) says that they feel the "pressure of having too much to do."

So what are the consequences of lower job satisfaction? We examine this question below.

Job Satisfaction and Individual Productivity

The evidence suggests that the link between an individual's job satisfaction and his or her productivity is slightly positive.[58] It turns out the productivity can be affected as much by external conditions as it is by job satisfaction. For instance, a stockbroker's productivity is largely affected by the general movement of the stock market. When the market is moving up and volume is high, both satisfied and dissatisfied brokers will earn lots of commissions. Conversely, when the market is down, the level of broker satisfaction is not likely to mean much. One's position in the organization also seems to be an important moderating variable.

The relationship between job satisfaction and productivity is stronger when the employee's behaviour is not linked to outside factors. An employee's productivity on machine-paced jobs, for instance, will be much more influenced by the speed of the machine than by his or her level of satisfaction.

The evidence also shows that the satisfaction-productivity correlation is stronger for higher-level employees. Thus, we might expect the relationship to be more relevant for individuals in professional, supervisory, and managerial positions.

There is another complication in the satisfaction-productivity link. Some studies have found that productivity leads to satisfaction rather than the other way around.[59] If you do a good job, you feel good about it. Additionally, assuming that the organization rewards productivity, higher productivity should increase verbal recognition, pay level, and probabilities for promotion. These rewards, in turn, increase the level of satisfaction with the job.

Our *Point/Counterpoint* discussion on page 102 investigates the debate on whether job satisfaction is created by the situation or by an individual's characteristics.

Job Satisfaction and Organizational Productivity

The link between job satisfaction and productivity is much stronger when we look not at individuals, but at the organization as a whole.[60] When satisfaction and productivity data are gathered for the organization as a whole, rather than at the individual level, we find that organizations with more satisfied employees tend to be more effective than organizations with less satisfied employees. For instance, Paul Walters, former chair and CEO of Toronto-based Sears Canada, thinks "there's a definite link between employee satisfaction and customer satisfaction. You can't have cranky employees and happy customers."[61]

job satisfaction An individual's general attitude toward his or her job.

Sears Canada
www.sears.ca

Fortune magazine studied the link between job satisfaction and productivity for the 100 Best Companies to Work for in America. "Of the 61 firms in the group that have been publicly traded for the past five years, 45 yielded higher returns to the shareholders than the Russell 3000, an index of large and small companies that mirrors our 100 Best. The 61 companies averaged annual returns of 27.5 percent, compared with 17.3 percent for the Russell 3000."[62] That's a substantial difference in return, all for having happy workers. Happy workers don't guarantee financial gains, however. Both Southwest Airlines and Nordstrom, which were included in the 100 Best list, had lower annual rates of return, but also faced very competitive economic climates.

The *Fortune* study identified four attitudes that, when taken together, correlated with higher profits: "Workers feel they are given the opportunity to do what they do best every day; they believe their opinions count; they sense that other workers are committed to quality; and they've made a direct connection between their work and the company's mission."[63] Managers can help the development of these attitudes by actively seeking employee input into decisions and clarifying organizational goals so that employees understand how their work relates to the overall direction of the company.

The *Fortune* study, coupled with previous research on organizational productivity, suggests that the reason we have not received strong support for the *satisfaction-causes-productivity* thesis is twofold: Studies have focused on individuals rather than on the organization, and individual-level measures of productivity don't take into consideration all the interactions and complexities in the work process.

Job Satisfaction and Organizational Citizenship Behaviour

organizational citizenship behaviour (OCB) Discretionary behaviour that is not part of an employee's formal job requirements, but that nevertheless promotes the effective functioning of the organization.

In Chapter 1, we defined **organizational citizenship behaviour (OCB)** as discretionary behaviour that is not part of an employee's formal job requirements and is not usually rewarded, but that nevertheless promotes the effective functioning of the organization.[64] Individuals who are high in OCB will go beyond their usual job duties, providing performance that is beyond expectations. Examples of such behaviour include helping colleagues with their workloads, taking only limited breaks, and alerting others to work-related problems.[65] More recently OCB has been associated with the following workplace behaviours: "altruism, conscientiousness, loyalty, civic virtue, voice, functional participation, sportsmanship, courtesy, and advocacy participation."[66] Organizational citizenship is important, as it can help the organization function more efficiently and more effectively.[67]

It seems logical to assume that job satisfaction should be a major determinant of an employee's OCB.[68] Satisfied employees would seem more likely to talk positively about an organization, help others, and go beyond the normal expectations in their jobs.[69] Moreover, satisfied employees might be more prone to go beyond the call of duty because they want to reciprocate their positive experiences. Consistent with this thinking, early discussions of OCB assumed that it was closely linked with satisfaction.[70] Some evidence, however, suggests that satisfaction does influence OCB, but through perceptions of fairness.[71]

There is, then, a modest overall relationship between job satisfaction and OCB.[72] But job satisfaction is unrelated to OCB when fairness is considered.[73] What does this mean? Basically, job satisfaction comes down to a belief that there are fair outcomes, treatment, and procedures in the workplace.[74] If you don't feel that your manager, the organization's procedures, or its pay policies are fair, your job satisfaction is likely to suffer significantly. However, when you perceive organizational processes and outcomes to be fair, trust is developed. When you trust your employer, your job satisfaction increases, and you are more willing to voluntarily engage in behaviours that go beyond your formal job requirements.

Job Satisfaction and Customer Satisfaction

Employees in service jobs often interact with customers. Since the management of service organizations should be concerned with pleasing those customers, it is reasonable to ask: Is employee satisfaction related to positive customer outcomes? For front-line employees who have regular contact with customers, the answer is yes.

The evidence indicates that satisfied employees increase customer satisfaction and loyalty.[75] Why? In service organizations, customer retention and defection are highly dependent on how front-line employees deal with customers. Satisfied employees are more likely to be friendly, upbeat, and responsive—which customers appreciate. Because satisfied employees are less prone to turnover, customers are more likely to encounter familiar faces and receive experienced service. These qualities build customer satisfaction and loyalty. In addition, the relationship seems to apply in reverse: Dissatisfied customers can increase an employee's job dissatisfaction. Employees who have regular contact with customers report that rude, thoughtless, or unreasonably demanding customers adversely affect the employees' job satisfaction.[76]

A number of companies are acting on this evidence. Service-oriented businesses such as FedEx, WestJet Airlines, and Office Depot obsess about pleasing their customers. Toward that end, they also focus on building employee satisfaction—recognizing that employee satisfaction will go a long way toward contributing to their goal of having happy customers. These firms seek to hire upbeat and friendly employees, they train employees in the importance of customer service, they reward customer service, they provide positive employee work climates, and they regularly track employee satisfaction through attitude surveys.

How Employees Can Express Dissatisfaction

Dissatisfied employees are more likely to miss work, but the correlation is moderate—usually less than −0.40.[77] Dissatisfied employees are also more likely to quit their jobs, and the correlation is stronger than what we found for absenteeism.[78] However, a person's general disposition toward life moderates the job satisfaction–turnover relationship.[79] Some individuals gripe more than others, and such individuals, when dissatisfied with their jobs, are less likely to quit than those who are more positively disposed toward life. So if two employees are equally dissatisfied, the one most likely to quit is the one with the highest predisposition to be happy or satisfied with life in general. Likely these individuals do not feel trapped and are willing to exert more control over the situation and look for another job.

The evidence suggests that employees express dissatisfaction in a number of ways.[80] For example, rather than quit, employees can complain, be insubordinate, steal organizational property, or slow down performing their work responsibilities. Exhibit 3-5 illustrates a model that can be used to examine individual responses to dissatisfaction along two dimensions: whether they are constructive or destructive and whether they are active or passive. Four types of behaviour result:[81]

- *Exit.* Actively attempting to leave the organization, including looking for a new position as well as resigning. This is a destructive action from the point of view of the organization.

- *Voice.* Actively and constructively attempting to improve conditions, including suggesting improvements, discussing problems with superiors, and some forms of union activity.

- *Loyalty.* Passively but optimistically waiting for conditions to improve, including speaking up for the organization in the face of external criticism and trusting the organization and its management to "do the right thing."

exit Dissatisfaction expressed by actively attempting to leaving the organization.

voice Dissatisfaction expressed by actively and constructively attempting to improve conditions.

loyalty Dissatisfaction expressed by passively waiting for conditions to improve.

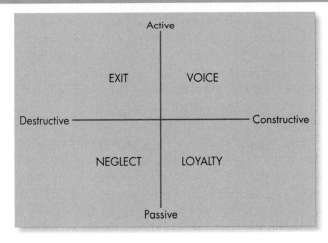

neglect Dissatisfaction expressed by passively allowing conditions to worsen.

- *Neglect.* Passively allowing conditions to worsen, including chronic absenteeism or lateness, reduced effort, and increased error rate. This is a destructive action from the point of view of the organization.

Exit and neglect behaviours reflect employee choices of lowered productivity, absenteeism, and turnover in the face of dissatisfaction. But this model also presents constructive behaviours that allow individuals to tolerate unpleasant situations or to work toward satisfactory working conditions. It helps us understand situations, such as those sometimes found among unionized workers, where low job satisfaction is coupled with low turnover.[82] Union members often express dissatisfaction through the grievance procedure or through formal contract negotiations. These voice mechanisms allow union members to continue in their jobs while convincing themselves that they are acting to improve the situation.

Organizational Commitment

organizational commitment A state in which an employee identifies with a particular organization and its goals, and wishes to maintain membership in the organization.

affective commitment An individual's emotional attachment to, identification with, and involvement in the organization.

normative commitment The obligation an individual feels to staying with the organization.

continuance commitment An individual's calculation to stay with the organization based on the perceived costs of leaving the organization.

Organizational commitment is defined as a state in which an employee identifies with a particular organization and its goals, and wishes to maintain membership in the organization.[83]

Professor John Meyer at the University of Western Ontario and his colleagues have identified and developed measures for three types of commitment:[84]

- *Affective commitment.* An individual's relationship to the organization: his or her emotional attachment to, identification with, and involvement in the organization.

- *Normative commitment.* The obligation an individual feels to staying with the organization.

- *Continuance commitment.* An individual's calculation that it is in his or her best interest to stay with the organization based on the perceived costs of leaving the organization.

Affective commitment is strongly associated with positive work behaviours such as performance, attendance, and citizenship. Normative commitment is less strongly associated with positive work behaviours. Because continuance commitment reflects an individual's calculation that it is in his or her best interest to stay with the organization (perhaps because it would be difficult to find a job elsewhere), it is often associated with negative work behaviours.[85]

The notion of organizational commitment has changed in recent years. Twenty years ago, employees and employers had an unwritten loyalty contract, with employees typically remaining with a single organization for most of their career. This notion has become increasingly obsolete. As such, "measures of employee-firm attachment, such as commitment, are problematic for new employment relations."[86] Canadian business consultant Barbara Moses notes that "40-somethings still value loyalty: they think people should be prepared to make sacrifices, to earn their way. The 20-somethings are saying, 'No, I want to be paid for my work; I have no belief in the goodness of organizations, so I'm going to be here as long as my work is meaningful.'"[87]

Arnold Carbone (centre) receives a high level of job satisfaction and has a positive attitude about his job. Carbone, "Conductor of Bizarre and D" at Ben & Jerry's, travels the world and eats as many desserts as he can in his job as developer of new ice-cream flavours for Ben & Jerry's. Carbone created flavours such as Phish Food and Wavy Gravy.

A recent study found that employees who are highly committed to their organization (about 11 percent of the workforce) exert 57 percent more discretionary effort—that is, willingness to go beyond their usual job duties—than employees who lack commitment. Individuals who show very little commitment to their organization (about 13 percent of the workforce) are four times more likely to quit their jobs than the average employee.[88]

How can companies increase organizational commitment? Research on a number of companies known for employees with high organizational commitment identified five reasons why employees commit themselves:[89]

- They are proud of [the company's] aspirations, accomplishments, and legacy; they share its values.

- They know what each person is expected to do, how performance is measured, and why it matters.

- They are in control of their own destinies; they savour the high-risk, high-reward work environment.

- They are recognized mostly for the quality of their individual performance.

- They have fun and enjoy the supportive and highly interactive environment.

These findings suggest a variety of ways for organizations to increase the commitment of employees. Earlier in the chapter, we discussed the role of satisfaction on organizational citizenship behaviour (OCB). We should also note that when individuals have high organizational commitment, they are likely to engage in more OCB.

MANAGING DIVERSITY IN THE WORKPLACE

Procter & Gamble Canada has a strong commitment to diversity in its workplace. For instance, the company changed its recruiting practices to ensure diversity in hiring. P&G broadened the number of universities from which they recruit, included French universities in Quebec in their recruiting, and targeted several campuses with high representation of visible minority students to ensure geographical, language, racial, and ethnic diversity. This resulted in a stronger and more diverse workforce at P&G. Why does managing diversity well make a difference?

5 How do we respond to diversity in the workplace?

Organizations are increasingly having to face diversity concerns as workplaces become more heterogeneous. Earlier in the chapter, we discussed cultural and generational differences and their implications in the Canadian workplace. Exhibit 3-6 identifies some of the major categories of workforce diversity and suggests how organizations might accommodate the needs of employees within each category.

Many organizations have attempted to incorporate workforce diversity initiatives into their workplaces to improve relations among co-workers. For example, IBM Canada is one of a number of companies in Canada that have developed diversity polices for their workplace. IBM Canada's policy states the following:

At IBM we acknowledge, value and respect diversity.... At IBM we recognize individual differences and appreciate how these differences provide a powerful competitive advantage and a source of great pride and opportunity in the workplace and marketplace.[90]

The company's statement on diversity is representative of the types of statements that organizations often include in their annual reports and employee information packets. These statements signal corporate values to both employees and other people who might do business with the company. Some corporations choose to signal the value of diversity because they think it is an important strategic goal. Other organizations recognize that the purchasing power of diverse groups is substantial.

EXHIBIT 3-6   Major Workforce Diversity Categories

GENDER

Nearly half of the Canadian workforce is now made up of women, and women are a growing percentage of the workforce in most countries throughout the world. Organizations need to ensure that hiring and employment policies create equal access and opportunities to individuals regardless of gender.

NATIONAL ORIGIN

A growing percentage of Canadian workers are immigrants or come from homes where English is not the primary language spoken. Because employers in Canada have the right to demand that English be spoken at the workplace on job-related activities except in bilingual parts of the country (i.e., the Ottawa region; all of New Brunswick; parts of Northern and Eastern Ontario; and within Quebec, the Montreal area and parts of the Eastern Townships, Gaspé, and West Quebec), communication problems can occur when employees' English-language skills are weak.

AGE

The Canadian workforce is aging, and recent polls indicate that an increasing percentage of employees expect to work past the traditional retirement age of 65. Though the rules vary somewhat by province, in general organizations cannot discriminate on the basis of an employee's age until that employee reaches the age of 65, and they are obligated to accommodate the needs of older workers.

DISABILITY

Organizations need to ensure that jobs and workplaces are accessible to people who have mental or physical disabilities, as well as to those who have health challenges.

DOMESTIC PARTNERS

An increasing number of gay and lesbian employees, as well as employees with live-in partners of the opposite sex, are demanding the same rights and benefits for their partners that organizations have provided for traditional married couples.

NON-CHRISTIAN

Organizations need to be sensitive to the customs, rituals, and holidays, as well as the appearance and attire, of individuals of non-Christian faiths such as Sikhism, Hinduism, Judaism, Islam, and Buddhism, and ensure that these individuals suffer no adverse impact as a result of their appearance or practices.

When companies design and then publicize statements about the importance of diversity. they are essentially producing value statements. The hope, of course, is that the statements will influence the behaviour of members of the organization. Interestingly enough, however, there is little research showing that values can be changed successfully.[91] Because values tend to be relatively stable, workplaces try to address diversity issues through education aimed at changing attitudes. In *HR Implications* on pages 103–104, we discuss a variety of diversity training programs designed by organizations to change employee attitudes toward diversity.

Ben Barry (left), president of Ben Barry Agency, received the 2002 bizSmart Student Entrepreneur of the Year award while a full-time business management student at the University of Toronto. Barry is trying to change the attitudes toward waif-like models through his modelling agency. Sixty percent of his models are atypical: bigger, shorter, older, or different from what the public usually expects.

Responses to Diversity Initiatives

Michael Adams' *Sex in the Snow* provides some information to help us understand how diversity initiatives might fare in the workplace in light of generational values. First, he notes that Generation Xers "eagerly embrace a number of egalitarian and pluralistic values."[92] This point might suggest that as Generation Xers move through the workplace, some of the tensions currently surrounding the introduction of diversity initiatives might lessen. On the other hand, Adams also notes that there are 4.3 million Baby Boomers who belong to the disengaged Darwinists group, and many of these tend to be the younger Boomers (that is, closer to their mid-40s than their mid-50s). This group, together with the rational traditionalists of the Elders group (representing 3.5 million Canadians), tends to be very conservative. As Adams notes, "Among the men in this group are a large number of what have come to be known as 'angry white guys.'" They find that society has changed too much, too quickly, and for the worse. "They do not support the idea of women's equality or alternative family structures. They brand programs of affirmative action or employment equity for women or visible minorities as 'reverse discrimination.'"[93] As a result of these generational differences, it is conceivable that tensions in the workplace over diversity initiatives will remain for some time to come. *Focus on Diversity* encourages you to think about whether changing behaviour without changing attitudes is really enough.

FOCUS ON **DIVERSITY**

Complying With Equity Legislation

What can companies do to change behaviour if not attitude? Nicole Chénier-Cullen is the director-general of the employment equity branch of the Canadian Human Rights Commission.[94] Her job is to see that Canadian organizations follow the laws regarding employment equity. She notes that companies need to be more proactive in the way they recruit visible minority job candidates. Placing an ad in the *Globe and Mail*, for example, often draws applicants who are similar to those placing the ad.

Still, Chénier-Cullen finds that organizations can change the way they recruit more easily than they can change employee attitudes. "That's one of the toughest barriers to admit, and one of the biggest to overcome," she says.

Renée Bazile-Jones is president of Toronto-based Unparalleled, a consulting firm that offers training programs to address discrimination, diversity, and sexual harassment. She encourages companies to go outside their comfort zone when they recruit, to help visible minorities get the message that they will be welcome in the company. Bazile-Jones agrees with Chénier-Cullen that "We can't force people to change their beliefs, but we can force them to change their behaviour."

Individuals or companies may or may not value workforce diversity. A company that values diversity may actively work to increase the diversity of the employees hired. A company that does not value diversity may try to skirt the law, or do the very minimum required by employment equity legislation. However, just because the company's managers may value diversity, this does not mean that all employees will share that value. Consequently, even if they are required to attend diversity training, employees may exhibit negative attitudes toward individuals because of their gender or ethnicity. Additionally, what attitudes are appropriate outside of the workplace may be questioned by some employers, as you will discover in *Case Incident—You Can't Do That* on page 107.

Cultural Intelligence

Are some individuals better than others at dealing with people from different cultures? Management professors Christopher Earley of the London School of Business and Elaine Mosakowski of the University of Colorado at Boulder have recently introduced the idea of **cultural intelligence**, or CQ, to suggest that people vary in how they deal with other cultures. This term is defined as "the seemingly natural ability to interpret someone's unfamiliar and ambiguous gestures in just the way that person's compatriots and colleagues would, even to mirror them."[95]

cultural intelligence The ability to understand someone's unfamiliar and ambiguous gestures in the same way as would people from his or her culture.

Earley and Mosakowski suggest that CQ "picks up where emotional intelligence leaves off." Those with CQ try to figure out whether a person's behaviour is representative of all members of a group, or just that person. Thus, for example, a person with high CQ who encounters two German engineers would be able to determine which of the engineers' conduct is explained by the fact of being an engineer, by being German, and by behaviour that is simply particular to the individual.

 RESEARCH FINDINGS

According to the researchers, "cultural intelligence resides in the body [the physical] and the heart [the emotional/motivational], as well as the head [the cognitive]." Individuals who have high *cognitive* CQ look for clues to help them identify a culture's shared understandings. Specifically, an individual does this by looking for consistencies in behaviours across a variety of people from the same cultural background. Individuals with high *physical* CQ learn the customs and gestures of those from other cultures and therefore act more like them. This increases understanding, trust, and openness between people of different cultures. One study found that job candidates who used some of the mannerisms of recruiters who had different cultural backgrounds from themselves were more likely to receive job offers than those who did not do so.[96] Those with high *emotional/motivational* CQ believe that they are capable of understanding people from other cultures, and will keep trying to do so, even if they are faced with difficulties in doing so.

Based on their research, Earley and Mosakowski have discovered that most managers fall into the following cultural intelligence profiles:

- *Provincial.* They work best with people of similar background, but have difficulties working with those from different backgrounds.

- *Analyst.* They analyze a foreign culture's rules and expectations to figure out how to interact with others.

- *Natural.* They use intuition rather than systematic study to understand those from other cultural backgrounds.

- *Ambassador.* They communicate convincingly that they fit in, even if they do not know much about the foreign culture.

- *Mimic.* They control actions and behaviours to match others, even if they do not understand the significance of the cultural cues observed.

EXHIBIT 3-7   Measuring Your Cultural Intelligence

Rate the extent to which you agree with each statement, using the following scale:

> 1 = strongly disagree
> 2 = disagree
> 3 = neutral
> 4 = agree
> 5 = strongly agree

_____ Before I interact with people from a new culture, I ask myself what I hope to achieve.

_____ If I encounter something unexpected while working in a new culture, I use this experience to figure out new ways to approach other cultures in the future.

_____ I plan how I'm going to relate to people from a different culture before I meet them.

_____ When I come into a new cultural situation, I can immediately sense whether something is going well or something is wrong.

Total _____ ÷ 4 = **Cognitive CQ**

_____ It's easy for me to change my body language (for example, eye contact or posture) to suit people from a different culture.

_____ I can alter my expression when a cultural encounter requires it.

_____ I modify my speech style (for example, accent or tone) to suit people from a different culture.

_____ I easily change the way I act when a cross-cultural encounter seems to require it.

Total _____ ÷ 4 = **Physical CQ**

_____ I have confidence that I can deal well with people from a different culture.

_____ I am certain that I can befriend people whose cultural backgrounds are different from mine.

_____ I can adapt to the lifestyle of a different culture with relative ease.

_____ I am confident that I can deal with a cultural situation that is unfamiliar.

Total _____ ÷ 4 = **Emotional/motivational CQ**

Interpretation: Generally, an average of less than 3 would indicate an area calling for improvement, while an average of greater than 4.5 reflects a true CQ strength.

Source: P. C. Earley and E. Mosakowski, "Cultural Intelligence," *Harvard Business Review* 82, no. 10 (October 2004), pp. 139–146. With permission.

- *Chameleon.* They have high levels of all three CQ components. They could be mistaken as being from the foreign culture. According to research, only about 5 percent of managers fit this profile.

Exhibit 3-7 can help you assess your own CQ.

SUMMARY AND IMPLICATIONS

1 **What are values?** Values guide how we make decisions about and evaluations of behaviours and events. They represent basic convictions about what is important, right, and good to the individual. Although they do not have a direct impact on behaviour, values strongly influence a person's attitudes. So knowledge of an individual's values can provide insight into his or her attitudes.

2 **How can we understand values across cultures?** Geert Hofstede found that managers and employees vary on five value dimensions of national culture. His insights were expanded by the GLOBE program, an ongoing cross-cultural investigation of leadership and national culture. That study has identified nine dimensions on which cultures can vary: assertiveness, future orientation, gender differentiation, uncertainty avoidance, power distance, individualism/collectivism, in-group collectivism, performance orientation, and humane orientation.

3 **Are there unique Canadian values?** In his recent books, pollster Michael Adams identified the social values of today's Canadians. He found that within three broad age groups of adult Canadians—the Elders (those over 60), Baby Boomers (born between the mid-1940s and mid-1960s), and Generation Xers (born between the mid-1960s and the early 1980s)—there are at least 12 quite distinct "value tribes." More recently, discussion has turned to the Net Generation—whose members are now in their early 20s—the newest entrants to the workplace. Canada is a multicultural country, and there are a number of groups that contribute to its diverse values, such as Aboriginal people, French Canadians, and various immigrant groups. Canadian values differ from American values and those of its other trading partners in a variety of ways.

4 **What are attitudes and why are they important?** Attitudes are positive or negative feelings about objects, people, or events. Attitudes affect the way people respond to situations. When I say, "I like my job," I am expressing my attitude to work and I am likely to be more committed in my behaviour than if my attitude was one of not liking my job. A person can have thousands of attitudes, but OB focuses our attention on a limited number of job-related attitudes. These job-related attitudes tap positive or negative evaluations that employees hold about aspects of their work environment. Most of the research in OB has been concerned with two attitudes: job satisfaction and organizational commitment.

5 **How do we respond to diversity in the workplace?** Many organizations have attempted to incorporate workforce diversity initiatives into their workplaces to improve relations among co-workers. Organizations have introduced diversity training programs to improve cultural awareness. Recent research suggests that individuals who score high on cultural intelligence have an easier time dealing with people from other cultures.

For Review

1. How does ethics relate to values?

2. Describe the G_OBE project's nine dimensions of national culture.

3. How might differences in generational values affect the workplace?

4. Compare Aboriginal and non-Aboriginal values.

5. What might explain low levels of employee job satisfaction in recent years?

6. Are satisfied workers productive workers? Explain your answer.

7. What is the relationship between job satisfaction and absenteeism? Job satisfaction and turnover? Which is the stronger relationship?

8. Contrast exit, voice, loyalty, and neglect as employee responses to job satisfaction.

9. What is cultural intelligence? How do its three dimensions relate to understanding people from other cultures?

10. How can managers get employees to more readily accept working with colleagues who are different from themselves?

For Critical Thinking

1. "Thirty-five years ago, young employees we hired were ambitious, conscientious, hard-working, and honest. Today's young workers don't have the same values." Do you agree or disagree with this manager's comments? Support your position.

2. Do you think there might be any relationship between the possession of certain personal values and successful career progression in organizations such as Merrill Lynch, the Canadian Union of Postal Workers (CUPW), and the City of Regina's police department? Discuss.

3. "Managers should do everything they can to enhance the job satisfaction of their employees." Do you agree or disagree? Support your position.

4. "Organizations should do everything they can to encourage organizational citizenship behaviour." Do you agree or disagree? Support your position.

5. When employees are asked whether they would again choose the same work or whether they would want their children to follow in their footsteps, fewer than half typically answer "yes." What, if anything, do you think this implies about employee job satisfaction?

OB for You

- You will encounter many people who have values different from yours in the classroom and in various kinds of activities in which you participate, as well as in the workplace. You should try to understand value differences, and to figure out ways to work positively with people who are different from you.

- We indicated that many Canadians were satisfied with their jobs, and we mentioned the sources of some of the satisfactions. We also identified areas in which people were dissatisfied with their jobs. This information may help you understand your own feelings about whether you are satisfied with your job.

- You may be able to use some of the information on attitudes to think about how to better work with people from different cultures. An understanding of how cultures differ may provide insight when you observe people doing things differently from the way you do them.

POINT

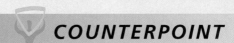

COUNTERPOINT

Managers Create Job Satisfaction

A review of the evidence has identified four factors conducive to high levels of employee job satisfaction: mentally challenging work, equitable rewards, supportive working conditions, and supportive colleagues.[97] Importantly, each of these factors is controllable by management.

Mentally challenging work. People prefer jobs that give them opportunities to use their skills and abilities and offer a variety of tasks, freedom, and feedback on how well they are doing. These characteristics make work mentally challenging.

Equitable rewards. Employees want pay systems and promotion policies that they perceive as being just, unambiguous, and in line with their expectations. When pay is seen as fair based on job demands, individual skill level, and community pay standards, job satisfaction is likely to result. Similarly, employees seek fair promotion policies and practices. Promotions provide opportunities for personal growth, more responsibilities, and increased social status. Individuals who perceive that promotion decisions are made in a fair and just manner, therefore, are likely to experience satisfaction from their jobs.

Supportive working conditions. Employees want work environments that support personal comfort and doing a good job too. Studies demonstrate that employees prefer physical surroundings that are not dangerous or uncomfortable. Additionally, most employees prefer working relatively close to home, in clean and relatively modern facilities, and with adequate tools and equipment.

Supportive colleagues. People get more out of work than merely money or tangible achievements. For most employees, work also fills the need for social interaction. Not surprisingly, therefore, having friendly and supportive co-workers leads to increased job satisfaction. The behaviour of an employee's boss is also a major determinant of satisfaction. Studies generally find that employee satisfaction increases when the immediate supervisor is understanding and friendly, offers praise for good performance, listens to employees' opinions, and shows a personal interest in them.

Satisfaction Is Individually Determined

The notion that managers and organizations can control the level of employee job satisfaction is inherently attractive. It fits nicely with the view that managers directly influence organizational processes and outcomes. Unfortunately there is a growing body of evidence challenging the notion that managers control the factors that influence employee job satisfaction. Contemporary research indicates that employee job satisfaction is largely genetically determined.[98]

Whether people are happy or not is essentially determined by their gene structure. You either have happy genes or you don't. Approximately 80 percent of people's differences in happiness, or subjective well-being, has been found to be attributable to their different genes.

Analysis of satisfaction data for a selected sample of individuals over a 50-year period found that individual results were consistently stable over time, even when these people changed employers and occupations. This and other research suggests that an individual's disposition toward life—positive or negative—is established by his or her genetic makeup, holds over time, and carries over into his or her disposition toward work.

Given these findings, there is probably little that most managers can do to influence employee satisfaction. In spite of the fact that managers and organizations go to extensive lengths to try to improve employee job satisfaction through actions such as manipulating job characteristics, working conditions, and rewards, these actions are likely to have little effect. The only place where managers will have significant influence is through their control of the selection process. If managers want satisfied employees, they need to make sure their selection process screens out the negative, maladjusted, troublemaking fault-finders who derive little satisfaction in anything about their jobs. This is probably best achieved through personality testing, in-depth interviewing, and careful checking of applicants' previous work records.

HR IMPLICATIONS

Attitude Surveys and Diversity Training

Our *HR Implications* considers two key facets of this chapter.

First, it is important for organizations to find out about the attitudes of employees. To do this, organizations sometimes conduct attitude surveys. Second, sometimes organizations want to try to change the attitudes of their employees. A number of firms have made this attempt with respect to diversity issues, trying to encourage employees to see that meeting employment equity targets is not about imposed quotas, but is about an opportunity to increase the number of viewpoints and add to the range of skills available.

Determining Attitudes: Attitude Surveys

How does management get information about employee attitudes? The most popular method is through the use of *attitude surveys*.[99]

Exhibit 3-8 illustrates what an attitude survey might look like. Typically, attitude surveys present the employee with a set of statements or questions. Ideally, the items are tailored to obtain the specific information that management desires. An attitude score is achieved by summing up responses to individual questionnaire items. These scores can then be averaged for job groups, departments, divisions, or the organization as a whole.

Results from attitude surveys can frequently surprise management.

For instance, managers at the heavy-duty division of Springfield Remanufacturing thought everything was great.[100] Since employees were actively involved in division decisions and profitability was the highest within the entire company, management assumed morale was high. To confirm their beliefs, they conducted a short attitude survey. Employees were asked if they agreed or disagreed with the following statements: (1) At work, your opinions count; (2) those of you who want to be a leader in this company have the opportunity to become one; and (3) in the past six months someone has talked to you about your personal development. In the survey, 43 percent disagreed with the first statement, 48 percent with the second, and 62 percent with the third. Management was astounded. How could this be? The division had been holding shop floor meetings to review the numbers every week for more than 12 years. Further, most of the managers had come up through the ranks. Management responded by creating a committee made up of representatives from every department in the division and all three shifts. The committee quickly found that there were lots of little things the division was doing that were alienating employees. Out of this committee came a large number of suggestions which, after implementation, significantly improved employees' perceptions of their decision-making influence and their career opportunities in the division.

EXHIBIT 3-8   **Sample Attitude Survey**

Please answer each of the following statements using the following rating scale:

1 = Strongly agree	4 = Disagree	
2 = Agree	5 = Strongly disagree	
3 = Undecided		

Statement	Rating
1. This company is a pretty good place to work.	_____
2. I can get ahead in this company if I make the effort.	_____
3. This company's wage rates are competitive with those of other companies.	_____
4. Employee promotion decisions are handled fairly.	_____
5. I understand the various fringe benefits the company offers.	_____
6. My job makes the best use of my abilities.	_____
7. My workload is challenging but not burdensome.	_____
8. I have trust and confidence in my boss.	_____
9. I feel free to tell my boss what I think.	_____
10. I know what my boss expects of me.	_____

Using attitude surveys on a regular basis provides managers with valuable feedback on how employees perceive their working conditions.[101] Policies and practices that management views as objective and fair may be seen as inequitable by employees in general or by certain groups of employees. That these distorted perceptions have led to negative attitudes toward the job and organization should be important to management. This is because employee behaviours are based on perceptions, not reality. Remember, the employee who quits because she believes she is underpaid—when, in fact, management has objective data to support that her salary is highly competitive—is just as gone as if she had actually been underpaid.

Modifying Attitudes: Diversity Training

The centrepiece of most diversity programs is training. For instance, a relatively recent survey found that, among companies with diversity initiatives, 93 percent used training as part of their programs.[102] Diversity training programs are generally intended to provide a vehicle for increasing awareness and examining stereotypes. Participants learn to value individual differences, increase their cross-cultural understanding, and confront stereotypes.[103] In today's global economy, diversity training can be particularly helpful in accelerating cooperation in multinational work teams, facilitating group learning, and reducing cultural misunderstandings.[104]

Trevor Wilson, president of Toronto-based TWI, has presented employment equity programs to such clients as Coca-Cola, Ernst & Young, NASA, Nike, Ottawa Police Service, and Halton Regional Police Service. His approach has been popular because it supports a "no-guilt, no-blame, everybody's-not-the-same, business-friendly, all-inclusive" approach to equity, thus reducing the barriers that sometimes accompany equity training.[105] He refuses to work with clients who don't see diversity training as "part of a broader, proactive strategy to change a corporation's culture."[106] The core issues tackled in the actual training include the following: "that people tend to hire people like themselves; that we all harbour stereotypes; that cultural differences can lead you to misunderstand someone's qualifications; that continually talking to a colleague's breasts instead of her face is demeaning as well as illegal, and how would you like your wife or daughter to go through that?"[107]

What do these diversity programs look like, and how do they address attitude change?[108] They almost all include a self-evaluation phase. People are pressed to examine themselves and to confront ethnic and cultural stereotypes they might hold. Then participants typically take part in group discussions or panels with representatives from diverse groups. So, for instance, a Hmong man might describe his family's life in Southeast Asia and explain why they resettled in British Columbia; a lesbian might describe how she discovered her sexual identity and the reaction of her friends and family when she "came out."

There are additional activities designed to change attitudes. These include arranging for people to do volunteer work in community or social service centres in order to meet face to face with individuals and groups from diverse backgrounds, and using exercises that let participants feel what it's like to be different. For example, when shown the film *Eye of the Beholder*, where people are segregated and stereotyped according to their eye colour, participants realize what it's like to be judged by something over which they have no control.

The typical program lasts from half a day to three days and includes role-playing exercises, lectures, discussions, and group experiences. For example, in the United States, Xerox has worked with Cornell University's theatre department to create a set of short plays that increases awareness of work-related racial and gender conflicts. The show has been presented to more than 1300 Xerox managers.[109]

A training exercise at one insurance company that sought to increase sensitivity to aging asked participants to respond to the following four questions:

1. If you didn't know how old you are, how old would you guess you are? In other words, how old do you feel inside?

2. When I was 18, I thought middle age began at age _____.

3. Today, I think middle age begins at age _____.

4. What would be your first reaction if someone called you an older worker?[110]

Answers to these questions were then used to analyze age-related stereotypes. In another program designed to raise awareness of the power of stereotypes, each participant was asked to write an anonymous paper detailing all groups—women, born-again Christians, Blacks, gays, men, etc.—to which they had attached stereotypes.[111] They were also asked to explain why they'd had trouble working with certain groups in the past. Based on the responses, guest speakers were brought into the class to shatter the stereotypes directed at each group. This was followed by extensive discussion.

What Do You Value?

There are 16 items in the list below. Rate how important each one is to you on a scale of 0 (not important) to 100 (very important). Write a number between 0 and 100 on the line to the left of each item.

Not Important				**Somewhat Important**						**Very Important**
0	10	20	30	40	50	60	70	80	90	100

_____	**1.** An enjoyable, satisfying job.
_____	**2.** A high-paying job.
_____	**3.** A good marriage.
_____	**4.** Meeting new people; social events.
_____	**5.** Involvement in community activities.
_____	**6.** My religion.
_____	**7.** Exercising, playing sports.
_____	**8.** Intellectual development.
_____	**9.** A career with challenging opportunities.
_____	**10.** Nice cars, clothes, home, and so on.
_____	**11.** Spending time with family.
_____	**12.** Having several close friends.
_____	**13.** Volunteer work for nonprofit organizations, such as the Canadian Cancer Society.
_____	**14.** Meditation, quiet time to think, pray, and so on.
_____	**15.** A healthy, balanced diet.
_____	**16.** Educational reading, television, self-improvement programs, and so on.

Scoring Key:

Transfer the numbers for each of the 16 items to the appropriate column; then add up the 2 numbers in each column.

	Professional	**Financial**	**Family**	**Social**
	1. _____	2. _____	3. _____	4. _____
	9. _____	10. _____	11. _____	12. _____
Totals	_____	_____	_____	_____

	Community	**Spiritual**	**Physical**	**Intellectual**
	5. _____	6. _____	7. _____	8. _____
	13. _____	14. _____	15. _____	16. _____
Totals	_____	_____	_____	_____

The higher the total in any value dimension, the higher the importance you place on that value set. The closer the numbers are in all 8 dimensions, the more well rounded you are.

Source: R. N. Lussier, *Human Relations in Organizations: A Skill Building Approach,* 2nd ed. (Homewood, IL: Richard D. Irwin, 1993). Reprinted by permission of the McGraw-Hill Companies, Inc.

BREAKOUT **GROUP** EXERCISES

Form small groups to discuss the following topics, as assigned by your instructor. Each person in the group should first identify 3 to 5 key personal values.

1. Identify the extent to which values overlap in your group.

2. Try to uncover with your group members the source of some of your key values (e.g., parents, peer group, teachers, church).

3. What kind of workplace would be most suitable for the values that you hold most closely?

WORKING WITH **OTHERS** EXERCISE

Understanding Cultural Values

Objective   To compare the cultural values of two countries, and determine how differences might affect group behaviour.

Time   Approximately 30 minutes.

Procedure

1. Break into groups of 5 or 6.

2. Pretend that you are a group of students working on a project. Half of you are from Canada and hold typically "Canadian" cultural values, the other half are from the country assigned and hold that country's cultural values.

3. Consider the values of power distance, individualism, and uncertainty avoidance, and discuss the differences between Canadian cultural values and the values of the country assigned to you.

4. Answer the following questions:

What challenges might you expect in working together?

What steps could be taken to work together more effectively?

ETHICAL **DILEMMA** EXERCISE

Is It a Bribe or a Gift?

The Corruption of Foreign Public Officials Act prohibits Canadian firms from making payments to foreign government officials with the aim of gaining or maintaining business. But payments are acceptable if they don't violate local laws. For instance, payments to officers working for foreign corporations are legal. Many countries don't have such legal guidelines.

Bribery is a common way of doing business in many underdeveloped countries. Government jobs there often don't pay very well, so it's tempting for officials to supplement their income with bribes. In addition, in many countries, the penalties for demanding and receiving bribes are few or nonexistent.

You are a Canadian who works for a large European multinational computer manufacturer. You are currently working to sell a $5-million system to a government agency in Nigeria. The Nigerian official who heads up the team that will decide who gets this contract has asked you for a payment of $20 000. He said this payment will not guarantee you get the order, but without it he could not be very encouraging. Your company's policy is very flexible on the issue of "gifts" to facilitate sales. Your boss says that it's OK to pay the $20 000, but only if you can be relatively assured of the order.

You are not sure what you should do. The Nigerian official has told you specifically that any payment to him is not to be mentioned to anyone else on the Nigerian team. You know for certain that three other companies are also nego-

tiating, but it's unconfirmed that two of those companies have turned down the payment request.

What would you do?

Source: This exercise is based on M. Allen, "Here Comes the Bribe," *Entrepreneur,* October 2000, p. 48.

CASE INCIDENTS

You Can't Do That

Paul Fromm is a high school teacher employed in one of the most ethnically diverse school districts in Canada. He is an excellent teacher, and receives high ratings from his students.

During weekends and summer holidays, when he is not working, he participates in conferences held by white supremacists and anti-Semitic groups. For instance, he attended a conference at which swastikas were waving, and individuals gave Nazi salutes. Fromm also attended a celebration of Adolf Hitler's birthday.

Though it is known that Fromm attends these conferences, he has never expressed racist views in the classroom or discriminated against any student. "I am here to teach English, not to make a political statement. This is my job, that's what I do. And I do it very well," he says.

The school board and some of the teachers are upset with Fromm's behaviour. They feel that what he does, even though outside of work time, is not consistent with the school board's values of encouraging multicultural diversity.

Questions

1. What, if anything, should the school board do in this instance?

2. Should Fromm consider not going to further conferences of this sort?

Source: Reconstructed, based on H. Sokoloff, "Firing of Teacher Upheld for His Opinions on Race," *National Post,* March 13, 2002, pp. A1, A11.

Gourmet Foods Works on Employee Attitudes

Gourmet Foods is a huge grocery and drug company. It has more than 2400 supermarkets, and its Premier and Polar brands make it the fifth-largest drugstore company in North America. In a typical year, shoppers will make 1.4 billion trips through its stores.

Gourmet Foods competes against tough businesses. Wal-Mart, in particular, has been eating away at its market share. In 2001, with revenues flat and profits falling, the company hired Larry Johnston to turn the business around.

Johnston came to Gourmet Foods from General Living Medical Systems. It was while he was at General Living that Johnston met a training specialist named Roger Nelson. Nelson endeared himself to Johnston when the latter hired Nelson to help him with a serious problem. At the time, Johnston had been sent to Paris to fix General

Living's European division. The division made CT scanners. Over the previous decade, four executives had been brought in to turn the division around and try to make it profitable. All had failed. Johnston responded to the challenge by initiating some important changes—he made a number of acquisitions, he closed down inefficient plants, and he moved factories to Eastern European countries to take advantage of lower labour costs. Then he brought in Nelson to charge up the troops. "After we got Roger in," says Johnston, "people began to live their lives differently. They came to work with a spring in their step." In three years, the division was bringing in annual profits of $100 million. Johnston gives a large part of the credit for this turnaround to Nelson.

What is Nelson's secret? He provides motivation and attitude training. Here is an example of Nelson's primary program—called the Successful Life Course. It lasts three days and begins each morning at 6 a.m. The first day begins with a chapter from an inspirational handout, followed by 12 minutes of yoga-like stretching. Then participants march up a hill, chanting, "I know I can, I know I can." This is followed by breakfast and then a variety of lectures on attitude, diet, and exercise. But the primary focus of the program is on attitude. Says Nelson, "It's your attitude, not your aptitude, that determines your altitude." Other parts of the program include group hugs, team activities, and mind-control relaxation exercises.

Johnston believes strongly in Nelson's program. "Positive attitude is the single biggest thing that can change a business," says Johnston. He sees Nelson's program as being a critical bridge linking employees with customers: "We're in the business of maintenance and acquisition of customers." With so many shoppers going through his stores, Johnston says there are "a lot of opportunities for customer service. We've got to energize the associates." To prove he is willing to put his money where his mouth is, Johnston has committed $10 million to this training. By the end of 2006, 10 000 managers will have taken the course. They, in turn, will train all 190 000 Gourmet Foods "associates," with the help of tapes and books.

Nelson claims his program works. He cites success at companies such as Allstate, Milliken & Co., and Abbott Labs. "The goal is to improve mental, physical, and emotional well-being," he says. "We as individuals determine the success of our lives. Positive thoughts create positive actions."

Questions

1. Explain the logic as to how Nelson's three-day course could positively influence Gourmet Foods' profitability.

2. Johnston says, "Positive attitude is the single biggest thing that can change a business." How valid and generalizable do you think this statement is?

3. If you were Johnston, what could you do to evaluate the effectiveness of your $10-million investment in Nelson's training program?

4. If you were a Gourmet Foods employee, how would you feel about going through Nelson's course? Explain your position.

Source: Based on M. Burke, "The Guru in the Vegetable Bin," *Forbes,* March 3, 2003, pp. 56–58.

From **Concepts** to **Skills**

Changing Attitudes

Can you change unfavourable employee attitudes? Sometimes! It depends on who you are, the strength of the employee's attitude, the magnitude of the change, and the technique you choose to try to change the attitude.

People are most likely to respond to changes suggested by someone who is liked, credible, and convincing. If people like you, they are more apt to identify and adopt your message. Credibility implies trust, expertise, and objectivity. So you are more likely to change someone's attitude if that person views you as believable, knowledgeable about what you are saying, and unbiased in your presentation. Finally, successful attitude change is enhanced when you present your arguments clearly and persuasively.

It's easier to change a person's attitude if he or she is not strongly committed to it. Conversely, the stronger the belief in the attitude, the harder it is to change it. Also, attitudes that have been expressed publicly are more difficult to change because doing so requires admitting having made a mistake.

It's also easier to change attitudes when the change required is not very significant. To get a person to accept a new attitude that varies greatly from his or her current position requires more effort. It may also threaten other deeply held attitudes.

All attitude-change techniques are not equally effective across situations. Oral persuasion techniques are most effective when you use a positive, tactful tone; present strong evidence to support your position; tailor your argument to the listener; use logic; and support your evidence by appealing to the person's fears, frustrations, and other emotions. But people are more likely to embrace change when they can experience it. The use of training sessions where employees share and personalize experiences, and practise new behaviours, can be powerful stimulants for change. Consistent with self-perception theory, changes in behaviour can lead to changes in attitudes.

Assessing Skills

After you've read this chapter, take the following Self-Assessments on your enclosed CD-ROM:

6. What Do I Value?

7. How Involved Am I in My Job?

8. How Satisfied Am I With My Job?

9. What Are My Attitudes Toward Workplace Diversity?

16. What's My Attitude Toward Achievement?

45. How Committed Am I to My Organization?

Practising Skills

Form groups of 2. Person A is to choose any topic that he or she feels strongly about and state his or her position on the topic in 30 words or less. Person B's task will be to try to change Person A's attitude on this topic. Person B will have 10 minutes to make his or her case. When the time is up, the roles are reversed. Person B picks the topic and Person A has 10 minutes to try to change Person B's attitude.

Potential topics (you can choose *either* side of a topic) include the following: politics; the economy; world events; social practices; or specific management issues, such as that organizations should require all employees to undergo regular drug testing, there is no such thing as organizational loyalty any more, the customer is always right, and layoffs are an indication of management failures.

Questions

1. Were you successful at changing the other person's attitude? Why or why not?

2. Was the other person successful at changing your attitude? Why or why not?

3. What conclusions can you draw about changing the attitudes of yourself and others?

Reinforcing Skills

1. Try to convince a friend or relative to go with you to see a movie or play that you know he or she does not want to see.

2. Try to convince a friend or relative to try a different brand of toothpaste.

OB ON THE EDGE

Stress at Work

Celebrated clothing designer and entrepreneur Linda Lundström (shown relaxing above), founder of Toronto-based Linda Lundström, knew she was under too much stress the day she started crying uncontrollably after she couldn't find a parking spot near her doctor's office.[1] "It was the proverbial last straw," she says about the parking incident. At the time, she was dealing with success, recognition, a growing business, and two small children. She had started to develop physical symptoms: skin rashes, intestinal disorders, neuralgia, and insomnia. That day, she walked into her doctor's office chanting over and over again, "I can't do it any more." Lundström has since learned to manage her stress and help her employees do the same..

Calgary school bus driver Marvin Franks had a much more negative response to stress.[2] Franks was arrested in March 2002 when a scared student on his bus phoned 911 from her cellphone after smelling alcohol on his breath and finding his driving erratic. When police stopped Franks, his blood alcohol level was three times the legal limit. Franks' excuse? "If you had these kids on your bus, you'd drink too." He admitted that he was unable to control the children, but said that he smelled of alcohol only because he had a hangover, and had drunk only two beers before starting his route.

Are We Overstressed?

Stress appears to be a major factor in the lives of many Canadians. A recent survey conducted by Statistics Canada found that Canadians experience a great deal of stress, with those from Quebec topping the list.[3] The survey also found that women were more stressed than men. The inset *Stress Across the Country, 2001–2002* reports the findings.

For employees, stress is also a fact of life—and it continues to increase over time. Recent research conducted at the University of Montreal found that of the 12 job categories examined, including unskilled white- and blue-collar employees and semi-skilled blue-collar employees, only upper-level managers reported no increase in stress levels from 1987 to 1998.[4] A 2001 survey done by Ipsos-Reid of 1500 Canadians with employer-sponsored health care plans found that 62 percent reported experiencing "a great deal of stress on the job." Workplace stress was bad enough to cause 34 percent of those surveyed to say that it had made them physically ill.[5] In a 2000 Statistics Canada survey, one-third of employees blamed long hours or overwork for their stress, while 15 percent blamed "poor inter-personal relations," and 13 percent blamed risk of accident or injury.[6] Front-line employees are not the only members of the organization who experience stress, however. In a study conducted by researchers Darren Larose and Bernadette Schell at Ontario's Laurentian University, 88 percent of the executives surveyed indicated elevated levels of stress and/or unhealthy personality traits.[7] They also had higher levels of predisposition to serious illnesses such as cancer and heart disease.

Perhaps one of the biggest problems for employees is that they are increasingly asked to donate labour to their employers, according to Professor Linda Duxbury of Carleton University's Sprott School of Business and Professor Chris Higgins of the Richard Ivey School of Business at the University of Western Ontario. Their survey of 31 571 Canadians found that in the previous month half of them had worked an extra 2.5 days of unpaid overtime, and more than half had donated 3.5 days of working at home to catch up.[8] Canadians are frequently reporting that they want more balance in their work and family lives.[9]

The Most Stressful Jobs

How do jobs rate in terms of stress? The inset *The Most Stressful Jobs* shows how selected occupations ranked in an evaluation of 250 jobs. Among the criteria used in the rankings were overtime, quotas, deadlines, competitiveness, physical demands, environmental conditions, hazards encountered, initiative required, stamina required, win-lose situations, and working in the public eye.

Stress is not something that can be ignored in the workplace. A 2005 poll by Ipsos-Reid found that 66 percent of the CEOs surveyed said that "stress, burnout or other physical and mental health issues" have a negative effect on productivity.[10] A 2001 study conducted in 15 developed countries found that individuals who report that they are stressed in their jobs are 25 percent more likely to quit and 25 percent more likely to miss days of work.[11] Canadian, French, and Swedish employees reported the highest stress levels. In Canada, 41 percent of employees noted that they "often" or "always" experience stress at work, while only 31 percent of employees in Denmark and Switzerland reported stress levels this high. "In the wake of years of fiscal downsizing, workers across all sectors are working harder and longer than ever while trying to balance family responsibilities," said Scott Morris, former head of the Vancouver-based consulting firm Priority Management Systems.[12] Daniel Ondrack, a professor at the University of Toronto's Joseph L. Rotman School of Management, notes that "one of the major reasons for absenteeism is the logistical problems workers face in just getting to work, including transporting children to school and finding daycare. Single parents, especially female, have to juggle all the daycare and family responsibilities, and that makes it extremely difficult for people to keep up with work demands."[13]

Stress Across the Country, 2001–2002

Region	% with no life stresses	% with quite a lot of stress
Alberta	9.8	26.0
Atlantic Canada	14.6	18.7
British Columbia	12.0	23.6
Ontario	10.7	25.7
The Prairies	8.7	24.5
Quebec	18.0	30.0

Source: Compiled using data from Statistics Canada, "Life Stress, by Sex, Household Population Aged 18 and Over, Canada, Provinces, Territories, Health Regions and Peer Groups, 2000/01," www.statcan.ca/english/freepub/82-221-XIE/00503/tables/html/2336.htm (accessed August 4, 2005).

OB ON THE EDGE

The Most Stressful Jobs

How do jobs rate in terms of stress? The following shows how selected occupations ranked in an evaluation of 250 jobs. Criteria used in the rankings included overtime, quotas, deadlines, competitiveness, physical demands, environmental conditions, hazards encountered, initiative required, stamina required, win-lose situations, and working in the public eye.

Rank	Stress Score	Rank	Stress Score
1. US president	176.6	47. Auto salesperson	56.3
2. Firefighter	110.9	50. College professor	54.2
3. Senior executive	108.6	60. School principal	51.7
6. Surgeon	99.5	103. Market research analyst	42.1
10. Air traffic controller	83.1	104. Personnel recruiter	41.8
12. Public relations executive	78.5	113. Hospital administrator	39.6
16. Advertising account executive	74.6	119. Economist	38.7
17. Real estate agent	73.1	122. Mechanical engineer	38.3
20. Stockbroker	71.7	124. Chiropractor	37.9
22. Pilot	68.7	132. Technical writer	36.5
25. Architect	66.9	149. Retail salesperson	34.9
31. Lawyer	64.3	173. Accountant	31.1
33. General physician	64.0	193. Purchasing agent	28.9
35. Insurance agent	63.3	229. Broadcast technician	24.2
42. Advertising salesperson	59.9	245. Actuary	20.2

Source: Reprinted by permission of the *Wall Street Journal*, © 1996 Dow Jones & Company. All rights reserved worldwide.

What Is Stress?

Stress is usually defined in terms of a situation that creates excessive psychological or physiological demands on a person. Thus the situation, often referred to as the stressor, and the response *together* create the stress that an individual experiences. This distinction is important because what is stressful to one person may be enjoyable or at least viewed as neutral by another. Although almost anyone might feel stress if followed by a stranger in a dark alley, not everyone feels stressed when given the opportunity for public speaking.

Dr. Hans Selye, a Montreal-based researcher, pioneered the study of stress and its effects. His model, the general adaptation syndrome (GAS), suggests that stress occurs in three stages: alarm, resistance, and exhaustion.[14] The alarm stage occurs when the body tries to meet the initial challenge of the stressor. The brain reacts by sending a message to the rest of the body's systems, causing such symptoms as increased respiration, raised blood pressure, dilated pupils, and tensed muscles.

The resistance stage occurs if the stressor continues. At this stage, a person feels such symptoms as fatigue, anxiety, and tension due to the body's attempt to fight the stressor. The exhaustion stage occurs from prolonged and continual exposure to the same stressor. The important thing to remember about how GAS works is that it puts heavy demands on the body. The more that GAS is activated and the longer that it goes on, the more wear and tear your body experiences. Individuals who frequently go through alarm, resistance, and exhaustion cycles are more likely to be susceptible to fatigue, disease, aging, and other negative physical and psychological consequences.

Stress is not necessarily bad in and of itself. It is typically discussed in a negative context, but it also has a positive value. Consider, for example, athletes or stage performers who use stress positively to rise to the occasion and perform at or near their maximum potential. On the other hand, students who put off studying for exams until the last moment and then develop the flu are not able to use their stress to perform at a maximum level.

Causes of Stress

A variety of sources of stress have been identified, including "work overload; role conflict; ineffective, hostile and incompetent bosses; lack of personal fit with a job; lack of recognition; lack of a clear job description or chain of command; fear, uncertainty, and doubt about career progress; and prejudice based on age, gender, ethnicity or religion."[15] In their research on stress, Professors Duxbury and Higgins found that more than 50 percent of employees feel they will not advance unless they put in long hours, and that turning down extra work is unacceptable.[16] They also found that although only 10 percent of employees worked 50 or more hours a week in 1991, 25 percent were working those hours in 2001.[17]

A variety of changes in the workplace have resulted in additional causes of stress. We identify some of these key changes below:[18]

- *Competition and change.* With globalization has come increasing pressure to compete and innovate, which has led to an increase in re-engineering and restructuring. Alicja Muszynski, a sociology professor at the University of Waterloo, notes that "as corporations, including universities, have been asked to tighten their belts, there are fewer jobs and people that are left have to take on more responsibility."[19] Meanwhile, she adds, "people are afraid to take on less in the workplace, or to complain, because they're afraid they're going to get downsized."

- *Technological change.* Employees are often expected to learn new technologies without being given adequate training. Or they are not consulted when new technology is introduced. In addition, employees at all levels are flooded with information because of technological changes. As well, employees are frequently asked to be "on" for their jobs more hours each day: Pagers, voice mail, faxes, email, the Internet, and intranets make it possible to stay in touch with the workplace 24 hours a day. Research by Professor Christina Cavanagh of the Richard Ivey School of Business at the University of Western Ontario shows that email is an increasing cause of stress. Individuals receive an average of 80 or 90 emails daily, and devote an hour more each day to handling it than they did two years ago. The frustration is not just with quantity or time. When Cavanagh asked 10 middle managers to keep track of their emails, she discovered that nearly half of the messages were "junk or notes with little relevance."[20]

- *Increasingly diverse workforce.* "If diversity is not managed effectively it may lead to interpersonal stress, competition among different groups for attention and resources, and decreased interaction because of the perceived need for political correctness in speech, interaction, and recognition." In diverse groups, individuals experience differences in beliefs and values, differences in role expectations, and differences in perceptions about fairness in procedures.

- *Downsizing.* With downsizing seemingly a routine procedure in many companies, even the threat of layoffs can be stressful. Moreover, after downsizing, firms often increase the workload of remaining employees, which leads to more stress.

- *Employee empowerment and teamwork.* Both empowerment and teamwork require greater decision-making responsibility and interaction skills from employees. Although this alone is stressful, it is particularly stressful for individuals who "have little or no interest in empowerment or teamwork structures and processes. Many people do not function well in a group setting, and they and their work may suffer if forced into a team environment."

- *Work/home conflict.* Trying to balance work life and family life is difficult at the best of times, but more employees are finding that their jobs are demanding longer hours, either formally or informally. This makes it difficult to manage the nonwork parts of life. Families with children where both parents work, or where parents are raising children alone, often have the added stress of managing childcare arrangements.

About one in eight workers was responsible for providing some form of care for aging parents in 1997, and one survey found that one in three was doing so in 2002.[21] Being a caregiver is an additional stress both at home and at work. Studies indicate that those who have difficulties finding effective child care or eldercare have lower work performance and increased absenteeism, decreased satisfaction, and lower physical and psychological well-being.[22] A fact that tends to be overlooked when stressors are reviewed individually is that stress is an additive phenomenon.[23] Stress builds up. Each new and persistent stressor adds to an individual's stress level. A single stressor may seem relatively unimportant in and of itself, but if it is added to an already high level of stress, it can be "the straw that breaks the camel's back." You may recall that the final straw for Linda Lundström was not being able to find a parking space.

Consequences of Stress

Stress manifests itself in a number of ways. For instance, an individual who is experiencing a high level of stress may develop high blood pressure, ulcers, irritability, difficulty in making routine decisions, loss of appetite, accident proneness, and the like. These symptoms can be placed under three general categories: physiological, psychological, and behavioural symptoms.[24]

- *Physiological symptoms.* Most of the research on stress suggests that it can create changes in metabolism, increase heart and breathing rates, increase blood pressure, cause headaches, and induce heart attacks. An interesting aspect of illness in today's workplace is the considerable change in how stress shows up. In the past, older workers were the ones claiming sick leave, workers' compensation, and short- and long-term disability—most often in cases of catastrophic illness such as heart attacks, cancer, and major back surgeries. These days, however, it is not unusual for long-term disability programs to be filled with employees in their 20s, 30s, and 40s. Employees are claiming illnesses that are either psychiatric (such as depression) or more difficult to diagnose (such as chronic fatigue syndrome or fibromyalgia, a musculoskeletal discomfort). The increase in disability claims may be the result of downsizing taking its toll on the psyches of those in the workforce.[25]

- *Psychological symptoms.* Job dissatisfaction is "the simplest and most obvious psychological effect" of stress.[26] However, stress also manifests itself in other psychological states—for instance, tension, anxiety, irritability, boredom, and procrastination.

The evidence indicates that when people are placed in jobs that make multiple and conflicting demands or in which there is a lack of clarity as to the person's duties, authority, and responsibilities, both stress and dissatisfaction increase.[27] Similarly, the less control that people have over the pace of their work, the greater the stress and dissatisfaction. More research is needed to clarify the relationship, but the evidence suggests that jobs providing a low level of variety, significance, autonomy, feedback, and identity create stress and reduce satisfaction and involvement in the job.[28]

- *Behavioural symptoms.* Behaviourally related stress symptoms include changes in productivity, absence, and turnover, as well as changes in eating habits, increased smoking or consumption of alcohol, rapid speech, fidgeting, and sleep dis-

orders. More recently stress has been linked to aggression and violence in the workplace.

Why Do Individuals Differ in Their Experience of Stress?

Some people thrive on stressful situations, while others are overwhelmed by them. What is it that differentiates people in terms of their ability to handle stress? What individual difference variables moderate the relationship between *potential* stressors and *experienced* stress? At least five variables—perception, job experience, social support, belief in locus of control, and hostility—have been found to be relevant moderators.

- *Perception.* Individuals react in response to their *perception* of reality rather than to reality itself. Perception, therefore, moderates the relationship between a potential stress condition and an employee's reaction to it. For example, one person might fear losing his job because the company is laying off staff, while another might perceive the situation as an opportunity to receive a large severance allowance and start a small business. Similarly, what one employee perceives as a challenging job may be viewed as threatening and demanding by others.[29] So the stress potential in environmental, organizational, and individual factors does not lie in objective conditions. Rather, it lies in an employee's interpretation of those factors.

- *Job experience.* Experience on the job tends to be negatively related to work stress. Two

explanations have been offered.[30] First, people who experience more stress on the job when they are first hired may be more likely to quit. Therefore, people who remain with the organization longer are those with more stress-resistant traits or those who are more resistant to the stress characteristics of their organization. Second, people eventually develop coping mechanisms to deal with stress. Because this takes time, senior members of the organization are more likely to be fully adapted and should experience less stress.

- *Social support.* There is increasing evidence that social support— that is, collegial relationships with co-workers or supervisors— can buffer the impact of stress.[31] The logic underlying this moderating variable is that social support helps ease the negative effects of even high-strain jobs.

For individuals whose work associates are unhelpful or even actively hostile, social support may be found outside the job. Involvement with family, friends, and community can provide the support—especially for those with a high social need—that is missing at work, and this can make job stressors more tolerable.

- *Belief in locus of control.* The personality trait locus of control determines the extent to which individuals believe they have control over the things that happen in their lives. Those with an internal locus of control believe they control their own destiny. Those with an external locus of control believe their lives are controlled by outside forces. Evidence indicates that internals perceive their jobs to be less stressful than do externals.[32]

When internals and externals confront a similar stressful situation, the internals are likely to believe that they can have a significant effect on the results. They therefore act to take control of events. Externals are more likely to experience stress because they frequently act helpless, often by being passive and defensive, while feeling helpless.

- *Hostility.* Some people's personality includes a high degree of hostility and anger. These people are chronically suspicious and mistrustful of others. Recent evidence indicates that such *hostility* significantly increases a person's stress and risk for heart disease.[33] More specifically, people who are quick to anger, maintain a persistently hostile outlook, and project a cynical mistrust of others are more likely to experience stress in situations.

How Do We Manage Stress?

Both the individual and the organization can take steps to help the individual manage stress. Below we discuss ways that individuals can manage stress, and then we examine programs that organizations use to help employees manage stress.

Individual Approaches

An employee can take personal responsibility for reducing his or her stress level. Individual strategies that have proven effective include time management techniques, physical exercise, relaxation training, and a close social support network.

- *Time management.* Many people manage their time poorly. The things we have to accomplish in any given day or week are not necessarily beyond completion if we manage our time properly.

The well-organized employee, like the well-organized student, can often accomplish twice as much as the person who is poorly organized. So understanding and using basic *time management* principles can help individuals cope better with tensions created by job demands.[34] A few of the more well-known time management principles are: (1) making daily lists of activities to be accomplished; (2) prioritizing activities by importance and urgency; (3) scheduling activities according to the priorities set; and (4) knowing your daily cycle and handling the most demanding parts of your job during the high part of your cycle, when you are most alert and productive.[35]

- *Physical activity.* Noncompetitive physical exercise, such as aerobics, walking, jogging, swimming, and riding a bicycle, has long been recommended by physicians as a way to deal with excessive stress levels. These forms of *physical exercise* increase heart capacity, lower at-rest heart rate, provide a mental diversion from work pressures, and offer a means to "let off steam."[36]

- *Relaxation techniques.* Individuals can teach themselves to reduce tension through *relaxation techniques* such as meditation, hypnosis, and biofeedback. The objective is to reach a state of deep relaxation, where you feel physically relaxed, somewhat detached from the immediate environment, and detached from body sensations.[37] Fifteen or 20 minutes a day of deep relaxation releases tension and provides a person with a pronounced sense of peacefulness. Importantly, significant changes

FactBox[38]

- One in three Canadians between the ages of 25 and 44 claims to be a workaholic.

- 38% of people in management report being workaholics.

- 85% of married women who are employed full-time and have at least one child at home, and 75% of similarly situated men, say that weekdays are too short to accomplish what needs to get done.

- The financial cost to companies because employees are trying to balance work and family obligations is estimated to be at least $2.7 billion a year.

- 1/3 of Canadians don't take all of their vacation days, saving their employers $8 billion a year.

- When Canadians do go on holiday, 36% of them take work, and check their office voice mail and email.

in heart rate, blood pressure, and other physiological factors result from achieving the deep relaxation condition.

- *Building social supports.* Having friends, family, or colleagues to talk to provides an outlet when stress levels become excessive. Expanding your *social support network*, therefore, can be a means for tension reduction. It provides you with someone to listen to your problems and to offer a more objective perspective on the situation. Research also demonstrates that social support moderates the stress-burnout relationship.[39] That is, high support reduces the likelihood that heavy work stress will result in job burnout.

OB ON THE EDGE

The inset *Tips for Reducing Stress* offers additional ideas for reducing stress.

Organizational Approaches

Employees who work at Toronto-based BCS Communications, a publishing, advertising, and public relations agency, receive biweekly shiatsu massages, paid for by the company. The company spends about $700 a month for the massages, equivalent to the amount it used to spend providing coffee to the employees. "It's in my company's best interest to have my employees be healthy," says Caroline Tapp-McDougall, the BCS group publisher.[40]

Vancouver-based QLT, which develops pharmaceuticals that are activated when exposed to light, has an in-house gym and offers aerobics and stretch classes and Friday-morning shiatsu massage treatments to its employees. QLT's cafeteria has healthy food choices, and Weight Watchers products. Robyn Crisanti, a QLT spokesperson, explains the company's investment in wellness: "Corporate wellness is good for employees and there is a lot of research that shows healthy employees take fewer sick days and are more productive."[41] The programs also make it easier for QLT to attract talented employees.

Most firms that have introduced wellness programs have found significant benefits. Health Canada reports that businesses get back $3.39 for each corporate dollar they invest in wellness initiatives. For individuals with three to five risk factors (such as high cholesterol, being overweight, or smoking) the return was $2.04 for each dollar spent.[42] The savings come about because there is less turnover, greater productivity, and reduced medical claims.[43] About 64 percent of Canadian companies surveyed by Health Canada offered some sort of wellness initiative, including stop-smoking programs, stress courses, and back-pain management programs; 17.5 percent of companies offered on-site wellness programs.[44]

So what can organizations do to reduce employee stress? In general, strategies to reduce stress include improved processes for choosing employees, placement of employees in appropriate jobs, realistic goal setting, designing jobs with employee needs and skills in mind, increased employee involvement, improved organizational communication, and, as mentioned, establishment of corporate wellness programs.

Certain jobs are more stressful than others, but individuals also differ in their response to stress situations. We know, for example, that individuals with little experience or an external locus of control tend to be more prone to stress. Selection and placement decisions should take these facts into consideration. Although management should not restrict hiring to only experienced individuals with an internal locus of control, such individuals may adapt better to high-stress jobs and perform those jobs more effectively.

Research shows that individuals perform better when they have specific and challenging goals and receive feedback on how well they are progressing toward them.[45] The use of goals can reduce stress as well as provide motivation. Specific goals that are perceived as attainable clarify performance expectations. Additionally, goal feedback reduces uncertainties as to actual job performance. The result is less employee frustration, role ambiguity, and stress.

Creating jobs that give employees more responsibility, more meaningful work, more autonomy, and increased feedback can reduce stress because these factors give the employee greater control over work activities and lessen dependence on others. Of course, not all employees want jobs with increased responsibility. The right job for employees with a low need for growth might be less responsibility and increased specialization. If individuals prefer structure and routine, more structured jobs should also reduce uncertainties and stress levels.

One idea that has received considerable recent attention is allowing employees to take short naps during the workday.[46] Nap time, apparently, isn't just for preschool kids any more! An increasing number of companies are finding that allowing employees to catch 10 to 30 minutes of sleep in the afternoon

Tips for Reducing Stress

- At least two or three times a week, spend time with supportive friends or family.

- Ask for support when you are under pressure. This is a sign of health, not weakness.

- If you have spiritual or religious beliefs, increase or maintain your involvement.

- Use a variety of methods to reduce stress. Consider exercise, nutrition, hobbies, positive thinking, and relaxation techniques such as meditation or yoga.

Source: J. Lee, "How to Fight That Debilitating Stress in Your Workplace," *The Vancouver Sun*, April 5, 1999, p. C3. Reprinted with permission.

Reducing Stress in the Workplace

- Avoid electronic monitoring of staff. Personal supervision generates considerably less stress.

- Allow workers time to recharge after periods of intense or demanding work.

- Deliver important information that significantly affects employees face to face.

- Encourage positive social interactions between staff to promote problem-solving around work issues and increase emotional support.

- Keep in mind that staff need to balance privacy and social interaction at work. Extremes can generate stress.

Source: J. Lee, "How to Fight That Debilitating Stress in Your Workplace," *Vancouver Sun*, April 5, 1999, p. C3. Reprinted with permission of the *Vancouver Sun*.

increases productivity and makes them less prone to errors.

Increasing formal organizational communication with employees reduces uncertainty by lessening role ambiguity and role conflict. Given the importance that perceptions play in moderating the stress-response relationship, management can also use effective communications as a means to shape employee perceptions. Remember that what employees categorize as demands, threats, or opportunities are merely interpretations, and those interpretations can be affected by the symbols and actions communicated by management.

Our final suggestion is to offer organizationally supported wellness programs, such as those provided by QLT and BCS Communications. These programs focus on the employee's total physical and mental condition.[47] For example, they typically include workshops to help people quit smoking, control alcohol use, lose weight, eat better, and develop a regular exercise program. The assumption underlying most wellness programs is that employees need to take personal responsibility for their physical and mental health. The organi-zation is merely a vehicle to make this happen. The inset *Reducing Stress in the Workplace* offers additional ideas.

Research Exercises

1. Look for data on stress levels in other countries. How do these data compare with the Canadian data presented above? Are the sources of stress the same in different countries? What might you conclude about how stress affects people in different cultures?

2. Find out what three Canadian organizations in three different industries have done to help employees manage stress. Are there common themes in these programs? Did you find any unusual programs? To what extent are these programs tailored to the needs of the employees in those industries?

Your Perspective

1. Think of all of the technological changes that have happened in the workplace in recent years, including email, BlackBerrys, and intranets. What are the positive benefits of this change? What are the downsides? As an employee facing the demand to "stay connected" to your workplace, how would you try to maintain a balance in your life?

2. How much responsibility should individuals take for managing their own stress? To what extent should organizations become involved in the personal lives of their employees when trying to help them manage stress? What are the pros and cons for whether employees or organizations take responsibility for managing stress?

Want to Know More?

If you are wondering how stressed you are, go to **www.heartandstroke.ca** and click on "Your Heart & Stroke Risk Assessment." The site also offers tips on how to relax and manage stress.

FACEOFF

When organizations provide on-site daycare facilities, they are filling a needed role in parents' lives, and making it easier for parents to attend to their job demands rather than worry about child-care arrangements.

When employees expect organizations to provide child care, they are shifting their responsibilities to their employers, rather than keeping their family needs and concerns private. Moreover, it is unfair to give child-care benefits when not all employees have children.

CHAPTER 4
Theories of
Motivation

The 2005 BC Lions football team started the
season with one of the longest winning
streaks in CFL history. How does motivation
affect how the team performs?

1 What is motivation?

2 How do needs motivate people?

3 Are there other ways to motivate people?

4 Do equity and fairness matter?

5 What role does reinforcement play in motivation?

6 What are the ethics behind motivation theories?

By most accounts, Vancouver-based BC Lions head coach Wally Buono is not a particularly warm person.[1] Buono is a hard taskmaster with his BC Lions players and coaches, and is not afraid to make tough decisions. He replaced many players and assistant coaches after the Lions lost in the Grey Cup Final in 2004.

Buono wants to coach winners, not losers. As a coach, Buono has one of the winningest records in the Canadian Football League (CFL). His teams have been to seven Grey Cups, and the BC Lions had the third-longest winning streak in CFL history by the middle of the season in 2005. But then they started losing games.

Buono seems to motivate by being tough. He's not afraid to criticize his players publicly, and will give them a long list of their faults during contract negotiations. He claims that he gives only two performance reviews to players: "Once when I warn you and once when I cut you."

Buono's players may not like him personally, but at the beginning of the season they performed well.

Players spent hours in training each day because "guys wanna get better," explained slotback Geroy Simon. Then the team fell apart.

In this chapter, we examine the subjects of motivation and rewards. We look at what motivation is, and how needs can be used to motivate individuals. We also present theories of motivation, and then consider the roles that fairness, reinforcement, and ethics play in motivation.

WHAT IS MOTIVATION?

We define **motivation** as the intensity, direction, and persistence of effort a person shows in reaching a goal.[2]

The three key elements in our definition are intensity, direction, and persistence. *Intensity* is concerned with how hard a person tries. This is the element most of us focus on when we talk about motivation. However, high intensity is unlikely to lead to favourable job-performance outcomes unless the effort is channelled in a *direction* that is beneficial. Finally, the effort requires *persistence*. This is a measure of how long a person can maintain his or her effort. Motivated individuals stay with a task long enough to achieve their goal.

Many people incorrectly view motivation as a personal trait—something some people have and others don't. Along these lines, Douglas McGregor proposed two distinct views of human beings. **Theory X**, which is basically negative, suggests that employees dislike work, will attempt to avoid it, and must be coerced, controlled, or threatened with punishment to achieve goals. **Theory Y**, which is basically positive, suggests that employees like work, are creative, seek responsibility, and will exercise self-direction and self-control if they are committed to the objectives.[3]

Our knowledge of motivation tells us that neither theory alone fully accounts for employee behaviour. What we know is that motivation is the result of the interaction of the individual and the situation. Certainly, individuals differ in their basic motivational drive. But the same employee who is quickly bored when pulling the lever on a drill press

1 What is motivation?

BC Lions
www.bclions.com

motivation The intensity, direction, and persistence of effort a person shows in reaching a goal.

Theory X The assumption that employees dislike work, will attempt to avoid it, and must be coerced, controlled, or threatened with punishment to achieve goals.

Theory Y The assumption that employees like work, are creative, seek responsibility, and will exercise self-direction and self-control if they are committed to the objectives.

may enthusiastically pull a slot machine lever in Casino Windsor for hours on end. You may read a thriller at one sitting, yet find it difficult to concentrate on a textbook for more than 20 minutes. It's not necessarily you—it's the situation. So as we analyze the concept of motivation, keep in mind that the level of motivation varies both *among* individuals and *within* individuals at different times.

You should also realize that what motivates individuals will also vary among individuals and situations. Motivation theorists talk about **intrinsic motivators** and **extrinsic motivators**. Extrinsic motivators come from outside the person and include such things as pay, bonuses, and other tangible rewards. Intrinsic motivators come from a person's internal desire to do something, due to such things as interest, challenge, and personal satisfaction. Individuals are intrinsically motivated when they genuinely care about their work, look for better ways to do it, and are energized and fulfilled by doing it well.[4] The rewards the individual gets from intrinsic motivation come from the work itself rather than from external factors such as increases in pay or compliments from the boss.

Are individuals primarily intrinsically or extrinsically motivated? Theory X suggests that people are almost exclusively driven by extrinsic motivators. However, Theory Y suggests that people are more intrinsically motivated. This view is consistent with that of Alfie Kohn, author of *Punished by Rewards*, who suggests that it's only necessary to provide the right environment, and people will be motivated.[5] We discuss his ideas further in Chapter 5.

Intrinsic and extrinsic motivation may reflect the situation, however, rather than individual personalities. For example, suppose your mother has asked you or your brother to take her to a meeting an hour away. You may be willing to drive her, without any thought of compensation, because it will make you feel good to do something for her. That is intrinsic motivation. But if you have a love-hate relationship with your brother, you may insist that he buy you lunch for helping out. Lunch would then be an extrinsic motivator—something that came from outside yourself and motivated you to do the task. Later in the chapter, we review the evidence regarding the significance of extrinsic vs. intrinsic motivators, and also examine how to increase intrinsic motivation.

intrinsic motivators A person's internal desire to do something, due to such things as interest, challenge, and personal satisfaction.

extrinsic motivators Motivation that comes from outsice the person and includes such things as pay, bonuses, and other tangible rewards.

NEEDS THEORIES OF MOTIVATION

2 How do needs motivate people?

The main theories of motivation fall into one of two categories: needs theories and process theories. Needs theories describe the types of needs that must be met in order to motivate individuals. Process theories (described later in the chapter) help us understand the actual ways in which we and others can be motivated. There are a variety of needs theories, including Maslow's hierarchy of needs, Herzberg's motivation-hygiene theory (sometimes called the two-factor theory), Alderfer's ERG theory, and McClelland's theory of needs. We briefly review these to illustrate the basic properties of needs theories.

Maslow's Hierarchy of Needs Theory

It's probably safe to say that the most well-known theory of motivation is Abraham Maslow's hierarchy of needs.[6] Maslow hypothesized that within every human being there exists a hierarchy of five needs:

- *Physiological.* Includes hunger, thirst, shelter, sex, and other bodily needs.

- *Safety.* Includes security and protection from physical and emotional harm.

- *Social.* Includes affection, belongingness, acceptance, and friendship.

- *Esteem.* Includes internal esteem factors such as self-respect, autonomy, and achievement; and external esteem factors such as status, recognition, and attention.

- *Self-actualization.* Includes growth, achieving one's potential, and self-fulfillment. This is the drive to become what one is capable of becoming.

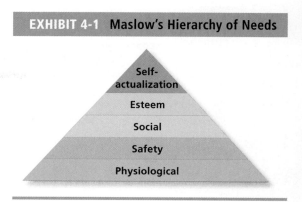

EXHIBIT 4-1   Maslow's Hierarchy of Needs

As each of these needs becomes substantially satisfied, the next need becomes dominant. In terms of Exhibit 4-1, the individual moves up the steps of the hierarchy. From the perspective of motivation, the theory would say that although no need is ever fully met, a substantially satisfied need no longer motivates. So if you want to motivate someone, according to Maslow, you need to understand what level of the hierarchy that person is currently on and focus on satisfying those needs at or above that level.

Maslow separated the five needs into higher and lower orders. Physiological and safety needs were described as lower-order, and social, esteem, and self-actualization as higher-order needs. The differentiation between the two orders was made on the premise that higher-order needs are satisfied internally (within the person), whereas lower-order needs are mainly satisfied externally (by such things as pay, union contracts, and tenure). In fact, the natural conclusion to be drawn from Maslow's classification is that in times of economic plenty, almost all permanently employed workers have their lower-order needs substantially met.

Maslow's needs theory continues to receive wide recognition, particularly among practising managers. This can be attributed to the theory's intuitive logic and ease of understanding. Unfortunately, however, research does not generally validate the theory. Maslow himself provided no empirical evidence, and several studies that sought to validate the theory found little support for the prediction that need structures are organized along the dimensions proposed by Maslow, that unsatisfied needs motivate, or that a satisfied need activates movement to a new need level.[7]

Motivation-Hygiene Theory

The motivation-hygiene theory was proposed by psychologist Frederick Herzberg.[8] In the belief that an individual's relationship to work is a basic one and that an individual's attitude toward this work can very well determine the individual's success or failure, Herzberg investigated the question, "What do people want from their jobs?" He asked people to describe, in detail, situations when they felt exceptionally good and bad about their jobs. These responses were tabulated and categorized. Exhibit 4-2 illustrates factors affecting job attitudes, as reported in 12 investigations conducted by Herzberg.

From the categorized responses, Herzberg concluded that the replies people gave when they felt good about their jobs were significantly different from the replies given when they felt bad. As seen in Exhibit 4-2, certain characteristics tend to be consistently related to job satisfaction (factors on the right side of the figure), and others to job dissatisfaction (the left side of the figure). Intrinsic factors, such as achievement, recognition, the work itself, responsibility, advancement, and growth, seem to be related to job satisfaction. When those questioned felt good about their work, they tended to attribute these characteristics to themselves. On the other hand, when they were dissatisfied, they tended to cite extrinsic factors, such as company policy and administration, supervision, interpersonal relations, and work conditions.

According to Herzberg, the data suggest that the opposite of satisfaction is not dissatisfaction, as was traditionally believed. Removing dissatisfying characteristics from a job does not necessarily make the job satisfying. As illustrated in Exhibit 4-3, Herzberg proposes that his findings indicate the existence of a dual continuum: the opposite of "Satisfaction" is "No Satisfaction," and the opposite of "Dissatisfaction" is "No Dissatisfaction."

Herzberg explained that the factors leading to job satisfaction (motivators) are separate and distinct from those that lead to job dissatisfaction (hygiene factors). Therefore,

EXHIBIT 4-2 Comparison of Satisfiers and Dissatisfiers

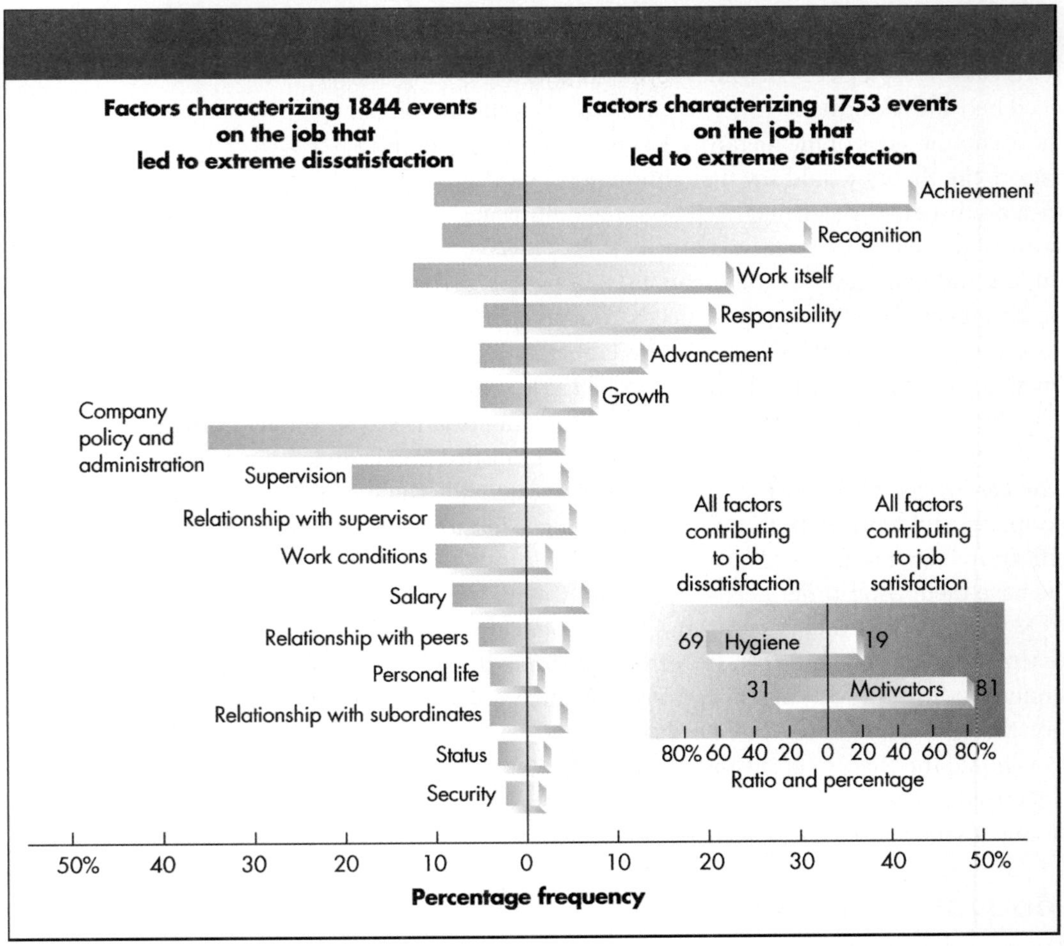

Factors characterizing 1844 events
on the job that
led to extreme dissatisfaction

Factors characterizing 1753 events
on the job that
led to extreme satisfaction

Achievement
Recognition
Work itself
Responsibility
Advancement
Growth

Company
policy and
administration
Supervision
Relationship with supervisor
Work conditions
Salary
Relationship with peers
Personal life
Relationship with subordinates
Status
Security

All factors
contributing
to job
dissatisfaction

All factors
contributing
to job
satisfaction

69 Hygiene   19
31 Motivators   81

80% 60 40 20 0 20 40 60 80%
Ratio and percentage

50%   40   30   20   10   0   10   20   30   40   50%

Percentage frequency

Source: Reprinted by permission of *Harvard Business Review.* An exhibit from Frederick Herzberg, "One More Time: How Do You Motivate Employees?" *Harvard Business Review* 81, no. 1 (January 2003), p. 90. Copyright © 1987 by the President and Fellows of Harvard College; all rights reserved.

managers who seek to eliminate factors that create job dissatisfaction can create more pleasant workplaces, but not necessarily more motivated ones. That is, they will be placating employees rather than motivating them. As a result, such characteristics as company policy and administration, supervision, interpersonal relations, work conditions, and salary have been characterized by Herzberg as *hygiene factors*. When these factors are adequate, people will not be dissatisfied; however, neither will they be satisfied. If we want to motivate people in their jobs, Herzberg suggests emphasizing achievement, recognition, the work itself, responsibility, and growth. These are the *motivation factors* that people find intrinsically rewarding or motivating. In this chapter's *Working With Others Exercise* on page 155, you will have an opportunity to discover what motivates both you and others with respect to one's job.

The motivation-hygiene theory is not without its critics, who suggest the following:[9]

EXHIBIT 4-3 Contrasting Views of Satisfaction and Dissatisfaction

Traditional view

Dissatisfaction   Satisfaction

Herzberg's view

Hygiene Factors

Dissatisfaction   No Dissatisfaction

Motivators

No Satisfaction   Satisfaction

- *The procedure that Herzberg used is limited by its methodology.* When things are going well, people tend to take credit themselves. Contrarily, they blame failure on the external environment.

- *The reliability of Herzberg's methodology is questionable.* Since raters had to make interpretations, it is possible that they contaminated the findings by interpreting one response in one manner while treating another similar response differently.

- *Herzberg did not really produce a theory of motivation.* Instead, the theory, to the degree that it is valid, provides an explanation of job satisfaction.

- *No overall measure of satisfaction was used.* In other words, individuals may dislike parts of their jobs, yet still think the jobs are acceptable.

- *The theory is inconsistent with previous research.* The motivation-hygiene theory ignores situational variables.

Herzberg assumed that there is a relationship between satisfaction and productivity. But the research methodology he used looked only at satisfaction, not at productivity. To make such research relevant, one must assume a high relationship between satisfaction and productivity.[10]

Regardless of these criticisms, Herzberg's theory has been widely read and few managers are unfamiliar with his recommendations. The popularity of vertically expanding jobs to allow employees greater responsibility in planning and controlling their work can probably be largely attributed to Herzberg's findings and recommendations.

ERG Theory

Clayton Alderfer has reworked Maslow's hierarchy of needs to align it more closely with the empirical research. His revised need hierarchy is called ERG theory.[11]

Alderfer argues that there are three groups of core needs—existence, relatedness, and growth—hence, the name: ERG theory. The *existence* group is concerned with our basic material existence requirements. They include the items that Maslow considered to be physiological and safety needs. The *relatedness* group is concerned with our desire for maintaining important interpersonal relationships. These social and status desires require interaction with others if they are to be satisfied, and they align with Maslow's social need and the external component of Maslow's esteem need. Finally, the *growth* group is concerned with our intrinsic desire for personal development. These include the intrinsic component of Maslow's esteem need and the characteristics included under self-actualization.

Aside from substituting three needs for five, how does Alderfer's ERG theory differ from Maslow's? In contrast to the hierarchy of needs theory, the ERG theory demonstrates that (1) more than one need may be working at the same time, and (2) if the gratification of a higher-level need is blocked, the desire to satisfy a lower-level need increases. ERG theory is more consistent with our knowledge of individual differences among people. Variables such as education, family background, and cultural environment can alter the importance or driving force that a group of needs holds for a particular person.

According to ERG theory, a core group of needs is relatedness needs. At Wesbury United Methodist Retirement Community, co-workers maintain interpersonal relationships by participating in regular jam sessions using drums and a keyboard. Popular among employees, these jam sessions have motivated employees in team building and have reduced employee turnover by 18 percent.

Several studies have supported ERG theory,[12] but there is also evidence that it doesn't work in some organizations.[13] Overall, however, ERG theory represents a more valid version of the need hierarchy.

McClelland's Theory of Needs

McClelland's theory of needs

McClelland's theory of needs
Achievement, power, and affiliation are three important needs that help explain motivation.

McClelland's theory of needs was developed by David McClelland and his associates to help explain motivation.[14] The theory focuses on three needs: achievement, power, and affiliation. They are defined as follows:

- *Need for achievement.* The drive to excel, to achieve in relation to a set of standards, to strive to succeed.

- *Need for power.* The need to make others behave in a way that they would not have behaved otherwise.

- *Need for affiliation.* The desire for friendly and close interpersonal relationships.

need for achievement The drive to excel, to achieve in relation to a set of standards, to strive to succeed.

Some people have a compelling drive to succeed. They are striving for personal achievement rather than the rewards of success per se. They have a desire to do something better or more efficiently than it has been done before. This drive is the achievement need (*nAch*). From research into the achievement need, McClelland found that high achievers differentiate themselves from others by their desire to do things better.[15] They seek situations in which they can attain personal responsibility for finding solutions to problems, in which they can receive rapid feedback on their performance so they can determine easily whether they are improving or not, and in which they can set moderately challenging goals. High achievers are not gamblers; they dislike succeeding by chance. They prefer the challenge of working at a problem and accepting the personal responsibility for success or failure rather than leaving the outcome to chance or the actions of others. Importantly, they avoid what they perceive to be very easy or very difficult tasks. They prefer tasks of intermediate difficulty.

need for power The need to make others behave in a way that they would not have behaved otherwise.

The need for power (*nPow*) is the desire to have impact, to be influential, and to control others. Individuals high in nPow enjoy being "in charge," strive for influence over others, prefer to be placed into competitive and status-oriented situations, and tend to be more concerned with prestige and gaining influence over others than with effective performance.

need for affiliation The desire for friendly and close interpersonal relationships.

The third need isolated by McClelland is affiliation (*nAff*). This need has received the least attention from researchers. Individuals with a high affiliation motive strive for friendship, prefer cooperative situations rather than competitive ones, and desire relationships that involve a high degree of mutual understanding.

Relying on an extensive amount of research, some reasonably well-supported predictions can be made based on the relationship of these needs to job performance. First, individuals with a high need to achieve prefer and will be motivated by job situations with personal responsibility, feedback, and an intermediate degree of risk. Second, people with a high achievement need are interested in how well they do personally and not in influencing others to do well. Thus, they may not make good managers.[16] Third, the best managers are high in their need for power and low in their need for affiliation.[17]

Summarizing Needs Theories

All needs theories of motivation, including Maslow's hierarchy of needs, Herzberg's motivation-hygiene theory (or the two-factor theory), Alderfer's ERG (existence, relatedness, growth) theory, and McClelland's theory of needs (need for achievement, need for power, need for affiliation), propose a similar idea: Individuals have needs that,

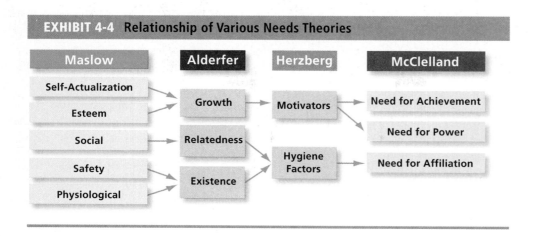

EXHIBIT 4-4 Relationship of Various Needs Theories

when unsatisfied, will result in motivation. For instance, if you have a need to be praised, you may work harder at your task in order to receive recognition from your manager or other co-workers. Similarly, if you need money and you are asked to do something, within reason, that offers money as a reward, you will be motivated to complete the task in order to earn the money.

Where needs theories differ is in the types of needs they consider, and whether they propose a hierarchy of needs (where some needs have to be satisfied before others) or simply a list of needs. Exhibit 4-4 illustrates the relationship of the four needs theories we discussed to each other. While the theories use different names for the needs, and also have different numbers of needs, we can see that they are somewhat consistent in the types of needs addressed. Exhibit 4-5 on page 126 indicates whether the theory proposes a hierarchy of needs, and the contribution of and empirical support for each theory.

What can we conclude from the needs theories? We can safely say that individuals do have needs, and that they can be highly motivated to achieve those needs. The types of needs, and their importance, vary by individual, and probably vary over time for the same individual as well. When rewarding individuals, you should consider their specific needs. Obviously, in a workplace, it would be difficult to design a reward structure that could completely take into account the specific needs of every employee. The *Point/Counterpoint* discussion on page 146 considers whether professional employees have needs that are different from those of other employees. To better understand what might motivate you in the workplace, look at this chapter's *Learning About Yourself Exercise* on page 154. This chapter's *CBC Video Case* suggests that considering people's needs for balance might help motivate them.

Workplace Stress

PROCESS THEORIES OF MOTIVATION

What is the life of a CFL assistant coach like? It's definitely not glamorous.[18] Assistant coaches work long hours, they can be fired readily if the team's owner or the head coach thinks they are responsible for the poor play of the team, and they work long hours without pensions or benefits.

Dan Dorazio, an offensive line coach with the BC Lions, faced a choice after his team beat the Calgary Stampeders in August 2005: stay in Calgary overnight or drive home to Abbotsford, BC, and arrive just before midnight. Tired after a long day of coaching, he still wasn't able to rest. He was expected to have the Calgary game tape analyzed before sunrise so the coaches could plan the post-game practice with the players later in the afternoon. Dorazio chose to drive home, and, after a brief nap, go to his office at 4 a.m.

What would make an assistant coach show up for work, day after day, under these conditions?

While needs theories identify the different needs that could be used to motivate individuals, process theories focus on the broader picture of *how* someone can set about

3 Are there other ways to motivate people?

EXHIBIT 4-5	Summarizing the Various Needs Theories			
Theory	**Maslow**	**Herzberg**	**Alderfer**	**McClelland**
Is there a hierarchy of needs?	The theory argues that lower-order needs must be satisfied before one progresses to higher-order needs.	Hygiene factors must be met if a person is not to be dissatisfied. They will not lead to satisfaction, however. Motivators lead to satisfaction.	More than one need can be important at the same time. If a higher-order need is not being met, the desire to satisfy a lower-level need increases.	People vary in the types of needs they have. Their motivation and how well they perform in a work situation are related to whether they have a need for achievement, power, or affiliation.
What is the theory's impact/ contribution?	The theory enjoys wide recognition among practising managers. Most managers are familiar with it.	The popularity of giving workers greater responsibility for planning and controlling their work can be attributed to his findings (see, for instance, the Job Characteristics Model in Chapter 5). It shows that more than one need may operate at the same time.	The theory is seen as a more valid version of the need hierarchy. Tells us that achievers will be motivated by jobs that offer personal responsibility, feedback, and moderate risks.	The theory tells us that high need achievers do not necessarily make good managers, since high achievers are more interested in how they do personally.
What empirical support/ criticisms exist?	Research does not generally validate the theory. In particular, there is little support for the hierarchical nature of needs. The theory is criticized for how data were collected and interpreted.	It is not really a *theory* of motivation: It assumes a link between satisfaction and productivity that was not measured or demonstrated.	It ignores situational variables.	It has mixed empirical support, but the theory is consistent with our knowledge of individual differences among people. Good empirical support exists on needs achievement in particular.

motivating another individual. Process theories include expectancy theory, goal-setting theory (and its application, management by objectives), equity theory, and fair process. By focusing greater attention on these process theories, we will help you understand how you might actually motivate either yourself or someone else.

Expectancy Theory

Currently, one of the most widely accepted explanations of motivation is Victor Vroom's **expectancy theory**.[19]

From a practical perspective, expectancy theory says that an employee will be motivated to exert a high level of effort when he or she believes the following:

- That the effort will lead to good performance

- That good performance will lead to organizational rewards, such as a bonus, a salary increase, or a promotion

- That the rewards will satisfy his or her personal goals

The theory, therefore, focuses on the three relationships (expectancy, instrumentality, and valence), illustrated in Exhibit 4-6 and described in the following pages. This

expectancy theory The theory that individuals act depending upon their evaluation of whether their effort will lead to good performance, whether good performance will be followed by a given outcome, and whether that outcome is attractive to them.

EXHIBIT 4-6   How Does Expectancy Theory Work?

My professor offers me $1 million if I memorize the textbook by tomorrow morning.

Expectancy	Instrumentality	Valence
Effort → Performance Link	Performance → Rewards Link	Rewards → Personal Goals Link
No matter how much effort I put in, probably not possible to memorize the text in 24 hours.	My professor does not look like someone who has $1 million.	There are a lot of wonderful things I could do with $1 million.
E = 0	I = 0	V = 1

Conclusion: Though I value the reward, I will not be motivated to do this task.

exhibit also provides an example of how you might apply the theory. You might also consider the question asked at the start of this section: Why would offensive line coach Dan Dorazio work such long hours for the BC Lions for moderate compensation? Dorazio obviously believes that if he puts effort into coaching, the effort will result in good performance by the team. He must believe that there will be some reward for his efforts, with some of the reward being his compensation, but some of it might be the intrinsic satisfaction of watching the team develop. These rewards then satisfy his personal goals. As he points out "It's really not work. I've never worked a day in my life in football." Dorazio enjoys his work, and that's what keeps him motivated.[20]

Effort-Performance Relationship

The effort-performance relationship is commonly called **expectancy**. It refers to the individual's perception of how probable it is that exerting a given amount of effort will lead to good performance. For example, employees are sometimes asked to do things for which they do not have the appropriate skills or training. When that is the case, they will be less motivated to try hard, because they already believe that they will not be able to accomplish the required task. Expectancy can be expressed as a probability, and ranges from 0 to 1.

> **expectancy** The belief that effort is related to performance.

In the opening vignette, we saw that the BC Lions players were willing to work hard for a demanding coach. These players likely felt that their efforts, such as spending extra time training, would lead to good performance. In general, an employee's expectancy is influenced by the following:

- Self-esteem
- Previous success
- Help from supervisors and subordinates
- Information
- Proper materials and equipment[21]

Performance-Rewards Relationship

The performance-rewards relationship is commonly called **instrumentality**. It refers to the individual's perception of whether performing at a particular level will lead to the attainment of a desired outcome. In particular, will the performance be acknowledged by those who have the power to allocate rewards? Instrumentality ranges from −1 to

> **instrumentality** The belief that performance is related to rewards.

> *Are managers manipulating employees when they link rewards to productivity? Is this ethical?*

+1. A negative instrumentality indicates that high performance reduces the chances of getting the desired outcome. An instrumentality of 0 indicates that there is no relationship between performance and receiving the desired outcome.

In a study by the Angus Reid Group, only 44 percent of employees said that the workplace recognizes employees who excel at their job.[22] Therefore, one possible source of low motivation is employees' belief that no matter how hard they work, the performance won't be recognized. BC Lions offensive line coach Dan Dorazio works long hours at his job because he does feel that his efforts are recognized by the head coach, and by the players on the team.

Rewards–Personal Goals Relationship

valence The value or importance an individual places on a reward.

> *Why do some managers do a better job of motivating people than others?*

The rewards–personal goals relationship is commonly called **valence**. It refers to the degree to which organizational rewards satisfy an individual's personal goals or needs, and the attractiveness of those potential rewards for the individual. Unfortunately, many managers are limited in the rewards they can distribute, which makes it difficult to personalize rewards. Moreover, some managers incorrectly assume that all employees want the same thing. They overlook the motivational effects of differentiating rewards. In either case, employee motivation may be lower because the specific need the employee has is not being met through the reward structure. Valence ranges from –1 (very undesirable reward) to +1 (very desirable reward).

Vancouver-based Radical Entertainment, creator of such digital entertainment as the *Hulk* and *The Simpsons: Road Rage,* makes sure the company meets the needs of its employees, because it doesn't want to lose them to the United States.[23] The company employs a "Radical fun guru" whose job is to make the workplace so much fun no one wants to leave. The company provides free food all day, including catered lunches a few times a week, and there is a log cabin on site, fitted out with big screens, DVDs, and gaming equipment, where employees can take time out to recharge during their long workdays. Radical Entertainment offers these benefits to meet the needs of its young employees, who find greater motivation from being part of a cool workplace than having a bigger pension plan.

Radical Entertainment
www.radical.ca

Expectancy Theory in the Workplace

Does expectancy theory work? Although it has its critics,[24] most of the research evidence supports the theory.[25] Research in cross-cultural settings has also indicated support for expectancy theory.[26]

Exhibit 4-7 gives some suggestions for what a manager can do to increase the motivation of employees, using insights from expectancy theory. To appreciate how expectancy

EXHIBIT 4-7   Steps to Increasing Motivation, Using Expectancy Theory

Improving Expectancy	Improving Instrumentality	Improving Valence
Improve the ability of the individual to perform.	Increase the individual's belief that performance will lead to reward.	Make sure that the reward is meaningful to the individual.
• Make sure employees have skills for the task. • Provide training. • Assign reasonable tasks and goals.	• Observe and recognize performance. • Deliver rewards as promised. • Indicate to employees how previous good performance led to greater rewards.	• Ask employees what rewards they value. • Give rewards that are valued.

theory might apply in the workplace, see this chapter's *Case Incident—Wage Reduction Proposal* on page 157 for an example of what happens when expected rewards are withdrawn.

Goal-Setting Theory

You have heard the phrase a number of times: "Just do your best. That's all anyone can ask for." But what does "do your best" mean? Do we ever know if we've achieved that vague goal? Might you have done better in your high school English class if your parents had said, "You should strive for 75 percent or higher on all your work in English" instead of "do your best"?

The research on goal setting by Edwin Locke and his colleague Professor Gary Latham at the University of Toronto shows that intentions to work toward a goal are a major source of work motivation.[27] A **goal** is "what an individual is trying to accomplish; it is the object or aim of an action."[28] Goals tell an employee what needs to be done and how much effort will need to be expended.[29] **Management by objectives (MBO)** is one approach to goal setting that has been applied in the workplace.[30] In MBO, managers and employees jointly set performance goals that are tangible, verifiable, and measurable; progress on goals is periodically reviewed, and rewards are allocated on the basis of this progress.

Golfers such as Prince Edward Island's Lorie Kane illustrate the effectiveness of the expectancy theory of motivation, where rewards are tied to effort and outcome. Players on the LPGA tour are paid strictly according to their performance, unlike members of professional sports teams. Kane's first LPGA tour victory came in 2000 at the Michelob Light Classic. It ended a string of nine runner-up finishes. As Kane has put more effort into her play, she has been increasing her earnings each year. By the end of July 2005, she had earned $612 362, which exceeded her total earnings of $530 078 for 2004.

How Does Goal Setting Motivate?

According to Locke, goal setting motivates in four ways (see Exhibit 4-8) on page 130:[31]

- *Goals direct attention.* Goals indicate where individuals should direct their efforts when they are choosing among things to do. For instance, recognizing that an important assignment is due in a few days, goal setting may encourage you to say no when friends invite you to a movie this evening.

- *Goals regulate effort.* Goals suggest how much effort an individual should put into a given task. For instance, If earning a high mark in accounting is more important to you than earning a high mark in organizational behaviour, you will likely put more effort into studying accounting.

- *Goals increase persistence.* Persistence represents the effort spent on a task over time. When people keep goals in mind, they will work hard on them, even in the face of obstacles.

- *Goals encourage the development of strategies and action plans.* Once goals are set, individuals can develop plans for achieving those goals. For instance, a goal to become more fit may include plans to join a gym, work out with friends, and change eating habits.

In order for goals to be effective, they should be "SMART." SMART stands for

- Specific: Individuals know exactly what is to be achieved.

- Measurable: The goals proposed can be tracked and reviewed.

- Attainable: The goals, even if difficult, are reasonable and achievable.

- Results-oriented: The goals should support the vision of the organization.

- Time-bound: The goals are to be achieved within a stated time.

From Concepts to Skills on page 158 gives further ideas of how to effectively engage in goal setting.

goal What an individual is trying to accomplish.

management by objectives (MBO) An approach to goal setting in which specific measurable goals are jointly set by managers and employees; progress on goals is periodically reviewed, and rewards are allocated on the basis of this progress.

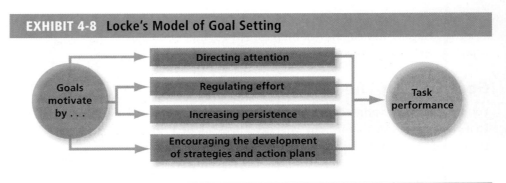

EXHIBIT 4-8   Locke's Model of Goal Setting

Source: Adapted from E. A. Locke and G. P. Latham, *A Theory of Goal Setting and Task Performance* (Englewood Cliffs, NJ: Prentice Hall, 1980). Reprinted by permission of Edwin A. Locke.

 ## RESEARCH FINDINGS

Locke and his colleagues have spent considerable time studying the effect of goal setting in various situations. The evidence strongly supports the value of goals. More to the point, we can say that

- *Specific goals increase performance, under certain conditions.* In early research, specific goals were linked to better performance.[32] However, more recent research indicates that specific goals can lead to poorer performance in complex tasks. Employees may be too goal-focused on complex tasks, and therefore not consider alternative and better solutions to such tasks.[33]

- *Difficult goals, when accepted, result in higher performance than do easy goals.* Research clearly shows that goal difficulty leads to positive performance.[34] This relationship does not hold when employees view the goals as impossible, rather than just difficult.[35]

- *Feedback leads to higher performance.* Feedback allows individuals to know how they are doing, relative to their goals. Thus feedback is an important part of goal setting.[36] Feedback encourages individuals to adjust their direction, effort, and action plans if they are falling short of their goals. We examine the process of performance evaluation in detail in *HR Implications* on pages 147–153.

- *Goals are equally effective whether participatively set, assigned, or self-set.* Research indicates that how goals are set is not clearly related to performance.[37] Managers may want to consider whether individuals want to participate in goal setting, and whether there is time to do so. Managers should also consider whether individuals need to accept the goals. Employees are more likely to accept goals if they are participatively set.

- *Goal commitment and financial incentives affect whether goals are achieved.* Research suggests that the level of commitment one has to a goal moderates the relationship between goal difficulty and accomplishment.[38] Individuals are more likely to be persistent if they are committed to their goals. Research also indicates that financial incentives can lower commitment to difficult goals. Individuals may fear that they will not achieve difficult goals if these are linked to financial rewards. Financial incentives for difficult goals can also inspire individuals to refuse to help co-workers, or neglect tasks not directly related to goals that will be financially rewarded.[39] For instance, employees may help their own customers, but not help customers who are linked to other co-workers. Quality can also be affected when employees have quantity goals to meet.[40]

One intriguing new approach to looking at how time affects goal setting is the idea that more frequent exposure to challenging goals can "give momentum to new ideas and prevent degradation of skills."[41] While research suggests that frequent exposure to demanding goals can stress people out,[42] some scientists suggest that facing a variety of challenging tasks can lead people to be engrossed and absorbed in what they are doing.[43] Employees can respond quite positively to frequent goal setting, as *OB in the Workplace* shows.

OB IN THE WORKPLACE

Employees Hold Meetings to Achieve Goals

Will employees police themselves to meet goals? Raj Narayanaswamy, CEO of Calgary-based Replicon, which develops time management software, thinks so.[44] He offered his employees a deal in the last quarter of 1998. His employees wanted him to close the office over Christmas holidays. He wanted to make sure all of his shipments got out on time. "Meet these goals before then, and we will think about it," he told them.

Replicon
www.replicon.com

To achieve this goal, the employees developed a plan, and scheduled daily 10-minute meetings to make sure everything stayed on track. They ended up surpassing their goal, and getting the vacation days they wanted.

Narayanaswamy has encouraged his employees to set departmental and personal goals to increase revenue and solve problems each quarter ever since. He rewards them with trips and events when goals are met. The employees continue to hold daily meetings to assess how well the goals are being met, and Narayanaswamy thinks the "cringe factor" motivates individuals. "It's difficult for someone to attend a daily meeting and say every day, 'I didn't get it done,'" he points out. Because the employees set the goals, they are also more likely to work hard to achieve them.

Goal-setting theory is consistent with expectancy theory. The goals can be considered the effort-performance link—in other words, the goals determine what must be done. Feedback can be considered the performance-reward relationship, where the individual's efforts are recognized. Finally, the implication of goal setting is that the achievement of the goals will result in intrinsic satisfaction (and may of course be linked to external rewards).

Contingency Factors in Goal Setting

Are there any contingencies in goal-setting theory, or can we take it as a universal truth that difficult and specific goals will always lead to higher performance? In addition to feedback, four other factors have been found to influence the goals-performance relationship. These are goal commitment, adequate self-efficacy, task characteristics, and national culture. Goal-setting theory presupposes that an individual is committed to the goal, that is, he or she is determined not to lower or abandon the goal. This is most likely to occur when goals are made public, when the individual has an internal locus of control, and when the goals are self-set rather than assigned.[45]

Self-efficacy refers to an individual's belief that he or she is capable of performing a task.[46] The higher your self-efficacy, the more confidence you have in your ability to succeed in a task. So, in difficult situations, we find that people with low self-efficacy are more likely to lessen their effort or give up altogether, while those with high self-efficacy will try harder to master the challenge.[47] In addition,

Goal setting works well for Pat Cavanaugh, CEO and top salesman of his promotional products company. He sets specific goals for himself and his sales team each year and has a long-term company goal of $100 million by 2010. By never missing a goal, the firm has grown 4000 percent in its first seven years. For Cavanaugh, well-learned tasks are the key to meeting goals. He trains his staff to prepare for client meetings, to listen to the client's needs, and to read people well.

self-efficacy An individual's belief that he or she is capable of performing a task.

individuals high in self-efficacy seem to respond to negative feedback with increased effort and motivation, whereas those low in self-efficacy are likely to lessen their effort when given negative feedback.[48]

Research indicates that individual goal setting doesn't work equally well on all tasks. The evidence suggests that goals seem to have a more substantial effect on performance when tasks are simple rather than complex, well learned rather than novel, and independent rather than interdependent.[49] On interdependent tasks, group goals are preferable. Finally, goal-setting theory is culture-bound. It's well adapted to countries like Canada and the United States because its key components align reasonably well with North American cultures. Following the GLOBE measures from Chapter 3, it assumes that employees will be reasonably independent (not too high a score on power distance), that managers and employees will seek challenging goals (low in uncertainty avoidance), and that performance is considered important by both (high in performance orientation). So don't expect goal setting to necessarily lead to higher employee performance in countries such as Portugal or Chile, where the opposite conditions exist.

Our overall conclusion is that intentions—as articulated in terms of hard and specific goals—are a potent motivating force. Under the proper conditions, they can lead to higher performance.

RESPONSES TO THE REWARD SYSTEM

Casey Printers, one of four quarterbacks for the BC Lions football team, was not a happy player when the football season started in summer 2005.[50] He was the CFL's most outstanding player in the 2004 season, after stepping in when starting quarterback Dave Dickenson was injured. Subsequently, Printers led the Lions to an eight-game winning streak, and he thought that should have entitled him to a better contract for 2005.

Printers signed his first contract with the Lions in 2004, for $65 000 a year. At the end of the season, he asked for a four-year contract from the Lions that would pay him more than $400 000 a year. The team turned him down, countering with an offer of $1 million over three years. Printers turned that down.

Printer's rationale for the seemingly high salary demand is that his teammate and fellow quarterback Dave Dickenson makes $400 000 a year, as does Edmonton Eskimos quarterback Ricky Ray and Montreal Alouettes quarterback Anthony Calvillo. "My value is just as equal as these guys, so why not try to get equal or more? It just makes perfect business sense," he explains. Will Printers continue to be motivated to play for the Lions? Is he making the right salary comparisons?

4 Do equity and fairness matter?

To a large extent, motivation theories are about rewards. The theories suggest that individuals have needs and will exert effort in order to have those needs met. The needs theories specifically identify those needs. Goal-setting and expectancy theories portray processes by which individuals act and then receive desirable rewards (intrinsic or extrinsic) for their behaviour.

Three additional process theories ask us to consider how individuals respond to rewards. Equity theory suggests that individuals evaluate and interpret rewards. Fair process goes one step further, suggesting that employees are sensitive to a variety of fairness issues in the workplace that extend beyond the reward system but also affect employee motivation. Cognitive evaluation theory examines how individuals respond to the introduction of extrinsic rewards for intrinsically satisfying activities.

Equity Theory

Jane Pearson graduated from university last year with a degree in accounting. After interviews with a number of organizations on campus, she accepted an articling position with one of the nation's largest public accounting firms and was assigned to the company's Edmonton office. Jane was very pleased with the offer she received: challenging work with a prestigious firm, an excellent opportunity to gain valuable experience, and the highest salary any accounting major at her university was offered last year—$4500 a month. But Jane was the top student in her class; she was ambitious and articulate, and fully expected to receive a commensurate salary.

How important is fairness to you?

Twelve months have passed since Jane joined her employer. The work has proved to be as challenging and satisfying as she had hoped. Her employer is extremely pleased with her performance; in fact, she recently received a $200-a-month raise. However, Jane's motivational level has dropped dramatically in the past few weeks. Why? Her employer has just hired a new graduate from Jane's university, who lacks the one-year experience Jane has gained, for $4750 a month—$50 more than Jane now makes! It would be an understatement to describe Jane as irate. Jane is even talking about looking for another job.

Jane's situation illustrates the role that equity plays in motivation. **Equity theory** suggests that individuals compare their job inputs (effort, experience, education, competence, creativity, etc.) and outcomes (salary levels, raises, recognition, challenging assignments, working conditions, etc.) with those of others. We perceive what we get from a job situation (outcomes) in relation to what we put into it (inputs), and then we compare our outcome-input ratio with the outcome-input ratio of relevant others. (This idea is illustrated in Exhibit 4-9.) If we perceive our ratio to be equal to that of the relevant others with whom we compare ourselves, a state of equity is said to exist. We perceive our situation as fair—justice prevails. When we see the ratio as unequal, we experience this as inequity.

For instance, suppose you wrote a case analysis for your marketing professor and spent 18 hours researching and writing it up. Your classmate spent six hours preparing the same analysis. Each of you received a mark of 75 percent. It is likely that you would perceive this as unfair, as you worked considerably harder (that is, exerted more effort) than your classmate. J. Stacy Adams has proposed that those experiencing inequity are motivated to do something to

Because of the financial crisis in Russia, many firms do not have money to pay their employees. Instead of receiving a salary, employees get paid in goods the factories produce. Velta Company, a bicycle maker in Russia, gives workers one bicycle a month instead of a paycheque. Workers then have to sell their bike for cash or barter it for food. Some workers deal with the inequity of not getting a salary by using a different referent. "We are luckier than people over at the chemical plant," says one Velta employee. "At least our factory gives us something we can sell."

equity theory Individuals compare their job inputs and outcomes with those of others and then respond so as to eliminate any inequities.

EXHIBIT 4-9 Equity Theory

Ratio of Output to Input	Person 1s Perception
Person 1 / Person 2	Inequity, underrewarded
Person 1 / Person 2	Equity
Person 1 / Person 2	Inequity, overrewarded

correct it.[51] Thus, you might be inclined to spend considerably less time on your next assignment for your marketing professor.

To Whom Do We Compare Ourselves?

In the case of the marketing assignment, the obvious referent is your classmate. However, in the workplace, the referent that an employee selects when making comparisons adds to the complexity of equity theory. Recall that Casey Printers chose three people to whom to compare his salary. All three were quarterbacks, the same position he played. One, Dave Dickenson, was quarterback for the same team on which Printers played. The other two played for other teams. Evidence indicates that the referent chosen is an important variable in equity theory.[52] There are four referent comparisons that an employee can use:

- *Self-inside.* An employee's experiences in a different position inside his or her current organization.

- *Self-outside.* An employee's experiences in a situation or position outside his or her current organization.

- *Other-inside.* Another individual or group of individuals inside the employee's organization. Printers made this type of comparison when he considered Dave Dickenson's salary.

- *Other-outside.* Another individual or group of individuals outside the employee's organization. Printers made this type of comparison when he considered the salaries of Ricky Ray and Anthony Calvillo.

Employees might compare themselves with friends, neighbours, co-workers, colleagues in other organizations, or their own situations in previous jobs. Which referent an employee chooses will be influenced by the information the employee holds about referents, as well as by the attractiveness of the referent. Research has focused on four moderating variables—gender, length of tenure, level in the organization, and amount of education or professionalism.[53]

Gender Research shows that both men and women often make same-sex comparisons. Research also demonstrates that women are typically paid less than men in comparable jobs and have lower pay expectations than men for the same work. For instance, Statistics Canada reports that in 2000 the gap between the full-time wages of men and women was the lowest ever, with full-time female employees earning, on average, 72.1 cents for every dollar earned by full-time male employees.[54] So a woman who uses another woman as a referent tends to have a lower comparative standard for pay than a woman who uses a man as the referent. If women are to be paid equally to men in comparable jobs, the standard of comparison—as used by both employees and employers—needs to be expanded to include both sexes.

Length of Tenure Employees with short tenure in their current organizations tend to have little information about others inside the organization, so they rely on their own personal experiences. On the other hand, employees with long tenure rely more heavily on co-workers for comparison.

Level in the Organization and Amount of Education Upper-level employees, those in the professional ranks, and those with more education tend to be more cosmopolitan and have better information about people in other organizations. Therefore, these types of employees will make more other-outside comparisons.

The choice of comparison can be quite important. Employees of Victoria's Empress Hotel went on strike to demand wages equal to those paid to employees at downtown

Vancouver's Hotel Vancouver. The Empress employees claimed that they were doing the same work as those in Vancouver. Management rejected this argument, noting that the cost of living in Victoria was lower. Ian Powell, the Empress Hotel's general manager, said that "Within the Victoria marketplace, the employees are the best paid in the city."[55]

What Happens When We Feel Treated Inequitably?

What can you do if you think your salary is "unfair"?

Based on equity theory, when employees perceive an inequity, they can be predicted to make one of six choices.[56] We can illustrate these by considering possible responses that BC Lions quarterback Casey Printers can make, if he thinks it's unfair to receive a lower salary than the three other quarterbacks in his reference group.

- *Change their inputs* (for example, Printers can decide to exert less effort—as some claimed he did in the 2005 season).

- *Change their outcomes* (for example, Printers can work harder than ever to show that he really does deserve higher pay).

- *Adjust perceptions of self* (for example, Printers could think to himself, "I've only been in the league for two years. Maybe I don't really have the same experience as the other guys").

- *Adjust perceptions of others* (for example, Printers could think, "Anthony Calvillo of the Alouettes has worked at this job a lot longer, and may deserve greater pay").

- *Choose a different referent* (for example, Printers could consider what other quarterbacks who have only been in the league for two years receive).

- *Leave the field* (for example, Printers could start looking at other teams, hoping that he can be picked up by one of them at the end of the season).

Case Incident—Frustrated at Age 32 on page 156 describes what happens when a Generation Xer feels he does not have the same opportunities in the workplace as a Baby Boomer.

Bear in mind that being treated equitably is not the same as being treated equally. Equity theory tells us that people who perform better should observe that they are rewarded better than those who do not perform as well. Thus, poor performers should also observe that they are getting smaller rewards than better performers. Paying equally would mean that everyone is paid the same, regardless of performance. Many employees in the nonprofit sector do not feel that they are being paid fairly, compared with people working in other sectors of the economy, as *OB in the Workplace* shows.

OB IN THE WORKPLACE

Money Matters!

Is intrinsic motivation ever enough? A recent study by the Canadian Policy Research Networks found that employees who work in the nonprofit sector are finding their pay low compared with those in other sectors.[57] Managers in the nonprofit sector (e.g., museums, professional associations, food banks, community health clinics, and group homes) make about $8 to $10 less than managers in other fields. The researchers used data collected by Statistics Canada to evaluate wage differences.

The researchers also found that one-third of employees in the nonprofit sector are unhappy with their pay. "One might expect that satisfaction derived from socially valuable or 'morally palatable' work could start to wear thin if juxtaposed against low wages, poor benefits and job insecurity over the longer term," researchers Kathryn McMullen and Grant Schellenberg wrote. The employees are aware that individuals doing similar work in other sectors get paid better.

Unlike for-profit organizations, nonprofit organizations often have very little money to pay their employees. This can cause crises when employees demand better pay. For instance, five group-home workers in Montague, PEI, went on strike for more than eight months to get higher wages and benefits. One employee, Kim MacKenzie, noted that employees were expected to work unpaid overtime so that they could provide round-the-clock care for residents of the home. "Basically we are just determined, we want to take a stand," said Ms. MacKenzie. "This may be the profession we have chosen, it's what we want to do. But this does not mean we should work 54 hours a week and only get paid for 44." MacKenzie's complaint underscores that not all employees are expected to work such long hours without pay.

The plight of workers in the nonprofit sector tells us that employees do compare what others around them are making to determine whether they are paid fairly.

RESEARCH FINDINGS

Equity theory establishes the following propositions relating to inequitable pay:

- *When paid by time worked, overrewarded employees will produce more than will equitably paid employees.* Hourly and salaried employees will generate high quantity or quality of production in order to increase the input side of the ratio and bring about equity.

- *When paid by number of units produced, overrewarded employees will produce fewer, but higher quality, units than will equitably paid employees.* Individuals paid on a piece-rate basis will increase their effort to achieve equity, which can result in greater quality or quantity. However, increases in quantity will only increase inequity, since every unit produced results in further overpayment. Therefore, effort is directed toward increasing quality rather than increasing quantity.

- *When paid by time worked, underrewarded employees will produce less or poorer quality output.* Effort will be decreased, which will bring about lower productivity or poorer quality output than that of equitably paid subjects.

- *When paid by number of units produced, underrewarded employees will produce a large number of low quality units in comparison with equitably paid employees.* Employees paid on a piece-rate basis can bring about equity because trading off quality of output for quantity will result in an increase in rewards, with little or no increase in contributions.

These propositions have generally been supported, with a few minor qualifications.[58] First, those who are overrewarded do not seem to change their behaviour. Apparently, people have a great deal more tolerance of overpayment inequities than of underpayment inequities, or are better able to rationalize them. Second, not all people are equity sensitive.[59] For example, some individuals simply do not worry about how their rewards compare with those of others. Predictions from equity theory are unlikely to be accurate with these individuals.

These propositions also suggest that when organizations reward only senior managers after a year of increased profitability and performance, lower-level employees receive a powerful message. They learn that only shareholders and senior management matter. This can lead to employees withholding effort and initiative.

It is important to note that while most research on equity theory has focused on pay, employees also look for equity in the distribution of other organizational rewards. For instance, it's been shown that the use of high-status job titles, as well as large and lavishly furnished offices, may function as desirable outcomes for some employees in their equity equation.[60]

In conclusion, equity theory demonstrates that, for most employees, motivation is influenced significantly by relative rewards, as well as by absolute rewards. However, some key issues are still unclear.[61] For instance, how do employees handle conflicting equity signals, such as when unions point to other employee groups who are substantially *better off*, while management argues how much things have *improved*? How do employees define inputs and outcomes? How do they combine and weigh their inputs and outcomes to arrive at totals? When and how do the factors change over time? Regardless of these problems, equity theory continues to offer some important insights into employee motivation.

BC Lions head coach Wally Buono talks to quarterbacks Dave Dickenson and Casey Printers during practice before the 2004 CFL Grey Cup game. After the season ended, Printers wanted a similar salary to his teammate Dickenson, based on his performance during the year.

Fair Process and Treatment

Recent research has been directed at redefining what is meant by equity, or fairness.[62] Historically, equity theory focused on **distributive justice**, or the perceived fairness of the *amount* and *allocation* of rewards among individuals. But people also care about **procedural justice**—the perceived fairness of the *process* used to determine the distribution of rewards. (This includes having a voice in a decision and finding accuracy in decision making). They care, too, about **interactional justice**—the quality of the interpersonal treatment received from a manager. (Being treated sensitively and being provided an explanation for decisions are examples.)

The evidence indicates that distributive justice has a greater influence on employee satisfaction than procedural justice, while procedural and interactional justice tend to affect an employee's organizational commitment, trust in his or her boss, and intention to quit.[63] Researchers have found that when managers and employees believed that the company's processes were fair, they were more likely to show a high level of trust and commitment to the organization. Employees engaged in negative behaviour when they felt the process was unfair.[64]

For example, employees at Volkswagen's Puebla, Mexico, plant staged a lengthy walkout *after* being offered a 20 percent raise because their union leaders had agreed to work-rule concessions without consulting them. The employees, even though happy about the raise, did not believe that the process leading to the change in the work rules was fair. This behaviour is consistent with economist Alan Blinder's findings that "Changing the way workers are *treated* may boost productivity more than changing the way they are *paid*."[65]

To increase employees' perception of procedural justice, managers should consider openly sharing information on how allocation decisions are made and follow consistent and unbiased procedures. With increased procedural and interactional fairness, employees are likely to view their managers and the organization as positive, even if they are dissatisfied with pay, promotions, and other personal outcomes. Professor Daniel Skarlicki of the Sauder School of Business at the University of British Columbia has found that it is when unfavourable outcomes are combined with unfair procedures or poor interpersonal treatment that resentment and retaliation (for example, theft, bad-mouthing, sabotage) are most likely.[66]

distributive justice The perceived fairness of the *amount* and *allocation* of rewards among individuals.

procedural justice The perceived fairness of the *process* used to determine the distribution of rewards.

interactional justice The quality of the interpersonal treatment received from a manager.

Cognitive Evaluation Theory

Several researchers suggest that the introduction of extrinsic rewards, such as pay, for work effort that was *previously rewarding intrinsically* (i.e., that was personally satisfying) will

cognitive evaluation theory
Offering extrinsic rewards (e.g., pay) for work effort that was previously rewarding intrinsically will tend to decrease the overall level of a person's motivation.

tend to decrease the overall level of a person's motivation.[67] This proposal—which has come to be called **cognitive evaluation theory**—has been extensively researched, and a large number of studies have been supportive.[68] Additionally, Alfie Kohn, often cited for his work on rewards, argues that people are actually punished by rewards, and do inferior work when they are enticed by money, grades, or other incentives. His extensive review of incentive studies concluded that "rewards usually improve performance only at extremely simple—indeed, mindless—tasks, and even then they improve only quantitative performance."[69]

Extrinsic vs. Intrinsic Rewards

Historically, motivation theorists have generally assumed that intrinsic motivators are independent of extrinsic motivators. That is, the stimulation of one would not affect the other. But cognitive evaluation theory suggests otherwise. It argues that when extrinsic rewards are used by organizations as payoffs for superior performance, the intrinsic rewards, which are derived from individuals doing what they like, are reduced.

In other words, when extrinsic rewards are given to someone for performing an interesting task, it causes intrinsic interest in the task itself to decline. For instance, although a taxi driver expects to be paid for taking your best friend to the airport, you do not expect your friend to pay you if you volunteer to drive her to the airport. In fact, the offer of pay might diminish your pleasure in doing a favour for your friend.

Why would such an outcome occur? The popular explanation is that the individual experiences a loss of control over his or her own behaviour when it is being rewarded by external sources. This causes the previous intrinsic motivation to diminish. Extrinsic rewards can produce a shift—from an internal to an external explanation—in an individual's perception of why he or she works on a task. If you're reading a novel a week because your contemporary literature instructor requires you to, you can attribute your reading behaviour to an external source. If you stop reading novels the moment the course ends, this is more evidence that your behaviour was due to an external source. However, if you find yourself continuing to read a novel a week when the course ends, your natural inclination is to say, "I must enjoy reading novels because I'm still reading one a week!"

If cognitive evaluation theory is valid, it should have major implications for managerial practices. Compensation specialists argue that motivation comes from extrinsic rewards tied to performance. But cognitive evaluation theorists suggest that introducing extrinsic rewards will tend to decrease the internal satisfaction that the individual receives from doing the job. So, if cognitive evaluation theory is correct, it would make sense to make an individual's pay *noncontingent* on performance in order to avoid decreasing intrinsic motivation. Instead, simply pay fairly, and then allow the individual's intrinsic motivation to guide performance.

 RESEARCH FINDINGS

Although further research is needed to clarify some of the current ambiguity, the evidence does lead us to conclude that the interdependence of extrinsic and intrinsic rewards is a real phenomenon.[70] A large body of research shows that large external rewards can undermine the positive performance of employees.[71] When employees work for a large reward, they will explain their behaviour through that reward—"I did it for the money." However, in the absence of large rewards, employees are more likely to reflect on the interesting nature of the work or the positive benefits of being an organizational member to explain their behaviour. When an organization provides employees with intrinsically interesting work, they will often work longer and harder than one might predict from the actual external rewards.

In studies dating back to the 1940s, employees have always ranked other items, such as being shown appreciation for work done, feeling "in" on things, and having interesting work, as being more important to them than their salaries.[72] Employees at both Southwest Airlines and AES, an independent producer of electrical power with offices in the United States, Argentina, China, Hungary, and other countries, indicated that they appreciated the positive working climates of these organizations more than the specific financial rewards they received.[73]

Jeffrey Pfeffer of Stanford University is one of the leaders in the field of organizational behaviour. In his 1998 book *The Human Equation*, he encourages organizations to examine the messages they are sending to employees through the rewards they offer. Pfeffer argues that relying exclusively on financial incentives does not work and notes that people will work hard if the atmosphere is fun. As he points out, "At Apple Computer in its early days, employees didn't work 80 or 90 hours a week to maximize the expected value of some discounted stream of future earnings or to maximize shareholder wealth; they did it because the work was fun and challenging and because they were changing how the world viewed personal computers."[74]

W. L. Gore, maker of Gore-Tex fabric and Elixir guitar strings, has a compensation and reward system based on procedural justice. At Gore, motivation comes from approval of co-workers. Compensation is determined by employees, who rank their team members each year. Gore openly shares information about how pay decisions are made based on consistent procedures. Procedural fairness helps create a strong organizational commitment among employees.

Of course, organizations cannot simply ignore financial rewards. When people feel they are being treated unfairly in the workplace, pay often becomes a focal point of their concerns. If tasks are dull or unpleasant, extrinsic rewards will probably increase intrinsic motivation.[75] Even when a job is inherently interesting, there still exists a powerful norm for extrinsic payment.[76] But creating fun, challenging, and empowered workplaces may do more for motivation and performance than focusing simply on the compensation system.

Southwest Airlines
www.southwest.com

AES
www.aes.com

Apple Computer
www.apple.com/ca

Increasing Intrinsic Motivation

Our discussion of motivation theories and our discussion of how to apply motivation theories in the workplace has focused mainly on improving extrinsic motivation. Professor Kenneth Thomas of the Naval Postgraduate School in Monterey, California, developed a model of intrinsic motivation that draws from the job characteristics model and cognitive evaluation theory.[77] He identified four key rewards that increase an individual's intrinsic motivation:

- *Sense of choice.* The opportunity to select what one will do and perform the way one thinks best. Individuals can use their own judgment to carry out the task.

- *Sense of competence.* The feeling of accomplishment for doing a good job. Individuals are more likely to feel a sense of accomplishment when they carry out challenging tasks.

- *Sense of meaningfulness.* The opportunity to pursue worthwhile tasks. Individuals feel good about what they are doing and believe that what they are doing matters.

- *Sense of progress.* The feeling of accomplishment that one is making progress on a task, and that it is moving forward. Individuals feel that they are spending their time wisely in doing their jobs.

Thomas also identified four sets of behaviours managers can use to build intrinsic rewards for their employees:

EXHIBIT 4-10   Building Blocks for Intrinsic Rewards

Leading for Choice	Leading for Competence
• Delegated authority • Trust in workers • Security (no punishment) for honest mistakes • A clear purpose • Information	• Knowledge • Positive feedback • Skill recognition • Challenge • High, non-comparative standards
Leading for Meaningfulness	**Leading for Progress**
• A noncynical climate • Clearly identified passions • An exciting vision • Relevant task purposes • Whole tasks	• A collaborative climate • Milestones • Celebrations • Access to customers • Measurement of improvement

Source: Reprinted with permission of the publisher. From *Intrinsic Motivation at Work: Building Energy and Commitment.* Copyright © K. Thomas. Berrett-Koehler Publishers Inc., San Francisco, CA. All rights reserved. www.bkconnection.com.

- *Leading for choice.* Empowering employees and delegating tasks.
- *Leading for competence.* Supporting and coaching employees.
- *Leading for meaningfulness.* Inspiring employees and modelling desired behaviours.
- *Leading for progress.* Monitoring and rewarding employees.

Exhibit 4-10 describes what managers can do to increase the likelihood that the intrinsic rewards are motivational.

MOTIVATING EMPLOYEES THROUGH REINFORCEMENT

BC Lions coach Wally Buono doesn't want his team making costly mistakes on game day, and losing yards in penalties.[78] The coach started the 2005 season by illustrating to the players that many of their touchdowns and big plays from the previous year were wiped out by penalties. Then he introduced reinforcement for not making mistakes. If a player receives a penalty during a game, the entire team has to do sprints across the field the next day, for four times as many yards as the penalty received. The players call these runs "gassers," and they don't like doing them.

The players say that Buono's punishment for penalties has paid off: "Guys are making a more conscious decision not to take a stupid penalty," says linebacker Barrin Simpson.

The gassers improved player performance at the start of the season. The team saw a 42 percent drop in penalties in the first nine games of 2005, compared with the first nine games in 2004. Then the team started having morale problems and confusion over who was the team's quarterback. So how does reinforcement work, and does it motivate?

5 What role does reinforcement play in motivation?

operant conditioning A type of conditioning in which desired voluntary behaviour leads to a reward or prevents a punishment.

The motivation theories we have covered to this point emphasize how people's needs and thought processes can be used to motivate them. As a behaviourist, B. F. Skinner found it "pointless to explain behaviour in terms of unobservable inner states such as needs, drives, attitudes, or thought processes."[79]

Skinner's view of motivation is much simpler. He suggested that people learn how to behave to get something they want or to avoid something they don't want.[80] This idea is known as **operant conditioning**, which means behaviour is influenced by the reinforcement or lack of reinforcement brought about by the consequences of the behaviour.

The BC Lions players, for instance, want to avoid doing "gassers," so they avoid getting penalties on game day.

Skinner argued that creating pleasing consequences to follow specific forms of behaviour would increase the frequency of that behaviour. People will most likely engage in desired behaviours if they are positively reinforced for doing so. Rewards are most effective if they immediately follow the desired behaviour. In addition, behaviour that is not rewarded, or is punished, is less likely to be repeated.

You see illustrations of operant conditioning everywhere. For example, any situation in which it is either explicitly stated or implicitly suggested that reinforcements are contingent on some action on your part involves the use of operant conditioning. Your instructor says that if you want a high grade in the course, you must supply correct answers on the test. A commissioned salesperson wanting to earn a sizable income finds that doing so is contingent on generating high sales in her territory. Of course, the linkage can also work to teach the individual to engage in behaviours that work against the best interests of the organization. Assume that your boss tells you that if you will work overtime during the next three-week busy season, you will be compensated for it at the next performance appraisal. However, when performance appraisal time comes, you find that you are given no positive reinforcement for your overtime work. The next time your manager asks you to work overtime, what will you do? You will probably decline! Your behaviour can be explained by operant conditioning: If a behaviour fails to be positively reinforced, the probability that the behaviour will be repeated declines.

Methods of Shaping Behaviour

There are four ways in which to shape behaviour: through positive reinforcement, negative reinforcement, punishment, and extinction.

Following a response with something pleasant is called *positive reinforcement.* Following a response by the termination or withdrawal of something unpleasant is called *negative reinforcement. Punishment* is causing an unpleasant condition in an attempt to eliminate an undesirable behaviour. Eliminating any reinforcement that is maintaining a behaviour is called *extinction.* Exhibit 4-11 gives examples of each type of reinforcement. Negative reinforcement should not be confused with punishment: negative reinforcement strengthens a behaviour because it takes away an unpleasant situation.

Schedules of Reinforcement

While consequences have an effect on behaviour, the timing of those consequences or reinforcements is also important. The two major types of reinforcement schedules are *continuous* and *intermittent.* A **continuous reinforcement** schedule reinforces the desired behaviour each and every time it is demonstrated. Take, for example, the case of someone who has historically had trouble arriving at work on time. Every time he is not

continuous reinforcement A desired behaviour is reinforced each and every time it is demonstrated.

EXHIBIT 4-11	Types of Reinforcement
Reinforcement Type	**Example**
Positive reinforcement	A manager praises an employee for a job well done.
Negative reinforcement	An instructor asks a question and a student looks through her lecture notes to avoid being called on. She has learned that looking busily through her notes prevents the instructor from calling on her.
Punishment	A manager gives an employee a two-day suspension from work without pay for showing up drunk.
Extinction	An instructor ignores students who raise their hands to ask questions. Hand-raising becomes extinct.

EXHIBIT 4-12	Schedules of Reinforcement		
Reinforcement Schedule	Nature of Reinforcement	Effect on Behaviour	Example
Continuous	Reward given after each desired behaviour	Fast learning of new behaviour but rapid extinction	Compliments
Fixed-interval	Reward given at fixed time intervals	Average and irregular performance with rapid extinction	Weekly paycheques
Variable-interval	Reward given at variable time intervals	Moderately high and stable performance with slow extinction	Pop quizzes
Fixed-ratio	Reward given at fixed amounts of output	High and stable performance attained quickly but also with rapid extinction	Piece-rate pay
Variable-ratio	Reward given at variable amounts of output	Very high performance with slow extinction	Commissioned sales

intermittent reinforcement A desired behaviour is reinforced often enough to make the behaviour worth repeating, but not every time it is demonstrated.

fixed-interval schedule The reward is given at fixed time intervals.

variable-interval schedule The reward is given at variable time intervals.

fixed-ratio schedule The reward is given at fixed amounts of output.

variable-ratio schedule The reward is given at variable amounts of output.

tardy his manager might compliment him on his desirable behaviour. In an intermittent schedule, on the other hand, not every instance of the desirable behaviour is reinforced, but reinforcement is given often enough to make the behaviour worth repeating. Evidence indicates that the intermittent, or varied, form of reinforcement tends to promote more resistance to extinction than does the continuous form.[81]

An **intermittent reinforcement** schedule can be of a ratio or interval type. *Ratio schedules* depend on how many responses the subject makes. The individual is reinforced after giving a certain number of specific types of behaviour. *Interval schedules* depend on how much time has passed since the previous reinforcement. With interval schedules, the individual is reinforced on the first appropriate behaviour after a particular time has elapsed. A reinforcement can also be classified as fixed or variable. When these factors are combined, four types of intermittent schedules of reinforcement result: **fixed-interval schedule**, **variable-interval schedule**, **fixed-ratio schedule**, and **variable-ratio schedule**.

Exhibit 4-12 summarizes the five schedules of reinforcement and their effects on behaviour.

Reinforcement in the Workplace

Managers want employees to behave in ways that most benefit the organization. Therefore, they look for ways to reinforce positive behaviour and extinguish negative behaviour. Consider the situation in which an employee's behaviour is significantly different from that sought by management. If management rewarded the individual only when he or she showed desirable responses, there might be very little reinforcement taking place. Instead, managers can reinforce each successive step that moves the individual closer to the desired response. If an employee who usually turns in his work two days late succeeds in turning in his work only one day late, managers can reinforce that improvement. Reinforcement would increase as responses more closely approximated the desired behaviour.

While variable-ratio and variable-interval reinforcement schedules produce the best results for improving behaviour, most work organizations rely on fixed-interval (weekly or monthly pay) or fixed-ratio (piece rate) pay. In the next chapter, we will discuss the idea of variable pay, as well as reactions to it. We will also look at how rewards in general are used in the workplace.

MOTIVATION FOR WHOM?

6 What are the ethics behind motivation theories?

A current debate among organizational behaviour scholars is, Who benefits from the theories of motivation?[82] Some argue that motivation theories are only intended to help managers get more productivity out of employees, and are little concerned with employees beyond improvements in productivity. Thus needs theories, process theories, and theories concerned with fairness could be interpreted not as ways to help employees get what they want or need, but rather as means to help managers get what they want from employees. In his review of "meaningful work" literature, Professor Christopher Michaelson of the Wharton School at the University of Pennsylvania finds that researchers propose that organizations have a moral obligation to provide employees with "free choice to enter, honest communication, fair and respectful treatment, intellectual challenge, considerable independence to determine work methods, democratic participation in decision making, moral development, due process and justice, nonpaternalism, and fair compensation."[83]

Michaelson suggests that scholars concerned with meaningful work should focus on the conditions of the workplace and improving those conditions. He also suggests that researchers have a moral obligation to make workplaces better for employees. While productivity may be a by-product of better work conditions, the important thing is for employers to treat employees well, and to consider the needs of employees as an end in itself. By contrast, he argues, mainstream motivation theory does not consider the moral obligation of employers to their employees, but it does consider ways to ensure employees are more productive.

While this debate is not easily resolved, and may well guide the elaboration of motivation theories in years to come, it does inspire a provocative analysis of why employers provide the workplace conditions they do. To further provoke your thoughts on this matter, the *Ethical Dilemma Exercise* on page 156 asks you to consider whether motivation is just manipulation.

Putting It All Together

While it's always dangerous to synthesize a large number of complex ideas into a few simple guidelines, the following suggestions summarize the essence of what we know about motivating employees in organizations:

- *Recognize individual differences.* Employees have different needs and should not be treated alike. Managers should spend the time necessary to understand what is important to each employee and then align goals, level of involvement, and rewards with individual needs.

- *Use goals and feedback.* Employees should have challenging, specific goals, as well as feedback on how well they are doing in pursuit of those goals.

- *Allow employees to participate in decisions that affect them.* Employees can contribute to a number of decisions that affect them: setting work goals, choosing their own benefits packages, solving productivity and quality problems, and the like. This can increase employee productivity, commitment to work goals, motivation, and job satisfaction.

- *When giving rewards, be sure that they reward desired performance.* Rewards should be linked to the type of performance expected. It is important that employees perceive a clear linkage. How closely rewards are actually correlated to performance criteria is less important than the perception of this relationship. If individuals perceive this relationship to be low, the results will be low performance, a decrease in job satisfaction, and an increase in turnover and absenteeism.

- *Check the system for equity.* Employees should be able to perceive rewards as equating with the inputs they bring to the job. At a simplistic level, this means that experience, skills, abilities, effort, and other obvious inputs should explain differences in performance and, hence, pay, job assignments, and other obvious rewards.

SUMMARY AND IMPLICATIONS

1 **What is motivation?** Motivation is the process that accounts for an individual's intensity, direction, and persistence of effort toward reaching a goal. *Intensity* is concerned with how hard a person tries. This is the element most of us focus on when we talk about motivation. However, high intensity is unlikely to lead to good job performance unless the effort is channelled in a useful *direction*. Finally, the effort requires *persistence*.

2 **How do needs motivate people?** All needs theories of motivation, including Maslow's hierarchy of needs, Herzberg's motivation-hygiene theory (sometimes called the two-factor theory), Alderfer's ERG theory, and McClelland's theory of needs, propose a similar idea: Individuals have needs that, when unsatisfied, will result in motivation. Needs theories suggest that motivation will be high to the degree that the rewards individuals receive for high performance satisfy their dominant needs.

3 **Are there other ways to motivate people?** Process theories focus on the broader picture of how someone can set about motivating another individual. Process theories include expectancy theory and goal-setting theory (and its application, management by objectives). Expectancy theory says that an employee will be motivated to exert a high level of effort when he or she believes (1) that effort will lead to good performance; (2) that good performance will lead to organizational rewards, such as a bonus, a salary increase, or a promotion; and (3) that the rewards will satisfy his or her personal goals.

Goal-setting theory suggests that intentions to work toward a goal are a major source of work motivation. That is, goals tell an employee what needs to be done and how much effort will need to be expended. Specific goals increase performance; difficult goals, when accepted, result in higher performance than do easy goals; and feedback leads to higher performance than does nonfeedback.

4 **Do equity and fairness matter?** Individuals look for fairness in the reward system. Rewards should be perceived by employees as related to the inputs they bring to the job. Simply stated, employees expect that experience, skills, abilities, effort, and other job inputs should explain differences in performance and, hence, pay, job assignments, and other obvious rewards.

5 **What role does reinforcement play in motivation?** B. F. Skinner suggested that behaviour is influenced by whether or not it is reinforced. Managers might consider how their actions toward employees reinforce (or do not reinforce) employee behaviour. For example, when an employee goes above and beyond the call of duty, but that action is not recognized (or reinforced), that employee may be reluctant to exert great effort at a later time. Skinner also noted that schedules of reinforcement affect behaviour. For instance, individuals are less likely to perform well when they are continuously reinforced than when they are randomly reinforced.

6 **What are the ethics behind motivation theories?** A current debate among organizational behaviour scholars is about who benefits from the theories of motivation. Some argue that motivation theories are only intended to help managers get more productivity out of employees, and are little concerned with employees beyond improvements in productivity. The theories can thus be interpreted as a means to help managers get what they want from employees. Although this debate is certainly controversial, motivation theories can also be applied in nonwork settings, and can just as easily help individuals figure out how to motivate themselves.

For Review

1. Does motivation come from within a person, or is it a result of the situation? Explain.

2. What are the implications of Theories X and Y for motivation practices?

3. Compare and contrast Maslow's hierarchy theory of needs with Herzberg's motivation-hygiene (two-factor) theory.

4. Explain the difference between hygiene factors and motivators in Herzberg's motivation-hygiene (two-factor) theory.

5. Identify the variables in expectancy theory.

6. What is the role of self-efficacy in goal setting?

7. Contrast distributive and procedural justice. What implications might they have for designing pay systems in different countries?

8. Explain cognitive evaluation theory. How applicable is it to management practice?

9. Describe the four types of intermittent reinforcers.

For Critical Thinking

1. Identify three activities you really enjoy (for example, playing tennis, reading a novel, going shopping). Next, identify three activities you really dislike (for example, visiting the dentist, cleaning the house, following a low-fat diet). Using the expectancy model, analyze each of your answers to assess why some activities stimulate your effort while others don't.

2. Expectancy theory argues that for people to be motivated, they have to value the rewards that they will receive for their effort. This suggests the need for recognizing individual differences. Does this view contradict the principles of equity theory? Discuss.

3. To what extent will you be motivated to study under the following circumstances:

    a. The instructor gives only one test—a final examination at the end of the course.

    b. The instructor gives four exams during the term, all of which are announced on the first day of class.

    c. The student's grade is based on the results of numerous exams, none of which are announced by the instructor ahead of time.

4. "The cognitive evaluation theory is contradictory to reinforcement and expectancy theories." Do you agree or disagree? Explain

5. Analyze the application of Maslow's and Herzberg's theories to an African or Caribbean nation where more than a quarter of the population is unemployed.

OB for You

- Don't think of motivation as something that should be done for you. Think about motivating others and yourself as well. How can you motivate yourself? After finishing a particularly long and dry chapter in a text, you could take a snack break. Or you might buy yourself a new CD once that major accounting assignment is finished.

- Be aware of the kinds of things that motivate you, so you can choose jobs and activities that suit you best.

- When working in a group, keep in mind that you and the other members can think of ways to make sure everyone feels motivated throughout the project.

POINT

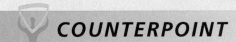

COUNTERPOINT

Professional Employees Are More Difficult to Motivate

Professional employees are different from your average employees. They are also more difficult to motivate. Why? Because professionals don't respond to the same stimuli that nonprofessionals do.

Professionals like engineers, accountants, lawyers, nurses, and software designers are different from non-professionals. They have a strong and long-term commitment to their field of expertise. Typical rewards, like money and promotions, are rarely effective in encouraging professionals to exert high levels of effort.

Professionals see their allegiance to their profession, not to the organization that employs them. A nurse, for instance, may work for Mercy Hospital, but she reads nursing journals, belongs to nursing associations, attends nursing conferences, and hangs around with other nurses during her breaks at work. When asked what she does for a living, she's more apt to respond, "I'm a registered nurse" than "I work at Mercy Hospital."

Money and promotions are typically low on the professional's priority list. Why? Because they tend to be well paid already and they enjoy what they do. For instance, professionals are not typically anxious to give up their work to take on managerial responsibilities. They have invested a great deal of time and effort in developing their professional skills. They have typically gone to professional schools for several years and undergone specialized training to build their proficiencies. They also invest regularly—in terms of reading, taking courses, attending conferences, and the like—to keep their skills current. Moving into management often means cutting their ties to their profession, losing touch with the latest advances in their field, and having to let the skills that they have spent years developing become obsolete.

This loyalty to the profession and less interest in typical organizational rewards makes motivating professionals more challenging and complex. They don't respond to traditional rewards. Because they tend to give their primary allegiance to their profession rather than to their employer, they are more likely to quit if they are dissatisfied. As an employer, you might be justified in deciding not to exert the effort to develop and keep professionals because they are unlikely to reciprocate the loyalty efforts you make.

Professional Employees Are Easier to Motivate

Let's first address the question of whether professionals with advanced degrees are really that different from non-professionals. One of the differences often cited regarding professionals is their allegiance to their profession. But this isn't unique to the so-called degreed professionals. For instance, plumbers, electricians, and similar trades-people aren't considered professionals, but they typically see themselves as affiliated to their trade or union rather than to their employer. Similarly, many auto workers at Ford and GM give their primary allegiance to the Canadian Auto Workers union.

Even if you accept that professionals are different from nonprofessionals, these differences may make it easier to motivate professionals rather than harder. For a large proportion of professionals, their work is their life. They rarely define their workweek in terms of 8 to 5 and five days a week. Working 60 hours a week or more is often common. They love what they do and often prefer to be working rather than doing anything else. So as long as they enjoy their work, they are likely to be self-motivated.

What factors are likely to determine if professionals enjoy their work? Job challenge tends to be ranked high. They like to tackle problems and find solutions. They prefer jobs that score high on the job characteristics model; that is, they want jobs that provide variety, identity, significance, autonomy, and feedback. Professionals also value support, recognition, and opportunities to improve and expand their professional expertise.

So how do you motivate professionals? Provide them with ongoing challenging projects. Give them autonomy to follow their interests, and allow them to structure their work in ways that they find productive. Provide them with lateral moves that allow them to broaden their experience. Reward them with educational opportunities—training, workshops, attending conferences—that allow them to keep current in their field. In addition, reward them with recognition. As well, consider creating alternative career paths that allow them to earn more money and status, without assuming managerial responsibilities. At Merck, IBM, and AT&T, for instance, the best scientists, engineers, and researchers gain titles such as fellow and senior scientists. They carry pay and prestige comparable to those of managers without the corresponding authority or responsibility.

HR IMPLICATIONS

Performance Evaluation

This chapter has demonstrated that there are a variety of incentives to encourage employees to perform in accordance with an organization's goals. One of the roles of the HR specialist in an organization is to determine how to actually evaluate that performance. We remind you that the use of performance appraisals should be carefully considered, and care should also be used in ensuring that the purpose of performance appraisals is understood by employees. Watson Wyatt Worldwide, an international consulting firm, recently surveyed employees from a variety of industrial sectors and found that many employees distrusted the performance appraisal process.[84] This is not surprising, considering that University of Toronto management professor Maria Rotundo found in her study of 504 North American managers that "Two employees may engage in the same behaviour on the job, yet receive completely different ratings of their performance depending on who their rater is."[85] Key findings of the Watson Wyatt survey are as follows:[86]

- In all, 70 percent of employees do not believe the performance appraisal process helps them improve their performance.

- Less than 40 percent say their company has clear performance goals.

- Only 39 percent of employees see the connection between their day-to-day work and company goals.

- Only 44 percent feel that people are held accountable for their performance.

Unfortunately, much research indicates that performance appraisals have not been particularly good at either developing or motivating people.[87] Often appraisals try to do too many things: serving as both feedback and information about raises. Below we describe the performance appraisal process to illustrate ways that individual resistance to the process might be lessened.

Performance Evaluation and Motivation

A vital component of the expectancy model is performance, specifically the effort-performance and performance-reward linkages.

The expectancy model can help us understand how performance evaluation might affect an individual's motivation. Specifically, the theory implies that to maximize motivation, people need to perceive that the effort they exert leads to a favourable performance evaluation, and that the favourable evaluation will lead to the rewards that they value.

Following the expectancy model of motivation, we can expect individuals to work considerably below their potential under the following circumstances: (1) if the objectives that employees are expected to achieve are unclear; (2) if the criteria for measuring those objectives are vague; (3) if the employees lack confidence that their efforts will lead to a satisfactory appraisal of their performance; and/or (4) if employees believe that there will be an unsatisfactory payoff by the organization when their performance objectives are achieved.

What Do We Evaluate?

Performance appraisal is not easy to do, and many managers do it poorly. Both managers and employees often dread the appraisal process. A recent survey found that 41 percent of employees report having had a least one incident of being demotivated after feedback from their manager.[88] Performance appraisal can also be subject to politics, not unlike the 2000 Olympics ice skating controversy where the French judge was accused of manipulating her scores to allow the Russian skaters to win the gold medal over Jamie Salé and David Pelletier.

Management's choice of criteria or a criterion to evaluate when appraising employee performance will have a major influence on what employees do. Two examples illustrate this point.

In a public employment agency, which served workers seeking employment and employers seeking workers, employment interviewers were appraised by the *number* of interviews they conducted. Consistent with the thesis that the evaluating criteria influence behaviour, interviewers emphasized the number of interviews conducted rather than the *placements* of clients in jobs.[89]

A management consultant specializing in police research noticed that, in one community, officers would come on duty for their shift, proceed to get into their police cars, drive to the highway that cut through the town, and speed back and forth along that highway for their entire shift. Clearly this fast cruising had little to do with good police work, but this behaviour made considerably more sense once the consultant learned that the community's city council used kilometrage on police vehicles as an evaluative measure of police effectiveness.[90]

These examples demonstrate the importance of criteria in performance evaluation. This, of course, begs the question, What should management evaluate? The three most popular sets of criteria are individual task outcomes, behaviours, and traits.

Individual Task Outcomes If ends count, rather than means, then management should evaluate an employee's task outcomes. Using task outcomes, a plant manager could be judged on criteria such as quantity produced, scrap generated, and cost per unit of production. Similarly, a salesperson could be assessed on overall sales volume in his or her territory, dollar increase in sales, and number of new accounts established.

Behaviours In many cases, it's difficult to identify specific outcomes that can be directly attributable to an employee's actions. This is particularly true of employees in staff positions, and individuals whose work assignments are intrinsically part of a group effort. In the latter case, the group's performance may be readily evaluated, but the contribution of each group member may be difficult or impossible to identify clearly. In such instances, it is not unusual for management to evaluate the employee's behaviour. Drawing on the previous examples, behaviours of a plant manager that could be used for performance evaluation purposes might include promptness in submitting his or her monthly reports, or the leadership style that the manager exhibits. Pertinent salesperson behaviours could be average number of contact calls made per day or sick days used per year.

Note that these behaviours need not be limited to those directly related to individual productivity.[91] As we pointed out in our previous discussion on organizational citizenship behaviour (see specifically Chapters 1 and 3), helping others, making suggestions for improvements, and volunteering for extra duties make work groups and organizations more effective. So including subjective or contextual factors in a performance evaluation—as long as they contribute to organizational effectiveness—may not only make sense, they may also improve coordination, teamwork, cooperation, and overall organizational performance.

Traits The weakest set of criteria, yet one that is still widely used by organizations, is individual traits.[92] We say such traits are weaker than either task outcomes or behaviours because they are furthest removed from the actual performance of the job itself. Traits such as having "a good attitude," showing "confidence," being "dependable" or "cooperative," "looking busy," or possessing "a wealth of experience" may or may not be highly correlated with positive task outcomes, but only the naive would ignore the reality that such traits are frequently used in organizations as criteria for assessing an employee's level of performance.

Who Should Do the Evaluating?

Who should evaluate an employee's performance? The obvious answer would seem to be his or her immediate manager! By tradition, a manager's authority has typically included appraising employees' performances. The logic behind this tradition seems to be that since managers are held responsible for their employees' performances, it only makes sense that these managers evaluate that performance. But that logic may be flawed. Others may actually be able to do the job better.

Immediate Manager While an employee's immediate boss was once the most popular source of evaluations, this is no longer true, largely because it has several major limitations. For instance, many managers feel unqualified to evaluate the unique contributions of each of their employees. Others resent being asked to "play God" with their employees' careers. Additionally, many of today's organizations are using self-managed teams, telecommuting, and other organizing devices that distance managers from their employees. For this reason, an employee's immediate manager may not be a reliable judge of that employee's performance.

Peers Peer evaluations are one of the most reliable sources of appraisal data. Why? First, peers are close to the action. Daily interactions provide them with a comprehensive view of an employee's job performance. Second, using peers as raters results in a number of independent judgments. A boss can offer only a single evaluation, but peers can provide multiple appraisals. The average of several ratings is often more reliable than a single evaluation. On the downside, peer evaluations can suffer from co-workers' unwillingness to evaluate one another and from biases based on friendship or animosity.

Self-Evaluation Having employees evaluate their own performance is consistent with values such as self-management and empowerment. Self-evaluations get high marks from employees themselves; they tend to lessen employees' defensiveness about the appraisal process; and they make excellent vehicles for stimulating job performance discussions between employees and their managers. This point helps explain their increased popularity. For instance, a recent survey found that about half of executives and 53 percent of employees now have input into their performance evaluations.[93]

As you might guess, self-evaluations suffer from over-inflated assessment and self-serving bias. Moreover, they are often low in agreement with managers' ratings.[94] There is some evidence that women are more likely to underestimate their performance than men. In addition, with increasing diversity in the workplace, there are some cultural differences in how self-evaluation might be handled. Because of these serious drawbacks, self-evaluations are probably better suited to developmental uses than evaluative purposes, or combined with other sources to reduce rating errors.

Immediate Subordinates A fourth judgment source is an employee's immediate subordinates. Its proponents argue that eliciting these opinions is consistent with recent trends toward enhancing honesty, openness, and empowerment in the workplace.

Immediate subordinates' evaluations can provide accurate and detailed information about a manager's behaviour because the evaluators typically have frequent contact with the evaluatee. The obvious problem with this form of rating is fear of reprisal from managers given unfavourable evaluations. Therefore, respondent anonymity is crucial if these evaluations are to be accurate.

360-Degree Evaluations The latest approach to performance evaluation is the use of 360-degree evaluations.[95] They provide performance feedback from the full circle of daily contacts that an employee might have, ranging from mailroom workers to customers to managers to peers (see Exhibit 4-13). The number of appraisals can be as few as 3 or 4 evaluations, or as many as 25; most organizations collect 5 to 10 per employee.

What's the appeal of 360-degree evaluations? They fit well into organizations that have introduced teams, employee involvement, and Total Quality Management (TQM) programs. By relying on feedback from co-workers, customers, and employees, these organizations are hoping to give everyone more of a sense of participation in the review process and gain more accurate readings on employee performance. On this latter point, 360-degree evaluations are consistent with evidence that employee performance varies across contexts and that people behave differently with different constituencies.[96] The use of multiple sources, therefore, is more likely to capture this variety of behaviour accurately.

The evidence on the effectiveness of 360-degree evaluations is mixed.[97] It provides employees with a wider perspective of their performance. However, when it is used as simple feedback, the ratings from employees and

---

EXHIBIT 4-13 360-Degree Evaluations

The primary objective of the 360-degree performance evaluation is to pool feedback from all of the employee's customers

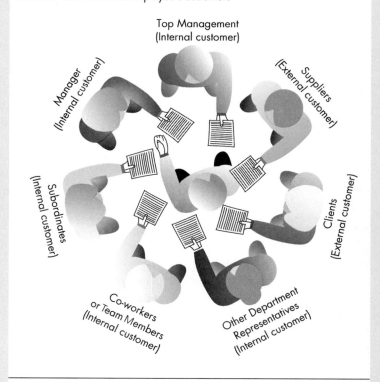

Source: J. F. Milliman, R. A. Zawacki, C. Norman, L. Powell, and J. Kirksey, "Companies Evaluate Employees From All Perspectives," *Personnel Journal,* November 1994, p. 100.

peers are different than when it is used as evidence for performance evaluation.[98] Moreover, others have found that when managers received lower ratings, they tended to discount the feedback,[99] which might suggest that those most likely to need feedback will be least likely to pay attention to it.

This type of feedback has the potential for being misused. For instance, to minimize costs, many organizations don't spend the time to train evaluators in how to give constructive criticism. Other problems include the potential for receiving artificially inflated feedback when employees choose the peers and subordinates they want to evaluate them, and the difficulty of reconciling disagreements and contradictions between rater groups. Managers using 360-degree appraisals and feedback also have to carefully consider the pros and cons of using anonymous evaluations.[100]

Of the 101 large Canadian organizations surveyed by professors Mehrdad Debrayen and Stephane Brutus of the John Molson School of Business at Concordia University, 43 percent used 360-degree feedback.[101] Sixty percent of the *PROFIT* 100 Canada's Fastest Growing Companies for 2005 also use this feedback.[102] Toronto-based Hill and Knowlton, a public relations firm, uses 360-degree feedback to help employees learn what they need to get to the next level of the organization. The feedback has had the added benefit of reducing turnover to 18 percent.[103]

Methods of Performance Evaluation

The previous sections explained *what* we evaluate and *who* should be the evaluating. Now we ask: *How* do we evaluate an employee's performance? That is, what are the specific techniques for evaluation? This section reviews the major performance evaluation methods.

Written Essays Probably the simplest method of evaluation is to write a narrative describing an employee's strengths, weaknesses, past performance, potential, and suggestions for improvement. The written essay requires no complex forms or extensive training to complete. But the results often reflect the ability of the writer. A good or bad appraisal may be determined as much by the evaluator's writing skill as by the employee's actual level of performance.

Critical Incidents Critical incidents focus the evaluator's attention on those behaviours that are key in making the difference between executing a job effectively and executing it ineffectively. That is, the appraiser writes down anec-

dotes that describe what the employee did that was especially effective or ineffective. The key here is that only specific behaviours, not vaguely defined personality traits, are cited. A list of critical incidents provides a rich set of examples from which the employee can be shown those behaviours that are desirable and those that call for improvement.

Graphic Rating Scales One of the oldest and most popular methods of evaluation is the use of graphic rating scales. In this method, a set of performance factors, such as quantity and quality of work, depth of knowledge, cooperation, loyalty, attendance, honesty, and initiative, is listed. The evaluator then goes down the list and rates each on incremental scales. The scales typically specify 5 points, so a factor such as job knowledge might be rated 1 ("poorly informed about work duties") to 5 ("has complete mastery of all phases of the job").

Why are graphic rating scales so popular? Though they don't provide the depth of information that essays or critical incidents do, they are less time-consuming to develop and administer. They also allow for quantitative analysis and comparison.

Behaviourally Anchored Rating Scales Behaviourally anchored rating scales (BARS) combine major elements from the critical incident and graphic rating scale approaches: The appraiser rates the employees based on items along a continuum, but the points are examples of actual behaviour on the given job rather than general descriptions or traits.

BARS specify definite, observable, and measurable job behaviour. Examples of job-related behaviour and performance dimensions are found by asking participants to give specific illustrations of effective and ineffective behaviour regarding each performance dimension. These behavioural examples are then translated into a set of performance dimensions, each dimension having varying levels of performance. The results of this process are behavioural descriptions, such as *anticipates, plans, executes, solves immediate problems, carries out orders,* and *handles emergency situations*.

Forced Comparisons Forced comparisons evaluate one individual's performance against the performance of one or more others. They are a relative rather than an absolute measuring device. The three most popular comparisons are group order ranking, individual ranking, and paired comparisons.

The *group order ranking* requires the evaluator to place employees into a particular classification, such as top one-fifth or second one-fifth. This method is often used in recommending students to graduate schools. Evaluators are asked whether the student ranks in the top 5 percent of the class, the next 5 percent, the next 15 percent, and so forth. When managers use this system to appraise employees, they deal with all their employees. Therefore, if a rater has 20 employees, only 4 can be in the top fifth and, of course, 4 must also be relegated to the bottom fifth.

The *individual ranking* approach rank-orders employees from best to worst. If the manager is required to appraise 30 employees, this approach assumes that the difference between the 1st and 2nd employee is the same as that between the 21st and 22nd. Even though some of the employees may be closely grouped, this approach allows for no ties. The result is a clear ordering of employees, from the highest performer down to the lowest.

Multiperson comparisons can be combined with one of the other methods to blend the best from both absolute and relative standards. For example, recent studies of Ivy League universities have found widespread evidence of grade inflation.[104] In one recent year, 46 percent of all undergraduate grades at Harvard were As. At Princeton, 43 percent of all undergraduate grades were As, with only 12 percent below the B range. One way for these universities to deal with this problem would be to require instructors to include not only an absolute letter grade but also relative data on class size and rank. So a prospective employer or graduate school could look at two students who each got an "A" in their physical geology courses and draw considerably different conclusions about each because next to one grade it says "ranked 2nd out of 26," while the other says "ranked 14th out of 30." Obviously, the former student performed better, relatively, than did the latter.

Potential Problems

While organizations may seek to make the performance evaluation process free from personal biases, prejudices, and idiosyncrasies, a number of potential problems can creep into the process. To the degree that the following factors are prevalent, an employee's evaluation is likely to be distorted.

Single Criterion The typical employee's job is made up of a number of tasks. A flight attendant's job, for example, includes welcoming passengers, seeing to their comfort, serving meals, and offering safety advice. If performance on this job were assessed by a single crite-

rion measure—say, the time it took to provide food and beverages to 100 passengers—the result would be a limited evaluation of that job. More important, flight attendants whose performance evaluation included assessment on only this single criterion would be motivated to ignore the other tasks in their job. Similarly, if a football quarterback were appraised only on his percentage of completed passes, he would be likely to throw short passes and only in situations where he felt assured that they would be caught. Our point is that where employees are evaluated on a single job criterion, and where successful performance on that job requires good performance on a number of criteria, employees will emphasize the single criterion to the exclusion of other job-relevant factors.

Recency Effect A month before the annual performance appraisal, an employee has a spectacular sales success. Or an employee has the worst month of performance on record. Because these events happened shortly before the performance appraisal was due, some managers may give undue weight to these events. This is known as the recency effect, which means that undue weight is given to the most recent events that have occurred. Managers are supposed to give equal weight to the employee's performance during the entire year, but it is often difficult for them to keep track of everything an employee does. Therefore, the manager may rely too heavily on recent events that may not even be representative of the employee's performance overall.

Leniency Error Every evaluator has his or her own value system that acts as a standard against which appraisals are made. Relative to the true or actual performance an individual exhibits, some evaluators mark high and others low. The former is referred to as positive leniency error, and the latter as negative leniency error. When evaluators are positively lenient in their appraisal, an individual's performance becomes overstated, that is, rated higher than it actually should be. This results in inflated evaluations, a problem widely acknowledged to exist in North American organizations.[105] A negative leniency error understates performance, giving the individual a lower appraisal than deserved.

If all individuals in an organization were appraised by the same person, there would be no problem. Although there would be an error factor, it would be applied equally to everyone. The difficulty arises when we have different raters with different leniency errors making judgments. For example, assume that Jones and Smith are performing the same job for different managers, but they have absolutely identical job performance. If Jones' manager tends to err toward positive leniency, while Smith's manager errs toward negative leniency, we might be confronted with two dramatically different evaluations.

Halo Effect The halo effect, as we noted in Chapter 2, is the tendency for an evaluator to let the assessment of an individual on one trait influence his or her evaluation of that person on other traits. For example, if an employee tends to be dependable, we might become biased toward that individual to the extent that we will rate him or her high on many desirable attributes.[106]

People who design teaching appraisal forms for university students to fill out to evaluate the effectiveness of their instructors each semester must confront the halo effect. Students tend to rate a faculty member as outstanding on all criteria when they are particularly appreciative of a few things he or she does in the classroom. Similarly, such habits as being slow in returning papers or assigning an extremely demanding reading requirement might result in students' evaluating the instructor as "lousy" across the board.

Similarity Error When evaluators give special consideration to those qualities in other people that they perceive in themselves, they are making a similarity error. For example, evaluators who perceive themselves as aggressive may evaluate others by looking for aggressiveness. Those who demonstrate this characteristic tend to benefit, while others are penalized.[107]

Again, this error would tend to wash out if the same evaluator appraised all the people in the organization. However, interrater reliability obviously suffers when various evaluators are using their own similarity criteria.

Low Differentiation It's possible that, regardless of whom the appraiser evaluates and what traits are used, the pattern of evaluation remains the same. It has been suggested that evaluators may be classified as (1) high differentiators, who use all or most of the scale; or (2) low differentiators, who use a limited range of the scale.[108]

Low differentiators tend to ignore or suppress differences, perceiving the universe as being more uniform than it really is. High differentiators, on the other hand, tend to utilize all available information to the utmost extent and thus are better able to perceptually define anomalies and contradictions than are low differentiators.[109]

This finding tells us that evaluations made by low differentiators need to be carefully inspected and that the people working for a low differentiator have a high probability of being appraised as being significantly more homogeneous than they really are.

Forcing Information to Match Nonperformance Criteria Although rarely advocated, it is not an infrequent practice to find the formal evaluation taking place *following* the decision as to how the individual has been performing. This may sound illogical, but it merely recognizes that subjective, yet formal, decisions are often arrived at before the gathering of objective information to support those decisions.[110] For example, if the evaluator believes that the evaluation should not be based on performance, but rather on seniority, he or she may be unknowingly adjusting each "performance" evaluation so as to bring it into line with the employee's seniority rank. In this and other similar cases, the evaluator is increasing or decreasing performance appraisals to align with the nonperformance criteria actually being utilized.

So how do these biases occur? One review of 24 studies of performance appraisals found that when supervisors felt more positive toward their employees, they were more likely to be lenient in their ratings, more prone to halo effects, were less accurate in their reviews, and less inclined to punish poor performance.[111]

Overcoming the Problems

Just because organizations can encounter problems with performance evaluations, managers should not give up on the process. Some things can be done to overcome most of the problems we have identified.[112] Performance appraisals seem to be less affected by bias when managers follow clear standards and have more closely observed the performance of subordinates.[113] Below we outline some of the most useful approaches.

Emphasize Behaviours Rather than Traits Many traits that are often considered to be related to good performance may, in fact, have little or no performance relationship. For example, loyalty, initiative, courage, reliability, and self-expression are intuitively appealing as desirable characteristics in employees. But the relevant question is this: Are individuals who are evaluated as high on those traits higher performers than those who rate low? We cannot answer this question easily. We know that there are employees who rate high on these characteristics and are poor performers. We can find others who are excellent performers but do not score well on traits such as these. Our conclusion is that traits such as loyalty and initiative may be prized by managers, but there is no evidence that certain traits will be adequate synonyms for performance in a large cross-section of jobs.

Another weakness of trait evaluation is the judgment itself. What is "loyalty"? When is an employee "reliable"? What you consider "loyalty," I may not. So traits suffer from weak interrater agreement.

Document Performance Behaviours in a Diary Keeping a diary of specific critical incidents for each employee tends to make evaluations more accurate.[114] Diaries, for instance, tend to reduce leniency and halo effects because they encourage the evaluator to focus on performance-related behaviours rather than traits. Appropriate documentation may also be useful for legal questions that may arise when an employee is dismissed due to poor performance. Most important, it is good to establish an ongoing routine to record behaviours at regular intervals.

Use Multiple Evaluators As the number of evaluators increases, the probability of attaining more accurate information increases. If rater error tends to follow a normal curve, an increase in the number of appraisers will tend to find the majority congregating about the middle. You see this approach being used in athletic competitions in such sports as diving and gymnastics. A set of evaluators judges a performance, the highest and lowest scores are dropped, and the final performance evaluation is made up from the cumulative scores of those remaining. The logic of multiple evaluators applies to organizations as well.

If an employee has had 10 managers, 9 having rated her excellent and 1 poor, we can discount the value of the 1 poor evaluation. Therefore, by moving employees about within the organization so as to gain a number of evaluations or by using multiple assessors (as provided in 360-degree appraisals), we increase the probability of achieving more valid and reliable evaluations.

Evaluate Selectively Appraisers should evaluate in only those areas in which they have some expertise.[115] If raters make evaluations on only those dimensions on which they are in a good position to rate, we increase the interrater agreement and make the evaluation a more valid process. This approach also recognizes that different organizational levels often have different orientations toward ratees and observe them in different settings. In general, therefore, we would recommend that appraisers should be as close as possible, in terms of organizational level, to the individual being evaluated. Conversely, the more levels that separate the evaluator and evaluatee, the less opportunity the evaluator has to observe the individual's behaviour and, not surprisingly, the greater the possibility for inaccuracies.

Train Evaluators If you cannot find good evaluators, the alternative is to make good evaluators. There is substantial evidence that training evaluators can make them more accurate raters.[116]

Common errors such as the halo effect and leniency have been minimized or eliminated in workshops where managers practise observing and rating behaviours. These workshops typically run from one to three days, but allocating many hours to training may not always be necessary. One case has been cited where both halo and leniency errors were decreased immediately after exposing evaluators to explanatory training sessions lasting only five minutes.[117] But the effects of training do appear to diminish over time.[118] This suggests the need for regular refresher sessions.

Provide Employees With Due Process The concept of due process can be applied to appraisals to increase the perception that employees are treated fairly.[119] Three features characterize due-process systems: (1) Individuals are provided with adequate notice of what is expected of them; (2) all relevant evidence to a proposed violation is aired in a fair hearing so individuals affected can respond; and (3) the final decision is based on the evidence and free from bias.

There is considerable evidence that evaluation systems often violate employees' due process by providing them with infrequent and relatively general performance feedback, allowing them little input into the appraisal process, and knowingly introducing bias into performance ratings. However, where due process has been part of the evaluation system, employees report positive reactions to the appraisal process, perceive the evaluation results as more accurate, and express increased intent to remain with the organization.

OB *AT WORK*

What Motivates You?

Circle the number that most closely agrees with how you feel. Consider your answers in the context of your current job or a past work experience.

		Strongly Disagree				Strongly Agree
1.	I try very hard to improve on my past performance at work.	1	2	3	4	5
2.	I enjoy competition and winning.	1	2	3	4	5
3.	I often find myself talking to those around me about nonwork matters.	1	2	3	4	5
4.	I enjoy a difficult challenge.	1	2	3	4	5
5.	I enjoy being in charge.	1	2	3	4	5
6.	I want to be liked by others.	1	2	3	4	5
7.	I want to know how I am progressing as I complete tasks.	1	2	3	4	5
8.	I confront people who do things I disagree with.	1	2	3	4	5
9.	I tend to build close relationships with co-workers.	1	2	3	4	5
10.	I enjoy setting and achieving realistic goals.	1	2	3	4	5
11.	I enjoy influencing other people to get my way.	1	2	3	4	5
12.	I enjoy belonging to groups and organizations.	1	2	3	4	5
13.	I enjoy the satisfaction of completing a difficult task.	1	2	3	4	5
14.	I often work to gain more control over the events around me.	1	2	3	4	5
15.	I enjoy working with others more than working alone.	1	2	3	4	5

Scoring Key:

To determine your dominant needs—and what motivates you—place the number 1 through 5 that represents your score for each statement next to the number for that statement.

Achievement	Power	Affiliation
1. _____	2. _____	3. _____
4. _____	5. _____	6. _____
7. _____	8. _____	9. _____
10. _____	11. _____	12. _____
13. _____	14. _____	15. _____
Totals: _____	_____	_____

Add up the total of each column. The sum of the numbers in each column will be between 5 and 25 points. The column with the highest score tells you your dominant need.

Source: Based on R. Steers and D. Braunstein, "A Behaviorally Based Measure of Manifest Needs in Work Settings," *Journal of Vocational Behavior,* October 1976, p. 254; and R. N. Lussier, *Human Relations in Organizations: A Skill Building Approach* (Homewood, IL: Richard D. Irwin, 1990), p. 120.

BREAKOUT **GROUP** EXERCISES

Form small groups to discuss the following topics, as assigned by your instructor:

1. One of the members of your team continually arrives late for meetings and does not turn drafts of assignments in on time. Choose one of the available theories and indicate how the theory explains the member's current behaviour and how the theory could be used to motivate the group member to perform more responsibly.

2. You are unhappy with the performance of one of your instructors and would like to encourage the instructor to present more lively classes. Choose one of the available theories and indicate how the theory explains the instructor's current behaviour. How could you as a student use the theory to motivate the instructor to present more lively classes?

3. Harvard University recently changed its grading policy to recommend to instructors that the average course mark should be a B. This was the result of a study showing that more than 50 percent of students were receiving an A or A– for coursework. Harvard students are often referred to as "the best and the brightest," and they pay $27 000 (US) for their education, so they expect high grades. Discuss the impact of this change in policy on the motivation of Harvard students to study harder.

WORKING WITH **OTHERS** EXERCISE

Positive Reinforcement vs. Punishment

This 10-step exercise takes approximately 20 minutes.

Exercise Overview (Steps 1–4)

1. Two volunteers are selected to receive reinforcement or punishment from the class while performing a particular task. The volunteers leave the room.

2. The instructor identifies an object for the student volunteers to locate when they return to the room. (The object should be unobstructed but clearly visible to the class. Examples that have worked well include a small triangular piece of paper that was left behind when a notice was torn off a classroom bulletin board, a smudge on the chalkboard, and a chip in the plaster of a classroom wall.)

3. The instructor specifies the actions that will be in effect when the volunteers return to the room. For punishment, students should hiss or boo when the first volunteer is moving away from the object. For positive reinforcement, they should cheer and applaud when the second volunteer is getting closer to the object.

4. The instructor should assign a student to keep a record of the time it takes each of the volunteers to locate the object.

Volunteer 1 (Steps 5 and 6)

5. Volunteer 1 is brought back into the room and is told, "Your task is to locate and touch a particular object in the room and the class has agreed to help you. You cannot use words or ask questions. Begin."

6. Volunteer 1 continues to look for the object until it is found, while the class engages in the punishing behaviour.

Volunteer 2 (Steps 7 and 8)

7. Volunteer 2 is brought back into the room and is told, "Your task is to locate and touch a particular object in the room and the class has agreed to help you. You cannot use words or ask questions. Begin."

8. Volunteer 2 continues to look for the object until it is found, while the class assists by giving positive reinforcement.

Class Review (Steps 9 and 10)

9. The timekeeper will present the results on how long it took each volunteer to find the object.

10. The class will discuss the following: What was the difference in behaviour of the two volunteers? What are the implications of this exercise for shaping behaviour in organizations?

Source: Adapted from an exercise developed by Larry Michaelson of the University of Oklahoma. With permission.

ETHICAL **DILEMMA** EXERCISE

Is Motivation Manipulation?

Managers are interested in the subject of motivation because they are concerned with learning how to get the most effort from their employees. Is this ethical? For example, when managers link rewards to productivity, aren't they manipulating employees?

"To manipulate" is defined as "(1) to handle, manage, or use, especially with skill, in some process of treatment or performance; (2) to manage or influence by artful skill; (3) to adapt or change to suit one's purpose or advantage."

Aren't one or more of these definitions compatible with the notion of managers skillfully seeking to influence employee productivity for the benefit of the manager and the organization?

Do managers have the right to seek control over their employees? Does anyone, for that matter, have the right to control others? Does control imply manipulation? Is there anything wrong with managers manipulating employees?

CASE INCIDENTS

Frustrated at Age 32

Bob Wood is 32. But if you listened to him, you would think he was 65 and washed up. "I graduated from university at a great time. It was 1996. I started as an analyst for Accenture, worked as a health care IT consultant for two other firms, and then became chief technology officer at Claimshop.com, a medical claims processor." By 2001, Bob was making $80 000 a year plus bonus, driving an expensive European sports car, and optimistic about his future. But Bob Wood has become a statistic. He's one of the Canadians born between 1966 and 1975 whose peak earnings may be behind them. Bob now makes $44 000 as a technology analyst at a hospital and is trying

to adjust to the fact that the go-go years of the late 1990s are history.

Like many of his generation, Bob is mired in debt. He owes $23 000 on his university loans and has run up more than $4500 on his credit cards. He faces a world very different from the one his father found when he graduated college in the early 1960s.

"The rules have changed. And we Generation Xers are getting hit hard. We had to go to university to get a decent job. But the majority of us graduated with tuition debt. The good news was that when we graduated, the job market was great. I got a $5000 hiring bonus on my first job! The competition by employers for good people drove salaries up. When I was 28, I was making more money than my dad, who had been with the same company for over 20 years. But my dad has job security. And he has a nice retirement plan that will pay him a guaranteed pension when he turns 58. Now look at me. I don't know if I'll ever make $80 000 again. If I do, it'll be in 20 or more years. I have no job security. I'm paying $350 a month on my university loans. I'm paying another $250 in payments on my BMW. And my girlfriend says it's time for us to settle down and get married. It would be nice to own a house, but how can I commit myself to a 30-year mortgage when I don't know if I'll have a job in six months?"

"I'm very frustrated. I feel like my generation got a bad deal. We initially got great jobs with unrealistically high pay. I admit it; we were spoiled. We got used to working one job for six months, quitting, then taking another and getting ourselves a 25 or 30 percent raise. We thought we'd be rich and retired by 40. The truth is that we're now lucky to have a job and, if we do, it probably pays half what we were making a few years ago. We have no job security. The competition for jobs, combined with pressures by business to keep costs down, means a future with minimal salary increases. It is pretty weird to be only 32 years old and to have your best years behind you!"

Questions

1. Analyze Bob using Maslow's hierarchy of needs.

2. Analyze Bob's lack of motivation using equity theory and expectancy theory.

3. If you were Bob's boss, what could you do to positively influence his motivation?

4. What are the implications of this case for employers hiring Generation Xers?

Source: Ideas for this case are based on N. Watson, "Generation Wrecked," *Fortune,* October 14, 2002, pp. 183–190.

Wage Reduction Proposal

The following proposal was made to employees of Montreal-based Quebecor's Vidéotron cable division:

> *Employees are asked to increase the number of hours worked per week to 40 from 35, while receiving the same pay as working the shorter work week. In addition, they are asked to accept less paid holiday time.*

Quebecor spokesman Luc Lavoie justified the request made to the employees by saying: "They have the richest work contract in the country, including eight weeks of holiday and high absenteeism."

The company made it clear that if this proposal were not accepted, it would sell its cable television and Internet installation and repair operations to Entourage Technology Solutions.

The employees, members of Canadian Union of Public Employees (CUPE) Local 2815, were reluctant to agree to these conditions. If they accepted, 300 to 400 employees were likely to be laid off, and the company could still consider outsourcing the work later.

Questions

1. Analyze this proposal in terms of motivation concepts.

2. As an employee, how would you respond if you received this proposal?

3. If you were the executive vice-president of the company and a number of your non-unionized employees asked you for a holiday cash gift, would you have responded differently? Why or why not?

Sources: "Quebecor Plays Hardball With Defiant Union: Videotron 'Ready to Listen': Aims to Sell Cable Installation Operations," *Financial Post (National Post),* March 5, 2002, p. FP6; and S. Silcoff, "Quebecor and Union in Showdown Over Costs," *Financial Post (National Post),* February 28, 2002, p. FP3.

From **Concepts**
to **Skills**

Setting Goals

You can be more effective at setting goals if you use the following eight suggestions:

1. *Identify your key tasks.* Goal setting begins by defining what it is that you want to accomplish.

2. *Establish specific and challenging goals for each key task.* Identify the level of performance expected. Specify the target toward which you will work.

3. *Specify the deadlines for each goal.* Putting deadlines on each goal reduces ambiguity. Deadlines, however, should not be set arbitrarily. Rather, they need to be realistic given the tasks to be completed.

4. *Allow the employee to participate actively.* When employees participate in goal setting, they are more likely to accept the goals. However, it must be sincere participation. That is, employees must perceive that you are truly seeking their input, not just going through the motions.

5. *Prioritize goals.* When you have more than one goal, it's important for you to rank the goals in order of importance. The purpose of prioritizing is to encourage you to take action and expend effort on each goal in proportion to its importance.

6. *Rate goals for difficulty and importance.* Goal setting should not encourage people to choose easy goals. Instead, goals should be rated for their difficulty and importance. When goals are rated, individuals can be given credit for trying difficult goals, even if they don't fully achieve them.

7. *Build in feedback mechanisms to assess goal progress.* Feedback lets you know whether your level of effort is sufficient to attain the goal. Feedback should be frequent and recurring.

8. *Link rewards to goal attainment.* Linking rewards to the achievement of goals will help motivate you.

Source: Based on S. P. Robbins and D. A. DeCenzo, *Fundamentals of Management,* 4th ed. (Upper Saddle River, NJ: Prentice Hall, 2004), p. 85.

Assessing Skills

After you've read this chapter, take the following Self-Assessments on your enclosed CD-ROM:

10. What Motivates Me?
11. What Are My Dominant Needs?
12. What Rewards Do I Value Most?
13. What's My View on the Nature of People?
14. What Are My Course Performance Goals?
17. How Sensitive Am I to Equity Differences?

Practising Skills

You worked your way through college while holding down a part-time job bagging groceries at the Food Town supermarket chain. You liked working in the food industry, and when you graduated, you accepted a position with Food Town as a management trainee. Three years have passed and you have gained experience in the grocery store industry and in operating a large supermarket. About a year ago, you received a promotion to store manager at one of the chain's locations. One of the things you have liked about Food Town is that it gives store managers a great deal of autonomy in running their stores. The company provides very general guidelines to its managers. Top management is concerned with the bottom line; for the most part, how you get there is up to you. Now that you're finally a store manager, you want to establish an MBO-type program in your store. You like the idea that everyone should have clear goals to work toward and then be evaluated against those goals.

Your store employs 70 people, although except for the managers, most work only 20 to 30 hours per week. You have six people reporting to you: an assistant manager; a weekend manager; and grocery, produce, meat, and bakery managers. The only highly skilled jobs belong to the butchers, who have strict training and regulatory guidelines. Other less-skilled jobs include cashier, shelf stocker, maintenance worker, and grocery bagger.

Specifically describe how you would go about setting goals in your new position. Include examples of goals for the jobs of butcher, cashier, and bakery manager.

Reinforcing Skills

1. Set personal and academic goals you want to achieve by the end of this term. Prioritize and rate them for difficulty.

2. Where do you want to be in five years? Do you have specific five-year goals? Establish three goals you want to achieve in five years. Make sure these goals are specific, challenging, and measurable.

CHAPTER 5
Motivation
in Action

A chocolate store seems the ideal place to work. Does the company need to offer employees anything more than lots of chocolate to motivate them?

1 Is money an important motivator?

2 What does an effective reward system look like?

3 What kinds of mistakes are made in reward systems?

4 Are rewards overrated?

5 How can jobs be designed to increase motivation?

6 How can flexible workplaces increase motivation?

Employees who work for Vancouver-based Purdy's Chocolates, a chocolate manufacturer and retailer, might not be surprised to hear some people would envy their jobs.[1] The employees are paid about 20 percent higher than the industry average, and receive medical and dental benefits. They also get a 30 percent discount on any chocolate they buy.

The company was voted by its 600 employees as a "Best Company to Work for in Canada" in 2002 and 2004, in surveys conducted by Hewitt Associates. Employees report that they love working for the company: Production supervisor Jessie Senghera says, "I wouldn't do anything else, even if anyone asked. It's been a privilege for me." Turnover at the company is low. The average employee has been with the company for nine years, a long time when 58 percent of the employees are retail workers. What makes Purdy's employees so motivated?

In this chapter, we focus on how to apply motivation concepts. We review a number of reward programs and consider whether rewards are overrated. We also discuss how to create more motivating jobs

and workplaces, both of which have been shown to be alternatives to rewards in motivating individuals.

FROM THEORY TO PRACTICE: THE ROLE OF MONEY

The most commonly used reward in organizations is money. As one author notes, "Money is probably the most emotionally meaningful object in contemporary life: only food and sex are its close competitors as common carriers of such strong and diverse feelings, significance, and strivings."[2]

The motivation theories we have presented only give us vague ideas of how money relates to individual motivation. For instance, Theory X suggests that individuals need to be extrinsically motivated. Money is certainly one such extrinsic motivator. According to Maslow's hierarchy of needs, individuals' basic needs must be met, including food, shelter, and safety. Generally, money can be used to satisfy those needs. Herzberg's motivation-hygiene theory, on the other hand, suggests that money (and other extrinsic motivators) are necessary but not sufficient conditions for individuals to be motivated. Process theories are relatively silent about the role of money specifically, indicating more how rewards motivate, without specifying particular types of rewards. Expectancy theory does note that individuals need to value the reward, or it won't be very motivational.

Despite the importance of money in attracting and retaining employees, and rewarding and recognizing them, little attention has been given to individual differences in people's feelings about money.[3] Some studies indicate that money is not the top priority of employees. Professor Graham Lowe at the University of Alberta and a colleague

1 Is money an important motivator?

Purdy's Chocolates
www.purdys.com

conducted a survey of 2500 Canadians and discovered that relationships in the workplace mattered more than pay or benefits when it came to employee satisfaction.[4] One respondent explained, "Of course money is important, but that's not what's going to make you jump out of bed in the morning." Another noted, "Everyone here would take more money and more time off—that's a given. But some of the things that really make the job a good or bad one are your relations with your boss."

A number of studies suggest that there are personality traits and demographic factors that correlate with an individual's attitude toward money.[5] People who value money highly score higher on "attributes like sensation seeking, competitiveness, materialism, and control." People who desire money score higher on self-esteem, need for achievement, and Type A personality measures. Men seem to value money more than women.

What these findings suggest is that when organizations develop reward programs, they need to consider very carefully the importance to the individual of the specific rewards offered. You will find a longer discussion of whether money really motivates in *Point/Counterpoint* on page 191. The *Ethical Dilemma Exercise* on page 196 gives you an intriguing look at the amount of money needed to motivate some Canadian CEOs.

CREATING EFFECTIVE REWARD SYSTEMS

> Purdy's Chocolates is a family-owned business. Charles Flavelle bought the company in 1964, and daughter Karen joined the firm in 1994. She became CEO in 1997. The company tries to preserve a family feeling among employees. Karen believes that treating employees well is the key to having a motivated workforce.[6] "We've worked hard to listen to people, respond to people, to treat people with respect—a lot of the things that are the history of the business and that my father did," she notes.
>
> Purdy's pays its employees higher than the industry average, the company has profit-sharing plans, and it promotes people from within. Experienced managers get higher wages if they serve as training managers, helping newer employees learn the culture of the organization.
>
> The company also has a variety of recognition programs. Employees are recognized for birthdays, moving, getting married, or having children. Employees who reach their five-year anniversary with the company are recognized at an annual luncheon, with out-of-town employees flown in for the event. All of these activities signal to employees that they are valued as important contributors to the company's success. What else can a company do to make sure its employees feel valued?

2 What does an effective reward system look like?

Organizations use specific incentives to motivate individuals, teams, and the entire organization to achieve organizational goals such as productivity, reduced turnover, and leadership effectiveness. These include employee recognition, variable pay, and other programs we describe in the following pages.

Employee Recognition

Expectancy theory tells us that a key component of motivation is the link between performance and reward (that is, having your behaviour recognized). Employee recognition programs cover a wide spectrum of activities. They range from a spontaneous and private "thank you" on up to widely publicized formal programs in which specific types of behaviour are encouraged and the procedures for attaining recognition are clearly identified.[7]

For instance, Aimia Foods, a British bottler of soft drinks and syrups, has a comprehensive recognition program.[8] The central hallway in its production area is lined with "bragging boards," where the accomplishments of various individuals and teams are regularly updated. Monthly awards are presented to people who have been nominated by peers for extraordinary effort on the job. Monthly award winners are eligible for further recognition at an annual off-site meeting for all employees. In contrast, most managers use a far more informal approach. As a case in point, Julia Stewart, former president of Applebee's restaurants, would frequently leave sealed notes on the chairs of employees after everyone had gone home.[9] These notes explained how critical Stewart thought the person's work was or how much she appreciated the completion of a recent project. Stewart also relied heavily on voice mail messages left after office hours to tell employees how appreciative she was for a job well done.

Recognition may not be enough for some jobs, however, as Exhibit 5-1 suggests.

Linking Employee Recognition Programs and Reinforcement Theory

A few years ago, 1500 employees were surveyed in a variety of work settings to find out what they considered to be the most powerful workplace motivator. Their response? Recognition, recognition, and more recognition![10]

Consistent with reinforcement theory, rewarding a behaviour with recognition immediately following that behaviour is likely to encourage its repetition.[11] As previously noted, recognition can take many forms. You can personally congratulate an employee in private for a good job. You can send a handwritten note or an email message acknowledging something positive that the employee has done. For employees with a strong need for social acceptance, you can publicly recognize accomplishments. To enhance group cohesiveness and motivation, you can celebrate team successes. For instance, you can throw a team pizza party to celebrate a team's accomplishments. Or, as illustrated in Exhibit 5-2, you can follow the example of Phoenix Inn Suites, a chain of small hotels. They encourage employees to smile by letting customers identify this desirable behaviour, then recognize those employees who are identified most often with rewards and publicity.

Employee Recognition in Practice

In today's highly competitive global economy, most organizations are under severe cost pressures. That makes recognition programs particularly attractive. Recognizing an employee's superior performance often costs little or no money.

A survey of Canadian firms in 2004 by Hewitt Associates found that 34 percent of companies recognized individual or group achievements with cash or merchandise.[12] Organizations can recognize employees in numerous ways. The *Globe and Mail* awards the Stephen Godfrey Prize for Newsroom Citizenship. Other ways of recognizing performance include sending employees personal thank-you notes or emails for good performance, putting employees on prestigious committees, sending employees for training, and giving an employee an assistant for a day to help clear backlogs.

Employee recognition may reduce turnover in organizations, particularly that of good employees. When executives were asked the reasons why employees left for jobs with other companies, 34 percent said it was due to lack of recognition and praise, compared with 29 percent who mentioned low compensation, 13 percent who mentioned limited authority, and 8 percent who cited personality problems.[13]

EXHIBIT 5-1

Source: From the *Wall Street Journal,* October 21, 1997. Reprinted by permission of Cartoon Features Syndicate.

EXHIBIT 5-2

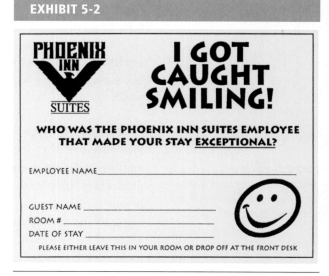

Source: Courtesy of Phoenix Inn Suites. Reprinted with permission of VIP's Industries, Inc.

Variable-Pay Programs

When organizations want to improve productivity, they typically introduce a **variable-pay program**, where a portion of an employee's pay is based on some individual and/or organizational measure of performance. With variable pay, earnings fluctuate up and down with the measure of performance.[14] Thus, there is no guarantee that just because you made $60 000 last year, you will make the same amount this year.

The number of employees who have variable-pay programs has been rising in Canada. A 2004 survey of 360 firms by Hewitt Associates found that 82 percent of them have variable-pay programs in place, compared with 43 percent in 1994.[15] These programs are more common among non-unionized companies, although more than 30 percent of unionized companies had such plans in 2002.[16] That same year, 80 percent of large US companies had some form of variable-pay program.[17] About 22 percent of Japanese companies have company-wide pay-for-performance (or variable pay) programs.[18]

Variable-pay programs do not guarantee employees specific annual wages, which makes the work experience a bit riskier. Employees may worry that they cannot predict their wages ahead of time. When the Hudson's Bay Company in Montreal tried to introduce merit pay (a form of variable pay), 800 employees were so upset that they went on strike for two weeks. Management had to back away from merit pay, and return to a simple wage system. Randy Ross, the spokesman for the union that led the strike (Local 1000 of the Canadian Auto Workers), noted that merit pay "causes nothing but trouble in your store." He was concerned about the fairness of merit pay. "You think you're doing a good job, and then you find some little sweetheart gets more money than you," Mr. Ross said. "Nobody is going to work very hard after that."[19] *Case Incident—When the Perks Fade* on page 197 further addresses what happens when bonuses fall.

Despite some reservations by employees, management professor Maria Rotundo of the Joseph L. Rotman School of Management at the University of Toronto noted that merit pay can work. "It all hinges on fair measures" during the performance appraisal. Managers need to explain why people get different amounts of money, or people "get angry, jealous and disenchanted."[20] At Purdy's Chocolates, employees are given written job descriptions that tell them exactly what is expected of them in their job. They also receive a manual that outlines "what they need to learn and by when."[21] Performance reviews are carried out for all staff annually.

Below we describe pay-for-performance programs that are designed for different circumstances: motivating individuals, motivating groups, or motivating the entire workforce of an organization.

Individual-Based Incentives

There are two major forms of individual-based pay-for-performance programs: piece-rate wages and bonuses.

Piece-Rate Wages Piece-rate wages are one of the earliest forms of individual performance pay. They have long been popular as a means for compensating production employees. In a **piece-rate pay plan**, employees are paid a fixed sum for each unit of production completed. When an employee gets no base salary and is paid only for what he or she produces, this is a pure piece-rate plan. People who work at baseball parks selling peanuts and soft drinks frequently are paid this way. They might get to keep 25 cents for every bag of peanuts they sell. If they sell 200 bags during a game, they make $50. If they sell only 40 bags, their take is a mere $10.

Many organizations use a modified piece-rate plan, where employees earn a base hourly wage plus a piece-rate differential. So a data entry clerk might be paid $8.50 an hour plus 30 cents per page. Such modified plans provide a basic security net while still offering a productivity incentive. Sales associates who are paid commissions based on sales also have a form of individual-based incentive plan.

Bonuses Bonuses are becoming an increasingly popular form of individual incentive in Canada.[22] Bonuses are more likely to be viewed as one-time rewards for defined work rather than ongoing entitlements. They are used by such companies as Molson Coors Brewing Company, Ontario Hydro Energy, and the Bank of Montreal. Incentive-based pay is less common in Canada than it is in the United States, where more employees receive it and larger rewards are given.[23] This is because Canada has a more unionized economy, a relative lack of competition, and a large public sector. Until recently, the only bonus for federal civil servants was $800, awarded to those in bilingual jobs. More recently, both federal and provincial governments introduced bonuses for public sector employees as a way to acknowledge superior performance. For instance, the Alberta government, which already had performance bonuses for senior administrators and employees in colleges and universities, introduced them for public school teachers and administrators in March 1999.[24] In August 1999, federal executives were introduced to a new bonus plan, with part of their performance evaluated against business plans and corporate priorities of their departments. Their pay also depends on their "leadership qualities, ethics, values and how they treat their staff."[25]

At Toronto-based Snap Promotions, rewards are given spontaneously for extraordinary effort. CEO Warren Kotler (kneeling at right, with employees Leilani Nolan and Mez Lalji) shows his deep appreciation for his entire team by giving them tickets to shows and concerts, buying them lunch, and even sending a masseuse to someone's home. Kotler recently organized a "Steak & Beans" contest, dividing the company into two teams that received points for meetings set, quotes generated, and sales achieved. At the end of the period, the losing team ate beans at Morton's Steak House in Toronto (a well-known upscale restaurant) while watching the winners feast on steak.

Bonuses are not free from organizational politics (which we discuss in Chapter 8), and they can sometimes result in negative behaviour. When using bonuses, managers should be mindful of potential unexpected behaviours that may arise when employees try to ensure they will receive bonuses. *Focus on Ethics* raises the possibility that part of Enron's failure was due to the way bonuses were awarded to executives.

FOCUS ON **ETHICS**

Huge Bonuses, Disastrous Results at Enron

Can compensation schemes encourage employees to adopt criminal strategies? When Enron collapsed in 2002, everyone wanted to know who knew what when. Many could not believe that such a large corporation could fall into bankruptcy so suddenly and unexpectedly.

The company's compensation strategy may have encouraged questionable behaviour by Enron executives. In 2001 executives received huge one-time bonuses because Enron's stock price hit various targets during 2000. Investigators have suggested that during 2000, those same executives were inflating the company's profits by as much as a billion dollars. Legal experts suggest that the bonuses tied to stock price goals may have provided a motive for executives to distort the company's performance. The stock price target likely would not have been achieved without the distorted reports of company performance.

How large were these bonuses? Well, Andrew S. Fastow, the former CFO, received more than $3 million (US) in bonuses over a one-month period! In the words of a former federal prosecutor, "The levels of compensation that we are talking about here would certainly seem to be a powerful incentive for anyone to do anything."[26] 🏃

The experience at Enron suggests that rewarding individuals based on financial measures can cause problems.

Group-Based Incentives

There is one major form of group-based pay-for-performance program: gainsharing.

Gainsharing The variable-pay program that has received the most attention in recent years is undoubtedly **gainsharing**.[27] It is a formula-based group incentive plan. Improvements in group productivity—from one period to another—determine the total amount of money to be shared. For instance, if last month a company produced 1000 items using 10 000 person hours, and this month production of the same number of items was produced with only 9000 person hours, the company experiences a savings of 1000 person hours, at the average cost per hour to hire a person. Productivity savings can be divided between the company and employees in any number of ways, but 50-50 is fairly typical.

Gainsharing differs from profit-sharing, discussed below. Gainsharing focuses on productivity gains rather than profits, and so it rewards specific behaviours that are less influenced by external factors. Employees in a gainsharing plan can receive incentive awards even when the organization isn't profitable.

Gainsharing's popularity was initially limited to large unionized manufacturing companies,[28] such as Montreal-based Molson Coors Brewing Company and Montreal-based Hydro-Québec. This has changed in recent years. More than 1500 organizations have now introduced it,[29] including smaller companies, such as Delta, BC-based Avcorp Industries, and governments, such as Ontario's Town of Ajax and Kingston Township. Gainsharing has been found to improve productivity in a majority of cases and often has a positive impact on employee attitudes.[30]

Organizational-Based Incentives

There are two major forms of organizational-based pay-for-performance programs: profit-sharing and stock option plans, including employee stock ownership plans.

Profit-Sharing Plans A **profit-sharing plan** is an organization-wide plan in which the employer shares profits with employees based on a predetermined formula. The plan can distribute direct cash outlays or stock options. Though senior executives are most likely to be rewarded through profit-sharing plans, employees at any level can be recipients. IKEA divided every penny rung up in its 152 stores on October 8, 1999, among its 44 000 staffers in 28 countries. This amounted to $2500 for each employee.[31] At Purdy's Chocolates, profit sharing was introduced in 1990 "to have people more conscious of what things cost, and paying attention to not wasting." Profit sharing is provided to all full- and part-time staff who are non-unionized. The practice has been successful. The amount paid is determined by the profits of the company, and is based on a percentage of the employee's salary. In 2003, Purdy's employees received about 5.5 percent bonuses from profit sharing.[32]

Be aware that profit-sharing plans focus on past financial results. They don't necessarily focus employees on the future, because employees and managers look for ways to cut costs today, without considering longer-term organizational needs. They also tend to ignore factors such as customer service and employee development, which may not be seen as having a direct link to profits. In addition, employees who work in companies in cyclical industries would see inconsistent rewards with such a plan. For example, a financial services company would offer few or no rewards during slumping economic periods, and substantial rewards during times of economic growth. Fluctuating rewards may not work for all employees. Employees at St. John's, Newfoundland-based Fishery Products International (FPI) were quite upset when the $750 profit-sharing cheques

gainsharing A group-based incentive plan in which improvements in group productivity determine the total amount of money to be shared.

profit-sharing plan An organization-wide plan in which the employer shares profits with employees based on a predetermined formula.

Fishery Products International
www.fpil.com

they received in 2000 were reduced to just 10 percent of that for 2001 because of lower profits. Allan Moulton, a union representative of the employees, said, "It's extremely hard for [workers]. . . to see that [the company] realized profits, and they expected to see some benefits from the profits they generated."[33]

From an expectancy theory perspective, employees who have a profit-sharing plan will be less motivated during economic downturns because they know that the likelihood of receiving significant bonuses is low. According to expectancy theory, for employees to be motivated, performance must be directly linked to rewards.

Three Canadian studies by Professor Richard J. Long of the University of Saskatchewan's College of Commerce show that a profit-sharing plan is most effective in workplaces where there is more involvement by employees, more teamwork, and a managerial philosophy that encourages participation.[34]

Stock Options and Employee Stock Ownership Plans Some companies try to encourage employees to adopt the perspective of top management by making them owners of their firms. The idea is that employees will be more likely to think about the consequences of their behaviour on the bottom line if they own part of the company. Employees can become owners of the company either through being granted stock options, or through an **employee stock ownership plan (ESOP)**.[35] Stock options give employees the right to buy stocks in the company at a later date for a guaranteed price. ESOPs are company-established benefit plans in which employees acquire stock as part of their benefits.

Canadian companies lag far behind the United States in the use of ESOPs because Canada's tax environment is less conducive to such plans. More recently, both the dot-com meltdown and the high-tech meltdown have made employees more reluctant to accept stock options instead of cash. Lisa Slipp, head of executive compensation at Toronto-based consulting firm Mercer Human Resource Consulting, noted that "people are recognizing the reality of stock options, that they are attractive in an up market and less so in a down market."[36]

RESEARCH FINDINGS

The research on ESOPs indicates that they increase employee satisfaction.[37] But their impact on performance is less clear. For instance, one study compared 45 companies with ESOPs against 238 companies without ESOPs.[38] Companies with ESOPs outperformed those without, both in terms of employment and sales growth. Other studies have shown disappointing results.[39]

ESOPs have the potential to increase employee job satisfaction and work motivation. For this potential to be realized, employees need to psychologically experience ownership.[40] So in addition to merely having a financial stake in the company, employees need to be kept regularly informed on the status of the business, and also have the opportunity to exercise influence over the business.

The evidence consistently indicates that it takes ownership and a participative style of management to achieve significant improvements in an organization's performance.[41] Research by Queen's University professor Carol Beatty shows why employee ownership matters, as reported in *Focus on Research*.

employee stock ownership plan (ESOP) A company-established benefit plan in which employees acquire stock as part of their benefits.

Mercer Human Resource Consulting
www.mercerhr.com

FOCUS ON **RESEARCH**

Owning Shares of Companies

Does owning a piece of the company really matter to employees? Professor Carol Beatty of Queen's University has examined employee ownership in a variety of companies. She concludes that employee ownership "has the potential to create a great deal of wealth within a company, and for the workers who hold shares."[42] She suggests that when employees own the company, they are more focused on making the company a success. Beatty doesn't argue that employee ownership is the answer to all company problems, but it can be a way of increasing productivity when companies also have good strategies.

Despite some evidence that stock options can make a positive difference in performance, a number of analysts started warning in 2002 that stock options may lead to questionable behaviour by managers who hold them, as the examples of Xerox, Kmart, Enron, America Online, WorldCom, and Cisco Systems illustrate. A CEO holding $100 million in stock options may focus more on the short term, recognizing that considerable wealth is available by cashing in the options. "Now, beating quarterly earnings becomes very important to you, because you have $50-million or $100-million of value tied up in these things," says Tom Caldwell, chairman of Caldwell Securities in Toronto.[43] Also, individuals holding stock options have not actually invested any money, so when share prices fall, they have only lost potential gains, not real money. So this may not induce them to work in the best interests of the company.

Challenges to Pay-for-Performance Programs

There are a variety of challenges related to pay-for-performance programs. Using pay for performance can be difficult for some managers. They worry about what should constitute performance and how it should be measured. There is also some belief by managers and employees alike that wages should keep pace with inflation, independent of performance issues. Other barriers include salary scales keyed to what the competition is paying, traditional compensation systems that rely heavily on specific pay grades with relatively narrow pay ranges, and performance appraisal practices that produce inflated evaluations and expectations of full rewards.

Of course, from the employees' perspective, the major concern about pay-for-performance programs is a potential drop in earnings. *Pay for performance* means employees must share in the risks as well as the rewards of their employer's business. They are not guaranteed the same salary year in and year out under this system. A recent Conference Board of Canada study may ease some fears about this particular concern. There was no evidence that pay for performance led to a reduction in salary in unionized settings. Instead, it "is used as an 'add-on' to the employees' base salary."[44]

Teamwork, unions, public sector employees, and ethical considerations present additional challenges to pay-for-performance programs.

Teamwork Incentive pay, especially when it is awarded to individuals, can have a negative effect on group cohesiveness and productivity, and in some cases it may not offer significant benefits to a company.[45] For example, Montreal-based National Bank of Canada offered a $5 employee bonus for every time employees referred clients for loans, mutual funds, or other bank products. But the bonus so upset employees that the plan was abandoned after just three months.[46] Tellers complained that the bonus caused colleagues to compete against one another. Meanwhile, the bank could not determine whether the referrals actually generated new business.

If an organization wants a group of individuals to function as a "team" (which we define in Chapter 6), emphasis needs to be on team-based rewards, rather than individual rewards. We will discuss the nature of team-based rewards in Chapter 6.

Unions In Canada, there are considerably more unionized workplaces than there are in the United States. Consequently, the unionized context must be considered when motivation theories and practices are examined. Unionized employees are typically

National Bank of Canada
www.nbc.ca

paid on the basis of seniority and job categories, with very little range within a category, and few opportunities to receive performance-based pay.

> *What is the impact of unions on pay for performance?*

Moreover, organized labour is, in general, cool to the idea of pay for performance. Prem Benimadhu, an analyst at the Conference Board of Canada, notes, "Canadian unions have been very allergic to variable compensation."[47] Andrew Jackson, senior economist for the Canadian Labour Congress in Ottawa, adds that "it hurts co-operation in the workplace. It can lead to competition between workers, speeding up the pace of work. It's a bad thing if it creates a stressful work environment where older workers can't keep up."[48] Union members are also concerned that factors out of their control might affect whether bonuses are awarded. *OB in the Workplace* illustrates one union's view of rewards that recognize performance.

OB IN THE WORKPLACE

No Toronto Hydro Jackets for Union Members

Why would unions oppose rewards for their members? Toronto Hydro discovered that rewarding its unionized employees for a job well done can be a tricky business.[49] A 2002 ruling by an arbitrator brought in to settle a dispute between Toronto Hydro and the Canadian Union of Public Employees (CUPE) Local 1 stopped the practice of free lunches, dinners, and such rewards as tickets to events, pen and pencil sets, extra breaks, cellphones, and Toronto Hydro jackets.

Bruno Silano, the local's president, argued that it is demoralizing for employees of some departments to get extra rewards, while other employees do not. Robert Herman, the arbitrator, agreed, stating "the rewards, bestowed at the discretion of management, violated the union's right as exclusive bargaining agent on behalf of its members."

The arbitrator's ruling does not apply to other companies operating with collective agreements, unless the union specifically objects to extra rewards for its members. Toronto labour lawyer Stewart Saxe noted that most unions go along with company reward plans "for obvious political reasons." Toronto Hydro will still give the forbidden perks to non-union employees.

Toronto Hydro
www.torontohydro.com

Still, not all unions share similar views to CUPE, and the benefits and drawbacks of incentive plans must be carefully considered before implementing them in a unionized environment. The ability of managers to hand out rewards of any sort may be limited because of the collective agreement. For instance, at Purdy's Chocolates, unionized employees do not participate in the profit-sharing plan. However, collective agreements do not prevent managers from creating better work environments. Showing appreciation in less tangible ways, providing opportunities for training and advancement, and listening to employees' concerns all help create a more positive environment. (Later in the chapter, we consider ways of improving the overall work environment to enhance performance.)

Public Sector Employees There are special challenges in pay-for-performance programs for public sector employees (those who work for local, provincial, or federal governments). Because public sector work is often of a service nature, it can be hard to measure productivity in the same way manufacturing or retail firms do. One might be able to count how many children an employee places in foster homes, but this might not really address the quality of those placements. Therefore, it becomes more difficult to make a meaningful link between rewards and productivity.

Because pay-for-performance programs can be difficult to administer in the public sector, several researchers have suggested that goal-setting theory be used to improve performance in public sector organizations instead.[50] More recently, another researcher found that goal difficulty and goal specificity, as well as the belief that the goal could be achieved, significantly improved motivation of public sector employees.[51] Because many public sector employees are also unionized, the challenges faced in motivating unionized employees also apply to government employees.

Ethical Considerations Organizations also need to consider the ethical implications of their performance-based plans. The recent Enron scandal provides one example of employees manipulating performance results to increase their bonuses. Wal-Mart has been accused by a number of employees of demanding that they work many unpaid hours.[52] According to company policy, Wal-Mart does not allow store managers to schedule employees for overtime, and they are reprimanded if they do so. At the same time, store managers are told to keep payroll costs below fixed targets. They face reprimands and possible demotion or dismissal when they miss their target. To maintain positive evaluations, store managers pressure employees to do work without recording the hours on time sheets. This behaviour, while unethical, is rational from the store managers' perspective, as they are simply following practices to ensure that they will be rewarded for performance by their superiors.

RESEARCH FINDINGS

Variable-pay programs are consistent with expectancy theory predictions. Specifically, under such programs, one would expect individuals to perceive a strong relationship between their performance and the rewards they receive, and thus be more motivated.

However, the evidence is mixed, at best. One study of 400 manufacturing firms found that those companies with wage incentive plans achieved 43 to 64 percent greater productivity than those without such plans.[53] Other studies generally support that organizations with profit-sharing plans or gainsharing have higher levels of profitability and productivity than those without.[54] But there are studies that question effectiveness of pay-for-performance approaches, suggesting they can lead to less group cohesiveness in the workplace.[55] Some researchers note that much of the evidence supporting pay for performance "is based on anecdotal testimonials and one-time company cases, rather than on methodologically more rigorous empirical studies."[56] The most recent study in Canada, however, examined both unionized and non-unionized workplaces, and found that variable-pay programs result in "increased productivity, a safer work environment, a better understanding of the business by employees, and little risk of employees losing base pay," according to Prem Benimadhu of the Conference Board of Canada.[57]

Motivating Beyond Productivity

In recent years, organizations have been paying for performance on bases other than strict productivity. Compensation experts Patricia Zingheim and Jay Schuster note the following activities merit additional compensation:[58]

- *Commissions beyond sales.* Commissions might be determined by customer satisfaction and/or sales team outcomes, such as meeting revenue or profit targets.

- *Leadership effectiveness.* Rewards can be determined by employee satisfaction, or measures of how the manager handles his or her employees.

- *New goals.* Rewards go to all employees who contribute to achieving specific new organizational goals, such as customer satisfaction, cycle time, or quality measures.

EXHIBIT 5-3 Comparing Various Pay Programs

Approach	Strengths	Weaknesses
Variable pay	• Motivates for performance. • Cost-effective. • Makes a clear link between organizational goals and individual rewards.	• Individuals do not always have control over factors that affect productivity. • Earnings vary from year to year. • Can cause unhealthy competition among employees.
Team-based rewards	• Encourages individuals to work together effectively. • Promotes goal of team-based work.	• Difficult to evaluate team performance sometimes. • Equity problems could arise if all members paid equally.
Skill-based pay	• Increases the skill levels of employees. • Increases the flexibility of the workforce. • Can reduce the number of employees needed.	• Employers may end up paying for unneeded skills. • Employees may not be able to learn some skills, and thus feel demotivated.

- *Knowledge workers in teams.* Rewards are linked to the performance of knowledge workers and/or professional employees who work on teams.

- *Competency and/or skills.* Rewards are based on employees' abstract knowledge or competencies—for example, knowledge of technology, the international business context, customer service, or social skills.

Exhibit 5-3 compares the strengths and weaknesses of variable-pay programs, team-based rewards, and skill-based pay programs. **Skill-based pay** is based on how many skills an employee has, or how many jobs he or she can do. While rewarding individuals for things other than performance may make sense in some instances, not everyone agrees that these rewards are fair. *OB in the Street* examines the question of athletic scholarships given just for athletic skills, rather than academic merit.

skill-based pay Pay based on how many skills an employee has or how many jobs he or she can do.

OB IN THE STREET

Scholarships for Jocks: Skills or Smarts?

Should university athletes be awarded money just for their athletic abilities? Jack Drover, athletic director at Mount Allison University in Sackville, New Brunswick, thinks not.[59] He objects to student-athlete awards that are often offered because of what coaches and teams need, rather than what the individual student needs.

Many university presidents react negatively to schools using financial rewards to recruit athletes. Some high school athletes can get full-tuition scholarships to university, even though they have not achieved high marks in school. While not every university finds this problematic, some feel awarding scholarships that don't recognize academic achievement or financial need is "an affront to the values of higher education."

Schools across the country interpret the rules for scholarships differently, which may affect the quality of school sports teams. Universities in Ontario (which rarely give scholarships to first-year students) have had particular difficulty competing with schools across the country. For example, since 1995 the only football team in Ontario to win the Vanier Cup was the Ottawa Gee Gees; the University of Ottawa is one of the few schools in the province that gives many athletic scholarships. Some members of Canadian Interuniversity Sport (CIS) suggest that a level playing field, with no scholarships granted to first-year athletes except in cases of financial need and academic merit, would be fairer to all teams. CIS president Marg MacGregor, however, argues that "we're asking a lot of our students when we say compete every weekend and practise all the time without any support." 🏃

CAVEAT EMPTOR: APPLY MOTIVATION THEORIES WISELY

3 What kinds of mistakes are made in reward systems?

While motivation theories generally work well in Canada and the United States, they don't always work successfully in other cultures. In addition, when managers are not careful, they can send the wrong signals with how they use rewards. We examine both of these issues below.

Motivation Theories Are Culture-Bound

Motivation theories do not necessarily work equally well throughout the world. Take, for instance, a study comparing sales representatives at a large electronics company in the United States with one in Japan. The study found that although Rolex watches, expensive dinners, and fancy vacations were appropriate rewards for star performers in the United States, taking the whole sales team bowling was more appreciated in Japan. The study's authors found that "being a member of a successful team with shared goals and values, rather than financial rewards, is what drives Japanese sales representatives to succeed."[60] *OB Around the Globe* discusses the use of rewards in Russia, China, and Mexico.

OB AROUND THE GLOBE

Foreign Employees Meet North American Rewards

What motivates employees in other countries? At a cotton mill 140 kilometres northwest of Moscow, a small group of employees were given either highly valued extrinsic rewards (North American T-shirts with logos, children's sweatpants, tapes of North American music, and a variety of other North American articles) or praise and recognition. Both types of rewards significantly increased employee productivity, with more top-grade fabric produced when rewards were delivered.

Interestingly enough, however, the rewards did not increase the productivity very significantly for those who worked the Saturday shift. These findings show that while rewards have some use in Russia, the conditions of work also affect productivity. Because the Russian employees did not want to work the Saturday shift, the rewards had less impact on their productivity.[61] Expectancy theory would tell us that the rewards offered for Saturday work were not valued highly enough by employees to increase their productivity.

In China, the reward structure is undergoing a fundamental shift. During the Cultural Revolution (1966–1976), equal pay for everyone, regardless of productivity, was the rule. Since 1978, however, there has been more openness toward paying for productivity.[62] However, it is still the case that some companies pay everyone a bonus, regardless of individual productivity, and there is debate among Chinese employees about the standards set for performance.

When Dell went to Xiamen, China, in August 1998 to produce computers for the Chinese market, it offered each employee 200 shares of Dell stock, which was then trading at $60.[63] Three months later, with shares trading at $110, each

Dell Canada
www.dell.ca

employee had a paper gain of $10 000, roughly a year's salary for the average Xiamen employee. But the Chinese employees had no idea what stock options were. Once these were explained to them, the productivity increased. Nevertheless, Dell has had to deal with the Chinese expectation of employment for life, even though that is no longer a guarantee. Dell executives say that "at first a little 'reeducation' was necessary in Xiamen so that workers understood that their jobs depended on their performance."

A researcher studying an American-owned manufacturing plant in Mexico noted that Mexican employees prefer immediate feedback on their work. Thus a daily incentive system with automatic bonuses for production exceeding quotas is preferable.[64] This is equivalent to piece-rate wages paid daily. Employers often add extra incentives that are meaningful to employees, including weekly food baskets, free meals, bus service, and daycare.

A study that examined how cultural differences affect choice of pay and benefit practices gives us further information about reward practices in different countries.[65] This study linked reward preferences to a country's ratings on GLOBE/Hofstede cultural dimensions, which we discussed in Chapter 3. In Exhibit 5-4, we show the link between a country's rating on particular cultural dimensions, and its preferences for particular types of rewards. Countries that put a high value on uncertainty avoidance prefer pay based on objective measures, such as skill or seniority, because the outcomes are more certain. Countries that put a high value on individualism place more emphasis on an individual's responsibility for performance that leads to rewards. Countries that put a high value on humane orientation offer social benefits and programs that provide work-family balance, such as child care, maternity leave, and sabbaticals. Managers who receive overseas assignments should consider a country's cultural orientation when designing and implementing reward practices.

Evaluating Motivation Theories Cross-Culturally

Why do our motivation theories perform less well when we look at their implementation in countries beyond Canada and the United States? Most current motivation theories were developed in the United States and so take American cultural norms for granted.[66] That may account for why Canada and the United States rely more heavily on

EXHIBIT 5-4 Reward Preferences in Different Countries

GLOBE/Hofstede Cultural Dimension	Reward Preference	Examples
High uncertainty avoidance	Certainty in compensation systems: • Seniority-based pay • Skill-based pay	Greece, Portugal, Japan
Individualism	Compensation based on individual performance: • Pay for performance • Individual incentives • Stock options	Australia, United Kingdom, United States
Humane orientation (Hofstede's quality-of-life dimension)	Social benefits and programs: • Flexible benefits • Workplace child-care programs • Career-break schemes • Maternity leave programs	Sweden, Norway, the Netherlands

Source: Based on R. S. Schuler and N. Rogovsky, "Understanding Compensation Practice Variations Across Firms: The Impact of National Culture," *Journal of International Business Studies* 29, no. 1 (First Quarter 1998), pp. 159–177. Reprinted by permission of Palgrave/Macmillan.

extrinsic motivating factors than some other countries.[67] Japanese and German firms rarely make use of individual-based incentives.[68]

Many of the social-psychological theories of motivation rely heavily on the notion of motivating the individual through individual rewards. Therefore they emphasize, particularly in an organizational context, the meaning of pay, and give little attention to the informal rewards that come from group norms and prestige from peers.[69] In contrast, Japanese organizations do not emphasize motivating each individual one at a time, but rely more heavily on group processes providing motivation to employees.

Motivation theories also assume some consistency in needs across society. For instance, Maslow's hierarchy of needs argues that people start at the physiological level and then move progressively up the hierarchy in this order: physiological, safety, social, esteem, and self-actualization. This hierarchy, if it has any application at all, aligns well with American culture and reasonably well with Canadian culture. However, in countries such as Japan, Greece, and Portugal, where uncertainty avoidance characteristics are strong, security needs would be at the top of the need hierarchy. Countries that score high on humane orientation characteristics—Denmark, Norway, the Netherlands, and Finland—would have social needs on top.[70] We would predict, for instance, that teamwork will motivate employees more when the country's culture scores high on the humane orientation criterion.

Equity theory has gained a relatively strong following in Canada and the United States. That's not surprising, since North American reward systems assume that employees are highly sensitive to equity in reward allocations, and expect pay to be tied closely to performance. However, recent evidence suggests that in collectivist cultures, especially in the former socialist countries of Central and Eastern Europe, employees expect rewards to reflect their individual needs as well as their performance.[71] Moreover, consistent with a legacy of Communism and centrally planned economies, employees exhibit an entitlement attitude—that is, they expect outcomes to be *greater* than their inputs.[72] These findings suggest that Canadian- and US-style pay practices may need modification, especially in Russia and former Communist countries, in order to be perceived as fair by employees.

These cross-cultural findings indicate that it is important to consider the internal norms of a country when developing an incentive plan rather than simply import a plan that is effective in Canada and the United States.

Beware the Signals That Are Sent by Rewards

Ever wonder why employees do some strange things?

In 1998, Vancouver's bus drivers claimed, on average, 18.6 sick days. Victoria's bus drivers averaged only 16.6 sick days.[73] Are Vancouver's drivers more likely to catch cold than Victoria's? Not likely! Rather, differences in the way that sick days are paid may account for the differences. Victoria's drivers get paid in full for six sick days, no matter how they're taken. But once Vancouver drivers take their second "sick time," they aren't paid unless they're off more than three days for their illness, so it makes sense for them to stay home sick longer. At Carignan, Quebec-based hardware store Centre de rénovation Pointe et Meunier, owner Daniel Blais had to revise his plan to give commissions to employees based on profit per sales. An "employee [who] happened to be near someone who was looking at a big-ticket item tended to shadow that person rather than going to help the next customer who was looking at something less costly," says Blais. He found that employees gave better overall service when he switched the performance plan to a group commission divided evenly among staff and based on overall profits for the department.[74]

"Odd" behaviour is not confined to employees in Canada, however, as this *OB Around the Globe* shows.

OB AROUND THE GLOBE

Planting Seeds in Russia

Why would someone plant something that can't grow? Peter Gorelkin worked as a tractor operator planting grain at a farm in the Russian region of Siberia.[75] His supervisor was paid by the number of hectares Gorelkin was able to plant. The grain was supposed to be planted at a depth of 6 cm to ensure it would germinate, but Gorelkin's supervisor insisted that the grain be planted at a depth of only 3 cm.

Why such apparently irrational behaviour? The supervisor knew that a tractor set to plant at 6 cm could only cover 4 hectares per day, whereas at a setting of 3 cm, 10 hectares could be planted. As Gorelkin reports, "The fact that we were able to plant more land meant nothing directly to us trainees, but not only did it mean more pay for our supervisor, it also meant the possibility of a bonus at the end of the job. The fact that most of the seeds might not survive the spring did not disturb him at all."

Perhaps more often than we would like, organizations engage in what has been called "the folly of rewarding A, while hoping for B."[76] Organizations do this when they hope that employees will engage in one type of behaviour, but they reward for another type. Hoping for the behaviour you are not rewarding is unlikely to ensure it is carried out. In fact, as expectancy theory suggests, individuals will generally perform in ways that raise the probability of receiving the rewards offered.

Exhibit 5-5 provides further examples of common management reward follies. Research suggests that there are three major obstacles to ending these follies:[77]

1. *Individuals are unable to break out of old ways of thinking about reward and recognition practices.* This approach is demonstrated when management emphasizes

EXHIBIT 5-5 **Management Reward Follies**	
We hope for . . .	**But we reward . . .**
Teamwork and collaboration	The best team members
Innovative thinking and risk-taking	Proven methods and not making mistakes
Development of people skills	Technical achievements and accomplishments
Employee involvement and empowerment	Tight control over operations and resources
High achievement	Another year's effort
Long-term growth; environmental responsibility	Quarterly earnings
Commitment to total quality	Shipping on schedule, even with defects
Candour; surfacing bad news early	Reporting good news, whether it's true or not; agreeing with the manager, whether or not (s)he's right

Sources: Constructed from S. Kerr, "On the Folly of Rewarding A, While Hoping for B," *Academy of Management Executive* 9, no. 1 (1995), pp. 7–14; and "More on the Folly," *Academy of Management Executive* 9, no. 1 (1995), pp. 15–16. Reprinted by permission.

quantifiable behaviours to the exclusion of nonquantifiable behaviours; when management is reluctant to change the existing performance system; and when employees have an entitlement mentality (that is, they don't support changing the reward system because they are comfortable with the current behaviours that are rewarded).

2. *Organizations often don't look at the big picture of their performance system.* Consequently, rewards are allocated at subunit levels, with the result that units often compete against each other.

3. *Both management and shareholders often focus on short-term results.* They don't reward employees for longer-range planning.

Organizations would do well to ensure that they do not send the wrong message when offering rewards. When organizations outline an organizational objective of "team performance," for example, but reward each employee according to individual productivity, does this send a message that teams are valued? Or when a retailer tells commissioned employees that they are responsible for monitoring and replacing stock as necessary, are employees more likely to concentrate on making sales or stocking the floor? Employees motivated by the promise of rewards will do those things that earn them the rewards they value.

CAN WE JUST ELIMINATE REWARDS?

Karen Flavelle, CEO of Purdy's Chocolates, doesn't just rely on salary to keep employees involved in the company.[78] New employees are given extensive training so that they will have enough product knowledge to answer any question a customer might ask. Even temporary holiday employees, who typically only work four weeks, receive a full-day's instruction in company policies and product.

Flavelle holds townhall meetings for employees so that she can outline company results and announce company events. Employees receive a company newsletter every two months. Head managers, including Flavelle, visit stores regularly. "It reduces the gap between head office and the stores," says Carmen Grant, Purdy's director of human resources. "In other companies, it can become 'us versus them,' and I don't see that in this company." What else can companies do, beyond rewards, to create a more motivating workplace?

4 Are rewards overrated?

Alfie Kohn, in his book *Punished by Rewards,* argues that "the desire to do something, much less to do it well, simply cannot be imposed; in this sense, it is a mistake to talk about motivating other people. All we can do is set up certain conditions that will maximize the probability of their developing an interest in what they are doing and remove the conditions that function as constraints."[79]

Employee commitment would benefit many organizations. People will work hard if the job captures their passion and their imagination. They will put in much more energy and devotion than they would if they were simply waiting to be rewarded every step of the way, and they generally do not require a lot of supervision in those situations. *HR Implications* on page 192 discusses how companies can help employees with career development, a way of engaging them more in the organization rather than focusing simply on rewards.

Creating a Motivating Work Environment

Based on his research and consulting experience, Kohn proposes a number of actions that organizations can take to create a motivating work environment.[80]

Abolish Incentive Pay   Paying employees generously and fairly makes sure they don't feel exploited, and takes pay off their minds. As a result, employees will be more able to focus on the goals of the organization, rather than have their paycheque as their main goal.

Re-evaluate Evaluation Instead of making performance appraisals look and feel like a punitive effort—who gets raises, who gets promoted, who is told they are performing poorly—the performance evaluation system might be structured more like a two-way conversation to trade ideas and questions, done continuously, not as a competition. The discussion of performance should not be tied to compensation. "Providing feedback that employees can use to do a better job ought never to be confused or combined with controlling them by offering (or withholding) rewards."[81]

Create the Conditions for Authentic Motivation A noted economist recently summarized the evidence about pay for productivity as follows: "Changing the way workers are *treated* may boost productivity more than changing the way they are *paid*."[82] There is some consensus about what the conditions for authentic motivation might be: helping employees rather than putting them under surveillance; listening to employee concerns and thinking about problems from their viewpoint; and providing plenty of feedback so they know what they have done right and what they need to improve.[83]

Encourage Collaboration People are more likely to perform better in well-functioning groups where they can get feedback and learn from each other.[84] Therefore, it's important to provide the necessary supports to create well-functioning teams.

Enhance Content People are generally the most motivated when their jobs give them an opportunity to learn new skills, provide variety in the tasks that are performed, and enable them to demonstrate competence. Some of this can be fostered by carefully matching people to their jobs, and by giving them the opportunity to try new jobs. It's also possible to increase the meaningfulness of many jobs, as we discuss later in this chapter.

But what about jobs that don't seem inherently interesting? One psychologist suggests that in cases where the jobs are fundamentally unappealing, the manager might acknowledge frankly that the task is not fun, give a meaningful rationale for why it must be done, and then give people as much choice as possible in how the task is completed.[85] One sociologist studying a group of garbage collectors in San Francisco discovered that they were quite satisfied with their work.[86] Their satisfaction came from the way the work and the company were organized: Relationships among the crew were important, the tasks and routes were varied to provide interest, and the company was set up as a cooperative, so that each worker owned a share of the company, and thus felt "pride of ownership."

Provide Choice "We are most likely to become enthusiastic about what we are doing—and all else being equal, to do it well—when we are free to make decisions about the way we carry out a task."[87] Extrinsic rewards (and punishments too) actually remove choice, because they focus us on rewards, rather than on tasks or goals. Research suggests that burnout, dissatisfaction, absenteeism, stress, and coronary heart disease are related to situations where individuals did not have enough control over their work situations.[88] By choice we do not mean lack of management, but rather, involving people in the decisions that are to be made. A number of case studies indicate that participative management, when it includes full participation by everyone, is successful.[89]

These actions represent an alternative to simply providing more and different kinds of incentives to try to induce people to work more effectively. They suggest that providing the proper environment may be more important than the reward structure.

It would be difficult for many organizations to implement these ideas immediately and expect that they would work. Doing so would require managers to be willing to relinquish control and instead take on the job of coaching. It would require employees to truly believe that their participation and input mattered, and that might require breaking down some of the suspicion that employees feel when managers give directives to employees, rather than seek collaborative input. Nevertheless, these actions, when implemented, can lead to quite a different workplace than what we often see. Moreover, Kohn suggests that sometimes it's not the type or amount of rewards that makes a difference as much as whether the work itself is intrinsically interesting.

Below we examine how to create more motivating jobs and workplaces in order to make work itself more intrinsically rewarding for employees.

JOB REDESIGN

At Purdy's Chocolates, managers emphasize the need to learn about the different jobs required in the organization.[90] Flavelle believes in promoting from within, signalling that employees are valued members of her team. In order to get employees ready for promotions, she uses job rotation. This helps employees evaluate opportunities for different jobs and gain the skills they might need to be promoted. For example, a warehouse employee was given a temporary job managing a Christmas packaging project. The employee was promoted to the production office later, in recognition of a job well done. What can employers do to make jobs more interesting for employees?

5 How can jobs be designed to increase motivation?

job design How tasks are assigned to form a job.

The writings of Maslow, McGregor, Herzberg, and Kohn all touched on the importance of looking at the work itself as a possible source of motivation. Recent research in **job design** (how tasks are assigned to form a job) provides stronger evidence that the way the elements in a job are organized can increase or decrease effort. This research also offers detailed insights into just what those elements are.

In this section, we look at some of the ways that jobs can be reshaped in order to make them more motivating. We look at three job redesign options—job rotation, job enlargement, and job enrichment, and show how the job characteristics model can be used to help us understand job enrichment.

Job Rotation

job rotation The periodic shifting of an employee from one task to another.

If employees suffer from overroutinization, one alternative is to use **job rotation** (or what many now call *cross-training*). We define this practice as the periodic shifting of an employee from one task to another. When an activity is no longer challenging, the employee is rotated to another job at the same level that has similar skill requirements.[91]

At McDonald's, this approach is used as a way to make sure that the new employees learn all of the tasks associated with making, packaging, and serving hamburgers and other items. Similarly, at DaimlerChrysler's Toledo North assembly plant, job rotation helps give employees in different areas a sense of the big picture. Employees are organized in teams of 10, and each learns the jobs of the others. Absenteeism is less of a problem, because team members can fill in for each other. Rotating jobs also decreases the frequency of repetitive stress injuries.[92]

A recent Statistics Canada survey found that about 19 percent of firms with 10 or more employees engaged in job rotation.[93] Employees in technical trades and clerical and administrative positions were more likely to rotate jobs than managerial and professional employees.

The strengths of job rotation are that it reduces boredom and increases motivation by diversifying the employee's activities. Of course, it can also have indirect benefits for the organization, since employees with a wider range of skills give management more flexibility in scheduling work, adapting to changes, and filling vacancies.

On the other hand, job rotation has drawbacks. Training costs are increased. Productivity is reduced because a worker moves into a new position just when his or her efficiency at the prior job achieves economies for the organization. Job rotation also creates disruptions. Members of the work group must adjust to the new employee. The manager may also have to spend more time answering questions and monitoring the work of the recently rotated employee. Finally, job rotation can demotivate intelligent and ambitious trainees who seek specific responsibilities in their chosen specialty.

Job Enlargement

The idea of expanding jobs horizontally, or what we call **job enlargement**, became popular more than 35 years ago. Increasing the number and variety of tasks that an individual performed resulted in jobs with more diversity. Instead of only sorting the incoming mail by department, for instance, a mail sorter's job could be enlarged to include delivering the mail to the various departments or running outgoing letters through the postage meter.

Control over the production line is not restricted to non-union environments. At the Honeywell plant in Scarborough, Ontario, unionized employees have the authority to shut down the production line to correct production defects. The work team meets to review the schedule and check quality as part of its daily responsibilities. This enriches the workers' jobs over many assembly-line jobs.

job enlargement The horizontal expansion of jobs.

Efforts at job enlargement have sometimes met with less than enthusiastic results.[94] As one employee who experienced such a redesign on his job remarked, "Before I had *one* lousy job. Now, through enlargement, I have *three*!"

However, there have been some successful applications of job enlargement. For example, GM Canada's Synchronous Administration through Managerial Excellence (SAME) system ensures that all of the employees in a work unit can perform each of the tasks of any of the individuals in the unit. The system significantly reduces the need for meetings, halves the cost of office equipment, and allows job continuity when workers leave the company or go on holiday.[95] The Candour unit of Montreal-based Bombardier's aerospace group introduced job enlargement to get away from having a large number of highly specialized manufacturing jobs.[96] Serge Perron, vice-president and general manager of operations, notes that the move gave Bombardier more flexibility, with workers installing several types of parts instead of just one, and also led to productivity improvements.

GM Canada
www.gmcanada.com

Bombardier
www.bombardier.com

While job enlargement attacks the lack of diversity in overspecialized jobs, it does little to add challenge or meaningfulness to a worker's activities. Job enrichment was developed to deal with the shortcomings of enlargement.

Job Enrichment and the Job Characteristics Model

OB researchers Richard Hackman from Harvard University and Greg Oldham from the University of Illinois explored the nature of good jobs through their **job characteristics model (JCM)**.[97] The JCM identifies five core job dimensions and their relationship to personal and work outcomes. Building on Herzberg's motivation-hygiene theory, the JCM focuses on the content of jobs, rather than the context of jobs, and can be considered as a way of motivating employees and increasing job satisfaction.

Job enrichment, an application of the JCM, refers to the vertical expansion of jobs. It increases the degree to which workers control the planning, execution, and evaluation

job characteristics model (JCM) A model that identifies five core job dimensions and their relationship to personal and work outcomes.

job enrichment The vertical expansion of jobs.

EXHIBIT 5-6	Examples of High and Low Job Characteristics
Skill Variety	
High variety	The owner-operator of a garage who does electrical repair, rebuilds engines, does body work, and interacts with customers
Low variety	A body shop worker who sprays paint eight hours a day
Task Identity	
High identity	A cabinet maker who designs a piece of furniture, selects the wood, builds the object, and finishes it to perfection
Low identity	A worker in a furniture factory who operates a lathe solely to make table legs
Task Significance	
High significance	Nursing the sick in a hospital intensive care unit
Low significance	Sweeping hospital floors
Autonomy	
High autonomy	A telephone installer who schedules his or her own work for the day, makes visits without supervision, and decides on the most effective techniques for a particular installation
Low autonomy	A telephone operator who must handle calls as they come according to a routine, highly specified procedure
Feedback	
High feedback	An electronics factory worker who assembles a radio and then tests it to determine if it operates properly
Low feedback	An electronics factory worker who assembles a radio and then routes it to a quality control inspector who tests it for proper operation and makes needed adjustments

Source: G. Johns, *Organizational Behavior: Understanding and Managing Life at Work,* 4th ed. Copyright © 1997. Adapted by permission of Pearson Education, Inc. Upper Saddle River, NJ.

of their work. An enriched job organizes tasks so that an employee does a complete activity. It expands employees' freedom and independence, increases responsibility, and provides feedback, so individuals will be able to assess and correct their own performance.[98] To find out whether an enriched job matches your own work preferences, see the *Learning About Yourself Exercise* on page 194.

Core Job Dimensions

According to the JCM, any job can be described in terms of five core job dimensions:

skill variety The degree to which the job requires a variety of different activities.

- *Skill variety.* The degree to which the job requires a variety of different activities so the employee can use a number of different skills and talents.

task identity The degree to which the job requires completion of a whole and identifiable piece of work.

- *Task identity.* The degree to which the job requires completion of a whole and identifiable piece of work.

task significance The degree to which the job has a substantial impact on the lives or work of other people.

- *Task significance.* The degree to which the job has a substantial impact on the lives or work of other people.

- *Autonomy.* The degree to which the job provides substantial freedom, independence, and discretion to the individual in scheduling the work and determining the procedures to be used in carrying it out.

- *Feedback.* The degree to which carrying out the work activities required by the job results in the individual obtaining direct and clear information about the effectiveness of his or her performance.

Jobs can be rated as high or low on these dimensions. Examples of jobs with high and low ratings appear in Exhibit 5-6. You might want to consider how these dimensions relate to call centre work shown in this chapter's *CBC Video Case.*

Critical Psychological States

The JCM, presented in Exhibit 5-7, links the five core job dimensions to three critical psychological states:[99]

- *Experienced meaningfulness.* The model predicts that if an employee's task is meaningful, the employee will view the job as important, valuable, and worthwhile. (Notice how in Exhibit 5-7 skill variety, task identity, and task significance combine to create meaningful work.)

- *Experienced responsibility for outcomes.* Employees feel a sense of personal responsibility for results when their jobs give them greater autonomy.

- *Knowledge of the actual results.* Feedback helps employees know whether they are performing effectively.

The model suggests that the more employees experience meaningfulness, responsibility, and knowledge of the actual results, the greater their motivation, performance, and satisfaction, and the lower their absenteeism and likelihood of leaving the organization.[100] As Exhibit 5-7 shows, the links between the job dimensions and the outcomes are moderated or adjusted by the strength of the individual's growth need—in

CBC

Hold Those Phones

autonomy The degree to which the job provides substantial freedom, independence, and discretion to the individual in scheduling the work and determining the procedures to be used in carrying it out.

feedback The degree to which carrying out the work activities required by the job results in the individual obtaining direct and clear information about the effectiveness of his or her performance.

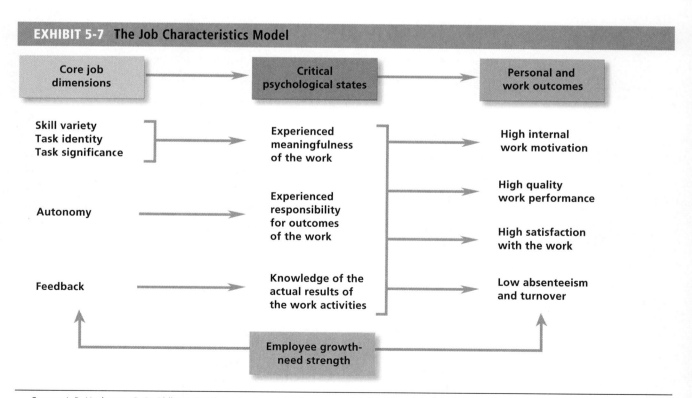

EXHIBIT 5-7 The Job Characteristics Model

Core job dimensions	Critical psychological states	Personal and work outcomes
Skill variety / Task identity / Task significance	Experienced meaningfulness of the work	High internal work motivation
Autonomy	Experienced responsibility for outcomes of the work	High quality work performance / High satisfaction with the work
Feedback	Knowledge of the actual results of the work activities	Low absenteeism and turnover

Employee growth-need strength

Source: J. R. Hackman, G. R. Oldham, *Work Design* (excerpted from pages 78–80). Copyright ©1980 by Addison-Wesley Publishing Co. Reprinted by permission of Addison-Wesley Longman.

other words, the employee's desire for self-esteem and self-actualization. This means, for example, that not every employee will respond favourably to a job with skill variety, task identity, task significance, autonomy, or feedback. Those with high self-esteem and self-actualization needs will respond more favourably than others with different needs.

A survey of college and university students highlights the underlying theme of the JCM. When the students were asked about what was most important to them as they thought about their careers, their top four answers were as follows:

- Having idealistic and committed co-workers (very important to 68 percent of the respondents)

- Doing work that helps others (very important to 65 percent)

- Doing work that requires creativity (very important to 47 percent)

- Having a lot of responsibility (very important to 39 percent)[101]

Salary and prestige ranked lower in importance than these four job characteristics.

Motivating Potential Score

The JCM can be viewed as a model of how to increase employee motivation by creating better jobs. The core job dimensions can be combined into a single predictive index, called the **motivating potential score (MPS)**. Its computation is shown in Exhibit 5-8.

motivating potential score (MPS) A predictive index suggesting the motivation potential in a job.

Jobs that are high on motivating potential must be high on at least one of the three factors that lead to experienced meaningfulness, and they must be high on both autonomy and feedback. If jobs score high on motivating potential, the model predicts that motivation, performance, and satisfaction will be positively affected, while the likelihood of absenteeism and turnover will be lessened.

The first part of the *Working With Others Exercise* on page 195 provides an opportunity for you to apply the JCM to a job of your choice. You will also calculate the job's MPS. In the second part of the *Working With Others Exercise,* you can redesign the job to show how you might increase its motivating potential. *From Concepts to Skills* on page 198 provides specific guidelines on the kinds of changes that can help increase the motivating potential of jobs.

 RESEARCH FINDINGS

The JCM has been well researched. Most of the evidence supports the general framework of the theory—that is, there is a multiple set of job characteristics, and these characteristics impact behavioural outcomes.[102] But there is still considerable debate over the five specific core dimensions in the JCM; whether you can simply multiply the scores for dimensions to determine the MPS; and the validity of growth-need strength as a moderating variable.

EXHIBIT 5-8   Computing a Motivating Potential Score

$$\text{Motivating Potential Score (MPS)} = \left[\frac{\text{Skill variety} + \text{Task identity} + \text{Task significance}}{3} \right] \times \text{Autonomy} \times \text{Feedback}$$

When might job redesign be most appropriate?

There is some question as to whether task identity adds to the model's predictive ability,[103] and there is evidence suggesting that skill variety may be redundant with autonomy.[104] Furthermore, a number of studies have found that by adding all the variables in the MPS, rather than adding some and multiplying by others, the MPS becomes a better predictor of work outcomes.[105] Finally, the strength of an individual's growth needs as a meaningful moderating variable has been called into question.[106] Other variables, such as the presence or absence of social cues, perceived equity with comparison groups, and tendency to assimilate work experience,[107] may be more valid in moderating the job characteristics–outcome relationship.

So where does the discussion of the JCM leave us? Given the current state of evidence, we can make the following statements with relative confidence:

- People who work on jobs with high core job dimensions are generally more motivated, satisfied, and productive than are those who do not.

- Job dimensions operate through critical psychological states in influencing personal and work outcomes rather than influencing them directly.[108]

The JCM gives relatively clear advice concerning how managers can enrich the jobs of employees. *OB in the Workplace* describes how First Chicago enriched the jobs of its employees.

Working on a fish-processing line requires being comfortable with job specialization. One person cuts off heads, another guts the fish, a third removes the scales. Each person performs the same task repetitively as fish move down the line. Such jobs are low on skill variety, task identity, task significance, autonomy, and feedback.

OB IN THE WORKPLACE

Enriching Jobs at First Chicago

How does a bank enrich jobs? Lawrence Buettner enriched the jobs of employees in his international trade banking department at First Chicago.[109] His department's chief product is commercial letters of credit—essentially a bank guarantee to stand behind huge import and export transactions. When he took over the department of 300 employees, he found paperwork crawling along a document "assembly line," with errors creeping in at each handoff. Employees did little to hide the boredom they were experiencing in their jobs.

Buettner replaced the narrow, specialized tasks that employees were doing with enriched jobs. Each clerk is now a trade expert who can handle a customer from start to finish. After 200 hours of training in finance and law, the clerks became full-service advisers who could turn around documents in a day while advising clients on such arcane matters as bank procedures in Turkey and US munitions export controls.

The result? Productivity has more than tripled, employee satisfaction has soared, and transaction volume has risen more than 10 percent a year. Additionally, increased skills have translated into higher pay for the employees who are performing the enriched jobs. These trade-service representatives, some of whom had come to the bank directly out of high school, now earn from $52 000 to $90 000 a year. 🏃

The First Chicago example shouldn't be taken as a blanket endorsement of job enrichment. The overall evidence generally shows that job enrichment reduces absenteeism and turnover costs and increases satisfaction, but on the critical issue of productivity, the evidence is inconclusive.[110] In some situations, such as First Chicago's, job enrichment increases productivity; in others, it decreases productivity. However, even when productivity goes down, there does seem to be consistently more conscientious use of resources and a higher quality of product or service.

Job Redesign in the Canadian Context: The Role of Unions

Until recently, labour unions have been largely resistant to participating in discussions with management over job redesign issues. Redesigns often result in loss of jobs, and labour unions try to prevent job loss. Union head offices, however, can sometimes be at odds with their membership over the acceptance of job redesign. Some members value the opportunity for skill development and more interesting work.

During the 1990s, some of the larger unions became more open to discussions about job redesign. This was reflected, for instance, in the position taken by the Communications, Energy and Paperworkers Union of Canada (CEP).[111] The CEP asserts that unions should be involved in the decisions and share in the benefits of work redesign. It calls for negotiated workplace changes, with greater union input into the conception, development, and implementation of work reorganization initiatives. The CEP also believes that basic wages, negotiated through a collective agreement, must remain the primary form of compensation, although it is open to other forms of compensation as long as they do not detract from basic wages determined through collective bargaining.

While managers may regard job redesign as more difficult under a collective agreement, the reality is that for change to be effective in the workplace, management must gain employees' acceptance of the plan whether or not they are unionized.

CREATING MORE FLEXIBLE WORKPLACES

The previous section examined how to make jobs more motivating. In this section, we examine practices that workplaces can use to address the needs of their employees, especially the need for work-life balance. Gay Bank, vice-president of human resources at the Royal Bank of Canada, notes that "it is estimated that as many as three in four working Canadians have responsibility for caring for children or aging parents."[112] A recent survey of work arrangements found that only 39 percent of employed Canadians have "normal" schedules in which they work Monday to Friday at regular starting times.[113] About 24 percent of employees have some sort of flexible work arrangement. Such arrangements help employees ease the stress of juggling family needs alongside work demands. Below we consider how a compressed workweek, flextime, job sharing, and telecommuting might address the idea that Kohn had for increasing motivation: creating better work environments for people. *Case Incident—Working at Bob's in Rio* on page 198 asks you to look at various possibilities for making the work setting better for employees.

Communications, Energy and Paperworkers Union of Canada (CEP)
www.cep.ca

6 How can flexible workplaces increase motivation?

Royal Bank of Canada
www.royalbank.com

EXHIBIT 5-9 **Example of a Flextime Schedule**

Flexible hours	Common core	Lunch	Common core	Flexible hours

6 a.m.   9 a.m.   12 noon   1 p.m.   3 p.m.   6 p.m.

Time during the day

Compressed Workweek

There are two common forms of a **compressed workweek**:

- The four 10-hour days per week plan (known as the 4–40 program)

- The nine days over two weeks plan (employees get either a Friday or Monday off once every two weeks in exchange for working slightly longer hours the other days)

These compressed workweek programs were conceived to allow employees more leisure and shopping time, and to permit them to travel to and from work outside rush hour. Supporters suggest that such programs can increase employee enthusiasm, morale, and commitment to the organization. Compressed workweek programs should make it easier for the organization to recruit employees. These programs also can provide additional support for employees to manage work and family conflicts.

compressed workweek A four-day week, with employees working 10 hours a day; or nine days of work over two weeks.

Flextime

Do employers really like flexible arrangements?

Flextime is short for *flexible work hours*. It allows employees some discretion over when they arrive at and leave work. Employees must work a specific number of hours a week, but they are free to vary the hours of work within certain limits. As shown in Exhibit 5-9, each day consists of a common core, usually six hours, with a flexibility band surrounding the core. (For example, exclusive of a one-hour lunch break, the core may be 9 a.m. to 3 p.m., with the office actually opening at 6 a.m. and closing at 6 p.m.) All employees are required to be at their jobs during the common core period, but they are allowed to accumulate their other two hours before and/or after the core time. Some flextime programs allow extra hours to be accumulated and turned into a free day off each month.

flextime An arrangement where employees work during a common core period each day but can form their total workday from a flexible set of hours outside the core.

Flextime has become an extremely popular scheduling option, although in Canada women are less likely than men to have flexible work schedules. About 30 percent of women have flexible work schedules, compared with 40 percent of men.[114] This compares with about 28 percent of the US full-time workforce who have flexibility in their daily arrival and departure times.[115] But flextime isn't available to all employees equally. More managers (42.4 percent) enjoy the freedom of flextime than do manufacturing employees (23.3 percent).[116]

A survey of Royal Bank of Canada employees shows strong support for flextime arrangements:[117]

- 94 percent of flex employees are very satisfied with their work arrangements

- 70 percent of flex employees reported less stress

- 81 percent of flex employees said they were more effective at balancing work and their outside lives

- 63 percent of managers would highly recommend flex work arrangements (This is notable because a similar survey conducted in 1994 found that only 34 percent of managers would have highly recommended flex work at that time.)

- 37 percent of managers reported that flex work led to an increase in employee efficiency

- 48 percent of employees use flex work to deal with family responsibilities and child care and/or eldercare

- 36 percent of employees said they would leave the company if flex work were not available

- 78 percent of employees on flex work said their opportunities for advancement were the same or better than when they worked a traditional schedule

Most of the performance evidence looking at the impact of flextime stacks up favourably. Flextime tends to reduce absenteeism and frequently improves employee productivity and satisfaction,[118] probably for several reasons. Employees can schedule their work hours to align with personal demands, thus reducing tardiness and absences, and employees can adjust their work activities to those hours in which they are individually more productive. Other research on the impact of flextime on the Canadian workplace has found that employees have positive attitudes and view it as their most preferred option.[119] Managers are in favour,[120] and women with flextime suffer less stress.[121]

Flextime's major drawback is that it is not applicable to every job. It works well with clerical tasks where an employee's interaction with people outside his or her department is limited. It is not a viable option for receptionists, salespeople in retail stores, or similar jobs where people must be at their workstations at fixed times that suit the needs of customers and clients.

Job Sharing

job sharing The practice of having two or more people spl t a 40-hour-a-week job.

Ceridian Canada
www.ceridian.ca

Job sharing is a fairly recent phenomenon in the workplace, and more companies are starting to permit such arrangements. It is the practice of having two or more people split a 40-hour-a-week job. About 48 percent of larger Canadian organizations offer this option.

Job sharing allows the organization to draw upon the talents of more than one individual in a given job. A bank manager who oversees two job sharers describes it as an opportunity to get two heads, but "pay for one."[122] It also opens up the opportunity to acquire skilled workers—for instance, women with young children, retirees, and others desiring flexibility—who might not be available on a full-time basis.[123] Consequently, it can increase motivation and satisfaction for those for whom a 40-hour-a-week job is just not practical. The major difficulty of job sharing is finding compatible pairs of employees who can successfully coordinate the demands of one job.[124]

Job sharing can be a creative solution to some organizational problems. For example, Nunavut has had great difficulty finding doctors willing to commit to serving the territory for more than short periods of time.[125] Dr. Sandy MacDonald, director of Medical Affairs and Telehealth for Nunavut, has tried to increase physician retention by allowing doctors to work for three months at a time. "In the past, the government was trying to get some of them to sign up for two or three years, and most people don't want to do that initially, or they would leave positions unfilled because someone would only come for two or three weeks or a month," he says. Meanwhile, doc-

Jennifer Hong and Beatrice Gauthier share a job at Ceridian Canada. They also share a chair, desk, telephone, and wastebasket! Hong and Gauthier work at the Vancouver office of Manitoba-based Ceridian Canada, a payroll management company. Their arrangement started when Hong half-jokingly asked her friend and colleague Gauthier if she wanted to share a job. Hong was a new mom and wanted to spend time with her young daughter. Gauthier had been looking for such an arrangement for several years.

tors working in Nunavut were overworked because there weren't enough doctors on call. MacDonald's approach has changed that—now more doctors are available because of the job sharing solution.

Telecommuting

It might be close to the ideal job for many people. No commuting, flexible hours, freedom to dress as you please, and few or no interruptions from colleagues. It's called **telecommuting** and refers to employees who do their work at home at least two days a week on a computer that is linked to their office.[126] (A closely related term—*the virtual office*—is increasingly being used to describe employees who work out of their home on a relatively permanent basis).

Telecommuting is on the rise in Canada. In 2004, about 1 million Canadians worked from home at least once a week.[127] Companies vary in their telecommuting policies, of course. Some do not permit much telecommuting. Others have more generous policies, including Brampton, Ontario-based Nortel Networks, where 13 percent of the workforce can work full-time from home and 36 percent can work part-time from home.[128]

Internationally, too, the concept is catching on. The number of Americans who reported working from home at least one day a year grew from 41.3 million in 2003 to 44.4 million in 2004. Another study found that 8.9 million Americans who were not self-employed worked at home at least three days a month in 2004.[129]

Telecommuting: How and Why It Works

If you want to telecommute, what kind of job should you consider?

The idea of having a home office appeals to many, but telecommuters do not always work from home. In one Telus program, for example, workers avoid up to a three-hour-a-day commute to and from downtown Vancouver by reporting for work at a specially established satellite office in suburban Langley, nearer to their homes. Telecommuting employees are more productive than they had previously been because of the reduced commute and fewer disruptions.[130]

Firms must make appropriate arrangements when employees working away from the office need routine administrative support. At North Vancouver, BC-based law firm Ratcliff and Company, one lawyer occasionally works from Bowen Island, while two others work from Vancouver Island. When they need documents typed, they email their dictated audio files to their support staff.[131]

We've been looking at examples from the Vancouver area, but telecommuting does not take place on just a local level, as this *OB Around the Globe* indicates.

OB AROUND THE GLOBE

Liz Codling Manages Long Distance

Can a manager be effective from five time zones away? Liz Codling, a senior manager at Bank of Montreal in Toronto, manages her staff from the United Kingdom.[132] After running the bank's staff education centre for four years and overseeing a team of eight people, she decided to return home to the United Kingdom with her husband. But Codling's bosses didn't want to lose her, so she became the bank's first transatlantic telecommuter. Although separated from her staff by five time zones and more than 4800 kilometres, she is able to manage her team by relying on communication technology—phone, fax, computer, modem, email, voice mail, video conferencing, and the Internet.

---

telecommuting An arrangement where employees do their work at home on a computer that is linked to their office.

Ratcliff and Company
www.ratcliff.com

Bank of Montreal
www.bmo.com

Some adjustments were needed. For instance, Codling has had to adjust her workday to align with Toronto hours, and her colleagues now know to schedule meetings in the mornings so she can be included. 🕱

What kinds of jobs lend themselves to telecommuting? Three categories have been identified as most appropriate: routine information-handling tasks, mobile activities, and professional and other knowledge-related tasks.[133] Writers, attorneys, analysts, and employees who spend the majority of their time on computers or the phone are natural candidates for telecommuting. Telemarketers, customer-service representatives, reservation agents, and product-support specialists can access information on their computer screens at home as easily as on the company screen in any office.

A recent EKOS Research study found that 55 percent of Canadians want to telecommute, and 43 percent would leave their current jobs if offered one where telecommuting were an option. Thirty-three percent of those surveyed said they would choose the opportunity to telecommute rather than a 10 percent raise. Other researchers looking at teleworking in Canada have found that it results in increased productivity,[134] decreased stress,[135] and better service to customers and clients.[136] Telecommuting has been found to reduce turnover[137] and decrease absenteeism.[138]

Telecommuting: The Downside

Not all employees embrace the idea of telecommuting, however. Some workers complain that they miss out on important meetings and informal interactions that lead to new policies and ideas. They also miss the social contact that occurs at work. Teleworking can decrease commitment to the organization,[139] and increase feelings of isolation[140] and burnout.[141] Telecommuters may be less likely or able to function as team players as well.[142] Typically, telecommuters are also remote from their managers.

The long-term future of telecommuting depends on some questions for which we don't yet have definitive answers. For instance, will employees who do their work at home be at a disadvantage in office politics? Might they be less likely to be considered for salary increases and promotions? Is being out of sight equivalent to being out of mind? Will nonwork distractions, such as children, neighbours, and the proximity of the television set and refrigerator, significantly reduce productivity for those without superior willpower and discipline?

We also do not know what the effect of working day after day in somewhat isolated circumstances has on individuals who do most of their work away from the office. Experts agree that home telecommuters in particular should come in to the central office at least once a week. As Ernie Gauvreau, chief operating officer for law firm Ratcliff and Company, explains, it is unlikely that Ratcliff's lawyers will work from home every day. "We need to bounce ideas off each other. And if you're at home, that doesn't exist."[143]

The strategies for work redesign that we have described have already had a profound impact on the ways Canadians perform and think about their jobs. Some even argue that "jobs" as we know them are becoming obsolete—that demands by employers and workers alike for greater flexibility and autonomy will result in the development of a contingent workforce with very little resemblance to job holders of the past.

SUMMARY AND IMPLICATIONS

1 **Is money an important motivator?** The most commonly used reward in organizations is money. The motivation theories we have presented only give us vague ideas of how money relates to individual motivation, however. Despite the importance of money in attracting and retaining employees, and rewarding and recognizing them, little attention has been given to individual differences in people's feelings about money.[144] Some studies indicate that money is not employees' top priority. A number of studies suggest that there are personality traits and demographic factors that correlate with an individual's attitude toward money.[145] People who value money highly score higher on "attributes like sensation seeking, competitiveness, materialism, and control." People who desire money score higher on self-esteem, need for achievement, and Type A personality measures. Men seem to value money more than women.

What these findings suggest is that when organizations develop reward programs, they need to consider very carefully the importance to the individual of the specific rewards offered.

2 **What does an effective reward system look like?** In general, an effective reward system links pay to performance, which is consistent with expectancy theory predictions. Recognition programs try to acknowledge individual efforts in concrete ways, with things like thank-you notes, employee-of-the-month programs, and public acknowledgments. In variable-pay or pay-for-performance programs, companies operate reward programs at three levels: individual (piece-rate wages and bonuses), group (gainsharing), and organizational (profit-sharing and stock option plans, including employee stock ownership plans). Under variable-pay programs, individuals should perceive a strong relationship between their performance and the rewards they receive, and thus be more motivated. The most recent research in Canada, which studied both unionized and non-unionized workplaces, found that variable-pay programs result in "increased productivity, a safer work environment, a better understanding of the business by employees, and little risk of employees losing base pay."[146]

3 **What kinds of mistakes are made in reward systems?** Individuals are responsive to the signals sent out by organizations, and if they determine that some activities are not valued, they may not engage in them, even when the firm expects employees to do so. Rewards should be linked to the type of performance expected. It is important that employees perceive a clear linkage between rewards and performance. If individuals perceive this relationship to be low, the results will be low performance, a decrease in job satisfaction, and an increase in turnover and absenteeism. Rewards are also culture-bound. Individuals respond to rewards in general, and specific rewards, differently, depending upon what culture they come from.

4 **Are rewards overrated?** In the right context, individuals often motivate themselves intrinsically and can achieve quite high levels of performance. We also know that giving rewards for things that were previously done for intrinsic motivation will decrease motivation.

5 **How can jobs be designed to increase motivation?** An understanding of work design can help managers design jobs that affect employee motivation positively. Managers can add more variety to jobs through job rotation and enlargement. They can also enrich jobs, increasing autonomy, following the job characteristics model. The model looks at a job's skill variety, task identity, task significance, autonomy, and feedback. It tells us that jobs in which employees have control over key elements in their work score higher in motivating potential than jobs in which employees don't have such control. Jobs that offer autonomy, feedback, and similar complex task characteristics tend to be more motivating for employees.

6 **How can flexible workplaces increase motivation?** Alternative work schedule options such as the compressed workweek, flextime, job sharing, and telecommuting have grown in popularity in recent years. They have become an important strategic tool as organizations try to increase the flexibility their employees need in a changing workplace.

For Review

1. What role, if any, does money play in employee recognition and job redesign?

2. Why is employee recognition an important reward?

3. What are the pluses and minuses of variable-pay programs from an employee's viewpoint? From management's viewpoint?

4. What is the difference between gainsharing and profit sharing?

5. What is an ESOP? How might it positively influence employee motivation?

6. What can firms do to create more motivating environments for their employees?

7. Describe three jobs that score high on the JCM. Describe three jobs that score low.

8. What are the advantages of flextime from an employee's perspective? From management's perspective?

9. What are the advantages of job sharing from an employee's perspective? From management's perspective?

10. From an employee's perspective, what are the pros and cons of telecommuting?

For Critical Thinking

1. "Employee recognition may be motivational for the moment, but it doesn't have any staying power. Why? Because employees can't take recognition to Roots or The Bay!" Do you agree or disagree? Discuss.

2. "Performance can't be measured, so any effort to link pay with performance is a fantasy. Differences in performance are often caused by the system, which means the organization ends up rewarding the circumstances. It's the same thing as rewarding the weather forecaster for a pleasant day." Do you agree or disagree with this statement? Support your position.

3. Describe five different bases (other than productivity) by which organizations can compensate employees. Based on your knowledge and experience, do you think productivity is the basis most used in practice? Discuss.

4. "Job redesign is a way of exploiting employees by increasing their responsibilities." Comment on this statement, and explain whether you agree with it or not.

5. What can management do to improve employees' perceptions that their jobs are interesting and challenging?

OB for You

■ Because the people you interact with appreciate recognition, consider including a brief note on a nice card to show thanks for a job well done. Or you might send a basket of flowers. Sometimes just sending a pleasant, thankful email is enough to make a person feel valued. All of these things are easy enough to do, and appreciated greatly by the recipient.

■ If you are working on a team or in a volunteer organization, try to find ways to motivate co-workers using the job characteristics model. For instance, make sure that everyone has some tasks over which they have autonomy, and make sure people get feedback on their work.

■ When you are working on a team project, think about whether everyone on the team should get the same reward, or whether rewards should be allocated according to performance. Individual-based performance rewards may decrease team cohesiveness if individuals do not cooperate with each other.

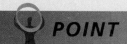

POINT

Money Motivates!

The importance of money as a motivator has been consistently downplayed by most behavioural scientists. They prefer to point out the value of challenging jobs, goals, participation in decision making, feedback, cohesive work teams, and other nonmonetary factors as stimulants to employee motivation. We argue otherwise here—that money is the crucial incentive to work motivation. As a medium of exchange, it is the vehicle by which employees can purchase the numerous need-satisfying things they desire. Furthermore, money also performs the function of a scorecard, by which employees assess the value that the organization places on their services and by which employees can compare their value to others.[147]

Money's value as a medium of exchange is obvious. People may not work only for money, but remove the money and how many people would come to work? A study of nearly 2500 employees found that while these people disagreed over what their primary motivator was, they unanimously ranked money as their number two.[148] This study reaffirms that for the vast majority of the workforce, a regular paycheque is absolutely necessary in order to meet basic physiological and safety needs.

The best case for money as a motivator is a review of studies done by Ed Locke at the University of Maryland.[149] Locke looked at four methods of motivating employee performance: money, goal setting, participation in decision making, and redesigning jobs to give employees more challenge and responsibility. He found that the average improvement from money was 30 percent; goal setting increased performance 16 percent; participation improved performance by less than 1 percent; and job redesign positively impacted performance by an average of 17 percent. Moreover, every study Locke reviewed that used money as a method of motivation resulted in some improvement in employee performance. Such evidence demonstrates that money may not be the only motivator, but it is difficult to argue that it doesn't motivate!

COUNTERPOINT

Money Doesn't Motivate Most Employees Today!

Money can motivate some people under some conditions, so the issue isn't really whether money can motivate. The answer to that is, "It can!" The more relevant question is this: Does money motivate most employees in the workforce today to higher performance? The answer to this question, we will argue, is "no."[150]

For money to motivate an individual's performance, certain conditions must be met. First, money must be important to the individual. Second, money must be perceived by the individual as being a direct reward for performance. Third, the marginal amount of money offered for the performance must be perceived by the individual as being significant. Finally, management must have the discretion to reward high performers with more money. Let's take a look at each of these conditions.

Money is not important to all employees. High achievers, for instance, are intrinsically motivated. Money should have little impact on these people. Similarly, money is relevant to those individuals with strong lower-order needs; but for most of the workforce, lower-order needs are substantially satisfied.

Money would motivate if employees perceived a strong linkage between performance and rewards in organizations. Unfortunately, pay increases are far more often determined by levels of skills and experience, community pay standards, the consumer price index, and the organization's current and future financial prospects than by each employee's level of performance.

For money to motivate, the marginal difference in pay increases between a high performer and an average performer must be significant. In practice, it rarely is. How much motivation is there in knowing that if you work really hard, you are going to end up with $20 a week more than someone who is doing just enough to get by? For a large number of people, not much! Research indicates that merit raises must be at least 7 percent of base pay for employees to perceive them as motivating. Unfortunately, recent surveys find nonmanagerial employees averaging merit increases of only 4.9 percent.[151]

In most organizations, managers have a very small area of discretion within which they can reward their higher-performing employees. So money might be theoretically capable of motivating employees to higher levels of performance, but most managers are not given enough flexibility to do much about it.

HR IMPLICATIONS

Developing Careers

Employees are likely to move from employer to employer over time, changing jobs and finding new workplace conditions. How to manage a career thus becomes an important issue.

First, let's define what we mean by the term *career*. A *career* is "the evolving sequence of a person's work experiences over time."[152] This definition does not imply advancement or success or failure. Any work, paid or unpaid, pursued over an extended period of time, can constitute a career. In addition to formal job work, it may include school work, homemaking, or volunteer work.[153]

Few human resource issues have changed as much in the past couple of decades as the role an organization has in developing its employees' careers.[154] Twenty years ago, when people were more likely to spend their entire work years with the same employer, most medium-sized and large organizations engaged in extensive employee career planning. Such planning focused exclusively on developing employees for opportunities within the specific organization. For instance, organizations would develop sophisticated placement charts to identify potential promotion candidates for key internal positions. They would also offer a wide range of in-house career development programs to prepare employees for promotions.

Today, many more organizations are engaged in nearly continuous restructuring through downsizing their operations, re-engineering processes, and increasing flexibility. Mergers lead to layoffs and duplicate jobs are eliminated. New technologies make it possible to do more work with fewer people. Because of globalization, companies are increasingly taking their labour-intensive work to countries with lower labour costs, resulting in fewer jobs within the corporation at home.

As a result of all these developments, individuals are far more likely to change jobs over time, and thus need to spend more time thinking about how their careers will evolve. Both organizations and individuals require much more flexibility in their approach to jobs and careers. Below, we discuss career development issues for organizations and individuals.

The Organization's Responsibilities for Career Development

There are a number of benefits that organizations gain by offering career development programs.[155] These include ensuring the right people will be available to meet changing staffing requirements, increasing workforce diversity, and providing employees with more realistic job expectations. The essence of a progressive career development program is built on providing support for employees to continually add to their skills, abilities, and knowledge. This support includes the following:

1. *Clearly communicating the organization's goals and future strategies.* When people know where the organization is headed, they are better able to develop a personal plan to share in that future.

2. *Creating growth opportunities.* Employees should have the opportunity to get new, interesting, and professionally challenging work experiences.

3. *Offering financial assistance.* The organization should offer tuition reimbursement to help employees keep their skills and knowledge current.

4. *Providing the time for employees to learn.* The organization should be generous in providing paid time off from work for off-the-job training. Additionally, workloads should not be so demanding that they preclude employees having the time to develop new skills, abilities, and knowledge.

The Employee's Responsibilities for Career Development

Although some employers do provide training and education, not all do. Therefore, today's employees should manage their own careers like entrepreneurs managing a small business. They should think of themselves as self-employed, even if employed in a large organization.[156] In a world of "free agency," the successful worker will build his or her career by maintaining flexibility and keeping skills and knowledge up-to-date. The following suggestions will help you become a career activist by taking charge of your own career:[157]

1. *Ensure your employability.* Make sure you have alternatives, should you lose your job. Acquire new skills; pursue opportunities that will stretch you.

2. *Have a fallback position.* Be sure to have multiple options for your career, and try to see yourself in multiple roles. Thus you could be an employee, a contract worker, or a freelance consultant using a wider skill set.

3. *Know your key skills.* Know how to package your current skills and experience in new ways. (For example, an architect who has a hobby as a gardener may start a business designing and building greenhouses.) Look carefully to identify your key talents and skills, and don't limit yourself to your job title.

4. *Market! market! market!* Even while performing at your highest level, always keep your eyes open for new work assignments, and position yourself for these. Let key people know your skills and how you can bring value to the organization. Also be sure to network. Be sure to treat everyone you meet as a potential client.

5. *Act Type A, be Type B.* While it's important, often, to have the drive and achievement orientation of Type As, it's also important to have the more relaxed Type B attitude of feeling good about yourself, even if you are not producing at a mile a minute. It's important that your sense of self not be completely tied to your job and the workplace.

6. *Stay culturally current.* Make sure that you are aware of world and cultural events through reading books, magazines, and other professional publications, and even participating in online discussion groups. Being in the know helps you

establish relationships with other people and can help you manage your career effectively.

7. *Be a compelling communicator.* Everyone is busy these days, so it's important to communicate effectively and efficiently. You may be communicating with people halfway around the globe or individuals who know little about the technical details of what you do, so being clear is important.

8. *Manage your finances.* To reduce your dependence on employment, make sure that you have your finances in order, as this will give you greater opportunities to explore change.

9. *Act like an insider, think like an outsider.* You need to be able to work as a team player, but also to be self-aware and able to evaluate your performance with some objectivity. It's important to be able to think independently. There will be times when you have to make decisions without the benefit of a group.

10. *Be capable of rewarding yourself.* With increased demands on everyone, you may not receive all of the external feedback you might like. Thus, you have to be able to give yourself a pat on the back when you do things well. Celebrate your successes, and take time to nourish yourself.

Career development pays off for both employees and organizations by increasing the skill levels available to do different jobs. The job characteristics model suggests that individuals would score higher on motivation when jobs require greater skill variety. Career development ensures that employees are always building additional skills, enabling them to take on jobs with greater skill variety.

LEARNING ABOUT **YOURSELF** EXERCISE

Is an Enriched Job for You?

People differ in what they like and dislike in their jobs. Listed below are 12 pairs of jobs. For each pair, indicate which job you would prefer. Assume that everything else about the jobs is the same—pay attention only to the characteristics actually listed for each pair of jobs. If you would prefer the job in Column A, indicate how much you prefer it by putting a checkmark in a blank to the left of the Neutral point. If you prefer the job in Column B, check 1 of the blanks to the right of Neutral. Check the Neutral blank only if you find the 2 jobs equally attractive or unattractive. Try to use the Neutral blank rarely.

Column A   **Column B**

1. A job that offers little or no challenge.

   Strongly prefer A — Neutral — Strongly prefer B

   A job that requires you to be completely isolated from co-workers.

2. A job that pays well.

   Strongly prefer A — Neutral — Strongly prefer B

   A job that allows considerable opportunity to be creative and innovative.

3. A job that often requires you to make important decisions.

   Strongly prefer A — Neutral — Strongly prefer B

   A job in which there are many pleasant people to work with.

4. A job with little security in a somewhat unstable organization.

   Strongly prefer A — Neutral — Strongly prefer B

   A job in which you have little or no opportunity to participate in decisions that affect your work.

5. A job in which greater responsibility is given to those who do the best work.

   Strongly prefer A — Neutral — Strongly prefer B

   A job in which greater responsibility is given to loyal employees who have the most seniority.

6. A job with a manager who sometimes is highly critical.

   Strongly prefer A — Neutral — Strongly prefer B

   A job that does not require you to use much of your talent.

7. A very routine job.

   Strongly prefer A — Neutral — Strongly prefer B

   A job in which your co-workers are not very friendly.

8. A job with a manager who respects you and treats you fairly.

   Strongly prefer A — Neutral — Strongly prefer B

   A job that provides constant opportunities for you to learn new and interesting things.

9. A job that gives you a real chance to develop yourself personally.

   Strongly prefer A — Neutral — Strongly prefer B

   A job with excellent vacation and fringe benefits.

10. A job in which there is a real chance you could be laid off.

    Strongly prefer A — Neutral — Strongly prefer B

    A job with very little chance to do challenging work.

11. A job with little freedom and independence to do your work in the way you think best.

    Strongly prefer A — Neutral — Strongly prefer B

    A job with poor working conditions.

12. A job with very satisfying teamwork.

    Strongly prefer A — Neutral — Strongly prefer B

    A job that allows you to use your skills and abilities to the fullest extent.

Scoring Key:

This questionnaire taps the degree to which you have a strong vs. weak desire to obtain growth satisfaction from your work. Each item on the questionnaire yields a score from 1 to 7 (that is, "Strongly prefer A" is scored 1; "Neutral" is scored 4; and "Strongly prefer B" is scored 7). To obtain your individual growth-need strength score, average the 12 items as follows:

Numbers 1, 2, 7, 8, 11, 12 (direct scoring, where "Strongly prefer A" is scored 1)

Numbers 3, 4, 5, 6, 9, 10 (reverse scoring, where "Strongly prefer B" is scored 1)

Average scores for typical respondents are close to the midpoint of 4. Research indicates that if you score high on this measure, you will respond positively to an enriched job. Conversely, if you score low, you will tend not to find enriched jobs satisfying or motivating.

You can use this questionnaire to identify areas where you can improve your interview skills. If you scored 3 or less on any statement, you should consider what you can do to improve that score.

Source: J. R. Hackman and G. R. Oldham, *Work Redesign* (Reading, MA: Addison-Wesley, 1980). Reprinted with permission.

BREAKOUT **GROUP** EXERCISES

Form small groups to discuss the following topics, as assigned by your instructor:

1. How might the job of student be redesigned to make it more motivating?

2. What is your ideal job? To what extent does it match up with the elements of the JCM?

3. Would you prefer working from home or working at the office? Why?

WORKING WITH **OTHERS** EXERCISE

Analyzing and Redesigning Jobs

Break into groups of 5 to 7 members each. Each student should describe the worst job he or she has ever had. Use any criteria you want to select 1 of these jobs for analysis by the group.

Members of the group will analyze the job selected by determining how well it scores on the job characteristics model. Use the following scale for your analysis of each job dimension:

7 = **Very high**

6 = **High**

5 = **Somewhat high**

4 = **Moderate**

3 = **Somewhat low**

2 = **Low**

1 = **Very low**

The following sample questions can guide the group in its analysis of the job in question:

- *Skill variety.* Describe the different identifiable skills required to do this job. What is the nature of the oral, written, and/or quantitative skills needed? Physical skills? Does the job holder get the opportunity to use all of his or her skills?

- *Task identity.* What is the product that the job holder creates? Is he or she involved in its production from beginning to end? If not, is he or she involved in a particular phase of its production from beginning to end?

- *Task significance.* How important is the product? How important is the job holder's role in producing it? How important is the job holder's contribution to the people he or she works with? If the job holder's job were eliminated, how inferior would the product be?

- *Autonomy.* How much independence does the job holder have? Does he or she have to follow a strict schedule? How closely is he or she supervised?

- *Feedback.* Does the job holder get regular feedback from his or her manager? From peers? From his or her staff? From customers? How about intrinsic performance feedback when doing the job?

Using the formula in Exhibit 5-8 on page 182, calculate the job's motivating potential score. Then, using the suggestions offered in the chapter for redesigning jobs, describe specific actions that management could take to increase this job's motivating potential.

Calculate the costs to management of redesigning the job in question. Do the benefits exceed the costs?

Conclude the exercise by having a representative of each group share his or her group's analysis and redesign suggestions with the entire class. Possible topics for class discussion might include similarities in the jobs chosen, problems in rating job dimensions, and the cost-benefit assessment of design changes.

Source: This exercise is based on W. P. Ferris, "Enlivening the Job Characteristics Model," in *Proceedings of the 29th Annual Eastern Academy of Management Meeting,* ed. C. Harris and C. C. Lundberg (Baltimore, MD: May 1992), pp. 125–128.

ETHICAL **DILEMMA** EXERCISE

Are CEOs Paid Too Much?

Critics have described the astronomical pay packages given to Canadian and American CEOs as "rampant greed." In 2004, the average compensation of CEOs of Canadian companies that make up the S&P/TSX index was $5.5 million, nearly doubling the $3.5 million in compensation awarded in 2003. By comparison, the S&P/TSX index rose 14.5 percent in 2004 and profits at TSX companies were up 30 percent.

How do you explain such large pay packages to CEOs? Some say this represents a classic economic response to a situation in which the demand is great for high quality top-executive talent, and the supply is low. Other arguments in favour of paying executives millions a year are the need to compensate people for the tremendous responsibilities and stress that go with such jobs; the motivating potential that seven- and eight-figure annual incomes provide to senior executives and those who might aspire to be; and the influence of senior executives on the company's bottom line. (For example, research findings cited on page 401 of Chapter 11 attribute a 15 to 25 percent variation in profitability to the leadership quality of CEOs.)

Critics of executive pay practices in Canada and the United States argue that CEOs choose board members whom they can count on to support ever-increasing pay for top management. If board members fail to "play along," they risk losing their positions, their fees, and the prestige and power inherent in board membership.

In addition, it is not clear that executive compensation is tied to firm performance. For instance, KPMG found in one survey that for 40 percent of the respondents, there was no correlation between the size of the bonus and how poorly or well the company fared. Consider the data in Exhibit 5-10, which illustrates the disconnect that can sometimes happen between CEO compensation and firm performance. *National Post Business* writers calculated that the CEOs noted in that exhibit were overpaid, based on their company's performance in 2004.

Is high compensation of CEOs a problem? If so, does the blame for the problem lie with CEOs or with the shareholders and boards that knowingly allow the practice? Are Canadian and American CEOs greedy? Are these CEOs acting unethically? Should their pay reflect more closely some multiple of their employees' wages? What do you think?

Sources: E. Church, "Market Recovery Delivers Executive Payout Bonanza," *Globe and Mail,* May 4, 2005, pp. B1, B9; "Gimme Gimme: Greed, the Most Insidious of Sins, Has Once Again Embraced a Decade," *Financial Post,* September 28/30, 1996, pp. 24–25; I. McGugan, "A Crapshoot Called Compensation," *Canadian Business,* July 1995, pp. 67–70.

EXHIBIT 5-10 2004 Compensation of Canada's "Most Overpaid" CEOs[*]

CEO(s)	Was Paid (3-Yr Avg.)	Should Have Been Paid	Amount Overpaid
1. Jozef Straus/Kevin Kennedy JDS Uniphase Ottawa, Ontario	$76 871 000	$1 537 000	$75 334 000
2. E. Melnyk/D. Squires Biovail Mississauga, Ontario	$63 216 000	$1 264 000	$61 952 000
3. Robert McEwen Goldcorp Vancouver, British Columbia	$33 053 000	$1 322 000	$31 731 000
4. Frank Weise III/J. Sheppard Cott Toronto, Ontario	$14 573 000	$4 080 000	$10 492 000
5. Gerald Schwartz Onex Toronto, Ontario	$17 109 000	$7 357 000	$9 752 000

[*]*National Post Business* calculated a "Bang for the Buck" formula, taking into account CEO performance variables.

Source: D. Dias, "Bang for Your Buck: Which CEOs are Really Worth Their Pay? Our Exclusive Tells All," *National Post Business*, November 1, 2004, p. 77. Material reprinted with the express permission of National Post Company, a CanWest Partnership.

CASE INCIDENTS

When the Perks Fade

Sean Neale is facing a dilemma. And he's not alone. Like many managers, Sean is struggling to find creative ways to keep his employees motivated.

Sean is CEO of a robotics manufacturing firm located in Montreal. The company prospered in the 1990s—sales revenue nearly tripled and the company's workforce doubled. The price of the company's stock rose form under $8 a share to more than $60. And his employees prospered because the firm had a pay-for-performance compensation system. Specifically, every year, 20 percent of the company's profits were set aside in a bonus pool and used to reward employees. Profit sharing provided the typical employee with an extra $7800 in 1998 and $9400 in 1999. Then it dropped to just $2750 in 2000. The company lost money in 2001 and 2002, so there were no profits to spare. Meanwhile, Sean's executive team was not spared from watching its profit-sharing bonuses disappear. The average executive bonus in 1999 was over $150 000. Like the company's operating employees, in 2001 and 2002, executives got nothing over and above their basic salaries.

Sean's situation seems to be common among many firms. While employees in 2002 and 2003 were often glad to just have a job, the incentives they enjoyed in the 1990s were eroding. For instance, Ford Motor Company suspended contributions to pension plans and merit raises for about 2200 salaried senior executives; media company Tribune froze wages and cut 140 senior managers' pay by 5 percent; and Hewlett-Packard eliminated profit sharing in 2001. A 2002 survey of 391 companies found that 48 percent planned to lower performance-based rewards for both managers and workers in the next 12 months.

Questions

1. What implications can you draw from this case regarding pay-for-performance programs?

2. If you were Sean Neale, what can you offer employees as an alternative to compensation that will not place an undue hardship on your organization's bottom line? Be specific.

Source: This case is based on S. Jones, "When the Perks Fade," *Wall Street Journal*, April 11, 2002, p. B12.

Working at Bob's in Rio

Bob's is one of the largest fast-food chains in Latin America. It's a McDonald's clone, with headquarters in Rio de Janeiro and more than half of its 225 outlets located in Brazil. What's it like to work at Bob's? A day at an outlet in a mall in São Paulo provides some insights.

The most notable characteristic of this fast-food restaurant is the youth of the 12 employees. Silvana, who supervises the training of new hires, has had two promotions in her four years on the job. Yet she's only 21 years old. Levy, the short-order cook, is 20 and has been doing his job for a year. Elisangela is 21 and has been a Bob's employee for two years. The restaurant's manager, who has seven years at Bob's, is 23. Simone is one of the oldest employees at 25.

Bob's employees have another commonality besides their youth. They are all from a humble social background. Middle-class kids want to avoid working in fast-food places.

The jobs at Bob's have a highly structured routine. For instance, if you are working the grill, you need to know that a Big Bob gets two slices of beef, 11 grams of lettuce, and 7 grams of sliced onions on a sesame seed bun; a Bob's Burger is also two slices of beef with special sauce but only a slice of tomato on a plain bun; and a Franburgao gets a chicken breast, tomato, and curry sauce on a sesame seed bun. If you are working the french fryer,

you need to check the temperature of the oil, make sure it's 174 degrees Celsius, put one package of fries into the bin, push it down slowly into the oil until you hear the click, wait for the machine to bring it back up, shake the bin three times, and pour the fries into the steel container.

Employees seem generally content with their jobs. In spite of having to wear a silly red tie, a blue and red baseball cap, and an apron that says *Bob's,* these people are glad to have a job in a country where as many as one in five is unemployed. Standard employees earn 500 *reals* (less than $450 Cdn. a month). The manager's salary is around 1300 *reals* a month.

Questions

1. Describe an entry-level job at Bob's in JCM terms.

2. What type of employee do you think would fit well at Bob's?

3. Could jobs at Bob's be enriched to make employees more productive?

4. Could flextime work at Bob's? Explain.

Source: T. Ogier, "Life as a Burger King," *Latin Trade,* December 2000, pp. 44–47.

From **Concepts** to **Skills**

Designing Enriched Jobs

How does management enrich an employee's job? The following suggestions, based on the JCM, specify the types of changes in jobs that are most likely to lead to improving their motivating potential.[158]

1. *Combine tasks.* Managers should seek to take existing and fractionalized tasks and put them back together to form a new and larger module of work. This increases skill variety and task identity.

2. *Create natural work units.* The creation of natural work units means that the tasks an employee does form an identifiable and meaningful whole. This

increases employee "ownership" of the work and improves the likelihood that employees will view their work as meaningful and important rather than as irrelevant and boring.

3. *Establish client relationships.* The client is the user of the product or service that the employee works on (and may be an "internal customer" as well as someone outside the organization). Wherever possible, managers should try to establish direct relationships between workers and their clients. This increases skill variety, autonomy, and feedback for the employee.

4. *Expand jobs vertically.* Vertical expansion gives employees responsibilities and control that were formerly reserved for management. It seeks to partially close the gap between the "doing" and the "controlling" aspects of the job, and it increases employee autonomy.

5. *Open feedback channels.* By increasing feedback, employees not only learn how well they are performing their jobs, but also whether their performance is improving, deteriorating, or remaining at a constant level. Ideally, this feedback about performance should be received directly as the employee does the job, rather than from management on an occasional basis. For instance, at many restaurants you can find feedback cards on the table to indicate the quality of service received during the meal.

Assessing Skills

After you've read this chapter, take the following Self-Assessments on your enclosed CD-ROM:

18. What's My Job Motivating Potential?

19. Do I Want an Enriched Job?

24. What Time of Day Am I Most Productive?

46. Am I Experiencing Work/Family Conflict?

50. How Stressful Is My Life?

51. Am I Burned Out?

Practising Skills

You own and manage Sunrise Deliveries, a small freight transportation company that makes local deliveries of products for your customers. You have a total of nine employees—an administrative assistant, two warehouse personnel, and six delivery drivers.

The drivers' job is pretty straightforward. Each morning they come in at 7:30 a.m., pick up their daily schedule, and then drive off in their preloaded trucks to make their stops. They occasionally will also pick up packages and return them to the Sunrise warehouse, where they will be unloaded and redirected by the warehouse workers.

You have become very concerned with the high turnover among your drivers. Of your current six drivers, three have been working for you less than two months and only one's tenure exceeds six months. This is frustrating because you are paying your drivers more than many of the larger delivery companies like UPS and FedEx. This turnover is getting expensive because you are constantly having to spend time finding and training replacements. It's also hard to develop a quality customer-service program when customers constantly see new faces. When you have asked departing drivers why they are quitting, common complaints include: "There's no room for advancement," "the job is boring," and "all we do is drive." What should you do to solve this problem?

Reinforcing Skills

1. Think of the worst job you have ever had. Analyze the job according to the five dimensions identified in the JCM. Redesign the job in order to make it more satisfying and motivating.

2. Spend one to three hours at various times observing employees in your college dining hall. What actions would you recommend to make these jobs more motivating?

CHAPTER 6

Groups and Teamwork

How do you get teenagers to devote their spare time to learning more about science and technology? Make it a competition that puts them on a team.

1 What are teams and groups?

2 Does everyone use teams?

3 What kinds of teams are there?

4 How does one become a team player?

5 Do teams go through stages while they work?

6 How do we create effective teams?

7 Are teams always the answer?

The students at Glenforest Secondary School in Mississauga, Ontario, took part in the ninth annual Canada FIRST Robotics Competition in spring 2002. They had eight weeks to design and build a remotely operated robot that would compete with other robots built by secondary school teams across the country. The students wanted to do a better job than they had in 2001. Their previous robot moved well, but it could not meet the challenge of firing balls at pie plates. The students suspected that to improve their entry, they needed a better team and more coaching from adults. Although they knew little about teamwork, they had support and encouragement from teachers, engineering mentors, and corporate sponsors. What factors could help the students have a better team and build a better robot the second time around?

For teams to excel, a number of conditions need to be met. Effective teams need wise leadership, a variety of resources, and a way to solve problems. Team members need to be dedicated, and they need to build trust. In this chapter, we examine when it's best to have a team, how to create effective teams, and how to deal with diversity on teams.

TEAMS VS. GROUPS: WHAT'S THE DIFFERENCE?

There is some debate whether groups and teams are really separate concepts, or whether the terms can be used interchangeably. We think that there is a subtle difference between the terms. A **group** is two or more people with a common relationship. Thus a group could be co-workers, or people meeting for lunch or standing at the bus stop. Unlike teams, groups do not necessarily engage in collective work that requires interdependent effort.

A **team** is "a small number of people with complementary skills who are committed to a common purpose, performance goals, and approach for which they hold themselves mutually accountable."[1] Groups become teams when they meet the following conditions:[2]

- Team members share *leadership*.

- Both individuals and the team as a whole share *accountability* for the work of the team.

- The team develops its own *purpose* or *mission*.

- The team works on *problem-solving* continuously, rather than just at scheduled meeting times.

- The team's measure of *effectiveness* is the team's outcomes and goals, not individual outcomes and goals.

1 What are teams and groups?

group Two or more people with a common relationship.

team A small number of people who work closely together toward a common objective and are accountable to one another.

Glenforest Secondary School
www.peel.edu.on.ca/schools/
rapidfacts/glenfor.htm

Thus, while not all groups are teams, all teams can be considered groups. Much of what we discuss in this chapter applies equally well to both. We will offer some suggestions on creating effective teams later in the chapter.

WHY HAVE TEAMS BECOME SO POPULAR?

> When Glenforest Secondary School teachers decided that students should enter the Canada FIRST Robotics Competition, they could have asked each of the smartest kids in the science class to build their own robots. This is not what the teachers and students chose to do, however. Instead, they created a team. Was this a reasonable way for Glenforest Secondary to proceed?

2 Does everyone use teams?

Pick up almost any business magazine today and you will read how teams have become an essential part of the way business is being done in companies such as Zellers, Xerox, Sears Canada, General Electric, AT&T, Hewlett-Packard, Motorola, Apple Computer, DaimlerChrysler AG, 3M, Australian Airlines, London Life Insurance Company, and Johnson & Johnson. A Conference Board of Canada report found that more than 80 percent of its 109 respondents used teams in the workplace.[3] This finding is similar to the United States, where 80 percent of *Fortune* 500 companies have half or more of their employees on teams.[4] As well, 68 percent of small US manufacturers use teams in their production areas.[5]

The extensive use of teams creates the *potential* for an organization to generate greater outputs with no increase in inputs. Notice, however, we said "potential." There is nothing inherently magical in the creation of teams that ensures the achievement of greater output. As we will show later in this chapter, successful, high-performing teams have certain common characteristics. If management hopes to increase organizational performance through the use of teams, it must ensure that its teams possess these characteristics.

Do teams work? The evidence suggests that teams typically outperform individuals when the tasks being done require multiple skills, judgment, and experience.[6] As organizations have restructured to compete more effectively and efficiently, they have turned to teams as a way to better utilize employee talents. Management has found that teams are more flexible and responsive to changing events than traditional departments or other forms of permanent groupings. Teams can quickly assemble, deploy, refocus, and disband. Teams also can be more motivational. Recall from the job characteristics model in Chapter 5 that having greater task identity is one way of increasing motivation. Teams allow for greater task identity, with team members working on tasks together.

Quaker Oats Company of Canada
www.quakeroats.ca

Peterborough, Ontario-based Quaker Oats Company of Canada is quite pleased with the way teamwork was introduced in its facilities in the mid-1990s. Plant manager Scott Baker noted that "in terms of productivity gains, every single year, our productivity has been improving in the facility."[7] The teams make their own schedules and order supplies. This has cut management costs by two-thirds. Still, Baker notes that teamwork is a challenge, and team members need to engage in continual learning.

Teams are not necessarily appropriate in every situation, however. Read this chapter's *Point/Counterpoint* for a debate on whether sports teams are good models for thinking about teams in the workplace.

TYPES OF TEAMS

3 What kinds of teams are there?

Teams can be classified based on their objective. The four most common kinds of teams you are likely to find in an organization are

- Problem-solving (or process-improvement) teams
- Self-managed (or self-directed) teams

- Cross-functional (or project) teams

- Virtual teams

The types of relationships that members within each team have to one another are shown in Exhibit 6-1.

Problem-Solving Teams

A **problem-solving (or process-improvement) team** is typically made up of 5 to 12 employees from the same department who meet for a few hours each week to discuss ways of improving quality, efficiency, and the work environment.[8] Such teams can also be planning teams, task forces, or committees that are organized to get tasks done. During meetings, members share ideas or offer suggestions on how to improve work processes and methods. Rarely, however, are these teams given the authority to unilaterally implement any of their suggested actions. Montreal-based Clairol Canada is an exception. When a Clairol employee identifies a problem, he or she has the authority to call together an ad hoc group to investigate, and then define and implement solutions. Clairol presents GOC (Group Operating Committee) Awards to teams for their efforts.

The 1998–1999 Workplace and Employee Survey (WES) found that the use of teamwork varies by organizational size. For companies with 500 or more employees, 50 percent had problem-solving teams, whereas only 25 percent of companies with 20 to 99 employees had problem-solving teams.[9]

problem-solving (or process-improvement) team A group of 5 to 12 employees from the same department who meet for a few hours each week to discuss ways of improving quality, efficiency, and the work environment.

Clairol Canada
www.clairol.ca

Quality Circles

A **quality circle** is a work group of 8 to 10 employees and managers who share an area of responsibility. They meet regularly—typically once a week, on company time and on company premises—to discuss their *quality problems,* investigate causes of the problems, recommend solutions, and take corrective actions. They assume responsibility for solving quality problems, and generate and evaluate their own feedback. Management typically retains control over the final decision regarding implementation of recommended solutions.

Part of the quality circle concept includes teaching participating employees group communication skills, various quality strategies, and measurement and problem analysis techniques. Exhibit 6-2 on page 204 describes a typical quality circle process.

quality circle A work group of 8 to 10 employees and managers who meet regularly to discuss their *quality problems,* investigate causes of the problems, recommend solutions, and take corrective actions.

Quality Circles and Productivity Do quality circles improve employee productivity and satisfaction? A review of the evidence is mixed. Quality circles tend to show little or no effect on employee satisfaction; many studies report positive results from quality circles on productivity, but these results are by no means guaranteed.[10] The failure of many quality circle programs to produce measurable benefits has also led to the discontinuation of a large number of them.

EXHIBIT 6-1 Four Types of Teams

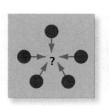 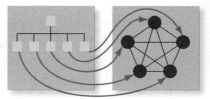 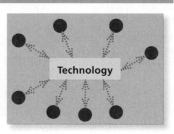

| Problem-solving | Self-managed | Cross-functional | Virtual |

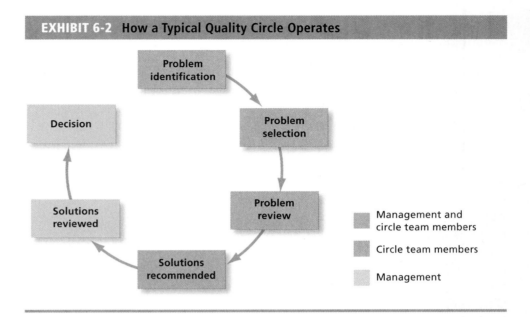

EXHIBIT 6-2 How a Typical Quality Circle Operates

Problem identification → Problem selection → Problem review → Solutions recommended → Solutions reviewed → Decision

■ Management and circle team members
■ Circle team members
□ Management

The Canadian Auto Workers (CAW) union has not been entirely pleased with quality circles, as workers have been asked to assume more responsibility for work when the circles are introduced. Ken Lewenza, president of a Windsor-area CAW local, explains: "A key change has been to transfer responsibility for monitoring and resolving quality problems at the minivan and truck plants from management employees to teams of unionized workers."[11] But he adds that the union "is resisting company efforts to establish Japanese-style cells of assembly workers because of concerns that the concept could lead to job losses through increased efficiency."

Quality circles were the management fad of the 1980s but have "become a flop," suggests J. L. Cotton.[12] He points out that in places that used them, little time was spent in quality circles, which were often viewed as a simple device that could be added on to the organization with few changes required outside the program itself.

However, failure does not have to be inevitable for quality circles. A case in point involves Montreal-based CAE, which showed that a company can overcome some of the failures associated with quality circles.[13] CAE's success with quality circles indicates that they can work even where they have previously failed if management introduces the proper supports. White Rock, BC-based Canadian Autoparts Toyota (CAPTIN), a wheel-manufacturing plant, has also used quality circles for many years with good results.

Self-Managed Teams

Problem-solving teams were on the right track, but they didn't go far enough in involving employees in work-related decisions and processes. This led to experiments with truly autonomous teams that could not only solve problems but also implement solutions and assume responsibility for outcomes.

A **self-managed (or self-directed) team** is typically made up of 10 to 15 employees. The employees perform highly related or interdependent jobs and take on many of the responsibilities of their former managers.[14] Typically, this includes planning and scheduling of work, assigning tasks to members, collectively controlling the pace of work, making operating decisions, and taking action on problems. Fully self-managed teams even select their own members and leader and have the members evaluate each other's performance. The evidence indicates that self-managed teams often perform better than teams with formally appointed leaders.[15] Under self-managed teams, external managerial positions can take on decreased importance and may even be eliminated. Leaders who interfere with self-managed teams can block high performance.[16]

self-managed (or self-directed) team A group of 10 to 15 employees who take on many of the responsibilities of their former managers.

A recent Statistics Canada study found that men were more likely than women to be part of self-directed teams (36 percent vs. 29 percent).[17] This may be explained by a Conference Board of Canada study that found self-directed teams are used more typically in a variety of manufacturing industries (such as the auto industry, chemicals, equipment repair) and service environments (such as hotels, banks, and airlines).[18] It should be noted that some organizations have been disappointed with the results from self-managed teams. The introduction of these teams is sometimes viewed negatively by workers who fear that increased use of teams will lead to layoffs. Their concerns may be well founded. At Honeywell's Scarborough plant, one-third of the 75 salaried positions were eliminated between 1991 and 1994 as a result of the shift to self-managed teams.[19] The plant was able to run with 40 percent fewer employees—and with no drop in production after doing this.

Many employees are asked to work in teams in order to accomplish their tasks. In a self-managed team, such as the one from Xerox shown here, members make decisions about how to manage and schedule production, and also monitor the quality of their output.

Honeywell
www.honeywell.ca

The research on self-managed teams is not extensive at this time. However, meta-analyses covering existing studies found a positive effect on productivity, and no significant impact on job satisfaction, organizational commitment, absenteeism or turnover.[20] Care needs to be taken when introducing self-managed teams globally, however. For instance, evidence suggests that these types of teams have not fared well in Mexico largely due to that culture's low tolerance of ambiguity and uncertainty and employees' strong respect for hierarchical authority.[21]

Cross-Functional Teams

The Boeing Company used **cross-functional (or project) teams** when it developed its 777 jet. Such teams are made up of employees from about the same hierarchical level, but from different work areas, who come together to accomplish a task.[22] For instance, if a business school wanted to design a new integrated curriculum in business for undergraduates, it might bring together a group of faculty members, each of whom represents one discipline (for example, finance, accounting, marketing, and organizational behaviour) to work together to design the new program. Each individual would be expected to contribute knowledge of his or her field, and ways to package together the knowledge in a more integrated fashion.

Many organizations have used groups formed from members of different departments for years. Such groups include **task forces** (temporary cross-functional teams) and **committees** (groups composed of members from different departments). But the popularity of cross-discipline work teams exploded in the late 1980s. All the major automobile manufacturers—including Toyota, Honda, Nissan, BMW, GM, Ford, and DaimlerChrysler AG—have turned to this form of team to coordinate complex projects. Calgary-based Canadian Pacific Railway (CPR) uses cross-functional teams to figure out ways to cut costs. Individuals from all of the functional areas affected by the spending review (such as supply services, operations, and finance) make up the team.[23]

Cross-functional teams are an effective means for allowing people from diverse areas within an organization (or even between organizations) to exchange information, develop new ideas, solve problems, and coordinate complex projects. Of course, cross-functional teams are not easy to manage.[24] Their early stages of development are often time-consuming as members learn to work with diversity and complexity. It takes time to build trust and teamwork, especially among people from different backgrounds,

cross-functional (or project) team A group of employees at about the same hierarchical level, but from different work areas, who come together to accomplish a task.

task force A temporary cross-functional team.

committee A group composed of members from different departments.

Canadian Pacific Railway
www.cpr.ca

with different experiences and perspectives. In *HR Implications* on page 235, we look at measures organizations can take to turn individuals into team players.

Skunkworks

Skunkworks are cross-functional teams that develop spontaneously to create new products or work on complex problems. Such teams are typically found in the high-tech sector, and are generally sheltered from other organizational members. This gives the team the ability to work on new ideas in isolation, without being watched over by organization members, during creative stages. Skunkworks are thus able to ignore the structure and bureaucratic rules of the organization while they work.

Lockheed Martin Canada
www.lockheedmartin.com/canada/

The first skunkworks team appeared in the 1940s, at Lockheed Aerospace Corporation.[25] The team was to create a jet fighter as fast as possible, and avoid bureaucratic delays. In just 43 days, the team of 23 engineers and a group of support personnel put together the first American fighter to fly at more than 800 kilometres an hour.

Not all skunkworks projects are as successful. Many companies, including IBM and Xerox, have had mixed results in using them. Still, skunkworks do offer companies an alternative approach to teamwork when speed is an important factor.

Virtual Teams

virtual team A team that uses computer technology to tie together physically dispersed members in order to achieve a common goal.

Problem-solving, self-managed, and cross-functional teams do their work face to face. **Virtual teams** use computer technology to tie together physically dispersed members in order to achieve a common goal.[26] They allow people to collaborate online—using communication links such as wide-area networks, video conferencing, and email—whether they are only a room away or continents apart. With greater availability of technology and increasing globalization, virtual teams become not only possible, but necessary. To the extent that work is knowledge-based rather than production-oriented, virtual teams are also more possible.

Virtual teams can do all the things that other teams do—share information, make decisions, complete tasks. They can include members from the same organization or link an organization's members with employees from other organizations (suppliers and joint partners, for example). They can convene for a few days to solve a problem or a few months to complete a project, or exist permanently.[27] Often they can be more efficient at tasks as well, because of the ease of sharing information through email and voice mail. Virtual teams also make it possible for people who are in different geographical and time zones to work together.

Virtual teams can suffer from the limited social contact of team members and the absence of paraverbal and nonverbal cues in their communications. In face-to-face conversation, people use paraverbal (tone of voice, inflection, voice volume) and nonverbal (eye movement, facial expression, hand gestures, and other body language) cues to provide increased meaning. In virtual communications, team members are not able to duplicate the normal give and take of face-to-face discussion. As a result, virtual team members often have less social rapport and are more at risk of misunderstanding one another. An additional concern about virtual teams is whether members are able to build the same kind of trust that face-to-face teams build. *Focus on Research* explores the trust issue.

Sheila Goldgrab coaches virtual teams from the comfort of her home in Toronto. She can do that coaching via teleconference, video conference, or email. She gets hired as a consultant to help virtual teams work together more smoothly. As one recipient of her coaching said, "Sheila was the rudder of the planning group. While we were going at high speed in different directions, she ensured there was a link among the group that kept us focused on the task at hand."

FOCUS ON **RESEARCH**

If I Can't See You, Can I Trust You?

Can teams build trust if they've never met each other face to face? A study examining how virtual teams work on projects indicates that virtual teams can develop close inter-action and trust.[28] These qualities simply evolve differently than in face-to-face groups.

In face-to-face groups, trust comes from direct interaction, over time. In virtual teams, trust is either established at the outset or it generally doesn't develop. The researchers found that initial electronic messages set the tone for how interactions occurred throughout the project.

In one team, for instance, when the appointed leader sent an introductory mes-sage that had a distrustful tone, the team suffered low morale and poor performance throughout the project. The researchers suggest that virtual teams should start with an electronic "courtship," where members provide some personal information. Then the teams should assign clear roles to members, helping members to identify with each other.

Finally, the researchers emphasized the impor-tance of a positive outlook. They noted that teams that had the best attitude (eagerness, enthusiasm, and intense action orientation in messages) did con-siderably better than teams that had one or more pes-simists among them.

Creating Virtual Workspaces

It's obvious that virtual teams must rely on technology to communicate. But what is the best way to do this? Team members can become overwhelmed with email, drowning in messages to the point of failing to read them. To better understand the problem, a recent study looked at 54 teams from 26 companies operating in a wide variety of industries.[29] The researchers found that 83 percent of the teams they studied used virtual work-spaces to communicate. The virtual workspace is a team website on a company's intranet, but was designed to help remind team members of their "decisions, ratio-nales, and commitments." The virtual workspace can have "walls" or links to information about each person, and discussion forums with topic threads that cover important issues and problems. The discussion forums can also serve as places to post work-in-progress to get feedback. Exhibit 6-3 shows an example of a virtual workspace for a project at Shell.

Some additional tips for improving the way that virtual teams function include the following: making sure that the team addresses feelings of isolation that members might have; making sure that team members have a mix of interpersonal and technical skills; and paying careful attention to evaluating performance and providing recog-nition and feedback.[30] For even more tips, see *OB in Action—Managing Virtual Teams.*

OB IN ACTION

Managing Virtual Teams

Establishing trust and commitment, encouraging communica-tion, and assessing team members pose tremendous challenges for virtual team managers. Here are a few tips to make the process easier:

→ Establish **regular times** for group interaction.

→ Set up **firm rules** for communication.

→ Use **visual forms of communication** where possible.

→ **Emulate** the attributes of co-located **teams**. For example, allow time for informal chitchat and socializing, and cele-brate achievements.

→ **Give and receive feedback** and offer assistance on a regular basis. Be persistent with people who are not com-municating with you or each other.

→ Agree on **standard technology** so all team members can work together easily.

→ Consider using **360-degree feedback** to better under-stand and evaluate team members.

→ Provide a **virtual meeting room** via an intranet, website, or bulletin board.

→ Note which employees **effectively use email** to build team rapport.

→ **Smooth the way for the next assignment** if member-ship on the team, or the team itself, is not permanent.

→ **Be available** to employees, but don't wait for them to seek you out.

→ Encourage **informal, off-line conversation** between team members.

Source: C. Joinson, "Managing Virtual Teams," *HR Magazine,* June 2002, p. 71. Reprinted with the permission of *HR Magazine,* published by the Society for Human Resource Management, Alexandria, VA.

EXHIBIT 6-3 **An Illustration of a Virtual Workspace**

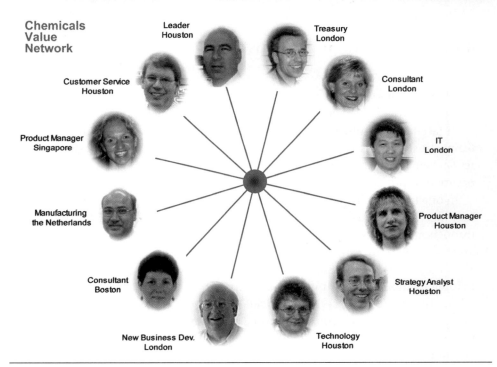

Chemicals Value Network

Leader Houston

Treasury London

Consultant London

IT London

Product Manager Houston

Strategy Analyst Houston

Technology Houston

New Business Dev. London

Consultant Boston

Manufacturing the Netherlands

Product Manager Singapore

Customer Service Houston

Source: Reprinted by permission of Shell Chemical LP.

Case Incident—A Virtual Team at T. A. Sterns on page 241 provides further exploration of how virtual teams work.

FROM INDIVIDUAL TO TEAM MEMBER

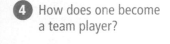

4 How does one become a team player?

In order for either a group or a team to function, individuals have to achieve some balance between their own needs and the needs of the group. When individuals come together to form groups and teams, they bring with them their personalities and all their previous experiences. They also bring their tendencies to act in different ways at different times, depending on the effects that different situations and different people have on them.

One way to think of these differences is in terms of possible pressures that individual group members put on each other through roles, norms, and status expectations. As we consider the process of how individuals learn to work in groups and teams, we will use the terms interchangeably. Many of the processes that each go through are the same, with the major difference being that teams within the workplace are often set up on a nonpermanent basis, in order to accomplish projects. Becoming a team player is not easy, as *OB in the Street* demonstrates.

OB IN THE STREET

Skeleton Racer Finds Teamwork a Real Challenge

Is being a team player really all that tough? Jeff Pain spent much of the 2000s trying his best not to be a team player.[31] Pain is the top skeleton racer in Canada, and a likely medal contender for the 2006 Olympic Winter Games.

Much of Pain's negativity toward teamwork was directed at team member Duff Gibson, who is also an Olympics contender. The two have been intense rivals for over five years.

"When Duff started skeleton [in 1999], I had a difficult time with my team dynamics because I felt that I knew a lot more than the people I was sliding with," says Pain. "I didn't want to share information with them and I carried that mistaken belief right up to last year [2004]. That was probably my and Duff's worst year."[32]

In summer 2004, Pain, Gibson, and fellow team member Paul Boehm decided to work together to share information about the tracks they are competing on, and then try to help each other out.

Pain and Gibson improved their times and reached the top of international standings. Pain admits that learning how to be more of a team player has helped him improve in a sport that he was thinking of quitting because of his unhappiness related to interactions with other team members. "I really insulated myself, and that didn't create a good environment for me or the team," Pain admits.[33]

As Jeff Pain shows, being a team member requires working together, sharing information, and being willing to take on the role of being a team member. We discuss roles below.

Roles

Shakespeare said, "All the world's a stage, and all the men and women merely players." Using the same metaphor, all group members are actors, each playing a **role**. By this term, we mean a set of expected behaviour patterns of a person in a given position in a social unit. The understanding of role behaviour would be dramatically simplified if each of us chose one role and "played it out" regularly and consistently. Unfortunately, we are required to play a number of diverse roles, both on and off our jobs.

As we will see, one of the tasks in understanding behaviour is grasping the role that a person is currently playing. For example, on the job a person might have the roles of electrical engineer, member of middle management, and primary company spokesperson in the community. Off the job, there are still more roles: spouse, parent, church member, food bank volunteer, and coach of the softball team. Many of these roles are compatible; some create conflicts. For instance, how does one's religious involvement influence managerial decisions regarding meeting with clients on the Sabbath? We address role conflict below.

Role Conflict

Most roles are governed by **role expectations**, that is, how others believe a person should act in a given situation. When an individual is confronted by conflicting role expectations, the result is role conflict. **Role conflict** exists when an individual finds that complying with one role requirement may make it more difficult to comply with another.[34] At the extreme, it can include situations in which two or more role expectations are mutually contradictory!

All of us have faced and will continue to face role conflicts. The critical issue, from our standpoint, is how conflicts imposed by different expectations within the organization affect behaviour. Certainly, they increase internal tension and frustration. There are a number of behavioural responses individuals may engage in. They may, for example,

role A set of expected behaviours of a person in a given position in a social unit.

role expectations How others believe a person should act in a given situation.

role conflict A situation in which an individual finds that complying with one role requirement may make it more difficult to comply with another.

Soccer star David Beckham, a husband and father of three young children, plays many different roles in several different jobs. Beckham is a key player as central midfielder for Spain's Real Madrid soccer team. In another job, he plays the role of an actor as celebrity endorser in advertising campaigns. In this photo, we see Beckham in a different role—as an author promoting his autobiography, *My Side*, at a book-signing session. Beckham's behaviour varies with the roles he plays on and off the job.

give a formalized bureaucratic response. The conflict is then resolved by relying on the rules, regulations, and procedures that govern organizational activities.

For example, an employee faced with the conflicting requirements imposed by the corporate controller's office and his own plant manager decides in favour of his immediate boss—the plant manager. Other behavioural responses may include withdrawal, stalling, negotiation, or redefining the facts or the situation to make them appear congruent. *Case Incident—Role Conflict Among Telephone Service Employees* on page 240 looks at how role conflict can affect one's worklife.

Role Ambiguity

role ambiguity A person is unclear about his or her role.

Role ambiguity exists when a person is unclear about the expectations of his or her role. In teams, role ambiguity can lead to confusion, stress, and even bad feelings. For instance, suppose two group members each think that the other one is responsible for preparing the first draft of a report. At the next group meeting, neither brings a draft report and both are annoyed that the other person did not do the work.

role overload Too much is expected of someone.

role underload Too little is expected of someone, and that person feels that he or she is not contributing to the group.

Groups benefit when individuals know their roles. Roles within groups and teams should be balanced. Edgar Schein suggests that **role overload** occurs when what is expected of a person "far exceeds what he or she is able to do."[35] **Role underload** occurs when too little is expected of someone, and that person feels that he or she is not contributing to the group.

Norms

Have you ever noticed that golfers don't speak while their partners are putting on the green, or that employees don't criticize their bosses in public? Why? The answer is "norms!"

norms Acceptable standards of behaviour within a group that are shared by the group's members.

Norms are acceptable standards of behaviour within a group that are shared by the group's members. All groups have established norms that tell members what they ought and ought not to do under certain circumstances. When agreed to and accepted by the group, norms act as a means of influencing the behaviour of group members with a minimum of external controls. Norms differ among groups, communities, and societies, but all of these entities have norms.[36]

Formalized norms are written up in organizational manuals that set out rules and procedures for employees to follow. But by far, most norms in organizations are informal. You don't need someone to tell you that throwing paper airplanes or engaging in prolonged gossip sessions at the water cooler is an unacceptable behaviour when the "big boss from Toronto" is touring the office. Similarly, we all know that when we are in an employment interview discussing what we didn't like about our previous job, there are certain things we should not talk about (such as difficulty in getting along with co-workers or our manager). There are other things it's appropriate to talk about (inadequate opportunities for advancement, or unimportant and meaningless work).

Norms for both groups and organizations cover a wide variety of circumstances. Some of the most common norms have to do with issues such as

Being a gracious team member can make a difference. When Atlanta-based CNN decided to revise its morning program *American Morning* in summer 2005, CNN/US President Jonathan Klein decided to replace co-anchor Bill Hemmer, who had held the anchor position for several years. In explaining the decision, Klein noted that he wanted a male anchor who would work with female co-anchor Soledad O'Brien and help her look good too, rather than trying to take all the attention himself.

- *Performance.* How hard to work, what kind of quality, levels of tardiness

- *Appearance.* Personal dress, when to look busy, when to "goof off," how to show loyalty

- *Social arrangement.* How team members interact

- *Allocation of resources.* Pay, assignments, allocation of tools and equipment

OB in Action—Creating a Team Charter presents a way for teams to develop norms when the team first forms.

The "How" and "Why" of Norms

How do norms develop? Why are they enforced? A review of the research allows us to answer these questions.[37]

Norms typically develop gradually as group members learn what behaviours are necessary for the team to function effectively. Of course, critical events in the group might short-circuit the process and quickly prompt new norms. Most norms develop in one or more of the following four ways:

- *Explicit statements made by a group member.* Often instructions from the group's supervisor or a powerful member establish norms. The team leader might specifically say that no personal phone calls are allowed during working hours or that coffee breaks must be no longer than 10 minutes.

- *Critical events in the group's history.* These set important precedents. A bystander is injured while standing too close to a machine and, from that point on, members of the work group regularly monitor each other to ensure that no one other than the operator gets within two metres of any machine.

- *Primacy.* The first behaviour pattern that emerges in a group frequently sets team expectations. Groups of students who are friends often choose seats near each other on the first day of class and become upset if an outsider takes "their" seats in a later class.

- *Carry-over behaviours from past situations.* Group members bring expectations with them from other groups to which they have belonged. Thus, work groups typically prefer to add new members who are similar to current ones in background and experience. This is likely to increase the probability that the expectations they bring are consistent with those already held by the group.

Groups don't establish or enforce norms for every conceivable situation, however. The norms that the groups will enforce tend to be those that are important to them.[38] What makes a norm important?

- *It facilitates the group's survival.* Groups don't like to fail, so they seek to enforce any norm that increases their chances for success. This means that groups try to protect themselves from interference from other groups or individuals.

- *It increases the predictability of group members' behaviours.* Norms that increase predictability enable group members to anticipate each other's actions and to prepare appropriate responses.

OB IN ACTION

Creating a Team Charter

When you form a new team, you may want to develop a team charter, so that everyone agrees on the basic norms for group performance. Consider including answers to the following in your charter:

→ What are team members' **names and contact information** (e.g., phone, email)?

→ How will **communication** among team members take place (e.g., phone, email)?

→ What will the **team ground rules** be (e.g., where and when to meet, attendance expectations, workload expectations)?

→ How will **decisions** be made (e.g., consensus, majority vote, leader rules)?

→ What **potential conflicts** may arise in the team? Among team members?

→ How will **conflicts be resolved** by the group?

Source: Submitted by Don Miskiman, Chair and U-C Professor of Management, Malaspina University College, Nanaimo, BC. With permission.

- *It reduces embarrassing interpersonal problems for group members.* Norms are important if they ensure the satisfaction of their members and prevent as much interpersonal discomfort as possible.

- *It allows members to express the central values of the group and clarify what is distinctive about the group's identity.* Norms that encourage expression of the group's values and distinctive identity help solidify and maintain the group.

Conformity

As a group member, you desire acceptance by the group. Because of your desire for acceptance, you are susceptible to conforming to the group's norms. Considerable evidence shows that the group can place strong pressures on individual members to change their attitudes and behaviours to conform to the group's standard.[39]

conformity Adjusting one's behaviour to align with the norms of the group.

The impact that group pressures for **conformity** can have on an individual member's judgment and attitudes was demonstrated in the now classic studies of noted social psychologist Solomon Asch.[40] Asch found that subjects gave answers that they knew were wrong, but that were consistent with the replies of other group members, about 35 percent of the time. The results suggest that group norms can pressure us toward conformity. We desire to be one of the group and avoid being visibly different.

Research by University of British Columbia professor Sandra Robinson and colleague Anne O'Leary-Kelly indicates that conformity may explain why some work groups are more prone to antisocial behaviour than others.[41] Individuals working with others who exhibited antisocial behaviour at work were more likely to engage in antisocial behaviour themselves. Of course, not all conformity leads to negative behaviour. Other research has indicated that work groups can have more positive influences, leading to more prosocial behaviour in the workplace.[42]

Overall, research continues to indicate that conformity to norms is a powerful force in groups and teams. The *Ethical Dilemma Exercise* on page 240 asks you to consider whether it is ethical to force employees to be team players.

STAGES OF GROUP AND TEAM DEVELOPMENT

Consider when the Glenforest Secondary School students first started working together to build the robot. If they were anything like most ordinary teams, they might not have known each other, or trusted each other. They might not have known who should be the leader or how to form the plans for what they had to do. Besides building a successful robot, they had to raise $16 000 to take part in the Canada FIRST Robotics Competition. They also had several deadlines to meet. To build a successful team that would achieve their goals, the students would have had to go through several stages. So what stages do teams go through as they develop?

5 Do teams go through stages while they work?

When people get together for the first time with the purpose of achieving some objective, they discover that acting as a team is not something simple, easy, or genetically programmed. Working in a group or team is often difficult, particularly in the initial stages, when people don't necessarily know each other. As time passes, groups and teams go through various stages of development, although the stages are not necessarily exactly the same for each group or team. In this section, we discuss two models of group development. The five-stage model describes the standardized sequence of stages groups pass through. The recently discovered punctuated-equilibrium model describes the pattern of development specific to temporary groups with deadlines. These models can be applied equally to groups and teams.

EXHIBIT 6-4 Stages of Group Development and Accompanying Issues

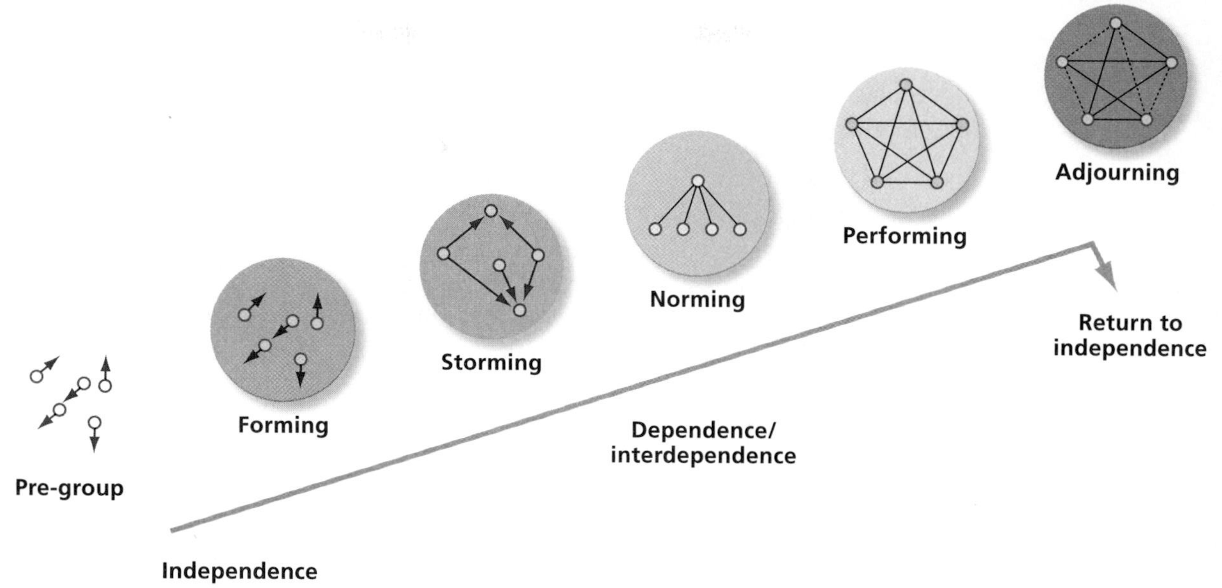

	Forming	Storming	Norming	Performing	Adjourning
Individual issues	"How do I fit in?"	"What's my role here?"	"What do the others expect of me?"	"How do I best perform?"	"What's next?"
Group issues	"Why are we here?"	"Who is in charge and who does what?"	"Can we agree on roles and work as a team?"	"Can we do the job properly?"	"How do we disband?"

The Five-Stage Model

From the mid-1960s, it was believed that groups passed through a standard sequence of five stages.[43] As shown in Exhibit 6-4, these five stages have been labelled *forming, storming, norming, performing,* and *adjourning.* Although we now know that not all groups pass through these stages in a linear fashion, the five-stage model of group development can still help in addressing your anxieties about working in groups and teams. The model shows how individuals move from being independent to working interdependently with group members.

- *Stage I: Forming.* Think about the first time you met with a new team. Do you remember how some people seemed silent and others felt confused about the task you were to accomplish? Those feelings arise during the first stage of group development, know as **forming**. Forming is characterized by a great deal of uncertainty about the team's purpose, structure, and leadership. Members are "testing the waters" to determine what types of behaviour are acceptable. This stage is complete when members have begun to think of themselves as part of a team.

  forming The first stage in group development, characterized by much uncertainty.

- *Stage II: Storming.* Do you remember how some people in your team just didn't seem to get along, and sometimes power struggles even emerged? These reactions are typical of the **storming** stage, which is one of intragroup conflict. Members accept the existence of the team, but resist the constraints that the team imposes on individuality. Furthermore, there is conflict over who will

  storming The second stage in group development, characterized by intragroup conflict.

control the team. When this stage is complete, a relatively clear hierarchy of leadership will emerge within the team.

Some teams never really emerge from the storming stage, or they move back and forth through storming and the other stages. A team that remains forever planted in the storming stage may have less ability to complete the task because of all the interpersonal problems.

- *Stage III: Norming.* Many teams resolve the interpersonal conflict and reach the third stage, in which close relationships develop and the team demonstrates cohesiveness. There is now a strong sense of team identity and camaraderie. This **norming** stage is complete when the team structure solidifies, and the team has assimilated a common set of expectations of what defines correct member behaviour.

- *Stage IV: Performing.* Next, and you may have noticed this in some of your own team interactions, some teams just seem to come together well and start to do their work. This fourth stage, when significant task progress is being made, is called **performing**. The structure at this point is fully functional and accepted. Team energy has moved from getting to know and understand each other to performing the task at hand. In this chapter's vignette, when Glenforest Secondary School raced its robot in the Canada FIRST Robotics Competition, it was performing.

- *Stage V: Adjourning.* For permanent work groups and teams, performing is the last stage in their development. However, for temporary committees, teams, task forces, and similar groups that have a limited task to perform, there is an **adjourning** stage. In this stage, the group prepares for its disbandment. High task performance is no longer the group's top priority. Instead, attention is directed toward wrapping up activities. Group members' responses vary at this stage. Some members are upbeat, basking in the group's accomplishments. Others may be depressed over the loss of camaraderie and friendships gained during the work group's life.

For some teams, the end of one project may mean the beginning of another. In this case, a team has to transform itself in order to get on with a new project that may need a different focus, different skills, and may need to take on new members. Thus the adjourning stage may lead to renewal of the team to get the next project started.

Putting the Five-Stage Model into Perspective

Many interpreters of the five-stage model have assumed that a group becomes more effective as it progresses through the first four stages. This assumption may be generally true, but what makes a group effective is more complex than this model acknowledges. Under some conditions, high levels of conflict are conducive to high group performance, as long as the conflict is directed toward the task and not toward group members. So we might expect to find situations where groups in Stage II outperform those in Stages III or IV. Similarly, groups do not always proceed clearly from one stage to the next. Sometimes, in fact, several stages go on simultaneously, as when groups are storming and performing at the same time. Teams even occasionally go backwards to previous stages. Therefore, you should not assume that all groups follow the five-stage process precisely, or that Stage IV is always the most preferable.

The five-stage model also ignores organizational context.[44] For instance, a study of a cockpit crew in an airliner found that, within 10 minutes, three strangers assigned to fly together for the first time had become a high-performing team. How could a team come together so quickly? The answer lies in the strong organizational context

norming The third stage in group development, characterized by close relationships and cohesiveness.

performing The fourth stage in group development, when the group is fully functional.

adjourning The final stage in group development for temporary groups, where attention is directed toward wrapping up activities rather than task performance.

surrounding the tasks of the cockpit crew. This context provided the rules, task definitions, information, and resources needed for the team to perform. They did not need to develop plans, assign roles, determine and allocate resources, resolve conflicts, and set norms the way the five-stage model predicts.

Within the workplace, some group behaviour takes place within a strong organizational context, and it would appear that the five-stage model has limited applicability for those groups. However, there are a variety of situations in the workplace where groups are assigned to tasks and the individuals do not know each other. They must therefore work out interpersonal differences at the same time that they work through the assigned tasks.

The Punctuated-Equilibrium Model

Temporary groups with deadlines don't seem to follow the previous model. Studies indicate that temporary groups with deadlines have their own unique sequence of action (or inaction):[45]

- The first meeting sets the group's direction.

- The first phase of group activity is one of inertia.

- A transition takes place at the end of the first phase, which occurs exactly when the group has used up half its allotted time.

- The transition initiates major changes.

- A second phase of inertia follows the transition.

- The group's last meeting is characterized by markedly accelerated activity.

Ever wonder what causes flurries of activity in groups?

This pattern is called the punctuated-equilibrium model, developed by Professor Connie Gersick, a Visiting Scholar at the Yale University School of Management, and is shown in Exhibit 6-5.[46] It is important for you to understand these shifts in group behaviour, if for no other reason than when you are in a group that is not working well or one that has gotten off to a slow start, you can start to think of ways to help the group move to a more productive phase.

Phase 1

As both a team member and possibly a team leader, it's important that you recognize that the first meeting sets the team's direction. A framework of behavioural patterns and

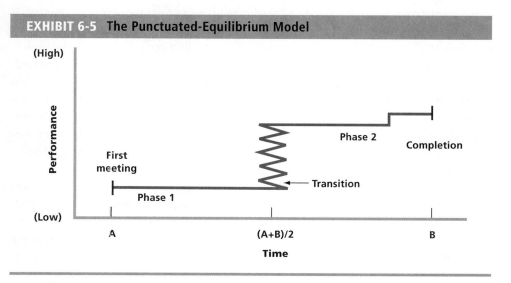

EXHIBIT 6-5 The Punctuated-Equilibrium Model

assumptions through which the team will approach its project emerges in this first meeting. These lasting patterns can appear as early as the first few seconds of the team's life.

Once set, the team's direction becomes "written in stone" and is unlikely to be re-examined throughout the first half of the team's life. This is a period of inertia—that is, the team tends to stand still or become locked into a fixed course of action. Even if it gains new insights that challenge initial patterns and assumptions, the team is incapable of acting on these new insights in Phase 1. You may recognize that in some teams, during the early period of trying to get things accomplished, no one really did his or her assigned tasks. You may also recognize this phase as one where everyone carries out the tasks, but not in a very coordinated fashion. Thus, the team is performing at a relatively low state. This does not necessarily mean that it is doing nothing at all, however.

Phase 2

At some point, the team moves out of the inertia stage and recognizes that work needs to get completed. One of the more interesting discoveries made in these studies was that each team experienced its transition at the same point in its calendar—precisely halfway between its first meeting and its official deadline. The similarity occurred despite the fact that some teams spent as little as an hour on their project while others spent six months. It was as if the teams universally experienced a mid-life crisis at this point. The midpoint appears to work like an alarm clock, heightening members' awareness that their time is limited and that they need to "get moving." When you work on your next team project, you might want to examine when your team starts to "get moving."

This transition ends Phase 1 and is characterized by a concentrated burst of changes, dropping of old patterns, and adoption of new perspectives. The transition sets a revised direction for Phase 2, which is a new equilibrium or period of inertia. In this phase, the team executes plans created during the transition period. The team's last meeting is characterized by a final burst of activity to finish its work. There have been a number of studies that support the basic premise of punctuated equilibrium, though not all of them found that the transition in the team occurred exactly at the midpoint.[47]

Applying the Punctuated-Equilibrium Model

We can use this model to describe typical experiences of student teams created for doing group term projects. At the first meeting, a basic timetable is established. Members size up one another. They agree they have nine weeks to do their project. The instructor's requirements are discussed and debated. From that point, the group meets regularly to carry out its activities. About four or five weeks into the project, however, problems are confronted. Criticism begins to be taken seriously. Discussion becomes more open. The group reassesses where it has been and aggressively moves to make necessary changes. If the right changes are made, the next four or five weeks find the group developing a first-rate project. The group's last meeting, which will probably occur just before the project is due, lasts longer than the others. In it, all final issues are discussed and details resolved.

In summary, the punctuated-equilibrium model characterizes deadline-oriented teams as exhibiting long periods of inertia, interspersed with brief revolutionary changes triggered primarily by their members' awareness of time and deadlines. To use the terminology of the five-stage model, the team begins by combining the *forming* and *norming* stages, then goes through a period of *low performing*, followed by *storming*, then a period of *high performing*, and, finally, *adjourning*.

Several researchers have suggested that the five-stage and punctuated-equilibrium models are at odds with each other.[48] However, it makes more sense to view the models as complementary: The five-stage model considers the interpersonal process of the group, while the punctuated-equilibrium model considers the time challenges that the group faces.[49]

CREATING EFFECTIVE TEAMS

Beatrice Sze, Glenforest Secondary School's team co-captain, gave her teammates a sense of responsibility and ownership over their work. For example, when a team member came to her with questions about what to do next, she would say encouragingly, "Use your brain. You can figure this out. You know how to do this."

The students at Glenforest Secondary also had to be resourceful. One team member's parents provided the family basement for a team gathering place. That enabled the students to get extra parts from the family's snowblower and dehumidifier. Sometimes they worked so late into the evening that they had sleepovers on the basement floor, huddled in sleeping bags. The also got a mentor—a computer and electrical engineer with Bell Mobility—who tried to guide the students in the right direction, without telling them what to do. What other factors might have contributed to the effectiveness of Glenforest Secondary's robotics team?

When we consider team effectiveness, we refer to such objective measures as the team's productivity, managers' ratings of the team's performance, and aggregate measures of member satisfaction. Some of the considerations necessary to create effective teams are outlined next. However, we are also interested in team process. Exhibit 6-6 on page 218 provides a checklist of the characteristics of an effective team.

There is no shortage of efforts that try to identify the factors that lead to team effectiveness.[50] However, studies have taken what was once a "veritable laundry list of characteristics"[51] and organized them into a relatively focused model with four general categories summarized in Exhibit 6-7, page 218:[52]

6 How do we create effective teams?

- Resources and other contextual influences that make teams effective

- The team's composition

- Work design

- Process variables (those things that go on in the team that influence how effective the team is).

Keep in mind two caveats as you review the issues that lead to effective teams:

- First, teams differ in form and structure. Since the model we present attempts to generalize across all varieties of teams, you need to be careful not to rigidly apply the model's predictions to all teams.[53] The model should be used as a guide, not as an inflexible prescription.

- Second, the model assumes that it's already been determined that teamwork is preferable over individual work. Creating "effective" teams in situations wherein individuals can do the job better is equivalent to solving the wrong problem perfectly.

OB in Action—Harming Your Team on page 219 presents activities that can make a team ineffective. You might want to evaluate your own team experience against this checklist to give you some idea of how well your team is functioning, or to understand what might be causing problems for your team. Then consider the factors that lead to more effective teams below. For an applied look at the process of building an effective team, see the *Working With Others Exercise* on page 239, which asks you to build a paper tower with teammates and then analyze how the team performed.

Kerri Molinaro, president of Burlington, Ontario-based IKEA Canada, believes that teams are the best way to bring employees together. IKEA's leadership style is informal, and the company values people who are humble and trustworthy. This also makes them good team members.

EXHIBIT 6-6   Characteristics of an Effective Team

1.	**Clear purpose**	The vision, mission, goal, or task of the team has been defined and is now accepted by everyone. There is an action plan.
2.	**Informality**	The climate tends to be informal, comfortable, and relaxed. There are no obvious tensions or signs of boredom.
3.	**Participation**	There is much discussion, and everyone is encouraged to participate.
4.	**Listening**	The members use effective listening techniques such as questioning, paraphrasing, and summarizing to get out ideas.
5.	**Civilized disagreement**	There is disagreement, but the team is comfortable with this and shows no signs of avoiding, smoothing over, or suppressing conflict.
6.	**Consensus decisions**	For important decisions, the goal is substantial but not necessarily unanimous agreement through open discussion of everyone's ideas, avoidance of formal voting, or easy compromises.
7.	**Open communication**	Team members feel free to express their feelings on the tasks as well as on the group's operation. There are few hidden agendas. Communication takes place outside of meetings.
8.	**Clear rules and work assignments**	There are clear expectations about the roles played by each team member. When action is taken, clear assignments are made, accepted, and carried out. Work is distributed among team members.
9.	**Shared leadership**	While the team has a formal leader, leadership functions shift from time to time depending on the circumstances, the needs of the group, and the skills of the members. The formal leader models the appropriate behaviour and helps establish positive norms.
10.	**External relations**	The team spends time developing key outside relationships, mobilizing resources, and building credibility with important players in other parts of the organization.
11.	**Style diversity**	The team has a broad spectrum of team-player types including members who emphasize attention to task, goal setting, focus on process, and questions about how the team is functioning.
12.	**Self-assessment**	Periodically, the team stops to examine how well it is functioning and what may be interfering with its effectiveness.

Source: G. M. Parker, *Team Players and Teamwork: The New Competitive Business Strategy* (San Francisco: Jossey-Bass, 1990), Table 2, p. 33. Copyright © 1990 by Jossey-Bass Inc., Publishers. Reprinted by permission of John Wiley & Sons, Inc.

EXHIBIT 6-7   A Model of Team Effectiveness

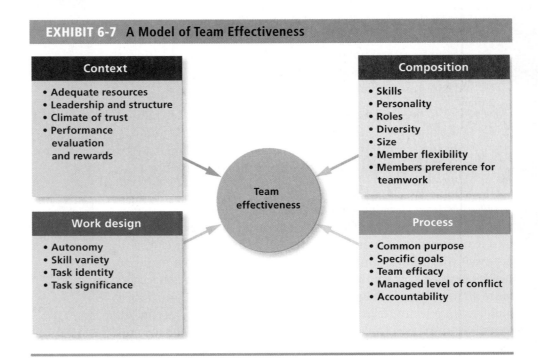

Context
- Adequate resources
- Leadership and structure
- Climate of trust
- Performance evaluation and rewards

Composition
- Skills
- Personality
- Roles
- Diversity
- Size
- Member flexibility
- Members preference for teamwork

Work design
- Autonomy
- Skill variety
- Task identity
- Task significance

Process
- Common purpose
- Specific goals
- Team efficacy
- Managed level of conflict
- Accountability

Team effectiveness

Context

Teams can require a great deal of maintenance to function properly. They need management support as well as an organizational structure that supports teamwork. The four contextual factors that appear to be most significantly related to team performance are the presence of adequate resources, effective leadership, a climate of trust, and a performance evaluation and reward system that reflects team contributions. Hamilton, Ontario-based Dofasco is a clear example of getting the context right for team performance. Dofasco started using teams in the early 1990s, by putting almost 7000 employees through team-building exercises. Today, multidisciplinary teams are given improvement goals; the teams assume responsibility for developing plans to reach the goals. To a large extent, the teams are self-managed. "The supervisor became less of an ass-kicker and more of a resource person," explained former CEO John Mayberry.[54] Pay is partly tied to how well Dofasco does each year, which helps motivate employees to work with their teams, rather than as individuals.

Adequate Resources

All work teams rely on resources outside the team to sustain them. A scarcity of resources directly reduces the ability of a team to perform its job effectively. As one set of researchers concluded, after looking at 13 factors potentially related to team performance, "perhaps one of the most important characteristics of an effective work group is the support the group receives from the organization."[55] This includes such support as technology, adequate staffing, administrative assistance, encouragement, and timely information.

Teams must receive the necessary support from management and the larger organization if they are going to succeed in achieving their goals. You may recall from the opening vignette that one of the reasons for the Glenforest Secondary School team's failure in 2001 was that it didn't have the kind of coaching it needed to build a great robot. For the 2002 competition, the team found a mentor, and also created a workshop at one of the team member's homes.

Leadership and Structure

Leadership plays a crucial role in the development and success of teams. Professor Richard Hackman of Harvard University, who is the leading expert on teams, suggests that the role of team leader involves the following:[56]

- Creating a real team rather than a team in name only
- Setting a clear and meaningful direction for the team's work
- Making sure that the team structure will support working effectively
- Ensuring that the team operates within a supportive organizational context
- Providing expert coaching

There are some practical problems that must be resolved when a team first starts working together. Team members must agree on who is to do what, and ensure that all members contribute equally in sharing the workload. The team also needs to determine how schedules will be set, what skills need to be developed, how the team will

OB IN ACTION

Harming Your Team

→ **Refuse to share** issues and concerns. Team members refuse to share information and engage in silence, avoidance, and meetings behind closed doors where not all members are included.

→ **Depend** too much **on the leader**. Members rely too much on the leader and do not carry out their responsibilities.

→ **Fail to follow through** on decisions. Teams do not take action after decision making, showing that the needs of the team have low priority, or members are not committed to the decisions that were made.

→ **Hide conflict**. Team members do not reveal that they have a difference of opinion and this causes tension.

→ **Fail at conflict resolution**. Infighting, put-downs, and attempts to hurt other members damage the team.

→ **Form subgroups**. The team breaks up into smaller groups that put their needs ahead of the team as a whole.

Source: Based on W. G. Dyer, R. H. Daines, and W. C. Giauque, *The Challenge of Management* (New York: Harcourt Brace Jovanovich, 1990), p. 343.

Dofasco
www.dofasco.ca

resolve conflicts, and how the team will make and modify decisions. Agreeing on the specifics of work and how they fit together to integrate individual skills requires team leadership and structure. This, incidentally, can be provided directly by management or by the team members themselves. In the case of the Glenforest Secondary School students in this chapter's vignette, the team was led by two student co-captains. The adult advisers did not try to tell the students what to do.

On traditionally managed teams, we find that two factors seem to be important in influencing team performance—the leader's expectations and his or her mood. Leaders who expect good things from their team are more likely to get them! For instance, military platoons under leaders who held high expectations performed significantly better in training than platoons whose leaders did not set expectations.[57] Additionally, studies have found that leaders who exhibit positive moods get better team performance and lower turnover.[58] The *Learning About Yourself Exercise* on page 237 will help you evaluate how suited you are to building and leading a team.

Recent research suggests that women may make better team leaders than men, as *Focus on Research* shows.

FOCUS ON **RESEARCH**

Team Leadership Can Affect Grades

How much leadership does a team need? "The more women participating equally in a project, the better the outcome," suggests Professor Jennifer Berdahl of the Joseph L. Rotman School of Management at the University of Toronto.[59] Berdahl's research looked at 169 students enrolled in her organizational behaviour courses.[60] She found that all of the teams started out with one person taking a leadership role. However, if the groups were predominantly males, the same person stayed in charge the entire time. In predominantly female teams, women shared leadership roles, and were more egalitarian in how they worked. Male-led teams, whether they were predominantly male groups or mixed-gender groups, received poorer grades on their projects than teams where women shared leadership roles.

Berdahl gives this advice to students: "In a creative project team, it's really important to ensure there is equal opportunity for participation."

A leader, of course, isn't always needed. For instance, the evidence indicates that self-managed teams often perform better than teams with formally appointed leaders.[61] Leaders can also obstruct high performance when they interfere with self-managed teams.[62] On self-managed teams, team members absorb many of the duties typically assumed by managers.

Climate of Trust

Members of effective teams trust each other. They also exhibit trust in their leaders.[63] Interpersonal trust among team members facilitates cooperation, reduces the need to monitor each others' behaviour, and bonds members around the belief that others on the team won't take advantage of them. Team members, for instance, are more likely to take risks and expose vulnerabilities when they believe they can trust others on their team. Trust in leadership is important in that it allows the team to be willing to accept and commit to their leader's goals and decisions.

Performance Evaluation and Rewards

How do you get team members to be both individually and jointly accountable? The traditional individually oriented evaluation must be modified to reflect team performance.[64]

Should individuals be paid for their "teamwork" or their individual performance?

Individual performance evaluations, fixed hourly wages, individual incentives, and the like are not consistent with the development of high-performance teams. So in addition to evaluating and rewarding employees for their individual contributions, management should consider group-based appraisals, profit sharing, gainsharing, small-group incentives, and other system modifications that will reinforce team effort and commitment.

One additional consideration when deciding whether and how to reward team members is the effect of pay dispersion on team performance. Research by Nancy Langton, your Vancouver-based author, shows that when there is a large discrepancy in wages among group members, collaboration is lowered.[65] A study of baseball player salaries also found that teams where players were paid more similarly often outperformed teams with highly paid "stars" and lowly paid "scrubs."[66]

Composition

This category includes variables that relate to how teams should be staffed. In this section, we will address the skills, personality, and roles of team members, the diversity and size of the team, member flexibility, and members' preference for teamwork.

Skills

To perform effectively, a team requires three different types of skills:

1. It needs people with *technical expertise.*

2. It needs people with the *problem-solving* and *decision-making skills* to be able to identify problems, generate alternatives, evaluate those alternatives, and make competent choices.

3. It needs people with good listening, feedback, conflict resolution, and other *interpersonal skills.*[67]

Why do some groups seem to get along better than others?

No team can achieve its performance potential without developing all three types of skills. The right mix is crucial. Too much of one at the expense of others will result in lower team performance. But teams don't need to have all the complementary skills in place at the beginning. It's not uncommon for one or more members to take responsibility to learn the skills in which the group is deficient, thereby allowing the team to reach its full potential.

Personality

Teams have different needs, and people should be selected for the team on the basis of their personalities and preferences, as well as the team's needs for diversity and specific roles. We demonstrated in Chapter 2 that personality has a significant influence on individual employee behaviour. Personality also influences team behaviour. Many of the dimensions identified in the Big Five model of personality have been shown to be

The top management team of Toronto-based Pursuit, a consulting firm, performs effectively because it has the right mix of technical, problem-solving, and interpersonal skills. With backgrounds in different marketing disciplines and training in personal awareness, each team member brings a particular technical skill to the team and a unique approach for solving clients' problems. "As a team, we collaborate like no other that I know," says Wayne Clark (left), "and I've worked with a lot of teams."

relevant to team effectiveness. Specifically, teams that rate higher in mean levels of extraversion, agreeableness, conscientiousness, and emotional stability tend to receive higher managerial ratings for team performance.[68]

Very interestingly, the evidence indicates that the variance in personality characteristics may be more important than the mean.[69] So, for example, although higher mean levels of conscientiousness on a team are desirable, mixing both conscientious and not-so-conscientious members tends to lower performance. Including just one person who is low on agreeableness, conscientiousness, or extraversion can result in strained internal processes and decreased overall performance.[70]

Roles

task-oriented roles Roles performed by group members to ensure that the tasks of the group are accomplished.

maintenance roles Roles performed by group members to maintain good relations within the group.

Earlier in the chapter we discussed how individuals fill roles within groups. Within almost any group, two sets of role relationships need to be considered: task-oriented roles and maintenance roles. **Task-oriented roles** are performed by group members to ensure that the tasks of the group are accomplished. These roles include initiators, information seekers, information providers, elaborators, summarizers, and consensus makers. **Maintenance roles** are carried out to ensure that group members maintain good relations. These roles include harmonizers, compromisers, gatekeepers, and encouragers. You may recall from this chapter's vignette that Beatrice Sze was an encourager—helping team members achieve their best.

Effective teams maintain some balance between task orientation and maintenance of relations. Exhibit 6-8 identifies a number of task-oriented and maintenance behaviours in the key roles that you might find in a team.

On many teams, there are individuals who will be flexible enough to play multiple roles and/or complete each other's tasks. This is an obvious plus to a team because it greatly improves its adaptability and makes it less reliant on any single member.[71] Selecting members who themselves value flexibility, and then cross-training them to be able to do each other's jobs, should lead to higher team performance over time.

individual roles Rcles performed by group members that are not productive for keeping the team on task.

Occasionally within teams, you will see people take on **individual roles** that are not productive for keeping the team on task. When this happens, the individual is demonstrating more concern for himself or herself than the team as a whole.

Diversity

group diversity The presence of a heterogeneous mix of individuals within a group.

Group diversity refers to the presence of a heterogeneous mix of individuals within a group.[72] Individuals can be different not only in functional characteristics (e.g., jobs, positions, or work experiences) but also in demographic or cultural characteristics (e.g., age, race, sex, and citizenship). Recent studies have examined the effect of heterogeneous values on performance, and suggested that value differences may have a greater influence than functional, demographic, or cultural differences.[73] *Focus on Research* describes one of those studies.

FOCUS ON **RESEARCH**

Diversity Can Improve or Hurt Teams

How do different types of diversity influence performance? When we talk about team diversity, we often mean demographic differences like race, gender, or age diversity.[74] Professor Margaret Neale of Stanford University's Graduate School of Business has looked at the impact of three types of diversity on group performance: informational, demographic, and value-goal diversity.

Her research did not find a direct effect of diversity on performance. Instead, different forms of diversity generate different types of conflict. The type of conflict and how the team deals with it are what affect the team's performance.

	Function	Description	Example
Roles that build task accomplishment	*Initiating*	Stating the goal or problem, making proposals about how to work on it, setting time limits.	"Let's set up an agenda for discussing each of the problems we have to consider."
	Seeking information and opinions	Asking group members for specific factual information related to the task or problem, or for their opinions about it.	"What do you think would be the best approach to this, Jack?"
	Providing information and opinions	Sharing information or opinions related to the task or problems.	"I worked on a similar problem last year and found. . ."
	Clarifying	Helping one another understand ideas and suggestions that come up in the group.	"What you mean, Sue, is that we could. . .?"
	Elaborating	Building on one another's ideas and suggestions.	"Building on Don's idea, I think we could. . ."
	Summarizing	Reviewing the points covered by the group and the different ideas stated so that decisions can be based on full information.	Appointing a recorder to take notes on a blackboard.
	Consensus testing	Providing periodic testing on whether the group is nearing a decision or needs to continue discussion.	"Is the group ready to decide about this?"
Roles that build and maintain a team	*Harmonizing*	Mediating conflict among other members, reconciling disagreements, relieving tensions.	"Don, I don't think you and Sue really see the question that differently."
	Compromising	Admitting error at times of group conflict.	"Well, I'd be willing to change if you provided some help on. . ."
	Gatekeeping	Making sure all members have a chance to express their ideas and feelings and preventing members from being interrupted.	"Sue, we haven't heard from you on this issue."
	Encouraging	Helping a group member make his or her point. Establishing a climate of acceptance in the group.	"I think what you started to say is important, Jack. Please continue."

EXHIBIT 6-8 Roles Required for Effective Team Functioning

Source: "Team Processes," in *Managing for the Future,* ed. D. Ancona, T. Kochan, M. Scully, J. Van Maanen, and D. E. Westney (Cincinnati, OH: South-Western College Publishing, 1996), p. 9.

Informational diversity was associated with constructive conflict, with team members debating about the best course of action. Neale considers this positive conflict. Demographic diversity can result in interpersonal conflict. If group members think, "I have a different opinion than you. I don't like what you do or how you do it. I don't like you," Neale says, it can destroy the group.

Groups that have value-goal diversity may face the most damage from the diversity. When team members do not agree on the values and goals, it is hard for them to function. However, if a team works through differences to reach consensus on values and goals, team members then know each other's intentions.

Neale and her colleagues conducted their research through a field study of work teams in a relocation company. They surveyed employees to measure their informational and value-goal diversity. They also collected group performance data and supervisor assessments of the teams' work.

RESEARCH FINDINGS

Managing diversity on teams is a balancing act (see Exhibit 6-9). On the one hand, a number of researchers have suggested that diversity brings a greater number of ideas, perspectives, knowledge, and skills to the group, which can be used to perform at a higher level.[75] On the other hand, researchers have suggested that diversity can lead people to recall stereotypes and therefore bring bias into their evaluation of people who are different from them.[76] Diversity can thus make it more difficult to unify the team and reach agreements. We consider some of the evidence to help us resolve these opposing views.

Ever wonder whether having a team built just from people who are friends is desirable?

In a study examining the effectiveness of teams of strangers and teams of friends on bargaining, researchers found that teams of strangers gained greater profit than teams of friends, when teams reported to a supervisor.[77] However, teams of friends were more cohesive than teams of strangers. Another study of 60 teams found that in effective teams, about 50 percent of the individuals considered themselves friends, which underscores the importance of teams developing friendships.[78] However, the researchers also found that in teams that reported almost 100 percent friendship, performance was much lower. These groups tended to isolate themselves from others, and not seek outside influences. The research on friendships in teams suggests that teams of friends may be less concerned with productivity and more concerned with maintaining their relationship than are teams of strangers.

Overall, studies suggest that the strongest case for diversity on work teams can be made when these teams are engaged in problem-solving and decision-making tasks.[79] Heterogeneous teams may have qualities that lead to creative or unique solutions.[80] The lack of a common perspective also means diverse teams usually spend more time discussing issues, which decreases the possibility that a weak alternative will be chosen. Although diverse groups have more difficulty working together and solving problems, this goes away with time as the members come to know each other.

EXHIBIT 6-9　Advantages and Disadvantages of Diversity	
Advantages	**Disadvantages**
Multiple perspectives	Ambiguity
Greater openness to new ideas	Complexity
Multiple interpretations	Confusion
Increased creativity	Miscommunication
Increased flexibility	Difficulty in reaching a single agreement
Increased problem-solving skills	Difficulty in agreeing on specific actions

Source: Adapted from N. J. Adler, *International Dimensions of Organizational Behavior,* 4th ed., p. 109. Copyright © 2002. By permission of South-Western College publishing, a division of International Thomson Publishing, Cincinnati, OH 45227.

Recent research suggests that if team members share a common belief that diversity will positively affect their performance, this sets the foundation for the team to manage the diversity in a positive way. Specifically, if team members set out early on trying to learn about each other in order to understand and use their differences, this will have a positive effect on the team.[81] Laurie Milton, at the Haskayne School of Business at the University of Calgary, and several co-authors found that even 10 minutes spent sharing personal information when a group first started working together lowered subsequent group conflict and improved creative performance.[82] When groups didn't share personal information at the beginning of their work, they were less likely to do so later.

The research findings, taken as a whole, suggest that diversity can bring increased benefits to the team, but to do so, teams must have some commonality in values, and they need to be willing to share information about themselves early on. We can thus expect that the value-added component of diverse teams increases as members become more familiar with each other and the team becomes more cohesive. *Focus on Diversity* examines the impact of diversity on learning to work together in teams.

FOCUS ON **DIVERSITY**

Questioning the Impact of Diversity

Do diverse teams really have more difficulty learning how to work together? The late Professor Barbara Kelsey of Ryerson University studied groups of Caucasian and Chinese men living in Canada to see how being a token ethnic member in a group (the only Chinese or the only Caucasian) would affect participation and influence levels in groups.[83] Some groups worked face to face, others by computer only.

What Kelsey found for the face-to-face groups was that Caucasian males, whether tokens or dominants in their groups, had higher participation levels, on average, than Chinese males. However, in face-to-face groups dominated by Chinese males, the Chinese males also had relatively high participation rates. Only the token Chinese males were low on participation or influence on their groups.

In the computer-only groups, the ethnicity of group members could be determined in some groups, while for others it could not. In those groups where the ethnicity of team members was unknown, there were no differences in participation rates of Chinese and Caucasian men.

Kelsey's research suggests that participation and influence may be less a cultural issue, and more related to how individuals respond to visible differences when interacting with diverse team members. 🕴

Size

Generally speaking, the most effective teams have fewer than 10 members. And experts suggest using the smallest number of people who can do the task. Unfortunately, there is a pervasive tendency for managers to err on the side of making teams too large. While a minimum of four or five may be necessary to develop diversity of views and skills, managers seem to seriously underestimate how coordination problems can geometrically increase as team members are added. When teams have excess members, cohesiveness and mutual accountability declines, social loafing increases, and more and more people do less talking relative to others. So in designing effective teams, managers should try to keep them under 10. If a natural working unit is larger and you want a team effort, consider breaking the group into subteams. Uneven numbers in teams may help provide a mechanism to break ties and resolve conflicts, while an even number of team members may foster the need to create more consensus.

Separated workstations, such as these at a Hong Kong toy factory, reduce work group interactions.

social loafing The tendency for individuals to expend less effort when working collectively than when working individually.

Size and Social Loafing One of the most important findings related to the size of a team has been labelled **social loafing**. Social loafing is the tendency for individuals to expend less effort when working collectively than when working individually.[84] It directly challenges the logic that the productivity of the team as a whole should at least equal the sum of the productivity of each individual in that team. *Focus on Research* explains how social loafing occurs.

FOCUS ON **RESEARCH**

Teams Are Not Always the Sum of Their Parts

Do individuals exert less effort when they're on teams? A common stereotype is that team spirit spurs individual effort and enhances the team's overall productivity. In the late 1920s, German psychologist Max Ringelmann compared the results of individual and team performance on a rope-pulling task.[85] He expected that the team's effort would be equal to the sum of the efforts of individuals within the team. That is, three people pulling together should exert three times as much pull on the rope as one person, and eight people should exert eight times as much pull. Ringelmann's results, however, did not confirm his expectations. One person pulling on a rope alone exerted an average of 63 kilograms of force. In groups of three, per-person force dropped to 53 kilograms. And in groups of eight, it fell to only 31 kilograms per person.

Replications of Ringelmann's research with similar tasks have generally supported his findings.[86] Increases in team size are inversely related to individual performance. More may be better in the sense that the total productivity of a group of four is greater than that of one or two people, but the individual productivity of each group member declines.

What causes this social loafing effect? It may be due to a belief that others in the team are not carrying their fair share. If you view others as lazy or inept, you can re-

Ever notice that some group members don't seem to pull their weight?

establish equity by reducing your effort. Another explanation is the dispersion of responsibility. Because the results of the team cannot be attributed to any single person, the relationship between an individual's input and the team's output is clouded. In such situations, individuals may be tempted to become "free riders" and coast on the team's efforts. In other words, there will be a reduction in efficiency when individuals believe that their contribution cannot be measured. To reduce social loafing, teams should not be larger than necessary, and individuals should be held accountable for their actions.

Member Flexibility

Teams made up of flexible individuals have members who can complete each other's tasks. This is an obvious plus to a team because it greatly improves its adaptability and makes it less reliant on any single member.[87] So selecting members who themselves value flexibility, then cross-training them to be able to do each other's jobs, should lead to higher team performance over time.

Members' Preference for Teamwork

Not every employee is a team player. Given the option, many employees will "select themselves out" of team participation. When people who would prefer to work alone are required to team up, there is a direct threat to the team's morale.[88] This suggests that, when selecting team members, individual preferences should be considered, as well as abilities, personalities, and skills. High-performing teams are likely to be composed of people who prefer working as part of a team.

A recent study of 23 National Basketball Association teams found that "shared experience"—tenure on the team and time on court—tended to improve turnover and boost win-loss performance significantly. Why do you think teams that stay together longer tend to play better?

Work Design

Effective teams need to work together and take collective responsibility to complete significant tasks. They must be more than a "team-in-name-only."[89] The work design category includes variables such as freedom and autonomy, the opportunity to utilize different skills and talents, the ability to complete a whole and identifiable task or product, and the participation in a task or project that has a substantial impact on others. The evidence indicates that these characteristics enhance member motivation and increase team effectiveness.[90] These work design characteristics motivate teams because they increase members' sense of responsibility and ownership over the work, and because they make the work more interesting to perform.[91] These recommendations are consistent with the job characteristics model we presented in Chapter 5.

Process

Process variables make up the final component of team effectiveness. The process category includes member commitment to a common purpose, establishment of specific goals, team efficacy, a managed level of conflict, and a system of accountability.

Common Purpose

Effective teams have a common and meaningful purpose that provides direction, momentum, and commitment for members.[92] This purpose is a vision. It's broader than specific goals.

Members of successful teams put a tremendous amount of time and effort into discussing, shaping, and agreeing upon a purpose that belongs to them both collectively and individually. This common purpose, when accepted by the team, becomes the equivalent of what celestial navigation is to a ship captain—it provides direction and guidance under any and all conditions.

Specific Goals

Successful teams translate their common purpose into specific, measurable, and realistic performance goals. Just as we demonstrated in Chapter 4 how goals lead individuals to higher performance, goals also energize teams. These specific goals facilitate clear communication. They also help teams maintain their focus on achieving results.

Consistent with the research on individual goals, team goals should be challenging. Difficult goals have been found to raise team performance on those criteria for which they're set. So, for instance, goals for quantity tend to raise quantity, goals for speed tend to raise speed, goals for accuracy tend to raise accuracy, and so on.[93]

Teams should also be encouraged to develop milestones—tangible steps toward completion of the project. This allows teams to focus on their goal and evaluate progress toward the goal. The milestones should be sufficiently important and readily accomplished so that teams can celebrate some of their accomplishments along the way.

Team Efficacy

Effective teams have confidence in themselves. They believe they can succeed. We call this *team efficacy*.[94]

Success breeds success. Teams that have been successful raise their beliefs about future success, which, in turn, motivates them to work harder. One of the factors that helps teams build their efficacy is **cohesiveness**—the degree to which members are attracted to each other and are motivated to stay on the team.[95] Though teams differ in their cohesiveness, it is important because it has been found to be related to the team's productivity.[96]

Studies consistently show that the relationship of cohesiveness and productivity depends on the performance-related norms established by the group.[97] If performance-related norms are high (for example, high output, quality work, cooperation with individuals outside the group), a cohesive group will be more productive than a less cohesive group. If cohesiveness is high and performance norms are low, productivity will be low. If cohesiveness is low and performance norms are high, productivity increases—but less than in the high cohesiveness–high norms situation. Where cohesiveness and performance-related norms are both low, productivity will tend to fall into the low-to-moderate range. These conclusions are summarized in Exhibit 6-10.

Most studies of cohesiveness focus on *socio-emotional cohesiveness*, the "sense of togetherness that develops when individuals derive emotional satisfaction from group participation."[98] There is also *instrumental cohesiveness*: the "sense of togetherness that develops when group members are mutually dependent on one another because they believe they could not achieve the group's goal by acting separately." Teams need to achieve a balance of these two types of cohesiveness to function well. *OB in Action— Increasing Group Cohesiveness* indicates how to increase both socio-emotional and instrumental cohesiveness.

What, if anything, can management do to increase team efficacy? Two possible options are helping the team to achieve small successes and skill training. Small successes build team confidence. As a team develops an increasingly stronger performance record, it also increases the collective belief that future efforts will lead to success. In addition, managers should consider providing training to improve members' technical and inter-

cohesiveness The degree to which team members are attracted to each other and are motivated to stay on the team.

EXHIBIT 6-10   **Relationship Between Team Cohesiveness, Performance Norms, and Productivity**

Cohesiveness

	High	Low
High Performance Norms	High productivity	Moderate productivity
Low	Low productivity	Moderate to low productivity

personal skills. The greater the abilities of team members, the greater the likelihood that the team will develop confidence and the capability to deliver on that confidence.

Managed Level of Conflict

Conflict on a team isn't necessarily bad. Though relationship conflicts—those based on interpersonal incompatibilities, tension, and animosity toward others—are almost always dysfunctional, teams that are completely void of conflict are likely to be less effective, with the members becoming withdrawn and only superficially harmonious. Often, if there is no conflict, the alternative is not agreement, but apathy and disengagement. Teams that avoid conflict also tend to have lower performance levels, forget to consider key issues, or remain unaware of important aspects of their situation.[99] So effective teams are characterized by an appropriate level of conflict.[100]

Kathleen Eisenhardt of the Stanford Graduate School of Business and her colleagues studied top management teams in technology-based companies to understand how they manage conflict.[101] Their research identified six tactics that helped teams successfully manage the interpersonal conflict that can accompany group interactions. These are presented in *OB in Action—Reducing Team Conflict* on page 230. By handling the interpersonal conflict well, these groups were able to achieve their goals without letting conflict get in the way.

Groups need mechanisms by which they can manage the conflict, however. From the research reported above, we could conclude that sharing information and goals, and striving to be open and get along are helpful strategies for negotiating our way through the maze of conflict. A sense of humour, and a willingness to understand the points of others without insisting that everyone agree on all points, are also important. Group members should try to focus on the issues, rather than on personalities, and strive to achieve fairness and equity in the group process.

OB IN ACTION

Increasing Group Cohesiveness

Increasing socio-emotional cohesiveness

→ Keep the group relatively **small**.

→ Strive for a **favourable public image** to increase the status and prestige of belonging.

→ Encourage **interaction** and **cooperation**.

→ Emphasize members' **common characteristics** and interests.

→ **Point out environmental threats** (e.g., competitors' achievements) to rally the group.

Increasing instrumental cohesiveness

→ Regularly update and **clarify the group's goal(s)**.

→ Give every group member a **vital "piece of the action."**

→ Channel each group member's special talents toward the **common goal(s)**.

→ **Recognize** and equitably reinforce **every member's contributions**.

→ Frequently remind group members they **need each other** to get the job done.

Source: R. Kreitner and A. Kinicki, *Organizational Behavior,* 6th ed. (New York: Irwin, 2004), p. 460. Reprinted by permission of McGraw Hill Education.

Accountability

Successful teams make members individually and jointly accountable for the team's purpose, goals, and approach.[102] They clearly define what they are individually responsible for and what they are jointly responsible for. *From Concepts to Skills* on page 242 discusses how to conduct effective team meetings.

BEWARE! TEAMS AREN'T ALWAYS THE ANSWER

When the Glenforest Secondary School students got together to build a robot, it made sense for them to form a team. No student had all the knowledge and skills required to complete the task, as we saw in the opening vignette. But does every task need a team?

7 Are teams always the answer?

Despite considerable success in the use of teams, they are not necessarily appropriate in all situations, as Exhibit 6-11 suggests. Teamwork takes more time and often more resources than individual work. Teams, for instance, have increased communication demands, conflicts to be managed, and meetings to be run. In the excitement to enjoy the benefits of teams, some managers have introduced them into situations where the work is better done by individuals. A 2003 study done by Statistics Canada found that the introduction of teamwork lowered turnover in the service industries, for both high- and low-skilled employees. However, manufacturing companies experienced higher turnover if they introduced teamwork and formal teamwork training, compared with not doing so (15.8 percent vs. 10.7 percent).[103]

How do you know if the work of your group would be better done in teams? It's been suggested that three tests be applied to see if a team fits the situation:[104]

1. *Can the work be done better by more than one person?* Simple tasks that don't require diverse input are probably better left to individuals.

2. *Does the work create a common purpose or set of goals for the people in the group that is more than the aggregate of individual goals?* For instance, many new-car-dealer service departments have introduced teams that link customer service personnel, mechanics, parts specialists, and sales representatives. Such teams can better manage collective responsibility for ensuring that customer needs are properly met.

3. *Are the members of the group interdependent?* Teams make sense where there is inter-dependence between tasks—where the success of the whole depends on the success of each one, and the success of each one depends on the success of the others. Soccer, for instance, is an obvious team sport because of the interdependence of the players. Swim teams, by contrast, rely heavily on individual performance to win a meet.

Other studies have outlined the conditions under which organizations would find teams more useful: "when work processes cut across functional lines; when speed is important (and complex relationships are involved); when the organization mirrors a complex, differentiated and rapidly changing market environment; when innovation and learning have priority; when the tasks that have to be done require online

O B IN ACTION

Reducing Team Conflict

→ Work with **more, rather than less, information**, and debate on the basis of **facts**.

→ Develop **multiple alternatives** to enrich the level of debate.

→ Develop commonly agreed-upon **goals**.

→ Use **humour** when making tough decisions.

→ Maintain a **balanced power** structure.

→ Resolve issues **without forcing consensus**.

Source: Based on K. M. Eisenhardt, J. L. Kahwajy, and L. J. Bourgeois III, "How Management Teams Can Have a Good Fight," *Harvard Business Review,* July–August 1997, p. 78.

EXHIBIT 6-11

Source: S. Adams, *Build a Better Life by Stealing Office Supplies* (Kansas City, MO: Andrews and McMeal. 1991), p. 31. Dilbert reprinted with permission of United Features Syndicate.

integration of highly interdependent performers."[105] This chapter's *CBC Video Case* explores some additional difficulties with teams

Another Team? Oh No!

SUMMARY AND IMPLICATIONS

1 **What are teams and groups?** Groups and teams differ. Groups are simply the sum of individual efforts. A team generates positive synergy through coordinated effort. The combined individual efforts result in a level of performance that is greater than the sum of those individual inputs.

2 **Does everyone use teams?** Teams have become an essential part of the way business is being done these days. A Conference Board of Canada report found that more than 80 percent of its 109 respondents used teams in the workplace. This finding is similar to the United States, where 80 percent of *Fortune* 500 companies have half or more of their employees on teams. As well, 68 percent of small US manufacturers are using teams in their production areas.

3 **What kinds of teams are there?** Teams can be classified based on their objective. The four most common forms of teams you're likely to find in an organization are problem-solving (or process-improvement) teams; self-managed (or self-directed) teams; cross-functional (or project) teams; and virtual teams. A problem-solving team meets for a few hours each week to discuss ways of improving quality, efficiency, and the work environment. A self-managed (self-directed) work team consists of members who take on many responsibilities of their former managers and direct themselves. A cross-functional team consists of employees from about the same hierarchical level, but from different work areas, who come together to accomplish a task. A virtual team uses computer technology to tie together physically dispersed members in order to achieve a common goal.

4 **How does one become a team player?** In order for either a group or a team to function, individuals have to achieve some balance between their own needs and the needs of the group. Individuals on the team need to understand their roles, and then work together to create a set of group norms.

5 **Do teams go through stages while they work?** Two different models illustrate how teams develop. The first, the five-stage model, describes the standardized sequence of stages groups pass through: forming, storming, norming, performing, and adjourning. Through these stages, group members learn how to settle conflicts and develop norms, which enable them to perform. The second, the punctuated-equilibrium model, describes the pattern of development specific to temporary groups with deadlines. In this model, the group shows two great periods of activity, first midway through the project, after which it performs at a higher level than it did previously. The second peak in activity takes place right before the project comes due.

6 **How do we create effective teams?** For teams to be effective, careful consideration must be given to resources, the team's composition, work design, and process variables. The four contextual factors that appear to be most significantly related to team performance are the presence of adequate resources, effective leadership, a climate of trust, and a performance evaluation and reward system that reflects team contributions. Effective teams are neither too large nor too small—typically they range in size from 5 to 12 people. They have members who fill role demands, are flexible, and who prefer to be part of a group. Teams will be more effective if members have freedom and opportunity to do their tasks and believe that the task will have a substantial impact on others. Finally, effective teams have members committed to a common purpose and specific team goals.

7 **Are teams always the answer?** Teams are not necessarily appropriate in every situation. How do you know if the work of your group would be better done in teams? It's been suggested that three tests be applied to see if a team fits the situation: (1) Can the work be done better by more than one person? (2) Does the work create a common purpose or set of goals for the people in the group that is more than the aggregate of individual goals? and (3) Are the members of the group interdependent? This third test asks whether the success of the whole depends on the success of each one *and* the success of each one depends on the success of the others.

For Review

1. Contrast self-managed and cross-functional teams.

2. Contrast virtual and face-to-face teams.

3. How do norms develop in a team?

4. What are the characteristics of important norms?

5. Describe the five-stage model of group development.

6. Describe the punctuated-equilibrium model of group development.

7. What is the difference between task-oriented roles and maintenance roles?

8. Contrast the pros and cons of having diverse teams.

9. What are the effects of team size on performance?

10. How can a team minimize social loafing?

For Critical Thinking

1. Identify five roles you play. What behaviours do they require? Are any of these roles in conflict? If so, in what way? How do you resolve these conflicts?

2. How could you use the punctuated-equilibrium model to better understand team behaviour?

3. Have you experienced social loafing as a team member? What did you do to prevent this problem?

4. Would you prefer to work alone or as part of a team? Why? How do you think your answer compares with that of others in your class?

5. What effect, if any, do you think workforce diversity has on a team's performance and satisfaction?

OB for You

- Know that you will be asked to work on teams and groups both during your undergraduate years and later on in life, so understanding how teams work is an important skill to have.

- Think about the roles that you play on teams. Teams need task-oriented people to get the job done, but they also need maintenance-oriented people who help keep people working together and feeling committed to the team.

- Help your team set specific, measurable, realistic goals, as this leads to more successful outcomes.

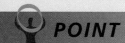

POINT

Sports Teams Are Good Models for Workplace Teams

Studies from hockey, football, soccer, basketball, and baseball have found a number of elements that successful sports teams have that can be extrapolated to successful work teams:[106]

Successful teams integrate cooperation and competition. Effective team coaches get athletes to help one another but also push one another to perform at their best. Sports teams with the best win-loss record had coaches who promoted a strong spirit of cooperation and a high level of healthy competition among their players.

Successful teams score early wins. Early successes build teammates' faith in themselves and their capacity as a team. For instance, research on hockey teams of relatively equal ability found that 72 percent of the time the team that was ahead at the end of the first period went on to win the game. So managers should give teams early tasks that are simple as well as "easy wins."

Successful teams avoid losing streaks. Losing can become a self-fulfilling prophecy. A couple of failures can lead to a downward spiral if a team becomes demoralized and believes it is helpless to end its losing streak. Managers need to instill confidence in team members that they can turn things around when they encounter setbacks.

Practice makes perfect. Successful sports teams execute on game day but learn from their mistakes in practice. A wise manager carves out time and space in which work teams can experiment and learn.

Successful teams use halftime breaks. The best coaches in basketball and football use halftime during a game to reassess what is working and what isn't. Managers of work teams should similarly build in assessments at around the halfway point in a team project to evaluate how the team can improve.

Winning teams have a stable membership. Studies of professional basketball teams have found that the more stable a team's membership, the more likely the team is to win. The more time teammates have together, the more able they are to anticipate one another's moves and the clearer they are about one another's roles.

Successful teams debrief after failures and successes. The best sports teams study the game video. Similarly, work teams need to take time to routinely reflect on both their successes and failures and to learn from them.

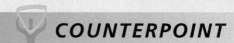

COUNTERPOINT

Sports Teams Are Not the Model for All Teams

There are flaws in using sports as a model for developing effective work teams. Here are just four caveats:[107]

All sport teams are not alike. In baseball, for instance, there is little interaction among teammates. Rarely are more than two or three players directly involved in a play. The performance of the team is largely the sum of the performance of the individual players. In contrast, basketball has much more interdependence among players. Geographic distribution is dense. Usually all players are involved in every play, team members have to be able to switch from offence to defence at a moment's notice, and there is continuous movement by all, not just the player with the ball. The performance of the team is more than the sum of its individual players. So when using sports teams as a model for work teams, you have to make sure you are making the correct comparison.

Work teams are more varied and complex. In an athletic league, teams vary little in their context, their individual design, and the design of the task. But in work teams these variables can differ greatly. As a result, coaching plays a much more significant part in a sports team's performance than a work team's. Performance of work teams is more a function of getting the teams' structural and design variables right. So, in contrast to sports, managers of work teams should focus more on getting the team set up for success than on coaching.

A lot of employees cannot relate to sports metaphors. Not everyone on work teams is conversant with sports. Women are still breaking down barriers for equal treatment in many sports, for example, so individuals may well have very different personal sports experience to draw from. Team members from different cultures also may not know the sports terms you are using. Most Canadians, for instance, know little about the rules of Australian football.

Work team outcomes are not easily defined in terms of wins and losses. Sports teams typically measure success in terms of wins and losses. Such measures of success are rarely as clear for work teams. Managers who try to define success in wins and losses might imply that the workplace is ethically no more complex than the playing field, which is rarely true.

HR IMPLICATIONS

Turning Individuals into Team Players

In this chapter, we have made a strong case for the value and growing popularity of teams. But many people are not inherently team players. Instead, they are loners or people who want to be recognized for their individual achievements. There are also many organizations that have historically nurtured individual accomplishments. Additionally, as we discussed in Chapter 3, countries differ in terms of how they rate on individualism and collectivism. Teams fit more naturally with cultures that score high on collectivism.[108]

But what if an organization wants to introduce teams into a work population that is composed largely of individuals born and raised in a highly individualistic society, such as Canada, the United States, the United Kingdom, or Australia? James Mitchell, president of Markham, Ontario-based Steelcase, sums up the difficulties of introducing teams to the workplace: "People talk about teams, but very few operate in a pure team sense. They tend to think that if they get cross-functional groups together—a person out of marketing, one out of sales, one out of product development, another out of engineering—somehow they've got a team-based organization. But they haven't. They have a committee."[109]

The Challenge

The previous points are meant to highlight two substantial barriers to using work teams: individual resistance and management resistance.

When an employee is assigned to a team, his or her success is no longer defined in terms of individual performance. To perform well as team members, individuals must be able to communicate openly and honestly, to confront differences and resolve conflicts, and to sublimate personal goals for the good of the team. For many employees, this is a difficult, if not impossible, task. The challenge of creating team players will be greatest where (1) the national culture is highly individualistic, and (2) the teams are being introduced into an established organization that has historically valued individual achievement. This context describes, for instance, what managers faced at AT&T, Ford, Motorola, and other large Canadian- and US-based companies. These firms prospered by hiring and rewarding corporate stars, and they bred a competitive climate that encouraged individual achievement and recognition. Employees in these types of firms can be jolted by this sudden shift to the importance of team play.[110] A veteran employee of a large company, who had done well working alone, described the experience of joining a team: "I'm learning my lesson. I just had my first negative performance appraisal in 20 years."[111]

As part of her training to become an astronaut, Julie Payette worked with other NASA astronauts to become a team player. Members of shuttle crews have to work harmoniously with other crew members to achieve the mission's goals. By stressing that the mission's success depends on teamwork, NASA teaches astronauts how to compromise and make decisions that benefit the entire team.

On the other hand, the challenge for management is less demanding when teams are introduced where employees have strong collectivist values—such as in Japan or Mexico—or in new organizations that use teams as their initial form for structuring work. For example, when Toyota opened plants in Canada, the working environment was designed around teams from the inception. Employees were hired with the knowledge that they would be working in teams. The ability to be a good

Outward Bound training programs provide organizations with the ability to develop team players. Training experiences, such as participating in a sailing exercise, teach employees the value of teamwork and give them the practical skills for working in teams.

team player was a basic hiring qualification that all new employees had to meet.

While it might seem easy enough to blame individual resistance as the cause of team failure, in many organizations there is no genuine infrastructure created to build teams. When organizations focus their rewards at the individual level, employees have no incentive to operate within a team structure. In some situations, managers are quite reluctant to give up their power and, in fact, share power with the other team members. This also makes it difficult for a real team to develop. As we mentioned in our extensive discussion of incentive programs in Chapter 5, organizations must align their incentives with their goals. If team behaviour is important to the organization, the incentive system must reflect this objective.

Below we discuss some individual and organizational factors that can be carried out through the human resource function of the organization to improve team performance.

Shaping Team Players

The following summarizes the primary options managers have for trying to turn individuals into team players.

Selection

Some people already possess the interpersonal skills to be effective team players. When hiring team members, managers naturally look for people with the technical skills required to fill the job. But managers also need to ensure that candidates can fulfill their team roles, as well as the technical requirements.[112]

Many job candidates don't have team skills. This is especially true for those socialized around individual contributions. When faced with such candidates, managers have three options. The candidates can undergo training to "make them into team players." If this isn't possible or doesn't work, the other two options are to transfer the individual to another unit within the organization, without teams (if this possibility exists); or not to hire the candidate. In established organizations that decide to redesign jobs around teams, it should be expected that some employees will resist being team players and may be untrainable. Unfortunately, such people typically become casualties of the team approach.

John Schram, President and CEO of Toronto-based We Care Home Health Services indicates the importance of emphasizing team skills, if that's what is wanted by the organization. "I believe in a team approach. I believe in

collaboration and co-operation. That is a fundamental value of mine," he says. "I can live with unproductive or just barely productive people. I cannot live with counter-productive people. And those are the ones I get rid of right away. If they are not team players I cannot live with them."[113]

Training

On a more optimistic note, a large proportion of people raised on the importance of individual accomplishment can be trained to become team players. Vancouver-based Purdy's Chocolates has built a loyal workforce because of the company's dedication to training its employees to be better team members through team-building exercises. Employee Dolores Gammon, who has worked for the company for 22 years, says, "If I could, I'd be here till I'm 99 and it's all over," she says. "It's like my home. I would go down with the ship—I would."[114]

Companies can hire others to help them with team building. What kind of team-building exercises are available? Guelph, Ontario-based Eagle's Flight puts teams of two to six through a treasure hunt, where teams compete with each other. Such exercises are meant to help participants develop skills in "planning, goal-setting and learning to take necessary risks."[115] Toronto-based The Second City uses improvisational techniques to generate team-building skills. Participants learn to work in a team environment, to create and build ideas, and to listen effectively.

Performance Evaluation

Performance evaluation concepts have been almost exclusively developed with only individual employees in mind. This reflects the historical belief that individuals are the core building block around which organizations are built. But as we have described throughout this textbook, more and more organizations are restructuring themselves around teams. How should organizations that use teams evaluate performance? Four suggestions have been offered for designing a system that supports and improves the performance of teams:[116]

1. *Tie the team's results to the organization's goals.* It's important to find measurements that apply to important goals that the team is supposed to accomplish.

2. *Begin with the team's customers and the work process that the team follows to satisfy customers' needs.* The final product the customer receives can be evaluated in terms of the

customer's requirements. The transactions between teams can be evaluated based on delivery and quality. The process steps can be evaluated based on waste and cycle time.

3. *Measure both team and individual performance.* Define the roles of each team member in terms of accomplishments that support the team's work process. Then assess each member's contribution and the team's overall performance. Remember that individual skills are necessary for team success but are not sufficient for good team performance.[117]

4. *Train the team to create its own measures.* Having the team define its objectives and those of each member ensures everyone understands his or her role on the team and helps the team develop into a more cohesive unit.

Rewards

The reward system should be reworked to encourage cooperative efforts rather than competitive ones. For instance, Hallmark Cards added an annual bonus, based on achievement of team goals, to its basic individual-incentive system. Imperial Oil adjusted its system to reward both individual goals and team behaviours.

If companies value teamwork, then promotions, pay raises, and other forms of recognition should be given to individuals for how effectively they work as a collaborative team member. This doesn't mean individual contribu-tion is ignored; rather, it is balanced with selfless contributions to the team. Examples of behaviours that should be rewarded include training new colleagues, sharing information with teammates, helping to resolve team conflicts, and mastering new skills that the team needs but in which it is deficient.

However, Canadian organizations that use teams have been slow to link team performance to rewards in a clear way. The Conference Board of Canada reported that only 10 percent of respondents assessed contribution to team performance as part of the regular performance appraisal. Of the 45 companies that evaluated contributions to team performance as part of an employee's performance appraisal, only 19 included peer review as part of the appraisal system, with 10 more reporting that they were considering implementing it.[118]

Although explicit links between team performance and extrinsic rewards are important, don't forget the intrinsic rewards that employees can receive from teamwork. Teams provide camaraderie. It's exciting and satisfying to be an integral part of a successful team. The opportunity to engage in personal development and to help teammates grow can also be a very satisfying and rewarding experience for employees. For instance, at Steelcase, teams are invited to conferences to present their successes to delegates and top company management. Teams are encouraged to celebrate when they reach their goals, and they design the celebration themselves.

LEARNING ABOUT **YOURSELF** EXERCISE

How Good Am I at Building and Leading a Team?

Use the following rating scale to respond to the 18 questions on building and leading an effective team.

Strongly Disagree	Disagree	Slightly Disagree	Slightly Agree	Agree	Strongly Agree
1	2	3	4	5	6

1. I am knowledgeable about the different stages of development that teams can go through in their life cycles.   1 2 3 4 5 6

2. When a team forms, I make certain that all team members are introduced to one another at the outset.   1 2 3 4 5 6

3. When the team first comes together, I provide directions, answer team members' questions, and clarify goals, expectations, and procedures.   1 2 3 4 5 6

4. I help team members establish a foundation of trust among one another and between themselves and me.   1 2 3 4 5 6

LEARNING ABOUT **YOURSELF** EXERCISE (Continued)

5.	I ensure that standards of excellence, not mediocrity or mere acceptability, characterize the team's work.	1	2	3	4	5	6
6.	I provide a great deal of feedback to team members regarding their performance.	1	2	3	4	5	6
7.	I encourage team members to balance individual autonomy with interdependence among other team members.	1	2	3	4	5	6
8.	I help team members become at least as committed to the success of the team as to their own personal success.	1	2	3	4	5	6
9.	I help team members learn to play roles that assist the team in accomplishing its tasks, as well as building strong interpersonal relationships.	1	2	3	4	5	6
10.	I articulate a clear, exciting, passionate vision of what the team can achieve.	1	2	3	4	5	6
11.	I help team members become committed to the team vision.	1	2	3	4	5	6
12.	I encourage a win-win philosophy in the team; that is, when one member wins, every member wins.	1	2	3	4	5	6
13.	I help the team avoid making the group's survival more important than accomplishing its goal.	1	2	3	4	5	6
14.	I use formal process-management procedures to help the group become faster, more efficient, and more productive, and to prevent errors.	1	2	3	4	5	6
15.	I encourage team members to represent the team's vision, goals, and accomplishments to outsiders.	1	2	3	4	5	6
16.	I diagnose and capitalize on the team's core competence.	1	2	3	4	5	6
17.	I encourage the team to achieve dramatic breakthrough innovations, as well as small continuous improvements.	1	2	3	4	5	6
18.	I help the team work toward preventing mistakes, not just correcting them after the fact.	1	2	3	4	5	6

Scoring Key:

This instrument assesses team development behaviours in five areas: diagnosing team development (items 1, 16); managing the forming stage (items 2–4); managing the storming stage (items 10–12, 14, 15); managing the norming stage (items 6–9, 13); and managing the performing stage (items 5, 17, 18). Add up your score. Your total score will range between 18 and 108.

Based on a norm group of 500 business students, the following can help estimate where you are relative to others:

95 or above = You're in the top quartile of being able to build and lead a team

72–94 = You're in the second quartile

60–71 = You're in the third quartile

Below 60 = You're in the bottom quartile

Source: Adapted from D. A. Whetten and K. S. Cameron, *Developing Management Skills,* 3rd ed. © 1995, pp. 534–535. Adapted by permission of Pearson Education, Inc. Upper Saddle River, NJ.

Form small groups to discuss the following topics, as assigned by your instructor:

1. One of the members of your team continually arrives late for meetings and does not turn drafts of assign_in_
   on time. In general this group member is engaging in social loafing. What can the members of your grou
   reduce social loafing?

2. Consider a team with which you've worked. Was there more emphasis on task-oriented or maintenance-
   roles? What impact did this have on the group's performance?

3. Identify 4 or 5 norms that a team could put into place near the beginning of its life that might help the te
   tion better over time.

WORKING WITH OTHERS EXERCISE

The Paper Tower Exercise

Step 1   Each group will receive 20 index cards, 12 paper clips, and 2 marking pens. Groups have 10 m
                plan a paper tower that will be judged on the basis of 3 criteria: height, stability, and beauty. No
                work (building) is allowed during this planning period.

Step 2   Each group has 15 minutes for the actual construction of the paper tower.

Step 3   Each tower will be identified by a number assigned by your instructor. Each student is to ind
                examine all the paper towers. Your group is then to come to a consensus as to which tower is t
                ner (5 minutes). A spokesperson from your group should report its decision and the criteria the
                used in reaching it.

Step 4   In your small groups, discuss the following questions (your instructor may choose to have you discuss
                a subset of these questions):

    a. What percentage of the plan did each member of your group contribute, on average?

    b. Did your group have a leader? Why or why not?

    c. How did the group generally respond to the ideas that were expressed during the planning
    period?

    d. To what extent did your group follow the five-stage model of group development?

    e. List specific behaviours exhibited during the planning and building sessions that you felt were
    helpful to the group. Explain why you found them to be helpful.

    f. List specific behaviours exhibited during the planning and building sessions that you felt were
    dysfunctional to the group. Explain why you found them dysfunctional.

Source: This exercise is based on *The Paper Tower Exercise: Experiencing Leadership and Group Dynamics,* by Phillip L. Hunsaker and Johanna S. Hunsaker, unpublished manuscript. A brief description is included in "Exchange," *The Organizational Behavior Teaching Journal* 4, no. 2 (1979), p. 49. Reprinted by permission of the authors. The materials list was suggested by Professor Sally Maitlis, Sauder School of Business, University of British Columbia.

Pressure to Be a Team Player

dmit it. I'm not a team player. I work best when I
one and am left alone," says Zach Sanders.

's employer, an office furniture manufacturer, recently
nized around teams. All production in the company's
peg factory is now done in teams. Zach's design
tment has been broken up into three design teams.

've worked here for four years. I'm very good at what
And my performance reviews confirm that. I've scored
ercent or higher on my evaluations every year I've been
e. But now everything is changing. I'm expected to be
t of our modular-office design team. My evaluations and

pay raises are going to depend on how well the team dose.
And, get this, 50 percent of my evaluation will be on how
well I facilitate the performance of the team. I'm really frustrated and demoralized. They hired me for my design skills.
They knew I wasn't a social type. Now they're forcing me to
be a team player. This doesn't play to my strengths at all."

Is it unethical for Zach's employer to force him to be a
team player? Is this firm breaking an implied contract that it
made with him at the time he was hired? Does this employer
have any responsibility to provide Zach with an alternative
that would allow him to continue to work independently?

Role Conflict Among Telephone Service Employees

All supervisory jobs aren't alike. Maggie Beckhard is just
learning this fact. After having spent three years as a production-scheduling supervisor at a Procter & Gamble
(P&G) manufacturing plant, she recently took a position
as manager of telephone services at Halifax Provident
Insurance (HPI). In her new job, Maggie supervises 20
telephone service employees. These people have direct
contact with customers—providing quotes, answering
questions, following up on claims, and the like.

At P&G, Maggie's employees knew they had only one
constituency to please. That was management. But Maggie
is discovering that her employees at HPI find it more
difficult. As service employees, they have to serve two
masters—management and the customer. And at least
from comments her employees have made, they seem to
think there is a discrepancy between what they believe
customers want them to do and what they believe management wants them to do. A frequent complaint, for
instance, is that customers want the telephone rep's undivided attention and to spend as much time as necessary to
solve their problem. But the reps see management as wanting them to handle as many calls as possible per day and
to keep each call as short as possible.

This morning, a rep came into Maggie's office complaining of severe headaches. "The more I try to please
our customers, the more stress I feel," the rep told Maggie.

"I want to do the best job I can for our customers, but I
don't feel like I can devote the time that's necessary. You
constantly remind us that 'it's customers that provide our
paycheques' and how important it is to give reliable, courteous, and responsive service, but then we feel the pressure
to handle more calls per hour."

Maggie is well aware of studies that have shown that
role conflict is related to reduced job satisfaction, increased
turnover and absenteeism, and fewer organizational citizenship behaviours. Severe role conflict is also likely to
lead to poor customer service—the antithesis of her department's goals.

After talking with her staff, Maggie concluded that
regardless of whether their perceptions were accurate, her
people certainly believed them to be. They were reading
one set of expectations through their interactions with
customers, and another set through what the company
conveyed during the selection process, in training sessions, and through the behaviours that management
rewarded.

Questions

1. What's the source of role conflict here?

2. Are there functional benefits to management from
   role conflict? Explain.

3. Should role conflict among these telephone service employees be any greater than it is for a typical employee who works as part of a team and has to meet the expectations of a boss as well as his or her team members? Explain.

4. What can Maggie do to manage this role conflict?

Source: This case is based on information in B. G. Chung and B. Schneider, "Serving Multiple Masters: Role Conflict Experienced by Service Employees," *Journal of Services Marketing* 16, 2, pp. 70–88.

A Virtual Team at T. A. Stearns

T. A. Stearns is a national tax accounting firm whose main business is tax preparation services for individuals. Stearns' superior reputation is based on the high quality of its advice and the excellence of its service. Key to the achievement of its reputation are the state-of-the-art computer databases and analysis tools that its people use when counselling clients. These programs were developed by highly trained individuals.

The programs are highly technical, both in terms of the tax laws they cover and the code in which they are written. Perfecting them requires high levels of programming skill as well as the ability to understand the law. New laws and interpretations of existing laws have to be integrated quickly and flawlessly into the existing regulations and analysis tools.

The creation of these programs is carried out in a virtual environment by four programmers in the greater Vancouver area. The four work at home and are connected to each other and to the company by email, telephone, and conference software. Formal on-site meetings among all of the programmers take place only a few times a year, although the workers sometimes meet informally at other times. The four members of the team are Tom Andrews, Cy Crane, Marge Dector, and Megan Harris.

These four people exchange email messages many times every day. In fact, it's not unusual for them to step away from guests or family to log on and check in with the others. Often their emails are amusing as well as work-related. Sometimes, for instance, when they were facing a deadline and one of Marge's kids was home sick, they helped each other with the work. Tom has occasionally invited the others to visit his farm; and Marge and Cy have got their families together several times for dinner. About once a month the whole team gets together for lunch.

All four of these Stearns employees are on salary, which, consistent with company custom, is negotiated separately and secretly with management. Although each is required to check in regularly during every workday,

they were told when they were hired they coul wherever they wanted. Clearly, flexibility is one pluses of these jobs. When the four get together, they joke about the managers and workers who are tied office, referring to them as "face timers" and to th selves as "free agents."

When the programmers are asked to make a major p gram change, they often develop programming tools call macros to help them do their work more efficiently. Thes macros greatly enhance the speed at which a change can be written into the programs. Cy, in particular, really enjoys hacking around with macros. On one recent project, for instance, he became obsessed with the prospect of creating a shortcut that could save him a huge amount of time. One week after turning in his code and his release notes to the company, Cy bragged to Tom that he had created a new macro that had saved him eight hours of work that week. Tom was skeptical of the shortcut, but after trying it out, he found that it actually saved him many hours too.

Stearns has a suggestion program that rewards employees for innovations that save the company money. The program gives an employee 5 percent of the savings generated by his or her innovation over three months. The company also has a profit-sharing plan. Tom and Cy felt that the small amount of money that would be generated by a company reward would not offset the free time that they gained using their new macro. They wanted the time for leisure or consulting work. They also feared their group might suffer if management learned about the innovation. It would allow three people to do the work of four, which could lead to one of them being let go. So they didn't share their innovative macro with management.

Although Tom and Cy would not share the innovation with management, they were concerned that they were entering their busy season and knew everyone in the team would be stressed by the heavy workload. They decided to distribute the macro to the other members of their team and swore them to secrecy.

Over lnch one day, the team set itself a level of production it it felt would not arouse management's suspicion. veral months passed and the four used some of their e time to push the quality of their work even higher t they also now had more time to pursue their own nal interests.

Regan, the in-house manager of the work group, p on the innovation several weeks after it was plemented. He had wondered why production time ne down a bit, while quality had shot up, and he s first inkling of an answer when he saw an email Marge to Cy thanking him for saving her so much e with his "brilliant mind." Not wanting to embarrass employees, the manager hinted to Tom that he wanted know what was happening, but he got nowhere. He did not tell his own manager about his suspicions, reasoning that since both quality and productivity were up he did not really need to pursue the matter further.

Dave has just learned that Cy has boasted about his trick to a member of another virtual work group in the company. Suddenly, the situation seems to have got out of control. Dave decided to take Cy to lunch. During the meal, Dave asked Cy to explain what was happening. Cy told him about the innovation, but he insisted the group's actions had been justified to protect itself.

Dave knew that his own boss would soon hear of the situation and that he would be looking for answers—from him.

Questions

1. Is this group a team?

2. What role have norms played in how this team acted?

3. Has anyone in this case acted unethically?

4. What should Dave do now?

Source: Adapted from "The Virtual Environment Work Team," a case prepared by R. Andre, professor, Northeastern University. With permission.

From **Concepts** to **Skills**

Conducting a Team Meeting

Team meetings have a reputation for inefficiency. For instance, noted Canadian-born economist John Kenneth Galbraith has said, "Meetings are indispensable when you don't want to do anything."

When you are responsible for conducting a meeting, what can you do to make it more efficient and effective? Follow these 12 steps:[119]

1. *Prepare a meeting agenda.* An agenda defines what you hope to accomplish at the meeting. It should state the meeting's purpose; who will be in attendance; what, if any, preparation is required of each participant; a detailed list of items to be covered; the specific time and location of the meeting; and a specific finishing time.

2. *Distribute the agenda in advance.* Participants should have the agenda sufficiently in advance so they can adequately prepare for the meeting.

3. *Consult with participants before the meeting.* An unprepared participant cannot contribute to his or her full potential. It is your responsibility to ensure that members are prepared, so check with them ahead of time.

4. *Get participants to go over the agenda.* The first thing to do at the meeting is to have participants review the agenda, make any changes, then approve the final agenda.

5. *Establish specific time parameters.* Meetings should begin on time and have a specific time for completion. It is your responsibility to specify these time parameters and to hold to them.

6. *Maintain focused discussion.* It is your responsibility to give direction to the discussion; to keep it focused on the issues; and to minimize interruptions, disruptions, and irrelevant comments.

7. *Encourage and support participation of all members.* To maximize the effectiveness of problem-oriented meetings, each participant must be encouraged to contribute. Quiet or reserved personalities need to be drawn out so their ideas can be heard.

8. *Maintain a balanced style.* The effective group leader pushes when necessary and is passive when need be.

9. *Encourage the clash of ideas.* You need to encourage different points of view, critical thinking, and constructive disagreement.

10. *Discourage the clash of personalities.* An effective meeting is characterized by the critical assessment of ideas, not attacks on people. When running a meeting, you must quickly intercede to stop personal attacks or other forms of verbal insult.

11. *Be an effective listener.* You need to listen with intensity, empathy, and objectivity, and do whatever is necessary to get the full intended meaning from each participant's comments.

12. *Bring proper closure.* You should close a meeting by summarizing the group's accomplishments. Clarify what actions, if any, need to follow the meeting and allocate follow-up assignments. If any decisions are made, you also need to determine who will be responsible for communicating and implementing them.

Assessing Skills

After you've read this chapter, take the following Self-Assessment on your enclosed CD-ROM:

34. How Good Am I at Building and Leading a Team?

Practising Skills

Jameel Saumur is the leader of a five-member project team that has been assigned the task of moving his engineering firm into the booming area of high-speed intercity rail construction. Saumur and his team members have been researching the field, identifying specific business opportunities, negotiating alliances with equipment vendors, and evaluating high-speed rail experts and consultants from around the world. Throughout the process, Tonya Eckler, a highly qualified and respected engineer, has challenged a number of things Saumur said during team meetings and in the workplace. For example, at a meeting two weeks ago, Saumur presented the team with a list of 10 possible high-speed rail projects and started evaluating the company's ability to compete for them. Eckler contradicted virtually all of Saumur's comments, questioned his statistics, and was quite pessimistic about the possibility of getting contracts on these projects. After this latest display of displeasure, two other group members, Bryan Worth and Maggie Ames, are complaining that Eckler's actions are damaging the team's effectiveness. Eckler was originally assigned to the team for her unique expertise and insight. If you had to advise this team, what suggestions would you make to get the team on the right track to achieve its fullest potential?

Reinforcing Skills

1. Interview three managers at different organizations. Ask them about their experiences in managing teams. Have each describe teams that they thought were effective and why they succeeded. Have each also describe teams that they thought were ineffective and the reasons that might have caused this.

2. Contrast a team you have been in where members trusted each other with another team you have been in where members lacked trust in each other. How did the conditions in each team develop? What were the consequences in terms of interaction patterns and performance?

Trust

Martha Stewart built her company, Martha Stewart Living Omnimedia (MSO), on her image as much as her homemaking ideas.[1] The Martha Stewart brand is the company, which is composed of four divisions: publishing, television, merchandising, and Internet/direct commerce. As Robert Kahn, executive vice-president of New York-based Enterprise IG, a brand consultancy firm, notes: "Martha Stewart really has become an American icon. What she has accomplished is to demonstrate that with a little helpful advice, ordinary people can do great things at home."

Stewart's credibility was challenged because of her personal ties to former ImClone Systems CEO Sam Waksal. He pleaded guilty to securities fraud in October 2002, and she was accused of insider trading for selling her ImClone shares when she did. Even before Stewart was charged, investors responded to the accusations. MSO shares plunged by two-thirds to around $7 (US) between March 2002, when an announcement of a probe of Stewart was made, and late October of that year. Her everyday fans also showed a lack of confidence in Stewart. Sales of her books and magazines dropped, and viewership for her syndicated TV show, *Martha Stewart Living*, fell from an average of 1.7 million in May 2002 to 1.3 million six months later.

The situation worsened after Stewart was convicted in 2004 of lying to authorities about a stock sale. She was ordered to serve a five-month jail term in a West Virginia prison. That was followed by nearly six months of home confinement, where she could only make limited trips to the outside world, and was forced to wear an ankle bracelet that monitored her movements. Her television show was cancelled in 2004 because of poor ratings. Her magazine *Martha Stewart Living* saw ad sales drop significantly in 2004, to $71.7 million, less than a third of the $234.4 million sold in 2002.[2] Revenues for the company dropped steadily from when the accusations were first made into 2005. MSO's president and CEO, Susan Lyne, told shareholders in May 2005 that "returning the company to profitability will take some time."[3] The company is hoping its fortunes will return with Stewart now able to work again. However the launch of her new TV show, *Martha*, in September 2005 was not well received.

As Martha Stewart no doubt has learned, trust is fragile. It takes a long time to build, can be easily destroyed, and is hard to regain.[4] MSO suffered significant losses, even though questions about Stewart's honesty and integrity were not even linked to actions directly related to the company. Instead, it was her actions as an individual, possibly engaging in insider trading, that created her difficulties. The problem for fans wasn't whether or not Stewart was more aggressive and ruthless than her caring, homemaker image suggested. What they were not necessarily willing to support was an appearance of greed or the misuse of privileged information.

Shareholders and fans are not the only people questioning whether they can trust corporations these days.

Many Canadian and US organizations have created a lack of trust in their employees because of the massive layoffs they embarked on in the 1990s. A 1998 survey of Canadian workers concluded that three out of four Canadians do not trust the people for whom they work.[5]

Lack of trust in an organization is a serious problem. Professors Linda Duxbury of the Carleton University School of Business and Christopher Higgins of the University of Western Ontario's Richard Ivey School of Business found that employees who work in environments characterized by trust and respect report less stress and greater productivity than those who work in environments where trust is lacking.[6]

What Is Trust?

Trust is a positive expectation (or belief) that another will not—through words, actions, or decisions—act opportunistically.[7] Trust involves making oneself vulnerable, such as when we disclose intimate information or rely on another's promises.[8] By its very nature, trust provides the opportunity for disappointment or to be taken advantage of.[9] When we trust someone, we expect that person will not take advantage of us.

What Determines Trust?

What are the key dimensions of trust? Research has identified five important criteria: integrity, competence, consistency, loyalty, and openness.[10] These dimensions of trust are presented in the illustration on the right and listed in their order of importance in determining one's trustworthiness.

- *Integrity.* Honesty and truthfulness. Of all five dimensions, integrity seems to be most critical when someone assesses

another's trustworthiness. "Without a perception of the other's 'moral character' and 'basic honesty,' other dimensions of trust [are] meaningless."[11]

- *Competence.* Technical and interpersonal knowledge and skills. Does the person know what he or she is talking about? You are unlikely to listen to or depend upon someone whose abilities you don't respect. You need to believe that the person has the skills and abilities to carry out what he or she promises to do.

- *Consistency.* Reliability, predictability, and good judgment in handling situations. "Inconsistencies between words and action decrease trust."[12] Individuals notice if one does not practise what one preaches.[13]

- *Loyalty.* Willingness to protect and save face for another person. Trust requires that you can depend on someone not to act opportunistically.

- *Openness.* Willingness to share ideas and information freely. Can you rely on the person to give you the full truth?

In addition to these factors, a review of the findings for the effects of leadership on building trust indicates that several characteristics of leadership are most likely to build trust. Leaders who engage in procedural justice (ensuring fair proce-

dures and outcomes) and interactional justice (treating people fairly when procedures are carried out), and who encourage participative decision making and use a transformational leadership style are most successful at building trust.[14]

Does Trust Really Make a Difference?

A variety of studies demonstrate the impact of trust on organizational performance.

At the organizational level, a study of relationships between auto manufacturers and suppliers in the United States, Japan, and Korea found that the relationships that had the highest levels of trust also had substantially lower transaction costs. These parties spent far less time negotiating with each other to achieve agreement.[15] Suppliers and automakers in the United States had the least amount of trust, and this resulted in substantially higher amounts of time spent on "unproductive transaction-oriented matters." Purchasers at the most trusted automaker in the United States spent less time checking up on the suppliers and handled "twice as many goods in dollar value" as the least trusted automaker.

The manufacturers who were least trusted often received lower prices than the less aggressive manufacturers, usually because they pitted suppliers against each other to get the best price. However, suppliers were less likely to share information with automakers whom they did not trust. In relationships of trust, suppliers were more likely to "offer ideas on designing and manufacturing components," and this often benefited the manufacturer over time. Similarly, manufacturers in trusting relationships gave ideas to suppliers about how to improve their manufacturing and distribution processes.

Trust thus brings important additional benefits to both parties. The researchers say their findings show "that trust, by keeping one side from taking advantage of the other, is not just an alternative to contracts and other rigid governance mechanisms. Trust actually adds value to the relationship because it encourages the sharing of resources."[16]

In an overview of employee responses to trust, a meta-analysis of 99 studies examining how trust in leadership developed and the effects of that trust found that when employees trusted their leaders, they were more likely to engage in altruism, civic virtue, conscientiousness, courtesy, and sportsmanship.[17] Employees who trusted their leaders showed greater job performance ($r = .16$), job satisfaction ($r = .53$) and organizational commitment ($r = .49$). Trusting employees were also less likely to express a desire to quit their job ($r = -.40$).

Profits are also higher when organizations show more trust in their employees. Professor Tony Simons of Cornell University's School of Hotel Administration surveyed more than 6500 employees at 76 Canadian and US Holiday Inns to find out whether their views on their managers' integrity correlated with the hotels' customer satisfaction surveys, personnel records, and financial records.[18] When employees strongly believed that their managers followed through on promises and practised what they preached, the hotel profits were substantially higher. In fact, a one-eighth of a point increase in a hotel's score on the integrity scale was linked to an increase in profits of more than $250 000 annually. The study found no other managerial characteristics that had such an impact on profits.

If integrity can have such a large benefit for organizations, why is it so

FactBox[19]

- Only 21% of Canadians surveyed thought CEOs were trustworthy or extremely trustworthy.
- Only 16% of Canadians surveyed thought that information conveyed by CEOs and CFOs was credible.
- 83% of Canadians surveyed thought corporate executives were somewhat or very likely to lie when making statements to the news media.
- 91% of Canadians surveyed thought politicians were somewhat or very likely to lie when making statements to the news media.
- 80% of Canadians surveyed "agree distrust is growing," while 87% "agree people are less trusting than in the past."

difficult for managers to appear to have integrity? Employees tend to look toward organizational outcomes to evaluate whether they trust top management. Therefore outcomes are weighed at least as heavily as a manager's character, words, and actions.[20] The inset *Why Integrity Is Questioned by Employees* shows some of the issues that cause employees to wonder about the integrity of their managers.

Maintaining integrity in organizations is a way of building social capital among members of the organization. Scholars use the term *social capital* to refer to strong relationships within organizations that help organizations function smoothly.[21] Social capital is built on trust, and allows deals to move faster, teams to be more productive, and people to perform more creatively.[22]

When Massachusetts-based Malden Mills, manufacturer of Polarfleece, burnt down in 1995, owner Aaron Feuerstein made what seemed a remarkable decision. He

Why Integrity Is Questioned by Employees

Employees are often distrustful of a manager's integrity for the following reasons:

Sticky labels. It is easy for a manager to get branded a "liar," but difficult to build a reputation as a person who is totally trustworthy. Generally people require far more evidence of positive behaviour than negative behaviour.

Competing stakeholders. Managers often send different messages to different stakeholders. So they might tell employees that "customers always come first," and yet the staff interpret downsizing as sending the opposite message. Meanwhile, shareholders believe that cuts to staff can increase profitability, and the value of their shares.

Shifting policies. When new managers take the place of old ones, employees can sometimes see changes in behaviour as being inconsistent with the previous management's message. This can cause employees to become cynical.

Changing fashions. Employees often become cynical when managers try out new fads in management techniques. New ways of managing can send a message to employees that management doesn't really know how to manage.

Unclear priorities. When managers are uncertain about the priorities of the company or their job, this uncertainty can appear to employees to be a lack of integrity.

Blind spots. Sometimes managers are not aware of their own integrity problems. This happens when what a manager says does not match up with what he or she does. For instance, managers might say that employees should be empowered, but then not give up some of their own power so that this happens.

Source: Based on information in T. Simons, "The High Cost of Lost Trust," *Harvard Business Review,* September 2002, pp. 18–19.

announced that he would rebuild the plant, and all employees would be kept on the payroll while waiting for the plant to reopen. Feuerstein could have used the fire as an opportunity to relocate to a developing country where costs would be lower; instead he chose to recognize the social capital he had already built up with his employees. After the fire the employees pitched in and cleaned up the site and did whatever else was necessary to help Feuerstein in the rebuilding process, even though they weren't required to do so.

Social capital shows up in less dramatic ways than what employees do after a fire. UPS drivers serving the same area often meet for lunch in a park or café, where they exchange missorted packages or redistribute the workload if necessary. This informal gathering is organized by the drivers, not management. Nevertheless, management supports this activity. One driver reported, "Our supervisor knows we meet here. . . . If he wants to talk to us together, he'll show up."[23]

Some companies seem better able to build social capital than others. The inset *How Do Companies Destroy Social Capital?* indicates ways that organizations decrease the level of trust available internally.

Basic Principles of Trust

Research offers a few principles that help us better understand how trust and mistrust are created:[24]

Mistrust drives out trust. People who are trusting demonstrate their trust by increasing their openness to others, disclosing relevant information, and expressing their true intentions. People who mistrust conceal information and act opportunistically to take advantage of others. A few mistrusting people can poison an entire organization.

Trust begets trust. Exhibiting trust in others tends to encourage reciprocity.

Growth often masks mistrust. Growth gives leaders opportunities for rapid promotion, and for increased power and responsibility. In this environment, leaders tend to solve problems with quick fixes that elude immediate detection and create later problems.

Decline or downsizing tests the highest levels of trust. Decline or downsizing tends to undermine even the most trusting environment. When employers break the loyalty bond by laying off employees, there is less willingness among workers who remain to trust what management says.

Trust increases cohesion. Trust holds people together. If one person needs help or falters, that person knows that the others will be there to fill in.

Mistrusting groups self-destruct. When group members mistrust each other, they repel and separate. They pursue their own interests rather than the group's. Members of mistrusting groups tend to be suspicious of each other, are constantly on guard against exploitation, and restrict communication with others in the group.

Mistrust generally reduces productivity. Mistrust focuses attention on the differences in member interests, making it difficult for

OB ON THE EDGE

How Do Companies Destroy Social Capital?

Hotelling. Hotelling takes away employees' individual desks, and assigns space to individuals on the days they show up for work. This decreases the amount of office space needed, but makes it difficult for employees to network, develop trust, and learn organizational culture. Individuals are not able to personalize their workspaces, which would allow others to get to know them better.

Re-engineering. Re-engineering encourages efficiency, often at the expense of the time needed to get to know people better and to form human connections.

The leader as superstar. When some individuals are praised as superstars it can take away from the trust, collaboration, and perceived fairness that helps to build relationships.

Hypocrisy. When organizations praise teamwork, but promote individuals who act alone, this sends a strong statement about what organizations really value. Whenever an organization says one thing, but does another, it is acting in a hypocritical manner.

Source: Based on information in L. Prusak and D. Cohen, "How to Invest in Social Capital," *Harvard Business Review,* June 2001, p. 92.

people to visualize common goals. People respond by concealing information and secretly pursuing their own interests.

What Can Leaders Do to Increase Trust on Teams?

Professor Kurt Dirks of Washington University in St. Louis studied the effect of trust in one's coach on team performance during basketball season for 30 teams in Division I and Division III of the NCAA (National Collegiate Athletic Association).[25] His findings show that basketball players' trust in their coach improves team performance. The two teams with the highest level of trust in their coach had outstanding records for the season he studied. The team with the lowest level of trust won only 10 percent of its games, and the coach was fired at the end of the season.

As these results indicate, team leaders have a significant impact on a team's trust climate. The following points summarize ways to build team trust:[26]

- *Demonstrate that you are working for others' interests as well as your own.* All of us are concerned with our own self-interest, but if others see you using them, your job, or the organization for your personal goals to the exclusion of your team's, department's, and organization's interests, your credibility will be undermined.

- *Be a team player.* Support your work team both through words and actions. Defend the team and team members when they're attacked by outsiders. This will demonstrate your loyalty to your work group.

- *Practise openness.* Mistrust comes as much from what people don't know as from what they do know. Openness leads to confidence and trust. So keep people informed, explain your decisions, be candid about problems, and fully disclose relevant information.

- *Be fair.* Before making decisions or taking actions, consider how others will perceive them in terms of objectivity and fairness.

Give credit where it's due, be objective and impartial in performance evaluations, and pay attention to equity perceptions in reward distributions.

- *Speak your feelings.* Managers and leaders who convey only hard facts come across as cold and distant. By sharing your feelings, you will encourage others to view you as real and human. They will know who you are and their respect for you will increase.

- *Show consistency in the basic values that guide your decision making.* Mistrust comes from not knowing what to expect. Take the time to think about your values and beliefs. Then let them consistently guide your decisions. When you know your central purpose, your actions will follow accordingly, and you will project a consistency that earns trust.

- *Maintain confidences.* You trust those you can confide in and rely on. So if people tell you something in confidence, they need to feel assured that you won't discuss it with others or betray that confidence. If people perceive you as someone who "leaks" personal confidences or someone who cannot be depended upon, you won't be perceived as trustworthy.

- *Demonstrate competence.* Develop the admiration and respect of others by demonstrating technical and professional ability and good business sense. Pay particular attention to developing and displaying your communication, team-building, and other interpersonal skills.

- *Work on continuous improvement.* Teams should approach their own development as part of a search for continuous improvement.

Making Your Paranoia More Prudent

Gather data relentlessly. Gather all the facts, not just the ones that support your hypotheses.

Question your interpretations. Leave room for other interpretations. Don't jump to conclusions; ask trusted advisers for their interpretations of the data.

Embrace your enemies. Do your best to keep your enemies on your side.

Trust the shuffler, but cut the deck anyway. Signal that you trust the other person, but also be sure to protect yourself from being tricked.

Be unpredictable. Unexpected behaviour can lead competitors to question themselves, giving you an edge.

Disregard all the rules. Don't be afraid to go with your instinct, rather than the rules.

Source: Based on information in R. M. Kramer, "When Paranoia Makes Sense," *Harvard Business Review,* July 2002, p. 68.

High-performance teams are characterized by high mutual trust among members. That is, members believe in the integrity, character, and ability of each other. Since trust begets trust and distrust begets distrust, maintaining trust requires careful attention by leaders and team members. High trust can have a downside, though, if it inspires team members to not pay attention to each other's work. Team members with high trust may not monitor each other, and if the low monitoring is accompanied by high individual autonomy, the team can perform poorly.[27]

Does Distrust Ever Pay Off?

Professor Roderick Kramer of the Graduate School of Business at Stanford University suggests that always being trusting may not be a desirable strategy. Instead, he offers "prudent paranoia" as a better way for individuals to act. His views are quite contrary to most management literature, which discusses the benefits of trust. Essentially, Kramer argues that distrust can be beneficial.[28]

So what does Kramer mean by *prudent paranoia?* "Prudent paranoia is a form of constructive suspicion regarding the intentions and actions of people and organizations."[29] Kramer argues that such paranoia can be an early warning signal during difficult times. For instance, during times of mergers and acquisitions, employees are naturally distrustful of other departments, and wonder whether they will lose their jobs. Managers may watch out to see who may be threatening their power base. Those with high emotional intelligence are most likely to practise prudent paranoia; after all, one of the signs of emotional intelligence is paying attention to one's environment and responding accordingly.

So how can you demonstrate prudent paranoia? The inset *Making Your Paranoia More Prudent* gives you some tips.

Research Exercises

1. Look for data on the extent to which companies in other countries are trusted by the citizens of those countries. How does this compare to the extent to which Canadians trust companies? Can you draw any inferences about what leads to greater or less trust of corporations?

2. Identify three Canadian organizations that are trying to improve their image to be more trustworthy. What effect is this having on the organizations' bottom lines?

Your Perspective

1. Why might corporations be willing to neglect the importance of trust and instead engage in behaviours such as those that led to recent corporate scandals?

2. What steps can organizations take to make sure that they are seen as trustworthy by the rest of society?

Want to Know More?

If you'd like to read more on this topic, see S. A. Joni, "The Geography of Trust," *Harvard Business Review,* March 2004, pp. 82–88; R. M. Kramer, "When Paranoia Makes Sense," *Harvard Business Review,* July 2002, pp. 62–69; and L. Prusak and D. Cohen, "How to Invest in Social Capital," *Harvard Business Review,* June 2001, pp. 86–93.

FACE**OFF**

Trust in others can be dangerous. If you get too close to someone else, that person could take advantage of you, and possibly hurt your chances to get ahead.

Trust improves relationships among individuals. Through trust, productivity can be increased and more creative ideas are likely to come forward.

CHAPTER 7

Communication

An employer faces a group of former employees who think they have been treated unfairly, while current employees are thinking about joining a union. Will communication help reduce tensions?

1 How does communication work?

2 What are the barriers to communication?

3 How does communication flow in organizations?

4 What are other issues in communication?

In late 1997, mill employees of Hamilton, Ontario-based Dofasco were unhappy with the company.[1] The number of jobs had fallen from 10 300 to 7000 in the previous five years. Former employees had started a group called SHAFT (So How Many Are Fired Tomorrow) to press grievances against the company for what they claimed was unfair dismissal. The Canadian Auto Workers and the United Steelworkers unions were approached by employees with requests to form a union at Dofasco.

John Mayberry, then CEO, showed little respect for his employees. From his early days as a manager, he was not popular: He was disliked "for his habit of springing surprise inspections, and there were rumours that he had threatened to fire employees he thought were malingering."

The culture at Dofasco in the early 1990s did not support open communication, and there was a great deal of conflict between Mayberry and his employees. Mayberry tended to use one-way communication: He would talk and employees were to listen.

In this chapter, we explore the foundations of communication. By learning how to communicate effectively with others, we can improve our relationships with those around us, and work more effectively on teams.

THE COMMUNICATION PROCESS

Research indicates that poor communication is probably the most frequently cited source of interpersonal conflict.[2] Individuals spend nearly 70 percent of their waking hours communicating—writing, reading, speaking, listening—which means that they have many opportunities in which to engage in poor communication. A WorkCanada survey of 2039 Canadians in six industrial and service categories explored the state of communication in Canadian businesses.[3] The survey found that 61 percent of senior executives believed that they did a good job of communicating with employees. However, those who worked below the senior executives failed to share this feeling; only 33 percent of the managers and department heads believed that senior executives were effective communicators. Lower-level employees reported that communication was even worse: Only 22 percent of hourly workers, 27 percent of clerical employees, and 22 percent of professional staff reported that senior executives did a good job of communicating with them. Moreover, another study found that Canadians reported less favourable perceptions about their company's communications than did Americans.[4]

1 How does communication work?

Dofasco
www.dofasco.ca

251

The Dofasco case and the survey of communication practices in the Canadian workplace point to the same reality: Communication is an important problem and a consideration for organizations and individuals alike. Communication is a foundation for many things that happen among groups and within the workplace—from motivating, to providing information, to controlling behaviour, to expressing emotion.

No group can exist without **communication**, which is the transfer and understanding of a message between two or more people. Communication can be thought of as a process, or flow, as shown in Exhibit 7-1. The model indicates that both the sender and the receiver are part of the communication process, with the sender establishing a message, encoding the message, and choosing the channel to send it, and the receiver decoding the message and providing feedback to the sender. Communication problems occur when something disrupts the flow during encoding, channel selection, decoding, or feedback.

The model indicates that communication is both an interactive and iterative process. The sender has to keep in mind the receiver (or audience) and in finalizing the communication, may decide to revisit decisions about the message, the encoding, and/or the feedback. For instance, a manager may want to convey a message face to face, and then is not able to do so for some reason. The message sent by email or voice mail may need to be framed differently than the message that would have been delivered face to face. Similarly, you may decide on a message, and then realize the medium that you have chosen will make the message too complicated. Writing 10 emails to set up a simple lunch appointment may convince you midway through the communication process to pick up the telephone to finalize the details.

We discussed perception in Chapter 2. The communication process is significantly affected by the sender's perception of the receiver and the receiver's perception of the sender. For instance, if the receiver does not trust the sender, he or she may interpret intended positive statements in a negative manner. This chapter's *CBC Video Case* gives you tips for building trust in communication.

Encoding and Decoding

Messages are **encoded** (converted to symbolic form) by a sender and **decoded** (interpreted) by a receiver. Four factors have been described that affect message encoding and decoding: skill, attitudes, knowledge, and the socio-cultural system. For example, our success in communicating to you depends upon our writing skills and your reading skills. Communicative success also includes speaking, listening, and reasoning skills. As we discussed in Chapter 3, our interactions with others are affected by our attitudes, values, and beliefs. Thus, the attitudes of the sender and receiver toward each other will affect how the message is transmitted and how it is received. As well, the amount of knowledge the source and receiver hold about the subject will affect the clarity of the message that is transferred. Finally, our rank in any hierarchy in which we operate affects our ability to successfully engage in communication. Messages sent and received by peo-

communication The transfer and understanding of a message between two or more people.

Small Talk

encoding Converting a message to symbolic form.

decoding Interpreting a sender's message.

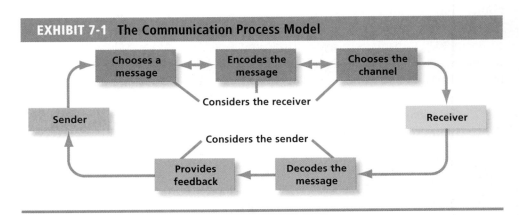

EXHIBIT 7-1   The Communication Process Model

ple of equal rank are sometimes interpreted differently than messages sent and received by people in very different ranks.

The Message

The **message** is the actual physical product from the source after it is encoded. "When we speak, the speech is the message. When we write, the writing is the message. When we paint, the picture is the message. When we gesture, the movements of our arms, the expressions on our face are the message."[5] Our message is affected by the code, or group of symbols, we use to transfer meaning; the content of the message itself; and the decisions that we make in selecting and arranging both codes and content. A poor choice of symbols, and confusion in the content of the message, can cause problems. McDonald's recently settled a lawsuit over its choice of words, as *Focus on Ethics* reveals.

message What is communicated.

FOCUS ON **ETHICS**

Vegetarian or Not Vegetarian?

Does "no beef" really mean what it implies? In March 2002, Oak Brook, Illinois-based McDonald's Corporation agreed to pay $19 million to settle lawsuits from vegetarians who suggested the company had deceived them about how it produced french fries.[6] The agreement requires McDonald's to pay $10 million to charities that support vegetarianism. The company also had to publicly apologize, and consult more to learn about vegetarian dietary issues.

McDonald's Canada
www.mcdonalds.ca

McDonald's communication practices were questioned in the lawsuit. In 1990, the company had announced that its restaurants would no longer use beef fat to cook french fries. Instead, only pure vegetable oil would be used. What the company did not say was that it would continue to add beef tallow to the fries as a flavouring agent.

When vegetarians discovered that they had been unwittingly eating beef-flavoured fries, they were upset. McDonald's claimed that it never said the french fries were vegetarian. The company did apologize for any confusion its announcement caused, however.

Messages can also get "lost in translation" when two parties formalize their understanding through contracts. Contracts are meant to be written in legal terms, for lawyers, and may not always capture the underlying meaning of the parties' understandings. Collective agreements written between management and unions sometimes suffer from this problem as well. When either management or union leaders point to the collective agreement for every interaction in the workplace, they are relying on the encoding of their negotiations, but this may not permit some of the flexibility that was intended in some cases.

The Channel

The **channel** is the medium through which a message travels. It is selected by the source, who must determine which channel is formal and which is informal. Formal channels are established by the organization and transmit messages that pertain to the job-related activities of members. Traditionally, they follow the authority network within the organization. Other forms of messages, such as personal or social messages, follow the informal channels in the organization. Examples of channels are formal memos, voice mail, email, meetings, and so on. The channel can distort a communication if a poor one is selected or if the noise level is high.

channel The medium through which a message travels.

Why do people choose one channel of communication over another; for instance, a phone call instead of a face-to-face talk? One answer might be anxiety! An estimated

communication apprehension
Undue tension and anxiety about oral communication, written communication, or both.

5 to 20 percent of the population[7] suffers from debilitating **communication apprehension**, or anxiety, which is undue tension and anxiety about oral communication, written communication, or both. We all know people who dread speaking in front of a group, but some people may find it extremely difficult to talk with others face to face or become extremely anxious when they have to use the telephone. As a result, they may rely on memos, letters, or email to convey messages when a phone call would not only be faster but also more appropriate.

But what about the 80 to 95 percent of the population who don't suffer from this problem? Is there any general insight we might be able to provide regarding choice of communication channel? The answer is a qualified "yes." A model of media richness has been developed to explain channel selection among managers.[8]

Research has found that channels differ in their capacity to convey information. Some are rich in that they have the ability to (1) handle multiple cues simultaneously, (2) facilitate rapid feedback, and (3) be very personal. Others are lean in that they score low on these three factors. As Exhibit 7-2 illustrates, face-to-face conversation scores highest in terms of **channel richness** because it provides for the maximum amount of information to be transmitted during a communication episode. That is, it offers multiple information cues (words, postures, facial expressions, gestures, intonations), immediate feedback (both verbal and nonverbal), and the personal touch of "being there." Impersonal written media such as formal reports and bulletins rate lowest in richness.

channel richness The amount of information that can be transmitted during a communication episode.

The choice of one channel over another depends on whether the message is routine or nonroutine. Routine messages tend to be straightforward and have a minimum of ambiguity. Nonroutine messages are likely to be complicated and have the potential for misunderstanding. Individuals can communicate routine messages efficiently through channels that are lower in richness. However, they communicate nonroutine messages more effectively by selecting rich channels. Evidence indicates that high-performing managers tend to be more media sensitive than low-performing managers.[9] That is, they are better able to match appropriate media richness with the ambiguity involved in the communication.

A 1999 study at Boston University revealed that managers found it easier to deliver bad news (layoffs, promotion denials, and negative feedback) via email, and that the mes-

EXHIBIT 7-2   Information Richness of Communication Channels

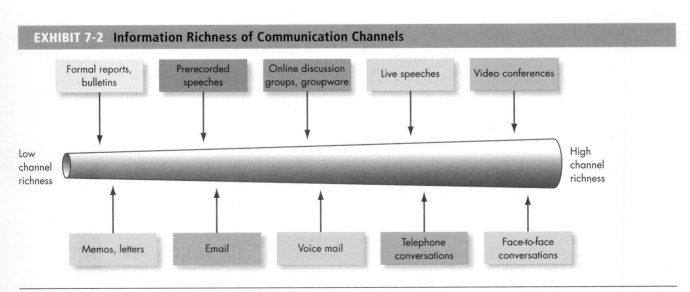

Sources: Based on R. H. Lengel and R. L. Daft, "The Selection of Communication Media as an Executive Skill," *Academy of Management Executive,* August 1988, pp. 225–232; and R. L. Daft and R. H. Lengel, "Organizational Information Requirements, Media Richness, and Structural Design," *Managerial Science,* May 1996, pp. 554–572. Reproduced from R. L. Daft and R. A. Noe, *Organizational Behavior* (Fort Worth, TX: Harcourt, 2001), p. 311.

sages were delivered more accurately this way. This does not mean that sending negative information through email is always recommended. One of the co-authors of the study noted that "offering negative comments face-to-face is often taken as a sign that the news is important and the deliverer cares about the recipient."[10] *Case Incident—Emailing "Lazy" Employees* on page 277 asks you to evaluate one manager's use of email to tell his employees to work harder.

It is not just coincidence that more and more senior managers have been using meetings for easier communication and are regularly leaving the isolated sanctuary of their executive offices to manage by walking around. Effective executives rely on richer channels of communication to transmit the more ambiguous nonroutine messages they need to convey about closing facilities, imposing large layoffs, restructuring, merging, consolidating, and introducing new products and services at an accelerated pace.

The Feedback Loop

The final link in the communication process is the **feedback loop**. Feedback lets us know whether understanding has been achieved. If the feedback loop is to succeed in preventing miscommunication, the receiver needs to give feedback and the sender needs to check for it. Many receivers forget that there is a responsibility involved in communication: to give feedback. For instance, if you sit in a boring lecture, but never discuss with the instructor ways that the delivery could be improved, you have not engaged in communication with your instructor.

When either the sender or the receiver fails to engage in the feedback process, the communication is effectively one-way communication. Two-way communication involves both talking and listening. Many managers communicate badly because they fail to use two-way communication.[11] The *Learning About Yourself Exercise* on page 274 will help you determine whether you are a good listener.

feedback loop The final link in the communication process; it puts the message back into the system as a check against misunderstandings.

The Context

All communication takes place within a context, and violations of that context may create additional problems in sending and receiving messages. For instance, the context of a workplace presents different expectations about how to interact with people than does the context of a bus stop. The workplace may demand more formal interaction, while communication at a bus stop is generally expected to be informal. In some situations, informal communication can look unprofessional, and thus be viewed negatively. In other situations, formal communication can make others feel awkward, if the formality is out of place. Thus, it is important to consider context in both encoding the message and choosing the channel. One of the greatest communication challenges managers have is providing performance feedback to employees. This chapter's *HR Implications* on page 273 presents suggestions on how to give feedback more effectively.

BARRIERS TO EFFECTIVE COMMUNICATION

Dofasco's former CEO, John Mayberry, initially had difficulty communicating with his employees. He didn't really respect them, because he felt they represented an entitlement culture ("good day's work, a day's pay, nice retirement package").[12] Thus, he used selective perception when evaluating their concerns. Because he carried out surprise inspections, employees worried they would be fired for any little problem. This caused them to be defensive. What are other ways that communication can be negatively affected?

A number of factors have been identified as barriers to communication. The more prominent ones are filtering, selective perception, defensiveness, information overload, and language.

2 What are the barriers to communication?

Filtering

Filtering refers to a sender manipulating information so that the receiver will view it more favourably. For example, when a manager tells a senior executive what the manager feels the executive wants to hear, the manager is filtering information. Does this happen much in organizations? Sure! As information is passed up to senior executives, employees must condense and synthesize it so that those on top don't become overloaded with information. The personal interests of those doing the synthesizing, as well as their perceptions of what is important, will result in filtering.

The major determinant of filtering is the number of levels an organization has. The more levels in an organization's hierarchy, the more opportunities there are for filtering information. The *Ethical Dilemma Exercise* on page 276 asks you to consider whether lying is ever a reasonable strategy.

Selective Perception

Receivers in the communication process selectively see and hear based on their needs, motivations, experience, background, and other personal characteristics. Receivers also project their interests and expectations into communications as they decode them. For example, the employment interviewer who believes that young people are more interested in spending time on leisure and social activities than working extra hours to further their careers is likely to be influenced by that stereotype when interviewing young job applicants. As we discussed in Chapter 2, we don't see reality; rather, we interpret what we see and call it "reality."

Enron's former CEO Jeff Skilling is a good example of a person with selective perception. When he was interviewed in November 2001 as information about Enron's accounting problems was just starting to emerge, he refused to acknowledge that anything wrong had gone on at the company. Enron's "a totally different way of thinking about business—we got it," he said.[13] His implication was that it was everyone else who was using selective perception in failing to recognize Enron's greatness. As the scandal continued to unfold, it became obvious that it was Skilling who was using selective perception.

Defensiveness

When people feel that they are being threatened, they tend to react in ways that reduce their ability to achieve mutual understanding. That is, they become defensive—engaging in behaviours such as verbally attacking others, making sarcastic remarks, being overly judgmental, and questioning others' motives. So when individuals interpret another's message as threatening, they often respond in ways that hinder effective communication. *OB in the Workplace* shows how defensiveness between the new head of FPI and its employees led to the breakdown of an acquisitions deal.

OB IN THE WORKPLACE

Seafood Companies Fail to Reach Acquisition Agreement

Why does defensiveness harm communication? John Risley, CEO of Halifax-based Clearwater Fine Foods, aimed to create a seafood giant by acquiring St. John's, Newfoundland-based Fishery Products International (FPI).[14]

At first Risley was successful in his goal, when in May 2001 he engineered a takeover of the FPI board. Immediately, he promised Newfoundlanders that they would lose no jobs. This was a relief to the fishery workers, who had seen jobs tumble by two-thirds in the previous decades.

However, in January 2002 union representatives were told that to cut costs, up to 580 jobs would be lost from three rural Newfoundland plants. This announcement angered workers and politicians alike. Risley defensively argued that the culture of Newfoundland was the real problem: "This is a culture in which people think there's value in the number of jobs that become eligible for unemployment insurance," he said.

Allan Moulton, a union leader and worker at FPI's Marystown plant for 30 years, spoke up at a public hearing on the FPI-Clearwater acquisition. "We're not the only seasonal workers in Canada and it's unfortunate Newfoundland really got pegged with this," he added. "We worked long hours in this industry and every single worker worked hard to save Fishery Products International, and we were successful and we want to get back to doing that."

During 2002, the acquisition was called off because the two companies could not reach agreement and plans to modernize FPI's plants were scrapped. In mid-2005, FPI was still having difficulties and hoping that the Newfoundland legislature would pass a bill to allow it to sell off some of its holdings.

More considerate communication by Risley might have led to fewer problems and less defensiveness, and might have allowed his planned acquisition to go through. ⊠

> **information overload** A condition in which information inflow exceeds an individual's processing capacity.

Information Overload

Individuals have a finite capacity for processing data. As noted in our previous discussion of email, when the information we have to work with exceeds our processing capacity, the result is **information overload**. With emails, phone calls, faxes, meetings, and the need to keep current in one's field, more and more managers and professionals are complaining that they are suffering from too much information. A related issue is the question of how much information managers should share with employees. *Point/Counterpoint* on page 272 examines the issue of open-book management, a practice of letting employees know everything about a company's financial status.

What happens when individuals have more information than they can sort out and use? They tend to select out, ignore, pass over, or forget information. Or they may put off further processing until the overload situation is over. Regardless, the result is lost information and less effective communication.

Language

Words mean different things to different people. "The meanings of words are not in the words; they are in us."[15] Age, education, and cultural background are three of the obvious variables that influence the language we use and the definitions we give to words. For instance, when Alanis Morissette sang, "Isn't it ironic?" middle-aged English professors complained that she completely misunderstood the meaning of "irony"—but the millions who bought her CD understood what she meant.

In an organization, employees usually come from diverse backgrounds and, therefore, have different patterns of speech. Additionally, the grouping of employees into departments creates specialists who develop their own jargon or technical language. In large organizations, members are also frequently widely dispersed geographically—even operating in different countries—and individuals in each locale will use terms and phrases that are unique to their area. The existence of vertical levels can also

Selective perception worked against C. Richard Cowan (in photo), founder and president of Los Angeles-based Power Lift, a distributor of fork-lift trucks. After a year in business, Cowan bought a competitor, where most employees had worked at least 15 years. Perceiving their new boss as young and inexperienced, 40 of the 200 employees quit their jobs, which caused rumours that Power Lift had financial problems. Cowan blamed the situation on poor communication, admitting that he should have met with his new employees to reassure them of the importance of their roles at Power Lift and of the firm's financial soundness. Now Cowan has made communication his top priority, talking personally with each employee to learn about his or her concerns.

cause language problems. The language of senior executives, for instance, can be mystifying to operative employees who are unfamiliar with management jargon.

The point is that even with a common language, such as English, our use of that language is far from uniform. Senders tend to assume that the words and terms they use mean the same to the receiver as they do to them. This, of course, is often incorrect, which creates communication difficulties. The multicultural environment of many of today's workplaces makes communication issues even more complex. In many workplaces, there are people whose first language is something other than English. This means that even more opportunities arise for confusion about meaning. It is therefore important to be aware that your understanding of the particular meaning of a word or phrase may not be shared similarly. Exhibit 7-3 shows individuals who have very different views on what words to use. To learn about effective listening skills, see *From Concepts to Skills* on page 278.

Communicating Under Stress

How can you communicate better when you're stressed out?

One of the most difficult times to communicate properly is when one is under stress. One consultant has identified several tips for communicating under stress. These tips are also appropriate for less stressful communication.[16]

- *Speak clearly.* Be direct about what you want to say, and avoid hiding behind words. For instance, as difficult as it might be to say, "You did not receive the position," the listener is better able to process the information when it is spoken that directly.

- *Be aware of the nonverbal part of communicating.* Tone, facial expression, and body language send signals that may or may not be consistent with your message. In a stressful situation, it is best to speak in a neutral manner.

- *Think carefully about how you state things.* In many situations, it is better to be restrained so that you do not offend your listener. For instance, when you threaten someone if they do not do exactly what you want ("I insist on speaking to your manager this minute"), you simply escalate the situation. It is better to state what you want calmly, so that you can be heard accurately.

Case Incident—Jeremy W. Caputo Has Communication Problems on page 277 indicates what happens when a person does not communicate effectively.

Organizational Communication

John Mayberry may have started off on the wrong foot when he took over as Dofasco CEO in 1993. But things turned around considerably over the next few years. Fast-forward to December 2001. Unionization efforts of previous years were not successful. No employees were laid off during all of the year, and the employees were looking forward to a lavish company Christmas party. Mayberry reported, "The employees have kept the company out of deep doo-doo this year. They deserve a celebration."

How does change like this happen? Mayberry said that he had to get people "working together and communicating." He organized people into a flatter organizational structure and got them to work together to solve problems. Communication has clearly helped the company survive, and even thrive in a troubled economic period. He worked hard at team building with his nearly 7000 employees, and all of them were taken in small groups over time for "experiential learning" exercises at a ski resort.

In 2000, Mayberry informed his employees that the company had to cut production costs by $100 million over the next year to stay in the black. The employees worked together in their various teams and came up with a plan that exceeded Mayberry's target. "Five years ago, we'd still be arguing about whether or not we had a problem—let alone how to go about fixing it." Employees at Dofasco are more confident these days that management will keep them informed of what's happening with the company, which makes them more likely to work together to solve company problems. So what can managers do to make communication more effective?

In this section, we explore ways that communication occurs in organizations, including the direction of communication, formal small-group networks, the grapevine, and electronic communications.

3 How does communication flow in organizations?

Direction of Communication

Communication can flow downward, upward, and/or laterally in organizations.[17] We will explore each of these directional flows and their implications.

Downward

Communication that flows from one level of a group or organization to a lower level is downward communication.

When we think of managers communicating with employees, the downward pattern is the one we usually have in mind. Group leaders and managers use this approach to assign goals, provide job instructions, inform employees of policies and procedures, identify problems that need attention, and offer feedback about performance.

Upward

Upward communication flows to a higher level in the group or organization.

Some organizational examples of upward communication are performance reports prepared by lower management for review by middle and top management; suggestion boxes; employee attitude surveys; grievance procedures; manager-employee discussions; and informal sessions where employees have the opportunity to identify and discuss problems with their direct manager or representatives of higher management.

In general, few Canadian firms rely on upward communication. In their study of 375 Canadian organizations, David Saunders, dean of Queen's School of Business, and Joanne Leck, associate dean (research) at the University of Ottawa School of Management, found that unionized organizations were more likely to use upward communication.[18] The form of upward communication most used was grievance procedures.

Lateral

When communication occurs among members of the same work group, among members of work groups at the same level, among managers at the same level, or among any horizontally equivalent employees, we describe it as lateral (or horizontal) communication.

Horizontal communication is often necessary to save time and to ease coordination. In some cases, lateral relationships are formally sanctioned. Often, they are informally created to short-circuit the vertical hierarchy and speed up action. So lateral communication can, from management's perspective, be good or bad. Because strict adherence to the formal vertical structure for all communications can slow the efficient and accurate transfer of information, lateral communication can be beneficial. In such cases, it occurs with the knowledge and support of managers. But it can create dysfunctional conflicts when the formal vertical channels are breached, when members go

EXHIBIT 7-3

THE FAR SIDE   BY GARY LARSON

© 1994 FarWorks, Inc. All Rights Reserved/Dist. by Creators Syndicate

"Well, actually, Doreen, I rather resent being called a 'swamp thing.' ... I prefer the term 'wetlands-challenged-mutant.'"

Source: The Far Side by Gary Larson, Copyright © 1994 for Works, Inc. All rights reserved. Used with permission.

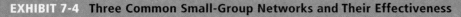

EXHIBIT 7-4   Three Common Small-Group Networks and Their Effectiveness

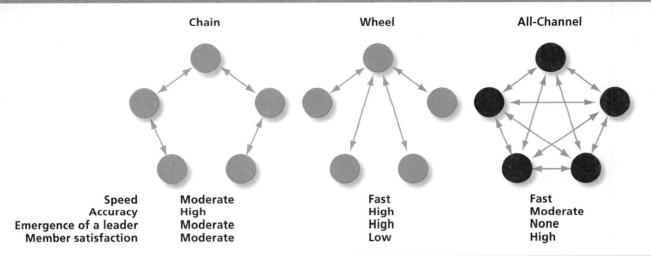

	Chain	Wheel	All-Channel
Speed	Moderate	Fast	Fast
Accuracy	High	High	Moderate
Emergence of a leader	Moderate	High	None
Member satisfaction	Moderate	Low	High

above or around their managers to get things done, or when employers find out that actions have been taken or decisions made without their knowledge.

Small-Group Networks

communication networks
Channels by which information flows.

formal networks Task-related communications that follow the authority chain.

Communication networks define the channels by which information flows. These channels are one of two varieties—either formal or informal. **Formal networks** are typically vertical, follow the authority chain, and are limited to task-related communications. Exhibit 7-4 illustrates three common formal small-group networks: the *chain, wheel,* and *all-channel.* The chain network rigidly follows the formal chain of command. The wheel network relies on the leader to act as the central conduit for all the group's communication. The all-channel network permits all group members to communicate actively with each other. As Exhibit 7-4 illustrates, the effectiveness of each network depends on the dependent variable you are concerned about. For instance, the structure of the wheel network facilitates the emergence of a leader, the all-channel network is best if high member satisfaction is most important, and the chain network is best if accuracy is most important. Thus, we conclude that no single network is appropriate for all occasions.

The Grapevine

informal networks
Communications that flow along social and relational lines.

grapevine The organization's most common informal network.

The previous discussion of networks emphasized formal communication patterns. In contrast, in **informal networks**, communication flows along social and relational lines. Communication is free to move in any direction, skip authority levels, and is as likely to satisfy group members' social needs as it is to help with task accomplishments.

The most common informal network in the organization is the **grapevine**. Research has found that 75 percent of employees hear about matters first through rumours on the grapevine.[19] Thus it is an important source of information for many employees.

Is the information that flows along the grapevine accurate? The evidence indicates that about 75 percent of what is carried is accurate.[20] But what conditions foster an active grapevine? What gets the rumour mill rolling?

It is frequently assumed that rumours start because they make titillating gossip. However, this is rarely the case. Rumours have at least four purposes:

1. To structure and reduce anxiety

2. To make sense of limited or fragmented information

3. To serve as a vehicle to organize group members, and possibly outsiders, into coalitions

4. To signal a sender's status ("I'm an insider and, with respect to this rumour, you're an outsider") or power ("I have the power to make you into an insider")[21]

Research indicates that rumours emerge as a response to situations that are important to us, where there is ambiguity, and under conditions that arouse anxiety.[22] The secrecy and competition that typically prevail in large organizations around such issues as the appointment of new senior managers, the relocation of offices, and the realignment of work assignments create conditions that encourage and sustain rumours on the grapevine. A rumour will persist either until the wants and expectations creating the uncertainty underlying the rumour are fulfilled or until the anxiety is reduced.

Grapevine Patterns

Communication through grapevines can take several different patterns, as illustrated in Exhibit 7-5. In the single strand, each person tells information to just one other person (somewhat like the child's game "Whisper Down the Lane"). In the gossip pattern, one person tells everyone the information. These people are commonly called gossips, and make up about 10 percent of organizational members.[23]

The probability and cluster patterns may appear to be similar, but they function quite differently. In the probability pattern, individuals are randomly told information, with no apparent pattern. In the cluster pattern, individuals selectively choose individuals to whom they will relay information. Individuals may strategically select to whom to pass on information, to ensure that it gets spread around. Not everyone passes along information that they hear, but those who consistently do are called liaison individuals: "Usually these liaisons are friendly, outgoing people who are in positions that allow them to cross departmental lines. For example, [administrative assistants] tend to

---

EXHIBIT 7-5 Grapevine Patterns

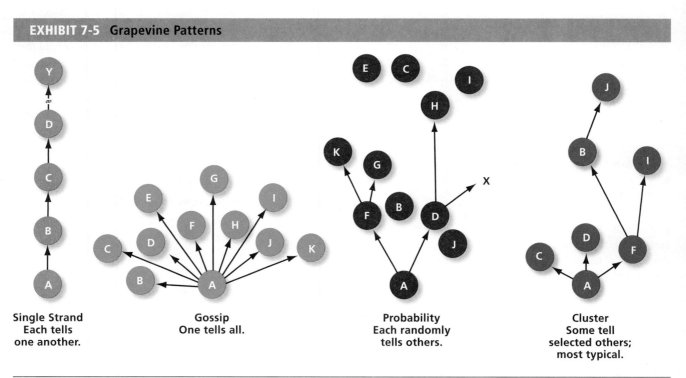

Single Strand
Each tells
one another.

Gossip
One tells all.

Probability
Each randomly
tells others.

Cluster
Some tell
selected others;
most typical.

Source: K. Davis and J. W. Newstrom, *Human Behavior at Work: Organizational Behavior,* 7th ed. (New York: McGraw-Hill, 1985), p. 317. Reprinted by permission.

be liaisons because they can communicate with the top executive, the janitor, and everyone in between without raising eyebrows."[24]

What can we conclude from this discussion? Certainly the grapevine is an important part of any group's or organization's communication network and well worth understanding.[25] It identifies for managers those confusing issues that employees consider important and anxiety-provoking. It acts, therefore, as both a filter and a feedback mechanism, picking up the issues that employees consider relevant. Managers can reduce the negative consequence of rumours by explaining decisions and openly discussing worst-case possibilities.[26]

Electronic Communications

Since the early 1980s, we have been subjected to an onslaught of new electronic ways to communicate. Electronic communications (including pagers, fax machines, videoconferencing, electronic meetings, email, cellphones, voice mail, and BlackBerrys) make it possible for you to work, even if you are away from your workstation. These technologies are largely reshaping the way we communicate in organizations.[27] You can be reached when you are in a meeting, having a lunch break, visiting a customer's office across town, watching a movie in a crowded theatre, or playing golf on a Saturday morning. The line between an employee's work and nonwork life is no longer distinct, meaning all employees theoretically can be "on call" 24 hours a day.

Organizational boundaries become less relevant as a result of electronic communications. Why? Because networked computers allow employees to jump vertical levels within the organization, work full-time at home or someplace other than "the office," and have ongoing communications with people in other organizations.

Email

Ever notice that communicating via email can lead to misunderstandings?

Email has added considerably to the number of hours worked per week, according to a recent study by Christina Cavanagh, professor of management communications at the Richard Ivey School of Business, University of Western Ontario. Between 2000 and 2002, business professionals and executives said they were working six more hours a week, responding to email.[28]

Email also does not provide either the verbal or nonverbal nuances that a face-to-face meeting does. There has been some attempt to remedy this through the development of "emoticons" (for example, the smiley face :-)) to indicate a friendly tone, and abbreviations (for example, IMHO, "in my humble opinion") to indicate that individuals are respectfully trying to convey their own viewpoint. There is also the standard warning not to write emails in ALL CAPS, as doing so is an indication that one is shouting. Exhibit 7-6 illustrates some of the conventional symbols used in email.

The information overload caused by the use of email in the workplace deserves greater consideration by managers and employees alike. Individuals may use email to hide from direct interaction, to protect their power, or to create a one-way communication tool. Email has also become a tool to create paper trails for interaction, allowing people to avoid face-to-face communication on difficult topics. Moreover, for people with a high need for social contact, a heavy reliance on electronic communications is likely to lead to lower job satisfaction.

Considerations for Writing and Sending Email Despite many advantages to email, it is important to realize that it is vir-

---

EXHIBIT 7-6	**Emoticons: Showing Emotions in Email**

Electronic mail need not be emotion-free. Over the years, email users have developed a set of symbols *(emoticons)* for expressing emotions. For instance, the use of all caps (as in THIS PROJECT NEEDS YOUR IMMEDIATE ATTENTION!) is the email equivalent of shouting. The following highlights some emoticons:

:)	Smile	:-e	Disappointed
<g>	Grin	:-@	Scream
:(	Frown	:-0	Yell
;)	Wink	:-D	Shock or surprise
:-[	Really sad face	:'(	Crying

tually indestructible once it gets backed up on your company's server. Also, its very speed and accessibility can cause miscommunication and misdirected messages. With these issues in mind, consider the following tips for writing and sending email offered by business professor Cavanagh:[29]

- Don't send emails without a subject line.

- Be careful in your use of emoticons and acronyms for business communication.

- Write your message clearly, and briefly.

- Copy emails to others only if they really need the information.

- Sleep on angry emails before sending to be sure you are sending the right message.

Employees should also be aware that email is not necessarily private, and companies often take the position that they have the right to read your email. Some wonder, however, whether reading employee email is ethical. *Focus on Ethics* illustrates that employees cannot assume that their email is private.

David Breda, co-owner of Leader Plumbing and Heating, a mechanical contractor in Woodbridge, Ontario, finds online collaboration a major boon to his business. His employees, mostly plumbers, are able to exchange real-time information, and thus be more efficient in their work.

FOCUS ON **ETHICS**

Your Email Can Get You Fired

Should your email be safe from your manager's eyes? The Canadian Auto Workers (CAW) union expressed outrage in early 1998 when it discovered that Montreal-based Canadian National Railway (CN) was reading employees' email messages.[30] "Our people feel violated. You're given an email address and you have a password, and it's yours. It's personal," is the view of Abe Rosner, a national CAW representative. CN, however, disagrees: "Email is to be used for CN business-approved activities only. Flowing from this is that any communication exchanged on the system is viewed as company property," explains Mark Hallman, a CN spokesperson.

While most employees do not think managers should listen to their subordinates' voice mail messages or read their emails, some managers disagree. More than 20 percent of managers surveyed recently said that they monitored their employees' voice mail, email, and/or computer files. The managers argue that the company owns the systems used to produce this material, and therefore, they should have access to the information.

Fred Jones (not his real name) was fired from a Canadian company for forwarding dirty jokes to his clients.[31] Until this incident, Jones had been a high-performing employee who sold network computers for his company. Jones thought that he was only sending the jokes to clients who liked them, and assumed the clients would tell him if they didn't want to receive the jokes. Instead, a client complained to the company about receiving the dirty jokes. After an investigation, the company fired Jones. Jones is still puzzled about being fired. He views his email as private; to him, sending jokes is the same as telling them at the water cooler.

Jones was not aware that under current law, employee information, including email, is not necessarily private. Most federal employees, provincial public sector employees, and employees working for federally regulated industries are covered by the federal Privacy Act and Access to Information Act, in place since 1985. Many private sector employees are not covered by privacy legislation, however.

Canadian Auto Workers (CAW)
www.caw.ca

Canadian National Railway (CN)
www.cn.ca

Ann Cavoukian, Information and Privacy Commissioner of Ontario, notes that "employees deserve to be treated like adults and companies should limit surveillance to rare instances, such as when there is suspicion of criminal activity or harassment."[32] She suggests that employers use respect and courtesy when dealing with employees' email, and she likens email to office phone calls, which generally are not monitored by the employer. It is clearly important, in any event, that employees be aware of their company's policy on email.

Instant Messaging

Instant messaging (IM), which has been popular among teens for more than a decade, is now rapidly moving into business.[33]

Instant messaging is essentially real-time email. Its growth has been spectacular. In 2002 Canadians sent 174 million text messages, in 2003 they sent 352 million text messages, and in 2004 they sent more than 710 million text messages.[34] Experts estimate that by 2005, more people will be using IM than email as their primary communication tool at work.[35]

IM is a fast and inexpensive means for managers to stay in touch with employees and for employees to stay in touch with each other. It also provides several advantages over email. There's no delay, no inbox clutter of messages, and no uncertainty as to whether the message was received. Managers also find that IM is an excellent means for monitoring employees' physical presence at their work stations. "With a glance at their contact lists, users can tell who's logged on and available right now."[36] Service technicians at Ajax, Ontario-based Pitney Bowes Canada started using IM rather than pagers, because "it's cheaper and it's two-way."[37] The company knows if messages are received.

IM isn't going to replace email. Email is still probably a better device for conveying long messages that need to be saved. IM is preferred for sending one- or two-line messages that would just clutter up an email inbox. On the downside, some IM users find the technology intrusive and distracting. IM's continual online presence can make it hard for employees to concentrate and stay focused. Managers also indicate concern that IM will be used by employees to chat with friends and colleagues about nonwork issues. Finally, because instant messages are easily broken into, many organizations are concerned about IM security.[38]

OTHER ISSUES IN COMMUNICATION

4 What are other issues in communication?

How important is nonverbal communication? What does silence have to do with communicating? Why do men and women often have difficulty communicating with each other? How can individuals improve their cross-cultural communication? We address each of these issues next.

Nonverbal Communication

Anyone who has ever paid a visit to a singles bar or a nightclub is aware that communication need not be verbal in order to convey a message. A glance, a stare, a smile, a frown, a provocative body movement—they all convey meaning. This example illustrates that no discussion of communication would be complete without a discussion of **nonverbal communication**. This includes body movements, facial expressions, and the physical distance between the sender and receiver.

Does body language really make a difference?

The academic study of body motions has been labelled **kinesics**. It refers to gestures, facial configurations, and other movements of the body. Because it is a relatively new field, there isn't complete agree-

nonverbal communication Messages conveyed through body movements, facial expressions, and the physical distance between the sender and receiver.

kinesics The study of body motions, such as gestures, facial configurations, and other movements of the body.

ment on findings. Still, body movement is an important segment of the study of communication.

It has been argued that every body movement has a meaning and that no movement is accidental.[39] Through body language, we can say such things as, "Help me, I'm confused," or "Leave me alone, I'm really angry." Rarely do we send our messages consciously. We act out our state of being with nonverbal body language, even if we are not aware of doing so. We lift one eyebrow for disbelief. We rub our noses for puzzlement. We clasp our arms to isolate ourselves or to protect ourselves. We shrug our shoulders for indifference, wink one eye for intimacy, tap our fingers for impatience, slap our forehead for forgetfulness.[40] Babies and young children provide another good illustration of effective use of nonverbal communication. Although they lack developed language skills, they often use fairly sophisticated body language to communicate their physical and emotional needs. Such use of body language underscores its importance in communicating needs throughout life.

While we may disagree with the specific meaning of these movements, body language adds to and often complicates verbal communication. For instance, if you read the transcript of a meeting, you do not grasp the impact of what was said in the same way you would if you had been there or had seen the meeting on video. Why? There is no record of nonverbal communication. The *intonations*, or emphasis, given to words or phrases is missing.

The *facial expression* of a person also conveys meaning. A snarling face says something different from a smile. Facial expressions, along with intonations, can show arrogance, aggressiveness, fear, shyness, and other characteristics that would never be communicated if you read a transcript of the meeting.

Studies indicate that those who maintain *eye contact* while speaking are viewed with more credibility than those whose eye contact wanders. People who make eye contact are also deemed more competent than those who do not.

The way individuals space themselves in terms of *physical distance*, commonly called **proxemics**, also has meaning. What is considered proper spacing is largely dependent on cultural norms. For instance, studies have shown that those from "contact" cultures (e.g., Arabs, Latin Americans, southern Europeans) are more comfortable with body closeness and touch than those from "noncontact" cultures (e.g., Asians, North Americans, northern Europeans).[41] These differences can lead to confusion. If someone stands closer to you than expected according to your cultural norms, you may interpret the action as an expression of aggressiveness or sexual interest. However, if the person stands farther away than you expect, you might think he or she is displeased with you or uninterested. Someone whose cultural norms differ from yours might be very surprised by your interpretation.

proxemics The study of physical space in interpersonal relationships.

Environmental factors such as seating arrangements or the conditions of the room can also send intended or unintended messages. A person whose desk faces the doorway demonstrates command of his or her physical space, while perhaps also conveying that others should not come too close.

It's important for the receiver to be alert to these nonverbal aspects of communication. You should look for nonverbal cues, as well as listen to the literal meaning of a sender's words. In particular, you should be aware of contradictions between the messages. The manager may say that she is free to talk to you about that raise you have

You can tell from his body language that David Weinberg likes his employees. Rather than talking down to them, he crouches to talk face to face with them. His smile is genuine. Weinberg is co-chairman of Fel-Pro, a Skokie, Illinois-based manufacturer of auto parts. Fel-Pro is well known in the business world as a company that treats its employees exceptionally well. It gives employees profit sharing, above-market wages, $1000 (US) in Treasury bonds when they have a new baby, and a $3500-a-year (US) scholarship for children's college tuition. Weinberg's nonverbal messages are in sync with his verbal messages. Both express his sincere concern for employees.

been seeking, but you may see nonverbal signals (such as looking at her watch) that suggest this is not the time to discuss the subject. It's not uncommon for people to express one emotion verbally and another nonverbally. These contradictions often suggest that actions speak louder (and more accurately) than words. The *Working With Others Exercise* on page 275 will help you see the value of nonverbal communication in interpersonal relations.

We should also monitor body language with some care. For instance, while it is often thought that people who cross their arms in front of their chest are showing resistance to a message, individuals might also do this if they're feeling cold, regardless of their reaction to a message.

Silence as Communication

Sherlock Holmes once solved a murder mystery based not on what happened but on what *didn't* happen. Holmes remarked to his assistant, Dr. Watson, about "the curious incident of the dog in the nighttime." Watson, surprised, responds, "But the dog did nothing in the nighttime." To which Holmes replied, "That was the curious incident." Holmes concluded the crime had to be committed by someone with whom the dog was familiar because the watchdog did not bark.

The dog that did not bark in the night is often used as a metaphor for an event that is significant by reason of its absence. That story is also an excellent illustration of the importance of silence in communication.

Professors Craig Pinder of the University of Victoria and Karen Harlos of McGill University have noted that silence—defined here as an absence of speech or noise—generally has been ignored as a form of communication in organizational behaviour because it represents *in*action or *non*behaviour. But silence is not necessarily inaction. Nor is it, as many believe, a failure to communicate. Silence can, in fact, be a powerful form of communication.[42] It can mean someone is thinking or contemplating a response to a question. It can mean a person is anxious and fearful of speaking. It can signal agreement, dissent, frustration, or anger.

In terms of organizational behaviour, we can see several links between silence and work-related behaviour. For instance, silence is a critical element of groupthink, in which it implies agreement with the majority. It can be a way for employees to express dissatisfaction, as when they "suffer in silence." It can be a sign that someone is upset, as when a typically talkative person suddenly says nothing—"What's the matter with him? Is he all right?" It's a powerful tool used by individuals to signal disfavour by shunning or ignoring someone with "silent insults." As well, it's a crucial element of group decision making, allowing individuals to think over and contemplate what others have said.

Failing to pay close attention to the silent portion of a conversation can result in missing a vital part of the message. Astute communicators watch for gaps, pauses, and hesitations. They hear and interpret silence. They treat pauses, for instance, as analogous to a flashing yellow light at an intersection—they pay attention to what comes next. Is the person thinking, deciding how to frame an answer? Is the person suffering from communication apprehension? Sometimes the real message in a communication is buried in the silence.

Communication Barriers Between Women and Men

Research by Deborah Tannen provides us with some important insights into the differences between men and women in terms of conversational styles.[43] In particular, Tannen has been able to explain why gender often creates oral communication barriers. Her research does not suggest that *all* men or *all* women behave as a gendered class in their communication; rather, she illustrates some important generalizations.

The essence of Tannen's research is that men use talk to emphasize status, while women use it to create connection. According to Tannen, women speak and hear a language of connection and intimacy while men speak and hear a language of status and independence. So, for many men, conversations are primarily a means to preserve independence and maintain status in a hierarchical social order. For many women, however, conversations are negotiations for closeness in which people try to seek and give confirmation and support. The following examples will illustrate Tannen's thesis.

Men frequently complain that women talk on and on about their problems. Women criticize men for not listening. What's happening is that when men hear a problem, they frequently assert their desire for independence and control by offering solutions. Many women, on the other hand, view telling a problem as a means to promote closeness. The women present the problem to gain support and connection, not to get the male's advice. Mutual understanding, as sought by women, is symmetrical. But giving advice is asymmetrical—it sets up the (male) advice giver as more knowledgeable, more reasonable, and more in control. This contributes to distancing men and women in their efforts to communicate.

In conversation, women and men tend to approach points of conflict in different ways. A woman might say, "Have you looked at the marketing department's research on that point?" (the implication being that the report will show the error). Rather than simply relying on her own knowledge or beliefs, she presents the supporting evidence. A man might say, "I think you're wrong on that point," and not even provide documented evidence. These lead to gendered interpretations of the communication. Men frequently view female indirectness as "covert" or "sneaky," and they also interpret weakness when women won't take definitive stands, whereas women interpret male directness as an assertion of status and one-upmanship. Neither position is correct. It is helpful, though, to begin to understand the ways that females and males sometimes interpret the same dialogue differently.

Finally, men often criticize women for seeming to apologize all the time. Men tend to see the phrase "I'm sorry" as a weakness because they interpret the phrase to mean the woman is accepting blame. However, women typically use "I'm sorry" to express empathy: "I know you must feel bad about this; I probably would too in the same position."

While Tannen has received wide acknowledgment of her work, some suggest that it is anecdotal and/or based on faulty research. Goldsmith and Fulfs argue that men and women have more similarities than differences as communicators, although they acknowledge that when communication difficulties do appear, it is appealing to attribute them to gender.[44] Despite this, Nancy Langton has noted, based on evidence from role plays, that men and women make requests for raises differently, and men are more likely to state that men were more effective at making requests, while women are more likely to indicate that it was women who handled the interaction more favourably.[45]

Research indicates that women use language to create connection while men use language to emphasize status and power. The businesswomen conversing here illustrate that women speak and hear a language of connection and intimacy.

Cross-Cultural Communication

Effective communication is difficult under the best of conditions. Cross-cultural factors clearly create the potential for increased communication problems.

Cultural Barriers

One author has identified four specific problems related to language difficulties in cross-cultural communication.[46] First, there are *barriers caused by semantics*. As we have

What factors hinder cross–cultural communication?

noted previously, words mean different things to different people. This is particularly true for people from different national cultures. Some words, for instance, don't translate between cultures. Understanding the word *sisu* will help you communicate with people from Finland, but this word does not have an exact translation in English. It means something akin to "guts" or "dogged persistence." Similarly, the new capitalists in Russia may have difficulty communicating with their English-speaking counterparts because English terms such as *efficiency, free market,* and *regulation* cannot be directly translated into Russian.

Second, there are *barriers caused by word connotations.* Words imply different things in different languages. The Japanese word *hai* translates as "yes," but its connotation may be "yes, I'm listening," rather than "yes, I agree." Western executives may be hampered in their negotiations if they don't understand this connotation.

Third are *barriers caused by tone differences.* In some cultures, language is formal; in others, it's informal. In some cultures, the tone changes depending on the context: People speak differently at home, in social situations, and at work. Using a personal, informal style in a situation where a more formal style is expected can be embarrassing and offensive.

Fourth, there are *barriers caused by differences among perceptions.* People who speak different languages actually view the world in different ways. The Inuit perceive snow differently because they have many words for it. They also perceive "no" differently from English speakers because the Inuit have no such word in their vocabulary.

Cultural Context

A better understanding of these cultural barriers and their implications for communicating across cultures can be achieved by considering the concepts of high- and low-context cultures.[47]

high-context cultures Cultures that rely heavily on nonverbal and subtle situational cues in communication.

low-context cultures Cultures that rely heavily on words to convey meaning in communication.

Cultures tend to differ in the importance of context in influencing the meaning that individuals take from what is actually said or written vs. who the other person is. Countries like China, Vietnam, and Saudi Arabia are **high-context cultures**. Their people rely heavily on nonverbal and subtle situational cues when communicating with others. What is not said may be more significant than what is said. A person's official status, place in society, and reputation carry considerable weight in communications. In contrast, people from Europe and North America reflect their **low-context cultures**. They rely essentially on words to convey meaning. Body language or formal titles are secondary to spoken and written words (see Exhibit 7-7).

What do these contextual differences mean in terms of communication? Actually, quite a lot! Communication in high-context cultures implies considerably more trust by both parties. What may appear, to an outsider, as a casual and insignificant conversation is important because it reflects the desire to build a relationship and create trust. Oral agreements imply strong commitments in high-context cultures. Also, who you are—your age, seniority, rank in the organization—are highly valued and heavily influence your credibility. But in low-context cultures, enforceable contracts will tend to be in writing, precisely worded, and highly legalistic. Similarly, low-context cultures value directness. Managers are expected to be explicit and precise in conveying intended meaning. It's quite different in high-context cultures, where managers tend to "make suggestions" rather than give orders.

Overcoming Cross-Cultural Difficulties

When communicating with people from a different culture, what can you do to reduce misperceptions, misinterpretations, and misevaluations? Following these four rules can be helpful:[48]

- *Assume differences until similarity is proven.* Most of us assume that others are more similar to us than they actually are. But people from different countries

EXHIBIT 7-7   High- vs. Low-Context Cultures

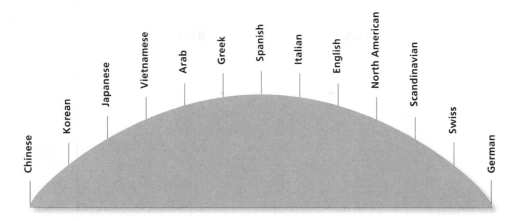

High Context
Strong social bonds
Social hierarchy governs communication
Communication builds connection
Avoidance of direct confrontation

Low Context
High individualism
Little social hierarchy observed
Communication is explicit and impersonal
Comfortable with open confrontation

Source: Based on the work of E. T. Hall. From R. E. Duleck, J.S. Fielden, and J. S. Hill, "International Communication: An Executive Primer," *Business Horizons,* January–February 1991, p. 21.

often are very different from us. So you are far less likely to make an error if you assume others are different from you rather than assuming similarity until difference is proven.

- *Emphasize description rather than interpretation or evaluation.* Interpreting or evaluating what someone has said or done, in contrast with describing, is based more on the observer's culture and background than on the observed situation. As a result, delay judgment until you have had sufficient time to observe and interpret the situation from the differing perspectives of all the cultures involved.

- *Practise empathy.* Before sending a message, put yourself in the recipient's shoes. What are his or her values, experiences, and frames of reference? What do you know about his or her education, upbringing, and background that can give you added insight? Try to see the other person as he or she really is.

- *Treat your interpretations as a working hypothesis.* Once you have developed an explanation for a new situation or think you empathize with someone from a foreign culture, treat your interpretation as a hypothesis that needs further testing rather than as a certainty. Carefully assess the feedback provided by recipients to see if it confirms your hypothesis. For important decisions or communiqués, you can also

Ottawa-based Donna Cona made history when it designed and installed the computer network for the government of the new Nunavut territory. Two-thirds of the firm's software engineers are Aboriginal. Peter Baril, Nunavut's director of information technology operations, notes: "Donna Cona's quiet and knowledgeable approach was perhaps the most important skill brought to our project. No other style could have worked in this predominantly Aboriginal environment."

check with other foreign and home-country colleagues to ensure that your interpretations are on target.

SUMMARY AND IMPLICATIONS

1 **How does communication work?** Findings in the chapter suggest that the goal of perfect communication is unattainable. Yet there is evidence that demonstrates a positive relationship between effective communication (which includes factors such as perceived trust, perceived accuracy, desire for interaction, top-management receptiveness, and upward information requirements) and employee productivity.[49] Therefore, choosing the correct channel, being an effective listener, and using feedback well may make for more effective communication.

2 **What are the barriers to communication?** Human beings will always be subject to errors in communication because of filtering, selective perception, defensiveness, information overload, and language. What is said may not be what is heard. Whatever the sender's expectations, the decoded message in the mind of the receiver represents the receiver's reality. This "reality" will determine the individual's reactions, including performance, motivation, and degree of satisfaction in the workplace.

3 **How does communication flow in organizations?** Communication can flow vertically and laterally, and by formal and informal channels in organizations. We noted that there are three common formal small-group networks: the *chain*, *wheel*, and *all-channel*. The most common informal network in the organization is the *grapevine*. Greater use of informal channels will increase communication flow, reduce uncertainty, and improve group performance and satisfaction. We also noted that email, among other electronic communications, has become far more prevalent, is causing more stress, and can be misused, so it is not always the most effective means of communication.

4 **What are the other issues in communication?** The big topics in communication are the importance of nonverbal communication and silence, gender differences in communication, and cross-cultural differences in communication. As we saw in this chapter, nonverbal cues help provide a clearer picture of what someone is trying to say. Silence can be an important communication clue, and failing to pay attention to silence can result in missing some or all of a message. Good communicators hear and interpret silence. We can make some generalizations about differences in the conversational style of men and women; men are more likely to use talk to emphasize status, while women use talk to create connection. We noted that there are a variety of barriers when communicating with someone from a different culture, and that it's best to assume differences until similarity is proven, emphasize description rather than *interpretation or evaluation*, practise empathy, and treat your interpretation as a working hypothesis.

For Review

1. Describe the communication process and identify its key components. Give an example of how this process operates with both oral and written messages.

2. Contrast encoding and decoding.

3. Identify three common formal small-group networks and give the advantages of each.

4. What conditions stimulate the emergence of rumours?

5. What are the advantages and disadvantages of email? Of instant messaging?

6. What is nonverbal communication? Does it aid or hinder verbal communication?

7. What does the expression "sometimes the real message in a communication is buried in the silence" mean?

8. What are the managerial implications from the research contrasting male and female communication styles?

9. List four specific problems related to language difficulties in cross-cultural communication.

10. Contrast high- and low-context cultures. What do the differences mean for communication?

For Critical Thinking

1. "Ineffective communication is the fault of the sender." Do you agree or disagree? Discuss.

2. What can you do to improve the likelihood that your message will be received and understood as you intended?

3. How might managers use the grapevine for their benefit?

4. Using the concept of channel richness, give examples of messages best conveyed by email, in face-to-face communication, and on the company bulletin board.

5. "Most people are poor listeners." Do you agree or disagree? Defend your position.

OB for You

- If you are having difficulty communicating with someone, you might consider that both you and the other person are contributing something to that breakdown. This tends to be true even if you are inclined to believe that the other person is the party more responsible for the breakdown.

- Often either selective perception or defensiveness gets in the way of communication. As you work in your groups on student projects, try to observe communication flows more critically to help you understand ways that communication can be improved and dysfunctional conflict avoided.

POINT

COUNTERPOINT

Open-Book Management Improves the Bottom Line

Open-book management (OBM) seeks to get every employee to think and behave like an owner.[50] It throws out the notion that bosses run things and employees do what they are told. In the open-book approach, employees are given the information that historically was kept strictly within the management ranks.

There are three key elements to any OBM program. First, management shares detailed financial and operating information with employees. If employees don't know how the company makes money, how can they be expected to make the firm more successful? Second, employees need to be taught to understand the company's financial statements, including how to read and interpret income statements, balance sheets, and cash flow statements. Third, management needs to show employees how their work influences financial results. Showing employees the impact of their jobs on the bottom line makes financial statement analysis relevant.

A growing number of companies are using OBM, including 67 percent of the *PROFIT* 100 Canada's Fastest Growing Companies.[51] Yves Poire, president of Montreal-based Fjord Interactive, believes that OBM helps his employees share the vision and dreams of the company.[52]

Why should it work? Access to financial information, and the ability to understand that information, makes employees think like owners. As a result, they make decisions that are best for the organization, not just for themselves.

Does it work? Most firms that have introduced OBM offer evidence that it has significantly helped the business. For instance, when Mississauga, Ontario-based Creditron was facing financial problems in 2001, the employees were aware of the situation, because CEO Wally Vogel kept them informed through his OBM practices. A manager let him know that employees were willing to take a pay cut to help the company out. As a consequence, Vogel only had to lay off five employees, and six months later two of them were rehired. Meanwhile, sales increased 25 percent that year. Vogel opens his books to his employees and has monthly meetings to outline how money is spent. "We've found it's a great way to get cross-pollination of ideas and have everybody in the office feel that they're part of a team," says Vogel, "as opposed to working in their little area, without knowing what's going on beyond them."[53]

Open-Book Management Can Ruin Relationships

Robert Herjavec, former CEO and president of Mississauga, Ontario-based BRAK Systems, says OBM doesn't work. When the company went through a bad quarter after a history of many good quarters, employees panicked, thinking the company would not survive. This led some employees to quit and then made it harder to recruit new employees. Herjavec believes that managers should filter the information they give out, providing only share revenues and overall numbers.[54]

As the above illustrates, part of the downside to OBM is that employees may misinterpret the information they get or misuse it against management.[55] Another potential problem is leaking of confidential information to competitors. In the hands of the competition, detailed information on the company's operations and financial position may undermine a firm's competitive advantage.

When OBM succeeds, two factors seem to exist. First, the organization or unit where it's implemented tends to be small. It's a lot easier to introduce OBM in a small start-up company than in a large, geographically dispersed company that has operated for years with closed books and little employee involvement. Second, there needs to be a mutually trusting relationship between management and workers. In organizational cultures where management doesn't trust employees to act selflessly or where managers and accountants have been trained to keep information under lock and key, OBM is not likely to work. Nor will it succeed where employees believe any new change program is only likely to further manipulate or exploit them for management's advantage.

HR IMPLICATIONS

Providing Performance Feedback

One of the most difficult communication challenges for individuals is providing feedback to others. For instance, in a study conducted by Watson Wyatt Worldwide, only 60 percent of Canadian employees said they understood the measures used to evaluate their performance; only 47 percent said that their managers clearly expressed goals and assignments.[56] We review some of these communication difficulties next.

Performance Feedback

For many managers, few activities are more unpleasant than providing performance feedback to employees.[57] In fact, unless pressured by organizational policies and controls, managers are likely to ignore this responsibility.[58]

Why the reluctance to give performance feedback? There seem to be at least three reasons. First, managers are often uncomfortable discussing performance weaknesses directly with employees. Given that almost every employee could undoubtedly improve in some areas, managers fear a confrontation when presenting negative feedback. This discomfort apparently applies even when people give negative feedback to a computer! Bill Gates reports that Microsoft recently conducted a project requiring users to rate their experience with a computer. "When we had the computer the users had worked with ask for an evaluation of its performance, the responses tended to be positive. But when we had a second computer ask the same people to evaluate their encounters with the first machine, the people were significantly more critical. Their reluctance to criticize the first computer 'to its face' suggested that they didn't want to hurt its feelings, even though they knew it was only a machine."[59]

Second, many employees tend to become defensive when their weaknesses are pointed out. Instead of accepting the feedback as constructive and a basis for improving performance, some employees challenge the evaluation by criticizing the manager or redirecting blame to someone else.

Finally, employees tend to have an inflated assessment of their own performance. Statistically speaking, half of all employees must be below-average performers. But the evidence indicates that the average employee's estimate of his or her own performance level generally falls around the 75th percentile.[60] So even when managers are providing good news, employees are likely to perceive it as not good enough!

The solution to the performance feedback problem is not to ignore it, but to train managers in how to conduct constructive feedback sessions. An effective review in which the employee perceives the appraisal as fair, the manager as sincere, and the climate as constructive can result in the employee leaving the interview in an upbeat mood. The employee will be informed about the performance areas in which he or she needs to improve, and feel determined to correct the deficiencies.[61] In addition, the performance review should be designed more as a counselling activity than a judgmental process. This can best be accomplished by allowing the review to evolve out of the employee's own self-evaluation, but be aware of the caveats of self-evaluation discussed in Chapter 4 on pages 148–149.

Managers can use the following tips to give more effective feedback:[62]

- Relate feedback to existing performance *goals* and clear *expectations*.

- Give *specific* feedback tied to observable behaviour or measurable results.

- Channel feedback toward *key result areas*.

- Give feedback as *soon* as possible.

- Give positive feedback for *improvement*, not just final results.

- Focus feedback on *performance*, not personalities.

- Base feedback on *accurate* and *credible* information.

360-Degree Feedback

Toronto-based Enbridge Gas Distribution has gone one step further with its employee performance appraisal, using one of the newest management trends—360-degree feedback assessment.[63] In this type of assessment, not just your manager, but also your colleagues, employees, customers, and other people with whom you deal regularly are part of the evaluation process. Enbridge has been working toward using 360-degree feedback for all of its employees.

At first, employees can feel anxious about 360-degree feedback, as they learn perhaps more than they ever wanted to know about what others think of them. However, the human resource manager at Edmonton-based Millar Western Industries, a family-owned forestry company that introduced 360-degree feedback for its 250 supervisory and managerial staff 10 years ago, found that employees actually liked knowing where they stood and how they were doing. A variety of companies, including Mississauga, Ontario-based Ciba Vision Canada; Toronto-based Hudson's Bay Company; Guelph, Ontario-based Co-operators General Insurance Company; and Toronto-based Royal Bank of Canada use 360-degree feedback. This type of feedback emphasizes the importance of communication to all levels of employees, not just the manager. It also shows customers and suppliers that they have a voice in the company.

Researchers agree that 360-degree feedback is best used in the following circumstances:[64]

- For employee development rather than for personnel decisions
- As part of a formal goal-setting system
- On a regular basis and not just once

They also suggest the following methods for making the feedback more effective:

- Feedback to those being evaluated should be anonymous and summarized.
- Raters should only evaluate employee behaviour that they know about and have experienced first-hand.
- Raters should receive orientation and training to do the evaluations.
- Recipients should receive guidance on how to interpret the feedback.

LEARNING ABOUT **YOURSELF** EXERCISE

Listening Self-Inventory

Go through this 15-item questionnaire twice. The first time, mark yes or no next to each question. Mark as truthfully as you can in light of your behaviour in recent meetings or gatherings you attended. The second time, mark a plus (+) next to your answer if you are satisfied with that answer, or a minus (–) next to the answer if you wish you could have answered that question differently.

	Yes	No	+ or –
1. I frequently attempt to listen to several conversations at the same time.	___	___	___
2. I like people to give me only the facts and then let me make my own interpretations.	___	___	___
3. I sometimes pretend to pay attention to people.	___	___	___
4. I consider myself a good judge of nonverbal communications.	___	___	___
5. I usually know what another person is going to say before he or she says it.	___	___	___
6. I usually end conversations that don't interest me by diverting my attention from the speaker.	___	___	___
7. I frequently nod, frown, or whatever to let the speaker know how I feel about what he or she is saying.	___	___	___
8. I usually respond immediately when someone has finished talking.	___	___	___
9. I evaluate what is being said while it is being said.	___	___	___
10. I usually formulate a response while the other person is still talking.	___	___	___

11. The speaker's delivery style frequently keeps me from listening to content. _____ _____ _____

12. I usually ask people to clarify what they have said rather than guess at the meaning. _____ _____ _____

13. I make a concerted effort to understand other people's point of view. _____ _____ _____

14. I frequently hear what I expect to hear rather than what is said. _____ _____ _____

15. Most people feel that I have understood their point of view when we disagree. _____ _____ _____

Scoring Key:

The correct answers to the 15 questions, based on listening theory, are as follows: (1) No; (2) No; (3) No; (4) Yes; (5) No; (6) No; (7) No; (8) No; (9) No; (10) No; (11) No; (12) Yes; (13) Yes; (14) No; (15) Yes. To determine your score, add up the number of incorrect answers, multiply by 7, and subtract that total from 105. If you scored between 91 and 105, you have good listening habits. Scores of 77 to 90 suggest significant room for improvement. Scores below 76 indicate that you are a poor listener and need to work hard on improving this skill.

Source: E. C. Glenn and E. A. Pood, "Listening Self-Inventory," *Supervisory Management,* January 1989, pp. 12–15. Reprinted by permission.

BREAKOUT **GROUP** EXERCISES

Form small groups to discuss the following topics, as assigned by your instructor:

1. What differences have you observed in the ways that men and women communicate?

2. How do you know when a person is listening to you? When someone is ignoring you?

3. Describe a situation in which you ignored someone. What impact did it have on that person's subsequent communication behaviours?

WORKING WITH **OTHERS** EXERCISE

An Absence of Nonverbal Communication

This exercise will help you see the value of nonverbal communication in interpersonal relations.

1. The class is to divide into pairs (Party A and Party B).

2. Party A is to select a topic from the following list:

   a. Managing in the Middle East is significantly different from managing in North America.

   b. Bureaucracies are frustrating to work in.

   c. An employer has a responsibility to provide every employee with an interesting and challenging job.

   d. Organizations should require all employees to undergo regular AIDS testing.

   e. Organizations should require all employees to undergo regular drug testing.

   f. Individuals who have majored in business or economics make better employees than those who have majored in history or English.

g. The place where you get your college or university degree is more important in determining career success than what you learn while you're there.

h. Effective managers often have to lie as part of their job.

i. It's unethical for a manager to purposely distort communications to get a favourable outcome.

3. Party B is to choose his or her position on this topic (for example, arguing *against* the view that "employers have a responsibility to provide every employee with an interesting and challenging job"). Party A now must automatically take the opposite position.

4. The 2 parties have 10 minutes in which to debate their topic. The catch is that individuals can only communicate verbally. They may *not* use gestures, facial movements, body movements, or any other nonverbal communication. It may help for both parties to maintain an expressionless look and to sit on their hands to remind them of these restrictions.

5. After the debate is over, the class should discuss the following:

a. How effective was communication during these debates?

b. What barriers to communication existed?

c. What purposes does nonverbal communication serve?

d. Relate the lessons learned in this exercise to problems that might occur when communicating on the telephone or through email.

ETHICAL **DILEMMA** EXERCISE

Is It Wrong to Tell a Lie?

When we were children, our parents told us, "It's wrong to tell a lie." Yet we all have told lies at one time or another. If most of us agree that telling lies is wrong, how do we justify continuing to do it? The answer is this: Most of us differentiate between "real lies" and "little white lies"—the latter being an acceptable, even necessary, part of social interaction.

A recent survey of 10 000 people 18 to 50 years old provides some insights into people's attitudes toward lying. Eighty percent described honesty as important, but nearly one-quarter said that they would lie to an employer "if necessary." More than 15 percent admitted to lying on a résumé or job application. And more than 45 percent said they would happily tell you a "little white lie."

Since lying is so closely intertwined with interpersonal communication, let's look at an issue many managers confront: Does a sound purpose justify intentionally distorting information? Consider the following situation:

An employee who works for you asks you about a rumour she has heard that your department and all its employees will be transferred from Calgary to Edmonton. You know the rumour is true, but you would rather not let the information out just yet. You're fearful it could hurt departmental morale and lead to premature resignations. What do you say to your employee? Do you lie, evade the question, distort your answer, or tell the truth?

In a larger context, where do you draw the line between the truth and lying? And if you are in a managerial position, how does your answer to the previous question fit with your desire to be trusted by those who work for you?

Source: Cited in "Who's Lying Now?" *Training*, October 2000, p. 34.

CASE INCIDENTS

Emailing "Lazy" Employees

Imagine receiving the following email from your CEO:

We are getting less than 40 hours of work from a large number of our EMPLOYEES. The parking lot is sparsely used at 8 a.m.; likewise at 5 p.m. As managers, you either do not know what your EMPLOYEES are doing or you do not CARE. In either case, you have a problem and you will fix it or I will replace you.

NEVER in my career have I allowed a team which worked for me to think they had a 40-hour job. I have allowed YOU to create a culture which is permitting this. NO LONGER.

The note [paraphrased] continues: "Hell will freeze over before any more employee benefits are given out. I will be watching the parking lot and expect it to be substantially full at 7:30 a.m. and 6:30 p.m. on weekdays and half full on Saturdays. You have two weeks. Tick, tock."

Questions

1. What impact would this message have on you if you received it?

2. Is email the best way to convey such a message?

3. What problems might arise if people outside the organization saw this email?

4. What suggestions, if any, would you make to the CEO to help improve communication effectiveness?

Sources: Based on E. Wong, "Stinging Office E-Mail Lights 'Firestorm,'" *Globe and Mail,* April 9, 2001, p. M1; P. D. Broughton, "Boss's Angry Email Sends Shares Plunging," *Daily Telegraph of London,* April 6, 2001; D. Stafford, "Shattering the Illusion of Respect," *Kansas City Star,* March 29, 2001, p. C1.

Jeremy W. Caputo Has Communication Problems

Jeremy W. Caputo has only four employees at his public relations firm, Message Out. But he seems to have done a pretty good job of alienating them.

According to his employees, Caputo, 47, is a brilliant guy who has a lot to learn in terms of being a better communicator. His communication style appears to be a regular source of conflict in his firm. Caputo admits he has a problem. "I'm probably not as verbally reinforcing [as I could be] when someone is doing a good job. I'm a very self-confident person. I don't need to be told I'm doing a good job—but there are people who do."

Caputo's employees had no problem listing off things that he does that bother them. He doesn't meet deadlines; he does a poor job of communicating with clients (which often puts the employees in an uncomfortable position); he does not listen fully to employee ideas before dismissing them; his voice tone is frequently condescending; and he is often quick to criticize employees and is stingy with praise.

Questions

1. A lot of bosses are accused of being "poor communicators." Why do you think this is?

2. What does this case suggest regarding the relationship between reinforcement theory and communication?

3. What, specifically, do you think Caputo needs to do to improve his communication skills?

4. Assuming Caputo wants to improve, how would you suggest he go about learning to be a better communicator?

Source: This case is based on N. J. Torres, "Playing Well With Others," *Entrepreneur,* February 2003, p. 30.

From **Concepts**
                to **Skills**

Effective Listening

Too many people take listening skills for granted.[65] They confuse hearing with listening.

What's the difference? Hearing is merely picking up sound vibrations. Listening is making sense out of what we hear. That is, listening requires paying attention, interpreting, and remembering sound stimuli.

The average person normally speaks at a rate of 125 to 200 words per minute. However, the average listener can comprehend up to 400 words per minute. This leaves a lot of time for idle mind-wandering while listening. For most people, it also means they have acquired a number of bad listening habits to fill in the "idle time."

The following eight behaviours are associated with effective listening skills. If you want to improve your listening skills, look to these behaviours as guides:

1. *Make eye contact.* How do you feel when somebody doesn't look at you when you are speaking? If you are like most people, you are likely to interpret this behaviour as aloofness or lack of interest. We may listen with our ears, but others tend to judge whether we are really listening by looking at our eyes.

2. *Exhibit affirmative head nods and appropriate facial expressions.* The effective listener shows interest in what is being said. How? Through nonverbal signals. Affirmative head nods and appropriate facial expressions, when added to good eye contact, convey to the speaker that you are listening.

3. *Avoid distracting actions or gestures.* The other side of showing interest is avoiding actions that suggest your mind is somewhere else. When listening, don't look at your watch, shuffle papers, play with your pencil, or engage in similar distractions. They make the speaker feel you're bored or uninterested. Maybe more important, they indicate that you are not fully attentive and may be missing part of the message that the speaker wants to convey.

4. *Ask questions.* The critical listener analyzes what he or she hears and asks questions. This behaviour provides clarification, ensures understanding, and assures the speaker that you are listening.

5. *Paraphrase.* Paraphrasing means restating what the speaker has said in your own words. The effective listener uses phrases such as "What I hear you saying is . . ." or "Do you mean . . .?" Why rephrase what has already been said? Two reasons! First, it's an excellent control device to check on whether you are listening carefully. You cannot paraphrase accurately if your mind is wandering or if you are thinking about what you are going to say next. Second, it's a control for accuracy. By rephrasing what the speaker has said in your own words and feeding it back to the speaker, you verify the accuracy of your understanding.

6. *Avoid interrupting the speaker.* Let the speaker complete his or her thought before you try to respond. Don't try to second-guess where the speaker's thoughts are going. When the speaker is finished, you will know!

7. *Don't overtalk.* Most of us would rather voice our own ideas than listen to what someone else says. Too many of us listen only because it's the price we have to pay to get people to let us talk. While talking may be more fun and silence may be uncomfortable, you cannot talk and listen at the same time. The good listener recognizes this fact and doesn't overtalk.

8. *Make smooth transitions between the roles of speaker and listener.* When you are a student sitting in a lecture hall, you find it relatively easy to get into an effective listening frame of mind. Why? Because communication is essentially one-way: The teacher talks and you listen. But the teacher-student dyad is not typical. In most work situations, you are continually shifting back and forth between the roles of speaker and listener. The effective listener, therefore, makes transitions smoothly from speaker to listener and back to speaker. From a listening perspective, this means concentrating on what a speaker has to say and practising not thinking about what you are going to say as soon as you get an opportunity.

Assessing Skills

After you've read this chapter, take the following Self-Assessments on your enclosed CD-ROM:

27. What's My Face-to-Face Communication Style?

28. How Good Are My Listening Skills?

43. How Good Am I at Giving Performance Feedback?

Practising Skills

Form groups of 2. This exercise is a debate. Person A can choose any contemporary issue. Some examples: business ethics, value of unions, stiffer grading policies, same-sex marriage, money as a motivator. Person B then selects a position on this issue. Person A must automatically take the counter-position. The debate is to proceed for 8 to 10 minutes, with only one catch. Before each person speaks, he or she must first summarize, in his or her own words and without notes, what the other has said. If the summary

doesn't satisfy the speaker, it must be corrected until it does. What impact do the summaries have on the quality of the debate?

Reinforcing Skills

1. In another class—preferably one with a lecture format—practise active listening. Ask questions, paraphrase, exhibit affirming nonverbal behaviours. Then ask yourself: Was this harder for me than a normal lecture? Did it affect my note taking? Did I ask more questions? Did it improve my understanding of the lecture's content? What was the instructor's response?

2. Spend an entire day fighting your urge to talk. Listen as carefully as you can to everyone you talk to and respond as appropriately as possible to understand, not to make your own point. What, if anything, did you learn from this exercise?

CHAPTER 8

Power and Politics

How could Jamie Salé and David Pelletier first lose and later win the 2002 Winter Olympics gold medal for figure skating? Power and politics tell much of the story.

1 What is power?

2 How does one get power?

3 How does dependency affect power?

4 What tactics can be used to increase power?

5 What does it mean to be empowered?

6 How are power and harassment related?

7 Why do people engage in politics?

Any Canadian, and many Americans, watching the pairs figure skating competition in the 2002 Winter Olympics seemed sure they had watched a gold-medal performance when Jamie Salé and David Pelletier gave their final bow.[1] Moments later, however, fans looked on in horror as the gold medal was awarded to Russian skaters Yelena Berezhnaya and Anton Sikharulidze. North Americans were shocked: What they remembered was a flawed performance by the Russians, with Sikharulidze shaky on a double axel and Berezhnaya stiff in some of her landings, and a perfect performance by the Canadian duo.

Figure skating has long been considered a political rather than an artistic event, where the Soviet Union influenced its allies to support Russian skaters, while Western judges tended to side with US skaters. Thus it was not surprising that charges of politics and abuse of power surfaced quickly. The French figure skating judge, Marie-Reine Le Gougne, was accused of improper voting. She initially said that she had been put under too much pressure. Jacques Rogge used his power as president of the International Olympic Committee (IOC) to pressure the International Skating Union (ISU) to reconsider the judgment and award gold medals for each pair of skaters.

A major theme throughout this chapter is that power and politics are a natural process in any group or organization. Although you might have heard the saying "Power corrupts, and absolute power corrupts absolutely," power is not always bad. Understanding how to use power and politics effectively makes organizational life more manageable, because it can help you gain the support you need to do your job effectively.

A DEFINITION OF POWER

Power refers to the capacity that A has to influence the behaviour of B, so that B acts in accordance with A's wishes.[2] This definition implies that there is a *potential* for power if someone is dependent on another. But one can have power and not impose it.

Probably the most important aspect of power is that it is a function of **dependency**. The more that B depends on A, the more power A has in the relationship. Dependence, in turn, is based on the alternatives that B perceives and the importance that B places on the alternative(s) that A controls. A person can have power over you only if he or she controls something you desire. If you are attending college or university on funds totally provided by your parents, you probably recognize the power that your parents hold over you. You are dependent on them for financial support. But once you are out of school, have a job, and are making a good income, your parents' power is reduced significantly. Who among us, though, has not known or heard of the rich relative who is able to control a large number of family members merely through the implicit or explicit threat of "writing them out of the will"?

 What is power?

International Olympics Committee (IOC)
www.olympic.org

International Skating Union (ISU)
www.isu.org

power A capacity that A has to influence the behaviour of B, so that B acts in accordance with A's wishes.

dependency B's relationship to A when A possesses something that B needs.

Within larger organizations, the information technology (IT) group often has considerable power, because everyone, right up to the CEO, is dependent on this group keeping computers and networks running. Since few people have the technical expertise to do so, IT personnel end up being viewed as irreplaceable. This gives them a lot of power within the organization.

Power should not be considered a bad thing, however. "Power, if used appropriately, should actually be a positive influence in your organization," says Professor Patricia Bradshaw of the Schulich School of Business at York University. "Having more power doesn't necessarily turn you into a Machiavellian monster. It can help your team and your organization achieve its goals and increase its potential."[3]

BASES OF POWER

> As the figure skating controversy swirled, ISU president Ottavio Cinquanta tried to contain the uproar by announcing three days after the event that "We cannot change the result of the competition." He was sending out a signal to the Americans, who had taken to the airwaves to protest the results of the competition, that lobbying could not turn judges' scores around, or change ISU procedures. Forty-eight hours later, however, he changed his mind and announced that the results would be changed, and Salé and Pelletier would receive gold medals as well. How could Cinquanta have been forced to change his decision so quickly?

2 How does one get power?

Where does power come from? What is it that gives an individual or a group influence over others? The answer to these questions was developed by social scientists John French and Bertrand Raven, who first presented a five-category classification scheme of sources or bases of power: coercive, reward, legitimate, expert, and referent.[4] They subsequently added information power.[5] Their scheme is described in Exhibit 8-1.

Coercive Power

coercive power Power that is based on fear.

Coercive power is defined by French and Raven as being dependent on fear. You react to this power base out of fear of the negative results that might occur if you fail to com-

---

EXHIBIT 8-1	**Measuring Bases of Power**

Does a person have one or more of the six bases of power? These descriptions help identify the person's power base.

Power Base	Statement
Coercive	The person can make things difficult for people, and you want to avoid getting him or her angry.
Reward	The person is able to give special benefits or rewards to people, and you find it advantageous to trade favours with him or her.
Legitimate	The person has the right, considering his or her position and your job responsibilities, to expect you to comply with legitimate requests.
Expert	The person has the experience and knowledge to earn your respect, and you defer to his or her judgment in some matters.
Referent	You like the person and enjoy doing things for him or her.
Information	The person has data or knowledge that you need.

Source: Adapted from G. Yukl and C. M. Falbe, "Importance of Different Power Sources in Downward and Lateral Relations," *Journal of Applied Psychology,* June 1991, p. 417. With permission.

ply. It rests on the application, or the threat of the application, of physical sanctions such as the infliction of pain, the generation of frustration through restriction of movement, or the controlling by force of basic physiological or safety needs. When Jacques Rogge, as president of the International Olympic Committee (IOC), threatened to ban judged sports from the Olympics, he was using a form of coercion. He was trying to intimidate the International Skating Union (ISU), making them fear that if the controversy was not ended quickly, figure skaters would no longer compete in the Olympics.

Of all the bases of power available, the power to hurt others is possibly the most often used, most often condemned, and most difficult to control: The state relies on its military and legal resources to intimidate nations, or even its own citizens; businesses rely upon the control of economic resources to request tax reductions; religious institutions threaten individuals with dire consequences in the afterlife if they do not conduct themselves properly in this life. At the personal level, individuals exercise coercive power through a reliance upon physical strength, verbal facility, or the ability to grant emotional support or withhold emotional support from others. These bases provide the individual with the means to physically harm, bully, humiliate, or deny love to others.[6]

At the organizational level, A has coercive power over B if A can dismiss, suspend, or demote B, assuming that B values his or her job. Similarly, if A can assign B work activities that B finds unpleasant or treat B in a manner that B finds embarrassing, A possesses coercive power over B.

Reward Power

The opposite of coercive power is **reward power**. People will go along with the wishes or directives of another if doing so produces positive benefits; therefore, someone who can distribute rewards that others view as valuable will have power over those others. These rewards can be anything that another person values. In an organizational context, we think of money, favourable performance appraisals, promotions, interesting work assignments, friendly colleagues, important information, and preferred work shifts or sales territories. As with coercive power, you don't have to be a manager to be able to exert influence through rewards. Rewards such as friendliness, acceptance, and praise are available to everyone in an organization. To the degree that an individual seeks such rewards, your ability to give or withhold them gives you power over that individual.

reward power Power that achieves compliance based on the ability to distribute rewards that others view as valuable.

legitimate power Power that a person receives as a result of his or her position in the formal hierarchy of an organization.

Legitimate Power

In formal groups and organizations, probably the most frequent access to one or more of the bases of power is through a person's structural position. This is called **legitimate power**. It represents the power a person receives as a result of his or her position in the formal hierarchy of an organization.

Positions of authority include coercive and reward powers. Legitimate power, however, is broader than the power to coerce and reward. Specifically, it includes acceptance by members of an organization of the authority of a position. When school principals, bank presidents, or generals speak (assuming that their directives are viewed to be within the authority of their positions), teachers, tellers, and privates listen and usually comply. You will note in Exhibit 8-2 that one of the men in the meeting identifies himself as the rule maker, which means that he has legitimate power. Because Jacques Rogge was IOC president, he was one of the few individuals who had legitimate power to try to bring resolution to the skating controversy. The Milgram experiment, discussed in *Focus on Research*, looks at the extremes individuals sometimes go to in order to comply with authority figures.

In India, Naina Lal Kidwai is a powerful woman in the banking industry. She derives her power as managing director and vice chairman of HSBC Securities and Capital Markets, a group within the Hongkong and Shanghai Banking Corporation. Kidwai's formal power is based on her position at the bank.

"*I was just going to say 'Well, I don't make the rules.' But, of course, I do make the rules.*"

Source: Drawing by Leo Cullum in *The New Yorker.* Copyright © 1986 *The New Yorker Magazine.* Reprinted by permission.

FOCUS ON **RESEARCH**

A Shocking Experiment

Would you shock someone if you were told to do so? A classic experiment conducted by Stanley Milgram studied the extent to which people are willing to obey those in authority.[7] Subjects were recruited for an experiment that asked them to administer electric shocks to a "student" who was supposed to learn a list of words. The experiments were conducted at Yale University, and subjects were assured by the experimenter, who was dressed in a white lab coat, that punishment was an effective way to learn. The subjects were placed in front of an instrument panel that indicated the shocks could go from 15 volts to 450 volts. With each wrong answer, subjects were to administer the next highest shock level. After the shocks reached a middle level, the "student" started to cry out in pain. The experimenter would instruct the subject to continue administering shocks. What the experimenter was trying to find out was the level at which subjects would stop administering the electric shock. No subject stopped before 300 volts, and 65 percent of the subjects continued to the end of the experiment, even though, at the upper levels, the instrument panel was marked "Danger XXX." It should be noted that subjects were not actually administering shocks, and that the "student" was actually a confederate, and simply acting as if in pain. However, the subjects believed that they were administering electric shocks. This experiment suggests that many people will obey those who appear to have legitimate authority, even in questionable circumstances.

Expert Power

Expert power is influence based on expertise, special skill, or knowledge. Expertise has become one of the most powerful sources of influence as the world has become more technologically oriented. While it is generally acknowledged that physicians have expertise and hence expert power—most of us follow the advice that our doctor gives us—you should also recognize that computer specialists, tax accountants, economists, and other specialists can have power as a result of their expertise. Young people may find they have increased power in the workplace these days because of their technical knowledge and expertise that their Baby Boomer managers may not have.

Expert power relies on trust that all relevant information is given out honestly and completely. Of course, since knowledge is power, the more that information is shared, the less expert power a person has. Thus, some individuals try to protect their power by withholding information.[8] This tactic can result in poor-quality performance by those who need the information.[9] The *Working With Others Exercise* on page 308 gives you the opportunity to explore the effectiveness of different bases of power in changing someone's behaviour.

expert power Influence based on special skills or knowledge.

Referent Power

Referent power develops out of admiration of another and a desire to be like that person. In a sense, it is a lot like charisma. If you admire someone to the point of modelling your behaviour and attitudes after him or her, that person possesses referent power over you. Sometimes teachers and coaches have referent power because of our admiration of them. Referent power explains why celebrities are paid millions of dollars to endorse products in commercials. Advertisers such as Toronto-based Roots Canada have developed advertising themes around popular Canadians such as "bad boy" Olympic gold-medallist and snowboarder Ross Rebagliati and Canadian R & B diva Deborah Cox to convince people to buy specific products.[10] Similarly, Nike has used sports celebrities such as former Toronto Raptors' star centre Vince Carter to promote its products.

referent power Influence based on possession by an individual of desirable resources or personal traits.

Roots Canada
www.roots.ca

Information Power

Information power comes from access to and control over information. People in an organization who have data or knowledge that others need can make those others dependent on them. Managers, for instance, because of their access to privileged sales, cost, salary, profit, and similar data, can use this information to control and shape subordinates' behaviour. Similarly, departments that possess information that is critical to a company's performance in times of high uncertainty—for example, the legal department when a firm faces a major lawsuit or the human resource department during critical labour negotiations—will gain increased power in their organization until those uncertainties are resolved. This chapter's *Case Incident—The Power of Bill Fowler at Blackmer/Dover Resources* on page 311 shows the information power that one man can have in a manufacturing organization.

information power Power that comes from access to and control over information.

Evaluating the Bases of Power

Generally, people will respond in one of three ways when faced with those who use the bases of power described above:

- *Commitment.* The person is enthusiastic about the request, and shows initiative and persistence in carrying it out.

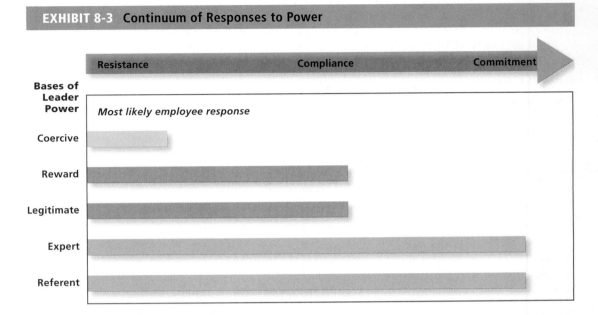

EXHIBIT 8-3   **Continuum of Responses to Power**

Source: R. M. Steers and J. S. Black, *Organizational Behavior,* 5th ed. (New York: HarperCollins, 1994, p. 487. Reprinted by permission of Pearson Education Inc., Upper Saddle River, New Jersey.

- *Compliance.* The person goes along with the request grudgingly, puts in minimal effort, and takes little initiative in carrying out the request.

- *Resistance.* The person is opposed to the request and tries to avoid it with such tactics as refusing, stalling, or arguing about it.[11]

A review of the research on the effectiveness of these forms of power finds that they differ in their impact on a person's performance.[12] Exhibit 8-3 summarizes some of this research. Coercive power leads to resistance from individuals, decreased satisfaction, and increased mistrust. Reward power results in compliance if the rewards are consistent with what individuals want as rewards, something the *Ethical Dilemma Exercise* on page 309 shows clearly. Legitimate power also results in compliance, but it does not generally result in increased commitment. In other words, legitimate power does not inspire individuals to act beyond the basic level. Expert and referent powers are the most likely to lead to commitment from individuals. Ironically, the least effective bases of power for improving commitment—coercive, reward, and legitimate—are the ones most often used by managers, perhaps because they are the easiest to introduce.[13] Research shows that deadline pressure increases group members' reliance on individuals with expert and information power.[14]

DEPENDENCY: THE KEY TO POWER

As the 2002 Winter Olympics figure skating furor unfolded, some claimed that French judge Marie-Reine Le Gougne was pressured by the French figure skating federation to vote for the Russians, in exchange for which the Russian judge would vote for the French skaters in the Olympic ice dancing competition. In August 2002, a Russian mobster was arrested for possible bribery charges in the case, suggesting that external pressures were applied to higher-ups in the skating organizations who then pressured judges to fix votes. "Though it doesn't excuse them for not judging honestly, it suggests that individuals highly ranked within their federations are indeed setting the tone for their [the judges'] behaviour," noted US dance judge Sharon Rogers.[15] The French judge was dependent on her superiors to keep her judging job, something she valued very much. Meanwhile, a dependence on bribes from the Russian mobster made higher-ups pressure their judges. What factors might lead to one person having greater power over another?

In this section, we show how an understanding of dependency is central to furthering your understanding of power itself.

3 How does dependency affect power?

The General Dependency Postulate

Let's begin with a general postulate: *The greater B's dependency on A, the greater the power A has over B.* When you possess anything that others require but that you alone control, you make them dependent upon you and, therefore, you gain power over them.[16] Another way to frame dependency is to think about a relationship in terms of "who needs whom?" The person who has most need is the one most dependent on the relationship.[17]

Dependency is inversely proportional to the alternative sources of supply. If something is plentiful, possession of it will not increase your power. If everyone is intelligent, intelligence gives no special advantage. Similarly, in the circles of the super rich, money does not result in power. But, if you can create a monopoly by controlling information, prestige, or anything that others crave, they become dependent on you. Alternatively, the more options you have, the less power you place in the hands of others. This explains, for example, why most organizations develop multiple suppliers rather than give their business to only one.

What Creates Dependency?

Dependency is increased when the resource you control is important, scarce, and non-substitutable.[18]

Importance

Have you ever wondered how you might increase your power?

If nobody wants what you have, there is no dependency. To create dependency, the thing(s) you control must be perceived as being important. In some organizations, people who control the budget have a great deal of importance. In other organizations, those who possess the knowledge to keep technology working smoothly are viewed as important. What's important is situational. It varies among organizations and undoubtedly also varies over time within any given organization. Individuals or organizations that are regarded as important may pressure others to engage in unethical behaviour, however, as *Focus on Ethics* suggests.

FOCUS ON **ETHICS**

Enron Requests Action From UBS PaineWebber

Did Enron use its power to cause a UBS PaineWebber employee to be fired? In August 2001, months before the Enron scandal broke, executives of Enron pressured UBS PaineWebber (now UBS Financial Services) to discipline one of its brokers.[19] The broker, Chung Wu, had advised Enron employees to sell their stock options. Within hours of the complaint, the broker was fired.

When the Enron executive in charge of the stock option program learned that Wu had warned employees that the company's "financial situation is deteriorating," he notified PaineWebber immediately via email. His message stated: "Please handle this situation. This is extremely disturbing to me."

PaineWebber went even further than firing Wu, however. It also sent his clients a report that Enron was "likely heading higher than lower from here on out."

PaineWebber has since suggested that Wu acted unethically because his emails to Enron clients were unauthorized, and because he didn't tell them that PaineWebber's research analyst rated Enron a "strong buy."

One might question PaineWebber's behaviour, however. When Wu sent the emails, the stock was worth $36. Only a few months later, it was worthless. PaineWebber managed Enron's stock option program and handled large personal accounts for many of Enron's executives. It also did investment banking for Enron. Thus, it did not want to risk losing Enron's business by suggesting the stock was in trouble. 🏃

Scarcity

As noted previously, if something is plentiful, possession of it will not increase your power. A resource must be perceived as being scarce to create dependency.

Scarcity can help explain how low-ranking employees who have important knowledge not available to high-ranking employees gain power. Possession of a scarce resource—in this case, important knowledge—makes those who don't have it dependent on those who do. Thus, an individual might refuse to show others how to do a job, or might refuse to share information, thereby increasing their importance.

The scarcity-dependency relationship can further be seen in the differing power of occupational categories. For example, college and university administrators have no problem finding English instructors to staff classes. There are more individuals who have degrees enabling them to work as English instructors than there are positions available in Canada. The market for corporate finance professors, by contrast, is extremely tight, with the demand high and the supply limited. The result is that the bargaining power of finance faculty allows them to negotiate higher salaries, lighter teaching loads, and other benefits.

Nonsubstitutability

Steve Jobs
www.apple.com/pr/bios/jobs.html

The fewer substitutes for a resource, the more power comes from the control of that resource. In the case of Apple Computer, most observers, as well as the board, believed that no one other than Steve Jobs could turn the company around when they returned him to the role of CEO in 1997. Thus the board willingly accepted many of his turnaround suggestions quickly, even though some were controversial. In another example, when a union goes on strike, and management is not permitted to replace the striking employees, the union has considerable control over the organization's ability to carry out its tasks.

People are often able to ask for special rewards (higher pay or better assignments) because they have skills that others do not. This chapter's *Point/Counterpoint* feature on page 304 considers the fairness of rewarding some people better than others.

INFLUENCE TACTICS

> Looking at the 2002 Winter Olympics figure skating controversy, we can find a number of instances where the various people involved in the controversy used influence tactics to get their way. There is some evidence that the French and Russian judges formed a coalition to ensure that the French ice dancers would get a gold medal in a later event. The Russian mobster used bargaining, trading bribes for votes. IOC president Jacques Rogge used assertiveness to convince Ottavio Cinquanta, ISU president, that in fact there would be two gold medals. He also threatened the ISU with sanctions, including banning judged sports from the Olympics, if they did not award the second medal. So how and why do influence tactics work?

4 What influence tactics can be used to increase power?

How do individuals translate their bases of power into specific, desired actions? Research indicates that people use common tactics to influence outcomes.[20] One study identified the nine influence tactics managers and employees use to increase their power:[21]

1. *Rational persuasion.* Using facts and data to make a logical or rational presentation of ideas.

2. *Inspirational appeals.* Appealing to the values, ideals, and goals when making a request.

3. *Consultation.* Getting others involved to support one's objectives.

4. *Ingratiation.* Using flattery, creating goodwill, and being friendly prior to making a request.

5. *Personal appeals.* Appealing to loyalty and friendship when asking for something.

6. *Exchange.* Offering favours or benefits in exchange for support.

7. *Coalition tactics.* Getting the support of other people to provide backing when making a request.

8. *Pressure.* Using demands, threats, and reminders to get someone to do something.

9. *Legitimating tactics.* Claiming the authority or right to make a request, or showing that it supports organizational goals or policies.

The location of power varies among organizations. At Walt Disney, enormous power is held by high-tech scientists in the research and development group of Walt Disney Imagineering, a division formed by Walt Disney in 1952 to create Disneyland. Today, the company relies on Bran Ferren (upper left), who heads the R & D unit, and his highly skilled and creative staffers to develop cyberland fantasies such as virtual-reality theme parks, websites for kids, and smart TV sets that learn viewers' programming preferences and automatically record programs they forget to watch.

You may want to review the opening vignette to see whether you can identify examples of the influence tactics used by participants in the ice-skating controversy.

Researchers found that there are significant differences in the tactics used to influence actions, depending upon whether one is interacting with someone above or below them in rank. While all individuals favour rational persuasion, those managing upward are even more likely to use it (77 percent vs. 52 percent of those managing downward). Those managing downward are next most likely to use pressure (22 percent) or ingratiation (15 percent). The other favoured choices of those managing upward were coalition tactics (15 percent) and pressure (15 percent).[22]

EMPOWERMENT: GIVING POWER TO EMPLOYEES

Thus far our discussion has implied, at least to some extent, that power is something that is more likely to reside in the hands of management, to be used as part of their interaction with employees. However, in today's workplace, there is a movement toward sharing more power with employees by putting them in teams and also by making them responsible for some of the decisions regarding their jobs. Organizational specialists refer to this increasing responsibility as *empowerment.* As we briefly mention in Chapter 11, one of the current trends in leadership is empowering workers. Between 1995 and 2005, nearly 50 000 articles about empowerment have appeared in the print media in the United States and Canada, with almost 6000 articles appearing in Canadian newspapers during that time.[23]

5 What does it mean to be empowered?

Definition of Empowerment

The definition of **empowerment** that we use here refers to the freedom and the ability of employees to make decisions and commitments.[24] Unfortunately, the definition of

empowerment The freedom and the ability of employees to make decisions and commitments.

Management at Flextronics plants in China used legitimating tactics and rational persuasion in establishing a series of rigid rules and procedures to guard against the threat of severe acute respiratory syndrome (SARS). Workers complied with the rules—such as twice-daily hand washing after eating meals in the company canteen—because they understood the mandates were made to protect their safety.

empowerment is not agreed upon by either managers or researchers. Robert E. Quinn and Gretchen M. Spreitzer, in their consulting work with a *Fortune* 50 manufacturing company, found that executives were split about 50-50 in their definition.[25] One group of executives "believed that empowerment was about delegating decision making within a set of clear boundaries." Empowerment would start at the top, specific goals and tasks would be assigned, responsibility would be delegated, and people would be held accountable for their results. The other group believed that empowerment was "a process of risk-taking and personal growth." This type of empowerment starts at the bottom, considering the employees' needs, showing them what empowered behaviour looks like, building teams, encouraging risk-taking, and demonstrating trust in employees' ability to perform.

Much of the press on empowerment has been positive, with both executives and employees applauding the ability of front-line workers to make and execute important decisions.[26] However, not all reports are favourable. One management expert noted that much of the talk about empowerment is simply lip service,[27] with organizations telling employees that they have decision-making responsibility, but not giving them the authority to carry out their decisions. In order for an employee to be fully empowered, he or she needs access to the information required to make decisions; rewards for acting in appropriate, responsible ways; and authority to make the necessary decisions. Empowerment means that employees understand how their job fits into the organization and are able to make decisions regarding job action guided by the organization's purpose and mission. Managers at Montague, PEI-based Durabelt recognize that to be empowered, employees need to have the appropriate skills to handle their jobs. The company sells customized conveyor belts used to harvest some vegetable and fruit crops. Employees need to be responsive to customer concerns when manufacturing the belts. In order to empower employees to manage customer relations successfully, Durabelt created Duraschool, an ongoing training program that provides employees with the skills they need to be more effective.[28]

The concept of empowerment has caused much cynicism in many workplaces. Employees are told that they are empowered, and yet they do not feel that they have the authority to act, or they feel that their manager still micromanages their performance. Some managers are reluctant to empower their employees, because this means sharing or even relinquishing their own power. Other managers worry that empowered employees may decide to work on goals and jobs that are not as closely aligned to organizational goals. Some managers, of course, do not fully understand how to go about empowering their employees. Sometimes empowerment can even make employees ill, as *Focus on Research* shows.

FOCUS ON **RESEARCH**

Empowerment Can Make You Ill

Why would having more power negatively affect an employee? A study carried out by Professor Jia Lin Xie, of the Joseph L. Rotman School of Management at the University of Toronto, and colleagues found that when people are put in charge at work, but don't have the confidence to handle their responsibilities, they can become ill.[29]

Specifically, people who blame themselves when things go wrong are more likely to suffer colds and infections if they have high levels of control at work.

This finding by Professor Xie and her colleagues was somewhat unexpected, as some have hypothesized that greater control at work would lead to less stress. The study showed, instead, that the impact of empowerment depended on personality and job factors. Those who had control, but did not blame themselves when things went wrong, suffered less stress, even if the job was demanding. The study's findings suggest the importance of choosing carefully which employees to empower when doing so.

The findings are also consistent with the Hackman-Oldham job characteristics model presented in Chapter 5.[30] Empowerment will be positive if a person has high growth-need strengths (see Exhibit 5-7 on page 181) but those with low growth-need strengths may be more likely to experience stress when empowered. 🏃

Degrees of Empowerment

What do you need to be truly empowered?

One study that helps us understand the degrees of empowerment looks at jobs in terms of both their context and their content.[31] The **job content** represents the tasks and procedures necessary for carrying out a particular job. The **job context** is the reason for the job being done and reflects the organizational mission, objectives, and setting. The context of the job would also include the organization's structure, culture, and reward systems.

job content The tasks and procedures necessary for carrying out a particular job.

job context The reason for the job being done; it reflects the organizational mission, objectives, and setting.

When employees are empowered, as we noted above, they are given decision-making authority over some aspect of their job.

Exhibit 8-4 on page 292 indicates three examples of employee power based on job context and content:[32]

- *No Discretion* (Point A) is the typical assembly-line job—highly routine and repetitive. The employee is assigned the task, given no discretion, and most likely monitored by a supervisor. When employees have no power, they are less likely to be satisfied with their jobs. They can also be less productive because the lack of discretion may cause a "rule mentality" where the employee chooses to operate strictly by the rules, rather than showing initiative.

- *Participatory Empowerment* (Point B) represents the situation of autonomous work groups that are given some decision-making authority over both job content and job context. There is some evidence of higher job satisfaction and productivity in such groups.[33]

- *Self-Management* (Point C) represents employees who have total decision-making power for both job content and job context. Granting an employee

At Vancouver-based Great Little Box Company (GLBC), which designs and manufactures corrugated containers, employees are given the freedom to do whatever they feel is necessary and appropriate to make customers happy. If a customer is dissatisfied with the product, the employee can say, "OK, I'll bring this product back and return it for you," without having to get prior authorization.

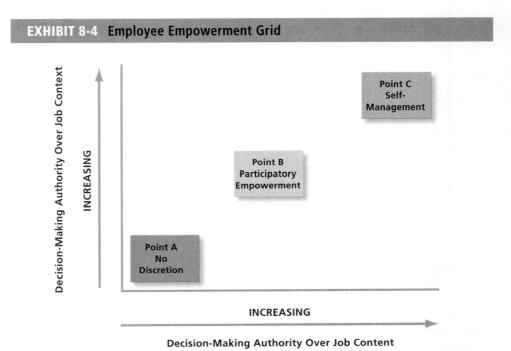

EXHIBIT 8-4   Employee Empowerment Grid

Source: Based on R. C. Ford and M. D. Fottler, "Empowerment: A Matter of Degree," *Academy of Management Executive,* August 1995, p. 24. Reprinted by permission.

this much power requires considerable faith on the part of management that the employee will carry out the goals and mission of the organization in an effective manner. Generally this sort of power is reserved for those in top management, although it is also sometimes granted to high-level salespeople. Obviously this kind of power can be very rewarding to those who hold it.

When employees are empowered, it means that they are expected to act, at least in a small way, as owners of the company, rather than just employees. Ownership is not necessary in the financial sense, but in terms of identifying with the goals and mission of the organization. For employees to be empowered, however, and have an ownership mentality, four conditions need to be met, according to Professor Dan Ondrack at the Rotman School of Management at the University of Toronto:[34]

1. There must be a clear definition of the values and mission of the company.

2. The company must help employees acquire the relevant skills.

3. Employees need to be supported in their decision making, and not criticized when they try to do something extraordinary.

4. Employees need to be recognized for their efforts.

Exhibit 8-5 outlines what two researchers discovered in studying the characteristics of empowered workers.

Effects of Empowerment

Does empowerment work? Researchers have shown that at both the individual level[35] and the team level,[36] empowerment leads to greater productivity. For instance, Vancouver-based Dominion Information Services, publisher of the BC Yellow Pages, cut customer complaints by 40 percent in three years.[37] The company also reduced the time it takes to fix

---

EXHIBIT 8-5 **Characteristics of Empowered People**

Robert E. Quinn and Gretchen M. Spreitzer, in their research on the characteristics of empowered people (through both in-depth interviews and survey analysis), found four characteristics that most empowered people have in common:

- Empowered people have a sense of *self-determination* (this means that they are free to choose how to do their work; they are not micromanaged).

- Empowered people have a sense of *meaning* (they feel that their work is important to them; they care about what they are doing).

- Empowered people have a sense of *competence* (this means that they are confident about their ability to do their work well; they know they can perform).

- Empowered people have a sense of *impact* (this means that people believe they can have influence on their work unit; others listen to their ideas).

Source: R. E. Quinn and G. M. Spreitzer, "The Road to Empowerment: Seven Questions Every Leader Should Consider," *Organizational Dynamics,* Autumn 1997, p. 41.

---

complaints from 27 days down to 48 hours. Not ready to rest on this accomplishment, however, Dominion is aiming for same-day complaint resolution. Dominion reports that its employee-empowerment efforts also led to revenues that have grown by 40 percent in six years and an annual turnover that is the lowest in the business at 5.27 percent. *OB Around the Globe* considers whether empowerment affects all employees equally.

OB AROUND THE GLOBE

Empowerment in the United States, Mexico, India, and Poland

Does empowerment work the same way around the world? Four US researchers investigated the effects of empowerment on employees of a multinational firm by looking at four of the company's comparable plants: one in the midwestern US, one in central Mexico, one in west-central India, and one in the south of Poland.[38] These four locations were chosen because they differed on power distance and individualism (concepts we discussed in Chapter 3). India and Mexico are considered high in power distance, and the United States is considered the lowest in power distance. Mexico and India are high in collectivity, the United States is highly individualistic, and Poland is moderately individualistic.

The findings showed that Indian employees gave their supervisors low ratings when empowerment was high, while employees in the other three countries rated their supervisors favourably when empowerment was high. In both the United States and Mexico, empowerment had no effect on satisfaction with co-workers. However, satisfaction with co-workers was higher when employees were empowered in Poland. In India, empowerment led to lower satisfaction with co-workers.

Similar findings in a study comparing empowerment in the United States, Brazil, and Argentina suggest that in hierarchical societies, empowerment may need to be introduced with care.[39] Employees in those countries may be more used to working in teams, but they also expect their manager to be the person with all the answers. 👤

Our discussion of empowerment suggests that a number of problems can arise when organizations decide they want to empower employees. First, some managers do not want empowered employees, because this can take away some of their own base of power. Second, some employees have little or no interest in being empowered, and therefore resist any attempts to be empowered. And finally, empowerment is not something that works well in every workplace throughout the world.

THE ABUSE OF POWER: HARASSMENT IN THE WORKPLACE

6 How are power and harassment related?

People who engage in harassment in the workplace are typically abusing their power position. The manager-employee relationship best characterizes an unequal power relationship, where position power gives the manager the capacity to reward and coerce. Managers give employees their assignments, evaluate their performance, make recommendations for salary adjustments and promotions, and even decide whether employees retain their job. These decisions give a manager power. Since employees want favourable performance reviews, salary increases, and the like, it's clear that managers control the resources that most employees consider important and scarce. It's also worth noting that individuals who occupy high-status roles (such as management positions) sometimes believe that harassing employees is merely an extension of their right to make demands on lower-status individuals.

Although co-workers do not have position power, they can have influence and use it to harass peers. In fact, although co-workers appear to engage in somewhat less severe forms of harassment than do managers, co-workers are the most frequent perpetrators of harassment, particularly sexual harassment, in organizations. How do co-workers exercise power? Most often it's by providing or withholding information, cooperation, and support. For example, the effective performance of most jobs requires interaction and support from co-workers. This is especially true these days as work is assigned to teams. By threatening to withhold or delay providing information that is necessary for the successful achievement of your work goals, co-workers can exert power over you.

Some categories of harassment have long been held to be illegal, including those based on race, religion, and national origin, as well as sexual harassment. Unfortunately, some types of harassment that occur in the workplace are not deemed illegal, even if they create problems for employees and managers. We focus here on two types of harassment that have received considerable attention in the press: workplace bullying and sexual harassment.

Workplace Bullying

Many of us are aware, anecdotally if not personally, of managers who harass employees, demanding overtime without pay or excessive work performance. Further, some of the recent stories of workplace violence have reportedly been the result of an employee feeling intimidated at work. In research conducted in the private and public sector in southern Saskatchewan, Céleste Brotheridge, a professor at the Université du Québec à Montréal, found that bullying was rather prevalent in the workplace. Forty percent of the respondents noted that they had experienced one or more forms of bullying weekly in the past six months. Ten percent experienced bullying at a much greater level: five or more incidents a week. Brotheridge notes that bullying has a negative effect on the workplace: "Given bullying's deleterious effects on employee health, it is reason for concern."[40]

There is no clear definition of workplace bullying, and Marilyn Noble, a Fredericton-based adult educator, remarks that in some instances there can be a fine line between managing and bullying. However, Noble, who co-chaired a research team on workplace violence and abuse at the University of New Brunswick, notes that "when it becomes a question of shaming people, embarrassing people, holding them up to ridicule, just constantly being on their case for no apparent reason, then [management] is becoming unreasonable." Moreover, "A bully often acts by isolating an individual. And they may be a serial bully, who always has a victim on the go. They may, in fact, have multiple victims on the go, but their strategy is to isolate them from one another."[41]

Sexual Harassment

The issue of sexual harassment has received increasing attention from corporations and the media because of the growing ranks of female employees, especially in nontraditional work environments, and because of a number of high-profile cases. For example, the Canadian Armed Forces was subject to intense media scrutiny during 1998 for alleged cover-ups of sexual harassment. A survey by York University found that 48 percent of working women in Canada reported they had experienced some form of "gender harassment" in the year before they were surveyed.[42] Barbara Orser, a research affiliate with the Conference Board of Canada, notes that "sexual harassment is more likely to occur in workplace environments that tolerate bullying, intimidation, yelling, innuendo and other forms of discourteous behaviour."[43] These behaviours indicate one person trying to use power over another.

The Supreme Court of Canada defines **sexual harassment** as unwelcome behaviour of a sexual nature in the workplace that negatively affects the work environment or leads to adverse job-related consequences for the employee.[44] Despite the legal framework for defining sexual harassment, there continues to be disagreement as to what *specifically* constitutes sexual harassment. Sexual harassment includes unwanted physical touching, recurring requests for dates when it is made clear the person isn't interested, and coercive threats that a person will lose her or his job if she or he refuses a sexual proposition. The problems of interpreting sexual harassment often surface around some of its more subtle forms—unwanted looks or comments; off-colour jokes; sexual artifacts such as nude calendars in the workplace; sexual innuendo; or misinterpretations of where the line between "being friendly" ends and "harassment" begins. *Case Incident— Damned If You Do: Damned If You Don't* on page 310 illustrates how these problems can make people feel uncomfortable in the workplace. Most studies confirm that the concept of power is central to understanding sexual harassment.[45] This seems to be true whether the harassment comes from a manager, a co-worker, or even an employee.

Because of power inequities, sexual harassment by a manager typically creates great difficulty for an employee being harassed. If there are no witnesses, it's the manager's word against the employee's word. Are there others whom this manager has harassed, and if so, will they come forward? Because of the manager's control over resources, many of those who are harassed are afraid of speaking out for fear of retaliation by the manager.

One of the places where there has been a dramatic increase in the number of sexual harassment complaints is at university campuses across Canada, according to Paddy Stamp, sexual harassment officer at the University of Toronto.[46] However, agreement on what constitutes sexual harassment, and how it should be investigated, is no clearer for universities than for industry.

While nonconsensual sex between professors and students is rape and subject to criminal charges, it's harder to evaluate apparently consensual relationships that occur outside the classroom. There is some argument over whether truly consensual sex is ever possible between students and professors. In an effort to underscore the power discrepancy and potential for abuse of it by professors, in the late 1990s Yale University decided that there could be no sexual relations between students and professors. In 2003, the University of California, which includes Berkeley, implemented a policy that went further, forbidding romantic relationships between professors and their students as well.[47] Most universities have been unwilling to adopt such an extreme stance. However, this issue is certainly one of concern, as the power difference between professors and students is considerable.

sexual harassment Unwelcome behaviour of a sexual nature in the workplace that negatively affects the work environment or leads to adverse job-related consequences for the employee.

Supreme Court of Canada
www.scc-csc.gc.ca

In concluding this discussion, we would like to point out that harassment is about power. It's about an individual controlling or threatening another individual. This chapter's *HR Implications* on pages 305–307 further explores issues of sexual harassment in the workplace.

POLITICS: POWER IN ACTION

> As the Olympic figure skating controversy unfolded, both Jacques Rogge, IOC president, and Ottavio Cinquanta, ISU president, paid a lot of attention to what the media said about the event. The event had happened in the United States, and Americans made it clear that they were dismayed when the Canadians lost. As a result, the controversy was discussed on a variety of talk shows and news programs and in newspapers. This was a way of keeping the controversy alive, and trying to persuade the Olympics' head that the decision needed to be changed. Rogge arguably was affected by the pressure, fearing that the negative publicity surrounding the skating controversy was harming the rest of the Olympics. Thus, when he decided to award the unprecedented second gold medal, it may have been less about making the "right" decision, and more about making a political decision to silence dissent. So why is politics so prevalent? Is it merely a fact of life?

7 Why do people engage in politics?

Organizational behaviour researchers have learned a lot in recent years about how people gain and use power in organizations. Part of using power in organizations is engaging in organizational politics to influence others to help you achieve your personal objectives. Lobbying others to get them to vote with you on a particular decision is engaging in organizational politics.

When people get together in groups, power will be exerted. People want to carve out a niche from which to exert influence, to earn awards, and to advance their careers.[48] When employees in organizations convert their power into action, we describe them as being engaged in politics. Those with good political skills have the ability to use their bases of power effectively.[49] In this section, we cover impression management and the types of political activity people use to try to influence others. Political skills aren't confined to adults, of course. When your Vancouver author's six-year-old nephew wanted the latest Game Boy knowing full well his parents didn't approve, he waged a careful, deliberate campaign to wear them down, explaining how he would use the toy only at assigned times, etc. His politicking paid off: Within six weeks, he succeeded in getting the toy.

Definition of Political Behaviour

There has been no shortage of definitions for organizational politics. One clever definition of politics comes from Tom Jakobek, Toronto's former budget chief, who said: "In politics, you may have to go from A to C to D to E to F to G and then to B."[50]

political behaviour Those activities that influence, or attempt to influence, the distribution of advantages and disadvantages within the organization.

For our purposes, we will define **political behaviour** in organizations as those activities that are outside one's formal role, and that influence, or attempt to influence, the distribution of advantages and disadvantages within the organization.[51]

This definition encompasses key elements from what most people mean when they talk about organizational politics. Political behaviour is *outside* one's specified job requirements. The behaviour requires some attempt to use one's *bases of power*. Our definition also encompasses efforts to influence the goals, criteria, or processes used for decision making when we state that politics is concerned with "the distribution of advantages and disadvantages within the organization." Our definition is broad enough to include such varied political behaviours as withholding key information from decision makers, spreading rumours, leaking confidential information about organizational activities to the media, exchanging favours with others in the organization for mutual benefit, and lobbying on behalf of or against a particular individual or decision alternative. Exhibit 8-6 provides a quick measure to help you assess how political your workplace is.

EXHIBIT 8-6 A Quick Measure of How Political Your Workplace Is

How political is your workplace? Answer the 12 questions using the following scale:

SD = **Strongly disagree**

D = **Disagree**

U = **Uncertain**

A = **Agree**

SA = **Strongly agree**

1. Managers often use the selection system to hire only people who can help them in their future. _____

2. The rules and policies concerning promotion and pay are fair; it's how managers carry out the policies that is unfair and self-serving. _____

3. The performance ratings people receive from their managers reflect more of the managers' "own agenda" than the actual performance of the employee. _____

4. Although a lot of what my manager does around here appears to be directed at helping employees, it's actually intended to protect my manager. _____

5. There are cliques or "in-groups" that hinder effectiveness around here. _____

6. My co-workers help themselves, not others. _____

7. I have seen people deliberately distort information requested by others for purposes of personal gain, either by withholding it or by selectively reporting it. _____

8. If co-workers offer to lend some assistance, it is because they expect to get something out of it. _____

9. Favouritism rather than merit determines who gets ahead around here. _____

10. You can usually get what you want around here if you know the right person to ask. _____

11. Overall, the rules and policies concerning promotion and pay are specific and well-defined. _____

12. Pay and promotion policies are generally clearly communicated in this organization. _____

This questionnaire taps the three salient dimensions that have been found to be related to perceptions of politics: manager behaviour; co-worker behaviour; and organizational policies and practices. To calculate your score for items 1–10, give yourself 1 point for Strongly disagree; 2 points for Disagree; and so forth (through 5 points for Strongly agree). For items 11 and 12, reverse the score (that is, 1 point for Strongly agree, etc.). Sum up the total: The higher the total score, the greater the degree of perceived organizational politics.

Source: G. R. Ferris, D. D. Frink, D. P. S. Bhawuk, J. Zhou, and D. C. Gilmore, "Reactions of Diverse Groups to Politics in the Workplace," *Journal of Management* 22, no. 1 (1996), pp. 32–33.

Now that you have learned a bit about political behaviour, you may want to assess your own political behaviour in *Learning About Yourself Exercise* on page 307.

Political behaviour is not confined to just individual hopes and goals. Politics might also be used to achieve organizational goals. For instance, if a CEO wants to change the way employees are paid, say from salaries to commissions, this might not be a popular choice for employees. While it might make good organizational sense to make this change (perhaps the CEO believes this will increase productivity), simply imposing the change through the use of power (e.g., go along with this or you're fired) might not be very popular. Instead, the CEO may try to pitch the reasons for the change to sympathetic managers and employees, trying to get them to understand the necessity for the change. Vancouver-based Telus used a direct approach with its employees after four and a half years of unsuccessful bargaining with union leaders. Management became frustrated with the impasse and explained their wage and benefit offer directly to employees in the hopes of getting the employees to side with management rather than their union leaders. The union was outraged by this behaviour, and it took several more months for union members and management to finally complete a new collective agreement in fall 2005.

The Reality of Politics

Why, you may wonder, must politics exist? Isn't it possible for an organization to be politics-free? It's *possible*, but most unlikely. Organizations are made up of individuals and groups with different values, goals, and interests.[52] This sets up the potential for conflict over resources. Organizational members sometimes disagree about the allocation of resources such as departmental budgets, space allocations, project responsibilities, and salary adjustments.

Resources in organizations are also limited, which often turns potential conflict into real conflict. If resources were abundant, all the constituencies within the organization could satisfy their goals. Because they are limited, not everyone's interests can be provided for. Furthermore, whether true or not, gains by one individual or group are often *perceived* as being at the expense of others within the organization. These forces create a competition among members for the organization's limited resources. Peter Godsoe, former chair and CEO of Toronto-based Scotiabank, demonstrated his awareness of how to get the most resources for whatever unit he headed while enhancing his own career, as *OB in the Workplace* shows.

OB IN THE WORKPLACE

Godsoe Makes the Most of Resources to Become CEO of Scotiabank

Can you ensure your way to the top? Peter Godsoe was determined to become CEO of Scotiabank. In his quest for this job, he learned how to "outlast and outwit other hopefuls."[53] When he was put in charge of the bank's lending in the United States and Latin America, he made the operation his own by giving it a new name, the Western Hemisphere International Regional Office (WHIRO). While heading WHIRO, he reported to Scott McDonald, who was regarded as a potential successor to then CEO Ced Ritchie. In order to raise his profile, Godsoe built "a loyal following by making WHIRO the hot shop," thus making himself look better than McDonald. Godsoe developed cartoons, WHIRO hero awards, a logo, jackets, and a Latin motto that translated, "If you don't have a hernia, you're not pulling your weight," all with the aim of strengthening his unit's culture and making it more prominent within the bank. After his time at WHIRO, Godsoe had the remarkable knack for getting himself appointed the head of every organizational division created. Eventually, McDonald ended up leaving the bank, and Godsoe replaced Ritchie (but not before he threatened that he would leave for another job offer).

Maybe the most important factor leading to politics within organizations is the realization that most of the "facts" that are used to allocate the limited resources are open to interpretation. What, for instance, is *good* performance? What's an *adequate* improvement? What constitutes an *unsatisfactory* job? It's in this large and ambiguous middle ground of organizational life—where the facts *don't* speak for themselves—that politics flourishes.

Finally, because most decisions must be made in a climate of ambiguity—where facts are rarely fully objective, and thus are open to interpretation—people within organizations will use whatever influence they can to spin the facts to support their goals and interests. That, of course, creates the activities we call politicking. For more about how one engages in politicking, see *From Concepts to Skills* on page 312.

Therefore, to answer the earlier question about whether it is possible for an organization to be politics-free, we can say "yes" if all members of that organization hold the same goals and interests, if organizational resources are not scarce, and if performance outcomes are completely clear and objective. However, that doesn't describe the organizational world that most of us live in!

RESEARCH FINDINGS

Our earlier discussion focused on the favourable outcomes for individuals who successfully engage in politicking. But for most people—who have modest political skills or are unwilling to play the politics game—outcomes tend to be predominantly negative.[54] There is, for instance, very strong evidence indicating that perceptions of organizational politics are negatively related to job satisfaction.[55] The perception of politics also tends to increase job anxiety and stress. This seems to be because of the perception that, by not engaging in politics, a person may be losing ground to others who are active politickers, or, conversely, because of the additional pressures individuals feel because of having entered into and competing in the political arena.[56] Not surprisingly, when politicking becomes too much to handle, it can lead to employees quitting.[57] Finally, there is preliminary evidence suggesting that politics leads to self-reported declines in employee performance.[58] Perceived organizational politics appears to have a demotivating effect on individuals, and thus leads to decreased performance levels.

President and CEO Aris Kaplanis of Toronto-based high-tech firm Teranet (shown here at far right with his senior management group) discourages negative office politics by his employees. The company employs the golden rule of "do unto others as you would have others do unto you." He tells his employees, "If you're here to play a game, you're in the wrong business."

Types of Political Activity

Within organizations, we can find a variety of political activities in which people engage. These include the following:[59]

- *Attacking or blaming others.* Used when trying to avoid responsibility for failure.

- *Using information.* Withholding or distorting information, particularly to hide negative information.

- *Managing impressions.* Bringing positive attention to one's self or taking credit for positive accomplishments of others.

- *Building support for ideas.* Making sure that others will support one's ideas before they are presented.

- *Praising others.* Making important people feel good.

- *Building coalitions.* Joining with other people to create a powerful group.

- *Associating with influential people.* Building support networks.

- *Creating obligations.* Doing favours for others so they will owe you favours later.

Individuals will use these political activities for different purposes. Some of these activities are more likely to be used to defend one's position (such as attacking or blaming others), while other activities are meant to enhance one's image (such as building support for ideas and managing impressions). This chapter's *CBC Video Case* explores how whistle-blowing can become a political act in some organizations.

Impression Management

impression management The process by which individuals attempt to control the impression others form of them.

> *Why do some people seem to engage in politics more than others?*

The process by which individuals attempt to control the impression others form of them is called **impression management**.[60] Being perceived positively by others should have benefits for people in organizations. It might, for instance, help them initially to get the jobs they want in an organization and, once hired, to get favourable evaluations, superior salary increases, and more rapid promotions. In a political context, it might help bring more advantages their way. For instance, during the Olympics figure skating controversy, Jamie Salé and David Pelletier were seen in many television shows and news conferences, always giving the impression that they were not lobbying for a gold medal after the fact, and presenting an image of clean-cut, soft-spoken individuals. This led to even more sympathy for their plight.

Impression management does not imply that the impressions people convey are necessarily false (although, of course, they sometimes are).[61] Some activities may be done with great sincerity. For instance, you may *actually* believe that ads contribute little to sales in your region or that you are the key to the tripling of your division's sales. However, if the image claimed is false, you may be discredited.[62] The impression manager must be cautious not to be perceived as insincere or manipulative.[63]

 RESEARCH FINDINGS

Below we explore research findings in two areas: the *use* of impression management and the *effectiveness* of impression management.

Use of Impression Management Impression management is more likely to be used by high self-monitors than low self-monitors.[64] Low self-monitors tend to present images of themselves that are consistent with their personalities, regardless of the beneficial or detrimental effects for them. In contrast, high self-monitors are skilled at reading situations and moulding their appearances and behaviour to fit each situation. Research by Marc-David Seidel at the Sauder School of Business, University of British Columbia, and his colleagues suggests that impression management is engaged in more frequently by those who spend at least some time telecommuting. These employees feel the need to keep their supervisor more informed about their activities, because they are physically absent.[65]

Effectiveness of Impression Management A number of studies have examined the effectiveness of impression management techniques in a variety of work situations. Studies show that impression management behaviour is positively associated with job-interview success.[66] For instance, one study found that recent university graduates who used more self-promotion tactics got higher evaluations by interviewers and more follow-up job-site visits, even after adjusting for grade point average, gender, and

> *In what situations does impression management work best?*

job type.[67] Other studies have found that those using impression management techniques received better performance evaluations from their managers,[68] were liked more by their managers,[69] and criticized less.[70] Impression management effects seem to work more strongly when the measures of performance are subjective, however, than when they can be measured more objectively.[71] For instance, those using impression management techniques were rated more highly for interpersonal effectiveness, but they could be more negatively evaluated on their business competence.[72] Overall, the findings of these studies suggest that there is some advantage to engaging in impression management, as long as the person delivers on the objective measures of performance as well. For those who intend to become leaders, engaging in impression management techniques makes it more likely that they will be chosen.[73]

Making Office Politics Work

One thing to be aware of is that extreme office politics can have a negative effect on employees. Researchers have found that organizational politics is associated with less organizational commitment,[74] lower job satisfaction,[75] and decreased job performance.[76] Individuals who experience greater organizational politics are more likely to report higher levels of job anxiety,[77] and they are more likely to consider leaving the organization.[78]

Is there an effective way to engage in office politics that is less likely to be disruptive or negative? We discuss different negotiation strategies in Chapter 9, including a "win-lose" strategy, which means if I win, you lose, and a "win-win" strategy, which means creating situations where both of us can win. *Fast Company*, an online business magazine, identifies several rules that may help improve the climate of the organization while negotiating through the office politics maze:[79]

Fast Company
www.fastcompany.com

- *Nobody wins unless everybody wins.* The most successful proposals look for ways to acknowledge, if not include, the interests of others. This requires building support for your ideas across the organization. "Real political skill isn't about campaign tactics," says Lou Di Natale, a veteran political consultant at the University of Massachusetts. "It's about pulling people toward your ideas and then pushing those ideas through to other people." When ideas are packaged to look like they're best for the organization as a whole and will help others, it is harder for others to counteract your proposal.

- *Don't just ask for opinions—change them.* It's helpful to find out what people think and then, if necessary, set out to change their opinions so that they can see what you want to do. It's also important to seek out the opinions of those you don't know well, or who are less likely to agree with you. Gathering together people who always support you is often not enough to build an effective coalition.

- *Everyone expects to be paid back.* In organizations, as in life, we develop personal relationships with those around us. It's those personal relationships that affect much of the behaviour in organizations. By building good relationships with colleagues, supporting them in their endeavours, and showing appreciation for what they accomplish, you are building a foundation of support for your own ideas.

General Electric (GE) wants its managers to share their power with employees. GE is breaking down autocratic barriers between labour and management that "cramp people, inhibit creativity, waste time, restrict visions, smother dreams, and above all, slow things down." GE expects managers to behave more democratically by fostering teamwork and rewarding employees who suggest ideas for improvement. This photo illustrates GE's move toward democracy, as a manager and an employee at the company's plant in Louisville, Kentucky, work together to improve the plant's profitability.

- *Success can create opposition.* As part of the office politics, success can be viewed as a "win-lose" strategy, which we identified above. Some people may feel that your success comes at their expense. So, for instance, your higher profile may mean that a project of theirs will be received less favourably. You have to be prepared to deal with this opposition.

SUMMARY AND IMPLICATIONS

1 **What is power?** Power refers to a capacity that A has to influence the behaviour of B, so that B acts in accordance with A's wishes.

2 **How does one get power?** There are six bases or sources of power: coercive, reward, legitimate, expert, referent, and information. These forms of power differ in their ability to improve a person's performance. *Coercive power* tends to result in negative performance responses from individuals; it decreases satisfaction, increases mistrust, and creates fear. *Reward power* may improve performance, but it can also lead to unethical behaviour. *Legitimate power* does not have a negative effect, but does not generally stimulate employees to improve their attitudes or performance, and it does not generally result in increased commitment. Ironically, the least effective bases of power—coercive, legitimate, and reward—are the ones most likely to be used by managers, perhaps because they are the easiest to implement. By contrast, effective leaders use *expert* and/or *referent power*; these forms of power are not derived from the person's position. *Information power* comes from access to and control over information and can be used in both positive (sharing) and negative (withholding) ways in the organization.

3 **How does dependency affect power?** To maximize your power, you will want to increase others' dependence on you. You can, for instance, increase your power in relation to your employer by developing knowledge or a skill that he or she needs and for which there is no ready substitute. However, you will not be alone in attempting to build your bases of power. Others, particularly employees and peers, will seek to make you dependent on them. The result is a continual struggle for power.

4 **What tactics can be used to increase power?** One particular study identified nine tactics, or strategies, that managers and employees use to increase their power: rational persuasion, inspirational appeals, consultation, ingratiation, personal appeals, exchange, coalition tactics, pressure, and legitimating tactics.[80]

5 **What does it mean to be empowered?** Empowerment refers to the freedom and the ability of employees to make decisions and commitments. There is a lot of positive press on empowerment. However, much of the talk in organizations about empowerment does not result in employees being empowered. Some managers do not fully understand how to go about empowering their employees, and others find it difficult to share their power with employees.

6 **How are power and harassment related?** People who engage in harassment in the workplace are typically abusing their power position. Harassment can come in many forms, from gross abuse of power toward anyone of lower rank, to abuse of individuals because of their personal characteristics, such as race, religion, national origin, and gender.

7 **Why do people engage in politics?** People use politics to influence others to help them achieve their personal objectives. Whenever people get together in groups, power will be exerted. People also use impression management to influence people. Impression management is the process by which individuals attempt to control the impression others form of them. Though politics is a natural occurrence in organizations, when it is carried to an extreme it can damage relationships among individuals.

For Review

1. What is power? How do you get it?

2. Contrast the bases of power with influence tactics.

3. What are some of the key contingency variables that determine which tactic a power holder is likely to use?

4. Which of the six bases of power lie with the individual? Which are derived from the organization?

5. State the general dependency postulate. What does it mean?

6. What creates dependency? Give an applied example.

7. Identify the range of empowerment that might be available to employees.

8. How are power and politics related?

9. Define political behaviour. Why is politics a fact of life in organizations?

10. Define sexual harassment. Who is most likely to harass an employee: a boss, a co-worker, or a subordinate? Explain.

For Critical Thinking

1. Based on the information presented in this chapter, what would you do as a recent graduate entering a new job to maximize your power and accelerate your career progress?

2. "Politics isn't inherently bad. It's merely a way to get things accomplished within organizations." Do you agree or disagree? Defend your position.

3. You are a sales representative for an international software company. After four excellent years, sales in your territory are off 30 percent this year. Describe three impression management techniques you might use to convince your manager that your sales record is better than should be expected under the circumstances.

4. "Sexual harassment should not be tolerated at the workplace." "Workplace romances are a natural occurrence in organizations." Are both of these statements true? Can they be reconciled?

5. Which impression management techniques have you used? What ethical implications, if any, are there in using impression management?

OB for You

■ Power and politics should not simply be viewed as a win-lose situation. Through power and politics, one builds coalitions to work together effectively. It's possible to make sure that everyone is included.

■ There are a variety of ways to increase your power in an organization. As an example, you could acquire more knowledge about a situation and then use that information to negotiate a bonus with your employer. Even if you don't get the bonus, the knowledge may help you in other ways.

■ You could also consider how dependent others are on you, when seeking to increase your power. Dependency is affected by your importance, substitutability, and scarcity options. If you have needed skills that no one else has, you will have more power.

■ Politics is a reality of most organizations. Being comfortable with politics is important. Politics is often about making deals with other people for mutual gain.

■ Political skills can be developed. Remembering to take time to join in an office birthday celebration for someone is part of developing the skill of working with others effectively.

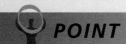

POINT

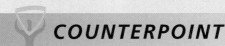

COUNTERPOINT

"Special Deals" for "Special Employees" Make Sense

In countries such as France, Belgium, and the Netherlands, terms of employment are largely mandated by law and hence highly standardized.[81] In contrast, in countries such as Canada, the United States, the United Kingdom, and New Zealand, managers have considerable leeway to negotiate individual deals with employees. And in these latter countries, managers are increasingly using this latitude to customize their treatment of "special" individuals.

Two trends help explain the growth in special deals for certain employees. First, the demand for knowledge workers with distinctive competencies in a competitive market means workers have greater power to negotiate employment conditions suited to their tastes and preferences. Second, the decline in unionization and the weakening of the job security–based model of organizational careers have led to less standardized conditions of employment.

In order to hire, motivate, and keep highly skilled workers, managers are negotiating special treatment for certain employees. Examples of this special treatment include higher pay than others for doing similar work, allowing an employee to work from home several days a week, permitting an employee to leave early to fulfill family obligations, upgrading travel arrangements, and allowing certain employees to spend time on personal projects during work time.

What do these employees have that allow them to make unique arrangements? It can be unique credentials, special skills, high status, important contacts, or high marketability. But it must also include the willingness of an employee or prospective employee to speak up and ask for special treatment. These deals are typically offered as bargaining chips when negotiating initial employment terms or after the employee has been on the job a while, built a trusting relationship with his or her manager, and become a valued performer.

These special deals have advantages for both employees and managers. They provide greater rewards for employees and allow them to tailor their job to better meet their personal needs. They also give individual managers greater latitude in motivating their employees and flexibility to adapt to changing circumstances.

"Special Deals" Hurt the Work Environment

Making special deals with certain employees is bound to undermine whatever trust there is in an organization. Although management may desire flexibility in its relationships with employees, maintaining standardized practices is more likely to provide the appearance of fairness that is needed to create a climate of trust. Customization of employment relationships, under the guise of flexibility, only increases politics in the workplace.

There is no shortage of arguments against special deals for special employees. Here are just a few:

- *Special deals give too much power to managers.* They allow managers to negotiate favourable treatment with employees they like, politicizing the work environment.

- *Special deals are unlikely to be perceived as fair by those who don't receive them.* One person's merit is another's favouritism.

- *Special deals reward the wrong behaviours.* They encourage employees to "kiss up" to their boss and to treat every attempt to get a raise or time off as a bargaining opportunity.

- *Special deals tend to go to aggressive employees, whether or not they're contributing the most.* Shy, quiet, and less demanding employees who are good performers are likely to be excluded.

- *Special deals aren't cost-free.* One employee's gain is often at another's expense. So allowing one employee in a department to take off two hours early every Thursday afternoon to coach his son's baseball team often means others in that department will have to take up some of his work. This has the potential to create conflicts. For instance, evidence indicates that many single and childless employees resent the "family-friendly" benefits—such as helping to find an employee's spouse employment or paid day-care—that many companies offer to married workers and those with children.

Our position is that special deals undermine trust and cooperation at work. We've spent three-quarters of a century building formalized human resource systems that ensure consistent treatment of the workforce. These systems are critical to promoting fairness, cooperation, and efficiency. Using idiosyncratic deals to supposedly enhance flexibility is a major step toward trashing these systems.

HR IMPLICATIONS

Dealing With Harassment in the Workplace

Workplace Bullying

British journalist Andrea Adams was the first to use the term *workplace bullying*, back in 1992.[82] The term was introduced to the US popular press in 1998 by psychologist Gary and Ruth Namie. They define workplace bullying as "status-blind" interpersonal hostility that is deliberate, repeated, and sufficiently severe as to harm the targeted person's health or economic status.[83] Further, it's driven by perpetrators' need to control another individual, often undermining legitimate business interests in the process.

Though researchers initially focused on workplace violence as an issue, more recent work has found that verbal passive-aggressive behaviour makes up much of the hostile behaviour in the workplace. Professor Julian Barling of Queen's School of Business has labelled these behaviours *psychological aggression*,[84] but they have also been termed *emotional abuse*[85] and *generalized workplace abuse*.[86]

Women are more likely to be the bulliers, according to one study that found 58 percent of the perpetrators to be women.[87] Much of the bullying is also "same sex." Women were bullied by other women in 63 percent of cases, and men were bullied by other men in 62 percent of the cases. Because legislation and workplace policies do not refer to same-sex harassment, this type of bullying tends not to be addressed.

Noting that there are a variety of bullying behaviours in the workplace, one researcher divided bullies into four categories:[88]

- *The Screaming Mimi.* Characterized by mood swings and unpredictable displays of anger. This type of bully publicly humiliates his or her victims to send the message that he or she should be feared.

- *The Constant Critic.* Characterized by being a hyper-critical nitpicker and name-caller. Tends to act behind closed doors, but can berate targets in public.

- *The Two-Headed Snake.* Characterized by moving up the organization while spreading negative stories about co-workers. Often tries to turn others against specific targets.

- *The Gatekeeper.* Characterized by being obsessed with control. Tries to ensure the target's failure by taking away resources, or otherwise making it difficult for the person to perform well.

Federal and provincial labour codes, human rights codes, and occupational health and safety acts have been written to protect employees from workplace harassment. However, these acts only cover harassment that is directed at an individual on the basis of race, creed, religion, colour, sex, sexual orientation, marital status, family status, disability, physical size or weight, age, nationality, and ancestry or place or origin. Much harassment in the workplace is not specifically directed on the basis of these protected categories, and thus is not covered by legislation.

Quebec introduced the first anti-bullying labour legislation in North America on June 1, 2004. The legislation defines psychological harassment as "any vexatious behaviour in the form of repeated and hostile or unwanted conduct, verbal comments, actions or gestures that affect an employee's dignity or psychological or physical integrity and that results in a harmful work environment for the employee."[89] Under the Quebec law, bullying allegations will be sent to mediation, where the accuser and the accused will work with an independent third party to try to resolve the problem. If mediation fails, employers who have allowed psychological harassment can be fined up to $10 000 and ordered to pay financial damages to the victim.

While other provinces have yet to introduce similar legislation, research on the impact of workplace aggression suggests that even without legislation, employers might want to take more direct action on this issue. A recent study indicates that nonsexual aggression in the workplace has a greater negative effect on job satisfaction than sexual aggression, and that this result is even stronger for female victims.[90]

Sexual Harassment and Canadian Law

The Supreme Court of Canada defines *sexual harassment* as unwelcome behaviour of a sexual nature in the workplace that negatively affects the work environment or leads to adverse job-related consequences for the employee. Protection from sexual harassment is governed by human rights legislation, which prohibits discrimination on the basis of sex (and age, ethnic origin, race, disability, religion, and sexual orientation, among other things). At the provincial/territorial and federal levels, these laws have been widely interpreted to mean both quid pro quo harassment involving exchange of sexual acts for job-related benefits, and a range of behaviours that create a hostile work environment for the person to whom the attention is directed.

In 1987, the court ruled that employers will be held responsible for sexual harassment by their employees. The court also said the employer is in the best position to stop harassment and should promote a workplace that is free of it. The court recommended that employers have clear guidelines to prevent sexual harassment, which included procedures to investigate complaints.

Dealing With Sexual Harassment in the Workplace

Several cases can be used to illustrate how to reduce sexual harassment in the workplace. For instance, in 2002 the Canadian Human Rights Tribunal fined a manager from Brandon, Manitoba-based Skycable for sexually harassing four of his female subordinates.[91] He was accused of making "inappropriate remarks, sexual advances, and derogatory comments to them on an ongoing basis." All four women first went on sick leave and then quit their jobs as a result of the harassment. The manager's fines included damages for lost wages to each woman (ranging from $698 to $13 979), compensation for hurt feelings to each woman (ranging from $6000 to $8000), and $10 000 for each woman due to reckless or willful conduct. He was also ordered to take training in harassment issues, seek counselling, and write letters of apology to three of the women.

Researchers representing Women in Trades and Technology interviewed a number of women who worked on the Hibernia offshore oil project based in Bull Arm, Newfoundland, in 1995. The women interviewed expressed concerns ranging from "not being allowed to do the heavy work they were trained and hired to do" to "degrading and sexual remarks made by male co-workers." The women reported being uncomfortable bringing the problems to their unions or management, and they received little support or help when they did. The researchers made a number of recommendations for the Hibernia project, which has since been completed, as well as for future projects, such as the Terra Nova offshore oil development and the Voisey's Bay nickel discovery in Labrador. These recommendations include the following:[92]

- Developing formal avenues to consult with women about integrating into nontraditional jobs

- Planning work camps with the needs of women in mind

- Providing better on-site education about sexual harassment

- Creating an employment equity plan covering recruitment, training, and promotion

In another example, Aurora, Ontario-based Magna International faced a sexual harassment suit in the United States, brought by a former saleswoman in the parts maker's Detroit sales office.[93] The woman alleged that she faced harassment in the office, and that her male co-workers regularly entertained customers at area strip clubs. One of the allegations in the complaint was that a Magna sales manager spent $23 000 entertaining customers at strip joints and other bars and restaurants. Magna denied the charges and issued a memo to customers and employees in the Detroit area that the company "does not tolerate any form of sexual discrimination or harassment."

However, auto industry executives and observers agree that the auto business remains male-dominated, and that some purchasing executives are entertained at strip clubs. Scott Upham, president of Providata, an analyst firm located in Southgate, Michigan, said that entertaining this way "is less prevalent than it used to be. I used to work at suppliers where this sort of conduct was commonplace. There are certain customers who want to be entertained that way, just like some like to go to the ball game."

The Magna example raises questions for both employers and employees about appropriate client and customer relationships, particularly with more women in the workplace and more women in the roles of clients and customers. Behaviour that might have once been tolerated because it was restricted to interactions between males is less tolerated in today's working environment.

Sears Canada faced a sexual harassment issue that turned into a murder-suicide at a Sears store in Chatham, Ontario. Theresa Vince, a human resource supervisor, was killed by her store manager, Russell Davis, on June 2, 1996. Davis, who had been sexually harassing her, then turned the gun on himself. A coroner's inquest into the murder-suicide released recommendations in December 1997 to various groups involved in dealing with sexual harassment in Ontario. These recommendations could equally apply to the other provinces and territories in Canada:[94]

Employers: Should have effective workplace harassment and discrimination policies and procedures in place. Confidential sources of help should be offered.

Ontario Human Rights Commission: Should develop an advertising campaign, encouraging victims to come forward with their complaints. The commission's services should be periodically reviewed by an outside audit.

Ontario Ministry of Labour: Should make a priority of the ongoing study of sexual harassment as a health and safety issue, so an informed decision about including it under labour legislation can be made.

Province: Should make funds available to the Human Rights Commission, allowing it to increase its investigation capabilities and "prevent cases from falling through the cracks."

Though sexual harassment is defined by the law, and there are procedures for dealing with it through human rights tribunals, organizations are still trying to define their own policies and procedures. Vancouver-based lawyer Heather MacKenzie notes that "Companies have a direct financial interest in ensuring they have a comprehensive policy in place. The courts have said you also have to educate all members of the organization about how the policy works."[95] In a move that will be watched by employers in both Canada and the United States, the Supreme Court of California ruled in July 2005 that employees can sue for sexual harassment if a colleague receives repeated preferential treatment (for example, raises, promotions, better assignments) for sleeping with the boss.[96]

LEARNING ABOUT **YOURSELF** EXERCISE

How Political Are You?

To determine your political tendencies, please review the following statements. Check the answer that best represents your behaviour or belief, even if that particular behaviour or belief is not present all the time.

	True	False
1. You should make others feel important through an open appreciation of their ideas and work.	___	___
2. Because people tend to judge you when they first meet you, always try to make a good first impression.	___	___
3. Try to let others do most of the talking, be sympathetic to their problems, and resist telling people that they are totally wrong.	___	___
4. Praise the good traits of the people you meet and always give people an opportunity to save face if they are wrong or make a mistake.	___	___
5. Spreading false rumours, planting misleading information, and backstabbing are necessary, if somewhat unpleasant, methods to deal with your enemies.	___	___
6. Sometimes it is necessary to make promises that you know you will not or cannot keep.	___	___
7. It's important to get along with everybody, even with those who are generally recognized as windbags, abrasive, or constant complainers.	___	___
8. It's vital to do favours for others so that you can call in these IOUs at times when they will do you the most good.	___	___
9. Be willing to compromise, particularly on issues that are minor to you but major to others.	___	___
10. On controversial issues, it's important to delay or avoid your involvement if possible.	___	___

OB *AT WORK*

Scoring Key:

According to the author of this instrument, a complete organizational politician will answer "true" to all 10 questions. Organizational politicians with fundamental ethical standards will answer "false" to questions 5 and 6, which deal with deliberate lies and uncharitable behaviour. Individuals who regard manipulation, incomplete disclosure, and self-serving behaviour as unacceptable will answer "false" to all or almost all of the questions.

Source: J. F. Byrnes, "The Political Behavior Inventory." Reprinted by permission of Dr. Joseph F. Byrnes, Bentley College, Waltham, Massachusetts.

BREAKOUT **GROUP** EXERCISES

Form small groups to discuss the following topics, as assigned by your instructor:

1. Describe an incident where you tried to use political behaviour in order to get something you wanted. What influence tactics did you use?

2. In thinking about the incident described above, were your influence tactics effective? Why?

3. Describe an incident where you saw someone engaging in politics. What was your reaction to observing the political behaviour? Under what circumstances do you think political behaviour is appropriate?

WORKING WITH **OTHERS** EXERCISE

Understanding Bases of Power

Step 1: Your instructor will divide the class into groups of about 5 or 6 (making sure there are at least 5 groups). Each group will be assigned 1 of the following bases of power: (1) coercive, (2) reward, (3) legitimate, (4) expert, and (5) referent. Refer to your text for discussion of these terms.

Step 2: Each group is to develop a role play that highlights the use of the power assigned. The role play should be developed using the following scenario:

You are the leader of a group that is trying to develop a website for a new client. One of your group members, who was assigned the task of researching and analyzing the websites of your client's competition, has twice failed to bring the analysis to scheduled meetings, even though the member knew the assignment was due. Consequently, your group is falling behind in getting the website developed. As leader of the group, you have decided to speak with this team member, and to use your specific brand of power to influence the individual's behaviour.

Step 3: Each group should select 1 person to play the group leader, and another to play the member who has not done the assignment. You have 10 minutes to prepare an influence plan.

Step 4: Each group will conduct its role play. In the event of multiple groups assigned the same power base, 1 of the groups may be asked to volunteer. While you are watching the other groups' role plays, try to put yourself in the place of the person being influenced, to see whether that type of influence would cause you to change your behaviour.

Immediately after each role play, while the next one is being set up, you should pretend that you were the person being influenced, and then record your reaction using the questionnaire below. To do this, take out a sheet of paper and tear it into 5 (or 6) pieces. At the top of each piece of paper, write the type of influence that was used. Then write the letters A, B, C, and D in a column, and indicate which number on the scale (see opposite) reflects the influence attempt.

Reaction to Influence Questionnaire

For each role play, think of yourself as being on the receiving end of the influence attempt described, and record your own reaction.

Type of power used _____

A. As a result of the influence attempt, I will . . .

| **definitely not comply** | 1 | 2 | 3 | 4 | 5 | **definitely comply** |

B. Any change that does come about will be . . .

| **temporary** | 1 | 2 | 3 | 4 | 5 | **long-lasting** |

C. My own personal reaction is . . .

| **resistant** | 1 | 2 | 3 | 4 | 5 | **accepting** |

D. As a result of this influence attempt, my relationship with my group leader will probably be . . .

| **worse** | 1 | 2 | 3 | 4 | 5 | **better** |

Step 5: For each influence type, 1 member of each group will take the pieces of paper from group members and calculate the average group score for each of the 4 questions. For efficiency, this should be done while the role plays are being conducted.

Step 6: Your instructor will collect the summaries from each group, and then lead a discussion based on these results.

Step 7: Discussion.

1. Which kind of influence is most likely to immediately result in the desired behaviour?
2. Which will have the most long-lasting effects?
3. What effect will using a particular base of power have on the ongoing relationship?
4. Which form of power will others find most acceptable? Least acceptable? Why?
5. Are there some situations where a particular type of influence strategy might be more effective than others?

Source: This exercise was inspired by one found in Judith R. Gordon, *Organizational Behavior,* 2nd ed. (Englewood Cliffs, NJ: Prentice Hall, 1992), pp. 499–502.

ETHICAL DILEMMA EXERCISE

Swapping Personal Favours?

Jack Grubman was a powerful man on Wall Street. As a star analyst of telecom companies for the Salomon Smith Barney unit of Citigroup, his recommendations carried a lot of weight with investors.

For years, Grubman had been negative on the stock of AT&T. But in November 1999, he upgraded his opinion on the stock. Based on email evidence, it appears that Grubman's decision to upgrade AT&T was not based on the stock's fundamentals. There were other factors involved.

At the time, his boss at Citigroup, Sanford Weill, was in the midst of a power struggle with co-CEO John Reed to become the single head of the company. Meanwhile, Salomon was looking for additional business to increase its revenues. Getting investment banking business fees from AT&T would be a big plus toward improving revenues. Salomon's efforts at getting that AT&T business would definitely be improved if Grubman would upgrade his opinion on the stock. Furthermore, Weill sought

Grubman's upgrade to win favour with AT&T CEO Michael Armstrong, who sat on Citigroup's board. Weill wanted Armstrong's backing in his efforts to oust Reed.

Grubman had his own concerns. Although he was earning tens of millions a year in his job, he was a man of modest background. He was the son of a city worker in Philadelphia. He wanted the best for his twin daughters, which included entry to an exclusive New York City nursery school—a school that a year earlier had reportedly turned down Madonna's daughter. Weill made a call on Grubman's behalf to the school and pledged a $1-million donation from Citigroup.

At approximately the same time, Weill also asked Grubman to "take a fresh look" at his neutral rating on AT&T. Shortly after being asked to review his rating, Grubman turned positive, raised his rating, and AT&T awarded Salomon an investment-banking job worth nearly $45 million.

Did Sanford Weill do anything unethical? How about Jack Grubman? What do you think?

Source: Based on D. Kadlec, "Did Sandy Play Dirty?" *Time Online Edition,* November 25, 2002.

CASE INCIDENTS

Damned If You Do; Damned If You Don't

Fran Gill has spent 15 years with the Thompson Grocery Company, starting out as a part-time cashier and rising up through the ranks of the grocery store chain.* Today, at 34, she is a regional manager, overseeing seven stores and earning nearly $110 000 a year. About five weeks ago, she was contacted by an executive-search firm inquiring about her interest in the position of vice-president and regional manager for a national drugstore chain. The position would be responsible for more than 100 stores in five provinces. After two meetings with top executives at the drugstore chain, she was notified two days ago that she was one of two finalists for the job.

The only person at Thompson who knows this news is Fran's good friend and colleague Ken Hamilton. Ken is director of finance for the grocery chain. "It's a dream job, with a lot more responsibility," Fran told Ken. "The pay is almost double what I earn here and I'd be their only female vice-president. The job would allow me to be a more visible role model for young women and give me a bigger voice in opening up doors for women and ethnic minorities in retail management."

Since Fran wanted to keep the fact that she was looking at another job secret, she asked Ken, whom she trusted completely, to be one of her references. He promised to write a great recommendation for her. Fran made it very clear to the recruiter that Ken was the only person at Thompson who knew she was considering another job. She knew that if anyone heard she was talking to another company, it might seriously jeopardize her chances for promotion. It's against this backdrop that this morning's incident became more than just a question of sexual harassment. It became a full-blown ethical and political dilemma for Fran.

Jennifer Chung has been a financial analyst in Ken's department for five months. Fran met Jennifer through Ken, and her impression of Jennifer is quite positive. In many ways, Jennifer strikes Fran as a lot like she was 10 years ago. This morning, Jennifer came into Fran's office. It was immediately evident that something was wrong. Jennifer was very nervous and uncomfortable, which was most unlike her. Jennifer said that about a month after she joined Thompson, Ken began making off-colour comments to her when they were alone. From there the behaviour escalated further. Ken would leer at her, put his arm over her shoulder when they were reviewing reports, even pat her bum. Every time one of these occurrences happened, Jennifer would ask him to stop and not do it again, but this fell on deaf ears. Yesterday, Ken reminded Jennifer that her six-month probationary review was coming up. "He told me that if I didn't sleep with him, I couldn't expect a very favourable evaluation."

Jennifer said that she had come to Fran because she didn't know what to do or to whom to turn. "I came to you, Fran, because you're a friend of Ken's and the highest-ranking woman here. Will you help me?" Fran had never heard anything like this about Ken before, but neither did she have any reason to suspect that Jennifer was lying.

Questions

1. Analyze Fran's situation in a purely legal sense.

2. Analyze Fran's dilemma in political terms.

3. Analyze Fran's situation in an ethical sense. What is the ethically right thing for her to do? Is that also the politically right thing to do?

4. If you were Fran, what would you do?

---

* The identity of this organization and the people described are disguised for obvious reasons.

▶

The Power of Bill Fowler at Blackmer/Dover Resources

Blackmer/Dover Resources' plant makes heavy-duty pumps designed to move commodities such as refined oil and chocolate. The plant employs 160 workers.

Historically, management assigned employees to operate the same machine for months or even years at a time. In this way, each worker became intimately familiar with a narrow task. Workers used their expertise to earn more money. Until 1997, about half the workers at the plant earned a premium, on top of their hourly wage, based on the number of pumps or pump parts they produced. The old system gave them a strong incentive to conceal output-enhancing tricks they had learned, even from co-workers.

Today, the plant's workers receive a straight hourly wage. To make the plant more flexible, management encourages workers to learn a variety of jobs and accept moves to different parts of the factory floor. Many of the plant's older workers, however, have not welcomed the change. One of those is Bill Fowler.

Fowler is 56 years old and has worked at the Blackmer plant for 24 years. Fowler doesn't like changing jobs, and he doesn't like telling anyone anything about what he does. "I don't want to move around," he says, "because I love my routine—it helps me get through the day."

Fowler's job is cutting metal shafts for industrial pumps. It's a precision task: A minor error could render a pump useless. And Fowler is outstanding at what he does. He is known for the accuracy of his cuts. His bosses also say he can be hours faster than anyone else in readying his giant cutting machines to shift from making one type of pump shaft to another. Management would love to incorporate Fowler's know-how into the manufacturing process, but he refuses to share his secrets even with fellow workers. "If I gave away my tricks, management could use [them] to speed things up and keep me at a flat-out pace all day long," says Fowler.

Employees like Fowler worry when they read about companies soliciting workers' expert advice in the name of making their plants more competitive, and then turning around and moving jobs to lower-wage locations abroad. Blackmer's top management, however, says they have no plans to relocate jobs or otherwise hurt workers. They merely want to pool workers' knowledge to make the plant stronger. "We've realized that to get competitive, we need to start asking these guys what they know," says Blackmer's president.

Questions

1. Explain Bill Fowler's behaviour in power terms.

2. What, if anything, does this case say about trust and power?

3. What does this case say regarding implementing knowledge-management systems?

4. What, if anything, can management do to change Fowler's behaviour?

Source: Based on T. Aeppel, "On Factory Floors, Top Workers Hide Secrets to Success," *Wall Street Journal,* July 1, 2002, p. A1.

OB *AT WORK*

From **Concepts** to **Skills**

Politicking

Forget, for a moment, the ethics of politicking and any negative impressions you may have of people who engage in organizational politics.[97] If you wanted to be more politically adept in your organization, what could you do? The following eight suggestions are likely to improve your political effectiveness.

1. *Frame arguments in terms of organizational goals.* Effective politicking requires camouflaging your self-interest. No matter that your objective is self-serving; all the arguments you marshal in support of it must be framed in terms of the benefits that the organization will gain. People whose actions appear to blatantly further their own interests at the expense of the organization's are almost universally denounced, are likely to lose influence, and often suffer the ultimate penalty of being expelled from the organization.

2. *Develop the right image.* If you know your organization's culture, you understand what the organization wants and values from its employees—in terms of dress; associates to cultivate, and those to avoid; whether to appear risk-taking or risk-aversive; the preferred leadership style; the importance placed on getting along well with others; and so forth. Then you are equipped to project the appropriate image. Because the assessment of your performance is not a fully objective process, both style and substance must be addressed.

3. *Gain control of organizational resources.* The control of organizational resources that are scarce and important is a source of power. Knowledge and expertise are particularly effective resources to control. They make you more valuable to the organization and, therefore, more likely to gain security, advancement, and a receptive audience for your ideas.

4. *Make yourself appear indispensable.* Because we are dealing with appearances rather than objective facts, you can enhance your power by appearing to be indispensable. That is, you don't have to really be indispensable as long as key people in the organization believe that you are. If the organization's prime decision makers believe there is no ready substitute for what you are giving the organization, they are likely to go to great lengths to ensure that your desires are satisfied.

5. *Be visible.* Because performance evaluation has a substantial subjective component, it's important that your manager and those in power in the organization be made aware of your contribution. If you are fortunate enough to have a job that brings your accomplishments to the attention of others, it may not be necessary to take direct measures to increase your visibility. But your job may require you to handle activities that are low in visibility, or your specific contribution may be indistinguishable because you are part of a team endeavour. In such cases—without appearing to be tooting your own horn or creating the image of a braggart—you will want to call attention to yourself by highlighting your successes in routine reports, having satisfied customers relay their appreciation to senior executives in your organization, being seen at social functions, being active in your professional associations, developing powerful allies who speak positively about your accomplishments, and similar tactics. Of course, the skilled politician actively and successfully lobbies to get those projects that will increase his or her visibility.

6. *Develop powerful allies.* It helps to have powerful people in your camp. Cultivate contacts with potentially influential people above you, at your own level, and in the lower ranks. They can provide you with important information that may not be available through normal channels. There will be times, too, when decisions will be made in favour of those with the greatest support. Having powerful allies can provide you with a coalition of support if and when you need it.

7. *Avoid "tainted" members.* In almost every organization, there are fringe members whose status is questionable. Their performance and/or loyalty is suspect. Keep your distance from such individuals. Given the reality that effectiveness has a large subjective component, your own effective-

ness might be called into question if you are perceived as being too closely associated with tainted members.

8. *Support your manager.* Your immediate future is in the hands of your current manager. Since he or she evaluates your performance, you will typically want to do whatever is necessary to have your manager on your side. You should make every effort to help your manager succeed, make her look good, support her if she is under siege, and spend the time to find out what criteria she will be using to assess your effectiveness. Do not undermine your manager, and do not speak negatively of her to others.

Assessing Skills

After you've read this chapter, take the following Self-Assessments on your enclosed CD-ROM:

35. How Power-Oriented Am I?

36. What's My Preferred Type of Power?

37. How Good Am I at Playing Politics?

38. How Well Do I Manage Impressions?

Practising Skills

You used to be the star marketing manager for Hilton Electronics Corporation. But for the past year, you have been outpaced again and again by Sean, a new manager in the design department who has been accomplishing everything expected of him and more. Meanwhile, your best efforts to do your job well have been sabotaged and undercut by Maria—your and Sean's manager. For example, before last year's international consumer electronics show, Maria moved $30 000 from your budget to Sean's. Despite your best efforts, your marketing team could not complete all the marketing materials normally developed to showcase all of your organization's new products at this important industry show. Also, Maria has chipped away at your staff and budget ever since. Although you have been able to meet most of your goals with less staff and budget, Maria has continued to slice away resources from your group. Just last week, she eliminated two positions in your team of eight marketing specialists to make room for a new designer and some extra equipment for Sean. Maria is clearly taking away your resources while giving Sean whatever he wants and more. You think it's time to do something or soon you will not have any team or resources left. What do you need to do to make sure your division has the resources to survive and grow?

Reinforcing Skills

1. Keep a one-week journal of your behaviour describing incidents when you tried to influence others around you. Assess each incident by asking: Were you successful at these attempts to influence them? Why or why not? What could you have done differently?

2. Outline a specific action plan, based on concepts in this module, that would improve your career progression in the organization in which you currently work or an organization in which you think you would like to be employed.

CHAPTER 9
Conflict and
Negotiation

The National Hockey League and the National Hockey League Players' Association needed to negotiate a new collective bargaining agreement. What difficulties led them to take so long to reach a deal?

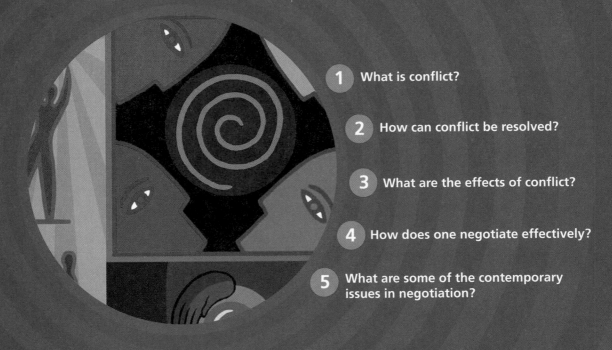

1 What is conflict?

2 How can conflict be resolved?

3 What are the effects of conflict?

4 How does one negotiate effectively?

5 What are some of the contemporary issues in negotiation?

In early February 2005, Gary Bettman, National Hockey League (NHL) commissioner, was signalling to hockey fans throughout North America that the 2004–2005 hockey season was about to be called off.[1] Hockey players had been trying to negotiate a new collective bargaining agreement with NHL management since 2003, meeting 14 times in 2003, 14 in 2004, and 9 times by early February to try to resolve their differences. Little success had been made, despite all of those meetings.

Each side blamed the other for the stalemate.

"Their [the hockey players] outright rejection of our proposal yesterday [February 9] I think speaks more to the fact that the union is never, ever, ever, ever—under any circumstances—prepared to play under any kind of cost-certain, economic partnership, salary cap—you pick the term—type of system," said Bill Daly, executive vice-president and chief legal officer of the NHL.

Hockey players saw the issue somewhat differently. "They [management] have made it clear they have only one way of doing things, and that's through their hard-

cap system," claimed National Hockey League Players' Association (NHLPA) senior director Ted Saskin.

The NHL and the NHLPA were locked in a conflict that led them to cancel an entire hockey season. In this chapter, we look at sources of conflict and strategies for resolving conflict, including negotiation.

CONFLICT DEFINED

Several common themes underlie most definitions of conflict.[2] Conflict must be *perceived* by the parties to it; if no one is aware of a conflict, then it is generally agreed that no conflict exists. Conflict also involves opposition or incompatibility, and some form of interaction between the parties.[3] These factors set the conditions that determine the beginning point of the conflict process. We can define **conflict**, then, as a process that begins when one party perceives that another party has negatively affected, or is about to negatively affect, something that the first party cares about.[4]

This definition is deliberately broad. It describes that point in any ongoing activity when an interaction "crosses over" to become an interparty conflict. It encompasses the wide range of conflicts that people experience in groups and organizations—incompatibility of goals, differences over interpretations of facts, disagreements based on behavioural expectations, and the like. Finally, our definition is flexible enough to cover the full range of conflict levels—from subtle forms of disagreement to overt and violent acts. Conflict has positive sides and negative sides, which we will discuss further when we cover functional and dysfunctional conflict. For more on this debate, refer to the *Point/Counterpoint* discussion on page 337.

Functional vs. Dysfunctional Conflict

Not all conflict is bad. Some conflicts support the goals of the group and improve its performance; these are **functional**, or constructive, forms of conflict. But there are

1 What is conflict?

conflict A process that begins when one party perceives that another party has negatively affected, or is about to negatively affect, something that the first party cares about.

National Hockey League www.nhl.com

National Hockey League Players' Association www.nhlpa.com

functional conflict Conflict that supports the goals of the group and improves its performance.

315

dysfunctional conflict Conflict that hinders group performance.

Buggy Wars

cognitive conflict Conflict that is task-oriented and related to differences in perspectives and judgments.

affective conflict Conflict that is emotional and aimed at a person rather than an issue.

Is conflict always bad?

conflicts that hinder group performance; these are **dysfunctional**, or destructive, forms of conflict. The criterion that differentiates functional from dysfunctional conflict is group performance. If a group is unable to achieve its goals because of conflict, then the conflict is dysfunctional.

Exhibit 9-1 provides a way of visualizing conflict behaviour. All conflicts exist somewhere along this continuum. At the lower part of the continuum, we have conflicts characterized by subtle, indirect, and highly controlled forms of tension. An illustration might be a student politely objecting to a point the instructor has just made in class. Conflict intensities escalate as they move upward along the continuum, until they become highly destructive. Strikes and lockouts, riots, and wars clearly fall in this upper range. For the most part, you should assume that conflicts that reach the upper ranges of the continuum are almost always dysfunctional. Functional conflicts are typically confined to the lower range of the continuum. This chapter's *CBC Video Case* explores the conflict that arises when two neighbours go into business together and then become bitter business rivals.

 RESEARCH FINDINGS

Research on conflict has yet to clearly identify those situations where conflict is more likely to be constructive than destructive. However, there is growing evidence that the source of the conflict is a significant factor determining functionality.[5] **Cognitive conflict**, which is task-oriented and occurs because of differences in perspectives and judgments, can often result in identifying potential solutions to problems. Thus it would be regarded as functional conflict. **Affective conflict**, which is emotional and aimed at a person rather than an issue, tends to be dysfunctional conflict.

One study of 53 teams found that cognitive conflict, because it generates more alternatives, led to better decisions, more acceptance of the decisions, and ownership of the decisions. Teams experiencing affective conflict, where members had personality incompatibilities and disputes, had poorer decisions and lower levels of acceptance of the decisions.[6]

Because conflict can involve our emotions in a variety of ways, it can also lead to stress. You may want to refer to the *OB on the Edge—Stress at Work* on pages 110–117 to get some ideas on how to manage the stress that might arise from conflicts you experience.

Sources of Conflict

There are a number of conditions that can give rise to conflict. They *need not* lead directly to conflict, but at least one of these conditions is necessary if conflict is to surface. For simplicity's sake, these conditions (which also may be looked at as causes or sources of conflict) have been condensed into three general categories: communication, structure, and personal variables.[7]

Communication

As we saw in Chapter 7, communication can be a source of conflict through semantic difficulties, misunderstandings, and "noise" in the communication channels.

Research has demonstrated a surprising finding: The potential for conflict increases when either too little or too much communication takes place. Apparently, an increase in communication is functional up to a point, whereupon it is possible to overcommunicate, with a resultant increase in the potential for conflict. Furthermore, the channel chosen for communicating can have an influence on stimulating opposition. Poor communication is certainly not the source of all conflicts, however.

Structure

Conflicts between two people can be structural in nature; that is, they can be the consequence of the requirements of the job or the workplace more than personality. For instance, it is not uncommon for the sales department to be in conflict with the production department, if sales perceives that products will be delivered late to customers. The term *structure* in this context includes variables such as size of the group, degree of specialization in the tasks assigned to group members, composition of the group, jurisdictional clarity, reward systems, leadership style, goal compatibility, and the degree of dependence between groups.

A review of structural variables that can lead to conflict in the workplace suggests the following:

- *Size, specialization, and composition* of the group act as forces to stimulate conflict. The larger the group and the more specialized its activities, the greater the likelihood of conflict. The potential for conflict tends to be greatest where group members are younger and where turnover is high.

- *The greater the ambiguity* in precisely defining where responsibility for actions lies, the greater the potential for conflict to emerge. Such jurisdictional ambiguities increase intergroup fighting for control of resources and territory.

- *Reward systems* create conflict when one member's gain is at another's expense. Similarly, the performance evaluation process can create conflict when individuals feel that they are unfairly evaluated, or when managers and employees have differing ideas about the employees' job responsibilities.

- *Leadership style* can create conflict if managers tightly control and oversee the work of employees, allowing employees little discretion in how they carry out tasks.

- *The diversity of goals* among groups is a major source of conflict. When groups within an organization seek diverse ends, some of which are inherently at odds—such as when the sales team promises products that the development team has not yet finalized—opportunities for conflict increase.

- *If one group is dependent on another* (in contrast to the two being mutually independent), or if interdependence allows one group to gain at another's expense, opposing forces are stimulated.

Focus on Diversity illustrates how York University's goal of having all exams marked in the same time period conflicted with the religious needs of some students. Rather than address the different religious needs of students, the university chose to treat everyone equally.

EXHIBIT 9-1	**Conflict Intensity Continuum**

Annihilatory conflict — Overt efforts to destroy the other party

Aggressive physical attacks

Threats and ultimatums

Assertive verbal attacks

Overt questioning or challenging of others

Minor disagreements or misunderstandings

No conflict

Sources: Based on S. P. Robbins, *Managing Organizational Conflict: A Nontraditional Approach* (Upper Saddle River, NJ: Prentice Hall, 1974), pp. 93–97; and F. Glasl, "The Process of Conflict Escalation and the Roles of Third Parties," in *Conflict Management and Industrial Relations,* ed. G. B. J. Bomers and R. Peterson (Boston: Kluwer-Nijhoff, 1982), pp. 119–140.

FOCUS ON **DIVERSITY**

Exam-Taking Students Faced With Sabbath Dilemma

Should students be accommodated, or should they have to ask for accommodation? Sabbath-observant Jewish students at York University had a choice to make during the final exam period of spring 2002.[8] They could take exams that were scheduled on the Sabbath, something they would not ordinarily expect to do, or ask for special arrangements to take their exams on another day.

The University of Toronto, McGill University, and York University, which all have significant Jewish faculty and student populations, had not previously scheduled exams on Saturdays. Administrators at York University decided that they could no longer follow this practice, and scheduled final exams for two Saturdays.

York's student population had been growing faster than the capacity of the existing space, which was one reason for scheduling exams on Saturdays, according to Deborah Hobson, York's vice-president of enrolment and student services. More professors were also giving exams rather than term papers to prevent the use of Internet-purchased papers.

Hobson noted that no special accommodation had been made for Christian or Muslim students regarding exam scheduling. Instead, groups had to ask for accommodation if religious constraints caused a conflict. "In scheduling exams on the Jewish Sabbath, it was felt that all religions would be treated fairly," Hobson said.

The Sabbath does present limitations on exam writing that most other religions do not, but Hobson felt that providing alternative arrangements upon the request of students would pose little difficulty.

Professor Martin Lockshin, director of the Centre for Jewish Studies at York University, worried that Jewish students might not want to ask for special accommodation. Some students fear that asking professors for makeup exams not only burdens professors, but could also harm the students. It means extra work for professors, and the concern is that students' marks might be affected. The students' concerns in this matter reflect power issues that we discussed in Chapter 8. Students recognize that there is a power imbalance in their relationship with professors, which makes them reluctant to ask for special exam accommodation.

Some faculty members also wondered whether "the way to demonstrate tolerance to . . . various multicultural communities is by not giving religious accommodation to anyone." 👤

Centre for Jewish Studies at
York University
www.yorku.ca/cjs/

Personal Variables

Have you ever met people to whom you take an immediate dislike? You disagree with most of their opinions. The sound of their voice, their smirk when they smile, and their personality annoy you. We have all met people like that. When you have to work with such individuals, there is often the potential for conflict.

Our last category of potential sources of conflict is personal variables. These variables include the individual value system that each person has, and the personality characteristics that account for individual idiosyncrasies and differences.

The evidence indicates that certain personality types—for example, individuals who are highly authoritarian and dogmatic, and who demonstrate low self-esteem—lead to potential conflict. Most important, and probably the most overlooked variable in the study of social conflict, is differing value systems. For example, value differences are the best explanation of such diverse issues as prejudice, disagreements over an individual's contribution to the group and the rewards the individual deserves, and assessments of whether this particular textbook is any good. That an employee thinks he is worth $60 000 a year but his manager believes him to be worth $55 000 are value judgments. Differences in value systems are important sources for creating the potential for conflict.

CONFLICT RESOLUTION

When the 2004–2005 hockey season was cancelled on February 16, 2005, the NHL and the NHLPA were quick to suggest that the other side was to blame for the conflict not being resolved.[9] Dave Elenbaas, who was once a backup goaltender with the Montreal Canadiens and now works for

Toronto-based law firm McMillan Binch as a labour relations expert, summarized the two positions: "So [Bob] Goodenow [NHLPA executive director] would certainly say that the league never really wanted to bargain in good faith, that the [players] made all the moves, and therefore we just couldn't make a deal. And [Gary] Bettman [NHL commissioner] would say that we made it clear from the get-go what we needed to get and until you came to there, there was nothing for us to talk about."

The NHL and NHLPA were unable to resolve their conflict because each party was more interested in maintaining its own position, rather than searching for a way to reach a compromise. What are other ways that the NHL and the NHLPA might have tried to resolve their conflict?

Conflict in the workplace can affect the effectiveness of individuals, teams, and the entire organization.[10] One study found 20 percent of managers' time is spent managing conflict.[11]

Once conflict arises, what can be done to resolve it? The way a conflict is defined goes a long way toward establishing the sort of outcomes that might settle it. For instance, if I define our salary disagreement as a zero-sum or *win-lose situation*—that is, if you get the increase in pay you want, there will be just that amount less for me—I am going to be far less willing to look for mutual solutions than if I frame the conflict as a potential *win-win situation.* So individual attitudes toward a conflict are important, because attitudes typically define the set of possible settlements.

2 How can conflict be resolved?

Conflict Management Strategies

A common way that conflict researchers summarize conflict management strategies is based on dual concern theory.[12] Using two dimensions—*cooperativeness* (the degree to which one party attempts to satisfy the other party's concerns) and *assertiveness* (the degree to which one party attempts to satisfy his or her own concerns)—five conflict-handling strategies can be identified:[13]

- *Forcing.* Imposing one's will on the other party.

- *Problem solving.* Trying to reach an agreement that satisfies both one's own and the other party's aspirations as much as possible.

- *Avoiding.* Ignoring or minimizing the importance of the issues creating the conflict.

- *Yielding.* Accepting and incorporating the will of the other party.

- *Compromising.* Balancing concern for oneself with concern for the other party in order to reach a solution.

Forcing is a win-lose solution, as is yielding, while problem solving seeks a win-win solution. Avoiding conflict and pretending it doesn't exist, and compromising, so that neither person gets what they want, can yield lose-lose solutions. Exhibit 9-2 on page 320 illustrates these five strategies, along with specific actions that one might take when using them.

Choosing a particular strategy for resolving conflict depends on a variety of factors. Research shows that while people may choose among the strategies, they have an underlying disposition to handle conflicts in

Positive emotions played a key role in shaping perceptions when a new member joined the world-famous Tokyo String Quartet. The chemistry among the original members, all Japanese musicians, was incredibly strong, as they had practised and performed together for decades. When one of the original artists left the group, the remaining members—Kazukide Isomura, Sadao Harada, and Kikuei Ikeda—asked Canadian violinist Peter Oundjian to take his place. With an outsider's perspective, Oundjian began questioning everything the ensemble did, from musical selections to tour destinations. Rather than perceiving the new violinist's ideas in a negative way, the other members framed the conflict as a potential win-win situation. They took a positive approach, viewing the situation as an opportunity to make the group more creative and innovative.

EXHIBIT 9-2   Conflict-Handling Strategies and Accompanying Behaviours

Sources: Based on K. W. Thomas, "Conflict and Negotiation Processes in Organizations," in *Handbook of Industrial and Organizational Psychology,* vol. 3, 2nd ed., ed. M. D. Dunnette and L. M. Hough (Palo Alto, CA: Consulting Psychologists Press, 1992), p. 668; C. K. W. De Dreu, A. Evers, B. Beersma, E. S. Kluwer, and A. Nauta, "A Theory-Based Measure of Conflict Management Strategies in the Workplace," *Journal of Organizational Behavior* 22, no. 6 (September 2001), pp. 645–668; and D. G. Pruitt and J. Rubin, *Social Conflict: Escalation, Stalemate and Settlement* (New York: Random House, 1986).

certain ways.[14] In addition, some situations call for particular strategies. For instance, when a small child insists on trying to run into the street, a parent may need a forcing strategy to restrain the child. Co-workers who are having a conflict over setting deadlines to complete a project on time may decide that problem solving is the best strategy to use.

This chapter's *Learning About Yourself Exercise* on page 339 gives you the opportunity to discover your preferred conflict-handling strategy. *OB in Action—Choosing Strategies to Deal With Conflicts* indicates the situations in which each strategy is best used.

The disagreement between the City of Vancouver and developer Peter Wall produced a compromise that could be called a lose-lose solution, as the following *OB in the Street* shows.

OB IN THE STREET

One Wall Centre Goes Two-Toned

Is compromise necessarily the best way to go? When developer Peter Wall hired architect Peter Busby to design One Wall Centre in downtown Vancouver, the two planned a massive glass skyscraper.[15] City council reviewed the plans and okayed the design, even granting a building height considerably higher than those in the surrounding neighbourhood.

The plans made the building look translucent, but as the tower went up, the glass looked black and impenetrable. Complaints started coming in to City Hall, because the assumption had been that the building would use clear glass. The architect said that Wall had changed his mind about the colour of the glass once construction started. Wall claimed, however, that the city had approved the darker glass sample in use. Unfortunately, no one could find the glass samples.

A planned lawsuit by the city was stopped for lack of evidence. So the two sides reached a compromise: The 48-storey building would have its lower levels in blackened glass, and the top 17 floors in lighter glass, rather than tearing down the building and starting over. Neither the city nor the developer obtained their preferred solution, and meanwhile, residents of Vancouver will have the two-toned building, a visible reminder of the outcome of compromise, towering over them for many years to come. ⚐

What Can Individuals Do to Manage Conflict?

There are a number of conflict resolution techniques that individuals can use to try to defuse conflict inside and outside of the workplace. These include the following:[16]

- *Problem solving.* Requesting a face-to-face meeting to identify the problem and resolve it through open discussion.

- *Developing superordinate goals.* Creating a shared goal that requires both parties to work together, and motivates them to do so.

- *Smoothing.* Playing down differences while emphasizing common interests with the other party.

- *Compromising.* Agreeing with the other party that each will give up something of value to reach an accord.

- *Avoidance.* Withdrawing from, or suppressing, the conflict.

The choice of technique may depend on how serious the issue is to you, whether you take a win-win or a win-lose approach, and your preferred conflict management style.

When the conflict is specifically work-related, there are additional techniques that might be used:

- *Expansion of resources.* The scarcity of a resource—say, money, promotion opportunities, office space—can create conflict. Expansion of the resource can create a win-win solution.

OB IN ACTION
Choosing Strategies to Deal With Conflicts

Forcing
- → In emergencies
- → On important but unpopular issues
- → On vital issues when you know you're right
- → Against people who take advantage of noncompetitive behaviour

Problem solving
- → If both sets of concerns are too important to be compromised
- → To merge different perspectives
- → To gain commitment through a consensus
- → To mend a relationship

Avoiding
- → When an issue is trivial
- → When your concerns won't be met
- → When potential disruption outweighs the benefits of resolution
- → To let people cool down and regain perspective

Yielding
- → When you find you're wrong
- → To show your reasonableness
- → When issues are more important to others than yourself
- → To build social credits for later issues
- → When harmony and stability are especially important

Compromising
- → When goals are important but not worth more assertive approaches
- → When opponents are committed to mutually exclusive goals
- → To achieve temporary settlements to complex issues
- → To arrive at expedient solutions under time pressure

Sources: Based on K. W. Thomas, "Toward Multidimensional Values in Teaching: The Example of Conflict Behaviors," *Academy of Management Review,* July 1977, p. 487; and C. K. W. De Dreu, A. Evers, B. Beersma, E. S. Kluwer, and A. Nauta, "A Theory-Based Measure of Conflict Management Strategies in the Workplace," *Journal of Organizational Behavior* 22, no. 6 (September 2001), pp. 645–668.

- *Authoritative command.* Management can use its formal authority to resolve the conflict and then communicate its desires to the parties involved.

- *Altering the human variable.* Behavioural change techniques such as human relations training can alter attitudes and behaviours that cause conflict.

- *Altering the structural variables.* The formal organization structure and the inter-action patterns of conflicting parties can be changed through job redesign, transfers, creation of coordinating positions, and the like.

Resolving Personality Conflicts

Personality conflicts are an everyday occurrence in the workplace. While there is no available data for Canada, supervisors in the United States spend about 18 percent of their time handling personality conflicts among employees.[17] A variety of factors lead to per-sonality conflicts, including the following:[18]

- Misunderstandings based on age, race, or cultural differences

- Intolerance, prejudice, discrimination, or bigotry

- Perceived inequities

- Misunderstandings, rumours, or falsehoods about an individual or group

- Blaming for mistakes or mishaps (finger-pointing)

Personality conflicts can result in lowered productivity when people find it difficult to work together. The individuals experiencing the conflict may seek sympathy from other members of the work group, causing co-workers to take sides. The ideal solution would be for the two people having a conflict to work it out between themselves, with-out involving others, but this does not always happen. *OB in Action—Handling Personality Conflicts* suggests ways of dealing with personality conflicts in the workplace.

Resolving Intercultural Conflicts

While personality conflicts may be stimulated by cultural differences, it's important to consider intercultural conflicts as a separate form of conflict. Not only is Canada a mul-ticultural society, but also its organizations are increasingly interacting in a global envi-ronment, setting up alliances and joint ventures with partners from other parts of the world. Greater contact with people from other cultures can lead to greater understand-ing, but it can also lead to misunderstanding when individuals ignore the different per-spectives that might result from cultural differences.

In Chapter 7, we discussed the idea that people from high- and low-context cultures have different expectations about how to interact with one another. In high-context cultures, communication is based on nonverbal and subtle situational cues. Status and one's place in society are also very important. Low-context cultures, such as those in North America, rely more on words and less on subtle situational cues. In low-context cultures, there is also less formality when communicating with people of different sta-tus. As a result of these differences, people from one cultural context may misinterpret the actions of those from another, which could produce conflict.

 RESEARCH FINDINGS

Across cultures, people have different ideas about the appropriateness and effects of conflict. For instance, Mexicans expect conflict to be kept private, while Americans expect conflict to be dealt with directly and openly.[19] We suggest in Exhibit 9-3 that there is an optimal level of conflict in the workplace to maximize productivity, but this is decidedly a North American viewpoint. Many Asian cultures believe that conflict almost always has a negative effect on the work unit.[20]

Collectivist cultures value harmony among members more than individualistic cultures do. Consistent with this, research shows that those from Asian cultures show a preference for conflict avoidance, compared with Americans and Britons.[21] Research also shows that Chinese and East Asian managers prefer compromising as a strategy,[22] even though from a North American perspective, this might be viewed as suboptimal. Compromise may be viewed as a way of saving face, so that each party gets to preserve pride and dignity.[23]

Studies show that North Americans prefer a problem-solving approach to conflicts, because this presents both parties with a win-win solution.[24] Win-win solutions are less likely to be achieved in Asian cultures, however. East Asian managers tend to ignore conflict rather than make it public,[25] and more often than not, Japanese managers tend to choose nonconfrontational styles.[26] These preferences make it difficult to negotiate a win-win solution. In general, Westerners are more comfortable with competition, which may explain why research finds that Westerners are more likely to choose forcing as a strategy than Asians.[27]

Taken together, these research findings suggest the importance of being aware of cultural preferences with respect to conflict. Using one's own culture's conflict resolution strategies may result in even greater conflict.[28] Some individuals and some cultures prefer harmonious relations over asserting themselves, and may not react well to the confrontational dynamics more common among North Americans. Similarly, North Americans expect that negotiations may lead to a legal contract, whereas Asian cultures rely less on legal contracts and more on relational contracts.

OB ACTION

Handling Personality Conflicts

Tips for employees having a personality conflict

→ **Communicate directly** with the other person to resolve the perceived conflict (emphasize problem solving and common objectives, not personalities).

→ **Avoid dragging** co-workers into the conflict.

→ If dysfunctional conflict persists, **seek help** from direct supervisors or human resource specialists.

Tips for third-party observers of a personality conflict

→ **Do not take sides** in someone else's personality conflict.

→ **Suggest the parties work things out** themselves in a constructive and positive way.

→ If dysfunctional conflict persists, **refer the problem to parties' direct supervisors**.

Tips for managers whose employees are having a personality conflict

→ **Investigate and document** conflict.

→ If appropriate, **take corrective action** (e.g., feedback or behaviour shaping).

→ If necessary, **attempt informal dispute resolution**.

→ **Refer difficult conflicts** to human resource specialists or hired counsellors for formal resolution attempts and other interventions.

Source: R. Kreitner and A. Kinicki, *Organizational Behavior,* 6th ed. (New York: McGraw-Hill, 2004), p. 492, Table 14-1. Reprinted by permission of McGraw Hill Education.

EXHIBIT 9-3   Conflict and Unit Performance

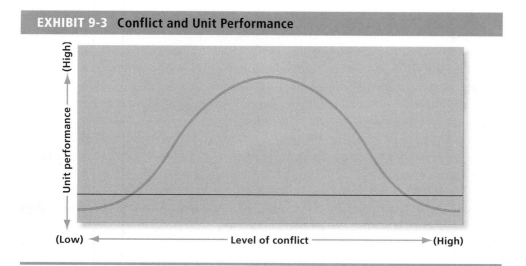

Third-Party Conflict Resolution

Can someone else be asked to help resolve a conflict?

Occasionally, individuals or group representatives reach a stalemate and are unable to resolve their differences. In such cases, they may turn to alternative dispute resolution (ADR), where a third party helps both sides find a solution outside a courtroom. Toronto-based labour lawyers Bernard Morrow and Lauren M. Bernardi note that ADR "uses faster, more user-friendly methods of dispute resolution, instead of traditional, adversarial approaches (such as unilateral decision making or litigation."[29] ADR encompasses a variety of strategies, from more simple to more complex, including facilitation, conciliation, an ombudsperson, peer review, mediation, and arbitration[30]

Facilitation

A facilitator, generally acquainted with both parties, suggests that the two parties work together to resolve the issue. This is an informal solution that is aimed at getting both parties to talk directly with each other.

Conciliation

conciliator A trusted third party who provides an informal communication link between the negotiator and the opponent.

A **conciliator** is a trusted third party who provides an informal communication link between the negotiator and the opponent. Conciliation is used extensively in international, labour, family, and community disputes. In practice, conciliators typically act as more than mere communication conduits. They also engage in fact-finding, interpreting messages, and persuading disputants to develop agreements.

The first step in trying to resolve a labour relations dispute can be to bring in a conciliation officer when agreement cannot be reached. This may be a good faith effort to resolve the dispute. Sometimes, however, it is used so that the union can reach a legal strike position or management can engage in a lockout. Once the conciliation officer determines that the dispute cannot be resolved through conciliation, the clock starts ticking toward the strike or lockout deadline (14 days). A mediator can be called in at this point to use more power to solve the dispute.

Mediators are not always the answer to conflict resolution, however. Two mediators were appointed by the US Federal Mediation and Conciliation Service to help in the hockey dispute. However, they were unable to bring the two sides to an agreement. After meeting a number of times with both parties, "They didn't see how they could assist the process in reaching a resolution," NHL vice-president Bill Daly said.[31]

Ombudsperson

Organizations sometimes create an official role for a person to hear disputes between parties. An ombudsperson is impartial, widely respected, and trusted. He or she investigates the issue confidentially and tries to arrange a solution. The advantage to having an ombudsperson involved in a dispute is that the parties can avoid going through formal organizational channels for a resolution. Going through formal organizational channels can escalate the differences between the parties, leading to greater conflict. The ombudsperson thus acts as a way to resolve differences between two parties in the organization before formal procedures, which might have an impact on one's employment, are initiated.

Peer Review

A panel of peers is put together to hear both sides of the issue from the parties involved and to recommend a solution. The panel is expected to be objective in listening to the issues and in making a recommendation. The peer review panel's decision may or may not be binding on the parties, depending upon what was agreed to at the outset.

Mediation

A **mediator** is a neutral third party who facilitates a negotiated solution by using reasoning and persuasion, suggesting alternatives, and the like. Mediators can be much more aggressive in proposing solutions than conciliators. Mediators are widely used in labour-management negotiations and in civil-court disputes. In Vancouver, where there has been a "leaky condo crisis" in recent years, owners and builders can insist upon mediation with the aid of an independent mediator. British Columbia's Motor Vehicle Branch uses mediation to help settle accident claims. In Ontario, all disputes between companies and employees now go to mediation within 100 days. Pilot projects found that more than 60 percent of the disputes were partly or fully resolved within 60 days after the start of the mediation session.[32]

Mediation can also be used directly in the workplace. At Aurora, Ontario-based Magna International, some employees volunteer to be trained in dispute mediation, and are then selected for a "fairness" committee. Grievances are handled by the "fairness" committee, and decisions are generally accepted by management. Decisions have included asking management to remove a written warning from an employee's file, even though the employee had caused considerable damage while operating a lift truck.[33]

The overall effectiveness of mediated negotiations is fairly impressive. The settlement rate is approximately 60 percent, with satisfaction with the mediator at about 75 percent. But the situation is the key to whether mediation will succeed; the conflicting parties must be motivated to bargain and resolve their conflict. Additionally, conflict intensity cannot be too high; mediation is most effective under moderate levels of conflict. Finally, perceptions of the mediator are important; to be effective, the mediator must be perceived as neutral and noncoercive.

Arbitration

An **arbitrator** is a third party with the authority to dictate an agreement. Arbitration can be voluntary (requested) or compulsory (forced on the parties by law or contract).

The authority of the arbitrator varies according to the rules set by the negotiators. For instance, the arbitrator might be limited to choosing one of the negotiating parties' last offers or to suggesting an agreement point that is nonbinding. Or the arbitrator might be free to choose and make any judgment that he or she wishes.

The big advantage of arbitration over mediation is that it always results in a settlement. Whether or not there is a negative side depends on how "heavy-handed" the arbitrator appears. If one party is left feeling overwhelmingly defeated, that party is certain to be dissatisfied and unlikely to accept the arbitrator's decision graciously. Therefore, the conflict may resurface at a later time.

CONFLICT OUTCOMES

The NHL owners and the NHL players settled their differences in July 2005. However, the 2004–2005 season's 1230 regular-season games were cancelled, and there was no Stanley Cup champion for the first time since 1919, when the final between Montreal and Seattle was cancelled because of a flu epidemic.

In the end, the players agreed to a salary cap, something they had said they absolutely would not do throughout most of the negotiations. Many were angry at NHLPA executive director Bob Goodenow for giving in on the salary cap at the end, after insisting throughout the negotiations that this was a nonnegotiable issue. The players also directed some bad feelings toward the NHL owners. Meanwhile, both the owners and the players wondered what reaction the fans would have when hockey began again after a year's absence. While the hockey conflict appeared to have a number of negative consequences, is it possible for conflict to have positive outcomes?

mediator A neutral third party who facilitates a negotiated solution by using reasoning, persuasion, and suggestions for alternatives.

Magna International
www.magnaint.com

arbitrator A third party to a negotiation who has the authority to dictate an agreement.

What are the effects of conflict?

As Exhibit 9-3 on page 323 demonstrates, conflict can be functional and improve group performance, or it can be dysfunctional and hinder group performance. As well, we see there is an optimal level of conflict that results in the highest level of unit performance.

Conflict is constructive when it improves the quality of decisions, stimulates creativity and innovation, encourages interest and curiosity among group members, provides the medium through which problems can be aired and tensions released, and fosters an environment of self-evaluation and change. The evidence suggests that conflict can improve the quality of decision making by allowing all points, particularly the ones that are unusual or held by a minority, to be weighed in important decisions.[34] Conflict can prevent groupthink (discussed in Chapter 12). It doesn't allow the group passively to "rubber-stamp" decisions that may be based on weak assumptions, inadequate consideration of relevant alternatives, or other problems. Conflict challenges the status quo and therefore supports the creation of new ideas, promotes reassessment of group goals and activities, and increases the probability that the group will respond to change.

Dean Tjosvold of Simon Fraser University suggests three desired outcomes for conflict:[35]

- *Agreement.* Equitable and fair agreements are the best outcome. If agreement means that one party feels exploited or defeated, this will likely lead to further conflict later.

- *Stronger relationships.* When conflict is resolved positively, this can lead to better relationships and greater trust. If the parties trust each other, they are more likely to keep the agreements they make.

- *Learning.* Handling conflict successfully teaches one how to do it better next time. It gives an opportunity to practise the skills one has learned about handling conflict.

Unfortunately, not all conflict results in positive outcomes. There is a substantial body of literature to document how dysfunctional conflict can reduce group effectiveness.[36] Among the more undesirable outcomes are stopping communication, reducing group cohesiveness, and subordinating group goals due to infighting between members. At the extreme, conflict can bring group functioning to a halt and potentially threaten the group's survival. Below we examine what research tells us about the effects of conflict. *Case Incident—Managing Conflict at Schneider National* on page 343 describes how functional conflict improves an organization.

 RESEARCH FINDINGS

Research studies in diverse settings confirm that conflict can be functional and improve productivity. For instance, studies demonstrate that groups composed of members with different interests tend to produce higher quality solutions to a variety of problems than do homogeneous groups.[37] One study found that high-conflict groups improved their decision-making ability 73 percent more than groups characterized by low-conflict conditions.[38] An investigation of 22 teams of systems analysts found that the more incompatible teams were likely to be more productive.[39] Research and development scientists have been found to be most productive when a certain amount of intellectual conflict exists.[40] These findings suggest that conflict within a group can lead to strength rather than weakness.

You might want to review *Case Incident—Not Your Dream Team* on page 342 to help you determine situations where conflict needs to be reduced or increased.

NEGOTIATION

When the NHL collective bargaining agreement expired in September 2004, owners and players both had decisions to make regarding how they would negotiate a new collective agreement. Gary Bettman, the NHL commissioner, announced that there would be a lockout, with no more hockey games until owners and players negotiated a new agreement.

Both owners and players quickly became committed to their positions in the negotiations: The owners were determined to get an agreement that included a salary cap, and the players were just as determined that they would never agree to a salary cap. Because of those positions, it was very difficult to get negotiators from either party to make much progress during talks.

Both owners and players might have been better off focusing on their interests, rather than their positions. Hockey players want to make as much money as possible. Owners want to make as much profit as possible. So both sides had to figure out a way to share the revenue arising from the game. Because each side focused on the salary cap, neither side seriously considered other alternatives that might have achieved a similar goal: maintaining costs for the owners while paying good salaries to the players. It took almost 10 months for the two sides to reach a new collective agreement, and during that time, the entire 2004–2005 hockey season was lost. In the end, the players agreed to a salary cap, the one issue that they had been firm about not doing during much of the negotiation.

The hockey negotiations could be considered a win-lose situation: One side wins (the owners got the salary cap they wanted), and one side loses (the players have to live with a salary cap). Are there other ways to negotiate so that both sides can win?

Earlier in the chapter, we reviewed a number of conflict resolution strategies. One well-developed strategy is to negotiate a resolution. Negotiation permeates the interactions of almost everyone in groups and organizations: Labour bargains with management; managers negotiate with employees, peers, and senior management; salespeople negotiate with customers; purchasing agents negotiate with suppliers; employees agree to answer a colleague's phone for a few minutes in exchange for some past or future benefit. In today's team-based organizations, negotiation skills become critical for teams to work together effectively.

We define **negotiation** as a process in which two or more parties who offer goods or services try to agree upon the exchange rate for them.[41] Note that we use the terms *negotiation* and *bargaining* interchangeably.

Within a negotiation, be aware that individuals have issues, positions, and interests. *Issues* are items that are specifically placed on the bargaining table for discussion. *Positions* are the individual's stand on the issue. For instance, salary may be an issue for discussion. The salary you hope to receive is your position. Finally, *interests* are the underlying concerns that are affected by the negotiation resolution. For instance, the reason that you might want a six-figure salary is that you are trying to buy a house in Vancouver, and that is your only hope of being able to make mortgage payments.

Negotiators who recognize the underlying interests of themselves and the other party may have more flexibility in achieving a resolution. For instance, in the example just given, an employer who offers you a mortgage at a lower rate than the bank does, or who provides you with an interest-free loan that can be used against the mortgage, may be able to address your underlying interests, without actually meeting your salary position. You may be satisfied with this alternative, if you understand what your interest is.

4 How does one negotiate effectively?

negotiation A process in which two or more parties exchange goods or services and try to agree upon the exchange rate for them.

Negotiation skills are critical in the buyer-seller relationship. At this open-air cheese market in Alkmaar, Netherlands, two purchasing agents for food buyers taste a sample of Edam cheese before they negotiate prices with the seller of the cheese.

NorskeCanada
www.norskecanada.com

Interest-based bargaining enabled Vancouver-based NorskeCanada to sign a mutually beneficial five-year contract with the Communications, Energy and Paperworkers Union of Canada in fall 2002, after just nine days of negotiations.[42] While the union and NorskeCanada had experienced bitter conflict in previous negotiations, in this particular situation both sides agreed to focus more on the interests of the parties, rather than on demands and concessions. Both sides were pleased with the outcome. We discuss this settlement further in *HR Implications* on page 338. In the case of the hockey negotiations, neither side engaged in interest-based bargaining. Instead, each side tried to win its position on the salary cap. Even when the players finally agreed to consider a cap, the owners were only willing to consider the cap they wanted, not the cap the players suggested.

Below we discuss bargaining strategies and how to negotiate.

Bargaining Strategies

There are two general approaches to negotiation—*distributive bargaining* and *integrative bargaining*.[43] These are compared in Exhibit 9-4.

Distributive Bargaining

distributive bargaining
Negotiation that seeks to divide up a fixed amount of resources; a win-lose solution

Should you try to win at any cost when you bargain?

Distributive bargaining is a negotiating strategy that operates under zero-sum conditions. That is, any gain I make is at your expense, and vice versa. Probably the most widely cited example of distributive bargaining is labour-management negotiations over wages. Typically, labour representatives come to the bargaining table determined to get as much money as possible out of management. Since every cent more that labour negotiates increases management's costs, each party bargains aggressively and treats the other as an opponent who must be defeated.

When engaged in distributive bargaining, a party focuses on trying to get the opponent to agree to a specific target point, or to get as close to it as possible. Examples of such tactics are persuading your opponent of the impossibility of reaching his or her target point and the advisability of accepting a settlement near yours; arguing that your target is fair, while your opponent's isn't; and attempting to get your opponent to feel emotionally generous toward you and thus accept an outcome close to your target point.

Integrative Bargaining

integrative bargaining
Negotiation that seeks one or more settlements that can create a win-win solution.

In contrast to distributive bargaining, **integrative bargaining** operates under the assumption that there exists one or more settlements that can create a win-win solution. In terms of intraorganizational behaviour, all things being equal, integrative bargaining

EXHIBIT 9-4   Distributive vs. Integrative Bargaining

Bargaining Characteristic	Distributive Bargaining	Integrative Bargaining
Available resources	Fixed amount of resources to be divided	Variable amount of resources to be divided
Primary motivations	I win, you lose	I win, you win
Primary interests	Opposed to each other	Convergent or congruent with each other
Focus of relationships	Short-term	Long-term

Source: Based on R. J. Lewicki and J. A. Litterer, *Negotiation* (Homewood, IL: Irwin, 1985), p. 280.

is preferable to distributive bargaining. Why? Because the former builds long-term relationships and makes working together in the future easier. It bonds negotiators and allows both sides to leave the bargaining table feeling that they have achieved a victory. For instance, in union-management negotiations, both sides might sit down to figure out other ways to reduce costs within an organization, so that it is possible to have greater wage increases. Distributive bargaining, on the other hand, leaves one party a loser. It tends to build animosities and deepen divisions when people must work together on an ongoing basis.

For examples of effective approaches to conflict resolution through negotiation in Canadian businesses, see this chapter's *HR Implications* on page 338.

How to Negotiate

Exhibit 9-5 provides a simplified model of the negotiation process. It views negotiation as made up of five steps: (1) developing a strategy; (2) defining ground rules; (3) clarification and justification; (4) bargaining and problem solving; and (5) closure and implementation.

Developing a Strategy

Before you start negotiating, you need to do your homework. What is the nature of the conflict? What's the history leading up to this negotiation? Who is involved and what are their perceptions of the conflict?

What do you want from the negotiation? What are *your* goals? It often helps to put your goals in writing and develop a range of outcomes—from "most hopeful" to "minimally acceptable"—to keep your attention focused.

You also want to prepare an assessment of what you think the other party to your negotiation's goals are. What are they likely to ask for? How entrenched are they likely to be in their position? What intangible or hidden interests may be important to them? What might they be willing to settle on? When you can anticipate your opponent's position, you are better equipped to counter his or her arguments with the facts and figures that support your position.

In determining goals, parties are well advised to consider their "target and resistance" points, as well as their *best alternative to a negotiated agreement* (**BATNA**).[44] The buyer and the seller are examples of two negotiators. Each has a *target point* that defines what he or she would like to achieve. Each also has a *resistance point*, which marks the lowest outcome that is acceptable—the point below which each would break off negotiations rather than accept a less favourable settlement. The area between these two points makes up each negotiator's aspiration range. As long as there is some overlap between the buyer's and seller's aspiration ranges, there exists a **bargaining zone** where each side's aspirations can be met. Referring to Exhibit 9-6 on page 330, if the buyer's resistance point is $450, and the seller's resistance point is $500, then the two may not be able to reach agreement because there is no overlap in their aspiration ranges. In the negotiations between the NHLPA and the NHL owners, there was no overlap on where the salary cap should be set.

One's BATNA represents the alternative that an individual will face if negotiations fail. For instance, during the winter 2005 hockey negotiations, for both hockey players and owners, the BATNA was the loss of the 2004–2005 season. In the end, both sides must have concluded that they preferred not playing the season to trying to get the conflict resolved.

As part of your strategy, you should determine not only your BATNA, but some estimate of the other side's as well.[45] If you go into your negotiation having a good idea

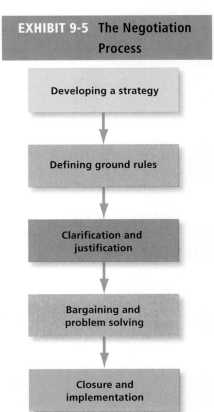

EXHIBIT 9-5 The Negotiation Process

- Developing a strategy
- Defining ground rules
- Clarification and justification
- Bargaining and problem solving
- Closure and implementation

Source: This model is based on R. J. Lewicki, "Bargaining and Negotiation," *Exchange: The Organizational Behavior Teaching Journal* 6, no. 2 (1981), pp. 39–40.

BATNA The *best alternative to a negotiated agreement*; the outcome an individual faces if negotiations fail.

bargaining zone The zone between each party's resistance point, assuming there is overlap in this range.

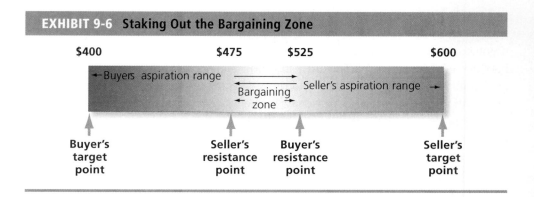

EXHIBIT 9-6   Staking Out the Bargaining Zone

of what the other party's BATNA is, even if you are not able to meet theirs, you might be able to get them to change it.

You can practise your negotiating skills in the *Working With Others Exercise* on page 340.

Defining Ground Rules

Once you've done your planning and developed a strategy, you're ready to begin defining the ground rules and procedures with the other party over the negotiation itself. Who will do the negotiating? Where will it take place? What time constraints, if any, will apply? To what issues will negotiation be limited? Will there be a specific procedure to follow if an impasse is reached? During this phase, the parties will also exchange their initial proposals or demands. *From Concepts to Skills* on page 344 directly addresses some of the actions you should take to improve the likelihood that you can achieve a good agreement. The *Ethical Dilemma Exercise* on page 341 considers whether it is ever appropriate to lie during negotiations.

Clarification and Justification

When initial positions have been exchanged, both you and the other party will explain, amplify, clarify, bolster, and justify your original demands. This part of the process need not be confrontational. Rather, it's an opportunity for educating and informing each other on the issues, why they are important, and how each arrived at their initial demands. This is the point at which you might want to provide the other party with any documentation that helps support your position.

Bargaining and Problem Solving

The essence of the negotiation process is the actual give and take in trying to hash out an agreement. It is here where concessions will undoubtedly need to be made by both parties. *OB in Action—Tips for Getting to Yes* gives you further ideas on how to make negotiating work for you, based on the popular book *Getting to Yes*.[46]

Closure and Implementation

The final step in the negotiation process is formalizing the agreement that has been worked out and developing procedures that are necessary for implementation and monitoring. For major negotiations—which would include everything from labour-management negotiations such as in the NHL situation, to bargaining over lease terms, to buying real estate, to negotiating a job offer for a senior management position—this will require hammering out the specifics in a formal contract. For most cases, however, closure of the negotiation process is nothing more formal than a handshake.

CONTEMPORARY ISSUES IN NEGOTIATION

We conclude our discussion of negotiation by reviewing two contemporary issues: gender differences in negotiating style and cultural differences in negotiating style.

⑤ What are some of the contemporary issues in negotiation?

Gender Differences in Negotiating Style

Do men and women negotiate differently? The answer appears to be "it depends."[47] It is difficult to generalize about gender differences in negotiating style, because the research yields many opinions, but few reliable conclusions. One review of a number of studies found no overall difference in effectiveness of men and women leaders in negotiation, although the study also indicated that men performed better when the negotiations were over male-stereotypical tasks (for example, negotiating for airplanes and turbo-engine parts), whereas women did better when the negotiations were over female-stereotypical tasks (for example, negotiations involving child care and caretaker issues).[48] Moreover, a review of 53 studies suggests that women receive lower gains than men after a negotiation process.[49] Let's look at four basic areas where interesting gender differences in bargaining have been found.[50]

Ever wonder if men and women negotiate differently?

First, women are more inclined to be concerned with feelings and perceptions, and thus take a longer-term view when negotiating. By contrast, men are more inclined to focus on resolving the matter at hand. Bill Forbes, president of Edmonton-based career management firm CDR Associates, observes that women assume they are not going to earn as much as men. They focus "on getting a position that utilizes their skills and gives them some challenge. When presented with the compensation range for their job classification, women generally aren't worried if they end up in the bottom half, whereas males might often be concerned if they're not in the top."[51] Unfortunately, employers may take advantage of these differing expectations to offer women lower wages when they first negotiate salary. This may be changing in recent times. For example, University of Waterloo psychology professor Serge Desmarais found that the narrowest pay gap between men and women existed with those who had graduated from university since 1992. The difference in wages for those men and women was only 6 percent.[52]

CDR Associates
www.mediate.org

Second, men view the bargaining session as a separate event, whereas women view it as part of the overall relationship with the individual. Women therefore put more weight on the importance of maintaining relationships after the bargaining session is over when considering their strategy.

Third, women tend to want all parties in the negotiation to be empowered, whereas men are more likely to use power as part of the bargaining strategy. In other words, women are less likely to negotiate solutions where one person is clearly the winner and the other is clearly the loser.

Finally, the researchers reported differences in dialogue. Men more often used dialogue to persuade other parties in the negotiation, whereas women were more likely to use dialogue to achieve understanding. Desmarais, whose work we noted above, suggests that

OB IN ACTION

Tips for Getting to Yes

R. Fisher and W. Ury present four principles for win-win negotiations in their book *Getting to Yes*:

→ **Separate** the **people from** the **problem**. Work on the issues at hand, rather than getting involved in personality issues between the parties.

→ Focus on **interests, not positions**. Try to identify what each person needs or wants, rather than coming up with an unmovable position.

→ Look for ways to achieve **mutual gains**. Rather than focusing on one "right" solution for your position, brainstorm for solutions that will satisfy the needs of both parties.

→ Use **objective criteria** to achieve a fair solution. Try to focus on fair standards, such as market value, expert opinion, norms, or laws to help guide decision making.

Source: R. Fisher and W. Ury, *Getting to Yes* (New York: Penguin Books, 1991).

In negotiating the creation of a theme park in France, the Walt Disney Company learned about cultural differences when it presented its plan to the French government. In France, a hierarchical country, decisions are made at the top. So the top leader in France, the late Prime Minister François Mitterand, was involved in the negotiations of Euro Disneyland. To navigate the levels of hierarchy, Disney hired local French people who were familiar with the rules of decision making to secure official approval of its project.

men are socialized to be more aggressive negotiators, which would account for some of the observed differences in men's and women's styles.[53]

One important thing to note is that even if a difference in style of negotiation exists, one style may not always be preferable to the other. The best style may, in fact, depend on the situation. For instance, in situations where trust, openness, and long-term relationships are critical, a woman's style may be more useful. However, when conflict, competition, and self-interest are an important part of the agenda, a man's style may be more effective.[54]

There is another thing worth noting: The belief that women are nicer than men in negotiations may well result not from gender, but from the lack of power typically held by women in most large organizations. The research indicates that low-power managers, regardless of gender, attempt to please their opponents and tend to use softly persuasive tactics rather than direct confrontation and threats. Where women and men have similar power bases, there may be less significant differences in their negotiation styles. There is still work to be done in this area, however. A study by two economists found that women were more likely than men to share some of the $10 they were given by researchers (53 percent vs. 40 percent), and women were also more likely than men to give away a larger portion ($1.60 vs. $0.82).[55]

Women's attitudes toward negotiation and toward themselves as negotiators also appear to be quite different from men's. Managerial women demonstrate less confidence in anticipation of negotiating and are less satisfied with their performance after the process is complete, even when their performance and the outcomes they achieve are similar to men's. This latter conclusion suggests that women may unduly penalize themselves by refusing to negotiate with confidence when such action would be in their best interests.

The outcomes of negotiations for women and men also seem to differ. One researcher found that when women negotiated to buy a car, the opening offer by the salesperson was higher than it was for men.[56] In a study of salary offers, researchers found that men were offered higher starting salaries in a negotiating process than were women.[57] While in each of these instances the opening offers were just that, offers to be negotiated, women also fared less well than men at the end of the negotiating process, even when they used the same negotiating tactics as men.

The results of these studies may shed some light on the pay and promotion discrepancies between men and women, which we discuss in Chapter 11. If women negotiate even slightly lower starting salaries, then over time, with raises based on percentages of salaries, the gap between men's and women's salaries can grow quite substantially.

Cultural Differences in Negotiating Style

Although there appears to be no significant direct relationship between an individual's personality and negotiation style, cultural background does seem to be relevant. Negotiating styles clearly do vary across national cultures, as the following examples suggest:[58]

- *France.* The French like conflict. They frequently gain recognition and develop their reputations by thinking and acting against others. As a result, the French tend to take a long time in negotiating agreements, and they aren't overly concerned about whether their opponents like or dislike them.[59]

EXHIBIT 9-7	Negotiating Attitude: Win-Win or Win-Lose?										
Country	Japan	China	Argentina	France	India	US	UK	Mexico	Germany	Nigeria	Brazil	Spain
Negotiator Focuses on Win-Win Solution (%)	100	82	81	80	78	71	59	50	55	47	44	37

Source: J. W. Salacuse, "Ten Ways That Culture Affects Negotiating Style: Some Survey Results," *Negotiation Journal,* July 1998, pp. 221–240.

- *China.* The Chinese draw out negotiations because they believe negotiations never end. Just when you think you've pinned down every detail and reached a final solution with a Chinese executive, that executive might smile and start the process all over again. The Chinese negotiate to develop a relationship and a commitment to work together rather than to tie up every loose end.[60]

- *Japan.* The Japanese also negotiate to develop relationships and a commitment to work together.

- *United States.* Americans are known around the world for their impatience and their desire to be liked. Astute negotiators from other countries often turn these characteristics to their advantage by dragging out negotiations and making friendship conditional on the final settlement.

The cultural context of the negotiation significantly influences the amount and type of preparation for bargaining, the relative emphasis on task vs. interpersonal relationships, the tactics used, and even the place where the negotiation should be conducted. Exhibit 9-7 helps you identify whether countries focus more on win-win or win-lose solutions. These findings are based on research on 300 negotiators in 12 countries. As you will note, 100 percent of Japanese negotiators said they focus on finding a win-win solution. By contrast, only 37 percent of Spanish negotiators said the same.[61] *OB Around the Globe* looks at more examples of cross-cultural differences in negotiating style.

OB AROUND THE GLOBE

The Many Styles of Negotiations

How different are bargaining styles cross-culturally? A study comparing North Americans, Arabs, and Russians looked at the groups' negotiating styles, their responses to an opponent's arguments, their approaches to making concessions, and their handling of negotiating deadlines.[62] The researchers found the following:

- North Americans tried to persuade by relying on facts and appealing to logic. They countered opponents' arguments with objective facts. They made small concessions early in the negotiation to establish a relationship, and usually reciprocated opponents' concessions. North Americans treated deadlines as very important.

- Arabs, however, tried to persuade by appealing to emotion. They countered opponents' arguments with subjective feelings. They made concessions throughout the bargaining process and almost always reciprocated opponents' concessions. The Arabs also approached deadlines very casually.

- Russians based their arguments on asserted ideals. They made few, if any, concessions. Any concession offered by an opponent was viewed as a weakness and almost never reciprocated. Finally, the Russians tended to ignore deadlines.

Another study looked at verbal and nonverbal negotiation tactics exhibited by North Americans, Japanese, and Brazilians during half-hour bargaining sessions.[63] Some of the differences were particularly interesting:

- Brazilians on average said "no" 83 times, compared with 5 times for the Japanese and 9 times for the North Americans.

- Japanese displayed more than 5 periods of silence lasting longer than 10 seconds during the 30-minute sessions. North Americans averaged 3.5 such periods; the Brazilians had none.

- Both Japanese and North Americans interrupted their opponent about the same number of times, but the Brazilians interrupted 2.5 to 3 times more often than the North Americans and the Japanese.

- While Japanese and North Americans had no physical contact with their opponents during negotiations except for handshaking, Brazilians touched each other almost 5 times every half-hour.

SUMMARY AND IMPLICATIONS

1 **What is conflict?** Conflict occurs when one party perceives that another party's actions will have a negative effect on something the first party cares about. Many people automatically assume that all conflict is bad. However, conflict can be either functional (constructive) or dysfunctional (destructive) to the performance of a group or unit. An optimal level of conflict encourages communication, prevents stagnation, stimulates creativity, allows tensions to be released, and plants the seeds of change, yet not so much as to be disruptive or to deter activities. For simplicity's sake, the sources of conflict have been condensed into three general categories: communication, structure, and personal variables.

2 **How can conflict be resolved?** The way a conflict is defined goes a long way toward establishing the sort of outcomes that might settle it. One can work toward a *win-lose solution* or a *win-win solution*. Conflict management strategies are determined by the extent to which one wants to cooperate with another party, and the extent to which one asserts his or her own concerns. Occasionally, individuals or group representatives reach a stalemate and are unable to resolve their differences through direct negotiations. In such cases, they may turn to alternative dispute resolution (ADR), where a third party helps both sides find a solution. ADR encompasses a variety of strategies, including facilitation, conciliation, an ombudsperson, peer review, mediation, and arbitration.

3 **What are the effects of conflict?** Conflict can be functional and improve group performance, or it can be dysfunctional and hinder group performance. There is a substantial body of literature to document how dysfunctional conflict can reduce group effectiveness. Among the more undesirable consequences of conflict are stopping communication, reducing group cohesiveness, and subordinating group goals due to infighting between members. At the extreme, conflict can bring group functioning to a halt and potentially threaten the group's survival.

4 **How does one negotiate effectively?** Negotiation is a process in which two or more parties who offer goods or services try to agree upon the exchange rate for these goods or services. Negotiation was shown to be an ongoing activity in groups and organizations. Distributive bargaining can resolve disputes, but it often negatively affects one or more negotiators' satisfaction because it is focused on the short term and because it is confrontational. Integrative bargaining, by contrast, tends to provide outcomes that satisfy all parties and build lasting relationships.

5 **What are some of the contemporary issues in negotiation?** Two contemporary issues are gender differences and cultural differences in negotiating style. The evidence suggests that men and women use somewhat different styles in negotiation, and also have somewhat different success rates. Cultural background does seem to be relevant to how negotiations are carried out. Moreover, negotiating styles vary across cultures.

For Review

1. What are the advantages to conflict? What are its disadvantages?

2. Under what conditions might conflict be beneficial to a group?

3. What is the difference between functional and dysfunctional conflict? What determines functionality?

4. What is dual concern theory?

5. What is the difference between a conciliator and a mediator?

6. What causes personality conflicts, and how can they be resolved?

7. What defines the bargaining zone in distributive bargaining?

8. Why isn't integrative bargaining more widely practised in organizations?

9. How do men and women differ, if at all, in their approaches to negotiations?

10. How can you improve your negotiating effectiveness?

For Critical Thinking

1. Do you think competition and conflict are different? Explain.

2. "Participation is an excellent method for identifying differences and resolving conflicts." Do you agree or disagree? Discuss.

3. From your own experience, describe a situation you were involved in where the conflict was dysfunctional. Describe another example, from your experience, where the conflict was functional. Now analyze how other parties in both conflicts might have interpreted the situation in terms of whether the conflicts were functional or dysfunctional.

4. Assume one of your co-workers had to negotiate a contract with someone from China. What problems might he or she face? If the co-worker asked for advice, what suggestions would you give to help facilitate a settlement?

5. Michael Eisner, former CEO at the Walt Disney Corporation, wanted to stimulate conflict inside his firm. But he wants to minimize conflict with outside parties—agents, contractors, unions, etc. What does this say about conflict levels, functional versus dysfunctional conflict, and managing conflict?

OB for You

- It may seem easier, but avoiding conflict does not necessarily have a more positive outcome than working with someone to resolve the conflict.

- Trying to achieve a win-win solution in a conflict situation tends to lead to better relationships and greater trust.

- It's not always possible to resolve conflict on one's own. There are alternative dispute resolution options, including having someone help mediate the conflict.

- It's better to focus more on interests rather than positions when engaged in a negotiation. Doing so gives you the ability to arrive at more flexible solutions.

 *POINT*

 COUNTERPOINT

Conflict Is Good for an Organization

We've made considerable progress in the past 25 years toward overcoming the negative stereotype given to conflict. Most behavioural scientists and an increasing number of practising managers now accept that the goal of effective management is not to eliminate conflict. Rather, it's to create the right intensity of conflict so as to reap its functional benefits.

Let's briefly review how stimulating conflict can provide benefits to the organization:[64]

- *Conflict is a means by which to bring about radical change.* It's an effective device by which management can drastically change the existing power structure, current interaction patterns, and entrenched attitudes.

- *Conflict facilitates group cohesiveness.* While conflict increases hostility between groups, external threats tend to cause a group to pull together as a unit. Intergroup conflicts raise the extent to which members identify with their own group and increase feelings of solidarity, while, at the same time, internal differences and irritations dissolve.

- *Conflict improves group and organizational effectiveness.* The stimulation of conflict initiates the search for new means and goals and clears the way for innovation. The successful solution of a conflict leads to greater effectiveness, to more trust and openness, to greater attraction of members for each other, and to depersonalization of future conflicts. In fact, it has been found that as the number of minor disagreements increases, the number of major clashes decreases.

- *Conflict brings about a slightly higher, more constructive level of tension.* Constructive levels of tension enhance the chances of solving the conflicts in a way satisfactory to all parties concerned. When the level of tension is very low, the parties are not sufficiently motivated to do something about a conflict.

These points are clearly not comprehensive. As noted in the chapter, conflict provides a number of benefits to an organization. However, groups or organizations that lack conflict are likely to suffer from apathy, stagnation, groupthink, and other serious problems. In fact, more organizations probably fail because they have too little conflict rather than too much.

All Conflicts Are Dysfunctional!

It may be true that conflict is an inherent part of any group or organization. It may not be possible to eliminate it completely. However, just because conflicts exist is no reason to glorify them. All conflicts are dysfunctional, and it is one of management's major responsibilities to keep conflict intensity as low as humanly possible. A few points will support this case:

- *The negative consequences from conflict can be devastating.* The list of negatives associated with conflict is awesome. The most obvious are increased turnover, decreased employee satisfaction, inefficiencies between work units, sabotage, labour grievances and strikes, and physical aggression.

- *Effective managers build teamwork.* A good manager builds a coordinated team. Conflict works against such an objective. A successful work group is like a successful sports team: Members all know their roles and support their teammates. When a team works well, the whole becomes greater than the sum of the parts. Management creates teamwork by minimizing internal conflicts and facilitating internal coordination.

- *Competition is good for an organization, but not conflict.* Competition and conflict should not be confused with each other. Conflict is behaviour directed against another party, whereas competition is behaviour aimed at obtaining a goal without interference from another party. Competition is healthy; it's the source of organizational vitality. Conflict, on the other hand, is destructive.

- *Managers who accept and stimulate conflict don't survive in organizations.* The whole argument on the value of conflict may be moot as long as most senior executives in organizations view conflict as bad. Since the evaluation of a manager's performance is made by higher-level executives, those managers who do not succeed in eliminating conflicts are likely to be appraised negatively. This, in turn, will reduce opportunities for advancement. Any manager who aspires to move up in such an environment will be wise to follow the traditional view and eliminate any outward signs of conflict. Failure to follow this advice might result in the premature departure of the manager.

HR IMPLICATIONS

Labour-Management Negotiations

Conflict in the workplace arises for a variety of reasons, but one major source of conflict in many of Canada's businesses is conflict between labour and management. Below we consider the importance of labour-management negotiations, noting that some negotiations are more positive than others. We also offer some tips for negotiating labour-management conflicts.

On the negative side of union-management negotiations, consider the example of Vancouver-based Telus and the union that organizes its employees, the Telecommunications Workers Union (TWU). As of spring 2005, the two sides had still not resolved an almost five-year dispute on settling a new contract. In desperation, Telus tried to appeal directly to its employees, going over the union's head, after first initiating limited lockout provisions that took away some union member benefits. Telus sought contract concessions it claimed it needed to compete successfully against rivals Bell Canada and Shaw. Telus and its union finally settled in mid-November 2005, but it took a second vote to have the contract accepted.

On the positive side of union-management negotiations, Vancouver-based NorskeCanada and the Communications, Energy and Paperworkers Union of Canada (CEP) came to an agreement in fall 2002 that each side said was a win-win solution. Though the union's contract with NorskeCanada did not expire until April 30, 2003, both sides recognized the need to settle conflict negotiations as early as possible. Doing so would mean ensuring labour peace, resulting in more orders from customers for NorskeCanada, and greater job security for CEP employees. In addition, NorskeCanada wanted to "bury the memory of the poor industrial relations we had between us."[65] Labour disputes had caused the company's returns to drop 8 percent in recent years, while CEP had spent $100 million in strike pay in the past four years.

So how do company negotiators plan when preparing to negotiate with a union? Susan Cassidy, vice-president of human resources with Calgary-based Calgary Laboratory Services, says that "A huge part of effective negotiations is in planning and preparing."[66] Cassidy prepares by having someone on her team role play the union negotiator and think of everything the union might bring to the table.

Cassidy cautions that one should be careful in presenting an initial offer. While high demands from union negotiators and low offers from management negotiators are part of the strategy for creating room to negotiate, an initial offer that seems unreasonable may have very negative effects. For instance, when the Alberta government proposed a 5 percent wage rollback to the province's nurses, the nurses refused to negotiate for three weeks.

Buzz Hargrove, president of the Canadian Auto Workers (CAW), notes that the union's strategy is to choose one automaker with which to bargain first, and then allow just 10 days to settle on a new contract. Hargrove says he prefers the intensity, suggesting that "short, intense, sometimes round-the-clock bargaining is actually helpful in getting an agreement."[67]

Genevieve Bich, vice-president of industrial relations for Bell Canada, notes the importance of trust. It's also important to manage emotions during negotiations, being aware of how one's tactics might affect the other side. She described a situation where one of her own negotiators was not paying attention to his impact on the other side: "We were at the table and one of the company spokespersons kept interrupting the union spokesperson. You could see the other person going through the stages of anger; trying to calm down then his face was getting red. Then he just blew out, 'Let me speak, you never let me speak.'"[68] The company spokesperson didn't realize that the union interpreted his interruptions as an example of not listening to employees.

These examples show just a few of the ways that groups that might naturally have conflicting interests can choose to work toward a more positive environment. In some cases, unions extend the olive branch; in others, management does so. Mechanisms for addressing conflict can range from formal programs, such as a conflict prevention program or consultation through an independent facilitator, to a short-term training seminar on mutual gains bargaining. Often these programs can help make the relationship considerably better.

Though our emphasis here has been on the union-management perspective, these negotiating tips don't have to be confined to that sector. In any conflict situation, it's helpful if at least one of the sides takes the opportunity to try to resolve the conflict by making an offer to work together.

What Is Your Primary Conflict-Handling Style?

Indicate how often you rely on each of the following tactics by circling the number you feel is most appropriate. When I have a conflict at work, I do the following:

	Not at All				Very Much
1. I give in to the wishes of the other party.	1	2	3	4	5
2. I try to realize a middle-of-the-road solution.	1	2	3	4	5
3. I push my own point of view.	1	2	3	4	5
4. I examine issues until I find a solution that really satisfies me and the other party.	1	2	3	4	5
5. I avoid a confrontation about our differences.	1	2	3	4	5
6. I concur with the other party.	1	2	3	4	5
7. I emphasize that we have to find a compromise solution.	1	2	3	4	5
8. I search for gains.	1	2	3	4	5
9. I stand for my own and the other party's goals and interests.	1	2	3	4	5
10. I avoid differences of opinion as much as possible.	1	2	3	4	5
11. I try to accommodate the other party.	1	2	3	4	5
12. I insist we both give in a little.	1	2	3	4	5
13. I fight for a good outcome for myself.	1	2	3	4	5
14. I examine ideas from both sides to find a mutually optimal solution.	1	2	3	4	5
15. I try to make differences loom less large.	1	2	3	4	5
16. I adapt to the other party's goals and interests.	1	2	3	4	5
17. I strive whenever possible toward a 50-50 compromise.	1	2	3	4	5
18. I do everything to win.	1	2	3	4	5
19. I work out a solution that serves my own, as well as the other party's, interests as well as possible.	1	2	3	4	5
20. I try to avoid a confrontation with the other party.	1	2	3	4	5

Scoring Key:

To determine your primary conflict-handling strategy, place the number 1 through 5 that represents your score for each statement next to the number for that statement. Then total up the columns.

(See next page.)

OB *AT WORK*

LEARNING ABOUT **YOURSELF** EXERCISE (Continued)

Yielding	Compromising	Forcing	Problem-solving	Avoiding
1. _____	2. _____	3. _____	4. _____	5. _____
6. _____	7. _____	8. _____	9. _____	10. _____
11. _____	12. _____	13. _____	14. _____	15. _____
16. _____	17. _____	18. _____	19. _____	20. _____
Totals _____	_____	_____	_____	_____

Your primary conflict-handling style is the category with the highest total. Your fallback intention is the category with the second-highest total.

Source: C. K. W. De Dreu, A. Evers, B. Beersma, E. S. Kluwer, and A. Nauta, "A Theory-Based Measure of Conflict Management Strategies in the Workplace," *Journal of Organizational Behavior* 22, no. 6 (September 2001), pp. 645–668. With permission.

BREAKOUT **GROUP** EXERCISES

Form small groups to discuss the following topics, as assigned by your instructor:

1. You and 2 other students carpool to school every day. The driver has recently taken to playing a new radio station quite loudly. You do not like the music, or the loudness. Using one of the conflict-handling strategies outlined in Exhibit 9-2, indicate how you might go about resolving this conflict.

2. Using the example above, identify a number of BATNAs (*best alternative to a negotiated agreement*) available to you, and then decide whether you should continue carpooling.

3. Which conflict-handling strategy is most consistent with how you deal with conflict? Is your strategy effective? Why or why not?

WORKING WITH **OTHERS** EXERCISE

A Negotiation Role Play

This role play is designed to help you develop your negotiating skills. The class is to break into pairs. One person will play the role of Terry, the department supervisor. The other person will play Dale, Terry's boss.

The Situation: Terry and Dale work for hockey-equipment manufacturer Bauer. Terry supervises a research laboratory. Dale is the manager of R & D. Terry and Dale are former skaters who have worked for Bauer for more than 6 years. Dale has been Terry's boss for 2 years.

One of Terry's employees has greatly impressed Terry. This employee is Lisa Roland. Lisa was hired 11 months ago. She is 24 years old and holds a master's degree in mechanical engineering. Her entry-level salary was $52 500 a year. She was told by Terry that, in accordance with corporation policy, she would receive an initial performance evaluation at 6 months and a comprehensive review after 1 year. Based on her performance record, Lisa was told she could expect a salary adjustment at the time of the 1-year review.

Terry's evaluation of Lisa after 6 months was very positive. Terry commented on the long hours Lisa was working, her cooperative spirit, the fact that others in the lab enjoyed working with her, and her immediate positive impact on the project she had been assigned. Now that Lisa's first anniversary is coming up, Terry has again reviewed Lisa's performance. Terry thinks Lisa may be the best new person the R & D group has ever hired. After only a year, Terry has ranked Lisa as the number three performer in a department of 11.

Salaries in the department vary greatly. Terry, for instance, has a basic salary of $93 800, plus eligibility for a bonus that might add another $7000 to $11 000 a year. The salary range of the 11 department members is $42 500 to $79 000. The lowest salary is a recent hire with a bachelor's degree in physics. The two people that Terry has rated above Lisa earn base salaries of $73 800 and $78 900. They are both 27 years old and have been at Bauer for 3 and 4 years, respectively. The median salary in Terry's department is $65 300.

Terry's Role: You want to give Lisa a big raise. While she's young, she has proven to be an excellent addition to the department. You don't want to lose her. More important, she knows in general what other people in the department are earning, and she thinks she's underpaid. The company typically gives 1-year raises of 5 percent, although 10 percent is not unusual and 20 to 30 percent increases have been approved on occasion. You would like to get Lisa as large an increase as Dale will approve.

Dale's Role: All your supervisors typically try to squeeze you for as much money as they can for their people. You understand this because you did the same thing when you were a supervisor, but your boss wants to keep a lid on costs. He wants you to keep raises for recent hires generally in the range of 5 to 8 percent. In fact, he has sent a memo to all managers and supervisors stating this objective. However, your boss is also very concerned with equity and paying people what they are worth. You feel assured that he will support any salary recommendation you make, as long as it can be justified. Your goal, consistent with cost reduction, is to keep salary increases as low as possible.

The Negotiation: Terry has a meeting scheduled with Dale to discuss Lisa's performance review and salary adjustment. Take a couple of minutes to think through the facts in this exercise and to prepare a strategy. Then you have up to 15 minutes to conduct your negotiation. When your negotiation is complete, the class will compare the various strategies used and the outcomes that resulted.

ETHICAL **DILEMMA** EXERCISE

Is It Unethical to Lie and Deceive During Negotiations?

In Chapter 7, we addressed lying in the context of communication. Here we return to the topic of lying but specifically as it relates to negotiation. We think this issue is important because, for many people, there is no such thing as lying when it comes to negotiating.

It's been said that the whole notion of negotiation is built on ethical quicksand: To succeed, you must deceive. Is this true? Apparently a lot of people think so. For instance, one study found that 28 percent of negotiators lied about a common-interest issue during negotiations, while another study found that 100 percent of negotiators either failed to reveal a problem or actively lied about it during negotiations if they were not directly asked about the issue.

Is it possible for someone to maintain high ethical standards and, at the same time, deal with the daily need to negotiate with bosses, peers, staff, people from other organizations, friends, and even relatives?

We can probably agree that bald-faced lies during negotiation are wrong. At least most ethicists would probably agree. The universal dilemma surrounds the little lies—the

omissions, evasions, and concealments that are often necessary to best an opponent.

During negotiations, when is a lie a lie? Is exaggerating benefits, downplaying negatives, ignoring flaws, or saying "I don't know" when in reality you do considered lying? Is declaring that "this is my final offer and nonnegotiable" (even when you are posturing) a lie? Is pretending to bend over backward to make meaningful concessions lying? Rather than being unethical practices, the use of these "lies" is considered by many as indicators that a negotiator is strong, smart, and savvy.

When is evasiveness and deception out of bounds? Is it naive to be completely honest and bare your soul during negotiations? Or are the rules of negotiations unique: Any tactic that will improve your chance of winning is acceptable?

Sources: Based on M. E. Schweitzer, "Deception in Negotiations," in *Wharton on Making Decisions*, ed. S. J. Hoch and H. C. Kunreuther (New York: Wiley, 2001), pp. 187–200; and M. Diener, "Fair Enough," *Entrepreneur*, January 2002, pp. 100–102.

CASE INCIDENTS

Not Your Dream Team

Mallory Murray hadn't had much experience working as part of a team. A recent graduate of the University of Saskatchewan, she had taken a business program focused primarily on individual projects and accomplishments. What little exposure she had had to teams was in her organizational behaviour, marketing research, and strategy formulation courses. When she interviewed with ThinkLink, an educational software firm, she didn't give much thought to the fact that ThinkLink made extensive use of cross-functional teams. During on-site interviews, she told interviewers and managers alike that she had limited experience on teams. But she did tell them that she worked well with people and thought that she could be an effective team player. Unfortunately, Murray didn't realize that working on a team is generally more complicated than simply working one-on-one with other people.

Murray joined ThinkLink as an assistant marketing manager for the company's high school core programs. These are essentially software programs designed to help students learn algebra and geometry. Murray's manager is Lin Chen (marketing manager). Other members of her team include Todd Schlotsky (senior programmer); Laura Willow (advertising); Sean Traynor (vice-president for strategic marketing); Joyce Rothman (a former high school math teacher who co-founded ThinkLink and is the formal leader of this project, although she now works only part-time in the company); and Harlow Gray (educational consultant).

After her first week on the job, Murray was seriously considering quitting. "I never imagined how difficult it would be working with people who are so opinionated and competitive. Every decision seems to be a power con-

test. Sean, Joyce, and Harlow are particularly troublesome. Sean thinks his rank entitles him to the last word. Joyce thinks her opinions should carry more weight because she was instrumental in creating the company. And Harlow views everyone as less knowledgeable than he is. Because he consults with a number of software firms and school districts, Harlow's a 'know-it-all.' To make things worse, Lin is passive and quiet. He rarely speaks up in meetings and appears to want to avoid any conflicts.

"What makes my job particularly difficult," Murray continued, "is that I don't have any specific job responsibilities. It seems that someone else is always interfering with what I'm doing or telling me how to do it. Our team has seven members—six chiefs and me!"

The project team that Murray is working on has a deadline to meet that is only six weeks away. Currently the team is at least two weeks behind schedule. Everyone is aware that there's a problem, but no one seems able to solve it. What is especially frustrating to Murray is that neither Lin Chen nor Joyce Rothman is showing any leadership. Chen is preoccupied with a number of other projects, and Rothman can't seem to control Traynor's and Gray's strong personalities.

Questions

1. Discuss the situation that has created the conflict.

2. What techniques or procedures might help reduce the conflict in this particular situation?

3. If you were Murray, could you do anything to lessen the conflict on the core project? Elaborate.

Managing Conflict at Schneider National

Schneider National is a transportation and logistics firm with locations in Canada, the United States, and Mexico. Begun in 1935, the private company now operates 14 000 trucks and 40 000 trailers that haul freight 8 million kilometres per day. Revenues are approximately $2.4 billion (US) a year.

The company has had only three leaders. The first was the founder; the second was his son, Donald; and in August 2002, the first nonfamily member took the helm when Chris Lofgren was made CEO, replacing Schneider, who was 67 years old. But it wasn't as if the company wasn't making preparations for executive leadership. Don Schneider told his board of directors in 1988 that their primary task was finding a successor. Lofgren joined the company in 1994 as a vice-president and became chief operating officer in 2000. After being appointed COO, Lofgren began to lay the framework for the six-person executive group that today shares many of the company's strategic responsibilities.

Everyone who knows Don Schneider concedes that he's a tough act to follow. "Don is an icon," says another top Schneider executive. "He probably commands more respect in transportation and logistics than anybody in the industry." Says Lofgren, "Our approach has been to put together an executive team that has a set of skills, perspectives and experiences that, when you put that team together, is broader and bigger than Don Schneider." The idea, according to Lofgren, is to have individuals with product line or functional focus, while maintaining their oversight of those areas, develop a sense of responsibility for the financial performance of the whole company. "If you have people who aren't taking an enterprise solution, their only role is their function or their business, then ultimately it has to go to someone who's going to referee the points of tension," says Lofgren. And Lofgren has no intention of playing the referee role.

To mediate the points of conflict, the executive group has had to learn how to work together. They have even brought in outside counsel to help them listen and understand one another better, and focus debate on critical issues. "Conflict between people or between groups of people is not positive. Conflict around business issues is the most wonderful, healthy thing," says Lofgren. "Any business without tension will fall to its lowest level of performance."

Questions

1. What view toward conflict does Lofgren support? Explain.

2. Explain why the transition in leadership from Don Schneider to Chris Lofgren was relatively conflict-free.

3. How does the organization of the executive group create conflict? How does it reduce conflict?

4. How does Lofgren manage conflict?

Source: Based on D. Drickhamer, "Rolling On," *IndustryWeek,* December 1, 2002.

OB *AT WORK*

From **Concepts**
to **Skills**

Negotiating

Once you've taken the time to assess your own goals, to consider the other party's goals and interests, and to develop a strategy, you're ready to begin actual negotiations. The following suggestions should improve your negotiating skills:[69]

Begin with a positive overture. Studies on negotiation show that concessions tend to be reciprocated and lead to agreements. As a result, begin bargaining with a positive overture—perhaps a small concession—and then reciprocate your opponent's concessions.

Address problems, not personalities. Concentrate on the negotiation issues, not on the personal characteristics of your opponent. When negotiations get tough, avoid the tendency to attack your opponent. It's your opponent's ideas or position that you disagree with, not him or her personally. Separate the people from the problem, and don't personalize differences.

Pay little attention to initial offers. Treat an initial offer as merely a point of departure. Everyone has to have an initial position. These initial offers tend to be extreme and idealistic. Treat them as such.

Emphasize win-win solutions. Inexperienced negotiators often assume that their gain must come at the expense of the other party. As noted with integrative bargaining, that need not be the case. There are often win-win solutions. But assuming a zero-sum game means missed opportunities for trade-offs that could benefit both sides. So if conditions are supportive, look for an integrative solution. Frame options in terms of your opponent's interests, and look for solutions that can allow your opponent, as well as yourself, to declare a victory.

Create an open and trusting climate. Skilled negotiators are better listeners, ask more questions, focus their arguments more directly, are less defensive, and have learned to avoid words and phrases that can irritate an opponent (for example, "generous offer," "fair price," "reasonable arrangement"). In other words, they are better at creating the open and trusting climate necessary for reaching an integrative settlement.

Assessing Skills

After you've read this chapter, take the following Self-Assessment on your enclosed CD-ROM:

   39. What's My Preferred Conflict-Handling Style?

   40. What's My Negotiating Style?

Practising Skills

As marketing director for Done Right, a regional home-repair chain, you have come up with a plan you believe has significant potential for future sales. Your plan involves a customer information service designed to help people make their homes more environmentally sensitive. Then, based on homeowners' assessments of their homes' environmental impact, your firm will be prepared to help them deal with problems or concerns they may uncover. You are really excited about the competitive potential of this new service. You envision pamphlets, in-store appearances by environmental experts, as well as contests for consumers and school kids. After several weeks of preparations, you make your pitch to your boss, Nick Castro. You point out how the market for environmentally sensitive products is growing and how this growing demand represents the perfect opportunity for Done Right. Nick seems impressed by your presentation, but he has expressed one major concern: He thinks your workload is already too heavy. He doesn't see how you are going to have enough time to start this new service *and* still be able to look after all of your other assigned marketing duties. You really want to start the new service. What strategy will you follow in your negotiation with Nick?

Reinforcing Skills

   1. Negotiate with a team member or work colleague to handle a small section of work that you are not going to be able to get done in time for an important deadline.

   2. The next time you purchase a relatively expensive item (e.g., automobile, apartment lease, appliance, jewellery), attempt to negotiate a better price and gain some concessions such as an extended warranty, smaller down payment, maintenance services, or the like.

OB ON THE EDGE

The Toxic Workplace

It's not unusual to find the following employee behaviours in today's workplace:

> *Answering the phone with a "yeah," neglecting to say thank you or please, using voice mail to screen calls, leaving a half cup of coffee behind to avoid having to brew the next pot, standing uninvited but impatiently over the desk of someone engaged in a telephone conversation, dropping trash on the floor and leaving it for the maintenance crew to clean up, and talking loudly on the phone about personal matters.*[1]

Some employers or managers fit the following descriptions:

> *In the months since [the new owner of the pharmacy] has been in charge [he] has made it clear that he is at liberty to fire employees at will . . . change their positions, decrease their bonus percentages, and refuse time-off and vacation choices. Furthermore, he has established an authoritarian work structure characterized by distrust, cut-backs on many items deemed essential to work comfort, disrespect, rigidity and poor-to-no-communication.*[2]

> *He walked all over people. He made fun of them; he intimidated them. He criticized work for no reason, and he changed his plans daily.*[3]

What's Happening in Our Workplaces?

Workplaces today are receiving highly critical reviews, being called everything from "uncivil" to "toxic."

Lynne Anderson and Christine Pearson, two management professors from St. Joseph's University and the University of North Carolina, respectively, note that "Historians may view the dawn of the twenty-first century as a time of thoughtless acts and rudeness: We tailgate, even in the slow lane; we dial wrong numbers and then slam the receiver on the innocent respondent; we break appointments with nonchalance."[4] The workplace has often been seen as one of the places where civility still ruled, with co-workers treating each other with a mixture of formality and friendliness, distance and politeness. However, with downsizing, re-engineering, budget cuts, pressures for increased productivity, autocratic work environments, and the use of part-time employees, there has been an increase in "uncivil and aggressive workplace behaviours."[5]

What does civility in the workplace mean? A simple definition of workplace civility is behaviour "involving politeness and regard for others in the workplace, within workplace norms for respect."[6] Workplace incivility then "involves acting with disregard for others in the workplace, in violation of workplace norms for respect."[7] Of course, different workplaces will have different norms for what determines mutual respect. For instance, in most restaurants, if the staff were rude to you when you were there for dinner, you would be annoyed, and perhaps even complain to the manager. However, at the Elbow Room Cafe in downtown Vancouver, if customers complain they are in a hurry, manager Patrick Savoie might well say, "If you're in a hurry, you should have gone to McDonald's.[8] Such a comeback is acceptable to the diners at the Elbow Room Cafe, because rudeness is its trademark.

Most work environments are not expected to be characterized by such rudeness. However, this has been changing in recent years. Robert Warren, a University of Manitoba marketing professor, notes that "simple courtesy has gone by the board."[9]

There is documented evidence of the rise of violence and threats of violence at work.[10] However, several studies have found that there is persistent negative behaviour in the workplace that is not of a violent nature.[11] For instance, a survey of 603 Toronto nurses found that 33 percent had experienced verbal abuse during the five previous days of work.[12]

Another study found that 78 percent of employees interviewed think that workplace incivility has increased in the past 10 years.[13] The researchers found that men are mostly to blame for this change: "Although men and women are targets of disrespect and rudeness in equal numbers . . . men instigate the rudeness 70 percent of the time."[14]

Rude behaviour is not confined to men, however. Professor André Roberge at Laval University suggests that some of the rudeness is generational. He finds that "young clerks often lack both knowledge and civility. Employers are having to train young people in simple manners because that is not being done at home."[15] Professor Warren backs this up: "One of the biggest complaints I hear from businesses when I go to talk about graduates is the lack of interpersonal skills."[16]

Workplace Violence

Recently, researchers have suggested that incivility may be the beginning of more negative behaviours in the workplace, including aggression and violence.[17]

Pierre Lebrun chose a deadly way to exhibit the anger he had stored up from his workplace.[18] He took a hunting rifle to Ottawa-Carleton–based OC Transpo and killed four public transit co-workers on April 6, 1999, before turning the gun on himself. Lebrun felt that he had been the target of harassment by his co-workers for years because of his stuttering. If this sounds like an unusual response for an irate employee, consider the circumstances at OC Transpo. "Quite apart from what's alleged or otherwise with Mr. Lebrun's situation, we know [OC Transpo's] had a very unhappy work environment for a long time," Al Loney, former chair of Ottawa-Carleton's transit commission, noted. A consultant's report produced the year before the shooting found a workplace with "rock-bottom morale and poor management." It was not uncommon for fights to break out in the unit where the four men were killed.

Workplace violence, according to the International Labour Organization (ILO), includes

> any incident in which a person is abused, threatened or assaulted in circumstances relating to [his or her] work. These behaviours would originate from customers or co-workers at any level of the organization. This definition would include all forms of harassment, bullying, intimidation, physical threats, assaults, robbery and other intrusive behaviour.[19]

No Canadian statistics on anger at work are available.[20] However, studies show that anger pervades the US workplace. While 25 percent of Americans reported being "generally at least somewhat angry at work," 49 percent say that they felt "at least 'a little angry' at work."[21] A 2000 Gallup poll conducted in the United States found that 25 percent of the working adults surveyed felt like screaming or shouting because of job stress, 14 percent had considered hitting a co-worker, and 10 percent worry about colleagues becoming violent. This worry is not unfounded. Twenty employees are murdered each week in the United States.[22]

Canadian workplaces are not murder-free, however. In 2001, 60 murders occurred at work, 10 percent of all murders for the year.[23] Most of these workplace incidents were carried out by male spouses and partners of female employees. Surprisingly, Canada scores higher than the United States on workplace violence. In a recent ILO study involving 130 000 workers in 32 countries, Argentina was ranked the most violent. Romania was second, France third, and Canada fourth. The United States placed ninth.[24]

Sixty-four percent of union representatives who were surveyed recently reported an increase in workplace aggression, based on their review of incident reports, grievance files, and other solid evidence.[25] The ILO, in a separate 1998 study, found that, per capita, the rate of assault at work for Canadian women is four times that of American women.[27] To understand the seriousness of this situation, consider that one quarter of Nova Scotia teachers surveyed reported that they faced physical violence at work during the 2001–2002 school year.[28]

What Causes Incivility (and Worse) in the Workplace?

If employers and employees are acting with less civility toward each other, what is causing this to happen?

Managers and employees often have different views of the employee's role in the organization. Jeffrey Pfeffer, a professor of organizational behaviour at the Graduate School of Business at Stanford University, notes that many companies don't really value their employees: "Most managers, if they're being honest with themselves, will admit it: When they look at their people, they see costs, they see salaries, they see benefits, they see overhead. Very few companies look at their people and see assets."[29]

Most employees, however, like to think that they are assets to their organization. The realization that they are simply costs and not valued members of an organization can cause frustration for employees.

In addition, "employers' excessive demands and top-down style of management are contributing to the rise of 'work rage,'" claims Gerry Smith of Toronto-based WarrenShepell Consultants.[30] He is the author of the recently released *Work Rage*.[31] He cites demands coming from a variety of sources: "overtime, downsizing, rapid technological changes, company restructuring and difficulty balancing the demands of job and home."[32] Smith worries about the consequences of these demands: "If you push people too hard, set unrealistic expectations and cut back their benefits, they're going to strike back."[33]

Smith's work supports the findings of a study that reported the most common cause of anger is the actions of supervisors or managers.[34] Other common causes of anger identified by the researchers include lack of productivity by co-workers and others; tight deadlines; heavy workload; interaction with the public; and bad treatment.

The Psychological Contract

Some researchers have looked at this frustration in terms of a breakdown of the psychological contract formed between employees and employers. Employers and employees begin to develop psychological contracts as they are first introduced to each other in the hiring process.[35] These continue over time as the employer and the employee come to understand each other's expectations about the amounts and quality of work to be performed and the types of rewards to be given. For instance, when an employee is continually asked to work late and/or be available at all hours through pagers and email, the employee may assume that doing so

FactBox[26]

- In 2000, only 49% of working Canadians said they were committed to their employer. In 1991, the level of commitment was 62%.

- More Americans report commitment to their employers than Canadians: 55% of Americans vs. 49% of Canadians.

- Of those who experience rudeness, 12% quit their jobs in response, 22% decrease their work effort, and 52% lose work time worrying about it.

- Employees over the age of 55 express the highest degree of commitment to their employers.

will result in greater rewards or faster promotion down the line. The employer may have had no such intention, and may even be thinking that the employee should be grateful simply to have a job. Later, when the employee does not get expected (though never promised) rewards, he or she is disappointed.

Sandra Robinson, an organizational behaviour professor at the Sauder School of Business at the University of British Columbia, and her colleagues have found that when a psychological contract is violated (perceptually or actually), the relationship between the employee and the employer is damaged. This can result in the loss of trust.[36] The breakdown in trust can cause employees to be less ready to accept decisions or obey rules.[37] The erosion of trust can also lead employees to take revenge on the employer. So they don't carry out their end of a task. Or they refuse to pass on messages. They engage in any number of subtle and not-so-subtle behaviours that affect the way work gets done—or prevents work from getting done.

The Toxic Organization

Pfeffer suggests that companies have become "toxic places to work.[38] He notes that companies, particularly in Silicon Valley, ask their employees to sign contracts on the first day of work indicating the employee's understanding that the company has the right to fire at will and for any reason. Some employers also ask their employees to choose between having a life and having a career. Pfeffer relates a joke people used to tell about Microsoft: "We offer flexible time—you can work any 18 hours you want."[39] This kind of attitude can be toxic to employees, though

this does not imply that Microsoft is a toxic employer.

What does it mean to be a toxic organization? The late professor Peter Frost of the Sauder School of Business at the University of British Columbia notes that there will always be pain in organizations, but that sometimes it becomes so intense or prolonged that conditions within the organization begin to break down. In other words, the situation becomes toxic. This is not dissimilar to what the liver or kidneys do when toxins become too intense in a human body.[40]

What causes organizations to be toxic? Like Pfeffer, professors Frost and Robinson identify a number of factors. Downsizing and organiza-

Do You Have a Toxic Manager?

Below are some of the toxic behaviours of managers and the workplace cultures that allow these behaviours to thrive.

Managerial Toxic Behaviour

Actor behaviour. These managers act out anger rather than discuss problems. They slam doors, sulk, and make it clear they are angry, but refuse to talk about it.

Fragmentor behaviour. These managers see no connection between what they do and the outcome, and take no responsibility for their behaviour.

Me-first behaviour. These managers make decisions based on their own convenience.

Mixed-messenger behaviour. These managers present themselves one way, but their behaviour doesn't match what they say.

Wooden-stick behaviour. These managers are extremely rigid and controlling.

Escape-artist behaviour. These managers don't deal with reality, often lying, or at the extreme, escaping through drugs or alcohol.

Workplace Culture That Fosters This Behaviour

- *Macho culture.* People don't discuss problems. The emphasis is to "take it like a man."

- *Specialist culture.* Employees who are technically gifted or great in their fields don't have to consider how their behaviour or work impacts anyone.

- *Elitist culture.* Promotions and rewards are not based on your work but on who your buddies are.

- *Office-politics culture.* Promotions and rewards are based on flattery and positioning.

- *Change-resistant culture.* Upper management struggles to maintain the status quo regardless of the outcome.

- *Workaholic culture.* Employees are forced to spend more time at the office than necessary.

Source: L. McClure, *Risky Business* (Binghamton, NY: Haworth Press, 1996).

tional change are two main factors, particularly in recent years. Sometimes organizations experience unexpected events—such as the sudden death of a key manager, an unwise move by senior management, strong competition from a start-up company—that lead to toxicity. Other organizations are toxic throughout their system due to policies and practices that create distress. Such factors as unreasonable stretch goals or performance targets, or unrelenting internal competition, can create toxicity. There are also toxic managers who lead through insensitivity, vindictiveness, and failure to take responsibility, or they are control freaks or are unethical. The inset *Do You Have a Toxic Manager?* on page 349 lists some types of toxic managers and the workplace culture that fosters their behaviour.

What Are the Effects of Incivility and Toxicity in the Workplace?

In general, researchers have found that the effects of workplace anger are sometimes subtle: a hostile work environment and the tendency to do only enough work to get by.[41]

Those who feel chronic anger in the workplace are more likely to report "feelings of betrayal by the organization, decreased feelings of loyalty, a decreased sense that respondent values and the organization's values are similar, a decreased sense that the employer treated the respondent with dignity and respect, and a decreased sense that employers had fulfilled promises made to respondents."[42] So do these feelings make a difference? Apparently so. Researchers have found that those who felt angry with their employers were less likely to put forth their best effort, more likely to be competitive toward other employees, and less likely to suggest "a quicker and better way to do their job.[43] All of these actions tend to decrease the productivity possible in the workplace.

It's not just those who work for an organization who are affected by incivility and toxicity. Poor service, from indifference to rudeness to outright hostility, characterizes many transactions in Canadian businesses. "Across the country, better business bureaus, provincial government consumer-help agencies and media ombudsmen report a lengthening litany of complaints about contractors, car dealers,

repair shops, moving companies, airlines and department stores."[44] This suggests that customers and clients may well be feeling the impact of internal workplace dynamics.

The Toxin Handler

Employees of toxic organizations suffer pain from their experiences in a toxic environment. In some organizations, mechanisms, often informal, are set up to deal with the results of toxicity.

Frost and Robinson identified a special role that some employees play in trying to relieve the toxicity within an organization: the toxin handler. This person tries to mitigate the pain by softening the blow of downsizing, or change, or the behaviour of the toxic leader. Essentially the toxin handler helps others around him or her deal with the strains of the organization, by counselling, advising, shielding employees from the wrath of angry managers, reinterpreting the managers' messages to make them less harsh, etc.

So who takes on this role? Certainly no organization to date has a line on its organizational chart for "the toxin handler." Often the role emerges as part of an individual's position in an organization, for instance, a manager in the human resource department. In many cases, however, handlers are pulled into the role "bit by bit—by their colleagues, who turn to them because they are trustworthy, calm, kind and nonjudgmental."[45] Frost and Robinson, in profiling these individuals, suggest that toxin handlers are predisposed to say yes, have a high tolerance for pain, a surplus of empathy, and when they notice people in pain, they have a need to make the situation right. But these are not individuals who thrive simply on dealing with the emotional needs of

---

How Toxin Handlers Alleviate Organizational Pain

- They listen empathically.
- They suggest solutions.
- They work behind the scenes to prevent pain.
- They carry the confidences of others.
- They reframe difficult messages.

Source: P. Frost and S. Robinson, "The Toxic Handler: Organizational Hero—and Casualty," *Harvard Business Review*, July–August 1999, p. 101 (Reprint 99406).

FACE**OFF**

Manners are an over-romanticized concept. The big issue isn't that employees need to be concerned about their manners. Rather, employers should be paying better wages.

The Golden Rule, "Do unto others as you would have others do unto you," should still have a role in today's workplace. Being nice pays off.

others. Quoting one of the managers in their study, Frost and Robinson cite the full range of activities of most toxin handlers: "These people are usually relentless in their drive to accomplish organizational targets and rarely lose focus on business issues. Managing emotional pain is one of their means."[46] The inset *How Toxin Handlers Alleviate Organizational Pain* identifies the many tasks that toxin handlers take on in an organization. Frost and Robinson suggest that these tasks will probably need to be handled forever, and they recommend that organizations take steps to actively support people performing this role.

Research Exercises

1. Look for data on violence and anger in the workplace in other countries. How do these data compare with the Canadian and American data presented here? What might you conclude about how violence and anger in the workplace are expressed in different cultures?

2. Identify three Canadian organizations that are trying to foster better and/or less toxic environments for their employees. What kind of effect is this having on the organizations' bottom lines?

Your Perspective

1. Is it reasonable to suggest, as some researchers have, that young people today have not learned to be civil to others, or do not place a high priority on doing so? Do you see this as one of the causes of incivility in the workplace?

2. What should be done about managers who create toxicity in the workplace while being rewarded because they achieve bottom-line results? Should bottom-line results justify their behaviour?

Want to Know More?

If you'd like to read more on this topic, see Peter Frost, *Toxic Emotions at Work* (Cambridge, MA: Harvard Business School Press, 2003); P. Frost and S. Robinson, "The Toxic Handler: Organizational Hero—and Casualty," *Harvard Business Review,* July–August 1999, pp. 96–106 (Reprint 99406); and A. M. Webber, "Danger: Toxic Company," *Fast Company,* November 1998, pp. 152–157. You can find the latter article at www.fastcompany.com/online/19/toxic.html. It contains an interview with Professor Jeffrey Pfeffer, who discusses examples of toxic organizations.

CHAPTER 10
Organizational Culture

How does a for-profit Crown corporation with a $7-million deficit get back in the black? Changing its culture is part of the answer.

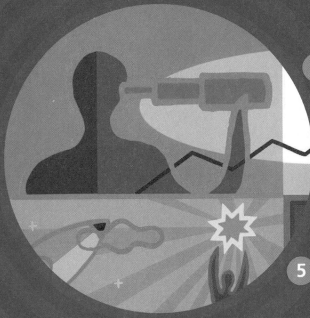

1 What is the purpose of organizational culture?

2 How do you read an organization's culture?

3 How do you create and maintain culture?

4 Can organizational culture have a downside?

5 How do you change culture?

When David Dingwall was appointed president and CEO of Ottawa-based Royal Canadian Mint in March 2003, the mint was a for-profit Crown corporation that had a $7-million deficit.[1] He described the culture that led to this deficit: "There was no discipline. There was no focus." He also noted that there was no urgency in wanting to help customers.

Dingwall noted that business processes "were essentially broken or non-existent. We had a very unprofitable jewellery line business; I'm talking about high-end jewellery that you or I would not buy for our spouses because we'd have to mortgage our house. In our foreign circulation coin we were floundering." Dingwall observed that the organization's culture needed to be changed if it was to become a profitable business.

Although Dingwall resigned amidst controversy in September 2005, most reports agreed that he had significantly turned around the fortunes of the Mint. Auditor-General Sheila Fraser, in her 2005 performance review of the Mint, gave "good marks to management for introducing a 'lean enterprise' initiative to control costs."

In this chapter, we show that every organization has a culture. We examine how that culture reveals itself and the impact it has on the attitudes and behaviours of members of that organization. An understanding of what makes up an organization's culture and how it's created, sustained, and learned enhances our ability to explain and predict the behaviour of people at work.

WHAT IS ORGANIZATIONAL CULTURE?

When Henry Mintzberg, professor at McGill University and one of the world's leading management experts, was asked to compare organizational structure and corporate culture, he said: "Culture is the soul of the organization—the beliefs and values, and how they are manifested. I think of the structure as the skeleton, and as the flesh and blood. And culture is the soul that holds the thing together and gives it life force."[2]

Mintzberg's culture metaphor provides a clear image of how to think about culture. Culture provides stability to an organization and gives employees a clear understanding of "the way things are done around here." Culture sets the tone for how an organization operates and how individuals within the organization interact. Think of the different impressions you have when a receptionist tells you that "Ms. Dettweiler" will be available in a moment, while at another organization you are told that "Emma" will be with you as soon as she gets off the phone. It's clear that in one organization the rules are more formal than in the other.

As we discuss organizational culture, you may want to remember that organizations differ considerably in the cultures they adopt. Consider the different cultures of Calgary-based WestJet Airlines and Montreal-based Air Canada. WestJet is viewed as having a "young, spunky, can-do environment, where customers will have more fun."[3] Air Canada, by contrast, is considered less helpful and friendly. One analyst even suggested that Air Canada staff "tend to make their customers feel stressed" by their confrontational behaviour.[4] Our discussion of culture should help you understand how these differences across organizations occur.

1 What is the purpose of organizational culture?

Royal Canadian Mint
www.mint.ca

WestJet Airlines
www.westjet.com

Air Canada
www.aircanada.com

As you start to think about different organizations where you might work, you will want to research their cultures. An organization that expects employees to work 15 hours a day may not be where you would like to work. To help you think more about culture and its impact on you, you may want to complete the *Learning About Yourself Exercise* on page 380, which assesses whether you would be more comfortable in a formal, rule-oriented culture or a more informal, flexible culture.

Definition of Organizational Culture

organizational culture The pattern of shared values, beliefs, and assumptions considered to be the appropriate way to think and act within an organization.

Organizational culture is the pattern of shared values, beliefs, and assumptions considered to be the appropriate way to think and act within an organization. The key features of culture are as follows:

- Culture is shared by the members of the organization.

- Culture helps members of the organization solve and understand the things that it encounters, both internally and externally.

- Because the assumptions, beliefs, and expectations that make up culture have worked over time, the organization's members believe they are valid. Therefore, they are taught to people who join the organization.

- These assumptions, beliefs, and expectations strongly influence how people perceive, think, feel, and behave within the organization.[5]

Not every group develops a culture, although any group that has existed for a while and has shared learnings will likely have a culture. Groups that experience high turnover (so that learnings are not really passed down to new members effectively) and groups that have not experienced any challenging events may not develop cultures.

Levels of Culture

artifacts Aspects of an organization's culture that you see, hear, and feel.

Exhibit 10-1 shows that culture is manifested at different levels within an organization. Culture is very visible at the level of **artifacts**. These are what you see, hear, and feel when you encounter an organization's culture. You may notice, for instance, that employees in two offices have very different dress policies, or one office displays great works of art while another posts company mottos on the wall. These visible artifacts emerge from the organization's culture.

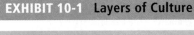

EXHIBIT 10-1   Layers of Culture

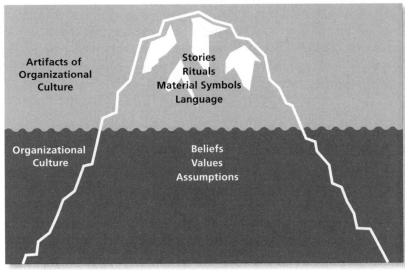

Artifacts of Organizational Culture

Stories
Rituals
Material Symbols
Language

Organizational Culture

Beliefs
Values
Assumptions

Below the surface of what you observe are the beliefs, values, and assumptions that make up the organizational culture. **Beliefs** are the understandings of how objects and ideas relate to each other. **Values** are the stable, long-lasting beliefs about what is important. For instance, Winnipeg-based Palliser Furniture, a manufacturer of wooden and upholstered furniture, promotes the following corporate values: "demonstrating integrity in all relationships, promoting the dignity and value of each other, and striving for excellence."[6] **Assumptions** are the taken-for-granted notions of how something should be. When basic assumptions are held by the entire group, members will have difficulty conceiving of another way of doing things. For instance, in Canada, some students hold a basic assumption that universities should not consider costs when setting tuition, and should keep tuition low for greater access by students.

The values and assumptions present in an organization are not always readily apparent. Therefore we rely on the organization's artifacts to help us uncover those values and assumptions.

Montreal-based PEAK Financial Group, which practically doubled its staff in 1999, worried that rapid growth might mean that not all employees would understand the company's culture. Therefore, PEAK established "The Academy," an intensive three-day orientation for all new hires. Afterward, all employees join together in a welcome ceremony, where new employees are asked to give a two-minute speech telling who they are and why they chose to work at PEAK. PEAK's programs make sure that employees feel part of the culture from day one and feel comfortable interacting with each other. Here we see Robert Frances, president and CEO, welcoming a new employee during a staff meeting.

Characteristics of Culture

Research suggests that seven primary characteristics capture the essence of an organization's culture:[7]

- *Innovation and risk-taking.* The degree to which employees are encouraged to be innovative and take risks.

- *Attention to detail.* The degree to which employees are expected to work with precision, analysis, and attention to detail.

- *Outcome orientation.* The degree to which management focuses on results, or outcomes, rather than on the techniques and processes used to achieve these outcomes.

- *People orientation.* The degree to which management decisions take into consideration the effect of outcomes on people within the organization.

- *Team orientation.* The degree to which work activities are organized around teams rather than individuals.

- *Aggressiveness.* The degree to which people are aggressive and competitive rather than easygoing and supportive.

- *Stability.* The degree to which organizational activities emphasize maintaining the status quo in contrast to growth.

Each of these characteristics exists on a continuum from low to high. For instance, the Royal Canadian Mint, discussed in this chapter's vignette, is high on innovation and risk-taking, and high on people orientation and team orientation. But the Mint is low on stability, as its goal is to be able to move quickly when opportunities arise.

When individuals consider their organization in terms of these seven characteristics, they get a composite picture of the organization's culture. This picture becomes the basis for feelings of shared understanding that members have about the organization, how things are done in it, and the way members are supposed to behave.

beliefs The understandings of how objects and ideas relate to each other.

values The stable, long-lasting beliefs about what is important.

assumptions The taken-for-granted notions of how something should be.

Exhibit 10-2 demonstrates how these characteristics can be mixed to create highly diverse organizations. To help you understand some of the characteristics of culture, you may want to look at the *Working With Others Exercise* on page 381, which asks you to rate your classroom culture.

Culture's Functions

Culture performs a number of functions within an organization:

- It has a boundary-defining role because it creates distinction between one organization and others.

- It conveys a sense of identity to organization members.

- It helps create commitment to something larger than an individual's self-interest.

- It enhances stability; it's the social glue that helps hold the organization together by providing appropriate standards for what employees should say and do.

- It serves as a control mechanism that guides and shapes the attitudes and behaviour of employees, and helps them make sense of the organization.

This last function is of particular interest to us.[8] As the following quotation makes clear, culture defines the rules of the game:

Culture by definition is elusive, intangible, implicit, and taken for granted. But every organization develops a core set of assumptions, understandings, and implicit rules that govern day-to-day behaviour in the workplace. Until newcomers learn the rules, they are not accepted as full-fledged members of the organization. Transgressions of the rules on the part of high-level executives or front-line employees result in universal disapproval and powerful penalties. Conformity to the rules becomes the primary basis for reward and upward mobility.[9]

What does culture do?

The role of culture in influencing employee behaviour appears to be increasingly important in today's workplace.[10] As organizations widen spans of control, flatten structures, introduce teams, reduce formalization, and empower employees, the *shared meaning* provided by a strong culture ensures that everyone is pointed in the same direction. Geoffrey Relph,

---

EXHIBIT 10-2   Contrasting Organizational Cultures

Organization A	Organization B
• Managers must fully document all decisions. • Creative decisions, change, and risks are not encouraged. • Extensive rules and regulations exist for all employees. • Productivity is valued over employee morale. • Employees are encouraged to stay within their own department. • Individual effort is encouraged.	• Management encourages and rewards risk-taking and change. • Employees are encouraged to "run with" ideas, and failures are treated as "learning experiences." • Employees have few rules and regulations to follow. • Productivity is balanced with treating its people right. • Team members are encouraged to interact with people at all levels and functions. • Many rewards are team-based.

IBM Canada's director of services marketing, compared the culture of his previous company (GE Appliances in Louisville, Kentucky) with that of IBM: "The priorities in GE are: 'Make the financial commitments. Make the financial commitments. Make the financial commitments.' At IBM, the company's attention is divided among customer satisfaction, employee morale, and positive financial results."[11] These two cultures give employees and managers different messages about where they should direct their attention.

Culture can also influence people's ethical behaviour. When lower-level employees see their managers padding expense reports, this sends a signal that the firm tolerates such dishonest behaviour. Firms that emphasize individual sales records may encourage unhealthy competition among sales staff, including "misplacing" phone messages, and not being helpful to someone else's client. Toronto-based GMP Securities, on the other hand, emphasizes the importance of a teamwork culture, so that individuals are not competing against one another and engaging in questionable activities. Founding partner Brad Griffiths notes that "the corporate culture is to make an environment where everybody feels they're involved. We want to be successful, but not at the expense of the individual."[12]

IBM Canada
www.ibm.com/ca/en/

GMP Securities
www.gmpsecurities.com

Do Organizations Have Uniform Cultures?

Organizational culture represents a common perception held by the organization's members. This was made explicit when we defined culture as a system of *shared* meaning. We should expect, therefore, that individuals with different backgrounds or at different levels in the organization will tend to describe the organization's culture in similar terms.[13]

However, the fact that organizational culture has common properties does not mean that there cannot be subcultures within it. Most large organizations have a dominant culture and numerous sets of subcultures.[14]

A **dominant culture** expresses the core values that are shared by a majority of the organization's members. When we talk about an *organization's* culture, we are referring to its dominant culture. It is this macro view of culture that gives an organization its distinct personality.[15] **Subcultures** tend to develop in large organizations to reflect common problems, situations, or experiences that members face. These subcultures are likely to be defined by department designations and geographical separation.

An organization's purchasing department, for example, can have a subculture that is uniquely shared by members of that department. It will include the **core values** of the dominant culture, plus additional values unique to members of the purchasing department. Similarly, an office or unit of the organization that is physically separated from the organization's main operations may take on a different personality. Again, the core values are essentially retained but modified to reflect the separated unit's distinct situation.

If organizations had no dominant culture and were composed only of numerous subcultures, the value of organizational culture as an explanatory variable for organizational behaviour would be significantly lessened. That is because there would be no uniform interpretation of what represented appropriate and inappropriate behaviour. It is the "shared meaning" aspect of culture that makes it such a potent device for guiding and shaping behaviour. This is what allows us to say that Microsoft's culture values aggressiveness and risk-taking,[16] and then to use that information to better understand the

dominant culture A system of shared meaning that expresses the core values shared by a majority of the organization's members.

subcultures Minicultures within an organization, typically defined by department designations and geographical separation.

core values The primary, or dominant, values that are accepted throughout the organization.

The core value of enhancing people's lives through sports and fitness is intensely held and widely shared by Nike employees. Nike founder Philip Knight has created a strong sports-oriented culture and promotes it through company practices such as paying employees extra for biking to work instead of driving. Nike is recognized worldwide as an athletes' company that hires former varsity, professional, and Olympic athletes to design and market its shoes and clothing for sports enthusiasts. Nike headquarters in Beaverton, Oregon, is a large campus with walking and jogging trails and buildings named for sports heroes, such as the Joan Benoit Samuelson Center, the Bo Jackson Fitness Center, and the Joe Paterno Day Care Center.

behaviour of Microsoft executives and employees. But we cannot ignore the reality that as well as a dominant culture, many organizations have subcultures that can influence the behaviour of members. Some strong subcultures can even make it difficult for managers to implement organizational change. This can happen in both unionized and non-unionized environments.

READING AN ORGANIZATION'S CULTURE

David Dingwall, former president and CEO of the Royal Canadian Mint, relates a story that highlights the culture of the Mint when he was in his early days of leading the organization.[17] In April 2003, representatives from Mike Weir's management company phoned the Mint to see if it could produce a commemorative coin should the Canadian golfer go on to win the Masters Tournament, which he was then leading. "Our staff person said, 'You will have to send in a letter and when we get the letter we will look at it. But obviously, we couldn't do anything this year,'" recalls Dingwall.

When Weir's rep asked how long he would have to wait for a decision, the Mint employee replied, "At least a year." Weir in fact won the Masters Tournament that year, but Dingwall didn't hear about the commemorative coin request for another month or two. When he did eventually find out, he realized "then and there that our business processes were not focused toward the customer or the market. So we took that as an example and turned [the culture] around." Why does culture have such a strong influence on people's behaviour?

2 How do you read an organization's culture?

strong culture Culture where the core values are intensely held and widely shared.

Nordstrom
www.nordstrom.com

Organizations differ in the extent to which they can be characterized as having strong or weak cultures.[18] In a **strong culture**, the organization's core values are both intensely held and widely shared.[19] The more members who accept the core values and the greater their commitment to those values, the stronger the culture is. A strong culture will have a great influence on the behaviour of its members because the high degree of shared experiences and intensity create an internal climate of high behavioural control. For example, American retailer Nordstrom has developed one of the strongest service cultures in the retailing industry. Nordstrom employees know what is expected of them, and these expectations go a long way in shaping their behaviour.

By contrast, the Royal Canadian Mint's employees did not recognize the opportunity that was presented to highlight the first time a Canadian won golfing's Masters Tournament. This suggests the Mint's employees were governed by a weak culture. In a weak culture, employees do not feel any great attachment to their organization or their co-workers. They may not take pride in their work. If you think about service and retail experiences you have had, if employees as a whole routinely seem to ignore customers, and the environment is unfriendly or unclean, this may be the result of a weak culture.

A strong culture demonstrates high agreement among members about what the organization stands for. Such unanimity of purpose builds cohesiveness, loyalty, and organizational commitment. These qualities, in turn, lessen employees' tendency to leave the organization.[20] This chapter's *HR Implications* on page 379 illustrates the creation of a specific type of strong culture, an ethical culture.

As we noted earlier in Exhibit 10-1, the artifacts of culture inform outsiders and employees about the underlying values and beliefs of the organization's culture. These artifacts, or physical manifestations of culture, include stories, rituals, material symbols, and language. The extent to which organizations have artifacts of their culture indicates whether they have strong or weak cultures. *From Concepts to Skills* on page 384 offers additional ideas on how to read an organization's culture.

Stories

Employees of Seattle-based Nordstrom are fond of a story that strongly conveys the company's policy toward customer returns. When this specialty retail chain was in its infancy, a customer came in and wanted to return a set of automobile tires. The salesperson was a bit uncertain how to handle the problem. As the customer and salesperson spoke, Mr. Nordstrom walked by and overheard the conversation. He immediately interceded, instructing the salesperson to take the tires back and provide a full cash refund. After the customer had received his refund and left, the perplexed salesperson looked at the boss. "But, Mr. Nordstrom, we don't sell tires!" "I know," replied Nordstrom, "but we do whatever we need to do to make the customer happy. I mean it when I say we have a no-questions-asked return policy." Nordstrom then picked up the telephone and called a friend in the auto-parts business to see how much he could get for the tires.

When publisher Hollinger International acquired Canada's Southam Newspapers, the story is that David Radler, Hollinger's president and COO, interrupted a local Canadian publisher's presentation on the paper's mission statement "and held up a bill from his wallet, pronouncing that 'from now on this is to be the mission.'"[21] This certainly sent the message that financial interests would be the bottom line for Canada's largest chain of newspapers.

Stories such as these circulate through many organizations. They typically tell about the organization's founders, rule breaking, rags-to-riches successes, reductions in the workforce, relocation of employees, reactions to past mistakes, and organizational coping.[22] These stories anchor the present in the past and provide explanations and legitimacy for current practices.[23]

Rituals

Rituals are repetitive sequences of activities that express and reinforce the key values of the organization; what goals are most important; and which people are important, and which ones are expendable.[24]

For example, college and university faculty members undergo a lengthy ritual in their quest for permanent employment, or tenure. Typically, the faculty member is on probation for six years. At the end of that period, the member's colleagues must make one of two choices: Extend a tenured appointment or issue a one-year terminal contract.

Faculty members who have been socialized properly prove themselves worthy of being granted tenure. But every year, hundreds of faculty members at colleges and universities are denied tenure. In some cases, this action is a result of overall poor performance. More often, however, the decision can be traced to the faculty member's not doing well in those areas that the tenured faculty believe are important. The instructor who spends dozens of hours each week preparing for class and achieves outstanding evaluations by students, but neglects research and publication activities, may be denied tenure. What has happened, simply, is that the instructor has failed to adapt to the norms set by the department. The astute faculty member will assess early on in the probationary period what attitudes and behaviours his or her colleagues want, and will then proceed to demonstrate them. By demanding certain attitudes and behaviours, the tenured faculty help bring about the standardization of tenure candidates.

One well-known corporate ritual is Wal-Mart's company chant. Begun by the company's founder, Sam Walton, as a way to motivate and unite his workforce, "Gimme a W, gimme an A, gimme an L, gimme a squiggle, give me an M, A, R, T!" has become a company ritual that bonds Wal-Mart workers and reinforces Sam Walton's belief in the importance of his employees to the company's success. Similar corporate chants are used by IBM, Ericsson, Novell, Deutsche Bank, and PricewaterhouseCoopers.[25]

Material Symbols

The layout of corporate headquarters, the types of cars given to top executives, and the presence or absence of corporate aircraft are a few examples of material symbols. Others include the size of offices, the elegance of furnishings, executive perks, and dress code,

rituals Repetitive sequences of activities that express and reinforce the key values of the organization; what goals are most important; and which people are important, and which ones are expendable.

Wal-Mart Canada
www.walmartcanada.ca

Ericsson Canada
www.ericsson.ca

Novell Canada
www.novell.com/offices/americas/canada/

including uniforms.[26] In addition, corporate logos, signs, brochures, and advertisements reveal aspects of the organization's culture.[27] These material symbols convey to employees, customers, and clients who is important, the degree of egalitarianism desired by top management, and the kinds of behaviour (for example, risk-taking, conservative, authoritarian, participative, individualistic, social) that are appropriate. For instance, pictures of all Creo employees hang in the Burnaby, BC-based company's entrance lobby, which visibly conveys Creo's anti-hierarchical culture.

Companies differ in how much separation they make between their executives and employees. This plays out in how material benefits are distributed to executives. Some companies provide their top executives with chauffeur-driven limousines and, when they travel by air, unlimited use of the corporate jet. Other companies might pay for car and air transportation for top executives, only the car is a Chevrolet with no driver, and the jet seat is in the economy section of a commercial airliner. At Bolton, Ontario-based Husky Injection Molding Systems, a more egalitarian culture is favoured. Employees and management share the parking lot, dining room, and even washrooms.

Husky Injection Molding Systems
www.husky.ca

Language

Many organizations and units within organizations use language as a way to identify members of a culture or subculture. By learning this language, members show their acceptance of the culture and, in so doing, help to preserve it.

Starbucks Coffee
www.starbucks.com

For example, *baristas* at Starbucks call drinks short, tall, or *grande*, not small, medium, or large, and they know the difference between a *half-decaf double tall almond skinny mocha* and an *iced short schizo skinny hazelnut cappuccino with wings*.[28] Students and employees at Grant MacEwan College are informed by the philosophy of the college's namesake. Dr. Grant MacEwan, historian, writer, politician, and environmentalist, was never a formal part of the management of the organization. However, many phrases from his writing and creed have found their way into formal college publications and calendars, as well as informal communications, including his most well known, "I have tried to leave things in the vineyard better than I found them."[29]

Grant MacEwan College
www.macewan.ca

Over time, organizations often develop unique terms to describe equipment, offices, key staff, suppliers, customers, or products that relate to their business. New employees are frequently overwhelmed with acronyms and jargon that, after six months on the job, have become fully part of their language. Once assimilated, this terminology acts as a common denominator that unites members of a given culture or subculture.

CREATING AND SUSTAINING CULTURE

To address the problems of the culture he faced when he became president and CEO at the Royal Canadian Mint, David Dingwall needed to make a number of changes.[30] He introduced a lean enterprise model and a new management team, including a new chief financial officer as well as a new vice-president of sales and marketing. He made $15 million in cuts, including getting rid of the jewellery business, reducing inventory by 50 percent, and lowering travel and advertising expenses. He also reduced the time it took to get a product to market from more than 460 days to just 150, with the aim of becoming even quicker in 2005. To show that he was intent on creating a new culture, Dingwall involved employees in the changes. He encouraged them to help figure out how to create better work processes. Employees helped map out the steps for change and then implemented them. Dingwall complimented the employees on the job they did. "We had inventory savings. We had time savings. We were able to redirect some of our labour to other projects."

Dingwall recognized the importance of acknowledging good performance from employees. He wanted employees to meet customer demands quickly and efficiently. He suggested that the old culture at the Mint was partially responsible for not encouraging new ideas and initiatives by employees. "One of the big things I found at the Mint was a real reluctance to celebrate," he said.

Dingwall gave each of his vice-presidents a budget for celebrating achievements. "I am sure there was some celebration in the past, but now if you don't have celebrations in your operations, I want to know why. That is the difference." What other ways might Dingwall have created a high-performance culture at the Mint?

> *Is culture the same as rules?*

An organization's culture does not pop out of thin air. Once established, it rarely fades away. Which forces influence the creation of a culture? What reinforces and sustains these forces once they are in place? Exhibit 10-3 on page 362 summarizes how an organization's culture is established and sustained. The original culture is derived from the philosophy of its founders. This, in turn, strongly influences the selection criteria used in hiring. The actions of the current top management set the general climate of what is acceptable behaviour and what is not. How employees are to be socialized will depend on the degree of success an organization achieves in matching new employees' values to its own in the selection process, and on top management's preference for socialization methods. We describe each part of this process next.

❸ How do you create and maintain culture?

How a Culture Begins

An organization's current customs, traditions, and general way of doing things are largely due to what it has done before and the degree of success it has had with those endeavours. This leads us to the ultimate source of an organization's culture: its founders.[31]

The founders of an organization traditionally have a major impact on its early culture. They have a vision of what the organization should be. They are unconstrained by previous customs or ideologies. Because new organizations are typically small, it's possible for the founders to impose their vision on all organizational members.

The process of culture creation occurs in three ways.[32] First, founders only hire and keep employees who think and feel the way they do. Second, they indoctrinate and socialize these employees to their way of thinking and feeling. Finally, the founders' behaviour acts as a role model, encouraging employees to identify with the founders and thereby internalize those beliefs, values, and assumptions. When the organization succeeds, the founders' vision is viewed as a primary determinant of that success. At that point, the founders' personality becomes embedded in the culture of the organization.

For example, Microsoft's culture is largely a reflection of its co-founder, chair, and chief software architect (and former CEO), Bill Gates. Gates is personally aggressive, competitive, and highly disciplined. Those are the same characteristics often used to describe the software giant he founded. Other contemporary examples of founders who have had an immeasurable impact on their organizations' cultures are Ted Rogers of Toronto-based Rogers Communications, Frank Stronach of Aurora, Ontario-based Magna International, Anita Roddick of UK-based The Body Shop, and Richard Branson of UK-based Virgin Group.

IKEA founder Ingvar Kamprad grew up in a poor farming area in Sweden where people worked hard and lived frugally. He combined the lessons he learned growing up with his vision of helping people live a better life at home by offering them affordable, functional, and well-designed furniture. He named his company IKEA by combining his initials plus the first letters of Elmtaryd and Agunnaryd, the farm and village where he grew up. The success of IKEA in expanding to over 200 stores in 35 countries stems from Kamprad's vision.

EXHIBIT 10-3 How Organizational Cultures Form

Keeping a Culture Alive

Once a culture is in place, there are human resource practices within the organization that act to maintain it by giving employees a set of similar experiences.[33] For example, the selection process, performance evaluation criteria, training and career development activities, and promotion procedures ensure that new employees fit in with the culture, rewarding those who support it and penalizing (even expelling) those who challenge it. Three forces play a particularly important part in sustaining a culture: selection criteria, the actions of top management, and socialization methods. Let's take a closer look at each.

Selection

The explicit goal of the selection process is to identify and hire individuals who have the knowledge, skills, and abilities to perform the jobs within the organization successfully. Typically, more than one candidate will meet any given job's requirements. The final decision as to who is hired is significantly influenced by the decision maker's judgment of how well each candidate will fit into the organization. This attempt to ensure a proper match, either deliberately or inadvertently, results in the hiring of people who have values essentially consistent with those of the organization, or at least a good portion of those values.[34]

At the same time, the selection process provides information about the organization to applicants. If they perceive a conflict between their values and those of the organization, they can remove themselves from the applicant pool. Selection, therefore, becomes a two-way street, allowing the employer or applicant to look elsewhere if there appears to be a mismatch. In this way, the selection process sustains an organization's culture by "selecting out" those individuals who might attack or undermine its core values. *OB in the Workplace* shows how one company's use of multiple interviews ensures that applicants are right for the job.

OB IN THE WORKPLACE

Surviving Procter & Gamble's Intensive Screening Process

Procter & Gamble Canada
www.pg.com/en_CA

How does a company make sure an applicant is right for the job? Applicants for entry-level positions in brand management at household products maker Procter & Gamble (P&G) experience an exhaustive application and screening process. Their interviewers are part of an elite group who have been selected and trained extensively via lectures, videos, practice interviews, and role plays to identify applicants who will successfully fit in at P&G. Applicants are interviewed in depth for such qualities as their ability to "turn out high volumes of excellent work," "identify and understand problems," and "reach thoroughly substantiated and well-reasoned conclusions that lead to action." P&G values rationality and seeks applicants who show that quality. University and college applicants receive two interviews and a general-knowledge test on campus before being flown back to head office for three more one-on-one interviews and a group interview at lunch. Each encounter seeks corroborating evidence of the traits that the firm believes correlate highly with "what counts" for success at P&G.[35] 🏃

Top Management

The actions of top management also have a major impact on the organization's culture.[36] Through what they say and how they behave, senior executives establish norms that filter down through the organization. These norms establish whether risk-taking is desirable, how much freedom managers should give their employees, what appropriate dress is, what actions will pay off in terms of pay raises, promotions, other rewards, and the like. As we noted earlier, managers at the Royal Canadian Mint didn't seem to value celebrating employees' positive actions prior to David Dingwall taking over. The manager of Sheraton Suites Calgary Eau Claire discovered how important changing the culture of the organization was to improving performance, as *OB in the Workplace* shows.

Markham, Ontario-based InSystems wants to be known as a high-performance culture and a hip place to work. Founder and CEO Michael Egan appears in one of his company's recruiting pamphlets atop his Harley-Davidson. To ensure that new hires will fit into the culture, he offers bonuses to his employees for recommending a successful hire. Recruits who meet the technical requirements for the job go through five to seven interviews "because the cultural fit is key."

OB IN THE WORKPLACE

Employees Have Feelings Too

Can a culture change help with turnover problems? Sheraton Suites Calgary Eau Claire had turnover problems almost from the time it opened.[37] Though the hotel ranked third out of 210 Sheratons across Canada in a 1999 customer satisfaction survey, its key employees kept leaving.

General manager Randy Zupanski wanted to improve employee morale and hired a consulting group to uncover problems in the workplace through a series of seminars. The consultants uncovered some interesting concerns. The hotel management had focused on team process, encouraging and rewarding team behaviour. However, the team culture was having a negative effect on many employees. They did not feel that they were being recognized and rewarded for what they were doing as individuals.

Zupanski and his managers introduced changes to the hotel's culture. They made the recognition program more personal, rewarding such things as attendance, performance, and extra work. Some employees received an extra day off with pay for their hard work.

The result, said the hotel's human resource manager, was an incredible change in atmosphere. Individual employees felt less stressed and more rewarded, which led to overall performance improvements by everyone. Customer satisfaction in turn improved so much that the Eau Claire Sheraton received the Highest Overall Guest Satisfaction award among 230 Sheratons in North America in 2001, 2002, 2003, and 2004. Zupanski noted that working together to change the hotel's culture brought "us together and brought trust and understanding into the team atmosphere." 🏃

Sheraton Suites Calgary Eau Claire
www.sheratonsuites.com

The example of Sheraton Suites Calgary Eau Claire shows that being aware of how culture affects individual performance can help managers identify specific practices that lead to lowered morale. However, we would not want to leave you with the impression that changing an organization's culture is easy. In fact, it's a difficult process. We discuss the process of reshaping culture in greater detail in Chapter 14.

Socialization

No matter how effectively the organization recruits and selects new employees, they are not fully indoctrinated in the organization's culture when they start their job. Because they are unfamiliar with the organization's culture, new employees are potentially likely to disturb the beliefs and customs that are in place. The organization will, therefore, want to help new employees adapt to its culture. This adaptation process is called **socialization**.[38]

socialization The process that adapts new employees to the organization's culture.

Sanyo Canada
www.sanyocanada.com

New employees at the Japanese electronics company Sanyo undergo an extensive training program. At their intensive five-month course, trainees eat and sleep together in company-subsidized dorms and are required to vacation together at company-owned resorts. They learn the Sanyo way of doing everything—from how to speak to managers to proper grooming and dress.[39] The company considers this program essential for transforming young employees, fresh out of school, into dedicated *kaisha senshi*, or corporate warriors.

Starbucks does not go to the extreme that Sanyo does, but it seeks the same outcome.[40] All new employees go through 24 hours of training. Classes cover everything necessary to transform new employees into brewing consultants. They learn the Starbucks philosophy, the company jargon, and even how to help customers make decisions about beans, grind, and espresso machines. The result is employees who understand Starbucks' culture and who project an enthusiastic and knowledgeable image to customers.

As we discuss socialization, keep in mind that the most critical socialization stage occurs when the new employee enters the organization. This is when the organization seeks to mould the outsider into an employee "in good standing." Employees who fail to learn the essential role behaviours risk being labelled "nonconformists" or "rebels," which often leads to expulsion. But the organization will continue to socialize all employees, though maybe not as explicitly, throughout their careers in the organization. This further contributes to sustaining the culture. (Sometimes, however, employees are not fully socialized. For instance, you will note in Exhibit 10-4 that employees had learned they were supposed to wear checkerboard caps to work, but clearly didn't know why.)

Socialization can be conceptualized as a process composed of three stages: prearrival, encounter, and metamorphosis.[41] The first stage, *prearrival*, encompasses all the learning that occurs before a new member joins the organization. In the second stage, *encounter*, the new employee sees what the organization is really like and confronts the possibility that expectations and reality may diverge. In the third stage, *metamorphosis*, the relatively long-lasting changes take place. The new employee masters the skills required for his or her job, successfully performs his or her new roles, and makes the adjustments to his or her work group's values and norms.[42] This three-stage process has an impact on the new employee's work productivity, commitment to the organization's objectives, and eventual decision to stay with the organization. Exhibit 10-5 depicts the socialization process.

Starbucks' international employees travel to Seattle headquarters to become immersed in the company's culture of caring for employees, customers, communities, and the environment. By socializing employees from other countries, Starbucks sustains its culture of treating others with respect, embracing diversity, and developing satisfied customers. Shown here are employees from Puerto Rico, Kuwait, China, and Australia learning about Starbucks' high coffee standards during a coffee-tasting session.

The Prearrival Stage The **prearrival stage** explicitly recognizes that each individual arrives with a set of values, attitudes, and expectations. These cover both the work to be done and the organization. For instance, in many jobs, particularly professional work, new members will have undergone a considerable degree of prior socialization in school and in training. One major purpose of a business school, for example, is to socialize business students to the attitudes and behaviours that business firms want. If business executives believe that successful employees value the profit ethic, are loyal, will work hard, and desire to achieve, they can hire individuals out of business schools who have been premoulded in this pattern.

But prearrival socialization goes beyond the specific job. The selection process is used in most organizations to inform prospective employees about the organization as a whole. In addition, as noted previously, the selection process also ensures the inclusion of the "right type"—those who will fit in. As one study notes, "Indeed, the ability of the individual to present the appropriate face during the selection process determines his or her ability to move into the organization in the first place. Thus, success depends on the degree to which the aspiring member has correctly anticipated the expectations and desires of those in the organization in charge of selection."[43]

EXHIBIT 10-4

"I don't know how it started, either. All I know is that it's part of our corporate culture."

Source: Drawing by Mick Stevens in *The New Yorker*, October 3, 1994. Copyright © 1994 by The New Yorker Magazine, Inc. Reprinted by permission.

prearrival stage The period of learning in the socialization process that occurs before a new employee joins the organization.

The Encounter Stage Upon entering the organization, the new employee begins the **encounter stage**. Here the individual confronts the possible gap between expectations—of the job, co-workers, boss, and the organization in general—and reality. If the employee's expectations are more or less accurate, the encounter stage merely provides a reaffirmation of the perceptions gained earlier.

However, this is often not the case. Where expectations and reality differ, the socialization period for the new employee should be designed to help him or her detach from previous assumptions and replace them with another set that the organization deems desirable. Of course, not all organizations that actively socialize their members are so successful that new employees completely adopt the new set of assumptions. At the extreme, new members may become totally disillusioned with the realities of their job and resign. Proper selection should significantly reduce the probability of this happening.

encounter stage The stage in the socialization process in which a new employee sees what the organization is really like and confronts the possibility that expectations and reality may diverge.

EXHIBIT 10-5   A Socialization Model

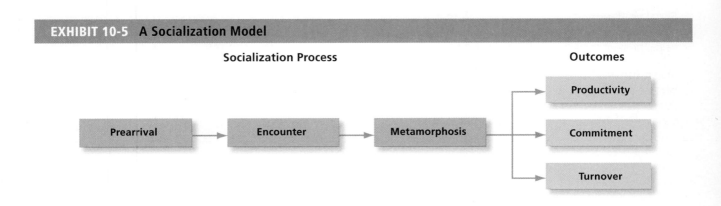

metamorphosis stage The stage in the socialization process in which a new employee adjusts to the work group's values and norms.

The Metamorphosis Stage Finally, the new employee must work out any problems discovered during the encounter stage. This may mean going through changes to adjust to the work group's values and norms—hence, we call this the **metamorphosis stage**. The socialization options presented in Exhibit 10-6 are designed to bring about the desired metamorphosis. Note, for example, that the more management relies on socialization programs that are formal, collective, fixed, serial, and emphasize divestiture, the greater the likelihood that newcomers' differences and perspectives will be stripped away and replaced by standardized and predictable behaviours. Management's careful selection of socialization experiences for newcomers can—at the extreme—create conformists who maintain traditions and customs, or inventive and creative individualists who consider no organizational practice sacred.

We can say that metamorphosis and the entry socialization process is complete when

- The new employee has become comfortable with the organization and his or her job

- The new employee has internalized the norms of the organization and the work group, and understands and accepts these norms

- The new employee feels accepted by his or her peers as a trusted and valued individual, is self-confident that he or she has the competence to complete the job successfully, and understands the system—not only his or her own tasks, but also the rules, procedures, and informally accepted practices

- The new employee understands how he or she will be evaluated and knows what criteria will be used to measure and appraise his or her work; he or she knows what is expected and what constitutes a job "well done"

EXHIBIT 10-6   Entry Socialization Options

Formal vs. Informal The more a new employee is segregated from the ongoing work setting and differentiated in some way to make explicit his or her newcomer's role, the more formal socialization is. Specific orientation and training programs are examples. Informal socialization puts the new employee directly into his or her job, with little or no special attention.

Individual vs. Collective New members can be socialized individually. This describes how it's done in many professional offices. They can also be grouped together and processed through an identical set of experiences, as in military boot camp.

Fixed vs. Variable This refers to the time schedule in which newcomers make the transition from outsider to insider. A fixed schedule establishes standardized stages of transition. This characterizes rotational training programs. It also includes probationary periods, such as the 8- to 10-year "associate" status accounting and law firms use before deciding whether to name a candidate as a partner. Variable schedules give no advance notice of their transition timetable. Variable schedules describe the typical promotion system, where individuals are not advanced to the next stage until they are "ready."

Serial vs. Random Serial socialization is characterized by the use of role models who train and encourage the newcomer. Apprenticeship and mentoring programs are examples. In random socialization, role models are deliberately withheld. The new employee is left on his or her own to figure things out.

Investiture vs. Divestiture Investiture socialization assumes that the newcomer's qualities and qualifications are the necessary ingredients for job success, so these qualities and qualifications are confirmed and supported. Divestiture socialization tries to strip away certain characteristics of the recruit. Fraternity and sorority "pledges" go through divestiture socialization to shape them into the proper role.

Sources: Based on J. Van Maanen, "People Processing: Strategies of Organizational Socialization," *Organizational Dynamics,* Summer 1978, pp. 19–36; and E. H. Schein, "Organizational Culture," *American Psychologist,* February 1990, p. 116.

As Exhibit 10-5 on page 365 shows, successful metamorphosis should have a positive impact on the new employee's productivity and commitment to the organization. It should reduce the tendency to leave the organization.

Some people, of course, do not fit well with the company culture. Doug Hobbes, director of product marketing for Globe Information Services (now Globe Interactive), lasted just four months at Toronto-based GlobeStar Systems.[44] In his words, "It was a culture thing." He did not enjoy going out for hamburgers after work or working late until 9 or 10 p.m. alongside the organization's key people. Because Hobbes' work habits differed from theirs, his co-workers viewed him as unenterprising and aloof. His story serves as a reminder that you should make sure you fit with the organization's culture before you accept a job. This chapter's *Ethical Dilemma Exercise* on page 381 considers whether some forms of socialization may be unethical.

GlobeStar Systems
www.globestarsystems.com

Effects of Layoffs

While the selection criteria, the actions of top management, and socialization methods all help to pass on the culture to new employees and keep the culture alive, the effects of layoffs on companies can be devastating. Layoffs can mean that people who know the culture best leave the organization. In addition, fear and stress about layoffs can seriously erode the company's culture.

Matching People With Cultures

What kind of culture would work best for you?

There is now a substantive body of evidence to demonstrate that organizations try to select new members who fit well with the organization's culture.[45] Most job candidates similarly try to find organizations where their values and personality will fit in.

Research by Goffee and Jones provides interesting insights on different organizational cultures and guidance for prospective employees.[46] The pair have identified four distinct cultural types. Let's take a look at their cultural framework and how you can use it to select an employer where you will best fit.

Goffee and Jones argue that two dimensions underlie organizational culture. The first dimension is *sociability.* This is a measure of friendliness. High sociability means people do kind things for one another without expecting something in return and relate to each other in a friendly, caring way. In terms of the characteristics of organizational culture presented at the beginning of this chapter, sociability is consistent with a high people orientation, high team orientation, and focus on processes rather than outcomes.

The second dimension is *solidarity.* It considers the strength of the group's task orientation. High solidarity means people can overlook personal biases and rally behind common interests and common goals. Again, referring back to our earlier discussion about the characteristics of culture, solidarity is consistent with high attention to detail and high aggressiveness.

Exhibit 10-7 on page 368 illustrates a matrix with these two dimensions rated as either high or low. They create four distinct culture types:

- *Networked culture (high on sociability, low on solidarity).* Organizations with this type of culture view members as family and friends. People know and like each other. People willingly give assistance to others and openly share information. The major downside to this culture is that the focus on friendships can lead to a tolerance for poor performance and creation of political cliques.

Unilever and Heineken are examples of companies with networked cultures. Heineken, for example, has more than 30 000 employees but retains the feeling of friendship and

Unilever Canada
www.unilever.ca

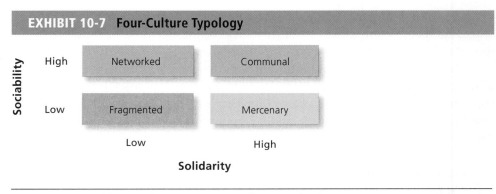

EXHIBIT 10-7   Four-Culture Typology

Source: Adapted from R. Goffee and G. Jones, *The Character of a Corporation: How Your Company's Culture Can Make or Break Your Business* (New York: HarperBusiness, 1998), p. 21.

family that is more typical at small firms. The company's highly social culture produces a strong sense of belonging and often a passionate identification with its product. Family businesses can often have this type of culture, although not all family businesses would have a networked culture.

- *Mercenary culture (low on sociability, high on solidarity).* Organizations with this type of culture are fiercely goal-focused. People are intense and determined to meet goals. They have a zest for getting things done quickly and a powerful sense of purpose. A mercenary culture is not just about winning; it is about destroying the enemy. This focus on goals and objectivity leads to a minimal degree of politicking. The major downside to this culture is that it can lead to an almost inhumane treatment of people who are perceived as low performers.

Campbell Company of Canada
www.campbellsoup.ca

Enron, Mars, Campbell Company of Canada, and Komatsu Canada (the Japanese heavy-equipment manufacturer) have classic mercenary cultures. At Virginia-based candy manufacturer Mars, for instance, meetings are almost totally concerned with work issues. There is little tolerance for socializing or small talk.

- *Fragmented culture (low on sociability, low on solidarity).* Organizations with this type of culture are made up of individualists. Commitment is first and foremost to individual members and their job tasks. There is little or no identification with the organization. In a fragmented culture, employees are judged solely on their productivity and the quality of their work. The major downside to this culture is that it can lead to excessive critiquing of others and an absence of collegiality and cooperation. Some large accounting and law firms have this type of culture.

Most top-tier universities and some large accounting and law firms take on the properties of fragmented cultures. Professors at major universities, for instance, are judged on their research and scholarship. Senior professors with big reputations don't need to be friendly to their peers or attend social functions to retain their status. Similarly, law partners who bring in new clients and win cases need to expend little energy getting to know co-workers or being visible in the office.

- *Communal culture (high on sociability, high on solidarity).* Organizations with this type of culture value both friendship and performance. People have a feeling of belonging, but there is still a ruthless focus on goal achievement. Leaders of these cultures tend to be inspirational and charismatic, with a clear vision of the organizations' future. The major downside to this culture is that it often consumes an employee's life. Its charismatic leaders frequently expect to create disciples rather than followers, resulting in a work climate that is almost "cult-like." Apple under Steve Jobs, particularly in its early years, is an example of a communal culture, as are Hewlett-Packard Canada, Johnson & Johnson Canada, and consulting firm Bain & Company. HP historically has been large and very goal-focused. Yet it's also a company known for its strong family feel. The "HP Way" is a set of values the company has developed that govern how people should behave and interact with each other. The HP Way's value of trust and community encourages loyalty to the company. The company returns that loyalty to employees as long as they perform well. Many start-ups exhibit a communal culture. During the height of the dot-com era, 20-something employees thought nothing of working around the clock, even sleeping and eating at their workplace.

OB IN ACTION
Finding Your Culture
How do you know which culture is a good fit for you?

✔ *You are cut out for a* **networked culture** if you possess good social skills and empathy; you like to forge close, work-related friendships; you thrive in a relaxed and convivial atmosphere; and you are not obsessed with efficiency and task performance.

✔ *You are well matched to a* **mercenary culture** if you are goal-oriented, thrive on competition, like clearly structured work tasks, enjoy risk-taking, and are able to deal openly with conflict.

✔ *You are likely to fit in well in a* **fragmented culture** if you are independent, have a low need to be part of a group atmosphere, are analytical rather than intuitive, and have a strong sense of self that is not easily undermined by criticism.

✔ *You might fit in with a* **communal culture** if you have a strong need to identify with something bigger than yourself; enjoy working in teams; and are willing to put the organization above family and personal life.

How important is the culture-person fit? In a study of accounting firms, new employees whose personalities meshed with the company were 20 percent less likely to leave their jobs in the first three years than those who did not fit as well.[47] *OB in Action—Finding Your Culture* provides a checklist to help you find the culture in which you might be most comfortable. This chapter's *From Concepts to Skills* on page 384 gives you some idea of factors that you might consider when trying to "read" an organization's culture.

The difficulties of matching people to organizational cultures becomes more important when organizations start operating in other countries. Toyota, for instance, faced challenges when it tried to bring its culture to its plant in Valenciennes, France. *OB Around the Globe* provides the details.

Hewlett-Packard Canada
welcome.hp.com/country/ca/en/welcome.html

Johnson & Johnson Canada
www.jnjcanada.com

OB AROUND THE GLOBE

No Chopsticks With Foie Gras

Can a company with a strong culture take that culture to another country? When Toyota opened its new plant in Valenciennes, France, both the French and the Japanese employees working there had to make some adjustments.[48] French workers had to give up red wine for lunch and, much to their surprise, do calisthenics at 8 a.m., before the first shift. Deferring to France's strong labour traditions, Japanese management had to accept four trade union representatives on their labour board.

Employees who had previously worked for French firms like Peugeot observed that instead of having early morning meetings to discuss the day's production run, Toyota insisted on having meetings whenever a problem arose. The culture of Toyota is different for French managers as well. They have no private office space and no executive dining room, perks they would have if they worked in French-based firms.

While some employees complain about too much rice in the cafeteria, and few use chopsticks, much of the food available is still "French": steak, pizza, pasta, and poached fish. But Toyota's greatest challenge is to develop a "Toyota identity" for the employees. Though Toyota provides free work clothing, most employees will not wear it. Toyota believes that a uniform look fosters identity and communication, but French workers strongly value individuality. 🕴

The experience of Toyota in France shows that an organization's culture does not always translate well to another country.

THE LIABILITIES OF CULTURE

When David Dingwall took over as president and CEO of the Royal Canadian Mint, he faced a large deficit and inefficient business processes.[49] Dingwall recognized the need to streamline the Mint's activities, but also knew that he might face great resistance by employees. The culture of the organization before he arrived was generally accepted by the employees.

Dingwall knew that part of what he had to do to change the culture was to get the employees onside with the changes. "I gave a commitment to all of our employees that nobody, but nobody, would lose their job as a result of the lean enterprise. And some of them didn't believe that, but when they saw that we were walking the walk, that we weren't laying people off as a result of lean enterprise [practices], then it became more believable. We started to see the exhilaration from employees in terms of improving our processes," he said.

At the end of 2004, just 20 months after Dingwall started, the Mint was set to have an unprecedented good year. The Winnipeg plant doubled its staff during 2004, allowing it to operate day and night. Revenue was $330 million, considerably higher than the Mint's $250-million revenue in 2003. Net income for 2004 was $13 million, wiping out the deficit Dingwall faced when he started. How does culture affect an employee's willingness to contribute to the organization?

4 Can organizational culture have a downside?

We have treated culture in a nonjudgmental manner thus far. We have not said that it is good or bad, only that it exists. Many of its functions, as outlined, are valuable for both the organization and the employee. Culture enhances organizational commitment and increases the consistency of employee behaviour. These are clearly benefits to an organization. From an employee's standpoint, culture is valuable because it reduces ambiguity. It tells employees how things are done and what's important. However, we should not ignore the potentially dysfunctional aspects of culture, especially of a strong culture, on an organization's effectiveness. The Royal Canadian Mint had faced a large deficit because of its previous organizational culture. *Focus on Ethics* discusses how Enron's pressure-cooker culture led to the company's ultimate collapse.

FOCUS ON **ETHICS**

Pressure-Cooker Culture Leads to Enron's Demise

Would employees knowingly do wrong for their employer? "At Enron, losers fell by the wayside but victors stayed in the game," report two *Washington Post* journalists.[50] The "winner-take-all" culture demanded that employees do whatever they could to make Enron's stock price continually rise. Executives thus took risks with investments and accounting procedures, inflating revenue and hiding debt. Those who could not (or would not) play this game were forced out. As the company's annual report stated, "We insist on results."

"The driver was this unbelievable desire to keep portraying Enron as something very, very different and keep the track record going and going," said Forrest Hoglund, a former senior manager.

Enron's culture set up an in-crowd and an out-crowd, and employees knew whether they were "in" or "out." Everyone wanted to be liked in the organization, according to Sally Ison, another employee. "You do everything you can do to keep that."

Employees were even willing to blatantly acknowledge—among themselves—that they were doing wrong, according to Margaret Ceconi, a former Enron Energy Services (EES) manager, who was only briefly employed by Enron. After she was laid off, she wrote a memo to Kenneth Lay, former chair of Enron, and phoned federal regulators twice. In her memo to Lay she said, "EES has knowingly misrepresented EES' earnings," and she wrote, "This is common knowledge among all the EES employees, and is actually joked about. . . . [Enron] must investigate all these going ons." 🏃

Enron's culture led its employees to engage in various unethical accounting practices. We also consider culture's impact on change, diversity, and mergers and acquisitions.

Culture as a Barrier to Change

Culture is a liability when the shared values are not in agreement with those that will further the organization's effectiveness. Employees are less likely to have shared values when the organization's environment is dynamic. When the environment is undergoing rapid change, the organization's entrenched culture may no longer be appropriate. Consistency of behaviour is an asset to an organization when the company faces a stable environment. However, it may burden the organization and make responding to changes in the environment difficult. For many organizations with strong cultures, practices that led to previous successes can lead to failure when those practices no longer match up well with environmental needs.[51] When employees at the Royal Canadian Mint failed to act rapidly to create a commemorative coin for Canadian golfer Mike Weir, president and CEO David Dingwall felt this underscored the Mint's reluctance to respond to a competitive environment.

Culture as a Barrier to Diversity

Hiring new employees who, because of race, gender, disability, or other differences, are not like the majority of the organization's members creates a paradox.[52] Management wants the new employees to accept the organization's core cultural values. Otherwise, these employees are unlikely to fit in or be accepted. But at the same time, management wants to openly acknowledge and demonstrate support for the differences that these employees bring to the workplace.

Strong cultures put considerable pressure on employees to conform. They limit the range of values and styles that are acceptable. It's not a coincidence that employees at Disney theme parks appear to be almost universally attractive, clean, and wholesome-looking, with bright smiles. That's the image Disney seeks. The company selects employees who will maintain that image. A strong culture, supported by formal rules and regulations, ensures that all Disney theme-park employees will act in a relatively uniform and predictable way.

A strong culture that condones prejudice can even undermine formal corporate diversity policies. A widely publicized example is the Texaco (now part of Chevron) case in the United States, where senior managers made disparaging remarks about minorities and, as a result of legal action on behalf of 1400 employees, paid a settlement of $246 mil-

Chevron
www.chevron.com

lion.[53] Organizations seek out and hire diverse individuals because of the new strengths these people bring to the workplace. Yet these diverse behaviours and strengths are likely to diminish in strong cultures as people try to fit in. Strong cultures, therefore, can be liabilities when they effectively eliminate the unique strengths that people of different backgrounds bring to the organization. Moreover, strong cultures can also be liabilities when they support institutional bias or become insensitive to people who are different.

Culture as a Barrier to Mergers and Acquisitions

Historically, the key factors that management looked at in making merger or acquisition decisions were related to financial advantages or product synergy. In recent years, cultural compatibility has become the primary concern.[54] A favourable financial statement or product line may be the initial attraction of a merger or acquisition candidate, but whether the merger or acquisition actually works seems to have more to do with how well the two organizations' cultures match up. Daimler-Benz and Chrysler have struggled to make their 1998 merger work, as *OB Around the Globe* shows.

DaimlerChrysler Canada
www.daimlerchrysler.ca

OB AROUND THE GLOBE

Mergers Across National Borders Are Challenging

What happens when two companies with very different cultures merge? When Daimler-Benz and Chrysler merged in 1998, some called it a "marriage made in heaven."[55] The merger was supposed to create a global automaker out of two respected companies. Instead, the merger has been a disaster, with the US-based Chrysler arm becoming a money loser in the years since the merger. In spring 2002, Daimler's stock was worth half what it had been on the day the merger was announced. By 2005, Daimler was still not doing as well financially as analysts and shareholders had hoped, although there had been slight improvements in overall profitability.

The Germans and the Americans blame each other for the failure, and the very different cultures of the two organizations no doubt led to many of the problems. Daimler-Benz was extremely hierarchical, while Chrysler, with its "cowboy culture," was more egalitarian. Chrysler's managers were independent and its middle managers were empowered. While this structure led to a lot of infighting, it also resulted in much creativity—for example, the development of the popular PT Cruiser.

Employees at Chrysler were very slow to trust the German management that took over the company in what was billed as a merger of equals. Juergen Schrempp, chair of the merged companies in the early years of the merger, admitted that he intended for the merger to be a takeover. Thus, to North American employees it's no surprise that he has slashed thousands of jobs in Canada and the United States after the merger.

Distrust went both ways: German management did not trust the American senior managers at Chrysler, and eventually Schrempp let them go. They were viewed as overpaid and lazy, unwilling to work overtime or miss their golf games by flying on weekends. These images of one another did not make it easy for managers from the two companies to work together, and created much uncertainty for the employees at Chrysler. In 2005, Chrysler was starting to recover from the initial changes imposed by Schrempp, under the leadership of Dieter Zetsche. In mid-2005, Schrempp stepped down, and Zetsche was given his responsibilities, perhaps in acknowledgment that the conflict in cultures had been a bigger problem than initially anticipated.

As the Daimler-Benz and Chrysler merger suggests, bringing employees from two different companies together is likely to cause friction. When the merger occurs under difficult circumstances, the problems can be greater. For instance, employees from Andersen Canada merged with Toronto-based Deloitte & Touche LLP Canada in June 2002 after they were essentially forced out of work with little notice when the Enron scandal unfolded. Colin Taylor, CEO of Deloitte in Canada, noted that "given the circumstances, you have a lot of employees worried, anxious, traumatized even. They are in shock that a professional service firm of this size would have this happen to them so quickly."[56] Andersen's employees were not in a very good bargaining position when accepted into Deloitte. Unlike mergers where the two merging organizations fight over the name of the new company, and who gets what titles, Andersen's employees were concerned about having any job at all. This may affect how comfortable Andersen employees feel with the Deloitte culture as time passes.

Deloitte
www.deloitte.com

Strategies for Merging Cultures

Organizations can use several strategies when considering how to merge the cultures of two organizations:[57]

- *Assimilation.* The entire new organization is determined to take on the culture of one of the merging organizations. This strategy works best when one of the organizations has a relatively weak culture. However, if a culture is simply imposed on an organization, it rarely works.

- *Separation.* The organizations remain separate, and keep their individual cultures. This strategy works best when the organizations have little overlap in the industries in which they operate.

- *Integration.* A new culture is formed by merging parts of each of the organizations. This strategy works best when aspects of each organization's culture need to be improved.

While an integration strategy may take a lot of work, it can pay off, as *OB in the Workplace* shows.

OB IN THE WORKPLACE

Agrium Creates Its Own Culture Through Blending

Can an organization successfully merge many companies together? Calgary-based Agrium, a fertilizer producer with production plants in Canada, the United States, and Argentina, grew aggressively during the 1990s through a series of mergers and acquisitions, which included companies such as Western Farm Services and Nu-West Industries.[58] Agrium grew out of the fertilizer division of Cominco (now Teck Cominco), and then absorbed fertilizer divisions and spinoff companies from the mining and oil-and-gas industries, including Esso, Sherritt, and Unocal.

Agrium
www.agrium.com

Since Agrium is the result of multiple mergers of companies, employees created a rule that if anyone mentions their former employer, they must contribute money to a fund. The fund is used for a "team-building event" where employees go out together for lunch or dinner.

CEO Michael Wilson's explanation of the company's approach to merging cultures suggests that Agrium has used an integration strategy. "We take the best of the mining culture, which is very proactive, decisive, willing to act, willing to take appropriate risks . . . We blend it with the oil-and-gas culture [which is] very thorough in its analysis, in dotting of the i's and crossing of the t's, in making sure everyone's marching at the same pace." Wilson adds the culture of Dow Chemicals to the mix, where he worked for 18 years and learned "how to build collaboration across very strong business units, how to get results when you don't have full accountability."

Agrium has performed well in recent years, and Wilson sees this as a measure of a successful organizational culture. However, he believes that success is more than just earnings: "I have a saying, 'You have to be happy, healthy, and wise,' in that order." Wilson goes on to say, "There's nothing nicer than when you're at a convention with all your competition. And you look over your team, it's the bottom of the cycle, business is tough, and they're smiling. And you look over to the competition and they're all depressed because business is tough. And that's one measure right there: Is your team happy?" ⟨⟩

bicultural audit An examination of the differences between two potential merger partners prior to a merger to determine whether the cultures will be able to work together.

Potential merger partners might do well to conduct a **bicultural audit** before concluding that a merger should occur. Through questionnaires, interviews, and/or focus groups, potential merger partners should examine differences in the "vision, values, structure, management practices and behaviours" of the merging parties.[59] This examination should indicate whether there are commonalities from which to build a successful merger, or differences that could cause extreme difficulties in merging the two organizations. If the decision after a bicultural audit is to merge, the management team should bridge any existing culture gaps by[60]

- Defining a structure that is appropriate for both organizations, along with a reorganization plan

- Identifying and implementing a management style that is appropriate for both organizations

- Reinforcing internal communication to make sure that employees are kept aware of changes that will occur

- Getting agreement on what will be considered in performance evaluations, including expected behaviours and performance criteria

For a specific example of the difficulties of merging two cultures, read this chapter's *Case Incident—EnCana Establishes a New Culture* on page 382.

CHANGING ORGANIZATIONAL CULTURE

When president and CEO David Dingwall decided to reshape the Royal Canadian Mint, he introduced changes at a number of levels. He eliminated two warehouses and concentrated the business lines.[61] He also changed much of the senior management team; encouraged employee participation in change activities; and introduced a broader recognition program.

Dingwall faced a potentially powerful obstacle to change. The Mint's employees are unionized, belonging to the Public Service Alliance of Canada (PSAC). Sometimes unions resist change, but Dingwall won the hearts of his unionized employees. Suzanne Lambert, an 18-year Mint employee who is vice-president of PSAC, praised Dingwall for his "down-to-earth style, [and for] listening to and mixing with the employees." She credited him with making employees feel "proud of their jobs again."

Mitch Sylvestre, a 20-year Mint employee and president of the Winnipeg local of PSAC, praised Dingwall. "Since David Dingwall's come in, he's definitely shaken up the senior management and the sales group," he said. "He's a motivator." Even in the face of his controversial resignation in September 2005, union members signed a petition for Dingwall to return to the Mint, indicating that he had a very positive impact on morale during his tenure. Why was Dingwall successful in changing the Mint's culture?

5 How do you change culture?

Trying to change the culture of an organization is quite difficult, and requires that many aspects of the organization change at the same time, especially the reward structure.

Culture is such a challenge to change because it often represents the established mindset of employees and managers.

The explosion of the space shuttle *Columbia* in February 2003 highlights how difficult changing culture has been for NASA. When the report on the investigation came out that summer, the reasons given for the failure were alarmingly similar to the reasons given for the *Challenger* disaster 20 years before.[62] Even though foam striking the shuttle was the technical cause of the explosion, the problem was rooted in NASA's organizational culture. NASA has again promised to change its culture, and create an atmosphere where employees are "encouraged to raise our hand and speak out when there are life-threatening hazards," said NASA administrator Sean O'Keefe. Joseph Grenny, a NASA engineer, is less certain. He notes that "the NASA culture does not accept being wrong." The culture doesn't accept that "there's no such thing as a stupid question." Instead, "the humiliation factor always runs high."[63]

John Kotter of the Harvard Business School created a more detailed approach to implementing change.[64] Kotter has noted common problems that occur when managers try to initiate change. These include the inability to create a sense of urgency about the need for change; failure to create a coalition for managing the change process; the absence of a vision for change and a failure to effectively communicate that vision; not removing obstacles that could impede the achievement of the vision; failure to provide short-term and achievable goals; the tendency to declare victory too soon; and not anchoring the changes in the organization's culture.

Kotter established eight sequential steps to changing organizational culture:[65]

1. Set the tone through management behaviour. Managers, particularly top management, need to be positive role models.

2. Create new stories, material symbols, and rituals to replace those currently in vogue.

3. Select, promote, and support employees who support the new values that are sought.

4. Redesign socialization processes to align with the new values.

5. Change the reward system to encourage acceptance of a new set of values.

6. Replace unwritten norms with formal rules and regulations that are tightly enforced.

7. Shake up current subcultures through transfers, job rotation, and/or terminations.

8. Work to get peer-group consensus through employee participation and creation of a climate with a high level of trust.

This chapter's *Point/Counterpoint* on page 378 outlines the conditions under which cultural change is most likely to occur. This chapter's *CBC Video Case* illustrates some of the difficulties in changing a culture.

Efforts directed at changing organizational culture do not usually yield immediate or dramatic results. Cultural change is actually a lengthy process—measured in years, not months. But we can ask the question, "Can culture be changed?" And the answer is "Yes!" when we consider such examples as the Royal Canadian Mint. For a specific example of the culture difficulties that organizations can face when the environment changes, read this chapter's *Case Incident—Southwest Airlines Faces New Challenges* on page 383.

CBC

Corporate Culture Meets G.A.P. Adventures

SUMMARY AND IMPLICATIONS

1 What is the purpose of organizational culture? Organizational culture is the pattern of shared values, beliefs, and assumptions considered to be the appropriate way to think and act within an organization. Culture provides stability to an organization and gives employees a clear understanding of "the way things are done around here." Culture performs a number of functions within an organization. First, it creates distinctions between one organization and others. Second, it conveys a sense of identity to organization members. Third, it helps create commitment to the organization. Fourth, it's the social glue that helps hold the organization together. Finally, it helps employees make sense of the organization. Organizations can have subcultures, with individual groups or teams creating their own cultures that may not completely reflect the overall organizational culture.

2 How do you read an organization's culture? Organizations differ in the extent to which they can be characterized as having strong or weak cultures. In a strong culture, the organization's core values are both intensely held and widely shared. In a weak culture, employees do not feel any great attachment to their organization or their co-workers. The artifacts of culture inform outsiders and employees about the underlying values and beliefs of the organization's culture. These artifacts— or aspects of an organization's culture that you see, hear, and feel—include stories, rituals, material symbols, and language, and can be used to help people read the organization's culture.

3 How do you create and maintain culture? The original culture of an organization is derived from the philosophy of its founders. That philosophy then influences what types of employees are hired. The culture of the organization is then reinforced by top management, who signal what is acceptable behaviour and what is not. Employees are socialized into the culture, and will be more easily socialized to the extent that the employee's values match those of the organization.

4 Can organizational culture have a downside? Many of culture's functions are valuable for both the organization and the employee. Culture enhances organizational commitment and increases the consistency of employee behaviour. Culture also reduces ambiguity for employees by telling them what's important and how things are done. However, a strong culture can have a negative effect, such as Enron's pressure-cooker culture, which led to the company's ultimate collapse. Culture can act as a barrier to change, it can make it difficult to create an inclusive environment, and it can hinder the success of mergers and acquisitions.

5 How do you change culture? Changing culture is not easy. It is not unusual for managers to try changing the structure, the technology, or the people, but this often isn't enough. Because culture is the shared beliefs within the organizations, it influences all of the activities in which people engage. Thus it's important to change the reward structure, and to work carefully to change employee beliefs in order to get real culture change.

For Review

1. What are the levels of organizational culture?

2. How can an outsider assess an organization's culture?

3. How is language related to organizational culture?

4. Can an employee survive in an organization if he or she rejects its core values? Explain.

5. What defines an organization's subcultures?

6. What benefits can socialization provide for the organization? For the new employee?

7. Describe four cultural types and the characteristics of employees who fit best with each.

8. How can culture be a liability to an organization?

9. How does a strong culture affect an organization's efforts to improve diversity?

10. Identify the steps a manager can take to implement culture change in an organization.

For Critical Thinking

1. Is socialization brainwashing? Explain.

2. If management sought a culture characterized as innovative and autonomous, what might its socialization program look like?

3. Can you identify a set of characteristics that describes your college's or university's culture? Compare them with what several of your peers have noted. How closely do they agree?

4. "We should be opposed to the manipulation of individuals for organizational purposes, but a degree of social uniformity enables organizations to work better." Do you agree or disagree with this statement? What are its implications for organizational culture? Discuss.

5. Today's workforce is increasingly made up of part-time or contingent employees. Is organizational culture really important if the workforce is mostly temporary employees?

OB for You

- Increase your understanding of culture by looking for similarities and differences across groups and organizations. For instance, do you have two courses where the classroom environment differs considerably? What does this suggest about the underlying assumptions in teaching students? Similarly, compare customer service at two local coffee shops or sandwich shops. What does the employee behaviour suggest about each organization's culture?

- Carefully consider the culture of any organization at which you are thinking of being employed. You will feel more comfortable in cultures that share your values and expectations. You may find yourself reacting very negatively if an organization's culture (and values) do not match your own.

- Keep in mind that groups create mini-cultures of their own. When you work in a group on a student project, be aware of the values and norms that are being supported early on in the group's life. These will greatly influence the group's culture.

 **POINT**

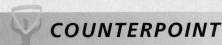 **COUNTERPOINT**

Organizational Culture Doesn't Change

An organization's culture develops over many years and is rooted in deeply held values to which employees are strongly committed. In addition, there are a number of forces continually operating to maintain a given culture. These would include written statements about the organization's mission and philosophy; the design of physical spaces and buildings; the dominant leadership style; hiring criteria; past promotion practices; entrenched rituals; popular stories about key people and events; the organization's historical performance evaluation criteria; and the organization's formal structure.

Selection and promotion policies are particularly important devices that work against cultural change. Employees chose the organization because they perceived their values to be a "good fit" with those of the organization. They become comfortable with that fit and will strongly resist efforts to disturb the equilibrium.

Those in control in organizations will also select senior managers who will continue the current culture. Even attempts to change a culture by going outside the organization to hire a new chief executive are unlikely to be effective. The evidence indicates that the culture is more likely to change the executive than the other way around. Why? It's too entrenched, and change becomes a potential threat to member self-interest. In fact, a more pragmatic view of the relationship between an organization's culture and its chief executive would be to note that the practice of filling senior-level management positions from the ranks of current managerial employees ensures that those who run the organization have been fully indoctrinated in the organization's culture. Promoting from within provides stability and lessens uncertainty. When a company's board of directors selects as a new chief executive officer an individual who has spent 30 years in the company, it virtually guarantees that the culture will continue unchanged.

Our argument, however, should not be viewed as saying that culture can never be changed. In the unusual case when an organization confronts a survival-threatening crisis—a crisis that is universally acknowledged as a true life-or-death situation—members of the organization will be responsive to efforts at cultural change. However, anything less than a crisis is unlikely to be effective in bringing about cultural change.

How to Change an Organization's Culture

Changing an organization's culture is extremely difficult, but cultures can be changed. The evidence suggests that cultural change is most likely to occur when most or all of the following conditions exist:

- *A dramatic crisis.* This is the shock that undermines the status quo and calls into question the relevance of the current culture. Examples of these crises might be a surprising financial setback, the loss of a major customer, or a dramatic technological breakthrough by a competitor. The *Columbia* disaster was a dramatic crisis for NASA. A $7-million deficit was a dramatic crisis for the Royal Canadian Mint.

- *Turnover in leadership.* New top leadership, which can provide an alternative set of key values, may be perceived as more capable of responding to the crisis. *Top leadership* definitely refers to the organization's chief executive, but also might need to include all senior management positions. The recent rush to hire outside CEOs after the Enron and WorldCom scandals illustrates attempts to create more ethical climates through the introduction of new leadership. At NASA, some of the top leadership was moved to other positions after the *Columbia* disaster. A new CEO at the Royal Canadian Mint, who was determined to turn around a deficit situation, brought about many changes to that organization.

- *Young and small organization.* The younger the organization is, the less entrenched its culture will be. Similarly, it's easier for management to communicate its new values when the organization is small. This point helps explain the difficulty that multibillion-dollar corporations have in changing their cultures.

- *Weak culture.* The more widely held a culture is and the higher the agreement among members on its values, the more difficult it will be to change. A strong culture has been one of the problems facing NASA. Conversely, weak cultures are more open to change than strong ones.

HR IMPLICATIONS

Creating an Ethical Culture

Organizations can introduce specific cultures that represent important values to the organization. For instance, culture can be used to signal that a company values an ethical climate and the ethical behaviour of its members.[66]

An organizational culture most likely to shape high ethical standards is one that's high in risk tolerance, low to moderate in aggressiveness, and focuses on means as well as outcomes. Managers in such a culture are supported for taking risks and innovating, are discouraged from engaging in unbridled competition, and will pay attention to how goals are achieved, as well as to what goals are achieved.

A strong organizational culture will exert more influence on employees than a weak one. If the culture is strong and supports high ethical standards, it should have a very powerful and positive influence on employee behaviour. Johnson & Johnson, for example, has a strong culture that has long stressed corporate obligations to customers, employees, the community, and shareholders, in that order. When poisoned Tylenol (a Johnson & Johnson product) was found on store shelves, employees at Johnson & Johnson across the United States independently pulled the product from these stores before management had ever issued a statement concerning the tamperings. No one had to tell these individuals what was morally right; they knew what Johnson & Johnson would expect them to do.

Brampton, Ontario-based Nortel Networks hired Susan Shepard to be its chief ethics officer in early 2005, after having to restate company earnings for 2001 to 2003. Shepard's job involves creating "a corporate culture which is very sensitive to ethics and doing things the right way. It involves training and it involves getting employees to come forward when they think there are problems. And it involves doing investigations and then coming into those problem areas as necessary and developing controls."[67] Nortel's previous ethics officer, Megan Barry, applauded the move. Barry was Nortel's first ethics officer and held the position from 1994 to 1999. By the end of that period, "Senior managers saw the ethics program as a cost and enthusiasm for it had 'diminished significantly,'" Barry noted. She also noticed that the sales and marketing departments sometimes did things that were "on the edge." When she left, she was not immediately replaced, "And you see where that got them," she noted.[68]

What can management do to create a more ethical culture? We suggest a combination of the following practices:

- *Be a visible role model.* Employees will look to top-management behaviour as a benchmark for defining appropriate behaviour. When senior managers are seen to be taking the ethical high road, they provide a positive message for all employees.

- *Communicate ethical expectations.* Ethical ambiguities can be minimized by creating and disseminating an organizational code of ethics. It should state the organization's primary values and the ethical rules that employees are expected to follow.

- *Provide ethics training.* Set up seminars, workshops, and similar ethics training programs. Use these training sessions to reinforce the organization's standards of conduct, to clarify what practices are and are not permissible, and to address possible ethical dilemmas.

- *Visibly reward ethical acts and punish unethical ones.* Performance appraisals of managers should include a point-by-point evaluation of how their decisions measured against the organization's code of ethics. Appraisals must include the means taken to achieve goals, as well as the ends themselves. People who act ethically should be visibly rewarded for their behaviour. Just as importantly, unethical acts should be conspicuously punished.

- *Provide protective mechanisms.* The organization needs to provide formal mechanisms so that employees can discuss ethical dilemmas and report unethical behaviour without fear of reprimand. This might include appointing an ethics counsellor, an ombudsperson, or an ethics officer.

LEARNING ABOUT **YOURSELF** EXERCISE

What Kind of Organizational Culture Fits You Best?

For each of the following statements, circle the level of agreement or disagreement that you personally feel:

SA = Strongly Agree

A = Agree

U = Uncertain

D = Disagree

SD = Strongly disagree

1. I like being part of a team and having my performance assessed in terms of my contribution to the team.	SA	A	U	D	SD
2. No person's needs should be compromised in order for a department to achieve its goals.	SA	A	U	D	SD
3. I like the thrill and excitement from taking risks.	SA	A	U	D	SD
4. If a person's job performance is inadequate, it's irrelevant how much effort he or she made.	SA	A	U	D	SD
5. I like things to be stable and predictable.	SA	A	U	D	SD
6. I prefer managers who provide detailed and rational explanations for their decisions.	SA	A	U	D	SD
7. I like to work where there isn't a great deal of pressure and where people are essentially easygoing.	SA	A	U	D	SD

Scoring Key:

For items 1, 2, 3, 4, and 7, score as follows: Strongly agree = +2 Agree = +1 Uncertain = 0 Disagree = −1 Strongly disagree = −2

For items 5 and 6, reverse the score (Strongly agree = −2, and so on). Add up your total. Your score will fall somewhere between +14 and −14.

What does your score mean? The lower your score, the more comfortable you will be in a formal, mechanistic, rule-oriented, and structured culture. This is often associated with large corporations and government agencies. Positive scores indicate a preference for informal, humanistic, flexible, and innovative cultures, which are more likely to be found in research units, advertising firms, high-tech companies, and small businesses.

BREAKOUT **GROUP** EXERCISES

Form small groups to discuss the following topics, as assigned by your instructor:

1. Choose two courses that you are taking this term, ideally in different faculties, and describe the culture of the classroom in each. What are the similarities and differences? What values about learning might you infer from your observations of culture?

2. Identify artifacts of culture in your current or previous workplace. From these artifacts, would you conclude that the organization had a strong or weak culture?

3. Have you or someone you know worked somewhere where the culture was strong? What was your reaction to that strong culture? Did you like that environment, or would you prefer to work where there is a weaker culture? Why?

Rate Your Classroom Culture

Listed here are 10 statements. Score each statement by indicating the degree to which you agree or disagree with it as follows:

Strongly agree= 5

Agree = 4

Uncertain = 3

Disagree = 2

Strongly disagree = 1

1. My classmates are friendly and supportive. _____

2. My instructor is friendly and supportive. _____

3. My instructor encourages me to question and challenge him or her, as well as other classmates. _____

4. My instructor clearly expresses his or her expectations to the class. _____

5. I think the grading system used by my instructor is based on clear standards of performance. _____

6. My instructor's behaviour during examinations demonstrates his or her belief that students are honest and trustworthy. _____

7. My instructor provides regular and rapid feedback on my performance. _____

8. My instructor uses a strict bell curve to allocate grades. _____

9. My instructor is open to suggestions on how the course might be improved. _____

10. My instructor makes me want to learn. _____

Scoring Key:

Add up your score for all the statements except number 8. For number 8, reverse the score (Strongly agree = 1; Agree = 2; Uncertain = 3; Disagree = 4; Strongly disagree = 5) and add it to your total. Your score will fall between 10 and 50.

A high score (37 or above) describes an open, warm, human, trusting, and supportive culture.

A low score (25 or below) describes a closed, cold, task-oriented, autocratic, and tense culture.

Form groups of 5 to 7 members each. Compare your scores. How closely do they align? Discuss and resolve discrepancies.

Is Involuntary Ethics Training Unethical?

A lot of companies rely on training as an essential part of their efforts to create an ethical culture. In some cases, this training is brief and requires little emotional investment by the employee. For instance, the training might require only reading a pamphlet describing the company's code of ethics, followed by an online quiz to ensure employee understanding. In contrast, some organizations' ethics train-ing is quite lengthy, requiring employees to seriously address their values and principles and to share them with their co-workers. For example, the Boeing Company's train-ing program, called Questions of Integrity: The Ethics Challenge, is conducted within an employee's work group. Led by their supervisor, employees discuss more than four dozen ethical situations. Each includes four possible ways of

▶

dealing with the problem. After the supervisor discusses each situation, employees are asked to choose the best outcome by holding up cards marked A, B, C, or D. Then the supervisor indicates the "ethically correct" answer.

Most of the evidence indicates that for ethics training to be effective, it needs to be intensive and frequently reinforced. So some of the best programs require participants to spend several days a year, every year, engaged in discussions and exercises designed to clarify the organization's ethical expectations.

Is it unethical to ask employees to share their deepest personal values regarding right and wrong with their boss and co-workers? Should employees have the right not to participate in ethics training programs that might require them to publicly vocalize their ethical standards, religious principles, or other personal beliefs?

CASE INCIDENTS

EnCana Establishes a New Culture

When Alberta Energy Company (AEC) and PanCanadian Energy merged on April 8, 2002, to form Calgary-based EnCana, they created arguably the largest producer of natural gas and the top exploration and production company in the world. The new company wanted to be taken seriously by institutional investors, so that its stock will be valued appropriately.

Getting EnCana recognized by institutional investors may have been one of the easier problems confronting the new company. AEC and PanCanadian were the largest natural gas producers in Canada, and they had competed against each other for years.

Gwyn Morgan, former head of AEC and president and CEO of EnCana at the time of the merger, knew the difficulties that lay ahead. He had overseen several other mergers at AEC. To get things off to a good start, his 1800 employees and PanCanadian's 2000 employees were given the booklet *The Employee Survival Guide to Mergers and Acquisitions*, by Price Pritchett, a US expert on organizational change. Morgan was determined to create a culture for the organization, rather than let one emerge over time.

He explained his approach as follows: "A business organization creates culture by establishing principles and expectations and aligning the incentive system with the results you want to achieve, and if you can do all of those things, whatever falls out of the resulting behavioural pattern in the company is something you call culture."

The two merging companies could not have been more different. AEC had an aggressive, entrepreneurial, results-oriented culture. PanCanadian's culture was risk-averse, hierarchical, and formal. Rather than focus on these differences, however, Morgan wanted employees to focus on commonalities: "We are all Canadian here, we work in Calgary, we work in the oil and gas business."

To steer employees in the right direction culturally, Morgan sent his employees emails even before the merger became official. In these, he explained the "basic principles and philosophies" of the new company. He particularly emphasized that in the new organizational structure, "Bureaucracy will be rooted out and distractions will be discouraged." Morgan's leadership style, which favoured a decentralized structure where employees are accountable for results, sought to discourage the desire for bureaucracy he anticipated from the PanCanadian employees.

Questions

1. What problems did Morgan face after the merger took place?

2. What did Morgan need to do to ensure that a new culture developed?

3. What difficulties do you think he faced in establishing the new culture?

Sources: Based on C. Cattaneo, "EnCana's Story Relevant for North America: AEC, PanCanadian Merger: Peers of New Firm Will Have to Find Way to Move Forward," *Financial Post (National Post),* April 11, 2002, p. FP6; and C. Cattaneo, "CEO Lays Out Path to AEC/PanCanadian Merger: Employee Booklet," *Financial Post (National Post),* March 1, 2002, p. FP3.

Southwest Airlines Faces New Challenges

For 32 years, Southwest Airlines has used the same formula to maintain its position as the most profitable airline in the United States. It offers low fares, frequent flights, and good service; it flies only Boeing 737s; it doesn't offer connecting flights, reserve seating, or free meals; it often relies on less expensive, secondary airports; and it prides itself on having the hardest-working and most productive employees in the industry. The company believes its true competitive advantage is its workforce.

Most of the major airlines' cost per seat-mile is nearly 100 percent higher than Southwest's. The company gets this cost advantage by paying its pilots and flight attendants considerably less than the competition and having them fly more hours. It has made up for the lower pay with generous profit-sharing and stock option plans. In addition, because of Southwest's rapid growth, it has provided its employees with something rare in the airline industry: job security. Because a large portion of Southwest employees' compensation comes in the form of stock options, they have worked harder and more flexibly than their peers at other airlines. For instance, pilots will often help ground crew move luggage and work extra hard to turn planes around fast. Of course, many Southwest employees originally joined the company and have stayed because of its spirit of fun. The company has always encouraged employees to work hard but to also have a good time. A sense of humour, for instance, has long been a basic criterion in the selection of new employees.

In the last couple of years, the environment has been changing for Southwest. First, it faces a number of new, upstart airlines in many of its markets. JetBlue, Frontier, AirTran, Song, and Ted are matching Southwest's low prices but offering benefits like reserved seating and free live-satellite TV. They are able to do this because they have newer, more fuel-efficient planes and young, lower-paid workforces. In many markets, Southwest's planes and service look dated. Second, the declining stock market of 2001–2002 took much of the air out of Southwest's stock. The company's stock option plan no longer looked so attractive to employees. Third, Southwest has to deal with the reality that it's no longer the underdog. For decades, employees enjoyed the challenge of competing against United, American, Delta, and other major airlines. They loved the role of being the underdogs and having to work harder to survive. Southwest's employees are increasingly vocal and aggressive in demanding higher wages and shorter hours. In the past, employees were willing to go beyond the call of duty to help the airline thrive. It's harder for management to motivate employees now by portraying the airline as the underdog. Finally, as the company has grown and matured, management has become more remote from the rank and file. When the company had a few hundred employees, it was easy for management to communicate its messages. Now, with 31 000 workers, it's much tougher.

Southwest's management realizes that times have changed. Now they face the question of whether they need to make changes in their basic strategy and, if they do, the effect it will have on the company's culture. For instance, the company considered adding in-flight entertainment to match its competitors, although it would cost millions to install and many more millions to maintain; and purchasing smaller jets to maintain competitiveness in smaller markets. The operating costs of these smaller jets would be 15 to 25 percent higher than those of its current fleet.

Questions

1. What has sustained Southwest's culture?

2. Do you think upstart airlines can successfully duplicate this culture?

3. No longer the underdog, what can Southwest's management do to retain its high-productivity culture?

4. What does this case imply about sustaining culture in a changing environment?

Sources: Based on S. B. Donnelly, "One Airline's Magic," *Time,* October 28, 2002, pp. 45–47; M. Trottman, "Inside Southwest Airlines, Storied Culture Feels Strains," *Wall Street Journal,* July 11, 2003, p. A1; M. Trottman, "Southwest Air Considers Shift in Its Approach," *Wall Street Journal,* December 23, 2003, p. B1; M. Maynard, "Low-Fare Airlines Decide Frills Maybe Aren't So Bad After All," *New York Times,* January 7, 2004, p. C1; and J. Helyar, "Southwest Finds Trouble in the Air," *Fortune,* August 9, 2004, p. 38.

From **Concepts** to **Skills**

How to "Read" an Organization's Culture

The ability to read and assess an organization's culture can be a valuable skill.[69] If you are looking for a job, you will want to choose an employer whose culture is compatible with your values and in which you will feel comfortable. If you can accurately assess a prospective employer's culture before you make your decision, you may be able to save yourself a lot of grief and reduce the likelihood of making a poor choice. Similarly, you will undoubtedly have business transactions with numerous organizations during your professional career. You will be trying to sell a product or service, negotiate a contract, arrange a joint venture, or you may merely be seeking out which individual in an organization controls certain decisions. The ability to assess another organization's culture can be a definite plus in successfully completing these pursuits.

For the sake of simplicity, we will approach the problem of reading an organization's culture from the point of view of a job applicant. We will assume you are interviewing for a job. Here is a list of things you can do to help learn about a potential employer's culture:

- Observe the physical surroundings. Pay attention to signs, pictures, style of dress, length of hair, degree of openness between offices, and office furnishings and arrangements.

- With whom did you meet? Just the person who would be your immediate manager? Or potential colleagues, managers from other departments, or senior executives? Based on what they revealed, to what degree do people other than the immediate manager have input into the hiring decision?

- How would you characterize the style of the people you met? Formal? Casual? Serious? Jovial?

- Does the organization have formal rules and regulations printed in a human resource policy manual? If so, how detailed are these policies?

- Ask questions of the people you meet. The most valid and reliable information tends to come from asking the same questions of many people (to see how closely

their responses align) and by talking with boundary spanners. *Boundary spanners* are employees whose work links them to the external environment and includes jobs such as human resource interviewer, salesperson, purchasing agent, labour negotiator, public relations specialist, and company lawyer. Questions that will give you insights into organizational processes and practices might include the following:

- What is the background of the founders?

- What is the background of current senior managers? What are their functional specializations? Were they promoted from within or hired from outside?

- How does the organization integrate new employees? Is there an orientation program? Training? If so, could you describe these features?

- How does your manager define his or her job success? (Amount of profit? Serving customers? Meeting deadlines? Acquiring budget increases?)

- How would you define fairness in terms of reward allocations?

- Can you identify some people here who are on the "fast track"? What do you think has put them on the fast track?

- Can you identify someone who seems to be considered a deviant in the organization? How has the organization responded to this person?

- Can you describe a decision that someone made here that was well received?

- Can you describe a decision that did not work out well? What were the consequences for the decision maker?

- Could you describe a crisis or critical event that has occurred recently in the organization? How did top management respond? What was learned from this experience?

Assessing Skills

After you've read this chapter, take the following Self-Assessments on your enclosed CD-ROM:

44. What's the Right Organizational Culture for Me?

Practising Skills

After spending your first three years after college graduation as a freelance graphic designer, you are looking at pursuing a job as an account executive at a graphic design firm. You feel that the scope of assignments and potential for technical training far exceed what you would be able to do on your own, and you are looking to expand your skills and meet a brand-new set of challenges. However, you want to make sure you "fit" in to the organization where you are going to be spending more than eight hours every workday. What's the best way for you to find a place where you will be happy, and where your style and personality will be appreciated?

Reinforcing Skills

1. Choose two courses that you are taking this term, ideally in different faculties, and describe the culture of the classroom in each. What are the simi-larities and differences? What values about learning might you infer from your observations of culture?

2. Do some comparisons of the atmosphere or feeling you get from various organizations. Because of the number and wide variety that you will find, it will probably be easiest for you to do this exercise using restaurants, retail stores, or banks. Based on the atmosphere that you observe, what type of organizational culture do you think these organizations might have? If you can, interview three employees at each organization for their descriptions of their organization's culture.

3. Think about changes (major and minor) that you have dealt with over the past year. Perhaps these changes involved other people and perhaps they were personal. Did you resist the change? Did others resist the change? How did you overcome your resistance or the resistance of others to the change?

4. Interview managers at three different organizations about changes they have introduced. What was their experience in bringing in the change? How did they manage resistance to the change?

CHAPTER 11
Leadership

A major US city is hit by a powerful hurricane and then suffers serious flooding. Does anyone have the leadership skills needed to rescue people and provide order?

1 What is the difference between a manager and a leader?

2 Are there specific traits, behaviours, and situations that affect how one leads?

3 How does a leader lead with vision?

4 Can a person be an informal leader?

5 What is self-leadership?

6 What are some of the contemporary issues in leadership?

Millions of people around the world were glued to their television sets in September 2005, watching the devastation of Hurricane Katrina unfold. While the storm damaged parts of Mississippi, Alabama, and Louisiana, it was the damage to New Orleans that got the most press coverage. The entire city had to be evacuated because of severe flooding, causing thousands of people, mostly poor and black, to be stranded at the city's Superdome and Convention Center.

For many of those watching people waving from rooftops begging to be rescued, and people from the Convention Center and Superdome begging for food and water, the questions that arose were, Who was in charge? Why wasn't help coming faster? There was plenty of blame to go around, and the obvious leaders, New Orleans mayor Ray Nagin, Louisiana governor Kathleen Blanco, and President George W. Bush, shown here, were all singled out for criticism.

In this chapter, we examine the various studies on leadership to determine what makes an effective leader. First we consider the traits, behaviours, and situations that affect one's ability to lead, and then we consider inspirational leadership. As well, we look at how leadership is spread throughout the organization, and how you might lead yourself, through self-management. Finally, we discuss contemporary issues in leadership.

ARE MANAGERS AND LEADERS THE SAME?

Leadership and *management* are two terms that are often confused. What is the difference between them?

John Kotter of the Harvard Business School argues that "managers promote stability while leaders press for change and only organizations that embrace both sides of the contradiction can survive in turbulent times."[1] McGill University professor Rabindra Kanungo notes there is a growing consensus emerging "among management scholars that the concept of 'leadership' must be distinguished from the concept of 'supervision/management.'"[2] Exhibit 11-1 on page 388 illustrates Kanungo's distinctions between leadership and management. Leaders provide vision and strategy; managers implement that vision and strategy, coordinate and staff the organization, and handle day-to-day problems.

In our discussion of leadership, we will focus on two major tasks of those who lead in organizations: managing those around them to get the day-to-day tasks done, and inspiring others to do the extraordinary. It will become clear that successful leaders rely on a variety of interpersonal skills in order to encourage others to perform at their best. It will also become clear that, no matter the place in the hierarchy, from CEO to team leader, a variety of individuals can be called on to perform leadership roles.

1. What is the difference between a manager and a leader?

Harvard Business School
www.hbs.edu

EXHIBIT 11-1 Distinguishing Leadership From Management	
Management	**Leadership**
1. Engages in day-to-day caretaker activities: Maintains and allocates resources	Formulates long-term objectives for reforming the system: Plans strategy and tactics
2. Exhibits supervisory behaviour: Acts to make others maintain standard job behaviour	Exhibits leading behaviour: Acts to bring about change in others congruent with long-term objectives
3. Administers subsystems within organizations	Innovates for the entire organization
4. Asks how and when to engage in standard practice	Asks what and why to change standard practice
5. Acts within established culture of the organization	Creates vision and meaning for the organization
6. Uses transactional influence: Induces compliance in manifest behaviour using rewards, sanctions, and formal authority	Uses transformational influence: Induces change in values, attitudes, and behaviour using personal examples and expertise
7. Relies on control strategies to get things done by subordinates	Uses empowering strategies to make followers internalize values
8. Status quo supporter and stabilizer	Status quo challenger and change creator

Source: R. N. Kanungo, "Leadership in Organizations: Looking Ahead to the 21st Century," *Canadian Psychology* 39, no. 1–2 (1998), p. 77.

LEADERSHIP AS SUPERVISION

As Hurricane Katrina rushed closer to the New Orleans coastline, people in authority in both Louisiana and Washington were trying to figure out how best to handle the situation. Some wondered whether hundreds of thousands of people should be evacuated from New Orleans before the storm hit, or whether everyone could simply ride out the storm. Michael Brown, then director of the Federal Emergency Management Agency (FEMA), sent a small emergency response team to Louisiana to review evacuation plans the weekend before the levees broke. Frustrated that Mayor Ray Nagin didn't seem to be acting quickly enough to get New Orleans evacuated, Brown called President George W. Bush to advise him of the situation. He also asked the president to phone the mayor directly to tell him to evacuate the people of New Orleans. The president's response, "Mike, you want me to call the Mayor?" illustrates the different roles of managers and leaders. The president was not expecting to micromanage an evacuation plan, and did not really consider it his role. As the "big picture person," his job might have been to make sure that strategies were developed for emergency situations, not to develop the strategies or implement them. Nevertheless, did President Bush do all that was needed to make sure his followers could carry out their tasks?

2 Are there specific traits, behaviours, and situations that affect how one leads?

In this section we discuss theories of leadership that were developed before 1980. These early theories focused on the supervisory nature of leadership, that is, how individuals managed the day-to-day functioning of employees. The theories took different approaches in understanding how best to lead in a supervisory capacity. The three general types of theories that emerged were (1) trait theories, which propose leaders have a particular set of traits that makes them different from nonleaders;

(2) behavioural theories, which propose that particular behaviours make for better leaders; and (3) contingency theories, which propose the situation has an effect on leaders. When you think about these theories, remember that although they have been considered "theories of leadership," they rely on an older understanding of what "leadership" means, and they don't convey Kanungo's distinction between leadership and supervision.

Trait Theories: Are Leaders Different From Others?

Have you ever wondered whether there's some fundamental personality difference that makes some people "born leaders"? Trait theories emerged in the hope that if it were possible to identify the traits of leaders, it would be easier to select people to fill leadership roles.

The media have long been believers in **trait theories of leadership**. They identify people such as Nelson Mandela, Richard Branson of the Virgin Group, and Steve Jobs of Apple as leaders, and then describe them in terms such as *charismatic, enthusiastic, decisive,* and *courageous*. The media aren't alone. The search for personality, social, physical, or intellectual attributes that would describe leaders and differentiate them from nonleaders goes back to research done by psychologists in the 1930s.

trait theories of leadership
Theories that propose traits—personality, social, physical, or intellectual—differentiate leaders from nonleaders.

Research efforts at isolating leadership traits resulted in a number of dead ends. For instance, a review in the late 1960s of 20 studies identified nearly 80 leadership traits, but only 5 of these traits were common to 4 or more of the investigations.[3] By the 1990s, after numerous studies and analyses, about the best thing that could be said was that the following seven traits seemed to differentiate leaders from nonleaders: ambition and energy, the desire to lead, honesty and integrity, self-confidence, intelligence, high self-monitoring, and job-relevant knowledge.[4] But the power of these traits to predict leadership continued to be modest.

A breakthrough, of sorts, came when researchers began organizing traits around the Big Five personality framework (see Chapter 2).[5] What became clear was that most of the dozens of traits that emerged in various leadership reviews could be subsumed under one of the Big Five factors, and that this approach resulted in consistent and strong support for traits as predictors of leadership. For instance, ambition and energy is part of extraversion and self-confidence is part of emotional stability.

Comprehensive reviews of the leadership literature, when organized around the Big Five, have found that extraversion is the most important trait of effective leaders.[6] But results show that extraversion is more strongly related to leader emergence than to leader effectiveness. This is not totally surprising, since sociable and dominant people are more likely to assert themselves in group situations. Conscientiousness and openness to experience also showed strong and consistent relationships to leadership, but not as strong as extraversion. The traits of agreeableness and emotional stability don't appear to offer much help in predicting leadership.

Meg Whitman, president and CEO of eBay, is a leader with high emotional intelligence. Since eBay founder Pierre Omidyar chose Whitman to transform his start-up into a global enterprise, she has emerged as a star performer in a job that demands a high degree of social interaction with employees and customers throughout the world. Whitman is described as self-confident, trustworthy, culturally sensitive, a high achiever, and expert at building teams and leading change. Shown here, Whitman interacts with customers during an eBay Live convention.

EXHIBIT 11-2 What CEOs Identity as Key Leadership Qualities	
Quality	**CEOs Rating It Most Important (%)**
Communication skills	52
Ability to motivate people	47
Honesty	34
Ability to listen	25
Team-building expertise	24
Analytical skills	19
Aggressiveness in business	10

Source: Survey conducted by American Express for the National Quality Institute. Reported in R. Nutt, "Survey Finds Leadership Key," *Vancouver Sun,* June 1, 2000, p. D6.

Based on the latest findings, we offer two conclusions. First, traits can predict leadership. Twenty years ago, the evidence suggested otherwise. But this was probably because of the lack of a valid framework for classifying and organizing traits. The Big Five seems to have rectified that. Second, traits do a better job at predicting the emergence of leaders and the appearance of leadership than in actually distinguishing between *effective* and *ineffective* leaders.[7] The fact that an individual exhibits the traits and others consider that person to be a leader does not necessarily mean that the leader is successful at getting his or her group to achieve its goals. Exhibit 11-2 shows the findings of a recent survey of 200 CEOs, and what they cited as the most important leadership qualities.

Emotional Intelligence and Leadership

Although trait theories in general have failed to find ways to identify good leaders, recent studies indicate that emotional intelligence (EI)—more than IQ, expertise, or any other single factor—is the best predictor of who will emerge as a leader.[8] Daniel Goleman has written a number of books and articles in this area, and in his book *Primal Leadership,*[9] he continues to argue that effective leadership needs people who are aware and in control of their emotions. He and his co-authors suggest that employees benefit most from leaders who show positive emotion and enthusiasm, and that fear and repression are harmful in the workplace. "Leaders who freely vent their anger, catastrophize or otherwise let their distressing emotions run amok can't also lead the group into a positive register, where the best work gets done," the authors say.

The work on EI suggests that leaders need more than the basic traits of intelligence and job-relevant knowledge.[10] It's the possession of the five components of emotional intelligence—self-awareness, self-management, self-motivation, empathy, and social skills—that allows an individual to become a star performer. Without EI, a person can have outstanding training, a highly analytical mind, a long-term vision, and an endless supply of terrific ideas, but still not make a great leader. This is especially true as individuals move up in an organization. The evidence indicates that the higher the rank of a person considered to be a star performer, the more that EI capabilities surface as the reason for his or her effectiveness. Specifically, when star performers were compared with average ones in senior management positions, nearly 90 percent of the difference in their effectiveness was attributable to EI factors rather than basic intelligence.

The recent evidence makes a strong case for concluding that EI is an essential element in leadership effectiveness. As such, it should probably be added to our earlier list of traits associated with leadership.

EXHIBIT 11-3 Leadership Attributes: A Cross-Cultural View		
Leader Attributes Universally Liked	**Leader Attributes Universally Disliked**	**Leader Attributes Over Which There Was Most Disagreement**
■ Trustworthy	■ Noncooperative	■ Subdued
■ Dynamic	■ Irritable	■ Intragroup conflict avoider
■ Motive arouser	■ Egocentric	■ Cunning
■ Decisive	■ Ruthless	■ Sensitive
■ Intelligent	■ Dictatorial	■ Provocateur
■ Dependable	■ Loner/self-centred	■ Self-effacing
■ Plans ahead		■ Willful
■ Excellence oriented		
■ Team builder		
■ Encouraging		

Source: D. N. Den Hartog, R. J. House, P. J. Hanges, S. A. Ruiz-Quintanilla, and P. W. Dorfman, "Culture Specific and Cross-culturally Generalizable Implicit Leadership Theories: Are Attributes of Charismatic/Transformational Leadership Universally Endorsed?" *Leadership Quarterly* 10, no. 2 (Summer 1999), pp. 219–256.

What Types of Traits are Preferred in Leaders?

Remember the GLOBE study we discussed in Chapter 3? As part of that study, researchers surveyed managers in 62 countries to find out what attributes they liked and disliked in leaders. The study uncovered 22 leader attributes that were universally liked, 8 that were universally disliked, and 35 over which there was a lot of disagreement.[11] Exhibit 11-3 identifies some of these different attributes.

The results of this study suggest that

- Universally liked attributes should be used by leaders working in any culture

- Universally disliked attributes should be avoided by leaders

- Attributes categorized by wide disagreement should be used cautiously, based on the demands of specific cultures

This chapter's *Point/Counterpoint* on page 418 raises further issues on the extent to which leadership is affected by national culture issues. *Case Incident—Moving From Colleague to Supervisor* on page 423 helps you think about the difficulties one has when moving from being a co-worker to taking on leadership responsibilities.

Behavioural Theories: Do Leaders Behave in Particular Ways?

The inability to strike "gold" in the trait "mines" led researchers to look at the behaviours that specific leaders exhibited. They wondered if there was something unique in the way that effective leaders behave. Trait theory, had it been successful, would have provided a basis for *selecting* the "right" people to assume formal positions in groups and organizations requiring leadership. In contrast, behavioural theories tried to identify critical behavioural determinants of leadership, in the hope that we could *train* people to be leaders.

The three most well-known **behavioural theories of leadership** are the Ohio State University studies conducted beginning in the late 1940s,[12] the University of Michigan studies conducted at about the same time, and Blake and Mouton's Managerial Grid, which

behavioural theories of leadership Theories that propose that specific behaviours differentiate leaders from nonleaders.

reflects the behavioural definitions of both the Ohio and Michigan studies. All three approaches consider two main dimensions by which managers can be characterized: attention to production and attention to people.

The Ohio State Studies

In the Ohio State studies, these two dimensions are known as *initiating structure* and *consideration*. **Initiating structure** refers to the extent to which a leader is likely to define and structure his or her role and the roles of employees in order to attain goals; it includes behaviour that attempts to organize work, work relationships, and goals. **Consideration** is defined as the extent to which a leader is likely to have job relationships characterized by mutual trust, respect for employees' ideas, and regard for their feelings. A leader who is high in consideration shows concern for employees' comfort, well-being, status, and satisfaction.

The Michigan Studies

Researchers at the University of Michigan also developed two dimensions of leadership behaviour that they labelled **employee oriented** and **production oriented**.[13] Their leaders who were employee oriented were described as emphasizing interpersonal relations. They took a personal interest in the needs of their subordinates and accepted individual differences among members. The production-oriented leaders, in contrast, tended to emphasize the technical or task aspects of the job. Their main concern was in accomplishing their group's tasks, and the group members were a means to that end.

The Managerial Grid

Blake and Mouton developed a graphic portrayal of a two-dimensional view of leadership style.[14] They proposed a **Managerial Grid** (now called a *Leadership Grid*)[15] based on the styles of "concern for people" and "concern for production," which essentially represent the Ohio State dimensions of consideration and initiating structure, or the Michigan dimensions of employee oriented and production oriented.

The grid, depicted in Exhibit 11-4, has 9 possible positions along each axis, creating 81 different positions in which the leader's style may fall, but emphasis has been placed on five: impoverished management (1,1); authority-obedience management (9,1); middle-of-the-road management (5,5); country club management (1,9); and team management (9,9). The grid shows the dominating factors in a leader's thinking with respect to getting results, rather than results produced.

◉ RESEARCH FINDINGS

While the results of the behavioural studies have been somewhat mixed,[16] a careful evaluation of the situations that leaders face provides some insights into when leaders should be production oriented and when they should be people oriented:[17]

- When subordinates experience a lot of pressure because of deadlines or unclear tasks, leaders who are people oriented will increase employee satisfaction and performance.

- When the task is interesting or satisfying, there is less need for leaders to be people oriented.

- When it's clear how to perform the task and what the goals are, leaders who are people oriented will increase employee satisfaction, while those who are task oriented will increase dissatisfaction.

- When people don't know what to do, or individuals don't have the knowledge or skills to do the job, it's more important for leaders to be production oriented than people oriented.

initiating structure The extent to which a leader is likely to define and structure his or her role and the roles of employees in order to attain goals.

consideration The extent to which a leader is likely to have job relationships characterized by mutual trust, respect for employees' ideas, and regard for their feelings.

employee-oriented leader A leader who emphasizes interpersonal relations.

production-oriented leader A leader who emphasizes the technical or task aspects of the job.

Managerial Grid A two-dimensional grid outlining 81 different leadership styles.

EXHIBIT 11-4   The Managerial Grid

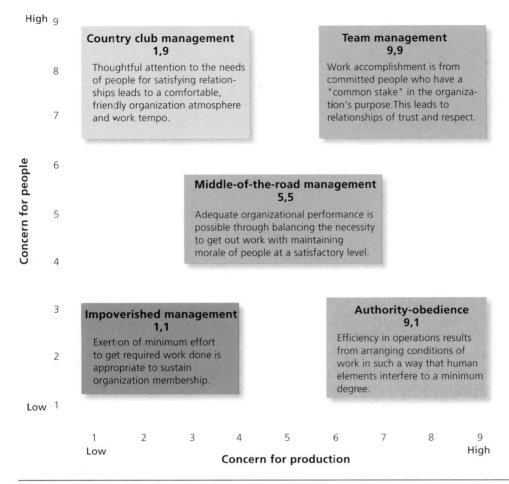

Country club management
1,9
Thoughtful attention to the needs of people for satisfying relationships leads to a comfortable, friendly organization atmosphere and work tempo.

Team management
9,9
Work accomplishment is from committed people who have a "common stake" in the organization's purpose. This leads to relationships of trust and respect.

Middle-of-the-road management
5,5
Adequate organizational performance is possible through balancing the necessity to get out work with maintaining morale of people at a satisfactory level.

Impoverished management
1,1
Exertion of minimum effort to get required work done is appropriate to sustain organization membership.

Authority-obedience
9,1
Efficiency in operations results from arranging conditions of work in such a way that human elements interfere to a minimum degree.

Concern for people (vertical axis, High 9 to Low 1)

Concern for production (horizontal axis, Low 1 to High 9)

Source: Reprinted by permission of *Harvard Business Review.* Based on an exhibit from "Breakthrough in Organization Development," by R. R. Blake, J. S. Mouton, L. B. Barnes, and L. E. Greiner (November–December 1964). Copyright © 1964 by the President and Fellows of Harvard College; all rights reserved.

Contingency Theories: Does the Situation Matter?

Have you ever wondered if there was one right way to lead?

It became increasingly clear to those who were studying the leadership phenomenon that predicting leadership success was more complex than simply isolating a few traits or preferable behaviours. The failure to obtain consistent results led to a focus on situational influences. For instance, Apple brought Steve Jobs back as leader in 1996 despite having dismissed him 11 years earlier. It is unlikely that his leadership skills changed that much during his absence, but the circumstances at Apple were quite different upon his return than when he left.

The relationship between leadership style and effectiveness suggests that there is no one right style, but that style *depends* upon the situation the leader faces. There has been no shortage of studies attempting to isolate critical situational factors that affect leadership effectiveness. The volume of studies is illustrated by the number of moderating variables that researchers have identified in their discussions of **situational, or contingency, theories**. These variables include the degree of structure in the task being

situational, or contingency, theories Theories that propose leadership effectiveness is dependent on the situation.

performed, the quality of leader-member relations; the leader's position power; employees' role clarity; group norms; information availability; employee acceptance of leader's decisions; and employee maturity.[18]

We consider four situational theories: the Fiedler contingency model, Hersey and Blanchard's situational leadership theory, path-goal theory, and substitutes for leadership.

Fiedler Contingency Model

The first comprehensive contingency model for leadership was developed by Fred Fiedler.[19] The **Fiedler contingency model** proposes that effective group performance depends upon the proper match between the leader's style and the degree to which the situation gives control to the leader.

Fiedler created the *least preferred co-worker (LPC) questionnaire* to determine whether individuals were primarily interested in good personal relations with co-workers, and thus *relationship oriented*, or primarily interested in productivity, and thus *task oriented*. Fiedler assumed that an individual's leadership style is fixed. Therefore, if a situation requires a task-oriented leader and the person in that leadership position is relationship oriented, either the situation has to be modified or the leader must be removed and replaced for optimum effectiveness to be achieved.

Fiedler identified three contingency dimensions that together define the situation a leader faces:

- *Leader-member relations.* The degree of confidence, trust, and respect members have in their leader.

- *Task structure.* The degree to which the job assignments are procedurized (that is, structured or unstructured).

- *Position power.* The degree of influence a leader has over power variables such as hiring, firing, discipline, promotions, and salary increases.

Fiedler stated that the better the leader-member relations, the more highly structured the job, and the stronger the position power, the more control the leader has. He suggested that task-oriented leaders perform best in situations of high and low control, while relationship-oriented leaders perform best in moderate control situations.[20] In a high control situation, a leader can "get away" with task orientation, because the relationships are good, and followers are easily influenced.[21] In a low control situation (which is characterized by poor relations, ill-defined task, and low influence), task orientation may be the only thing that makes it possible to get something done. In a moderate control situation, being relationship oriented may smooth the way to getting things done.

Hersey and Blanchard's Situational Leadership Theory

Paul Hersey and Ken Blanchard developed a leadership model that has gained a strong following among management development specialists.[22] This model—called **situational leadership theory (SLT)**—has been incorporated into leadership training programs at more than 400 of the *Fortune* 500 companies, and more than a million managers a year from a wide variety of organizations are being taught its basic elements.[23]

SLT essentially views the leader-follower relationship as analogous to that between a parent and child. Just as a parent needs to relinquish control as a child becomes more mature and responsible, so too should leaders. Hersey and Blanchard identify four specific leader behaviours—from highly directive to highly laissez-faire. The most effective behaviour depends on a follower's ability and motivation. This is illustrated in Exhibit 11-5. So SLT says if a follower is *unable and unwilling* to do a task, the leader needs to give clear and specific directions (in other words, be highly directive). If a follower is *unable and willing,* the leader needs to display high task orientation to compensate for the follower's lack of ability, and high relationship orientation to get the

Fiedler contingency model A theory that proposes effective group performance depends upon the proper match between the leader's style and the degree to which the situation gives control to the leader.

situational leadership theory (SLT) A theory that proposes effective leaders adapt their leadership style according to how willing and able a follower is to perform tasks.

EXHIBIT 11-5 Hersey and Blanchard's Situational Leadership Theory

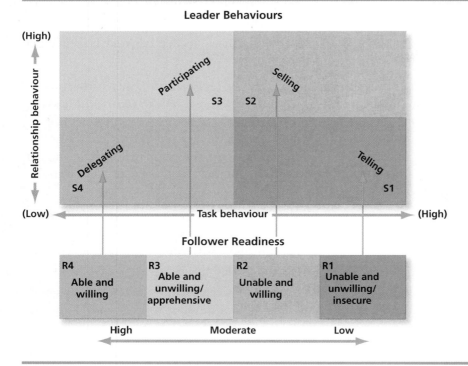

follower to "buy into" the leader's desires (in other words, "sell" the task). If the follower is *able and unwilling,* the leader needs to use a supportive and participative style. Finally, if the employee is both *able and willing,* the leader doesn't need to do much (in other words, a laissez-faire approach will work).

Both the Fiedler contingency model and Hersey and Blanchard's SLT have some intuitive appeal. Blanchard's work, for instance, is widely applied in the workplace. However, these approaches have received far less empirical support, and Fiedler's theory has been found to be more difficult to apply in the workplace than the next model we consider, path-goal theory.[24]

Path-Goal Theory

Currently, one of the most respected approaches to leadership is **path-goal theory**. Developed by University of Toronto professor Martin Evans in the late 1960s, it was subsequently expanded upon by Robert House (formerly at the University of Toronto, but now at the Wharton School of Business at the University of Pennsylvania). Path-goal theory is a contingency model of leadership that extracts key elements from the Ohio State leadership research on initiating structure and consideration, and from the expectancy theory of motivation.[25]

The essence of the theory is that it's the leader's job to assist followers in attaining their goals and to provide the necessary direction and/or support to ensure that their individual goals are compatible with the overall goals. The term *path-goal* derives from the belief that effective leaders clarify the path to help their followers get from where they are to the achievement of their work goals, and to make the journey along the path easier by reducing roadblocks and pitfalls. According to this theory, leaders should follow three guidelines to be effective:[26]

- *Determine the outcomes subordinates want.* These might include good pay, job security, interesting work, and autonomy to do one's job.

- *Reward individuals with their desired outcomes* when they perform well.

path-goal theory A theory that says it's the leader's job to assist followers in attaining their goals and to provide the necessary direction and/or support to ensure that their individual goals are compatible with the overall goals.

- *Let individuals know what they need to do to receive rewards* (that is, the path to the goal), remove any barriers that would prevent high performance, and express confidence that individuals have the ability to perform well.

Path-goal theory identifies four leadership behaviours that might be used in different situations to motivate individuals:

- The *directive leader* lets followers know what is expected of them, schedules work to be done, and gives specific guidance as to how to accomplish tasks. This closely parallels the Ohio State dimension of initiating structure. This behaviour is best used when individuals have difficulty doing tasks or the tasks are ambiguous. It would not be very helpful when used with individuals who are already highly motivated, have the skills and abilities to do the task, and understand the requirements of the task.

- The *supportive leader* is friendly and shows concern for the needs of followers. This is essentially synonymous with the Ohio State dimension of consideration. This behaviour is often recommended when individuals are under stress, or otherwise show that they need to be supported.

- The *participative leader* consults with followers and uses their suggestions before making a decision. This behaviour is most appropriate when individuals need to buy in to decisions.

- The *achievement-oriented leader* sets challenging goals and expects followers to perform at their highest level. This behaviour works well with individuals who like challenges and are highly motivated. It would be less effective with less capable individuals, or those who are highly stressed from overwork.

As Exhibit 11-6 illustrates, path-goal theory proposes two types of contingency variables that affect the leadership behaviour–outcome relationship: environmental variables that are outside the control of the employee and variables that are part of the personal characteristics of the employee. The theory proposes that employee

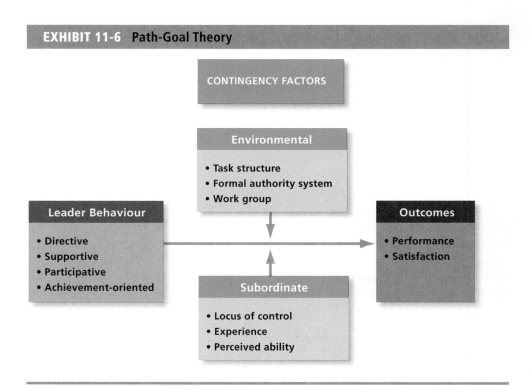

EXHIBIT 11-6   Path-Goal Theory

CONTINGENCY FACTORS

Environmental
- Task structure
- Formal authority system
- Work group

Leader Behaviour
- Directive
- Supportive
- Participative
- Achievement-oriented

Outcomes
- Performance
- Satisfaction

Subordinate
- Locus of control
- Experience
- Perceived ability

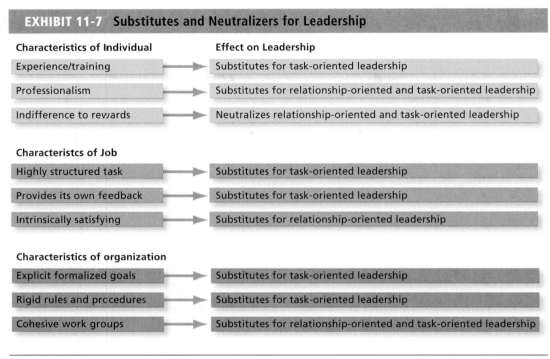

EXHIBIT 11-7 Substitutes and Neutralizers for Leadership

Characteristics of Individual	Effect on Leadership
Experience/training	Substitutes for task-oriented leadership
Professionalism	Substitutes for relationship-oriented and task-oriented leadership
Indifference to rewards	Neutralizes relationship-oriented and task-oriented leadership

Characteristcs of Job	
Highly structured task	Substitutes for task-oriented leadership
Provides its own feedback	Substitutes for task-oriented leadership
Intrinsically satisfying	Substitutes for relationship-oriented leadership

Characteristics of organization	
Explicit formalized goals	Substitutes for task-oriented leadership
Rigid rules and procedures	Substitutes for task-oriented leadership
Cohesive work groups	Substitutes for relationship-oriented and task-oriented leadership

Source: Based on S. Kerr and J. M. Jermier, "Substitutes for Leadership: Their Meaning and Measurement," *Organizational Behavior and Human Performance,* December 1978, p. 378.

performance and satisfaction are likely to be positively influenced when the leader compensates for what is lacking in either the employee or the work setting. However, the leader who spends time explaining tasks when those tasks are already clear or when the employee has the ability and experience to handle them without interference is likely to be ineffective because the employee will see such directive behaviour as redundant or even insulting.

House revised his path-goal theory in 1996 to include additional leadership behaviours that involve employees more in decisions, make sure that employees have the resources they need to carry out their tasks, and gain greater commitment from employees.[27]

One question that arises from contingency theories is whether leaders can actually adjust their behaviour to various situations. As we know, individuals differ in their behavioural flexibility. Some people show considerable ability to adjust their behaviour to external, situational factors: They are adaptable. Others, however, exhibit high levels of consistency regardless of the situation. High self-monitors are generally able to adjust their leadership style to suit changing situations better than low self-monitors.[28] Clearly, if an individual's leadership style range is very narrow and he or she cannot or will not adjust (that is, the person is a low self-monitor), that individual will only be successful in very specific situations suitable to his or her style. To find out more about your style of leadership, see the *Learning About Yourself Exercise* on page 421.

Substitutes for Leadership

The previous three theories argue that leaders are needed, but that leaders should consider the situation in determining which style of leadership to use. However, numerous studies collectively demonstrate that, in many situations, leaders' actions are irrelevant. Certain individual, job, and organizational variables can act as *substitutes* for leadership or *neutralize* the leader's ability to influence his or her followers as shown in Exhibit 11-7.[29]

If employees have appropriate experience, training, or "professional" orientation, or if employees are indifferent to organizational rewards, the effect of leadership can be replaced or neutralized. Experience and training, for instance, can replace the need for a leader's support or ability to create structure and reduce task ambiguity. Jobs that are inherently unambiguous and routine, provide their own feedback, or are intrinsically satisfying generally require less hands-on leadership. Organizational characteristics such as explicit formalized goals, rigid rules and procedures, and cohesive work groups can replace formal leadership.

Can You Be a Better Follower?

Thus far we have concentrated on how leaders must adapt their styles to the needs of their followers. This underscores the importance of the followers' role in how leadership is carried out. Only recently have we begun to recognize that in addition to having leaders who can lead, successful organizations need followers who can follow.[30] In fact, it's probably fair to say that all organizations have far more followers than leaders, so ineffective followers may be more of a handicap to an organization than ineffective leaders. The Far Side cartoon shown in Exhibit 11-8 gives you some indication of what can happen when someone finally realizes that he or she is "a follower, too."

An understanding of how to be a follower is important, because almost all roles in an organization require one to be a follower in some settings. Obviously, lower-level employees are followers to their supervisors. But the supervisor is a follower to his or her manager, who is a follower to the CEO. The CEO in a public corporation is a follower to the board of directors. Even the best leaders have to be followers at some times.

What qualities do effective followers have? One writer focuses on four:[31]

- *They manage themselves well.* They are able to think for themselves. They can work independently and without close supervision.

- *They are committed to a purpose outside themselves.* Effective followers are committed to something—a cause, a product, a work team, an organization, an idea—in addition to the care of their own lives. Most people like working with colleagues who are emotionally, as well as physically, committed to their work.

- *They build their competence and focus their efforts for maximum impact.* Effective followers master skills that will be useful to their organizations, and they hold higher performance standards than their job or work group requires.

- *They are courageous, honest, and credible.* Effective followers establish themselves as independent, critical thinkers whose knowledge and judgment can be trusted. They hold high ethical standards, give credit where credit is due, and aren't afraid to own up to their mistakes.

These points suggest that there is a relationship between leadership and followership, and that taking responsibility for your own behaviour is beneficial for both yourself and the organization.

EXHIBIT 11-8

THE FAR SIDE   By GARY LARSON

"Well, what d'ya know! . . . *I'm* a follower, too!"

Source: THE FAR SIDE copyright 1990 & 1991 Farworks, Inc./Dist. by Universal Press Syndicate. Reprinted with permission. All rights reserved.

INSPIRATIONAL LEADERSHIP

As people around the world watched the aftermath of Hurricane Katrina from the safety of their homes, many wondered, Why isn't anyone sending in food or water? The implicit question people were asking was, Why isn't someone just taking charge and doing something, rather than waiting for others to act? Both New Orleans mayor Ray Nagin and Louisiana governor Kathleen Blanco were quick to criticize President Bush, and the president's staff just as quickly tried to explain that it wasn't the role of the federal government to be the first responder. People who lead with vision do not wonder why someone else isn't acting—rather, they make sure action gets carried out. Without pointing any fingers of blame, it is easy to see that in the early days after the levees broke, none of the official leaders was prepared to rise to the occasion and lead with vision. What does it take for a person to lead with vision? What characteristics does such a person need?

3 How does a leader lead with vision?

The leadership theories reported above were developed at a time when most organizations were organized in traditional hierarchies where there were classic lines of command. While this form still dominates in Canada's "Most Respected Corporations,"[32] there are organizations trying to be more innovative, faster moving, and more responsive to employees who are highly educated and intelligent, and who want more say in the workplace. Thus, new styles of leadership are evolving to meet the demands of these organizations. The more recent approaches to leadership move away from the supervisory tasks of leaders and focus on vision-setting activities. Today, leadership theories also try to explain how certain leaders can get extraordinary levels of performance from their followers, and they stress symbolic and emotionally appealing leadership behaviours.[33] Below we consider transactional leadership, transformational leadership, and charismatic leadership.

From Transactional to Transformational Leadership

Most of the leadership theories presented thus far in this chapter have concerned **transactional leaders**. These kinds of leaders guide or motivate their followers in the direction of established goals by clarifying role and task requirements. In some styles of transactional leadership, the leader uses rewarding and recognizing behaviours. This approach results in performance that meets expectations, though rarely do we see results that exceed expectations.[34] In other styles of transactional leadership, the leader emphasizes correction and possibly punishment rather than rewards and recognition. This style "results in performance below expectations, and discourages innovation and initiative in the workplace."[35] Of course, leaders should not ignore poor performance, but effective leaders emphasize how to achieve expectations, rather than dwell on mistakes.

transactional leaders Leaders who guide or motivate their followers in the direction of established goals by clarifying role and task requirements.

Some leaders inspire followers to go beyond their own self-interests for the good of the organization, and have a profound and extraordinary effect on their followers. These are **transformational leaders**, such as Matthew Barrett, CEO of Barclays PLC, the United Kingdom's second-largest bank, and former CEO of Bank of Montreal; Frank Stronach of Aurora, Ontario-based Magna International; and Mogens Smed, CEO of Calgary-based DIRTT (Doing It Right This Time) and former CEO of SMED International. Other Canadians who have frequently been cited as being charismatic leaders include René Lévesque, former Quebec premier; Lucien Bouchard, former Bloc Québécois leader; Adrienne Clarkson, former Governor General; Robert Chisholm, former NDP leader for Nova Scotia; and Craig Kielburger, the Canadian teenager who founded Kids Can Free the Children to promote children's rights and combat exploitation of child labour. What links these individuals is that they pay attention to the concerns and developmental needs of individual followers; they change followers' awareness of issues by helping them look at old problems in new ways; and they are able to excite, arouse, and inspire followers to exert extra effort to achieve group goals. This chapter's *CBC Video Case* highlights the charismatic leadership of Richard Branson.

transformational leaders Leaders who inspire followers to go beyond their own self-interests for the good of the organization, and have a profound and extraordinary effect on their followers.

Richard Branson

charismatic leadership Leadership that critically examines the status quo with a view to developing and articulating future strategic goals or vision for the organization, and then leading organizational members to achieve these goals through empowering strategies.

Transformational leadership is sometimes identified separately from **charismatic leadership** in the literature, although McGill's Kanungo notes that the two formulations are not different in that charismatic leaders are also transformational leaders. Relying on his judgment, we use the two terms interchangeably. Kanungo's definition of the charismatic/transformational leader is one who "critically examines the status quo with a view to developing and articulating future strategic goals or vision for the organization and then leading organizational members to achieve these goals through empowering strategies."[36] Though we use these terms interchangeably, be aware that while all charismatic leaders are transformational, not all transformational leaders are charismatic in personality. Both, however, work to empower their followers to reach higher goals.

Transactional and transformational leadership should not be viewed as opposing approaches to getting things done.[37] Transformational leadership is built on top of transactional leadership—it produces levels of employee effort and performance that go beyond what would occur with a transactional approach alone. Exhibit 11-9 outlines the difference between transactional and transformational (or charismatic) leaders. Would you be able to be a charismatic leader? We give you tips in this chapter's *From Concepts to Skills* on page 425.

Next we discuss the importance of sharing a vision in transformational and charismatic leadership. We also look at the influence of culture on leadership style and the downside of charismatic leadership.

Sharing a Vision

Perhaps one of the key components of transformational and charismatic leadership is the ability to articulate a vision. A review of various definitions finds that a vision differs from other forms of direction setting in several ways:

> *A vision has clear and compelling imagery that offers an innovative way to improve, which recognizes and draws on traditions, and connects to actions that people can take to realize change. Vision taps people's emotions and energy. Properly articulated, a vision creates the enthusiasm that people have for sporting events and other leisure-time activities, bringing the energy and commitment to the workplace.*[38]

The key properties of a vision seem to be inspirational possibilities that are value-centred and realizable, with superior imagery and articulation.[39] Visions should be able to create possibilities that are inspirational and unique, and offer a new order that can produce organizational distinction. A vision is likely to fail if it doesn't offer a view of the future that is clearly and demonstrably better for the organization and its mem-

---

EXHIBIT 11-9   Characteristics of Transactional and Transformational Leaders

Transactional Leader

Contingent rewards: Contracts exchange of rewards for effort, promises rewards for good performance, recognizes accomplishments.

Management by exception (active): Watches and searches for deviations from rules and standards, takes corrective action.

Management by exception (passive): Intervenes only if standards are not met.

Laissez-faire: Abdicates responsibilities, avoids making decisions.

Transformational Leader

Charisma: Provides vision and sense of mission, instills pride, gains respect and trust.

Inspiration: Communicates high expectations, uses symbols to focus efforts, expresses important purposes in simple ways.

Intellectual stimulation: Promotes intelligence, rationality, and careful problem solving.

Individualized consideration: Gives personal attention, treats each employee individually, coaches, advises.

Source: B. M. Bass, "From Transactional to Transformational Leadership: Learning to Share the Vision," *Organizational Dynamics,* Winter 1990, p. 22. Reprinted by permission of the publisher. American Management Association, New York. All rights reserved.

bers. Desirable visions fit the times and circumstances and reflect the uniqueness of the organization. People in the organization must also believe that the vision is attainable. It should be perceived as challenging yet doable. Visions that have clear articulation and powerful imagery are more easily grasped and accepted. *Case Incident—Anne Mulcahy at Xerox* on page 424 discusses how visionary leadership helped turn Xerox around.

RESEARCH FINDINGS

A number of studies demonstrate the effectiveness of charismatic and transformational leadership. We consider the impact of this leadership style on company performance and individual performance.

Company Performance Do vision and charismatic leadership really make a difference? Several studies provide positive evidence that they do:

- One study contrasted 18 visionary companies with 18 comparable nonvisionary firms over a 65-year period.[40] The visionary companies performed 6 times better than the comparison group, based on standard financial criteria, and their stocks performed 15 times better than the general market.

- In a study of 250 executives and managers at a major financial services company, Jane Howell (at the Richard Ivey School of Business at the University of Western Ontario) and her colleagues found that "transformational leaders had 34 percent higher business unit performance results than other types of leaders."[41]

- An unpublished study by Robert House and some colleagues of 63 American and 49 Canadian companies (including Nortel Networks, Molson, Gulf Canada [now ConocoPhillips], and Manulife Financial) found that "between 15 and 25 percent of the variation in profitability among the companies was accounted for by the leadership qualities of their CEO."[42] That is, charismatic leaders led more profitable companies in the 1990s. This may explain the high compensation packages for CEOs that we discussed in Chapter 5.

Individual Performance An increasing body of research shows that people working for charismatic leaders are motivated to exert extra work effort and, because they like their leaders, they express greater satisfaction.[43] One of the most cited studies of the effects of charismatic leadership was done at the University of British Columbia in the early 1980s. It's discussed in *Focus on Research.*

Through his charismatic leadership, Steve Jobs achieved unwavering loyalty and commitment from the technical staff he oversaw at Apple Computer during the late 1970s and early 1980s. However, as the company grew, this style was less effective, and he was forced out of Apple in 1985. In 1996, with Apple doing poorly, Jobs was brought back to lead the company once again because of his vision and charisma. With such innovations as the iPod and the iPod shuffle, Jobs' visionary leadership continues to make Apple successful.

FedEx Canada
www.fedex.com/ca

FOCUS ON **RESEARCH**

The Effects of Charismatic Leaders

Do charismatic leaders really make a difference? Jane Howell and the late Peter Frost of the Sauder School of Business, University of British Columbia, compared the charismatic leadership style with structuring (that is, task-oriented) and considerate (that is, employee-oriented) styles.[44] They found that those who worked under a charismatic leader generated more ideas and reported higher job satisfaction than those working under structuring leaders. Charismatic leaders also produced better results than considerate leaders, with employees performing at a higher level. Those working under charismatic leaders also showed higher job satisfaction and stronger bonds of loyalty. Howell, in summarizing these results, says, "While it is true that considerate leaders make people feel good, that doesn't necessarily translate into increased productivity. In contrast, charismatic leaders know how to inspire people to think in new directions."[45] ✈

To learn more about how to be transformational/charismatic yourself, see the *Working With Others Exercise* on page 422.

The evidence supporting the superiority of transformational leadership over the transactional variety is overwhelmingly impressive. For instance, a number of studies with US, Canadian, and German military officers found, at every level, that transformational leaders were evaluated as more effective than their transactional counterparts.[46] Managers at FedEx who were rated by their followers as exhibiting more transformational leadership were evaluated by their immediate supervisors as higher performers and more promotable.[47]

In summary, the overall evidence indicates that transformational leadership is more strongly correlated than transactional leadership with lower turnover rates, higher productivity, and higher employee satisfaction.[48] One caveat to this research is a study by Professor Timothy DeGroot of McMaster University and his colleagues. They found that charismatic leadership had a greater impact on team performance than on individual performance, and suggest that the positive findings of previous studies are the result of charismatic leaders providing a better team environment for everyone, which then resulted in higher performance.[49]

Transformational Leadership Styles Across Cultures

While the idea of charismatic leadership was developed based on North American observations, professors Dale Carl of the Faculty of Management at Ryerson University and Mansour Javidan at the University of Calgary also propose that charismatic leadership is expressed relatively similarly in a variety of countries, including Canada, Hungary, India, Turkey, Austria, Singapore, Sweden, and Venezuela.[50] This suggests that there may be some universal aspects of this style of leadership.

Focus on Research provides additional insights on whether transformational leadership styles differ across cultures.

FOCUS ON **RESEARCH**

Leadership Around the World

Are there cross-cultural differences in leadership? Professor Joseph Di Stefano and one of his students, Nick Bontis, both of the Richard Ivey School of Business at the

University of Western Ontario, studied differences in leadership styles across cultures.[51] They were particularly interested in the behaviours that were used to generate exceptional performance by employees. In general, they reported that there were many similarities in managers from the United States, Northern Europe, Southern Europe, Latin America, the Far East, and Commonwealth countries, including Canada. In order to achieve exceptional performance from employees, leaders from all of these countries used visioning, coaching, and stimulating (encouraging new ideas) behaviours similarly, and as their chief strategies.

US leaders reported they were more likely to correct employees' behaviour than did Far Eastern or Latin managers. Americans also used team building more often than did Asian managers. Far Eastern managers were less likely to include recognition as part of how they encouraged their employees' exceptional performance than were Southern European leaders.

These findings suggest that there are some minor differences in how leaders throughout the world achieve exceptional performance from their employees. However, they also suggest a great degree of similarity in what it takes to get high-performing employees. 🏃

The Downside of Charismatic Leadership

When organizations are in need of great change, charismatic leaders are often able to inspire their followers to meet the challenges of change. Be aware that a charismatic leader may become a liability to an organization once the crisis is over and the need for dramatic change subsides.[52] Why? Because then the charismatic leader's overwhelming self-confidence can be a liability. He or she is unable to listen to others, becomes uncomfortable when challenged by aggressive employees, and begins to hold an unjustifiable belief in his or her "rightness" on issues. Some would argue that Jean Chrétien's behaviour leading up to his decision to announce that he would eventually step down as prime minister, thus preventing a divisive leadership review in February 2003, would fit this description.

Many have argued that the recent accounting scandals and high-profile bankruptcies facing North American companies, including Enron and WorldCom, point to some of the dangers of charismatic leadership. WorldCom's Bernard Ebbers and Enron's Kenneth Lay "seemed almost a breed apart, blessed with unique visionary powers" when their companies were increasing stock prices at phenomenal rates in the 1990s.[53]

Harvard Business School professor Rakesh Khurana argues that an inordinate number of today's chief executives have been "chosen for their ability to articulate messianic 'visions' for their companies; inspire employees to do whatever it takes to realize these grand designs; and imbue investors with faith in their own talents."[54] These traits, however, may have led to the corporate scandals that unfolded in recent years. Charismatic leadership, by its very nature, silences criticism. Thus, employees follow the lead of their visionary CEOs unquestioningly. Professor David Leighton, of the Richard Ivey School of Business at the University of Western Ontario, notes that even the boards of directors and auditors were reluctant to challenge these CEOs. He also suggests that Canada's "more balanced culture," which is less likely to turn CEOs into heroes, may help protect the country from some of the scandals that the United States faced.[55]

A recent study of 29 companies that went from good to great (their cumulative stock returns were all at least three times better than the general stock market over 15 years) found that a key difference in successful charismatic leaders may be the absence of being *ego-driven*.[56] Although the leaders of these firms were fiercely ambitious and driven, their ambition was directed toward their company rather than themselves. They generated extraordinary results, but with little fanfare or hoopla. They took responsibility for mistakes and poor results but gave credit for successes to other people. They also prided themselves on developing strong leaders inside the firm who could direct the company to greater heights after they were gone. These individuals have been called **level 5 leaders** because they have four basic leadership qualities—individual capability, team skills, managerial competence, and the ability to stimulate others to high performance—plus a fifth quality: a paradoxical blend of personal humility and professional will. Level 5 leaders channel their ego needs away from themselves and into the goal of building a great company. So, while level 5 leaders are highly effective, they tend to be people you have never heard of and who get little notoriety in the business press—people like Orin Smith at Starbucks, Kristine McDivitt of Patagonia, John Whitehead of Goldman Sachs, and Jack Brennan of Vanguard. This study is important because it confirms that leaders don't necessarily need to be charismatic to be effective, especially where charisma is enmeshed with an outsized ego.

The current mood seems to be for CEOs with less vision, and more ethical and corporate responsibility. It seems clear that future research on charismatic leadership will need to provide greater insight into how this style relates to ethical and business behaviour.

DISPERSED LEADERSHIP: SPREADING LEADERSHIP THROUGHOUT THE ORGANIZATION

US Army Lieutenant General Russel Honoré was perhaps the first leader to inspire calm in New Orleans, as people struggled to get help, and others struggled to help out.[57] Clear leadership, with clear statements of what people should do, had not come from the obvious leaders in the situation: President George W. Bush, Governor Kathleen Blanco, and Mayor Ray Nagin. While these latter were elected politicians, chosen by their constituents to lead them, Honoré had no direct connection to the people he was about to save. Instead, he was a no-nonsense military man. When he arrived on the scene in New Orleans, he didn't wait to find out what the other leaders wanted him to do: He assessed the situation and made decisions about the best way to get things under control.

One of the major issues facing Honoré when he arrived in Louisiana was how to evacuate the Superdome, where more than 20 000 people had gone to get away from the storm. Once there, they became stranded when the New Orleans levees broke. With no electricity, and little food and water, Mayor Nagin complained bitterly that no one was sending the buses that were needed to get the people relocated. Honoré's junior officers did not provide much hope that the job could be done quickly—they told him it would take days. Honoré was not prepared to wait that long, and 24 hours after he gave orders, he managed to clear the Superdome and put people on buses to shelters in other states. How is it that people who are not officially in charge can also be effective leaders?

4 Can a person be an informal leader?

Transformational leadership theory focuses on heroic leaders, leaders at the top echelons of the organization, and also on individuals rather than teams. The following sections aim to explain how leadership can be spread throughout the organization through mentoring and team leadership. Even if you are not a manager or someone thinking about leadership in a corporate situation, this discussion offers important insights into how you can take on a leadership role in an organization. Moreover, in today's flatter organizations, you may well be expected to show leadership characteristics, even if you are not a formal leader. The work of General Russel Honoré illustrates this point. Although he was a leader in the army, he had no formal authority to take charge in New Orleans. That was the job of politicians. Still, he saw what needed to be done and did it.

Can anyone be a leader?

As you consider the ways organizations distribute leadership to their employees, be aware that not all organizations engage in this practice, and even within organizations, not all managers are happy with the notion of sharing power or leadership. Gifted leaders often recognize that they actually have more power if they share power. That is, sharing power enables them to build coalitions and teams that work together for the overall good of the organization. There are other managers, though, who fear the loss of any power.

Mentoring

Many leaders create mentoring relationships. A **mentor** is often a senior employee who sponsors and supports a less-experienced employee (a protégé). The mentoring role includes coaching, counselling, and sponsorship.[58] As a coach, mentors help develop their protégés' skills. As counsellors, mentors provide support and help bolster protégés' self-confidence. And as sponsors, mentors actively intervene on behalf of their protégés, lobby to get their protégés visible assignments, and politic to get their protégés rewards such as promotions and salary increases.

Successful mentors are good teachers. They can present ideas clearly, listen well, and empathize with the problems of their protégés. They also share experiences with the protégé, act as role models, share contacts, and provide guidance through the political maze of the organization. They provide advice on how to survive and get ahead in the organization, and act as a sounding board for ideas that a protégé may be hesitant to share with his or her direct supervisor. A mentor vouches for a protégé, answers for him or her in the highest circles within the organization, and makes appropriate introductions.

Some organizations have formal mentoring programs, in which mentors are officially assigned to new or high-potential employees. For instance, Montreal-based Bell Canada introduced Mentor Match in late 2002 to bring together senior and junior employees. The mentors meet one-on-one for about an hour a month, to build a stronger understanding of leadership and organizational knowledge for the younger employees.[59] However, in contrast to Bell Canada's formal system, most organizations rely on informal mentoring—with senior managers personally selecting an employee and taking that employee on as a protégé.

The most effective mentoring relationships exist outside the immediate boss–subordinate interface.[60] The boss–subordinate context has an inherent conflict of interest and tension, mostly attributable to managers' directly evaluating the performance of subordinates, that limits openness and meaningful communication.

Why would a leader want to be a mentor? There are personal benefits to the leader as well as benefits for the organization. The mentor–protégé relationship gives the mentor unfiltered access to the attitudes and feelings of lower-ranking employees. Protégés can be an excellent source of information on potential problems; they can provide early warning signals to upper managers because they short-circuit the formal channels. So the mentor–protégé relationship is a valuable communication channel that allows mentors to have news of problems before they become common knowledge to others in upper management. In addition, in terms of leader self-interest, mentoring can provide personal satisfaction to senior executives. It gives them the opportunity to share with others the knowledge and experience that they have developed over many years.

From the organization's standpoint, mentoring provides a support system for high-potential employees. Where mentors exist, protégés are often more motivated, better grounded politically, and less likely to quit. A recent comprehensive review of the research, for instance, found that mentoring provided substantial benefits to protégés.[61] Specifically, mentored employees had higher compensation, a larger number of promotions, and were more satisfied with their careers than their nonmentored counterparts.

Are all employees in an organization equally likely to participate in a mentoring relationship? Unfortunately the answer is no.[62] The evidence indicates that minorities

mentor A senior employee who sponsors and supports a less-experienced employee.

Bell Canada
www.bell.ca

and women are less likely to be chosen as protégés than are white males and thus are less likely to accrue the benefits of mentorship. Mentors tend to select protégés who are similar to themselves on criteria such as background, education, gender, race, ethnicity, and religion. "People naturally move to mentor and can more easily communicate with those with whom they most closely identify."[63]

Procter & Gamble Canada
www.pg.com/en_CA

On a twist to the typical mentoring down idea, Procter & Gamble introduced a Mentoring Up program to help senior managers become more aware of what female managers can contribute to the organization. In its program, mid-level female managers mentor senior-level male executives. The program has led to fewer departures of female managers and has exposed women to top decision makers.[64]

Providing Team Leadership

Leadership is increasingly taking place within a team context. As teams grow in popularity, the role of the leader in guiding team members takes on heightened importance.[65] Also, because of its more collaborative nature, the role of team leader is different from the traditional leadership role performed by first-line supervisors.

Many leaders are not equipped to handle the change to team leader. As one prominent consultant noted, "Even the most capable managers have trouble making the transition because all the command-and-control type things they were encouraged to do before are no longer appropriate. There's no reason to have any skill or sense of this."[66] This same consultant estimated that "probably 15 percent of managers are natural team leaders; another 15 percent could never lead a team because it runs counter to their personality. [They're unable to sublimate their dominating style for the good of the team.] Then there's that huge group in the middle: team leadership doesn't come naturally to them, but they can learn it."[67]

Effective team leaders need to build commitment and confidence, remove obstacles, create opportunities, and be part of the team.[68] They have to learn skills such as the patience to share information, the willingness to trust others, the ability to give up authority, and an understanding of when to intervene. New team leaders may try to retain too much control at a time when team members need more autonomy, or they may abandon their teams at times when the teams need support and help.[69]

Roles of Team Leaders

A study of 20 organizations that reorganized themselves around teams found certain common responsibilities that all leaders had to assume. These included coaching, facilitating, training, communicating, handling disciplinary problems, and reviewing team/individual performance.[70] Many of these responsibilities apply to managers in general. A more meaningful way to describe the team leader's job is to focus on two priorities: managing the team's external boundary and facilitating the team process.[71] We have divided these priorities into four specific roles that team leaders play:

After Hurricane Katrina devastated many areas of the southern United States, Vancouver Urban Search and Rescue Team sent a group of 46 men to help with evacuations. The team is a self-contained unit that can bring all of its own supplies to a disaster area, in addition to supplies to help out others. The team members were the first rescuers to get to St. Bernard Parish in New Orleans. They received great praise for their team leadership in helping Americans in a time of real need.

EXHIBIT 11-10

Source: DILBERT reprinted by permission of United Features Syndicate, Inc.

- *Liaisons with external constituencies.* Outsiders include upper management, other internal teams, customers, and suppliers. The leader represents the team to other constituencies, secures needed resources, clarifies others' expectations of the team, gathers information from the outside, and shares this information with team members.

- *Troubleshooters.* When the team has problems and asks for assistance, team leaders sit in on meetings and try to help resolve the problems. This rarely relates to technical or operational issues because the team members typically know more about the tasks being done than does the team leader. The leader contributes by asking penetrating questions, by helping the team discuss problems, and by getting needed resources from external constituencies. For instance, when a team in an aerospace firm found itself short-handed, its team leader took responsibility for getting more staff. He presented the

  team's case to upper management and got the approval through the company's human resource department.

- *Conflict managers.* When disagreements surface, team leaders help process the conflict. What is the source of the conflict? Who is involved? What are the issues? What resolution options are available? What are the advantages and disadvantages of each? By getting team members to address questions such as these, the leader minimizes the disruptive aspects of intrateam conflicts.

- *Coaches.* They clarify expectations and roles, teach, offer support, cheerlead, and do whatever else is necessary to help team members improve their work performance.

Exhibit 11-10 offers a lighthearted look at what it means to be a team leader.

LEADING ONE'S SELF

When the death toll after Hurricane Katrina was around 900 in New Orleans and 1100 overall, rather than the tens of thousands officials had feared at the start of the catastrophe, most people breathed a sigh of relief. What kept the toll so low? Two factors were largely responsible. First, people took charge of themselves and their families, doing what they could to get themselves evacuated before the storm hit. People also did what they could to help others evacuate—making it their own responsibility to help their poor, sick, and elderly neighbours move to safety. That the death toll was so low illustrates the importance of individuals taking leadership responsibility when the situation demands. So, how can individuals practise leadership on a daily basis, even if they do not have official positions of leadership?

5 What is self-leadership?

Thus far we have discussed the role of leadership as if it were mainly a one-way street: Leadership is something someone at the top does, and hopefully, those at the bottom—the followers—follow. However, we would like to raise two provocative issues for you to consider when thinking about leadership. The first is the issue of self-leadership, or taking responsibility for your own actions. The second is learning how to be a leader, even if only in small areas of your work or personal life.

Self-Leadership (or Self-Management)

How do you manage yourself?

A growing trend in organizations is the focus on self-leadership,[72] or self-management. We saw this earlier when we discussed self-managed teams. With self-leadership, individuals and teams set goals, plan and implement tasks, evaluate performance, solve their own problems, and motivate themselves.

Several factors call for self-leadership: reduced levels of supervision; offices in the home; teamwork; and growth in service and professional employment where individuals are often required to make decisions on the spot. Following from our previous discussion on substitutes for leadership, self-management can also be a substitute or neutralizer for leadership from others.

Despite the lack of studies of self-management techniques in organizational settings, self-management strategies have been shown to be successful in nonorganizational settings.[73] Those who practise self-management look for opportunities to be more effective in the workplace and improve their career success. Their behaviour is self-reinforced; that is, they provide their own sense of reward and feedback after carrying out their accomplishments. Moreover, self-reinforced behaviour is often maintained at a higher rate than behaviour that is externally regulated.[74]

What does self-management look like? Though "individuals in organizations are regularly taught how to manage subordinates, groups, and even organizations, they rarely receive instruction on how to manage themselves."[75] Few empirical studies of this kind have been carried out in the workplace,[76] but a 1999 study of 305 managers at a large retailing organization in the Midwestern United States identified four behaviours that can be considered self-management: planning, access management, catch-up activities, and emotions management.[77] The *Learning About Yourself Exercise* on page 421 describes these behaviours in greater detail.

How do leaders create self-leaders? The following have been suggested:[78]

1. *Model self-leadership.* Practise self-observation, setting challenging personal goals, self-direction, and self-reinforcement. Then display these behaviours and encourage others to rehearse and then produce them.

2. *Encourage employees to create self-set goals.* Support employees in developing quantitative, specific goals; having such goals is the most important part of self-leadership.

3. *Encourage the use of self-rewards to strengthen and increase desirable behaviours.* By contrast, limit self-punishment only to occasions when the employee has been dishonest or destructive.

4. *Create positive thought patterns.* Encourage employees to use mental imagery and self-talk to further stimulate self-motivation.

5. *Create a climate of self-leadership.* Redesign the work to increase the natural rewards of a job and focus on these naturally rewarding features of work to increase motivation.

6. *Encourage self-criticism.* Encourage individuals to be critical of their own performance.

The underlying assumptions behind self-leadership are that people are responsible, capable, and able to exercise initiative without the external constraints of bosses, rules, or regulations. Given the proper support, individuals can monitor and control their own behaviour.

Leading Without Authority

Thus far in this section we have discussed how to manage yourself, but what if your goal is to be a leader, even if you don't have the authority (or formal appointment) to be one? For instance, what if you wanted to convince the dean of your school to introduce new business courses that were more relevant, or you wanted to convince the president of the company where you work that she should start thinking about more effective environmentally friendly strategies in dealing with waste? How do you effectively lead in a student group, when everyone is a peer?

Leadership at the grassroots level in organizations does happen. Rosabeth Moss Kanter, in her book *The Change Masters,*[79] discusses examples of people who saw something in their workplace that needed changing and took the responsibility to do so upon themselves. Employees were more likely to do this when organizations permitted initiative at all levels of the organization, rather than making it a tool of senior executives only.

Leading without authority simply means exhibiting leadership behaviour even though you do not have a formal position or title that might encourage others "to obey." Neither Martin Luther King Jr. nor Nelson Mandela operated from a position of authority, yet each was able to inspire many to follow him in the quest for social justice. The workplace can be an opportunity for leading without authority as well. As Ronald Heifetz of Harvard's Kennedy School of Government notes, "Leadership means taking responsibility for hard problems beyond anyone's expectations."[80] It also means not waiting for the coach's call.[81]

What are the benefits of leading without authority? Heifetz has identified three:[82]

- *Latitude for creative deviance.* When a person does not have authority, and the trappings that go with authority, it's easier to raise harder questions and look for less traditional solutions.

- *Issue focus.* Leading without authority means that individuals can focus on a single issue, rather than be concerned with the myriad issues that those in authority face.

- *Front-line information.* Leading without authority means that an individual is closer to the detailed experiences of some of the stakeholders. Thus, more information is available to this kind of leader.

Not all organizations will support this type of leadership, and some have been known to actively suppress it. Still others will look aside, not encouraging, but not discouraging either. Nevertheless, you may want to reflect on the possibility of engaging in leadership behaviour because you see a need, rather than because you are required to act.

CONTEMPORARY ISSUES IN LEADERSHIP

Louisiana governor Kathleen Blanco found herself under severe criticism in the wake of Hurricane Katrina. Louisiana seemed to have greater difficulties with its emergency evacuation plans compared with two other states faced with similar problems in the face of Hurricane Katrina: Mississippi and Alabama (states led by men).[83] Michael Brown, then director of the Federal Emergency Management Agency (FEMA), went so far as to describe Blanco's response to the disaster as "confused" compared with the governors of the two other states.

In the early days after the levees broke, Blanco expressed some frustration that aides to President George W. Bush did not seem to respond to her pleas for help in a timely manner. FEMA director Brown asked her, "What do you need? Help me help you." Blanco's communications director, Robert Mann, said Blanco could not believe that FEMA could not anticipate some of the state's needs. "It was like walking into an emergency room bleeding profusely and being expected to instruct the doctors how to treat you," he said. Could gender differences in leadership styles and communication have had any role in how the reactions to Hurricane Katrina played out?

6 What are some of the contemporary issues in leadership?

Is there a moral dimension to leadership? Do men and women rely on different leadership styles, and if so, is one style inherently superior to the other? What are the challenges of online leadership? In this section, we briefly address these contemporary issues in leadership.

Moral Leadership

The topic of leadership and ethics has received surprisingly little attention by scholars until very recently.[84] However, the corporate scandals that rocked financial markets, starting with the collapse of Enron in late 2001, have had nearly everyone questioning the ethics of leadership.

During much of the 1990s, CEOs were viewed as heroes, and achieved star status in the media. They received personal credit as their companies' stock prices increased, and they were rewarded lavishly for improving company bottom lines. Meanwhile, perceptions of executives' integrity have dropped significantly since the 1990s.[85] CEOs are now less able to justify their wealthy pay packages, and some are reconsidering how much compensation is enough. Former General Electric chair Jack Welch acknowledged in late 2002 that "perceptions" persuaded him to modify his retirement package so that he will repay the company $2 million to $2.5 million (US) annually for services provided under his contract.[86]

General Electric Canada
www.ge.com/ca

Ethics touches on leadership at a number of junctures. Transformational leaders, for instance, have been described by one authority as fostering moral virtue when they try to change the attitudes and behaviours of followers.[87] Charisma, too, has an ethical component. Unethical leaders are more likely to use their charisma to enhance power over followers, directed toward self-serving ends. Ethical leaders are considered to use their charisma in a socially constructive way to serve others.[88] There is also the issue of abuse of power by leaders—for example, when they give themselves large salaries and bonuses while also seeking to cut costs by laying off long-time employees.

Leadership effectiveness needs to address the means that a leader uses in trying to achieve goals, as well as the content of those goals. For instance, at Enron, employees were driven by the top executives to keep Enron stock prices up, at whatever cost. "The driver was this unbelievable desire to keep portraying Enron as something very different and keep the track record going and going," said Forrest Hoglund, who ran Enron's oil and gas exploration until 1999.[89] To achieve these goals, executives inflated revenues and hid debts. CEO and chair Kenneth Lay thus led his subordinates to achieve stock price goals irrespective of how this was accomplished. Anyone who questioned what the company was doing was ignored or dismissed.

Bill Young created Toronto-based Social Capital Partners to help businesses hire the hard to employ: youths, single mothers, Aboriginal people, new immigrants, and those with disabilities or substance abuse. His goal is to help people who are struggling get back into the economic mainstream.

George Cooke, CEO of Toronto-based Dominion of Canada General Insurance, believes in promoting women to senior positions. He is noteworthy for this: Dominion is well above the national average in the percentage of women who have made it to the executive ranks of Canada's top companies.

Additionally, ethical leadership must address the content of a leader's goals. Are the changes that the leader seeks for the organization morally acceptable? Is a business leader effective if he or she builds an organization's success by selling products that damage the health of their users, such as tobacco executives have done? Is a military leader successful when winning a war that should not have been fought in the first place?

Professor James Clawson of the Darden Graduate School of Business, University of Virginia, suggests that there are four cornerstones to a "moral foundation of leadership":[90]

- *Truth telling.* Leaders who tell the truth as they see it allow for a mutual, fair exchange to occur.

- *Promise keeping.* Leaders need to be careful of the commitments they make, and then careful of keeping those commitments.

- *Fairness.* Leaders who are equitable ensure that followers get their fair share for their contributions to the organization.

- *Respect for the individual.* Leaders who tell the truth, keep promises, and are fair show respect for followers. Respect means treating people with dignity.

Moral leadership comes from within the individual, and in general means treating people well, and with respect. This chapter's *Ethical Dilemma Exercise* on page 422 raises some provocative issues about whether we should consider just the ends toward which a leader strives, or the means as well.

Gender and Leadership

How Many Women Make It to the Top?

Women make up 46.2 percent of the labour force in Canada,[91] but they hold only 32 percent of managerial roles, 14 percent of the senior management roles, and 6.7 percent of the highest corporate titles—CEO, chief financial officer, or chief operating officer.[92] They make up 57 percent of graduate degree holders and 51 percent of the Canadian population. Half of Canada's companies have no women in the senior ranks at all.[93] Commenting on the low numbers of women in leadership positions at top companies in 2004, Toronto-based Catalyst Canada president Susan Black suggests that "at the pace of change we are reporting . . . women's overall representation in Corporate Canada will not reach 25 per cent until 2025. It will not reach parity until close to the end of the century."[94]

Despite women's lack of representation in large companies, they are highly involved in smaller companies. Industry Canada reports that in 2000, 45 percent of all small- to medium-sized enterprises had at least one female owner.[95] Moreover, women start almost half of all small businesses in Canada today and, among young people, women start almost 80 percent of small businesses.[96]

Promotion Similarities and Differences A study by the Center for Creative Leadership found that there were some differences, as well as many similarities, in the promotion processes for men and women.[97] This study is discussed in *Focus on Research*.

FOCUS ON **RESEARCH**

Promotions for Men and Women

Are men and women promoted for the same reasons? Researchers at the Center for Creative Leadership examined the promotions of 16 men and 13 women to middle and upper management.[98] The study was based on interviews with the person promoted, that person's promoting supervisor, the promoting supervisor's supervisor, and an HR representative. The researchers discovered that for both men and women to become candidates for promotion, "credentials, experience, track record, skills, work ethic, ability to work on a team, interpersonal skills, and growth potential" were important. The differences underlying the decision to promote were more subtle. The men's supervisors mentioned in 75 percent of the cases that they felt comfortable with the candidates at an interpersonal level, and that's what led to their promotions. This factor was cited in only 23 percent of the cases where women were promoted. For women to be promoted, it was more important that they exhibit personal strength and a willingness to take risks and accept responsibility. Continuity with the job (that is, moving up along the same career track) was cited in 38 percent of women's promotions, whereas this factor was cited in only 6 percent of men's promotions. This finding suggests that men are more likely to be promoted into new opportunities, whereas women are more likely to be promoted in areas where they can continue using their existing knowledge. To illustrate the significance of this point, in one case a supervisor waited to promote a woman until an opportunity appeared in the plant where she worked. The supervisor "thought it would be easier for the woman to succeed in a new job in a location where she already had credibility." The woman would have preferred to take a similar opportunity elsewhere sooner and "felt restricted by having to wait for the right opportunity to open up" in her own plant.

Do men and women get promoted differently?

Additional studies confirm that women and men are evaluated differently when in leadership positions. Deloitte found that its managers "rated men's lack of experience in any area as untested potential, while they often saw women with identical skills and career tracks as unprepared for promotion."[99] Debra Meyerson, a visiting professor at Stanford University's Center for Work, Technology, and Organization who has done extensive work on gender differences in organizations, finds that "for a woman, any slip-up is seen as evidence that you weren't up to the job, while men are more likely to be given the benefit of the doubt."[100]

Some research indicates that men and women view their workplaces differently. Linda Duxbury, a professor at the Sprott School of Business at Carleton University, found that 86 percent of men surveyed said that organizations actively communicate with employees, but only 65 percent of women agreed. Women were also less likely to state that their companies had established a policy of inclusion, with 44 percent of the women and 73 percent of the men agreeing with this statement.[101] Lorna Rosenstein, former general manager of Lotus Development Canada (which was bought by IBM Canada), explains additional difficulties women face: "Women have to be smarter, more creative, more focused, more bottom-line oriented, simply better than men overall if they want to rise as far."[102] Even so, women's wages are lower than men's on average. Statistics Canada reports that in 2001 (the most recent data available), women earned an average of $18.36 per hour, or 77 percent of the men's $23.75 per hour.[103]

Similarities and Differences in Women's and Men's Leadership Styles

Do men and women lead differently? An extensive review of the literature suggests two conclusions.[104] First, the similarities between men and women tend to outweigh the differences. Second, what differences there are seem to relate to women falling back on a more democratic leadership style and men feeling more comfortable with a directive style.

Emmie Wong Leung, founder and CEO of International Paper Industries (IPI) of North Vancouver, which collects, processes, and sells waste paper to offshore buyers, has been exporting to the United States, Hong Kong, Japan, China, the Philippines, India, and Indonesia for more than 20 years. She says: "I think an old-boys' network operates all over the world, but you can get them to accept you."

The similarities among men and women leaders should not be completely surprising. Almost all the studies on this issue have looked at managerial positions and considered them as synonymous with leadership roles. Both male and female managers have characteristics that set them apart from the general population. Just as people who choose careers in law enforcement or civil engineering have a lot in common, individuals who choose managerial careers also tend to have commonalities. People with traits associated with leadership—such as intelligence, confidence, and sociability—are more likely to be perceived as leaders and encouraged to pursue careers where they can exert leadership. This is true regardless of gender. Similarly, organizations tend to recruit and promote people into leadership positions who project leadership attributes. The result is that, regardless of gender, those who achieve formal leadership positions in organizations tend to be more alike than different.

Despite the previous conclusion, studies indicate some differences in the leadership styles between women and men. A recent Conference Board of Canada study found that "women are particularly strong in managing interpersonal relationships and their approach is more consensual."[105] Other studies indicate that women tend to adopt a style of shared leadership. They encourage participation, share power and information, and attempt to enhance followers' self-worth. They prefer to lead through inclusion and rely on their charisma, expertise, contacts, and interpersonal skills to influence others. Men, on the other hand, are more likely to use a directive command-and-control style. They rely on the formal authority of their position for their influence base. Differences in leadership style may account for some of the difficulties that Louisiana governor

---

EXHIBIT 11-11   **Where Female Managers Do Better: A Scorecard**

None of the five studies set out to find gender differences. They stumbled on them while compiling and analyzing performance evaluations.

Skill (Each check mark denotes which group scored higher on the respective studies)	MEN	WOMEN
Motivating others		✓ ✓ ✓ ✓
Fostering communication		✓ ✓ ✓ *
Producing high quality work		✓ ✓ ✓ ✓
Strategic planning	✓ ✓	✓ ✓ *
Listening to others		✓ ✓ ✓ ✓
Analyzing issues	✓ ✓	✓ ✓ *

* In one study, women's and men's scores in these categories were statistically even.

Data: Hagberg Consulting Group, Management Research Group, Lawrence A. Pfaff, Personnel Decisions International Inc., Advanced Teamware Inc.

Source: R. Sharpe, "As Leaders, Women Rule," *BusinessWeek,* November 20, 2000, p. 75. Reprinted by permission of Business Week.

Blanco faced in dealing with male federal government officials: She may have assumed that everyone would work collaboratively to resolve problems quickly, whereas the men she sought help from likely expected her to have a take-charge attitude.

Given that men have historically held the great majority of leadership positions in organizations, it's tempting to assume that the differences noted between men and women would automatically work in men's favour. They don't. In today's organizations, flexibility, teamwork, trust, and information sharing are replacing rigid structures, competitive individualism, control, and secrecy. The best managers listen, motivate, and provide support to their people. Many women seem to do those things better than men. As a specific example, the expanded use of cross-functional teams in organizations means that effective managers must become skilled negotiators. The leadership styles women typically use can make them better at negotiating, as they are less likely than men to focus on wins, losses, and competition. They tend to treat negotiations in the context of a continuing relationship—trying hard to make the other party a winner in their own and others' eyes. Chapter 9 discussed differences between men's and women's negotiating style in greater detail. In this chapter's *HR Implications* on page 419, in addition to discussing how to improve the leadership skills of all employees, we consider specific ways for organizations to prepare women for more leadership opportunities.

Although it's interesting to see how men's and women's leadership styles differ, a more important question is whether they differ in effectiveness. Although some researchers have shown that men and women tend to be equally effective as leaders,[106] an increasing number of studies have shown that women executives, when rated by their peers, employees, and bosses, score higher than their male counterparts on a wide variety of measures, including getting extra effort from subordinates and overall effectiveness in leading. Subordinates also reported more satisfaction with the leadership given by women.[107] See Exhibit 11-11 for a scorecard on where female managers do better, based on a summary of five studies. Why these differences? One possible explanation is that in organizations that value flexibility, teamwork and partnering, trust, and information sharing, effective managers must use more social and interpersonal behaviours. They must listen, motivate, and provide support to their people. They must inspire and influence rather than control. Women seem to do those things better than men.[108]

Although women seem to rate highly on those leadership skills needed to succeed in today's dynamic global environment, we don't want to fall into the same trap as the early leadership researchers who tried to find the "one best leadership style" for all situations. We know that there is no one *best* style for all situations. Instead, which leadership style is effective will depend on the situation. So even if men and women differ in their leadership styles, we should not assume that one is always preferable to the other.

Online Leadership

Organizations are facing more telecommuting by employees, more contracting out, more mergers, and increasing globalization. It's becoming more common, then, that the person doing the leading is not necessarily in the same building, let alone the same organization or country, as the person being led.

How do you lead people who are physically separated from you and for whom interactions are basically reduced to written digital communications? This is a question that, to date, has received minimal attention from organizational behaviour researchers.[109] Leadership research has been directed almost exclusively to face-to-face and verbal situations. But we cannot ignore the reality that today's managers and their employees are increasingly being linked by networks rather than geographical proximity. Obvious examples include managers who regularly use email to communicate with their staff, managers overseeing virtual projects or teams, and managers whose telecommuting employees are linked to the office by a computer and modem.

If leadership is important for inspiring and motivating dispersed employees, we need to offer some guidance as to how leadership might function in this context. Keep in mind, however, that there is limited research on this topic. So our intention here is not to provide you with definitive guidelines for leading online. Rather, it's to introduce you to an increasingly important issue and to get you to think about how leadership changes when relationships are defined by network interactions.

In face-to-face communications, harsh *words* can be softened by nonverbal action. A smile and comforting gestures, for instance, can lessen the blow behind strong words like *disappointed, unsatisfactory, inadequate,* or *below expectations.* That nonverbal component doesn't exist with online interactions. The *structure* of words in a digital communication has the power to motivate or demotivate the receiver.

Leaders need to be sure the *tone* of their email correctly reflects the emotions they want to send. Is the message formal or informal? Does it match the verbal style of the sender? Does it convey the appropriate level of importance or urgency? The fact that many people's writing style is very different from their interpersonal style is certainly a potential problem.

Jane Howell at the Richard Ivey School of Business, University of Western Ontario, and one of her students, Kate Hall-Merenda, have considered the issues of leading from a distance.[110] They note that physical distance can create many potential problems, with employees feeling isolated, forgotten, and perhaps not cared about. It may result in lowered productivity. Their study of 109 business leaders and 371 followers in a large financial institution found that physical distance makes it more difficult for managers and employees to develop high quality relationships.

Howell and Hall-Merenda suggest that some of the same characteristics of transformational leaders are appropriate for long-distance managing. In particular, they emphasize the need to articulate a compelling vision to employees and to communicate that vision in an inspiring way. Encouraging employees to think about ways to strive toward that vision is another important task of the leader. Their research also indicates that communication does not have to be done face to face, as long as the vision is communicated clearly in some fashion.

This discussion leads us to the tentative conclusion that, for an increasing number of managers, good interpersonal skills may include the abilities to communicate support and leadership through written words on a computer screen and to read emotions in others' messages. In this "new world" of communications, writing skills are likely to become an extension of interpersonal skills.

SUMMARY AND IMPLICATIONS

1 **What is the difference between a manager and a leader?** One theorist suggests that managers promote stability, while leaders press for change. Leaders provide vision and strategy; managers implement that vision and strategy, coordinate and staff the organization, and handle day-to-day problems.

2 **Are there specific traits, behaviours, and situations that affect how one leads?** Early leadership theories were concerned with supervision, and sought to find out if there were ways to identify leaders. Trait theories examined whether there were some traits that were universal to leaders. While there are some common traits, leaders are more different than similar in terms of traits. Further research led to behavioural theories that examined which particular behaviours make for better leaders. This body of research was mixed, suggesting that leaders need to be both task oriented and people oriented. The mixed findings led to contingency theories that considered the effect of situations in which leadership is applied. This research tells us that leaders need to adjust their behaviours, depending on the situation and the needs of employees. Contingency theories were an important contribution to the study of leadership.

3 **How does a leader lead with vision?** The more recent approaches to leadership move away from the supervisory tasks of leaders and focus on vision-setting activities. These theories try to explain how certain leaders can achieve extraordinary levels of performance from their followers, and they stress symbolic and emotionally appealing leadership behaviours. These leaders, known as *transformational* or *charismatic leaders,* inspire followers to go beyond their own self-interests for the good of the organization.

4 **Can a person be an informal leader?** There are several approaches to being a leader even if one does not have a formal position of leadership. Mentoring is one way to be an informal leader. Mentors sponsor and support less-experienced employees, coaching and counselling them about their jobs. A person can also act as an informal leader on a team.

5 **What is self-leadership?** With self-leadership, individuals and teams set goals, plan and implement tasks, evaluate performance, solve their own problems, and motivate themselves. The supervisor plays a much reduced role. Self-leadership can also include leadership at the grassroots level in an organization, where one does not have actual authority. Leading without authority simply means exhibiting leadership behaviour even though you do not have a formal position or title that might encourage others "to obey."

6 **What are some of the contemporary issues in leadership?** One of the major issues in leadership today is whether there is a moral dimension to leadership. Moral leadership comes from within the individual, and, in general, means treating people well and with respect. Another hot issue in leadership is the question of whether men and women rely on different leadership styles, and if that is the case, whether one style is inherently superior to the other. An extensive review of the literature suggests two conclusions.[111] First, the similarities between men and women tend to outweigh the differences. Second, what differences there are seem to relate to women falling back on a more democratic leadership style and men feeling more comfortable with a directive style. Providing leadership online to telecommuting and physically distant employees is another issue beginning to gain attention.

For Review

1. Trace the development of leadership research.

2. What traits predict leadership?

3. What is the Managerial Grid? Contrast its approach to leadership with the approaches of the Ohio State and Michigan studies.

4. What are the contingency variables in the path-goal theory?

5. When might leaders be irrelevant?

6. What characteristics define an effective follower?

7. What are the differences among transactional, transformational, and laissez-faire leaders?

8. Describe the strengths and weaknesses of a charismatic leader.

9. What is moral leadership?

10. Why do you think effective female and male managers often exhibit similar traits and behaviours?

For Critical Thinking

1. Reconcile path-goal theory and substitutes for leadership.

2. What kind of activities could a full-time college or university student pursue that might lead to the perception that he or she is a charismatic leader? In pursuing those activities, what might the student do to enhance this perception of being charismatic?

3. Based on the low representation of women in upper management, to what extent do you think that organizations should actively promote women into the senior ranks of management?

4. Is there an ethical problem if leaders focus more on looking like a leader than actually being one? Discuss.

5. "Leaders make a real difference in an organization's performance." Build an argument in support of this statement. Then build an argument against this statement.

OB for You

■ It's easy to imagine that theories of leadership are more important to those who are leaders or who plan in the near future to become leaders. However, leadership opportunities occur throughout an organization. You have no doubt seen a student leader who did not necessarily have any formal authority be extremely successful.

■ Leaders are not born, they learn how to lead by paying attention to the situation and what needs to be done.

■ There is no one best way to lead. It is important to consider the situation and the needs of the people who will be led.

■ Sometimes no leader is needed—the individuals in the group simply work well enough together that each takes turns at leadership without appointing a formal leader.

 *POINT*

Leadership Is Culturally Bound

Leaders must adapt their style to different national cultures. What works in China, for instance, isn't likely to work in Canada or France. Can you imagine, for instance, executives at a large Canadian department store chain, like The Bay, being effective by humiliating their employees? But that works at the Asia Department Store in central China.[112] Executives there blatantly brag about practising "heartless" management, requiring new employees to undergo two to four weeks of military-type training in order to increase their obedience, and conduct the store's in-house training sessions in a public place where employees can openly suffer embarrassment from their mistakes.

National culture affects leadership style by way of the follower. Leaders cannot choose their styles at will. They are constrained by the cultural conditions that their followers have come to expect. For instance, Korean leaders are expected to be paternalistic toward employees; Arab leaders who show kindness or generosity without being asked to do so are seen by other Arabs as weak; and Japanese leaders are expected to be humble and speak infrequently.[113]

Consistent with the contingency approach, leaders need to adjust their style to the unique cultural aspects of a country. For example, a manipulative or autocratic style is compatible with high power distance, and we find high power distance scores in Russia, Spain, Arab, Far Eastern, and most Latin countries. Power distance rankings should also be good indicators of employee willingness to accept participative leadership. Participation is likely to be most effective in low power distance cultures as exist in Norway, Finland, Denmark, and Sweden.

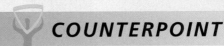 *COUNTERPOINT*

Leadership Transcends Culture

The GLOBE research program, which we introduced in Chapter 3, has gathered data on approximately 18 000 middle managers in 825 organizations, covering 62 countries. It's the most comprehensive cross-cultural study of leadership ever undertaken. So its findings should not be quickly dismissed. It's illuminating that one of the results coming from the GLOBE study is that there are some universal aspects to leadership. Specifically, a number of the elements making up transformational leadership appear to be associated with effective leadership regardless of what country the leader is in.[114] This conclusion is very important because it flies in the face of the contingency view that leadership style needs to adapt to cultural differences.

What elements of transformational leadership appear universal? Vision, foresight, providing encouragement, trustworthiness, dynamism, positiveness, and proactiveness. The results led two members of the GLOBE team to conclude that "effective business leaders in any country are expected by their subordinates to provide a powerful and proactive vision to guide the company into the future, strong motivational skills to stimulate all employees to fulfill the vision, and excellent planning skills to assist in implementing the vision."[115]

What might explain the universal appeal of these transformational leader attributes? It's been suggested that pressures toward common technologies and management practices, as a result of global competition and multinational influences, may make some aspects of leadership universally accepted. If this is true, we may be able to select and train leaders in a universal style and thus significantly raise the quality of leadership worldwide.

HR IMPLICATIONS

Developing Leadership Potential

Organizations, in aggregate, spend billions of dollars, yen, and euros on leadership training and development.[116] These efforts take many forms—from $50 000 executive leadership programs offered by universities such as Harvard to sailing experiences through Outward Bound Canada. Although much of the money spent on training may provide dubious benefits, our review suggests that there are some things management can do to get the maximum effect from leadership-training budgets.[117]

First, let's recognize the obvious. People are not equally trainable. Leadership training of any kind is likely to be more successful with individuals who are high self-monitors than with low self-monitors. Such individuals have the flexibility to change their behaviour.

What kinds of things can individuals learn that might be related to higher leader effectiveness? It may be a bit optimistic to believe that we can teach "vision creation," but we can teach implementation skills. We can train people to develop "an understanding about content themes critical to effective visions."[118] We also can teach skills such as trust building and mentoring. As well, leaders can be taught situation-analysis skills. They can learn how to evaluate situations, how to modify situations to make them fit better with their style, and how to assess which leader behaviours might be most effective in given situations. Below we discuss general management training, and then we follow that with some specific examples of what has been done to promote women's leadership skills and abilities.

General Management Training

Executives can choose from a variety of programs to increase their management skills. Some opt to go for their master of business administration degrees. "The executive MBA is the ultimate in self-improvement," says Don Nightingale, executive director of the executive MBA programs at Queen's School of Business.[119]

An MBA isn't the only educational option executives have, however. Senior and middle managers are taking everything from four- or five-day programs on specific topics to five- to six-week executive programs. They study such issues as managing change, strategic decision making, leadership, global management, and teamwork.

Traditionally, management development courses focused almost exclusively on budgeting, planning, and managing. More recently, the emphasis is on "personal development" courses, where those who attend are encouraged to learn more about themselves to help them become better people. As an example of this new trend, Vancouver-based Fletcher Challenge Canada (now NorskeCanada) sent some of its employees to a course called The Seven Habits of Highly Effective People, offered by the Covey Leadership Center, headquartered in Utah. Lois Nahirney, one of Fletcher Challenge's employees, found the course extremely useful, partly because it gave her time to reflect on her own goals in life. "It's very much about personal vision, personal mastery," she says. The Vancouver company believes programs such as these benefit both the individual and the organization, and more than 600 of its employees have been through such courses as leadership, communication, and facilitation.

HSBC Bank Canada sends two or three executives a year to external courses, often university-based. BCTV has sent senior managers to the Covey course. BC Hydro, Coast Hotels, and A&W have also sent managers to various programs. Vancouver-based a&b sound has sent more than a dozen people to Seattle's Pacific Institute "affirmation" program.

All of these companies believe that courses help their managers. For example, BC Hydro's Gary Rodford says course participants come back to work "better managers and better people." Lois Nahirney at Fletcher Challenge agrees: "The better you understand who you are and who you want to be, the better you can approach your job and the people you do it with. A company which helps its people do that is going to be more successful."[120]

Efforts to Develop Women's Leadership Capabilities

Some corporations have become increasingly aware that women do not seem to be making it into higher management positions as rapidly as men. As a result, some have started tying compensation directly to senior executives' identification and promotion of "high potential" women. Vancouver-based Telus has been doing this since 1994.[121] Telus also identified managers who were not prepared to support the new women-friendly environment, and they were encouraged to look for jobs elsewhere.

Toronto-based Deloitte introduced its Advancement and Retention of Talented People (ART) initiative in 1998. Among the goals of the program is to ensure equal opportunity for everyone to succeed and create a culture of work-life harmony. The ART program include Men and Women Working workshops. The workshops try to open communication between men and women, leading to greater understanding, and removing barriers for women to move ahead. Entire work groups attend the workshop together, to "discuss the different ways men and women operate and how the talents of the different members can be used to make a strong team."[122]

When Tony Comper became president of Bank of Montreal (BMO) in 1990 (he is now also CEO), he was determined to find out why 75 percent of the bank's employees were women but only 9 percent of women had made it into the executive ranks. He created a task force to investigate the problems and develop action plans for change. The task force's report, submitted in November 1991, found that women were held back by stereotypical attitudes, myths, and "conventional wisdoms." The following fictions and facts, highlighted in the report, illustrate some of those conventional wisdoms:[123]

Fiction: Women were less committed to their work, less educated than men, and tended to turn in weaker job performances.

Fact: Women in the bank turned out to be at least as fully qualified as men in every respect—just as educated and just as dedicated.

Fiction: Women had not been in the pipeline long enough.

Fact: Women had put in longer service than men at every level, except senior management, where their presence was a recent development.

Fiction: Child-rearing women tend to quit, and ergo, were not committed to their careers.

Fact: Ninety-eight percent of women returned to the company after giving birth.

Fiction: Time will take care of gender imbalances.

Fact: If the bank relied on time solving the problem, women's representation at executive and senior management levels would have risen to only 18 percent and 22 percent, respectively, by the year 2000.

The task force also determined that more direct involvement to promote women was necessary. The bank's women employees were well educated, had received better performance appraisals than men at all levels, and wanted advancement as much as men did, but they weren't making it. Comper recognized that simply waiting for things to right themselves would not work. In light of that fact, the task force concluded that the bank needed to act aggressively to move women up the ranks. In order to do that, the bank tied performance appraisals and compensation of managers to the promotion of women. The bank also created a more family-friendly environment to help employees manage the stress of work and home, and introduced such things as flex work arrangements and people-care days to the workplace. By late 1998, women held 25 percent of all executive positions at BMO, and by 2005 that proportion had increased to 33 percent.[124] Comper would still like to see 50 percent of the top offices held by women by the year 2007.

It might seem obvious from these examples that senior management needs to be involved in the training and development of women to ensure that they have the same access as men to leadership positions in organizations. However, this is not always an accepted view. Maria Ferris, manager of global workforce diversity initiatives at IBM, notes that in three European countries she visited, she found that "some women feel [IBM's diversity initiatives are] about women getting something they don't deserve. But when you can show that the goal is removing a disadvantage—just creating a level playing field, not granting special rights—everyone can understand."[125]

Even when companies have good policies in place, they can't simply relax their vigilance. Linda Scherr, a software engineer who has been with IBM for 26 years and chairs the IBM Women in Technology Steering Committee, notes that "while the vast majority of our managers both recognize and endorse the value of these programs," not all do. She adds, "we must be relentless until every manager is supportive."[126]

Are You a Self-Manager?

To determine your self-management initiative, rate each of the following items, from 1 ("Never Do This") to 7 ("Always Do This").

	Never Do This				**Always Do This**		

Planning

1. I plan out my day before beginning to work. 1 2 3 4 5 6 7
2. I try to schedule my work in advance. 1 2 3 4 5 6 7
3. I plan my career carefully. 1 2 3 4 5 6 7
4. I come to work early to plan my day. 1 2 3 4 5 6 7
5. I use lists and agendas to structure my workday. 1 2 3 4 5 6 7
6. I set specific job goals on a regular basis. 1 2 3 4 5 6 7
7. I set daily goals for myself. 1 2 3 4 5 6 7
8. I try to manage my time. 1 2 3 4 5 6 7

Access management

1. I control the access subordinates have to me in order to get my work done. 1 2 3 4 5 6 7
2. I use a special place at work where I can work uninterrupted. 1 2 3 4 5 6 7
3. I hold my telephone calls when I need to get things done. 1 2 3 4 5 6 7

Catch-up activities

1. I come in early or stay late at work to prevent distractions from interfering with my work. 1 2 3 4 5 6 7
2. I take my work home with me to make sure it gets done. 1 2 3 4 5 6 7
3. I come in on my days off to catch up on my work. 1 2 3 4 5 6 7

Emotions management

1. I have learned to manage my aggressiveness with my subordinates. 1 2 3 4 5 6 7
2. My facial expression and conversational tone are important in dealing with subordinates. 1 2 3 4 5 6 7
3. It's important for me to maintain a "professional" manager-subordinate relationship. 1 2 3 4 5 6 7
4. I try to keep my emotions under control. 1 2 3 4 5 6 7

Scoring Key:

Higher scores mean a higher degree of self-management. For the overall scale, scores of 100 or higher represent high scores. For each area, the following represent high scores: planning, scores of 48 or higher; access management, scores of 18 or higher; catch-up activities, scores of 18 or higher; and emotions management, scores of 24 or higher.

Source: M. Castaneda, T. A. Kolenko, and R. J. Aldag, "Self-Management Perceptions and Practices: A Structural Equations Analysis," *Journal of Organizational Behavior* 20, 1999. Table 4, pp. 114–115. Copyright © John Wiley & Sons, Inc. Reproduced with permission.

BREAKOUT **GROUP** EXERCISES

Form small groups to discuss the following topics, as assigned by your instructor:

1. Identify an example of someone you think of as a good leader (currently or in the past). What traits did he or she have? How did these traits differ from those in someone you identify as a bad leader?

2. Identify a situation when you were in a leadership position (in a group, in the workplace, within your family, etc.). To what extent were you able to use a contingency approach to leadership? What made that easier or more difficult for you?

3. When you've worked in student groups, how frequently have leaders emerged in the groups? What difficulties occur when leaders are leading peers? Are there ways to overcome these difficulties?

WORKING WITH **OTHERS** EXERCISE

Practising to Be Charismatic

From Concepts to Skills on page 425 indicates how to become charismatic. In this exercise, you will use that information to practise projecting charisma.

a. The class should break into pairs.

b. Student A's task is to "lead" Student B through a new-student orientation to your college or university. The orientation should last about 10 to 15 minutes. Assume Student B is new to your college or university and is unfamiliar with the campus. Student A should attempt to project himself or herself as charismatic.

c. Roles now reverse and Student B's task is to "lead" Student A in a 10- to 15-minute program on how to study more effectively for college or university exams. Take a few minutes to think about what has worked well for you, and assume that Student A is a new student interested in improving his or her study habits. Again, Student B should attempt to project himself or herself as charismatic.

d. When both role plays are complete, each pair should assess how well it did in projecting charisma and how it might improve.

Source: This exercise is based on J. M. Howell and P. J. Frost, "A Laboratory Study of Charismatic Leadership," *Organizational Behavior and Human Decision Processes,* April 1989, pp. 243–269.

ETHICAL **DILEMMA** EXERCISE

Do the Ends Justify the Means?

The power that comes from being a leader can be used for evil as well as for good. When you assume the benefits of leadership, you also assume ethical burdens. But many highly successful leaders have relied on questionable tactics to achieve their ends. These include manipulation, verbal attacks, physical intimidation, lying, fear, and control.

Consider a few examples:

- Bill Clinton was viewed as a charismatic US president. Yet he lied when necessary and "managed" the truth.

- Former Prime Minister Jean Chrétien successfully led Canada through 10 years of economic change. Those close to him were committed and loyal followers. Yet concerns were raised recently that he may have been willing to quietly spend millions of dollars in sponsorship money to manage the Quebec situation.

- Jack Welch, former head of General Electric (GE), provided the leadership that made GE the most valuable company in America. He also ruthlessly preached firing the lowest-performing 10 percent of the company's employees every year.

- Former IBM chair Lou Gerstner oversaw the re-emergence of IBM as a powerhouse in the computer industry. He

was not, however, easy to work for. He believed in never relaxing or in letting others enjoy life.

Should leaders be judged solely on their end achievements? Or do the means they choose also reflect on their leadership qualities? Are employees, shareholders, and society too quick to excuse leaders who use questionable means if they are successful in achieving their goals? Is it impossible for leaders to be ethical *and* successful?

Source: Based on C. E. Johnson, *Meeting the Ethical Challenges in Leadership* (Thousand Oaks, CA: Sage, 2001), pp. 4–5.

CASE INCIDENTS

Moving from Colleague to Supervisor

Cheryl Kahn, Rob Carstons, and Linda McGee have something in common. They all were promoted within their organizations into management positions. As well, each found the transition a challenge.

Kahn was promoted to director of catering for the Glazier Group of restaurants. With the promotion, she realized that things would never be the same again. No longer would she be able to participate in water-cooler gossip or shrug off an employee's chronic lateness. She says she found her new role to be daunting. "At first I was like a bulldozer knocking everyone over, and that was not well received. I was saying, 'It's my way or the highway.' And was forgetting that my friends were also in transition." She admits that this style alienated just about everyone with whom she worked.

Carstons, a technical manager at IBM, talks about the uncertainty he felt after being promoted to a manager from a junior programmer. "It was a little bit challenging to be suddenly giving directives to peers, when just the day before you were one of them. You try to be careful not to offend anyone. It's strange walking into a room and the whole conversation changes. People don't want to be as open with you when you become the boss."

McGee is now president of Medex Insurance Services. She started as a customer-service representative with the company, then leapfrogged over colleagues in a series of promotions. Her fast rise created problems. Colleagues "would say, 'Oh, here comes the big cheese now.' God only knows what they talked about behind my back."

Questions

1. A lot of new managers err in selecting the right leadership style when they move into management. Why do you think this happens?

2. If new managers don't know what leadership style to use, what does this say about leadership and leadership training?

3. Which leadership theories, if any, could help new leaders deal with this transition?

4. Do you think it's easier or harder to be promoted internally into a formal leadership position than to come into it as an outsider? Explain.

Source: Based on D. Koeppel, "A Tough Transition: Friend to Supervisor," *New York Times,* March 16, 2003, p. BU-12.

Anne Mulcahy at Xerox

Anne Mulcahy is the ultimate loyal employee. She joined Xerox when she was 23 years old. She spent her first 16 years in sales, then 8 years in an assortment of management assignments—director of human resources, head of the company's fledging desktop computer business, and chief of staff to Xerox's CEO. She never aspired to run Xerox, nor was she groomed to be the boss. So she was as surprised as anyone when Xerox's board chose her as CEO in August 2001.

Mulcahy accepted the job with mixed feelings: The company was in horrible financial shape. It had $17.1 billion (US) in debt and only $154 million (US) in cash. It was about to begin seven straight quarters of losses. The company had been slow to move from analog to digital copying, and from black and white to colour. Japanese competitors like Canon and Ricoh had taken a large chunk of its market share in copying machines. Prior executives had diversified the company into financial services and never leveraged Xerox's expertise in personal computers. Xerox's stock price had dropped from nearly $64 (US) in 2000 to $4.43 (US) at the time of her appointment. But Mulcahy felt a deep loyalty to the company. She felt an obligation to do everything in her power to save Xerox. Duty and loyalty compelled her to take a job that nobody else really wanted, despite the fact that she had zero preparation.

To say Mulcahy wasn't groomed for the CEO position is a true understatement. For instance, she didn't know financial analysis. She had no MBA and her undergraduate degree was in English/journalism. So she asked the company's director of corporate finance to give her a cram course in Balance Sheet 101. He helped her understand debt structure, inventory trends, and the impact of taxes and currency rates. This allowed her to see what would generate cash and how each of her decisions would affect the balance sheet. Mulcahy says now that her lack of training had its advantages. She had no preconceived notions, no time to develop bad habits.

Mulcahy and her executive team faced a difficult task from the beginning. Xerox is an old-fashioned company, and people resisted change. The average tenure of a Xerox employee is 14 years, double the overall corporate average. Although everyone knew the company was in trouble, there wasn't a lot of willingness to challenge the conventional wisdom. She appealed to employees with missionary zeal, in videos and in person, to "save each dollar as if it were your own." She rewarded those who stuck it out not only by refusing to abolish raises but with symbolic gestures as well; in 2002, for instance, she gave all employees their birthdays off. The gentle pressure was vintage Mulcahy: Work hard, measure the results, tell the truth, and be brutally honest.

After four years as CEO, Mulcahy had made startling progress in turning Xerox around. Employees appreciated her truthful and straightforward style. They also liked the fact that she was willing to work shoulder to shoulder with subordinates. Because she was working so hard, people felt obligated to work harder too. But Mulcahy is no softy. She's smart, energetic, and tough but compassionate. She has showed the ability to make hard decisions. For instance, she slashed costs in part by cutting Xerox's workforce by 30 percent, and she shut down the desktop division. She oversaw the streamlining of production, new investment in research and development, and restructured the sales force so vague lines of authority became clear. She met with bankers and customers. Most importantly, she travelled. She galvanized "the troops" by visiting Xerox offices—sometimes hitting three cities a day—and inspiring employees. Although many people were concerned that the company was headed for bankruptcy, she wouldn't consider that an option. By the summer of 2005, Xerox's debt was down to $9.6 billion (US) and the company had had operating profits in 11 of the previous 12 quarters. While Xerox's future is still far from secure, at least it's beginning to look like the company has a future.

Mulcahy explains the turnaround by saying she "simply took Xerox back to the roots of its corporate culture: innovation and customer care. You need to change and adapt . . . but you need to respect and bring forward the things that are why people came to the company."

Questions

1. How did Anne Mulcahy create trust with employees after becoming CEO?

2. Did Mulcahy have a vision for Xerox? Explain.

3. What qualities do you think helped Mulcahy effect the turnaround at Xerox?

4. What does this case say about leadership experience?

Sources: B. Morris, "The Accidental CEO," *Fortune,* June 23, 2003, pp. 58–66; and "Xerox Chief Anne Mulcahy Took Her Company Back to Its Roots—and Profitability," *Red Herring,* June 6, 2005, www.redherring.com/Article.aspx?a=12404&hed=Women+in+Tech%3A+Anne+Mulcahysector=Profiles&subsector=People (accessed September 23, 2005).

From **Concepts**
to **Skills**

Practising to Be Charismatic

In order to be charismatic in your leadership style, you need to engage in the following behaviours:[127]

1. *Project a powerful, confident, and dynamic presence.* This has both verbal and nonverbal components. Use a captivating and engaging voice tone. Convey confidence. Talk directly to people, maintain direct eye contact, and hold your body posture in a way that says you are sure of yourself. Speak clearly, avoid stammering, and avoid sprinkling your sentences with noncontent phrases such as "ahhh" and "you know."

2. *Articulate an overarching goal.* You need to share a vision for the future, develop an unconventional way of achieving the vision, and have the ability to communicate the vision to others.

   The vision is a clear statement of where you want to go and how you are going to get there. You need to persuade others that the achievement of this vision is in their self-interest.

   You need to look for fresh and radically different approaches to problems. The road to achieving your vision should be seen as novel but also appropriate to the context.

   Charismatic individuals not only have a vision, but they are also able to get others to buy into it. The real power of Martin Luther King Jr. was not that he had a dream, but that he could articulate it in terms that made it accessible to millions.

3. *Communicate high performance expectations and confidence in others' ability to meet these expectations.* You need to demonstrate your confidence in people by stating ambitious goals for them individually and as a group. You then convey absolute belief that they will achieve their expectations.

4. *Be sensitive to the needs of followers.* Charismatic leaders get to know their followers individually. You need to understand their individual needs and develop intensely personal relationships with each. This is done through encouraging followers to express their points of view, being approachable, genuinely listening to and caring about followers' concerns, and asking questions so that followers can learn what is really important to them.

Assessing Skills

After you've read this chapter, take the following Self-Assessments on your enclosed CD-ROM:

25. How Good Am I at Personal Planning?

29. What's My Leadership Style?

30. How Charismatic Am I?

32. Do Others See Me as Trustworthy?

Practising Skills

You are a manufacturing manager in a large electronics plant.[128] The company's management is always searching for ways to increase efficiency. They recently installed new machines and set up a new simplified work system, but to the surprise of everyone—including you—the expected increase in production was not realized. In fact, production has begun to drop, quality has fallen off, and the number of employee resignations has risen.

You do not think that there is anything wrong with the machines. You have had reports from other companies that are using them, and they confirm your opinion. You have also had representatives from the firm that built the machines go over them, and they report that the machines are operating at peak efficiency.

You know that some aspect of the new work system must be responsible for the change, but you are getting no help from your immediate team members—four first-line supervisors who report to you and who are each in charge of a section—or your supply manager. The drop in production has been variously attributed to poor training of the operators, lack of an adequate system of financial incentives, and poor morale. All of the individuals involved have deep feelings about this issue. Your team does not agree with you or with one another.

This morning you received a phone call from your division manager. He had just received your production figures for the past six months and was calling to express his concern. He indicated that the problem was yours to solve in any way that you think best but that he would like to know within a week what steps you plan to take.

You share your division manager's concern with the falling productivity and know that your employees are also concerned. Using your knowledge of leadership concepts, which leadership style would you choose? And why?

Reinforcing Skills

1. Think of a group or team to which you currently belong or of which you have been a part. What type of leadership style did the leader of this group appear to exhibit? Give some specific examples of the types of leadership behaviours he or she used. Evaluate the leadership style. Was it appropriate for the group? Why or why not? What would you have done differently? Why?

2. Observe two sports teams (either college/university or professional—one that you consider successful and the other unsuccessful). What leadership styles appear to be used in these team situations? Give some specific examples of the types of leadership behaviours you observe. How would you evaluate the leadership style? Was it appropriate for the team? Why or why not? To what degree do you think leadership style influenced the team's outcomes?

CHAPTER 12

Decision Making, Creativity, and Ethics

Nike's decision to manufacture shoes overseas has prompted critics to claim that it exploits workers in poor countries. Did Nike make a rational decision, and is the decision socially responsible?

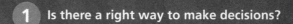

1 Is there a right way to make decisions?

2 How do people actually make decisions?

3 How can knowledge management improve decision making?

4 What factors affect group decision making?

5 Should the leader make the decision, or encourage the group to participate?

6 How can we get more creative decisions?

7 What is ethics, and how can it be used for better decision making?

8 What is corporate social responsibility?

ike's first Corporate Responsibility Report, published in October 2001, confessed that making Nike's runners is "tedious, hard and doesn't offer a wonderful future."[1] Readers may have been startled to learn that employees in overseas factories making Nike products were being harassed by supervisors. Employees were also asked to work far more overtime than rules permitted. Finally, the company admitted to knowing far too little about day-to-day life in the factories, because it was not monitoring the situation closely enough.

These admissions might have seemed shocking to anyone who would have expected Nike to deny what critics have been saying for years: Nike benefits from unfair labour practices in foreign-owned plants to which it subcontracts work.

Nike's decision to publish a corporate responsibility report is just one example of the many decisions companies face every day. The company has decided to improve conditions at its overseas operations.

In this chapter, we describe how decisions in organizations are made, as well as how creativity is linked to decision making. We also look at the ethical and socially responsible aspects of decision making as part of our discussion. Decision making affects people at all levels of the organization, and it is engaged in by both individuals and groups. Therefore, we also consider the special characteristics of group decision making.

HOW SHOULD DECISIONS BE MADE?

After publishing its first Corporate Responsibility Report, Nike increased training for both managers and employees at its overseas operations. Managers were told that treating employees properly will lead to "improved productivity, reduced labour turnover and less sick leave." Nike thus evaluated its problem, and came up with ways to resolve it in order to reduce criticism of its labour practices. How do individuals and companies make decisions?

Decisions are the choices made from two or more alternatives. Decision making occurs as a reaction to a *problem* or an *opportunity*. A problem is a discrepancy between some *current* state of affairs and some *desired* state, requiring consideration of alternative courses of action. Opportunities occur when something unplanned happens, giving rise to thoughts about new ways of proceeding.

Decision making happens at all levels of the organization. For instance, top managers such as those at Nike determine their organization's goals, what products or services to offer, how best to finance operations, or where to locate a new high-tech research and development facility. Middle- and lower-level managers determine production schedules, select new employees, and decide how pay raises are to be allocated. Nonmanagerial employees also make decisions such as whether to come to work on any given day, how much effort to put forward once at work, and whether to comply with a request made by the manager. In addition, an increasing number of organizations in

1 Is there a right way to make decisions?

Nike Canada
www.nike.com/canada/

decisions The choices made from two or more alternatives.

recent years have been empowering their nonmanagerial employees with job-related decision-making authority that was historically reserved for managers alone. Thus they may make decisions about initiating some new projects or solving some customer-related problems without consulting their managers.

Knowing how to make decisions is an important part of everyday life. Below we consider various decision-making models. Even though we discuss the special aspects of group decision making later in the chapter, these models apply, whether it is individuals or an entire group or team making a decision. We start with the rational model, which describes decision making in the ideal world, a situation that rarely exists. We then look at alternatives to the rational model, and how decisions actually get made.

The Rational Decision-Making Process

rational Refers to choices that are consistent and value-maximizing within specified constraints.

The **rational** decision maker makes consistent, value-maximizing choices within specified constraints.[2] These choices are made following a six-step **rational decision-making model**.[3] Moreover, specific assumptions underlie this model.

The Rational Model

rational decision-making model A six-step decision-making model that describes how individuals should behave in order to maximize some outcome.

The six steps in the rational decision-making model are presented in Exhibit 12-1.

First, the decision maker must *define the problem*. As noted previously, a problem exists when a discrepancy occurs between the current and a desired state of affairs.[4] If you calculate your monthly expenses and find you are spending $50 more than your monthly earnings, you have defined a problem. Many poor decisions can be traced to the decision maker overlooking a problem or defining the wrong problem.

Once a decision maker has defined the problem, he or she needs to *identify the criteria* that will be important in solving the problem. In this step, the decision maker determines what is relevant in making the decision. This step brings the decision maker's interests, values, and similar personal preferences into the process. Identifying criteria is important because what one person thinks is relevant, another person may not. Also keep in mind that any factors not identified in this step are considered irrelevant to the decision maker.

Canadian Imperial Bank of Commerce (CIBC)
www.cibc.com

To understand the types of criteria that might be used to make a decision, consider the many sponsorship requests that Toronto-based Canadian Imperial Bank of Commerce (CIBC) receives each year. In making a decision about whether or not to support a request, the bank considers the following criteria:[5]

- Strategic fit with CIBC's overall goals and objectives

- Ability to achieve marketing objectives for the youth customer segment

- Tangible and intangible benefits of the proposal, such as goodwill, reputation, and cost/potential revenue

- Organizational impact

- Business risks (if any)

If the sponsorship request does not meet these criteria, it is not funded.

The criteria identified are rarely all equal in importance. So the third step requires the decision maker to *allocate weights to the criteria* in order to give them the correct priority in the decision.

EXHIBIT 12-1 Steps in the Rational Decision-Making Model

1. Define the problem
2. Identify the criteria
3. Allocate weights to the criteria
4. Develop alternatives
5. Evaluate the alternatives
6. Select the best alternative

Making a Decision

The fourth step requires the decision maker to *develop alternatives* that could succeed in resolving the problem. No attempt is made in this step to appraise these alternatives, only to list them.

Once the alternatives have been generated, the decision maker must critically *evaluate the alternatives.* The strengths and weaknesses of each alternative become evident as they are compared with the criteria and weights established in the second and third steps.

The final step in this model requires the decision maker to *select the best alternative.* This is done by evaluating each alternative against the weighted criteria and selecting the alternative with the highest total score.

Assumptions of the Model

The rational decision-making model we just described contains a number of assumptions.[6] Let's briefly outline those assumptions:

- *Problem clarity.* The problem is clear and unambiguous. The decision maker is assumed to have complete information regarding the decision situation.

- *Known options.* It's assumed the decision maker can identify all the relevant criteria and can list all the workable alternatives. Furthermore, the decision maker is aware of all the possible consequences of each alternative.

- *Clear preferences.* Rationality assumes that the criteria and alternatives can be ranked and weighted to reflect their importance.

- *Constant preferences.* It's assumed that the specific decision criteria are constant and that the weights assigned to them are stable over time.

- *No time or cost constraints.* The decision maker can obtain full information about criteria and alternatives because it's assumed that there are no time or cost constraints.

- *Maximum payoff.* The decision maker will choose the alternative that yields the highest perceived value.

HOW DO INDIVIDUALS ACTUALLY MAKE DECISIONS?

Chaichana Homsombat, a 21-year-old employee at Pan Asia Footwear Public Company in Thailand, the world's third-largest Nike subcontractor factory, explains his job: "Each of us has to work constantly. The faster we meet the assigned quota, the earlier we can go home."[7] Homsombat's quota is to pack 1296 pairs of runners into boxes each workday.

The deputy managing director of the plant, Boonrawd Indamanee, says the quotas improve productivity. A human rights inspector at the plant wonders whether employees are really getting a fair day's pay under the quota system. The management does not want trade unions in the plant, but the inspector fears that "workers don't know their rights. They simply accept whatever is given to them." Thus, when asked if the company gives benefits to employees, one supervisor responded: "The uniform. We get three of them when we join the company and two more each year." If employees are not aware of their rights, or do not have full information about them, or have few alternatives, are they really able to make an informed decision about how to behave?

Do decision makers actually follow the rational model? Do they carefully assess problems, identify all relevant criteria, use their creativity to identify all workable alternatives, and painstakingly evaluate every alternative to find an optimizing choice?

When decision makers are faced with a simple problem with few alternative courses of action, and when the cost of searching out and evaluating alternatives is low, the

2 How do people actually make decisions?

rational model provides a fairly accurate description of the decision process.[8] However, such situations are the exception. Most decisions in the real world don't follow the rational model. For instance, people are usually content to find an acceptable or reasonable solution to their problem rather than an optimizing one. As such, decision makers generally make limited use of their creativity. Choices tend to be confined to the neighbourhood of the problem symptom and to the neighbourhood of the current alternative. As one expert in decision making concluded: "Most significant decisions are made by judgment, rather than by a defined prescriptive model."[9]

In the following sections, we indicate areas where the reality of decision making conflicts with the rational model.[10] None of these ways of making decisions should be considered *irrational*; they are simply departures from the rational model.

Problem Identification

Most of the decisions that get made reflect only the problems that decision makers see. Problems don't come with flashing neon lights to identify themselves. One person's *problem* may even be another person's *acceptable status quo*. So how do decision makers identify and select problems?

Problems that are visible tend to have a higher probability of being selected than ones that are important.[11] Why? We can offer at least two reasons. First, it's easier to recognize visible problems. They are more likely to catch a decision maker's attention. This explains why politicians are more likely to talk about the "crime problem" than the "illiteracy problem." Second, remember we are concerned with decision making in organizations. Decision makers want to appear competent and "on top of problems." This motivates them to focus attention on problems that are visible to others.

Don't ignore the decision maker's self-interest. If a decision maker faces a conflict between selecting a problem that is important to the organization and one that is important to the decision maker, self-interest tends to win out.[12] This also ties in with the issue of visibility. It's usually in a decision maker's best interest to attack high-profile problems. It conveys to others that things are under control. Moreover, when the decision maker's performance is later reviewed, the evaluator is more likely to give a high rating to someone who has been aggressively attacking visible problems than to someone whose actions have been less obvious.

Bounded Rationality in Considering Alternatives

Do people really consider every alternative?

When you considered which university or college to attend, did you look at *every* workable alternative? Did you carefully identify all the criteria that were important in your decision? Did you evaluate each alternative against the criteria in order to find the optimum school? The answer to these questions is probably "no." But don't feel bad, because few people selected their educational institution this way.

It's difficult for individuals to identify and consider every possible alternative available to them. Realistically speaking, people are bounded by their limitations in interpreting, processing, and acting on information. This is called **bounded rationality**.[13]

bounded rationality Limitations on a person's ability to interpret, process, and act on information.

Because of bounded rationality, individuals are not able to discover and consider every alternative for a decision. Instead, individuals identify a limited list of the more conspicuous choices. In most cases, the list will represent familiar criteria and previously tried-and-true solutions. Rather than carefully reviewing and evaluating each alternative in great detail, individuals will settle on an alternative that is "good enough"—one that meets an acceptable level of performance. The first alternative that meets the "good enough" criterion ends the search. So decision makers choose final solutions that **satisfice** rather

satisfice To provide a solution that is both satisfactory and sufficient.

than optimize; that is, they seek solutions that are both satisfactory and sufficient. In practice this might mean that rather than interviewing 10 job candidates for a position and then making a decision, a manager interviews individuals only until someone "good enough" is found, that is, the first job candidate encountered who meets the minimum criteria for the job. The federal government has proposed such a rule for its own hiring, as *OB in the Workplace* shows.

OB IN THE WORKPLACE

Ottawa May Stop Hiring "Best Qualified"

Is hiring the "best-qualified" person too much work? Executives and middle managers working in the federal government are starting to think so.[14] They argue that "being qualified and competent for a particular job should be enough" even though the person may not be the best possible candidate.

Civil servants asked for the rules on hiring to be loosened so that they could actually start hiring and filling positions rather than spending so much time finding the "best-qualified" person. They find those searches excruciating and exhausting. When managers follow the federal guidelines for hiring, it can take six months or more to fill a position.

Steve Hindle, president of The Professional Institute of the Public Service of Canada, explains why hiring someone who is qualified is probably good enough: "If people are honest, what they want is someone who is qualified, but the idea of finding the best? Do we have the time, tools and money needed to find the very best? You want someone competent and good, and if they're the best, that's great."

Not everyone agrees that changing the rules for hiring is a good idea, however. The public sector unions worry that favouritism may become more common. But they do agree that the current system has too much red tape. 🕴

Intuition

Is it okay to use intuition when making decisions?

Jessie Lam has just committed her corporation to spend more than $40 million to build a new plant in New Westminster, BC, to manufacture electronic components for satellite communication equipment. A vice-president of operations for her firm, Lam had before her a comprehensive analysis of five possible plant locations developed by a site-location consulting firm she had hired. This report ranked the New Westminster location third among the five alternatives. After carefully reading the report and its conclusions, Lam decided against the consultant's recommendation. When asked to explain her decision, Lam said, "I looked the report over very carefully. Despite its recommendation, I felt that the numbers didn't tell the whole story. Intuitively, I just sensed that New Westminster would prove to be the best bet over the long run."

Intuitive decision making, like that used by Jessie Lam, has recently come out of the closet and gained some respectability. Experts no longer automatically assume that using intuition to make decisions is irrational or ineffective.[15] There is growing recognition that rational analysis has been overemphasized and that, in certain instances, relying on intuition can improve decision making.

What do we mean by intuitive decision making? There are a number of ways to conceptualize intuition.[16] For instance, some consider it a form of extrasensory power or sixth sense, and some believe it is a personality trait that a limited number of people are

intuitive decision making A subconscious process created out of a person's many experiences.

born with. For our purposes, we define **intuitive decision making** as a subconscious process created out of a person's many experiences. It does not necessarily operate independently of rational analysis; rather, the two complement each other. Those who use intuition effectively often rely on their experiences to help guide and assess their intuitions. That is why many managers are able to rely on intuition, as *Focus on Research* shows.

FOCUS ON **RESEARCH**

Many Managers Add Intuition to Data Analysis

Do senior managers use intuition in their decision making? A recent study of 60 experienced professionals holding high-level positions in major US organizations found that many of them used intuition to help them make workplace decisions.[17] Twelve percent said they always used it; 47 percent said they often used it. Only 10 percent said they rarely or seldom used intuition. More than 90 percent of managers said they were likely to use a mix of intuition and data analysis when making decisions.

When asked the types of decisions where they most often used intuition, 40 percent reported that they used it to make people-related decisions such as hiring, performance appraisal, harassment complaints, and safety issues. The managers said they also used intuition for quick or unexpected decisions so they could avoid delays. They also were more likely to rely on intuition in novel situations that had a lot of uncertainty.

The results from this study suggest that intuitive decisions are best applied when time is short, when policies, rules, and guidelines do not give clear-cut advice, when there is a great deal of uncertainty, and when quantitative analysis needs a check and balance.

Intuition can be wrong, so it's important to develop your intuition. Often, good intuition is really the result of recognizing the pattern in a situation and drawing upon previously learned information associated with that pattern to arrive quickly at a decision. The result is that the intuitive decision maker can decide rapidly with what appears to be very limited information. Decision making can be improved by analyzing your decisions after the fact to develop a better understanding of when good and bad decisions have been made.

So what does all of this discussion about making decisions tell us? Based on our discussion above, you should consider the following when making decisions:

- Make sure that you define the problem as best you can.

- Be clear on the factors that you will use to make your decision.

- Be sure to collect enough alternatives that you can clearly differentiate among them.

Judgment Shortcuts

So why is it that we sometimes make bad decisions?

heuristics Judgment shortcuts in decision making.

In examining the ways that people make decisions, two eminent psychologists, Daniel Kahneman (the 2002 winner of the Nobel Prize in economic sciences) and Amos Tversky, discovered that individuals often rely on **heuristics**, or judgment shortcuts, to simplify the decision process, rather than going through all of the steps of the rational decision-making model.[18] We review some of these shortcuts next to alert you to mistakes that are often made when making decisions.

Framing

Kahneman and Tversky discovered that even when people are trying to be coldly logical, they give radically different answers to the same question if it's posed in different ways.[19] For instance, consider choices A and B in Scenario 1 in Exhibit 12-2. Most people come to opposite conclusions when faced with these two problems, even though they are identical. The only difference is that the first states the problem in terms of lives saved, while the second states it in terms of lives lost.

This judgment error is called **framing**, and refers to how the selective use of perspective alters the way we might view a situation in formulating a decision.

framing Error in judgment that arises from the selective use of perspective (that is, the way in which a set of ideas, facts, or information is presented) that alters the way we view a situation in formulating a decision.

Statistical Regression to the Mean

Sometimes people make judgments while ignoring **statistical regression to the mean**. This heuristic may be of particular interest to those trying to decide whether rewards or punishments work better with employees, colleagues, children, and even friends. Although many studies indicate that rewards are a more effective teaching tool than punishment, Kahneman was once faced with a student who begged to differ on this point. "I've often praised people warmly for beautifully executed manoeuvres, and the next time they almost always do worse. And I've screamed at people for badly executed manoeuvres, and by and large the next time they improve." Regression to the mean helps us understand that an exceptional performance is often followed by a lesser performance, while a poorer performance is more likely followed by a better performance. This happens because each person has an average performance level, so the highs and the lows balance out.

statistical regression to the mean The statistical observation that an above-average performance is often followed by a lesser performance, while a below-average performance is more likely followed by a better performance; the result is average performance over time.

Availability Heuristic

The **availability heuristic** is the tendency for people to base their judgments on information that is readily available to them rather than complete data. Events that evoke emotions, that are particularly vivid, or that have occurred more recently tend to be more available in our memory. As a result, we tend to overestimate unlikely events such as an airplane crash, compared with more likely events like car crashes. The availability heuristic

availability heuristic The tendency for people to base their judgments on information that is readily available to them rather than complete data.

EXHIBIT 12-2   Examples of Decision Biases

Scenario 1: Answer part A before reading part B.

A: Threatened by a superior enemy force, the general faces a dilemma. His intelligence officers say his soldiers will be caught in an ambush in which 600 of them will die unless he leads them to safety by one of two available routes. If he takes the first route, 200 soldiers will be saved. If he takes the second, there's a one-third chance that 600 soldiers will be saved and a two-thirds chance that none will be saved. Which route should he take?

B: The general again has to choose between two escape routes. But this time his aides tell him that if he takes the first, 400 soldiers will die. If he takes the second, there's a one-third chance that no soldiers will die, and a two-thirds chance that 600 soldiers will die. Which route should he take?

Scenario 2:

Linda is 31, single, outspoken, and very bright. She majored in philosophy in university. As a student, she was deeply concerned with discrimination and other social issues and participated in antinuclear demonstrations. Which statement is more likely:

a. Linda is a bank teller.

b. Linda is a bank teller and active in the feminist movement.

Source: K. McKean, "Decisions, Decisions," *Discover,* June 1985, pp. 22–31.

can also explain why managers, when doing annual performance appraisals, tend to give more weight to recent behaviours of an employee than to those behaviours of six or nine months ago.

Representative Heuristic

representative heuristic The tendency for people to assess the likelihood of an occurrence by trying to match it with a pre-existing category.

Many youngsters in Canada dream of playing hockey in the National Hockey League (NHL) when they grow up. In reality, they have a better chance of becoming medical doctors than they do of playing in the NHL, but these kids are suffering from a **representative heuristic**. They tend to assess the likelihood of an occurrence by trying to match it with a pre-existing category.[20] They heard about someone from their neighborhood who went to the NHL 25 years ago, and imagine that anyone from their neighborhood can do the same. In the workplace, individuals use this heuristic to make any number of decisions. For instance, if three graduates from the same university were hired and turned out to be poor performers, a manager might predict that a current job applicant from the same university would not be a good employee. The manager is assuming that the small sample of graduates previously employed represents all graduates from that university. Scenario 2 in Exhibit 12-2 gives an additional example of representativeness. In that case, Linda is assumed to be a bank teller and a feminist, given her concerns about social issues, even though the probability of both situations being true is much less than the probability that she is just a bank teller.

Ignoring the Base Rate

ignoring the base rate Error in judgment that arises from ignoring the statistical likelihood that an event might happen.

Yet another judgment error that people make is **ignoring the base rate**, which is ignoring the statistical likelihood that an event might happen. For instance, if you were planning to become an entrepreneur, and were asked whether your business would succeed, you would almost undoubtedly respond with a resounding "yes." Individuals believe they will beat the odds, even when, in the case of founding a business, the failure rate is close to 90 percent. Ignoring the base rate is not due to inexperience of the decision maker. Professors Glen Whyte of the Rotman School of Management (University of Toronto) and Christina Sue-Chan of the Asper School of Business (University of Manitoba) found that even experienced human resource managers ignore the base rate when asked to make hiring decisions in an experiment.[21] They suggest the importance of reminding people of what the base rate is before asking them to make decisions.

Escalation of commitment

escalation of commitment An increased commitment to a previous decision despite negative information.

Some decision makers escalate commitment to a failing course of action.[22] **Escalation of commitment** is an increased commitment to a previous decision despite negative information. For example, a friend had been dating a man for about four years. Although she admitted that things were not going too well in the relationship, she was determined to marry the man. When asked to explain this seemingly nonrational choice of action, she responded: "I have a lot invested in the relationship!"

Individuals escalate commitment to a failing course of action when they view themselves as responsible for the failure. That is, they "throw good money after bad" to demonstrate that their initial decision was not wrong and to avoid having to admit they made a mistake. Many organizations have suffered large losses because a manager was determined to prove his or her original decision was right by continuing to commit resources to what was a lost cause from the beginning.

When making decisions, you should consider whether you are falling into any of the judgment traps described above. In particular, understanding the base rates, and making sure that you collect information beyond that which is immediately available to you, will provide you with more alternatives from which to frame a decision. It is also useful to consider whether you are sticking with a decision simply because you have invested time in that particular alternative, even though it may not be wise to continue. *OB in Action—Reducing Biases and Errors in Decision Making* provides you with some ideas for improving your decision making. To learn more about your decision-making style, refer to the *Learning About Yourself Exercise* on page 462.

IMPROVING DECISION MAKING THROUGH KNOWLEDGE MANAGEMENT

The process of organizing and distributing an organization's collective wisdom so the right information gets to the right people at the right time is called **knowledge management** (KM).[23] When done properly, KM provides an organization with both a competitive edge and improved organizational performance because it makes its employees smarter.

A growing number of companies—including the Royal Bank of Canada, Cisco Systems, British Telecom, and Johnson & Johnson—have realized the value of knowledge management. In fact, a recent survey found that 81 percent of the leading organizations in Europe and the United States say they have, or are at least considering adopting, some kind of KM system.[24]

Knowledge management is increasingly important today for at least three reasons:[25]

1. Organizations that can quickly and efficiently tap into their employees' collective experience and wisdom are more likely to "outsmart" their competition.

2. As Baby Boomers begin to leave the workforce, there is an increasing awareness that they represent a wealth of knowledge that will be lost if there are no attempts to capture it.

3. A well-designed KM system reduces redundancy and makes the organization more efficient. For instance, when employees in a large organization undertake a new project, they need not start from scratch. They can access what previous employees have learned and avoid repeating previous mistakes.

How do organizations record the knowledge and expertise of their employees and make that information easily accessible? First, organizations need to develop *computer databases* of pertinent information that employees can readily access. This process includes identifying what knowledge matters to the organization.[26]

Second, organizations needs to create a *culture* that promotes, values, and rewards sharing knowledge. As we discussed in Chapter 8, information that is important and scarce can be a potent source of power. And people who hold that power are often reluctant to share it with others. KM won't work unless the culture supports sharing of information.[27]

Finally, organizations need to develop *mechanisms* that allow employees who have built up valuable expertise and insights to share them with others.[28] *More* knowledge is not necessarily *better* knowledge. Information overload needs to be avoided by designing the system to capture only pertinent information and then organizing it so it can be quickly accessed by the people whom it can help. Royal Bank of Canada, for instance, has created a KM system with customized email distribution lists

3 How can knowledge management improve decision making?

knowledge management The process of organizing and distributing an organization's collective wisdom so the right information gets to the right people at the right time.

OB IN ACTION

Reducing Biases and Errors in Decision Making

→ **Focus on goals**. Clear goals make decision making easier and help you eliminate options that are inconsistent with your interests.

→ Look for **information** that **disconfirms** your **beliefs**. When we deliberately consider various ways we could be wrong, we challenge our tendencies to think we are smarter than we actually are.

→ **Don't create meaning** out of random events. Ask yourself if patterns can be meaningfully explained or whether they are merely coincidence. Don't attempt to create meaning out of coincidence.

→ **Increase** your **options**. The more alternatives you can generate, and the more diverse those alternatives, the greater your chance of finding an outstanding one.

Source: S. P. Robbins, *Decide & Conquer: Making Winning Decisions and Taking Control of Your Life* (Upper Saddle River, NJ: Financial Times/Prentice Hall, 2004), pp. 164–168.

carefully broken down by employees' specialty, title, and area of interest; set aside a dedicated site on the company's intranet that serves as a central information repository; and created separate in-house websites featuring "lessons learned" summaries, where employees with various expertise can share new information with others.[29]

GROUP DECISION MAKING

4 What factors affect group decision making?

A variety of decisions in both life and organizations are made at the individual level. But the belief—characterized by juries—that two heads are better than one has long been accepted as a basic component of North American and many other countries' legal systems. This belief has expanded to the point that, today, many decisions in organizations are made by groups, teams, or committees. In this section, we will review group decision making and compare it with individual decision making.

Groups vs. the Individual

Decision-making groups may be widely used in organizations, but does that imply group decisions are preferable to those made by an individual alone? The answer to this question depends on a number of factors we consider below.[30] See Exhibit 12-3 for a summary of our major points.

Strengths of Group Decision Making

Groups generate *more complete information and knowledge.* By aggregating the resources of several individuals, groups bring more input into the decision process. In addition to more input, groups can bring heterogeneity to the decision process. They offer an *increased diversity of views,* and the opportunity to consider more approaches and alternatives. The evidence indicates that a group will almost always outperform even the best individual. So groups generate *higher quality decisions.* Groups also lead to *increased acceptance of a solution.*[31] Many decisions fail after they are made because people don't accept them. Group members who participated in making a decision are likely to enthusiastically support the decision and encourage others to accept it.

In terms of decision outcomes, group decisions tend to be more *accurate.* The evidence also indicates that, on average, groups make *better quality decisions* than individuals.[32] Finally, if *creativity* is important, groups tend to be more creative in their decisions than individuals.

Weaknesses of Group Decision Making

Despite the advantages noted, group decisions involve certain drawbacks. First, they are *time-consuming.* They typically take more time to reach a solution than would be the case if an individual were making the decision alone. Thus, group decisions are not

EXHIBIT 12-3 Group vs. Individual Decision Making		
Criteria of Effectiveness	**Groups**	**Individuals**
Accuracy	✔	
Speed		✔
Creativity	✔	
Degree of acceptance	✔	
Efficiency		✔

always efficient. Second, there are *conformity pressures* in groups. The desire by group members to be accepted and considered an asset to the group can result in squashing any overt disagreement. Third, group discussion can be *dominated by one or a few members*. If this dominant coalition is composed of low- and medium-ability members, the group's overall effectiveness will suffer. Finally, group decisions suffer from *ambiguous responsibility*. In an individual decision, it's clear who is accountable for the final outcome. In a group decision, the responsibility of any single member is watered down.

Groupthink and Groupshift

Two by-products of group decision making have received a considerable amount of attention by organizational behaviour (OB) researchers: groupthink and groupshift. As we will show, these two factors have the potential to affect the group's ability to appraise alternatives objectively and arrive at quality solutions.

Molly Mak was chosen president of a national information technology solutions provider, Calgary-based Onward Computer Systems, by other partners in the firm after she showed that she had the vision and determination to lead the company to greater growth and profits. She says that consensus is not always possible, especially when it's important to get things accomplished under tight time constraints.

Groupthink

Have you ever felt like speaking up in a meeting, classroom, or informal group, but decided against it? One reason may have been shyness. On the other hand, you may have been a victim of **groupthink**, a phenomenon in which group pressures for conformity prevent the group from critically appraising unusual, minority, or unpopular views. It describes a deterioration in an individual's mental efficiency, reality testing, and moral judgment as a result of group pressures.[33]

We have all seen the symptoms of the groupthink phenomenon:[34]

groupthink A phenomenon in which group pressures for conformity prevent the group from critically appraising unusual, minority, or unpopular views.

- *Illusion of invulnerability.* Group members become overconfident among themselves, allowing them to take extraordinary risks.

- *Assumption of morality.* Group members believe highly in the moral rightness of the group's objectives and do not feel the need to debate the ethics of their actions.

- *Rationalized resistance.* Group members rationalize any resistance to the assumptions they have made. No matter how strongly the evidence may contradict their basic assumptions, members behave so as to reinforce those assumptions continually.

- *Peer pressure.* Group members apply direct pressures on those who momentarily express doubts about any of the group's shared views or who question the validity of arguments supporting the alternative favoured by the majority.

- *Minimized doubts.* Those group members who have doubts or hold differing points of view seek to avoid deviating from what appears to be group consensus by keeping silent about misgivings and even minimizing to themselves the importance of their doubts.

- *Illusion of unanimity.* If someone doesn't speak, it's assumed that he or she is in full accord. In other words, abstention becomes viewed as a yes vote.

As the Bre-X scandal was unfolding in early 1997, many people who possibly should have known better refused to accept the initial evidence that there might not be any gold at Busang, Indonesia. Because investors and the companies involved had convinced themselves that they were sitting on the gold find of the twentieth century, they were reluctant to challenge their beliefs when the first evidence of tampered core samples was produced. More recently, forecasters seemed to be suffering from groupthink as they pronounced the economy in recession, as *OB in the Street* shows.

OB IN THE STREET

Recession: Are We There Yet?

How many economic forecasters does it take to change the economy? In early 2002, economic forecasters were absolutely surprised by all the good news they heard on the economic front in Canada and the United States.[35] They were surprised that the economies of both countries grew in the fourth quarter and by the job growth in Canada during January and February. They were even surprised that Canada's manufacturers and exporters had a great January. Their surprise came because they had been predicting either a recession, at worst, or a recession and jobless recovery, at best.

Forecasters started painting a gloomy picture after the September 11, 2001, terrorist attacks, anticipating that the US national crisis would have a long-lasting impact on the world economy. Even as evidence failed to support this gloomy picture, forecasters struggled to find evidence that they were right.

Groupthink may well explain the forecasters' lingering negative predictions. They were from the financial industry, which was harder hit than most industries, except for the technology sector. Wall Street economists also lived next door to the World Trade Center, so this had a greater impact. Rather than search more widely for evidence, they looked more locally, at the economy right around Wall Street.

Stock prices and corporate profits fell significantly during much of 2001, and this is what they focused on. Meanwhile, housing prices and consumer spending continued to rise. The analysts figured this was a temporary upturn before the large downturn they were predicting. They also failed to notice that personal income continued to rise throughout the year.

In short, forecasters were calling for a recession. They convinced each other it was coming. "[Those] who didn't buy the line, and suggested that maybe this was only a very sharp slowdown, invited ridicule."

The forecasters were suffering from some of the symptoms of groupthink. They rationalized resistance, suggesting it was everyone else who didn't understand the economic numbers. They applied peer pressure to each other, ridiculing those who suggested that a recession might not occur. This may have led some analysts to minimize their doubts, keeping silent. All of these behaviours led forecasters to appear unanimous in their views on the coming recession for 2002–2003.

Groupthink appears to be closely aligned with the conclusions Solomon Asch drew in his experiments with a lone dissenter, which we described in Chapter 6. Individuals who hold a position that is different from that of the dominant majority are under pressure to suppress, withhold, or modify their true feelings and beliefs. As members of a group, we find it more pleasant to be in agreement—to be a positive part of the group—than to be a disruptive force, even if disruption is necessary to improve the effectiveness of the group's decisions.

Do all groups suffer from groupthink? No. It seems to occur most often where there is a clear group identity, where members hold a positive image of their group, which they want to protect, and where the group perceives a collective threat to this positive image.[36]

So groupthink is less a dissenter-suppression mechanism than a means for a group to protect its positive image.

What can managers do to minimize groupthink?[37]

- Encourage group leaders to play an impartial role. Leaders should actively seek input from all members and avoid expressing their own opinions, especially in the early stages of deliberation.

- Appoint one group member to play the role of devil's advocate. This member's role is to overtly challenge the majority position and offer divergent perspectives.

- Stimulate active discussion of diverse alternatives to encourage dissenting views and more objective evaluations.

Despite considerable anecdotal evidence indicating the negative implications of groupthink in organizational settings, there has not been much actual empirical work conducted in organizations on this matter.[38] In fact, researchers on groupthink have been criticized for suggesting that its effect is uniformly negative[39] and for overestimating the link between the decision-making process and its outcome.[40] A 1999 study of groupthink using 30 teams from five large corporations suggests that elements of groupthink may affect decision making differently. For instance, the illusion of invulnerability, assumption of morality, and the illusion of unanimity were positively associated with team performance.[41] The most recent research suggests that we should be aware of groupthink conditions that lead to poor decisions, while realizing that not all groupthink symptoms harm decision making.

Groupshift

Research suggests that there are differences between the decisions groups make and the decisions that would be made by individual members within the group.[42] In some cases, group decisions are more conservative than individual decisions. More often, group decisions are riskier than individual decisions.[43] In either case, participants have engaged in **groupshift**, a phenomenon in which the initial positions of individual group members become exaggerated because of the interactions of the group.

What appears to happen in groups is that the discussion leads to a significant shift in the positions of members toward a more extreme position in the direction in which they were already leaning before the discussion. So conservative types become more cautious and more aggressive types assume more risk. The group discussion tends to exaggerate the initial position of the group.

Groupshift can be viewed as a special case of groupthink. The group's decision reflects the dominant decision-making norm that develops during the group's discussion. Whether the shift in the group's decision is toward greater caution or more risk depends on the dominant prediscussion norm.

The greater occurrence of the shift toward risk has generated several explanations for the phenomenon.[44] It's been argued, for instance, that discussion creates familiarization among the members. As they become more comfortable with each other, they also become more bold and daring. Another argument is that our society values risk, that we admire individuals who are willing to take risks, and that group discussion motivates members to show that they are at least as willing as their peers to take risks. The most plausible explanation of the shift toward risk, however, seems to be that the group diffuses responsibility. Group decisions free any single member from accountability for the group's final choice. Greater risk can be taken because even if the decision fails, no one member can be held wholly responsible.

How should you use the findings on groupshift? You should recognize that group decisions exaggerate the initial position of the individual members, that the shift has been

groupshift A phenomenon in which the initial positions of individual group members become exaggerated because of the interactions of the group.

shown more often to be toward greater risk, and that whether a group will shift toward greater risk or caution is a function of the members' prediscussion inclinations.

Group Decision-Making Techniques

Groups can use a variety of techniques to stimulate decision making. We outline four of them below.

Interacting Groups

The most common form of group decision making takes place in **interacting groups**. In these groups, members meet face to face and rely on both verbal and nonverbal interaction to communicate with each other. But as our discussion of groupthink demonstrated, interacting groups often censor themselves and pressure individual members toward conformity of opinion. Brainstorming, the nominal group technique, and electronic meetings have been proposed as ways to reduce many of the problems inherent in the traditional interacting group.

Brainstorming

Brainstorming is meant to overcome pressures for conformity in the interacting group that retard the development of creative alternatives.[45] It achieves this by using an idea-generation process that specifically encourages any and all alternatives, while withholding any criticism of those alternatives.

In a typical brainstorming session, 6 to 12 people sit around a table. The group leader states the problem in a clear manner so that all participants understand it. Members then "free-wheel" as many alternatives as they can in a given period of time. No criticism is allowed, and all the alternatives are recorded for later discussion and analysis. With one idea stimulating others and judgments of even the most bizarre suggestions withheld until later, group members are encouraged to "think the unusual."

A more recent variant of brainstorming is electronic brainstorming, which is done by people interacting on computers to generate ideas. For example, Calgary-based Jerilyn Wright & Associates uses electronic brainstorming to help clients design their workspaces through software that has been adapted for office-space design.[46]

The Executive Decision Centre at Queen's University was "one of the first electronic [decision making] facilities in North America and the first to be made accessible to the public."[47] Professor Brent Gallupe and another facilitator at the centre have conducted more than 600 decision-making sessions with a variety of North American organizations. The strength of Queen's system is that participants simultaneously interact via computer terminals, all responses are anonymous, and the speed allows numerous ideas to be generated in a short time. Whitby, Ontario-based McGraw-Hill Ryerson became a regular user when it found that one of its divisions experienced a surge in sales after visiting the Queen's centre. "They came up with a better, more soundly developed strategy, with more commitment on the part of the people. People feel very committed to the outcomes of the process because they don't feel like they've been strong-armed into the outcomes. They've had a voice in it," says John Dill, McGraw-Hill Ryerson's president and CEO.

However, brainstorming isn't always the right strategy to use. For example, Terry Graham, former president and CEO of Scarborough, Ontario-based Image Processing Systems, which won Canada's 1997 Export Award, saw brainstorming backfire when he was doing business in China. He says that meetings with Chinese business people "are definitely not for brainstorming. We learned this lesson the hard way. Our team thought we could show our creativity by placing fresh alternatives in front of an important manager. It was two years before the company would talk to us again."[48]

Brainstorming is merely a process for generating ideas. The following two techniques go further by offering methods of actually arriving at a preferred solution.[49]

Nominal Group Technique

The **nominal group technique** restricts discussion or interpersonal communication during the decision-making process, hence the term *nominal*. Group members are all physically present, as in a traditional committee meeting, but members operate independently. Specifically, a problem is presented and then the following steps take place:

- Members meet as a group, but before any discussion takes place, they independently write down their ideas on the problem.

- After this silent period, each member presents one idea to the group. Group members take turns presenting a single idea until all ideas have been presented and recorded. No discussion takes place until all ideas have been recorded.

- The group then discusses the ideas for clarity and evaluates them.

- Each group member silently and independently ranks the ideas. The idea with the highest aggregate ranking determines the final decision.

The steps of the nominal group technique are illustrated in Exhibit 12-4. The chief advantage of the technique is that it permits the group to meet formally but does not restrict independent thinking, as does the interacting group.

nominal group technique A group decision-making method in which individual members meet face to face to pool their judgments in a systematic but independent fashion.

Electronic Meetings

The most recent approach to group decision making blends the nominal group technique with sophisticated computer technology.[50] It's called the computer-assisted group, or **electronic meeting**. Up to 50 people sit around a horseshoe-shaped table, which is empty except for a series of computer terminals. Issues are presented to participants and they type their responses onto their computer monitors. Individual comments, as well as aggregate votes, are displayed on a projection screen in the room.

The major advantages of electronic meetings are anonymity, honesty, and speed. Participants can anonymously type any message they want, and it flashes on the screen for all to see at the push of a participant's keyboard. It also allows people to be brutally honest without penalty. And it's fast because chitchat is eliminated, discussions don't digress, and many participants can "talk" at once without stepping on one another's toes. The future of group meetings undoubtedly will include extensive use of this technology.

electronic meeting A meeting where members interact on computers, allowing for anonymity of comments and aggregation of votes.

Each of these four group decision techniques has its own strengths and weaknesses. The choice of one technique over another will depend on what criteria you want to emphasize and the cost-benefit trade-off. For instance, as Exhibit 12-5 indicates, the interacting group is effective for building group cohesiveness; brainstorming keeps social pressures to a minimum; the nominal group technique is an inexpensive means for generating a large number of ideas; and electronic meetings process ideas quickly.

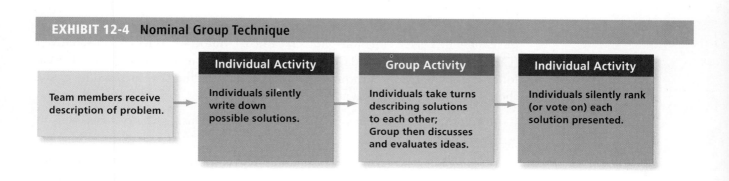

EXHIBIT 12-4 Nominal Group Technique

Team members receive description of problem. → **Individual Activity** Individuals silently write down possible solutions. → **Group Activity** Individuals take turns describing solutions to each other; Group then discusses and evaluates ideas. → **Individual Activity** Individuals silently rank (or vote on) each solution presented.

EXHIBIT 12-5 Evaluating Group Effectiveness

Effectiveness Criteria	Type of Group			
	Interacting	Brainstorming	Nominal	Electronic
Number of ideas	Low	Moderate	High	High
Quality of ideas	Low	Moderate	High	High
Social pressure	High	Low	Moderate	Low
Money costs	Low	Low	Low	High
Speed	Moderate	Moderate	Moderate	High
Task orientation	Low	High	High	High
Potential for interpersonal conflict	High	Low	Moderate	Low
Feelings of accomplishment	High to low	High	High	High
Commitment to solution	High	Not applicable	Moderate	Moderate
Develops group cohesiveness	High	High	Moderate	Low

Source: Based on J. K. Murnighan, "Group Decision Making: What Strategies Should You Use?" *Academy of Management Review,* February 1981, p. 61.

THE INFLUENCE OF THE LEADER ON GROUP DECISION MAKING

⑤ Should the leader make the decision, or encourage the group to participate?

You're the head of your own business, or you're the manager of your division at work, and you're trying to decide whether you should make a decision yourself, or involve the members of your team in the decision. Is there anything that informs you about whether it's better for the leader to make the decision, or to get everyone involved in the decision-making process?

leader-participation model A leadership theory that provides a set of rules to determine the form and amount of participative decision making in different situations.

Back in 1973, OB scholars Victor Vroom and Philip Yetton developed a **leader-participation model** to account for various actions the leader might take with respect to the decision-making processes of the group he or she led.[51] Vroom and Yetton's model was normative—it provided a sequential set of rules that should be followed for determining the form and amount of participation desirable by the manager or group leader in decision making, as dictated by different types of situations. The model was a complex decision tree incorporating seven contingencies (whose relevance could be identified by making "yes" or "no" choices) and five alternative leadership styles.

More recent work by Vroom and Arthur Jago has resulted in a revision of this model.[52] The new model retains the same five alternative leadership styles, but adds a set of problem types and expands the contingency variables to 12, 10 of which are answered along a five-point scale.

The model assumes that any of five possible behaviours that leaders could use might be feasible in a given situation—Autocratic I (AI), Autocratic II (AII), Consultative I (CI), Consultative II (CII), and Group II (GII). Thus the group leader or manager has the following alternatives from which to choose when deciding how involved he or she should be with decisions that affect a work group:

AI: You solve the problem or make a decision yourself using whatever facts you have at hand.

AII: You obtain the necessary information from employees and then decide on the solution to the problem yourself. You may or may not tell employees about the nature of the situation you face. You seek only relevant facts from them, not their advice or counsel.

CI: You share the problem with relevant employees one-on-one, getting their ideas and suggestions. However, the final decision is yours alone.

CII: You share the problem with your employees as a group, collectively obtaining their ideas and suggestions. Then you make the decision, which may or may not reflect your employees' influence.

GII: You share the problem with your employees as a group. Your goal is to help the group concur on a decision. Your ideas are not given any greater weight than those of others.

The original leader-participation model has been revised, and is too sophisticated and complex to describe in detail in a basic OB textbook. There is a computer program that cuts through the complexity of the new model. The variables identified in the decision tree in Exhibit 12-6 provide you with solid insights about when you as a leader should participate in a group decision, make the decision yourself, or delegate to someone else. The major decision factors include the quality of the decision required, the degree of commitment needed from participants, and the time available to make the decision.

To help you become more familiar with using these decision trees, the *Working With Others Exercise* on page 463 presents several cases for you to analyze.

EXHIBIT 12-6   The Revised Leadership-Participation Model (Time-Driven Decision Tree Group Problems)

QR	Quality requirement:	How important is the technical quality of this decision?
CR	Commitment requirement:	How important is subordinate commitment to the decision?
LI	Leader's information:	Do you have sufficient information to make a high quality decision?
ST	Problem structure:	Is the problem well structured?
CP	Commitment probability:	If you were to make the decision by yourself, is it reasonably certain that your subordinate(s) would be committed to the decision?
GC	Goal congruence:	Do subordinates share the organizational goals to be attained in solving this problem?
CO	Subordinate conflict:	Is conflict among subordinates over preferred solutions likely?
SI	Subordinate information:	Do subordinates have sufficient information to make a high quality decision?

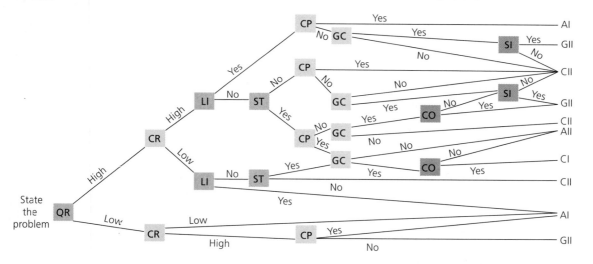

Source: Adapted and reprinted from *Leadership and Decision-Making,* by Victor H. Vroom and Philip W. Yetton, by permission of the University of Pittsburgh Press. Copyright © 1973 by University of Pittsburgh Press.

Research testing of the original leader-participation model was very encouraging.[53] We have every reason to believe that the revised model provides an excellent guide to help managers choose the most appropriate leadership style in different situations.

CREATIVITY IN ORGANIZATIONAL DECISION MAKING

6 How can we get more creative decisions?

"Canada is not a very creative culture," according to a National Research Council report written by Professor David Bentley of the English Department at the University of Western Ontario.[54] The report suggests that concrete steps need to be taken to promote a culture of innovation and improve the creativity of individuals. The report gives a number of suggestions for improving creativity, including using metaphors, empathetic thinking, and imagining to help see things in new ways.

Bentley's call for improving creativity is consistent with a contemporary survey showing that 58 percent of both large public companies and entrepreneurs recognize a link between creative thinking within the organization and having a competitive edge.[55] "It [creative thinking] will not necessarily spell the difference between success and failure. But it is one of those tangential issues that can add a few cents per share profit," noted the head of an Ontario agriproducts company, who was not identified by the survey. Moreover, research shows that the organizational benefits of individual creativity include "higher-quality products, more effective decision making, better group performance, and more innovative solutions to organizational problems."[56]

A variety of definitions exist for the concept of creativity; some view it as a characteristic of a person, and others view it as a process.[57] Most contemporary researchers and theorists use a definition that addresses either the product or the outcome of the product development process.[58] In the discussion below, we consider **creativity** as the process of creating novel products, ideas, or procedures that are potentially relevant or useful to an organization.[59]

creativity The process of creating novel products, ideas, or procedures that are potentially relevant or useful to an organization.

Factors That Affect Individual Creativity

Why are some people more creative than others?

People differ in their inherent creativity. Albert Einstein, Marie Curie, Thomas Edison, Pablo Picasso, and Wolfgang Amadeus Mozart were individuals of exceptional creativity. In more recent times, Canadian artist Emily Carr, legendary Canadian concert pianist Glenn Gould, Canadian author Carol Shields, and basketball star Michael Jordan have been noted for the creative contributions they made to their fields. Not surprisingly, exceptional creativity is scarce. For example, a study of lifetime creativity of 461 men and women found that less than 1 percent were exceptionally creative.[60] But 10 percent were highly creative and about 60 percent were somewhat creative. This suggests that most of us have creative potential, if we can learn to unleash it.

A large body of literature has examined the personal attributes associated with creative achievement.[61] In general, "these studies have demonstrated that a stable set of core personal characteristics, including broad interests, attraction to complexity, intuition, aesthetic sensitivity, toleration of ambiguity, and self-confidence relate positively and consistently to measures of creative performance across a variety of domains."[62]

While personality and cognitive skills are linked to creativity,[63] the task itself plays an important role. Individuals are more creative when they are motivated by intrinsic interest, challenge, task satisfaction, and self-set goals.[64] Those who are extrinsically motivated are more likely to look for the most efficient solution to a problem in order to receive the desired rewards. Those who are intrinsically motivated may take more time exploring issues and situations, which gives them the opportunity to see things in a different light.[65] The setting also makes a difference, and those settings that provide opportunities, absence of constraints,[66] and rewards[67] encourage creativity.

There is some evidence that the brain is set up to think linearly, rather than laterally, and yet lateral thinking is needed for creative thinking. Edward De Bono, a leading authority on creative and conceptual thinking for over 25 years, has written a number of books on this topic, including *Six Thinking Hats* and *The Mechanism of Mind*.[68] De Bono's "six thinking hats" concept is a simple yet powerful tool that is intended to change the way people think. He suggests that innovative and creative problem-solving can develop from working through decisions using each of the frameworks represented by individual hats. The hats are metaphors for different kinds of thinking.[69]

- The *white hat* represents impartial thinking, focusing strictly on the facts.

- The *red hat* represents expression of feelings, passions, intuitions, emotions.

- The *black hat* represents a critical, deliberate, evaluating outlook.

- The *yellow hat* represents an optimistic, upbeat, positive outlook.

- The *green hat* represents creativity, inspiration, imagination, and the free flow of new concepts.

- The *blue hat* represents control, an overall "managerial" perspective of the process.

Creativity and the bottom line can go hand in hand. In fact, at Vancouver-based Big House Communications, creativity rules. Big House develops communications, including websites, for other companies. It's known for giving clients several alternatives: traditional, wacky, and fun. The company must be doing something right. It's more than 16 years old, which makes it really old for its business.

From Concepts to Skills on page 466 points out how to solve problems creatively.

Each hat has its own place in the decision-making process. De Bono suggests that we use all six in order to fully develop our capacity to think more creatively. Groups could do the same by assigning each person to the role of one of the hats.

Organizational Factors That Affect Creativity

In two decades of research analyzing the links between work environment and creativity, six general categories have been found:[70]

Edward De Bono
www.edwdebono.com

- *Challenge.* When people are matched up with the right assignments, their expertise and skills can be brought to the task of creative thinking. Individuals should be stretched, but not overwhelmed.

- *Freedom.* To be creative, once a person is given a project, he or she needs the autonomy to determine the process. In other words, let the person decide how to tackle the problem. This heightens intrinsic motivation.

- *Resources.* Time and money are the two main resources that affect creativity. Thus, managers need to allot these resources carefully.

- *Work group features.* Our discussion of group composition and diversity concluded that heterogeneous groups were likely to come up with more creative solutions. In addition to ensuring a diverse group of people, team members need to share excitement over the goal, must be willing to support each other through difficult periods, and must recognize each other's unique knowledge and perspective.

- *Supervisory encouragement.* To sustain passion, most people need to feel that what they are doing matters to others. Managers can reward, collaborate, and communicate to nurture the creativity of individuals and teams.

- *Organizational support.* Creativity-supporting organizations reward creativity, and also make sure that there is information sharing and collaboration. They make sure that negative political problems do not get out of control.

The Swiss firm BrainStore takes advantage of group diversity to improve decision making in *Focus on Diversity*.

FOCUS ON **DIVERSITY**

Kids Improve Decision Making at BrainStore

BrainStore
www.brainstore.com

Can kids help organizations be more creative? BrainStore, an "idea factory" in Biel, Switzerland, recognizes the importance of diversity in putting together creative ideas.[71] It uses an international network of children to brainstorm its most challenging projects.

BrainStore manufactures and sells ideas. Clients include pharmaceuticals giant Novartis AG, which was looking for ideas for new food products; the Swiss Cancer Association, which wanted ideas on how to promote the use of sun-protection products; and a 70-year-old woman who wanted ideas to help her fall in love again.

The company vision of BrainStore founders Markus Mettler, 38, and Nadja Schnetzler, 32, is to "approach the manufacturing of ideas with as much rigour and as much discipline as you apply to the manufacturing of assembly-line products."

BrainStore calls in the BrainNet whenever it faces a really big creative challenge. BrainNet is a 1500-person global network of young people aged 13 to 20. The young people scour the world for new trends and offbeat sources of inspiration to help the company. "We're not looking for average ideas," says Mettler. "We're looking for crazy ideas. We use kids to find those ideas, because they know how to talk without letting their thinking get in the way."

Members of BrainNet join members of BrainStore's client teams during creative workshops. "One of the ideas behind the company was to blend the professionalism of experts with the unbridled enthusiasm of kids," says Schnetzler. It's not unusual for teens to work with such clients as Nestle SA and the Swiss railway.

Recently, nine kids helped five executives from Credit Suisse Group, one of Switzerland's top banks, to brainstorm ideas to get rid of its passbook savings accounts. Swiss families liked the accounts, but bank employees found them obsolete. After the cross-generational teams developed a set of raw ideas, they went through the remaining steps in the BrainStore assembly line: "compression (in which a team of in-house employees and outside experts sorts through ideas and picks out the best ones); testing (research and prototype); and finishing (marketing campaigns and positioning strategies)." Mettler suggests that it is this assembly-line process that keeps innovation flowing, by making sure that all parts of the decision-making process get carried out.

Videogame maker Electronic Arts (EA) created an on-site labyrinth to help employees unleash their creative potential. EA encourages video and computer game developers to wander the maze when their creativity levels are running low. While walking the maze, they can think about their challenges in divergent ways for designing innovative products.

Five organizational factors have been found to block your creativity at work:[72]

- *Expected evaluation.* Focusing on how your work is going to be evaluated.
- *Surveillance.* Being watched while you are working.
- *External motivators.* Focusing on external, tangible rewards.
- *Competition.* Facing win-lose situations with peers.
- *Constrained choice.* Being given limits on how you can do your work.

This chapter's *CBC Video Case* illustrates how one creativity specialist gets people to think more creatively.

Doug Hall, Creativity Guru

WHAT ABOUT ETHICS IN DECISION MAKING?

> At the Pan Asia Footwear Public Company in Thailand, managers set quotas in order to keep productivity high.[73] The difficulty, as one inspector points out, is "shoes with complex details sometimes can't be finished in eight hours. This means that staff might work 10 hours for an eight-hour wage." The company does not pay overtime when this happens, because the employee has not met the quota on time. Employees are not paid by the hour. They simply receive a flat fee for a day's work. How can we determine whether this is an ethical practice by the company?

No contemporary discussion of decision making would be complete without the inclusion of ethics, because ethical considerations should be an important criterion in organizational decision making. **Ethics** is the study of moral values or principles that guide our behaviour, and inform us whether actions are right or wrong. Ethical principles help us "do the right thing." In this section, we present three ways to ethically frame decisions and examine the factors that shape an individual's ethical decision-making behaviour. We also examine organizational responses to the demand for ethical behaviour, as well as consideration of ethical decisions when doing business in other cultures. To learn more about your ethical decision-making approach, see the *Ethical Dilemma Exercise* on page 464. To consider the extent to which ethical decision making blurs the lines between work and personal life, examine the *Case Incident—Bankers' Excess Gets Them Fired* on page 465.

7 What is ethics, and how can it be used for better decision making?

ethics The study of moral values or principles that guide our behaviour and inform us whether actions are right or wrong.

Four Ethical Decision Criteria

An individual can use four different criteria in making ethical choices.[74] The first is the *utilitarian* criterion, in which decisions are made solely on the basis of their outcomes or consequences. The goal of **utilitarianism** is to provide the greatest good for the greatest number. This view tends to dominate business decision making. It is consistent with goals such as efficiency, productivity, and high profits. By maximizing profits, for instance, business executives can argue that they are securing the greatest good for the greatest number—as they hand out dismissal notices to 15 percent of employees.

utilitarianism A decision focused on outcomes or consequences that emphasizes the greatest good for the greatest number.

BMO Nesbitt Burns ignored unethical behaviour by an employee because the company stood to gain from the behaviour, as *Focus on Ethics* shows.

FOCUS ON **ETHICS**

Making Profits at the Expense of Clients

Can profits really drive unethical decisions? In spring 2001, BMO Nesbitt Burns in Winnipeg agreed to pay the highest fine in Manitoba securities history ($100 000 plus $60 000 toward investigation costs) after being investigated by the Manitoba

BMO Nesbitt Burns
www.bmonesbittburns.com

Securities Commission, the Investment Dealers Association (IDA), and the Canadian Banking Ombudsman for ignoring unethical behaviour by one of its investment brokers over several years.[75] These investigations stemmed from continuing complaints about broker Randolph McDuff's behaviour, for which the company took little action. McDuff was first investigated by BMO Nesbitt Burns in March 1999 for trading in clients' accounts without their permission. McDuff admitted he had made unauthorized trades in client accounts; a compliance officer noted that "McDuff did not seem to understand that a client must be contacted prior to a trade being executed." The head of compliance at Nesbitt Burns' Toronto headquarters recommended that McDuff be fired.

However, McDuff was not fired. Instead he was fined $2000 and warned that "any further occurrences may result in termination of employment." This was not the first incident of unethical behaviour by McDuff. An internal document dated January 28, 1999, noted, "We have experienced a large increase in the amount of settlements [anticipated and settled]" regarding McDuff.

Nevertheless, Tom Waitt, senior vice-president of BMO Nesbitt Burns' Prairie division and McDuff's supervisor in Manitoba, urged the head office to avoid taking drastic action, and to keep McDuff under close supervision instead. A memo McDuff wrote to his supervisor in September 1999 may explain why the Winnipeg office was so interested in ignoring his behaviour: "I know there is this great big cloud over my head and that head office wants me out of here. Does head office forget about my contributions to this firm over the years? In addition to providing for more than 15% of the office revenue consistently over the past five years, I have been an advocate of Nesbitt Burns. . . . Rookies and marketers are still amazed at my work ethic. Some have said that it inspires them to work harder." 🏃

Decision makers, particularly in for-profit organizations, tend to feel safe and comfortable when they use utilitarianism. Many questionable actions can be justified when framed as being in the best interests of "the organization" and stockholders. But many critics of business decision makers argue that this perspective should change because it can result in ignoring the rights of some individuals, particularly those with minority representation in the organization.[76]

A second ethical criterion is to focus on *rights*. This criterion calls on individuals to make decisions consistent with fundamental liberties and privileges as set forth in documents such as the Canadian Charter of Rights and Freedoms. An emphasis on rights in decision making means respecting and protecting the basic rights of individuals, such as the right to privacy, to free speech, and to due process. For instance, use of this criterion would protect whistle-blowers when they report unethical or illegal practices by their organization to the media or to government agencies on the grounds of their right to free speech.

A third ethical criterion is to focus on *justice*. This requires individuals to impose and enforce rules fairly and impartially so there is an equitable distribution of benefits and costs. Union members typically favour this view. It justifies paying people the same wage for a given job, regardless of performance differences, and using seniority as the primary determination in making layoff decisions. A focus on justice protects the interests of the

Stewart Leibl, president of Perth's, a Winnipeg dry-cleaning chain, is a founding sponsor of the Koats for Kids program. The company's outlets are a drop-off point for no-longer-needed children's coats, which Perth's cleans free of charge before distributing them to children who don't have winter coats. Leibl is going beyond the utilitarian criterion when he says, "We all have a responsibility to contribute to the society that we live in." He is also looking at social justice.

underrepresented and less powerful, but it can encourage a sense of entitlement that reduces risk-taking, innovation, and productivity.

A fourth ethical criterion is to focus on *care*. The ethics of care can be stated as follows: "The morally correct action is the one that expresses care in protecting the special relationships that individuals have with each other."[77] Care as an ethical criterion came out of feminist literature[78] to address the idea that the male-dominated view of ethics was too impersonal and ignored the relationships among individuals.[79] The care criterion suggests that we should be aware of the needs, desires, and well-being of those to whom we are closely connected. Recent research does not suggest that men and women differ in their use of justice vs. care in making decisions.[80] However, this perspective does remind us of the difficulty of being impartial in all decisions.

Factors Influencing Ethical Decision-Making Behaviour

Why do some people make more ethical decisions than others?

What accounts for unethical behaviour in organizations? Is it immoral individuals or work environments that promote unethical activity? The answer is, *both!* The evidence indicates that ethical or unethical actions are largely a function of both the individual's characteristics and the environment in which he or she works.[81] The model in Exhibit 12-7 illustrates factors affecting ethical decision-making behaviour and emphasizes three factors: stage of moral development, locus of control, and the organizational environment.

Stages of Moral Development

Stages of moral development assess a person's capacity to judge what is morally right.[82] Research suggests that there are three levels of moral development, and each level has two stages.[83] The higher a person's moral development, the less dependent he or she is on outside influences and, hence, the more he or she will be predisposed to behave ethically. The first level is the preconventional level, the second is the conventional level, and the third, or highest, level is the principled level. These levels and their stages are described in Exhibit 12-8 on page 452.

Research indicates that people proceed through the stages one step at a time, though they do not necessarily reach the highest stage.[84] Most adults are at a mid-level of moral development—they are strongly influenced by peers and will follow an organization's rules and procedures. Those individuals who have progressed to the higher stages place increased value on the rights of others, regardless of the majority's opinion, and are likely to challenge organizational practices they personally believe are wrong. Those at the higher stages are most likely to make ethical decisions.

stages of moral development The developmental stages that explain a person's capacity to judge what is morally right.

EXHIBIT 12-7 Factors Affecting Ethical Decision-Making Behaviour

Stage of moral development

Locus of control

Organizational environment

→ Ethical decision-making behaviour

EXHIBIT 12-8 **Stages of Moral Development**

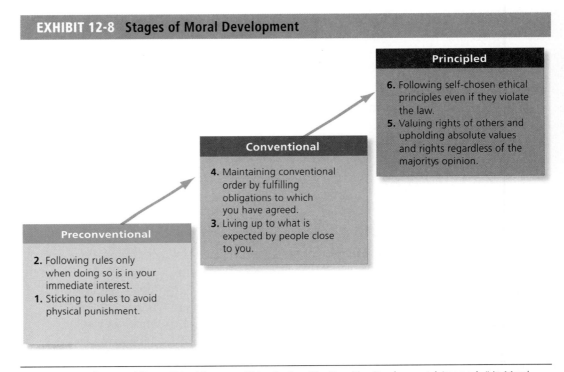

Source: Based on L. Kohlberg, "Moral Stages and Moralization: The Cognitive-Developmental Approach," in *Moral Development and Behaviour: Theory, Research, and Social Issues,* ed. T. Lickona (New York: Holt, Rinehart and Winston, 1976), pp. 34–35.

Locus of Control

Research indicates that people with an external *locus of control* (that is, they believe their lives are controlled by outside forces, such as luck or chance) are less likely to take responsibility for the consequences of their behaviour and are more likely to rely on external influences to determine their behaviour. Those with an internal locus of control (they believe they are responsible for their destiny), on the other hand, are more likely to rely on their own internal standards of right or wrong to guide their behaviour.

Organizational Environment

The *organizational environment* refers to an employee's perception of organizational expectations. Does the organizational culture encourage and support ethical behaviour by rewarding it or discourage unethical behaviour by punishing it? Characteristics of an organizational environment that are likely to foster high ethical decision making include written codes of ethics; high moral behaviour by senior management; realistic performance expectations; performance appraisals that evaluate means as well as ends; visible recognition and promotions for individuals who display high moral behaviour; and visible punishment for those who act unethically.

In summary, people who lack a strong moral sense are much less likely to make unethical decisions if they are constrained by an organizational environment that frowns on such behaviours. Conversely, righteous individuals can be corrupted by an organizational environment that permits or encourages unethical practices. In the next section, we consider how to formulate an ethical decision.

Making Ethical Decisions

While there are no clear-cut ways to differentiate ethical from unethical decision making, there are some questions you should consider.

Exhibit 12-9 illustrates a decision tree to guide ethical decisions.[85] This tree is built on the three ethical decision criteria—utilitarianism, rights, and justice—presented earlier. The first question you need to answer addresses self-interest vs. organizational goals.

The second question concerns the rights of other parties. If the decision violates the rights of someone else (the person's right to privacy, for instance), then the decision is unethical.

The final question that needs to be addressed relates to whether the decision conforms to standards of equity and justice. The department head who inflates the performance evaluation of a favoured employee and deflates the evaluation of a disfavoured employee—and then uses these evaluations to justify giving the former a big raise and nothing to the latter—has treated the disfavoured employee unfairly.

Unfortunately, the answers to the questions in Exhibit 12-9 are often argued in ways to make unethical decisions seem ethical. Powerful people, for example, can become very adept at explaining self-serving behaviours in terms of the organization's best interests. Similarly, they can persuasively argue that unfair actions are really fair and just. Our point is that immoral people can justify almost any behaviour. Those who are powerful, articulate, and persuasive are the most likely to be able to get away with unethical actions successfully. When faced with an ethical dilemma, try to answer the questions in Exhibit 12-9 truthfully.

Organizational Response to Demands for Ethical Behaviour

During the 1990s, an explosion in the demand for more ethics occurred in Canada and the United States. A second explosion occurred in 2002, after the Enron, WorldCom, and other accounting scandals. In Canada, more than 120 ethics specialists now offer services as in-house moral arbitrators, mediators, watchdogs, and listening posts. Some work at Canada's largest corporations, including CIBC, Canada Post, Magna International, Royal Bank of Canada, Nortel Networks, and McDonald's Canada. These corporate ethics officers hear about issues such as colleagues making phone calls on company time, managers yelling at their employees, product researchers being asked to fake data to meet a deadline, or a company wanting to terminate a contract because the costs are higher than anticipated. Ethics professor Wayne Norman of the Université de Montréal believes that ethics officers are a positive trend, noting, "All sorts of studies show the companies that take ethics seriously tend to be more successful."[86]

Canada Post
www.canadapost.ca

Magna International
www.magnaint.com

Nortel Networks
www.nortelnetworks.com

McDonald's Canada
www.mcdonalds.ca/en/

EXHIBIT 12-9 Is a Decision Ethical?

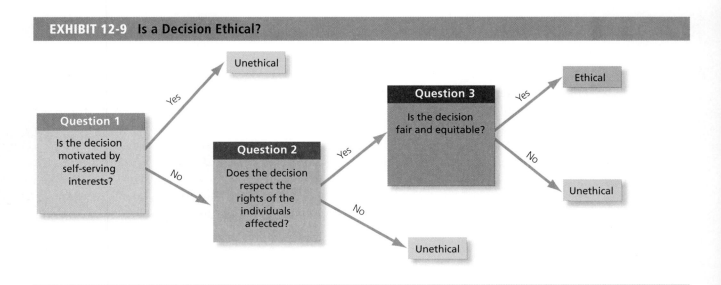

United Parcel Service (UPS) Canada, based in Moncton, New Brunswick, wants to make sure that its employees approach ethical dilemmas with the confidence to make the right decision. Therefore, the company conducts an ethics training program for all of its employees, from senior managers to the service providers.

United Parcel Services (UPS) Canada
www.ups.com/canada/

Many corporations are also developing codes of ethics. For example, about 66 percent of Canada's largest 1000 corporations have them,[87] while about 90 percent of the companies on the *Fortune* 500 index have them. Twenty percent of the top 300 Canadian organizations employ ethics specialists, compared with 30 percent of the *Fortune* 500 companies in the United States. Unlike the United States, however, Canada does not legally require companies to create an ethical culture. In the United States, when a company is sued for illegal practices, financial damages may be reduced considerably if the company has a fully functioning ethics program in place.

Having a corporate ethics policy is not enough; employees must be instructed in how to follow the policy. Yet only about 39 percent of Canadian firms provided training in ethical decision making in 2000, although this was up from 21 percent in 1997. United Parcel Services (UPS) Canada launched its ethics training program in July 1999. As David Cole, vice-president of human resources at UPS, noted, "We want to make sure that as people approach ethical dilemmas, they understand there is a support structure in place."[88] *OB in Action—Developing a Meaningful Code of Ethics* shows how to implement codes of ethics in organizations.

Only 14 percent of companies evaluate their ethics-related performance, suggesting that most are not focused on improving ethics in the workplace.[89] However, a small group of companies is starting a new trend in monitoring ethical practices—hiring an ethics auditor in much the same way as they would hire a financial auditor. The ethics auditor is hired to "double-check an organization's perception of its own morals."[90] Vancouver City Savings Credit Union (Vancity), Bell Canada, Tetra Pak, British Telecom, the University of Toronto, and The Body Shop have all brought in ethics auditors. This chapter's *HR Implications*, on page 461, contains further details about the types of ethical policies that organizations implement.

Another way to encourage ethical behaviour is to create mechanisms that encourage employees to speak up when they see wrongdoing. Toronto-based BBDO Canada encourages "candour moments." Employees are empowered "to call each other on behaviour that goes against company values, even junior employees who want to be candid with managers," says the ad agency's president and CEO, Gerry Frascione.[91]

What About National Culture?

We have already shown that there are differences between Canada and the United States in the legal treatment of ethics violations and the creation of an ethical corporate culture. However, it's important to note that what is considered unethical in one country may not be viewed similarly in another country. The reason is that there are no global ethical standards. Contrasts between Asia and the West provide an illustration.[92] In Japan, people doing business together often exchange gifts, even expensive ones. This is part of Japanese tradition. When North American and European companies started doing business in Japan, most North American executives were not aware of the Japanese tradition of exchanging gifts and wondered whether this was a form of bribery. Most have come to accept this tradition now and have even set different limits on gift giving in Japan than in other countries.[93]

In another example of the differences between Asia and North America, a manager of a large US company that operates in China caught an employee stealing. Following company policy, she fired the employee and turned him over to the local authorities for his act. Later she discovered, to her horror, that the former employee had been executed for the theft.[94] These examples indicate that standards for ethical behaviour and the consequences of particular acts are not universal. This presents a variety of problems for those doing business in other countries.

Companies operating branches in foreign countries are faced with tough decisions about how to conduct business under different ethical standards from those in Canada. For instance, Canadian companies must decide whether they want to operate in countries such as China, Burma, and Nigeria, which abuse human rights. Although the Canadian government permits investing in these countries, it also encourages companies to act ethically.

Although ethical standards may seem ambiguous in the West, criteria defining right and wrong are actually much clearer in the West than in Asia and the Middle East. Few issues are black and white there; most are grey. John B. McWilliams, senior vice-president and general counsel for Calgary-based Canadian Occidental Petroleum (now known as Nexen), notes that requests for bribes are not necessarily direct: "Usually, they don't say, 'Give me X thousands of dollars and you've got the deal.' It's a lot more subtle than that."[95] Michael Davies, vice-president and general counsel for Toronto-based General Electric Canada, offers an example: "A payment [is] made to an administrative official to do the job that he's supposed to do. In other words, you pay a fellow over the counter $10 when you're in the airport in Saudi Arabia to get on the flight you're supposed to get on, because, otherwise, he's going to keep you there for two days."[96]

The US government reported that between 1994 and 2001, bribery was uncovered in more than 400 competitions for international contracts.[97] The need for global organizations to establish ethical principles for decision makers in all countries may be critical if high standards are to be upheld and if consistent practices are to be achieved.

> ## O B IN ACTION
>
> ### Developing a Meaningful Code of Ethics
>
> → Clearly **state basic principles** and expectations.
> → Realistically **focus on potential ethical dilemmas** that employees face.
> → **Distribute** the **code** to all employees.
> → **Enforce violations** of the code.
>
> *Source:* Based on W. E. Stead, D. L. Worrell, and J. G. Stead, "An Integrative Model for Understanding and Managing Ethical Behavior in Business Organizations," *Journal of Business Ethics* 9, no. 3 (March 1990), pp. 233–242.

Nexen
www.nexen.inc.com

General Electric Canada
www.ge.com/ca

The Global Alliance for Workers and Communities
www.theglobalalliance.org

CORPORATE SOCIAL RESPONSIBILITY

> In 1999 Nike gave a $7.7-million (US) grant to the International Youth Foundation (IYF) to establish an organization called the Global Alliance for Workers and Communities (GA).[98] GA, founded to improve working conditions in overseas factories, has been critical of Nike, publishing a report in 2001 on abuses in Indonesian factories making Nike products. "Verbal abuse was the most marked, with 30 per cent of the workers having personally experienced and 56 per cent having observed the problem. An average of 7 per cent of workers reported receiving unwelcome sexual comments and 3 per cent reported being physically abused," the report said.
>
> Nike admitted that it was unaware of these problems when the report was published. The company has since increased training for both managers and employees at its overseas facilities to avoid some of the abuses that were happening in the factories. Maria Eitel, the company's vice-president for corporate responsibility, says: "The factory managers are telling us that as they increase their work around social responsibility, they are seeing improvements." To what extent should companies be socially responsible?

Corporate social responsibility is defined as an organization's responsibility to consider the impact of its decisions on society. Thus, organizations may try to better society, through such things as charitable contributions or providing better wages to employees working in offshore factories. Organizations may engage in these practices because they feel pressured by society to do so, or they may seek ways to improve society because they feel it is the right thing to do.

8 What is corporate social responsibility?

corporate social responsibility
An organization's responsibility to consider the impact of its decisions on society.

Halifax-based Nova Scotia Power wants its employees to be active in helping their communities. To encourage them to invest their time, the company started a Good Neighbour funding program. Employees apply to the Good Neighbour committee to receive up to $1000 for capital costs for a community project.

Eighty percent of Canadians feel that Ottawa should establish standards for corporate social responsibility, and require corporations to report on how they are meeting guidelines, according to a recent survey.[99] Many Canadian companies are feeling the pressure to act socially responsible as well. Environics Research Group recently found that 49 percent of the 25 000 consumers interviewed worldwide made product decisions on the basis of companies' social responsibility.[100] This exceeded the 40 percent who made decisions based on brand quality and reputation. Moreover, 23 percent said they had punished a company in the previous year for not meeting what they thought were the company's social obligations.

Not everyone agrees with the position of organizations assuming social responsibility. For example, economist Milton Friedman remarked in *Capitalism and Freedom* that "few trends could so thoroughly undermine the very foundations of our free society as the acceptance by corporate officials of a social responsibility other than to make as much money for their stockholders as possible."[101]

Joel Bakan, professor of law at the University of British Columbia, author of *The Corporation*,[102] and co-director of the documentary of the same name, is more critical of organizations than Friedman, though he finds that current laws support corporate behaviour that some might find troubling. Bakan suggests that today's corporations have many of the same characteristics as a psychopathic personality (e.g., self-interested, lacking empathy, manipulative, and reckless in their disregard of others). Bakan notes that even though companies have a tendency to act psychopathically, this is not why they are fixated on profits. Rather, the only legal responsibility corporations have is to maximize organizational profits for stockholders. He suggests more laws and more restraints need to be put in place if corporations are to behave more socially responsibly, as current laws direct corporations to be responsible to their shareholders, and make little mention of responsibility toward other stakeholders.

Interestingly enough, a recent study shows that MBA students change their views about social responsibility during the course of their program.[103] Students from 13 international business schools, including the Ivey School at the University of Western

Ontario and the Schulich School at York University, were asked at the beginning and the end of their MBA program about their attitudes toward corporate social responsibility. At the start of their program, 40 percent reported that one of the primary responsibilities of a company is to produce useful, high quality goods and services. By the time the students graduated, only 30 percent of them thought this was a valuable corporate goal; 75 percent suggested that a company's primary responsibility was to maximize shareholder value.

Some Canadian companies do practise social responsibility, however. Both Vancouver-based Vancity and Bolton, Ontario-based Husky Injection Molding Systems have "taken comprehensive steps to include customer, employee, community and environmental concerns in both long-term planning and day-to-day decision making."[104] Vancity's electronic banking arm, Citizens Bank, has an "Ethical Policy," which states, for instance, that the bank is against excessive environmental harm, and will not do business with companies that either violate the fundamental rights of children or are involved in weapons.[105] This chapter's *Case Incident—Syncrude Wants to be a Good Neighbour* on page 465 describes a socially responsible approach to running a business located near an Aboriginal community. For more on the debate about social responsibility vs. concentrating on the bottom line, see this chapter's *Point/Counterpoint* on page 460.

Vancity
www.vancity.com

Husky Injection Molding Systems
www.husky.ca

SUMMARY AND IMPLICATIONS

1 Is there a right way to make decisions? The rational decision-making model describes the six steps individuals take to make decisions: (1) Define the problem, (2) identify the criteria, (3) allocate weights to the criteria, (4) develop alternatives, (5) evaluate the alternatives, and (6) select the best alternative. This is an idealized model, and not every decision thoroughly follows these steps.

2 How do people actually make decisions? Most decisions in the real world don't follow the rational model. For instance, people are usually content to find an acceptable or reasonable solution to their problem rather than an optimizing one. Thus, decision makers may rely on bounded rationality, satisficing, and intuition in making decisions. There are a number of judgment shortcuts people use, including framing, statistical regression to the mean, the availability heuristic, the representative heuristic, ignoring the base rate, and escalation of commitment.

3 How can knowledge management improve decision making? Knowledge management makes employees smarter when it's carried out properly. By electronically storing information that employees have, organizations make it possible to share collective wisdom. As well, when new projects are started, individuals can see what others have done before them, to avoid going down unproductive paths.

4 What factors affect group decision making? Groups generate more complete information and knowledge, they offer increased diversity of views, they generate higher quality decisions, and they lead to increased acceptance of a solution. However, group decisions are time-consuming. They also lead to conformity pressures and the group discussion can be dominated by one or a few members. Finally, group decisions suffer from ambiguous responsibility, and the responsibility of any single member is watered down. Groups can suffer from groupthink and/or groupshift. Under groupthink, the group emphasizes agreement above everything else, often shutting down individuals who express any disagreement with the group's actions. In groupshift, the group takes a more extreme position (either more conservative or more risky) than individuals would take on their own.

5 **Should the leader make the decision, or encourage the group to participate?** The revised leadership-participation model uses a decision tree to determine whether the leader should make the decision alone or incorporate some level of group participation. The factors in the model include the quality of the decision required, the degree of commitment needed from participants, and the time available to make the decision.

6 **How can we get more creative decisions?** While there is some evidence that individuals vary in their ability to be creative, we also know that individuals are more creative when they are motivated by intrinsic interest, challenge, task satisfaction, and self-set goals. Five organizational factors have been found that can block creativity at work: (1) expected evaluation—focusing on how work is going to be evaluated; (2) surveillance—being watched while working; (3) external motivators—focusing on external, tangible rewards; (4) competition—facing win-lose situations with peers; and (5) constrained choice—being given limits on how to do the work.

7 **What is ethics, and how can it be used for better decision making?** Ethics is the study of moral values or principles that guide our behaviour, and inform us whether actions are right or wrong. Ethical principles help us "do the right thing." An individual can use four different criteria in making ethical choices. The first is the utilitarian criterion, in which decisions are made solely on the basis of their outcomes or consequences. The second ethical criterion is to focus on rights. This means respecting and protecting the basic rights of individuals. The third ethical criterion is to focus on justice. This requires individuals to impose and enforce rules fairly and impartially so there is an equitable distribution of benefits and costs. The fourth ethical criterion is to focus on care. The care criterion suggests that we should be aware of the needs, desires, and well-being of those to whom we are closely connected. There are advantages and disadvantages to each of these criteria.

8 **What is corporate social responsibility?** Corporate social responsibility is defined as an organization's responsibility to consider the impact of its decisions on society. Thus, organizations may try to better society, through such things as charitable contributions or providing better wages to employees working in offshore factories. Organizations may engage in these practices because they feel pressured by society to do so, or they may seek ways to improve society because they feel it is the right thing to do.

For Review

1. What is the rational decision-making model? Under what conditions is it applicable?

2. Describe organizational factors that might constrain decision makers.

3. What role does intuition play in effective decision making?

4. What is groupthink? What is its effect on decision-making quality?

5. What is groupshift? What is its effect on decision-making quality?

6. Identify five organizational factors that block creativity at work.

7. Describe the four criteria that individuals can use in making ethical decisions.

8. Are unethical decisions more a function of the individual decision maker or the decision maker's work environment? Explain.

For Critical Thinking

1. "For the most part, individual decision making in organizations is an irrational process." Do you agree or disagree? Discuss.

2. What factors do you think differentiate good decision makers from poor ones? Relate your answer to the six-step rational decision-making model.

3. Have you ever increased your commitment to a failed course of action? If so, analyze the follow-up decision to increase your commitment and explain why you behaved as you did.

4. If group decisions are of consistently better quality than individual decisions, how did the phrase "a camel is a horse designed by a committee" become so popular and ingrained in our culture?

OB for You

- In some decision situations, consider following the rational decision-making model. Doing so will ensure that you review a wider variety of options before committing to a particular decision.

- Analyze the decision situation and be aware of your biases. We all bring biases to the decisions we make. Combine rational analysis with intuition. As you gain experience, you should feel increasingly confident in imposing your intuitive processes on top of your rational analysis.

- Use creativity-stimulation techniques. You can improve your overall decision-making effectiveness by searching for innovative solutions to problems. This can be as basic as telling yourself to think creatively and to look specifically for unique alternatives.

- When making decisions, think about their ethical implications. A quick way to do this is to ask yourself: Would I be embarrassed if this action were printed on the front page of the newspaper?

OB *AT WORK*

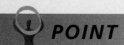

POINT

Organizations Should Just Stick to the Bottom Line

The major goals of organizations are and should be efficiency, productivity, and high profits. By maximizing profits, businesses ensure that they will survive and thus make it possible to provide employment. Doing so is in the best interests of the organization, employees, and stockholders. Moreover, it's up to individuals to show that they are concerned about the environment through their investment and purchasing activities, not for corporations to lead the way.

Let's examine some of the reasons why it's not economically feasible to place the entire burden of protecting the environment on the shoulders of big business.

Studies show that environmental regulations are too costly. The Conference Board of Canada suggested that environmental regulations cost Canadian companies $580 million to $600 million a year.[106] The Fraser Institute in Vancouver reported that all regulations, including those designed to protect the environment, cost Canadian industry $85 billion a year.[107]

Environmental regulations can also be harmful to jobs. In British Columbia, the Forest Practices Code is said to have added $1 billion a year to harvesting costs and resulted in a number of job cuts.

While businesses are concerned with the high cost that results from environmental regulations, the general public are not completely supportive of protecting the environment either, particularly if it will inconvenience them.[108]

Companies would be better off sticking to the bottom line, and governments should stay away from imposing costly environmental regulations on business. Stringent environmental standards cause trade distortions, and governments rarely consider the cost of complying with regulations. Companies should be allowed to take their lead from shareholders and customers. If these constituencies want businesses to pay for environmental protection, they will indicate this by investing in firms that do so. Until they do, the cost of environmental legislation is simply too high.

COUNTERPOINT

Environmental Responsibility Is Part of the Bottom Line

Going green makes good economic sense. The studies reported in the *Point* argument tend to overstate the cost of environmental regulations.[109] They do not consider the benefits to society of those regulations.

A closer look at a few companies that have devoted efforts to being more environmentally friendly will illustrate the benefits of this approach. When Quaker Oats Canada started working toward a "greener" work environment, its Peterborough, Ontario, plant saved more than $1 million in three years through various environmental initiatives.[110]

As another example, Inco spent $600 million to change the way it produces nickel at its Sudbury, Ontario, operations in order to be less devastating to the local environment. Its new smelting process is the most energy-efficient and environmentally friendly process in the world. Inco continues to work to restore the appearance of Sudbury. Trees have grown back, the wildlife has returned, and the air is clean. Sudbury has even been listed as one of the 10 most desirable places to live in Canada. While Inco invested a lot of money to change its production process, Doug Hamilton, controller at Inco's Ontario division in Sudbury, says, "Our Sulphur Dioxide Abatement Program was an awesome undertaking. Not only did this investment allow us to capture 90 percent of the sulphur in the ore we mine, but the new processes save the company $90 million a year in production costs. That strikes me as a pretty smart investment."[111]

London, Ontario-based 3M Canada started a Pollution Prevention Pays (3P) program more than 20 years ago.[112] The program emphasizes stopping pollution at the source to avoid the expense and effort of cleaning it up or treating it after the fact. The recycling program at 3M Canada's tape plant in Perth, Ontario, reduced its waste by 96 percent and saved the company about $650 000 annually. The capital cost for the program was only $30 000.

The examples of Quaker Oats, Inco, and 3M show that companies that are environmentally friendly have an advantage over their competitors. If organizations control their pollution costs better than their competitors, they will use their resources more efficiently and therefore increase profitability.

HR IMPLICATIONS

Developing Corporate Ethics Policies

Canadian corporations have chosen a variety of ways to implement ethics programs. These include developing training sessions, writing out explicit codes, making more general principles, or developing a culture of ethics. In the examples below, we indicate companies that have chosen one or more of these ways of developing their ethics approach.[113]

Brampton, Ontario-based Nortel Networks revised its "Guide to Ethical Business Practices" in 2004, in response to financial reporting issues in the telecom industry. The guide directs employees to act in accordance with the company's core values when trying to decide on ethical business practices. These core values are:[114]

- Customers are the driving force.

- People are our strength.

- Quality is in every aspect.

- Innovation fuels our future.

- Accountability brings clarity.

- Integrity underpins everything.

The guide is required reading for all employees, and copies of it are found on its intranet and Internet sites. Posting it on the Internet has alerted those outside Nortel to the importance the company places on corporate ethics.

Nortel hired a senior ethics adviser in 2005, several years after the previous one left in 1998. Nortel includes ethics training modules as part of its new employee training, and newly promoted managers receive ethics modules. Nortel produces the modules locally, so that the relevant business examples are provided in the proper cultural context.

In 1995, the Department of National Defence and Canadian Forces appointed a team headed by Rosalie Bernier to develop a statement of ethics that would apply across all ranks and divisions of the department, both military and bureaucratic. Bernier, who was manager of the Defence Ethics Program at the Department of Defence, noted that the team tried to take a positive approach by establishing a set of values rather than rules. The core values are loyalty, honesty, courage, diligence, fairness, and responsibility. There are also three principles to frame the values: "to respect the dignity of all persons; to serve Canada before self; and to obey and support lawful authority."[115] The Department's website provides extensive information about acting ethically, and includes a self-assessment tool to help leaders evaluate the ethical climate in their unit or section.[116]

At the Bank of Montreal (BMO), all employees are asked to read "First Principles," BMO's comprehensive code of business conduct and ethics, once a year, and sign a document indicating that this has been done. "First Principles" encourages employees to consider the questions "Is it fair? Is it right? Is it legal?" before engaging in any actions related to their job.[117]

Shell Canada's code of ethics states the following:

Shell Canada's reputation and credibility are based upon its total commitment to ethical business practices. To safeguard the Shell reputation, employees must conduct themselves in accordance with the highest ethical standards and also be perceived to be acting ethically at all times.[118]

Shell Canada's code requires the following conduct of all employees:

- Acting with honesty and integrity and being open in dealings with customers, employees, shareholders, and others with whom Shell does business.

- Treating others with fairness, dignity, and respect to create and protect a trusting environment free from harassment and discrimination.

- Striving for excellence and professionalism, taking pride in what we do individually and as part of a team.

It should be obvious from these examples that there is no one right way to introduce ethics to employees, and that it also takes some realistic planning to do so.

LEARNING ABOUT **YOURSELF** EXERCISE

Decision-Making Style Questionnaire

Circle the response that comes closest to how you usually feel or act. There are no right or wrong responses to any of these items.

1. I am more careful about

    a. people's feelings   **b.** their rights

2. I usually get along better with

    a. imaginative people   **b.** realistic people

3. It's a higher compliment to be called

    a. a person of real feeling   **b.** a consistently reasonable person

4. In doing something with other people, it appeals more to me

    a. to do it in the accepted way   **b.** to invent a way of my own

5. I get more annoyed at

    a. fancy theories   **b.** people who do not like theories

6. It's higher praise to call someone

    a. a person of vision   **b.** a person of common sense

7. I more often let

    a. my heart rule my head   **b.** my head rule my heart

8. I think it's a worse fault

    a. to show too much warmth   **b.** to be unsympathetic

9. If I were a teacher, I would rather teach

    a. courses involving theory   **b.** factual courses

Which word in the following pairs appeals to you more? Circle a or b.

10. **a.** Compassion   **b.** Foresight

11. **a.** Justice   **b.** Mercy

12. **a.** Production   **b.** Design

13. **a.** Gentle   **b.** Firm

14. **a.** Uncritical   **b.** Critical

15. **a.** Literal   **b.** Figurative

16. **a.** Imaginative   **b.** Matter-of-fact

Scoring Key:

Mark each of your responses on the following scales. Then use the point value column to arrive at your score. For example, if you answered a to the first question, you would check 1a in the Feeling column. This response receives zero points when you add up the point value column. Instructions for classifying your scores are indicated following the scales.

Sensation	Point Value	Intuition	Point Value	Thinking	Point Value	Feeling	Point Value
2b _____	1	2a _____	2	1b _____	1	1a _____	0
4a _____	1	4b _____	1	3b _____	2	3a _____	1
5a _____	1	5b _____	1	7b _____	1	7a _____	1
6b _____	1	6a _____	0	8a _____	0	8b _____	1
9b _____	2	9a _____	2	10b _____	2	10a _____	1
12a _____	1	12b _____	0	11a _____	2	11b _____	1
15a _____	1	15b _____	1	13b _____	1	13a _____	1
16b _____	2	16a _____	0	14b _____	0	14a _____	1

| Maximum Point Value | (10) | | (7) | | (9) | | (7) |

Circle *Intuition* if your Intuition score is equal to or greater than your Sensation score. Circle *Sensation* if your Sensation score is greater than your Intuition score. Circle *Feeling* if your Feeling score is greater than your Thinking score. Circle *Thinking* if your Thinking score is greater than your Feeling score.

A high score on *Intuition* indicates you see the world in holistic terms. You tend to be creative. A high score on *Sensation* indicates that you are realistic and see the world in terms of facts. A high score on *Feeling* means you make decisions based on gut feeling. A high score on *Thinking* indicates a highly logical and analytical approach to decision making.

Sources: Based on a personality scale developed by D. Hellriegel, J. Slocum, and R.W. Woodman, *Organizational Behavior,* 3rd ed. (St. Paul, MN: West Publishing, 1983), pp. 127–141, and reproduced in J. M. Ivancevich and M. T. Matteson, *Organizational Behavior and Management,* 2nd ed. (Homewood, IL: BPI/Irwin, 1990), pp. 538–539.

BREAKOUT **GROUP** EXERCISES

Form small groups to discuss the following topics, as assigned by your instructor:

1. Apply the rational decision-making model to deciding where your group might eat dinner this evening. How closely were you able to follow the rational model in making this decision?

2. The company that makes your favourite snack product has been accused of being weak in its social responsibility efforts. What impact will this have on your purchase of any more products from that company?

3. You've seen a classmate cheat on an exam or an assignment. Do you do something about this or ignore it?

WORKING WITH **OTHERS** EXERCISE

Individual vs. Group Decision Making

1. Read each of the cases on page 464, and using the revised leadership-participation model in Exhibit 12-6 on page 445, select the appropriate decision style for each case.

2. Your instructor will divide the class into small groups in which you will be asked to reach a consensus about the appropriate decision style.

3. A group spokesperson will be asked to present the group's response and the rationale for this decision.

Case 1

Assume that you are a production manager, and one of your responsibilities is to order the materials used by your employees to manufacture wheels. A large stockpile of material sitting idle is costly, but having idle workers because there are not enough materials also costs money. Based on past records, you have been able to determine with considerable accuracy which materials employees will need a few weeks in advance. The purchase orders are written up by the Purchasing Office, not by your employees.

How would you decide how much material you should order? Specifically, would you tell the Purchasing Office how much to order, or would you first ask your employees what they think? Why?

Case 2

Assume that you are the vice-president for production in a small computer-assembly company. Your plant is working close to capacity to fill current orders. You have just been offered a contract to assemble 25 computers for a new customer. If the customer is pleased with the way you handle this order, additional orders are likely and the new customer could become one of your company's largest clients. You are confident that your production supervisors can handle the job, but it would impose a heavy burden on them in terms of rescheduling production, hiring extra workers, and working extra hours.

How would you decide whether to accept the new contract? Specifically, would you make the decision yourself, or would you ask others for help? Why?

Case 3

Assume that you have been appointed the chair of a committee formed to coordinate the interdependent activities of the marketing, production, and design departments in the company. Coordination problems have interfered with the flow of work, causing bottlenecks, delays, and wasted effort. The coordination problems are complex, and solving them requires knowledge of ongoing events in the different departments. Even though you are the designated chair, you have no formal authority over the other members, who are not your employees. You depend on committee members to return to their respective departments and implement the decisions made by the committee. You are pleased that most members appear to be sincerely interested in improving coordination among departments.

How would you make decisions about coordination? Specifically, would you decide how best to coordinate among the departments yourself, or would you ask others for help? Why?

Your instructor will discuss with you possible answers to these cases.

ETHICAL **DILEMMA** EXERCISE

Five Ethical Decisions: What Would You Do?

Assume you are a middle manager in a company with about 1000 employees. How would you respond to each of the following situations?

1. You are negotiating a contract with a potentially very large customer whose representative has hinted that you could almost certainly be assured of getting his business if you gave him and his wife an all-expenses-paid cruise to the Caribbean. You know the representative's employer would not approve of such a "payoff," but you have the discretion to authorize such an expenditure. What would you do?

2. You have the opportunity to steal $100 000 from your company with absolute certainty that

you would not be detected or caught. Would you do it?

3. Your company policy on reimbursement for meals while travelling on company business is that you will be repaid for your out-of-pocket costs, which are not to exceed $50 a day. You don't need receipts for these expenses—the company will take your word. When travelling, you tend to eat at fast-food places and rarely spend in excess of $15 a day. Most of your colleagues submit reimbursement requests in the range of $40 to $45 a day regardless of what their actual expenses are. How much would you request for your meal reimbursements?

4. You want to get feedback from people who are using one of your competitor's products. You believe you will get much more honest responses from these people if you disguise the identity of your company. Your boss suggests you contact possible participants by using the fictitious name of the Consumer Marketing Research Corporation. What would you do?

5. You have discovered that one of your closest friends at work has stolen a large sum of money from the company. Would you do nothing? Go directly to an executive to report the incident before talking about it with the offender? Confront the individual before taking action? Make contact with the individual with the goal of persuading that person to return the money?

Source: Several of these scenarios are based on D. R. Altany, "Torn Between Halo and Horns," *IndustryWeek,* March 15, 1993, pp. 15–20.

Bankers' Excess Gets Them Fired

Five bond and derivatives specialists from Barclays PLC of London were dismissed after a dinner celebrating a major bond and derivatives deal. The dinner tab came to $97 736. Initial reports of the incident suggested that the investment bankers had purchased the dinners with their own funds. Most of the bill was for five bottles of vintage wine; one bottle alone cost $27 244.

Barclays knew about the dinner for nearly seven months before firing the employees. Petrus, the restaurant in London's St. James district where the dinner occurred, gave details of the bill to the media right after the meal. Initially, the bank suggested that "this is a matter on personal time, it didn't involve clients, it was personal money." Some press reports later suggested that the bankers tried to claim some of the meal expenses as client expenses, but these could not be confirmed.

In the wake of the Enron scandal, which led to massive cutbacks in the brokerage industry and concern about corporate excesses, Barclays rethought its decision. The dinner was viewed as outrageously extravagant, and reflecting poorly on Barclays' investment bankers.

Questions

1. Would you have fired the five investment bankers? Why or why not?

2. Did the bankers do anything unethical?

3. How can decision-making processes be used to explain why Barclays changed its initial response of "this is private" to something more serious later?

Sources: "Barclays Finds Lavish Dinner Indigestible, Lets Bankers Go," *Globe and Mail,* February 26, 2002, p. B2; and J. Lawless, "Bankers Hold Record for Most Costly Meal," *Salon,* February 26, 2002, www.salon.com/people/wire/2002/02/26/bankers_meal/index.html (accessed February 27, 2002).

Syncrude Wants to be a Good Neighbour

Fort McMurray, Alberta-based Syncrude is "the largest non-governmental employer of Aboriginal people in Canada." The company, the largest producer of light sweet crude oil from oil sand, is strongly committed to working with the Aboriginal community. According to Syncrude's website, "Commitment to the Aboriginal people of our region is not only motivated by our responsibility as a good corporate citizen, but by our desire to be a good neighbour."

In order to make sure that members of the Aboriginal community are employable, Syncrude provides them with skill training, before they are even considered for hiring.

This makes it possible for Aboriginal people to compete for jobs in the oil sands industry on an equal footing with non-Aboriginal people. Nora Flett, Syncrude's Aboriginal affairs representative, explains that companies cannot just hire Aboriginal people directly without training, "because you don't just take someone from a small community, put them in a big corporation environment and expect that people will survive there, because that's quite a bit of a culture shock."

In addition to being sensitive to the employment needs of the Aboriginal community, Syncrude is committed to being a good neighbour in the community. The company gives preference to local suppliers to help the local population benefit economically from Syncrude's presence. Syncrude supports literacy programs for schools. As well, employment counsellors offer advice about the company, helping Aboriginal families learn about the company and what is expected of its employees.

Questions

1. What benefits do you think Syncrude might derive from being a good neighbour in Fort McMurray?

2. Should the company engage in practices that help the Aboriginal community, even if it means that the return to shareholders isn't as large?

3. How does social responsibility explain what Syncrude does?

Sources: A. Kellogg, "Punch the Query 'Canada's Best Major Corporate Citizen' into Google on Your Computer and It's Likely the Image of Eric Newell Will Pop Up," *Calgary Herald,* November 30, 2003, p. C2; C. Petten, "Syncrude, Cameco Strike Gold With PAR," *Windspeaker,* March 2002, pp. B7–B8; www.syncrude.com/community/aboriginal.html; and www.syncrude.com/business/business_04.html#4b.

From **Concepts**
to **Skills**

Solving Problems Creatively

You can be more effective at solving problems creatively if you use the following 10 suggestions:[119]

1. *Think of yourself as creative.* Research shows that if you think you can't be creative, you won't be. Believing in your ability to be creative is the first step in becoming more creative.

2. *Pay attention to your intuition.* Every individual has a subconscious mind that works well. Sometimes answers will come to you when you least expect them. Listen to that "inner voice." In fact, most creative people will keep a notepad near their bed and write down ideas when the thoughts come to them.

3. *Move away from your comfort zone.* Every individual has a comfort zone in which certainty exists. But creativity and the known often do not mix. To be creative, you need to move away from the status quo and focus your mind on something new.

4. *Determine what you want to do.* This includes such things as taking time to understand a problem before beginning to try to resolve it, getting all the facts in mind, and trying to identify the most important facts.

5. *Think outside the box.* Use analogies whenever possible (e.g., could you approach your problem like a fish out of water and look at what the fish does to cope? Or can you use the things you

have to do to find your way when it's foggy to help you solve your problem?). Use different problem-solving strategies, such as verbal, visual, mathematical, or theatrical. Look at your problem from a different perspective or ask yourself what someone else, like your grandmother, might do if faced with the same situation.

6. *Look for ways to do things better.* This may involve trying consciously to be original, not worrying about looking foolish, keeping an open mind, being alert to odd or puzzling facts, thinking of unconventional ways to use objects and the environment, discarding usual or habitual ways of doing things, and striving for objectivity by being as critical of your own ideas as you would be of someone else's.

7. *Find several right answers.* Being creative means continuing to look for other solutions even when you think you have solved the problem. A better, more creative solution just might be found.

8. *Believe in finding a workable solution.* Like believing in yourself, you also need to believe in your ideas. If you don't think you can find a solution, you probably won't.

9. *Brainstorm with others.* Creativity is not an isolated activity. Bouncing ideas off of others creates a synergistic effect.

10. *Turn creative ideas into action.* Coming up with creative ideas is only part of the process. Once the ideas are generated, they must be implemented. Keeping great ideas in your mind, or on papers that no one will read, does little to expand your creative abilities.

Assessing Skills

After you've read this chapter, take the following Self-Assessments on your enclosed CD-ROM:

   5.   How Creative Am I?

   20.   What's My Decision-Making Style?

   22.   How Do My Ethics Rate?

Practising Skills

Every time the phone rings, your stomach clenches and your palms start to sweat. And it's no wonder! As sales manager for Brinkers, a machine tool parts manufacturer, you are besieged by calls from customers who are upset about late deliveries. Your boss, Carter Hererra, acts as both production manager and scheduler. Every time your sales representatives negotiate a sale, it's up to Carter to determine whether production can actually meet the delivery date the customer specifies. And Carter invariably says, "No problem." The good thing about this is that you make a lot of initial sales. The bad news is that production hardly ever meets the shipment dates that Carter authorizes. And he does not seem to be all that concerned about the aftermath of late deliveries. He says: "Our customers know they're getting outstanding quality at a great price. Just let them try to match that anywhere. It can't be done. So even if they have to wait a couple of extra days or weeks, they're still getting the best deal they can." Somehow the customers do not see it that way. And they let you know about their unhappiness. Then it's up to you to try to soothe the relationship. You know this problem has to be taken care of, but what possible solutions are there? After all, how are you going to keep from making your manager angry or making the customers angry? Use your knowledge of creative problem-solving to come up with solutions.

Reinforcing Skills

1.   Take 20 minutes to list as many medical or health-care-related jobs as you can that begin with the letter *r* (for instance, radiologist, registered nurse). If you run out of listings before time is up, it's OK to quit early. But try to be as creative as you can.

2.   List on a piece of paper some common terms that apply to both *water* and *finance*. How many were you able to come up with?

Spirituality in the Workplace

Entrepreneur Robin Kirby (shown above) represents clothing manufacturers; she meets with retailers to sell them clothes produced by the factories she represents.[1] She also markets a line of her own clothing on The Shopping Channel.

Kirby is passionate about spiritual connections and the healing arts. "I'm a reiki master and I do crystal bowl healing. I'm known as 'the white witch' among my menswear clients." Kirby sometimes carries a deep crystal bowl and a rubber striker, which she uses to create tones that she says clear "difficult energies from the spaces she visits."

Kirby recently cleared the energy at a client's knitwear factory and showroom, after she arrived to find the staff and the client looking stressed out. She used prayers, meditations, and bowl-ringing to do this. The employees later told her that the workplace stayed calm for a week after she did her energy clearing, and they wanted her to come back and do it again.

What Is Spirituality?

In a study to determine what people mean by *spirituality,* the following elements were identified:[2]

- Not formal, structured, or organized

- Nondenominational, above and beyond denominations

- Broadly inclusive, embracing everyone; universal and timeless

- The ultimate source and provider of meaning and purpose in life

- The awe we feel in the presence of the transcendent

- The sacredness of everything, the ordinariness of everyday life

- The deep feeling of the interconnectedness of everything

- Inner peace and calm

- An inexhaustible source of faith and willpower

- The ultimate end in itself

In general, three streams of definitions have been identified. One stream defines spirituality in terms of a personal inner experience based on "interconnectedness."[3] A second stream focuses on "principles, virtues, ethics, values, emotions, wisdom, and intuition."[4] Organizations are then considered spiritual to the extent that they hold these values. Finally, a third stream considers spirituality as the link between one's "personal inner experience" and how this is modelled in "outer behaviours, principles, and practices."[5]

Comparing Spirituality and Religion

Spirituality and religion are not the same thing, although it's sometimes difficult to reach precise definitions of each term. One of the few empirical studies of spirituality in the workplace was conducted by Ian Mitroff and Elizabeth Denton.[6] Though the response rate to their mailed survey was low, they corroborated many of their findings through interviews with human resource managers and senior managers at other organizations. They discovered that individuals fall into four patterns in terms of how they view the relationship between religion and spirituality:

- *A person can view religion and spirituality positively.* This person sees religion and spirituality as synonymous, with spirituality developed through religious practices. About 30 percent of the participants fell into this category.

- *A person can view religion positively but spirituality negatively.* This person focuses on the rituals and the practices of a particular religion. The emphasis is on salvation and being a member of a closely bound, shared community. About 2 percent of the participants fell into this category.

- *A person can view religion negatively, while viewing spirituality positively.* This person sees religion as "organized, close-minded, and intolerant." Spirituality, by contrast, is viewed as "open-minded, tolerant, and universal," and intended to be a bonding force. About 60 percent of the participants fell into this category.

- *Finally, a person can view both religion and spirituality negatively.* This person believes that "religion and spirituality have nothing to do with the modern, secular workplace." About 8 percent of the participants fell into this category.

These findings suggest that workplace spirituality is *not* about organized religious practices. It's not about God or theology. Workplace spirituality recognizes that people have an inner life that nourishes and is nourished by meaningful work that takes place in the context of community.[7] Organizations that promote a spiritual culture recognize that people have both a mind and a spirit, seek to find meaning and purpose in their work, and desire to connect with other human beings and be part of a community.

For instance, at Montreal-based Ouimet-Cordon Bleu Foods, a processed-foods company, CEO J.-Robert Ouimet has installed meditation rooms in all of his factories. He took his idea from a conversation he had with Mother Teresa. "There is no talking or eating allowed—only silence. The idea is to give the workplace a feeling of serenity and a sense of higher purpose," he explains.[8] Ouimet wants his workplace to be not only a place where goods are produced, but also where employees find their lives enriched. He believes such practices as meditation rooms, prayers before meetings, and other "soulful initiatives" increase "not only human happiness and well-being, but company profitability as well."[9]

Another company that tries to encourage employees to look beyond themselves is New Hampshire-based The Timberland Company, where boots symbolize what customers and employees are supposed to do: "Pull on your boots and make a difference."[10] The company pays its employees for up to 40 hours of volunteer work a year. It has also developed a plan for employees to apply for six-month paid sabbaticals if they want to give service to a nonprofit organization. Jeffrey B. Swartz, the company's president and CEO, believes that "doing well" and "doing good" help make this family-owned firm successful.

Why Spirituality Now?

Employees working for the District of North Vancouver take workshops to help them develop personal and professional effectiveness.[11] The workshops are led by Tanis Helliwell, a therapist in Vancouver, and are based on her book *Take Your Soul to Work*.[12] David Stuart, director of corporate services at the District of North Vancouver, read her book and decided that the municipality's 600 employees, be they ditch diggers or architects, would benefit from its practices.

Helliwell believes that employers should help their employees develop their whole person, rather than just the "nine-to-five person." "The more people look at what they need to do in order to develop their potential and find work that will encompass that, the more the employer is going to get in the workplace," she says.

Stuart says that the response to the workshops has been "spectacular." "Workers are expecting more from their employment situation. They need tools to give them a sense that they can in fact control what's happening in their lives and the changes happening around them and how they deal with them," he explains.

Workplace spirituality is a relatively new phenomenon. Historical models of management and organizational behaviour had no room for spirituality. The myth of rationality assumed that the well-run organization eliminated feelings. Similarly, concern about an employee's inner life had no role in the perfectly rational model. But just as we have now come to realize that the study

of emotions improves our understanding of organizational behaviour, an awareness of spirituality can help us better understand employee behaviour in the twenty-first century.

The Sobey School of Business at Saint Mary's University in Halifax has taken the lead in Canada for trying

Reasons for the Growing Interest in Spirituality

- Spirituality acts as a counterbalance to the pressures and stress of a turbulent pace of life. Contemporary lifestyles—single-parent families, geographic mobility, the temporary nature of jobs, new technologies that create distance between people—underscore the lack of community many people feel and increase the need for involvement and connection.

- Aging Baby Boomers, reaching mid-life, are looking for something meaningful in their lives.

- Formalized religion has not worked for many people, and they continue to look for anchors to replace lack of faith and to fill a growing feeling of emptiness.

- Job demands have made the workplace dominant in many people's lives, yet they continue to question the meaning of work.

- More people desire to integrate personal life values with their professional life.

- In times of economic plenty, more people have the luxury to engage in a search to reach their full potential.

to understand the implications of spirituality in the workplace. In fall 2004, the Sobey School of Business opened a centre devoted to teaching and studying spirituality in the workplace. The Centre for Spirituality in the Workplace is the first academic-based centre of its kind in Canada, though there are such centres in the United States and overseas.

"The centre is not devoted to religious dogma and theology," Allan Miciak, dean of the Sobey School of Business, explains. Spirituality at work is about "creating better workplaces," he adds.[13]

Martin Rutte, co-author of *Chicken Soup for the Soul at Work*,[14] who spoke at a conference that marked the centre's opening, notes that Baby Boomers are in the midst of questioning what life is all about, and "the corporate world has offered them fewer answers than ever."[15]

"Over the past several years, there have been dramatic changes in the world of work, such as corporate downsizing, that have forced people to do more with less, and technologies that have replaced people," Rutte says. "These things have broken the feeling of security that came with work and changed people's attitudes about their jobs."[16]

We summarize additional reasons why people are turning to spirituality in the inset *Reasons for the Growing Interest in Spirituality*.

Characteristics of a Spiritual Organization

Spiritual organizations are concerned with helping people develop and reach their full potential. This is analogous to Abraham Maslow's description of self-actualization that we discussed in relation to motivation. Similarly, organizations that are concerned with spirituality are more likely to directly address problems created by conflicts that occur in everyday life.

Sister Mangalam Lena, of the Franciscan Missionaries of Mary, started Ottawa-based Home-based Spiritual Care (HBSC) to help recovering patients in their homes. "[Traditional] home-care provides nursing, counselling, and physiotherapy for the home-bound. But who cares for their spiritual needs in the home?" she asked.[17] This led to the start of her business. Lena believes that "people who are spiritually healthy are also physically healthier." She has convinced researchers at the University of Ottawa, including Dian Prud'homme Brisson, assistant director of the university's nursing program, to study the effects of such care.

What differentiates spiritual organizations from their nonspiritual counterparts? Although research on this question is only preliminary, our review identified five cultural characteristics that tend to be evident in spiritual organizations.[18]

Strong Sense of Purpose

Spiritual organizations build their cultures around a meaningful purpose. While profits may be important, they are not necessarily the primary value of these organizations. Ben & Jerry's Homemade, for example, has closely intermeshed socially responsible behaviour with its producing and selling of ice cream. The company gives donations to environmental and civil rights causes in the developing world.

Charllotte Kwon, owner and CEO of Vancouver-based Maiwa Handprints, pays the artisans from developing countries who provide textiles for her retail stores substantially more than what others pay them. She wants to protect crafts-

people, so that they can continue to produce their artwork. She also notes that she doesn't need to pay minimum prices to survive: "I live okay. I don't need anything more."[19]

Focus on Individual Development

Spiritual organizations recognize the worth and value of people. They are not just providing jobs. They seek to create cultures in which employees can continually learn and grow.

Recognizing the importance of people, they also try to provide employment security.

Trust and Openness

Spiritual organizations are characterized by mutual trust, honesty, and openness. Managers are not afraid to admit mistakes. They tend to be extremely upfront with their employees, customers, and suppliers. The president of Wetherill Associates, a highly successful American auto parts distribution

---

Organizational Models for Fostering Spirituality

- **Religious-Based Organization:** Organization's practices are consistent with biblical teachings; emphasis on prayer as a primary form of intrafirm communication; employees expected to accept core Christian principles as guides to decision making.

- **Evolutionary Organization:** Spiritual openness is encouraged; the guiding texts are a mixture of Christian scriptures and philosophical works (Kant, Neibuhr, Buber); emphasis on serving the customer, preserving the environment, and respecting stakeholders.

- **Recovering Organization:** Organization models itself after the 12-step program of Alcoholics Anonymous; spirituality discussed in ways that are acceptable to the largest number of people. The 12-step program emphasizes confession (of failures), acceptance of God's will and guidance, and reliance on the help of others. Infrequently found in the business world.

- **Socially Responsible Organization:** Social concerns and values are part of everyday business activity; emphasizes expression of individual's "whole person" and soul; customers, suppliers, and other stakeholders are expected to bond more readily to the firm; spirituality and soul are explicit core business principles.

- **Values-Based Organization:** Organization firmly rejects all notions of religious doctrine; favours nonreligious and nonspiritual secular values or virtues (e.g., awareness, consciousness, dignity, honesty, openness, respect, integrity, and, above all, trust); values are guides for policy setting and decision making throughout the firm. The Golden Rule is the prime business principle.

- **Best-Practice Model:** Organization combines parts of all of the above models; emphasizes values-based secular orientation; adds an openly expressed spiritual dimension; emphasizes the importance of "a higher power," periodic moral audits, and a broadly inclusive approach to stakeholders.

Source: I. I. Mitroff and E. A. Denton, *A Spiritual Audit of Corporate America: A Hard Look at Spirituality, Religion, and Values in the Workplace* (San Francisco: Jossey-Bass, 1999).

firm, says, "We don't tell lies here, and everyone knows it. We are specific and honest about quality and suitability of the product for our customers' needs, even if we know they might not be able to detect any problem."[20]

Employee Empowerment

The high-trust climate in spiritual organizations, when combined with the desire to promote employee learning and growth, leads to management empowering employees to make many work-related decisions. Managers in such organizations are comfortable delegating authority to individual employees and teams. They trust their employees to make thoughtful and conscientious decisions. Southwest Airlines exhibits these kinds of values when its employees—including flight attendants, customer-service representatives, and baggage handlers—are encouraged to take whatever action they deem necessary to meet customer needs or help fellow employees, even if it means breaking company policies.

Toleration of Employee Expression

Finally, spiritual organizations don't stifle employee emotions. They allow people to be themselves—to express their moods and feelings without guilt or fear of reprimand. Employees at Southwest Airlines, for instance, are encouraged to express their sense of humour on the job, to act spontaneously, and to make their work fun.

At Ouimet-Cordon Bleu Foods, employees are encouraged to have annual one-on-one meetings with their managers, where employees can express any and all frustrations, without worrying that something nega-

tive will happen to them. When Ouimet first introduced this practice, employees were reluctant to voice their concerns. As Ouimet notes, "Over time, a sense of trust developed."[21] Ouimet's employees are also encouraged to engage in "gestures of reconciliation," where they apologize to one another when interpersonal conflicts arise. Ouimet says he sets the example by apologizing when he's "blown a gasket."

The inset *Organizational Models for Fostering Spirituality* describes models for spiritually based organizations.

Criticisms of Spirituality

Critics of organizations embracing spiritual values have focused on two issues. First is the question of legitimacy. Specifically, do organizations have the right to impose spiritual values on their employees? Second is the question of economics. Are spirituality and profits compatible?

On the first question, clearly it is possible that an emphasis on spirituality may make some employees uneasy. Critics might argue that secular institutions, especially business firms, have no business imposing spiritual values on employees. This criticism is undoubtedly valid when spirituality is defined as bringing religion and God into the workplace.[22] However, the criticism seems less stinging when the goal is limited to helping employees find meaning in their work lives. If the concerns listed in the inset *Reasons for the Growing Interest in Spirituality* truly characterize a growing segment of the workforce, maybe the time is right for more organizations to help employees find meaning and purpose in their work and to use the workplace as a source of community.

The issue of whether spirituality and profits are compatible objectives is certainly relevant for managers and investors in business. However limited it may be, there is evidence that the two objectives may be very compatible. A research study by a major consulting firm found that companies that introduced spiritually based techniques improved productivity and significantly reduced turnover.[23] Another study found organizations that provide their employees with opportunities for spiritual development outperformed those that did not.[24] Other studies also report that spirituality in organizations was positively related to creativity, employee satisfaction, team performance, and organizational commitment.[25]

The cynic will say that all this caring stuff is in fact merely good public relations. Even so, the results at both Southwest Airlines and Ouimet-Cordon Bleu Foods suggest that a caring organization is good for the bottom line. Southwest Airlines is strongly committed to providing the

FactBox

Maclean's year-end poll for 2001, which surveyed 1200 Canadians, found that since the terrorist attacks of September 11:

- 72% had become more appreciative of family life

- 26% had less interest in material wealth and possessions

- 23% felt a stronger need for religious beliefs

- 16% had a stronger desire to go to a place of worship

- 73% had not changed their view of the Islamic religion, for better or worse, because of the terrorist attacks

FACE**OFF**

Organizations that encourage spirituality as part of their culture are bound to have more positive bottom lines, as everyone in the organization will act more ethically.

An emphasis on spirituality at work distracts individuals from focusing on the demands of their job, and makes some people uncomfortable. It should not be encouraged.

lowest airfares, on-time service, and a pleasant experience for customers. Southwest employees have one of the lowest turnover rates in the airline industry, the company consistently has the lowest labour costs per miles flown of any major airline, and it has proven itself to be the most consistently profitable airline in the United States.[26] It is the only airline to remain profitable since the September 11, 2001, terrorist attacks.[27] Of Ouimet-Cordon Bleu Foods' 55 employees, 32 have been there for more than 20 years. Jacques Gingras, a production manager with the company, says Ouimet's practices really help the bottom line. "Obviously, people can't go to the silence rooms whenever they want, because we're running an assembly line. But they communicate well and respect one another. It makes the operation run more smoothly."[28]

Research Exercises

1. Look for data on the extent to which companies encourage spirituality in the workplace in the United States and Canada. Can you draw any inferences about whether there is a trend in this practice?

2. Identify three Canadian organizations or CEOs who have encouraged more openness toward spirituality in their organizations. What, if any, commonalities exist in these organizations?

Your Perspective

1. In this feature, we report on individuals' views on religion and spirituality. Do you see the two as linked or not linked?

2. What does spirituality mean to you?

Want to Know More?

Top brass at the Bank of Montreal read Ann Coombs' *The Living Workplace: Soul, Spirit and Success in the 21st Century* (Toronto: HarperCollins Canada, 2001), and were so impressed that they bought 800 copies, put the bank's logo on them, and started giving copies to their clients. Coombs is a Toronto-based corporate consultant, whose clients include Ford Canada, Campbell Soup Company, and Telus.

Other books to consider include Tom Chappel, *The Soul of a Business: Managing for Profit and the Common Good* (New York: Bantam Books, 1996); Matthew Fox, *The Reinvention of Work: A New Vision of Livelihood for Our Time* (New York: HarperCollins, 1994); and Herman Bryant Maynard Jr. and Susan E. Mehrtens, *The Fourth Wave: Business in the 21st Century* (San Francisco: Berrett-Koehler, 1993).

CHAPTER 13

Organizational Structure

What happens when an activity, such as filming a movie, needs to bring large groups of people together for a limited time? How do you design an organizational structure that will be flexible enough, yet ensure the work gets done?

1 What are the key elements of organizational structure?

2 How flexible can organizational structures be?

3 What are some examples of traditional organizational designs?

4 What do newer organizational structures look like?

5 Why do organizational structures differ?

Brollywood, the affectionate name given to the "new Hollywood North" located in Vancouver because of the frequent need for umbrellas (brollies) in the city, is just behind Los Angeles and New York in the size of its movie industry.[1] It's big in every way imaginable: more than a billion dollars a year, standard 60-hour weeks, substantia rewards. But, unlike the American c ties or Toronto or Montreal, Brollywood has no major entertainment ccmpany or television network attached to it.

Vancouver's film industry represents a new and unique form of organization. The entire industry is "made up of self-employed individuals, niche suppliers and production companies that start up and shut down in a matter of months." Companies don't get things done in Vancouver's film industry; teams of free agents do.

Brollywood's organizational structure is unique, although more organizations are developing flexible structures and developing long- and short-term partnerships to get specific tasks done.

The theme of this chapter is that organizations have different structures, determined by specific forces, and that these structures have a bearing on employee attitudes and behaviour. Organizations need to think carefully about the best way to organize how people inside and outside the organization are connected to each other. These connections form the basis for organizational structure.

WHAT IS ORGANIZATIONAL STRUCTURE?

An **organizational structure** defines how job tasks are formally divided, grouped, and coordinated. The structure can represent a tall pyramid, or it can be relatively flat. For instance, Exhibit 13-1 on page 476 shows a pyramidal organization with five layers (and some organizations have even more), while Exhibit 13-2 shows a flatter organization, with only three layers. The organizational structure can also be something intermediate between pyramid and flat. Among other things, the structure determines the reporting relationships of people. Thus, in a flat organization, if you have a problem, you can easily talk to the person at the top of the organization. In a pyramidal structure, you would talk to your manager, who might talk to his or her manager, who might talk to the manager above, until finally, if the message did actually reach the top of the organization, it might be very different from the original message you told your manager.

There are six key elements that managers need to address when they design their organization's structure: work specialization, departmentalization, chain of command, span of control, centralization and decentralization, and formalization.[2] Exhibit 13-3 on page 477 presents all of these elements as answers to an important structural question. The following sections describe these six elements of structure. Organizations do change their structures from time to time, which is known as *restructuring*. Often this involves layoffs. Despite the profound impact restructuring has on employees (discussed in detail in this chapter's *HR Implications* on page 503), managers realize that in a dynamic

1 What are the key elements of organizational structure?

organizational structure How job tasks are formally divided, grouped, and coordinated.

EXHIBIT 13-1 **Pyramidal Organizational Structure**

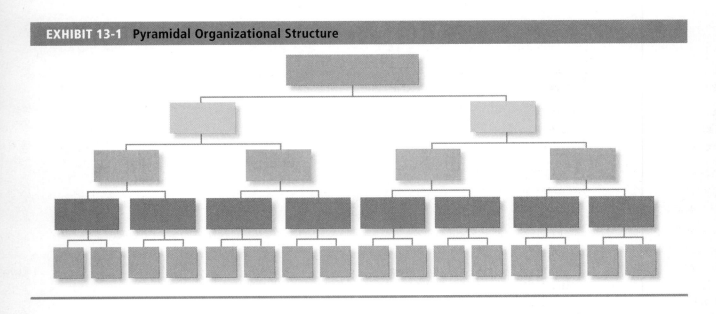

EXHIBIT 13-2 **Flat Organizational Structure**

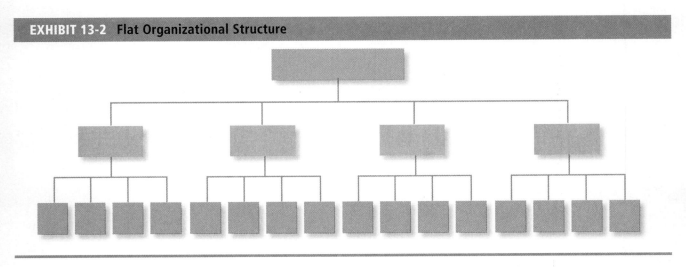

and changing environment, inflexible organizations end up as bankruptcy statistics. This chapter's *Case Incident—Ajax University Needs a New Structure* on page 507 provides an opportunity for you to consider how to change an organizational structure in order to resolve some of the problems the organization faces.

Work Specialization

work specialization The degree to which tasks in the organization are subdivided into separate jobs.

Wouldn't it be better if each person just did his or her same job over and over again?

We use the term **work specialization**, or *division of labour*, to describe the degree to which tasks in the organization are subdivided into separate jobs.

The essence of work specialization is that, rather than an entire job being completed by one individual, it's broken down into a number of steps, with each step being completed by a separate individual. In essence, individuals specialize in doing part of an activity rather than the entire activity.

Specialization can be efficient. Employee skills at performing a task improve through repetition. Less time is spent in changing tasks, in putting away tools and equipment from a prior step in the work process, and in preparing for another. It's easier and less costly to find and train workers to do specific and repetitive tasks. This is especially true of

EXHIBIT 13-3	Six Key Questions That Managers Need to Answer in Designing the Proper Organizational Structure	
The Key Question	**The Answer Is Provided By**
1. To what degree are tasks subdivided into separate jobs?	*Work specialization*
2. On what basis will jobs be grouped together?	*Departmentalization*
3. To whom do individuals and groups report?	*Chain of command*
4. How many individuals can a manager efficiently and effectively direct?	*Span of control*
5. Where does decision-making authority lie?	*Centralization and decentralization*
6. To what degree will there be rules and regulations to direct employees and managers?	*Formalization*

highly sophisticated and complex operations. For example, could Montreal-based Bombardier produce even one Canadian regional jet a year if one person had to build the entire plane alone? Not likely! Finally, work specialization increases efficiency and productivity by encouraging the creation of special inventions and machinery.

Specialization can lead to boredom, fatigue, stress, low productivity, poor quality, increased absenteeism, and high turnover, so it is not always the best way to organize employees. Giving employees a variety of activities to do, allowing them to do a whole and complete job, and putting them into teams with interchangeable skills can result in significantly higher output and increased employee satisfaction.

Organizations today exhibit a range of specialization. You will find, for example, high work specialization being used by McDonald's to make and sell hamburgers and fries efficiently, and by medical specialists in hospitals. On the other hand, companies such as Saturn have had success by broadening the scope of jobs and reducing specialization.

Individual Responses to Work Specialization

The evidence generally indicates that *work specialization* contributes to higher employee productivity but at the price of reduced job satisfaction. However, this statement ignores individual differences and the type of job tasks people do.

As we noted previously, productivity begins to suffer when the human diseconomies of doing repetitive and narrow tasks overtake the economies of specialization. As the workforce has become more highly educated and desirous of jobs that are intrinsically rewarding, the point where productivity begins to decline seems to be reached more quickly than in decades past.

However, some individuals want work that makes minimal intellectual demands and provides the security of routine. For these people, high work specialization is a source of job satisfaction.

Departmentalization

Once you've divided up jobs through work specialization, you need to group these jobs together so that common tasks can be coordinated. The basis on which jobs are grouped together is called **departmentalization**. One of the concerns in creating departmental groups is to prevent the creation of *silos* within the organization. Often departments start protecting their own turf, and not interacting well with other departments. This can lead to narrow vision with respect to organizational goals.

Bombardier
www.bombardier.com

McDonald's Canada
www.mcdonalds.ca/en/

Saturn Canada
www.saturncanada.com

departmentalization The basis on which jobs are grouped together.

Functional Departmentalization

One of the most popular ways to group activities is by *functions* performed. For example, a manufacturing company might separate engineering, accounting, manufacturing, human resource, and purchasing specialists into common departments. Similarly, a hospital might have departments devoted to research, patient care, accounting, and so forth. The major advantage to functional groupings is obtaining efficiencies from putting people with common skills and orientations together into common units. Exhibit 13-4 illustrates how the City of Kingston, in Ontario, organizes its departments by function. Note that the chart reveals four main functions: community services; operations; planning and development; and corporate services.

Product Departmentalization

Estée Lauder
www.esteelauder.com

Tasks can also be departmentalized by the type of *product* the organization produces. Estée Lauder, whose product lines include Clinique, Prescriptives, Origins, Canadian-created MAC Cosmetics, and Estée Lauder, operates each line as a distinct company. The major advantage to this type of grouping is increased accountability for product performance,

EXHIBIT 13-4   Departmentalization by Function

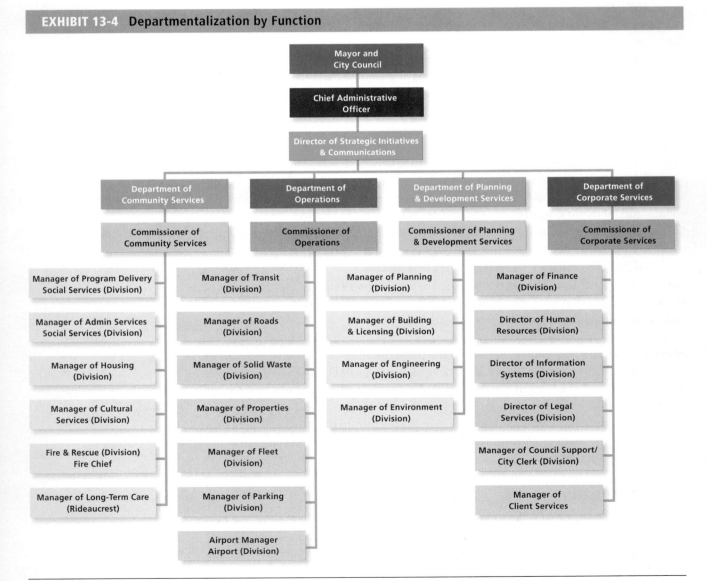

Source: www.cityofkingston.ca/pdf/cityhall/CityOrgChart2005.pdf. Reprinted by permission of the City of Kingston.

since all activities related to a specific product line are under the direction of a single manager. If an organization's activities are service—rather than product—related, each service would be grouped autonomously. For instance, many of the big accounting firms now call themselves "professional services firms" to reflect the variety of services they offer, including tax, management consulting, auditing, and the like. Each of the different services is under the direction of a product or service manager.

Exhibit 13-5 illustrates Brampton, Ontario-based Nortel Networks' four separate businesses, which are organized by product lines to make it easier to service very different customer needs. Wireless Networks is concerned with servicing wireless technologies and mobile networks. Enterprise Networks services Nortel's enterprise customers. Wireline Networks provides services to Nortel's service provider customers. Optical Networks provides optical transport and switching solutions and service to broadband services.

Geographic Departmentalization

Another way to departmentalize is on the basis of *geography*, or territory. The sales function, for instance, may be divided regionally with departments for British Columbia, the Prairies, Central Canada, and Atlantic Canada. Each of these regions is, in effect, a department organized around geography. If an organization's customers are scattered over a large geographic area and have similar needs based on their location, then this form of departmentalization can be valuable. Exhibit 13-6 on page 480 illustrates how the Royal Bank of Canada organizes itself by regional units (not all of its regional units are included in the exhibit, however).

Process Departmentalization

Some companies organize departments by the processing that occurs. For example, an aluminum tubing manufacturer might have the following departments: casting; press; tubing; finishing; and inspecting, packing, and shipping. This is an example of *process* departmentalization, because each department specializes in one specific phase in the production of aluminum tubing. Since each process requires different skills, this method offers a basis for the homogeneous categorizing of activities.

Process departmentalization can be used for processing customers, as well as products. For example, in some provinces, you may go through a series of steps handled by several departments before receiving your driver's licence: (1) validation by motor vehicles division; (2) processing by the licensing department; and (3) payment collection by the treasury department.

Until the mid-1990s, Montreal-based Hydro-Québec had been organized geographically, with each territory having its own business units responsible for production, transmission, and distribution for a total of 40 business units. However, they decided that being organized functionally made more sense. Now they have only six business units (Hydro-Québec Production, Hydro-Québec Pétrole et gaz, Hydro-Québec TransÉnergie, Hydro-Québec Distribution, Hydro-Québec Équipement, and Hydro-Québec Technologie et développement industriel). They expect this change in structure will lead to greater growth in business both inside and outside Quebec.

Hydro-Québec
www.hydroquebec.com/en/

Nortel Networks
www.nortelnetworks.com

Royal Bank of Canada
www.royalbank.com

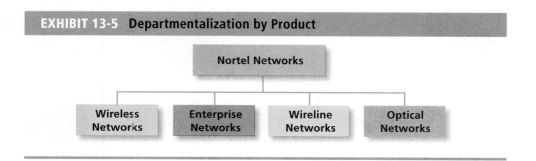

EXHIBIT 13-5 Departmentalization by Product

Nortel Networks — Wireless Networks, Enterprise Networks, Wireline Networks, Optical Networks

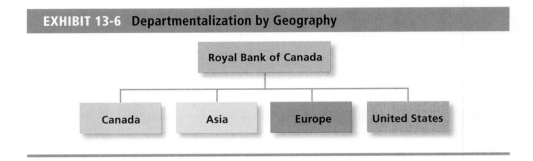

EXHIBIT 13-6 Departmentalization by Geography

Customer Departmentalization

Yet another way to departmentalize is on the basis of the particular type of *customer* the organization seeks to reach. The sales activities in an office supply firm, for instance, can be broken down into three departments to provide specialized service to different customer categories: service retail, wholesale, and government customers. A large law office can segment its staff on the basis of whether they service corporate or individual clients. The assumption underlying customer departmentalization is that customers of each department have a common set of problems and needs that can best be met by having specialists for each. Exhibit 13-7 illustrates how Dell Canada is divided into sales marketing units, according to the type of customer serviced.

Dell Canada
www.dell.ca

Organizational Variety in Departmentalization

Large organizations sometimes change their departmentalization to reflect new needs or emphases. In February 2002, Toronto-based TD Canada Trust announced that it would combine three of its businesses (full-service, discount brokerage, and financial planning) under the TD Waterhouse banner. The bank said that this move would help it better meet its customer needs. The former structure—with separate units for full-service, discount brokerage, and financial planning needs—was a product-oriented structure. Changing the structure to bring all of these units together to focus on customer needs may cause problems, some industry insiders have predicted, however. "The easy part is altering the structure. The challenge, however, is changing the behaviour of full-service brokers and other financial advisors. That behaviour is driven by compensation schemes."[3]

TD Canada Trust
www.tdcanadatrust.com

Not all changes in departmentalization end up meeting customer needs, however, as *OB in the Workplace* shows.

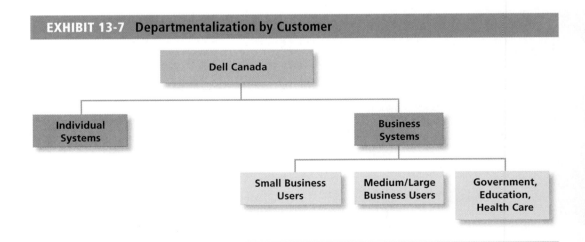

EXHIBIT 13-7 Departmentalization by Customer

OB IN THE WORKPLACE

Xerox Goes From Geography to Industry

Does it matter whether your customers are organized by geography or industry?
Xerox found out the hard way that sometimes it does.[4] In 2000, then CEO Richard
Thoman consolidated the company's 36 billing centres into 3. Then he changed the
reporting relationships of sales managers and field representatives. Previously, these
groups had been assigned to geographical areas. Over a large number of years, the sales
managers and representatives had built up close relationships with their customers.

Thoman proposed that efficiency would improve if customers could have specialized sales managers and field reps who knew the industry of their customers.
Thus, representatives were assigned by industry, such as financial services or education. Thoman was trying to change Xerox from "an old-economy firm . . . [that] sold
or leased copiers to familiar customers, to a 21st century company" with a technologically sophisticated salesforce that was expert in given business sectors.

Unfortunately, lack of communication in making the changes left customers
uncertain of whether their representatives cared about building the relationships
necessary to move forward. Previously, customers could ask their representatives to
handle any problem. By contrast, new procedures had decisions going through many
layers of decision makers, and not through each customer's representative. Thus the
change in departmentalization came at great cost to customers and Xerox alike.

Xerox Canada
www.xerox.ca

Large organizations may also use all of the forms of departmentalization that we
have described—at the same time. A major Japanese electronics firm, for instance, organizes each of its divisions along functional lines and its manufacturing units around
processes; it departmentalizes sales around seven geographic regions, and divides each
sales region into four customer groupings. Two general trends, however, seem to be
gaining momentum. First, many organizations have given greater emphasis to customer
departmentalization. Second, rigid, functional departmentalization is being increasingly complemented by teams that cross over traditional departmental lines. As we
described in Chapter 6, as tasks have become more complex, and more diverse skills are
needed to accomplish those tasks, management has turned to cross-functional teams.

Organizations may choose to go a step further than departmentalization and actually
turn departments into divisions that are separate profit centres. For instance, within
Estée Lauder's product-based departmentalization (discussed earlier), the Clinique,
Prescriptives, Origins, MAC Cosmetics, and Estée Lauder product lines are each separate
profit centres, responsible for setting their own strategic goals.

Chain of Command

The **chain of command** is an unbroken line of authority that extends from the top of
the organization to the lowest echelon and clarifies who reports to whom. It answers
questions for employees such as, "To whom do I go if I have a problem?" and "To whom
do I report?"

Twenty-five years ago, the chain-of-command concept was a basic cornerstone in
the design of organizations. Today's workplace is substantially different.

Because managers have limited time and knowledge, they may choose to delegate
some of their responsibilities to other employees. **Delegation** is the assignment of
authority to another person to carry out specific duties, allowing the employee to make
some of the decisions. Delegation is an important part of a manager's job, as it can
ensure that the right people are part of the decision-making process.

chain of command The unbroken
line of authority that extends from
the top of the organization to the
lowest echelon and clarifies who
reports to whom.

delegation Assignment of authority
to another person to carry out specific duties, allowing the employee
to make some of the decisions.

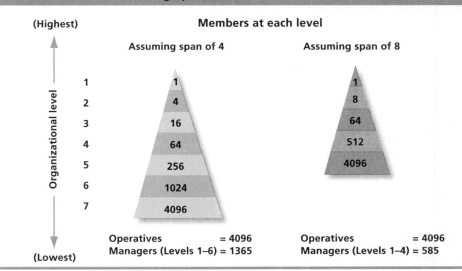

EXHIBIT 13-8   Contrasting Spans of Control

Members at each level

(Highest)

Organizational level

	Assuming span of 4	Assuming span of 8
1	1	1
2	4	8
3	16	64
4	64	512
5	256	4096
6	1024	
7	4096	

(Lowest)

Operatives = 4096
Managers (Levels 1–6) = 1365

Operatives = 4096
Managers (Levels 1–4) = 585

Through delegation, employees are being empowered to make decisions that previously were reserved for management. This chapter's *From Concepts to Skills* on page 508 presents strategies to be a better delegator.

Self-managed and cross-functional teams, along with new structural designs that include multiple bosses, have decreased the relevance of the chain-of-command concept. There are, of course, still many organizations that find they can be most productive by enforcing the chain of command. There just seem to be fewer of them nowadays.

Span of Control

span of control The number of employees that report to a manager.

Span of control refers to the number of employees that report to a manager. This number will vary by organization, and by unit within an organization, and is determined by the number of employees a manager can efficiently and effectively direct. In an assembly-line factory, a manager may be able to direct numerous employees, because the work is well defined and controlled by machinery. A sales manager, by contrast, might have to give one-on-one supervision to individual sales reps, and, therefore, fewer would report to the sales manager. All things being equal, the wider or larger the span, the more efficient the organization. An example can illustrate the validity of this statement.

Assume that we have two organizations, both of which have approximately 4100 operative-level employees. As Exhibit 13-8 illustrates, if one has a uniform span of 4 and the other a span of 8, the wider span would have 2 fewer levels and approximately 800 fewer managers. If the average manager earned $56 000 a year, the wider span would save about $45 million a year in management salaries! Obviously, wider spans are more efficient in terms of cost. However, at some point wider spans reduce effectiveness. That is, when the span becomes too large, employee performance suffers because managers no longer have the time to provide the necessary leadership and support.

Computer technology is increasing sales managers' span of control at Owens-Corning, a building-supply manufacturer and retailer. The company has equipped its salespeople with computers loaded with software that provides up-to-date information about products, customers, and marketplace trends. The information empowers salespeople to manage their territory by making on-the-spot decisions on their own. Regional sales manager Charles Causey (left) expects the computer system to increase his span of control from 9 salespeople to 15.

Narrow or small spans have their advocates. By keeping the span of control to 5 or 6 employees, a manager can maintain close control.[5] But narrow spans pose three major drawbacks. First, as already described, they are expensive because they add levels of management. Second, they make vertical communication in the organization more complex. The added levels of hierarchy slow down decision making and tend to isolate upper management. Third, narrow spans of control encourage overly tight supervision and discourage employee autonomy.

The trend in recent years has been toward wider spans of control, in part because of downsizing and the move to teamwork in some organizations.[6] Wider spans of control are also consistent with recent efforts by companies to reduce costs, cut overhead, speed up decision making, increase flexibility, get closer to customers, and empower employees. However, to ensure that performance does not suffer because of these wider spans, organizations have been investing heavily in employee training. Managers recognize that they can handle a wider span when employees know their jobs inside and out or can turn to their co-workers when they have questions.

When Surrey, BC, RCMP decentralized their offices, the results were positive. Merchants, local politicians, and police in Surrey say they are happy with the results. Some crime statistics have dropped, and the police feel that they are closer to the people they serve. The RCMP split their force into five units operating at regional stations, rather than out of one headquarters opposite Surrey's city hall. The advantage is that "regional offices can concentrate on the unique problems of the various areas."

Individual Responses to Span of Control

A review of the research indicates that it's probably safe to say that there is no evidence to support a relationship between span of control and employee performance. While it is intuitively attractive to argue that large spans might lead to higher employee performance because they provide more distant supervision and more opportunity for personal initiative, the research fails to support this notion. At this point it's impossible to state that any particular span of control is best for producing high performance or high satisfaction among employees. The reason is, again, probably individual differences. That is, some people like to be left alone, while others prefer the security of a manager who is quickly available at all times. Consistent with several of the contingency theories of leadership discussed in Chapter 11, we would expect factors such as employees' experiences and abilities, and the degree of structure in their tasks, to explain when wide or narrow spans of control are likely to contribute to employees' performance and job satisfaction. However, there is some evidence to indicate that a manager's job satisfaction increases as the number of employees he or she supervises increases.

BC RCMP
www.rcmp-grc.gc.ca/bc/

Centralization and Decentralization

The term **centralization** refers to the degree to which decision making is concentrated at a single point in the organization. The concept includes only formal authority, that is, the rights inherent in one's position. Typically, it's said that if top management makes the organization's key decisions with little or no input from lower-level employees, then the organization is centralized. In contrast, the more that lower-level employees provide input or are actually given the discretion to make decisions, the more **decentralization** there is. As Dilbert points out in Exhibit 13-9, however, some organizations do not seem able to decide upon an appropriate level of decentralization.

An organization characterized by centralization is a much different structural animal from one that is decentralized. In a decentralized organization, action can be taken more

centralization The degree to which decision making is concentrated at a single point in the organization.

decentralization The degree to which decision making is distributed to lower-level employees.

Source: S. Adams, *Dogbert's Big Book of Business,* DILBERT reprinted by permission of United Feature Syndicate, Inc.

quickly to solve problems, more people provide input into decisions, and employees are less likely to feel alienated from those who make the decisions that affect their work lives. Decentralized departments make it easier to address customer concerns as well.

Consistent with recent management efforts to make organizations more flexible and responsive, there has been a marked trend toward decentralizing decision making. A survey of 100 international corporations found that 36 percent of them are centrally structured today, compared with 53 percent in 1990.[7] The reason for decentralization in large companies is that lower-level managers are closer to "the action" and typically have more detailed knowledge about problems than do top managers. Big retailers such as The Bay and Sears Canada have given their store managers considerably more discretion in choosing what merchandise to stock. This allows those stores to compete more effectively against local merchants.

Individual Responses to Centralization
We find fairly strong evidence linking centralization and job satisfaction. In general, organizations that are less centralized have a greater amount of participative decision making. The evidence suggests that participative decision making is positively related to job satisfaction. But, again, individual differences surface. The decentralization-

Hudson's Bay Company
www.hbc.com

Sears Canada
www.sears.ca

satisfaction relationship is strongest with employees who have low self-esteem. Because individuals with low self-esteem have less confidence in their abilities, they place a higher value on shared decision making, which means that they are not held solely responsible for decision outcomes.

Formalization

Formalization refers to the degree to which jobs within the organization are standardized. If jobs are highly formalized, there are explicit job descriptions, lots of organizational rules, and clearly defined procedures covering work processes in organizations. Employees can be expected always to handle the same input in exactly the same way, resulting in a consistent and uniform output where there is high formalization. Where formalization is low, job behaviours are relatively nonprogrammed, and employees have a great deal of freedom to exercise discretion in their work. Because an individual's discretion on the job is inversely related to the amount of behaviour in that job that is preprogrammed by the organization, the greater the standardization, the less input the employee has into how his or her work is to be done. Standardization not only eliminates the possibility of employees engaging in alternative behaviours, but it also removes the need for employees to consider alternatives.

Employees' jobs at McDonald's restaurants are highly formalized. To provide customers with consistent product quality and fast service, workers are expected to follow defined food-preparation procedures. Learning these procedures is an important part of employee training at McDonald's Hamburger University training centre, shown here.

formalization The degree to which jobs within the organization are standardized.

McDonald's is an example of a company where employee routines are highly formalized. Employees are instructed in such things as how to greet the customer (smile, be sincere, make eye contact), ask for and receive payment (state amount of order clearly and loudly, announce the amount of money customer gives to the employee, count change out loud and efficiently), and thank the customer (give a sincere thank you, make eye contact, ask customer to come again). McDonald's includes this information in training and employee handbooks, and managers are given a checklist of these behaviours so that they can observe their employees to ensure that the proper procedures are followed.[8]

The degree of formalization can vary widely between organizations and within organizations. Certain jobs, for instance, are well known to have little formalization. University textbook sellers—the representatives of publishers who call on professors to inform them of their company's new publications—have a great deal of freedom in their jobs. They have no standard sales "spiel," and the extent of rules and procedures governing their behaviour may be little more than the requirement that they submit a weekly sales report and some suggestions on what to emphasize for the various new titles. At the other extreme, there are clerical and editorial positions in the same publishing houses where employees are required to "clock in" at their workstations by 8 a.m. or be docked a half-hour's pay and, once at that workstation, to follow a set of precise procedures dictated by management.

MECHANISTIC AND ORGANIC ORGANIZATIONS

When working in Vancouver, Hollywood film producers rely on line producers who manage the financial and logistical details of productions. Line producer Warren Carr sees himself as a facilitator of foreign productions. If a Hollywood studio decides to film in Vancouver, people like Carr hire heads of departments, who then hire staff. He sets up short-term office and studio space. He then oversees the project, and the executive producers may never come up from Hollywood at all. In other words, Carr sets up a very flexible operation to help get the filming done. Is a flexible organization really more effective than a highly structured organization?

2 How flexible can organizational structures be?

mechanistic model A structure characterized by extensive departmentalization, high formalization, a clear chain of command, narrow spans of control, a limited information network, and centralization.

organic model A structure that is flat, uses cross-hierarchical and cross-functional teams, has low formalization, possesses a comprehensive information network, and involves high participation in decision making.

In the previous section, we described six elements of organizational structure. If you think of these as design decisions that an owner or CEO makes about his or her organization, you begin to realize that a variety of organizational forms might emerge based on individual responses to each of the structural questions. Management in some firms may choose a highly formalized and centralized structure, while others might choose a structure that is looser and more amorphous. A variety of other designs exist somewhere between these two extremes.

Exhibit 13-10 presents two extreme models of organizational design. One extreme we will call the **mechanistic model**. It has extensive departmentalization, high formalization, a clear chain of command, narrow spans of control, a limited information network (mostly downward communication), and little participation by lower-level members in decision making. Historically, government bureaucracies have tended to operate at a more mechanistic level. At the other extreme is the **organic model**. This model is flat, uses cross-hierarchical and cross-functional teams, has low formalization, possesses a comprehensive information network (utilizing lateral and upward communication, as well as downward), and involves high participation in decision making.[9] High-tech firms, particularly those in their early years, operate in a more organic fashion, with individuals collaborating on many of the tasks. You may want to explore how different structures affect performance in this chapter's *Working With Others Exercise* on page 505.

Individual Responses to Organizational Structure

As we review the different design possibilities of organization, you might want to think about how organizational design would affect you. Your response to organizational design will be affected by factors such as your experience, personality, and the work task. For simplicity's sake, it might help to keep in mind that individuals with a high degree of bureaucratic orientation (see the *Learning About Yourself Exercise* on page 504) tend to place a heavy reliance on higher authority, prefer formalized and specific rules, and prefer formal relationships with others on the job. These people seem better suited

---

EXHIBIT 13-10 **Mechanistic vs. Organic Models**

The mechanistic model   **The organic model**

 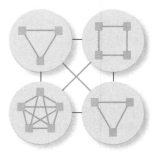

• High specialization   • Cross-functional teams
• Rigid departmentalization   • Cross-hierarchical teams
• Clear chain of command   • Free flow of information
• Narrow spans of control   • Wide spans of control
• Centralization   • Decentralization
• High formalization   • Low formalization

to mechanistic structures. Individuals with a low degree of bureaucratic orientation would probably fit better in organic structures. Additionally, cultural background influences preference for structure. Thus, employees from high power distance countries, such as Russia, Spain, and Thailand, will be much more accepting of mechanistic structures than will employees who come from low power distance countries. So you need to consider cultural differences along with individual differences when making predictions on how structure will affect employee performance and satisfaction. These same factors should be considered if you are ever in the position to design a new organization, for instance, if you choose to become an entrepreneur. Musicians with the Edmonton Symphony Orchestra were unhappy enough with their organizational structure that they went on strike for a month in early 2002, as *OB in the Workplace* discusses.

OB IN THE WORKPLACE

Musicians Given More Control Over Decisions

Do symphony orchestra members care about their organizational structure? Musicians with the Edmonton Symphony Orchestra were so frustrated that their views on how the orchestra should be run were not being heard that they went on strike in February 2002.[10] Decisions for the symphony orchestra were made by the Edmonton Symphony Society, which had 10 000 voting members, including subscribers, donors, musicians, and volunteers. The symphony also had a board of directors that made most management decisions without consulting with the members of the orchestra. The musicians argued that this structure gave too much control to outsiders, and no control to the musicians who had to perform.

During the dispute, the orchestra's CEO, Elaine Calder, said that the musicians were asking for too much change in the structure of the Edmonton Symphony Orchestra. The musicians' request for seats on the board would "disenfranchise our entire community and give them complete control of our orchestra."

After a month-long strike, the musicians were granted more involvement in the running of the orchestra. Following the lead of both the Toronto and the Winnipeg orchestras, musicians were to be added to the board, giving them more say in what performances would be held each year. With the strike over, Calder conceded some positive side to the changes. "Allowing musicians into the decision-making process will allow orchestras to use all their creativity. There's going to be a left-brain, right-brain aspect to that board and that can only help."

Bill Dimmer, a trumpeter with the orchestra, is also positive about the new structure. "Where I hope this goes is a new kind of structure with some really meaningful input from musicians, especially on artistic matters, and some real meaningful input from the community so the board is appropriately accountable to the musicians and the community."

Edmonton Symphony Orchestra
www.edmontonsymphony.com

The Edmonton Symphony Orchestra's structure is very different from many organizations in that the board—rather than an inside management team—makes many of the decisions. The conductor actually directs the musicians. Next we consider a variety of structures used by organizations.

TRADITIONAL ORGANIZATIONAL DESIGNS

With the extremes of mechanistic and organic models in mind, we now turn to describing some of the more common organizational designs found in use: the *simple structure*, the *bureaucracy*, and the *matrix structure*.

3 What are some examples of traditional organizational designs?

The Simple Structure

What do a small retail store, a start-up electronics firm run by a hard-driving entrepreneur, a new Planned Parenthood office, and an airline in the midst of a company-wide pilots' strike have in common? They probably all use the **simple structure**.

The simple structure is said to be characterized most by what it is *not* rather than by what it is. The simple structure is not elaborated.[11] It has a low degree of departmentalization, wide spans of control, authority centralized in a single person, and little formalization. The simple structure is a "flat" organization; it usually has only two or three vertical levels, a loose body of employees, and one individual in whom the decision-making authority is centralized.

The simple structure is most widely practised in small businesses in which the manager and the owner are one and the same, such as the local corner grocery store.

The strength of the simple structure lies in its simplicity. It's fast, flexible, inexpensive to maintain, and accountability is clear. One major weakness is that it's difficult to maintain in anything other than small organizations. It becomes increasingly inadequate as an organization grows because its low formalization and high centralization tend to create information overload at the top. As size increases, decision making typically becomes slower and can eventually come to a standstill as the single executive tries to continue making all the decisions. This often proves to be the undoing of many small businesses. When an organization begins to employ 50 or 100 people, it's very difficult for the owner-manager to make all the choices. If the structure is not changed and made more elaborate, the firm often loses momentum and can eventually fail. The simple structure's other weakness is that it's risky—everything depends on one person. One serious illness can literally destroy the organization's information and decision-making centre. This chapter's *CBC Video Case* shows some of the difficulties of a simple structure.

The Family Business

Family businesses represent 70 percent of Canadian employment and more than 30 percent of the gross domestic product. Some of the most prominent family businesses in Canada over the past 50 years include the Seagram Company (the Bronfman family), Eaton's (the Eaton family), Birks (the Birk family), Irving Paper (the Irving family), Molson Breweries (the Molson family), and McCain Foods (the McCain family). Not all family businesses are as large as these, however, and many have relatively simple structures.

Family businesses have more complex dynamics than nonfamily businesses, because they face both family/personal relations and business/management relations. These companies generally have shareholders (family members and perhaps others), although the businesses may or may not be public companies listed on the stock exchange. Unlike nonfamily businesses, family businesses must manage the conflicts found within families, as well as the normal business issues that arise for any business. As John Davis of Harvard Business School notes, "In a family business, the business, the family, and the ownership group all need governance."

Good governance structures can help family businesses manage the conflicts that may arise. Good governance includes "a sense of direction, values to live by or work by, and well-understood and accepted policies that tell organization members how they should behave."[12]

One area in which governance can play a key role is in CEO succession. Family businesses need to figure out rules of succession for when the CEO retires, and also rules for who in the family gets to work in the business. Succession in family-owned businesses often does not work "because personal and emotional factors determine who the next leader will be," rather than suitability.[13] For instance, a father may want his first-born son to take over the business, even if one of the daughters might make a better CEO.

The issues become more complex when second- and third-generation family members become involved in the family business. *OB in the Street* shows the difficulties the

simple structure An organizational design characterized by a low degree of departmentalization, wide spans of control, authority centralized in a single person, and little formalization.

Growing Big Can Be Hard To Do

McCain brothers had in deciding who would succeed them as head of McCain Foods and the fallout of their relationship as a consequence.

OB IN THE STREET

Brothers' Feud Leads to Breakup of Family

Does blood come before business? For 37 years, Wallace McCain and his older brother Harrison shared command of McCain Foods, the Florenceville, New Brunswick-based french-fry empire they had built together.[14] In August 1993, however, that partnership came to an end, after the *Financial Post* profiled Wallace's son Michael, referring to him as "the leading candidate to become the potato king." Apparently, it was that reference to Michael as successor that started what the newspapers called "the feud of the century."

The public display of animosity came as somewhat of a surprise. The brothers started McCain Foods in 1956, and "one brother never made a decision without consulting the other." Their offices were linked by an unlocked door. They seemed suited to working together. Harrison was the outgoing salesperson. Wallace was quieter, the number cruncher who managed the books. The partnership worked. In the first year, sales were $152 678. Sales of McCain Foods products are still growing; while the core of the business remains french fries, nonfood subsidiaries include a large trucking division and a national courier company.

What brought these two brothers down was a conflict, which had simmered quietly for 20 years, over who would succeed the brothers to run the family business. Harrison convinced other family members that Wallace and his sons would not share the business with the other McCains. The dispute ended up in a New Brunswick arbitration court, where Wallace was ousted as co-CEO. Eighteen months after the *Financial Post* article appeared, Wallace left McCain Foods and moved to Toronto to become chair of Maple Leaf Foods. Meanwhile, Harrison fired his nephew Michael, and ordered the locks changed on his office door. Michael joined his father at Maple Leaf, where he is now president and CEO. The brothers received a leadership award in 2001, but Harrison was too ill to attend the ceremony in Toronto. Wallace, however, indicated at the ceremony that troubles continued between the brothers: "I'm not going to candy-coat that situation," said Wallace. "It was a very hard thing for me to endure, to watch such a successful partnership go down the drain the way it did."

Harrison passed away in 2004, with no signs of a public reconciliation. However, Frank McKenna, the former premier of New Brunswick and friends with both McCain brothers, said that the relationship had improved prior to Harrison's death. "It's not commonly understood, but I think it's important now on Harrison's death to know that Wallace and Harrison had become very close," McKenna said.

McCain Foods
www.mccain.com

Maple Leaf Foods
www.mapleleaf.com

So what makes family businesses unique? Founders of family business seek to "build businesses that are also family institutions."[15] As a result, there is added pressure on the business, which needs to balance business needs and family needs. Family businesses may have different goals than nonfamily businesses as well, emphasizing the importance of family values in maintaining and growing the business rather than wealth maximization.

The Bureaucracy

Standardization! That's the key concept underlying all bureaucracies. Take a look at the bank where you keep your chequing account, the department store where you buy your

bureaucracy An organizational design with highly routine operating tasks achieved through specialization; formalized rules and regulations; tasks that are grouped into functional departments; centralized authority; narrow spans of control; and decision making that follows the chain of command.

clothes, or the government offices that collect your taxes, enforce health regulations, or provide local fire protection. They all rely on standardized work processes for coordination and control.

A **bureaucracy** is characterized by highly routine operating tasks achieved through specialization; formalized rules and regulations; tasks that are grouped into functional departments; centralized authority; narrow spans of control; and decision making that follows the chain of command.

Strengths of Bureaucracy

German sociologist Max Weber, writing in the early 1900s, described bureaucracy as an alternative to the traditional administrative form. In the traditional model, leaders could be quite arbitrary, with authority based on personal relations. There were no general rules, and no separation between the leader's "private" and "public" business. Bureaucracy solved some of the problems of leaders who took advantage of their situation.

The primary strength of the bureaucracy lies in its ability to perform standardized activities in a highly efficient manner. Putting together similar specialties in functional departments results in economies of scale, minimum duplication of staff and equipment, and employees who have the opportunity to talk "the same language" with their peers. Furthermore, bureaucracies can get by nicely with less talented—and, hence, less costly—middle- and lower-level managers. The pervasiveness of rules and regulations substitutes for managerial discretion. Standardized operations, coupled with high formalization, allow decision making to be centralized. There is little need, therefore, for innovative and experienced decision makers below the level of senior executives. In short, bureaucracy is an effective structure for ensuring consistent application of policies and practices and for ensuring accountability.

Weaknesses of Bureaucracy

Bureaucracy is not without its problems. One of its major weaknesses is that it can create subunit conflict. For instance, the production department believes that it has the most important role in the organization because nothing happens until something is produced. Meanwhile, the research and development department may believe that design provides added value to a product, while producing it is no big deal. At the same time, the marketing department views selling the product as the most important task in the organization. Finally, the accounting department sees itself in the central role of tallying up the results and making sure everything stays on budget. Thus, each department acts like a silo, focusing more on what it perceives as its own value and contribution to the organization. Each silo fails to understand that departments are really interdependent on each other, with each having to perform well for the company as a whole to survive. The conflict that can happen among functional units means that sometimes functional unit goals can override the overall goals of the organization.

Bureaucracy can sometimes lead to power being concentrated in the hands of just a few people, with others expected to follow their orders unquestioningly. This chapter's *Ethical Dilemma Exercise* on page 506 illustrates what can happen when someone higher in the authority chain pressures someone below them to perform unethical tasks.

In thinking about the possible conflicts that can arise in a bureaucracy, you might want to refer to Chapter 8, which discussed the relationship of dependency to power. That chapter pointed out that importance, scarcity, and nonsubstitutability will all affect the degree of power an individual or unit has.

The other major weakness of a bureaucracy is something we have all experienced at one time or another when dealing with people who work in these organizations: obsessive concern with following the rules. When cases arise that don't precisely fit the rules, there is no room for modification. The bureaucracy is efficient only as long as employees confront problems that they have previously encountered and for which programmed decision rules have already been established. This chapter's *Case Incident—"I Detest Bureaucracy"* on page 508 lets you consider alternatives to bureaucracy and how you might feel about these alternatives.

The Matrix Structure

Another popular organizational design option is the **matrix structure**. You will find it being used in advertising agencies, aerospace firms, research and development laboratories, construction companies, hospitals, government agencies, universities, management consulting firms, and entertainment companies.[16] Ideally, the matrix combines the benefits of two forms of departmentalization—functional and product—without their drawbacks. Specifically, functional departmentalization groups similar specialists, which minimizes the number necessary, while it allows the pooling and sharing of specialized resources across products. Product departmentalization facilitates coordination among specialties to achieve on-time completion and meet budget targets. Furthermore, it provides clear responsibility for all activities related to a product, but with duplication of activities and costs.

The most obvious structural characteristic of the matrix is that it breaks the unity-of-command concept. Employees in the matrix have two bosses—their functional department managers and their product managers. Therefore, the matrix has a dual chain of command.

Exhibit 13-11 shows the matrix form as used in a faculty of business administration. The academic departments of accounting, administrative studies, finance, and so forth are functional units. Additionally, specific programs (that is, products) are overlaid on the functions. In this way, members in a matrix structure have a dual assignment—to their functional department, and to their product groups. For instance, a professor of accounting who is teaching an undergraduate course reports to the director of undergraduate programs, as well as to the chair of the accounting department.

matrix structure An organizational design that combines functional and product departmentalization; it has a dual chain of command.

Advantages of a Matrix Structure

The strength of the matrix lies in its ability to foster coordination when the organization carries out many complex and interdependent activities. As an organization becomes larger, its information-processing capacity can become overloaded. In a bureaucracy,

EXHIBIT 13-11   Matrix Structure for a Faculty of Business Administration

Academic departments \ Programs	Undergraduate	Master's	PhD	Research	Executive development	Community service
Accounting						
Administrative studies						
Finance						
Information and decision sciences						
Marketing						
Organizational behaviour						
Quantitative methods						

complexity results in increased formalization. The direct and frequent contact between different specialties in the matrix can result in improved communication and more flexibility. Information permeates the organization and more quickly reaches those people who need to take account of it. Furthermore, the matrix reduces "bureau-pathologies." The dual lines of authority reduce tendencies of departmental members to become so busy protecting their little worlds that the organization's overall goals become secondary.

The matrix offers another fundamental advantage: It facilitates the efficient allocation of specialists. When individuals with highly specialized skills are lodged in one functional department or product group, their talents are monopolized and underused. The matrix achieves the advantages of economies of scale by providing the organization with both the best resources and an effective way of ensuring their efficient deployment.

Disadvantages of a Matrix Structure

What happens when you report to two bosses?

The major disadvantages of the matrix lie in the confusion it creates, its tendency to foster power struggles, and the stress it places on individuals.[17] For example, it's frequently unclear who reports to whom, and it's not unusual for product managers to fight over getting the best specialists assigned to their products. Confusion and ambiguity also create the seeds of power struggles. Bureaucracy reduces the potential for power grabs by defining the rules of the game. When those rules are "up for grabs," power struggles between functional and product managers result. For individuals who desire security and absence from ambiguity, this work climate can produce stress. Reporting to more than one manager introduces role conflict, and unclear expectations introduce role ambiguity. The comfort of bureaucracy's predictability is absent, replaced by insecurity and stress.

NEW DESIGN OPTIONS

Vancouver's film industry structure does not resemble the traditional corporate structure of large manufacturing organizations.[18] Single-purpose companies may start up, do several million dollars in business, and close down in a matter of months. This flexibility reflects the creative nature of the movie business, and allows people to move from project to project rather fluidly. Most people expect that companies will only operate for three or four months.

This corporate "structure" means there are few permanent jobs, but many people in the industry have long, productive careers. About 35 000 British Columbians have jobs in this industry. David Murphy, who recently studied the industry for his PhD from the University of British Columbia, called the structure "a network model of industrial organization." Small companies and suppliers work together on a project, and when it's finished, move on to another project. Ironically, the strong union presence in Vancouver helps the industry thrive. "The unions run training programs for many jobs in the industry and refer qualified members to producers when needed," according to Professor Mark Thompson of the Sauder School of Business at UBC. Essentially, the unions provide a corporate structure. Union representative Mark Adair finds the structure positive: "We have no history and no baggage. We adapt better." Can new forms of organization lead to better ways of getting things done?

4 What do newer organizational structures look like?

Organizational theorists Jay Galbraith and Edward Lawler have argued that there is a "new logic of organizing" for organizations.[19] They suggest that new-style organizations are considerably more flexible than older-style organizations. Exhibit 13-12 compares characteristics of new-style and old-style organizations.

The new structural options for organizations involve breaking down boundaries in some fashion, either internally, externally, or a combination of the two. In this section,

EXHIBIT 13-12   New-Style vs. Old-Style Organizations

New	Old
Dynamic, learning	Stable
Information rich	Information is scarce
Global	Local
Small and large	Large
Product/customer oriented	Functional oriented
Skills oriented	Job oriented
Team oriented	Individual oriented
Involvement oriented	Command/control oriented
Lateral/networked	Hierarchical
Customer oriented	Job requirements oriented

Source: J. R. Galbraith and E. E. Lawler III, "Effective Organizations: Using the New Logic of Organizing,"
in *Organizing for the Future: The New Logic for Managing Complex Organizations,* ed. J. R. Galbraith,
E. E. Lawler III, and associates (San Francisco: Jossey-Bass, 1993). Copyright © 1993 Jossey-Bass Inc.
Publishers. Reprinted with permission of John Wiley & Sons, Inc.

we describe four such designs: the *team structure,* which modifies internal boundaries; the *modular* and *virtual organizations,* both of which modify external organizational boundaries; and the *boundaryless organization,* which attempts to break down both internal and external boundaries.[20]

The Team Structure

As described in Chapter 6, teams have become an extremely popular means around which to organize work activities. When management uses teams as its central coordination device, you have a **team structure**. The primary characteristics of the team structure are that it breaks down departmental barriers and decentralizes decision making to the level of the work team. Team structures also require employees to be generalists as well as specialists.[21]

In smaller companies, the team structure can define the entire organization. For instance, Toyota Canada's parts distribution centre in Toronto reorganized its workforce into work teams in 1995. Workers have a team-focused mission statement, and the staff are split into six work teams, each with its own leader. Among larger organizations, such as Xerox Canada and GM Canada, the team structure often complements what is typically a bureaucratic structure. This allows the organization to achieve the efficiency of bureaucracy's standardization, while gaining the flexibility that teams provide.

The Modular Organization

Why do it all when sometimes someone else can do some of it better? That question captures the essence of the **modular organization**, which is typically a small core organization that outsources major business functions.[22]

Nike, Reebok, Liz Claiborne, Vancouver-based Mountain Equipment Co-op, and Dell Canada are just a few of the thousands of companies that have found that they can do hundreds of millions of dollars in business without owning manufacturing facilities.

team structure The use of teams as the central device to coordinate work activities.

Toyota Canada
www.toyota.ca

GM Canada
www.gmcanada.com

modular organization A small core organization that outsources major business functions.

Bruce Brown (wearing hat) operates a virtual organization. He publishes an online newsletter, *BugNet,* that provides subscribers with solutions for fixing computer bugs. Brown and employees are shown here at the firm's headquarters in Sumas, Washington. But most functions are outsourced to people throughout the country and as far away as London, England. They are managed through an intranet that contains editorial guidelines, deadlines, contact information, and photos. Brown has never met most of his employees, including a senior editor in Cleveland whom he has worked with for five years.

These organizations have created networks of relationships that allow them to contract out manufacturing, distribution, marketing, or any other business function where management believes that others can do it better or more cheaply. The modular organization, however, outsources many functions and concentrates on what it does best. For many Canadian firms, that means focusing on design or marketing rather than production.

Exhibit 13-13 shows a modular structure in which management outsources the marketing, sales, and service functions of the business. Top management directly oversees the activities that are done in-house and coordinates relationships with the other organizations that perform the sales, marketing, and service functions for the modular organization. Managers in modular structures spend some of their time coordinating and controlling external relations, typically by way of computer network links.

There are several advantages to modular organizations. Organizations can devote their technical and managerial talent to their most critical activities. They can respond more quickly to environmental changes, and there is increased focus on customers and markets. The primary drawback to this structure is that it reduces management's control over key parts of its business. The organization is forced to rely on outsiders, which decreases operational control. Additionally, Nike and several other companies have come under attack for relying on low-paid, exploited labourers, many of whom are children, in less-developed countries. These organizations are having to make decisions about the trade-offs between low-cost production strategies and criticisms from potential customers who are concerned about human rights.

The Virtual Organization

virtual organization A continually evolving network of independent companies—suppliers, customers, even competitors—linked together to share skills, costs, and access to one another's markets.

The **virtual organization** "is a continually evolving network of independent companies—suppliers, customers, even competitors—linked together to share skills, costs, and access to one another's markets."[23] Vancouver's film industry, described in this chapter's vignette, succeeds because of virtual organizations. In a virtual organization, units of different firms join together in an alliance to pursue common strategic objectives. While control in the modular structure remains with the core organization, in

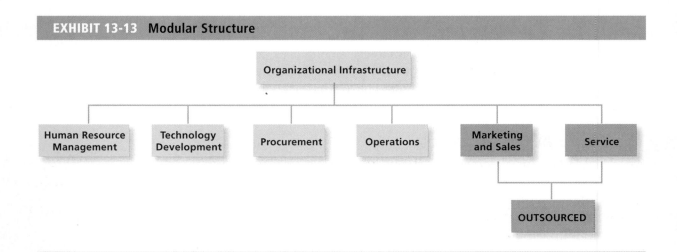

EXHIBIT 13-13   Modular Structure

Organizational Infrastructure

Human Resource Management · Technology Development · Procurement · Operations · Marketing and Sales · Service

OUTSOURCED

the virtual organization participants give up some of their control and act more interdependently. Virtual organizations may not have a central office, an organizational chart, or a hierarchy. Typically, the organizations come together to exploit specific opportunities or attain specific strategic objectives.

About one in nine Canadian companies engages in some sort of alliance. These alliances take many forms, ranging from precompetitive consortia to coproduction, cross-equity arrangements, and equity joint ventures with separate legal entities.[24] Exhibit 13-14 illustrates a possible virtual structure where the reference firm is responsible for technology development, and then works together with the alliance partners to complete the other functions. Another example of a virtual structure is Amazon.ca, which partners with Canada Post. Orders placed on Amazon.ca's Canadian website are fulfilled and shipped by Assured Logistics, which is part of Canada Post. Assured Logistics operates a Toronto-area warehouse that stores books, music, and movies so that they can be shipped when ordered, thus eliminating the need for Amazon.com to set up its own warehouse facility in Canada.

Amazon.ca
www.amazon.ca

Canada Post
www.canadapost.ca

There are several advantages to virtual organizations. They allow organizations to share costs and skills, provide access to global markets, and increase market responsiveness. However, there are also distinct disadvantages. The boundaries between companies become blurred due to interdependence. In order to work together, companies must relinquish operational and strategic control. This form of organization also requires new managerial skills. Managers must build relations with other companies, negotiate "win-win" deals, find compatible partners in terms of values and goals, and then develop appropriate communication systems to keep everyone informed.[25]

The Boundaryless Organization

Both the modular organization and the virtual organization break down external boundaries of the organization without generally affecting the internal workings of each of the cooperating organizations. Some organizations, however, strive to break down both the internal and external boundaries. Former General Electric (GE) chairman Jack Welch coined the term **boundaryless organization** to describe his idea of what he wanted GE to become. The boundaryless organization seeks to eliminate the chain of command, have limitless spans of control, and replace departments with empowered teams. Because it relies so heavily on information technology, some have turned to calling this structure the *T-form* (or technology-based) organization.[26]

boundaryless organization
An organization that seeks to eliminate the chain of command, have limitless spans of control, and replace departments with empowered teams.

Although GE has not yet achieved this boundaryless state—and probably never will—it has made significant progress toward this end. So have other companies such as Hewlett-Packard, AT&T, and Motorola. Let's explore what a boundaryless organization would look like and what some firms are doing to make it a reality.[27]

General Electric Canada
www.ge.com/ca

Hewlett-Packard Canada
http://welcome.hp.com/country/ca/en/welcome.html

EXHIBIT 13-14   Virtual Structure

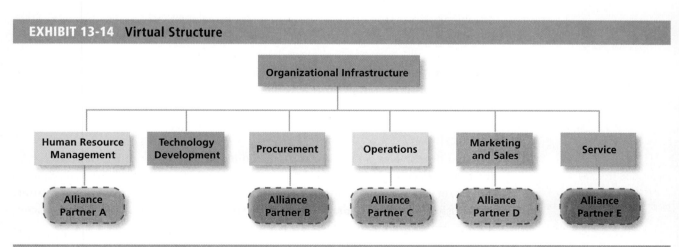

Can an organization really have no boundaries?

The boundaryless organization breaks down barriers internally by flattening the hierarchy, creating cross-hierarchical teams (which include top executives, middle managers, supervisors, and operative employees), and using participative decision-making practices and 360-degree performance appraisals (where peers and others above and below the employee evaluate his or her performance). The boundaryless organization also breaks down barriers to external constituencies (suppliers, customers, regulators, etc.) and barriers created by geography. Globalization, strategic alliances, supplier-organization and customer-organization linkages, and telecommuting are all examples of practices that reduce external boundaries.

The one common technological thread that makes the boundaryless organization possible is networked computers. They allow people to communicate across intraorganizational and interorganizational boundaries.[28] Additionally, many large companies, including the City of Richmond (BC), Procter & Gamble Canada, FedEx, AT&T, and 3M, have intranets to help with internal communication. Interorganizational networks now make it possible for Wal-Mart suppliers such as Procter & Gamble (P&G) to monitor inventory levels of laundry soap, because P&G's company computer system is networked to Wal-Mart's system.

One of the drawbacks of boundaryless organizations is that they are difficult to manage. It's difficult to overcome the political and authority boundaries inherent in many organizations. It can also be time-consuming and difficult to manage the coordination necessary with so many different stakeholders. That said, the well-managed boundaryless organization offers the best talents of employees across several different organizations; enhances cooperation across functions, divisions, and external groups; and potentially offers much quicker response time to the environment.

Procter & Gamble Canada
www.pg.com/en_CA

Wal-Mart Canada
www.walmartcanada.ca

WHAT MAJOR FORCES SHAPE AN ORGANIZATION'S STRUCTURE?

5 Why do organizational structures differ?

With an understanding of the various structures possible, we are now prepared to address the following questions: What are the forces that influence the design that is chosen? Why are some organizations structured along more mechanistic lines while others follow organic characteristics? In the following pages, we present the major forces that have been identified as causes, or determinants, of an organization's structure: strategy, organizational size, technology, and environment.[29]

Strategy

An organization's structure is a means to help management achieve its objectives. Since objectives are derived from the organization's overall strategy, it's only logical that the structure should support the strategy.[30]

Most current strategy frameworks focus on three strategy dimensions—innovation, cost minimization, and imitation—and the structural design that works best with each.[31]

Innovation Strategy

To what degree does an organization introduce major new products or services? An **innovation strategy** does not mean a strategy merely for simple or cosmetic changes from previous offerings, but rather one for meaningful and unique innovations. Obviously, not all firms pursue innovation. This strategy may appropriately characterize 3M, but it certainly is not a strategy pursued by McDonald's.

innovation strategy A strategy that emphasizes the introduction of major new products and services.

EXHIBIT 13-15 The Strategy-Structure Thesis	
Strategy	**Structural Option**
Innovation	*Organic:* A loose structure; low specialization, low formalization, decentralized
Cost minimization	*Mechanistic:* Tight control; extensive work specialization, high formalization, high centralization
Imitation	*Mechanistic and organic:* Mix of loose with tight properties; tight controls over current activities and looser controls for new undertakings

Cost-Minimization Strategy

An organization that is pursuing a **cost-minimization strategy** tightly controls costs, refrains from incurring unnecessary innovation or marketing expenses, and cuts prices in selling a basic product. This would describe the strategy pursued by Wal-Mart or the sellers of generic grocery products.

cost-minimization strategy A strategy that emphasizes tight cost controls, avoidance of unnecessary innovation or marketing expenses, and price cutting.

Imitation Strategy

Organizations following an **imitation strategy** try to capitalize on the best of both of the previous strategies. They seek to minimize risk and maximize opportunity for profit. Their strategy is to move into new products or new markets only after viability has been proven by innovators. They take the successful ideas of innovators and copy them. Manufacturers of mass-marketed fashion goods that are "rip-offs" of designer styles follow the imitation strategy. This label also probably characterizes such well-known firms as IBM and Caterpillar. They essentially follow their smaller and more innovative competitors with superior products, but only after their competitors have demonstrated that the market is there.

imitation strategy A strategy of moving into new products or new markets only after their viability has already been proven.

IBM Canada
www.ibm.com/ca/en/

Caterpillar
www.cat.com

Exhibit 13-15 describes the structural option that best matches each strategy. Innovators need the flexibility of the organic structure, while cost minimizers seek the efficiency and stability of the mechanistic structure. Imitators combine the two structures. They use a mechanistic structure in order to maintain tight controls and low costs in their current activities, while at the same time they create organic subunits in which to pursue new undertakings.

Organizational Size

There is considerable evidence to support the idea that an organization's size significantly affects its structure.[32] For instance, large organizations—those typically employing 2000 or more people—tend to have more specialization, more departmentalization, more vertical levels, and more rules and regulations than do small organizations. However, the relationship is not linear. Rather, size affects structure at a decreasing rate. The impact of size becomes less important as an organization expands. Why is this? Essentially, once an organization has around 2000 employees, it's already fairly mechanistic. An additional 500 employees will not have much impact. On the other hand, adding 500 employees to an organization that has only 300 members is likely to result in a shift toward a more mechanistic structure.

Technology

The term **technology** refers to the way in which an organization transfers its inputs into outputs. Every organization has at least one technology for converting financial,

technology The way in which an organization transfers its inputs into outputs.

human, and physical resources into products or services. The Ford Motor Company, for instance, predominantly uses an assembly-line process to make its products. On the other hand, universities may use a number of instruction technologies to develop coursework for students—the ever-popular formal lecture method, the case-analysis method, the experiential exercise method, the programmed learning method, and so forth. In this section, we show that organizational structures adapt to their technology.

Variations in Technology

So what does technology mean?

The common theme that differentiates technologies is their *degree of routineness.* By this we mean that technologies tend toward either routine or nonroutine activities. The former are characterized by automated and standardized operations, such as an assembly line, where one might affix a car door to a car at set intervals. Nonroutine activities are customized. They include such varied operations as furniture restoring, custom shoemaking, and genetic research.

The Relationship Between Technology and Structure

What relationship has been found between technology and structure? Although the relationship is not overwhelmingly strong, we find that routine tasks are associated with taller and more departmentalized structures. The relationship between technology and formalization, however, is stronger. Studies consistently show routineness to be associated with the presence of rule manuals, job descriptions, and other formalized documentation.

An interesting relationship has been found between technology and centralization. It seems logical that routine technologies would be associated with a centralized structure, whereas nonroutine technologies, which rely more heavily on the knowledge of specialists, would be characterized by delegated decision authority. This position has received some support. However, a more generalizable conclusion is that the technology-centralization relationship is moderated by the degree of formalization. Both formal regulations and centralized decision making are control mechanisms, and management can substitute one for the other. Routine technologies should be associated with centralized control if there is a minimum of rules and regulations. However, if formalization is high, routine technology can be accompanied by decentralization. So we would predict that routine technology would lead to centralization, but only if formalization is low.

The chapter's *Point/Counterpoint* on page 502 discusses whether technology drives rapid organizational change.

Environment

environment Those institutions or forces outside the organization that potentially affect the organization's performance.

An organization's **environment** is composed of those institutions or forces outside the organization that potentially affect the organization's performance. These typically include suppliers, customers, competitors, government regulatory agencies, public pressure groups, and the like.

Why should an organization's structure be affected by its environment? The answer is environmental uncertainty. Some organizations face relatively static environments—few forces in their environment are changing. There is, for example, no new competition, no new technological breakthroughs by current competitors, or little activity by public pressure groups to influence the organization. Other organizations face dynamic environments—rapidly changing government regulations affecting their business, new competitors, difficulties in acquiring raw materials, continually changing product preferences by customers, and so on. Static environments create significantly less uncertainty for managers than do dynamic ones. Since uncertainty is a threat to an organization's effectiveness, management will try to minimize it. One way to reduce environmental uncertainty is through adjustments in the organization's structure.[33]

Recent research has helped clarify what is meant by environmental uncertainty. It's been found that there are three key dimensions to any organization's environment: capacity, volatility, and complexity.[34]

Capacity

The *capacity* of an environment refers to the degree to which it can support growth. Rich and growing environments generate excess resources, which can buffer the organization in times of relative scarcity. Abundant capacity, for example, leaves room for an organization to make mistakes, while scarce capacity does not. In 2000, firms operating in the multimedia software business had relatively abundant environments, whereas those in the full-service brokerage business faced relative scarcity.

Volatility

The degree of instability in an environment is captured in the *volatility* dimension. Where there is a high degree of unpredictable change, the environment is dynamic. This makes it difficult for management to predict accurately the probabilities associated with various decision alternatives. At the other extreme is a stable environment. Turmoil in Asian financial markets caught many by surprise and created a lot of instability in the late 1990s, particularly in resource industries. Canada's resource exports suffered as demand shrank in Asia. This led to widespread layoffs in the BC lumber industry, for example, and Japan's steel producers demanded a cut in the price they paid for Canadian coal. The instability was not limited to the resource sector, however. Small manufacturers were also hit. The Asian crisis was a valuable reminder to all organizations that they are operating in a global environment.

Complexity

Finally, the environment needs to be assessed in terms of *complexity*; that is, the degree of heterogeneity and concentration among environmental elements. Simple environments are homogeneous and concentrated. This might describe the tobacco industry, since there are relatively few players. It's easy for firms in this industry to keep a close eye on the competition. In contrast, environments characterized by heterogeneity and dispersion are called *complex*. This term sums up the current environment for firms competing in the cellular connection business. Every day, there seems to be another "new kid on the block" with whom current cellphone providers must deal.

Exhibit 13-16 summarizes our definition of the environment along its three dimensions. The arrows in this figure are meant to indicate movement toward higher uncertainty. Organizations that operate in environments characterized as scarce, dynamic, and complex face the greatest degree of uncertainty. Why? They have high unpredictability, little room for error, and a diverse set of elements in the environment to monitor constantly.

Given this three-dimensional definition of environment, we can offer some general conclusions. There is evidence that relates the degrees of environmental uncertainty to different structural arrangements. Specifically, the more scarce, dynamic, and complex the environment, the more organic a structure should be. The more abundant, stable, and simple the environment, the more mechanistic a structure should be.

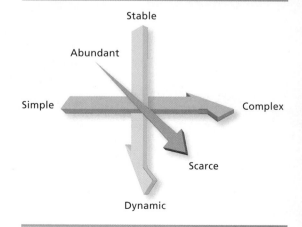

EXHIBIT 13-16 Three-Dimensional Model of the Environment

SUMMARY AND IMPLICATIONS

1 **What are the key elements of organizational structure?** An organizational structure defines how job tasks are formally divided, grouped, and coordinated. There are six key elements that managers need to address when they design their organization's structure: work specialization, departmentalization, chain of command, span of control, centralization and decentralization, and formalization. Organizations structured around high levels of formalization and specialization, strict adherence to the chain of command, limited delegation of authority, and narrow spans of control give employees little autonomy. Organizations that are structured around limited specialization, low formalization, wide spans of control, and the like give employees greater autonomy.

2 **How flexible can organizational structures be?** For simplicity's sake, we can classify the extent to which organizations are flexible around one of two models: mechanistic or organic. A mechanistic organization has extensive departmentalization, high formalization, a limited information network (mostly downward communication), and little participation by lower-level members in decision making. Historically, government bureaucracies have tended to operate at a more mechanistic level. At the other extreme is the organic organization, which is flat, uses cross-hierarchical and cross-functional teams, has low formalization, possesses a comprehensive information network (utilizing lateral and upward communication, as well as downward), and involves high participation in decision making. High-tech firms, particularly those in their early years, operate in a more organic fashion, with individuals collaborating on many of the tasks.

3 **What are some examples of traditional organizational designs?** Some of the more common organizational designs found in use are the *simple structure*, the *bureaucracy*, and the *matrix structure*. The simple structure has a low degree of departmentalization, wide spans of control, authority centralized in a single person, little formalization, and one individual in whom the decision-making authority is centralized. Bureaucracy is characterized by highly routine operating tasks achieved through specialization; formalized rules and regulations; tasks that are grouped into functional departments; centralized authority; narrow spans of control; and decision making that follows the chain of command. The most obvious structural characteristic of the matrix is that it breaks the unity-of-command concept. Employees in the matrix have two bosses—their functional department managers and their product managers. Therefore, the matrix has a dual chain of command.

4 **What do newer organizational structures look like?** The new structural options for organizations involve breaking down the boundaries in some fashion, either internally, externally, or a combination of the two. We have illustrated four such structural designs: the *team structure*, which modifies internal boundaries; the *modular* and *virtual organizations*, which modify external organizational boundaries; and the *boundaryless organization*, which attempts to break down both internal and external boundaries.

5 **Why do organizational structures differ?** Strategy, organizational size, technology, and environment determine the type of structure an organization will have.

For Review

1. Why isn't work specialization an unending source of increased productivity?

2. What are the different forms of departmentalization?

3. All things being equal, which is more efficient, a wide or narrow span of control? Why?

4. What is a matrix structure? When would management use it?

5. How does a family business differ from other organizational structures?

6. Contrast the virtual organization with the boundaryless organization.

7. What type of structure works best with an innovation strategy? A cost-minimization strategy? An imitation strategy?

8. Summarize the size-structure relationship.

9. Define and give an example of what is meant by the term *technology*.

10. Summarize the environment-structure relationship.

For Critical Thinking

1. How is the typical large corporation of today organized, in contrast with how that same organization was probably organized in the 1960s?

2. Do you think most employees prefer high formalization? Support your position.

3. If you were an employee in a matrix structure, what pluses do you think the structure would provide? What about minuses?

4. What could management do to make a bureaucracy more like a boundaryless organization?

5. What behavioural predictions would you make about people who worked in a "pure" boundaryless organization (if such a structure were ever to exist)?

OB for You

- Think about the type of organizational structure that suits you best when you look for a job. You may prefer a structured workplace, like that of a mechanistic organization. Or you may prefer a much less structured workplace, like that of an organic organization.

- If you decide to start your own company, know the different structural considerations so that you can create an organization that meets your needs as both a business person and a person with additional interests.

- As a manager or as an entrepreneur, consider how much responsibility (centralization/decentralization) you want to take for yourself compared with how much you are willing to share with others in the organization.

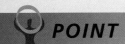 **POINT**

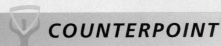 **COUNTERPOINT**

Technology Is Reshaping Organizations

In today's chaotic, uncertain, and high-tech world, there is essentially only one type of design that is going to survive. This is the electronically configured organic organization.[35]

We are undergoing a second Industrial Revolution, and it will change every aspect of people's lives. The changes the large corporations used to take a decade to implement now occur in one to two years. Companies that are successful will be designed to thrive on change, and the structure of those organizations will have common characteristics.

Ten years from now, there will be nothing but electronic organizations. Brick-and-mortar organizations won't go away, but bricks-and-clicks will become the only means to survival. In addition, every organization will need to keep its finger on the pulse of its customers. Customer priorities will change rapidly. Those who lose touch with their customers will be candidates for extinction. Consumers are gaining the ability to compare the prices of hundreds of competitors rather than just two or three. This is going to dramatically drive down prices. If firms don't improve their productivity to match these drops in prices, they will be out of business.

Technology allows firms to stay closer to the customer, to move jobs to where costs are lowest, and to make decisions much more rapidly. For instance, executives at Cisco Systems can monitor expenses, gross margins, the supply chain, and profitability in real time. Surprises need not exist. Every employee can make decisions that might have had to come from the top management ranks a few years ago. At the end of a quarter, an individual product manager at Cisco can see exactly what the gross margins are on his or her products, whether they are below expectations, and determine the cause of any discrepancy. Quicker decision making at lower levels will translate into higher profit margins. So instead of the CEO or chief financial officer making 50 to 100 different decisions in a quarter, managers throughout the organization can make millions of decisions. Companies that don't adjust to create this capability will be noncompetitive.

Technology Only Brings Gradual Change

There's a saying that every generation thinks it has discovered sex. This seems to be the case with technology and how it's going to change the world completely.

Technology will transform the structure of organizations at a much slower rate than many believe.[36] For instance, it's useful to go back and ask if the railroads changed the world. There were definitely changes in how commerce and industry were arranged. But life remained the same, and the way people related to each other remained the same.

There are changes occurring that will influence the way businesses organize. But the changes have been, and will continue to be, gradual. They may accelerate some, but we are not going to see a revolution in the design of organizations. Take the case of globalization. It's significant, but it's also evolutionary. Has the formation of the European Union abolished national borders in the largest continental society in the Western world? No. France is still France, and Germany is still Germany. Things have changed, but things have not changed.

The emphasis on speed has its limits. Brains don't speed up. The exchange of ideas does not really speed up, only the overhead that slowed down the exchange. When it comes down to the bulk of knowledge work, the twenty-first century works the same as the twentieth century: You can reach people around the clock, but they won't think any better or faster just because you have reached them faster. The give and take remains a limiting factor.

The virtual organization also has its limitations. When you outsource your data processing, manufacturing, and other functions, you make your capabilities available to your competitors. So virtualization of work diminishes competitive advantages. It leads to everything becoming a commodity. Any function that an organization uses to achieve a competitive advantage cannot be outsourced.

Look back over the past 40 years. People have not changed. Our fundamental organizations have not changed. On the fringes, there is more looseness in the organization. But a lot more has not changed than has. The changes we have seen have been slow and gradual. That pace is likely to continue into the future.

HR IMPLICATIONS

The Effects of Restructuring on Employees

Nearly every day, it seems, companies throughout the world announce that they are "restructuring" and laying off employees. In January 2005, Toronto-based Celestica announced that it would cut 5500 jobs in North America and Western Europe by mid-2006, and Montreal-based Bombardier announced job cuts of 2200.[37] In June 2005, General Motors announced that it was cutting 25 000 US jobs, raising concerns that the General Motors parts plant in St. Catharines, Ontario, would be closed as a result.[38] Brampton, Ontario-based Nortel Networks laid off 48 500 employees (half its workforce) in 2001. Restructuring often goes by various names, including *downsizing, rightsizing,* and *delayering,* but all these terms are really euphemisms for layoffs.

Restructuring happens in a variety of ways. Sometimes organizations decide to engage in work redesign. Whole divisions or business units might be combined, or disaggregated, or even spun off. Sometimes business functions, such as engineering, operations, and distribution, might be joined together. Or some of these functions might be contracted out. Delayering is another restructuring technique, which means that the organization reduces the number of layers, or hierarchical levels. Finally, restructuring can also involve downsizing, or layoffs.

While structural changes and work redesign may be a more planned approach to workforce change, generally the intent behind layoffs is not some planned approach to a new organizational structure. Rather it serves as an attempt to increase shareholder well-being.[39] For instance, when Longueuil, Quebec-based BCE Emergis, a subsidiary of BCE, announced in April 2002 it was cutting 550 jobs, including 440 in Canada, and eliminating 40 percent of its business operations, its shares climbed 15 percent.[40] These results are only short-term, however. A recent study found that organizations that cut 10 percent or more employees significantly underperform organizations that cut fewer employees.[41]

Canadians are concerned about the impact of layoffs and the responsibilities of corporations. When a *Maclean's*/CBC News poll asked respondents about the acceptability of profitable corporations laying off workers, 58 percent did not find this acceptable.[42] Negative reactions to downsizing were even higher in the regions experiencing the most difficult economic times, with Quebec (64 percent) and the Atlantic provinces (66 percent) giving the most unfavourable views. In Alberta, where the economy had been booming, fewer people were reluctant to criticize companies for layoffs (49 percent).

There are several options that the human resource department can recommend to senior executives as alternatives to downsizing.[43] A number of Canadian corporations have developed options such as job-sharing, voluntarily reduced work time, and phased-in retirement as ways to avoid downsizing. These companies have chosen these options as a way to preserve employee morale.

Professor Ronald Burke of the Schulich School of Business at York University and his co-author, Debra Nelson, proposed a three-stage guide for managing revitalization efforts:[44]

- *Initiation—planning and preparing for the transition.* During this stage, develop concrete goals, communicate the strategy clearly, look for alternatives to and criteria for downsizing, and develop timetables.

- *Implementation—moving toward change.* During this stage, involve the employees, communicate extensively, give support, and watch for stress.

- *Institutionalization—healing and refocusing.* During this stage, focus on why changes are needed, celebrate accomplishments, retrain employees as needed, and maintain individual and organizational health.

Burke and Nelson note that how managers treat employees during downsizing and restructuring makes a large difference in the results. For instance, telling employees that they are lucky to have survived the cuts does not necessarily instill goodwill.

LEARNING ABOUT **YOURSELF** EXERCISE

Bureaucratic Orientation Test

For each statement, check the response (either "Mostly Agree" or "Mostly Disagree") that best represents your feelings.

	Mostly Agree	Mostly Disagree
1. I value stability in my job.	_____	_____
2. I like a predictable organization.	_____	_____
3. The best job for me would be one in which the future is uncertain.	_____	_____
4. The federal government would be a nice place to work.	_____	_____
5. Rules, policies, and procedures tend to frustrate me.	_____	_____
6. I would enjoy working for a company that employs 85 000 people worldwide.	_____	_____
7. Being self-employed would involve more risk than I am willing to take.	_____	_____
8. Before accepting a job, I would like to see an exact job description.	_____	_____
9. I would prefer a job as a freelance house painter to one as a clerk for the Motor Vehicles Branch.	_____	_____
10. Seniority should be as important as performance in determining pay increases and promotion.	_____	_____
11. It would give me a feeling of pride to work for the largest and most successful company in its field.	_____	_____
12. Given a choice, I would prefer to make $70 000 per year as a vice-president in a small company than $85 000 as a staff specialist in a large company.	_____	_____
13. I would regard wearing an employee badge with a number on it as a degrading experience.	_____	_____
14. Parking spaces in a company lot should be assigned on the basis of job level.	_____	_____
15. If an accountant works for a large organization, he or she cannot be a true professional.	_____	_____
16. Before accepting a job (given a choice), I would want to make sure that the company had a very fine program of employee benefits.	_____	_____
17. A company will probably not be successful unless it establishes a clear set of rules and procedures.	_____	_____
18. Regular working hours and vacations are more important to me than finding thrills on the job.	_____	_____
19. You should respect people according to their rank.	_____	_____
20. Rules are meant to be broken.	_____	_____

Scoring Key:

Give yourself 1 point for each statement for which you responded in the bureaucratic direction:

Mostly agree: 1, 2, 4, 7, 8, 10, 11, 14, 16, 18, 19

Mostly disagree: 3, 5, 6, 9, 12, 13, 15, 17, 20

A very high score (15 or over) suggests that you would enjoy working in a bureaucracy. A very low score (5 or lower) suggests that you would be frustrated by working in a bureaucracy, especially a large one.

Source: Adapted from A. J. DuBrin, *Human Relations: A Job Oriented Approach,* 5th ed., 1992. Reprinted with permission of Prentice Hall, Inc., Upper Saddle River, NJ.

BREAKOUT **GROUP** EXERCISES

Form small groups to discuss the following topics, as assigned by your instructor:

1. Describe the structure of an organization in which you worked. Was the structure appropriate for the tasks being done?

2. Have you ever worked in an organization with a structure that seemed inappropriate to the task? What would have improved the structure?

3. You are considering opening up a coffee bar with several of your friends. What kind of structure might you use? After the coffee bar becomes successful, you decide that expanding the number of branches might be a good idea. What changes to the structure might you make?

WORKING WITH **OTHERS** EXERCISE

Words-in-Sentences Company

Overview: You are a small company that

1. manufactures words; and

2. packages them into meaningful English-language sentences.[45]

Market research has established that sentences of at least 3 words but not more than 6 words are in demand. Therefore, packaging, distribution, and sales should be set up for **3- to 6-word sentences**.

Time: Approximately 30 minutes. (Note: A production run takes 10 minutes. While the game is more effective if 2 [or more] production runs are completed, even 1 production run will generate effective discussion about how organizational structure affects performance.)

Group Task: Your group must design and participate in running a W-I-S company. You will be competing with other companies in your industry. The success of your company will depend on (a) your objectives, (b) planning, (c) organizational structure, and (d) quality control. You should design your organization to be as efficient as possible during each 10-minute production run. After the first production run, you will have an opportunity to reorganize your company if you want.

Raw Materials: For each production run, you will be given a **"raw material phrase."** The letters found in the phrase serve as the raw materials available to produce new words in sentences. For example, if the raw material phrase is "organizational behaviour is fun," you could produce the words and sentence "Nat ran to a zoo." One way to think of your raw material phrase is to take all the letters appearing in the phrase and write them down as many times as they appear in the phrase. Thus, for the phrase "organizational behaviour is fun" you have: a-4; b-1; c-0; d-0; e-1; f-1; g-1; h-1; i-4; j-0; k-0; l-1; m-0; n-3; o-3; p-0; q-0; r-2; s-1; t-1; u-1; v-1; w-0; x-0; y-0; z-1 for a total of 28 raw material letters.

Production Standards: There are several rules that have to be followed in producing "words-in-sentences." **If these rules are not followed, your output will not meet production specifications and will not pass quality-control inspection.**

▶

1. A letter may appear only as often in a manufactured word as it appears in the raw material phrase; for example, "organizational behaviour is fun" has 1 letter *l* and 1 letter *e*. Thus "steal" is legitimate, but not "teller." It has too many *l*'s and *e*'s.

2. Raw material letters can be used again in different manufactured words.

3. A manufactured **word** may be used only **once** during a production run; once a word—for example, "the"—is used in a sentence, it is out of stock for the rest of the production run. No other sentence may use the word "the."

4. A new word may not be made by adding *s* to form the plural of an already used manufactured word.

5. Sentences must make grammatical and logical sense.

6. All words must be in the English language.

7. Names and places are acceptable.

8. Slang is not acceptable.

9. Writing must be legible. Any illegible sentence will be disqualified.

10. Only sentences that have a minimum of 3 words and a maximum of 6 words will be considered.

Directions:

Step 1   Production Run 1. The instructor will place a raw material phrase on the board or overhead. When the instructor announces, "Begin production," you are to manufacture as many words as possible and package them in sentences for delivery to the Quality Control Review Board. You will have 10 minutes.

Step 2   When the instructor announces, "Stop production," you will have 30 seconds to deliver your output to the Quality Control Review Board. Output received after 30 seconds does not meet the delivery schedule and will not be counted. You may use up to 2 sheets of paper and each sheet of paper must identify your group.

Step 3   Your output should be delivered by your quality-control representative, who will work with the other representatives to evaluate the performance of each of the groups.

Measuring Performance: The output of your W-I-S company is measured by the total number of acceptable words that are packaged in sentences of 3 to 6 words only.

Quality Control: If any word in a sentence does not meet the standards set forth above, all the words in the sentence will be rejected. The Quality Control Review Board (composed of 1 member from each company) is the final arbiter of acceptability. In the event of a tie vote on the Review Board, a coin toss will determine the outcome.

Step 4   While the output is being evaluated, you should make plans for organizing the 2nd production run.

Step 5   Production Run 2.

Step 6   The results are presented.

Step 7   Discussion.

ETHICAL **DILEMMA** EXERCISE

Just Following Orders

In 1996, Betty Vinson took a job as a mid-level accountant for $50 000 a year with a small long-distance company in Jackson, Mississippi. Within five years, that long-distance company had grown up to become telecom giant WorldCom.

Hard-working and diligent, within two years Ms. Vinson was promoted to a senior manager in WorldCom's corpo-rate accounting division. In her new job, she helped compile quarterly results, along with 10 employees who reported to her. Soon after taking the new position, her bosses asked her to make false accounting entries. At first, she said "no." But continued pressure led to her finally caving in. Her decision to make the false entries came after the company's chief financial officer assured her that he would assume all responsibility.

Over the course of six quarters, Ms. Vinson made illegal entries to bolster WorldCom's profits at the request of her superiors. At the end of 18 months, she had helped falsify at least $3.7 billion in profits. Of course, the whole scheme unravelled in 2002, in what became the largest fraud case in corporate history.

Ms. Vinson pleaded guilty to two criminal counts of conspiracy and securities fraud, charges that carry a maximum sentence of 15 years in prison. In the summer of 2005, she was sentenced to five months in prison and five months of house arrest.

What would you have done had you been in Ms. Vinson's job? Is "just following orders" an acceptable excuse for breaking the law? If your livelihood is on the line, do you say no to a powerful boss? What can organizations do to lessen the chance that employees might capitulate to unethical pressures imposed by their boss?

Sources: Based on S. Pulliam, "A Staffer Ordered to Commit Fraud Balked, Then Caved," *Wall Street Journal,* June 23, 2003, p. A1; and E. McClam, "Ex-WorldCom Exec Gets 5-Month Term, House Arrest," Clarion-Ledger, August 5, 2005, www.clarionledger.com/apps/pbcs.dll/article?AID=/20050805/NEWS0108/50805011/1002/NEWS01 (accessed September 29, 2005).

CASE INCIDENTS

Ajax University Needs a New Structure

Ajax University has recently been in the news for scandals within its athletics department. The athletics department admits to doctoring athletes' transcripts so these athletes can gain admission or maintain eligibility; coaches have been charged with recruiting violations; and alumni have been found to be providing athletes with cars and illegal cash payments.

Despite widespread criticism of these practices, little seems to be done to implement changes to deal with these abuses. Why? There's a lot of money and prestige involved, and university administrators seem willing to look the other way so as not to upset the system.

Within the current structure of the university, the athletics department is responsible for all sports programs. The head of the department, the athletics director, reports to the president of the university, at least on paper. In practice, because the department brings so much money into the university, the athletics director is given free rein to do whatever he wants within his department. The separate and special status given to the athletics department makes abuse rather easy.

Gordon Gee, the chancellor at Vanderbilt University, in reflecting on the problems at Ajax University, believes that the problems are structural: "For too long, athletics has been segregated from the core mission of the university. As a result, we have created a culture, both on campus and nationally, that is disconnected from students, faculty and other constituents, where responsibility is diffused, the potential abuse considerable, and the costs—both financial and academic—unsustainable."

Ajax University needs a new organizational structure for its athletics department that would help eliminate much of the abuse that has happened. The department currently oversees 14 varsity sports, 37 club sports, and various intramural sports.

Varsity sports are elite programs; the significant amount of revenue they bring in not only covers the costs of all club and intramural sports, but also contributes to the general operating budget of the university. One of the problems facing varsity sports is how to recruit students who fit the profile of the university. Ajax athletes are typically admitted with a grade point average of 60 percent. The overall student average for those admitted to Ajax is 70 percent.

Intramural sports provide opportunities to students, faculty, and staff to participate in sports on a league basis with post-secondary schools in the region. Rules for intramural sports are determined by representatives of league teams. Club sports provide a co-ed, competitive, recreational program for students, faculty, and staff. Students coordinate and administer the programs and find coaches to participate on a volunteer basis.

Questions

1. How would you classify Ajax University's structure with respect to the athletics department? Defend your choice.

2. Is Ajax University's problem one of poor leadership or inadequate structural design? Explain.

3. If you were a consultant advising Ajax University, what would you suggest to fix the problems noted?

Sources: Based on "Major Changes for Vanderbilt Athletics," *New York Times,* September 10, 2003, p. C19; M. Cass, "Vanderbilt Realigns Management," *USA Today,* September 10, 2003, p. 7C; and "Vanderbilt University Is Not Getting Rid of Sports," *Chronicle of Higher Education,* September 19, 2003, p. A35.

OB *AT WORK*

"I Detest Bureaucracy"

Greg Strakosch, founder and CEO of interactive media company TechTarget, hates bureaucracy. So he has created a workplace where his 210 employees are free to come and go as they please. There are no set policies mandating working hours or detailing sick, personal, or vacation days. Employees are free to take as much vacation as they want and to work the hours when they are most productive—even if it's between midnight and 4 a.m. And if you need a day off to take your kid to camp? No problem. Strakosch says ideas like setting a specific number of sick days "strike me as arbitrary and dumb." He trusts his employees to act responsibly.

Strakosch is quick to state that "this isn't a country club." A painstaking hiring process is designed to weed out all but the most autonomous. Managers set ambitious quarterly goals, and employees are given plenty of independence to achieve them. But there is little tolerance for failure. In the most recent 12 months, for instance, Strakosch had fired 7 percent of his workforce for underachieving.

And while hours are flexible, employees frequently put in at least 50 hours a week. In addition, regardless of hours worked, employees are required to remain accessible via email, cellphones, instant messaging, or laptops.

Strakosch's approach seems to be working. Started in 1999, sales in 2003 were expected to hit $35 million—up nearly 30 percent from 2002.

Questions

1. What type of organization is this?

2. Why does this type of structure work at TechTarget?

3. How transferable is this structure to other organizations?

4. Would you want to work at TechTarget? Why or why not?

Source: Based on P. J. Sauer, "Open-Door Management," *Inc.,* June 2003, p. 44.

From **Concepts** to **Skills**

Delegating Authority

Managers get things done through other people. Because there are limits to any manager's time and knowledge, effective managers need to understand how to delegate. *Delegation* is the assignment of authority to another person to carry out specific duties. It allows an employee to make decisions. Delegation should not be confused with participation. In participative decision making, there is a sharing of authority. In delegation, employees make decisions on their own.

A number of actions differentiate the effective delegator from the ineffective delegator. There are five behaviours that effective delegators will use:[46]

1. *Clarify the assignment.* The place to begin is to determine what is to be delegated and to whom. You need to identify the person most capable of doing the task, then determine if he or she has the time and motivation to do the job.

    Assuming you have a willing and able employee, it is your responsibility to provide clear information on what is being delegated, the results you expect, and any time or performance expectations you hold.

    Unless there is an overriding need to adhere to specific methods, you should delegate only the end results. That is, get agreement on what is to be done and the end results expected, but let the employee decide on the means.

2. *Specify the employee's range of discretion.* Every act of delegation comes with constraints. You are delegating authority to act, but not unlimited authority. What you are delegating is authority to

act on certain issues and, on those issues, within certain parameters. You need to specify what those parameters are so employees know, in no uncertain terms, the range of their discretion.

3. *Allow the employee to participate.* One of the best sources for determining how much authority will be necessary to accomplish a task is the employee who will be held accountable for that task. If you allow employees to participate in determining what is delegated, how much authority is needed to get the job done, and the standards by which they will be judged, you increase employee motivation, satisfaction, and accountability for performance.

4. *Inform others that delegation has occurred.* Delegation should not occur in a vacuum. Not only do you and the employee need to know specifically what has been delegated and how much authority has been granted, but anyone else who may be affected by the delegation act also needs to be informed.

5. *Establish feedback controls.* The establishment of controls to monitor the employee's progress increases the likelihood that important problems will be identified early and that the task will be completed on time and to the desired specifications. For instance, agree on a specific time for completion of the task, and then set progress dates when the employee will report back on how well he or she is doing and any major problems that have surfaced. This can be supplemented with periodic spot checks to ensure that authority guidelines are not being abused, organization policies are being followed, and proper procedures are being met.

Assessing Skills

After you've read this chapter, take the following Self-Assessment on your enclosed CD-ROM:

41. What Type of Organization Structure Do I Prefer?

42. How Willing Am I to Delegate?

Practising Skills

You are the director of research and development for a large pharmaceutical manufacturer. You have six people who report directly to you: Sue (your secretary), Dale (laboratory manager), Todd (quality standards manager), Linda (patent coordination manager), Ruben (market coordina-

tion manager), and Marjorie (senior projects manager). Dale is the most senior of the five managers and is generally acknowledged as the chief candidate to replace you if you are promoted or leave.

You have received your annual instructions from the CEO to develop next year's budget for your area. The task is relatively routine but takes quite a bit of time. In the past, you have always done the annual budget yourself. But this year, because your workload is exceptionally heavy, you have decided to try something different. You are going to assign budget preparation to one of your subordinate managers. The obvious choice is Dale. Dale has been with the company longest, is highly dependable, and, as your probable successor, is most likely to gain from the experience. The budget is due on your boss's desk in eight weeks. Last year it took you about 30 to 35 hours to complete. However, you have done a budget many times before. For a novice, it might take double that amount of time.

The budget process is generally straightforward. You start with last year's budget and modify it to reflect inflation and changes in departmental objectives. All the data that Dale will need are in your files, online, or can be obtained from your other managers.

You have just walked over to Dale's office and informed him of your decision. He seemed enthusiastic about doing the budget, but he also has a heavy workload. He told you, "I'm regularly coming in around 7 a.m. and it's unusual for me to leave before 7 p.m. For the past five weekends, I've even come in on Saturday mornings to get my work done. I can do my best to try to find time to do the budget." Specify exactly what you would say to Dale and the actions you would take if Dale agrees to do the budget.

Reinforcing Skills

1. When watching a video of a classic movie that has examples of "managers" delegating assignments, pay explicit attention to the incidence of delegation. Was delegating done effectively? What was good about the practice? How might it have been improved? Examples of movies with delegation examples include *The Godfather, The Firm, Star Trek, Nine-to-Five,* and *Working Girl.*

2. The next time you have to do a group project for a class, pay explicit attention to how tasks are delegated. Does someone assume a leadership role? If so, note how closely the delegation process is followed. Is delegation different in project or study groups than in typical work groups?

CHAPTER 14
Organizational Change

All around it, competitors are closing or losing money. How can Canadian Tire make the changes needed to survive?

1 **What are the forces for change?**

2 **How do organizations manage change?**

3 **Why do people and organizations resist change?**

4 **What are some of the contemporary issues in managing change?**

S tephen Bachand, former CEO of Toronto-based Canadian Tire, created a remarkable turnaround between taking over in 1994 and announcing his resignation in 2000.[1] Although Eaton's liquidated and Marks & Spencer closed its Canadian stores in 1999, Canadian Tire turned in a record profit of $167 million in 1998, a 3000 percent improvement over five years. Between 1994 and late 1999, Canadian Tire's stock price quadrupled. In 1999, total retail sales were up 7.7 percent over 1998, following an increase of 7.5 percent in 1998 over 1997.

During his tenure, Bachand worked to change both the employees and the stores. Canadian Tire wanted improvements in customer service and employee training. To do this, the company "outlined core company values—like honesty, respect and responsibility—and established a long-term training program for employees to develop leadership and customer relationship skills."

Canadian Tire faced a new set of challenges in 2001, after Bachand announced his retirement. The stock price fell dramatically. Would the company be able to recover from the change in leadership?

Canadian Tire is just one of the many organizations that need to reinvent themselves often if they are to survive in a challenging business environment. Engaging in any kind of change in an organization is not easy. In this chapter, we examine the forces for change, managing change, and contemporary change issues.

WHAT CAUSES CHANGE?

A study of 309 human resource executives across a variety of industries found that *all* respondents were going through at least one of the following changes: mergers, acquisitions, divestitures, global competition, management and/or organizational structure.[2] A Statistics Canada Workplace and Employee Survey further identified types of changes that Canadian businesses went through recently: "integrating different functional areas; modifying the degree of centralisation; downsizing; relying more on temporary and/or part-time workers; re-engineering; increasing overtime hours; adopting flexible working hours; reducing the number of managerial levels; relying on job rotation and/or multi-skilling; implementing Total Quality Management; outsourcing; and collaborating more on interfirm research and development, production, or marketing."[3] The extent to which businesses undergo change varies by organizational size. More than 80 percent of companies that employed 100 or more people underwent at least one of these changes. Only 40 percent of the smaller companies underwent change.

Organizational change is not just confined to larger organizations; 18 percent of self-employed individuals also reported organizational change. The same study identified the following types of changes for the self-employed: engaging in "collaborative work, new inventory systems, introducing sub-contracting, new financial management

1 What are the forces for change?

Canadian Tire
www.canadiantire.ca

techniques, computerisation of organisational practices, introduction of new corporate strategic orientation or redefining operating hours."[4]

What brings about change in organizations? Organizations face continuously changing environments. As a result, organizations must not only be aware of opportunities for change, but also consider how best to respond to them. They must also appoint people to help them manage organizational change efforts.

Forces for Change

As recently as the late 1990s, music retailers Virgin Records and Vancouver-based a&b sound were rapidly growing and profitable companies. Young people were flocking to their superstores because they offered a wide selection and competitive prices. But the market changed, and these chains and others like them suffered the consequences. Downloading, legal and otherwise, cut hard into CD sales, and growing competition from Indigo.com and Amazon.ca, as well as discounters such as Wal-Mart and Costco, stole a sizable part of their market share.

More and more organizations today face a dynamic and changing environment. This, in turn, is requiring these organizations to adapt. "Change or die!" is the rallying cry among today's managers worldwide. Exhibit 14-1 summarizes six specific forces that are acting as stimulants for change.

In a number of places in this textbook, we have discussed the changing *nature of the workforce*. For instance, almost every organization is having to adjust to a multicultural environment. Human resource policies and practices have to change to reflect the needs of an aging labour force. Many companies are having to spend large amounts of money on employee training to upgrade reading, math, computer, and other skills.

Technology is changing jobs and organizations. For instance, computers are now commonplace in almost every organization, and cellphones and hand-held PDAs are increasingly being perceived as necessities by a large segment of the population. The music

EXHIBIT 14-1 Forces for Change	
Force	**Examples**
Nature of the workforce	More cultural diversity Aging population Many new entrants with inadequate skills
Technology	Faster, cheaper, and more mobile computers Online music sharing Deciphering of the human genetic code
Economic shocks	Rise and fall of dot-com stocks 2000–2002 stock market collapse Record low interest rates
Competition	Global competitors Mergers and consolidations Growth of e-commerce
Social trends	Internet chat rooms Retirement of Baby Boomers Rise in discount and "big box" retailers
World politics	Iraq–US war Opening of markets in China Hurricane disasters in US in September 2005

business, as a case in point, is now struggling to cope with the economic consequences of widespread online music sharing. For the longer term, recent breakthroughs in deciphering the human genetic code offer the potential for pharmaceutical companies to produce drugs designed for specific individuals, which creates serious ethical dilemmas for insurance companies as to who is insurable and who is not.

Beginning in the early 1970s, with the overnight quadrupling of world oil prices, *economic shocks* have continued to impose changes on organizations. In recent years, for instance, new dot-com businesses have been created, turned tens of thousands of investors into overnight millionaires, and then crashed. The stock market decline from 2000 to 2002 eroded approximately 40 percent of the average employee's retirement account, which may force many employees to postpone their anticipated retirement date. Record low interest rates have stimulated a rapid rise in home values, helped sustain consumer spending, and proven a spur to home builders and remodellers, furniture retailers, mortgage bankers, and other home-related businesses.

Competition is changing. In the global economy, competitors are as likely to come from across the ocean as from across town. Heightened competition also makes it necessary for established organizations to defend themselves against both traditional competitors who develop new products and services, and small, entrepreneurial firms with innovative offerings.

Social trends don't remain static. For instance, in contrast to just 15 years ago, people are meeting and sharing information in Internet chat rooms; Baby Boomers have begun to retire; and consumers are increasingly doing their shopping at discount warehouses and "big box" retailers such as The Home Depot and Future Shop.

Throughout this textbook, we have argued strongly for the importance of seeing organizational behaviour in a global context. Business schools have been preaching a global perspective since the early 1980s, but no one—not even the strongest proponents of globalization—could have imagined how *world politics* would change in recent years. We have seen the breakup of the Soviet Union; the opening up of South Africa and China; almost daily suicide bombings in the Middle East; and, of course, the rise of Muslim fundamentalism. The unilateral invasion of Iraq by the United States has led to an expensive postwar rebuilding program and an increase in anti-American attitudes in much of the world.

This chapter's *CBC Video Case* illustrates some of the conditions that Fairmont Hotels and Resorts faced that forced it to change.

Fairmont Hotels and Resorts

Opportunities for Change

Organizations have many opportunities to engage in change. For instance, we noted the importance of motivating employees and discussed a variety of programs that could be used to motivate individuals for specific outcomes. We described job redesign as a way of motivating employees and indicated that increasing factors such as autonomy and feedback generally increases job satisfaction. We looked at the greater emphasis on teamwork in organizations. We suggested that organizations are moving toward becoming more ethically and socially responsible. We discussed the leadership challenges of sharing power with employees, as well as the need for employees to be good followers when necessary. We discussed reorganizing the workplace, noting how recent changes in organizational structure have, in some instances, led to more flattened organizations and more interconnections with other organizations. We also noted that the culture of an organization is like the glue that holds the organization together, and that sometimes the entire culture of the organization needs to change in order for organizational change to be successful. Exhibit 14-2 on page 514 summarizes the range of change targets available to organizations.

As we discussed the workplace in this textbook, and talked about possible change, we might have implied that change happens easily, perhaps overnight, and does not require careful thought or planning. This implication exists because we did not discuss how these changes actually happen in the workplace, what has to be done to achieve change,

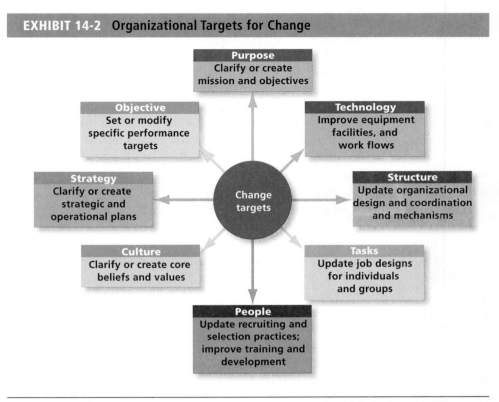

EXHIBIT 14-2   Organizational Targets for Change

Purpose
Clarify or create mission and objectives

Objective
Set or modify specific performance targets

Technology
Improve equipment facilities, and work flows

Strategy
Clarify or create strategic and operational plans

Change targets

Structure
Update organizational design and coordination and mechanisms

Culture
Clarify or create core beliefs and values

Tasks
Update job designs for individuals and groups

People
Update recruiting and selection practices; improve training and development

Source: J. R. Schermerhorn Jr., J. G. Hunt, and R. N. Osborn, *Organizational Behavior,* 9th ed., 2005, p. 363, Figure 16.1. Copyright © 2005 John Wiley & Sons, Inc. Reprinted with permission of John Wiley & Sons, Inc.

and how difficult change actually is. We wanted you to understand what changes were possible before we actually discussed how to carry them out.

Change Agents

Who is responsible for managing change activities in an organization? The answer is **change agents**.[5] Change agents can be managers or nonmanagers, employees of the organization, or outside consultants. A contemporary example of an internal change agent is Lawrence Summers, president of Harvard University.[6] Since accepting the presidency in 2001, Summers has aggressively sought to shake up the complacent institution by, among other things, leading the battle to reshape the undergraduate curriculum, proposing that the university be more directly engaged with problems in education and public health, and reorganizing to consolidate more power in the president's office. While his critics admit that he has "offended nearly everyone," he is bringing about revolutionary changes at Harvard that many thought were not possible. It has come at some cost, however, with some faculty members complaining bitterly about his leadership.

In some instances, internal management will hire the services of outside consultants to provide advice and assistance with major change efforts. Because they are from the outside, these individuals can offer an objective perspective often unavailable to insiders. Outside consultants, however, are disadvantaged because they usually have an inadequate understanding of the organization's history, culture, operating procedures, and personnel. Outside consultants also may be prone to initiating more drastic changes—which can be a benefit or a disadvantage—because they don't have to live with the repercussions after the change is implemented. In contrast, internal staff specialists or managers, when acting as change agents, may be more thoughtful (and possibly more cautious) because they have to live with the consequences of their actions.

change agents People who act as catalysts and assume the responsibility for managing change activities.

APPROACHES TO MANAGING CHANGE

Now we turn to several approaches to managing change: Lewin's classic three-step model of the change process, Kotter's eight-step plan for implementing change, action research, and appreciative inquiry.

2 How do organizations manage change?

Lewin's Three-Step Model

To this point, we have discussed the kinds of changes organizations can make. Assuming that an organization has uncovered a need for change, how does it engage in the change process? Kurt Lewin argued that successful change in organizations should follow three steps, which are illustrated in Exhibit 14-3: **unfreezing** the status quo, **moving** to a new state, and **refreezing** the new change to make it permanent.[7]

unfreezing Change efforts to overcome the pressures of both individual resistance and group conformity.

moving Efforts to get employees involved in the change process.

refreezing Stabilizing a change intervention by balancing driving and restraining forces.

The value of this model can be seen through the example of a large oil company whose management decided to reorganize its marketing function in Western Canada.

The oil company had three divisional marketing offices in the West, located in Winnipeg, Calgary, and Vancouver. The decision was made to consolidate the marketing divisions into a single regional office in Calgary. The reorganization meant transferring more than 150 employees, eliminating some duplicate managerial positions, and instituting a new hierarchy of command. As you might guess, keeping such a big move secret was difficult. The rumour that it would take place preceded the announcement by several months. The decision itself was made unilaterally. It came from the executive offices in Toronto. The people affected had no say whatsoever in the choice. For those in Vancouver or Winnipeg who disliked the decision and its consequences—the problems inherent in transferring to another city, pulling youngsters out of school, making new friends, having new co-workers, undergoing the reassignment of responsibilities—the only recourse was to quit. The status quo was about to change.

The status quo can be considered to be an equilibrium state. To move from this equilibrium—to overcome the pressures of both individual resistance and group conformity—unfreezing is necessary. Exhibit 14-4 on page 516 shows that unfreezing can occur in one of three ways. The **driving forces**, which direct behaviour away from the status quo, can be increased. The **restraining forces**, which hinder movement from the existing equilibrium, can be decreased. A third alternative is to *combine the first two approaches.*

driving forces Forces that direct behaviour away from the status quo.

restraining forces Forces that hinder movement away from the status quo

The oil company's management expected employee resistance to the consolidation and outlined its alternatives. Management could use positive incentives to encourage employees to accept the change. The company could offer pay increases to those who accept the transfer or liberal moving expenses. Management might offer low-cost mortgage funds to allow employees to buy new homes in Calgary. Of course, management might also consider unfreezing acceptance of the status quo by removing restraining forces. Employees could be counselled individually. Each employee's concerns and apprehensions could be heard and specifically clarified. Assuming that most of the fears are unjustified, the counsellor could assure the employees that there was nothing to fear and then demonstrate, through tangible evidence, that restraining forces are unwarranted. If resistance is extremely high, management may have to resort to both reducing resistance and increasing the attractiveness of the alternative if the unfreezing is to be successful.

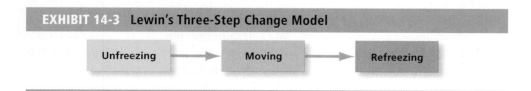

EXHIBIT 14-3   Lewin's Three-Step Change Model

Unfreezing → Moving → Refreezing

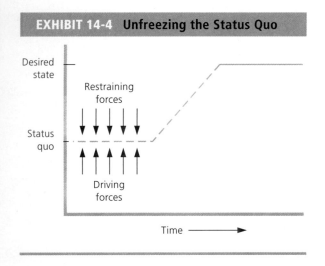

EXHIBIT 14-4   Unfreezing the Status Quo

Once the consolidation change has been implemented, if it is to be successful, the new situation must be refrozen so that it can be sustained over time. Unless this last step is taken, there is a high chance that the change will be short-lived and that employees will try to revert to the previous equilibrium state. The objective of refreezing, then, is to stabilize the new situation by balancing the driving and restraining forces.

How could the oil company's management refreeze its consolidation change? It could systematically replace temporary forces with permanent ones. For instance, management might impose a new bonus system tied to the specific changes desired. The formal rules and regulations governing behaviour of those affected by the change should also be revised to reinforce the new situation. Over time, of course, the work group's own norms will evolve to sustain the new equilibrium. But until that point is reached, management will have to rely on more formal mechanisms.

A key feature of Lewin's three-step model is its conception of change as an episodic activity. For a debate about whether change can continue to be implemented as an activity with a beginning, middle, and end, or whether the structure of twenty-first-century workplaces will require change to take place as an ongoing if not chaotic process, see this chapter's *Point/Counterpoint* on page 532.

Kotter's Eight-Step Plan for Implementing Change

John Kotter, professor of leadership at Harvard Business School, built on Lewin's three-step model to create a more detailed approach for implementing change.[8]

Kotter began by listing common failures that occur when managers try to initiate change. These include the inability to create a sense of urgency about the need for change; failure to create a coalition for managing the change process; the absence of a vision for change and to effectively communicate that vision; not removing obstacles that could impede the achievement of the vision; failure to provide short-term and achievable goals; the tendency to declare victory too soon; and not anchoring the changes in the organization's culture.

Kotter then established eight sequential steps to overcome these problems. These steps are listed in Exhibit 14-5.

Notice how Exhibit 14-5 builds on Lewin's model. Kotter's first four steps essentially represent the "unfreezing" stage. Steps 5 through 7 represent "moving." The final step works on "refreezing." Kotter's contribution lies in providing managers and change agents with a more detailed guide for successfully implementing change.

Action Research

action research A change process based on the systematic collection of data and then selection of a change action based on what the analyzed data indicate.

Action research refers to a change process based on the systematic collection of data and then selection of a change action based on what the analyzed data indicate.[9] The importance of this approach is that it provides a scientific method for managing planned change.

The process of action research consists of five steps: diagnosis, analysis, feedback, action, and evaluation. The change agent, often an outside consultant in action research, begins by gathering information about problems, concerns, and needed changes from members of the organization. This *diagnosis* is analogous to the physician's search to find specifically what ails a patient. In action research, the change agent asks questions, interviews employees, reviews records, and listens to the concerns of employees.

Diagnosis is followed by *analysis.* What problems do people key in on? What patterns do these problems seem to take? The change agent synthesizes this information into primary concerns, problem areas, and possible actions.

EXHIBIT 14-5   Kotter's Eight-Step Plan for Implementing Change
1.   Establish a sense of urgency by creating a compelling reason for why change is needed.
2.   Form a coalition with enough power to lead the change.
3.   Create a new vision to direct the change and strategies for achieving the vision.
4.   Communicate the vision throughout the organization.
5.   Empower others to act on the vision by removing barriers to change and encouraging risk-taking and creative problem-solving.
6.   Plan for, create, and reward short-term "wins" that move the organization toward the new vision.
7.   Consolidate improvements, reassess changes, and make necessary adjustments in the new programs.
8.   Reinforce the changes by demonstrating the relationship between new behaviours and organizational success.

Source: Based on J. P. Kotter, *Leading Change* (Boston: Harvard Business School Press, 1996).

Action research includes extensive involvement of the change targets. That is, the people who will be involved in any change program must be actively involved in determining what the problem is and participating in creating the solution. So the third step—*feedback*—requires sharing with employees what has been found from steps one and two. The employees, with the help of the change agent, develop action plans for bringing about any needed change.

Now the *action* part of action research is set in motion. The employees and the change agent carry out the specific actions to correct the problems that have been identified.

The final step, consistent with the scientific underpinnings of action research, is *evaluation* of the action plan's effectiveness. Using the initial data gathered as a benchmark, any subsequent changes can be compared and evaluated.

Action research provides at least two specific benefits for an organization. First, it is problem-focused. The change agent objectively looks for problems, and the type of problem determines the type of change action. While this may seem intuitively obvious, a lot of change activities are not done this way. Rather, they are solution-centred. The change agent has a favourite solution—for example, implementing flextime, teams, or a process re-engineering program—and then seeks out problems that his or her solution fits. Second, because action research so heavily involves employees in the process, resistance to change is reduced. In fact, once employees have actively participated in the feedback stage, the change process typically takes on a momentum of its own. The employees and groups that have been involved become an internal source of sustained pressure to bring about the change.

Appreciative Inquiry

Most organizational change approaches are problem-centred. They identify a problem or set of problems, then look for a solution. **Appreciative inquiry** accentuates the positive.[10] Rather than looking for problems to fix, this approach seeks to identify the unique qualities and special strengths of an organization, which can then be built on to improve performance. That is, it focuses on an organization's successes rather than on its problems.

Advocates of appreciative inquiry argue that problem-solving approaches always ask people to look backward at yesterday's failures, to focus on shortcomings, and rarely result

appreciative inquiry An approach to change that seeks to identify the unique qualities and special strengths of an organization, which can then be built on to improve performance.

in new visions. Instead of creating a climate for positive change, action research and organizational development techniques such as survey feedback and process consultation end up placing blame and generating defensiveness. Proponents of appreciative inquiry claim it makes more sense to refine and enhance what the organization is already doing well. This allows the organization to change by playing to its strengths and competitive advantages.

The appreciate inquiry process essentially consists of four steps, or "Four *D*'s," often played out in a large-group meeting over a two- or three-day time period, and overseen by a trained change agent:

- *Discovery.* The idea is to find out what people think are the strengths of the organization. For instance, employees are asked to recount times they felt the organization worked best or when they specifically felt most satisfied with their jobs.

- *Dreaming.* The information from the discovery phase is used to speculate on possible futures for the organization. For instance, people are asked to envision the organization in five years and describe what's different.

- *Design.* Based on the dream articulation, participants focus on finding a common vision of how the organization will look and agree on its unique qualities.

- *Destiny.* In this final step, participants discuss how the organization is going to fulfill its dream. This typically includes the writing of action plans and the development of implementation strategies.

Appreciate inquiry has proven to be an effective change strategy in organizations such as Toronto-based Orchestras Canada, Ajax, Ontario-based Nokia Canada, Vancouver-based Telus, Calgary-based EnCana, and Toronto-based CBC.

Nokia Canada
www.nokia.ca

Nokia Canada employees consider the future, envision the perfect solutions to the future, and then identify what needs to happen to get to the future as envisioned. Of their appreciative inquiry work, general manager Nathalie Le Prohon says, "It's very unstructured, very open to innovation and imagination, and very powerful as a tool for developing new thought leadership, new ways to approach business problems."[11]

Telus
www.telus.com

Telus' Go East division in Calgary has used appreciative inquiry to increase positive ideas among customer-care employees. Barbara Armstrong, a senior manager, explains the positive impact of the process: "The fact that [front-line workers] are being heard completely changes the way they view things."[12]

The use of appreciative inquiry in organizations is relatively recent, and it has not yet been determined when it is most appropriately used for organizational change.[13] However, it does give us the opportunity of viewing change from a much more positive perspective.

RESISTANCE TO CHANGE

3 Why do people and organizations resist change?

One of the most well-documented findings from studies of individual and organizational behaviour is that organizations and their members resist change. In a sense, this is positive. It provides a degree of stability and predictability to behaviour. If there weren't some resistance, organizational behaviour would take on characteristics of chaotic randomness. Resistance to change can also be a source of functional conflict. For example, resistance to a reorganization plan or a change in a product line can stimulate a healthy debate over the merits of the idea and result in a better decision.

However, there is a definite downside to resistance to change: It hinders adaptation and progress.

Resistance to change doesn't necessarily surface in standardized ways. Resistance can be overt, implicit, immediate, or deferred. It is easiest for management to deal with resistance when it is overt and immediate. For instance, a change is proposed, and employees respond immediately by voicing complaints, engaging in a work slowdown, threatening to go on strike, or the like. The greater challenge is managing resistance that is implicit or deferred. Implicit resistance efforts are more subtle—loss of loyalty to the organization, loss of motivation to work, increased errors or mistakes, increased absenteeism due to "sickness"—and hence more difficult to recognize. Similarly, deferred actions cloud the link between the source of the resistance and the reaction to it. A change may produce what appears to be only a minimal reaction at the time it is initiated, but then resistance surfaces weeks, months, or even years later. Or a single change that in and of itself might have little impact becomes "the straw that breaks the camel's back." Reactions to change can build up and then explode in some response that seems totally out of proportion to the change itself. The resistance, of course, has merely been deferred and stockpiled. What surfaces is a response to an accumulation of previous changes.

Let's look at the sources of resistance. For analytical purposes, we have categorized them by individual and organizational sources. In the real world, the sources often overlap.

Individual Resistance

How do you respond to change?

Individual sources of resistance to change reside in basic human characteristics such as perceptions, personalities, and needs. This chapter's *Case Incident—GreyStar Art & Greetings Makes Technological Changes* on page 538 looks at an individual who resists change in the workplace. Exhibit 14-6 on page 520 summarizes five reasons why individuals may resist change:

- *Habit.* To cope with life's complexities, we rely on habits or programmed responses. But when confronted with change, this tendency to respond in our accustomed ways becomes a source of resistance.

- *Security.* People with a high need for security are likely to resist change because it threatens their feelings of safety.

- *Economic factors.* Changes in job tasks or established work routines can arouse economic fears if people are concerned that they won't be able to perform the new tasks or routines to their previous standards, especially when pay is closely tied to productivity.

- *Fear of the unknown.* Change substitutes ambiguity and uncertainty for the known.

- *Selective information processing.* Individuals are guilty of selectively processing information in order to keep their perceptions intact. They hear what they want to hear, and they ignore information that challenges the world they have created.

Cynicism

In addition to simple resistance to change, employees often feel cynical about the change process, particularly if they have been through several rounds of "change," and nothing appears (to them) to have changed. In a 1997 study, three researchers from Ohio State

EXHIBIT 14-6   Sources of Individual Resistance to Change

University identified sources of cynicism in the change process of a large unionized manufacturing plant.[14] The major elements contributing to the cynicism were as follows:

- Feeling uninformed about what was happening
- Lack of communication and respect from one's manager
- Lack of communication and respect from one's union representative
- Lack of opportunity for meaningful participation in decision making

The researchers also found that employees with negative personalities were more likely to be cynical about change. While organizations might not be able to change an individual's personality, they certainly have the ability to provide greater communication and respect, as well as opportunities to participate in decision making. The researchers found that cynicism about change led to such outcomes as lower commitment, less satisfaction, and reduced motivation to work hard. Exhibit 14-7 illustrates why some employees, particularly Dilbert, may have reason to feel cynical about organizational change. You can discover more about how comfortable you are with change by taking the test in this chapter's *Learning About Yourself Exercise* on page 534. *HR Implications* on page 533 specifically deals with managing change in a unionized environment.

Organizational Resistance

What makes organizations resist change?

Organizations, by their very nature, are conservative.[15] They actively resist change. You don't have to look far to see evidence of this phenomenon. Government agencies want to continue doing what they have been doing for years, whether the need for their service changes or remains the same. Organized religions are deeply entrenched in their history. Attempts to change church doctrine require great persistence and patience. Educational institutions, which exist to open minds and challenge established ways of thinking, are themselves extremely resistant to change. Most school systems are using essentially the same teaching technologies today as they were 50 years ago. Similarly, most business firms appear highly resistant to change. Half of the 309 human resource executives of Canadian firms surveyed rated their companies' ability to manage change as "fair."[16] One-third of them said that their ability to manage change was their weakest skill, and only 25 percent of the companies make a strong effort to train leaders

EXHIBIT 14-7

Source: Dilbert, by Scott Adams. August 3, 1996. DILBERT reprinted by permission of United Feature Syndicate, Inc.

in the change process. When organizations refuse to change with the times, they can fail, as was the case with Eaton's, which never really adjusted to the arrival of Wal-Mart. When Eaton's was founded in 1869 by Irish immigrant Timothy Eaton, it was regarded as a "new wave" department store. Eaton's continued to set that pace for many years, but by the early 1980s, the store was considered dowdy rather than fashionable.[17]

Six major sources of organizational resistance (shown in Exhibit 14-8) on page 522 have been identified:[18]

Advantech AMT
www.advantechamt.com

- *Structural inertia.* Organizations have built-in mechanisms—such as their selection processes and formalized regulations—to produce stability. When an organization is confronted with change, this structural inertia acts as a counterbalance to sustain stability.

- *Limited focus of change.* Organizations are made up of a number of interdependent subsystems. One cannot be changed without affecting the others. So limited changes in subsystems tend to be nullified by the larger system.

- *Group inertia.* Even if individuals want to change their behaviour, group norms may act as a constraint.

- *Threat to expertise.* Changes in organizational patterns may threaten the expertise of specialized groups.

- *Threat to established power relationships.* Any redistribution of decision-making authority can threaten long-established power relationships within the organization.

- *Threat to established resource allocations.* Groups in the organization that control sizable resources often see change as a threat. They tend to be content with the way things are.

The *Working With Others Exercise* on page 536 asks you to identify how power relationships are affected by organizational change.

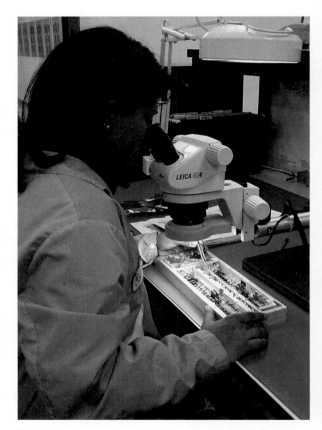

Though most people and organizations resist change, at Advantech AMT, located in Dorval, Quebec, change is the norm. Françoise Binette, vice-president of finance, says that "managing change forms an intrinsic part of our corporate DNA, and it is this environment that has allowed us to consistently develop unique and innovative products."

EXHIBIT 14-8   Sources of Organizational Resistance to Change

Overcoming Resistance to Change

Environics Research Group
erg.environics.net

Michael Adams, president of Environics Research Group in Toronto, has noted that Canadians may have become more resistant to change in recent years.[19] Between 1983 and the mid-1990s, Canadians increasingly reported that they "felt confident in their ability to cope with change." This trend has reversed in recent years. Half of Canadians aged 15 to 33 now "feel left behind and overwhelmed by the pace of life and the prevalence of technology." Those who feel left behind tend to be those who are not college- or university-educated, highly skilled, or adaptive.

This chapter's *Case Incident—GE's Work-Out* on page 538 looks at one organization's attempt to reduce resistance to change. *From Concepts to Skills* on page 539 provides additional tips for carrying out organizational change.

It probably cannot be emphasized enough that in order to break down resistance to change, it is essential to communicate a sense of urgency in the need for change. This provides a framework for people to understand why the change is occurring. Also, it is important to communicate and celebrate early successes to keep the momentum going, as change is a lengthy process. John Kotter and Leonard Schlesinger have identified six tactics organizations use to deal with resistance to change:[20]

- *Education and communication.* Resistance can be reduced through communicating with employees to help them see the logic of a change. Communication can be achieved through one-on-one discussions, memos, group presentations, or reports.

- *Participation and involvement.* It's difficult for individuals to resist a change decision in which they participated. Before making a change, those opposed can be brought into the decision process. Assuming that the participants have the expertise to make a meaningful contribution, their involvement can reduce resistance, obtain commitment, and increase the quality of the change decision.

- *Facilitation and support.* Organizations undergoing change can offer a range of supportive efforts to reduce resistance, such as employee counselling and therapy, new-skills training, or a short paid leave of absence.

- *Negotiation and agreement.* Another way for organizations to deal with potential resistance to change is to exchange something of value for a decrease in resistance. For instance, if the resistance is centred in a few powerful individuals, a specific reward package can be negotiated that will meet their individual needs.

- *Manipulation and co-optation.* Manipulation refers to covert influence attempts. Twisting and distorting facts to make them appear more attractive, withholding undesirable information, and creating false rumours to get employees to accept a change are all examples of manipulation. Co-optation, on the other hand, is a form of both manipulation and participation. It seeks to "buy off" the leaders of a resistance group by giving them a key role in the change decision.

- *Explicit and implicit coercion.* Coercion is the application of direct threats or force upon the resisters. If the corporate management is determined to close a manufacturing plant should employees not acquiesce to a pay cut, then coercion would be the label attached to its change tactic. Other examples of coercion are threats of transfer, loss of promotions, negative performance evaluations, and a poor letter of recommendation.

Exhibit 14-9 describes when each of these approaches is best used, and the advantages and drawbacks of each.

Michael Ying, chair of Esprit Asia Holdings, learned that communications can help overcome resistance to change. Ying, in trying to integrate Esprit's Asian and European operations, recognized major differences in the way they managed people and the business. The European operation was nationalistic, autocratic, and had rigid structures, whereas the Asian operation was more open-minded and willing to learn. During visits with the European managers, Ying communicated his common-sense approach to problem-solving and listened to the Europeans' concerns. This communication helped the Europeans to become receptive to Ying's plan of merging the two operations.

EXHIBIT 14-9   Strategies for Overcoming Resistance to Change

Approach	Commonly Used in Situations	Advantages	Drawbacks
Education + communication	Where there is a lack of information or inaccurate information and analysis.	Once persuaded, people will often help with the implementation of the change.	Can be very time-consuming if lots of people are involved
Participation + involvement	Where the initiators do not have all the information they need to design the change, and where others have considerable power to resist.	People who participate will be committed to implementing change, and any relevant information they have will be integrated into the change plan.	Can be very time-consuming if participators design an inappropriate change.
Facilitation + support	Where people are resisting because of adjustment problems.	No other approach works as well with adjustment problems.	Can be time-consuming, expensive, and still fail.
Negotiation + agreement	Where someone or some group will clearly lose out in a change, and where that group has considerable power to resist.	Sometimes it is a relatively easy way to avoid major resistance.	Can be too expensive in many cases if it alerts others to negotiate for compliance.
Manipulation + co-optation	Where other tactics will not work, or are too expensive.	It can be a relatively quick and inexpensive solution to resistance problems.	Can lead to future problems if people feel manipulated.
Explicit + implicit coercion	Where speed is essential, and the change initiators possess considerable power.	It is speedy, and can overcome any kind of resistance.	Can be risky if it leaves people mad at the initiators.

Source: Methods for dealing with resistance to change, J. P. Kotter and L. A. Schlesinger, "Choosing Strategies for Change," *Harvard Business Review,* March–April 1979, p. 111, Exhibit 1. Reprinted with permission.

The Politics of Change

No discussion of resistance to change would be complete without a brief mention of the politics of change. Because change invariably threatens the status quo, it inherently implies political activity.[21]

Politics suggests that the push for change is more likely to come from employees who are new to the organization (and have less invested in the status quo) or managers who are slightly removed from the main power structure. Those managers who have spent their entire careers with a single organization and eventually achieve a senior position in the hierarchy are often major impediments to change. Change itself is a very real threat to their status and position. Yet they may be expected to implement changes to demonstrate that they are not merely caretakers. By trying to bring about change, they can symbolically convey to various constituencies—stockholders, suppliers, employees, customers—that they are on top of problems and adapting to a dynamic environment. Of course, as you might guess, when forced to introduce change, these long-time power holders tend to implement **first-order change** (change that is linear and continuous). Radical change is too threatening. This, incidentally, explains why boards of directors that recognize the need for the rapid introduction of **second-order change** (change that is multidimensional, multilevel, discontinuous, and radical) in their organizations frequently turn to outside candidates for new leadership.[22]

You may remember that we discussed politics in Chapter 8 and suggested ways to more effectively encourage people to go along with your ideas. That chapter also indicated how individuals acquire power, which provides further insight into the ability of some individuals to resist change.

first-order change Change that is linear and continuous.

second-order change Change that is multidimensional, multilevel, discontinuous, and radical.

Contemporary Change Issues for Today's Managers

In April 2005, in the fifth year of his first five-year plan, Wayne Sales, Canadian Tire's CEO, announced an ambitious second five-year plan to increase the retailer's profile throughout the country. For Sales, change is a continuous process. In 2004, the company achieved record profitability, but that was not enough for him. "Our plan is designed to enable us to grow from our strengths and develop new ones, emphasizing and improving on those things we do best," Sales said.[23]

Sales also wants to improve customer loyalty. He plans to launch a "customer for life" campaign across the country. "We want to be the first choice of customers, not just this week, but for a lifetime," Sales said.[24] Sales' challenge is to keep the company innovative as it moves forward, a plan he hopes to achieve by renovating over half of its stores, making them bigger, with more products directed toward women and younger shoppers. How can Sales introduce more innovation to Canadian Tire and also help the organization continue to learn and adapt?

4 What are some of the contemporary issues in managing change?

How are changes in technology affecting the work lives of employees? What can managers do to help their organizations become more innovative? How do managers create organizations that continually learn and adapt? Is managing change culture-bound? In this section, we briefly address these four contemporary change issues.

Technology in the Workplace

Recent advances in technology are changing the workplace and affecting the work lives of employees. In this section, we will look at two specific issues related to process technology and work. These are continuous improvement processes and process re-engineering.

Continuous Improvement Processes

Quality management seeks to preserve customer satisfaction by continually improving all organizational processes. This search for continuous improvement recognizes that *good* isn't *good enough* and that even excellent performance can, and should, be improved on.

Quality management programs seek to reduce variability in outcomes and performance. When you eliminate variations, you increase the uniformity of the product or service. Increasing uniformity, in turn, results in lower costs and higher quality.

As tens of thousands of organizations introduce continuous improvement processes, how will employees be affected? They will no longer be able to rest on their previous accomplishments and successes. So some people may experience more stress in a work climate that no longer accepts complacency with the status quo. This tension may be positive for the organization (remember *functional conflict* from Chapter 9?), but the pressures from an unrelenting search for process improvements can create anxiety and stress in some employees.

At Toronto-based NRI Industries, which takes tires and waste rubber and makes parts for the auto industry, workers play with Lego to get a feeling for how continuous process improvement works. The company, which is already a stellar performer for its low rate of defective parts, does not want to rest on its laurels. So it engages in continuous improvement to make sure that it will still be stellar in the years to come.

NRI Industries
www.nriindustries.com

Process Re-engineering

The term *re-engineering* comes from the process of taking apart an electronic product and designing a better version. As applied to organizations, process re-engineering means that management should start with a clean sheet of paper—rethinking and redesigning the processes by which the organization creates value and does work, ridding itself of operations that have become antiquated.[25] The three key elements of process re-engineering are identifying an organization's distinctive competencies, assessing core processes, and reorganizing horizontally by process.

An organization's **distinctive competencies** define what it is that the organization does better than its competition. Examples might include better store locations, a more efficient distribution system, higher quality products, more knowledgeable sales personnel, or superior technical support. Dell, for instance, differentiates itself from its competitors by emphasizing high quality hardware, comprehensive service and technical support, and low prices. Why is identifying distinctive competencies so important? Because it guides decisions regarding what activities are crucial to the organization's success.

distinctive competencies What an organization delivers better than its competition.

Dell Canada
www.dell.ca

Management also needs to assess the core processes that clearly add value to the organization's distinctive competencies. These are the processes that transform materials, capital, information, and labour into products and services that the customer values. When the organization is viewed as a series of processes, ranging from strategic planning to after-sales customer support, management can determine to what degree each adds value. This process-value analysis typically uncovers a lot of activities that add little or nothing of value and whose only justification is "we've always done it this way."

Process re-engineering requires management to reorganize around horizontal processes. This means using cross-functional and self-managed teams. It means focusing on processes rather than on functions. It also means cutting out unnecessary levels of middle management.

Process re-engineering has been popular since the early 1990s. Almost all major companies—in the United States, Asia, and Europe—have re-engineered at least some

Top management at Union Carbide's industrial chemicals division led the drive to re-engineer work processes in plant and equipment maintenance, which accounted for 30 percent of costs. Directed to work in teams and to set ambitious cost-cutting goals, employees (shown here) worked out the details of their new work process by developing new repair and maintenance procedures. The re-engineering effort saved Union Carbide $38 million, 50 percent more than management's target. Company-wide, Union Carbide used re-engineering to cut $560 million out of fixed costs over a recent three-year period.

of their processes. The result has been that a lot of people have lost their jobs. Staff support jobs, especially middle managers, have been particularly vulnerable to process re-engineering efforts. So, too, have clerical jobs in service industries.

Employees who keep their jobs after process re-engineering have typically found that they are no longer the same jobs. These new jobs typically require a wider range of skills, including more interaction with customers and suppliers, greater challenge, increased responsibilities, and higher pay. However, the three- to five-year period it takes to implement process re-engineering is usually tough on employees. They suffer from uncertainty and anxiety associated with taking on new tasks and having to discard long-established work practices and formal social networks. The *Ethical Dilemma Exercise* on page 537 asks you to consider the stress that employees face after downsizing occurs in the workplace, and the pressure to take on more tasks increases.

Stimulating Innovation

How can an organization become more innovative? Although there is no guaranteed formula, certain characteristics surface again and again when researchers study innovative organizations. We have grouped them into structural, cultural, and human resource categories. Our message to change agents is that they should consider introducing these characteristics into their organization if they want to create an innovative climate. Before we look at these characteristics, however, let's clarify what we mean by innovation.

Definition of Innovation

innovation A new idea applied to initiating or improving a product, process, or service.

We said change refers to making things different. **Innovation** is a more specialized kind of change. Innovation is a new idea applied to initiating or improving a product, process, or service.[26] So all innovations involve change, but not all changes necessarily involve new ideas or lead to significant improvements. Innovations in organizations can range from small incremental improvements, such as Nabisco's extension of the Oreo product line to include double stuffs and chocolate-covered Oreos, up to radical breakthroughs, such as Jeff Bezos' idea in 1994 to create the online bookstore Amazon.com. Keep in mind that while there are many product innovations, the concept of innovation also encompasses new production process technologies, new structures or administrative systems, and new plans or programs pertaining to organizational members.

Sources of Innovation

Structural variables have been the most studied potential source of innovation.[27] A comprehensive review of the structure–innovation relationship leads to the following conclusions:[28]

- *Organic structures positively influence innovation.* Because they are lower in vertical differentiation, formalization, and centralization, organic organizations facilitate the flexibility, adaptation, and cross-fertilization that make the adoption of innovations easier.

- *Long tenure in management is associated with innovation.* Managerial tenure apparently provides legitimacy and knowledge of how to accomplish tasks and obtain desired outcomes.

- *Innovation is nurtured when there are slack resources.* Having an abundance of resources allows an organization to afford to purchase innovations, bear the cost of instituting innovations, and absorb failures.

- *Interunit communication is high in innovative organizations.*[29] Innovative organizations are high users of committees, task forces, cross-functional teams, and other mechanisms that facilitate interaction across departmental lines.

Innovative organizations tend to have similar *cultures*. They encourage experimentation. They reward both successes and failures. They celebrate mistakes. Unfortunately, in too many organizations, people are rewarded for the absence of failures rather than for the presence of successes. Such cultures extinguish risk-taking and innovation. People will suggest and try new ideas only when they feel such behaviours exact no penalties. Managers in innovative organizations recognize that failures are a natural by-product of venturing into the unknown. 3M is known for its culture of innovation, as *OB in the Workplace* describes.

OB IN THE WORKPLACE

3M Is a Leader in Innovation

What does it take to be a leader in innovation? Many organizations strive to achieve the standard of innovation reached by 3M, the company responsible for the development of waterproof sandpaper, masking tape, and Post-it® notes.[30] 3M has developed a reputation for being able to stimulate innovation over a long period of time. It has a stated objective that 30 percent of its sales are to come from products less than four years old. In one recent year alone, 3M launched more than 200 new products.

The company encourages its employees to take risks—and rewards the failures as well as the successes. 3M's management has the patience to see ideas through to successful products. It invests nearly 7 percent of company sales revenue (more than $1.4 billion a year) in research and development, yet management tells its R & D people that not everything will work. It also fosters a culture that allows people to defy their managers. For instance, each new employee and his or her manager take a one-day orientation class where, among other things, stories are told of victories won by employees despite the opposition of their boss.

All of 3M's scientists and managers are challenged to "keep current." Idea champions are created and encouraged by allowing scientists and engineers to spend up to 15 percent of their time on projects of their own choosing. And if a 3M scientist comes up with a new idea but finds resistance within the researcher's own division, he or she can apply for a $70 000 grant from an internal venture-capital fund to further develop the idea.

Within the *human resource* category, we find that innovative organizations actively promote the training and development of their members so that they keep current, offer high job security so employees don't fear getting fired for making mistakes, and encourage individuals to become champions of change. Once a new idea is developed, **idea champions** actively and enthusiastically promote the idea, build support for it,

idea champions Individuals who actively and enthusiastically promote an idea, build support for it, overcome resistance to it, and ensure that the innovation is implemented.

overcome resistance to it, and ensure that the innovation is implemented.[31] The evidence indicates that champions have common personality characteristics: extremely high self-confidence, persistence, energy, and a tendency to take risks. Idea champions also display characteristics associated with transformational leadership. They inspire and energize others with their vision of the potential of an innovation and through their strong personal conviction in their mission. They are also good at gaining the commitment of others to support their mission. In addition, idea champions have jobs that provide considerable decision-making discretion. This autonomy helps them introduce and implement innovations in organizations.[32]

Creating a Learning Organization

The learning organization has recently developed a groundswell of interest from managers and organization theorists looking for new ways to successfully respond to a world of interdependence and change.[33] In this section, we describe what a learning organization looks like and methods for managing learning.

What Is a Learning Organization?

learning organization An organization that has developed the continuous capacity to adapt and change.

A **learning organization** is an organization that has developed the continuous capacity to adapt and change. Just as individuals learn, so too do organizations. "All organizations learn, whether they consciously choose to or not—it is a fundamental requirement for their sustained existence."[34] However, some organizations do it better than others. Canadian Tire is an example of a company that has worked hard to learn how to improve itself from year to year.

single-loop learning Errors are corrected using past routines and present policies.

double-loop learning Errors are corrected by modifying the organization's objectives, policies, and standard routines.

Most organizations engage in what has been called **single-loop learning**.[35] When errors are detected, the correction process relies on past routines and present policies. This type of learning has been likened to a thermostat, which, once set at 17°C, simply turns on and off to keep the room at the set temperature. It does not question whether the temperature should be set at 17°C. In contrast, learning organizations use **double-loop learning**. When an error is detected, it's corrected in ways that involve the modification of the organization's objectives, policies, and standard routines. Double-loop learning challenges deeply rooted assumptions and norms within an organization. In this way, it provides opportunities for radically different solutions to problems and dramatic jumps in improvement. To draw on the thermostat analogy, a thermostat using double-loop learning would try to determine whether the correct policy is 17°C, and whether changes might be necessitated by the change in season.

Exhibit 14-10 summarizes the five basic characteristics of a learning organization. It's an organization in which people put aside their old ways of thinking, learn to be open with each other, understand how their organization really works, form a plan or vision on which everyone can agree, and then work together to achieve that vision.[36]

Managing Learning

How do you change an organization to make it into a continual learner? What can managers do to make their firms learning organizations?

- *Establish a strategy.* Managers need to make their commitment to change, innovation, and continuous improvement explicit.

- *Redesign the organization's structure.* The formal structure can be a serious impediment to learning. By flattening the structure, eliminating or combining departments, and increasing the use of cross-functional teams, interdependence is reinforced and boundaries between people are reduced.

- *Reshape the organization's culture.* Learning organizations are characterized by risk-taking, openness, and growth. Managers set the tone for the organization's culture

---

EXHIBIT 14-10 Characteristics of a Learning Organization

1. The organization has a shared vision that everyone agrees on.

2. People discard their old ways of thinking and the standard routines they use for solving problems or doing their jobs.

3. Members think of all organizational processes, activities, functions, and interactions with the environment as part of a system of interrelationships.

4. People openly communicate with each other (across vertical and horizontal boundaries) without fear of criticism or punishment.

5. People suppress their personal self-interest and fragmented departmental interests to work together to achieve the organization's shared vision.

Source: Based on P. M. Senge, *The Fifth Discipline* (New York: Doubleday, 1990).

---

both by what they say (strategy) and what they do (behaviour). Managers need to demonstrate by their actions that taking risks and admitting failures are desirable traits. That means rewarding people who take chances and make mistakes. Managers also need to encourage functional conflict. "The key to unlocking real openness at work," says one expert on learning organizations, "is to teach people to give up having to be in agreement. We think agreement is so important. Who cares? You have to bring paradoxes, conflicts, and dilemmas out in the open, so collectively we can be more intelligent than we can be individually."[37]

Managing Change: It's Culture-Bound

A number of change issues we have discussed in this chapter are culture-bound, meaning that they do not necessarily apply well cross-culturally. To illustrate, let's briefly look at five questions:

- *Do people believe change is possible?* Remember that cultures vary in terms of beliefs about their ability to control their environment. In cultures in which people believe that they can dominate their environment, individuals will take a proactive view of change. This, for example, would describe the United States and Canada. In many other countries, such as Iran and Saudi Arabia, people see themselves as subjugated to their environment and thus will tend to take a passive approach toward change.

- *If change is possible, how long will it take to bring it about?* A culture's time orientation can help us answer this question. Societies that focus on the long term, such as Japan, will demonstrate considerable patience while waiting for positive outcomes from change efforts. In societies with a short-term focus, such as the United States and Canada, people expect quick improvements and will seek change programs that promise fast results.

- *Is resistance to change greater in some cultures than in others?* Resistance to change will be influenced by a society's reliance on tradition. Italians, as

Middle Eastern countries tend to take a passive approach toward change. In banking centres like Bahrain, a state on the Persian Gulf, culture dictates gender separations, so banks continue to have special sections for women.

an example, focus on the past, whereas Americans emphasize the present. Italians, therefore, should generally be more resistant to change efforts than their American counterparts.

- *Does culture influence how change efforts will be implemented?* Power distance can help with this issue. In high power distance cultures, such as Spain or Thailand, change efforts will tend to be autocratically implemented by top management. In contrast, low power distance cultures value democratic methods. We would predict, therefore, a greater use of participation in countries such as Denmark and the Netherlands.

- *Do successful idea champions do things differently in different cultures?* The evidence indicates that the answer is yes.[38] People in collectivist cultures, in contrast to individualistic cultures, prefer appeals for cross-functional support for innovation efforts; people in high power distance cultures prefer champions to work closely with those in authority to approve innovative activities before work is conducted on them; and the higher the uncertainty avoidance of a society, the more champions should work within the organization's rules and procedures to develop the innovation. These findings suggest that effective managers will alter their organization's championing strategies to reflect cultural values. So, for instance, while idea champions in Russia might succeed by ignoring budgetary limitations and working around confining procedures, idea champions in Austria, Denmark, Germany, or other cultures high in uncertainty avoidance will be more effective by closely following budgets and procedures.

SUMMARY AND IMPLICATIONS

1 **What are the forces for change?** The nature of the workforce, technology, economic shocks, competition, social trends, and world politics are all forces for change. Organizations have had to respond to these forces by making organizational changes, such as changing their reward structure, redesigning jobs, introducing teams, and meeting ethical challenges. To carry out change, organizations need to appoint change agents, individuals who manage change activities for the organization.

2 **How do organizations manage change?** Kurt Lewin argued that successful change in organizations should follow three steps: *unfreezing* the status quo, *moving* to a new state, and *refreezing* the new change to make it permanent. John Kotter built on Lewin's three-step model to create a more detailed eight-step plan for implementing change. Another approach to managing change is action research. *Action research* refers to a change process based on the systematic collection of data and then selection of a change action based on what the analyzed data indicate. Some organizations use appreciative inquiry to manage change. Appreciative inquiry seeks to identify the unique qualities and special strengths of an organization, which can then be built on to improve performance.

3 **Why do people and organizations resist change?** Individuals resist change because of basic human characteristics such as perceptions, personalities, and needs. Organizations resist change because they are conservative, and because change is difficult. The status quo is often preferred by those who feel they have the most to lose if change goes ahead.

4 **What are some of the contemporary issues in managing change?** Some of the contemporary issues include helping employees deal with technological change, making organizations more innovative, creating learning organizations, and understanding the influence of culture on managing change.

For Review

1. "Resistance to change is an irrational response." Do you agree or disagree? Explain.

2. Why is participation considered such an effective technique for lessening resistance to change?

3. How does Lewin's three-step change model deal with resistance to change?

4. What is the difference between driving forces and restraining forces?

5. What are the factors that lead individuals to resist change?

6. What are the factors that lead organizations to resist change?

7. Why does change so frequently become a political issue in organizations?

8. How does Kotter's eight-step plan for implementing change deal with resistance to change?

9. What are the implications for employees of a continuous improvement process?

10. In an organization that has a history of "following the leader," what changes can be made to foster innovation?

For Critical Thinking

1. How have changes in the workforce during the past 20 years affected organizational policies?

2. "Managing today is easier than at the start of the twentieth century, because the years of real change took place between Confederation and World War I." Do you agree or disagree? Discuss.

3. What is meant by the phrase "We live in an age of discontinuity"?

4. Are all managers change agents?

OB for You

■ Not everyone is comfortable with change, but you should realize that change is a fact of life. It is difficult to avoid, and can result in negative consequences when it is avoided.

■ If you need to change something in yourself, be aware of the importance of creating new systems to replace the old. Saying you want to be healthier, without specifying that you intend to go to the gym three times a week, or eat five servings of fruits and vegetables a day, means that change likely will not occur. It's important to specify goals and behaviours as part of change.

■ Consider focusing on positive aspects of change, rather than negative ones. For instance, rather than noting that you didn't study hard enough, acknowledge the effort you put into studying, and how that helped your performance, and then set positive goals as a result.

OB *AT WORK*

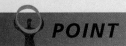

POINT

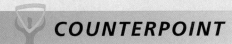

COUNTERPOINT

Organizations Are More Like Calm Waters

Organizational change is an episodic activity. That is, it starts at some point, proceeds through a series of steps, and culminates in some outcome that those involved hope is an improvement over the starting point. It has a beginning, a middle, and an end.

Lewin's three-step change model represents a classic illustration of this perspective. Change is seen as a break in the organization's equilibrium. The status quo has been disturbed, and change is necessary to establish a new equilibrium state. The objective of refreezing is to stabilize the new situation by balancing the driving and restraining forces.

Some experts have argued that organizational change should be thought of as balancing a system made up of five interacting variables within the organization—people, tasks, technology, structure, and strategy. A change in any one variable has repercussions on one or more of the others. This perspective is episodic in that it treats organizational change as essentially an effort to sustain an equilibrium. A change in one variable begins a chain of events that, if properly managed, requires adjustments in the other variables to achieve a new state of equilibrium.

Another way to conceptualize the episodic view of looking at change is to think of managing change as analogous to captaining a ship. The organization is like a large ship travelling across the calm Mediterranean Sea to a specific port. The ship's captain has made this exact trip hundreds of times before with the same crew. Every once in a while, however, a storm will appear, and the crew has to respond. The captain will make the appropriate adjustments—that is, implement changes—and, having manoeuvred through the storm, will return to calm waters. Like this ship's voyage, managing an organization should be seen as a journey with a beginning and an end, and implementing change as a response to a break in the status quo that is needed only occasionally.

Organizations Are More Like Whitewater Rafting

The episodic approach may be the dominant paradigm for handling organizational change, but it has become obsolete. It applies to a world of certainty and predictability. The episodic approach was developed in the 1950s and 1960s, and it reflects the environment of those times. It treats change as the occasional disturbance in an otherwise peaceful world. However, this paradigm has little resemblance to today's environment of constant and chaotic change.[39]

If you want to understand what it's like to manage change in today's organizations, think of it as equivalent to permanent whitewater rafting.[40] The organization is not a large ship, but more akin to a 40-foot raft. Rather than sailing a calm sea, this raft must traverse a racing river made up of an uninterrupted flow of whitewater rapids. To make things worse, the raft has 10 paddlers who have never worked together or travelled the river before, much of the trip is in the dark, the river is dotted by unexpected turns and obstacles, the exact destination of the raft is not clear, and at irregular intervals the raft needs to pull to shore, where some new crew members are added and others leave. Change is a natural state and managing change is a continual process. That is, managers never get the luxury of escaping the whitewater rapids.

The stability and predictability characterized by the episodic perspective no longer captures the world we live in. Disruptions in the status quo are not occasional, temporary, and followed by a return to an equilibrium state. There is, in fact, no equilibrium state. Managers today face constant change, bordering on chaos. They are being forced to play a game they have never played before, governed by rules that are created as the game progresses.

HR IMPLICATIONS

Managing Change in a Unionized Environment

More companies are looking for ways to ensure labour peace, particularly after a World Bank study found that a stable labour environment brings about economic growth.[41] Canada loses more days to labour disputes than most other developed countries, except Spain and Iceland. Faced with increased globalization, and a much lower unionization rate in the United States (12 percent in the United States compared with about 35 percent in Canada), some Canadian businesses want to assure their customers that labour stability is possible.

One of the most successful companies on this front is Vancouver-based NorskeCanada.[42] In summer 2002, Norske started negotiations with its union, the Communications, Energy and Paperworkers Union of Canada, a year early. In just nine days, labour and management had worked out a five-year agreement for labour peace, and created a corporate-worker partnership that had not been seen in BC's paper industry before. The deal was approved by 82 percent of the union's members.

"Right off the bat they told us they understood that labour was an important part of society and they intended to treat us with respect," says Dave Coles, as lead West Coast negotiator for the union. "After our history with this industry, that just blew us away."

To win over union members, Norske management started taking workplace safety seriously, something union members at the plant had complained about for years. Management also set up meetings between union members and customers, so that the employees could hear the concerns customers had about labour disruptions. The company told the union that they were not interested in confrontation. "We told them we wanted to avoid the kind of power bargaining that has plagued the industry for decades," Ron Buchhorn, Norske's chief negotiator and vice-president of human resources, recalls.

Part of Norske's strategy is to increase the amount of information provided to employees. Union members participate in the annual business review, and they are invited to help with the budget and long-term planning.

Saint John, New Brunswick-based Irving Pulp and Paper's closer relationship with its union started to develop in 1991, following a prolonged strike.[43] Management at Irving recognized that without signifi-

cant change in the relationship, the company would suffer. In 1997, Irving Pulp and Paper was able to sign a six-year contract with its two locals of the Communications, Energy and Paperworkers Union of Canada, in part because it chose to share more information with its employees about its financial status.

Instead of simply giving the information to union leaders, management erected information bulletin boards and production boards to ensure that all employees knew how much money the company was making and whether productivity quotas were being met. Management also took union members to visit other mills to show them what change might look like, and to make them more comfortable with engaging in the change process at Irving.

Peter McIntyre, manager of human resources, states that it takes a lot of time and costs money to keep the union-management relationship working, but it also improves the organization's performance. "There's an expense, but there's also a payback, and the payback is we have a reasonably content workforce." Absenteeism is down, production is up, and quality is improved in recent years.

The Conference Board of Canada suggests the following conditions are needed to build better union-management partnerships:[44]

- Effective union and management leadership

- Trust

- Common values and goals

- Formalized partnership agreement

- Strategic planning

- Commitment to process improvement

- A change in roles

- Commitment to employee development

- Relationship management

Two consultants who have worked with a number of Canadian organizations note four essential elements for managing change in a unionized environment:[45]

- *An effective system for resolving day-to-day issues.* Employees should feel that they do not have to go through the formal grievance process in order to be heard. Instead, the workplace should be open to hearing employees' issues, as this will underscore a commitment to participation and empowerment.

- *A jointly administered business education process.* Union leaders and their members become uneasy about the future, particularly as Canadian organizations have gone through prolonged periods of downsizing. An education process that allows employees to understand the financial statements of the company and understand how their performance affects the bottom line helps them better understand the decisions the company makes.

- *A jointly developed strategic vision for the organization.* When union members are involved in setting the vision, they are more likely to focus on how

change can be made, rather than whether it should be made. The vision "should describe performance expectations, work design, organizational structure, the supply chain, governance, pay and rewards, technology, education and training, operating processes, employee involvement, employment security, and union-management roles and relations."[46]

- *A nontraditional problem-solving method of negotiating collective agreements.* It's important to promote an atmosphere of tolerance and willingness to listen, where issues are problems to be solved rather than victories to be claimed. It's also helpful to expand the traditional scope of bargaining to include complex issues such as strategic plans. Generally, management does not want to bargain over these issues, but when they do, it signals further commitment to working jointly with unionized employees.

LEARNING ABOUT **YOURSELF** EXERCISE

Managing-in-a-Turbulent-World Tolerance Test

Listed below are some statements a 37-year-old manager made about his job at a large, successful corporation. If your job had these characteristics, how would you react to them? After each statement are 5 letters, A to E. Circle the letter that best describes how you think you would react according to the following scale:

A   I would enjoy this very much; it's completely acceptable.

B   This would be enjoyable and acceptable most of the time.

C   I would have no reaction to this feature one way or another, or it would be about equally enjoyable and unpleasant.

D   This feature would be somewhat unpleasant for me.

E   This feature would be very unpleasant for me.

1.	I regularly spend 30 to 40 percent of my time in meetings.	A	B	C	D	E
2.	A year and a half ago, my job did not exist, and I have been essentially inventing it as I go along.	A	B	C	D	E
3.	The responsibilities I either assume or am assigned consistently exceed the authority I have for discharging them.	A	B	C	D	E
4.	At any given moment in my job, I have on the average about a dozen phone calls to be returned.	A	B	C	D	E
5.	There seems to be very little relation in my job between the quality of my performance and my actual pay and fringe benefits.	A	B	C	D	E
6.	About 2 weeks a year of formal management training is needed in my job just to stay current.	A	B	C	D	E

7. Because we have very effective employment equity in my company, and because it is thoroughly multinational, my job brings me into close working contact at a professional level with people of many races, ethnic groups, and nationalities and of both sexes.   A   B   C   D   E

8. There is no objective way to measure my effectiveness.   A   B   C   D   E

9. I report to 3 different bosses for different aspects of my job, and each has an equal say in my performance appraisal.   A   B   C   D   E

10. On average, about a third of my time is spent dealing with unexpected emergencies that force all scheduled work to be postponed.   A   B   C   D   E

11. When I must have a meeting of the people who report to me, it takes my secretary most of a day to find a time when we are all available, and even then, I have yet to have a meeting where everyone is present for the entire meeting.   A   B   C   D   E

12. The university degree I earned in preparation for this type of work is now obsolete, and I probably should go back for another degree.   A   B   C   D   E

13. My job requires that I absorb 100 to 200 pages per week of technical materials.   A   B   C   D   E

14. I am out of town overnight at least 1 night per week.   A   B   C   D   E

15. My department is so interdependent with several other departments in the company that all distinctions about which departments are responsible for which tasks are quite arbitrary.   A   B   C   D   E

16. I will probably get a promotion in about a year to a job in another division that has most of these same characteristics.   A   B   C   D   E

17. During the period of my employment here, either the entire company or the division I worked in has been reorganized every year or so.   A   B   C   D   E

18. Although there are several possible promotions I can see ahead of me, I have no real career path in an objective sense.   A   B   C   D   E

19. Although there are several possible promotions I can see ahead of me, I think I have no realistic chance of reaching the top levels of the company.   A   B   C   D   E

20. Although I have many ideas about how to make things work better, I have no direct influence on either the business policies or the personnel policies that govern my division.   A   B   C   D   E

21. My company has recently put in an "assessment centre" where I and all other managers will be required to go through an extensive battery of psychological tests to assess our potential.   A   B   C   D   E

22. My company is a defendant in an antitrust suit, and if the case comes to trial, I will probably have to testify about some decisions that were made a few years ago.   A   B   C   D   E

23. Advanced computer and other electronic office technology are continually being introduced into my division, necessitating constant learning on my part.   A   B   C   D   E

24. The computer terminal and screen I have in my office can be monitored in my bosses' offices without my knowledge.   A   B   C   D   E

Scoring Key:

Score 4 points for each A, 3 for each B, 2 for each C, 1 for each D, and 0 for each E. Add up the points, divide by 24, and round to 1 decimal place.

While the results are not intended to be more than suggestive, the higher your score, the more comfortable you seem to be with change. The test's author suggests analyzing scores as if they were grade point averages. In this way, a 4.0 average is an A, a 2.0 is a C, and scores below 1.0 flunk.

▶

Using replies from nearly 500 MBA students and young managers, the range of scores was found to be narrow— between 1.0 and 2.2. The average score was between 1.5 and 1.6—equivalent to a D+/C– grade! If these scores are generalizable to the work population, clearly people are not very tolerant of the kind of changes that come with a turbulent environment. However, this sample is now over a decade old. We should expect average scores today to be higher, as people have become more accustomed to living in a dynamic environment.

Source: From P. B. Vaill, *Managing as a Performing Art: New Ideas for a World of Chaotic Change* (San Francisco: Jossey-Bass, 1989), pp. 8–9. Reproduced with permission of the publisher. All rights reserved.

BREAKOUT **GROUP** EXERCISES

Form small groups to discuss the following topics, as assigned by your instructor:

1. Identify a local company that you think needs to undergo change. What factors suggest that change is necessary?

2. Have you ever tried to change the behaviour of someone you worked with (for instance, someone in one of your project groups)? How effective were you in getting change to occur? How would you explain this?

3. Identify a recent change that your college or university introduced, and its effects on the students. Did the students accept the change or fight it? How would you explain this?

WORKING WITH **OTHERS** EXERCISE

Power and the Changing Environment

Objectives

1. To describe the forces for change influencing power differentials in organizational and interpersonal relationships.

2. To understand the effect of technological, legal/political, economic, and social changes on the power of individuals within an organization.

The Situation

Your organization manufactures golf carts and sells them to country clubs, golf courses, and consumers. Your team is faced with the task of assessing how environmental changes will affect individuals' organizational power. Read each of the five scenarios and then, for each, identify the 5 members in the organization whose power will increase most in light of the environmental condition(s).

Advertising expert (m)	Accountant-CGA (m)	Product designer (m)
Chief financial officer (f)	General manager (m)	In-house counsel (m)
Securities analyst (m)	Marketing manager (f)	Public relations expert (m)
Operations manager (f)	Computer programmer (f)	Human resource manager (f)
Corporate trainer (m)	Industrial engineer (m)	Chemist (m)

(m) = male   (f) = female

1. New computer-aided manufacturing technologies are being introduced in the workplace during the upcoming 2 to 18 months.

2. New federal emission standards are being legislated by the government.

3. Sales are way down; the industry appears to be shrinking.

4. The company is planning to go international in the next 12 to 18 months.

5. The Human Rights Commission is applying pressure to balance the male–female population in the organization's upper hierarchy by threatening to publicize the predominance of men in upper management.

The Procedure

1. Divide the class into teams of 3 to 4 students each.

2. Teams should read each scenario and identify the 5 members whose power will increase most in light of the external environmental condition described.

3. Teams should then address the question: Assuming that the 5 environmental changes are taking place at once, which 5 members of the organization will now have the most power?

4. After 20 to 30 minutes, representatives of each team will be selected to present and justify their conclusions to the entire class. Discussion will begin with scenario 1 and proceed through to scenario 5. Then the class will look at what might happen if all 5 environmental changes happened at once.

Source: Adapted from J. E. Barbuto Jr., "Power and the Changing Environment," *Journal of Management Education,* April 2000, pp. 288–296.

ETHICAL **DILEMMA** EXERCISE

Increasing Employee Productivity and Stress

Ellen West supervises a staff of 15 people handling back-office functions for a regional brokerage firm in Saskatoon. With company revenues down, Ellen's boss has put increasing pressure on her to improve her department's productivity.

The quickest way for Ellen to increase productivity in her department is to lay off two or three employees and fill the gap by asking the rest of the staff to work harder and put in more time on the job. Since all her employees are on salary, they are not paid for overtime. So if Ellen let three people go and asked her remaining staff to each put in an additional 10 hours a week on the job, she could effectively handle the same workload with 20 percent fewer employees.

As Ellen considered this idea, she had mixed feelings. Reducing her staff and asking people to work more hours would please her boss and increase job security for those people remaining. On the other hand, she was fearful that she was taking advantage of a weak labour market. Her employees knew that jobs were scarce and would be hard put to find comparable positions elsewhere in the securities industry. The people laid off would have a tough time finding work. Moreover, she knew that her current staff was unlikely to openly complain about working longer hours for fear that they, too, would be let go. But was it fair to increase the department's productivity on the backs of already hard-working employees? Was it unethical to ask her employees to put in 10 hours more a week, for no additional money, because the current weak labour market worked to her advantage? If you were Ellen West, what would you do?

CASE INCIDENTS

GreyStar Art & Greetings Makes Technological Changes

Tammy Reinhold didn't believe the rumours. Now that the rumours were confirmed, she was in denial. "I can't believe it," she said. "I've worked as a greeting-card artist here for 17 years. I love what I do. Now they tell me that I'm going to have to do all my work on a computer."

Tammy was not alone in her fear. The company's other two artists, Mike Tomaski and Maggie Lyall, were just as concerned. Each had graduated from art school near the top of his or her class. They came to work for GreyStar Art & Greetings right out of school—Mike in 1979, Tammy in 1986, and Maggie in 1991. They chose the company, which had been around for more than 50 years, because of its reputation as a good place to work. The company also had never had a layoff.

GreyStar Art & Greetings is a small maker of greeting cards and specialty wrapping paper. It has modest resources and modest ambitions. Management has always pursued progress slowly. Artists do much of their work by hand. Today, however, the company installed three high-powered Mac computers equipped with the latest graphics and photo-manipulation software, including Photoshop, Quark, and Illustrator.

Courtland Grey, the company's owner, called Tammy, Mike, and Maggie into his office this morning. He told them about the changes that were going to be made. Grey acknowledged that the three were going to have a lot to learn to be able to do all their work on computers. But he stressed that the changes would dramatically speed up the art-production and photo-layout processes and eventually result in significant cost savings. He offered to send the three to a one-week course specifically designed to train artists in the new technology. He also said he expected all of the company's art and photo operations to be completely digitalized within three months.

Tammy is not stupid. She's been following the trends in graphic art. More and more work is being done on computers. She just thought, as did Mike and Maggie, that she might escape having to learn these programs. After all, GreyStar Art & Greetings is not Hallmark. But Tammy was wrong. Technology is coming to GreyStar Art & Greetings and there isn't much she can do about it. Other than complain or look for another job!

Questions

1. Explain Tammy's resistance.

2. Evaluate the way Courtland Grey handled this change.

3. What, if anything, would you have done differently if you had been Grey?

GE's Work-Out

General Electric (GE) established its Work-Out process in the early 1990s. It continues to be a mainstay in GE's efforts to initiate change. In the interim years, the Work-Out process has also been adopted by such diverse organizations as General Motors, The Home Depot, and the World Bank.

The impetus for the Work-Out was the belief by GE's CEO that the company's culture was too bureaucratic and slow to respond to change. He wanted to create a vehicle that would effectively engage and empower GE employees.

Essentially, Work-Out brings together employees and managers from many different functions and levels within an organization for an informal three-day meeting to discuss and solve problems that have been identified by employees or senior management. Set into small teams, people are encouraged to challenge prevailing assumptions about "the way we have always done things" and develop recommendations for significant improvements in organizational processes. The Work-Out teams then present their recommendations to a senior manager in a public gathering called a Town Meeting.

At the Town Meeting, the manager in charge oversees a discussion about the recommendation and then is required to make a yes-or-no decision on the spot. Only in unusual circumstances can a recommendation be tabled for further study. Recommendations that are accepted are assigned to managers who have volunteered to carry them out. Typically, a recommendation will move from inception to implementation in 90 days or less.

The logic behind the Work-Out is to identify problems, stimulate diverse input, and provide a mechanism for speedy decision and action.

Questions

1. What type of change process would you call this? Explain.

2. Why should it work?

3. What negative consequences do you think might result from this process?

Source: Based on D. Ulrich, S. Kerr, and R. Ashkenas, *The GE Work-Out* (New York: McGraw-Hill, 2002).

From **Concepts** to **Skills**

Carrying Out Organizational Change

In reviewing three US organizations that effectively underwent major changes (Sears, Roebuck & Company, Royal Dutch/Shell, and the US Army), three organizational change consultants used the US Army's After Action Review to summarize how an effective change process can be carried out in both business and the military.[47] The After Action Review is a nonhierarchical team debriefing to help participants understand performance. The consultants identified seven disciplines embedded in the After Action Review that help create effective change:

- *Build an intricate understanding of the business.* Organizational members need to have the big picture revealed to them so they know why change is needed and what is happening in the industry. Let organizational members know what is expected of them as the change proceeds.

- *Encourage uncompromising straight talk.* Communication cannot be based on hierarchy, but must allow everyone to contribute freely to the discussion.

- *Manage from the future.* Rather than setting goals that are directed toward a specific future point in time (and thus encouraging everyone to stop when the goal is achieved), manage from the perspective of always looking toward the future and future needs.

- *Harness setbacks.* When things do not go as planned, and there are setbacks, it's natural to blame yourself, others, or bad luck. Instead, teach everyone to view setbacks as learning opportunities and opportunities for improvement.

- *Promote inventive accountability.* While employees know what the specific targets and goals are, they should also be encouraged in the change process to be inventive and take initiative when new opportunities arise.

- *Understand the quid pro quo.* When organizations undergo change processes, employees are put under a lot of stress and strain. Organizations must ensure that employees are rewarded for their efforts. To build appropriate commitment, organizations must develop four levels of incentives:

  a. Reward and recognition for effort

  b. Training and skill development that will make the employee marketable

  c. Meaningful work that provides intrinsic satisfaction

  d. Communication about where the organization is going and some say in the process for employees

- *Create relentless discomfort with the status quo.* People are more willing to change when the current situation looks less attractive than the new situation.

These points indicate that effective change is a comprehensive process, requiring a lot of commitment from both the organization's leaders and its members.

Assessing Skills

After you've read this chapter, take the following Self-Assessments on your enclosed CD-ROM:

4. How Well Do I Handle Ambiguity?

49. How Well Do I Respond to Turbulent Change?

50. How Stressful Is My Life?

51. Am I Burned Out?

Practising Skills

You are the nursing supervisor at a local hospital that employs both emergency room and floor nurses. Each of these teams of nurses tends to work almost exclusively with others doing the same job. In your professional reading, you have come across the concept of cross-training nursing teams and giving them more varied responsibilities, which in turn has been shown to improve patient care while lowering costs. You call the two team leaders, Sue and Scott, into your office to explain that you want the nursing teams to move to this approach. To your surprise, they are both opposed to the idea. Sue says she and the other emergency room nurses feel they are needed in the ER, where they fill the most vital role in the hospital. They work special hours when needed, do whatever tasks are required, and often work in difficult and stressful circumstances. They think the floor nurses have relatively easy jobs for the pay they receive. Scott, the leader of the floor nurse team, tells you that his group believes the ER nurses lack the special training and extra experience that the floor nurses bring to the hospital. The floor nurses claim they have the heaviest responsibilities and do the most exacting work. Because they have ongoing contact with patients and families, they believe they should not be called away from vital floor duties to help the ER nurses complete their tasks. What should you do about your idea to introduce more cross-training for the nursing teams?

Reinforcing Skills

1. Think about a change (major and minor) that you have dealt with over the last year. Perhaps the change involved other people and perhaps it was personal. Did you resist the change? Did others resist the change? How did you overcome your resistance or the resistance of others to the change?

2. Interview a manager at three different organizations about a change he or she implemented. What was the manager's experience in implementing the change? How did the manager manage resistance to the change?

VIDEO CASE INCIDENTS

CBC

CHAPTER 1 Under 21 and Self-Employed

There is a growing trend in this country: business start-ups.

Between 2001 and 2002, start-ups by Canadian entrepreneurs between the ages of 15 and 24 rose 25 percent. These young entrepreneurs compare the risks of starting a new business against the risk of climbing the traditional corporate ladder, and decide to strike out on their own. They are a motivated group—and this new generation also wants to better the world they live in.

Take, for instance, Evan Clifford and Alexandra Hickey, two Canadian entrepreneurs who are part of this trend.

Evan Clifford is hip, urban, 21, and has already made his mark on his community as the owner of Parallel, an upbeat store located on trendy Queen Street West in Toronto. In the middle of grade 13, he decided to quit school and devote his time to something more interesting—designing his own line of casual clothing. Clifford's hard work paid off fast when he landed a few major contracts. He quickly established a client base and opened his own store. Clifford's creativity and drive have also allowed him to contribute to his community. Clifford has teamed up with a Canadian rap artist to introduce a new clothing line. Proceeds go to a charity and to help street kids during the Christmas season. Clifford distributes phone cards to street kids, hoping that they will get in touch with someone they love and care about, and who cares about them.

Alexandra Hickey is yet another creative young entrepreneur. Hickey, who has a diploma as a trained chef, made a life-changing decision to leave her secure yet unfulfilling government job. Hickey wanted a job that would inspire her—and a job that would allow her to express her social awareness. She took the risk and is now a personal chef, running her own business her own way. Hickey is out to give back to her community, too. Cleaner air is important to her—so important that she does not own a car and rides a bicycle to serve her clients instead of driving. She says giving up the convenience and comfort of driving a car is a small price to pay for cleaner air.

More than ever in Canada, young entrepreneurs are not only building their businesses, but also building their communities. They are bringing a new set of ideals to the business environment while charting their own path to success. With young entrepreneurs like Clifford and Hickey, business isn't just about the money, it's "capitalism with a conscience."

Questions

1. What are Clifford and Hickey looking for in their work?

2. What explanation do you have for the rising trend of young entrepreneurs?

3. How can we link the study of organizational behaviour to the challenges facing managers of today's organizations?

Sources: Based on "Under 21," *CBC Venture*, December 1, 2002, 856; Young Entrepreneurs Association of Canada, www.yea.ca (accessed January 13, 2006); Advancing Canadian Entrepreneurship (ACE), www.acecanada.ca (accessed January 13, 2006).

CHAPTER 2 NovaScotian Crystal

Do opposites attract? Meet Denis Ryan and Rod McCulloch—partners in NovaScotian Crystal, a small company situated on the quaint waterfront of Halifax.

NovaScotian Crystal makes fine crystal the traditional, old-fashioned, expensive way, with trained craftspeople. It is the only company in Canada that produces mouth-blown, hand-cut crystal.

Ryan started the company in the late 1990s on an impulse. He had already had successful careers in the entertainment and the financial services sectors. With a vision, intrigue, creativity,

an impulsive nature, and a contagious enthusiasm for making crystal the traditional way, Ryan set up his glassworks. He even convinced craftspeople to come from Ireland to work for him.

After a few years of making crystal, but not many sales, Ryan found himself facing a serious financial crisis and possible bankruptcy. He needed someone who could focus on the financial side of the business. On another impulse, Ryan hired Rod McCulloch and a new partnership was born. Ryan took on the role of chair, figurehead, and liaison, while McCulloch became president.

McCulloch—a details, numbers, cost-conscious, organized kind of guy—looked for ways to turn the company around. Using his years of experience as an accountant, he thought about how to manage the company better, make it more efficient, and iron out production. He then began searching for more ways to cut costs and increase sales.

With each man taking on different roles, Ryan and McCulloch worked well together. While McCulloch presented tough cost-cutting measures, Ryan brought impulsive ideas about new markets and, often, much-needed personal and emotional support. Even in the face of continuous failures and disappointments, the team never gave up. Out on the waterfront, over a mug of tea, Ryan could often be found giving McCulloch encouragement, a moment of peace, inspiration, and yet more creative, impulsive ideas for meeting their challenges. Take, for instance, how Ryan encouraged McCulloch to call investors for more money, or the suggestion to market their product to a high-end retail store in Toronto.

At long last, after a spring trade show, creative selling strategies, an expanded product line, and a Christmas craft show, NovaScotian Crystal finally turned a profit in the fall of 2001. Ryan and McCulloch celebrated their success over something

stronger than tea. And wouldn't you know it: They didn't drink the same brand of beer.

Today, after years of operating near bankruptcy, NovaScotian Crystal has expanded its product lines, launched a series of online catalogues, and markets its products worldwide.

Questions

1. How would you describe the personalities of Ryan and McCulloch? Describe the extent to which personality plays a role in how Ryan and McCulloch run NovaScotian Crystal.

2. Evaluate the emotional side of running the business. How do Ryan and McCulloch each deal with the stress of running the business?

3. Explain the perceptions of each of these men. What role do these perceptions play in how each runs the company?

Sources: Based on "NovaScotian Crystal," *CBC Venture*, April, 2002, 822; NovaScotian Crystal, "About Us," www.novascotiancrystal.com (accessed January 13, 2006).

CHAPTER 3 Managing in a Cross-Cultural World

Canadians are doing business in more and more countries. So exactly how *do* companies manage in a cross-cultural world?

The more we travel and interact, the more we need to understand how to manage across cultures.

Understanding culture means understanding differences in values and beliefs. But understanding culture is more than a few tips and helpful hints on global etiquette or how to avoid culture clash. Success in crossing cultures in business takes research and basic awareness of what culture is.

So just what makes people from different cultures different? Is it differences in religion, future orientation, language, behaviour, power distance, or values? How do cultural differences affect your work? These are just some of the questions corporate owners should ask.

Cultural differences can baffle people in business. Try these on for size: If you want to lose a contract in Japan, take a lawyer along. In India, yes may mean no; there are different degrees of assent. "Yes" could mean maybe, God willing, or certainly. In Indonesia, they say, "The stronger your handshake, the emptier your mind." In southern Japan, they say, "Only dead fish have their mouths open." Hugs and kisses in the Dominican Republic mean warmth and acceptance, and are not a violation of personal space.

How about marketing your product? Do you brag and give specifications on how great it is? Not in Germany. As the Dutch say, "Good wine doesn't need boasting."

When asked in a survey if they would paint their boss's house, 28 percent in China said "no," but in Japan a resounding 83 percent said "no." The difference? In China, you do everything for your boss. In Japan, even the question is misplaced—they don't paint houses there.

And just look at this contrast: In Canada, when asked in a survey, 96 percent of individuals said they would tell the truth rather than lie to protect a friend. They would put the law above friendship. In Korea, only 26 percent said they would not support their friend by telling the truth. The Koreans clearly valued friendship over truth and the law.

There may be only two expressions that work across all cultures: "Sorry" and "Thank you"!

Questions

1. To what extent does national culture affect the way you interact with others? Consider differences in future orientation, language, values, religion, and your personal power distance.

2. What can organizations and managers do to promote a greater understanding of cultural differences among employees?

3. Should managers and organizations attempt to change the values of their employees, the business's values, or the values of the country they are in? Give reasons for your answer.

Source: Based on "Cross-Culture," *CBC Venture*, August 6, 1995, 552.

CHAPTER 4 Workplace Stress

There is a crisis in the Canadian workforce. Canadian workers are struggling—and failing—to balance the demands of home life with the demands of their job. They're stressed out.

Canadians are under more pressure than ever before. A recent report called *Voices of Canadians: Seeking Work-Life Balance* shows that people are

- Working evenings and weekends to keep ahead,
- Dealing with workplaces that are underfunded and understaffed,
- Working 60-hour weeks to get promoted,
- Suffering from job stress caused by supervisors, and
- Working 12-hour days to become a member of the executive team.

Study after study tells us Canadians are cracking under the strain. More people are working 50-hour weeks, more employers are forking out millions in benefits for antidepressants and anti-anxiety drugs, and absenteeism is costing the Canadian economy $3 billion a year.

Management expert Linda Duxbury of the School of Business at Carleton University surveyed 33 000 Canadians and found startling results. Only 5 percent of those surveyed could say anything good about their organizations. Duxbury stresses that employees are tired of downsizing, restructuring, and changes in the workplace. Employers cannot treat employees like a commodity and expect them to think they have wonderful jobs and workplaces. Employers should be focusing on ways for employees to balance work and life as a way of attracting and keeping good people.

Duxbury's survey also showed that while some organizations have worker-friendly policies and benefits, such as telecommuting and flextime, few employers actually encourage staff to use them. Employees, she found, are tired of business's rhetoric. They are tired of hearing how organizations care about their people, about how they're employers of choice, about the importance of balancing home, work, and lifestyle, and yet, in reality, failing to carry out these ideals.

Duxbury is out to change all of this. She says that it isn't that hard for employers to adjust the work schedules to employee needs and that the real challenge is to change the attitudes of employers so that productivity, not face time, is rewarded.

Chris Duffy, who runs a small consulting business in Fredericton, says that being a supportive manager is not always that easy—you still have to make money while being flexible and letting employees take leaves.

Bob Howe, who started a small law firm in Toronto, is one of those employers who is flexible and rewards productivity. Bob Howe and his partners have escaped face time and 12-hour days with flextime—and less stress. Partners can take extra personal time in the morning and come in later if they need to. They take their children to school and put in fewer hours than the typical partner in a large firm. Partners in this law firm will tell you that the quality of their work is high and that even though they have a friendly, more relaxed work environment, they take home the same pay as their workaholic counterparts on Bay Street.

The federal government has also made changes. Parental leave was recently extended to 12 months, and the government is now considering paid compassionate leave for caregivers of gravely ill family members.

Has corporate Canada woken up to the high cost of stress and job burnout? Linda Duxbury says it has to. Changes have to be made. Business has to do what is right for the long-term health of the workforce.

Questions

1. Using the motivational theories outlined in Chapter 4, explain what is meant by the need for employees to meet the demands of their homes and their jobs, and to balance home, life, and job.

2. What can companies do to create a more balanced and fulfilling work environment for their employees?

3. How well are Canadian firms doing in the process of creating a more balanced work environment?

Source: Based on "Workplace: The Delicate Balance," *CBC Venture*, April 7, 2002, 822.

CHAPTER 5 Hold Those Phones

Telemarketers sell everything from memberships in fitness clubs, to charities, to long-distance calling plans. And Canadians spend almost $6 billion a year over the phone.

We all get these calls—but we don't all hear them out. Sitel Corporation, for instance, had a 34 percent contact rate when it was marketing a new product, Tracker. Only 34 percent of placed calls resulted in a sales pitch, and of course fewer sales. In this industry, turnover can be high—and costly. Motivating call centre employees is a large part of what makes a telemarketing company successful.

The sales representatives at call centres have little flexibility. The work pace is automated, with computers feeding the calls to the rep at a relentless pace. Grabbing the customer's attention at the start of the sales pitch is a tricky business. People at the other end of the line can be nasty. Supervisors and business clients monitor calls whenever they choose. Targeted sale levels are high, predetermined, and often hard to reach. Pay is often at a minimum.

So how *does* a telemarketing company keep its sales reps motivated and committed to selling a product? How does Sitel motivate its phone reps in a job that isn't easy and is extremely tiring?

Energetic young trainers coach the telephone sales reps on the ABCs of telemarketing. They are told to "always be closing" the sale. Intense training and role playing energizes them.

Scripts are carefully written and memorized. Every possible customer objection has a written comeback. Positive attitude is encouraged in the office. Carefully positioned mirrors reflect back the smile the reps always "give" to the customer. Telephone sales reps always know the customer's name—and they use it often, to keep the customer's attention *and* to keep themselves motivated. Muscles get tense, but massages and the supervisor's pep talks are free. It takes teamwork, too. Sales targets are set for the team, and it's everybody's job to achieve the team's goal. Results are fed back to the reps. Success is shared at the end of every sales campaign. It's a real boost, especially when sales have been down.

Telemarketing is the new assembly-line job, and as long as customers buy, telemarketing will be here to stay.

Questions

1. Using the concepts of job design, describe the job of the telephone sales rep.

2. Explain how Sitel and other telemarketing companies motivate their telephone sales representatives.

3. Using the Hackman-Oldham model of job design, explain how you would redesign the sales rep's job.

Source: Based on "Telemarketing," *CBC Venture*, March 31, 1996, 584.

CHAPTER 6 Another Team? Oh No!

Teamwork turned into a buzzword in the 1980s. Authoritarian structures were out; people power was in. Today, you'd be hard pressed to find a company that does not use one kind of team or another.

Quaker Canada has found success and challenges with teams too. At Quaker Canada, workers switch jobs from packing to quality control. Productivity has improved and management costs have been cut by two-thirds since workers started to carry out supervisory decisions like scheduling and ordering supplies.

But consider another example. The five equal partners of Kingston, Ontario-based ESG Canada used teamwork to capture the entrepreneurial spirit of their company. The partners believed

they could achieve a better outcome working as a team than they could if each person worked individually. Five years ago, they laid out their company plan on a roll of brown paper. Since then, their product, a sound-monitoring system used in underground mines, has been a big success. Business has grown astronomically. Now their problem is how to make the team work. They are finding that teamwork takes a lot of effort, slows them down, and sometimes makes achieving consensus difficult, leading to bad decisions. They are considering a change.

Some of those first promoters of teams are now saying teams don't work. Peter Drucker, the late management guru, who once advised companies that they had to have teams, more recently preached that leaders are everything. Researchers at the Massachusetts Institute of Technology (MIT) who used to advocate teamwork are now saying that there isn't proof of better performance from teams.

The car industry was the first to embrace teams back in the early 1980s. The North American automakers were fighting for their lives against the Japanese imports. Many of the North American management gurus believed that the key to Japan's success was a form of teamwork. The Japanese did not work on traditional assembly lines, but in small groups, making productivity suggestions and taking turns doing different jobs. By 1989, GM was turning Japanese, and the movement spread to the rest of the automotive sector, other manufacturers, and then to corporations at large. But now it turns out that the automakers have not been able to use teams as much as they'd planned.

So why are the gurus changing their minds? Why are companies finding that teams just don't work?

A study at MIT of European parts manufacturers found that the most productive manufacturer was in Spain, where there were no teams. Wayne Lewchuk of McMaster University says that workers who spend their time training for other jobs and in team meetings are not producing the product. Natalie Allen of the University of Western Ontario also says teams don't work. Our culture is very individualistic, and corporations rank stars above true team players, she says. They reward individual players through career advancement, promotions, and raises. One other note of caution, she adds, is that success in the early days does not guarantee success in the long term. There is just not enough evidence to conclude that teams increase performance over the long run.

Questions

1. Consider the team management at ESG Canada, the teams at Quaker Canada, and the use of teams in the auto manufacturing sector. What are the advantages and disadvantages of teams?

2. Explain why teams may or may not improve company performance. Consider both the short-run and the long-run performance of the company.

3. What can be done to improve the performance of a team?

Source: Based on "The Trouble with Teams," *CBC Venture*, October 28, 1998, 703.

CHAPTER 7   Small Talk

Try this paradox: Small talk can be a big deal. For the corporate hopeful, chitchat just might be the way to success—small talk sets the tone for negotiations and could lead to bigger things. Read on for some helpful tips.

First impressions *are* important. Recruiters can tell in the first four minutes if you are eligible for the job. Standing with one hand in your pocket and the other out helps portray confidence. And don't forget the smile! Use a handshake that's genuine, and hold it for the length of time it takes to remember the colour of the person's eyes. As for introductions, first and last names will do—no need for a résumé now! Remember to close it with, "A pleasure to meet you."

Give your small talk substance—it will help build rapport. Use some good opening lines to establish a commonality with the other person. Know something about sports, a positive current event, or a human-interest story. Stay away from topics like politics, race, religion, and gender differences.

And remember to practise!

Small talk—it isn't so small.

Questions

1. What tips did you pick up from this case? How will they be useful to you?

2. Describe your most successful experiences in engaging in small talk with strangers. What tips can you give to others?

3. What else can you do to make others feel at ease when first meeting and communicating with you?

Source: Based on "Small Talk," *CBC Venture*, October 26, 1999, 726.

CHAPTER 8 Whistle-Blowers

BusinessWeek called 2002 the year of the whistle-blower, citing the role corporate insiders played in the downfall of a number of companies, including Enron and WorldCom. A number of high-profile cases of people willing to expose questionable activities within their organizations continue to appear in the media.

All the attention and glory a few whistle-blowers have received might make you think that standing up to a corporation—or the system—is a rewarding experience. Whistle-blowing could certainly be regarded as a noble act. However, before you start planning to blow the whistle on your own organization, there is something you ought to know. Most of the time, those who say negative things publicly about their employers are seen as troublemakers or maybe even as psychologically unstable. They are not seen as heroes, but as people who have messed up others' lives.

Two Canadians have discovered the challenges related to being a whistle-blower.

Joanna Gualtieri was in charge of the real estate portfolio for Foreign Affairs Canada when she blew the whistle on wasteful spending in her department. Her job was to ensure that residences for diplomats abroad were cost-effective. She thought some were not. For example, Gualtieri was uncomfortable when she realized that a $20-million residence in Tokyo was sitting empty because the diplomat who was supposed to live there preferred a $350 000 apartment instead. Gualtieri complained to her employer, but got nowhere. She says Foreign Affairs refused to deal with the issue, and then ostracized her in the workplace. In response, she hired a lawyer and reported the issue to the media. The battle has been draining for Gualtieri. She suffered a breakdown, her emotional and physical health have suffered, and she eventually took an unpaid leave from her job. Gualtieri now runs the Federal Accountability Initiative for Reform (FAIR) to help other federal employees who wish to speak out about government wrongdoings.

In 1995, accountant Mike Hilson blew the whistle on the unethical practices of his former employer, Philip Services—a Hamilton, Ontario-based waste disposal services company that was a stock market darling at the time. In 1993, when he was employed by Philip Services, Hilson noted that the company was stockpiling waste, some of it hazardous, and not recording the liability to get rid of it. Hilson told his supervisor numerous times about the matter, but nothing was done about it. Instead, Hilson was told to look for another job, and in 1994 he was fired. A year later, Hilson discovered that the company was seeking approval for a landfill site near his parent's home. Hilson felt strongly that the company would eventually go bankrupt,

and he didn't feel he could sit and watch the landfill site ruin the neighbourhood where he grew up. So he chose to expose his knowledge of the company. He wrote a letter to Ontario's Minister of the Environment, citing examples of the company's deceptive bookkeeping and suggesting the company might not be around to deal with any future problems that might arise at the landfill site. Unfortunately, the government allowed Philip Services to go ahead with the landfill site. The company sold even more shares and served Hilson with a $300-million libel suit and a restraining order. Even those who had read Hilson's letter were served with a restraining order.

Hilson eventually found himself dealing with a company attempting to discredit his character. The company went so far as to publicize bouts of drinking and depression, both consequences of the economic and psychological stress caused by Hilson's conflict with Philip Services. By 1999, Philip Services had filed for bankruptcy protection and was also facing a class-action lawsuit filed by investors who had lost a lot of money with the company. The libel suit against Hilson was eventually dropped, but he still wonders why no one took him seriously.

Why are whistle-blowers not taken seriously? Why are their claims discounted? Why are the authorities, co-workers, and the media so skeptical? Professor Mark Wexler at SFU business has interviewed more than 200 whistle-blowers. He says many cases are far from clear-cut, and sometimes the whistle-blower exaggerates what the employer has been doing.

Although many countries offer legal protection for whistle-blowers, the risk of some form of employer and co-worker retaliation is high. At the same time, as Gualtieri says, "There is no more important thing in the modern workplace than to be able to express yourself freely and do the right thing."

Questions

1. How do power and politics influence whistle-blowing and the consequences whistle-blowers face?

2. Would you blow the whistle on your organization if you discovered it was undertaking activities that are wrong, dangerous, or illegal? Give reasons for your answer.

3. What advice would you give others about blowing the whistle on their organization's activities?

Sources: Based on "Whistle-Blowers," *CBC Venture*, January 5, 2003, 861; www.businessweek.com/magazine/content/02_50/b3812094.htm (accessed January 13, 2006); and www.workopolis.com/servlet/Content/tprinter/20030609/whistleblower (accessed January 13, 2006).

CHAPTER 9 Buggy Wars

Two friends and neighbours arrange to go into business together and then become bitter rivals: This is the story of Bob Bell and Michael Sharpe, who once lived just four houses apart on Oxford Street in Guelph, Ontario.

Bell and Sharpe thought they had a good idea for a new business venture—a bicycle trailer—but the good idea turned into a long, sizzling struggle.

Bell invented the bicycle trailer. Shortly after coming up with the idea, he began to design and build the bicycle trailer in his garage. Once he shared his idea with Sharpe, both thought they could form a successful partnership by drawing upon each other's expertise. Bell, an engineer by trade, would take on research and development; Sharpe, a former computer software sales manager and career manager, would focus on marketing. Sharpe put together the business plan—but before it was finalized, the deal fell apart.

The major point of conflict between Bell and Sharpe was royalties. Bell wanted to license the bicycle trailer design to Sharpe and collect a fee for each bicycle trailer produced. Sharpe wanted Bell to invest more into the venture and share the financial risk. However, Bell did not see any grounds for negotiation. Bell considered the bicycle trailer to be his idea. He had designed it, he had bought the materials to build it, and he had put in the time to develop the final product. When both parties hired lawyers and Bell demanded intellectual property rights, the great Canadian buggy war began.

Bell planned a slow, steady campaign, working from the basement of his home with one employee. He started selling his cargo trailer, the WIKE, at the local farmers' market. His goal was to sell 20 trailers the first year and 500 in the coming year. Bell continued his "go slow, get it right campaign," selling locally and fine-tuning his trailer to carry children. However, he eventually decided that making every bicycle trailer himself was not a good strategy. By 2002, Bell just wanted his life back.

Meanwhile, Sharpe had his own grand plan. He established his new company, Greenways, mortgaged his home, took a bank loan, rented a factory, and hired five employees. Sharpe began mass production of his version of the trailer, the Wonder Wagon, which accommodated small children. He projected sales of 2500 nationwide for the coming year. By the spring of 1994, Sharpe was selling to big specialty retailers and Toronto's largest sporting goods store. Later, bike shops across the country and two national retailers were selling his wagon. He was even a corporate sponsor in Vancouver's Ride for Life.

So how did this end? Bell won the patent infringement case against Sharpe. Bell's company has expanded to six different versions of the bicycle trailer. It also has a licensed manufacturer in China, from whom Bell collects royalties. Sharpe eventually abandoned the whole buggy idea, and switched careers to . . . the fitness industry.

Questions

1. What were the sources of conflict between Bell and Sharpe?

2. Discuss the conflict resolution methods used by the parties. How could negotiation strategies have been used to resolve this conflict?

3. How would you have handled the conflict? How would your personality have affected your approach to resolving the conflict?

Source: Based on "Buggy Wars," *CBC Venture*, August 18, 2002, 841.

CHAPTER 10 Corporate Culture Meets G.A.P Adventures

Bruce Poon Tip, owner of G.A.P Adventures, is one of Canada's most successful entrepreneurs. G.A.P Adventures is a travel company that offers eco-friendly tours with a difference—adventure and adrenaline. Its tour destinations are located in over 100 countries. According to one of its brochures, "If you want the comforts of home, stay home."

Poon Tip has managed to take G.A.P Adventures from a business with 2 employees to one with more than 70 employees—and over $12 million in annual sales—in 10 years.

Since the company's beginnings, Poon Tip has run G.A.P Adventures as more of a family business than a corporation. He considers himself better at building rather than maintaining businesses and wants to move on to new challenges in expanding and diversifying G.A.P Adventures' operations. Poon Tip believes it's time to take G.A.P Adventures to a new corporate level.

It's the 1990s. G.A.P Adventures' staff is at the annual spring retreat in Ontario's cottage country. To the surprise of all, Poon Tip announces a new division and the development of a travel TV show, and introduces a new "hired gun." Poon Tip has hired Dave Bowen, an aggressive marketing director with a corporate background, from one of G.A.P Adventures' biggest competitors. He wants Bowen to shake up the company, which he is concerned is not putting enough emphasis on the customer.

Bowen's challenge is to bring corporate discipline to the company *without* losing employee enthusiasm. Bowen uses his New York savvy and southern charm to transform G.A.P Adventures' corporate culture. The inefficient, handwritten reservation system is organized and converted to a high-tech reservation system, and reservation policies are formalized. The company's annual brochure will include more large, glossy pictures, and more exciting titles and tour descriptions. Bowen decides the brochure will not include a warning about long bus rides in uncomfortable settings or the slogan "If you want the comforts of home, stay home." Bowen insists that it's important to gain the interest of the customer first with the positive aspects of the tour, and then give the details later.

How has G.A.P Adventures fared since the change to a corporate culture? Although some G.A.P employees have left the company, others have adjusted to a work environment that is more serious, more controlled, and less relaxed and open. G.A.P Adventures' 1999 sales were $12.9 million, up from just $500 000 five years earlier. The events of September 11 made 2001 a financially challenging year for many travel companies, yet it was a profitable year for G.A.P Adventures. Expansion, diversification, and leverage are in Poon Tip's blood, and Poon Tip continues to make changes and spring surprises.

This year's annual spring retreat is a bit different—the staff is staying in the executive suites of the upscale Blue Mountain resort. Poon Tip announces another surprise: The company will be split into two divisions: the G.A.P division and the Real Tours division. The G.A.P division will market the company's own brand: G.A.P tours. The new Real Tours division will market other contracted-out tours. G.A.P Adventures has also partnered with Signature Vacations to market G.A.P tours. The reservation system is also changing, with a new IT company supporting it. Where will G.A.P Adventures' journey in the world of corporate culture take it next?

Questions

1. Describe the organizational culture of G.A.P Adventures before and after the changes, and how the company has maintained the new culture.

2. What challenges might be expected in bringing corporate culture to G.A.P Adventures?

3. What type of employee would feel most comfortable working in a strong culture such as the one at G.A.P Adventures?

Sources: Based on "Corporate Culture Meets G.A.P Adventures," *CBC Venture,* June 23, 2002, 833; G.A.P Adventures: World Wide Adventure Travel and Eco Tour website, www.gap.ca (accessed January 13, 2006); www.profitguide.com/magazine/article.jsp?content=261 (accessed January 13, 2006).

CHAPTER 11   Richard Branson

British billionaire Richard Branson—owner and CEO of the Virgin Group, Britain's largest private company, and born thrill-seeker—is one of the world's most intriguing entrepreneurs. At 45, Branson has created an image for his business that matches his own. His companies are as free-spirited, innovative, and irreverent as he is. He relishes any opportunity to turn the establishment on its ear and loves to challenge bloated, complacent companies that don't motivate staff and charge too much for their products.

In the 1970s and 1980s, Branson created the Virgin brand as a music megastore. The Virgin Group has since expanded to approximately 200 companies with over 25 000 employees throughout the world involved in "planes, trains, finance, soft drinks, music, mobile phones, holidays, cars, wines, publishing, and bridal wear." Branson targets the giant companies in sectors where he can perform better than them—where he can offer a price and quality advantage over his competitors.

Branson's philosophy? To be a total-life company. His vision? For Virgin Group to be able to satisfy all the consumer's needs. His ambition and specialty? Taking on the giants in well-developed industries.

Branson operates the Virgin Group under a thin corporate structure. He is good at delegating. There is no bureaucracy, no corporate headquarters, only 150 small companies with managing directors who have lots of freedom to make decisions—and mistakes. Directors have a stake in the company and the freedom to run it as their own. Branson believes it his job to empower managers and employees. He loves to mingle with his customers and believes the managing directors should do the same.

Branson once took the Virgin Group public, but he took it private again when global challenges made its share prices plummet. True to his integrity and reputation, Branson bought back the shares at their original value—investors lost nothing. Branson says, "In the end, you only have your reputation," and "You can think more long-term, and do what is right for the company in the long term, when the company is private."

So what does the future hold for the Virgin Group? Branson says he will continue to be a force to be reckoned with—he will continue to pit himself against the industry giants.

Questions

1. Describe Branson's leadership style.

2. How does Branson use charisma to run the Virgin Group of companies?

3. Why is it possible for Branson to have almost no bureaucracy in his company?

Source: Based on "Richard Branson," *CBC Venture*, October 20, 1996, 613; www.virgin.com (accessed January 22, 2006).

CHAPTER 12 Doug Hall, Creativity Guru

Meet Doug Hall, leading creativity guru, entrepreneur, and master inventor. Doug runs the highly acclaimed Eureka Ranch just outside Cincinnati, Ohio. Hall and his team of coaches, called *trained brains,* help large corporate clients think smarter and more creatively about what they do, and invent new products.

The year is 2002, and Hall is in Summerside, PEI, on a tour to launch his new book, *Jump Start Your Business Brain.* Hall had been on the island the year before, helping small craft companies be more innovative marketers and lay out plans to become more profitable. His book features his on-the-road experience with the small business owners he consulted throughout the island.

So just what did Hall tell these Islanders that turned them into all-star entrepreneurs?

Hall says entrepreneurs should think smarter and more creatively about how to grow their business. He also says that entrepreneurs have a high urgency to do something different, but a high fear of doing anything. Too many Islanders are willing to work forever for no money and don't explain their product very well. With the help of his trained brains and a computer program that simulates a test market, Hall assesses each entrepreneur's chance of success.

Small business can be a lot more effective, says Hall. For instance, when the owners of a souvenir shop want to sell more upscale figurines, Hall suggests that they no longer call the shop a factory. He encourages them to showcase their locally produced figurines as heirloom collectibles, placing them in a high-profile glass cabinet, centre stage, rather than on the back wall, out of sight. Hall's advice? Focus on the idea and get it right, then get the communications right. First, find out what your product's obvious benefit is, then turn it into one concise concept and communicate clearly to customers the benefit of what they are buying.

Hall's second client is a sheep farmer located over 40 kilometres from Charlottetown that produces a variety of woolly wares, including felt slippers. Hall's advice? Pair down the line of items and really promote one "marquee" item. By communicating a product's dramatic difference, customers will be willing to drive the distance to the shop.

A third client has been making wind chimes in his barn for 20 years, but growing competition is putting him out of business. Hall's advice? Engage in marketing warfare and compete aggressively. Fight the competitor with quality products rather than cheap ones. Build wind chimes that withstand the gale-force winds of the island, and then prove that they work. Give customers a reason to believe in the product.

Hall's fourth client makes Mi'qmaq statues because she likes the legend behind them. Sales are sinking. Hall's advice? "Just because you can do something doesn't mean you should. Start over. Recreate the product; rename the company."

Creativity is the driving force behind Doug Hall's advice. As one PEI entrepreneur put it, Hall has a way of shaking "people out of their comfort zone!" which for business can mean greater profit.

Questions

1. What were Doug Hall and his trained brains able to do for the small business owners that they were not able to do for themselves?

2. How can a company get more creativity from its employees? Does it have to spend a lot of money to do so? Give reasons for your answers.

3. What prevents entrepreneurs from thinking creatively when it comes to growing their business?

Sources: Based on "Doug Hall," *CBC Venture*, September 29, 2002, 847; www.doughall.com (accessed January 13, 2006); http://www.eurekaranch.com (accessed January 13, 2006); Barnes & Noble, www.bn.com (accessed January 13, 2006); http://cbc.ca/business/programs/venture/onventure/090401.html (accessed January 13, 2006); and D. Hall, *Jump Start Your Business Brain* (Cincinnati, OH: Eureka! Institute, 2001).

CHAPTER 13 Growing Big Can Be Hard to Do

Debra Belinsky and Cheryl Benson-Guanci, originally from Winnipeg, are two of the most dynamic entrepreneurs in the sports entertainment industry.

Belinsky was a university athlete, and Benson-Guanci was a cheerleader, choreographer, and producer of minor pro basketball. In 1994, they joined forces to create DCB Group (formerly DCB Productions), which produces shows and entertainment for a number of Canadian and US organizations.

DCB Group has grown incredibly since its beginnings. Today it has three specialized divisions: Productions, Creative Communications, and Events. The company provides a range of operational, technical, and entertainment services for sporting and special events. The partners' philosophy is to provide clients, sponsors, and guests with a valued entertainment experience. A one-stop sports entertainment package may include anything from fireworks to trivia quizzes to dance contests to free pizzas—each package is designed to keep the audience excited, entertained, and in the game.

The DCB Group has captivated audiences of the Calgary Flames, Toronto Blue Jays, Edmonton World Figure Skating Championships, Anaheim Mighty Ducks, Los Angeles Clippers, Labatt Canada, World Team Tennis, and Disneyland Entertainment. The company has also won the contract for the John R. Wooden Classic basketball series consistently from 1995 to 2003.

Belinsky and Benson-Guanci started their business almost on a shoestring. After producing one show for the Winnipeg Jets—and borrowing $6000 from their parents—they went right to the top of the entertainment mega-business and approached Disney. Three years before, Disney had bought the Anaheim Mighty Ducks franchise and brought sports enter-

tainment to the hockey arena for the first time. Enter the DCB Group and two Canadians who know hockey. From there, the company took off.

Benson-Guanci is based in Anaheim, California, while Belinsky is based in Calgary, with an office in Toronto. The company researches local markets, finds sponsors for the games, and develops, produces, and provides hands-on delivery of each program. While the job is rewarding, it is also very demanding. Organizing face-to-face business meetings between the partners is difficult because of the physical distance between them, and clients expect either Belinsky or Benson-Guanci to run the show.

To maintain the growth of DCB Group, Belinsky and Benson-Guanci need to set strategic goals and consider a new company structure that would release them from managing daily organizational affairs. Their challenge is to select an organizational structure that will allow the company to continue their momentum of growth in a flourishing industry.

Questions

1. Describe the present organizational structure of the DCB Group.

2. How did the structure of the company change as the company grew?

3. What kind of organizational structure will the DCB Group need in the future to maintain the company's growth?

Source: Based on "Duck Ladies," *CBC Venture*, February 3, 1998, 593; http://thedcbgroup.com (accessed January 13, 2006).

CHAPTER 14 Fairmont Hotels and Resorts

Following the terrorist attacks of September 11, 2001, hotel bookings throughout North America were down almost as much as airline reservations. This was not a good time to launch a new Canadian hotel chain. Yet Bill Fatt, CEO of Fairmont Hotels and Resorts, did just that.

Fairmont Hotels and Resorts owns many of the hotels that Canadians know best, like the Château Frontenac and the Banff Springs Hotel. Canadians will likely still recognize these hotels as being under the CP (Canadian Pacific) name. Today, though, Fairmont Hotels and Resorts is a separate company, with no more ties to its parent company, Canadian Pacific.

Immediately before the terrorist attacks, Fatt was at the Toronto Stock Exchange, establishing Fairmont Hotels and Resorts as a publicly traded company. Immediately after the terrorist attacks, Fatt was at the Plaza Hotel in New York, calming analyst and investor fears about the fallout in the travel industry. At the time, Fatt said it was anyone's guess what business conditions would be like in 2002. Overall, the upscale hotel sector was facing uncertainty, with some hotels laying off thousands of employees, delaying major construction projects, and implementing a four-day workweek.

The Banff Springs Hotel is the jewel of Fairmont Hotels and Resorts. Many of its guests are from the United States, Europe, and Asia. Just after the terrorist attacks, cancellations poured in, restaurants were temporarily closed, and staff were laid off or given time off.

The entire Fairmont Hotels and Resorts chain was affected by the decreased number of travellers. The company froze all new renovation plans, cut staff across the country, lowered projections for profits, and told investors they could not predict where the business was going.

So just where *is* Fairmont Hotels and Resorts going now?

Bill Fatt plans to turn the Fairmont chain into a global player. Fatt has a long list of cities where he would like to establish his chain. Fairmont Hotels and Resorts has a clean balance sheet that might help Fatt do just that. The Fairmont chain came out a big winner when it separated from Canadian Pacific; it had almost all of its long-term debt wiped off its books. This is giving Fatt a distinct advantage. It means that Fairmont Hotels and Resorts can borrow and spend to improve the chain and gain new customers.

Fatt's ability to go shopping for the best hotels and resorts might indeed propel Fairmont Hotels and Resorts to one of the top places among the world's luxury hotel chains.

Questions

1. What external and internal business factors affected Fairmont Hotels and Resorts directly after the 2001 terrorist attacks? How did these factors impact the operation of the Fairmont chain?

2. How did uncertainty in the external business environment affect the Fairmont chain and the hotel industry in general?

3. What factors are working for and against Bill Fatt's plan to turn the Fairmont chain into a global player? Should he go forward with his plan? Explain your answer.

Source: Based on "Hotels in Crisis," *CBC Venture*, October 7, 2001, 796.

INTEGRATIVE OB CASES

Working at Wal-Mart

Claude has a problem.[1] His father is celebrating a major birthday with a special dinner this Saturday, and Claude is scheduled to work from 4:00 to 8:00 pm. Claude comes from a close-knit family where all family milestones are celebrated together over an extended meal. If Claude works his shift, he will have to miss his father's birthday dinner. If he calls in sick, he will feel like a liar since he is not actually ill; he does not even feel a cold coming on.

Claude is sure that his manager will not give him the time off. When he first started this job, he had asked that he not be scheduled to work on his day of Sabbath. His manager simply said that the auto scheduler, a computer program designed to create employee work schedules, could not accommodate this request, and then walked away. There was no room for discussion. "How much is this job worth to me, anyway?" Claude is asking himself.

Claude is a 22-year-old fourth year engineering student living at home. Wanting to avoid student loans, Claude applied to work at Wal-Mart as an associate processing film in the photo lab. Because the store was new, all the associates had to undergo orientation before the store could be opened. Groups of 30 to 40 associates met in the basement meeting room of a hotel. Each associate received a copy of the Wal-Mart associate handbook. The store manager reviewed portions of the handbook related to codes of conduct and told the associates, "At Wal-Mart, you should never hear the phrase 'it's not my job,' since associates are empowered by Wal-Mart." He explained the profit-sharing program and the stock-ownership plan along with the benefits.

The associates then watched a video entitled "You've Picked a Great Place to Work" that described Wal-Mart's success as a business and how it had grown from a single store that Sam Walton had opened to become the world's largest retailer. Various quotations from Sam Walton such as, "If you want a successful business, your people must feel that you are working for them—not that they are working for you" were sprinkled liberally throughout the videos.

The manager also outlined Sam Walton's guiding principles:[2]

1. Be committed to your work. Your passion will be contagious to those around you.
2. Treat associates as partners and be a servant leader.
3. Make your work exciting and motivational by setting high goals, using job rotation, and encouraging competition.
4. Communicate as much information as you can to associates. Associates with information feel empowered and care about the organization.
5. Demonstrate appreciation on a regular basis. Praise is priceless.
6. Have fun at work, show enthusiasm, and celebrate successes.
7. Listen to your associates. They know what the customers are thinking, and they have ideas about how to improve operations.
8. Go beyond meeting your customers' expectations.
9. Pay careful attention to expenses, and keep them to a minimum.
10. Be open to trying things that haven't been tried before. Take risks.

The manager then taught the associates the infamous Wal-Mart cheer:

Manager: "Give me a W"
Associates: "W"
Manager: "Give me an A"
Associates: "A"
Manager: "Give me an L"
Associates: "L"
Manager: "Give me a squiggly"
Associates: "Squiggly" (while doing something that resembles the twist)
Manager: "Give me an M"
Associates: "M"
Manager: "Give me an A"
Associates: "A"

Case study written by Céleste M. Brotheridge, École des sciences de la gestion, Université du Québec à Montréal. © Céleste M. Brotheridge. Reprinted by permission.

Manager: "Give me an R"
Associates: "R"
Manager: "Give me a T"
Associates: "T"
Manager: "What's that spell?"
Associates: "Wal-Mart!"
Manager: "Who's number one?"
Associates: "The customer always"
Manager: "What store is number one?"
Associates: "[Store number] 999 customer service all the time"

The associates are required to sing this song at every morning meeting and after the store closes for the evening. At these meetings, the associates are also informed of how the store is doing in terms of sales levels.

The orientation ended with a presentation in which each associate's name was called, and the associate was presented a nametag that doubled as a swipe card to be used for the time clock. Claude left the orientation session feeling excited about being part of the Wal-Mart team. It was his first real job, and he was impressed with the "family" approach that the managers talked about during the orientation. The managers had encouraged employees to become passionate about Wal-Mart, to share in Sam's vision, and to put Wal-Mart's needs first.

A few days after the orientation session, Claude began working in the photo lab. During his four-hour shift, he placed the film in one end of the developing machine and out the other end came the negatives. Next, he placed the negatives in a scanner, made adjustments for colour, and ordered prints. He then placed these prints and negatives in an envelope and started the process over again with another roll of film. Although Claude sometimes enjoyed looking at the prints, he found his job to be rather routine. He looked forward to troubleshooting when a machine would break down. He tried to process the film as quickly and perfectly as possible so that the customers would be happy with the service that Wal-Mart provided. As did other employees, he learned his job within a few days. There were very few skills to master, and the procedures were clearly laid out. Claude realized that employees could be easily replaced (and were), but having the right attitude—one of commitment and a sense of duty—seemed to be particularly important.

At first, having the right attitude was not a problem for Claude. Because he always thought the best of others and made light of any problems, he had simply dismissed any doubts that he had about his work as unimportant. After a few weeks, however, Claude began to notice that his co-workers were complaining about many things: shifts, management, procedures, and, especially, the song that they were taught as part of their orientation.

Ever since his manager criticized him for suggesting some new procedures (or "complaining" as his manager called it), Claude thought that it was best to keep quiet. When he

had an idea, he thought of a line from a poem that he had read in high school, "The Charge of the Light Brigade": "Theirs not to make reply, Theirs not to reason why, Theirs but to do and die." Whereas Claude used to "go the extra mile," now he did only as much as he needed to keep his job. He would tell himself that Wal-Mart was a means to an end, just like he was a means for Wal-Mart. He was glad that he was getting an education so that he wouldn't have to be Wal-Mart "lifer." He almost felt bad for the lifers. In a year or two, he'd be a professional engineer, a prestigious occupation paying more than they could every dream about. More importantly, he had choices; they did not.

Claude noticed that there was a lot of turnover at Wal-Mart. Within a year, most of the people that had started with him had left. There seemed to be an increased focus on following rules. For example, although they brought water into the photo lab for the equipment, associates were not permitted to bring in water or other beverages for themselves. Also, although the photo lab employees were able to develop a workable holiday schedule for themselves, the manager refused to accept this schedule because the auto scheduler "would not permit it." Exceptions, negotiation, and relaxation of the rules were not possible.

There were four additional incidents along the same theme that stood out for Claude. After doing an inventory count for several hours, an associate named Roger stepped outside the store for his coffee break. Once back on the job, he noticed that he had left his electronic inventory scanner outside. So, Roger went outside and found his scanner where he left it. However, when he went back into the store, his manager confronted him, indicating that it was inappropriate for an associate to take two coffee breaks and that this formal warning would be placed on Roger's personnel record. Roger quit his job that afternoon.

On her last day of work, another associate, Judy, came into the store wearing a pair of khaki shorts. Her manager rushed toward Judy, stopped her within a few feet from the door, used his badge to measure her shorts, and told her to go home and change her clothes because her shorts were more than the length of a badge above her knees. Judy did go home but did not return to work.

Similarly, Colette, a cashier, had joined the Canadian Forces and then informed Wal-Mart that she would require every third weekend off. Colette thought that this minor unavailability could be input into the auto scheduler and that all would be fine. Even during weeks in which she could not work weekends, she was available for 30 hours of work. However, Colette was informed by her manager that he would not be able to schedule her for the minimum 12 hours per week and that she would have to make a choice between the Forces and Wal-Mart. Colette then requested a leave of absence that was also denied by her manager. Although she was only one of a handful of employees to receive the Four-Star Cashier Award for excellent work and customer service, Colette was subsequently dismissed.

Claude thought about another incident in which Michel, a high school student, requested holidays during the first week of August so that he could participate in an annual family camping trip. Although Michel had submitted his request four months in advance, his manager waited until the middle of July to inform him that he could not find anyone to cover for Michel and, that, as a result, he would have to either work those days or lose his job. Michel decided to miss his family holiday. He didn't want to work at McDonald's or some other place that paid new employees about two dollars less per hour than Wal-Mart did.

On this day at work, Claude is especially apprehensive. Besides having to make a decision regarding his father's birthday dinner, Claude is also concerned about some material that he came across while surfing the net. Several websites reported that Wal-Mart is sued, on average, two to five times per day by customers, employees, and other parties.[3] The case that really stands out for Claude deals with the issue of religious discrimination.[4] A store manager who was displeased with the unwillingness of a Seventh Day Adventist to work during her Sabbath made negative comments about the plaintiff's religion. He also provided an inaccurate account of the activities of the plaintiff and another employee who had both accessed the company's computer system using a management password. Although he fired the plaintiff, he did not fire the other employee who did not practice the plaintiff's religion.

Even though most of these sources contain actual court documents, Claude is skeptical. After all, it is reasonable to expect that any organization would experience these sorts of issues, especially one as visible and as large as Wal-Mart. The retailer had $285.2 billion in sales in the 2004–2005 fiscal year, more than 1.6 million associates worldwide, over 3700 facilities in the United States and 2400 units in other countries, and more than 138 million customers per week.[5] In fact, it may well be that Wal-Mart is the target of even fewer lawsuits than other companies its size. And, after all, Claude thinks to himself, Wal-Mart earned the titles of "Top Corporate Citizen" by the 2000 Cone/Roper Report of philanthropy and "Most Admired Company in America" by *Fortune* magazine in 2003 and 2004.[6] However, after reflecting on what was happening in his own workplace, Claude does not know what to think.

As he walks into the store, Claude feels as though hundreds of eyes are watching him from every direction. He ducks into the restroom, but this only reminds him of a case in which a Wal-Mart manager had secretly set up a camera in a unisex restroom in an attempt to catch potential shoplifters in the act.[7] Two employees, however, found this to be invasive, and the courts agreed. Although the camera did not actually record anything, the jury considered this irrelevant. "Rightly so," Claude thinks, "The restroom is the last sanctuary of mankind." After glancing at the ceiling, Claude slips into the employee lunchroom.

The walls of the lunchroom are plastered with posters containing slogans such as "Our people make the difference" and "Associates are partners." On the table is an open can of cashews. Although Claude and the other associates normally enjoy eating whatever food is on the lunchroom table, on this occasion, Claude mutters, "I'd have to be nuts to eat any of those!" He is reminded of another case in which Wal-Mart was ordered to pay 20 million dollars in damages to four employees for defamation, eavesdropping, and outrageous conduct.[8] A manager who was concerned about theft in the store had set up a video camera in the employee break room and placed several open packages of nuts and candy on the table as bait. After the manager viewed the tape, he fired four employees without notice. During the resulting trial, another Wal-Mart manager testified that opened packages of nuts and candy were regularly donated to charity or given to employees.

Claude normally has a friendly chat with Monique, a visible minority woman who works in electronics, but "not today. Why take chances?" he thinks. Claude is referring to a case in which Wal-Mart was fined $40 000 for secretly recording employee conversations.[9] He waves at Monique as he proceeds to the photo lab.

Claude also thinks about a case in which a manager fired a white female employee, telling her that she "would never move up with the company being associated with a black man."[10] Wal-Mart was subsequently ordered to pay her $94 000 in damages. "What's the deal here?" Claude thinks. "Wal-Mart seems to concern itself with associates' choice of marital partners, elimination of bodily fluids, and religion. If this is how the world's largest retailer treats its employees, what do I have to look forward to in the rest of my career? Maybe, I'm expecting too much. After all, this is just a job."

Having reached the photo lab, Claude starts loading film into the processor, something he will do for his entire shift. He tries to block out all the questions that he has about his workplace. One question that he is unable to stop thinking about, however, is what he should do about his father's birthday dinner. "Should I not go to dad's birthday party at all, should I try to ask my manager for time off (and, if so, how), should I pretend to have a cough and ask to go home early on Saturday?" While contemplating his options, another possibility enters his mind, "Or... should I just leave for 20 minutes or so and get my co-workers to cover for me?"

Trouble at City Zoo

City Zoo has been an important visitor destination for generations of children. Locally, provincially, and nationally, City Zoo has had a remarkable reputation for providing a high quality environment for its animals while enabling children of all ages to learn about animals and see them in natural environments. The zoo operates with a dedicated staff, as well as a large number of volunteers. Over half of its revenues come from a special tax levy on city property owners who vote on whether to renew the levy during city elections held every three years.

Despite its sterling reputation, the zoo went through a year of unpleasant publicity in 2005, after the board of directors dismissed head veterinarian Tim Bernardino. Newspaper reports of the dismissal suggested that Bernardino had been dismissed for speaking up about harm to some of the zoo's animals. The publicity forced zoo management to respond to many tough questions regarding its practices and operations regarding both animals and staff. City Council acted swiftly in the face of continued negative press coverage of the zoo, feeling a responsibility to the taxpayers. In order to answer all of the questions raised by the press, council created a special Citizens' Task Force to review the zoo's finances and operations, including animal care.

It is February 2006, and Emma Breslin has just been hired by the board of directors to take over as executive director of the zoo. She is reviewing the many concerns raised by the task force and wondering how she might restore employees' and the public's confidence in the zoo. She will be meeting with the board in two weeks to present her recommendations for moving forward. The board has asked her to act quickly because city residents will vote on the next tax levy in just three months. A "no" vote would substantially reduce the zoo's revenues for the next several years. (Exhibit 1 outlines the revenues and expenses of the zoo for fiscal year 2005.)

Background

The City Zoological Gardens got its start in 1905, when Samantha Fraser donated a hedgehog to the city's Parks Board. Building on that first donation, the zoo has grown to be one of the most comprehensive zoological institutions in the country. The zoo's African Savannah recreates the look of Africa's plains and jungles. The Savannah houses the world-famous Hippoquarium, the first natural hippo habitat to be created in a zoo. The zoo includes exhibits for Siberian tigers, Asian sloth bears, and the endangered African wild dogs. The zoo has also renovated the Aviary and the Primate Forest. More recent improvements include a new parking lot and gift shop. The zoo is a top tourist attraction for the city, and the number of annual visitors to the zoo has nearly tripled from 1982 (364 000 visitors) to 2004 (more than 1 million visitors). In the past five years, the zoo has twice been ranked as one of the top 10 zoos in North America for children and families. It was also voted one of the top five zoos in North America in the "North America's Favorite Zoo" contest sponsored by Microsoft. The zoo's vision and mission statements (see Exhibit 2) are widely credited with helping the zoo achieve these awards.

Until 1982, the zoo was run by the city. That year, ownership was transferred to the City Zoological Society, a private nonprofit organization. Because of its dedication, the Society was able to introduce a number of improvements that the city had not been able to accomplish. The zoo has since doubled in size and now contributes significantly to the local economy. A recent study by a local university found that the zoo generates almost $8 in local economic activity for each tax dollar it receives.

The zoo employs 157 full-time staff members and more than 550 part-time and seasonal employees. There are also more than 300 volunteers who assist with programs, events, and community outreach. Donors and members provide financial support for animal conservation and educational programming.

The Ministry of Natural Resources Inquiry

The 2001 Inquiry

In December 2000, Medusa, a female sloth bear mistakenly believed to be pregnant, was put into isolation, where it died. Zoo officials later admitted that they had misunderstood how to properly care for sloth bears. Tim French, the curator of Large Mammals at the time, made the decision to put the bear in isolation on his own, without reporting this to his supervisors. The bear's zookeeper, Melissa Fox, who reported to French, objected to his decision, but no one would listen to her, including acting head veterinarian Wynona Singh (who was in charge while Dr. Bernardino was away on research). Fox's daily notes, which she was required to file with her supervisor, described her worries about the bear. Fox finally became so upset with the bear's condition that she asked to be transferred to another part of the zoo. French resigned after the bear's death.

As a result of the investigation, the zoo was fined $1450 by the Ministry of Natural Resources for violating federal

This case was prepared by Nancy Langton, Sauder School of Business. This case is based on an actual set of events, although all names have been changed. © 2006 by Nancy Langton.

EXHIBIT 1   City Zoo Revenues and Expenses, Fiscal Year 2005

Public Support

Property Tax Levy Receipts	$6 466 860
Grants	$174 780
Education Program Revenue	$344 110
Total Public Support	**$6 985 750**

Development Revenue

Membership	$3 903 420
Friends of the Zoo	$214 397
Annual Fundraising	$130 852
Corporate Support	$302 952
Development Events	$391 565
Total Development Revenue	**$4 943 186**

Earned Revenue

Admissions	$3 253 355
Advanced Sales	$337 908
Gross Revenue From Concessions and Gift Shop Operations	$7 153 483
Rides, Parking, and Tours	$1 560 727
Facility Rentals	$116 520
Total Earned Revenue	**$12 421 993**
Other Revenue	**$34 956**

Total Public Support and Revenue	**$24 385 885**

Expenses

Cost of Goods Sold	$2 448 164
Wages and Benefits	$13 900 524
Supplies, Maintenance, and Utilities	$4 387 642
Professional Services	$2 246 560
Other Expenses	$714 487
Conservation—Project Support	$45 093
Animal Purchases	$76 542
Special Exhibits	$293 630

Total Operating Expenses	**$24 112 642**
Excess (Deficit)	**$273 243**

animal welfare regulations. The zoo also agreed to create an animal reporting system so that employees could raise any concerns they had about animal welfare, although nothing ever resulted from this agreement.

The 2004 Inquiry

In February 2004, the Ministry of Natural Resources began an investigation of animal deaths that had occurred at the zoo over the past several years:

- Cupid, a hippopotamus, died in the summer of 2003 at the age of 49. While the veterinary staff raised some questionable circumstances concerning the death, zoo officials dismissed the animal's death as "old age."

- George, a 14-year-old giraffe, died in 2001 from tetanus three weeks after he was gored by a kudu when the two were put in an enclosure together.

- Medusa, the female sloth bear, died in December 2000.

Zoo officials were puzzled about why the Ministry of Natural Resources had decided to investigate these deaths.

"Initially, my gut reaction was that the Ministry of Natural Resources was just stepping things up because of what had transpired at that other zoo," a zoo spokesperson said. The spokesperson was referring to several suspicious animal deaths, including an orangutan euthanized by mistake, at a large zoo in another part of the country.

As the Ministry of Natural Resources investigation progressed, however, many zoo staff became nervous about the way it was being conducted. Inspectors did not reveal the exact reason for their inspection, but they asked specific questions about the giraffe and the hippopotamus. The inspectors requested to speak to some employees, while refusing to speak with others. Zoo officials later said the surprise inspection was "unusual, unprecedented, and aggressive."

"As you can imagine, it was a very upsetting and confusing time. We've never had this kind of inspection, and the frustrating thing was they would not tell us what they were inspecting for," said William Lau, the zoo's executive director.

Before the Ministry of Natural Resources could issue a report, zoo officials decided to conduct their own internal investigation into the deaths of George, the giraffe, and Cupid, the hippopotamus. Officials were concerned that someone at the zoo had made a call to the Ministry of Natural Resources that led to the surprise inspection. Lau claimed that the investigation was not a "witch hunt," and

that officials were not trying to find out if anyone had acted as a whistle-blower. "We simply want to understand what the Ministry of Natural Resources is worried about," he said.

The Ministry of Natural Resources issued a report on its investigation the following month. In it, the inspectors noted that the zoo had ignored the warnings of Dr. Tim Bernardino, City Zoo's head veterinarian, about animal care. "From the review of numerous documents and interviews, it is clear that these veterinary recommendations from the attending veterinarian [Dr. Bernardino] have not been addressed in a reasonable time. The licensee [the City Zoo] has failed to provide the attending veterinarian with adequate authority to ensure the provision of adequate veterinary care," the report stated.

Zoo Management

Board of Directors

The board of directors oversees City Zoo's business affairs and strategic plan, but day-to-day operations are left in the hands of the executive director. There are 18 people on the board. Each board member serves a three-year term. The term can be renewed up to two times, if the board member is nominated by the Nominating Committee and approved by the board of directors. The board in recent years has been mostly hands-off, allowing the executive director a great deal of latitude in running the zoo.

Executive Director

The executive director is effectively the CEO of the zoo, carrying out the strategic plan of the board. William (Bill) Lau was appointed executive director in 1980, when the zoo was still run by the city. Under his leadership, the zoo expanded considerably, won numerous awards, and significantly increased its revenues.

Lau did a good job of raising the zoo profile externally, particularly in leading fundraising efforts that brought numerous exotic animals to the zoo. He was not necessarily seen as a good internal leader, however. The board's Executive Management Committee reported at a March 13, 2002 board meeting that the zoo's work environment was characterized by numerous disagreements. The minutes of this meeting showed that the board discussed "'open warfare' between managers; backbiting and rude behaviour during meetings; and problems in managers' relationships with Mr. Lau." The minutes also reported that "Working with Bill is experienced by some as difficult, intimidating, or scary." Some staff had complained that Lau frequently yelled at staff and failed to acknowledge their value. "There is a fear of repercussion, and some people are afraid they will be... seen as stupid, belittled in meetings, [and] blamed and shamed in front of others," the minutes state.

Chief Operating Officer

The chief operating officer (COO) is second in command at the zoo, reporting to the executive director. The COO responsibilities include most of the operational functions of the zoo: finance, human resources, maintenance and horticulture, interpretive services, and education. The Department of Veterinary Care was the only nonoperational function that also reported to the COO. All other animal-related departments, including the curators, reported to the executive director.

In early 2002, the zoo hired Robert (Bob) Stellenbosch to be the new COO. Unlike the COO he replaced, Stellenbosch had no animal care experience in his previous positions. Before coming to the zoo, he had been executive director of the National Funeral Directors Association for 14 years. Prior to that, he had been executive director of the Provincial Bankers Association. Nevertheless, veterinary care still fell under Stellenbosch's mandate, and the head veterinarian reported to him. Stellenbosch did not see this as a problem. As Stellenbosch pointed out, he often had to oversee "departments in areas I know very little about. The secret [is] having a strong line of communication with the people who report to you."

The zoo's executive director also did not see Stellenbosch's lack of animal-care experience as a problem. "We were looking for anybody with a background that could run a zoo on a day-to-day basis. We didn't find anybody with an animal background who could do that. We chose Bob Stellenbosch because he was the best candidate," Lau said.

Caring for the Animals

Three sets of employees work closely with the animals: veterinarians, curators, and zookeepers.

The Veterinarians

Dr. Tim Bernardino

Dr. Tim Bernardino, Director of Animal Health and Nutrition at City Zoo, was the zoo's head veterinarian, and had been a zoo employee for 22 years. Eight full- and part-time employees in the animal health and nutrition department reported to him. Veterinarians are responsible for the health care program for the animals, and they also maintain all health records. Bernardino was also the "attending veterinarian" for the zoo, a position that carries with it the responsibility to communicate on a regular basis with the Ministry of Natural Resources. Part of this responsibility involved bringing questionable animal deaths to the attention of the Ministry of Natural Resources.

Bernardino was well respected by the international veterinarian community, and well-liked by the zookeepers. He was known to deeply care for all of the animals in the zoo, and kept up with the latest literature on the best ways to manage and display animals to maximize their comfort and well-being.

Bernardino's performance as head veterinarian was generally applauded by senior management. He had received glowing ratings in his annual performance reviews throughout his career. For instance, at the end of 2004, Bernardino received one of his best performance reviews ever. Robert Stellenbosch, his direct supervisor, wrote that Bernardino maintained "the highest quality of work!" He also wrote that "Tim is well respected throughout the zoo." Stellenbosch praised the veterinarian's technical skills, his dependability, and his tremendous work ethic.

There were occasional negative comments in his reviews, although these did not seem to weigh heavily in his overall evaluations. For instance, in his 2000 review a former supervisor wrote, "Tim can be intense and inflexible, causing strained relations with fellow employees." Still, the supervisor noted that Bernardino "gets along reasonably well" with other zoo employees. In his 2004 review, the veterinarian was specifically asked to "focus more on people skills in the department and with curators." The review also noted that "Tim is strong in his beliefs, and sometimes needs to temper that once a final decision is made."

The negative performance appraisal comments were related to Bernardino's relationships with the curators and zookeepers. He was well respected by the zookeepers, and maintained good relations with them because their observations of the animals helped the animals stay healthy. However, some of the curators felt that Bernardino empowered the zookeepers too much, so that the zookeepers would sometimes go around their curators to make complaints about animal care. Bernardino worried that some of the zookeepers were disciplined by their curators when they spoke with him about their concerns regarding the animals. "People don't feel free to be open. Discussions don't happen. [There is] control of information, control of communications, control of decision making [by the curators]," he said.

Beth Else, curator of Conservation and Research, saw it differently. "I think he empowered the keepers to go around the supervisors and go to him when they didn't get the answer that they liked," she said, echoing comments of the other curators.

Despite his generally good reviews, Bernardino also felt that he was "alienated from the decision-making process... with the curatorial staff and with other administrators." He sometimes complained the curators were given more weight than the veterinary staff in decision making about the animals, even when the health of the animals was in question. He also felt that his role as attending veterinarian, where he was accountable to the Ministry of Natural Resources, was "not well defined or understood by those in the zoo community."

Bernardino's reviews took a turn for the worse after the Ministry of Natural Resources released the report of its 2004 surprise investigation. Just two months later, in May 2004, Stellenbosch gave Bernardino, in writing, what was termed a "verbal" reprimand about his performance. "We need to have team players, and you need to work through these issues in a more professional, less 'attacking' manner," the COO's warning stated. Bernardino was also told that he lacked "team attitude, professionalism, and judgment."

This warning was closely followed by the announcement that Bernardino would share the "attending veterinarian" position with two others: his subordinate, veterinarian Wynona Singh, and Mammals curator Randi Walker. Though Walker was also a veterinarian, she was not licensed to practise as one in the province. In August 2004, Bernardino was told that he would no longer serve as an "attending veterinarian," and that Singh would be the sole "attending veterinarian." At about the same time, Bernardino received a written reprimand, in which he was accused of "steadily undermining animal curator Dr. Walker, poor communication skills, and intimidating other employees."

Dr. Wynona Singh

Dr. Wynona Singh, who reported to Dr. Bernardino, had been a full-time veterinarian at the zoo since 1999. She first joined the zoo in 1989 as a part-time veterinarian. Singh was the veterinarian on call when the giraffe died in 2001 and the sloth bear died in 2000, although she was not implicated in either death.

Bernardino and Singh often butted heads. In his 2003 evaluation of her, Bernardino recommended that she receive no salary increase. In January 2004, Bernardino told the zoo's human resources director that "if she doesn't improve and we keep her, I'm out of here."

Bernardino was reflecting on a survey of her performance he had conducted with the veterinary and animal food staff. Only 29 percent of them gave her favourable ratings, while 61 percent noted that she had big communication problems. The zookeepers specifically complained that Singh did not relate well to them and was not always open to their concerns. This led Bernardino to tell her that she "had to continue to improve some management skills, including communication." Despite negative reviews from her immediate staff and subordinates, Singh received high marks from the curators and associate curators, who indicated their full and unambiguous support of her.

The Curators and Zookeepers

Curators make recommendations such as what animals to acquire, whether animals should be bred, and whether animals should be lent to other zoos for either breeding or display purposes. Curators are also responsible for the designing and planning of animal exhibits, including coming up with ideas for new exhibits that might be of interest to the public. Though curators are responsible for the overall well-being of the animals, they are certainly aware of the marketing and public relations functions of animal exhibits.

The general curator at a zoo oversees the entire animal collection and animal management and is responsible for strategic collection planning. Zoos also have animal curators who manage a specific section of the animal collection. City Zoo had four area curators: curator of Fishes, curator of Reptiles, curator of Birds, and curator of Mammals. Some areas also had associate curators, such as the assistant curator of Large Mammals and the assistant curator of Small Mammals.

Senior zookeepers and zookeepers (also called *keepers*) report to the curators and work with individual animals, feeding them, handling them, keeping their cages clean, and looking after their welfare on a day-to-day basis. Keepers often work with the same animals for a number of years, so they can grow quite attached to their animals. Keepers can feel that they understand more about the welfare of their animals than the curators.

At City Zoo there was significant tension between the curators and the keepers. The keepers complained that curators did not listen to their concerns, and curators complained that the keepers often went around them to share concerns about animals with Dr. Bernardino. The curators felt that the keepers should raise all concerns with them, rather than with the veterinarian.

Randi Walker

Randi Walker was curator of Mammals at the zoo. The Mammals department's 22 full-time employees (including 14 zookeepers) took care of the zoo's apes, great cats, bears, elephants, and all hoofed animals. This was the largest animal department at the zoo, and was twice the size of the next largest department, the Birds department. All of the deaths investigated by the Ministry of Natural Resources had happened in Walker's unit.

The assistant curator of Large Mammals and the assistant curator of Small Mammals worked under Walker. The assistant curators were two of the most liked curators at the zoo. They had excellent animal-care backgrounds, were very aware of the zoo's communication problems, and knew how to work effectively with the other employees. They were also respected by the zookeepers and other curators.

Although curators do not usually have veterinary training, Walker had completed her veterinary studies. However, she was not licensed to practise veterinary medicine in the province. Her background may have led to her difficult relationship with Bernardino. Sometimes she tried to second guess him, and other times she attempted to overrule his decisions.

Walker was particularly uncomfortable with the relationship that Bernardino had with the Mammals zookeepers. She felt that his close relationship to them undermined her. "There are communication problems with mammal keepers and [Mammals curator Randi Walker]," one keeper said. "Some people can talk; other people, if they open their mouth, she jumps on them. That's the underlying thing why people talk to Dr. Tim."

Gorilla keeper Dale Petiniot noted that while she had no problem discussing issues with Walker, sometimes keepers needed to discuss issues with a neutral third party. "It's not always that we're justified, but sometimes you need to talk about things, and you don't have a next step, other than the vet," Ms. Petiniot said.

When zoo officials, responding to the Ministry of Natural Resources' surprise investigation, tried to investigate the death of George the giraffe, they quickly discovered that most employees in the Mammals department would simply not talk about the event, saying that they feared retribution by Walker. Even though zoo officials offered immunity from any disciplinary action in exchange for clarification about what had happened, no one came forth to take responsibility for putting the two animals together. "Nobody claimed responsibility," Andy Yang, curator of Reptiles and head of the internal investigation, said.

The report of the internal investigation concluded, "The apparent failure of the mammal keeper staff to inform, discuss, and plan this introduction with the veterinary staff prior to any action was unacceptable and compromised the welfare of the giraffe." Yang's committee made a pointed observation regarding the Mammals department: "There are significant communication problems in the Mammals department that need attention. These communications problems have negatively affected animal welfare."

Xavier Tolson, a human resource consultant hired by the zoo at the end of 2004 to analyze workplace problems in the Mammals department, reached many of the same conclusions. "I do not believe I have ever seen a department as dysfunctional as the Mammals department" at City Zoo. He noted that there was a lot of conflict between the head curator and the zookeepers. Tolson suggested that the keepers had a tendency to try to bully Walker into seeing their point of view about animal concerns.

Though most of her subordinates were quite critical of Walker's performance, managers at the most senior levels in the zoo were strongly supportive of her. She was always deferential to their views, and they felt she was right not to cave in to employee concerns.

The Biological Program Committee

In most zoos, the general curator oversees the work of the curators, zookeepers, and veterinarians and attempts to resolve any issue that might come up amongst the three groups. However, City Zoo had no general curator. When the zoo hired Robert Stellenbosch as COO in 2002, he was unable to serve as general curator, a role his predecessor had filled, because he had no previous animal experience.

Shortly after Stellenbosch was hired, William Lau, the executive director, announced that the newly created Biological Program Committee (BPC) would perform the duties normally handled by the general curator. The committee consisted of the curators of Mammals, Birds, Reptiles, and Fishes, an animal behaviour specialist, and members of the zoo's veterinary staff. Only the four curators and the animal behaviour specialist had voting rights on the committee, however. The curators took turns chairing the monthly committee, rotating the position every few months. No one else was allowed to chair the committee.

Not everyone was happy with the new management committee meetings. Bernardino, who had had a very good relationship with the former general curator, felt that his authority was diminished because of the BPC structure. Bernardino also objected that he was not able to rotate into the role of committee chair. He complained that the curators did not pay enough attention to animal-care issues. He also complained that the curators treated members of the veterinary staff who were on the committee like second-class citizens. After trying to get along with the new management structure for about six months, Bernardino took his concerns about the BPC to the executive director. Lau dismissed the veterinarian's concerns, suggesting that communication amongst committee members was good, except for some "troublemakers," which Bernardino took to be a reference to himself.

Beth Else, curator of Conservation and Research at the zoo, noticed a change in Bernardino's demeanor after the creation of the BPC. "It seemed in the past that Tim relied on gentle persuasion to bring people over to his way of thinking. In recent years, particularly in the past year, Tim has been more of a disruptive influence at the zoo," Else said. "I don't want to give the impression that I think Tim is malicious, because I don't," Else said. "Tim, in his own mind, thinks he is doing what is right."

Other employees must have agreed with Else that Bernardino was trying to do the right things at the zoo. On February 23, 2005, the zoo staff voted on nominees for "Outstanding Employee" of the year. Bernardino received the most votes.

Shockwaves at the Zoo
Head Veterinarian Fired

On February 28, 2005, City Zoo dismissed Bernardino from his $102 000-a-year position as head veterinarian. The executive director said that the dismissal had nothing to do with the 2004 Ministry of Natural Resources inspection, or with issues about animal care. "There is no question in my mind that he raised the level of animal care here at the zoo," Lau explained. "And while I do have a problem with the way Bernardino dealt with the Ministry of Natural Resources in the past, the termination was a result of our concerns over Dr. Bernardino's administrative and management skills that we had worked with him to address over the last several years."

Bernardino's dismissal created shockwaves both inside and outside of the zoo. The local newspaper contacted several well-known veterinarians throughout the country to find out what they could do about Bernardino. All of the contacted veterinarians spoke with great regard for the dismissed veterinarian. Reporters also uncovered previous performance reviews of Bernardino, which indicated that Bernardino had performed exceptionally in his work with the animals. Reporters concluded from their investigation that "The firing of Dr. Bernardino in late February was the culmination of a year-long struggle between him and zoo administrators beginning, it appears, with the veterinarian's frank comments last year during a routine animal-care inspection by the Ministry of Natural Resources. Those comments led to an admonition by the Ministry of Natural Resources that the zoo failed to heed warnings about its animal-care practices."

The intense press coverage prompted the city to start its own investigation of zoo administration. City Council felt an obligation to protect taxpayers' money, and recognized that public confidence in the zoo was at an all-time low because of all the negative publicity. Council appointed a 14-member Citizens' Task Force in mid-March. The mandate of the task force was to review zoo finances and operations, including animal care, and to issue a report within 100 days.

As the task force was getting underway, more scandal struck the zoo. The local newspaper reported that Executive Director William Lau had traded in the Jeep he had been given at zoo expense for a luxury Volvo, also paid for by the zoo. Similarly, COO Robert Stellenbosch had traded in his Dodge. The two Volvos were costing taxpayers $700 per month.

Members of the public were outraged by this news, coming just two weeks after Bernardino's firing. One long-standing zoo member emailed the local newspaper that he was disgusted with zoo administrators: "The firing of the whistleblowing vet is enough to make one wonder if the chimpanzees could not do a better job of running the place. If anything would make me stop supporting the zoo, it is the attitude of the zoo director and [chief operating officer]. To rent Volvos for themselves, to be so wasteful with the dollars of the taxpayers is tantamount to being part of the low-down reptile exhibit."

A Settlement and Resignations at the Top

After his dismissal, Bernardino approached the board of directors, requesting that they meet with him and give him back his job. The board was feeling under siege because of all the negative publicity. Bernardino's dismissal seemed to mobilize community sentiment toward the veterinarian, and against the zoo's senior management.

In an effort to quiet speculation by community members about zoo leadership, the board of directors made a settlement with Dr. Bernardino on May 1, 2005. The agreement reinstated him to his position of director of Animal Health and Nutrition of the zoo effective immediately, although he would serve in this role only as a "consultant," on an "as-needed basis." The agreement stated that Bernardino was not allowed to be on zoo grounds while performing his job, and could not enter the zoo as a private citizen for six months. The agreement prohibited him from discussing "his opinions as to the welfare of the animals at the Zoo, the circumstances of his termination or reinstatement of employment, his opinions regarding personnel at the Zoo, or any other matters pertaining to the Zoo" with anyone unless subpoenaed.

Bernardino's consulting position was to last for 18 months. He would be paid $105 000, plus health and retirement benefits during that time. Under the settlement, he would also receive $42 815 in back pay, benefits, and attorney's fees. The board agreed to remove all negative evaluations that were added to his file in 2004. Bernardino agreed that he would not file claims of wrongful discharge or breach of contract against the zoo.

Two weeks after the settlement with Bernardino, the zoo board announced that Executive Director William Lau would retire immediately, after 25 years at the zoo. The board also announced that COO Robert Stellenbosch would resign once a new management team was in place.

The Findings of the Citizens' Task Force

The Citizens' Task Force presented its findings to City Council at a public meeting held on July 8, 2005. The task force divided its presentation into three parts: a discussion of the employee survey they had commissioned; a presentation of what they had learned about the politics of zookeeping; and a discussion of other observations about how the zoo operated.

Employee Survey

The Citizen's Task Force asked Maynard & Associates, a Toronto-based employee relations consulting firm, to determine employee morale. Exhibit 3 summarizes the results of the survey, including separate results for the Mammals department. Maynard & Associates have collected baseline data as a result of their many employee surveys, and that data is also included.

On many dimensions, City Zoo employees were more critical than the average employee in Maynard's surveys.

Zoo employees complained about the lack of effective leadership, poor communication, and the scarcity of teamwork. Only half of the employees said there was open and honest communication at the zoo, and many employees noted that this lack of communication led to rumours and myths that spread throughout the zoo.

Employees said that they did not feel that they could talk freely to their supervisors about job-related problems, and they gave low marks to supervisors for resolving employee problems. Employees also gave low marks to

EXHIBIT 3	Employee Attitude Survey of City Zoo, and Some Comparisons				
		Percentage of Employees Who Agree or Strongly Agree With Statement			
Category	Question	City Zoo	Mammals Department	Other Zoos	Other Organizations
Pay	My compensation is satisfactory and fair compared with that of other employees who work here.	80	81	82	75
	My compensation is satisfactory and fair compared with what I would earn at similar companies.	81	81	82	74
Recognition	My supervisor recognizes and provides positive feedback for work well done.	63	57	68	72
Supervision	My supervisor treats me fairly.	43	43	63	63
	My supervisor helps me perform my work effectively.	41	39	70	70
Communication	I feel comfortable expressing my ideas to my supervisor and other leaders in the company.	41	35	71	73
	Leaders communicate pertinent information to employees.	51	48	55	74
Empowerment	I am free to make decisions that affect my work without consulting with my supervisor.	55	45	67	69
	My ideas are used when managers make decisions that affect the company.	49	41	65	70
Job Satisfaction	Overall, the company is a good place to work.	68	60	70	77
Management	The managers here are honest, fair, and ethical.	45	39	76	79
Participation	Managers seek employee input into the way work is done here.	53	45	68	77
Teamwork	Employees work together as a team here.	59	53	79	79
	Teamwork is encouraged here.	55	50	75	75
Training	I receive adequate job-related training to do my job.	85	83	81	76
	There are plenty of opportunities here to learn additional skills.	85	78	81	74
Work Demands	The workload is fair and reasonable.	75	74	73	79

supervisors for letting employees know what was expected of them. Supervisors were also criticized for not considering differing opinions, and a number of employees noted that they feared punishment if they expressed contrary opinions. Employees also expressed the expectation many employees placed on each other that "if you are not with us; you are against us," which created a lot of divisiveness across the zoo.

Despite the low morale uncovered by the survey, results indicated that employees loved working at the zoo, were fairly paid, and felt that they had been trained appropriately to do their jobs. However, they wanted to see an end to the political, communication, and leadership problems that dominated day-to-day work at the zoo.

The Politics of Zookeeping

Three members of the Citizens' Task Force were asked to discuss the events that had occurred at City Zoo with respected members of the zoo community throughout North America. Dr. Christopher Bondar, the associate veterinarian at the Central Canada zoo, suggested that it was not surprising that there were tensions between zoo management and the veterinarians. "The zoo business in general, because people's emotions tend to run high about animals and their welfare and because it is a small community, tends to have a lot of politics," said Dr. Bondar, who added that he has not encountered such problems at his own zoo. It can be hard to understand all of the politics at zoos because "so many businesses are about paperwork or industry or goods that don't spawn the type of passion people have for living animals."

Members of the task force spoke with Dr. Philip Robinson, a former director of veterinary services at the San Diego Zoo, and author of the book, *Life at the Zoo: Behind the Scenes with the Animal Doctors,* and asked him about the relationship between curators and veterinarians. "The perception that [veterinarians] should stick to sick animals and leave the other issues to the other people on staff—traditionally, this is sort of a turf battle that has more to do with management style than anything that benefits the animals," he told them.

Other experts supported Dr. Robinson's position. They told the task force that it is crucial for veterinarians to interact with keepers to understand the needs of individual animals. "If the curator says to the keeper, 'You only tell *me* what's happening,' then the veterinarian is sort of between a rock and a hard place to know when the animal is on the road to a problem, or already is there and has the problem," said Randolph Stuart, the executive director of the Canadian Association of Zoo Veterinarians. "That's why most vets will keep a good rapport with keepers."

Experts in the area of zoo administration suggested that many zoo administrators don't appreciate the passion that

veterinarians bring to their work. Veterinarians are chiefly concerned with animal welfare, while the zoo administration is also concerned with fundraising, providing an experience for zoo visitors, running successful gift shops and snack bars, and making sure parking lots are adequately designed for visitor load.

Dr. Mark Cornwall, the director of animal health and attending veterinarian at the Maple Leaf Zoo stressed the need for good communication among all zoo employees. The Maple Leaf Zoo was sued by an employee under whistle-blower protection legislation. The employee was demoted and harassed after she complained to government officials about unsafe conditions at the zoo. "Everybody kind of learned something from that," said Dr. Cornwall. "Animal welfare comes first," he said. "Zoo veterinarians are really the ones who are in charge of that. Veterinarians tend to champion those causes because that is what they are expected to do. You have different perspectives and opinions on those things, but the key is to sit down with all the folks." He added, "Zoos are complicated organisms and organizations. Open communication can improve the situation, however."

Other Issues Raised by the Task Force

During its presentation, the Citizens' Task Force identified a number of other issues of concern, and they briefly reviewed these for council.

Organizational Culture The task force found that lack of trust was a big issue among staff. They also found a "culture of fear" and noted that even though retaliation was often subtle, it was definitely there. In particular, keepers were afraid to admit actions or mistakes, even when immunity was offered. The task force expressed concern that many of the zookeepers were too focused on their own specific job duties and did not "see or support the 'big picture' of the zoo as both a wildlife conservation facility and a business."

Relationship Between Curators, Veterinarians, and Zookeepers Some curators were found to be good at managing animals but weak at managing people. The keepers complained that curators did not always respond in a timely manner to their proposals and suggestions for improving animal care. Veterinarians had some of the same complaints as the keepers—that curators did not always see the need to consult with veterinarians on animal management issues. The task force also noted that some keepers and curators held grudges that they might not be able to put behind them.

Curators complained that veterinarians undermined them through direct contact with the keepers. However, the task force noted that there was no defined communication path for keepers to raise concern with the veterinary staff. Moreover, experts throughout the zoo veterinary world stressed the importance of open communication between keepers and veterinarians so that vets can fulfill their obligations under the Fish and Wildlife Conservation Act.

The task force concluded that there was a lack of communication among keepers, veterinarians, and curators that led to questionable care standards for the animals. Because departments of the zoo did not work closely together, there was not a good system of checks and balances to maintain appropriate care.

The Biological Program Committee The Citizens' Task Force was particularly critical of the BPC, suggesting that many of the zoo's problems resulted from the creation of the BPC. The BPC created a mutual admiration society for the curators, and allowed the curators to overlook the concerns of keepers and the veterinarian staff. The board also found that there was no real accountability for decisions because of the committee structure.

Organizational Structure The task force raised a number of questions about the current structure of the zoo, noting that communication issues, lack of teamwork, and lack of coordination were all factors that resulted in animal deaths, and were likely related to the current structure. During their investigation, they had asked Lau whether all individuals directly involved with animal care had reported to him. He claimed they did, until a member of the task force, pointing to the organizational chart (see Exhibit 4), noted that the veterinarians and veterinarian technicians reported to the COO.

"It was largely the size of the group, and the number of people reporting to different people. We were trying to divide the zoo up so that neither Bob nor I [had too many]," Lau explained. "Money being what it is, we didn't want another high management position."

Employee Conduct The task force found that there was a "lack of consistency, uniformity, accountability, and decisiveness in the enforcement of standards of conduct across departments" and that the Employee Relations department was not good at enforcing standards of conduct. A number of employees complained that those who worked hard were often expected to compensate for employees who underperformed.

Employees are disciplined through a "five step" process. An employee can be terminated if he or she receives five written infractions within a 12-month period. The task force found this process so burdensome that employees were almost never terminated. In fact, Jennifer Fisher, employee relations director, told the task force that "no animal keepers or other non-managerial employees had been fired in the past 20 years."

A New Executive Director Takes Over

Emma Breslin began her position as the new executive director last week, eight months after the resignation of the previous executive director.

Breslin's previous position was as executive director for the past 10 years at Maritimes Zoo, a smaller zoo with 51 employees, a general curator, and two contract veterinarians. Breslin had been hired by Maritimes Zoo to reunite a divided staff. She is known as a consensus leader, and at Maritimes Zoo she increased communication, improved supervisory skills, and taught employees to value each other's contributions to the successful operation of the zoo. Breslin was also successful in raising awareness among the community about why financial support from the public was so important to the zoo.

Breslin faces a large public relations problem as she begins her new job. She knows that much of the zoo's revenue is dependent upon public support. The next tax levy vote is three months from now. The zoo also raises significant revenue through the "Friends of the Zoo" program, an annual subscription program where people donate money to the zoo. She needs to restore community trust. At the same time, she needs to grow zoo attendance levels, which have fallen in the past six months, and develop a strategic plan for the zoo.

Breslin also faces a very divided and demoralized staff. She has reviewed what was written in the press and familiarized herself with the Citizens' Task Force review. She knows she needs to bring some peace and stability to employee relations. Her most difficult task will be to unite the staff. She needs to build staff morale and gain their trust. She wonders how she will accomplish these goals over the next year. The outline of what she intends to do over the next six months to get things back on track is to be presented to the board in two weeks.

Sources: "Zoo Mulls Qualities Sought in Next Director," *toledoblade.com,* September 9, 2005, http://toledoblade.com (accessed January 17, 2006); S. Eder, "Zoo Task Force Sets 100-Day Target for Submitting Investigation Report," *toledoblade.com,* March 25, 2005, http://toledoblade.com (accessed January 17, 2006); S. Eder, "Experience With Animals Lacking for Operations Chief," *toledoblade.com,* March 13, 2005, http:// toledoblade.com (accessed January 17, 2006); S. Eder, "Reichard Held in High Esteem by Fellow Zoo Veterinarians," *toledoblade.com,* March 9, 2005, http://toledoblade.com (accessed January 17, 2006); M Greenwell, "Zoo Sees New Job As Way to Fix Problems," *toledoblade.com,* June 23, 2005, http://toledoblade.com (accessed January 17, 2006); J. Laidman, "Employee Relations Top Zoo Leaders' List," *toledoblade.com,* May 22, 2005, http://toledoblade.com (accessed January 17, 2006); J. Laidman, "Embattled Zoo Leaders Quit," *toledoblade.com,* May 5, 2005, http://toledoblade.com (accessed January 17, 2006); J. Laidman, "Clash of Philosophies, Loss of Animals Triggered Turmoil," *toledoblade.com,* March 13, 2005, http://toledoblade.com (accessed January 17, 2006); J. Laidman, "Fired Zoo Veterinarian's File Mostly Positive, With a Few Concerns," *toledoblade.com,* March 9, 2005, http://toledoblade.com (accessed January 17, 2006); J. Laidman, "Toledo Zoo Veterinarian Blames Firing on His Warnings to USDA," *toledoblade.com,* March 8, 2005,

EXHIBIT 4   Organizational Chart of City Zoo, January 2005

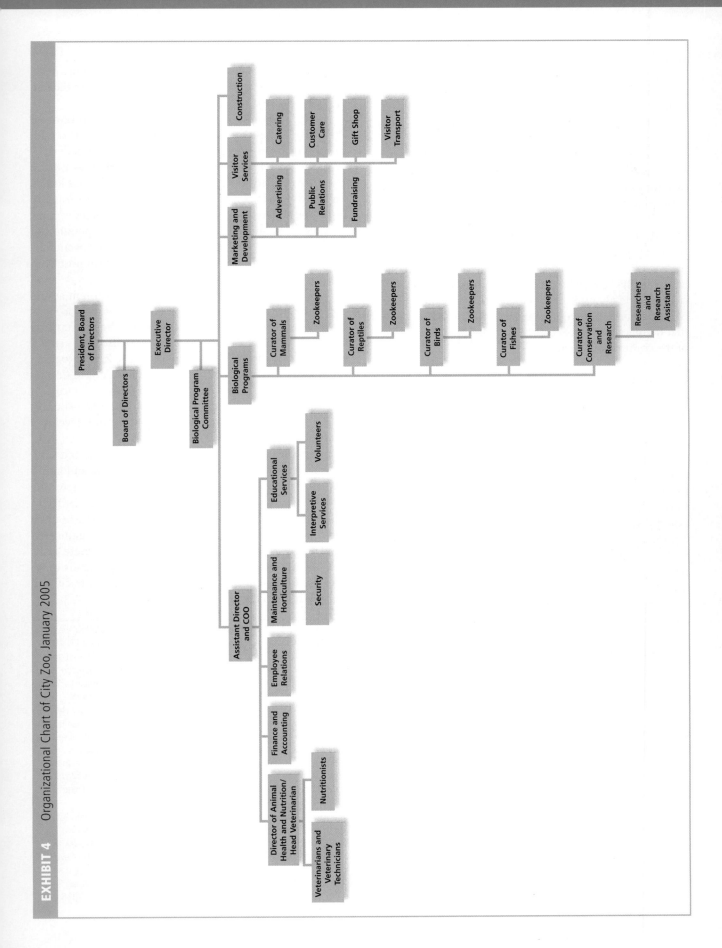

http://toledoblade.com (accessed January 17, 2006); J. Laidman, "Feds Probe 2 Animal Deaths at Toledo Zoo," *toledoblade.com,* February 24, 2004, http://toledoblade.com (accessed January 17, 2006); J. Laidman and T. Vezner, "Staff Offers Criticism, Praise in Zoo Survey," *toledoblade.com,* May 27, 2005, http://toledoblade.com (accessed January 17, 2006); J. Laidman and T. Vezner, "Vet's Deal Isn't First to Silence Ex-Official," *toledoblade.com,* May 2, 2005, http://toledoblade.com (accessed January 17, 2006); J. Laidman and T. Vezner, "Internal Battles Plunge Zoo into a Caldron of Discontent," *toledoblade.com,* March 20, 2005, http://toledoblade.com (accessed January 17, 2006); S. H. Staelin, "Zoo Board Tackles Challenges," *toledoblade.com,* April 16, 2005, http://toledoblade.com (accessed January 17, 2006); T. Vezner, "Zoo Names Chief Veterinarian, Ignoring Task Force's Proposal," *toledoblade.com,* December 17, 2005, http://toledoblade.com (accessed January 17, 2006); T. Vezner, "Consultant Hired to Oversee Zoo Administration," *toledoblade.com,* July 20, 2005, http://toledoblade.com (accessed January 17, 2006); T. Vezner, "Zoo's Ex-Vet on Hand for Report," *toledoblade.com,* July 9, 2005, http://toledoblade.com (accessed January 17, 2006); T. Vezner, "Zoo Task Force Report Demands Broad Changes," *toledoblade.com,* July 7, 2005, http://toledoblade.com (accessed January 17, 2006); T. Vezner and J. Laidman, "Flurry of Changes Leaves Workers Reeling," *toledoblade.com,* May 6, 2005, http://toledoblade.com (accessed January 17, 2006); T. Vezner, "Settlement Bars Zoo Vet From Speaking to Panel," *toledoblade.com,* May 1, 2005, http://toledoblade.com (accessed January 17, 2006); T. Vezner, "Zoo Task Force's Questions for Dennler Hit Time Limit," *toledoblade.com,* April 1, 2005, http://toledoblade.com (accessed January 17, 2006); T. Vezner, "Inquiry in 2004 Disclosed Problems," *toledoblade.com,* March 27, 2005, http://toledoblade.com (accessed January 17, 2006); Lucas County Commissioners Special Citizens Task Force for the Zoo, *Final Report,* July 8, 2005, http://www.co.lucas.oh.us/commissioners/Final_Report_Zoo_Task_Force.pdf (accessed January 17, 2006); www.toledozoo.org (accessed January 17, 2006); and www.doctortim.org (accessed January 17, 2006).

ENDNOTES

Chapter 1

1 Opening vignette based on Social Capital Partners, "Launching a Social Enterprise: Early Learnings from Inner City Renovation," ICR Learnings Report.

2 T. Belford, "Strategy for the New Economy," *Financial Post (National Post)*, March 14, 2005, p. FP9.

3 C. R. Farquhar and J. A. Longair, *Creating High-Performance Organizations With People*, Report R164–96 (Ottawa: The Conference Board of Canada, 1996).

4 Based on Social Capital Partners, "Launching a Social Enterprise: Early Learnings from Inner City Renovation," ICR Learnings Report.

5 T. A. Wright, R. Cropanzano, P. J. Denney, and G. L. Moline, "When a Happy Worker Is a Productive Worker: A Preliminary Examination of Three Models," *Canadian Journal of Behavioural Science* 34, no. 3 (July 2002), pp. 146–150.

6 Angus Reid Group, *Workplace 2000: Working Toward the Millennium*, Fall 1997.

7 B. Dumaine, "The New Non-Manager Managers," *Fortune*, February 22, 1993, pp. 80–84.

8 "Wanted: Teammates, Crew Members, and Cast Members: But No Employees," *Wall Street Journal*, April 30, 1996, p. A1.

9 M. Sashkin, "Participative Management Is an Ethical Imperative," *Organizational Dynamics*, Spring 1984, pp. 5–22.

10 See "What Self-Managing Teams Manage," *Training*, October 1995, p. 72.

11 S. Ross, "U.S. Managers Fail to Fit the Bill in New Workplace: Study," *Reuters News Agency*, November 19, 1999.

12 P. Verburg, "Prepare for Takeoff," *Canadian Business*, December 25, 2000, pp. 94–96+.

13 The Conference Board of Canada, *Employability Skills Profile*, 1998.

14 T. Belford, "Strategy for the New Economy," *Financial Post (National Post)*, March 14, 2005, p. FP9.

15 D. Nebenzahl, "People Skills Matter Most," *The Gazette* (Montreal), September 20, 2004, p. B.1.

16 See, for instance, R. R. Thomas Jr., "From Affirmative Action to Affirming Diversity," *Harvard Business Review*, March–April 1990, pp. 107–117; B. Mandrell and S. Kohler-Gray, "Management Development That Values Diversity," *Personnel*, March 1990, pp. 41–47; J. Dreyfuss, "Get Ready for the New Work Force," *Fortune*, April 23, 1990, pp. 165–181; and I. Wielawski, "Diversity Makes Both Dollars and Sense," *Los Angeles Times*, May 16, 1994, p. II-3.

17 Based on M. O'Brien, "Heritage Room for Native Cadets," *Leader-Post* (Regina), December 5, 2000, p. A3.

18 See, for instance, E. E. Kossek and S. A. Lobel, eds., *Managing Diversity* (Cambridge, MA: Blackwell, 1996); J. A. Segal, "Diversify for Dollars," *HR Magazine*, April 1997, pp. 134–140; and "Strength Through Diversity for Bottom-Line Success," *Working Women*, March 1999, pp. 67–77.

19 D. W. Organ, *Organizational Citizenship Behavior: The Good Soldier Syndrome* (Lexington, MA: Lexington Books, 1988), p. 4.

20 M. G. Ehrhart and S. E. Naumann, "Organizational Citizenship Behavior in Work Groups: A Group Norms Approach," *Journal of Applied Psychology* 89, no. 6 (December 1, 2004), pp. 960–974.

21 "Corporate Culture," *Canadian HR Reporter* 17, no. 21 (December 6, 2004), pp. 7–11.

22 See, for example, P. M. Podsakoff and S. B. MacKenzie, "Organizational Citizenship Behavior and Sales Unit Effectiveness," *Journal of Marketing Research*, August 1994, pp. 351–363; P. M. Podsakoff, M. Ahearne, and S. B. MacKenzie, "Organizational Citizenship Behavior and the Quantity and Quality of Work Group Performance," *Journal of Applied Psychology*, April 1997, pp. 262–270; L. A. Bettencourt, K. Gwinner, and M. L. Meuter, "A Comparison of Attitude, Personality, and Knowledge Predictors of Service-Oriented Organizational Citizenship Behaviors," *Journal of Applied Psychology* 86, 2001, pp. 29–41; and E. W. Morrison, "Organizational Citizenship Behavior as a Critical Link Between HRM Practices and Service Quality," *Human Resource Management* 35, 1996, pp. 493–512.

23 J. Pfeffer, and J. F. Veiga, "Putting People First for Organizational Success," *Academy of Management Executive* 13, no. 2 (May 1999), pp. 37–48. See also L. Bassi and D. McMurrer, "How's Your Return on People?" *Harvard Business Review* 82, no. 3 (March 2004), p. 18.

24 M. A. Huselid, "The Impact of Human Resource Management Practices on Turnover, Productivity, and Corporate Financial Performance," *Academy of Management Journal* 38, 1995, p. 647.

25 L. Blimes, K. Wetzker, and P. Xhonneux, "Value in Human Resources," *Financial Times*, February 1997, p. 10.

26 M. Kaeter, "The Age of the Specialized Generalist," *Training*, December 1993, pp. 48–53; and N. Templin, "Auto Plants, Hiring Again, Are Demanding Higher-Skilled Labor," *Wall Street Journal*, March 11, 1994, p. A1.

27 J. Lee, "Family Business Has Nerves of Steel," *Vancouver Sun*, December 22, 1997, pp. D1, D3.

28 J. H. Eggers, "The Dynamics of Asian Business, Culture," *Globe and Mail*, March 13, 1998, p. C5.

29 The following examples are derived from M. P. Mangaliso, "Building Competitive Advantage From *Ubuntu*, Management Practices From South Africa," *Academy of Management Executive* 15, no. 3 (2001), pp. 23–33.

30 Based on Social Capital Partners, "Launching a Social Enterprise: Early Learnings from Inner City Renovation," ICR Learnings Report.

31 M. Warner, "Organizational Behavior Revisited," *Human Relations*, October 1994, pp. 1151–1166.

32 See, for example, M. J. Driver, "Cognitive Psychology: An Interactionist View," R. H. Hall, "Organizational Behavior: A Sociological Perspective," and C. Hardy, "The Contribution of Political Science to Organizational Behavior," all in *Handbook of Organizational Behavior*, ed. J. W. Lorsch (Englewood Cliffs, NJ: Prentice Hall, 1987), pp. 62–108.

33 R. Weinberg and W. Nord, "Coping With 'It's All Common Sense,'" *Exchange* 7, no. 2 (1982), pp. 29–33; R. P. Vecchio, "Some Popular (But Misguided) Criticisms of the Organizational Sciences," *Organizational Behavior Teaching Review* 10, no. 1 (1986–87), pp. 28–34; and M. L. Lynn, "Organizational Behavior and Common Sense: Philosophical Implications for Teaching and Thinking" (paper presented at the 14th Annual Organizational Behavior Teaching Conference, Waltham, MA, May 1987).

34 R. E. Quinn, *Beyond Rational Management: Mastering the Paradoxes and Competing Demands of High Performance* (San Francisco: Jossey-Bass, 1991); R. E. Quinn, S. R. Faerman, M. P. Thompson, and M. R. McGrath, *Becoming a Master Manager: A Competency Framework* (New York: Wiley, 1990); K. Cameron and R. E. Quinn, *Diagnosing and Changing Organizational Culture: Based on the Competing Values Framework* (Reading, MA: Addison Wesley Longman, 1999).

35 R. E. Quinn, S. R. Faerman, M. P. Thompson, and M. R. McGrath, *Becoming a Master Manager: A Competency Framework* (New York: Wiley, 1990).

36 D. Maley, "Canada's Top Women CEOs," *Maclean's,* October 20, 1997, pp. 52 passim.

37 Written by Nancy Langton and Joy Begley, copyright 1999. (The events described are based on an actual situation, although the participants, as well as the centre, have been disguised.)

Chapter 2

1 Opening vignette based on P. Stock, "Mutual Back-Scratchers: Longstanding Liberal Policies Are Linked to the Feds' Civil Service Morale Crisis," *Report Newsmagazine,* June 25, 2001, pp. 17–18; A. Thompson, "Who Protects the Protectors?" *Toronto Star,* May 26, 2001, pp. K1, K4; "Canada's Human Rights Watchdog Considers Changes in Wake of Scathing Report," *Canadian Press Newswire,* May 18, 2001; and "Women Working at Canadian Human Rights Watchdog Face Discrimination: Report," *Canadian Press Newswire,* May 12, 2001.

2 A. Thompson, "Who Protects the Protectors?" *Toronto Star,* May 26, 2001, pp. K1, K4.

3 T. Cole, "Who Loves Ya?" *Report on Business Magazine,* April 1999, pp. 44–60.

4 P. Stock, "Mutual Back-Scratchers: Longstanding Liberal Policies Are Linked to the Feds' Civil Service Morale Crisis," *Report Newsmagazine,* June 25, 2001, pp. 17–18.

5 A. Thompson, "Who Protects the Protectors?" *Toronto Star,* May 26, 2001, pp. K1, K4.

6 H. H. Kelley, "Attribution in Social Interaction," in *Attribution: Perceiving the Causes of Behavior,* ed. E. Jones, D. Kanouse, H. Kelley, N. Nisbett, S. Valins, and B. Weiner (Morristown, NJ: General Learning Press, 1972).

7 See L. Ross, "The Intuitive Psychologist and His Shortcomings," in *Advances in Experimental Social Psychology,* 10, ed. L. Berkowitz (Orlando, FL: Academic Press, 1977), pp. 174–220; and A. G. Miller and T. Lawson, "The Effect of an Informational Option on the Fundamental Attribution Error," *Personality and Social Psychology Bulletin,* June 1989, pp. 194–204.

8 N. Epley and D. Dunning, "Feeling 'Holier Than Thou': Are Self-Serving Assessments Produced by Errors in Self- or Social Predictions?" *Journal of Personality and Social Psychology,* 79, no. 6 (2000), pp. 861–875.

9 *Focus on Diversity* based on A. Kerr, "Illness Can Be a Workplace Handicap," *Globe and Mail,* July 15, 2002.

10 S. E. Asch, "Forming Impressions of Personality," *Journal of Abnormal and Social Psychology,* July 1946, pp. 258–290.

11 J. S. Bruner and R. Tagiuri, "The Perception of People," in *Handbook of Social Psychology,* ed. E. Lindzey (Reading, MA: Addison Wesley, 1954), p. 641.

12 See, for example, C. M. Judd and B. Park, "Definition and Assessment of Accuracy in Social Stereotypes," *Psychological Review,* January 1993, pp. 109–128.

13 K. D. Elsbach, and R. M. Kramer, "Assessing Creativity in Hollywood Pitch Meetings: Evidence for a Dual-Process Model of Creativity Judgments," *Academy of Management Journal* 46, no. 3 (2003), pp. 283–301.

14 J. T. Jost and A. C. Kay, "Complementary Justice: Effects of 'Poor But Happy' and 'Poor But Honest' Stereotype Exemplars on System Justification and Implicit Activation of the Justice Motive," *Journal of Personality and Social Psychology* 85, no. 5 (2003), p. 823–837.

15 K. May, "Action Vowed on Unrest: Agency Head Refuses to Quit," *Calgary Herald,* May 19, 2001, p. A13.

16 See, for example, E. C. Webster, *Decision Making in the Employment Interview* (Montreal: McGill University, Industrial Relations Centre, 1964).

17 See, for example, R. D. Bretz Jr., G. T. Milkovich, and W. Read, "The Current State of Performance Appraisal Research and Practice: Concerns, Directions, and Implications," *Journal of Management,* June 1992, pp. 323–324; and P. M. Swiercz, M. L. Icenogle, N. B. Bryan, and R. W. Renn, "Do Perceptions of Performance Appraisal Fairness Predict Employee Attitudes and Performance?" in *Proceedings of the Academy of Management,* ed. D. P. Moore (Atlanta: Academy of Management, 1993), pp. 304–308.

18 J. Schaubroeck and S. S. K. Lam, "How Similarity to Peers and Supervisor Influences Organizational Advancement in Different Cultures," *Academy of Management Journal* 45, no. 6 (2002), pp. 1120–1136.

19 M. Owens, "People Who Exercise Are More Highly Regarded: Study," *National Post,* February 10, 2001, p. A2.

20 See, for example, D. Eden, *Pygmalion in Management* (Lexington, MA: Lexington Books, 1990); D. Eden, "Leadership and Expectations: Pygmalion Effects and Other Self-Fulfilling Prophecies," *Leadership Quarterly,* Winter 1992, pp. 271–305; D. B. McNatt, "Ancient Pygmalion Joins Contemporary Management: A Meta-Analysis of the Result," *Journal of Applied Psychology,* April 2000, pp. 314–322; and O. B. Davidson and D. Eden, "Remedial Self-Fulfilling Prophecy: Two Field Experiments to Prevent Golem Effects Among Disadvantaged Women," *Journal of Applied Psychology,* June 2000, pp. 386–398.

21 D. Eden and A. B. Shani, "Pygmalion Goes to Boot Camp: Expectancy, Leadership, and Trainee Performance," *Journal of Applied Psychology,* April 1982, pp. 194–199.

22 G. W. Allport, *Personality: A Psychological Interpretation* (New York: Holt, Rinehart and Winston, 1937), p. 48.

23 Reported in R. L. Hotz, "Genetics, Not Parenting, Key to Temperament, Studies Say," *Los Angeles Times,* February 20, 1994, p. A1.

24 See D. T. Lykken, T. J. Bouchard Jr., M. McGue, and A. Tellegen, "Heritability of Interests: A Twin Study," *Journal of Applied Psychology,* August 1993, pp. 649–661; R. D. Arvey and T. J. Bouchard Jr., "Genetics, Twins, and Organizational Behavior," in *Research in Organizational Behavior,* vol. 16, ed. B. M. Staw and L. L. Cummings (Greenwich, CT: JAI Press, 1994), pp. 65–66; D. Lykken and A. Tellegen, "Happiness Is a Stochastic

Phenomenon," *Psychological Science,* May 1996, pp. 186–189; and W. Wright, *Born That Way: Genes, Behavior, Personality* (New York: Knopf, 1998).

25 R. C. Carson, "Personality," in *Annual Review of Psychology,* 40, ed. M. R. Rosenzweig and L. W. Porter (Palo Alto, CA: Annual Reviews, 1989), pp. 228–229.

26 L. Sechrest, "Personality," in *Annual Review of Psychology,* 27, ed. M. R. Rosenzweig and L. W. Porter (Palo Alto, CA: Annual Reviews, 1976), p. 10.

27 W. Mischel, "The Interaction of Person and Situation," in *Personality at the Crossroads: Current Issues in Interactional Psychology,* ed. D. Magnusson and N. S. Endler (Hillsdale, NJ: Erlbaum, 1977), pp. 166–207.

28 See A. H. Buss, "Personality as Traits," *American Psychologist,* November 1989, pp. 1378–1388; and D. G. Winter, O. P. John, A. J. Stewart, E. C. Klohnen, and L. E. Duncan, "Traits and Motives: Toward an Integration of Two Traditions in Personality Research," *Psychological Review,* April 1998, pp. 230–250.

29 R. B. Catell, "Personality Pinned Down," *Psychology Today,* July 1973, pp. 40–46.

30 See R. R. McCrae and P. T. Costa Jr., "Reinterpreting the Myers-Briggs Type Indicator From the Perspective of the Five Factor Model of Personality," *Journal of Personality,* March 1989, pp. 17–40; and C. Fitzgerald and L. K. Kirby, eds., *Developing Leaders: Research and Applications in Psychological Type and Leadership Development* (Palo Alto, CA: Davies-Black Publishing, 1997).

31 G. N. Landrum, *Profiles of Genius* (New York: Prometheus, 1993).

32 See, for example, J. M. Digman, "Personality Structure: Emergence of the Five-Factor Model," in *Annual Review of Psychology,* 41, ed. M. R. Rosenzweig and L. W. Porter (Palo Alto, CA: Annual Reviews, 1990), pp. 417–440; R. R. McCrae and O. P. John, "An Introduction to the Five-Factor Model and Its Applications," *Journal of Personality,* June 1992, pp. 175–215; L. R. Goldberg, "The Structure of Phenotypic Personality Traits," *American Psychologist,* January 1993, pp. 26–34; P. H. Raymark, M. J. Schmit, and R. M. Guion, "Identifying Potentially Useful Personality Constructs for Employee Selection," *Personnel Psychology,* Autumn 1997, pp. 723–736; and O. Behling, "Employee Selection: Will Intelligence and Conscientiousness Do the Job?" *Academy of Management Executive* 12, 1998, pp. 77–86.

33 See, for instance, M. R. Barrick and M. K. Mount, "The Big Five Personality Dimensions and Job Performance: A Meta-Analysis," *Personnel Psychology* 44, 1991, pp. 1–26; R. P. Tett, D. N. Jackson, and M. Rothstein, "Personality Measures as Predictors of Job Performance: A Meta-Analytic Review," *Personnel Psychology,* Winter 1991, pp. 703–742; T. A. Judge, J. J. Martocchio, and C. J. Thoresen, "Five-Factor Model of Personality and Employee Absence," *Journal of Applied Psychology,* October 1997, pp. 745–755; O. Behling, "Employee Selection: Will Intelligence and Conscientiousness Do the Job?" *Academy of Management Executive,* February 1998, pp. 77–86; and F. S. Switzer III and P. L. Roth, "A Meta-Analytic Review of Predictors of Job Performance for Salespeople," *Journal of Applied Psychology,* August 1998, pp. 586–597.

34 See, for instance, S. L. Kichuk and W. H. Wiesner, "Work Teams: Selecting Members for Optimal Performance," *Canadian Psychology* 39, no. 1–2 (February–May 1998), pp. 23–32; M. R. Barrick and M. K. Mount, "The Big Five Personality Dimensions and Job Performance: A Meta-Analysis," *Personnel Psychology* 44, 1991, pp. 1–26; D. Ones, C. Viswesvaran, and F. Schmidt, "Meta-Analysis of Integrity Test Validities: Findings and Implications for Personnel Selection and Theories of Job Performance [Monograph]," *Journal of Applied Psychology* 47, no. 1 (1993), pp. 147–156; and R. T. Hogan, J. Hogan, and B. W. Roberts, "Personality Measurement and Employment Decisions: Questions and Answers, *American Psychologist* 51, no. 5 (1996), pp. 469–477.

35 P. Thoms, "The Relationship Between Self-Efficacy for Participating in Self-Managed Work Groups and the Big Five Personality Dimensions," *Journal of Applied Psychology* 82, 1996, pp. 472–484; R. A. Guzzo, P. R. Yost, R. J. Campbell, and G. P. Shea, "Potency in Groups: Articulating a Construct," *British Journal of Social Psychology* 32, 1993, pp. 87–106; and G. A. Neuman and J. Wright, "Team Effectiveness: Beyond Skills and Cognitive Ability," *Journal of Applied Psychology* 84, 1999, pp. 376–389. See also S. L. Kichuk and W. H. Wiesner, "Work Teams: Selecting Members for Optimal Performance," *Canadian Psychology* 39, no. 1–2 (February–May 1998), pp. 23–32, who summarize a wide body of literature on this topic. You might also be interested in B. Barry and G. L. Stewart, "Compositions, Process and Performance in Self-Managed Groups: The Role of Personality," *Journal of Applied Psychology* 82, 1997, pp. 62–78, for an opposing look at the conscientiousness-performance link.

36 T. A. Judge and R. Ilies, "Relationship of Personality to Performance Motivation: A Meta-Analytic Review," *Journal of Applied Psychology* 87, no. 4 (2002), pp. 797–807.

37 D. W. Organ, "Personality and Organizational Citizenship Behavior," *Journal of Management,* Summer 1994, pp. 465–478; D. W. Organ and K. Ryan, "A Meta-Analytic Review of Attitudinal and Dispositional Predictors of Organizational Citizenship Behavior," *Personnel Psychology,* Winter 1995, pp. 775–802; and M. A. Konovsky and D. W. Organ, "Dispositional and Contextual Determinants of Organizational Citizenship Behavior," *Journal of Organizational Behavior,* May 1996, pp. 253–266.

38 J. B. Rotter, "Generalized Expectancies for Internal Versus External Control of Reinforcement," *Psychological Monographs* 80, no. 609 (1966).

39 P. E. Spector, C. L. Cooper, J. I. Sanchez, et al., "Locus of Control and Well-Being at Work: How Generalizable Are Western Findings?" *Academy of Management Journal* 45, no. 2 (2002), pp. 453–456, present the results of studies done in five continents.

40 P. E. Spector, "Behavior in Organizations as a Function of Employee's Locus of Control," *Psychological Bulletin,* May 1982, p. 493; D. R. Norris and R. E. Niebuhr, "Attributional Influences on the Job Performance-Job Satisfaction Relationship," *Academy of Management Journal,* June 1984, pp. 424–431; and P. C. Nystrom, "Managers' Salaries and Their Beliefs About Reinforcement Control," *Journal of Social Psychology,* August 1983, pp. 291–292.

41 J. B. Rotter, "Generalized Expectancies for Internal Versus External Control of Reinforcement," *Psychological Monographs* 80, no. 609 (1966).

42 R. G. Vleeming, "Machiavellianism: A Preliminary Review," *Psychological Reports,* February 1979, pp. 295–310.

43 R. Christie and F. L. Geis, *Studies in Machiavellianism* (New York: Academic Press, 1970), p. 312; and N. V. Ramanaiah, A. Byravan, and F. R. J. Detwiler, "Revised Neo Personality Inventory Profiles of Machiavellian and Non-Machiavellian People," *Psychological Reports,* October 1994, pp. 937–938.

44 R. Christie and F. L. Geis, *Studies in Machiavellianism* (New York: Academic Press, 1970).

45 Based on J. Brockner, *Self-Esteem at Work* (Lexington, MA: Lexington Books, 1988), Chapters 1–4; and N. Branden, *Self-Esteem at Work* (San Francisco: Jossey-Bass, 1998).

46 See M. Snyder, *Public Appearances/Private Realities: The Psychology of Self-Monitoring* (New York: W. H. Freeman, 1987).

47 See M. Snyder, *Public Appearances/Private Realities: The Psychology of Self-Monitoring* (New York: W. H. Freeman, 1987).

48 M. Kilduff and D. V. Day, "Do Chameleons Get Ahead? The Effects of Self-Monitoring on Managerial Careers," *Academy of Management Journal*, August 1994, pp. 1047–1060.

49 D. V. Day, D. J. Schleicher, A. L. Unckless, and N. J. Hiller, "Self-Monitoring Personality at Work: A Meta-Analytic Investigation of Construct Validity," *Journal of Applied Psychology*, April 2002, pp. 390–401.

50 R. N. Taylor and M. D. Dunnette, "Influence of Dogmatism, Risk-Taking Propensity, and Intelligence on Decision-Making Strategies for a Sample of Industrial Managers," *Journal of Applied Psychology*, August 1974, pp. 420–423.

51 I. L. Janis and L. Mann, *Decision Making: A Psychological Analysis of Conflict, Choice, and Commitment* (New York: Free Press, 1977).

52 N. Kogan and M. A. Wallach, "Group Risk Taking as a Function of Members' Anxiety and Defensiveness," *Journal of Personality*, March 1967, pp. 50–63.

53 M. Friedman and R. H. Rosenman, *Type A Behavior and Your Heart* (New York: Knopf, 1974), p. 84.

54 M. Friedman and R. H. Rosenman, *Type A Behavior and Your Heart* (New York: Knopf, 1974), pp. 84–85.

55 K. A. Matthews, "Assessment of Type A Behavior, Anger, and Hostility in Epidemiological Studies of Cardiovascular Disease," in *Measuring Psychological Variables in Epidemiologic Studies of Cardiovascular Disease*, NIH Publication No. 85–2270, ed. A. M. Ostfield and E. D. Eaker (Washington, DC: US Department of Health and Human Services, 1985).

56 M. Friedman and R. H. Rosenman, *Type A Behavior and Your Heart* (New York: Knopf, 1974), p. 86.

57 D. C. Ganster, W. E. Sime, and B. T. Mayes, "Type A Behavior in the Work Setting: A Review and Some New Data," in *In Search of Coronary-Prone Behavior: Beyond Type A*, ed. A. W. Siegman and T. M. Dembroski (Hillsdale, NJ: Erlbaum, 1989), pp. 117–118; and B. K. Houston, "Cardiovascular and Neuroendocrine Reactivity, Global Type A, and Components of Type A," in *Type A Behavior Pattern: Research, Theory, and Intervention*, ed. B. K. Houston and C. R. Snyder (New York: Wiley, 1988), pp. 212–253.

58 A. Rozanski, J. A. Blumenthal, and J. Kaplan, "Impact of Psychological Factors on the Pathogenesis of Cardiovascular Disease and Implications for Therapy," *Circulation* 99, 1999, pp. 2192–2217; and J. Schaubroeck, D. C. Ganster, and B. E. Kemmerer, "Job Complexity, 'Type A' Behavior, and Cardiovascular Disorder," *Academy of Management Journal* 37, April 1994, pp. 426–439.

59 J. M. Crant, "Proactive Behavior in Organizations," *Journal of Management* 26, no. 3 (2000), p. 436.

60 S. E. Seibert, M. L. Kraimer, and J. M. Crant, "What Do Proactive People Do? A Longitudinal Model Linking Proactive Personality and Career Success," *Personnel Psychology*, Winter 2001, p. 850.

61 T. S. Bateman and J. M. Crant, "The Proactive Component of Organizational Behavior: A Measure and Correlates," *Journal of Organizational Behavior*, March 1993, pp. 103–118; A. L. Frohman, "Igniting Organizational Change From Below: The Power of Personal Initiative," *Organizational Dynamics*, Winter 1997, pp. 39–53; and J. M. Crant and T. S. Bateman, "Charismatic Leadership Viewed From Above: The Impact of Proactive Personality," *Journal of Organizational Behavior*, February 2000, pp. 63–75.

62 J. M. Crant, "Proactive Behavior in Organizations," *Journal of Management* 26, no. 3 (2000), p. 436.

63 See, for instance, R. C. Becherer and J. G. Maurer, "The Proactive Personality Disposition and Entrepreneurial Behavior Among Small Company Presidents," *Journal of Small Business Management*, January 1999, pp. 28–36.

64 S. E. Seibert, J. M. Crant, and M. L. Kraimer, "Proactive Personality and Career Success," *Journal of Applied Psychology*, June 1999, pp. 416–427; and S. E. Seibert, M. L. Kraimer, and J. M. Crant, "What Do Proactive People Do? A Longitudinal Model Linking Proactive Personality and Career Success," *Personnel Psychology*, Winter 2001, p. 850.

65 F. Kluckhohn and F. L. Strodtbeck, *Variations in Value Orientations* (Evanston, IL: Row Peterson, 1961).

66 J. Pickard, "Misuse of Tests Leads to Unfair Recruitment," *People Management* 2, no. 25 (December 1996), p. 7.

67 J. Pickard, "Misuse of Tests Leads to Unfair Recruitment," *People Management* 2, no. 25 (December 1996), p. 7.

68 J. A. LePine, J. A. Colquitt, and A. Erez, "Adaptability to Changing Task Contexts: Effects of General Cognitive Ability, Conscientiousness, and Openness to Experience," *Personnel Psychology* 53, 2000, pp. 563–593.

69 M. Barrick and M. K. Mount, "The Big Five Personality Factors and Job Performance: A Meta-Analysis," *Personnel Psychology* 44, 1991, pp. 1–26; M. Kilduff and D. V. Day, "Do Chameleons Get Ahead: The Effects of Self-Monitoring on Managerial Careers," *Academy of Management Journal* 37, 1994, pp. 1047–1060; A. Mehra, M. Kilduff, and D. J. Brass, "The Social Networks of High and Low Self-Monitors: Implications for Workplace Performance," *Administrative Science Quarterly* 46, 2001, pp. 121–146; and C. A. O'Reilly and J. A. Chatman, "Working Smarter and Harder: A Longitudinal Study of Managerial Success," *Administrative Science Quarterly* 39, 1994, pp. 603–627.

70 F. J. Flynn, J. A. Chatman, and S. E. Spataro, "Getting to Know You: The Influence of Personality on Impressions and Performance of Demographically Different People in Organizations," *Administrative Science Quarterly* 46, 2001, pp. 414–442.

71 O. P. John, "The 'Big Five' Factor Taxonomy: Dimensions of Personality in the Natural Language and in Questionnaires," in *Handbook of Personality Theory and Practice*, ed. L. A. Pervin (New York: Guilford Press, 1990), pp. 66–96.

72 M. Snyder, *Public Appearances, Private Realities* (New York: W. H. Freeman, 1987).

73 M. Snyder and J. Copeland, "Self-Monitoring Processes in Organizational Settings," in *Impression Management in the Organization*, ed. R. A. Giacolone and P. Rosenfeld (Hillsdale, NJ: Erlbaum, 1989), p. 16.

74 F. J. Flynn, J. A. Chatman, and S. E. Spataro, "Getting to Know You: The Influence of Personality on Impressions and Performance of Demographically Different People in Organizations," *Administrative Science Quarterly* 46, 2001, pp. 414–442.

75 K. Howlett, "Accidental Chairman," *Globe and Mail*, August 30, 2002, pp. 46–54.

76 S. D. Gosling, S.-J. Ko, T. Mannarelli, and M. E. Morris, "A Room with a Cue: Personality Judgements Based on Offices and Bedrooms," *Journal of Personality and Social Psychology* 82, no. 3 (March 2002), pp. 379–398.

77 See N. H. Frijda, "Moods, Emotion Episodes and Emotions," in *Handbook of Emotions*, ed. M. Lewis and J. M. Haviland (New York: Guildford Press, 1993), pp. 381–403.

78 H. M. Weiss and R. Cropanzano, "Affective Events Theory," in *Research in Organizational Behavior,* vol. 18, ed. B. M. Staw and L. L. Cummings (Greenwich, CT: JAI Press, 1996), pp. 17–19.

79 N. H. Frijda, "Moods, Emotion Episodes and Emotions," in *Handbook of Emotions,* ed. M. Lewis and J. M. Haviland (New York: Guildford Press, 1993), p. 381.

80 H. M. Weiss and R. Cropanzano, "Affective Events Theory," in *Research in Organizational Behavior,* vol. 18, ed. B. M. Staw and L. L. Cummings (Greenwich, CT: JAI Press, 1996), pp. 20–22.

81 A. Hochschild, *The Managed Heart: The Commercialization of Human Feeling* (Berkeley: University of California Press, 1983); J. Van Maanen and G. Kunda, "Real Feelings: Emotional Expression and Organizational Culture," in *Research in Organizational Behavior,* vol. 11, ed. L. L. Cummings and B. M. Staw (Greenwich, CT: JAI Press, 1989), pp. 43–103; and B. A. Turner, "Sociological Aspects of Organizational Symbolism," *Organization Studies* 7, 1986, pp. 101–115.

82 A. Hochschild, *The Managed Heart: The Commercialization of Human Feeling* (Berkeley, CA: University of California Press, 1983).

83 A. Hochschild, *The Managed Heart: The Commercialization of Human Feeling* (Berkeley: University of California Press, 1983); R. I. Sutton and A. Rafaeli, "Untangling the Relationship Between Displayed Emotions and Organizational Sales: The Case of Convenience Stores," *Academy of Management Journal* 31, 1988, pp. 461–487; A. Rafaeli, "When Cashiers Meet Customers: An Analysis of the Role of Supermarket Cashiers," *Academy of Management Journal* 32, 1989, pp. 245–273; A. Rafaeli and R. I. Sutton, "The Expression of Emotion in Organizational Life," in *Research in Organizational Behavior,* vol. 11, ed. L. L. Cummings and B. M. Staw (Greenwich, CT: JAI Press, 1989), pp. 1–42; A. Rafaeli and R. I. Sutton, "Busy Stores and Demanding Customers: How Do They Affect the Display of Positive Emotion?" *Academy of Management Journal* 33, 1990, pp. 623–637; A. Rafaeli and R. I. Sutton, "Emotional Contrast Strategies as Means of Social Influence: Lessons From Criminal Interrogators and Bill Collectors," *Academy of Management Journal* 34, 1991, pp. 749–775; and R. I. Sutton, "Maintaining Norms About Expressed Emotions: The Case of Bill Collectors," *Administrative Science Quarterly* 36, 1991, pp. 245–268.

84 A. A. Grandey, "When 'The Show Must Go On': Surface Acting and Deep Acting as Determinants of Emotional Exhaustion and Peer-Rated Service Delivery," *Academy of Management Journal* 46, no. 1 (2003), pp. 86–96.

85 H. Willmott, "Strength Is Ignorance; Slavery Is Freedom: Managing Culture in Modern Organizations," *Journal of Management Studies* 30, 1993, pp. 515–552; and S. Fineman, "Emotion and Organizing," in *Handbook of Organizational Studies,* ed. S. Clegg (London: Sage, 1996), pp. 543–564.

86 A. Hochschild, *The Managed Heart: The Commercialization of Human Feeling* (Berkeley: University of California Press, 1983).

87 J. Van Maanen and G. Kunda, "Real Feelings: Emotional Expression and Organizational Culture," in *Research in Organizational Behavior,* vol. 11, ed. L. L. Cummings and B. M. Staw (Greenwich, CT: JAI Press, 1989), pp. 43–103.

88 V. Waldron and K. Krone, "The Experience and Expression of Emotion in the Workplace: A Study of a Corrections Organization," *Management Communication Quarterly* 4, 1991, pp. 287–309.

89 C. Bains, "Safeway Clerks' Forced Smiles Seen as Flirtation," *Vancouver Sun,* September 3, 1998, pp. A1, A2.

90 K. Deaux, "Sex Differences," in *Annual Review of Psychology,* 26, ed. M. R. Rosenzweig and L. W. Porter (Palo Alto, CA: Annual Reviews, 1985), pp. 48–82; M. LaFrance and M. Banaji, "Toward a Reconsideration of the Gender-Emotion Relationship," in *Review of Personality and Social Psychology,* 14, ed. M. Clark (Newbury Park, CA: Sage, 1992), pp. 178–197; and A. M. Kring and A. H. Gordon, "Sex Differences in Emotion: Expression, Experience, and Physiology," *Journal of Personality and Social Psychology,* March 1998, pp. 686–703.

91 L. R. Brody and J. A. Hall, "Gender and Emotion," in *Handbook of Emotions,* ed. M. Lewis and J. M. Haviland (New York: Guilford Press, 1993), pp. 447–460; and M. Grossman and W. Wood, "Sex Differences in Intensity of Emotional Experience: A Social Role Interpretation," *Journal of Personality and Social Psychology,* November 1992, pp. 1010–1022.

92 J. A. Hall, *Nonverbal Sex Differences: Communication Accuracy and Expressive Style* (Baltimore: Johns Hopkins Press, 1984).

93 N. James, "Emotional Labour: Skill and Work in the Social Regulations of Feelings," *Sociological Review,* February 1989, pp. 15–42; A. Hochschild, *The Second Shift* (New York: Viking, 1989); and F. M. Deutsch, "Status, Sex, and Smiling: The Effect of Role on Smiling in Men and Women," *Personality and Social Psychology Bulletin,* September 1990, pp. 531–540.

94 A. Rafaeli, "When Clerks Meet Customers: A Test of Variables Related to Emotional Expression on the Job," *Journal of Applied Psychology,* June 1989, pp. 385–393; and M. LaFrance and M. Banaji, "Toward a Reconsideration of the Gender-Emotion Relationship," in *Emotion and Social Behavior: Review of Personality and Social Psychology,* 14, ed. M. S. Clark (Newbury Park, CA: Sage, 1992), pp. 178, 201.

95 L. W. Hoffman, "Early Childhood Experiences and Women's Achievement Motives," *Journal of Social Issues* 28, no. 2 (1972), pp. 129–155.

96 N. M. Ashkanasy and C. S. Daus, "Emotion in the Workplace: The New Challenge for Managers," *Academy of Management Executive* 16, no. 1 (2002), pp. 76–86.

97 This section is based on Daniel Goleman, *Emotional Intelligence* (New York: Bantam, 1995); J. D. Mayer and G. Geher, "Emotional Intelligence and the Identification of Emotion," *Intelligence,* March–April 1996, pp. 89–113; J. Stuller, "EQ: Edging Toward Respectability," *Training,* June 1997, pp. 43–48; R. K. Cooper, "Applying Emotional Intelligence in the Workplace," *Training & Development,* December 1997, pp. 31–38; "HR Pulse: Emotional Intelligence," *HR Magazine,* January 1998, p. 19; M. Davies, L. Stankov, and R. D. Roberts, "Emotional Intelligence: In Search of an Elusive Construct," *Journal of Personality and Social Psychology,* October 1998, pp. 989–1015; and D. Goleman, *Working With Emotional Intelligence* (New York: Bantam, 1999).

98 D. Goleman, *Emotional Intelligence* (New York: Bantam, 1995).

99 R. Bar-On, "Emotional and Social Intelligence: Insights From the Emotional Quotient Inventory," in *Handbook of Emotional Intelligence,* ed. R. Bar-On and J. Parker (San Francisco: Jossey-Bass, 2000).

100 J. Rowlands, "Soft Skills Give Hard Edge," *Globe and Mail,* June 9, 2004, p. C8.

101 D. Goleman, *Working With Emotional Intelligence* (New York: Bantam, 1999).

102 R. McQueen, "New CEO Brings Fresh Style to BMO: Tony Comper Slowly Stepping out of the Shadows," *Financial Post (National Post),* November 10, 1999, p. C3.

103 S. L. Robinson and R. J. Bennett, "A Typology of Deviant Workplace Behaviors: A Multidimensional Scaling Study," *Academy of Management Journal,* April 1995, p. 556.

104 S. L. Robinson and R. J. Bennett, "A Typology of Deviant Workplace Behaviors: A Multidimensional Scaling Study," *Academy of Management Journal,* April 1995, pp. 555–572.

105 Based on A. G. Bedeian, "Workplace Envy," *Organizational Dynamics,* Spring 1995, p. 50.

106 A. G. Bedeian, "Workplace Envy," *Organizational Dynamics,* Spring 1995, p. 54.

107 *Focus on Research* based on C. A. Bartela and R. Saavedra, "The Collective Construction of Work Group Moods," *Administrative Science Quarterly* 45, no. 2 (June 2000), pp. 197–231.

108 H. M. Weiss and R. Cropanzano, "Affective Events Theory: A Theoretical Discussion of the Structure, Causes and Consequences of Affective Experiences at Work," in *Research in Organizational Behavior,* vol. 18, ed. B. M. Staw and L. L. Cummings (Greenwich, CT: JAI Press, 1996), pp. 17–19.

109 J. Basch and C. D. Fisher, "Affective Events-Emotions Matrix: A Classification of Work Events and Associated Emotions," in *Emotions in the Workplace,* ed. N. M. Ashkanasy, C. E. J. Hartel, and W. J. Zerbe (Westport, CN: Quorum Books, 2000), pp. 36–48.

110 See, for example, H. M. Weiss and R. Cropanzano, "Affective Events Theory: A Theoretical Discussion of the Structure, Causes and Consequences of Affective Experiences at Work," in *Research in Organizational Behavior,* vol. 18, ed. B. M. Staw and L. L. Cummings (Greenwich, CT: JAI Press, 1996), pp. 17–19; and C. D. Fisher, "Antecedents and Consequences of Real-Time Affective Reactions at Work," *Motivation and Emotion,* March 2002, pp. 3–30.

111 Based on H. M. Weiss and R. Cropanzano, "Affective Events Theory: A Theoretical Discussion of the Structure, Causes and Consequences of Affective Experiences at Work," in *Research in Organizational Behavior,* vol. 18, ed. B. M. Staw and L. L. Cummings (Greenwich, CT: JAI Press, 1996), p. 42.

112 N. M. Ashkanasy, C. E. J. Hartel, and C. S. Daus, "Diversity and Emotion: The New Frontiers in Organizational Behavior Research," *Journal of Management* 28, no. 3 (2002), p. 324.

113 H. M. Weiss and R. Cropanzano, "Affective Events Theory," in *Research in Organizational Behavior,* vol. 18, ed. B. M. Staw and L. L. Cummings (Greenwich, CT: JAI Press, 1996), p. 55.

114 Some of the points in this argument are from R. J. House, S. A. Shane, and D. M. Herold, "Rumors of the Death of Dispositional Research Are Vastly Exaggerated," *Academy of Management Review,* January 1996, pp. 203–224.

115 Based on A. Davis-Blake and J. Pfeffer, "Just a Mirage: The Search for Dispositional Effects in Organizational Research," *Academy of Management Review,* July 1989, pp. 385–400.

116 Based on V. P. Richmond, J. C. McCroskey, and S. K. Payne, *Nonverbal Behavior in Interpersonal Relations,* 2nd ed. (Englewood Cliffs, NJ: Prentice Hall, 1991), pp. 117–138; and L. A. King, "Ambivalence Over Emotional Expression and Reading Emotions in Situations and Faces," *Journal of Personality and Social Psychology,* March 1998, pp. 753–762.

Chapter 3

1 Taken from the website of Procter & Gamble at www.pg.com.

2 S. H. Schwartz, "Universals in the Content and Structure of Values: Theoretical Advances and Empirical Tests in 20 Countries," in *Advances in Experimental Social Psychology,* ed. M. P. Zanna (New York: Academic Press, 1992), p. 4.

3 M. Rokeach and S. J. Ball-Rokeach, "Stability and Change in American Value Priorities, 1968–1981," *American Psychologist,* May 1989, pp. 775–784.

4 M. Rokeach, *The Nature of Human Values* (New York: Free Press, 1973), p. 6.

5 J. M. Munson and B. Z. Posner, "The Factorial Validity of a Modified Rokeach Value Survey for Four Diverse Samples," *Educational and Psychological Measurement,* Winter 1980, pp. 1073–1079; and W. C. Frederick and J. Weber, "The Values of Corporate Managers and Their Critics: An Empirical Description and Normative Implications," in *Business Ethics: Research Issues and Empirical Studies,* ed. W. C. Frederick and L. E. Preston (Greenwich, CT: JAI Press, 1990), pp. 123–144.

6 W. C. Frederick and J. Weber, "The Values of Corporate Managers and Their Critics: An Empirical Description and Normative Implications," in *Business Ethics: Research Issues and Empirical Studies,* ed. W. C. Frederick and L. E. Preston (Greenwich, CT: JAI Press, 1990), pp. 123–144.

7 W. C. Frederick and J. Weber, "The Values of Corporate Managers and Their Critics: An Empirical Description and Normative Implications," in *Business Ethics: Research Issues and Empirical Studies,* ed. W. C. Frederick and L. E. Preston (Greenwich, CT: JAI Press, 1990), p. 132.

8 K. Hodgson, *A Rock and a Hard Place: How to Make Ethical Business Decisions When the Choices Are Tough,* (New York: AMACOM, 1992), pp. 66–67.

9 G. Hofstede, *Culture's Consequences: International Differences in Work Related Values* (Beverly Hills, CA: Sage, 1980); G. Hofstede, *Cultures and Organizations: Software of the Mind* (London: McGraw-Hill, 1991); and G. Hofstede, "Cultural Constraints in Management Theories," *Academy of Management Executive,* February 1993, pp. 81–94.

10 G. Hofstede and M. H. Bond, "The Confucius Connection: From Cultural Roots to Economic Growth," *Organizational Dynamics,* Spring 1988, pp. 12–13.

11 R. J. House, P. J. Hanges, M. Javidan, P. W. Dorfman, and V. Gupta, *Culture, Leadership, and Organizations: The GLOBE Study of 62 Societies,* (Thousand Oaks, CA: Sage, 2004).

12 G. Hofstede and M. H. Bond, "The Confucius Connection: From Cultural Roots to Economic Growth," *Organizational Dynamics,* Spring 1988, pp. 12–13; and G. Hofstede, "Cultural Constraints in Management Theories," *Academy of Management Executive,* February 1993, pp. 81–94.

13 B, Meglino, E. C. Ravlin, and C. L. Adkins, "A Work Values Approach to Corporate Culture: A Field Test of the Value Congruence Process and Its Relationship to Individual Outcomes," *Journal of Applied Psychology* 74, 1989, pp. 424–432.

14 B. Z. Posner, J. M. Kouzes, and W. H. Schmidt, "Shared Values Make a Difference: An Empirical Test of Corporate Culture," *Human Resource Management* 24, 1985, pp. 293–310; and A. L. Balazas, "Value Congruency: The Case of the 'Socially Responsible' Firm," *Journal of Business Research* 20, 1990, pp. 171–181.

15 C. A. O'Reilly, J. Chatman, and D. Caldwell: "People and Organizational Culture: A Q-Sort Approach to Assessing Person-Organizational Fit," *Academy of Management Journal* 34, 1991, pp. 487–516.

16 C. Enz and C. K. Schwenk, "Performance and Sharing of Organizational Values" (paper presented at the annual meeting of the Academy of Management, Washington, DC, 1989).

17 Material in this section based on the work of M. Adams, *Sex in the Snow* (Toronto: Penguin, 1997); and M. Adams, *Fire and Ice: The*

United States, Canada and the Myth of Converging Values (Toronto: Penguin, 2003).

18 D. Tapscott, *Growing up Digital: The Rise of the Net Generation* (New York: McGraw-Hill, 1998).

19 W. Howe and N. Strauss, *Millennials Rising: The Next Great Generation* (New York: Vintage, 2001).

20 "Get Used to It: The Net Generation Knows More Than Its Parents," *Financial Post (National Post)*, February 8, 2000, p. C10.

21 W. Howe and N. Strauss, *Millennials Rising: The Next Great Generation* (New York: Vintage, 2001).

22 Statistics Canada, "Census of Population," *The Daily*, February 11, 2003.

23 E. Anderssen and M. Valpy, "Face the Nation: Canada Remade," *Globe and Mail*, June 7, 2003, pp. A10–A11.

24 G. Schellenberg, *Immigrants in Canada's Census Metropolitan Areas*, Catalogue no. 89-613-MIE—No. 003 (Ottawa: Statistics Canada, August 2004).

25 Statistics Canada, "2001 Census: *Census of Population: Language, Mobility and Migration*," *The Daily*, December 10, 2002.

26 Statistics Canada, "2001 Census: *Census of Population: Language, Mobility and Migration*," *The Daily*, December 10, 2002.

27 Statistics Canada, "Ethnic Diversity Survey, 2002," *The Daily*, September 29, 2003.

28 The Pew Research Center For The People & The Press, *Views of a Changing World 2003* (Washington, DC: The Pew Research Center For The People & The Press, June 2003).

29 M. Adams, *Fire and Ice: The United States, Canada and the Myth of Converging Values* (Toronto: Penguin, 2003).

30 M. Adams, *Fire and Ice: The United States, Canada and the Myth of Converging Values* (Toronto: Penguin, 2003).

31 R. N. Kanungo and J. K. Bhatnagar, "Achievement Orientation and Occupational Values: A Comparative Study of Young French and English Canadians," *Canadian Journal of Behavioural Science* 12, 1978, pp. 384–392; M. W. McCarrey, S. Edwards, and R. Jones, "The Influence of Ethnolinguistic Group Membership, Sex and Position Level on Motivational Orientation of Canadian Anglophone and Francophone Employees," *Canadian Journal of Behavioural Science* 9, 1977, pp. 274–282; M. W. McCarrey, S. Edwards, and R. Jones, "Personal Values of Canadian Anglophone and Francophone Employees and Ethnolinguistic Group Membership, Sex and Position Level," *Journal of Psychology* 104, 1978, pp. 175–184; S. Richer and P. Laporte, "Culture, Cognition and English-French Competition," in *Readings in Social Psychology: Focus on Canada*, ed. D. Koulack and D. Perlman (Toronto: Wiley, 1973); and L. Shapiro and D. Perlman, "Value Differences Between English and French Canadian High School Students," *Canadian Ethnic Studies* 8, 1976, pp. 50–55.

32 R. N. Kanungo and J. K. Bhatnagar, "Achievement Orientation and Occupational Values: A Comparative Study of Young French and English Canadians," *Canadian Journal of Behavioural Science* 12, 1978, pp. 384–392.

33 V. Mann-Feder and V. Savicki, "Burnout in Anglophone and Francophone Child and Youth Workers in Canada: A Cross-Cultural Comparison," *Child & Youth Care Forum* 32, no. 6 (December 2003), p. 345.

34 R. N. Kanungo and J. K. Bhatnagar, "Achievement Orientation and Occupational Values: A Comparative Study of Young French and English Canadians," *Canadian Journal of Behavioural Science* 12, 1978, pp. 384–392.

35 V. Mann-Feder and V. Savicki, "Burnout in Anglophone and Francophone Child and Youth Workers in Canada: A Cross-Cultural Comparison," *Child & Youth Care Forum* 32, no. 6 (December 2003), pp. 337–354.

36 H. C. Jain, J. Normand, and R. N. Kanungo, "Job Motivation of Canadian Anglophone and Francophone Hospital Employees," *Canadian Journal of Behavioural Science*, April 1979, pp. 160–163; and R. N. Kanungo, G. J. Gorn, and H. J. Dauderis, "Motivational Orientation of Canadian Anglophone and Francophone Managers," *Canadian Journal of Behavioural Science*, April 1976, pp. 107–121.

37 M. Major, M. McCarrey, P. Mercier, and Y. Gasse, "Meanings of Work and Personal Values of Canadian Anglophone and Francophone Middle Managers," *Canadian Journal of Administrative Sciences*, September 1994, pp. 251–263.

38 G. Bouchard, F. Rocher, and G. Rocher, *Les Francophones Québécois* (Montreal: Bowne de Montréal, 1991).

39 A. Derfel, "Boy, Are We Stressed Out! Quebec Has Highest Rate of Work Absenteeism," *The Gazette* (Montreal), May 29, 2003, www.canada.com/montreal/montrealgazette/story.asp?id=5D0D7AF8-DFCB-44D5-ABE4-DA4DACA11DEA (accessed May 29, 2003).

40 P. La Novara, "Culture Participation: Does Language Make a Difference?" *Focus on Culture*, 13, no. 3, Catalogue no. 87-004-XIE (Ottawa: Statistics Canada, 2002).

41 J. Paulson, "First Nations Bank Launches First Branch With Sweetgrass Ceremony," *Canadian Press Newswire*, September 23, 1997.

42 L. Redpath and M. O. Nielsen, "A Comparison of Native Culture, Non-Native Culture and New Management Ideology," *Canadian Journal of Administrative Sciences* 14, no. 3 (1997), p. 327.

43 G. C. Anders and K. K. Anders, "Incompatible Goals in Unconventional Organizations: The Politics of Alaska Native Corporations," *Organization Studies* 7, 1986, pp. 213–233; G. Dacks, "Worker-Controlled Native Enterprises: A Vehicle for Community Development in Northern Canada?" *Canadian Journal of Native Studies* 3, 1983, pp. 289–310; and L. P. Dana, "Self-Employment in the Canadian Sub-Arctic: An Exploratory Study," *Canadian Journal of Administrative Sciences* 13, 1996, pp. 65–77.

44 L. Redpath and M. O. Nielsen, "A Comparison of Native Culture, Non-Native Culture and New Management Ideology," *Canadian Journal of Administrative Sciences* 14, no. 3 (1997), p. 327.

45 R. B. Anderson, "The Business Economy of the First Nations in Saskatchewan: A Contingency Perspective," *Canadian Journal of Native Studies* 2, 1995, pp. 309–345.

46 E. Struzik, "'Win-Win Scenario' Possible for Resource Industry, Aboriginals," *Edmonton Journal*, April 6, 2003, p. A12.

47 Discussion based on L. Redpath and M. O. Nielsen, "A Comparison of Native Culture, Non-Native Culture and New Management Ideology," *Canadian Journal of Administrative Sciences* 14, no. 3 (1997), pp. 327–339.

48 Discussion based on L. Redpath and M. O. Nielsen, "A Comparison of Native Culture, Non-Native Culture and New Management Ideology," *Canadian Journal of Administrative Sciences* 14, no. 3 (1997), pp. 327–339.

49 D. Grigg and J. Newman, "Five Ways to Foster Bonds, Win Trust in Business," *Ottawa Citizen*, April 23, 2003, p. F12.

50 T. Chui, K. Tran, and J. Flanders, "Chinese Canadians: Enriching the Cultural Mosaic," *Canadian Social Trends*, no. 76, Spring 2005, pp. 26–34.

51 Statistics Canada, "Canada's Visible Minority Population in 2017," *The Daily*, March 22, 2005.

52 I. Y. M. Yeung and R. L. Tung, "Achieving Business Success in Confucian Societies: The Importance of *Guanxi* (Connections)," *Organizational Dynamics, Special Report*, 1998, pp. 72–83.

53 I. Y. M. Yeung and R. L. Tung, "Achieving Business Success in Confucian Societies: The Importance of *Guanxi* (Connections)," *Organizational Dynamics, Special Report*, 1998, p. 73.

54 See www.pg.com/en_CA.

55 A. Kerr, "Female Architects Seen Running for Exits," *Globe and Mail*, May 6, 2002, p. B11.

56 Vignette based on E. Louie "She Has a Knife And She Knows How to Use It," *New York Times*, June 5, 2002, p. F1.

57 G. Shaw, "Canada Lags World On Job Quality," *Vancouver Sun*, September 18, 2004, p. F5.

58 V. H. Vroom, *Work and Motivation* (New York: Wiley, 1964); and M. T. Iaffaldano and P. M. Muchinsky, "Job Satisfaction and Job Performance: A Meta-Analysis," *Psychological Bulletin*, March 1985, pp. 251–273.

59 C. N. Greene, "The Satisfaction-Performance Controversy," *Business Horizons*, February 1972, pp. 31–41; E. E. Lawler III, *Motivation in Organizations* (Monterey, CA: Brooks/Cole, 1973); and M. M. Petty, G. W. McGee, and J. W. Cavender, "A Meta-Analysis of the Relationship Between Individual Job Satisfaction and Individual Performance," *Academy of Management Review*, October 1984, pp. 712–721.

60 C. Ostroff, "The Relationship Between Satisfaction, Attitudes, and Performance: An Organizational Level Analysis," *Journal of Applied Psychology*, December 1992, pp. 963–974.

61 "Sears Chief Sees 'Definite Link' Between Employee and Customer Satisfaction," *Financial Post (National Post)*, May 4, 1999, p. C5.

62 L. Grant, "Happy Workers, High Returns," *Fortune*, January 12, 1998, p. 81.

63 L. Grant, "Happy Workers, High Returns," *Fortune*, January 12, 1998, p. 81.

64 D. W. Organ, *Organizational Citizenship Behavior: The Good Soldier Syndrome* (Lexington, MA: Lexington Books, 1988), p. 4.

65 D. W. Organ, *Organizational Citizenship Behavior: The Good Soldier Syndrome* (Lexington, MA: Lexington Books, 1988); C. A. Smith, D. W. Organ, and J. P. Near, "Organizational Citizenship Behavior: Its Nature and Antecedents," *Journal of Applied Psychology*, 1983, pp. 653–663.

66 J. Farh, C. Zhong, and D. W. Organ, "Organizational Citizenship Behavior in the People's Republic of China," *Academy of Management Proceedings*, 2000, pp. OB: D1–D6.

67 J. M. George and A. P. Brief, "Feeling Good-Doing Good: A Conceptual Analysis of the Mood at Work–Organizational Spontaneity Relationship," *Psychological Bulletin* 112, 2002, pp. 310–329; and S. Wagner and M. Rush, "Altruistic Organizational Citizenship Behavior: Context, Disposition and Age," *Journal of Social Psychology* 140, 2002, pp. 379–391.

68 P. E. Spector, *Job Satisfaction: Application, Assessment, Causes, and Consequences* (Thousand Oaks, CA: Sage, 1997), pp. 57–58.

69 P. M. Podsakoff, S. B. MacKenzie, J. B. Paine, and D. G. Bachrach, "Organizational Citizenship Behaviors: A Critical Review of the Theoretical and Empirical Literature and Suggestions for Future Research," *Journal of Management* 26, no. 3 (2000), pp. 513–563.

70 See T. S. Bateman and D. W. Organ, "Job Satisfaction and the Good Soldier: The Relationship Between Affect and Employee 'Citizenship,'" *Academy of Management Journal*, December 1983, pp. 587–595; C. A. Smith, D. W. Organ, and J. P. Near, "Organizational Citizenship Behavior: Its Nature and Antecedents," *Journal of Applied Psychology*, October 1983, pp. 653–663; and A. P. Brief, *Attitudes in and Around Organizations* (Thousand Oaks, CA: Sage, 1998), pp. 44–45.

71 D. W. Organ and R. H. Moorman, "Fairness and Organizational Citizenship Behavior: What Are the Connections?" *Social Justice Research* 6, no. 1 (March 1993), pp. 5–18.

72 D. W. Organ and K. Ryan, "A Meta-Analytic Review of Attitudinal and Dispositional Predictors of Organizational Citizenship Behavior," *Personnel Psychology*, Winter 1995, p. 791.

73 J. Fahr, P. M. Podsakoff, and D. W. Organ, "Accounting for Organizational Citizenship Behavior: Leader Fairness and Task Scope Versus Satisfaction," *Journal of Management*, December 1990, pp. 705–722; R. H. Moorman, "Relationship Between Organizational Justice and Organizational Citizenship Behaviors: Do Fairness Perceptions Influence Employee Citizenship?" *Journal of Applied Psychology*, December 1991, pp. 845–855; and M. A. Konovsky and D. W. Organ, "Dispositional and Contextual Determinants of Organizational Citizenship Behavior," *Journal of Organizational Behavior*, May 1996, pp. 253–266.

74 D. W. Organ, "Personality and Organizational Citizenship Behavior," *Journal of Management*, Summer 1994, p. 466.

75 See, for instance, E. Naumann and D. W. Jackson Jr., "One More Time: How Do You Satisfy Customers?" *Business Horizons*, May–June 1999, pp. 71–76; D. J. Koys, "The Effects of Employee Satisfaction, Organizational Citizenship Behavior, and Turnover on Organizational Effectiveness: A Unit-Level, Longitudinal Study," *Personnel Psychology*, Spring 2001, pp. 101–114; and J. Griffith, "Do Satisfied Employees Satisfy Customers? Support-Services Staff Morale and Satisfaction among Public School Administrators, Students, and Parents," *Journal of Applied Social Psychology*, August 2001, pp. 1627–1658.

76 M. J. Bitner, B. H. Booms, and L. A. Mohr, "Critical Service Encounters: The Employee's Viewpoint," *Journal of Marketing*, October 1994, pp. 95–106.

77 E. A. Locke, "The Nature and Causes of Job Satisfaction," in *Handbook of Industrial and Organizational Psychology*, ed. M. D. Dunnette (Chicago: Rand McNally, 1976), p. 1331; S. L. McShane, "Job Satisfaction and Absenteeism: A Meta-Analytic Re-Examination," *Canadian Journal of Administrative Science*, June 1984, pp. 61–77; R. D. Hackett and R. M. Guion, "A Reevaluation of the Absenteeism-Job Satisfaction Relationship," *Organizational Behavior and Human Decision Processes*, June 1985, pp. 340–381; K. D. Scott and G. S. Taylor, "An Examination of Conflicting Findings on the Relationship Between Job Satisfaction and Absenteeism: A Meta-Analysis," *Academy of Management Journal*, September 1985, pp. 599–612; R. D. Hackett, "Work Attitudes and Employee Absenteeism: A Synthesis of the Literature" (paper presented at the 1988 National Academy of Management Conference, Anaheim, CA, August 1988); and R. P. Steel and J. R. Rentsch, "Influence of Cumulation Strategies on the Long-Range Prediction of Absenteeism," *Academy of Management Journal*, December 1995, pp. 1616–1634.

78 J. L. Cotton and J. M. Tuttle, "Employee Turnover: A Meta-Analysis and Review With Implications for Research," *Academy of Management Review* 11, 1986, pp. 55–70; R. W. Griffeth and P. W. Hom, "The Employee Turnover Process," *Research in Personnel and Human Resources Management* 13, 1995, pp. 245–293; P. W. Hom, F. Caranikas-Walker, G. E. Prussia, and R. W. Griffeth, "A Meta-Analytical Structural Equations Analysis of a Model of Employee Turnover," *Journal of Applied Psychology* 77, 1992, pp. 890–909; P. W. Hom, and R. W. Griffeth, *Employee Turnover*

(Cincinnati, OH: South-Western College, 1995); W. H. Mobley, R. W. Griffeth, H. H. Hand, and B. Meglino, "Review and Conceptual Analysis of the Employee Turnover Process," *Psychological Bulletin* 86, 1979, pp. 493–522; J. L. Price, *The Study of Turnover* (Ames: Iowa State University Press, 1977); R. P. Steel and N. K. Ovalle, "A Review and Metaanalysis of Research on the Relationship Between Behavioral Intentions and Employee Turnover," *Journal of Applied Psychology* 69, 1984, pp. 673–686; and R. P. Tett and J. P. Meyer, "Job Satisfaction, Organizational Commitment, Turnover Intention, and Turnover: Path Analyses Based on Meta-Analytical Findings," *Personnel Psychology* 46, 1993, pp. 259–293.

79 T. A. Judge, "Does Affective Disposition Moderate the Relationship Between Job Satisfaction and Voluntary Turnover?" *Journal of Applied Psychology*, June 1993, pp. 395–401.

80 S. M. Puffer, "Prosocial Behavior, Noncompliant Behavior, and Work Performance Among Commission Salespeople," *Journal of Applied Psychology*, November 1987, pp. 615–621; J. Hogan and R. Hogan, "How to Measure Employee Reliability," *Journal of Applied Psychology*, May 1989, pp. 273–279; and C. D. Fisher and E. A. Locke, "The New Look in Job Satisfaction Research and Theory," in *Job Satisfaction*. ed. C. J. Cranny, P. C. Smith, and E. F. Stone (New York: Lexington Books, 1992), pp. 165–194.

81 S. M. Puffer, "Prosocial Behavior, Noncompliant Behavior, and Work Performance Among Commission Salespeople," *Journal of Applied Psychology*, November 1987, pp. 615–621; J. Hogan and R. Hogan, "How to Measure Employee Reliability," *Journal of Applied Psychology*, May 1989, pp. 273–279; and C. D. Fisher and E. A. Locke, "The New Look in Job Satisfaction Research and Theory," in *Job Satisfaction*, ed. C. J. Cranny, P. C. Smith, and E. F. Stone (New York: Lexington Books, 1992), pp. 165–194.

82 R. B. Freeman, "Job Satisfaction as an Economic Variable," *American Economic Review*, January 1978, pp. 135–141.

83 G. J. Blau and K. R. Boal, "Conceptualizing How Job Involvement and Organizational Commitment Affect Turnover and Absenteeism," *Academy of Management Review*, April 1987, p. 290.

84 N. J. Allen and J. P. Meyer, "The Measurement and Antecedents of Affective, Continuance, and Normative Commitment to the Organization," *Journal of Occupational Psychology* 63, 1990, pp. 1–18; and J. P. Meyer, N. J. Allen, and C. A. Smith, "Commitment to Organizations and Occupations: Extension and Test of a Three-Component Conceptualization," *Journal of Applied Psychology* 78, 1993, pp. 538–551.

85 J. P. Meyer, S. V. Paumonen, I. R. Gellatly, R. D. Goffin, and D. N. Jackson, "Organizational Commitment and Job Performance: It's the Nature of the Commitment That Counts," *Journal of Applied Psychology* 74, 1989, pp. 152–156; L. M. Shore and S. J. Wayne, "Commitment and Employee Behavior: Comparison of Affective and Continuance Commitment With Perceived Organizational Support," *Journal of Applied Psychology* 78, 1993, pp. 774–780.

86 D. M. Rousseau, "Organizational Behavior in the New Organizational Era," in *Annual Review of Psychology*, 48, ed. J. T. Spence, J. M. Darley, and D. J. Foss (Palo Alto, CA: Annual Reviews, 1997), p. 523.

87 "Do as I Do," *Canadian Business*, March 12, 1999, p. 35.

88 Corporate Leadership Council, "Driving Performance and Retention Through Employee Engagement," news release, September 2004.

89 J. R. Katzenback and J. A. Santamaria, "Firing up the Front Line," *Harvard Business Review*, May–June 1999, p. 109.

90 See www.can.ibm.com/employment/ca/en/diversity.html.

91 R. A. Roe and P. Ester, "Values and Work: Empirical Findings and Theoretical Perspective," *Applied Psychology: An International Review* 48, 1999, pp. 1–21.

92 M. Adams, *Sex in the Snow* (Toronto: Penguin, 1997), p. 102.

93 M. Adams, *Sex in the Snow* (Toronto: Penguin, 1997), p. 102.

94 *Focus on Diversity* based on D. Calleja, "Equity or Else," *Canadian Business*, March 19, 2001, pp. 29–34.

95 P. C. Earley and E. Mosakowski, "Cultural Intelligence," *Harvard Business Review* 82, no. 10 (October 2004), pp. 139–146.

96 J. Sanchez-Burks, F. Lee, R. Nisbett, I. Choi, S. Zhao, and J. Koo, "Conversing Across Cultures: East-West Communication Styles in Work and Nonwork Contexts," *Journal of Personality and Social Psychology* 85, no. 2 (August 2003), pp. 363–372.

97 E. A. Locke, "The Nature and Causes of Job Satisfaction," in *Handbook of Industrial and Organizational Psychology*, ed. M. D. Dunnette (Chicago: Rand McNally, 1976), pp. 1319–1328.

98 See, for instance, T. A. Judge and S. Watanabe, "Another Look at the Job Satisfaction–Life Satisfaction Relationship," *Journal of Applied Psychology*, December 1993, pp. 939–948; R. D. Arvey, B. P. McCall, T. J. Bouchard Jr., and P. Taubman, "Genetic Influences on Job Satisfaction and Work Values," *Personality and Individual Differences*, July 1994, pp. 21–33; and D. Lykken and A. Tellegen, "Happiness Is a Stochastic Phenomenon," *Psychological Science*, May 1996, pp. 186–189.

99 See, for example, B. Fishel, "A New Perspective: How to Get the Real Story From Attitude Surveys," *Training*, February 1998, pp. 91–94.

100 J. Stack, "Measuring Morale," *Inc.*, January 1997, pp. 29–30.

101 T. Lammers, "The Essential Employee Survey," *Inc.*, December 1992, pp. 159–161; and S. Shellenbarger, "Companies Are Finding It Really Pays to Be Nice to Employees," *Wall Street Journal*, July 22, 1998, p. B1.

102 Cited in "Survey Shows 75% of Large Corporations Support Diversity Programs," *Fortune*, July 6, 1998, p. S14.

103 See, for example, J. K. Ford and S. Fisher, "The Role of Training in a Changing Workplace and Workforce: New Perspectives and Approaches," in *Managing Diversity*, ed. E. E. Kossek and S. A. Lobel (Cambridge, MA: Blackwell Publishers, 1996), pp. 164–193; and J. Barbian, "Moving Toward Diversity," *Training*, February 2003, pp. 44–48.

104 R. Koonce, "Redefining Diversity," *Training & Development*, December 2001, p. 25; and M. D. Lee, "Post-9/11 Training," *Training & Development*, September 2002, pp. 32–35.

105 "Selling Equity," *Financial Post Magazine*, September 1994, pp. 20–25.

106 P. Preville, "What Exactly Is Sensitivity Training?" *Saturday Night*, January 27, 2001, p. 14.

107 "Selling Equity," *Financial Post Magazine*, September 1994, pp. 20–25; and www.wiley.co.uk/products/worldwide/canada/diversityatwork/about_author.htm.

108 This section is based on A. Rossett and T. Bickham, "Diversity Training: Hope, Faith and Cynicism," *Training*, January 1994, pp. 40–46.

109 L. E. Wynter, "Theatre Program Tackles Issues of Diversity," *Wall Street Journal*, April 18, 1991, p. B1.

110 B. Hynes-Grace, "To Thrive, Not Merely Survive," in *Textbook Authors Conference Presentations* (Washington, DC: October 21, 1992), sponsored by the American Association of Retired Persons, p. 12.

111 "Teaching Diversity: Business Schools Search for Model Approaches," *Newsline,* Fall 1992, p. 21.

OB on the Edge: Stress at Work

1 Information in this paragraph based on S. McKay, "The Work-Family Conundrum," *Financial Post Magazine,* December 1997, pp. 78–81; and J. Mawhinney, "Style With Heart and Soul," *Toronto Star,* September 1, 2005, p. E04.

2 Paragraph based on "'You'd Drink Too,' Charged School Bus Driver Says," *National Post,* March 4, 2002, p. A7.

3 Statistics Canada, "Life Stress, by Sex, Household Population Aged 18 and Over, Canada, Provinces, Territories, Health Regions and Peer Groups, 2000/01," www.statcan.ca/english/freepub/82-221-XIE/00503/tables/html/2336.htm (accessed August 4, 2005).

4 A. Marchand, P. Durand, and A. Demers, "Work and Mental Health: The Experience of the Quebec Workforce Between 1987 and 1998," *Work* 25, no. 2, 2005, pp. 135–142.

5 I. Phaneuf, "Drug Company Study Finds Rise in Work-Related Stress," *Vancouver Sun,* May 5, 2001, p. D15.

6 V. Galt, "Statscan Studies Workplace Stress," *Globe and Mail,* June 26, 2003, p. B3.

7 R. B. Mason, "Taking Health Care to Factory Floor Proves Smart Move for Growing Ontario Company," *Canadian Medical Association Journal,* November 15, 1997, pp. 1423–1424.

8 L. Duxbury and C. Higgins, *2001 National Work-Life Conflict Study,* as reported in J. Campbell, "'Organizational Anorexia' Puts Stress on Employees," *Ottawa Citizen,* July 4, 2002.

9 K. Harding, "Balance Tops List of Job Desires," *Globe and Mail,* May 7, 2003, pp. C1, C6.

10 V. Galt, "Productivity Buckling Under the Strain of Stress, CEOs Say," *Globe and Mail,* June 9, 2005, p. B1.

11 "Canadian Workers Among Most Stressed," *Worklife Report* 14, no. 2 (2002), pp. 8–9.

12 N. Ayed, "Absenteeism Up Since 1993," *Canadian Press Newswire,* March 25, 1998.

13 N. Ayed, "Absenteeism Up Since 1993," *Canadian Press Newswire,* March 25, 1998.

14 H. Selye, *The Stress of Life* (New York: McGraw-Hill, 1976); and H. Selye, *Stress Without Distress* (Philadelphia, PA: J. B. Lippincott, 1974).

15 R. DeFrank and J. M. Ivancevich, "Stress on the Job: An Executive Update," *Academy of Management Executive,* August 1998, pp. 55–66.

16 E. Church, "Work Winning Out Over Family in the Struggle for Balance," *Globe and Mail,* February 13, 2002, pp. B1, B2.

17 W. Stueck, "Firms Not 'Family Friendly': Study," *Globe and Mail,* July 4, 2002, p. B4.

18 These key changes and the unattributed quotations in this section are taken from R. DeFrank and J. M. Ivancevich, "Stress on the Job: An Executive Update," *Academy of Management Executive,* August 1998, pp. 55–66.

19 P. Demont and A. M. Tobin, "One in Three Canadians Say They're Workaholics," *Vancouver Sun,* November 10, 1999, pp. A1, A2.

20 D. Stonehouse, "Caught in the E-Mailstrom: You Know Things Are Getting out of Hand When a Guy With an Online Newsletter Pulls the Plug," *Vancouver Sun,* June 8, 2002, pp. H3, H4.

21 S. McKay, "The Work-Family Conundrum," *Financial Post Magazine,* December 1997, pp. 78–81; and A. Davis, "Respect Your Elders: Pressure on the Healthcare System Means Elderly Patients Aren't Staying in Hospitals as Long as They Used To," *Benefits Canada* 26, no. 8 (2002), p. 13.

22 L. T. Thomas and D. C. Ganster, "Impact of Family-Supportive Work Variables on Work-Family Conflict and Strain: A Control Perspective," *Journal of Applied Psychology* 80, 1995, pp. 6–15.

23 H. Selye, *The Stress of Life* (New York: McGraw-Hill, 1976).

24 R. S. Schuler, "Definition and Conceptualization of Stress in Organizations," *Organizational Behavior and Human Performance,* April 1980, p. 191; and R. L. Kahn and P. Byosiere, "Stress in Organizations," *Organizational Behavior and Human Performance,* April 1980, pp. 604–610.

25 KPMG Canada, compensation letter, July 1998.

26 B. D. Steffy and J. W. Jones, "Workplace Stress and Indicators of Coronary-Disease Risk," *Academy of Management Journal* 31, 1988, p. 687.

27 C. L. Cooper and J. Marshall, "Occupational Sources of Stress: A Review of the Literature Relating to Coronary Heart Disease and Mental Ill Health," *Journal of Occupational Psychology* 49, no. 1 (1976), pp. 11–28.

28 J. R. Hackman and G. R. Oldham, "Development of the Job Diagnostic Survey," *Journal of Applied Psychology,* April 1975, pp. 159–170.

29 J. L. Xie and G. Johns, "Job Scope and Stress: Can Job Scope Be Too High?" *Academy of Management Journal,* October 1995, pp. 1288–1309.

30 S. J. Motowidlo, J. S. Packard, and M. R. Manning, "Occupational Stress: Its Causes and Consequences for Job Performance," *Journal of Applied Psychology,* November 1987, pp. 619–620.

31 See, for instance, R. C. Cummings, "Job Stress and the Buffering Effect of Supervisory Support," *Group & Organization Studies,* March 1990, pp. 92–104; M. R. Manning, C. N. Jackson, and M. R. Fusilier, "Occupational Stress, Social Support, and the Cost of Health Care," *Academy of Management Journal,* June 1996, pp. 738–750; and P. D. Bliese and T. W. Britt, "Social Support, Group Consensus and Stressor-Strain Relationships: Social Context Matters," *Journal of Organizational Behavior,* June 2001, pp. 425–436.

32 See L. R. Murphy, "A Review of Organizational Stress Management Research," *Journal of Organizational Behavior Management,* Fall–Winter 1986, pp. 215–227.

33 R. Williams, *The Trusting Heart: Great News About Type A Behavior* (New York: Times Books, 1989).

34 T. H. Macan, "Time Management: Test of a Process Model," *Journal of Applied Psychology,* June 1994, pp. 381–391.

35 See, for example, G. Lawrence-Ell, *The Invisible Clock: A Practical Revolution in Finding Time for Everyone and Everything* (Seaside Park, NJ: Kingsland Hall, 2002).

36 J. Kiely and G. Hodgson, "Stress in the Prison Service: The Benefits of Exercise Programs," *Human Relations,* June 1990, pp. 551–572.

37 E. J. Forbes and R. J. Pekala, "Psychophysiological Effects of Several Stress Management Techniques," *Psychological Reports,* February 1993, pp. 19–27; and G. Smith, "Meditation, the New Balm for Corporate Stress," *BusinessWeek,* May 10, 1993, pp. 86–87.

38 *FactBox* based on P. Demont and A. M. Tobin, "One in Three Canadians Say They're Workaholics," *Vancouver Sun,* November 10, 1999, pp. A1, A2; E. Beauchesne, "Lost Work Cost Placed at $10b: Growing Stress Levels Are Cited as a Leading Factor in the Rise in Absenteeism in Canada," *Vancouver Sun,* September 2, 1999,

p. A3; L. Ramsay "Caught Between the Potty and the PC," *National Post*, November 9, 1998, p. D9; V. Galt, "Just Don't Call Them 'Workaholics'" *Globe and Mail*, April 8, 2002, pp. B1, B2; S. McGovern, "No Rest for the Weary," *The Gazette* (Montreal), August 19, 2003, p. B1; and D. McMurdy, "People Get Stress Relief Express-Style," *Financial Post (National Post)*, January 15, 2005, p. IN1.

39 D. Etzion, "Moderating Effects of Social Support on the Stress-Burnout Relationship," *Journal of Applied Psychology*, November 1984, pp. 615–622; and S. Jackson, R. Schwab, and R. Schuler, "Toward an Understanding of the Burnout Phenomenon," *Journal of Applied Psychology* 71, no. 4 (November 1986), pp. 630–640.

40 H. Staseson, "Can Perk Help Massage Bottom Line? On-Site Therapeutic Sessions Are Used by an Increasingly Diverse Group of Employers Hoping to Improve Staff Performance," *Globe and Mail*, July 3, 2002, p. C1.

41 B. Bouw, "Employers Embrace Wellness at Work: Fitness Programs Gaining Popularity as Companies Look to Boost Productivity With Healthier Staff," *Globe and Mail*, April 10, 2002, p. C1.

42 "Wellness Programs Offer Healthy Return, Study Finds," *Report Bulletin*, #224, October 2001, p. 1.

43 H. Staseson, "Can Perk Help Massage Bottom Line? On-Site Therapeutic Sessions Are Used by an Increasingly Diverse Group of Employers Hoping to Improve Staff Performance," *Globe and Mail*, July 3, 2002, p. C1.

44 B. Bouw, "Employers Embrace Wellness at Work: Fitness Programs Gaining Popularity as Companies Look to Boost Productivity With Healthier Staff," *Globe and Mail*, April 10, 2002, p. C1.

45 P. M. Wright, "Operationalization of Goal Difficulty as a Moderator of the Goal Difficulty-Performance Relationship," *Journal of Applied Psychology*, June 1990, pp. 227–234; E. A. Locke and G. P. Latham, "Building a Practically Useful Theory of Goal Setting and Task Motivation: A 35-Year Odyssey," *American Psychologist* 57, no. 9 (2002), pp. 705–717; K. L. Langeland, C. M. Johnson, and T. C. Mawhinney, "Improving Staff Performance in a Community Mental Health Setting: Job Analysis, Training, Goal Setting, Feedback, and Years of Data," *Journal of Organizational Behavior Management*, 1998, pp. 21–43.

46 See W. A. Anthony and C. W. Anthony, *The Art of Napping at Work* (Burdett, NY: Larson Publications, 2000); J. E. Brody, "New Respect for the Nap, A Pause That Refreshes," *New York Times*, January 4, 2000, p. D7; and "Nappers of the World, Lie Down and Be Counted!" *Training*, May 2000, p. 24.

47 See, for instance. R. A. Wolfe, D. O. Ulrich, and D. F. Parker, "Employee Health Management Programs: Review, Critique, and Research Agenda," *Journal of Management*, Winter 1987, pp. 603–615; D. L. Gebhardt and C. E. Crump, "Employee Fitness and Wellness Programs in the Workplace," *American Psychologist*, February 1990, pp. 262–272; and C. E. Beadle, "And Let's Save 'Wellness.' It Works," *New York Times*, July 24, 1994, p. F9.

Chapter 4

1 Opening vignette based on M. Beamish, "Lions Know Practice Makes Perfect," *Nanaimo Daily News*, August 23, 2005, p. B3; and M. Sekeres, "Two Sides to Buono," *Kamloops Daily News*, September 8, 2005, p. A13.

2 See, for instance, T. R. Mitchell, "Matching Motivational Strategies With Organizational Contexts," in *Research in Organizational Behavior*, vol. 19, ed. L. L. Cummings and B. M. Staw (Greenwich, CT: JAI Press, 1997), pp. 60–62.

3 D. McGregor, *The Human Side of Enterprise* (New York: McGraw-Hill, 1960). For an updated analysis of Theory X and Theory Y constructs, see R. J. Summers and S. F. Cronshaw, "A Study of McGregor's Theory X, Theory Y and the Influence of Theory X, Theory Y Assumptions on Causal Attributions for Instances of Worker Poor Performance," in *Organizational Behavior*, ed. S. L. McShane, ASAC Conference Proceedings, vol. 9, part 5, Halifax, 1988, pp. 115–123.

4 K. W. Thomas, *Intrinsic Motivation at Work* (San Francisco: Berrett-Koehler, 2000); and K. W. Thomas, "Intrinsic Motivation and How It Works," *Training*, October 2000, pp. 130–135.

5 A. Kohn, *Punished by Rewards* (Boston: Houghton Mifflin, 1993).

6 A. H. Maslow, *Motivation and Personality* (New York: Harper and Row, 1954).

7 K. Korman, J. H. Greenhaus, and I. J. Badin, "Personnel Attitudes and Motivation," in *Annual Review of Psychology*, ed. M. R. Rosenzweig and L. W. Porter (Palo Alto, CA: Annual Reviews, 1977), p. 178; and M. A. Wahba and L. G. Bridwell, "Maslow Reconsidered: A Review of Research on the Need Hierarchy Theory," *Organizational Behavior and Human Performance*, April 1976, pp. 212–240.

8 F. Herzberg, B. Mausner, and B. Snyderman, *The Motivation to Work* (New York: Wiley, 1959).

9 R. J. House and L. A. Wigdor, "Herzberg's Dual-Factor Theory of Job Satisfaction and Motivations: A Review of the Evidence and Criticism," *Personnel Psychology*, Winter 1967, pp. 369–389; D. P. Schwab and L. L. Cummings, "Theories of Performance and Satisfaction: A Review," *Industrial Relations*, October 1970, pp. 403–430; R. J. Caston and R. Braito, "A Specification Issue in Job Satisfaction Research," *Sociological Perspectives*, April 1985, pp. 175–197; and J. Phillipchuk and J. Whittaker, "An Inquiry into the Continuing Relevance of Herzberg's Motivation Theory," *Engineering Management Journal* 8, no. 1 (1996), pp. 15–20.

10 R. J. House and L. A. Wigdor, "Herzberg's Dual-Factor Theory of Job Satisfaction and Motivations: A Review of the Evidence and Criticism," *Personnel Psychology*, Winter 1967, pp. 369–389; D. P. Schwab and L. L. Cummings, "Theories of Performance and Satisfaction: A Review," *Industrial Relations*, October 1970, pp. 403–430; and R. J. Caston and R. Braito, "A Specification Issue in Job Satisfaction Research," *Sociological Perspectives*, April 1985, pp. 175–197.

11 C. P. Alderfer, "An Empirical Test of a New Theory of Human Needs," *Organizational Behavior and Human Performance*, May 1969, pp. 142–175.

12 C. P. Schneider and C. P. Alderfer, "Three Studies of Measures of Need Satisfaction in Organizations," *Administrative Science Quarterly*, December 1973, pp. 489–505; and I. Borg and M. Braun, "Work Values in East and West Germany: Different Weights, but Identical Structures," *Journal of Organizational Behavior* 17, special issue (1996), pp. 541–555.

13 J. P. Wanous and A. Zwany, "A Cross-Sectional Test of Need Hierarchy Theory," *Organizational Behavior and Human Performance*, May 1977, pp. 78–97.

14 D. C. McClelland, *The Achieving Society* (New York: Van Nostrand Reinhold, 1961); J. W. Atkinson and J. O. Raynor, *Motivation and Achievement* (Washington, DC: Winston, 1974); D. C. McClelland, *Power: The Inner Experience* (New York: Irvington, 1975); and M. J. Stahl, *Managerial and Technical Motivation: Assessing Needs for Achievement, Power, and Affiliation* (New York: Praeger, 1986).

15 D. C. McClelland, *The Achieving Society* (New York: Van Nostrand Reinhold, 1961).

16 D. C. McClelland, *Power: The Inner Experience* (New York: Irvington, 1975); D. C. McClelland and D. H. Burnham, "Power Is the Great Motivator," *Harvard Business Review*, March–April 1976, pp. 100–110; and R. E. Boyatzis, "The Need for Close Relationships and the Manager's Job," in *Organizational Psychology: Readings on Human Behavior in Organizations*, 4th ed., ed. D. A. Kolb, I. M. Rubin, and J. M. McIntyre (Upper Saddle River, NJ: Prentice Hall, 1984), pp. 81–86.

17 D. G. Winter, "The Motivational Dimensions of Leadership: Power, Achievement, and Affiliation," in *Multiple Intelligences and Leadership*, ed. R. E. Riggio, S. E. Murphy, and F. J. Pirozzolo (Mahwah, NJ: Erlbaum, 2002), pp. 119–138.

18 Based on L. Ullrich. "Anything But Glamorous at 4 a.m.: No Security, Insane Hours, No Pension and Zero Benefits," *Province* (Vancouver), August 3, 2005, p. A40.

19 V. H. Vroom, *Work and Motivation* (New York: Wiley, 1964).

20 L. Ullrich. "Anything But Glamorous at 4 a.m.: No Security, Insane Hours, No Pension and Zero Benefits," *Province* (Vancouver), August 3, 2005, p. A40.

21 J. Choudhury, "The Motivational Impact of Sales Quotas on Effort," *Journal of Marketing Research*, February 1993, pp. 28–41; and C. C. Pinder, *Work Motivation* (Glenview, IL: Scott Foresman, 1984), Chapter 7.

22 Angus Reid Group, *Workplace 2000: Working Toward the Millennium*, Fall 1997, p. 14.

23 See www.radical.ca.

24 See, for example, H. G. Heneman III and D. P. Schwab, "Evaluation of Research on Expectancy Theory Prediction of Employee Performance," *Psychological Bulletin*, July 1972, pp. 1–9; T. R. Mitchell, "Expectancy Models of Job Satisfaction, Occupational Preference and Effort: A Theoretical, Methodological and Empirical Appraisal," *Psychological Bulletin*, November 1974, pp. 1053–1077; and L. Reinharth and M. A. Wahba, "Expectancy Theory as a Predictor of Work Motivation, Effort Expenditure, and Job Performance," *Academy of Management Journal*, September 1975, pp. 502–537.

25 See, for example, L. W. Porter and E. E. Lawler III, *Managerial Attitudes and Performance* (Homewood, IL: Richard D. Irwin, 1968); D. F. Parker and L. Dyer, "Expectancy Theory as a Within-Person Behavioral Choice Model: An Empirical Test of Some Conceptual and Methodological Refinements," *Organizational Behavior and Human Performance*, October 1976, pp. 97–117; H. J. Arnold, "A Test of the Multiplicative Hypothesis of Expectancy-Valence Theories of Work Motivation," *Academy of Management Journal*, April 1981, pp. 128–141; and W. Van Eerde and H. Thierry, "Vroom's Expectancy Models and Work-Related Criteria: A Meta-Analysis," *Journal of Applied Psychology*, October 1996, pp. 575–586.

26 P. C. Earley, *Face, Harmony, and Social Structure: An Analysis of Organizational Behavior Across Cultures* (New York: Oxford University Press, 1997); R. M. Steers and C. Sanchez-Runde, "Culture, Motivation, and Work Behavior," in *Handbook of Cross-Cultural Management*, ed. M. Gannon and K. Newman (London: Blackwell, 2001), pp. 190–215; and H. C. Triandis, "Motivation and Achievement in Collectivist and Individualistic Cultures," in *Advances in Motivation and Achievement*, vol. 9, ed. M. Maehr and P. Pintrich (Greenwich, CT: JAI Press, 1995), pp. 1–30.

27 E. A. Locke, "Toward a Theory of Task Motivation and Incentives," *Organizational Behavior and Human Performance*, May 1968, pp. 157–189.

28 E. A. Locke, K. N. Shaw, L. M. Saari, and G. P. Latham, "Goal Setting and Task Performance: 1969–1980," *Psychological Bulletin*, July 1981, p. 126.

29 P. C. Earley, P. Wojnaroski, and W. Prest, "Task Planning and Energy Expended: Exploration of How Goals Influence Performance," *Journal of Applied Psychology*, February 1987, pp. 107–114.

30 See, for instance, S. J. Carroll and H. L. Tosi, *Management by Objectives: Applications and Research* (New York: Macmillan, 1973); and R. Rodgers and J. E. Hunter, "Impact of Management by Objectives on Organizational Productivity," *Journal of Applied Psychology*, April 1991, pp. 322–336.

31 E. A. Locke and G. P. Latham, *A Theory of Goal Setting and Task Performance* (Englewood Cliffs, NJ: Prentice Hall, 1980).

32 E. A. Locke, K. N. Shaw, L. M. Saari, and G. P. Latham, "Goal Setting and Task Performance," *Psychological Bulletin*, January 1981, pp. 125–152; and A. J. Mento, R. P. Steel, and R. J. Karren, "A Meta-Analytic Study of the Effects of Goal Setting on Task Performance: 1966–1984," *Organizational Behavior and Human Decision Processes*, February 1987, pp. 52–83.

33 R. E. Wood, A. J. Mento, and E. A. Locke, "Task Complexity as a Moderator of Goal Effects: A Meta-Analysis," *Journal of Applied Psychology*, August 1987, pp. 416–425.

34 P. M. Wright, "Operationalization of Goal Difficulty as a Moderator of the Goal Difficulty-Performance Relationship," *Journal of Applied Psychology*, June 1990, pp. 227–234; E. A. Locke and G. P. Latham, "Building a Practically Useful Theory of Goal Setting and Task Motivation: A 35-Year Odyssey," *American Psychologist* 57, no. 9 (2002), pp. 705–717.

35 P. M. Wright, J. R. Hollenbeck, S. Wolf, and G. C. McMahan, "The Effects of Varying Goal Difficulty Operationalizations on Goal Setting Outcomes and Processes," *Organizational Behavior and Human Decision Processes*, January 1995, pp. 28–43.

36 K. L. Langeland, C. M. Johnson, and T. C. Mawhinney, "Improving Staff Performance in a Community Mental Health Setting: Job Analysis, Training, Goal Setting, Feedback, and Years of Data," *Journal of Organizational Behavior Management*, 1998, pp. 21–43.

37 E. A. Locke and G. P. Latham, *A Theory of Goal Setting and Task Performance* (Englewood Cliffs, NJ: Prentice Hall, 1990).

38 J. J. Donovan and D. J. Radosevich, "The Moderating Role of Goal Commitment on the Goal Difficulty-Performance Relationship: A Meta-Analytic Review and Critical Reanalysis," *Journal of Applied Psychology*, April 1998, pp. 308–315.

39 P. M. Wright, J. M. George, S. R. Farnsworth, and G. C. McMahan, "Productivity and Extra-Role Behavior: The Effects of Goals and Incentives on Spontaneous Helping," *Journal of Applied Psychology*, October 1992, pp. 672–681.

40 S. W. Gilliland and R. S. Landis, "Quality and Quantity Goals in a Complex Decision Task: Strategies and Outcomes," *Journal of Applied Psychology*, October 1992, pp. 672–681.

41 C. Mainemelis, "When the Muse Takes It All: A Model for the Experience of Timelessness in Organizations," *Academy of Management Review* 26, no. 4 (2001), pp. 548–565.

42 Y. Fried, S. Melamed, and A. Ben-David, "The Joint Effects of Noise, Job Complexity, and Gender on Employee Sickness Absence: An Exploratory Study Across 21 Organizations—The Cordes Study," *Journal of Occupational and Organizational Psychology* 75, 2002, pp. 131–144; and R. L. Kahn and P. Byosiere, "Stress in Organizations," in *Handbook of Industrial and Organizational Psychology*, vol. 3, ed. M. D. Dunnette and L. M. Hough (Palo Alto, CA: Consulting Psychologists Press, 1992), pp. 571–650.

43 M. Csikszentmihalyi, *Flow: The Psychology of Optimal Experience,* (New York: Harper and Row, 1990); C. Mainemelis, "When the Muse Takes it All: A Model for the Experience of Timelessness in Organizations," *Academy of Management Review* 26, no. 4 (2001), pp. 548–565.

44 Based on www.profitguide.com/profit100/2005/article.asp?ID= 1328&page=3 (accessed September 10, 2005).

45 J. R. Hollenbeck, C. R. Williams, and H. J. Klein, "An Empirical Examination of the Antecedents of Commitment to Difficult Goals," *Journal of Applied Psychology,* February 1989, pp. 18–23. See also J. C. Wofford, V. L. Goodwin, and S. Premack, "Meta-Analysis of the Antecedents of Personal Goal Level and of the Antecedents and Consequences of Goal Commitment," *Journal of Management,* September 1992, pp. 595–615; and M. E. Tubbs, "Commitment as a Moderator of the Goal-Performance Relation: A Case for Clearer Construct Definition," *Journal of Applied Psychology,* February 1993, pp. 86–97.

46 A. Bandura, *Self-Efficacy: The Exercise of Control* (New York: Freeman, 1997).

47 E. A. Locke, E. Frederick, C. Lee, and P. Bobko, "Effect of Self-Efficacy, Goals, and Task Strategies on Task Performance," *Journal of Applied Psychology,* May 1984, pp. 241–251; M. E. Gist and T. R. Mitchell, "Self-Efficacy: A Theoretical Analysis of Its Determinants and Malleability," *Academy of Management Review,* April 1992, pp. 183–211; and A. D. Stajkovic and F. Luthans, "Self-Efficacy and Work-Related Performance: A Meta-Analysis," *Psychological Bulletin,* September 1998, pp. 240–261.

48 A. Bandura and D. Cervone, "Differential Engagement in Self-Reactive Influences in Cognitively-Based Motivation," *Organizational Behavior and Human Decision Processes,* August 1986, pp. 92–113.

49 See R. E. Wood, A. J. Mento, and E. A. Locke, "Task Complexity as a Moderator of Goal Effects: A Meta Analysis," *Journal of Applied Psychology,* August 1987, pp. 416–425; R. Kanfer and P. L. Ackerman, "Motivation and Cognitive Abilities: An Integrative/Aptitude-Treatment Interaction Approach to Skill Acquisition," *Journal of Applied Psychology* 74, monograph (1989), pp. 657–690; T. R. Mitchell and W. S. Silver, "Individual and Group Goals When Workers Are Interdependent: Effects on Task Strategies and Performance," *Journal of Applied Psychology,* April 1990, pp. 185–193; and A. M. O'Leary-Kelly, J. J. Martocchio, and D. D. Frink, "A Review of the Influence of Group Goals on Group Performance," *Academy of Management Journal,* October 1994, pp. 1285–1301.

50 Based on J. Morris, "QB Controversy Hits Lions," *Nelson Daily News,* August 8, 2005, p. 7; and M. Beamish, "Casey Printers Grumpy Over Contract Talk," *Nanaimo Daily News,* June 20, 2005, p. B3.

51 J. S. Adams, "Inequity in Social Exchanges," in *Advances in Experimental Social Psychology,* ed. L. Berkowitz (New York: Academic Press, 1965), pp. 267–300.

52 P. S. Goodman, "An Examination of Referents Used in the Evaluation of Pay," *Organizational Behavior and Human Performance,* October 1974, pp. 170–195; S. Ronen, "Equity Perception in Multiple Comparisons: A Field Study," *Human Relations,* April 1986, pp. 333–346; R. W. Scholl, E. A. Cooper, and J. F. McKenna, "Referent Selection in Determining Equity Perception: Differential Effects on Behavioral and Attitudinal Outcomes," *Personnel Psychology,* Spring 1987, pp. 113–127; T. P. Summers and A. S. DeNisi, "In Search of Adams' Other: Reexamination of Referents Used in the Evaluation of Pay," *Human Relations,* June 1990, pp. 497–511; S. Werner and N. P. Mero, "Fair or Foul? The Effects of External, Internal, and Employee Equity on Changes in

Performance of Major League Baseball Players," *Human Relations,* October 1999, pp. 1291–1312; and R. W. Griffeth and S. Gaertner, "A Role for Equity Theory in the Turnover Process: An Empirical Test," *Journal of Applied Social Psychology,* May 2001, pp. 1017–1037.

53 C. T. Kulik and M. L. Ambrose, "Personal and Situational Determinants of Referent Choice," *Academy of Management Review,* April 1992, pp. 212–237.

54 I. Bailey, "B.C. Women's Groups Call for Minister's Resignation," *National Post,* February 22, 2002, p. A4.

55 C. McInnes, "Strike Interrupts Empress' Historic Tea Party," *Vancouver Sun,* September 21, 1999, p. A1.

56 See, for example, E. Walster, G. W. Walster, and W. G. Scott, *Equity: Theory and Research* (Boston: Allyn and Bacon, 1978); and J. Greenberg, "Cognitive Reevaluation of Outcomes in Response to Underpayment Inequity," *Academy of Management Journal,* March 1989, pp. 174–184.

57 *OB in the Workplace* based on V. Galt, "Low Pay Stresses Staff At Non-Profits: Study," *Globe and Mail,* January 10, 2003, p. B2.

58 P. S. Goodman and A. Friedman, "An Examination of Adams' Theory of Inequity," *Administrative Science Quarterly,* September 1971, pp. 271–288; R. P. Vecchio, "An Individual-Differences Interpretation of the Conflicting Predictions Generated by Equity Theory and Expectancy Theory," *Journal of Applied Psychology,* August 1981, pp. 470–481; J. Greenberg, "Approaching Equity and Avoiding Inequity in Groups and Organizations," in *Equity and Justice in Social Behavior,* ed. J. Greenberg and R. L. Cohen (New York: Academic Press, 1982), pp. 389–435; E. W. Miles, J. D. Hatfield, and R. C. Huseman, "The Equity Sensitive Construct: Potential Implications for Worker Performance," *Journal of Management,* December 1989, pp. 581–588; R. T. Mowday, "Equity Theory Predictions of Behavior in Organizations," in *Motivation and Work Behavior,* 5th ed., ed. R. Steers and L. W. Porter (New York: McGraw-Hill, 1991), pp. 111–131; and R. T. Mowday and K. A. Colwell, "Employee Reactions to Unfair Outcomes in the Workplace: The Contributions of Adams' Equity Theory to Understanding Work Motivation," in *Motivation and Work Behavior,* 7th ed., ed. L. W. Porter, G. A. Bigley, and R. M. Steers (Burr Ridge, IL: Irwin/McGraw-Hill, 2003), pp. 65–82.

59 See, for example, K. S. Sauley and A. G. Bedeian, "Equity Sensitivity: Construction of a Measure and Examination of Its Psychometric Properties," *Journal of Management* 26, no. 5 (2000), pp. 885–910; and M. N. Bing and S. M. Burroughs, "The Predictive and Interactive Effects of Equity Sensitivity in Teamwork-Oriented Organizations," *Journal of Organizational Behavior,* May 2001, pp. 271–290.

60 J. Greenberg and S. Ornstein, "High Status Job Title as Compensation for Underpayment: A Test of Equity Theory," *Journal of Applied Psychology,* May 1983, pp. 285–297; and J. Greenberg, "Equity and Workplace Status: A Field Experiment," *Journal of Applied Psychology,* November 1988, pp. 606–613.

61 P. S. Goodman, "Social Comparison Process in Organizations," in *New Directions in Organizational Behavior,* ed. B. M. Staw and G. R. Salancik (Chicago: St. Clair, 1977), pp. 97–132; and J. Greenberg, "A Taxonomy of Organizational Justice Theories," *Academy of Management Review,* January 1987, pp. 9–22.

62 See, for instance, J. Greenberg, *The Quest for Justice on the Job* (Thousand Oaks, CA: Sage, 1996); R. Cropanzano and J. Greenberg, "Progress in Organizational Justice: Tunneling Through the Maze," in *International Review of Industrial and Organizational Psychology,* vol. 12, ed. C. L. Cooper and I. T. Robertson (New York: Wiley, 1997); and J. A. Colquitt, D. E. Conlon, M. J. Wesson, C. O. L. H. Porter, and K. Y. Ng, "Justice at the Millennium: A

Meta-Analytic Review of the 25 Years of Organizational Justice Research," *Journal of Applied Psychology,* June 2001, pp. 425–445.

63 See, for example, R. C. Dailey and D. J. Kirk, "Distributive and Procedural Justice as Antecedents of Job Dissatisfaction and Intent to Turnover," *Human Relations,* March 1992, pp. 305–316; D. B. McFarlin and P. D. Sweeney, "Distributive and Procedural Justice as Predictors of Satisfaction With Personal and Organizational Outcomes," *Academy of Management Journal,* August 1992, pp. 626–637; M. A. Korsgaard, D. M. Schweiger, and H. J. Sapienza, "Building Commitment, Attachment, and Trust in Strategic Decision-Making Teams: The Role of Procedural Justice," *Academy of Management Journal,* February 1995, pp. 60–84; M. A. Konovsky, "Understanding Procedural Justice and Its Impact on Business Organizations," *Journal of Management* 26, no. 3 (2000), pp. 489–511; and R. Cropanzano and D. E, Rupp, "An Overview of Organizational Justice: Implications for Work Motivation," in *Motivation and Work Behavior,* 7th ed. ed. L. W. Porter, G. A. Bigley, and R. M. Steers (Burr Ridge, IL: Irwin/McGraw-Hill, 2003), pp. 82–95.

64 The remainder of this paragraph based on W. Chan Kim and R. Mauborgne, "Fair Process: Managing in the Knowledge Economy," *Harvard Business Review,* July–August 1997, pp. 65–76.

65 A. S. Blinder, "Introduction," in *Paying for Productivity: A Look at the Evidence,* ed. A. S. Blinder (Washington, DC: Brookings Institution, 1990), p. 30.

66 D. P. Skarlicki and R. Folger, "Retaliation in the Workplace: The Roles of Distributive, Procedural and Interactional Justice," *Journal of Applied Psychology* 82, no. 3 (1997), pp. 434–443.

67 R. de Charms, *Personal Causation: The Internal Affective Determinants of Behavior* (New York: Academic Press, 1968).

68 E. L. Deci, *Intrinsic Motivation* (New York: Plenum, 1975); R. D. Pritchard, K. M. Campbell, and D. J. Campbell, "Effects of Extrinsic Financial Rewards on Intrinsic Motivation," *Journal of Applied Psychology,* February 1977, pp. 9–15; E. L. Deci, G. Betly, J. Kahle, L. Abrams, and J. Porac, "When Trying to Win: Competition and Intrinsic Motivation,"*Personality and Social Psychology Bulletin,* March 1981, pp. 79–83; and P. C. Jordan, "Effects of an Extrinsic Reward on Intrinsic Motivation: A Field Experiment," *Academy of Management Journal,* June 1986, pp. 405–412. See also J. M. Schrof, "Tarnished Trophies," *U.S. News & World Report,* October 25, 1993, pp. 52–59.

69 A. Kohn, *Punished by Rewards* (Boston: Houghton Mifflin, 1993).

70 J. B. Miner, *Theories of Organizational Behavior* (Hinsdale, IL: Dryden Press, 1980), p. 157; and A. Kohn, *Punished by Rewards* (Boston: Houghton Mifflin, 1993).

71 A. Kohn, *Punished by Rewards* (Boston: Houghton Mifflin, 1993).

72 B. Nelson, "Dump the Cash, Load on the Praise," *Personnel Journal* 75, July 1996, pp. 65–66.

73 J. Pfeffer, *The Human Equation: Building Profits by Putting People First* (Boston: Harvard Business School Press, 1998).

74 J. Pfeffer, *The Human Equation: Building Profits by Putting People First* (Boston: Harvard Business School Press, 1998).

75 B. J. Calder and B. M. Staw, "Self-Perception of Intrinsic and Extrinsic Motivation," *Journal of Personality and Social Psychology,* April 1975, pp. 599–605; J. Pfeffer, *The Human Equation: Building Profits by Putting People First* (Boston: Harvard Business School Press, 1998), p. 217.

76 B. M. Staw, "Motivation in Organizations: Toward Synthesis and Redirection," in *New Directions in Organizational Behavior,* ed. B. M. Staw and G. R. Salancik (Chicago: St. Clair, 1977), p. 76.

77 K. W. Thomas, E. Jansen, and W. G. Tymon Jr., "Navigating in the Realm of Theory: An Empowering View of Construct Development," in *Research in Organizational Change and Development,* vol. 10, ed. W. A. Pasmore and R. W. Woodman (Greenwich, CT: JAI Press, 1997), pp. 1–30.

78 Based on Lowell Ullrich. "'Gassers a Reminder That Penalties Hurt the Whole Team,'" *Province* (Vancouver), September 6, 2005, p. A48.

79 R. Kreitner and A. Kinicki, *Organizational Behavior,* 6th ed. (New York: McGraw-Hill, 2004), p. 345. See also J. W. Donahoe, "The Unconventional Wisdom of B F Skinner: The Analysis-Interpretation Distinction," *Journal of the Experimental Analysis of Behavior,* September 1993, pp. 453–456.

80 B. F. Skinner, *Contingencies of Reinforcement* (East Norwalk, CT: Appleton-Century-Crofts, 1971).

81 F. Luthans and R. Kreitner, *Organizational Behavior Modification and Beyond,* 2nd ed. (Glenview, IL: Scott, Foresman, 1985); and A. D. Stajkovic and F. Luthans, "A Meta-Analysis of the Effects of Organizational Behavior Modification on Task Performance, 1975–95," *Academy of Management Journal,* October 1997, pp. 1122–1149.

82 This section based on C. Michaelson, "Meaningful Motivation for Work Motivation Theory," *Academy of Management Review* 30, no. 2 (2005), pp. 235–238; and R. M. Steers, R. T. Mowday, and D. L. Shapiro, "Response to Meaningful Motivation for Work Motivation Theory," *Academy of Management Review* 30, no. 2 (2005), p. 238.

83 C. Michaelson, "Meaningful Motivation for Work Motivation Theory," *Academy of Management Review* 30, no. 2 (2005), p. 237.

84 Watson Wyatt Worldwide, "WorkUSA® 2004: An Ongoing Study of Employee Attitudes and Opinions," Watson Wyatt Worldwide, www.watsonwyatt.com/research/resrender.asp?id=ONL011&page=1 (accessed June 9, 2005).

85 V. Galt, "Job Reviews Rife With Bias: Study," *Globe and Mail,* February 27, 2002, p. C1.

86 Watson Wyatt Worldwide, "WorkUSA® 2004: An Ongoing Study of Employee Attitudes and Opinions," Watson Wyatt Worldwide, www.watsonwyatt.com/research/resrender.asp?id=ONL011&page=1 (accessed June 9, 2005).

87 C. Fletcher, "Performance Appraisal and Management: The Developing Research Agenda," *Journal of Occupational and Organizational Psychology,* November 2001, pp. 473–487. See also A. N. Kluger and A. DeNisi, "The Effects of Feedback Interventions on Performance: A Historical Review, a Meta-Analysis, and a Preliminary Feedback Intervention Theory," *Psychological Bulletin* 119, 1996, pp. 254–284.

88 S. Purba, "When Reviews Deserve a Failing Grade," *Globe and Mail,* June 11, 2004, p. C1.

89 P. M. Blau, *The Dynamics of Bureaucracy,* rev. ed. (Chicago: University of Chicago Press, 1963).

90 "The Cop-Out Cops," *National Observer,* August 3, 1974.

91 See W. C. Borman and S. J. Motowidlo, "Expanding the Criterion Domain to Include Elements of Contextual Performance," in *Personnel Selection in Organizations,* ed. N. Schmitt and W. C. Borman (San Francisco: Jossey-Bass, 1993), pp. 71–98; and W. H. Bommer, J. L. Johnson, G. A. Rich, P. M. Podsakoff, and S. B. MacKenzie, "On the Interchangeability of Objective and Subjective Measures of Employee Performance: A Meta-Analysis," *Personnel Psychology,* Autumn 1995, pp. 587–605.

92 A. H. Locher and K. S. Teel, "Appraisal Trends," *Personnel Journal,* September 1988, pp. 139–145.

93 Cited in S. Armour, "Job Reviews Take on Added Significance in Down Times," *USA Today*, July 23, 2003, p. 4B.

94 See review in R. D. Bretz Jr., G. T. Milkovich, and W. Read, "The Current State of Performance Appraisal Research and Practice: Concerns, Directions, and Implications," *Journal of Management*, June 1992, p. 326.

95 See, for instance, J. F. Milliman, R. A. Zawacki, C. Norman, L. Powell, and J. Kirksey, "Companies Evaluate Employees From All Perspectives," *Personnel Journal*, November 1994, pp. 99–103; G. Yukl and R. Lepsinger, "How to Get the Most Out of 360-Degree Feedback," *Training*, December 1995, pp. 45–50; H. Lancaster, "Performance Reviews Are More Valuable When More Join In," *Wall Street Journal*, July 9, 1996, p. B1; and D. Antonioni, "Designing an Effective 360-Degree Appraisal Feedback Process," *Organizational Dynamics*, Autumn 1996, pp. 24–38.

96 D. V. Day, "Leadership Development: A Review in Context," *Leadership Quarterly*, Winter 2000, pp. 587–589.

97 P. W. B. Atkins and R. E. Wood, "Self Versus Others' Ratings as Predictors of Assessment Center Ratings: Validation Evidence for 360-Degree Feedback Programs," *Personnel Psychology*, Winter 2002, pp. 871–904; B. Pfau, I. Kay, K. M. Nowack, and J. Ghorpade, "Does 360-Degree Feedback Negatively Affect Company Performance?" *HR Magazine*, June 2002, pp. 54–59.

98 D. A. Waldman, L. E. Atwater, and D. Antonioni, "Has 360 Degree Feedback Gone Amok?" *Academy of Management Executive* 12, no. 2 (1998), pp. 86–94.

99 C. L. Facteau, J. D. Facteau, L. C. Schoel, J. E. A. Russell, and M. L Poteet, "Reactions of Leaders to 360-Degree Feedback From Subordinates and Peers," *Leadership Quarterly* 9, no. 4 (1998), pp. 427–448.

100 M. A. Peiperl, "Getting 360° Feedback Right," *Harvard Business Review*, January 2001, 142–147.

101 M. Debrayen and S. Brutus, "Learning From Others' 360-Degree Experiences," *Canadian HR Reporter*, February 10, 2003, pp. 18–19.

102 www.profitguide.com/profit100/2005/article.asp?ID=1332&page=2 (accessed September 10, 2005).

103 M. Johne, "It's Good PR to Keep Employees Loyal," *Globe and Mail*, September 20, 2002, p. C1.

104 "Ivy League Grade Inflation," *USA Today*, February 8, 2002, p. 11A.

105 R. D. Bretz Jr., G. T. Milkovich, and W. Read, "The Current State of Performance Appraisal Research and Practice: Concerns, Directions, and Implications," *Journal of Management*, June 1992, p. 333. See also J. S. Kanne, H. J. Bernardin, P. Villanova, and J. Peyrefitte, "Stability of Rater Leniency: Three Studies," *Academy of Management Journal*, August 1995, pp. 1036–1051.

106 For a review of the role of halo effect in performance evaluation, see W. K. Balzer and L. M. Sulsky, "Halo and Performance Appraisal Research: A Critical Evaluation," *Journal of Applied Psychology*, December 1992, pp. 975–985.

107 See T. A. Judge and G. R. Ferris, "Social Context of Performance Evaluation Decisions," *Academy of Management Journal*, February 1993, pp. 80–105.

108 A. Pizam, "Social Differentiation—A New Psychological Barrier to Performance Appraisal," *Public Personnel Management*, July–August 1975, pp. 244–247.

109 A. Pizam, "Social Differentiation—A New Psychological Barrier to Performance Appraisal," *Public Personnel Management*, July–August 1975, pp. 245–247.

110 See D. J. Woehr and J. Feldman, "Processing Objective and Question Order Effects on the Causal Relation Between Memory and Judgment in Performance Appraisal: The Tip of the Iceberg," *Journal of Applied Psychology*, April 1993, pp. 232–241.

111 J. Lefkowitz, "The Role of Interpersonal Affective Regard in Supervisory Performance Ratings: A Literature Review and Proposed Causal Model," *Journal of Occupational and Organizational Psychology* 73, 2000, pp. 67–85.

112 See, for example, W. M. Fox, "Improving Performance Appraisal Systems," *National Productivity Review*, Winter 1987–1988, pp. 20–27.

113 A. Varma, A. S. DeNisi, and L. H. Peters, "Interpersonal Affect and Performance Appraisal: A Field Study," *Personnel Psychology* 49, 1996, pp. 341–360.

114 See J. Greenberg, "Determinants of Perceived Fairness of Performance Evaluations," *Journal of Applied Psychology*, May 1986, pp. 340–342; and B. P. Maroney and M. R. Buckley, "Does Research in Performance Appraisal Influence the Practice of Performance Appraisal? Regretfully Not!" *Public Personnel Management*, Summer 1992, pp. 185–196.

115 W. C. Borman, "The Rating of Individuals in Organizations: An Alternate Approach," *Organizational Behavior and Human Performance*, August 1974, pp. 105–124.

116 See, for instance, D. E. Smith, "Training Programs for Performance Appraisal: A Review," *Academy of Management Review*, January 1986, pp. 22–40; D. C. Martin and K. Bartol, "Training the Raters: A Key to Effective Performance Appraisal," *Public Personnel Management*, Summer 1986, pp. 101–109; and T. R. Athey and R. M. McIntyre, "Effect of Rater Training on Rater Accuracy: Levels-of-Processing Theory and Social Facilitation Theory Perspectives," *Journal of Applied Psychology*, November 1987, pp. 567–572.

117 H. J. Bernardin, "The Effects of Rater Training on Leniency and Halo Errors in Student Rating of Instructors," *Journal of Applied Psychology*, June 1978, pp. 301–308.

118 H. J. Bernardin, "The Effects of Rater Training on Leniency and Halo Errors in Student Rating of Instructors," *Journal of Applied Psychology*, June 1978, pp. 301–308; and J. M. Ivancevich, "Longitudinal Study of the Effects of Rater Training on Psychometric Error in Ratings," *Journal of Applied Psychology*, October 1979, pp. 502–508.

119 M. S. Taylor, K. B. Tracy, M. K. Renard, J. K. Harrison, and S. J. Carroll, "Due Process in Performance Appraisal: A Quasi-Experiment in Procedural Justice," *Administrative Science Quarterly*, September 1995, pp. 495–523.

Chapter 5

1 Opening vignette based on S. Baille-Ruder, "Sweet Devotion: How Chocolatier R.C. Purdy Developed the Perfect Recipe for a Superstar Workforce," *PROFIT*, December 2004, pp. 44–51; L. Pratt, "Management Tip From the Top," *National Post*, July 26, 2004. p. FP9; B. Constantineau, "Staff Discounts Can Make a Good Employer Great," *Vancouver Sun*, July 16, 2005, p. A1; and www.purdys.com/employer.htm.

2 D. W. Krueger, "Money, Success, and Success Phobia," in *The Last Taboo: Money as a Symbol and Reality in Psychotherapy and Psychoanalysis*, ed. D. W. Krueger (New York: Brunner/Mazel, 1986), pp. 3–16.

3 T. R. Mitchell and A. E. Mickel, "The Meaning of Money: An Individual-Difference Perspective," *Academy of Management*, July 1999, pp. 568–578.

4 Information in this paragraph based on D. Grigg and J. Newman, "Labour Researchers Define Job Satisfaction," *Vancouver Sun*, February 16, 2002, p. E2.

5 This paragraph is based on T. R. Mitchell and A. E. Mickel, "The Meaning of Money: An Individual-Difference Perspective," *Academy of Management*, July 1999, pp. 568–578. The reader may want to refer to the myriad of references cited in the article.

6 Based on S. Baille-Ruder, "Sweet Devotion: How Chocolatier R.C. Purdy Developed the Perfect Recipe for a Superstar Workforce," *PROFIT*, December 2004, pp. 44–51.

7 Our definition of a formal recognition system is based on S. E. Markham, K. D. Scott, and G. H. McKee, "Recognizing Good Attendance: A Longitudinal, Quasi-Experimental Field Study," *Personnel Psychology*, Autumn 2002, p. 641.

8 D. Drickhamer, "Best Plant Winners: Nichols Foods Ltd.," *IndustryWeek*, October 1, 2001, pp. 17–19.

9 M. Littman, "Best Bosses Tell All," *Working Woman*, October 2000, p. 54.

10 Cited in S. Caudron, "The Top 20 Ways to Motivate Employees," *IndustryWeek*, April 3, 1995, pp. 15–16. See also B. Nelson, "Try Praise," *Inc.*, September 1996, p. 115.

11 S. Glasscock and K. Gram, *Workplace Recognition: Step-by-Step Examples of a Positive Reinforcement Strategy* (London: Brasseys, 1999).

12 Hewitt Associates, "Employers Willing to Pay for High Performance," news release, September 8, 2004, http://was4.hewitt.com/hewitt/resource/newsroom/pressrel/2004/09-08-04eng.htm (accessed October 9, 2004).

13 "Praise Beats Raise as Best Motivator, Survey Shows," *Vancouver Sun*, September 10, 1994.

14 Based on S. E. Gross and J. P. Bacher, "The New Variable Pay Programs: How Some Succeed, Why Some Don't," *Compensation & Benefits Review*, January–February 1993, p. 51; and J. R. Schuster and P. K. Zingheim, "The New Variable Pay: Key Design Issues," *Compensation & Benefits Review*, March–April 1993, p. 28.

15 Hewitt Associates, "Employers Willing to Pay for High Performance," news release, September 8, 2004, http://was4.hewitt.com/hewitt/resource/newsroom/pressrel/2004/09-08-04eng.htm (accessed October 9, 2004); and Peter Brieger, "Variable Pay Packages Gain Favour: Signing Bonuses, Profit Sharing Taking Place of Salary Hikes," *Financial Post (National Post)*, September 13, 2002, p. FP5.

16 E. Beauchesne, "Pay Bonuses Improve Productivity, Study Shows," *Vancouver Sun*, September 13, 2002, p. D5.

17 J. Smilko and K. Van Neck, "Rewarding Excellence Through Variable Pay," *Benefits Quarterly* 20, no. 3 (Third Quarter 2004), pp. 21–25.

18 "More Than 20 Percent of Japanese Firms Use Pay Systems Based on Performance," *Manpower Argus*, May 1998, p. 7; and "Bonus Pay in Canada," *Manpower Argus*, September 1996, p. 5.

19 O. Bertin, "Is There Any Merit in Giving Merit Pay?" *Globe and Mail*, January 31, 2003, pp. C1, C7.

20 O. Bertin, "Is There Any Merit in Giving Merit Pay?" *Globe and Mail*, January 31, 2003, pp. C1, C7.

21 S. Baille-Ruder, "Sweet Devotion: How Chocolatier R.C. Purdy Developed the Perfect Recipe for a Superstar Workforce," *PROFIT*, December 2004, pp. 44–51.

22 "Bonus Pay in Canada," *Manpower Argus*, September 1996, p. 5.

23 "Risk and Reward: More Canadian Companies Are Experimenting With Variable Pay," *Maclean's*, January 8, 1996, pp. 26–27.

24 C. Mandel, "Cash by the Numbers: The Vogue for 'Performance Incentives' Spreads to Primary Schools," *Alberta Report*, March 29, 1999, p. 33.

25 K. May, "New Pay Scheme Intended to Help Retain Canada's Top Bureaucrats," *Vancouver Sun*, August 3, 1999, p. A5.

26 K. Eichenwald, "Bonuses Seen as Enron Motive," *National Post*, pp. A1, A11.

27 See, for instance, S. C. Hanlon, D. G. Meyer, and R. R. Taylor, "Consequences of Gainsharing," *Group & Organization Management*, March 1994, pp. 87–111; J. G. Belcher Jr., "Gainsharing and Variable Pay: The State of the Art," *Compensation & Benefits Review*, May–June 1994, pp. 50–60; and T. M. Welbourne and L. R. Gomez Mejia, "Gainsharing: A Critical Review and a Future Research Agenda," *Journal of Management* 21, no. 3 (1995), pp. 559–609.

28 D. Beck, "Implementing a Gainsharing Plan: What Companies Need to Know," *Compensation & Benefits Review*, January–February 1992, p. 23.

29 W. Imberman, "Gainsharing Is a Concept Canadians Should Embrace," *Business in Vancouver*, March 20–26, 2001, p. 19.

30 T. M. Welbourne and L. R. Gomez-Mejia, "Gainsharing: A Critical Review and a Future Research Agenda," *Journal of Management* 21, no. 3 (1995), pp. 559–609.

31 M. Byfield, "Ikea's Boss Gives Away the Store for a Day," *Report Newsmagazine*, October 25, 1999, p. 47.

32 S. Baille-Ruder, "Sweet Devotion: How Chocolatier R.C. Purdy Developed the Perfect Recipe for a Superstar Workforce," *PROFIT*, December 2004, pp. 44–51.

33 K. Cox, "Power Struggle Cost FPI Millions," *Globe and Mail*, February 21, 2002, p. B3.

34 R. J. Long, "Patterns of Workplace Innovations in Canada," *Relations Industrielles* 44, no. 4 (1989), pp. 805–826; R. J. Long, "Motives for Profit Sharing: A Study of Canadian Chief Executive Officers," *Relations Industrielles* 52, no. 4 (1997), pp. 712–723; T. H. Wagar and R. J. Long, "Profit Sharing in Canada: Incidences and Predictors," *Proceedings of the Administrative Sciences Association of Canada (Human Resources Division)*, 1995, pp. 97–105.

35 See K. M. Young, ed., *The Expanding Role of ESOPs in Public Companies* (New York: Quorum, 1990); J. L. Pierce and C. A. Furo, "Employee Ownership: Implications for Management," *Organizational Dynamics*, Winter 1990, pp. 32–43; J. Blasi and D. L. Druse, *The New Owners: The Mass Emergence of Employee Ownership in Public Companies and What It Means to American Business* (Champaign, IL: Harper Business, 1991); F. T. Adams and G. B. Hansen, *Putting Democracy to Work: A Practical Guide for Starting and Managing Worker-Owned Businesses* (San Francisco: Berrett-Koehler, 1993); and A. A. Buchko, "The Effects of Employee Ownership on Employee Attitudes: An Integrated Causal Model and Path Analysis," *Journal of Management Studies*, July 1993, pp. 633–656.

36 A. Toulin, "Lowly Staff Join Bosses in Receiving Stock Options," *National Post*, March 1, 2001, pp. C1, C12.

37 A. A. Buchko, "The Effects of Employee Ownership on Employee Attitudes: An Integrated Causal Model and Path Analysis," *Journal of Management Studies*, July 1993, pp. 633–656.

38 C. M. Rosen and M. Quarrey, "How Well Is Employee Ownership Working?" *Harvard Business Review*, September–October 1987, pp. 126–132.

39 W. N. Davidson and D. L. Worrell, "ESOP's Fables: The Influence of Employee Stock Ownership Plans on Corporate Stock Prices

and Subsequent Operating Performance," *Human Resource Planning*, 1994 pp. 69–85.

40 J. L. Pierce and C. A. Furo, "Employee Ownership: Implications for Management," *Organizational Dynamics*, Winter 1990, pp. 32–43; and S. Kaufman, "ESOPs' Appeal on the Increase," *Nation's Business*, June 1997, p. 43.

41 See data in D. Stamps, "A Piece of the Action," *Training*, March 1996, p. 66.

42 E. Church, "Benefits of Being Worker and Boss," *Globe and Mail*, February 22, 2002, p. C1.

43 J. McFarland, "The Hidden Costs of Stock Options," *Globe and Mail*, July 10, 2002, pp. B1, B5.

44 E. Beauchesne, "Pay Bonuses Improve Productivity, Study Shows," *Vancouver Sun*, September 13, 2002, p. D5.

45 J. Pfeffer and N. Langton, "The Effects of Wage Dispersion on Satisfaction, Productivity, and Working Collaboratively: Evidence From College and University Faculty," *Administrative Science Quarterly* 38, no. 3 (1983), pp. 382–407.

46 "Risk and Reward: More Canadian Companies Are Experimenting With Variable Pay," *Maclean's*, January 8, 1996, pp. 26–27.

47 "Hope for Higher Pay: The Squeeze on Incomes Is Gradually Easing Up," *Maclean's*, November 25, 1996, pp. 100–101.

48 "Risk and Reward: More Canadian Companies Are Experimenting With Variable Pay," *Maclean's*, January 8, 1996, pp. 26–27.

49 Box based on V. Galt, "No More Freebies for Hydro Staff: Arbitrator," *Globe and Mail*, February 16, 2002, p. B3.

50 B. E. Wright, "Work Motivation in the Public Sector," *Academy of Management Proceedings*, 2001, pp. PNP: D1–5.

51 B. E. Wright, "Work Motivation in the Public Sector," *Academy of Management Proceedings*, 2001, pp. PNP: D1–5.

52 S. Greenhouse, "Suits Say Wal-Mart Forces Workers to Toil Off the Clock," *New York Times*, June 25, 2002, www.nytimes.com/2002/06/25/national/25WALM.html?pagewanted=1 (accessed June 25, 2002).

53 M. Fein, "Work Measurement and Wage Incentives," *Industrial Engineering*, September 1973, pp. 49–51. For an updated review of the effect of pay on performance, see G. D. Jenkins Jr., N. Gupta, A. Mitra, and J. D. Shaw, "Are Financial Incentives Related to Performance? A Meta-Analytic Review of Empirical Research," *Journal of Applied Psychology*, October 1998, pp. 777–787.

54 C. G. Hanson and W. D. Bell, *Profit Sharing and Profitability: How Profit Sharing Promotes Business Success* (London: Kogan Page, 1987); M. Magnan and S. St-Onge, "Profit Sharing and Firm Performance: A Comparative and Longitudinal Analysis" (paper presented at the 58th Annual Meeting of the Academy of Management, San Diego, CA, August 1998); E. M. Doherty, W. R. Nord, and J. L. McAdams, "Gainsharing and Organizational Development: A Productive Synergy," *Journal of Applied Behavioral Science*, August 1989, pp. 209–230; and T. C. McGrath, "How Three Screw Machine Companies Are Tapping Human Productivity Through Gainsharing," *Employment Relations Today* 20, no. 4 (1994), pp. 437–447.

55 S. Kerr, "Practical, Cost-Neutral Alternatives That You May Know, But Don't Practice," *Organizational Dynamics* 28, no. 1 (1999), pp. 61–70; E. E. Lawler, *Strategic Pay* (San Francisco: Jossey-Bass, 1990); and J. Pfeffer, *The Human Equation: Building Profits by Putting People First* (Boston: Harvard Business School Press, 1998).

56 A. D. Stajkovic and F. Luthans, "Differential Effects of Incentive Motivators on Work Performance," *Academy of Management Journal*, June 2001, pp. 580–590.

57 E. Beauchesne, "Pay Bonuses Improve Productivity, Study Shows," *Vancouver Sun*, September 13, 2002, p. D5.

58 P. K. Zingheim and J. R. Schuster, "Introduction: How Are the New Pay Tools Being Deployed?" *Compensation & Benefits Review*, July–August 1995, pp. 10–11.

59 *OB in the Street* based on "In Pursuit of Level Playing Fields," *Globe and Mail*, March 9, 2002, p. S1.

60 J. A. Ross, "Japan: Does Money Motivate?" *Harvard Business Review*, September–October 1997. See also R. Bruce Money and John L. Graham, "Salesperson Performance, Pay, and Job Satisfaction: Tests of a Model Using Data Collected in the U.S. and Japan" (working paper, University of South Carolina, 1997).

61 D. H. B. Welsh, F. Luthans, and S. M. Sommer, "Managing Russian Factory Workers: The Impact of U.S.-Based Behavioral and Participative Techniques," *Academy of Management Journal* 36, no. 1 (1993), pp. 58–79.

62 S. K. Saha, "Managing Human Resources: China vs. the West," *Canadian Journal of Administrative Sciences* 10, no. 2 (1998), pp. 167–177; Chao C. Chen, "New Trends in Reward Allocation Preference: A Sino/U.S. Comparison," *Academy of Management Journal* 38, no. 2 (1995), pp. 408–492.

63 N. Chowdhury, "Dell Cracks China," *Fortune*, June 21, 1999, pp. 120–124.

64 M. E. de Forest, "Thinking of a Plant in Mexico?" *Academy of Management Executive* 8, no. 1 (1994), pp. 33–40.

65 R. S. Schuler and N. Rogovsky, "Understanding Compensation Practice Variations Across Firms: The Impact of National Culture," *Journal of International Business Studies* 29, no. 1 (First Quarter 1998), pp. 159–177.

66 N. J. Adler, *International Dimensions of Organizational Behavior*, 4th ed. (Cincinnati, OH: South Western College, 2002), p. 174.

67 A. Kohn, *Punished by Rewards* (Boston: Houghton Mifflin, 1993).

68 W. G. Ouchi, *Theory Z* (New York: Avon Books, 1982); "Bosses' Pay," *Economist*, February 1, 1992, pp. 19–22; W. Edwards Deming, *Out of the Crisis* (Cambridge, MA: MIT Center for Advanced Engineering Study, 1986).

69 J. Pfeffer, *The Human Equation: Building Profits by Putting People First* (Boston: Harvard Business School Press, 1998).

70 G. Hofstede, "Motivation, Leadership, and Organization: Do American Theories Apply Abroad?" *Organizational Dynamics*, Summer 1980, p. 55.

71 J. K. Giacobbe-Miller, D. J. Miller, and V. I. Victorov, "A Comparison of Russian and U.S. Pay Allocation Decisions, Distributive Justice Judgments, and Productivity Under Different Payment Conditions," *Personnel Psychology*, Spring 1998, pp. 137–163.

72 S. L. Mueller and L. D. Clarke, "Political-Economic Context and Sensitivity to Equity: Differences Between the United States and the Transition Economies of Central and Eastern Europe," *Academy of Management Journal*, June 1998, pp. 319–329.

73 H. Munro, "Transit Drivers Taking Fewer Sick Days," *Vancouver Sun*, June 2, 1999, p. B3.

74 V. Sanderson, "Sweetening Their Slice: More Hardware and Lumberyard Dealers Are Investing in Profit-Sharing Programs as a Way to Promote Employee Loyalty," *Hardware Merchandising*, May–June 2003, p. 66.

75 Story based on M. Gorelkin, "Sowing Seeds of Discontent Back in the U.S.S.R," *Vancouver Sun*, June 9, 1990, pp. D3–4.

76 S. Kerr, "On the Folly of Rewarding A, While Hoping for B," *Academy of Management Executive* 9, no. 1 (1995), pp. 7–14.

77 "More on the Folly," *Academy of Management Executive* 9, no. 1 (1995), pp. 15–16.

78 Based on S. Baille-Ruder, "Sweet Devotion: How Chocolatier R.C. Purdy Developed the Perfect Recipe for a Superstar Workforce," *PROFIT*, December 2004, pp. 44–51.

79 A. Kohn, *Punished by Rewards* (Boston: Houghton Mifflin, 1993), p. 181.

80 A. Kohn, *Punished by Rewards* (Boston: Houghton Mifflin, 1993), p. 181.

81 A. Kohn, *Punished by Rewards* (Boston: Houghton Mifflin, 1993), p. 186; see also Peter R. Scholtes, "An Elaboration of Deming's Teachings on Performance Appraisal," in *Performance Appraisal: Perspectives on a Quality Management Approach*, ed. Gary N. McLean, Susan R. Damme, and Richard A. Swanson (Alexandria, VA: American Society for Training and Development, 1990); H. H. Meyer, E. Kay, and J. R. P. French Jr., "Split Roles in Performance Appraisal," *Harvard Business Review*, 1965, excerpts reprinted in "HBR Retrospect," *Harvard Business Review*, January–February 1989, p. 26; W.-U. Meyer, M. Bachmann, U. Biermann, M. Hempelmann, F.-O. Ploeger, and H. Spiller, "The Informational Value of Evaluative Behavior: Influences of Praise and Blame on Perceptions of Ability," *Journal of Educational Psychology* 71, 1979, pp. 259–268; and A. Halachmi and M. Holzer, "Merit Pay, Performance Targeting, and Productivity," *Review of Public Personnel Administration* 7, 1987, pp. 80–91.

82 A. S. Blinder, "Introduction," in *Paying for Productivity: A Look at the Evidence*, ed. A. S. Blinder (Washington, DC: Brookings Institution, 1990).

83 A. Kohn, *Punished by Rewards* (Boston: Houghton Mifflin, 1993), p. 187.

84 D. Tjosvold, *Working Together to Get Things Done: Managing for Organizational Productivity* (Lexington, MA: Lexington Books, 1986); P. R. Scholtes, *The Team Handbook: How to Use Teams to Improve Quality* (Madison, WI: Joiner Associates, 1988); A. Kohn, *No Contest: The Case Against Competition*, rev. ed. (Boston: Houghton Mifflin, 1992).

85 E. L. Deci, "Applications of Research on the Effects of Rewards," in *The Hidden Costs of Rewards: New Perspectives on the Psychology of Human Motivation*, ed. M. R. Lepper and D. Green (Hillsdale, NJ: Erlbaum, 1978).

86 S. E. Perry, *San Francisco Scavengers: Dirty Work and the Pride of Ownership* (Berkeley: University of California Press, 1978).

87 A. Kohn, *Punished by Rewards* (Boston: Houghton Mifflin, 1993), p. 192.

88 T. H. Naylor, "Redefining Corporate Motivation, Swedish Style," *Christian Century*, May 30–June 6, 1990, pp. 566–570; R. A. Karasek, T. Thorell, J. E. Schwartz, P. L. Schnall, C. F. Pieper, and J. L. Michela, "Job Characteristics in Relation to the Prevalence of Myocardial Infarction in the US Health Examination Survey (HES) and the Health and Nutrition Examination Survey (HANES)," *American Journal of Public Health* 78, 1988, pp. 910–916; D. P. Levin, "Toyota Plant in Kentucky Is Font of Ideas for the U.S.," *New York Times*, May 5, 1992, pp. A1, D8.

89 M. Bosquet, "The Prison Factory," reprinted from *Le Nouvel Observateur* in *Working Papers for a New Society*, Spring 1973, pp. 20–27; J. Holusha, "Grace Pastiak's 'Web of Inclusion,'" *New York Times*, May 5, 1991, pp. F1, F6; J. Simmons and W. Mares, *Working Together: Employee Participation in Action* (New York: New York University Press, 1985); D. I. Levine and L. D'Andrea Tyson, "Participation, Productivity, and the Firm's Environment," in *Paying for Productivity: A Look at the Evidence*, ed. A. S. Blinder (Washington, DC: Brookings Institution, 1990); and W. F. Whyte,

"Worker Participation: International and Historical Perspectives," *Journal of Applied Behavioral Science* 19, 1983, pp. 395–407.

90 Based on S. Baille-Ruder, "Sweet Devotion: How Chocolatier R.C. Purdy Developed the Perfect Recipe for a Superstar Workforce," *PROFIT*, December 2004, pp. 44–51.

91 J. E. Rigdon, "Using Lateral Moves to Spur Employees," *Wall Street Journal*, May 26, 1992, p. B1.

92 S. Ross, "New Ideas Take 'Grunt' From Assembly Lines: Worker Participation Eliminates All-Too-Common Waste of 'Human Ingenuity,'" *Vancouver Sun*, September 1, 2001, p. E1.

93 N. Leckie, A. Léonard, J. Turcotte, and D. Wallace, *Employer and Employee Perspectives on Human Resource Practices*, 71–584–MIE no. 1 (Ottawa: Ministry of Industry, 2001).

94 See, for instance, data on job enlargement described in M. A. Campion and C. L. McClelland, "Follow-up and Extension of the Interdisciplinary Costs and Benefits of Enlarged Jobs," *Journal of Applied Psychology*, June 1993, pp. 339–351.

95 B. Livesey, "Glitch Doctor," *Report on Business Magazine*, November 1997, pp. 97–102.

96 W. Karl, "Bombardier Reaches Lofty Heights: The Challenge Now Is Maintaining Cruise Altitude," *Plant*, August 11, 1997, pp. 1, 12 ff.

97 J. R. Hackman and G. R. Oldham, "Motivation Through the Design of Work: Test of a Theory," *Organizational Behavior and Human Performance*, August 1976, pp. 250–279.

98 J. R. Hackman and G. R. Oldham, *Work Redesign* (Reading, MA: Addison Wesley, 1980).

99 J. R. Hackman, "Work Design," in *Improving Life at Work*, ed. J. R. Hackman and J. L. Suttle (Santa Monica, CA: Goodyear, 1977), pp. 132–133.

100 J. R. Hackman, "Work Design," in *Improving Life at Work*, ed. J. R. Hackman and J. L. Suttle (Santa Monica, CA: Goodyear, 1977), p. 129.

101 D. A. Light, "Human Resources: Recruiting Generation 2001," *Harvard Business Review*, July–August 1998, pp. 13–16.

102 See "Job Characteristics Theory of Work Redesign," in *Theories of Organizational Behavior*, ed. J. B. Miner (Hinsdale, IL: Dryden Press, 1980), pp. 231–266; B. T. Loher, R. A. Noe, N. L. Moeller, and M. P. Fitzgerald, "A Meta-Analysis of the Relation of Job Characteristics to Job Satisfaction," *Journal of Applied Psychology*, May 1985, pp. 280–289; W. H. Glick, G. D. Jenkins Jr., and N. Gupta, "Method Versus Substance: How Strong Are Underlying Relationships Between Job Characteristics and Attitudinal Outcomes?" *Academy of Management Journal*, September 1986, pp. 441–464; Y. Fried and G. R. Ferris, "The Validity of the Job Characteristics Model: A Review and Meta-Analysis," *Personnel Psychology*, Summer 1987, pp. 287–322; S. J. Zaccaro and E. F. Stone, "Incremental Validity of an Empirically Based Measure of Job Characteristics," *Journal of Applied Psychology*, May 1988, pp. 245–252; R. W. Renn and R. J. Vandenberg, "The Critical Psychological States: An Underrepresented Component in Job Characteristics Model Research," *Journal of Management* 21, no. 2 (1995), pp. 279–303; and J. R. Rentsch and R. P. Steel, "Testing the Durability of Job Characteristics as Predictors of Absenteeism Over a Six-Year Period," *Personnel Psychology*, Spring 1998, pp. 165–190.

103 See R. B. Dunham, "Measurement and Dimensionality of Job Characteristics," *Journal of Applied Psychology*, August 1976, pp. 404–409; J. L. Pierce and R. B. Dunham, "Task Design: A Literature Review," *Academy of Management Review*, January 1976, pp. 83–97; D. M. Rousseau, "Technological Differences in Job

Characteristics, Employee Satisfaction, and Motivation: A Synthesis of Job Design Research and Sociotechnical Systems Theory," *Organizational Behavior and Human Performance*, October 1977, pp. 18–42; and Y. Fried and G. R. Ferris, "The Dimensionality of Job Characteristics: Some Neglected Issues," *Journal of Applied Psychology*, August 1986, pp. 419–426.

104 Y. Fried and G. R. Ferris, "The Dimensionality of Job Characteristics: Some Neglected Issues," *Journal of Applied Psychology*, August 1986, pp. 419–426.

105 See, for instance, Y. Fried and G. R. Ferris, "The Dimensionality of Job Characteristics: Some Neglected Issues," *Journal of Applied Psychology*, August 1986, pp. 419–426; and M. G. Evans and D. A. Ondrack, "The Motivational Potential of Jobs: Is a Multiplicative Model Really Necessary?" in *Organizational Behavior*, ed. S. L. McShane, ASAC Conference Proceedings, vol. 9, part 5, Halifax, 1988, pp. 31–39.

106 R. B. Tiegs, L. E. Tetrick, and Y. Fried, "Growth Need Strength and Context Satisfactions as Moderators of the Relations of the Job Characteristics Model," *Journal of Management*, September 1992, pp. 575–593.

107 C. A. O'Reilly and D. F. Caldwell, "Informational Influence as a Determinant of Perceived Task Characteristics and Job Satisfaction," *Journal of Applied Psychology*, April 1979, pp. 157–165; R. V. Montagno, "The Effects of Comparison Others and Prior Experience on Responses to Task Design," *Academy of Management Journal*, June 1985, pp. 491–498; and P. C. Bottger and I. K.-H. Chew, "The Job Characteristics Model and Growth Satisfaction: Main Effects of Assimilation of Work Experience and Context Satisfaction," *Human Relations*, June 1986, pp. 575–594.

108 J. R. Hackman, "Work Design," in *Improving Life at Work*, ed. J. R. Hackman and J. L. Suttle (Santa Monica, CA: Goodyear, 1977), pp. 132–133.

109 Cited in *U.S. News & World Report*, May 31, 1993, p. 63.

110 See, for example, J. R. Hackman and G. R. Oldham, *Work Redesign* (Reading, MA: Addison Wesley, 1980); J. B. Miner, *Theories of Organizational Behavior* (Hinsdale, IL: Dryden Press, 1980), pp. 231–266; R. W. Griffin, "Effects of Work Redesign on Employee Perceptions, Attitudes, and Behaviors: A Long-Term Investigation," *Academy of Management Journal*, June 1991, pp. 425–435; and J. L. Cotton, *Employee Involvement* (Newbury Park, CA: Sage, 1993), pp. 141–172.

111 F. Pomeroy, "Workplace Change: A Union Perspective," *Canadian Business Review* 22, no. 2 (1995), pp. 17–19.

112 M. Kane, "Flexwork Finds More Favour," *Vancouver Sun*, May 15, 1998, pp. F1, F2.

113 "Fewer Workers Had Jobs in June but They Made Slightly More Money," *Canadian Press Newswire*, August 29, 1996.

114 M. Kane, "Flexwork Finds More Favour," *Vancouver Sun*, May 15, 1998, pp. F1, F2.

115 L. Rubis, "Fourth of Full-Timers Enjoy Flexible Hours," *HR Magazine*, June 1998, pp. 26–28.

116 L. Rubis, "Fourth of Full-Timers Enjoy Flexible Hours," *HR Magazine*, June 1998, pp. 26–28.

117 M. Kane, "Flexwork Finds More Favour," *Vancouver Sun*, May 15, 1998, pp. F1, F2; M. Gibb-Clark, "Royal Bank Scores With Flexible Work Programs," *Globe and Mail*, May 15, 1998, p. B23.

118 See, for example, D. A. Ralston and M. F. Flanagan, "The Effect of Flextime on Absenteeism and Turnover for Male and Female Employees," *Journal of Vocational Behavior*, April 1985, pp. 206–217; D. A. Ralston, W. P. Anthony, and D. J. Gustafson, "Employees May Love Flextime, but What Does It Do to the Organization's Productivity?" *Journal of Applied Psychology*, May 1985, pp. 272–279; J. B. McGuire and J. R. Liro, "Flexible Work Schedules, Work Attitudes, and Perceptions of Productivity," *Public Personnel Management*, Spring 1986, pp. 65–73; P. Bernstein, "The Ultimate in Flextime: From Sweden, by Way of Volvo," *Personnel*, June 1988, pp. 70–74; and D. R. Dalton and D. J. Mesch, "The Impact of Flexible Scheduling on Employee Attendance and Turnover," *Administrative Science Quarterly*, June 1990, pp. 370–387.

119 D. Keevil, *The Flexible Workplace Study: Asking the Experts About Flexible Policies and Workplace Performance* (Halifax: Halifax YWCA in cooperation with Status of Women Canada, 1996).

120 L. Duxbury and G. Haines, "Predicting Alternative Work Arrangements From Salient Attitudes: A Study of Decision Makers in the Public Sector," *Journal of Business Research*, August 1991, pp. 83–97.

121 J. E. Fast and J. A. Frederick, "Working Arrangements and Time Stress," *Canadian Social Trends*, Winter 1996, pp. 14–19.

122 S. Shellenbarger, "Two People, One Job: It Can Really Work," *Wall Street Journal*, December 7, 1994, p. B1.

123 "Telecommuting in Europe," *Manpower Argus*, April 1997, p. 9.

124 S. Shellenbarger, "Two People, One Job: It Can Really Work," *Wall Street Journal*, December 7, 1994, p. B1.

125 D. Hodges, "New Nunavut: Canada's Newest Territory Faces the Daunting Task of Creating a New Health Bureaucracy While Dealing With Traditional Recruitment Problems in the Arctic," *Medical Post*, November 13, 2001, p. 31.

126 See, for example, T. H. Davenport and K. Pearlson, "Two Cheers for the Virtual Office," *Sloan Management Review*, Summer 1998, pp. 61–65; E. J. Hill, B. C. Miller, S. P. Weiner, and J. Colihan, "Influences of the Virtual Office on Aspects of Work and Work/Life Balance," *Personnel Psychology*, Autumn 1998, pp. 667–683; and K. E. Pearlson and C. S. Saunders, "There's No Place Like Home: Managing Telecommuting Paradoxes," *Academy of Management Executive*, May 2001, pp. 117–128; and S. J. Wells, "Making Telecommuting Work," *HR Magazine*, October 2001, pp. 34–45.

127 S. Mingail, "Computing Telework's Trade-offs," *Financial Post (National Post)*, August 9, 1999, p. C8.

128 D. Bruser, "Working at Home: Mistrust Still Rules; Cultural Barrier Holds Firms Back," *Toronto Star*, May 18, 2005, p. C01.

129 A. Joyce, "Telework a Productive Part of Many Companies," *Ottawa Citizen*, August 27, 2005, p. D12; and C. Said, "Work Is Where You Hang Your Coat," *National Post*, July 20, 2005, p. FP11.

130 J. Cote-O'Hara, "Sending Them Home to Work: Telecommuting," *Business Quarterly*, Spring, 1993, pp. 104–109.

131 N. Hulsman, "Farewell Corner Office," *BCBusiness Magazine*, June 1999, pp. 48–55.

132 R. Hearn, "First Banker in Space," *Canadian Business*, August 1997, p. 15.

133 Cited in R. W. Judy and C. D'Amico, *Workforce 2020* (Indianapolis, IL: Hudson Institute, 1997), p. 58.

134 L. Arnold, "Geographical, Organisational and Social Implications of Teleworking—Emphasis on the Social Perspectives" (paper presented at the 29th Annual Meeting of the Canadian Sociological and Anthropological Association, Calgary, June 1994); K. S. Devine, L. Taylor, and K. Haryett, "The Impact of Teleworking on Canadian Employment," in *Good Jobs, Bad Jobs, No Jobs: The Uncertain Future of Employment* in Canada, ed. A. Duffy, D. Glenday, and N. Pupo (Toronto : Harcourt Brace, 1997); C. A. Hamilton, "Telecommuting," *Personnel Journal*, April 1987, pp. 91–101; and I. U. Zeytinoglu, "Employment Conditions in

Telework: An Experiment in Ontario," *Proceedings of the 30th Conference of the Canadian Industrial Relations Association,* 1992, pp. 281–293.

135 L. Arnold, "Geographical, Organisational and Social Implications of Teleworking—Emphasis on the Social Perspectives" (paper presented at the 29th Annual Meeting of the Canadian Sociological and Anthropological Association, Calgary, June 1994).

136 I. U. Zeytinoglu, "Employment Conditions in Telework: An Experiment in Ontario," *Proceedings of the 30th Conference of the Canadian Industrial Relations Association,* 1992, pp. 281–293; and K. S. Devine, L. Taylor, and K. Haryett, "The Impact of Teleworking on Canadian Employment," in *Good Jobs, Bad Jobs, No Jobs: The Uncertain Future of Employment in Canada,* ed. A. Duffy, D. Glenday, and N. Pupo (Toronto: Harcourt Brace, 1997).

137 I. U. Zeytinoglu, "Employment Conditions in Telework: An Experiment in Ontario," *Proceedings of the 30th Conference of the Canadian Industrial Relations Association,* 1992, pp. 281–293.

138 K. S. Devine, L. Taylor, and K. Haryett, "The Impact of Teleworking on Canadian Employment," in *Good Jobs, Bad Jobs, No Jobs: The Uncertain Future of Employment in Canada,* ed. A. Duffy, D. Glenday, and N. Pupo (Toronto: Harcourt Brace, 1997); and C. A. Hamilton, "Telecommuting," *Personnel Journal,* April 1987, pp. 91–101.

139 K. S. Devine, L. Taylor, and K. Haryett, "The Impact of Teleworking on Canadian Employment," in *Good Jobs, Bad Jobs, No Jobs: The Uncertain Future of Employment in Canada,* ed. A. Duffy, D. Glenday, and N. Pupo (Toronto: Harcourt Brace, 1997).

140 K. S. Devine, L. Taylor, and K. Haryett, "The Impact of Teleworking on Canadian Employment," in *Good Jobs, Bad Jobs, No Jobs: The Uncertain Future of Employment in Canada,* ed. A. Duffy, D. Glenday, and N. Pupo (Toronto: Harcourt Brace, 1997).

141 C. A. Hamilton, "Telecommuting," *Personnel Journal,* April 1987, pp. 91–101.

142 L. Arnold, "Geographical, Organisational and Social Implications of Teleworking—Emphasis on the Social Perspectives" (paper presented at the 29th Annual Meeting of the Canadian Sociological and Anthropological Association, Calgary, June 1994).

143 N. Hulsman, "Farewell Corner Office," *BCBusiness Magazine,* June 1999, pp. 48–55.

144 T. R. Mitchell and A. E. Mickel, "The Meaning of Money: An Individual-Difference Perspective," *Academy of Management,* July 1999, pp. 568–578.

145 This paragraph is based on T. R. Mitchell and A. E. Mickel, "The Meaning of Money: An Individual-Difference Perspective," *Academy of Management,* July 1999, pp. 568–578. The reader may want to refer to the myriad of references cited in the article.

146 E. Beauchesne, "Pay Bonuses Improve Productivity, Study Shows," *Vancouver Sun,* September 13, 2002, p. D5.

147 K. O. Doyle, "Introduction: Money and the Behavioral Sciences," *American Behavioral Scientist,* July 1992, pp. 641–657.

148 S. Caudron, "Motivation? Money's Only No. 2," *IndustryWeek,* November 15, 1993, p. 33.

149 E. A. Locke, D. B. Feren, V. M. McCaleb, K. N. Shaw, and A. T. Denny, "The Relative Effectiveness of Four Methods of Motivating Employee Performance," in *Changes in Working Life,* ed. K. D. Duncan, M. M. Gruneberg, and D. Wallis (London: Wiley, 1980), pp. 363–383.

150 B. Filipczak, "Can't Buy Me Love," *Training,* January 1996, pp. 29–34.

151 See A. Mitra, N. Gupta, and G. D. Jenkins Jr., "The Case of the Invisible Merit Raise: How People See Their Pay Raises," *Compensation & Benefits Review,* May–June 1995, pp. 71–76.

152 M. B. Arthur, D. T. Hall, and B. S. Lawrence (eds.), *Handbook of Career Theory* (Cambridge: Cambridge University Press, 1989), p. 8.

153 D. T. Hall, *Careers in Organizations* (Santa Monica, CA: Goodyear, 1976), pp. 3–4.

154 See H. Lancaster, "You, and Only You, Must Stay in Charge of Your Employability," *Wall Street Journal,* November 15, 1994, p. B1; B. Filipczak, "You're on Your Own: Training, Employability, and the New Employment Contract," *Training,* January 1995, pp. 29–36; and M. B. Arthur, P. H. Claman, and R. J. DeFillippi, "Intelligent Enterprise, Intelligent Careers," *Executive,* November 1995, pp. 7–20.

155 See, for example, P. O. Benham Jr., "Developing Organizational Talent: The Key to Performance and Productivity," *SAM Advanced Management Journal,* January 1993, pp. 34–39.

156 G. Johns, *Organizational Behavior: Understanding and Managing Life at Work,* 4th ed. (New York: HarperCollins, 1996), p. 622.

157 For further elaboration of these points, see B. Moses, *Career Intelligence: Mastering the New Work and Personal Realities* (Toronto: Stoddart, 1997).

158 J. R. Hackman, "Work Design," in *Improving Life at Work,* ed. J. R. Hackman and J. L. Suttle (Santa Monica, CA: Goodyear, 1977), pp. 132–133.

Chapter 6

1 J. R. Katzenback and D. K. Smith, *The Wisdom of Teams: Creating the High-Performance Organization* (New York: Harper Business, 1999), p. 45.

2 J. R. Katzenback and D. K. Smith, *The Wisdom of Teams: Creating the High-Performance Organization* (New York: Harper Business, 1999), p. 214.

3 P. Booth, *Challenge and Change: Embracing the Team Concept,* Report 123-94 (Ottawa: The Conference Board of Canada, 1994).

4 Cited in C. Joinson, "Teams at Work," *HR Magazine,* May 1999, p. 30; and P. Strozniak, "Teams at Work," *IndustryWeek,* September 18, 2000, p. 47.

5 Cited in C. Joinson, "Teams at Work," *HR Magazine,* May 1999, p. 30; and P. Strozniak, "Teams at Work," *IndustryWeek,* September 18, 2000, p. 47.

6 See, for example, D. Tjosvold, *Team Organization: An Enduring Competitive Advantage* (Chichester, UK: Wiley, 1991); S. A. Mohrman, S. G. Cohen, and A. M. Mohrman Jr., *Designing Team-Based Organizations* (San Francisco: Jossey-Bass, 1995); P. MacMillan, *The Performance Factor: Unlocking the Secrets of Teamwork* (Nashville, TN: Broadman and Holman, 2001); and E. Salas, C. A. Bowers, and E. Edens, (eds.), *Improving Teamwork in Organizations: Applications of Resource Management Training* (Mahwah, NJ: Erlbaum, 2002).

7 "Teams in Business," *Venture,* CBC, November 10, 1998.

8 J. H. Shonk, *Team-Based Organizations* (Homewood, IL: Business One Irwin, 1992); and M. A. Verespej, "When Workers Get New Roles," *IndustryWeek,* February 3, 1992, p. 11.

9 L. Earl, *An Overview of Organisational and Technological Change in the Private Sector, 1998–2000*, Catalogue no. 88F0006XIE, no. 09 (Ottawa: Statistics Canada, June 2002), p. 14.

10 J. L. Cotton, *Employee Involvement* (Newbury Park, CA: Sage, 1993), p. 76.

11 "Corporate Culture Club: Companies Are Focusing on Employee Morale and Training to Boost the Bottom Line," *Maclean's*, December 12, 1994, pp. 42–43.

12 J. L. Cotton, *Employee Involvement* (Newbury Park, CA: Sage, 1993), p. 76.

13 J. L. Cotton, *Employee Involvement* (Newbury Park, CA: Sage, 1993), p. 3.

14 See, for example, C. C. Manz and H. P. Sims Jr., *Business Without Bosses: How Self-Managing Teams Are Building High Performance Companies* (New York: Wiley, 1993); J. R. Barker, "Tightening the Iron Cage: Concertive Control in Self-Managing Teams," *Administrative Science Quarterly*, September 1993, pp. 408–437; and S. G. Cohen, G. E. Ledford Jr., and G. M. Spreitzer, "A Predictive Model of Self-Managing Work Team Effectiveness," *Human Relations*, May 1996, pp. 643–676.

15 R. I. Beekun, "Assessing the Effectiveness of Sociotechnical Interventions: Antidote or Fad?" *Human Relations*, October 1989, pp. 877–897.

16 S. G. Cohen, G. E. Ledford, and G. M. Spreitzer, "A Predictive Model of Self-Managing Work Team Effectiveness," *Human Relations*, May 1996, pp. 643–676.

17 Statistics Canada, "Gender Pay Differentials: Impact of the Workplace, 1999," *The Daily*, June 19, 2002.

18 P. Booth, *Challenge and Change: Embracing the Team Concept*, Report 123-94 (Ottawa: The Conference Board of Canada, 1994).

19 P. Booth, *Challenge and Change: Embracing the Team Concept*, Report 123-94 (Ottawa: The Conference Board of Canada, 1994).

20 E. F. Rogers, W. Metlay, I. T. Kaplan, and T. Shapiro, "Self-Managing Work Teams: Do They Really Work?" *Human Resource Planning*, no. 2 (1995), pp. 53–57; and V. U. Druskat and S. B. Wolff, "Effects and Timing of Developmental Peer Appraisals in Self-Managing Work Groups," *Journal of Applied Psychology*, February 1999, pp. 58–74.

21 C. E. Nicholls, H. W. Lane, and M. Brehm Brechu, "Taking Self-Managed Teams to Mexico," *Academy of Management Executive*, August 1999, pp. 15–27.

22 G. Taninecz, "Team Players," *IndustryWeek*, July 15, 1996, pp. 28–32; D. R. Denison, S. L. Hart, and J. A. Kahn, "From Chimneys to Cross-Functional Teams: Developing and Validating a Diagnostic Model," *Academy of Management Journal*, August 1996, pp. 1005–1023; and A. R. Jassawalla, "Building Collaborative Cross-Functional New Product Teams," *Academy of Management Executive*, August 1999, pp. 50–63.

23 R. Lepine and K. Rawson, "Strategic Savings on the Right Track: How Canadian Pacific Railway Has Saved Millions of Dollars in the Past Four Years Through Strategic Sourcing," *CMA Management*, February 2003, pp. 20–23.

24 "Cross-Functional Obstacles," *Training*, May 1994, pp. 125–126.

25 P. Gwynne, "Skunk Works, 1990s-Style," *Research Technology Management*, July–August 1997, pp. 18–23.

26 See, for example, M. E. Warkentin, L. Sayeed, and R. Hightower, "Virtual Teams Versus Face-to-Face Teams: An Exploratory Study of a Web-Based Conference System," *Decision Sciences*, Fall 1997, pp. 975–993; A. M. Townsend, S. M. DeMarie, and A. R. Hendrickson, "Virtual Teams: Technology and the Workplace of the Future," *Academy of Management Executive*, August 1998, pp. 17–29; and D. Duarte and N. T. Snyder, *Mastering Virtual Teams: Strategies, Tools, and Techniques* (San Francisco: Jossey-Bass, 1999); M. L. Maznevski and K. M. Chudoba, "Bridging Space Over Time: Global Virtual Team Dynamics and Effectiveness," *Organization Science*, September–October 2000, pp. 473–492; and J. Katzenbach and D. Smith, "Virtual Teaming," *Forbes*, May 21, 2001, pp. 48–51.

27 K. Kiser, "Working on World Time," *Training*, March 1999, p. 30.

28 *Focus on Research* based on S. L. Jarvenpaa, K. Knoll, and D. E. Leidner, "Is Anybody out There? Antecedents of Trust in Global Virtual Teams," *Journal of Management Information Systems*, Spring 1998, pp. 29–64.

29 This section based on A. Majchrzak, A. Malhotra, J. Stamps, and J. Lipnack, "Can Absence Make a Team Grow Stronger?" *Harvard Business Review* 82, no. 5 (May 2004), pp. 131–136.

30 B. L. Kirkman, B. Rosen, C. B. Gibson, P. E. Tesluk, S. O. McPherson, "Five Challenges to Virtual Team Success: Lessons From Sabre, Inc.," *Academy of Management Executive* 16, no. 3 (2002), pp. 67–79.

31 *OB in the Street* based on M. Petrie, "Canada's Skeleton Crew Made Peace to Improve," *CanWest News Service*, February 21, 2005; and B. Graveland, "Pain Credits Team for Win," *Edmonton Journal*, February 22, 2005, p. D3.

32 M. Petrie, "Canada's Skeleton Crew Made Peace to Improve," *CanWest News Service*, February 21, 2005.

33 B. Graveland, "Pain Credits Team for Win," *Edmonton Journal*, February 22, 2005, p. D3.

34 See M. F. Peterson, P. B. Smith, A. Akande, S. Ayestaran, et al., "Role Conflict, Ambiguity, and Overload: A 21-Nation Study," *Academy of Management Journal*, April 1995, pp. 429–452.

35 E. H. Schein, *Organizational Psychology*, 3rd ed. (Englewood Cliffs, NJ: Prentice Hall, 1980), p. 145.

36 For a recent review of the research on group norms, see J. R. Hackman, "Group Influences on Individuals in Organizations," in *Handbook of Industrial & Organizational Psychology*, vol. 3, 2nd ed., ed. M. D. Dunnette and L. M. Hough (Palo Alto, CA: Consulting Psychologists Press, 1992), pp. 235–250.

37 D. C. Feldman, "The Development and Enforcement of Group Norms," *Academy of Management Journal*, January 1984, pp. 47–53; and K. L. Bettenhausen and J. K. Murnighan, "The Development of an Intragroup Norm and the Effects of Interpersonal and Structural Challenges," *Administrative Science Quarterly*, March 1991, pp. 20–35.

38 D. C. Feldman, "The Development and Enforcement of Group Norms," *Academy of Management Journal*, January 1984, pp. 47–53; and K. L. Bettenhausen and J. K. Murnighan, "The Development of an Intragroup Norm and the Effects of Interpersonal and Structural Challenges," *Administrative Science Quarterly*, March 1991, pp. 20–35.

39 C. A. Kiesler and S. B. Kiesler, *Conformity* (Reading, MA: Addison Wesley, 1969).

40 S. E. Asch, "Effects of Group Pressure Upon the Modification and Distortion of Judgments," in *Groups, Leadership and Men*, ed. H. Guetzkow (Pittsburgh, PA: Carnegie Press, 1951), pp. 177–190; and S. E. Asch, "Studies of Independence and Conformity: A Minority of One Against a Unanimous Majority," *Psychological Monographs: General and Applied* 70, no. 9 (1956), pp. 1–70.

41 S. L. Robinson and A. M. O'Leary-Kelly, "Monkey See, Monkey Do: The Influence of Work Groups on the Antisocial Behavior of Employees," *Academy of Management Journal* 41, 1998, pp. 658–672.

42 J. M. George, "Personality, Affect and Behavior in Groups," *Journal of Applied Psychology* 78, 1993, pp. 798–804; and J. M. George and L. R. James, "Personality, Affect, and Behavior in Groups Revisited: Comment on Aggregation, Levels of Analysis, and a Recent Application of Within and Between Analysis," *Journal of Applied Psychology* 78, 1993, pp. 798–804.

43 B. W. Tuckman, "Developmental Sequences in Small Groups," *Psychological Bulletin*, June 1965, pp. 384–399; B. W. Tuckman and M. C. Jensen, "Stages of Small-Group Development Revisited," *Group and Organizational Studies*, December 1977, pp. 419–427; and M. F. Maples, "Group Development: Extending Tuckman's Theory," *Journal for Specialists in Group Work*, Fall 1988, pp. 17–23.

44 R. C. Ginnett, "The Airline Cockpit Crew," in *Groups That Work (and Those That Don't)*, ed. J. R. Hackman (San Francisco: Jossey-Bass, 1990).

45 C. J. G. Gersick, "Time and Transition in Work Teams: Toward a New Model of Group Development," *Academy of Management Journal*, March 1988, pp. 9–41; C. J. G. Gersick, "Marking Time: Predictable Transitions in Task Groups," *Academy of Management Journal*, June 1989, pp. 274–309; E. Romanelli and M. L. Tushman, "Organizational Transformation as Punctuated Equilibrium: An Empirical Test," *Academy of Management Journal*, October 1994, pp. 1141–1166; B. M. Lichtenstein, "Evolution or Transformation: A Critique and Alternative to Punctuated Equilibrium," in *Academy of Management Best Paper Proceedings*, ed. D. P. Moore (National Academy of Management Conference, Vancouver, 1995), pp. 291–295; and A. Seers and S. Woodruff, "Temporal Pacing in Task Forces: Group Development or Deadline Pressure?" *Journal of Management* 23, no. 2 (1997), pp. 169–187.

46 C. J. G. Gersick, "Time and Transition in Work Teams: Toward a New Model of Group Development," *Academy of Management Journal*, March 1988, pp. 9–41; M. J. Waller, J. M. Conte, C. B. Gibson, and M. A. Carpenter, "The Effect of Individual Perceptions of Deadlines on Team Performance," *Academy of Management Review*, October 2001, pp. 586–600.

47 A. Chang, P. Bordia, and J. Duck, "Punctuated Equilibrium and Linear Progression: Toward a New Understanding of Group Development," *Academy of Management Journal* 46, no. 1 (2003), pp. 106–117.

48 K. L. Bettenhausen, "Five Years of Groups Research: What We Have Learned and What Needs to be Addressed," *Journal of Management* 17, 1991, pp. 345–381; and R. A. Guzzo and G. P. Shea, "Group Performance and Intergroup Relations in Organizations," in *Handbook of Industrial and Organizational Psychology*, vol. 3, 2nd ed., ed. M. D. Dunnette and L. M. Hough (Palo Alto, CA: Consulting Psychologists Press, 1992), pp. 269–313.

49 A. Chang, P. Bordia, and J. Duck, "Punctuated Equilibrium and Linear Progression: Toward a New Understanding of Group Development," *Academy of Management Journal* 46, no. 1 (2003), pp. 106–117; and S. G. S. Lim and J. K. Murnighan, "Phases, Deadlines, and the Bargaining Process," *Organizational Behavior and Human Decision Processes* 58, 1994, pp. 153–171.

50 See, for instance, D. L. Gladstein, "Groups in Context: A Model of Task Group Effectiveness," *Administrative Science Quarterly*, December 1984, pp. 499–517; J. R. Hackman, "The Design of Work Teams," in *Handbook of Organizational Behavior*, ed. J. W. Lorsch (Englewood Cliffs, NJ: Prentice Hall, 1987), pp. 315–342; M. A. Campion, G. J. Medsker, and C. A. Higgs, "Relations Between Work Group Characteristics and Effectiveness:

Implications for Designing Effective Work Groups," *Personnel Psychology*, 1993; and R. A. Guzzo and M. W. Dickson, "Teams in Organizations: Recent Research on Performance and Effectiveness," in *Annual Review of Psychology*, vol. 47, ed. J. T. Spence, J. M. Darley, and D. J. Foss, 1996, pp. 307–338.

51 D. E. Hyatt and T. M. Ruddy, "An Examination of the Relationship Between Work Group Characteristics and Performance: Once More into the Breech," *Personnel Psychology*, Autumn 1997, p. 555.

52 This model is based on M. A. Campion, E. M. Papper, and G. J. Medsker, "Relations Between Work Team Characteristics and Effectiveness: A Replication and Extension," *Personnel Psychology*, Summer 1996, pp. 429–452; D. E. Hyatt and T. M. Ruddy, "An Examination of the Relationship Between Work Group Characteristics and Performance: Once More into the Breech," *Personnel Psychology*, Autumn 1997, pp. 553–585; S. G. Cohen and D. E. Bailey, "What Makes Teams Work: Group Effectiveness Research From the Shop Floor to the Executive Suite," *Journal of Management* 23, no. 3 (1997), pp. 239–290; G. A. Neuman and J. Wright, "Team Effectiveness: Beyond Skills and Cognitive Ability," *Journal of Applied Psychology*, June 1999, pp. 376–389; and L. Thompson, *Making the Team* (Upper Saddle River, NJ: Prentice Hall, 2000), pp. 18–33.

53 See M. Mattson, T. V. Mumford, and G. S. Sintay, "Taking Teams to Task: A Normative Model for Designing or Recalibrating Work Teams" (paper presented at the National Academy of Management Conference, Chicago, August 1999); and G. L. Stewart and M. R. Barrick, "Team Structure and Performance: Assessing the Mediating Role of Intrateam Process and the Moderating Role of Task Type," *Academy of Management Journal*, April 2000, pp. 135–148.

54 G. Keenan, "Steely John: Dofasco Lifer John Mayberry Is Not Your Typical Steel CEO. He's Making Money," *Report on Business Magazine*, September 2002, pp. 12–15.

55 E. M. Stark, "Interdependence and Preference for Group Work: Main and Congruence Effects on the Satisfaction and Performance of Group Members," *Journal of Management* 26, no. 2 (2000), pp. 259–279; and J. W. Bishop, K. D. Scott, and S. M. Burroughs, "Support, Commitment, and Employee Outcomes in a Team Environment," *Journal of Management* 26, no. 6 (2000), pp. 1113–1132.

56 J. R. Hackman, *Leading Teams*. (Boston: Harvard Business School Press, 2002).

57 D. Eden, "Pygmalion Without Interpersonal Contrast Effects: Whole Groups Gain From Raising Manager Expectations," *Journal of Applied Psychology*, August 1990, pp. 394–398.

58 J. M. George and K. Bettenhausen, "Understanding Prosocial Behavior, Sales, Performance, and Turnover: A Group-Level Analysis in a Service Context," *Journal of Applied Psychology*, December 1990, pp. 698–709; and J. M. George, "State or Trait: Effects of Positive Mood on Prosocial Behaviors at Work, *Journal of Applied Social Psychology*, April 1991, pp. 299–307.

59 W. Immen, "The More Women in Groups, the Better," *Globe and Mail*, April 27, 2005, p. C3.

60 J. L. Berdahl and C. Anderson, "Men, Women, and Leadership Centralization in Groups Over Time," *Group Dynamics: Theory, Research, and Practice* 9, no. 1 (2005), pp. 45–57.

61 R. I. Beekun, "Assessing the Effectiveness of Sociotechnical Interventions: Antidote or Fad?" *Human Relations*, October 1989, pp. 877–897.

62 S. G. Cohen, G. E. Ledford, and G. M. Spreitzer, "A Predictive Model of Self-Managing Work Team Effectiveness," *Human Relations*, May 1996, pp. 643–676.

63 K. T. Dirks, "Trust in Leadership and Team Performance: Evidence from NCAA Basketball," *Journal of Applied Psychology,* December 2000, pp. 1004–1012; and M. Williams, "In Whom We Trust: Group Membership as an Affective Context for Trust Development," *Academy of Management Review,* July 2001, pp. 377–396.

64 See S. T. Johnson, "Work Teams: What's Ahead in Work Design and Rewards Management," *Compensation & Benefits Review,* March–April 1993, pp. 35–41; and A. M. Saunier and E. J. Hawk, "Realizing the Potential of Teams Through Team-Based Rewards," *Compensation & Benefits Review,* July–August 1994, pp. 24–33.

65 J. Pfeffer and N. Langton, "The Effect of Wage Dispersion on Satisfaction, Productivity, and Working Collaboratively: Evidence From College and University Faculty," *Administrative Science Quarterly* 38, 1993, pp. 382–407.

66 M. Bloom, "The Performance Effects of Pay Dispersion on Individuals and Organizations," *Academy of Management Journal* 42, 1999, pp. 25–40.

67 For a more detailed breakdown on team skills, see M. J. Stevens and M. A. Campion, "The Knowledge, Skill, and Ability Requirements for Teamwork: Implications for Human Resource Management," *Journal of Management,* Summer 1994, pp. 503–530.

68 M. R. Barrick, G. L. Stewart, M. J. Neubert, and M. K. Mount, "Relating Member Ability and Personality to Work-Team Processes and Team Effectiveness," *Journal of Applied Psychology,* June 1998, pp. 377–391.

69 M. R. Barrick, G. L. Stewart, M. J. Neubert, and M. K. Mount, "Relating Member Ability and Personality to Work-Team Processes and Team Effectiveness," *Journal of Applied Psychology,* June 1998, pp. 377–391.

70 M. R. Barrick, G. L. Stewart, M. J. Neubert, and M. K. Mount, "Relating Member Ability and Personality to Work-Team Processes and Team Effectiveness," *Journal of Applied Psychology,* June 1998, pp. 377–391.

71 E. Sundstrom, K. P. Meuse, and D. Futrell, "Work Teams: Applications and Effectiveness," *American Psychologist,* February 1990, pp. 120–133.

72 See, for instance M. Sashkin and K. J. Kiser, *Putting Total Quality Management to Work* (San Francisco: Berrett-Koehler, 1993); and J. R. Hackman and R. Wageman, "Total Quality Management: Empirical, Conceptual and Practical Issues," *Administrative Science Quarterly,* June 1995, pp. 309–342.

73 D. A. Harrison, K. H. Price, J. H. Gavin, and A. T. Florey, "Time, Teams, and Task Performance: Changing Effects of Surface- and Deep-Level Diversity on Group Functioning," *Academy of Management Journal* 45, no. 5 (2002), pp. 1029–1045; and J. S. Bunderson and K. M. Sutcliffe, "Comparing Alternative Conceptualizations of Functional Diversity in Management Teams: Process and Performance Effects," *Academy of Management Journal,* 45, no. 5 (2002), pp. 875–893.

74 M. A. Neale, G. B. Northcraft, and K. A. Jehn, "Exploring Pandora's Box: The Impact of Diversity and Conflict on Work Group Performance," *Performance Improvement Quarterly* 12, no. 1 (1999), pp. 113–126.

75 R. J. Ely and D. A. Thomas, "Cultural Diversity at Work: The Effects of Diversity Perspectives on Work Group Processes and Outcomes," *Administrative Science Quarterly* 46, 2001, pp. 229–273; K. A. Jehn, G. B. Northcraft, and M. A. Neale, "Why Some Differences Make a Difference: A Field Study of Diversity, Conflict, and Performance in Workgroups." *Administrative Science Quarterly* 44, 1999, pp. 741–763; and W. E. Watson, K. Kumar, and L. K. Michaelsen, "Cultural Diversity's Impact on Interaction Process and Performance: Comparing Homogeneous and Diverse Task Groups." *Academy of Management Journal* 36, 1993, pp. 590–602.

76 For a review, see K. Y. Williams and C. A. O'Reilly, "Demography and Diversity in Organizations: A Review of 40 Years of Research," in *Research in Organizational Behavior,* vol. 20, ed. B. M. Staw and L. L. Cummings (Greenwich, CT: JAI Press, 1998), pp. 77–140.

77 E. Peterson, "Negotiation Teamwork: The Impact of Information Distribution and Accountability on Performance Depends on the Relationship Among Team Members," *Organizational Behavior and Human Decision Processes* 72, 1997, pp. 364–384.

78 J. Labianca, "The Ties That Blind," *Harvard Business Review* 82, no. 10 (October 2004), p. 19.

79 See, for instance, M. Sashkin and K. J. Kiser, *Putting Total Quality Management to Work* (San Francisco: Berrett-Koehler, 1993); and J. R. Hackman and R. Wageman, "Total Quality Management: Empirical, Conceptual and Practical Issues," *Administrative Science Quarterly,* June 1995, pp. 309–342.

80 J. S. Bunderson and K. M. Sutcliffe, "Comparing Alternative Conceptualizations of Functional Diversity in Management Teams: Process and Performance Effects," *Academy of Management Journal* 45, no. 5 (2002), pp. 875–893, discusses some of the recent work in this area.

81 R. J. Ely and D. A. Thomas, "Cultural Diversity at Work: The Effects of Diversity Perspectives on Work Group Processes and Outcomes," *Administrative Science Quarterly* 46, 2001, pp. 229–273.

82 J. T. Polzer, L. P. Milton, and W. B. Swann Jr., "Capitalizing on Diversity: Interpersonal Congruence in Small Work Groups," *Administrative Science Quarterly* 47, no. 2 (2002), pp. 296–324.

83 *Focus on Diversity* based on B. L. Kelsey, "Increasing Minority Group Participation and Influence Using a Group Support System," *Canadian Journal of Administrative Sciences* 17, no. 1 (2000), pp. 63–75.

84 See D. R. Comer, "A Model of Social Loafing in Real Work Groups," *Human Relations,* June 1995, pp. 647–667.

85 W. Moede, "Die Richtlinien der Leistungs-Psychologie," *Industrielle Psychotechnik* 4, 1927, pp. 193–207. See also D. A. Kravitz and B. Martin, "Ringelmann Rediscovered: The Original Article," *Journal of Personality and Social Psychology,* May 1986, pp. 936–941.

86 See, for example, J. A. Shepperd, "Productivity Loss in Performance Groups: A Motivation Analysis," *Psychological Bulletin,* January 1993, pp. 67–81; and S. J. Karau and K. D. Williams, "Social Loafing: A Meta-Analytic Review and Theoretical Integration," *Journal of Personality and Social Psychology,* October 1993, pp. 681–706.

87 E. Sundstrom, K. P. Meuse, and D. Futrell, "Work Teams: Applications and Effectiveness," *American Psychologist,* February 1990, pp. 120–133.

88 D. E. Hyatt and T. M. Ruddy, "An Examination of the Relationship Between Work Group Characteristics and Performance: Once More into the Breech," *Personnel Psychology,* Autumn 1997, p. 555; and J. D. Shaw, M. K. Duffy, and E. M. Stark, "Interdependence and Preference for Group Work: Main and Congruence Effects on the Satisfaction and Performance of Group Members," *Journal of Management* 26, no. 2 (2000), pp. 259–279.

89 R. Wageman, "Critical Success Factors for Creating Superb Self-Managing Teams," *Organizational Dynamics,* Summer 1997, p. 55.

90 M. A. Campion, E. M. Papper, and G. J. Medsker, "Relations Between Work Team Characteristics and Effectiveness: A

Replication and Extension," *Personnel Psychology,* Summer 1996, p. 430.

91 M. A. Campion, E. M. Papper, and G. J. Medsker, "Relations Between Work Team Characteristics and Effectiveness: A Replication and Extension," *Personnel Psychology,* Summer 1996, p. 430.

92 K. Hess, *Creating the High-Performance Team* (New York: Wiley, 1987); J. R. Katzenbach and D. K. Smith, *The Wisdom of Teams* (Boston: Harvard Business School Press, 1993), pp. 43–64; and K. D. Scott and A. Townsend, "Teams: Why Some Succeed and Others Fail," *HR Magazine,* August 1994, pp. 62–67.

93 E. Weldon and L. R. Weingart, "Group Goals and Group Performance," *British Journal of Social Psychology,* Spring 1993, pp. 307–334.

94 R. A. Guzzo, P. R. Yost, R. J. Campbell, and G. P. Shea, "Potency in Groups: Articulating a Construct," *British Journal of Social Psychology,* March 1993, pp. 87–106; S. J. Zaccaro, V. Blair, C. Peterson, and M. Zazanis, "Collective Efficacy," in *Self-Efficacy, Adaptation and Adjustment: Theory, Research and Application,* ed. J. E. Maddux (New York: Plenum, 1995), pp. 308–330; and D. L. Feltz and C. D. Lirgg, "Perceived Team and Player Efficacy in Hockey," *Journal of Applied Psychology,* August 1998, pp. 557–564.

95 For some of the controversy surrounding the definition of cohesion, see J. Keyton and J. Springston, "Redefining Cohesiveness in Groups," *Small Group Research,* May 1990, pp. 234–254.

96 C. R. Evans and K. L. Dion, "Group Cohesion and Performance: A Meta-Analysis," *Small Group Research,* May 1991, pp. 175–186; B. Mullen and C. Cooper, "The Relation Between Group Cohesiveness and Performance: An Integration," *Psychological Bulletin,* March 1994, pp. 210–227; S. M. Gully, D. J. Devine, and D. J. Whitney, "A Meta-Analysis of Cohesion and Performance: Effects of Level of Analysis and Task Interdependence," *Small Group Research,* 1995, pp. 497–520; and P. M. Podsakoff, S. B. MacKenzie, and M. Ahearne, "Moderating Effects of Goal Acceptance on the Relationship Between Group Cohesiveness and Productivity," *Journal of Applied Psychology,* December 1997, pp. 974–983.

97 A. Chang and P. Bordia, "A Multidimensional Approach to the Group Cohesion-Group Performance Relationship," *Small Group Research,* August 2001, pp. 379–405.

98 Paragraph based on R. Kreitner and A. Kinicki, *Organizational Behavior,* 6th ed. (New York: Irwin, 2004), pp. 459–461.

99 K. M. Eisenhardt, J. L. Kahwajy, and L. J. Bourgeois III, "How Management Teams Can Have a Good Fight," *Harvard Business Review,* July–August 1997, p. 78.

100 K. Jehn, "A Multimethod Examination of the Benefits and Detriments of Intragroup Conflict," *Administrative Science Quarterly,* June 1995, pp. 256–282.

101 K. M. Eisenhardt, J. L. Kahwajy, and L. J. Bourgeois III, "How Management Teams Can Have a Good Fight," *Harvard Business Review,* July–August 1997, p. 78.

102 K. Hess, *Creating the High-Performance Team* (New York: Wiley, 1987).

103 D. Brown, "Innovative HR Ineffective in Manufacturing Firms," *Canadian HR Reporter,* April 7, 2003, pp. 1–2.

104 A. B. Drexler and R. Forrester, "Teamwork—Not Necessarily the Answer," *HR Magazine,* January 1998, pp. 55–58.

105 R. Forrester and A. B. Drexler, "A Model for Team-Based Organization Performance," *Academy of Management Executive,* August 1999, p. 47. See also S. A. Mohrman, with S. G. Cohen and A. M. Mohrman Jr., *Designing Team-Based Organizations* (San

Francisco: Jossey-Bass, 1995); and J. H. Shonk, *Team-Based Organizations* (Homewood, IL: Business One Irwin, 1992).

106 Based on N. Katz, "Sports Teams as a Model for Workplace Teams: Lessons and Liabilities," *Academy of Management Executive,* August 2001, pp. 56–67.

107 Based on N. Katz, "Sports Teams as a Model for Workplace Teams: Lessons and Liabilities," *Academy of Management Executive,* August 2001, pp. 56–67.

108 See, for instance, B. L. Kirkman and D. L. Shapiro, "The Impact of Cultural Values on Employee Resistance to Teams: Toward a Model of Globalized Self-Managing Work Team Effectiveness," *Academy of Management Review,* July 1997, pp. 730–757; and B. L. Kirkman, C. B. Gibson, and D. L. Shapiro, "'Exporting' Teams: Enhancing the Implementation and Effectiveness of Work Teams in Global Affiliates," *Organizational Dynamics* 30, no. 1 (2001), pp. 12–29.

109 D. B. Harrison and H. P. Conn, "Mobilizing Abilities Through Teamwork," *Canadian Business Review,* Autumn 1994, p. 21.

110 T. D. Schellhardt, "To Be a Star Among Equals, Be a Team Player," *Wall Street Journal,* April 20, 1994, p. B1.

111 T. D. Schellhardt, "To Be a Star Among Equals, Be a Team Player," *Wall Street Journal,* April 20, 1994, p. B1.

112 See, for instance, J. Prieto, "The Team Perspective in Selection and Assessment," in *Personnel Selection and Assessment: Industrial and Organizational Perspectives,* ed. H. Schuler, J. L. Farr, and M. Smith (Hillsdale, NJ: Erlbaum, 1994); and R. Klimoski and R. G. Jones, "Staffing for Effective Group Decision Making: Key Issues in Matching People and Teams," in *Team Effectiveness and Decision Making in Organizations,* ed. R. A. Guzzo and E. Salas (San Francisco: Jossey-Bass, 1995), pp. 307–326.

113 "Corporate Culture," *Canadian HR Reporter* 17, no. 21 (December 6, 2004), pp. 7–11.

114 S. Baillie-Ruder, "Sweet Devotion," *PROFIT,* December 2004, pp. 44–51.

115 "Teamwork That Works," *PROFIT,* March 2004, p. 12.

116 J. Zigon, "Making Performance Appraisal Work for Teams," *Training,* June 1994, pp. 58–63.

117 E. Salas, T. L. Dickinson, S. A. Converse, and S. I. Tannenbaum, "Toward an Understanding of Team Performance and Training," in *Teams: Their Training and Performance,* ed. R. W. Swezey and E. Salas (Norwood, NJ: Ablex, 1992), pp. 3–29.

118 P. Booth, *Challenge and Change: Embracing the Team Concept,* Report 123-94 (Ottawa: The Conference Board of Canada, 1994), p. 7.

119 S. P. Robbins and P. L. Hunsaker, *Training in Interpersonal Skills,* 2nd ed. (Upper Saddle River, NJ: Prentice Hall, 1996), pp. 168–184.

OB on the Edge: Trust

1 Vignette based on G. Khermouch, with T. Lowry and J. Muller, "What's Martha Minus Martha?" *BusinessWeek,* October 18, 2002, www.businessweek.com/bwdaily/dnflash/oct2002/nf20021018_1980.htm (accessed September 20, 2005); "Profile of the Day: Martha Stewart Living," *Hoover's Online,* October 25, 2002, www.hoovers.com/company/features/0,2960,8_3577,00.html (accessed October 25, 2002); and R. Tomkins, "The Bad News That Builds Brands," *Financial Times,* June 27, 2002, http://news.ft.com (accessed June 28, 2002).

2 "Martha Stewart Magazine Winning Back Advertisers," *Calgary Herald,* June 8, 2005, p. E2.

3 A. D'Innocenzio, "Stewart's Corporate Turnaround Pegged to September Shows," *Vancouver Sun*, May 11, 2005, p. D3.

4 F. K. Sonnenberg, "Trust Me, Trust Me Not," *IndustryWeek*, August 16, 1993, pp. 22–28; and L. T. Hosmer, "Trust: The Connecting Link Between Organizational Theory and Philosophical Ethics," *Academy of Management Review*, April 1995, pp. 379–403.

5 T. Davis and M. J. Landa, "The Trust Deficit," *Worklife Report* 4, 1999, pp. 6–7.

6 T. Davis and M. J. Landa, "The Trust Deficit," *Worklife Report* 4, 1999, pp. 6–7.

7 D. J. McAllister, "Affect- and Cognition-Based Trust as Foundations for Interpersonal Cooperation in Organizations," *Academy of Management Journal*, February 1995, p. 25; R. C. Mayer, J. H. Davis, and F. D. Schoorman, "An Integrative Model of Organizational Trust," *Academy of Management Review* 20, 1995, pp. 709–734; and D. M. Rousseau, S. B. Sitkin, R. S. Burt, and C. Camerer, "Not So Different After All: A Cross-Discipline View of Trust," *Academy of Management Review*, July 1998, pp. 393–404.

8 J. K. Rempel, J. G. Holmes, and M. P. Zanna, "Trust in Close Relationships," *Journal of Personality and Social Psychology*, July 1985, p. 96.

9 M. Granovetter, "Economic Action and Social Structure: The Problem of Embeddedness," *American Journal of Sociology*, November 1985, p. 491.

10 P. L. Schindler and C. C. Thomas, "The Structure of Interpersonal Trust in the Workplace," *Psychological Reports*, October 1993, pp. 563–573.

11 J. K. Butler Jr. and R. S. Cantrell, "A Behavioral Decision Theory Approach to Modeling Dyadic Trust in Superiors and Subordinates," *Psychological Reports*, August 1984, pp. 19–28.

12 D. McGregor, *The Professional Manager* (New York: McGraw-Hill, 1967), p. 164.

13 B. Nanus, *The Leader's Edge: The Seven Keys to Leadership in a Turbulent World* (Chicago: Contemporary Books, 1989), p. 102.

14 K. T. Dirks and D. L. Ferrin, "Trust in Leadership: Meta-Analytic Findings and Implications for Organizational Research," *Journal of Applied Psychology* 87, 2002, pp. 611–628.

15 J. H. Dyer and W. Chu, "The Determinants of Trust in Supplier-Automaker Relationships in the U.S., Japan, and Korea," *Journal of International Business Studies*, Second Quarter 2000, pp. 259–285.

16 J. H. Dyer and W. Chu, "The Determinants of Trust in Supplier-Automaker Relationships in the U.S., Japan, and Korea," *Journal of International Business Studies*, Second Quarter 2000, p. 283.

17 K. T. Dirks and D. L. Ferrin, "Trust in Leadership: Meta-Analytic Findings and Implications for Organizational Research," *Journal of Applied Psychology* 87, 2002, pp. 611–628.

18 T. Simons, "The High Cost of Lost Trust," *Harvard Business Review*, September 2002, pp. 18–19.

19 *FactBox* items cited in Z. Ezekiel, *Building Public Trust in Canadian Organizations: Preliminary Findings* (Ottawa: The Conference Board of Canada, May 2005), pp. 1–3.

20 R. D. Costigan, S. S. Ilter, and J. J. Berman, "A Multi-Dimensional Study of Trust in Organizations," *Journal of Managerial Issues* 10, no. 3, pp. 303–317.

21 L. Prusak and D. Cohen, "How to Invest in Social Capital," *Harvard Business Review*, June 2001, pp. 86–93.

22 L. Prusak and D. Cohen, "How to Invest in Social Capital," *Harvard Business Review*, June 2001, pp. 86–93.

23 L. Prusak and D. Cohen, "How to Invest in Social Capital," *Harvard Business Review*, June 2001, pp. 86–93.

24 This section is based on D. E. Zand, *The Leadership Triad: Knowledge, Trust, and Power* (New York: Oxford University Press, 1997), pp. 122–134; and A. M. Zak, J. A. Gold, R. M. Ryckman, and E. Lenney, "Assessments of Trust in Intimate Relationships and the Self-Perception Process," *Journal of Social Psychology*, April 1998, pp. 217–228.

25 K. T. Dirks, "Trust in Leadership and Team Performance: Evidence From NCAA Basketball," *Journal of Applied Psychology* 85, 2000, pp. 1004–1012.

26 Based on F. Bartolome, "Nobody Trusts the Boss Completely—Now What?" *Harvard Business Review*, March–April 1989, pp. 135–142; and P. Pascarella, "15 Ways to Win People's Trust," *IndustryWeek*, February 1, 1993, pp. 47–51.

27 C. W. Langfred, "Too Much of a Good Thing? Negative Effects of High Trust and Individual Autonomy in Self-Managing Teams," *Academy of Management Journal* 47, no. 3 (June 2004), pp. 385–399.

28 R. M. Kramer, "When Paranoia Makes Sense," *Harvard Business Review*, July 2002, pp. 62–69.

29 R. M. Kramer, "When Paranoia Makes Sense," *Harvard Business Review*, July 2002, p. 63.

Chapter 7

1 Opening vignette based on B. Livesey, "Heart of Steel," *Report on Business Magazine*, August 1997, pp. 20–27; D. McMurdy, "Dofasco Steel on Cutting Edge: Mayberry Banks on High-Tech to Boost Production," *Financial Post* (*National Post*), December 10, 2001, pp. FP1, FP7; J. Terrett, "Dofasco Engages Workforce to Profit in Tough Steel Market: Losses in Early 1990s Lead to Major Transformation, *Plant*, May 6, 2002, p 15; and G. Keenan, "Dofasco Head Leaves Winning Strategy for Steel Maker," *Globe and Mail*, May 3, 2003, p. B3.

2 See, for example, K. W. Thomas and W. H. Schmidt, "A Survey of Managerial Interests With Respect to Conflict," *Academy of Management Journal*, June 1976, p. 317.

3 L. Ramsay, "Communication Key to Workplace Happiness," *Financial Post*, December 6/8, 1997, p. 58.

4 See www.isrsurveys.com/default.asp (accessed March 14, 2002).

5 D. K. Berlo, *The Process of Communication* (New York: Holt, Rinehart and Winston, 1960), p. 54.

6 *Focus on Ethics* based on "Big Mac Said Close to Settling Fries Suit," *Toronto Star*, March 8, 2002, www.torontostar.com/NASApp/cs/ContentServer?pagename=thestar/Layout/Article_Type1&c=Article&cid=1015542115092&call_page=TS_Business&call_pageid=968350072197&call_pagepath=Business/News&col=969048863851 (accessed March 9, 2002).

7 J. C. McCroskey, J. A. Daly, and G. Sorenson, "Personality Correlates of Communication Apprehension," *Human Communication Research*, Spring 1976, pp. 376–380.

8 See R. L. Daft and R. H. Lengel, "Information Richness: A New Approach to Managerial Behavior and Organization Design," in *Research in Organizational Behavior*, vol. 6, ed. B. M. Staw and L. L. Cummings (Greenwich, CT: JAI Press, 1984), pp. 191–233; R. E. Rice and D. E. Shook, "Relationships of Job Categories and Organizational Levels to Use of Communication Channels, Including Electronic Mail: A Meta-Analysis and Extension," *Journal of Management Studies*, March 1990, pp. 195–229; R. E. Rice, "Task Analyzability, Use of New Media, and Effectiveness," *Organization*

Science, November 1992, pp. 475–500; S. G. Straus and J. E. McGrath, "Does the Medium Matter? The Interaction of Task Type and Technology on Group Performance and Member Reaction," *Journal of Applied Psychology*, February 1994, pp. 87–97; J. Webster and L. K. Trevino, "Rational and Social Theories as Complementary Explanations of Communication Media Choices: Two Policy-Capturing Studies," *Academy of Management Journal*, December 1995, pp. 1544–1572.

9   R. L. Daft, R. H. Lengel, and L. K. Trevino, "Message Equivocality, Media Selection, and Manager Performance: Implications for Information Systems," *MIS Quarterly*, September 1987, pp. 355–368.

10   "Virtual Pink Slips Start Coming Online," *Vancouver Sun*, July 3, 1999, p. D15.

11   Thanks are due to an anonymous reviewer for providing this elaboration.

12   J. Terrett, "Dofasco Engages Workforce to Profit in Tough Steel Market: Losses in Early 1990s Lead to Major Transformation," *Plant*, May 6, 2002, p. 15.

13   M. Swartz, "How Enron Blew It," *Texas Monthly*, November 2001.

14   *OB in the Workplace* based on K. Cox, "Risley's Wagging Tongue Doomed FPI Deal," *Globe and Mail*, February 19, 2002, p. B14; and C. Jackson, "Liberal Leader Has Doubts About Bill," *Telegram*, June 7, 2005, p. A1.

15   S. I. Hayakawa, *Language in Thought and Action* (New York: Harcourt Brace Jovanovich, 1949), p. 292.

16   H. Weeks, "Taking the Stress Out of Stressful Conversations," *Harvard Business Review*, July–August 2001, pp. 112–119.

17   R. L. Simpson, "Vertical and Horizontal Communication in Formal Organizations," *Administrative Science Quarterly*, September 1959, pp. 188–196; and B. Harriman, "Up and Down the Communications Ladder," *Harvard Business Review*, September–October 1974, pp. 143–151.

18   D. M. Saunders and J. D. Leck, "Formal Upward Communication Procedures: Organizational and Employee Perspectives," *Revue Canadienne des Sciences de l'Administration*, September 1993, pp. 255–268.

19   "Heard It Through the Grapevine," *Forbes*, February 10, 1997, p. 22.

20   K. Davis cited in R. Rowan, "Where Did That Rumor Come From?" *Fortune*, August 13, 1979, p. 134.

21   L. Hirschhorn, "Managing Rumors," in *Cutting Back*, ed. L. Hirschhorn (San Francisco: Jossey-Bass, 1983), pp. 49–52.

22   R. L. Rosnow and G. A. Fine, *Rumor and Gossip: The Social Psychology of Hearsay* (New York: Elsevier, 1976).

23   This section based on R. Kreitner and A. Kinicki, *Organizational Behavior*, 6th ed. (New York: McGraw-Hill, 2004), pp. 541–542.

24   H. B. Vickery III, "Tapping into the Employee Grapevine," *Association Management*, January 1984, pp. 59–60.

25   See, for instance, J. G. March and G. Sevon, "Gossip, Information and Decision Making," in *Decisions and Organizations*, ed. J. G. March (Oxford: Blackwell, 1988), pp. 429–442; M. Noon and R. Delbridge, "News From Behind My Hand: Gossip in Organizations," *Organization Studies* 14, no. 1 (1993), pp. 23–36; and N. DiFonzo, P. Bordia, and R. L. Rosnow, "Reining in Rumors," *Organizational Dynamics*, Summer 1994, pp. 47–62.

26   L. Hirschhorn, "Managing Rumors," in *Cutting Back*, ed. L. Hirschhorn (San Francisco: Jossey-Bass, 1983), pp. 54–56.

27   See, for instance, R. Hotch, "Communication Revolution," *Nation's Business*, May 1993, pp. 20–28; G. Brockhouse, "I Have Seen the Future," *Canadian Business*, August 1993, pp. 43–45; R. Hotch, "In Touch Through Technology," *Nation's Business*, January 1994, pp. 33–35; and P. LaBarre, "The Other Network," *IndustryWeek*, September 19, 1994, pp. 33–36.

28   T. Hamilton, "E-Mail Overload Swamps Workplace," *Toronto Star*, June 26, 2002, www.torontostar.com/NASApp/cs/ContentServer? pagename=thestar/Layout/ArticleType1&c=Article&cid=102210035 2728&call_page=TS_Business&call_pageid=968350072197&call_ pagepath=Business/News&col=969048863851 (accessed June 26, 2002).

29   Derived from P. Kuitenbrouwer, "Office E-Mail Runs Amok," *Financial Post (National Post)*, October 18, 2001, p. FP11.

30   E. Church, "Employers Read E-Mail as Fair Game," *Globe and Mail*, April 14, 1998, p. B16.

31   J. Kay, "Someone Will Watch Over Me: Think Your Office E-Mails Are Private? Think Again," *National Post Business*, January 2001, pp. 59–64.

32   E. Church, "Employers Read E-Mail as Fair Game," *Globe and Mail*, April 14, 1998, p. B16.

33   A. Harmon, "Appeal of Instant Messaging Extends into the Workplace," *New York Times*, March 11, 2003, p. A1.

34   Report released by the Canadian Wireless Telecommunications Association, as reported in P. Wilson, "Record Growth of Text Messaging Continues in Canada," *Vancouver Sun*, March 23, 2005, p. D2.

35   Cited in C. Y. Chen, "The IM Invasion," *Fortune*, May 26, 2003, pp. 135–138.

36   A. Stuart, "IM Is Here. RU Ready 2 Try It?" *Inc.*, July 2003, pp. 7–8.

37   G. Buckler, "Instant Messaging Replacing Pagers in the Enterprise," *Computing Canada* 30, no. 4 (March 26, 2004), p. 18.

38   R. O. Crockett, "'The Office Gossips' New Water Cooler," *BusinessWeek*, June 24, 2003, p. 14.

39   R. L. Birdwhistell, *Introduction to Kinesics* (Louisville, KY: University of Louisville Press, 1952).

40   J. Fast, *Body Language* (Philadelphia, PA: M. Evan, 1970), p. 7.

41   E. T. Hall, *The Hidden Dimension*, 2nd ed. (Garden City, NY: Anchor Books/Doubleday, 1966).

42   This section largely based on C. G. Pinder and K. P. Harlos, "Silent Organizational Behavior" (paper presented at the Western Academy of Management Conference, March 2000); and P. Mornell, "The Sounds of Silence," *Inc.*, February 2001, pp. 117–118.

43   See D. Tannen, *You Just Don't Understand: Women and Men in Conversation* (New York: Ballantine Books, 1991); and D. Tannen, *Talking From 9 to 5* (New York: William Morrow, 1995).

44   D. Goldsmith and P. Fulfs, "You Just Don't Have the Evidence: An Analysis of Claims and Evidence in Deborah Tannen's *You Just Don't Understand*," in *Communications Yearbook*, vol. 22, ed. M. Roloff (Thousand Oaks, CA: Sage, 1999).

45   N. Langton "Differences in Communication Styles: Asking for a Raise," in *Organizational Behavior: Experiences and Cases*, 4th ed., ed. D. Marcic (St. Paul, MN: West Publishing, 1995).

46   See M. Munter, "Cross-Cultural Communication for Managers," *Business Horizons*, May–June 1993, pp. 75–76.

47   See E. T. Hall, *Beyond Culture* (Garden City, NY: Anchor Press/Doubleday, 1976); E. T. Hall, "How Cultures Collide," *Psychology Today*, July 1976, pp. 67–74; E. T. Hall and M. R. Hall, *Understanding Cultural Differences* (Yarmouth, ME: Intercultural

Press, 1990); and R. E. Dulek, J. S. Fielden, and J. S. Hill, "International Communication: An Executive Primer," *Business Horizons*, January–February 1991, pp. 20–25.

48 N. Adler, *International Dimensions of Organizational Behavior*, 3rd ed. (Cincinnati. OH: South Western College, 1997), pp. 87–88.

49 S. A. Hellweg and S. L. Phillips, "Communication and Productivity in Organizations: A State-of-the-Art Review," in *Proceedings of the 40th Annual Academy of Management Conference*, Detroit, 1980, pp. 188–192.

50 Based on J. Case, "The Open-Book Revolution," *Inc.*, June 1995, pp. 26–50; and J. P. Schuster, J. Carpenter, and M. P. Kane, *The Power of Open-Book Management* (New York: Wiley, 1996).

51 www.profitguide.com/profit100/2005/article.asp?ID=1332&page=2 (accessed September 10, 2005).

52 R. Wright, "21 Ways to Build Great People [Profit 100 CEOs Reveal Their Best Tips for Finding and Keeping Top-Notch Talent]," *PROFIT*, June 2000, pp. 122–132.

53 J. Myers, "Dream Teams: Canada's Fastest-Growing Companies Are Powered by People," *Profit*, June 2003, pp. 24–32.

54 R. Wright, "21 Ways to Build Great People [Profit 100 CEOs Reveal Their Best Tips for Finding and Keeping Top-Notch Talent]," *PROFIT*, June 2000, pp. 122–132.

55 Based on S. L. Gruner, "Why Open the Books?" *Inc.*, November 1996, p. 95; and T. R. V. Davis, "Open-Book Management: Its Promise and Pitfalls," *Organizational Dynamics*, Winter 1997, pp. 7–20.

56 T. Davis and M. J. Landa, "A Contrary Look at Employee Performance Appraisal," *Canadian Manager*, Fall 1999, pp. 18–19+.

57 J. S. Lublin, "It's Shape-up Time for Performance Reviews," *Wall Street Journal*, October 3, 1994, p. B1.

58 Much of this section is based on H. H. Meyer, "A Solution to the Performance Appraisal Feedback Enigma," *Academy of Management Executive*, February 1991, pp. 68–76.

59 B. Gates, *The Road Ahead* (New York: Viking, 1995), p. 86.

60 R. J. Burke, "Why Performance Appraisal Systems Fail," *Personnel Administration*, June 1972, pp. 32–40.

61 B. R. Nathan, A. M. Mohrman Jr., and J. Milliman, "Interpersonal Relations as a Context for the Effects of Appraisal Interviews on Performance and Satisfaction: A Longitudinal Study," *Academy of Management Journal*, June 1991, pp. 352–369.

62 R. Kreitner and A. Kinicki, *Organizational Behavior*, 6th ed. (New York: McGraw-Hill/Irwin, 2004), p. 335. Reprinted by permission of McGraw Hill Education.

63 P. Booth, *Challenge and Change: Embracing the Team Concept*, Report 123–94 (Ottawa: The Conference Board of Canada, 1994), p. 10.

64 This list is adapted from S. G. Scott and W. O. Einstein, "Strategic Performance Appraisal in Team-Based Organizations: One Size Does Not Fit All," *Academy of Management Executive*, May 2001, pp. 107–116. They cite as the sources of the list A. S. DeNisi and A. N. Kluger, "Feedback Effectiveness: Can 360-Degree Appraisals Be Improved?" *Academy of Management Executive* 14, no. 1 (2000), pp. 129–139; W. W. Tornow, "Perceptions of Reality: Is Multi-Perspective Measurement a Means or an End?" *Human Resource Management* 32, 1993, pp. 221–229; and J. Ghorpade, "Managing Five Paradoxes of 360-Degree Feedback," *Academy of Management Executive* 14, no. 1 (2000), pp. 140–150.

65 *From Concepts to Skills* based on S. P. Robbins and P. L. Hunsaker, *Training in Interpersonal Skills: TIPs for Managing People at Work*, 2nd

ed. (Upper Saddle River, NJ: Prentice Hall, 1996), Chapter 3; and data in R. C. Huseman, J. M. Lahiff, and J. M. Penrose, *Business Communication: Strategies and Skills* (Chicago: Dryden Press, 1988), pp. 380, 425.

Chapter 8

1 Opening vignette based on T. Wharnsby, "How New IOC President Rogge Turned Scandalous Silver into Gold," *Globe and Mail*, February 17, 2002, www.globeandmail.com; "A Duo Deprived," *New York Times*, February 13, 2002, http://ea.nytimes.com/cgi-bin/email?REFURI=http://www.nytimes.com/2002/02/13/opinion/_13WED4.html (accessed February 17, 2002); and B. Smith, "Overhaul Proposed in Judging of Skaters, *Globe and Mail*, February 19, 2002, pp. A1, A10.

2 Based on B. M. Bass, *Bass & Stogdill's Handbook of Leadership*, 3rd ed. (New York: Free Press, 1990).

3 Sharda Prashad, "Fill Your Power Gap," *Globe and Mail*, July 23, 2003, p. C3.

4 J. R. P. French Jr. and B. Raven, "The Bases of Social Power," in *Studies in Social Power*, ed. D. Cartwright (Ann Arbor: University of Michigan, Institute for Social Research, 1959), pp. 150–167. For an update on French and Raven's work, see D. E. Frost and A. J. Stahelski, "The Systematic Measurement of French and Raven's Bases of Social Power in Workgroups," *Journal of Applied Social Psychology*, April 1988, pp. 375–389; T. R. Hinkin and C. A. Schriesheim, "Development and Application of New Scales to Measure the French and Raven (1959) Bases of Social Power," *Journal of Applied Psychology*, August 1989, pp. 561–567; and G. E. Littlepage, J. L. Van Hein, K. M. Cohen, and L. L. Janiec, "Evaluation and Comparison of Three Instruments Designed to Measure Organizational Power and Influence Tactics," *Journal of Applied Social Psychology*, January 16–31, 1993, pp. 107–125.

5 B. H. Raven, "Social Influence and Power," in *Current Studies in Social Psychology*, ed. I. D. Steiner and M. Fishbein (New York: Holt, Rinehart, Winston, 1965), pp. 371–382.

6 D. Kipnis, *The Powerholders* (Chicago: University of Chicago Press, 1976), pp. 77–78.

7 S. Milgram, *Obedience to Authority* (New York: Harper and Row, 1974).

8 D. Hickson, C. Hinings, C. Lee, R. Schneck, and J. Pennings, "A Strategic Contingencies Theory of Intra-Organizational Power," *Administrative Science Quarterly* 16, 1971, pp. 216–229.

9 J. W. Dean Jr. and J. R. Evans, *Total Quality: Management, Organization, and Strategy* (Minneapolis-St. Paul, MN: West, 1994).

10 M. Folb, "Cause Celeb: From Deborah Cox to Maestro, Homegrown Talent Is Hocking Retail Fashion," *Marketing Magazine*, April 5, 1999, p. 13.

11 G. Yukl, H. Kim, C. M. Falbe, "Antecedents of Influence Outcomes," *Journal of Applied Psychology* 81, no. 3 (June 1, 1996), pp. 309–317.

12 P. P. Carson, K. D. Carson, and C. W. Roe, "Social Power Bases: A Meta-Analytic Examination of Interrelationships and Outcomes," *Journal of Applied Social Psychology* 23, no. 14 (1993), pp. 1150–1169.

13 C. M. Falbe and G. Yukl, "Consequences for Managers of Using Single Tactics and Combinations of Tactics," *Academy of Management Journal* 35, 1992, pp. 638–652.

14 Cited in J. R. Carlson, D. S. Carlson, and L. L. Wadsworth, "The Relationship Between Individual Power Moves and Group

Agreement Type: An Examination and Model," *S.A.M. Advanced Management Journal* 65, no. 4 (2000), pp. 44–51.

15   B. Smith, "Russian Refuses Extradition," *Globe and Mail*, www.globeandmail.com (accessed August 7, 2002).

16   R. E. Emerson, "Power-Dependence Relations," *American Sociological Review* 27, 1962, pp. 31–41.

17   Thanks are due to an anonymous reviewer for supplying this insight.

18   H. Mintzberg, *Power in and Around Organizations* (Englewood Cliffs, NJ: Prentice Hall, 1983), p. 24.

19   Based on R. A. Oppel Jr., "The Man Who Paid the Price for Sizing Up Enron," *New York Times*, March 27, 2002, www.nytimes.com/2002/03/27/business/27ENRO.html?ex=1018242314&ei=1&en=84c572c79afa6b2c (accessed March 27, 2002).

20   See, for example, D. Kipnis, S. M. Schmidt, C. Swaffin-Smith, and I. Wilkinson, "Patterns of Managerial Influence: Shotgun Managers, Tacticians, and Bystanders," *Organizational Dynamics*, Winter 1984, pp. 58–67; T. Case, L. Dosier, G. Murkison, and B. Keys, "How Managers Influence Superiors: A Study of Upward Influence Tactics," *Leadership and Organization Development Journal* 9, no. 4 (1988), pp. 25–31; D. Kipnis and S. M. Schmidt, "Upward-Influence Styles: Relationship With Performance Evaluations, Salary, and Stress," *Administrative Science Quarterly*, December 1988, pp. 528–542; G. Yukl and C. M. Falbe, "Influence Tactics and Objectives in Upward, Downward, and Lateral Influence Attempts," *Journal of Applied Psychology*, April 1990, pp. 132–140; B. Keys and T. Case, "How to Become an Influential Manager," *Academy of Management Executive*, November 1990, pp. 38–51; D. A. Ralston, D. J. Gustafson, L. Mainiero, and D. Umstot, "Strategies of Upward Influence: A Cross-National Comparison of Hong Kong and American Managers," *Asia Pacific Journal of Management*, October 1993, pp. 157–175; G. Yukl, H. Kim, and C. M. Falbe, "Antecedents of Influence Outcomes," *Journal of Applied Psychology*, June 1996, pp. 309–317; K. E. Lauterbach and B. J. Weiner, "Dynamics of Upward Influence: How Male and Female Managers Get Their Way," *Leadership Quarterly*, Spring 1996, pp. 87–107; K. R. Xin and A. S. Tsui, "Different Strokes for Different Folks? Influence Tactics by Asian-American and Caucasian-American Managers," *Leadership Quarterly*, Spring 1996, pp. 109–132; and S. J. Wayne, R. C. Liden, I. K. Graf, and G. R. Ferris, "The Role of Upward Influence Tactics in Human Resource Decisions," *Personnel Psychology*, Winter 1997, pp. 979–1006.

21   This section adapted from G. Yukl, C. M. Falbe, and J. Y. Youn, "Patterns of Influence Behavior for Managers," *Group & Organization Studies* 18, no. 1 (March 1993), p. 7.

22   This section adapted from G. Yukl, C. M. Falbe, and J. Y. Youn, "Patterns of Influence Behavior for Managers," *Group & Organization Studies* 18, no. 1 (March 1993), p. 7.

23   Search of *Business Source Premier* and *Canadian Newsstand* articles conducted by the author, September 2005.

24   This is the definition given by R. Forrester, "Empowerment: Rejuvenating a Potent Idea," *Academy of Management Executive*, August 2000, pp. 67–80.

25   R. E. Quinn and G. M. Spreitzer, "The Road to Empowerment: Seven Questions Every Leader Should Consider," *Organizational Dynamics*, Autumn 1997, p. 38.

26   S. Wetlaufer, "Organizing for Empowerment: An Interview With AES's Roger Sant and Dennis Bakke," *Harvard Business Review*, January–February 1999, pp. 110–123.

27   C. Argyris, "Empowerment: The Emperor's New Clothes," *Harvard Business Review*, May–June 1998.

28   K. Kitagawa, *Empowering Employee–Learners with Essential Skills at Durabelt Inc.* (Ottawa: The Conference Board of Canada, March 2005).

29   J. Schaubroeck, J. R. Jones, and J. L. Xie, "Individual Differences in Utilizing Control to Cope with Job Demands: Effects on Susceptibility to Infectious Disease," *Journal of Applied Psychology* 86, no. 2 (2001), pp. 265–278.

30   Thanks are due to an anonymous reviewer for this insight.

31   R. C. Ford and M. D. Fottler, "Empowerment: A Matter of Degree," *Academy of Management Executive* 9, 1995, pp. 21–31.

32   Points are summarized from R. C. Ford and M. D. Fottler, "Empowerment: A Matter of Degree," *Academy of Management Executive* 9, 1995, pp. 23–25.

33   T. D. Wall, N. J. Kemp, P. R. Jackson, and W. W. Clegg, "Outcomes of Autonomous Work Groups: A Long-Term Field Experiment," *Academy of Management Journal* 29, 1986, pp. 280–304.

34   "Delta Promotes Empowerment," *Globe and Mail*, May 31, 1999, Advertising Supplement, p. C5.

35   G. M. Spreitzer, "Psychological Empowerment in the Workplace: Dimensions, Measurement, and Validation," *Academy of Management Journal* 38, 1995, pp. 1442–1465; G. M. Spreitzer, M. A. Kizilos, and S. W. Nason, "A Dimensional Analysis of the Relationship Between Psychological Empowerment and Effectiveness, Satisfaction, and Strain," *Journal of Management* 23, 1997, pp. 679–704; and K. W. Thomas and W. G. Tymon, "Does Empowerment Always Work: Understanding the Role of Intrinsic Motivation and Personal Interpretation," *Journal of Management Systems* 6, 1994, pp. 39–54.

36   D. E. Hyatt and T. M. Ruddy, "An Examination of the Relationship Between Work Group Characteristics and Performance: Once More into the Breech," *Personnel Psychology* 50, 1997, pp. 553–585; B. L. Kirkman and B. Rosen, "Beyond Self-Management: Antecedents and Consequences of Team Empowerment," *Academy of Management Journal* 42, 1999, pp. 58–74; P. E. Tesluck, D. J. Brass, and J. E. Mathieu, "An Examination of Empowerment Processes at Individual and Group Levels" (paper presented at the 11th annual conference of the Society of Industrial and Organizational Psychology, San Diego, 1996).

37   M. Kane, "Quality Control Can Save Firms Millions, New Data Suggests," *Vancouver Sun*, May 29, 1998, pp. H1, H6.

38   C. Robert, T. M. Probst, J. J. Martocchio, F. Drasgow, and J. J. Lawler, "Empowerment and Continuous Improvement in the United States, Mexico, Poland, and India: Predicting Fit on the Basis of the Dimensions of Power Distance and Individualism," *Journal of Applied Psychology* 85, 2000, pp. 643–658.

39   W. A. Randolph and M. Sashkin, "Can Organizational Empowerment Work in Multinational Settings?" *Academy of Management Executive*, February 2002, pp. 102–115.

40   T. Lee and C. M. Brotheridge, "When the Prey Becomes the Predator: Bullying as Predictor of Reciprocal Bullying, Coping, and Well-Being," working paper, University of Regina, 2005.

41   "More and More Workplaces Have Bullies," *Leader-Post* (Regina), December 14, 2004, p. A1.

42   "Employers Underestimate Extent of Sexual Harassment, Report Says," *Vancouver Sun*, March 8, 2001, p. D6.

43   "Employers Underestimate Extent of Sexual Harassment, Report Says," *Vancouver Sun*, March 8, 2001, p. D6.

44   *Janzen v. Platy Enterprises Ltd.* [1989] 10 C.H.R.R. D/6205 SCC.

45   The following section based on J. N. Cleveland and M. E. Kerst, "Sexual Harassment and Perceptions of Power: An Under-

Articulated Relationship," *Journal of Vocational Behavior,* February 1993, pp. 49–67.

46 J. Goddu, "Sexual Harassment Complaints Rise Dramatically," *Canadian Press Newswire,* March 6, 1998.

47 K. Von Hoffmann, "Forbidden Fruit: Student-Faculty Relationships," *Yale Herald,* October 17, 2003, p. 1.

48 S. A. Culbert and J. J. McDonough, *The Invisible War: Pursuing Self-Interest at Work* (New York: Wiley, 1980), p. 6.

49 H. Mintzberg, *Power in and Around Organizations* (Englewood Cliffs, NJ: Prentice Hall, 1983), p. 26.

50 T. Cole, "Who Loves Ya?" *Report on Business Magazine,* April 1999, p. 54.

51 D. Farrell and J. C. Petersen, "Patterns of Political Behavior in Organizations," *Academy of Management Review,* July 1982, p. 405. For a thoughtful analysis of the academic controversies underlying any definition of organizational politics, see A. Drory and T. Romm, "The Definition of Organizational Politics: A Review," *Human Relations,* November 1990, pp. 1133–1154.

52 J. Pfeffer, *Power in Organizations* (Marshfield, MA: Pittman, 1981).

53 R. McQueen, "Hard Truths: To Capture a Corner Office, You Have to Play Politics and Know When to Lie," *National Post Business,* September 2000, pp. 51–52.

54 G. R. Ferris, G. S. Russ, and P. M. Fandt, "Politics in Organizations," in *Impression Management in Organizations,* ed. R. A. Giacalone and P. Rosenfeld (Newbury Park, CA: Sage, 1989), pp. 143–170; and K. M. Kacmar, D. P. Bozeman, D. S. Carlson, and W. P. Anthony, "An Examination of the Perceptions of Organizational Politics Model: Replication and Extension," *Human Relations,* March 1999, pp. 383–416.

55 K. M. Kacmar and R. A. Baron, "Organizational Politics: The State of the Field, Links to Related Processes, and an Agenda for Future Research," in *Research in Personnel and Human Resources Management,* vol. 17, ed. G. R. Ferris (Greenwich, CT: JAI Press, 1999); and M. Valle and L. A. Witt, "The Moderating Effect of Teamwork Perceptions on the Organizational Politics-Job Satisfaction Relationship," *Journal of Social Psychology,* June 2001, pp. 379–388.

56 G. R. Ferris, D. D. Frink, M. C. Galang, J. Zhou, K. M. Kacmar, and J. L. Howard, "Perceptions of Organizational Politics: Prediction, Stress-Related Implications, and Outcomes," *Human Relations,* February 1996, pp. 233–266; K. M. Kacmar, D. P. Bozeman, D. S. Carlson, and W. P. Anthony, "An Examination of the Perceptions of Organizational Politics Model; Replication and Extension," *Human Relations,* March 1999, p. 388; and J. M. L. Poon, "Situational Antecedents and Outcomes of Organizational Politics Perceptions," *Journal of Managerial Psychology* 18, no. 2 (2003), pp. 138–155.

57 C. Kiewitz, W. A. Hochwarter, G. R. Ferris, and S. L. Castro, "The Role of Psychological Climate in Neutralizing the Effects of Organizational Politics on work Outcomes," *Journal of Applied Social Psychology,* June 2002, pp. 1189–1207; and J. M. L. Poon, "Situational Antecedents and Outcomes of Organizational Politics Perceptions," *Journal of Managerial Psychology* 18, no. 2 (2003), pp. 138–155.

58 K. M. Kacmar and R. A. Baron, "Organizational Politics: The State of the Field, Links to Related Processes, and an Agenda for Future Research," in *Research in Personnel and Human Resources Management,* vol. 17, ed. G. R. Ferris (Greenwich, CT: JAI Press, 1999); and M. Valle and L. A. Witt, "The Moderating Effect of Teamwork Perceptions on the Organizational Politics-Job Satisfaction Relationship," *Journal of Social Psychology,* June 2001, pp. 379–388.

59 R. W. Allen, D. L. Madison, L. W. Porter, P. A. Renwick, and B. T. Mayes, "Organizational Politics: Tactics and Characteristics of Its Actors," *California Management Review,* Fall 1979, pp. 77–83.

60 W. L. Gardner and M. J. Martinko, "Impression Management in Organizations," *Journal of Management,* June 1988, pp. 321–338; D. C. Gilmore and G. R. Ferris, "The Effects of Applicant Impression Management Tactics on Interviewer Judgments," *Journal of Management,* December 1989, pp. 557–564; M. R. Leary and R. M. Kowalski, "Impression Management: A Literature Review and Two-Component Model," *Psychological Bulletin,* January 1990, pp. 34–47; S. J. Wayne and K. M. Kacmar, "The Effects of Impression Management on the Performance Appraisal Process," *Organizational Behavior and Human Decision Processes,* February 1991, pp. 70–88; E. W. Morrison and R. J. Bies, "Impression Management in the Feedback-Seeking Process: A Literature Review and Research Agenda," *Academy of Management Review,* July 1991, pp. 522–541; S. J. Wayne and R. C. Liden, "Effects of Impression Management on Performance Ratings: A Longitudinal Study," *Academy of Management Journal,* February 1995, pp. 232–260; and C. K. Stevens and A. L. Kristof, "Making the Right Impression: A Field Study of Applicant Impression Management During Job Interviews," *Journal of Applied Psychology,* October 1995, pp. 587–606.

61 M. R. Leary and R. M. Kowalski, "Impression Management: A Literature Review and Two-Component Model," *Psychological Bulletin,* January 1990, p. 40.

62 W. L. Gardner and M. J. Martinko, "Impression Management in Organizations," *Journal of Management,* June 1988, p. 333.

63 R. A. Baron, "Impression Management by Applicants During Employment Interviews: The 'Too Much of a Good Thing' Effect," in *The Employment Interview: Theory, Research, and Practice,* ed. R. W. Eder and G. R. Ferris (Newbury Park, CA: Sage, 1989), pp. 204–215.

64 M. Snyder and J. Copeland, "Self-Monitoring Processes in Organizational Settings," in *Impression Management in the Organization,* ed. R. A. Giacalone and P. Rosenfeld (Hillsdale, NJ: Lawrence Erlbaum Associates, 1989), p. 11; E. D. Long and G. H. Dobbins, "Self-Monitoring, Impression Management, and Interview Ratings: A Field and Laboratory Study," in *Proceedings of the 52nd Annual Academy of Management Conference,* ed. J. L. Wall and L. R. Jauch (Las Vegas, August 1992), pp. 274–278; and A. Montagliani and R. A. Giacalone, "Impression Management and Cross-Cultural Adaption," *Journal of Social Psychology,* October 1998, pp. 598–608.

65 Z. I. Barsness, K. A. Diekmann, and M. D. L. Seidel, "Motivation and Opportunity: The Role of Remote Work, Demographic Dissimilarity, and Social Network Centrality in Impression Management." *Academy of Management Journal,* 48, 2005, pp. 401–419.

66 R. A. Baron, "Impression Management by Applicants During Employment Interviews: The 'Too Much of a Good Thing' Effect," in *The Employment Interview: Theory, Research, and Practice,* ed. R. W. Eder and G. R. Ferris (Newbury Park, CA: Sage, 1989), pp. 204–215; D. C. Gilmore and G. R. Ferris, "The Effects of Applicant Impression Management Tactics on Interviewer Judgments," *Journal of Management,* December 1989, pp. 557–564; and C. K. Stevens and A. L. Kristof, "Making the Right Impression: A Field Study of Applicant Impression Management During Job Interviews," *Journal of Applied Psychology,* October 1995, pp. 587–606.

67 C. K. Stevens and A. L. Kristof, "Making the Right Impression: A Field Study of Applicant Impression Management During Job

Interviews," *Journal of Applied Psychology,* October 1995, pp. 587–606.

68 S. J. Wayne and K. M. Kacmar, "The Effects of Impression Management on the Performance Appraisal Process," *Organizational Behavior and Human Decision Processes* 48, 1991, pp. 70–78; S. J. Wayne and G. R. Ferris, "Influence Tactics, Affect, and Exchange Quality in Supervisor-Subordinate Interactions," *Journal of Applied Psychology* 75, 1990, pp. 487–499; and G. R. Ferris, T. A. Judge, K. M. Rowland, and D. E. Fitzgibbons, "Subordinate Influence and the Performance Evaluation Process: Test of a Model," *Organizational Behavior and Human Decision Processes* 58, 1994, pp. 101–135.

69 S. J. Wayne and R. C. Liden, "Effects of Impression Management on Performance Ratings: A Longitudinal Study," *Academy of Management Journal* 38, 1995, pp. 232–260.

70 G. H. Dobbins and J. M. Russell, "The Biasing Effects of Subordinate Likeableness on Leaders' Responses to Poor Performers: A Laboratory and a Field Study," *Personnel Psychology* 39, 1986, pp. 759–777; and T. R. Mitchell and R. Wood, "Manager Behavior in a Social Context: The Impact of Impression Management on Attributions and Disciplinary Actions," *Organizational Behavior and Human Decision Processes,* December 1981, pp. 356–378.

71 D. V. Day, D. J. Schneider, and A. L. Unckless, "Self-Monitoring and Work-Related Outcomes: A Meta-Analysis" (paper presented at the 11th Annual Conference of the Society of Industrial and Organizational Psychology, San Diego, CA, 1996); and M. A. Warech, J. W. Smither, R. R. Reilly, R. E. Millsap, and S. P. Reilly, "Self-Monitoring and 360-Degree Ratings," *Leadership Quarterly* 9, 1998, pp. 449–473.

72 M. A. Warech, J. W. Smither, R. R. Reilly, R. E. Millsap, and S. P. Reilly, "Self-Monitoring and 360-Degree Ratings," *Leadership Quarterly* 9, 1998, pp. 449–473.

73 D. V. Day, D. J. Schneider, and A. L. Unckless, "Self-Monitoring and Work-Related Outcomes: A Meta-Analysis" (paper presented at the 11th Annual Conference of the Society of Industrial and Organizational Psychology, San Diego, CA, 1996).

74 J. M. Maslyn and D. B. Fedor, "Perceptions of Politics: Does Measuring Different Foci Matter?" *Journal of Applied Psychology* 84, 1998, pp. 645–653; L. G. Nye and L. A. Witt, "Dimensionality and Construct Validity of the Perceptions of Organizational Politics Scale," *Educational and Psychological Measurement* 53, 1993, pp. 821–829.

75 G. R. Ferris, D. D. Frink, D. Bhawuk, J. Zhou, and D. C. Gilmore, "Reactions of Diverse Groups to Politics in the Workplace," *Journal of Management* 22, 1996, pp. 23–44; K. M. Kacmar, D. P. Bozeman, D. S. Carlson, and W. P. Anthony, "An Examination of the Perceptions of Organizational Politics Model: Replication and Extension," *Human Relations* 52, 1999, pp. 383–416.

76 T. P. Anderson, "Creating Measures of Dysfunctional Office and Organizational Politics: The DOOP and Short-Form DOOP Scales," *Psychology: A Journal of Human Behavior* 31, 1994, pp. 24–34.

77 G. R. Ferris, D. D. Frink, D. Bhawuk, J. Zhou, and D. C. Gilmore, "Reactions of Diverse Groups to Politics in the Workplace," *Journal of Management* 22, 1996, pp. 23–44; K. M. Kacmar, D. P. Bozeman, D. S. Carlson, and W. P. Anthony, "An Examination of the Perceptions of Organizational Politics Model: Replication and Extension," *Human Relations* 52, 1999, pp. 383–416.

78 K. M. Kacmar, D. P. Bozeman, D. S. Carlson, and W. P. Anthony, "An Examination of the Perceptions of Organizational Politics Model: Replication and Extension," *Human Relations* 52, 1999,

pp. 383–416; J. M. Maslyn and D. B. Fedor, "Perceptions of Politics: Does Measuring Different Foci Matter?" *Journal of Applied Psychology* 84, 1998, pp. 645–653.

79 M. Warshaw, "The Good Guy's (and Gal's) Guide to Office Politics," *Fast Company,* April 1998, p. 156.

80 G. Yukl, C. M. Falbe, and J. Y. Youn, "Patterns of Influence Behavior for Managers," *Group & Organization Studies* 18, no. 1 (March 1993), p. 7.

81 This is largely based on D. M. Rousseau, "The Idiosyncratic Deal: Flexibility versus Fairness?" *Organizational Dynamics,* Spring 2001, pp. 260–273.

82 G. Namie, "Workplace Bullying: Escalated Incivility," *Ivey Business Journal,* November/December 2003.

83 G. Namie, "Workplace Bullying: Escalated Incivility," *Ivey Business Journal,* November/December 2003.

84 J. Barling, "The Prediction, Psychological Experience, and Consequences Of Workplace Violence," in *Violence on the Job: Identifying Risks and Developing Solutions,* ed. G. VandenBos and E. Q. Bulatao (Washington, DC: American Psychological Association, 1996).

85 L. Keashly, "Emotional Abuse in the Workplace: Conceptual and Empirical Issues," *Journal of Emotional Abuse,* 1, 1998, pp. 85–117.

86 J. A. Richman, K. M. Rospenda, S. J. Nawyn, J. A. Flaherty, M. Fendrich, M. L. Drum and T. P. Johnson, "Sexual Harassment and Generalized Workplace Abuse Among University Employees: Prevalence And Mental Health Correlates," *American Journal of Public Health* 89, no. 3 (1999), pp. 358–363.

87 G. Namie, "Workplace Bullying: Escalated Incivility," *Ivey Business Journal,* November/December 2003.

88 G. Namie, "Workplace Bullying: Escalated Incivility," *Ivey Business Journal,* November/December 2003.

89 *Quebec Labour Standards,* s. 81.18, Psychological Harassment at Work.

90 L. M. Lapierre, P. E. Spector, and J. D. Leck, "Sexual Versus Nonsexual Workplace Aggression and Victims' Overall Job Satisfaction: A Meta-Analysis," *Journal of Occupational Health Psychology* 10, no. 2 (April 2005), pp. 155–169.

91 www.chrc-ccdp.ca/media_room/news_releases-en.asp?highlight=1&id=240.

92 "Female Workers Mistreated at Hibernia, Study Says," *Plant,* September 2, 1996, p. 4.

93 Information in this and the following paragraph based on I. Jack, "Magna Suit Spotlights Auto Industry Practices," *Financial Post Daily,* September 10, 1997, p. 1.

94 "Harassment Inquest Doesn't Go Far Enough, Say Critics," *Canadian Press Newswire,* December 2, 1997.

95 M. Jiminez, "Sexual Harassment at Work Prevalent in B.C., Poll Shows," *Vancouver Sun,* May 4, 1998, pp. A1, A2.

96 M. Navarro, "California Gets Tough on Love at Work," *Gazette* (Montreal), July 30, 2005, p. B6.

97 *From Concepts to Skills* based on S. P. Robbins and P. L. Hunsaker, *Training in Interpersonal Skills: Tips for Managing People at Work,* 2nd ed. (Upper Saddle River, NJ: Prentice Hall, 1996), pp. 131–134.

Chapter 9

1 Opening vignette based on P. LeBrun, "Talks End Badly Thursday in Toronto," *Canadian Press,* February 10, 2005.

2 See, for instance, C. F. Fink, "Some Conceptual Difficulties in the Theory of Social Conflict," *Journal of Conflict Resolution*, December 1968, pp. 412–460. For an updated review of the conflict literature, see J. A. Wall Jr. and R. R. Callister, "Conflict and Its Management," *Journal of Management* 21, no. 3 (1995), pp. 515–558.

3 L. L. Putnam and M. S. Poole, "Conflict and Negotiation," in *Handbook of Organizational Communication: An Interdisciplinary Perspective*, ed. F. M. Jablin, L. L. Putnam, K. H. Roberts, and L. W. Porter (Newbury Park, CA: Sage, 1987), pp. 549–599.

4 K. W. Thomas, "Conflict and Negotiation Processes in Organizations," in *Handbook of Industrial and Organizational Psychology*, 2nd ed., vol. 3, ed. M. D. Dunnette and L. M. Hough (Palo Alto, CA: Consulting Psychologists Press, 1992), pp. 651–717.

5 K. Jehn, "A Multimethod Examination of the Benefits and Detriments of Intragroup Conflict," *Administrative Science Quarterly*, June 1995, pp. 256–282; K. A. Jehn, "A Qualitative Analysis of Conflict Types and Dimensions in Organizational Groups," *Administrative Science Quarterly*, September 1997, pp. 530–557; K. A. Jehn and E. A. Mannix, "The Dynamic Nature of Conflict: A Longitudinal Study of Intragroup Conflict and Group Performance," *Academy of Management Journal*, April 2001, pp. 238–251; C. K. W. De Dreu and A. E. M. Van Vianen, "Managing Relationship Conflict and the Effectiveness of Organizational Teams," *Journal of Organizational Behavior*, May 2001, pp. 309–328; and K. A. Jehn and C. Bendersky, "Intragroup Conflict in Organizations: A Contingency Perspective on the Conflict-Outcome Relationship," in *Research in Organizational Behavior*, vol. 25, ed. R. M. Kramer and B. M. Staw (Oxford, UK: Elsevier, 2003), pp. 199–210.

6 A. C. Amason, "Distinguishing the Effects of Functional and Dysfunctional Conflict on Strategic Decision Making: Resolving a Paradox for Top Management Teams," *Academy of Management Journal* 39, no. 1 (1996), pp. 123–148.

7 This section is based on S. P. Robbins, *Managing Organizational Conflict: A Nontraditional Approach* (Englewood Cliffs, NJ: Prentice Hall, 1974), pp. 31–55; and J. A. Wall Jr. and R. R. Callister, "Conflict and Its Management," *Journal of Management* 21, no. 3 (1995), pp. 517–523.

8 Based on A. Morgan, "York University Schedules Exams on Shabbat," *Canadian Jewish News*, April 11, 2002, p. 5.

9 Based on J. O'Connor, "I Wouldn't Be Optimistic," *National Post*, February 17, 2005, p. B4.

10 D. Tjosvold, "Cooperative and Competitive Goal Approach to Conflict: Accomplishments and Challenges," *Applied Psychology: An International Review* 47, no. 3 (1998), pp. 285–342.

11 K. W. Thomas, "Conflict and Negotiation Processes in Organizations," in *Handbook of Industrial and Organizational Psychology*, 2nd ed., vol. 3, ed. M. D. Dunnette and L. M. Hough (Palo Alto, CA: Consulting Psychologists Press, 1992), pp. 651–717.

12 C. K. W. De Dreu, A. Evers, B. Beersma, E. S. Kluwer, and A. Nauta, "A Theory-Based Measure of Conflict Management Strategies in the Workplace," *Journal of Organizational Behavior* 22, no. 6 (September 2001), pp. 645–668. See also D. G. Pruitt and J. Rubin, *Social Conflict: Escalation, Stalemate and Settlement* (New York: Random House, 1986).

13 C. K. W. De Dreu, A. Evers, B. Beersma, E. S. Kluwer, and A. Nauta, "A Theory-Based Measure of Conflict Management Strategies in the Workplace," *Journal of Organizational Behavior* 22, no. 6 (September 2001), pp. 645–668.

14 R. A. Baron, "Personality and Organizational Conflict: Effects of the Type A Behavior Pattern and Self-Monitoring," *Organizational Behavior and Human Decision Processes*, October 1989, pp. 281–296; A. Drory and I. Ritov, "Effects of Work Experience and Opponent's Power on Conflict Management Styles," *International Journal of Conflict Management* 8, 1997, pp. 148–161; R. J. Sternberg and L. J. Soriano, "Styles of Conflict Resolution," *Journal of Personality and Social Psychology*, July 1984, pp. 115–126; and R. J. Volkema and T. J. Bergmann, "Conflict Styles as Indicators of Behavioral Patterns in Interpersonal Conflicts," *Journal of Social Psychology*, February 1995, pp. 5–15.

15 *OB in the Street* based on "A Lesson in Design: Get It in Writing," *Vancouver Sun*, May 13, 2000, p. A22.

16 These ideas are based on S. P. Robbins, *Managing Organizational Conflict: A Nontraditional Approach* (Upper Saddle River, NJ: Prentice Hall, 1974), pp. 59–89.

17 R. D. Ramsey, "Interpersonal Conflicts," *SuperVision* 66, no. 4 (April 2005), pp. 14–17.

18 R. D. Ramsey, "Interpersonal Conflicts," *SuperVision* 66, no. 4 (April 2005), pp. 14–17.

19 "Negotiating South of the Border," *Harvard Management Communication Letter* 2, no. 8 (August 1999), p. 12.

20 F. W. Swierczek, "Culture and Conflict in Joint Ventures in Asia," *International Journal of Project Management* 12, no. 1 (1994), pp. 39–47.

21 P. S. Kirkbride, S. Tang, and R. I. Westwood, "Chinese Conflict Preferences and Negotiation Behavior: Cultural and Psychological Influences," *Organization Studies* 12, no. 3 (1991), pp. 365–386; S. Tang, P. Kirkbride, "Development of Conflict Management Skills in Hong Kong: An Analysis of Some Cross-cultural Implications," *Management Education and Development* 17, no. 3 (1986), pp. 287–301; P. Trubisky, S. Ting-Toomey, and S. L. Lin, "The Influence of Individualism-Collectivism and Self-monitoring on Conflict Styles," *International Journal of Intercultural Relations* 15, 1991, pp. 65–84; and K. I. Ohbuchi and Y. Takahashi, "Cultural Styles of Conflict Management in Japanese and Americans: Passivity, Covertness, and Effectiveness of Strategies," *Journal of Applied Social Psychology* 24, 1994, pp. 1345–1366.

22 P. S. Kirkbride, S. Tang, and R. I. Westwood, "Chinese Conflict Preferences and Negotiation Behavior: Cultural and Psychological Influences," *Organization Studies* 12, 1991, pp. 365–386; and F. W. Swierczek, "Culture and Conflict in Joint Ventures in Asia," *International Journal of Project Management* 12, 1994, pp. 39–47.

23 C. L. Wang, X. Lin, A. K. K. Chan, and Y. Shi, "Conflict Handling Styles in International Joint Ventures: A Cross-cultural and Cross-national Comparison," *Management International Review* 45, no. 1 (2005), pp. 3–21.

24 M. A. Rahim, "A Measure of Styles of Handling Interpersonal Conflict," *Academy of Management Journal* 26, 1983, pp. 368–376; and C. H. Tinsley, "Model of Conflict Resolution in Japanese, German, and American Cultures," *Journal of Applied Psychology* 83, 1998, pp. 316–323.

25 R. T. Moran, J. Allen, R. Wichman, T. Ando, and M. Sasano, "Japan," in *Global Perspectives on Organizational Conflict*, ed. M. A. Rahim and A. A. Blum (Westport, CT: Praeger 1994), pp. 33–52.

26 D. C. Barnlund, *Communicative Styles of Japanese and Americans: Images and Realities* (Belmont, CA: Wadsworth 1989); and K. I. Ohbuchi and Y. Takahashi, "Cultural Styles of Conflict Management in Japanese and Americans: Passivity, Covertness, and Effectiveness of Strategies," *Journal of Applied Social Psychology* 24, 1994, pp. 1345–1366.

27 K. Leung, " Some Determinants of Reactions to Procedural Models for Conflict Resolution: A Cross-national Study," *Journal of Personality and Social Psychology* 53, 1987, pp. 898–908; K. Leung and E. A. Lind, "Procedure and Culture: Effects of Culture, Gender, and Investigator Status on Procedural Preferences," *Journal of Personality and Social Psychology* 50, 1986, pp. 1134–1140; M. W. Morris, K. Y. Williams, K. Leung, R. Larrick, M. T. Mendoza, D. Bhatnagar, J. Li, M. Kondo, J. Luo, and J. Hu, "Conflict Management Style: Accounting for Cross-national Differences," *Journal of International Business Studies* 29, 1998, pp. 729–747; and F. W. Swierczek, "Culture and Conflict in Joint Ventures in Asia," *International Journal of Project Management* 12, 1994, pp. 39–47.

28 J. S. Black and M. Mendenhall, "Resolving Conflicts With the Japanese: Mission Impossible?," *Sloan Management Review* 34, 1993, pp. 49–59.

29 B. Morrow and L. M. Bernardi, "Resolving Workplace Disputes," *Canadian Manager*, Spring 1999, p. 17.

30 Based on A. F. Westin and A. G. Feliu, *Resolving Employment Disputes Without Litigation.* (Washington: Bureau of National Affairs, 1988); J. A. Wall Jr. and M. W. Blum, "Negotiations," *Journal of Management*, June 1991, pp. 283–287; and R. Kreitner and A. Kinicki, *Organizational Behavior*, 6th ed. (New York: McGraw-Hill, 2004), p. 502.

31 A. Woods, "Season Down to Final Hours," *National Post*, February 11, 2005, pp. B8, B11.

32 C. Olsheski, "Resolving Disputes Has Just Become More Efficient," *Financial Post (National Post)*, August 16, 1999, p. D9.

33 B. Simon, "Work Ethic and the Magna Carta," *Financial Post Daily*, March 20, 1997, p. 14.

34 See, for instance, R. A. Cosier and C. R. Schwenk, "Agreement and Thinking Alike: Ingredients for Poor Decisions," *Academy of Management Executive*, February 1990, pp. 69–74; K. A. Jehn, "Enhancing Effectiveness: An Investigation of Advantages and Disadvantages of Value-Based Intragroup Conflict," *International Journal of Conflict Management*, July 1994, pp. 223–238; R. L. Priem, D. A. Harrison, and N. K. Muir, "Structured Conflict and Consensus Outcomes in Group Decision Making," *Journal of Management* 21, no. 4 (1995), pp. 691–710; and K. A. Jehn and E. A. Mannix, "The Dynamic Nature of Conflict: A Longitudinal Study of Intragroup Conflict and Group Performance," *Academy of Management Journal*, April 2001, pp. 238–251.

35 Based on D. Tjosvold, *Learning to Manage Conflict: Getting People to Work Together Productively* (New York: Lexington Books, 1993), pp. 12–13.

36 See J. A. Wall Jr. and R. R. Callister, "Conflict and Its Management," *Journal of Management* 21, no. 3 (1995), pp. 523–526 for evidence supporting the argument that conflict is almost uniformly dysfunctional.

37 R. L. Hoffman, "Homogeneity of Member Personality and Its Effect on Group Problem-Solving," *Journal of Abnormal and Social Psychology*, January 1959, pp. 27–32; and R. L. Hoffman and N. R. F. Maier, "Quality and Acceptance of Problem Solutions by Members of Homogeneous and Heterogeneous Groups," *Journal of Abnormal and Social Psychology*, March 1961, pp. 401–407.

38 J. Hall and M. S. Williams, "A Comparison of Decision-Making Performances in Established and Ad-Hoc Groups," *Journal of Personality and Social Psychology*, February 1966, p. 217.

39 R. E. Hill, "Interpersonal Compatibility and Work Group Performance Among Systems Analysts: An Empirical Study," *Proceedings of the Seventeenth Annual Midwest Academy of Management Conference*, Kent, OH, April 1974, pp. 97–110.

40 D. C. Pelz and F. Andrews, *Scientists in Organizations* (New York: Wiley, 1966).

41 J. A. Wall Jr., *Negotiation: Theory and Practice* (Glenview, IL: Scott, Foresman, 1985).

42 K. Harding, "A New Language, a New Deal," *Globe and Mail*, October 30, 2002, pp. C1, C10.

43 This model is based on R. J. Lewicki, "Bargaining and Negotiation," *Exchange: The Organizational Behavior Teaching Journal* 6, no. 2 (1981), pp. 39–40; and B. S. Moskal, "The Art of the Deal," *IndustryWeek*, January 18, 1993, p. 23.

44 R. Fisher and W. Ury, *Getting to Yes: Negotiating Agreement Without Giving In*, 2nd ed. (New York: Penguin, 1991).

45 M. H. Bazerman and M. A. Neale, *Negotiating Rationally* (New York: Free Press, 1992), pp. 67–68.

46 R. Fisher and W. Ury, *Getting to Yes: Negotiating Agreement Without Giving In*, 2nd ed. (New York: Penguin, 1991).

47 For a negative answer to this question, see C. Watson and L. R. Hoffman, "Managers as Negotiators: A Test of Power Versus Gender as Predictors of Feelings, Behavior, and Outcomes," *Leadership Quarterly*, Spring 1996, pp. 63–85.

48 A. H. Eagley, S. J. Karau, and M. Makhijani, "Gender and the Effectiveness of Leaders: A Meta-Analysis," *Psychological Bulletin* 117, 1995, pp. 125–145.

49 A. F. Stuhlmacher and A. E. Walters, "Gender Differences in Negotiation Outcome: A Meta-Analysis," *Personnel Psychology* 52, 1992, pp. 653–677.

50 D. M. Kolb and G. G. Coolidge, "Her Place at the Table," *Journal of State Government* 64, no. 2 (April–June 1991), pp. 68–71.

51 "Women Must Be Ready to Negotiate for Equal Pay," *Financial Post*, October 5/7, 1996, p. 41.

52 "Women Must Be Ready to Negotiate for Equal Pay," *Financial Post*, October 5/7, 1996, p. 41.

53 "Women Must Be Ready to Negotiate for Equal Pay," *Financial Post*, October 5/7, 1996, p. 41.

54 "The Battle of the Sexes: Do Men and Women Really Have Different Negotiating Styles?" *CMA Management Accounting Magazine* 71, no. 1 (February 1997), p. 8.

55 C. C. Eckel and P. J. Grossman, "Are Women Less Selfish Than Men? Evidence From Dictator Experiments," *Economic Journal*, May 1998, pp. 726–735.

56 I. Ayres, "Further Evidence of Discrimination in New Car Negotiations and Estimates of Its Cause," *Michigan Law Review* 94, no. 1 (October 1995), pp. 109–147.

57 B. Gerhart and S. Rynes, "Determinants and Consequences of Salary Negotiations by Male and Female MBA Graduates," *Journal of Applied Psychology* 76, no. 2 (April 1991), pp. 256–262.

58 See N. J. Adler, *International Dimensions of Organizational Behavior*, 4th ed. (Cincinnati, OH: South Western, 2002), pp. 208–256; and W. L. Adair, T. Okurmura, and J. M. Brett, "Negotiation Behavior When Cultures Collide: The United States and Japan," *Journal of Applied Psychology*, June 2001, pp. 371–385.

59 K. D. Schmidt, *Doing Business in France* (Menlo Park, CA: SRI International, 1987).

60 S. Lubman, "Round and Round," *Wall Street Journal*, December 10, 1993, p. R3.

61 J. W. Salacuse, "Ten Ways That Culture Affects Negotiating Style: Some Survey Results," *Negotiation Journal*, July 1998, pp. 221–240.

62 E. S. Glenn, D. Witmeyer, and K. A. Stevenson, "Cultural Styles of Persuasion," *Journal of Intercultural Relations*, Fall 1977, pp. 52–66.

63 J. Graham, "The Influence of Culture on Business Negotiations," *Journal of International Business Studies,* Spring 1985, pp. 81–96.

64 The points presented here were influenced by E. Van de Vliert, "Escalative Intervention in Small-Group Conflicts," *Journal of Applied Behavioral Science,* Winter 1985, pp. 19–36.

65 G. Hamilton, "Norske Labour Pact Extolled," *Vancouver Sun,* September 6, 2002, p. F6.

66 D. Brown, "Table Talk—War Stories From the Negotiating Front," *Canadian HR Reporter,* September 9, 2002, pp. 7, 10–11.

67 D. Brown, "Table Talk—War Stories From the Negotiating Front," *Canadian HR Reporter,* September 9, 2002, pp. 7, 10–11.

68 D. Brown, "Table Talk—War Stories From the Negotiating Front," *Canadian HR Reporter,* September 9, 2002, pp. 7, 10–11.

69 These suggestions are based on J. A. Wall Jr. and M. W. Blum, "Negotiations," *Journal of Management,* June 1991, pp. 278–282; and J. S. Pouliot, "Eight Steps to Success in Negotiating," *Nation's Business,* April 1999, pp. 40–42.

OB on the Edge:
The Toxic Workplace

1 L. M. Anderson and C. M. Pearson, "Tit for Tat? The Spiraling Effect of Incivility in the Workplace," *Academy of Management Review* 24, no. 3 (1999), p. 453.

2 The source of this quotation is N. Giarrusso, "An Issue of Job Satisfaction," unpublished undergraduate term paper, Concordia University, Montreal, 1990. It is cited in B. E. Ashforth, "Petty Tyranny in Organizations: A Preliminary Examination of Antecedents and Consequences," *Canadian Journal of Administrative Sciences* 14, no. 2 (1997), pp. 126–140.

3 P. Frost and S. Robinson, "The Toxic Handler: Organizational Hero—and Casualty," *Harvard Business Review,* July–August 1999, p. 101 (Reprint 99406).

4 L. M. Anderson and C. M. Pearson, "Tit for Tat? The Spiraling Effect of Incivility in the Workplace," *Academy of Management Review* 24, no. 3 (1999), pp. 452–471.

5 L. M. Anderson and C. M. Pearson, "Tit for Tat? The Spiraling Effect of Incivility in the Workplace," *Academy of Management Review* 24, no. 3 (1999), pp. 452–471. For further discussion of this, see R. A. Baron and J. H. Neuman, "Workplace Violence and Workplace Aggression: Evidence on Their Relative Frequency and Potential Causes," *Aggressive Behavior* 22, 1996, pp. 161–173; C. C. Chen and W. Eastman, "Towards a Civic Culture for Multicultural Organizations," *Journal of Applied Behavioral Science* 33, 1997, pp. 454–470; J. H. Neuman and R. A. Baron, "Aggression in the Workplace," in *Antisocial Behavior in Organizations,* ed. R. A. Giacalone and J. Greenberg (Thousand Oaks, CA: Sage, 1997), pp. 37–67.

6 L. M. Anderson and C. M. Pearson, "Tit for Tat? The Spiraling Effect of Incivility in the Workplace," *Academy of Management Review* 24, no. 3 (1999), pp. 452–471.

7 L. M. Anderson and C. M. Pearson, "Tit for Tat? The Spiraling Effect of Incivility in the Workplace," *Academy of Management Review* 24, no. 3 (1999), pp. 452–471.

8 R. Corelli, "Dishing Out Rudeness: Complaints Abound as Customers Are Ignored, Berated," *Maclean's,* January 11, 1999, p. 44.

9 R. Corelli, "Dishing Out Rudeness: Complaints Abound as Customers Are Ignored, Berated," *Maclean's,* January 11, 1999, p. 44.

10 See, for example, "The National Labour Survey," The Canadian Initiative on Workplace Violence, March 2000, www.workplaceviolence.ca/research/survey1.pdf (accessed September 26, 2005).

11 R. A. Baron and J. H. Neuman, "Workplace Violence and Workplace Aggression: Evidence on Their Relative Frequency and Potential Causes," *Aggressive Behavior* 22, 1996, pp. 161–173; K. Bjorkqvist, K. Osterman, and M. Hjelt-Back, "Aggression Among University Employees," *Aggressive Behavior* 20, 1986, pp. 173–184; and H. J. Ehrlich and B. E. K. Larcom, *Ethnoviolence in the Workplace* (Baltimore, MD: Center for the Applied Study of Ethnoviolence, 1994).

12 J. Graydon, W. Kasta, and P. Khan, "Verbal and Physical Abuse of Nurses," *Canadian Journal of Nursing Administration,* November–December 1994, pp. 70–89.

13 C. M. Pearson and C. L. Porath, "Workplace Incivility: The Target's Eye View" (paper presented at the annual meetings of The Academy of Management, Chicago, August 10, 1999).

14 "Men More Likely to Be Rude in Workplace, Survey Shows," *Vancouver Sun,* August 16, 1999, p. B10.

15 R. Corelli, "Dishing Out Rudeness: Complaints Abound as Customers Are Ignored, Berated," *Maclean's,* January 11, 1999, p. 44.

16 R. Corelli, "Dishing Out Rudeness: Complaints Abound as Customers Are Ignored, Berated," *Maclean's,* January 11, 1999, p. 44.

17 R. A. Baron and J. H. Neuman, "Workplace Violence and Workplace Aggression: Evidence on Their Relative Frequency and Potential Causes," *Aggressive Behavior* 22, 1996, pp. 161–173; C. MacKinnon, *Only Words* (New York: Basic Books, 1994); J. Marks, "The American Uncivil Wars," *U.S. News & World Report,* April 22, 1996, pp. 66–72; and L. P. Spratlen, "Workplace Mistreatment: Its Relationship to Interpersonal Violence," *Journal of Psychosocial Nursing* 32, no. 12 (1994), pp. 5–6.

18 Information in this paragraph based on B. Branswell, "Death in Ottawa: The Capital Is Shocked by a Massacre That Leaves Five Dead," *Maclean's,* April 19, 1999, p. 18; "Four Employees Killed by Former Co-worker," *Occupational Health & Safety,* June 1999, pp. 14, 16; and "Preventing Workplace Violence," *Human Resources Advisor Newsletter, Western Edition,* May–June 1999, pp. 1–2.

19 W. M. Glenn, "An Employee's Survival Guide: An ILO Survey of Workplaces in 32 Countries Ranked Argentina the Most Violent, Followed by Romania, France and Then, Surprisingly, Canada," *Occupational Health & Safety,* April–May 2002, p. 28 passim.

20 D. Flavelle, "Managers Cited for Increase in 'Work Rage,'" *Vancouver Sun,* April 11, 2000, pp. D1, D11.

21 E. Girardet, "Office Rage Is on the Boil," *National Post,* August 11, 1999, p. B1.

22 S. James, "Long Hours Linked to Rising Toll From Stress," *Financial Post (National Post),* August 6, 2003, p. FP12.

23 S. Boyes, "Workplace Violence: Coping in a Dangerous World," *Canadian Consulting Engineer,* January–February 2002, pp. 51–52.

24 W. M. Glenn, "An Employee's Survival Guide: An ILO Survey of Workplaces in 32 Countries Ranked Argentina the Most Violent, Followed by Romania, France and Then, Surprisingly, Canada," *Occupational Health & Safety,* April–May 2002, p. 28 passim.

25 W. M. Glenn, "An Employee's Survival Guide: An ILO Survey of Workplaces in 32 Countries Ranked Argentina the Most Violent, Followed by Romania, France and Then, Surprisingly, Canada," *Occupational Health & Safety,* April–May 2002, p. 28 passim.

26 Information for *FactBox* based on "Breeding Loyalty Pays for Employers," *Vancouver Sun,* April 22, 2000, p. D14; and "Men

More Likely to Be Rude in Workplace, Survey Shows," *Vancouver Sun*, August 16, 1999, p. B10.

27 "Work Rage," *BCBusiness Magazine*, January 2001, p. 23.

28 "A Quarter of Nova Scotia Teachers Who Responded to a Recent Survey Said They Faced Physical Violence at Work During the 2001–02 School Year," *Canadian Press Newswire*, February 14, 2003.

29 A. M. Webber, "Danger: Toxic Company," *Fast Company*, November 1998, pp. 152–157.

30 D. Flavelle, "Managers Cited for Increase in 'Work Rage,'" *Vancouver Sun*, April 11, 2000, pp. D1, D11.

31 G. Smith, *Work Rage* (Toronto: HarperCollins Canada, 2000).

32 "Work Rage," *BCBusiness Magazine*, January 2001, p. 23.

33 D. Flavelle, "Managers Cited for Increase in 'Work Rage,'" *Vancouver Sun*, April 11, 2000, pp. D1, D11.

34 D. E. Gibson and S. G. Barsade, "The Experience of Anger at Work: Lessons From the Chronically Angry" (paper presented at the annual meetings of the Academy of Management, Chicago, August 11, 1999).

35 H. Levinson, *Emotional Health in the World of Work* (Boston: South End Press, 1964); E. Schein, *Organizational Psychology* (Englewood Cliffs, NJ: Prentice Hall, 1980).

36 E. W. Morrison and S. L. Robinson, "When Employees Feel Betrayed: A Model of How Psychological Contract Violation Develops," *Academy of Management Journal* 22, 1997, pp. 226–256; S. L. Robinson, "Trust and Breach of the Psychological Contract," *Administrative Science Quarterly* 41, 1996, pp. 574–599; and S. L. Robinson, M. S. Kraatz, and D. M. Rousseau, "Changing Obligations and the Psychological Contract: A Longitudinal Study," *Academy of Management Journal* 37, 1994, pp. 137–152.

37 T. R. Tyler and P. Dogoey, "Trust in Organizational Authorities: The Influence of Motive Attributions on Willingness to Accept Decisions," in *Trust in Organizations*, ed. R. M. Kramer and T. R. Tyler (Thousand Oaks, CA: Sage, 1996), pp. 246–260.

38 A. M. Webber, "Danger: Toxic Company," *Fast Company*, November 1998, pp. 152–157.

39 A. M. Webber, "Danger: Toxic Company," *Fast Company*, November 1998, pp. 152–157.

40 P. Frost, *Toxic Emotions at Work* (Cambridge, MA: Harvard Business School Press, 2003).

41 "Men More Likely to Be Rude in Workplace, Survey Shows," *Vancouver Sun*, August 16, 1999, p. B10.

42 D. E. Gibson and S. G. Barsade, "The Experience of Anger at Work: Lessons From the Chronically Angry" (paper presented at the annual meetings of the Academy of Management, Chicago, August 11, 1999).

43 D. E. Gibson and S. G. Barsade, "The Experience of Anger at Work: Lessons From the Chronically Angry" (paper presented at the annual meetings of the Academy of Management, Chicago, August 11, 1999).

44 R. Corelli, "Dishing Out Rudeness: Complaints Abound as Customers Are Ignored, Berated," *Maclean's*, January 11, 1999, p. 44.

45 P. Frost and S. Robinson, "The Toxic Handler: Organizational Hero—and Casualty," *Harvard Business Review*, July–August 1999, p. 101 (Reprint 99406).

46 P. Frost and S. Robinson, "The Toxic Handler: Organizational Hero—and Casualty," *Harvard Business Review*, July–August 1999, p. 101 (Reprint 99406).

Chapter 10

1 Opening vignette based on "Corporate Culture," *Canadian HR Reporter* 17, no. 21 (December 6, 2004), pp. 7–11; P. Kuitenbrouwer, "Making Money, and Enjoying It: Dingwall at the Mint," *Financial Post (National Post)*, December 29, 2004, p. FP1; and C. Clark, "Dingwall Severance in the Works," *Globe and Mail*, September 30, 2005, p. A5.

2 "Organization Man: Henry Mintzberg Has Some Common Sense Observations About the Ways We Run Companies," *Financial Post*, November 22/24, 1997, pp. 14–16.

3 K. McArthur, "Air Canada Tells Employees to Crack a Smile More Often," *Globe and Mail*, March 14, 2002, pp. B1, B2.

4 K. McArthur, "Air Canada Tells Employees to Crack a Smile More Often," *Globe and Mail*, March 14, 2002, pp. B1, B2.

5 C. O'Reilly, "Corporations, Culture and Commitment: Motivation and Social Control in Organizations," *California Management Review* 31, no. 4 (1989), pp. 9–25.

6 See www.palliser.com/companyinfo.html (accessed June 11, 2005).

7 This seven-item description is based on C. A. O'Reilly III, J. Chatman, and D. F. Caldwell, "People and Organizational Culture: A Profile Comparison Approach to Assessing Person-Organization Fit," *Academy of Management Journal*, September 1991, pp. 487–516; and J. A. Chatman and K. A. Jehn, "Assessing the Relationship Between Industry Characteristics and Organizational Culture: How Different Can You Be?" *Academy of Management Journal*, June 1994, pp. 522–553. For a description of other popular measures, see A. Xenikou and A. Furnham, "A Correlational and Factor Analytic Study of Four Questionnaire Measures of Organizational Culture," *Human Relations*, March 1996, pp. 349–371. For a review of cultural dimensions, see N. M. Ashkanasy, C. P. M. Wilderom, and M. F. Peterson, eds., *Handbook of Organizational Culture and Climate* (Thousand Oaks, CA: Sage, 2000), pp. 131–145.

8 See C. A. O'Reilly and J. A. Chatman, "Culture as Social Control: Corporations, Cultures, and Commitment," in *Research in Organizational Behavior*, vol. 18, ed. B. M. Staw and L. L. Cummings (Greenwich, CT: JAI Press, 1996), pp. 157–200.

9 T. E. Deal and A. A. Kennedy, "Culture: A New Look Through Old Lenses," *Journal of Applied Behavioral Science*, November 1983, p. 501.

10 J. Case, "Corporate Culture," *Inc.*, November 1996, pp. 42–53.

11 T. Cole, "How to Stay Hired," *Report on Business Magazine*, March 1995, pp. 46–48.

12 R. McQueen, "Bad Boys Make Good," *Financial Post*, April 4, 1998, p.6.

13 The view that there will be consistency among perceptions of organizational culture has been called the "integration" perspective. For a review of this perspective and conflicting approaches, see D. Meyerson and J. Martin, "Cultural Change: An Integration of Three Different Views," *Journal of Management Studies*, November 1987, pp. 623–647; and P. J. Frost, L. F. Moore, M. R. Louis, C. C. Lundberg, and J. Martin, eds., *Reframing Organizational Culture* (Newbury Park, CA: Sage, 1991).

14 See J. M. Jermier, J. W. Slocum Jr., L. W. Fry, and J. Gaines, "Organizational Subcultures in a Soft Bureaucracy: Resistance Behind the Myth and Facade of an Official Culture," *Organization Science*, May 1991, pp. 170–194; S. A. Sackmann, "Culture and Subcultures: An Analysis of Organizational Knowledge," *Administrative Science Quarterly*, March 1992, pp. 140–161; R. F. Zammuto, "Mapping Organizational Cultures and Subcultures:

Looking Inside and Across Hospitals" (paper presented at the 1995 National Academy of Management Conference, Vancouver, August 1995); and G. Hofstede, "Identifying Organizational Subcultures: An Empirical Approach," *Journal of Management Studies*, January 1998, pp. 1–12.

15 T. A. Timmerman, "Do Organizations Have Personalities?" (paper presented at the 1996 National Academy of Management Conference, Cincinnati, OH, August 1996).

16 S. Hamm, "No Letup—and No Apologies," *BusinessWeek*, October 26, 1998, pp. 58–64.

17 Based on "Corporate Culture," *Canadian HR Reporter* 17, no. 21 (December 6, 2004), pp. 7–11.

18 See, for example, G. G. Gordon and N. DiTomaso, "Predicting Corporate Performance From Organizational Culture," *Journal of Management Studies*, November 1992, pp. 793–798; and J. B. Sorensen, "The Strength of Corporate Culture and the Reliability of Firm Performance," *Administrative Science Quarterly*, March 2002, pp. 70–91.

19 Y. Wiener, "Forms of Value Systems: A Focus on Organizational Effectiveness and Cultural Change and Maintenance," *Academy of Management Review*, October 1988, p. 536.

20 R. T. Mowday, L. W. Porter, and R. M. Steers, *Employee-Organization Linkages: The Psychology of Commitment, Absenteeism, and Turnover* (New York: Academic Press, 1982).

21 K. W. Smith, "A Brand-New Culture for the Merged Firm," *Mergers and Acquisitions* 35, no. 6 (June 2000), pp. 45–50.

22 D. M. Boje, "The Storytelling Organization: A Study of Story Performance in an Office-Supply Firm," *Administrative Science Quarterly*, March 1991, pp. 106–126; and C. H. Deutsch, "The Parables of Corporate Culture," *New York Times*, October 13, 1991, p. F25.

23 A. M. Pettigrew, "On Studying Organizational Cultures," *Administrative Science Quarterly*, December 1979, p. 576.

24 A. M. Pettigrew, "On Studying Organizational Cultures," *Administrative Science Quarterly*, December 1979, p. 576. See also K. Kamoche, "Rhetoric, Ritualism, and Totemism in Human Resource Management," *Human Relations*, April 1995, pp. 367–385.

25 V. Matthews, "Starting Every Day With a Shout and a Song," *Financial Times*, May 2, 2001, p. 11; and M. Gimein, "Sam Walton Made Us a Promise," *Fortune*, March 18, 2002, pp. 121–130.

26 A. Rafaeli and M. G. Pratt, "Tailored Meanings: On the Meaning and Impact of Organizational Dress," *Academy of Management Review*, January 1993, pp. 32–55.

27 Thanks to an anonymous reviewer for adding these.

28 M. Pendergast, *Uncommon Grounds: The History of Coffee and How It Transformed Our World* (New York: Basic Books, 1999), p. 369.

29 Thanks to a reviewer for this story.

30 Based on "Corporate Culture," *Canadian HR Reporter* 17, no. 21 (December 6, 2004), pp. 7–11; and P. Kuitenbrouwer, "Making Money, and Enjoying It: Dingwall at the Mint," *Financial Post (National Post)*, December 29, 2004, p. FP1.

31 E. H. Schein, "The Role of the Founder in Creating Organizational Culture," *Organizational Dynamics*, Summer 1983, pp. 13–28.

32 E. H. Schein, "Leadership and Organizational Culture," in *The Leader of the Future*, ed. F. Hesselbein, M. Goldsmith, and R. Beckhard (San Francisco: Jossey-Bass, 1996), pp. 61–62.

33 See, for example, J. R. Harrison and G. R. Carroll, "Keeping the Faith: A Model of Cultural Transmission in Formal Organizations," *Administrative Science Quarterly*, December 1991, pp. 552–582.

34 See B. Schneider, "The People Make the Place," *Personnel Psychology*, Autumn 1987, pp. 437–453; J. A. Chatman, "Matching People and Organizations: Selection and Socialization in Public Accounting Firms," *Administrative Science Quarterly*, September 1991, pp. 459–484; D. E. Bowen, G. E. Ledford Jr., and B. R. Nathan, "Hiring for the Organization, Not the Job," *Academy of Management Executive*, November 1991, pp. 35–51; B. Schneider, H. W. Goldstein, and D. B. Smith, "The ASA Framework: An Update," *Personnel Psychology*, Winter 1995, pp. 747–773; A. L. Kristof, "Person-Organization Fit: An Integrative Review of Its Conceptualizations, Measurement, and Implications," *Personnel Psychology*, Spring 1996, pp. 1–49; and J. Harris and J. Brannick, *Finding and Keeping Great Employees* (New York: AMACOM, 1999).

35 R. Pascale, "The Paradox of 'Corporate Culture': Reconciling Ourselves to Socialization," *California Management Review*, Winter 1985, pp. 26–27.

36 D. C. Hambrick and P. A. Mason, "Upper Echelons: The Organization as a Reflection of Its Top Managers," *Academy of Management Review*, April 1984, pp. 193–206; B. P. Niehoff, C. A. Enz, and R. A. Grover, "The Impact of Top-Management Actions on Employee Attitudes and Perceptions," *Group and Organization Studies*, September 1990, pp. 337–352; and H. M. Trice and J. M. Beyer, "Cultural Leadership in Organizations," *Organization Science*, May 1991, pp. 149–169.

37 *OB in the Workplace* based on D. Sankey, "Listening to Employees Can Solve Most Workplace Woes," *Vancouver Sun*, December 2, 2000, p. D23.

38 See, for instance, J. P. Wanous, *Organizational Entry*, 2nd ed. (New York: Addison Wesley, 1992); G. T. Chao, A. M. O'Leary-Kelly, S. Wolf, H. J. Klein, and P. D. Gardner, "Organizational Socialization: Its Content and Consequences," *Journal of Applied Psychology*, October 1994, pp. 730–743; B. E. Ashforth, A. M. Saks, and R. T. Lee, "Socialization and Newcomer Adjustment: The Role of Organizational Context," *Human Relations*, July 1998, pp. 897–926; D. A. Major, "Effective Newcomer Socialization into High-Performance Organizational Cultures," in *Handbook of Organizational Culture & Climate*, ed. N. M. Ashkanasy, C. P. M. Wilderom, and M. F. Peterson (Thousand Oaks, CA: Sage, 2000), pp. 355–368; and D. M. Cable and C. K. Parsons, "Socialization Tactics and Person-Organization Fit," *Personnel Psychology*, Spring 2001, pp. 1–23.

39 J. Impoco, "Basic Training, Sanyo Style," *U.S. News & World Report*, July 13, 1992, pp. 46–48.

40 B. Filipczak, "Trained by Starbucks," *Training*, June 1995, pp. 73–79; and S. Gruner, "Lasting Impressions," *Inc.*, July 1998, p. 126.

41 J. Van Maanen and E. H. Schein, "Career Development," in *Improving Life at Work*, ed. J. R. Hackman and J. L. Suttle (Santa Monica, CA: Goodyear, 1977), pp. 58–62.

42 D. C. Feldman, "The Multiple Socialization of Organization Members," *Academy of Management Review*, April 1981, p. 310.

43 J. Van Maanen and E. H. Schein, "Career Development," in *Improving Life at Work*, ed. J. R. Hackman and J. L. Suttle (Santa Monica, CA: Goodyear, 1977), p. 59.

44 T. Cole, "How to Stay Hired," *Report on Business Magazine*, March 1995, pp. 46–48.

45 B. Schneider, "The People Make the Place," *Personnel Psychology*, Autumn 1987, pp. 437–453; D. E. Bowen, G. E. Ledford Jr., and B. R. Nathan, "Hiring for the Organization, Not the Job," *Academy of Management Executive*, November 1991, pp. 35–51; B. Schneider,

H. W. Goldstein, and D. B. Smith, "The ASA Framework: An Update," *Personnel Psychology*, Winter 1995, pp. 747–773; A. L. Kristof, "Person-Organization Fit: An Integrative Review of Its Conceptualizations, Measurement, and Implications," *Personnel Psychology*, Spring 1996, pp. 1–49; D. M. Cable and T. A. Judge, "Interviewers' Perceptions of Person-Organization Fit and Organizational Selection Decisions," *Journal of Applied Psychology*, August 1997, pp. 546–561; and J. Schaubroeck, D. C. Ganster, and J. R. Jones, "Organization and Occupation Influences in the Attraction-Selection-Attrition Process," *Journal of Applied Psychology*, December 1998, pp. 869–891.

46 This section is based on R. Goffee and G. Jones, *The Character of a Corporation: How Your Company's Culture Can Make or Break Your Business* (New York: HarperBusiness, 1998).

47 Jennifer Chatman's work, as reported in M. Siegel, "The Perils of Culture Conflict," *Fortune*, November 9, 1998, pp. 257–262.

48 J. Tagliabue, "At a French Factory, Culture Is a Two-Way Street," *New York Times*, February 25, 2001, p. BU4.

49 Vignette based on "Corporate Culture," *Canadian HR Reporter* 17, no. 21 (December 6, 2004), pp. 7–11; and P. Kuitenbrouwer, "Making Money, and Enjoying It: Dingwall at the Mint," *Financial Post (National Post)*, December 29, 2004, p. FP1.

50 J. Stephens and P. Behr, "Enron's Culture Fed Its Demise: Groupthink Promoted Foolhardy Risks," *Washington Post*, January 27, 2002, p. A01.

51 See, for instance, D. Miller, "What Happens After Success: The Perils of Excellence," *Journal of Management Studies*, May 1994, pp. 11–38.

52 See C. Lindsay, "Paradoxes of Organizational Diversity: Living Within the Paradoxes," in *Proceedings of the 50th Academy of Management Conference*, ed. L. R. Jauch and J. L. Wall, San Francisco, 1990, pp. 374–378; T. Cox Jr., *Cultural Diversity in Organizations: Theory, Research & Practice* (San Francisco: Berrett-Koehler, 1993), pp. 162–170; and L. Grensing-Pophal, "Hiring to Fit Your Corporate Culture," *HR Magazine*, August 1999, pp. 50–54.

53 "Texaco: Lessons From a Crisis-in-Progress," *BusinessWeek*, December 2, 1996, p. 44; and M. A. Verespej, "Zero Tolerance," *IndustryWeek*, January 6, 1997, pp. 24–28.

54 A. F. Buono and J. L. Bowditch, *The Human Side of Mergers and Acquisitions: Managing Collisions Between People, Cultures, and Organizations* (San Francisco: Jossey-Bass, 1989); S. Cartwright and C. L. Cooper, "The Role of Culture Compatibility in Successful Organizational Marriages," *Academy of Management Executive*, May 1993, pp. 57–70; D. Carey and D. Ogden, "A Match Made in Heaven? Find out Before You Merge," *Wall Street Journal*, November 30, 1998, p. A22; R. J. Grossman, "Irreconcilable Differences," *HR Magazine*, April 1999, pp. 42–48; J. Veiga, M. Lubatkin, R. Calori, and P. Very, "Measuring Organizational Culture Clashes: A Two-Nation Post-Hoc Analysis of a Cultural Compatibility Index," *Human Relations*, April 2000, pp. 539–557; and E. Krell, "Merging Corporate Cultures," *Training*, May 2001, pp. 68–78.

55 T. Watson, "In the Clutches of a Slowdown: Plant Closures Might Loom in DaimlerChrysler's Future as the Carmaker Tries to Correct Past Management Errors, a Misread of What Consumers Wanted to Drive off the Lot and a Clash of Cultures From Its Recent Merger," *Financial Post (National Post)*, December 23, 2000, p. D7; T. Watson, "Zetsche Runs into Perfect Storm: Chrysler's Crisis," *Financial Post (National Post)*, December 13, 2000, p. C1, C4; M. Steen, "Chrysler to Improve: Schrempp: Shareholders Are Embittered by Steep Losses and Imprecise

Earnings Forecasts: Better Operating Results," *Financial Post (National Post)*, April 11, 2002, p. FP12; and "DaimlerChrysler Boss to Step Down," BBC News World Edition, July 28, 2005.

56 E. Church, "Andersen Name Fades into Canadian History," *Globe and Mail*, June 12, 2002, pp. B1, B2.

57 K. W. Smith, "A Brand-New Culture for the Merged Firm," *Mergers and Acquisitions* 35, no. 6 (June 2000), pp. 45–50.

58 Based on "Corporate Culture," *Canadian HR Reporter* 17, no. 21 (December 6, 2004), pp. 7–11.

59 M. Raynaud and M. Teasdale, "Confusions & Acquisitions: Post-Merger Culture Shock and Some Remedies," *Communication World* 9, no. 6 (May–June 1992), pp. 44–45.

60 M. Raynaud and M. Teasdale, "Confusions & Acquisitions: Post-Merger Culture Shock and Some Remedies," *Communication World* 9, no. 6 (May–June 1992), pp. 44–45.

61 Vignette based on "Corporate Culture," *Canadian HR Reporter* 17, no. 21 (December 6, 2004), pp. 7–11; and P. Kuitenbrouwer, "Making Money, and Enjoying It: Dingwall at the Mint," *Financial Post (National Post)*, December 29, 2004, p. FP1; and C. Clark, "Dingwall Severance in the Works," *Globe and Mail*, September 30, 2005, p. A5.

62 M. L. Wald and J. Schwartz, "Shuttle Inquiry Uncovers Flaws in Communication," *New York Times*, August 4, 2003, www.nytimes.com.

63 M. L. Wald and J. Schwartz, "Shuttle Inquiry Uncovers Flaws in Communication," *New York Times*, August 4, 2003, www.nytimes.com.

64 J. P. Kotter, "Leading Changes: Why Transformation Efforts Fail," *Harvard Business Review*, March–April 1995, pp. 59–67; and J. P. Kotter, *Leading Change* (Boston: Harvard Business School Press, 1996).

65 Based on J. P. Kotter, *Leading Change* (Boston: Harvard Business School Press, 1996).

66 See B. Victor and J. B. Cullen, "The Organizational Bases of Ethical Work Climates," *Administrative Science Quarterly*, March 1988, pp. 101–125; L. K. Trevino, "A Cultural Perspective on Changing and Developing Organizational Ethics," in *Research in Organizational Change and Development*, vol. 4, ed. W. A. Pasmore and R. W. Woodman (Greenwich, CT: JAI Press, 1990); and M. W. Dickson, D. B. Smith, M. W. Grojean, and M. Ehrhart, "An Organizational Climate Regarding Ethics: The Outcome of Leader Values and the Practices That Reflect Them," *Leadership Quarterly*, Summer 2001, pp. 197–217.

67 Richard Starnes, "Nortel's New Ethics Chief Is Veteran Corruption Fighter," *Ottawa Citizen*, January 12, 2005, p. D1.

68 J. Laucius, "Ethics Weren't Valued at Old Nortel," *Ottawa Citizen*, August 21, 2004, p. D1.

69 Ideas in this feature were influenced by A. L. Wilkins, "The Culture Audit: A Tool for Understanding Organizations," *Organizational Dynamics*, Autumn 1983, pp. 24–38; H. M. Trice and J. M. Beyer, *The Cultures of Work Organizations* (Englewood Cliffs, NJ: Prentice Hall, 1993), pp. 358–362; H. Lancaster, "To Avoid a Job Failure, Learn the Culture of a Company First," *Wall Street Journal*, July 14, 1998, p. B1; and M. Belliveau, "4 Ways to Read a Company," *Fast Company*, October 1998, p. 158.

Chapter 11

1 J. P. Kotter, "What Leaders Really Do," *Harvard Business Review*, May–June 1990, pp. 103–111.

2 R. N. Kanungo, "Leadership in Organizations: Looking Ahead to the 21st Century," *Canadian Psychology* 39, no. 1–2 (1998), p. 77. For more evidence of this consensus, see N. Adler, *International Dimensions of Organizational Behavior*, 3rd ed. (Cincinnati, OH: South Western, 1997); R. J. House, "Leadership in the Twenty-First Century," in *The Changing Nature of Work*, ed. A. Howard (San Francisco: Jossey-Bass, 1995), pp. 411–450; R. N. Kanungo and M. Mendonca, *Ethical Dimensions of Leadership* (Thousand Oaks, CA: Sage. 1996); A. Zaleznik, "The Leadership Gap," *Academy of Management Executive* 4, no. 1 (1990), pp. 7–22.

3 J. G. Geier, "A Trait Approach to the Study of Leadership in Small Groups," *Journal of Communication*, December 1967, pp. 316–323.

4 S. A. Kirkpatrick and E. A. Locke, "Leadership: Do Traits Matter?" *Academy of Management Executive*, May 1991, pp. 48–60; and S. J. Zaccaro, R. J. Foti, and D. A. Kenny, "Self-Monitoring and Trait-Based Variance in Leadership: An Investigation of Leader Flexibility Across Multiple Group Situations," *Journal of Applied Psychology*, April 1991, pp. 308–315.

5 See T. A. Judge, J. E. Bono, R. Ilies, and M. Werner, "Personality and Leadership: A Review" (paper presented at the 15th Annual Conference of the Society for Industrial and Organizational Psychology, New Orleans, 2000); and T. A. Judge, J. E. Bono, R. Ilies, and M. W. Gerhardt, "Personality and Leadership: A Qualitative and Quantitative Review," *Journal of Applied Psychology*, August 2002, pp. 765–780.

6 T. A. Judge, J. E. Bono, R. Ilies, and M. Werner, "Personality and Leadership: A Review" (paper presented at the 15th Annual Conference of the Society for Industrial and Organizational Psychology, New Orleans, 2000).

7 T. A. Judge, J. E. Bono, R. Ilies, and M. Werner, "Personality and Leadership: A Review" (paper presented at the 15th Annual Conference of the Society for Industrial and Organizational Psychology, New Orleans, 2000); R. G. Lord, C. L. DeVader, and G. M. Alliger, "A Meta-Analysis of the Relation Between Personality Traits and Leadership Perceptions: An Application of Validity Generalization Procedures," *Journal of Applied Psychology*, August 1986, pp. 402–410; and J. A. Smith and R. J. Foti, "A Pattern Approach to the Study of Leader Emergence," *Leadership Quarterly*, Summer 1998, pp. 147–160.

8 This section is based on D. Goleman, *Working With Emotional Intelligence* (New York: Bantam, 1998); and D. Goleman, "What Makes a Leader?" *Harvard Business Review*, November–December 1998, pp. 93–102.

9 D. Goleman, R. Boyatzis, and A. McKee, *Primal Leadership: Realizing the Power of Emotional Intelligence* (Cambridge, MA: Harvard Business School Press, 2002).

10 N. M. Ashkanasy and C. S. Daus, "Emotion in the Workplace: The New Challenge for Managers," *Academy of Management Executive* 16, no. 1 (2002), pp. 76–86.

11 D. N. Den Hartog, R. J. House, P. J. Hanges, S. A. Ruiz-Quintanilla, and P. W. Dorfman, "Culture Specific and Cross-culturally Generalizable Implicit Leadership Theories: Are Attributes of Charismatic/Transformational Leadership Universally Endorsed?" *Leadership Quarterly* 10, no. 2 (Summer 1999), pp. 219–256.

12 R. M. Stogdill and A. E. Coons, eds., *Leader Behavior: Its Description and Measurement*, Research Monograph no. 88 (Columbus: Ohio State University, Bureau of Business Research, 1951). This research is updated in S. Kerr, C. A. Schriesheim, C. J. Murphy, and R. M. Stogdill, "Toward a Contingency Theory of Leadership Based Upon the Consideration and Initiating Structure Literature," *Organizational Behavior and Human Performance*, August 1974, pp. 62–82; and C. A. Schriesheim, C. C. Cogliser, and L. L. Neider,

"Is It 'Trustworthy'? A Multiple-Levels-of-Analysis Reexamination of an Ohio State Leadership Study, With Implications for Future Research," *Leadership Quarterly*, Summer 1995, pp. 111–145.

13 R. Kahn and D. Katz, "Leadership Practices in Relation to Productivity and Morale," in *Group Dynamics: Research and Theory*, 2nd ed., ed. D. Cartwright and A. Zander (Elmsford, NY: Row, Paterson, 1960).

14 R. R. Blake and J. S. Mouton, *The Managerial Grid* (Houston, TX: Gulf, 1964).

15 R. R. Blake and A. A. McCanse, *Leadership Dilemmas—Grid Solutions* (Houston, TX: Gulf Publishing Company, 1991); R. R. Blake and J. S. Mouton, "Management by Grid Principles or Situationalism: Which?" *Group and Organization Studies* 7, 1982, pp. 207–210.

16 For a critical review, see A. K. Korman, "'Consideration,' 'Initiating Structure' and Organizational Criteria—A Review," *Personnel Psychology* 19, 1966, pp. 349–361. For a more supportive review, see S. Kerr and C. Schriesheim, "Consideration, Initiating Structure, and Organizational Criteria—An Update of Korman's 1966 Review," *Personnel Psychology* 27, 1974, pp. 555–568.

17 Based on G. Johns and A. M. Saks, *Organizational Behaviour*, 5th ed. (Toronto: Pearson Education Canada, 2001), p. 276.

18 See, for instance, P. M. Podsakoff, S. B. MacKenzie, M. Ahearne, and W. H. Bommer, "Searching for a Needle in a Haystack: Trying to Identify the Illusive Moderators of Leadership Behavior," *Journal of Management* 1, no. 3 (1995), pp. 422–470.

19 F. E. Fiedler, *A Theory of Leadership Effectiveness* (New York: McGraw-Hill, 1967).

20 Cited in R. J. House and R. N. Aditya, "The Social Scientific Study of Leadership: Quo Vadis?" *Journal of Management* 23, no. 3 (1997), p. 422.

21 G. Johns and A. M. Saks, *Organizational Behaviour*, 5th ed. (Toronto: Pearson Education Canada, 2001), pp. 278– 279.

22 P. Hersey and K. H. Blanchard, "So You Want to Know Your Leadership Style?" *Training and Development Journal*, February 1974, pp. 1–15; and P. Hersey, K. H. Blanchard, and D. E. Johnson, *Management of Organizational Behavior: Leading Human Resources*, 8th ed. (Upper Saddle River, NJ: Prentice Hall, 2001).

23 Cited in C. F. Fernandez and R. P. Vecchio, "Situational Leadership Theory Revisited: A Test of an Across-Jobs Perspective," *Leadership Quarterly* 8, no. 1 (1997), p. 67.

24 **For controversy surrounding the Fiedler LPC scale, see** A. Bryman, "Leadership in Organizations," in *Handbook of Organization Studies*, ed. S. R. Clegg, C. Hardy, and W. R. Nord (London: Sage, 1996), pp. 279–280; A. Bryman, *Leadership and Organizations* (London: Routledge and Kegan Paul, 1986); and T. Peters and N. Austin, *A Passion for Excellence* (New York: Random House, 1985). **For supportive evidence on the Fiedler model, see** L. H. Peters, D. D. Hartke, and J. T. Pohlmann, "Fiedler's Contingency Theory of Leadership: An Application of the Meta-Analysis Procedures of Schmidt and Hunter," *Psychological Bulletin*, March 1985, pp. 274–285; C. A. Schriesheim, B. J. Tepper, and L. A. Tetrault, "Least Preferred Co-Worker Score, Situational Control, and Leadership Effectiveness: A Meta-Analysis of Contingency Model Performance Predictions," *Journal of Applied Psychology*, August 1994, pp. 561–573; and R. Ayman, M. M. Chemers, and F. Fiedler, "The Contingency Model of Leadership Effectiveness: Its Levels of Analysis," *Leadership Quarterly*, Summer 1995, pp. 147–167. **For evidence that LPC scores are not stable, see,** for instance, R. W. Rice, "Psychometric Properties of the Esteem for the Least Preferred Coworker (LPC) Scale," *Academy of Management Review*, January 1978, pp. 106–118; C. A. Schriesheim, B. D. Bannister, and W. H. Money, "Psychometric Properties of the LPC Scale: An Extension of Rice's Review," *Academy of Management Review,* April 1979, pp. 287–290; and J. K. Kennedy, J. M. Houston, M. A. Korgaard, and D. D. Gallo, "Construct Space of the Least Preferred Co-Worker (LPC) Scale," *Educational & Psychological Measurement,* Fall 1987, pp. 807–814. **For difficulty in applying Fiedler's model, see** E. H. Schein, *Organizational Psychology,* 3rd ed. (Englewood Cliffs, NJ: Prentice Hall, 1980), pp. 116–117; and B. Kabanoff, "A Critique of Leader Match and Its Implications for Leadership Research," *Personnel Psychology,* Winter 1981, pp. 749–764. **For evidence that Hersey and Blanchard's model has received little attention from researchers, see** R. K. Hambleton and R. Gumpert, "The Validity of Hersey and Blanchard's Theory of Leader Effectiveness," *Group & Organizational Studies,* June 1982, pp. 225–242; C. L. Graeff, "The Situational Leadership Theory: A Critical View," *Academy of Management Review,* April 1983, pp. 285–291; R. P. Vecchio, "Situational Leadership Theory: An Examination of a Prescriptive Theory," *Journal of Applied Psychology,* August 1987, pp. 444–451; J. R. Goodson, G. W. McGee, and J. F. Cashman, "Situational Leadership Theory: A Test of Leadership Prescriptions," *Group & Organization Studies,* December 1989, pp. 446–461; W. Blank, J. R. Weitzel, and S. G. Green, "A Test of the Situational Leadership Theory," *Personnel Psychology,* Autumn 1990, pp. 579–597; and W. R. Norris and R. P. Vecchio, "Situational Leadership Theory: A Replication," *Group & Organization Management,* September 1992, pp. 331–342. **For evidence of partial support for the theory, see** R. P. Vecchio, "Situational Leadership Theory: An Examination of a Prescriptive Theory," *Journal of Applied Psychology,* August 1987, pp. 444–451; and W. R. Norris and R. P. Vecchio, "Situational Leadership Theory: A Replication," *Group & Organization Management,* September 1992, pp. 331–342; and **for evidence of no support for Hersey and Blanchard, see** W. Blank, J. R. Weitzel, and S. G. Green, "A Test of the Situational Leadership Theory," *Personnel Psychology,* Autumn 1990, pp. 579–597.

25 M. G. Evans, "The Effects of Supervisory Behavior on the Path-Goal Relationship," *Organizational Behavior and Human Performance* 5, 1970, pp. 277–298; M. G. Evans, "Leadership and Motivation: A Core Concept," *Academy of Management Journal* 13, 1970, 91–102; R. J. House, "A Path-Goal Theory of Leader Effectiveness," *Administrative Science Quarterly,* September 1971, pp. 321–338; R. J. House and T. R. Mitchell, "Path-Goal Theory of Leadership," *Journal of Contemporary Business,* Autumn 1974, p. 86; M. G. Evans, "Leadership," in *Organizational Behavior,* ed. S. Kerr (Columbus, OH: Grid Publishing, 1979); R. J. House, "Retrospective Comment," in *The Great Writings in Management and Organizational Behavior,* 2nd ed., ed. L. E. Boone and D. D. Bowen (New York: Random House, 1987), pp. 354–364; and M. G. Evans, "Fuhrungstheorien, Weg-ziel-theorie," in *Handworterbuch Der Fuhrung,* 2nd ed., ed. A. Kieser, G. Reber, and R. Wunderer, trans. G. Reber (Stuttgart, Germany: Schaffer Poeschal Verlag, 1995), pp. 1075–1091.

26 G. R. Jones, J. M. George, C. W. L. Hill, and N. Langton, *Contemporary Management* (Toronto: McGraw-Hill Ryerson, 2002), p. 392.

27 R. J. House, "Path-Goal Theory of Leadership: Lessons, Legacy, and a Reformulated Theory," *Leadership Quarterly* 7, no. 3 (Fall 1996), pp. 323–352.

28 L. R. Anderson, "Toward a Two-Track Model of Leadership Training: Suggestions From Self-Monitoring Theory," *Small Group Research,* May 1990, pp. 147–167; G. H. Dobbins, W. S. Long, E. J. Dedrick, and T. C. Clemons, "The Role of Self-Monitoring and Gender on Leader Emergence: A Laboratory and Field Study," *Journal of Management,* September 1990, pp. 609–618; and S. J.

Zaccaro, R. J. Foti, and D. A. Kenny, "Self-Monitoring and Trait-Based Variance in Leadership: An Investigation of Leader Flexibility Across Multiple Group Situations," *Journal of Applied Psychology,* April 1991, pp. 308–315.

29 S. Kerr and J. M. Jermier, "Substitutes for Leadership: Their Meaning and Measurement," *Organizational Behavior and Human Performance,* December 1978, pp. 375–403; J. P. Howell and P. W. Dorfman, "Substitutes for Leadership: Test of a Construct," *Academy of Management Journal,* December 1981, pp. 714–728; J. P. Howell, P. W. Dorfman, and S. Kerr, "Leadership and Substitutes for Leadership," *Journal of Applied Behavioral Science* 22, no. 1 (1986), pp. 29–46; J. P. Howell, D. E. Bowen, P. W. Dorfman, S. Kerr, and P. M. Podsakoff, "Substitutes for Leadership: Effective Alternatives to Ineffective Leadership," *Organizational Dynamics,* Summer 1990, pp. 21–38; P. M. Podsakoff, B. P. Niehoff, S. B. MacKenzie, and M. L. Williams, "Do Substitutes for Leadership Really Substitute for Leadership? An Empirical Examination of Kerr and Jermier's Situational Leadership Model," *Organizational Behavior and Human Decision Processes,* February 1993, pp. 1–44; P. M. Podsakoff and S. B. MacKenzie, "An Examination of Substitutes for Leadership Within a Levels-of-Analysis Framework," *Leadership Quarterly,* Fall 1995, pp. 289–328; P. M. Podsakoff, S. B. MacKenzie, and W. H. Bommer, "Transformational Leader Behaviors and Substitutes for Leadership as Determinants of Employee Satisfaction, Commitment, Trust, and Organizational Citizenship Behaviors," *Journal of Management* 22, no. 2 (1996), pp. 259–298; P. M. Podsakoff, S. B. MacKenzie, and W. H. Bommer, "Meta-Analysis of the Relationships Between Kerr and Jermier's Substitutes for Leadership and Employee Attitudes, Role Perceptions, and Performance," *Journal of Applied Psychology,* August 1996, pp. 380–399; and J. M. Jermier and S. Kerr, "'Substitutes for Leadership: Their Meaning and Measurement'—Contextual Recollections and Current Observations," *Leadership Quarterly* 8, no. 2 (1997), pp. 95–101.

30 R. E. Kelley, "In Praise of Followers," *Harvard Business Review,* November–December 1988, pp. 142–148; E. P. Hollander, "Leadership, Followership, Self, and Others," *Leadership Quarterly,* Spring 1992, pp. 43–54; and I. Challeff, *The Courageous Follower: Standing up to and for Our Leaders* (San Francisco: Berrett-Koehler, 1995).

31 R. E. Kelley, "In Praise of Followers," *Harvard Business Review,* November–December 1988, pp. 142–148.

32 V. Smith, "Leading Us On," *Report on Business Magazine,* April 1999, pp. 91–96.

33 A. Bryman, "Leadership in Organizations," in *Handbook of Organization Studies,* ed. S. R. Clegg, C. Hardy, and W. R. Nord (London: Sage, 1996), pp. 276–292.

34 J. M. Howell and B. J. Avolio, "The Leverage of Leadership," in *Leadership: Achieving Exceptional Performance,* A Special Supplement Prepared by the Richard Ivey School of Business, *Globe and Mail,* May 15, 1998, pp. C1, C2.

35 J. M. Howell and B. J. Avolio, "The Leverage of Leadership," in *Leadership: Achieving Exceptional Performance,* A Special Supplement Prepared by the Richard Ivey School of Business, *Globe and Mail,* May 15, 1998, pp. C1, C2.

36 R. N. Kanungo, "Leadership in Organizations: Looking Ahead to the 21st Century," *Canadian Psychology* 39, no. 1–2 (1998), p. 78.

37 B. M. Bass, "Leadership: Good, Better, Best," *Organizational Dynamics,* Winter 1985, pp. 26–40; and J. Seltzer and B. M. Bass, "Transformational Leadership: Beyond Initiation and Consideration," *Journal of Management,* December 1990, pp. 693–703.

38 P. C. Nutt and R. W. Backoff, "Crafting Vision," *Journal of Management Inquiry,* December 1997, p. 309.

39 P. C. Nutt and R. W. Backoff, "Crafting Vision," *Journal of Management Inquiry,* December 1997, pp. 312–314.

40 J. C. Collins and J. I. Porras, *Built to Last: Successful Habits of Visionary Companies* (New York: HarperBusiness, 1994).

41 J. M. Howell and B. J. Avolio, "The Leverage of Leadership," in *Leadership: Achieving Exceptional Performance,* A Special Supplement Prepared by the Richard Ivey School of Business, *Globe and Mail,* May 15, 1998, p. C2.

42 "Building a Better Boss," *Maclean's,* September 30, 1996, p. 41.

43 T. Dvir, D. Eden, B. J. Avolio, and B. Shamir, "Impact of Transformational Leadership on Follower Development and Performance: A Field Experiment," *Academy of Management Journal* 45, no. 4 (2002), pp. 735–744; R. J. House, J. Woycke, and E. M. Fodor, "Charismatic and Noncharismatic Leaders: Differences in Behavior and Effectiveness," in *Charismatic Leadership in Organizations,* ed. J. A. Conger and R. N. Kanungo (Thousand Oaks, CA: Sage, 1998), pp. 103–104; D. A. Waldman, B. M. Bass, and F. J. Yammarino, "Adding to Contingent-Reward Behavior: The Augmenting Effect of Charismatic Leadership," *Group & Organization Studies,* December 1990, pp. 381–394; S. A. Kirkpatrick and E. A. Locke, "Direct and Indirect Effects of Three Core Charismatic Leadership Components on Performance and Attitudes," *Journal of Applied Psychology,* February 1996, pp. 36–51; and J. A. Conger, R. N. Kanungo, and S. T. Menon, "Charismatic Leadership and Follower Outcome Effects" (paper presented at the 58th Annual Academy of Management Meetings, San Diego, CA, August 1998).

44 J. M. Howell and P. J. Frost, "A Laboratory Study of Charismatic Leadership," *Organizational Behavior & Human Decision Processes* 43, no. 2 (April 1989), pp. 243–269.

45 "Building a Better Boss," *Maclean's,* September 30, 1996, p. 41.

46 Cited in B. M. Bass and B. J. Avolio, "Developing Transformational Leadership: 1992 and Beyond," *Journal of European Industrial Training,* January 1990, p. 23.

47 J. J. Hater and B. M. Bass, "Supervisors' Evaluation and Subordinates' Perceptions of Transformational and Transactional Leadership," *Journal of Applied Psychology,* November 1988, pp. 695–702.

48 B. M. Bass and B. J. Avolio, "Developing Transformational Leadership: 1992 and Beyond," *Journal of European Industrial Training,* January 1990, p. 23; and J. M. Howell and B. J. Avolio, "The Leverage of Leadership," in *Leadership: Achieving Exceptional Performance,* A Special Supplement Prepared by the Richard Ivey School of Business, *Globe and Mail,* May 15, 1998, pp. C1, C2.

49 T. DeGroot, D. S. Kiker, and T. C. Cross, "A Meta-Analysis to Review Organizational Outcomes Related to Charismatic Leadership," *Canadian Journal of Administrative Sciences* 17, no. 4 (2000), pp. 356–371.

50 D. E. Carl and M. Javidan, "Universality of Charismatic Leadership: A Multi-Nation Study," *Academy of Management Proceedings,* 2001, p. IM: B1–B6.

51 Information in this paragraph based on K. Boehnke, A. C. Di Stefano, J. J. Di Stefano, and N. Bontis, "Leadership for Extraordinary Performance," *Business Quarterly,* Summer 1997, pp. 57–63.

52 J. A. Conger, *The Charismatic Leader: Behind the Mystique of Exceptional Leadership* (San Francisco: Jossey-Bass, 1989); R. Hogan, R. Raskin, and D. Fazzini, "The Dark Side of Charisma," in *Measures of Leadership,* ed. K. E. Clark and M. B. Clark (West

Orange, NJ: Leadership Library of America, 1990); D. Sankowsky, "The Charismatic Leader as Narcissist: Understanding the Abuse of Power," *Organizational Dynamics,* Spring 1995, pp. 57–71; and J. O'Connor, M. D. Mumford, T. C. Clifton, T. L. Gessner, and M. S. Connelly, "Charismatic Leaders and Destructiveness: An Historiometric Study," *Leadership Quarterly,* Winter 1995, pp. 529–555.

53 A. Elsner, "The Era of CEO as Superhero Ends Amid Corporate Scandals," *Globe and Mail,* July 10, 2002, p. C1.

54 Rakesh Khurana, "Toward More Rational CEO Succession," *Chief Executive,* April 2003, p. 16.

55 G. Pitts, "Scandals Part of Natural Cycles of Excess," *Globe and Mail,* June 28, 2002, pp. B1, B5.

56 J. Collins, "Level 5 Leadership: The Triumph of Humility and Fierce Resolve," *Harvard Business Review,* January 2001, pp. 67–76; R. A. Hinde and J. Groebel, eds., *Cooperation, Prosocial Behavior, Trust and Commitment* (Cambridge, UK: Cambridge University Press, 1991), p. 194; D. J. McAllister, "Affect- and Cognition-Based Trust as Foundations for Interpersonal Cooperation in Organizations," *Academy of Management Journal,* February 1995, p. 25; and D. M. Rousseau, S. B. Sitkin, R. S. Burt, and C. Camerer, "Not So Different After All: A Cross-Discipline View of Trust," *Academy of Management Review,* July 1998, pp. 393–404.

57 Based on D. Montgomery, "To Task-Force Leader, Results, Not Excuses, Matter," *Star-Telegram.com,* September 12, 2005, www.dfw.com/mld/dfw/ (accessed September 22, 2005).

58 See, for example, L. J. Zachary, *The Mentor's Guide: Facilitating Effective Learning Relationships* (San Francisco: Jossey-Bass, 2000); M. Murray, *Beyond the Myths and Magic of Mentoring: How to Facilitate an Effective Mentoring Process,* rev. ed. (New York: Wiley, 2001); and F. Warner, "Inside Intel's Mentoring Movement," *Fast Company,* April 2002, pp. 116–120.

59 *Mentoring: Finding a Perfect Match for People Development Briefing* (Ottawa: The Conference Board of Canada, June 2003).

60 J. A. Wilson and N. S. Elman, "Organizational Benefits of Mentoring," *Academy of Management Executive,* November 1990, p. 90; and J. Reingold, "Want to Grow as a Leader? Get a Mentor?" *Fast Company,* January 2001, pp. 58–60.

61 T. D. Allen, L. T. Eby, M. L. Poteet, E. Lentz, and L. Lima, "Career Benefits Associated With Mentoring for Protégés: A Meta-Analysis," *Journal of Applied Psychology,* February 2004, pp. 127–136.

62 See, for example, D. A. Thomas, "The Impact of Race on Managers' Experiences of Developmental Relationships: An Intra-Organizational Study," *Journal of Organizational Behavior,* November 1990, pp. 479–492; K. E. Kram and D. T. Hall, "Mentoring in a Context of Diversity and Turbulence," in *Managing Diversity,* ed. E. E. Kossek and S. A. Lobel (Cambridge, MA: Blackwell, 1996), pp. 108–36; M. N. Ruderman and M. W. Hughes-James, "Leadership Development Across Race and Gender," in *The Center for Creative Leadership Handbook of Leadership Development,* ed. C. D. McCauley, R. S. Moxley, and E. Van Velsor (San Francisco: Jossey-Bass, 1998), pp. 291–335; and B. R. Ragins and J. L. Cotton, "Mentor Functions and Outcomes: A Comparison of Men and Women in Formal and Informal Mentoring Relationships," *Journal of Applied Psychology,* August 1999, pp. 529–550.

63 J. A. Wilson and N. S. Elman, "Organizational Benefits of Mentoring," *Academy of Management Executive,* November 1990, p. 90.

64 D. Zielinski, "Mentoring Up," *Training* 37, no. 10 (October 2000), pp. 136–141.

65 See, for instance, J. H. Zenger, E. Musselwhite, K. Hurson, and C. Perrin, *Leading Teams: Mastering the New Role* (Homewood, IL: Business One Irwin, 1994); and M. Frohman, "Nothing Kills Teams Like Ill-Prepared Leaders," *IndustryWeek*, October 2, 1995, pp. 72–76.

66 See, for instance, M. Frohman, "Nothing Kills Teams Like Ill-Prepared Leaders," *IndustryWeek*, October 2, 1995, p. 93.

67 See, for instance, M. Frohman, "Nothing Kills Teams Like Ill-Prepared Leaders," *IndustryWeek*, October 2, 1995, p. 100.

68 J. R. Katzenbach, and D. K. Smith, *The Wisdom of Teams: Creating the High-Performance Organization* (Boston: Harvard Business School Press, 1993).

69 N. Steckler and N. Fondas, "Building Team Leader Effectiveness: A Diagnostic Tool," *Organizational Dynamics*, Winter 1995, p. 20.

70 R. S. Wellins, W. C. Byham, and G. R. Dixon, *Inside Teams* (San Francisco: Jossey-Bass, 1994), p. 318.

71 N. Steckler and N. Fondas, "Building Team Leader Effectiveness: A Diagnostic Tool," *Organizational Dynamics*, Winter 1995, p. 21.

72 C. C. Manz and H. P. Sims Jr., *The New SuperLeadership: Leading Others to Lead Themselves* (San Francisco: Berrett-Koehler Publishers, 2001).

73 A. Bandura, "Self-Reinforcement: Theoretical and Methodological Considerations," *Behaviorism* 4, 1976, pp. 135–155; P. W. Corrigan, C. J. Wallace, and M. L. Schade, "Learning Medication Self-Management Skills in Schizophrenia; Relationships With Cognitive Deficits and Psychiatric Symptom," *Behavior Therapy*, Winter, 1994, pp. 5–15; A. S. Bellack, "A Comparison of Self-Reinforcement and Self-Monitoring in a Weight Reduction Program," *Behavior Therapy* 7, 1976, pp. 68–75; T. A. Eckman, W. C. Wirshing, and S. R. Marder, "Technique for Training Schizophrenic Patients in Illness Self-Management: A Controlled Trial," *American Journal of Psychiatry* 149, 1992, pp. 1549–1555; J. J. Felixbrod and K. D. O'Leary, "Effect of Reinforcement on Children's Academic Behavior as a Function of Self-Determined and Externally Imposed Contingencies," *Journal of Applied Behavior Analysis* 6, 1973, pp. 141–150; A. J. Litrownik, L. R. Franzini, and D. Skenderian, "The Effects of Locus of Reinforcement Control on a Concept Identification Task," *Psychological Reports* 39, 1976, pp. 159–165; P. D. McGorry, "Psychoeducation in First-Episode Psychosis: A Therapeutic Process," *Psychiatry*, November, 1995, pp. 313–328; G. S. Parcel, P. R. Swank, and M. J. Mariotto, "Self-Management of Cystic Fibrosis: A Structural Model for Educational and Behavioral Variables," *Social Science and Medicine* 38, 1994, pp. 1307–1315; G. E. Speidel, "Motivating Effect of Contingent Self-Reward," *Journal of Experimental Psychology* 102, 1974, pp. 528–530.

74 D. B. Jeffrey, "A Comparison of the Effects of External Control and Self-Control on the Modification and Maintenance of Weight," *Journal of Abnormal Psychology* 83, 1974, pp. 404–410.

75 M. Castaneda, T. A. Kolenko, and R. J. Aldag, "Self-Management Perceptions and Practices: A Structural Equations Analysis," *Journal of Organizational Behavior* 20, 1999, p. 102.

76 M. Castaneda, T. A. Kolenko, and R. J. Aldag, "Self-Management Perceptions and Practices: A Structural Equations Analysis," *Journal of Organizational Behavior* 20, 1999, p. 102.

77 M. Castaneda, T. A. Kolenko and R. J. Aldag, "Self-Management Perceptions and Practices: A Structural Equations Analysis," *Journal of Organizational Behavior* 20, 1999, p. 102.

78 C. C. Manz and H. P. Sims Jr., *The New SuperLeadership: Leading Others to Lead Themselves* (San Francisco: Berrett-Koehler, 2001).

79 R. M. Kanter, *The Change Masters, Innovation and Entrepreneurship in the American Corporation* (New York: Simon and Schuster, 1983).

80 R. A. Heifetz, *Leadership Without Easy Answers* (Cambridge, MA: Harvard University Press, 1996), p. 205.

81 R. A. Heifetz, *Leadership Without Easy Answers* (Cambridge, MA: Harvard University Press, 1996), p. 205.

82 R. A. Heifetz, *Leadership Without Easy Answers* (Cambridge, MA: Harvard University Press, 1996), p. 188.

83 Based on D. D. Kirkpatrick and S. Shane, "Ex-FEMA Chief Tells of Frustration and Chaos," *New York Times*, September 15, 2005, www.nytimes.com.

84 This section is based on R. B. Morgan, "Self- and Co-Worker Perceptions of Ethics and Their Relationships to Leadership and Salary," *Academy of Management Journal*, February 1993, pp. 200–214; J. B. Ciulla, "Leadership Ethics: Mapping the Territory," *Business Ethics Quarterly*, January 1995, pp. 5–28; E. P. Hollander, "Ethical Challenges in the Leader-Follower Relationship," *Business Ethics Quarterly*, January 1995, pp. 55–65; J. C. Rost, "Leadership: A Discussion About Ethics," *Business Ethics Quarterly*, January 1995, pp. 129–142; and R. N. Kanungo and M. Mendonca, *Ethical Dimensions of Leadership* (Thousand Oaks, CA: Sage, 1996).

85 D. Leonhardt, "The Imperial Chief Executive Is Suddenly in the Cross Hairs," *New York Times*, June 24, 2002, www.nytimes.com (accessed June 24, 2002).

86 P. Morton, "Welch Tries to Save Face in Post-Enron World: Regulators Circling," *National Post*, September 17, 2002, p. A1.

87 J. M. Burns, *Leadership* (New York: Harper and Row, 1978).

88 J. M. Howell and B. J. Avolio, "The Ethics of Charismatic Leadership: Submission or Liberation?" *Academy of Management Executive*, May 1992, pp. 43–55.

89 J. Stephens and P. Behr, "Enron's Culture Fed Its Demise: Groupthink Promoted Foolhardy Risks," *Washington Post*, January 27, 2002, p. A01.

90 J. G. Clawson, *Level Three Leadership* (Upper Saddle River, NJ: Prentice Hall, 1999), pp. 46–49.

91 B. Little, "It's True: Women Are Gaining Ground in Every Job Category," *Globe and Mail*, March 4, 2002, p. B8.

92 J. McFarland, "Women Still Find Slow Rise to Power Positions," *Globe and Mail*, March 13, 2003, pp. B1, B7.

93 R. McQueen, "Glitter Girls No More," *National Post Business*, March 2001, p. 68.

94 V. Galt, "Glass Ceiling Still Tough To Crack," *Globe and Mail*, May 4, 2005, pp. C1, C2.

95 L. Ramsay, "A League of Their Own," *Globe and Mail*, November 23, 2002, p. B11.

96 L. Ramsay, "A League of Their Own," *Globe and Mail*, November 23, 2002, p. B11.

97 Michelle Martinez, "Prepared for the Future: Training Women for Corporate Leadership," *HRM Magazine*, April 1997, pp. 80–87.

98 Information in this paragraph based on Michelle Martinez, "Prepared for the Future: Training Women for Corporate Leadership," *HRM Magazine*, April 1997, pp. 80–87.

99 M. McDonald, "They Love Me—Not: Once Hailed as Heroines, Female CEOs Now Face Harsh Critiques," *U.S. News & World Report*, June 24, 2002, www.usnews.com/usnews/issue/020624/biztech/24women.htm (accessed November 26, 2005).

100 M. McDonald, "They Love Me—Not: Once Hailed as Heroines, Female CEOs Now Face Harsh Critiques," *U.S. News & World*

Report, June 24, 2002, www.usnews.com/usnews/issue/
020624/biztech/24women.htm (accessed November 26, 2005).

101 J. Wells, "Stuck on the Ladder: Not Only Is the Glass Ceiling Still in Place, But Men and Women Have Very Different Views of the Problem," *Maclean's*, October 20, 1997, p. 60.

102 J. Wells, "Stuck on the Ladder: Not Only Is the Glass Ceiling Still in Place, But Men and Women Have Very Different Views of the Problem," *Maclean's*, October 20, 1997, p. 60.

103 Statistics Canada, "Workplace and Employee Survey Compendium," October 25, 2004, Catalogue no 71-585-XIE, p. 36.

104 The material in this section is based on J. Grant, "Women as Managers: What They Can Offer to Organizations," *Organizational Dynamics*, Winter 1988, pp. 56–63; S. Helgesen, *The Female Advantage: Women's Ways of Leadership* (New York: Doubleday, 1990); A. H. Eagly and B. T. Johnson, "Gender and Leadership Style: A Meta-Analysis," *Psychological Bulletin*, September 1990, pp. 233–256; A. H. Eagly and S. J. Karau, "Gender and the Emergence of Leaders: A Meta-Analysis," *Journal of Personality and Social Psychology*, May 1991, pp. 685–710; J. B. Rosener, "Ways Women Lead," *Harvard Business Review*, November–December 1990, pp. 119–125; "Debate: Ways Men and Women Lead," *Harvard Business Review*, January–February 1991, pp. 150–160; A. H. Eagly, M. G. Makhijani, and B. G. Klonsky, "Gender and the Evaluation of Leaders: A Meta-Analysis," *Psychological Bulletin*, January 1992, pp. 3–22; A. H. Eagly, S. J. Karau, and B. T. Johnson, "Gender and Leadership Style Among School Principals: A Meta-Analysis," *Educational Administration Quarterly*, February 1992, pp. 76–102; L. R. Offermann and C. Beil, "Achievement Styles of Women Leaders and Their Peers," *Psychology of Women Quarterly*, March 1992, pp. 37–56; T. Melamed and N. Bozionelos, "Gender Differences in the Personality Features of British Managers," *Psychological Reports*, December 1992, pp. 979–986; G. N. Powell, *Women & Men in Management*, 2nd ed. (Thousand Oaks, CA: Sage, 1993); R. L. Kent and S. E. Moss, "Effects of Size and Gender Role on Leader Emergence," *Academy of Management Journal*, October 1994, pp. 1335–1346; C. Lee, "The Feminization of Management," *Training*, November 1994, pp. 25–31; H. Collingwood, "Women as Managers: Not Just Different, Better," *Working Woman*, November 1995, p. 14; and J. B. Rosener, *America's Competitive Secret: Women Managers* (New York: Oxford University Press, 1995).

105 B. Orser, *Creating High Performance Organizations: Leveraging Women's Leadership* (Ottawa: The Conference Board of Canada, 2000).

106 J. M. Norvilitis and H. M. Reid, "Evidence for an Association Between Gender-Role Identity and a Measure of Executive Function," *Psychological Reports*, February 2002, pp. 35–45; W. H. Decker and D. M. Rotondo, "Relationships Among Gender, Type of Humor, and Perceived Leader Effectiveness," *Journal of Managerial Issues*, Winter 2001, pp. 450–465; H. Aguinis and S. K. R. Adams, "Social-Role Versus Structural Models of Gender and Influence Use in Organizations: A Strong Inference Approach," *Group & Organization Management*, December 1998, pp. 414–446; and A. H. Eagly, S. J. Karau, and M. G. Makhijani, "Gender and the Effectiveness of Leaders: A Meta-Analysis," *Psychological Bulletin* 117, 1995, pp. 125–145.

107 A. H. Eagly, M. C. Johannesen-Schmidt, and M. L. van Engen, "Transformational, Transactional, and Laissez-Faire Leadership Styles: A Meta-Analysis Comparing Women and Men," *Psychological Bulletin* 129, no. 4 (July 2003), pp. 569–591; K. M. Bartol, D. C. Martin, and J. A. Kromkowski, "Leadership and the Glass Ceiling: Gender and Ethnic Influences on Leader Behaviors

at Middle and Executive Managerial Levels," *Journal of Leadership & Organizational Studies*, Winter 2003, pp. 8–19; and R. Sharpe, "As Leaders, Women Rule," *BusinessWeek*, November 20, 2000, pp. 74–84.

108 K. M. Bartol, D. C. Martin, and J. A. Kromkowski, "Leadership and the Glass Ceiling: Gender and Ethnic Influences on Leader Behaviors at Middle and Executive Managerial Levels," *Journal of Leadership & Organizational Studies*, Winter 2003, pp. 8–19.

109 B. J. Avolio, S. Kahai, and G. E. Dodge, "E-Leadership: Implications for Theory, Research, and Practice," *Leadership Quarterly*, Winter 2000, pp. 615–668; and B. J. Avolio and S. S. Kahai, "Adding the 'E' to E-Leadership: How It May Impact Your Leadership," *Organizational Dynamics* 31, no. 4 (2003), 325–338.

110 J. Howell and K. Hall-Merenda, "Leading From a Distance," in *Leadership: Achieving Exceptional Performance*, A Special Supplement Prepared by the Richard Ivey School of Business, *Globe and Mail*, May 15, 1998, pp. C1, C2.

111 The material in this section is based on J. Grant, "Women as Managers: What They Can Offer to Organizations," *Organizational Dynamics*, Winter 1988, pp. 56–63; S. Helgesen, *The Female Advantage: Women's Ways of Leadership* (New York: Doubleday, 1990); A. H. Eagly and B. T. Johnson, "Gender and Leadership Style: A Meta-Analysis," *Psychological Bulletin*, September 1990, pp. 233–256; A. H. Eagly and S. J. Karau, "Gender and the Emergence of Leaders: A Meta-Analysis," *Journal of Personality and Social Psychology*, May 1991, pp. 685–710; J. B. Rosener, "Ways Women Lead," *Harvard Business Review*, November–December 1990, pp. 119–125; "Debate: Ways Men and Women Lead," *Harvard Business Review*, January–February 1991, pp. 150–160; A. H. Eagly, M. G. Makhijani, and B. G. Klonsky, "Gender and the Evaluation of Leaders: A Meta-Analysis," *Psychological Bulletin*, January 1992, pp. 3–22; A. H. Eagly, S. J. Karau, and B. T. Johnson, "Gender and Leadership Style Among School Principals: A Meta-Analysis," *Educational Administration Quarterly*, February 1992, pp. 76–102; L. R. Offermann and C. Beil, "Achievement Styles of Women Leaders and Their Peers," *Psychology of Women Quarterly*, March 1992, pp. 37–56; T. Melamed and N. Bozionelos, "Gender Differences in the Personality Features of British Managers," *Psychological Reports*, December 1992, pp. 979–986; G. N. Powell, *Women & Men in Management*, 2nd ed. (Thousand Oaks, CA: Sage, 1993); R. L. Kent and S. E. Moss, "Effects of Size and Gender Role on Leader Emergence," *Academy of Management Journal*, October 1994, pp. 1335–1346; C. Lee, "The Feminization of Management," *Training*, November 1994, pp. 25–31; H. Collingwood, "Women as Managers: Not Just Different: Better," *Working Woman*, November 1995, p. 14; and J. B. Rosener, *America's Competitive Secret: Women Managers* (New York: Oxford University Press, 1995).

112 "Military-Style Management in China," *Asia Inc.*, March 1995, p. 70.

113 R. J. House, "Leadership in the Twenty-First Century," in *The Changing Nature of Work*, ed. A. Howard (San Francisco: Jossey-Bass, 1995), pp. 442–444; and M. F. Peterson and J. G. Hunt, "International Perspectives on International Leadership," *Leadership Quarterly*, Fall 1997, pp. 203–231.

114 D. N. Den Hartog, R. J. House, P. J. Hanges, S. A. Ruiz-Quintanilla, and P. W. Dorfman, "Culture Specific and Cross-culturally Generalizable Implicit Leadership Theories: Are Attributes of Charismatic/Transformational Leadership Universally Endorsed?" *Leadership Quarterly* 10, no. 2 (Summer 1999), pp. 219–256.; and D. E. Carl and M. Javidan, "Universality of Charismatic Leadership: A Multi-Nation Study" (paper presented at the

115 D. E. Carl and M. Javidan, "Universality of Charismatic Leadership: A Multi-Nation Study" (paper presented at the National Academy of Management Conference, Washington, DC, August 2001).

National Academy of Management Conference, Washington, DC, August 2001), p. 29.

116 See, for instance, R. Lofthouse, "Herding the Cats," *EuroBusiness*, February 2001, pp. 64-65; M. Delahoussaye, "Leadership in the 21st Century," *Training*, September 2001, pp. 60-72; and K. Ellis, "Making Waves," *Training*, June 2003, pp. 16-21.

117 See, for instance, A. A. Vicere, "Executive Education: The Leading Edge," *Organizational Dynamics*, Autumn 1996, pp. 67–81; J. Barling, T. Weber, and E. K. Kelloway, "Effects of Transformational Leadership Training on Attitudinal and Financial Outcomes: A Field Experiment," *Journal of Applied Psychology*, December 1996, pp. 827–832; and D. V. Day, "Leadership Development: A Review in Context," *Leadership Quarterly*, Winter 2000, pp. 581–613.

118 M. Sashkin, "The Visionary Leader," in *Charismatic Leadership*, ed. J. A. Conger, R. N. Kanungo, and Associates (San Francisco: Jossey-Bass, 1988), p. 150.

119 J. Powell, "Forging Fearless Leaders," *Financial Post Daily*, March 13, 1997, pp. 14, 16.

120 "Camp Overhaul: Where BC Companies Send Their Best and Brightest for Management Development," *BCBusiness Magazine*, February 1995, pp. 27–30.

121 Information on Telus and Bank of Montreal based on Jennifer Wells, "Stuck on the Ladder: Not Only Is the Glass Ceiling Still in Place, but Men and Women Have Very Different Views of the Problem," *Maclean's*, October 20, 1997, p. 60.

122 P. Brady and D. McLean, *In the Pipeline or on the Sidelines: Is Your Leadership Development Working for Women? Gender Diversity Tool Kit—Resource No. 3* (Ottawa: The Conference Board of Canada, 2002).

123 J. Wells, "Stuck on the Ladder: Not Only Is the Glass Ceiling Still in Place, but Men and Women Have Very Different Views of the Problem," *Maclean's*, October 20, 1997, p. 60; and M. Barrett, "Workplace Equality: Pursuing a Goal That Makes the Best of Business Sense," *CMA Management Accounting Magazine*, September, 1993, p. 11.

124 W. Mclellan, "Companies Can't Ignore Diversity," *Sudbury Star*, August 27, 2005, p. C1.

125 M. B. White, "Women of the World: Diversity Goes Global at IBM," *Diversity Factor*, Summer 1999, pp. 13–16.

126 M. B. White, "Women of the World: Diversity Goes Global at IBM," *Diversity Factor*, Summer 1999, pp. 13–16.

127 Based on J. M. Howell and P. J. Frost, "A Laboratory Study of Charismatic Leadership," *Organizational Behavior and Human Decision Processes*, April 1989, pp. 243–269.

128 Based on V. H. Vroom, "A New Look at Managerial Decision Making," *Organizational Dynamics*, Spring 1973, pp. 66–80. With permission.

Chapter 12

1 Opening vignette based on M. Skapinker, "Why Nike Has Broken into a Sweat," *Financial Times*, March 6, 2002, http://news.ft.com/ft/gx.cgi/ftc?pagename=View&c=Article&cid=FT363BT GHYC&live=true (accessed March 12, 2002); D. Simpson, "Ethics and Corporate Social Responsibility," advertising supplement, *Report on Business Magazine*, February 2002.

2 See H. A. Simon, "Rationality in Psychology and Economics," *Journal of Business*, October 1986, pp. 209–224; and A. Langley, "In Search of Rationality: The Purposes Behind the Use of Formal Analysis in Organizations," *Administrative Science Quarterly*, December 1989, pp. 598–631.

3 For a review of the rational model, see E. F. Harrison, *The Managerial Decision Making Process*, 5th ed. (Boston: Houghton Mifflin, 1999), pp. 75–102.

4 W. Pounds, "The Process of Problem Finding," *Industrial Management Review*, Fall 1969, pp. 1–19.

5 T. Barry, "Smart Cookies: Why CIBC Said Yes to the Girl Guides," *Marketing Magazine*, May 31, 1999, pp. 11, 14.

6 J. G. March, *A Primer on Decision Making* (New York: Free Press, 1994), pp. 2–7.

7 Vignette based on "Quotas at Thailand Footwear Factory Promote Fast Work but Draw Fire," *Knight Ridder Tribune Business News*, March 18, 2002, p. 1.

8 D. L. Rados, "Selection and Evaluation of Alternatives in Repetitive Decision Making," *Administrative Science Quarterly*, June 1972, pp. 196–206.

9 M. Bazerman, *Judgment in Managerial Decision Making*, 3rd ed. (New York: Wiley, 1994), p. 5.

10 See, for instance, L. R. Beach, *The Psychology of Decision Making* (Thousand Oaks, CA: Sage, 1997).

11 See, for example, M. D. Cohen, J. G. March, and J. P. Olsen, "A Garbage Can Model of Organizational Choice," *Administrative Science Quarterly*, March 1972, pp. 1–25.

12 See J. G. Thompson, *Organizations in Action* (New York: McGraw-Hill, 1967), p. 123.

13 See H. A. Simon, *Administrative Behavior*, 4th ed. (New York: Free Press, 1997); and M. Augier, "Simon Says: Bounded Rationality Matters," *Journal of Management Inquiry*, September 2001, pp. 268–275.

14 Based on K. May, "Ottawa May Stop Hiring Best Qualified," *National Post*, March 4, 2002, p. A4.

15 W. H. Agor, "The Logic of Intuition: How Top Executives Make Important Decisions," *Organizational Dynamics*, Winter 1986, p. 5; W. H. Agor, ed., *Intuition in Organizations* (Newbury Park, CA: Sage, 1989); O. Behling and N. L. Eckel, "Making Sense Out of Intuition," *Academy of Management Executive*, February 1991, pp. 46–47; G. Klein, *Sources of Power: How People Make Decisions* (Cambridge, MA: MIT Press, 1998); P. E. Ross, "Flash of Genius," *Forbes*, November 16, 1998, pp. 98–104; L. A. Burke and M. K. Miller, "Taking the Mystery Out of Intuitive Decision Making," *Academy of Management Executive*, November 1999, pp. 91–99; and N. Khatri and H. A. Ng, "The Role of Intuition in Strategic Decision Making," *Human Relations*, January 2000, pp. 57–86.

16 O. Behling and N. L. Eckel, "Making Sense Out of Intuition," *Academy of Management Executive*, February 1991, pp. 46–54.

17 L. A. Burke and M. K. Miller, "Taking the Mystery Out of Intuitive Decision Making," *Academy of Management Executive*, November 1999, pp. 91–99.

18 A. Tversky and K. Kahneman, "Judgment Under Uncertainty: Heuristics and Biases," *Science*, September 1974, pp. 1124–1131.

19 A. Tversky and D. Kahneman, "Judgment Under Uncertainty: Heuristics and Biases," *Science*, September 1974, pp. 1124–1131; and J. S. Hammond, R. L. Keeney, and H. Raiffa, "The Hidden Traps in Decision Making," *Harvard Business Review*, September–October 1998, pp. 47–58.

20 See A. Tversky and D. Kahneman, "Availability: A Heuristic for Judging Frequency and Probability," in *Judgment Under Uncertainty: Heuristics and Biases*, ed. D. Kahneman, P. Slovic, and A. Tversky (Cambridge, UK: Cambridge University Press, 1982), pp. 163–78.

21 G. Whyte and C. Sue-Chan, "The Neglect of Base Rate Data by Human Resources Managers in Employee Selection," *Revue Canadienne des Sciences de l'Administration* 19, no. 1 (2002), pp. 1–11.

22 See B. M. Staw, "The Escalation of Commitment to a Course of Action," *Academy of Management Review*, October 1981, pp. 577–587; and H. Moon, "Looking Forward and Looking Back: Integrating Completion and Sunk-Cost Effects within an Escalation-of-Commitment Progress Decision," *Journal of Applied Psychology*, February 2001, pp. 104–113.

23 See S. A. Mohrman, D. Finegold, and J. A. Klein, "Designing the Knowledge Enterprise: Beyond Programs and Tools," *Organizational Dynamics* 31, no. 2 (2002), pp. 134–150; and H. Dolezalek, "Collaborating in Cyberspace," *Training*, April 2003, pp. 32–37.

24 Cited in A. Cabrera and E. F. Cabrera, "Knowledge-Sharing Dilemmas," *Organization Studies* 5, 2002, p. 687.

25 B. Roberts, "Pick Employees' Brains," *HR Magazine*, February 2000, pp. 115–116; B. Fryer, "Get Smart," *Inc.*, September 1999, p. 65; and D. Zielinski, "Have You Shared a Bright Idea Today?" *Training*, July 2000, p. 65.

26 B. Fryer, "Get Smart," *Inc.*, September 1999, p. 63.

27 E. Truch, "Managing Personal Knowledge: The Key to Tomorrow's Employability," *Journal of Change Management*, December 2001, pp. 102–105.

28 J. Gordon, "Intellectual Capital and You," *Training*, September 1999, p. 33.

29 D. Zielinski, "Have You Shared a Bright Idea Today?" *Training*, July 2000, pp. 65–67.

30 See N. R. F. Maier, "Assets and Liabilities in Group Problem Solving: The Need for an Integrative Function," *Psychological Review*, April 1967, pp. 239–249; G. W. Hill, "Group Versus Individual Performance: Are N+1 Heads Better Than One?" *Psychological Bulletin*, May 1982, pp. 517–539; and A. E. Schwartz and J. Levin, "Better Group Decision Making," *Supervisory Management*, June 1990, p. 4.

31 See, for example, W. C. Swap and Associates, *Group Decision Making* (Newbury Park, CA: Sage, 1984).

32 See, for example, R. A. Cooke and J. A. Kernaghan, "Estimating the Difference Between Group Versus Individual Performance on Problem-Solving Tasks," *Group & Organization Studies*, September 1987, pp. 319–342; and L. K. Michaelsen, W. E. Watson, and R. H. Black, "A Realistic Test of Individual Versus Group Consensus Decision Making," *Journal of Applied Psychology*, October 1989, pp. 834–839.

33 I. L. Janis, *Groupthink: Psychological Studies of Policy Decisions and Fiascoes*, 2nd ed. (Boston: Houghton Mifflin, 1982); W. Park, "A Review of Research on Groupthink," *Journal of Behavioral Decision Making*, July 1990, pp. 229–245; C. P. Neck and G. Moorhead, "Groupthink Remodeled: The Importance of Leadership, Time Pressure, and Methodical Decision Making Procedures," *Human Relations*, May 1995, pp. 537–558; and J. N. Choi and M. U. Kim, "The Organizational Application of Groupthink and Its Limits in Organizations," *Journal of Applied Psychology*, April 1999, pp. 297–306.

34 I. L. Janis, *Groupthink: Psychological Studies of Policy Decisions and Fiascoes*, 2nd ed. (Boston: Houghton Mifflin, 1982).

35 Based on B. Little, "Forecasters Were Lost in a Fog of Pessimism," *Globe and Mail*, March 21, 2002, p. B19.

36 M. E. Turner and A. R. Pratkanis, "Mitigating Groupthink by Stimulating Constructive Conflict," in *Using Conflict in Organizations*, ed. C. De Dreu and E. Van de Vliert (London: Sage, 1997), pp. 53–71.

37 See N. R. F. Maier, *Principles of Human Relations* (New York: Wiley, 1952); I. L. Janis, *Groupthink: Psychological Studies of Policy Decisions and Fiascoes*, 2nd ed. (Boston: Houghton Mifflin, 1982); and C. R. Leana, "A Partial Test of Janis' Groupthink Model: Effects of Group Cohesiveness and Leader Behavior on Defective Decision Making," *Journal of Management*, Spring 1985, pp. 5–17.

38 J. N. Choi and M. U. Kim, "The Organizational Application of Groupthink and Its Limitations in Organizations," *Journal of Applied Psychology* 84, 1999, pp. 297–306.

39 J. Longley and D. G. Pruitt, "Groupthink: A Critique of Janis' Theory," in *Review of Personality and Social Psychology*, ed. L. Wheeler (Newbury Park, CA: Sage, 1980), pp. 507–513; and J. A. Sniezek, "Groups Under Uncertainty: An Examination of Confidence in Group Decision Making," *Organizational Behavior & Human Decision Processes* 52, 1992, pp. 124–155.

40 C. McCauley, "The Nature of Social Influence in Groupthink: Compliance and Internalization," *Journal of Personality and Social Psychology* 57, 1989, pp. 250–260; P. E. Tetlock, R. S. Peterson, C. McGuire, S. Chang, and P. Feld, "Assessing Political Group Dynamics: A Test of the Groupthink Model," *Journal of Personality and Social Psychology* 63, 1992, pp. 781–796; S. Graham, "A Review of Attribution Theory in Achievement Contexts," *Educational Psychology Review* 3, 1991, pp. 5–39; and G. Moorhead and J. R. Montanari, "An Empirical Investigation of the Groupthink Phenomenon," *Human Relations* 39, 1986, pp. 399–410.

41 J. N. Choi and M. U. Kim, "The Organizational Application of Groupthink and Its Limitations in Organizations," *Journal of Applied Psychology* 84, 1999, pp. 297–306.

42 See D. J. Isenberg, "Group Polarization: A Critical Review and Meta-Analysis," *Journal of Personality and Social Psychology*, December 1986, pp. 1141–1151; J. L. Hale and F. J. Boster, "Comparing Effect Coded Models of Choice Shifts," *Communication Research Reports*, April 1988, pp. 180–186; and P. W. Paese, M. Bieser, and M. E. Tubbs, "Framing Effects and Choice Shifts in Group Decision Making," *Organizational Behavior & Human Decision Processes*, October 1993, pp. 149–165.

43 See, for example, N. Kogan and M. A. Wallach, "Risk Taking as a Function of the Situation, the Person, and the Group," in *New Directions in Psychology*, 3 (New York: Holt, Rinehart and Winston, 1967); and M. A. Wallach, N. Kogan, and D. J. Bem, "Group Influence on Individual Risk Taking," *Journal of Abnormal and Social Psychology* 65, 1962, pp. 75–86.

44 R. D. Clark III, "Group-Induced Shift Toward Risk: A Critical Appraisal," *Psychological Bulletin*, October 1971, pp. 251–270.

45 A. F. Osborn, *Applied Imagination: Principles and Procedures of Creative Thinking* (New York: Scribner's, 1941). See also P. B. Paulus, M. T. Dzindolet, G. Poletes, and L. M. Camacho, "Perception of Performance in Group Brainstorming: The Illusion of Group Productivity," *Personality and Social Psychology Bulletin*, February 1993, pp. 78–89.

46 I. Edwards, "Office Intrigue: By Design, Consultants Have Workers Conspire to Create Business Environments Tailored to Getting the Job Done," *Financial Post Daily*, December 16, 1997, p. 25.

47 Information in this paragraph from G. Crone, "Electrifying Brainstorms," *Financial Post (National Post)*, July 3, 1999, p. D11.

48 T. Graham, "The Keys to the Middle Kingdom: Experts Will Tell You It Takes Years of Patient Effort to Crack the Chinese Market, but That's Not Always the Case," *PROFIT*, December 1997/January 1998, p. 29.

49 See A. L. Delbecq, A. H. Van deVen, and D. H. Gustafson, *Group Techniques for Program Planning: A Guide to Nominal and Delphi Processes* (Glenview, IL: Scott, Foresman, 1975); and W. M. Fox, "Anonymity and Other Keys to Successful Problem-Solving Meetings," *National Productivity Review,* Spring 1989, pp. 145–156.

50 See, for instance, A. R. Dennis and J. S. Valacich, "Computer Brainstorms: More Heads Are Better Than One," *Journal of Applied Psychology,* August 1993, pp. 531–537; R. B. Gallupe and W. H. Cooper, "Brainstorming Electronically," *Sloan Management Review,* Fall 1993, pp. 27–36; and A. B. Hollingshead and J. E. McGrath, "Computer-Assisted Groups: A Critical Review of the Empirical Research," in *Team Effectiveness and Decision Making in Organizations,* ed. R. A. Guzzo and E. Salas (San Francisco: Jossey-Bass, 1995), pp. 46–78.

51 V. H. Vroom and P. W. Yetton, *Leadership and Decision Making* (Pittsburgh, PA: University of Pittsburgh Press, 1973).

52 V. H. Vroom and A. G. Jago, *The New Leadership: Managing Participation in Organizations* (Englewood Cliffs, NJ: Prentice Hall, 1988). See also V. H. Vroom and A. G. Jago, "Situation Effects and Levels of Analysis in the Study of Leader Participation," *Leadership Quarterly,* Summer 1995, pp. 169–181.

53 See, for example, R. H. G. Field, "A Test of the Vroom-Yetton Normative Model of Leadership," *Journal of Applied Psychology,* October 1982, pp. 523–532; C. R. Leana, "Power Relinquishment Versus Power Sharing: Theoretical Clarification and Empirical Comparison of Delegation and Participation," *Journal of Applied Psychology,* May 1987, pp. 228–233; J. T. Ettling and A. G. Jago, "Participation Under Conditions of Conflict: More on the Validity of the Vroom-Yetton Model," *Journal of Management Studies,* January 1988, pp. 73–83; and R. H. G. Field and R. J. House, "A Test of the Vroom-Yetton Model Using Manager and Subordinate Reports," *Journal of Applied Psychology,* June 1990, pp. 362–366.

54 W. Kondro, "Canada in Creativity Crisis: Study," *National Post,* May 25, 2001, pp. A2, A6.

55 "Theatrics in the Boardroom: Acting Classes Are Not Widely Accepted as Management Tools," *Financial Post,* March 4/6, 1995, pp. 24–25.

56 T. Kelley, *The Art of Innovation: Lessons in Creativity From IDEO, America's Leading Design Firm* (New York: Doubleday, 2001).

57 T. M. Amabile, "A Model of Creativity and Innovation in Organizations," in *Research in Organizational Behavior,* vol. 10, ed. B. M. Staw and L. L. Cummings (Greenwich, CT: JAI Press, 1988), pp. 123–167; and T. M. Amabile, "Motivating Creativity in Organizations," *California Management Review,* Fall 1997, p. 40.

58 T. M. Amabile, *The Social Psychology of Creativity* (New York: Springer-Verlag, 1983); T. M. Amabile, "A Model of Creativity and Innovation in Organizations," in *Research in Organizational Behavior,* vol. 10, ed. B. M. Staw and L. L. Cummings (Greenwich, CT: JAI Press, 1988), pp. 123–167; C. E. Shalley, "Effects of Productivity Goals, Creativity Goals, and Personal Discretion on Individual Creativity," *Journal of Applied Psychology* 76, 1991, pp. 179–185; R. W. Woodman, J. E. Sawyer, and R. W. Griffin, "Toward a Theory of Organizational Creativity," *Academy of Management Review* 18, 1993, pp. 293–321; G. Zaltman, R. Duncan, and J. Holbek, *Innovation and Organizations* (London: Wiley, 1973).

59 G. R. Oldham and A. Cummings, "Employee Creativity: Personal and Contextual Factors at Work," *Academy of Management Journal* 39, 1996, pp. 607–634.

60 Cited in C. G. Morris, *Psychology: An Introduction,* 9th ed. (Upper Saddle River, NJ: Prentice Hall, 1996), p. 344.

61 F. B. Barron and D. M. Harrington, "Creativity, Intelligence, and Personality," *Annual Review of Psychology* 32, 1981, pp. 439–476; G. A. Davis, "Testing for Creative Potential," *Contemporary Educational Psychology* 14, 1989, pp. 257–274; C. Martindale, "Personality, Situation, and Creativity," in *Handbook of Creativity,* ed. J. A. Glover, R. R. Ronning, and C. R. Reynolds (New York: Plenum, 1989), pp. 211–232.

62 G. R. Oldham and A. Cummings, "Employee Creativity: Personal and Contextual Factors at Work," *Academy of Management Journal* 39, 1996, pp. 607–634; see also F. B. Barron and D. M. Harrington, "Creativity, Intelligence, and Personality," *Annual Review of Psychology* 32, 1981, pp. 439–476; H. G. Gough, "A Creative Personality Scale for the Adjective Check List," *Journal of Personality and Social Psychology* 37, 1979, pp. 1398–1405; C. Martindale, "Personality, Situation, and Creativity," in *Handbook of Creativity,* ed. J. A. Glover, R. R. Ronning, and C. R. Reynolds (New York: Plenum, 1989), pp. 211–232; and R. J. Sternberg, *Handbook of Creativity* (New York: Cambridge University Press, 1999).

63 F. Barron and D. M. Harrington, "Creativity, Intelligence, and Personality," *Annual Review of Psychology* 32, 1981, pp. 439–476; M. Basadur and C. T. Finkbeiner, "Measuring Preference for Ideation in Creating Problem Solving Training," *Journal of Applied Behavioral Science* 21, 1985, pp. 37–49; M. Basadur, G. B. Graen, and S. G. Green, "Training in Creative Problem Solving: Effects on Ideation and Problem Finding and Solving in an Industrial Research Organization," *Organizational Behavior and Human Performance* 30, 1982, pp. 41–70; H. Gardner, *Frames of Mind* (New York: Basic Books, 1993); M. A. Glynn, "Innovative Genius: A Framework for Relating Individual and Organizational Intelligences to Innovation," *Academy of Management Review* 21, 1996, pp. 1081–1111; R. Helson, B. Roberts, and G. Agronick, "Enduringness and Change in Creative Personality and the Prediction of Occupational Creativity," *Journal of Personality and Social Psychology* 69, 1995, pp. 1173–1183; B. Singh, "Role of Personality Versus Biographical Factors in Creativity," *Psychological Studies* 31, 1986, pp. 90–92; and R. J. Sternberg, "A Three-Facet Model of Creativity," in *The Nature of Creativity: Contemporary Psychological Views,* ed. R. J. Sternberg (Cambridge, UK: Cambridge University Press, 1988), pp. 125–147.

64 T. M. Amabile, "A Model of Creativity and Innovation in Organizations," in *Research in Organizational Behavior,* vol. 10, ed. B. M. Staw, and L. L. Cummings (Greenwich, CT: JAI Press, 1988), pp. 123–167; T. M. Amabile, K. G. Hill, B. A. Hennessey, and E. M. Tighe, "The Work Preference Inventory; Assessing Intrinsic and Extrinsic Motivational Orientations," *Journal of Personality and Social Psychology* 66, 1994, pp. 950–967; M. A. Glynn and J. Webster, "Refining the Nomological Net of the Adult Playfulness Scale: Personality, Motivational, and Attitudinal Correlates for Highly Intelligent Adults," *Psychological Reports* 72, 1993, pp. 1023–1026; R. Kanfer, "Motivation Theory and Industrial/Organizational Psychology," in *Handbook of Industrial and Organizational Psychology,* vol. 1, ed. M. D. Dunnette (Palo Alto, CA: Consulting Psychologists Press, 1990), pp. 75–170; and R. Kanfer and P. L. Ackerman, "Motivation and Cognitive Abilities: An Integrative Aptitude-Treatment Interaction Approach to Skill Acquisition," *Journal of Applied Psychology* Monograph 74, 1989, pp. 657–690.

65 T. M. Amabile, "How to Kill Creativity," *Harvard Business Review,* September–October 1998, pp. 76–87.

66 T. M. Amabile, "A Model of Creativity and Innovation in Organizations," in *Research in Organizational Behavior*, vol. 10, ed. B. M. Staw and L. L. Cummings (Greenwich, CT: JAI Press, 1988), pp. 123–167; T. M. Amabile and S. S. Gryskiewicz, *Creativity in the R&D Laboratory*, Technical Report no. 10 (Greensboro, NC: Center for Creative Leadership, 1987); and G. R. Oldham and A. Cummings, "Employee Creativity: Personal and Contextual Factors at Work," *Academy of Management Journal* 39, 1996, pp. 607–634.

67 M. D. Mumford and S. B. Gustafson, "Creativity Syndrome: Integration, Application, and Innovation," *Psychological Bulletin* 103, 1988, pp. 27–43.

68 E. De Bono, *Six Thinking Hats* (Boston: Little, Brown, 1985); and E. De Bono, *The Mechanism of Mind* (New York: Simon and Schuster, 1969).

69 Adapted from E. De Bono, *Six Thinking Hats* (Boston: Little, Brown, 1985).

70 T. M. Amabile, "How to Kill Creativity," *Harvard Business Review*, September–October 1998, pp. 76–87.

71 Insight based on A. Muoio, "Brainstorming at Switzerland's BrainStore: Building an Assembly Line for Ideas," *Financial Post (National Post)*, April 12, 2000, p. C15.

72 Cited in T. Stevens, "Creativity Killers," *IndustryWeek*, January 23, 1995, p. 63.

73 Vignette based on "Quotas at Thailand Footwear Factory Promote Fast Work but Draw Fire," *Knight Ridder Tribune Business News*, March 18, 2002, p. 1.

74 P. L. Schumann, "A Moral Principles Framework for Human Resource Management Ethics," *Human Resource Management Review* 11, Spring–Summer 2001, pp. 93–111; M. G. Velasquez, *Business Ethics*, 4th ed. (Upper Saddle River, NJ: Prentice Hall, 1998), Chapter 2; and G. F. Cavanagh, D. J. Moberg, and M. Valasquez, "The Ethics of Organizational Politics," *Academy of Management Journal*, June 1981, pp. 363–374.

75 *Focus on Ethics* based on T. Tedesco, "Broker Shielded From Firing," *Financial Post (National Post)*, April 10, 2001, pp. C1, C10; P. Brieger, "Manitoba Hits Brokerage for Poor Supervision: $160,000 Fine," *National Post*, May 10, 2001, p. C1; and D. DeCloet, "Punished Broker Acted as an Advisor to Watchdog," *Financial Post (National Post)*, May 16, 2001, p. C4.

76 See, for example, T. Machan, ed., *Commerce and Morality* (Totowa, NJ: Rowman and Littlefield, 1988).

77 P. L. Schumann, "A Moral Principles Framework for Human Resource Management Ethics," *Human Resource Management Review* 11, Spring–Summer 2001, pp. 93–111.

78 See, for instance, R. S. Dillon, "Care and Respect," in *Explorations in Feminist Ethics: Theory and Practice*, ed. E. Browning Cole and S. Coultrap-McQuin (Bloomington, IN: Indiana University Press, 1992), pp. 69–81; C. Gilligan, *In a Different Voice: Psychological Theory and Women's Development* (Cambridge, MA: Harvard University Press, 1982); and M. C. Raugust, "Feminist Ethics and Workplace Values," in *Explorations in Feminist Ethics: Theory and Practice*, ed. E. Browning Cole and S. Coultrap-McQuin (Bloomington, IN: Indiana University Press, 1992), pp. 69–81.

79 P. L. Schumann, "A Moral Principles Framework for Human Resource Management Ethics," *Human Resource Management Review* 11, Spring–Summer 2001, pp. 93–111.

80 S. Jaffee and J. Hyde, "Gender Differences in Moral Orientation: A Meta-Analysis," *Psychological Bulletin*, September 2000, pp. 703–726.

81 L. K. Trevino, "Ethical Decision Making in Organizations: A Person-Situation Interactionist Model," *Academy of Management Review*, July 1986, pp. 601–617; and L. K. Trevino and S. A. Youngblood, "Bad Apples in Bad Barrels: A Causal Analysis of Ethical Decision Making Behavior," *Journal of Applied Psychology*, August 1990, pp. 378–385.

82 See L. Kohlberg, *Essays in Moral Development: The Philosophy of Moral Development*, 1 (New York: Harper and Row, 1981); L. Kohlberg, *Essays in Moral Development: The Psychology of Moral Development*, 2 (New York: Harper and Row, 1984); and R. S. Snell, "Complementing Kohlberg: Mapping the Ethical Reasoning Used by Managers for Their Own Dilemma Cases," *Human Relations*, January 1996, pp. 23–49.

83 L. Kohlberg, *Essays in Moral Development: The Philosophy of Moral Development*, 1 (New York: Harper and Row, 1981); L. Kohlberg, *Essays in Moral Development: The Philosophy of Moral Development*, 2 (New York: Harper and Row, 1984); and R. S. Snell, "Complementing Kohlberg: Mapping the Ethical Reasoning Used by Managers for Their Own Dilemma Cases," *Human Relations*, January 1996, pp. 23–49.

84 J. Weber, "Managers' Moral Reasoning: Assessing Their Responses to Three Moral Dilemmas," *Human Relations*, July 1990, pp. 687–702; and S. B. Knouse and R. A. Giacalone, "Ethical Decision-Making in Business: Behavioral Issues and Concerns," *Journal of Business Ethics*, May 1992, pp. 369–377.

85 This discussion is based on G. F. Cavanagh, D. J. Moberg, and M. Valasquez, "The Ethics of Organizational Politics," *Academy of Management Journal*, June 1981, pp. 363–374.

86 D. Todd, "Business Responds to Ethics Explosion," *Vancouver Sun*, April 27, 1998, pp. A1, A7.

87 L. Ramsay, "A Matter of Principle," *Financial Post (National Post)*, February 26, 1999, p. C18.

88 G. Crone, "UPS Rolls Out Ethics Program," *Financial Post (National Post)*, May 26, 1999, p. C4.

89 K. Doucet, "Canadian Organizations Not Meeting Ethics Expectations," *CMA Management* 74, no. 5 (2000), p. 10; and G. Crone, "UPS Rolls Out Ethics Program," *Financial Post (National Post)*, May 26, 1999, p. C4.

90 D. Todd, "Ethics Audit: Credit Union Reveals All," *Vancouver Sun*, October 19, 1998, p. A5.

91 "Corporate Culture," *Canadian HR Reporter* 17, no. 21 (December 6, 2004), pp. 7–11.

92 W. Chow Hou, "To Bribe or Not to Bribe?" *Asia, Inc.*, October 1996, p. 104; and T. Jackson, "Cultural Values and Management Ethics: A 10-Nation Study," *Human Relations*, October 2001, pp. 1267–1302.

93 T. Donaldson, "Values in Tension: Ethics Away From Home," *Harvard Business Review*, September–October 1996, pp. 48–62.

94 P. Digh, "Shades of Gray in the Global Marketplace," *HR Magazine*, April 1997, pp. 91–98.

95 A. Gillis, "How Can You Do Business in a Country Where Crooked Cops Will Kill You for a Song?" *Report on Business Magazine*, March 1998, p. 60.

96 A. Gillis, "How Can You Do Business in a Country Where Crooked Cops Will Kill You for a Song?" *Report on Business Magazine*, March 1998, p. 60.

97 M. McClearn, "African Adventure," *Canadian Business*, September 1, 2003, pp. 60–66.

98 Vignette based on M. Skapinker, "Why Nike Has Broken into a Sweat," *Financial Times*, March 6, 2002, http://news.ft.com/ft/gx.cgi/ftc?pagename=View&c=Article&cid=FT363BTGHYC&live=true (accessed March 12, 2002); and D. Simpson, "Ethics and

Corporate Social Responsibility, advertising supplement, *Report on Business Magazine*, February 2002.

99   "Many Canadian Businesses and Citizens Want to See Tougher Federal Rules Governing Corporate Responsibility and It's Time for the Government to Take Action, Says a Social Justice Coalition," *Canadian Press Newswire*, January 24, 2002.

100 R. Littlemore, "Do The Right Thing: Would a Socially Responsible Company Do This?" *BCBusiness Magazine*, October 2001, pp. 30–33+.

101 M. Friedman, *Capitalism and Freedom* (Chicago: University of Chicago Press, 1962).

102 J. Bakan, *The Corporation* (Toronto: Big Picture Media Corporation, 2003).

103 D. Bradshaw, "How to Make an Idealist Think Again," *Financial Times*, April 5, 2002, http://news.ft.com/ft/gx.cgi/ftc?pagename=View&c=Article&cid=FT39XM6AOZC&live=true (accessed April 11, 2002).

104 R. Walker and S. Flanagan, "The Ethical Imperative: If You Don't Talk About a Wider Range of Values, You May Not Have a Bottom Line," *Financial Post 500*, 1997, pp. 28–36.

105 P. Foster, "Social Responsibility, Corporate Humbug," *Financial Post (National Post)*, June 23, 1999, p. C7.

106 A. Howatson, *Lean Green: Benefits From a Streamlined Canadian Environmental Regulatory System* (Ottawa: The Conference Board of Canada, April 1996).

107 F. Mihlar, *Regulatory Overkill: The Cost of Regulation in Canada* (Vancouver: The Fraser Institute, September 1996).

108 R. Brunet, "To Survive and Thrive: Bled Dry by the NDP, BC Business Plots a New Course for the 21st Century," *British Columbia Report*, February 9, 1998, pp. 18–22.

109 G. Gallon, "Bunk Behind the Backlash: Highly Publicized Reports Exaggerate the Costs of Environmental Regulation," *Alternatives*, Fall 1997, pp. 14–15.

110 J. K. Grant, "Whatever Happened to Our Concern About the Environment?" *Canadian Speeches*, April 1997, pp. 37–42.

111 "The Business of Being Green," advertising supplement, *Canadian Business*, January 1996, pp. 41–56.

112 Minnesota Mining and Manufacturing Company (3M), *Pollution Prevention Pays: Moving Toward Environmental Sustainability*, Brochure #78-6900-3343-2, St. Paul, MN, 1998; and J. K. Grant, "Whatever Happened to Our Concern About the Environment?" *Canadian Speeches*, April 1997, pp. 37–42.

113 Information about these companies is based, except where noted below, on John Greenwood, "The Guardians: Six Portraits in the Emerging Discipline of Playing Watchdog Over a Company's Code of Conduct," *Financial Post 500*, 1997, pp. 40–50.

114 www.nortel.com/corporate/community/ethics/guide.html (accessed June 12, 2005).

115 www.dnd.ca/ethics/background_e.asp (accessed June 12, 2005).

116 www.dnd.ca/ethics/risk/assess_e.asp (accessed June 12, 2005).

117 www2.bmo.com/ar2003/lead_delivering.html (accessed June 12, 2005).

118 www.shell.ca/code/values/commitments/ethics.html (accessed June 12, 2005). Reprinted with permission of Shell Canada Limited.

119 Based on J. Calano and J. Salzman, "Ten Ways to Fire Up Your Creativity," *Working Woman*, July 1989, p. 94; J. V. Anderson, "Mind Mapping: A Tool for Creative Thinking," *Business Horizons*, January–February 1993, pp. 42–46; M. Loeb, "Ten Commandments for Managing Creative People," *Fortune*, January

16, 1995, pp. 135–136; and M. Henricks, "Good Thinking," *Entrepreneur*, May 1996, pp. 70–73.

OB on the Edge:
Spirituality in the Workplace

1   Vignette based on J. Mawhinney, "Style With Heart and Soul; Spiritual Beliefs Guide Their Work," *Toronto Star*, September 1, 2005, p. E4.

2   I. I. Mitroff and E. A. Denton, "A Study of Spirituality in the Workplace," *Sloan Management Review*, Summer 1999, pp. 83–92.

3   I. I. Mitroff and E. A. Denton, "A Study of Spirituality in the Workplace," *Sloan Management Review*, Summer 1999, pp. 83–92.

4   W. J. Harrington, R. C. Preziosi, and D. J. Gooden, "Perceptions of Workplace Spirituality Among Professionals and Executives," *Employee Responsibilities and Rights Journal* 13, no. 3 (2001), p. 156.

5   W. J. Harrington, R. C. Preziosi, and D. J. Gooden, "Perceptions of Workplace Spirituality Among Professionals and Executives," *Employee Responsibilities and Rights Journal* 13, no. 3 (2001), p. 156.

6   Information in this section based on I. I. Mitroff and E. A. Denton, "A Study of Spirituality in the Workplace," *Sloan Management Review*, Summer 1999, pp. 83–92.

7   D. P. Ashmos and D. Duchon, "Spirituality at Work: A Conceptualization and Measure," *Journal of Management Inquiry*, June 2000, p. 139.

8   P. Preville, "For God's Sake," *Canadian Business*, June 25–July 9, 1999, p. 58.

9   P. Preville, "For God's Sake," *Canadian Business*, June 25–July 9, 1999, p. 60.

10 A. Esposito, "Doing Well and Doing Good [Aaron Feuerstein Spirituality & Business Award]," *Financial Post (National Post)*, March 30, 2001, p. C2.

11 Example based on J. White, "Soul@Work: As We Begin a New Century, Do You Know How to Bring out the Best in Your Employees?" *Benefits Canada*, January 2000, p. 17.

12 T. Helliwell, *Take Your Soul to Work* (Toronto: Random House Canada, 1999).

13 L. Fowlie, "Spirituality Centre is Canadian First," *National Post*, November 22, 2004, p. FP10.

14 J. Canfield, M. V. Hansen, M. Rutte, M. Rogerson, and T. Clauss, *Chicken Soup for the Soul at Work* (Deerfield Beach, FL: HCI, 1996).

15 L. Fowlie, "Spirituality Centre is Canadian First," *National Post*, November 22, 2004, p. FP10.

16 L. Fowlie, "Spirituality Centre is Canadian First," *National Post*, November 22, 2004, p. FP10.

17 B. Harvey, "Sister Mangalam Lena Believes Spiritual Care Is an Essential Part of Health Care, in and out of the Hospital," *Canadian Press Newswire*, April 10, 2001.

18 This section is based on I. I. Mitroff and E. A. Denton, *A Spiritual Audit of Corporate America: A Hard Look at Spirituality, Religion, and Values in the Workplace* (San Francisco: Jossey-Bass, 1999); J. Milliman, J. Ferguson, D. Trickett, and B. Condemi, "Spirit and Community at Southwest Airlines: An Investigation of a Spiritual Values-Based Model," *Journal of Organizational Change Management* 12, no. 3 (1999), pp. 221–233; E. H. Burack, "Spirituality in the Workplace," *Journal of Organizational Change Management* 12, no. 3 (1999), pp. 280–291; and F. Wagner-Marsh and J. Conley, "The

Fourth Wave: The Spiritually-Based Firm," *Journal of Organizational Change Management* 12, no. 3 (1999), pp. 292–302.

19 A. Daniels, "Textile Importer Defends Artisans' Rights," *Vancouver Sun*, May 1, 2000, pp. C8, C10.

20 Cited in F. Wagner-Marsh and J. Conley, "The Fourth Wave: The Spiritually-Based Firm," *Journal of Organizational Change Management* 12, no. 3 (1999), p. 295.

21 M. Conlin, "Religion in the Workplace: The Growing Presence of Spirituality in Corporate America," *BusinessWeek*, November 1, 1999, pp. 151–158; and P. Paul, "A Holier Holiday Season," *American Demographics*, December 2001, pp. 41–45.

22 M. Conlin, "Religion in the Workplace: The Growing Presence of Spirituality in Corporate America," *BusinessWeek*, November 1, 1999, pp. 151–158; and P. Paul, "A Holier Holiday Season," *American Demographics*, December 2001, pp. 41–45.

23 Cited in M. Conlin, "Religion in the Workplace: The Growing Presence of Spirituality in Corporate America," *BusinessWeek*, November 1, 1999, p. 153.

24 C. P. Neck and J. F. Milliman, "Thought Self-Leadership: Finding Spiritual Fulfillment in Organizational Life," *Journal of Managerial Psychology* 9, no. 8 (1994), p. 9.

25 D. W. McCormick, "Spirituality and Management," *Journal of Managerial Psychology* 9, no. 6 (1994), p. 5; E. Brandt, "Corporate Pioneers Explore Spiritual Peace," *HR Magazine* 41, no. 4 (1996), p. 82; P. Leigh, "The New Spirit at Work," *Training and Development* 51, no. 3 (1997), p. 26; P. H. Mirvis, "Soul Work in Organizations," *Organization Science* 8, no. 2 (1997), p. 193; and J. Millman, A. Czaplewski, and J. Ferguson, "An Exploratory Empirical Assessment of the Relationship Between Spirituality and Employee Work Attitudes" (paper presented at the National Academy of Management Meeting, Washington, DC, August 2001).

26 Cited in J. Milliman, J. Ferguson, D. Trickett, and B. Condemi, "Spirit and Community at Southwest Airlines: An Investigation of a Spiritual Values-Based Model," *Journal of Organizational Change Management* 12, no. 3 (1999).

27 M. Schlangenstein, "Southwest Airlines Profit Jumps," *Washington Post*, April 15, 2005, p. E5.

28 P. Preville, "For God's Sake," *Canadian Business*, June 25–July 9, 1999, p. 61.

29 *FactBox* based on B. Wickens, "Our Changing Life: With the World Becoming a More Terrifying Place, Many of Us Are Asking, 'What Can I Do?'" *Maclean's*, December 17, 2001, p. 24.

Chapter 13

1 Opening vignette based on M. McCullough, "Virtual Tinseltown," *National Post Business*, June 2000, pp. 46–58.

2 See, for instance, R. L. Daft, *Organization Theory and Design*, 6th ed. (Cincinnati, OH: South Western College, 1998).

3 S. Stewart and K. Kalawsky, "TD Evergreen's Struggle for Well-Off Clients," *Financial Post*, February 12, 2002, p. SR9.

4 Based on K. McCoy and D. Jones, "The Fade-Out at the King of Copies," *Financial Post (National Post)*, October 24, 2000, p. C13.

5 See, for instance, L. Urwick, *The Elements of Administration* (New York: Harper and Row, 1944), pp. 52–53.

6 J. Child and R. G. McGrath, "Organizations Unfettered: Organizational Form in an Information-Intensive Economy," *Academy of Management Journal*, December 2001, pp. 1135–1148.

7 D. B. Harrison, "Shaping the Organization of the Future," *Canadian Business Review*, Winter 1995, pp. 13–16.

8 G. Morgan, *Images of Organization* (Newbury Park, CA: Sage, 1986), p. 21.

9 T. Burns and G. M. Stalker, *The Management of Innovation* (London: Tavistock, 1961); and J. A. Courtright, G. T. Fairhurst, and L. E. Rogers, "Interaction Patterns in Organic and Mechanistic Systems," *Academy of Management Journal*, December 1989, pp. 773–802.

10 Based on C. Gillis, "Musicians Launch Unexpected Strike," *National Post*, February 16, 2002, p. A5; and B. Weber, "Edmonton Orchestra Deal Part of Trend to Give Musicians More Control," *Canadian Press Newswire*, March 21, 2002.

11 H. Mintzberg, *Structure in Fives: Designing Effective Organizations* (Englewood Cliffs, NJ: Prentice Hall, 1983), p. 157.

12 J. Davis, "Governing the Family-Run Business," *Working Knowledge for Business Leaders* (Boston: Harvard Business School, September 4, 2001).

13 D. Miller, L. Steier, and I. Le Breton-Miller, "Lost in Time: Intergenerational Succession, Change, and Failure in Family Business," *Journal of Business Venturing*, July 2003, pp. 513–531.

14 Based on P. Kuitenbrouwer, "Simmer . . . Then Raise to a Boil: A Family Stew Over Succession at the McCain Foods Empire Spills into the Courts [1993 review]," *Financial Post Daily*, 10, no. 205A, F 2 '98, anniversary ed., p. 22; P. Newman, "Tales From a Mellower Harrison McCain: Four Years After Winning a Bitter Feud With His Brother, Harrison Acknowledges That 'Strained' Family Relations Still Exist," *Maclean's*, January 19, 1998, p. 50; and "Harrison McCain: King of the Frozen French Fry," *Calgary Herald*, March 28, 2004, p. B6.

15 J. J. Chrisman, J. H. Chua, and L. P. Steier, "An Introduction to Theories of Family Business," *Journal of Business Venturing*, July 2003, pp. 441–448.

16 K. Knight, "Matrix Organization: A Review," *Journal of Management Studies*, May 1976, pp. 111–130; and L. R. Burns and D. R. Wholey, "Adoption and Abandonment of Matrix Management Programs: Effects of Organizational Characteristics and Interorganizational Networks," *Academy of Management Journal*, February 1993, pp. 106–138.

17 See, for instance, S. M. Davis and P. R. Lawrence, "Problems of Matrix Organization," *Harvard Business Review*, May–June 1978, pp. 131–142.

18 Based on M. McCullough, "Virtual Tinseltown," *National Post Business*, June 2000, pp. 46–58.

19 J. R. Galbraith and E. E. Lawler III, "Effective Organizations: Using the New Logic of Organizing," in *Organizing for the Future: The New Logic for Managing Complex Organizations*, ed. J. R. Galbraith, E. E. Lawler III, and associates (San Francisco: Jossey-Bass, 1993).

20 G. G. Dess, A. M. A. Rasheed, K. J. McLaughlin, and R. Priem, "The New Corporate Architecture," *Academy of Management Executive*, August 1995, pp. 7–18; C. Y. Baldwin and K. B. Clark, "Managing in an Age of Modularity," *Harvard Business Review*, September–October 1997, pp. 84–93.

21 M. Kaeter, "The Age of the Specialized Generalist," *Training*, December 1993, pp. 48–53.

22 See, for instance, E. A. Gargan, "'Virtual' Companies Leave the Manufacturing to Others," *New York Times*, July 17, 1994, p. F5; D. W. Cravens, S. H. Shipp, and K. S. Cravens, "Reforming the Traditional Organization: The Mandate for Developing Networks," *Business Horizons*, July–August 1994, pp. 19–27; R. T. King Jr., "The Virtual Company," *Wall Street Journal*, November 14, 1994, p. 85; R. E. Miles and C. C. Snow, "The New Network Firm: A

Spherical Structure Built on Human Investment Philosophy," *Organizational* Dynamics, Spring 1995, pp. 5–18; G. G. Dess, A. M. A. Rasheed, K. J. McLaughlin, and R. L. Priem, "The New Corporate Architecture," *Academy of Management Executive*, August 1995, pp. 7–20; D. Pescovitz, "The Company Where Everybody's a Temp," *New York Times Magazine*, June 11, 2000, pp. 94–96; W. F. Cascio, "Managing a Virtual Workplace," *Academy of Management Executive*, August 2000, pp. 81–90; and D. Lyons, "Smart and Smarter," *Forbes*, March 18, 2002, pp. 40–41.

23 G. G. Dess, A. M. A. Rasheed, K. J. McLaughlin, and R. Priem, "The New Corporate Architecture," *Academy of Management Executive*, August 1995, pp. 7–18.

24 "Why Do Canadian Companies Opt for Cooperative Ventures?" *Micro: The Micro-Economic Research Bulletin* 4, no. 2 (1997), pp. 3–5.

25 G. G. Dess, A. M. A. Rasheed, K. J. McLaughlin, and R. Priem, "The New Corporate Architecture," *Academy of Management Executive*, August 1995, p. 13. See also P. Lorange and J. Roos, "Why Some Strategic Alliances Succeed and Why Others Fail," *Journal of Business Strategy*, January/February 1991, pp. 25–30; and G. Slowinski, "The Human Touch in Strategic Alliances," *Mergers and Acquisitions*, July/August 1992, pp. 44–47.

26 H. C. Lucas Jr., *The T-Form Organization: Using Technology to Design Organizations for the 21st Century* (San Francisco: Jossey-Bass, 1996).

27 This section is based on D. D. Davis, "Form, Function and Strategy in Boundaryless Organizations," in *The Changing Nature of Work*, ed. A. Howard (San Francisco: Jossey-Bass, 1995), pp. 112–138; P. Roberts, "We Are One Company, No Matter Where We Are. Time and Space Are Irrelevant," *Fast Company*, April–May 1998, pp. 122–128; R. L. Cross, A. Yan, and M. R. Louis, "Boundary Activities in 'Boundaryless' Organizations: A Case Study of a Transformation to a Team-Based Structure," *Human Relations*, June 2000, pp. 841–868; and R. Ashkenas, D. Ulrich, T. Jick, and S. Kerr, *The Boundaryless Organization: Breaking the Chains of Organizational Structure*, rev. ed. (San Francisco: Jossey-Bass, 2002).

28 See J. Lipnack and J. Stamps, *The TeamNet Factor* (Essex Junction, VT: Oliver Wight Publications, 1993); J. R. Wilke, "Computer Links Erode Hierarchical Nature of Workplace Culture," *Wall Street Journal*, December 9, 1993, p. A1; T. A. Stewart, "Managing in a Wired Company," *Fortune*, July 11, 1994, pp. 44–56; and M. Hammer, *The Agenda* (New York: Crown Business, 2001).

29 This analysis is referred to as a contingency approach to organization design. See, for instance, J. M. Pennings, "Structural Contingency Theory: A Reappraisal," in *Research in Organizational Behavior*, vol. 14, ed. B. M. Staw and L. L. Cummings (Greenwich, CT: JAI Press, 1992), pp. 267–309.

30 The strategy-structure thesis was originally proposed in A. D. Chandler Jr., *Strategy and Structure: Chapters in the History of the Industrial Enterprise* (Cambridge, MA: MIT Press, 1962). For an updated analysis, see T. L. Amburgey and T. Dacin, "As the Left Foot Follows the Right? The Dynamics of Strategic and Structural Change," *Academy of Management Journal*, December 1994, pp. 1427–1452.

31 See R. E. Miles and C. C. Snow, *Organizational Strategy, Structure, and Process* (New York: McGraw-Hill, 1978); D. Miller, "The Structural and Environmental Correlates of Business Strategy," *Strategic Management Journal*, January–February 1987, pp. 55–76; D. C. Galunic and K. M. Eisenhardt, "Renewing the Strategy-Structure-Performance Paradigm," in *Research in Organizational Behavior*, vol. 16, ed. B. M. Staw and L. L. Cummings (Greenwich, CT: JAI Press, 1994), pp. 215–255; and I. C. Harris and T. W. Ruefli, "The Strategy/Structure Debate: An Examination of the

Performance Implications," *Journal of Management Studies*, June 2000, pp. 587–603.

32 See, for instance, P. M. Blau and R. A. Schoenherr, *The Structure of Organizations* (New York: Basic Books, 1971); D. S. Pugh, "The Aston Program of Research: Retrospect and Prospect," in *Perspectives on Organization Design and Behavior*, ed. A. H. Van de Ven and W. F. Joyce (New York: Wiley, 1981), pp. 135–166; R. Z. Gooding and J. A. Wagner III, "A Meta-Analytic Review of the Relationship Between Size and Performance: The Productivity and Efficiency of Organizations and Their Subunits," *Administrative Science Quarterly*, December 1985, pp. 462–481; and A. C. Bluedorn, "Pilgrim's Progress: Trends and Convergence in Research on Organizational Size and Environments," *Journal of Management*, Summer 1993, pp. 163–192.

33 See F. E. Emery and E. Trist, "The Causal Texture of Organizational Environments," *Human Relations*, February 1965, pp. 21–32; P. Lawrence and J. W. Lorsch, *Organization and Environment: Managing Differentiation and Integration* (Boston: Harvard Business School, Division of Research, 1967); M. Yasai-Ardekani, "Structural Adaptations to Environments," *Academy of Management Review*, January 1986, pp. 9–21; and A. C. Bluedorn, "Pilgrim's Progress: Trends and Convergence in Research on Organizational Size and Environments," *Journal of Management*, Summer 1993, pp. 163–192.

34 G. G. Dess and D. W. Beard, "Dimensions of Organizational Task Environments," *Administrative Science Quarterly*, March 1984, pp. 52–73; E. A. Gerloff, N. K. Muir, and W. D. Bodensteiner, "Three Components of Perceived Environmental Uncertainty: An Exploratory Analysis of the Effects of Aggregation," *Journal of Management*, December 1991, pp. 749–768; and O. Shenkar, N. Aranya, and T. Almor, "Construct Dimensions in the Contingency Model: An Analysis Comparing Metric and Non-Metric Multivariate Instruments," *Human Relations*, May 1995, pp. 559–580.

35 This argument was presented by J. Chambers, "Nothing Except E-Companies," *BusinessWeek*, August 28, 2000, pp. 210–212.

36 This argument was presented by A. Grove, "I'm a Little Skeptical . . . Brains Don't Speed Up," *BusinessWeek*, August 28, 2000, pp. 212–214.

37 D. Paddon, "Celestica Cost-Cutting Starts to Show Results," *The Gazette* (Montreal), April 22, 2005, p. B7; and "Bombardier Announces More Job Cuts," *International Railway Journal* 45, no. 1 (January 2005), p. 2.

38 T. Van Alphen, "St. Catharines Workers Voice Apprehension," *Toronto Star*, June 8, 2005, p. D1.

39 R. W. Keidel, "Rethinking Organizational Design," *Academy of Management Executive* 8, 1994, pp. 12–30.

40 A. Swift, "BCE Emergis Chops 40 Per Cent of Its Business and 550 Employees; Shares Up," *Canadian Press Newswire*, April 2002.

41 K. P. De Meuse, T. J. Bergmann, P. A. Vanderheiden, and C. E. Roraff, "Corporate Downsizing: Separating Myth From Fact," *Journal of Management Inquiry* 6, no. 2 (2004), pp. 168–176.

42 "Haves & Have-nots: Canadians Look for Corporate Conscience," *Maclean's*, December 30, 1996/January 6, 1997, pp. 26, 37.

43 "Work Option Plans Can Soften Blows of Layoffs," *Financial Post*, May 4/6, 1996, p. 37.

44 D. L. Nelson and R. J. Burke, "Lessons Learned," *Canadian Journal of Administrative Sciences* 15, no. 4 (1998), pp. 372–381.

45 The source of this exercise is unknown.

46 Based on S. P. Robbins and P. L. Hunsaker, *Training in Interpersonal Skills*, 3rd ed. (Upper Saddle River, NJ: Prentice Hall, 2003), pp. 95–98.

Chapter 14

1 Opening vignette based on G. Crone, "Canadian Tire Chief Takes Home $2.1m," *Financial Post (National Post)*, April 7, 1999, p. C6; G. Livingston, "Managing Change Stressed for Retailers," *Vancouver Sun*, June 15, 1999, p. D2; S. Theobald, "Canadian Tire Store Makeovers Pay Off," *Canadian Press Newswire*, December 23, 1998; Z. Olijnyk, "Canadian Tire CEO Bachand Set to Retire," *Financial Post (National Post)*, January 12, 2000, pp. C1, C10; Z. Olijnyk, "Bachand Leaves CTC Corp with $4.5m: Retirement Package," *Financial Post (National Post)*, January 13, 2000, p. C6; G. Livingston, "With Higher Sales Defying the Economic Malaise, Canadian Tire Corp. Has Reported a 19.3 Per Cent Increase in Annual Profit and Forecast Continuing Earnings Gains in 2002," *Canadian Press Newswire*, February 7, 2002; H. Shaw, "Canadian Tire Sets Out on Building Program: 40 to 50 Stores: Greater Focus Placed on Gas Stations, Credit Card Business," *Financial Post (National Post)*, September 25, 2001, p. B6; and R. McQueen, "Canadian Tire at Crossroads, Once Again: Retailer Haunted by Past Attempts at Strategic Growth," *Financial Post (National Post)*, May 7, 2001, p. C7.

2 J. Lee, "Canadian Businesses Not Good at Adjusting, Survey Says," *Vancouver Sun*, December 14, 1998, pp. C1–2.

3 L. Earl, *An Overview of Organisational and Technological Change in the Private Sector, 1998–2000*, Catalogue no. 88F0006XIE no. 09 (Ottawa: Statistics Canada, June 2002), p. 13.

4 L. Earl, *An Overview of Organisational and Technological Change in the Private Sector, 1998–2000*, Catalogue no. 88F0006XIE no. 09 (Ottawa: Statistics Canada, June 2002), p. 13

5 See, for instance, K. H. Hammonds, "Practical Radicals," *Fast Company*, September 2000, pp. 162–174; and P. C. Judge, "Change Agents," *Fast Company*, November 2000, pp. 216–226.

6 J. Taub, "Harvard Radical," *New York Times Magazine*, August 24, 2003, pp. 28–45 ff.

7 K. Lewin, *Field Theory in Social Science* (New York: Harper and Row, 1951).

8 J. P. Kotter, "Leading Changes: Why Transformation Efforts Fail," *Harvard Business Review*, March–April 1995, pp. 59–67; and J. P. Kotter, *Leading Change* (Boston: Harvard Business School Press, 1996).

9 See, for example, A. B. Shani and W. A. Pasmore, "Organization Inquiry: Towards a New Model of the Action Research Process," in *Contemporary Organization Development: Current Thinking and Applications*, ed. D. D. Warrick (Glenview, IL: Scott, Foresman, 1985), pp. 438–448; and C. Eden and C. Huxham, "Action Research for the Study of Organizations," in *Handbook of Organization Studies*, ed. S. R. Clegg, C. Hardy, and W. R. Nord (London: Sage, 1996).

10 See, for example, G. R. Bushe, "Advances in Appreciative Inquiry as an Organization Development Intervention," *Organizational Development Journal*, Summer 1999, pp. 61–68; D. L. Cooperrider and D. Whitney, *Collaborating for Change: Appreciative Inquiry* (San Francisco: Berrett-Koehler, 2000); R. Fry, F. Barrett, J. Seiling, and D. Whitney, eds., *Appreciative Inquiry & Organizational Transformation: Reports From the Field* (Westport, CT: Quorum, 2002); J. K. Barge and C. Oliver, "Working With Appreciation in Managerial Practice," *Academy of Management Review*, January 2003, pp. 124–142; and D. van der Haar and D. M. Hosking,

"Evaluating Appreciative Inquiry: A Relational Constructionist Perspective," *Human Relations*, August 2004, pp. 1017–1036.

11 R. Rabinovitch, "Training and Development," *Canadian HR Reporter* 17, no. 10 (May 17, 2004), pp. 7–10.

12 D. Sankey, "New Tool Solves Firms' Problems," *Calgary Herald*, July 12, 2003, p. CR1F.

13 G. R. Bushe, "Advances in Appreciative Inquiry as an Organization Development Intervention," *Organization Development Journal* 17, no. 2 (Summer 1999), p. 61–68.

14 A. E. Reichers, J. P. Wanous, and J. T. Austin, "Understanding and Managing Cynicism About Organizational Change," *Academy of Management Executive* 11, 1997, pp. 48–59.

15 R. H. Hall, *Organizations: Structures, Processes, and Outcomes*, 4th ed. (Englewood Cliffs, NJ: Prentice Hall, 1987), p. 29.

16 J. Lee, "Canadian Businesses Not Good at Adjusting, Survey Says," *Vancouver Sun*, December 14, 1998, pp. C1, C2.

17 R. Starnes, "The Lucky Touch Wore Off: Timothy Eaton's Legacy Fell Victim to Its Conservative Image and Failure to Keep Pace With Trends," *Ottawa Citizen*, February 19, 2002, p. D.1.

18 D. Katz and R. L. Kahn, *The Social Psychology of Organizations*, 2nd ed. (New York: Wiley, 1978), pp. 714–715.

19 Paragraph based on M. Johne, "Wanted: A Few Good Egocentric, Self-Serving Risk-Takers," *Globe and Mail*, May 27, 2002, p. C1.

20 J. P. Kotter and L. A. Schlesinger, "Choosing Strategies for Change," *Harvard Business Review*, March–April 1979, pp. 106–114.

21 See J. Pfeffer, *Managing With Power: Politics and Influence in Organizations* (Boston: Harvard Business School Press, 1992), pp. 7 and 318–320; and D. Knights and D. McCabe, "When 'Life Is but a Dream': Obliterating Politics Through Business Process Reengineering?" *Human Relations*, June 1998, pp. 761–798.

22 See, for instance, W. Ocasio, "Political Dynamics and the Circulation of Power: CEO Succession in U.S. Industrial Corporations, 1960–1990," *Administrative Science Quarterly*, June 1994, pp. 285–312.

23 Vignette based on "Canadian Tire Unveils Five-Year Plan," *Daily News*, April 7, 2005, p. 15.

24 W. Mclellan, "CT's Goal: 'Lifetime Loyalty': Ambitious Expansion Plan Begins in the West," *Province* (Vancouver), April 7, 2005, p. A39.

25 M. Hammer and J. Champy, *Reengineering the Corporation: A Manifesto for Business Revolution* (New York: Harper Business, 1993).

26 See, for instance, A. Van de Ven, "Central Problems in the Management of Innovation," *Management Science* 32, 1986, 590–607; and R. M. Kanter, "When a Thousand Flowers Bloom: Structural, Collective and Social Conditions for Innovation in Organizations," in *Research in Organizational Behavior*, vol. 10, ed. B. M. Staw and L. L. Cummings (Greenwich, CT: JAI Press, 1988), pp. 169–211.

27 F. Damanpour, "Organizational Innovation: A Meta-Analysis of Effects of Determinants and Moderators," *Academy of Management Journal*, September 1991, p. 557.

28 F. Damanpour, "Organizational Innovation: A Meta-Analysis of Effects of Determinants and Moderators," *Academy of Management Journal*, September 1991, pp. 555–590.

29 See also P. R. Monge, M. D. Cozzens, and N. S. Contractor, "Communication and Motivational Predictors of the Dynamics of Organizational Innovation," *Organization Science*, May 1992, pp. 250–274.

30 Discussion of 3M is based on K. Labich, "The Innovators," *Fortune*, June 6, 1988, p. 49; R. Mitchell, "Masters of Innovation," *BusinessWeek*, April 10, 1989, p. 58; K. Kelly, "The Drought Is Over at 3M," *BusinessWeek*, November 7, 1994, pp. 140–141; T. A. Stewart, "3M Fights Back," *Fortune*, February 5, 1996, pp. 94–99; and T. D. Schellhardt, "David in Goliath," *Wall Street Journal*, May 23, 1996, p. R14.

31 J. M. Howell and C. A. Higgins, "Champions of Change," *Business Quarterly*, Spring 1990, pp. 31–32; and D. L. Day, "Raising Radicals: Different Processes for Championing Innovative Corporate Ventures," *Organization Science*, May 1994, pp. 148–172.

32 J. M. Howell and C. A. Higgins, "Champions of Change," *Business Quarterly*, Spring 1990, pp. 31–32.

33 See, for example, the special edition on organizational learning in *Organizational Dynamics*, Autumn 1998; P. Senge, *The Dance of Change: The Challenges to Sustaining Momentum in Learning Organizations* (New York: Doubleday/Currency, 1999); A. M. Webber, "Will Companies Ever Learn?" *Fast Company*, October 2000, pp. 275–282; R. Snell, "Moral Foundations of the Learning Organization," *Human Relations*, March 2001, pp. 319–342; and M. M. Brown and J. L. Brudney, "Learning Organizations in the Public Sector? A Study of Police Agencies Employing Information and Technology to Advance Knowledge," *Public Administration Review*, January–February 2003, pp. 30–43.

34 D. H. Kim, "The Link Between Individual and Organizational Learning," *Sloan Management Review*, Fall 1993, p. 37.

35 C. Argyris and D. A. Schon, *Organizational Learning* (Reading, MA: Addison-Wesley, 1978).

36 B. Dumaine, "Mr. Learning Organization," *Fortune*, October 17, 1994, p. 148.

37 B. Dumaine, "Mr. Learning Organization," *Fortune*, October 17, 1994, p. 154.

38 See S. Shane, S. Venkataraman, and I. MacMillan, "Cultural Differences in Innovation Championing Strategies," *Journal of Management* 21, no. 5 (1995), pp. 931–952.

39 For contrasting views on episodic and continuous change, see K. E. Weick and R. E. Quinn, "Organizational Change and Development," in *Annual Review of Psychology*, vol. 50, ed. J. T. Spence, J. M. Darley, and D. J. Foss (Palo Alto, CA: Annual Reviews, 1999), pp. 361–386.

40 This perspective is based on P. B. Vaill, *Managing as a Performing Art: New Ideas for a World of Chaotic Change* (San Francisco: Jossey-Bass, 1989).

41 T. Aidt and Z. Tzannatos, "Unions and Collective Bargaining," The World Bank, 2002.

42 Information on NorskeCanada based on D. Fischer, "Peace and Prosperity: Good Labour Relations Are Worth It," *Edmonton Journal*, July 2, 2003, p. G1.

43 Information on Irving Pulp and Paper based on A. Van den Broek, "All's Quiet on the Eastern Front: Times Have Changed for the Better at Historically Turbulent Irving Paper Inc," *Plant* 56, no. 17 (November 24, 1997), pp. 10–11; and D. Brown, "Can Unions,

Management Learn to Co-operate?" *Canadian HR Reporter*, November 6, 2000, pp. 1–2.

44 S. Ward and B. Chartrand, *Change Is Inevitable, but Growth Is Optional* (Ottawa: The Conference Board of Canada, August 2000).

45 J. R. Stepp and T. J. Schneider, "Fostering Change in a Unionized Environment," *Canadian Business Review*, Summer 1995, pp. 13–16.

46 J. R. Stepp and T. J. Schneider, "Fostering Change in a Unionized Environment," *Canadian Business Review*, Summer 1995, pp. 13–16.

47 R. Pascale, M. Millemann, and L. Gioja, "Changing the Way We Change," *Harvard Business Review*, November–December 1997, pp. 127–139. The actual names of the points based on the *After Action Review* are taken from the article, although the summaries are provided by the authors of this textbook.

Integrative OB Cases

1   An earlier version of this case study was co-authored with Brent McLain (University of Regina) and was presented at the annual meeting of the Administrative Sciences Association of Canada, Winnipeg, Manitoba, June 2002. The author thanks Tupper Cawsey for his helpful feedback on an earlier version of this case study.

2   S. Walton, *Made in America: My Story* (New York: Doubleday, 1992).

3   L. Laska, "99 Verdicts Against Wal-Mart," Wal-Mart Litigation Project, **http://www.wal-martlitigation.com/99verdic.htm** (accessed December 15, 2005).

4   *Tincher v. Wal-Mart*, 155 F.3d 1317, in L. Laska, "99 Verdicts Against Wal-Mart," Wal-Mart Litigation Project, **http://www.wal-martlitigation.com/99verdic.htm** (accessed December 15, 2005).

5   **www.walmartfacts.com/newsdesk/wal-mart-fact-sheets.aspx#a26** (accessed December 15, 2005).

6   **www.walmartfacts.com/newsdesk/wal-mart-fact-sheets.aspx#a26** (accessed December 15, 2005).

7   L. Pierce and B. Appell, *Jury Fed-up With Employer: Department Store Ordered to Pay $20 Million to Four Clerks Fired for Eating Candy.* **http://www.silver-freedman.com/library/mar_99_br5.html** (accessed December 15, 2005).

8   *Stringer v. Wal-Mart*, Wayne Co. (KY) Circuit Court, in L. Laska, "99 Verdicts Against Wal-Mart," Wal-Mart Litigation Project, **http://www.wal-martlitigation.com/99verdic.htm** (accessed December 15, 2005).

9   *Desilets v. Wal-Mart*, 171 F.3d 711 (1st Cir. 1999), in L. Laska, "99 Verdicts Against Wal-Mart," Wal-Mart Litigation Project, **http://www.wal-martlitigation.com/99verdic.htm** (accessed December 15, 2005).

10 *Deffenbaugh-Williams v. Wal-Mart*, 156 F.3d 581, in L. Laska, "99 Verdicts Against Wal-Mart," Wal-Mart Litigation Project, **http://www.wal-martlitigation.com/99verdic.htm** (accessed December 15, 2005).

GLOSSARY/SUBJECT INDEX

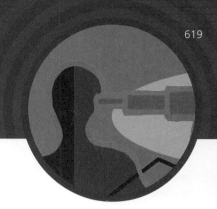

The page on which the key term is defined is printed in boldface; *f* denotes a figure.

M

NAME AND ORGANIZATION INDEX

The page on which a weblink appears is printed in boldface.

LIST OF CANADIAN COMPANIES

The page number indicates where the company is mentioned in the text.

ONTARIO

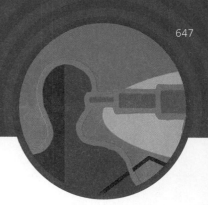

PHOTO CREDITS